CRIMINAL LAW AND ITS PROCESSES

CASES AND MATERIALS

EDITORIAL ADVISORS

Vicki Been
Elihu Root Professor of Law
New York University School of Law

Erwin Chemerinsky
Dean and Distinguished Professor of Law
University of California, Irvine, School of Law

Richard A. Epstein
Laurence A. Tisch Professor of Law
New York University School of Law
Peter and Kirsten Bedford Senior Fellow
The Hoover Institution
Senior Lecturer in Law
The University of Chicago

Ronald J. Gilson
Charles J. Meyers Professor of Law and Business
Stanford University
Marc and Eva Stern Professor of Law and Business
Columbia Law School

James E. Krier
Earl Warren DeLano Professor of Law
The University of Michigan Law School

Richard K. Neumann, Jr.
Professor of Law
Hofstra University School of Law

Robert H. Sitkoff
John L. Gray Professor of Law
Harvard Law School

David Alan Sklansky
Yosef Osheawich Professor of Law
University of California at Berkeley School of Law

Kent D. Syverud
Dean and Ethan A. H. Shepley University Professor
Washington University School of Law

Elizabeth Warren
Leo Gottlieb Professor of Law
Harvard Law School

ASPEN CASEBOOK SERIES

CRIMINAL LAW AND ITS PROCESSES

CASES AND MATERIALS

NINTH EDITION

Sanford H. Kadish

Alexander F. and May T. Morrison
Professor of Law, Emeritus
University of California, Berkeley

Stephen J. Schulhofer

Robert B. McKay Professor of Law
New York University

Carol S. Steiker

Henry J. Friendly Professor of Law
Harvard University

Rachel E. Barkow

Segal Family Professor of
Regulatory Law and Policy
New York University

Wolters Kluwer
Law & Business

Copyright © 2012 Sanford H. Kadish, Stephen J. Schulhofer, and Rachel E. Barkow.

Published by Wolters Kluwer Law & Business in New York.

Wolters Kluwer Law & Business serves customers worldwide with CCH, Aspen Publishers, and Kluwer Law International products. (www.wolterskluwerlb.com)

No part of this publication may be reproduced or transmitted in any form or by any means, electronic or mechanical, including photocopy, recording, or utilized by any information storage or retrieval system, without written permission from the publisher. For information about permissions or to request permissions online, visit us at www.wolterskluwerlb.com, or a written request may be faxed to our permissions department at 212-771-0803.

To contact Customer Service, e-mail customer.service@wolterskluwer.com, call 1-800-234-1660, fax 1-800-901-9075, or mail correspondence to:

    Wolters Kluwer Law & Business
    Attn: Order Department
    PO Box 990
    Frederick, MD 21705

Printed in the United States of America.

1 2 3 4 5 6 7 8 9 0

ISBN 978-1-4548-1755-0

Library of Congress Cataloging-in-Publication Data

    Criminal law and its processes : cases and materials / Sanford H. Kadish . . . [et al.].—9th ed.
        p. cm.
    Rev. ed. of: Criminal law and its processes : cases and materials / Sanford H. Kadish, Stephen J. Schulhofer, Carol S. Steiker. 8th ed. c2007.
    Includes index.
    "Appendix, American Law Institute, Model Penal Code."
    ISBN 978-1-4548-1755-0
   1. Criminal law—United States. I. Kadish, Sanford H. II. Kadish, Sanford H. Criminal law and its processes.
    KF9218.K3 2012
    345.73—dc23   2012015981

SUSTAINABLE FORESTRY INITIATIVE

Certified Sourcing

www.sfiprogram.org

SFI-01042

SFI label applies to the text stock

About Wolters Kluwer Law & Business

Wolters Kluwer Law & Business is a leading global provider of intelligent information and digital solutions for legal and business professionals in key specialty areas, and respected educational resources for professors and law students. Wolters Kluwer Law & Business connects legal and business professionals as well as those in the education market with timely, specialized authoritative content and information-enabled solutions to support success through productivity, accuracy and mobility.

Serving customers worldwide, Wolters Kluwer Law & Business products include those under the Aspen Publishers, CCH, Kluwer Law International, Loislaw, Best Case, ftwilliam.com and MediRegs family of products.

CCH products have been a trusted resource since 1913, and are highly regarded resources for legal, securities, antitrust and trade regulation, government contracting, banking, pension, payroll, employment and labor, and healthcare reimbursement and compliance professionals.

Aspen Publishers products provide essential information to attorneys, business professionals and law students. Written by preeminent authorities, the product line offers analytical and practical information in a range of specialty practice areas from securities law and intellectual property to mergers and acquisitions and pension/benefits. Aspen's trusted legal education resources provide professors and students with high-quality, up-to-date and effective resources for successful instruction and study in all areas of the law.

Kluwer Law International products provide the global business community with reliable international legal information in English. Legal practitioners, corporate counsel and business executives around the world rely on Kluwer Law journals, looseleafs, books, and electronic products for comprehensive information in many areas of international legal practice.

Loislaw is a comprehensive online legal research product providing legal content to law firm practitioners of various specializations. Loislaw provides attorneys with the ability to quickly and efficiently find the necessary legal information they need, when and where they need it, by facilitating access to primary law as well as state-specific law, records, forms and treatises.

Best Case Solutions is the leading bankruptcy software product to the bankruptcy industry. It provides software and workflow tools to flawlessly streamline petition preparation and the electronic filing process, while timely incorporating ever-changing court requirements.

ftwilliam.com offers employee benefits professionals the highest quality plan documents (retirement, welfare and non-qualified) and government forms (5500/PBGC, 1099 and IRS) software at highly competitive prices.

MediRegs products provide integrated health care compliance content and software solutions for professionals in healthcare, higher education and life sciences, including professionals in accounting, law and consulting.

Wolters Kluwer Law & Business, a division of Wolters Kluwer, is headquartered in New York. Wolters Kluwer is a market-leading global information services company focused on professionals.

Summary of Contents

Contents

CHAPTER 2

CHAPTER 3

DEFINING CRIMINAL CONDUCT—THE ELEMENTS OF JUST PUNISHMENT

149

CHAPTER 4

RAPE   331

CHAPTER 5

HOMICIDE   419

CHAPTER 6

THE SIGNIFICANCE OF RESULTING HARM 571

CHAPTER 7
GROUP CRIMINALITY   657

CHAPTER 8

EXCULPATION   817

CHAPTER 9

THEFT OFFENSES   1033

CHAPTER 10

DISCRETION   1111

Preface

This edition, while preserving continuity with its predecessors, introduces several changes in the content and sequencing of the material. We have retained the basic organization, tone, and perspective of the book. We have replaced relatively few of the major cases and have maintained the intellectual framework and concrete questions and problems that so many of our colleagues have found helpful vehicles for successful teaching. This Preface discusses the basic goals of the course before turning to the specific changes made for this edition.

Why substantive criminal law? We conceive of a criminal law course as serving the ends of both general legal education and training in the criminal law in particular. There are, as we see it, three chief ways the course can contribute to the general legal education of the law student. One way is to provide a vehicle for the close reading of statutory texts—primarily the Model Penal Code, but also state statutory formulations—to help balance the emphasis on case law in the first-year curriculum. The second way is to introduce the student to the operation of a system of rules and principles designed to apportion blame and responsibility in accordance with our moral norms, subject to the practical restraints of a functioning system. While the criminal law is the primary institution serving this function, fault and wrongdoing each play a role in determining liability throughout the law. Hence some understanding of the analytical elements in assessing blame for a person's conduct or for the conduct of another, and of the concepts of excuse and justification, is an important element in a lawyer's legal education.

The third way the criminal law course serves the purposes of general legal education is by enlarging insight into the potentialities and limitations of the law as an instrument of social control. We have in mind the hard problems encountered in using the law for this purpose: the difficulty of giving legal form to the compromises made necessary when goals conflict; the creation of institutional arrangements—judicial and administrative—appropriate to the goals sought; the limitations—moral and practical—on the use of the law as a means of social control; the relation of legal controls to other social processes.

The substantive criminal law provides an unusually suitable introduction to these pervasive problems of the law. The ends criminal law serves involve social and human values of the highest order. Its means, entailing the imposition of brute force on the lives of individuals, are potentially the most destructive and abusive to be found within the legal system. The issues it raises and the setting in which it raises them are compelling and vivid. Its institutions are acutely controversial and often controverted. And one of its underlying themes is the momentous issue of the reconciliation of authority and the individual. As Professor Herbert Wechsler has written:

> Whatever views one holds about the penal law, no one will question its importance in society. This is the law on which men place their ultimate reliance for protection against all the deepest injuries that human conduct can inflict on individuals and institutions. By the same token, penal law governs the strongest force that we permit official agencies to bring to bear on individuals. Its promise as an instrument of safety is matched only by its power to destroy. If penal law is weak or ineffective, basic human interests are in jeopardy. If it is harsh or arbitrary in its impact, it works a gross injustice on those caught within its toils. The law that carries such responsibilities should surely be as rational and just as law can be. Nowhere in the entire legal field is more at stake for the community or for the individual. Herbert Wechsler, The Challenge of a Model Penal Code, 65 Harv. L. Rev. 1097, 1087-98 (1952).

What of the course's narrower purpose of training students in the criminal law in particular? Here there are two main pedagogic objectives. One is to furnish a solid foundation for those who will, in greater or lesser degree, participate directly in the processes of the criminal law. This foundation does not require mastery of the full range of technical skills and information held by the practicing criminal lawyer, judge or administrator, but rather the development of confidence in handling principles and rules—judge-made or statutory—through knowledge about the larger implications of the doctrines and institutions of the criminal law. The second purpose is to create in law school graduates, who will have little occasion to practice criminal law, an understanding of the problems of the criminal law. As influential members of their communities—and more directly as judges, legislators, or teachers—lawyers versed in the principles of criminal law can bring an informed intelligence to the challenge of solving some of the most vexing problems of our times. For a fuller discussion of the role of the criminal law course in a law school curriculum, see Sanford H. Kadish, Why Substantive Criminal Law—A Dialogue, 29 Clev. St. L. Rev. 1 (1980).

Revisions for the ninth edition. As mentioned, this edition maintains the organization, intellectual perspectives, and pedagogical tools that have proved successful in previous editions. We reinforced the steps we took in the eighth edition to improve the book's organization and the accessibility of its notes and questions, in order to provide greater clarity and ease of teaching. For example, we have completely reorganized Chapter 7, on group criminality, one of the more difficult topics in criminal law, to aid students' understanding of this material. The chapter begins with accomplice liability, then tackles conspiracy, and concludes with corporate liability, an order we believe will facilitate comprehension and mastery of the material. We similarly reorganized and updated Chapter 5 to include a completely revised section on felony murder, in order to make it more accessible to readers. And throughout the book, we have included more roadmaps to guide students in their reading and to explain what the cases are designed to illustrate.

Beyond these revisions related to the presentation, our main substantive focus throughout the ninth edition has been to emphasize *contemporary* legal issues. In our consideration of *what* to punish, in Chapter 2, we now use bullying and emotional harm to raise questions about the appropriate scope of criminal law. In Chapter 4, on rape, we have added new material to address where the contemporary debates over consent are taking place, and we have added new sections on male rape victims and human trafficking. Chapter 7 has an updated section on corporate criminal liability that includes a new section on sanctioning corporations, including an analysis of deferred prosecution agreements and non-prosecution agreements and a principal case that raises the issue of how to approach sanctioning a company. Chapter 9, on theft, retains the traditional cases but streamlines that material to allow for more consideration of modern theft crimes such as honest services fraud and to include new examples and problems that test students' understanding of traditional theft offenses as applied to modern technology and intellectual property.

We have also included new principal cases and discussion material to reflect *advances in the doctrine*. Chapter 3's look at proportionality includes recent Supreme Court case law, including *Graham*, a new principal case on sentences of life without the possibility of parole for juveniles. Chapter 9's analysis of honest services fraud includes the Supreme Court's treatment of the issue in *Skilling*. Chapter 2 now analyzes the issue of sentence length by using Bernard Madoff's sentencing (replacing the Michael Milken material that previously covered this topic).

This edition also places greater emphasis throughout the book on the latest *empirical* research. Chapter 1 continues to provide an overview of the criminal justice system, with updated statistics on what that system looks like. Chapter 4's materials on rape similarly contain new data on the incidence and prevalence of this offense, including data on the often-overlooked problem of prison rape. Chapter 5's materials on the death penalty provide a wealth of new empirical information, including a more detailed look at the relationship between racial disparities and the death penalty. Chapter 10's analysis of discretion similarly provides up-to-date data on plea bargaining and sentencing.

The ninth edition also continues the eighth edition's efforts to acclimate the students with developments in the field of *international human rights*. We do not seek to examine this complex topic systematically, but we believe it is possible and desirable to give students an introduction to this increasingly significant area through one example (the rape case of *M.C. v. Bulgaria* that was in the eighth edition), along with shorter references elsewhere in the book.

Finally, the ninth edition continues to emphasize the importance of discretion in the criminal justice system. Chapter 10's materials on charging, plea bargaining, and sentencing have been expanded and updated. Because of major changes to sentencing jurisprudence at the federal level, we have included a more recent principal case, *Deegan*, that provides an illustration of the post-*Booker* sentencing regime as well as classic problems in sentencing, such as the tension between individualization and the desire for uniformity. We have added a new case on mandatory minimums and a section on cooperation. We believe this material grounds the study of criminal law in real-world institutions that should not be ignored.

As in previous editions, the substantive materials continue to focus on imparting an understanding of what is often called the general part of the criminal law—that is, those basic principles and doctrines that come into play across the range of specific offenses (for example, actus reus, mens rea, and the various justifications and excuses). We believe that mastery of the detailed elements of many particular crimes is not an appropriate goal for a basic criminal law course. Nevertheless, we have found that an understanding of the basic principles is enhanced by testing their applications and interactions in the context of particular offenses. Accordingly, we examine in detail three offense categories: rape (Chapter 4), homicide (Chapter 5), and theft (Chapter 9). The chapter on rape provides an opportunity to focus on the definitional elements of a major crime in a context that remains the focus of acute controversy because of changing perceptions and changing social values. The theme of the chapter on homicide is the task of legislative grading of punishment in a particularly challenging area. The chapter on theft explores the significance of history and the continued impact of old doctrinal categories on the resolution of thoroughly modern difficulties in defining the boundaries of the criminal law.

Use of the materials in diverse teaching formats. Over the years, law schools have experimented with a variety of formats for the basic criminal law course. Although the year-long five- or six-hour course remains common, some schools offer criminal law as a four- or even three-hour course, and some schedule the course in the first or second semester or even in the second or third years. Under these circumstances, a short book designed to be taught straight through, without adjustments or deletions, is bound to prove unsatisfactory for many users. In preparing the ninth edition, we have sought to edit the materials to avoid significant surplusage for the average course, without preempting all possible judgments about inclusion and exclusion. Rather, we thought it essential to allow for teachers to select topics that accord with their own interests and with the curricular arrangements at their own schools. Thus, we have aspired to create a flexible teaching tool, one that reflects the rich diversity of the subject. For the five- or six-hour, year-long course, the book can be taught straight through, perhaps with some minor deletions. For a four-hour course, and especially in the case of a three-hour course, substantial omissions will be necessary. The Teacher's Manual presents detailed suggestions for appropriate coverage and focus, together with specific suggestions for sequencing and class-by-class assignments.

Collateral Reading. There are a number of useful readings for students interested in pursuing further the questions developed in this casebook. Some of the suggestions that follow may no longer be in print, but they are available in virtually all law libraries.

Comprehensive Works: The following publications should be helpful to the student:

American Law Institute, Model Penal Code and Commentaries (1980-1985). This is a six-volume set containing the text and supporting commentaries of the Model Penal Code. The commentaries constitute the most comprehensive available examination of the American substantive criminal law.

Encyclopedia of Crime and Justice (J. Dressler ed., 2d ed. 2002). This work contains relatively short treatments, written by experts for the general lay reader, on virtually all the subjects covered in this casebook. It should prove particularly helpful for orientation and perspective.

Textbooks: There are several conventional textbooks that are useful for review purposes:

Wayne LaFave, *Criminal Law* (5th ed. 2010). A widely used hornbook; comprehensive and heavily footnoted.

Joshua Dressler, *Understanding Criminal Law* (5th ed. 2009). A shorter textbook, available in paperback; its coverage largely focuses on the subjects covered in this casebook.

Monographs: The following books deal selectively with aspects of the criminal law:

George Fletcher, *Rethinking Criminal Law* (1978). A comparative and theoretical treatment of the criminal law that is critical of dominant thinking in the field. See also Fletcher's more recent *Basic Concepts of Criminal Law* (1998).

H.L.A. Hart, *Punishment and Responsibility* (1968). A collection of powerfully argued essays that have had a great influence on contemporary thinking concerning issues of punishment and excuse.

Sanford H. Kadish, *Blame and Punishment—Essays in the Criminal Law* (1987). Authored by one of the editors of this casebook, a collection of essays, most of which grew out of the experience of teaching prior editions.

Herbert Packer, *The Limits of the Criminal Sanction* (1968). A classic treatment of the problems of criminalization and the theory of punishment.

Style. Citations in the footnotes and text of extracted material have been omitted when they did not seem useful for pedagogical purposes, and we have not used ellipses or other signals to indicate such deletions. Ellipses are used, however, to indicate omitted text material. Where we have retained footnotes in readings and quotations, the original footnote numbers are preserved. Our own footnotes to excerpts and quotations from other works are designated by letters, while footnotes to our own Notes are numbered consecutively throughout each chapter.

Acknowledgements. Half a century has passed since the first edition of *Criminal Law and Its Processes* appeared in 1962. This revision is the first in which Sanford Kadish has not fully participated in the research, writing, editorial judgments, and active collaboration that helped give his creation its extraordinary initial impact and its lasting influence—not only on the teaching of criminal law but as well on the profession's understanding of the law's conceptual structure and practical dynamics. His co-authors, and Stephen Schulhofer especially, have been exceptionally privileged to have had the opportunity to work closely with Sandy over the years, to learn from him, and to pursue with him the education of several generations of law students, many of them now law teachers themselves, and to absorb from Sandy his compelling vision of the essential predicates of a just system of criminal law. Although Sandy has chosen to claim his well-earned right to play a secondary role in the day-to-day details of this revision, his co-authors have benefited in countless ways from his continuing inspiration and guidance. Our acknowledgments therefore begin, first and foremost, with our incalculable debt of gratitude to him.

Sanford Kadish, Stephen Schulhofer, and Carol Steiker feel fortunate that this transition has been aided immeasurably by the valuable contributions of Rachel Barkow, who joins us in this edition as a collaborator. All four of us are grateful for the many thoughts and suggestions we have received from colleagues and users too numerous to acknowledge individually. But we want to express special thanks to several colleagues who have provided particularly extensive comments and suggestions: David Garland, Harry First, James Jacobs, Dan Markel, Erin Murphy, and Alec Walen. In addition, we are particularly grateful to Lara Maraziti for unfailingly helpful and efficient administrative support. For outstanding research assistance, we thank our students: Akari Atoyama, Yotam Barkai, Luke Berg, Zachary Briers, Sean Childers, Christine DiDomenico, Rachel Dizard, Kevin Friedl, Chad Harple, Laura Larsen, Alexander Li, David Lin, Jing-Yi Lu, Evelyn Malave, Michael Marco, David Mesrobian, Karl Mulloney-Radke, Jeff Oakley, Lauren Pedley, Chelsea Rosenthal, Zach Savage, Timothy Shepherd, Elliot Siegel, Cameron Tepfer, Michael Levi Thomas, David Tracey, and Kari Wohlschlegel. For inspiration, Rachel Barkow thanks Nate Barkow. For both intellectual and moral support, above and beyond the call of duty, Stephen Schulhofer thanks Laurie Wohl, Carol Steiker thanks Paul Holtzman, and Sanford Kadish thanks the late June Kadish.

SHK
SJS
CSS
REB

May 2012

Acknowledgments

The authors would like to acknowledge the authors, publishers, and copyright holders of the following publications for permission to reproduce excerpts herein:

Alschuler, Albert W., The Prosecutor's Role in Plea Bargaining, 36 University of Chicago Law Review 50 (1968). Reprinted by permission.

Alschuler, Albert W., The Supreme Court, The Defense Attorney and the Guilty Plea, 47 U. Colo. L. Rev. 1 (1975). Reprinted with permission of the University of Colorado Law Review, and the author.

American Law Institute, Model Penal Code, copyright 1985 by the American Law Institute. Reprinted with permission. All rights reserved.

Armour, Jody D., Race Ipsa Loquitur: Of Reasonable Racists, Intelligent Bayesians, and Involuntary Negrophobes, 46 Stanford Law Review 781 (1994). Copyright © 1994 by the Board of Trustees of the Leland Stanford Jr. University and reprinted with their permission and that of Fred B. Rothman & Co.

Austin, J.L., A Plea for Excuses, 57 Proceedings of the Aristotelian Society (1956-1957). Copyright © 1956 by The Aristotelian Society. Reprinted by courtesy of the editor.

Berger, Joseph, Goetz Case: Commentary on Nature of Urban Life, The New York Times, June 18, 1987. Copyright © 1987 by the New York Times Company. Reprinted by permission.

Bibas, Stephanos, Plea Bargaining Outside the Shadow of Trial, 117 Harv. L. Rev. (2004). Reprinted by permission of the author.

Bowman, Frank O., The Failure of the Federal Sentencing Guidelines: A Structural Analysis, 105 Columbia Law Review (2005). Reprinted by permission of the Columbia Law Review and the author.

Brickey, Kathleen, Rethinking Corporate Liability Under the Model Penal Code, 19 Rutgers Law Journal 593 (1988). Reprinted by permission.

Bryden, David P., Redefining Rape, 3 Buff. Crim. L. Rev. (2000). Reprinted by permission of the Buffalo Criminal Law Review.

Bucy, Pamela H., Corporate Ethos: A Standard for Imposing Corporate Criminal Liability, 75 Minnesota Law Review 1095 (1991). Reprinted by permission.

Butler, Paul, Racially Based Jury Nullification: Black Power in the Criminal Justice System, 105 Yale Law Journal 677 (1995). Reprinted by permission of The Yale Law Journal Company and William S. Hein Company from The Yale Law Journal, Vol. 105, pages 677-725.

Capers, I. Bennett, The Unintentional Rapist, 87 Wash. U. L. Rev. 1345, 1385 (2010).

Carter, Stephen L., When Victims Happen to Be Black, 97 Yale Law Journal 420 (1988). Reprinted by permission.

Chapman, Stephen, Court Upholds America's Right to Hang Out, excerpts from article appearing on June 13, 1999. Copyrighted 6/13/1999, Chicago Tribune Company. All rights reserved. Used with permission.

Coffee, Jr., John C., Hush!: The Criminal Status of Confidential Information After McNally and Carpenter and the Enduring Problem of Overcriminalization, 26 American Criminal Law Review 121 (1988). Reprinted with permission of the publisher, Georgetown University, and American Criminal Law Review. Copyright © 1988.

Coleman, Doriane, Individualizing Justice Through Multiculturalism: The Liberals' Dilemma. This article originally appeared at 96 Columbia Law Review 1093 (1996). Reprinted by permission.

Coughlin, Anne M., Excusing Women, 82 Cal. L. Rev. 1 (1994) © 1994 by the California Law Review, Inc. Reprinted from 82 Cal. L. Rev. 1 (1994) by permission of the California Law Review.

Dan-Cohen, Meir, Actus Reus. From Dressler (editor). Encyclopedia of Crime & Justice, 2E. © 2001 Gale, a part of Cengage Learning, Inc. Reproduced by permission. www.cengage.com/permissions.

Delgado, Richard, "Rotten Social Background": Should the Criminal Law Recognize a Defense of Severe Environmental Deprivation?, 3 Law and Inequality 9 (1985). Reprinted by permission.

Dilulio, Jr., John, Prisons Are a Bargain by Any Measure, excerpts from an article appearing January 16, 1996. Copyright © 1996 by The New York Times Company. Reprinted by permission.

Donohue, John J. & Peter Seligman, Allocating Resources Among Prisons and Social Programs in the Battle Against Crime, 27 J. Legal Stud. 1 (1998). Copyright © 1998 by The University of Chicago. All rights reserved.

Durkheim, Emile, The Division of Labor in Society (W.D. Halls translator, 1984). Copyright © 1984 by the Higher & Further Education Division of Macmillan Publishers, Ltd. Reprinted with permission.

Dworkin, G. & G. Blumenfeld, Punishments for Intentions, 75 Mind 396 (1966). Copyright © 1966 by Oxford University Press. Reprinted with permission of Oxford University Press.

Estrich, Susan R., Defending Women, 88 Michigan Law Review 1430 (1990). Reprinted by permission.

Ferzan, Kimberly Kessler, Defending Imminence: From Battered Women to Iraq, 46 Ariz. L. Rev. 213, 255-256, 260-262 (2004).

Fischel, Daniel R. & Alan O. Sykes, Civil RICO After Reves: An Economic Commentary, [1993] Supreme Court Review 157. Copyright © 1995 by The University of Chicago. All Rights Reserved. Reprinted by permission.

Fletcher, George P., Reflections on Felony-Murder, 12 Southwestern University Law Review 413 (1981). Reprinted by permission.

Fletcher, George P., Rethinking Criminal Law (1978). Copyright © 1978 by George P. Fletcher. Reprinted by permission of Aspen Law and Business Publishers and the author.

Frankel, Marvin, excerpts from Criminal Sentences: Law Without Order (1973). Copyright © 1972, 1973 by Marvin E. Frankel. Reprinted by permission of Hill & Wang, a division of Farrar, Straus & Giroux.

Gordon, Margaret T. and Stephanie Riger, The Female Fear: The Social Cost of Rape (1991). Reprinted with the permission of The Free Press, a division of Simon & Schuster, Inc. Copyright © 1989 by Margaret T. Gordon and Stephanie Riger.

Harcourt, Bernard, The Collapse of the Harm Principle, 90 Journal of Criminal Law and Criminology 109 (1999). Reprinted by special permission of Northwestern University School of Law, Journal of Criminal Law and Criminology.

Hart, H.L.A., Law, Liberty and Morality (1963). Reprinted by permission of Stanford University Press.

Hart, H.L.A., The Morality of the Criminal Law 52-53 (1965). Reprinted by permission of Oxford University Press.

Hart, H.L.A., Punishment and Responsibility 235 (1968). Reprinted by permission of Oxford University Press.

Hart, H. L. A. & A. Honoré, Causation in the Law (2d ed. 1985). Reprinted by permission of Oxford University Press.

Henriques, Diana B. and Jack Healy, Madoff Goes to Jail After Guilty Pleas, N.Y. Times, March 13, 2009.

Hughes, Graham, Criminal Responsibility, 16 Stanford Law Review 470 (1964). Copyright © 1964 by the Board of Trustees of the Leland Stanford, Jr. University and reprinted with their permission and that of Fred B. Rothman & Co.

Jeffries, John Calvin, Jr. & Paul B. Stephan, Defenses, Presumptions and Burdens of Proof in the Criminal Law, 88 Yale Law Journal 1325 (1979). Reprinted by permission of The Yale Law Journal Company and William S. Hein Company from The Yale Law Journal, Volume 88, pages 1325-1347.

Johnson, Phillip E., Strict Liability: The Prevalent View. From Dressler (editor). Encyclopedia of Crime & Justice, 2E. © 2001 Gale, a part of Cengage Learning, Inc. Reproduced by permission. www.cengage.com/permissions.

Johnson, Phillip E., The Unnecessary Crime of Conspiracy, 61 California Law Review 1137 (1973). Copyright © 1973 by the California Law Review, Inc. Reprinted from 61 Cal. L. Rev. 1137 (1973) by permission of the California Law Review.

Kadish, Sanford H., The Crisis of Overcriminalization, 374 Annals 157 (1967). Reprinted by permission of The American Academy of Political and Social Science.

Kadish, Sanford H., Excusing Crime, 75 Cal. L. Rev. 257, 263-265 (1987). Copyright © 1987 by the California Law Review, Inc. Reprinted from 75 Cal. L. Rev. 257 (1987) by permission of the California Law Review.

Kadish, Sanford H., A Theory of Complicity, in Issues in Contemporary Legal Philosophy, The Influence of H.L.A. Hart (R. Gavison ed. 1987). Copyright © 1987 Oxford University Press. Reprinted by permission of Oxford University Press.

Kalven, Harry & Hans Zeisel, The American Jury (1966). Reprinted by permission of Aspen Law & Business.

Katyal, Neal Kumar, Conspiracy Theory, 112 Yale Law Journal 1307 (2003). Reprinted by permission of The Yale Law Journal Company.

Kelman, Mark, Strict Liability: An Unorthodox View. From Dressler (editor). Encyclopedia of Crime & Justice, 2E. © 2001 Gale, a part of Cengage Learning, Inc. Reproduced by permission. www.cengage.com/permissions.

Kennedy, Randall L., Race, Crime and the Law (1997). Copyright © 1997 by Randall Kennedy. Used by permission of Pantheon Books, a Division of Random House, Inc.

Kiesel, D., Who Saw This Happen?—States Move to Make Crime Bystanders Responsible, 69 American Bar Association Journal 1208 (1983). Reprinted with permission from the ABA Journal. Copyright © 2012, ABA Journal. All rights reserved.

Kleinig, John, Good Samaritanism, Philosophy & Public Affairs 5, No. 4 (Summer 1976). Reprinted with permission of Blackwell Publishing (UK).

Lewis, Anthony, "Whisper Who Dares," excerpts from an article appearing in the New York Times (June 19, 1978). Copyright © 1978 by The New York Times Company. Reprinted by permission.

Lindgren, James, Unraveling the Paradox of Blackmail, 84 Colum. L. Rev. 670 (1984). This article originally appeared at 84 Columbia Law Review 670 (1984). Reprinted by permission.

Luban, David, Contrived Ignorance, 87 Georgetown Law Review 957 (1999). Reprinted with permission of the publisher, Georgetown University and Georgetown Law Journal. Copyright © 1999.

Lynch, David, The Impropriety of Plea Agreements: A Tale of Two Counties, 19 L. & Soc. Inquiry (1994). Reprinted with permission of Blackwell Publishers, UK.

Lynch, Gerard E., Our Administrative System of Criminal Justice, 66 Fordham L. Rev. (1998).

Lynch, Gerard E., RICO: The Crime of Being a Criminal, 661, 920, 932-955, 967-970, and Parts I & II, 87 Colum. L. Rev. 920 (1987). This article originally appeared at 87 Columbia Law Review 661 (1987). Reprinted by permission.

Mackie, J. L., Retributivism: A Test Case for Ethical Objectivity. Published by permission of Mrs. Joan Mackie. All rights to further publication reserved.

McCord, David & Sandra Lyons, Moral Reasoning and the Criminal Law: The Example of Self Defense, 30 American Criminal Law Review 97 (1992). Reprinted with permission of the publisher, Georgetown University and American Criminal Law Review. Copyright © 1992.

Michael, Jerome & Herbert Wechsler, A Rationale of the Law of Homicide, 37 Colum. L. Rev. 1261, 1281-1282 (1937).

Milhizer, Eugene R., Justification and Excuse: What They Were, What They Are, and What They Ought to Be, 78 St. John's L. Rev. 725, 816-818 (2004).

Moore, Michael S., Law and Psychiatry: Rethinking the Relationship (1984). Copyright © 1984 by Cambridge University Press. Reprinted with the permission of Cambridge University Press.

Moore, Michael, excerpts from The Moral Worth of Retributivism, in Responsibility, Character and Emotions 179 (F. Schoeman ed., 1987). Copyright © 1987 by Cambridge University Press. Reprinted by permission.

Morris, Herbert, On Guilt and Innocence (1976). Copyright © 1976 by The Regents of the University of California. Reprinted by permission of author.

Morris, Norval R., Somnambulistic Homicide: Ghosts, Spiders and North Koreans, 5 Res Judicatae 29 (1951). Reprinted by permission of the publisher.

Morse, Stephen J., Undiminished Confusion in Diminished Capacity, 75 Journal of Criminal Law and Criminology 1 (1984). Reprinted by special permission of Northwestern University School of Law, Journal of Criminal Law and Criminology and the author.

Murphy, Jeffrie, Marxism and Retribution, 2 Philosophy & Public Affairs 217 (Spring 1973). Copyright © 1973 Princeton University Press. Reprinted by permission of Princeton University Press.

Note, A Rationale of the Law Aggravated Theft, 54 Colum. L. Rev. 84 (1954). This article originally appeared at 54 Columbia Law Review 84 (1954). Reprinted by permission.

Note, Developments in the Law—Corporate Crime: Regulating Corporate Behavior Through Criminal Sanction, 92 Harvard L. Rev. 1227 (1979). Copyright © 1979 by the Harvard Law Review Association. Reprinted by permission.

Pillsbury, Samuel, Crimes of Indifference, 49 Rutgers Law Review 105 (1996). Reprinted by permission.

Restak, Richard, The Fiction of the "Reasonable Man," Washington Post, May 17, 1987. Reprinted by permission of the author.

Robertson, John, Respect for Life in Bioethical Dilemmas, 45 Cleveland State Law Review 329 (1997). Reprinted by permission.

Robinson, Paul H. & John Darley, The Utility of Desert, 91 NW. U. L. Rev. Reprinted by special permission of Northwestern University School of Law, Law Review, and the author. Copyright © Paul H. Robinson.

S.F. Chronicle, "A Man Who Withdrew $43,000 Mistakenly Credited to His Bank Account and Refused to Give It Back," Nov. 14, 1964, at 4.

Schulhofer, Stephen J., The Gender Question in Criminal Law, 7 Social Philosophy and Public Policy 105 (1990). © Social Philosophy & Policy 1990. Reprinted with permission of Blackwell Publishers.

Schulhofer, Stephen J., Unwanted Sex: The Culture of Intimidation and the Failure of the Law, by Stephen J. Schulhofer, pp. 91-93, 121-124, 163-164, Cambridge, Mass.: Harvard University Press, Copyright 1998 by the president and Fellows of Harvard College.

Sentelle, David D., RICO: The Monster That Ate Jurisprudence, pp. 5-13 of the Lecture to the CATO Institute, Oct. 18, 1989. Reprinted by permission.

Simons, Kenneth W., When Is Strict Criminal Liability Just?, 87 J. Crim. L. & Criminology 1075, 1121-1125 (1997). Reprinted by special permission of Northwestern University School of Law, The Journal of Criminal Law and Criminology.

Steiker, Carol S., Jordan M. Steiker, Sober Second Thoughts: Reflections on Two Decades of Constitutional Regulation of Capital Punishment, 109 Harvard Law Review 355 (1995). Reprinted by permission.

Stone, Alan A., Law, Psychiatry and Morality (1984). Reprinted by permission of the author and the American Psychiatric Press, Inc.

Tebo, Margaret, Guilty By Reason of Title, 70 American Bar Association Journal 44 (May 2000). Reprinted with permission from the 1983 issue of ABA Journal. Copyright 2012, ABA Journal. All rights reserved.

Thomas, Clarence, Crime and Punishment—and Personal Responsibility. Reprinted with permission.

Tomkovicz, James, The Endurance of the Felony-Murder Rule: A Study of the Forces That Shape Our Criminal Law, 51 Washington & Lee Law Review 1429 (1994). Reprinted by permission.

Vitiello, Michael, Reconsidering Rehabilitation, originally published in 65 Tul. L. Rev. 1011 (1991). Reprinted with the permission of the Tulane Law Review Association, which holds the copyright.

Von Hirsch, Andrew & Andrew Ashworth, Proportionate Sentencing: Exploring the Principles 132-135 (2005). Reprinted by permission of Oxford University Press.

Von Hirsch, Andrew, & Lisa Maher, Should Penal Rehabilitationism Be Revived, Criminal Justice Ethics, Vol. 11, No. 1 (Winter/Spring 1992), pages 25-30. Reprinted by permission of The Institute for Criminal Justice Ethics, 555 West 57th Street, Suite 601, New York, NY 10019-1029.

Wheeler, Stanton, "Adversarial Biography: Reflections on the Sentencing of Michael Milken," 3 Fed. Sent. Rev. 167 (1990).

Whitman, James Q., What Is Wrong with Inflicting Shame Sanctions?, 107 Yale Law Journal 1055 (1998). Reprinted by permission of The Yale Law Journal Company.

Williams, Glanville, Criminal Law: The General Part (2d ed. 1961). Reprinted by permission of Sweet & Maxwell Ltd.

Williams, Glanville, Finis for Novus Actus, 48 Cambridge Law Journal 391 (1989). Reprinted by permission of Cambridge University Press.

Williams, Glanville, The Mental Element in Crime (1965). Copyright © The Magnes Press. Reprinted by permission.

Williams, Glanville, The Unresolved Problem of Recklessness, 8 Legal Studies 74 (1988). Copyright Society of Public Teachers of Law. Reprinted by permission.

Wright, Richard A., Prisons: Prisoners. From Dressler (editor). Encyclopedia of Crime & Justice, 2E. Copyright © 2001 Gale, a part of Cengage Learning, Inc. Reproduced by permission. www.cengage.com/permissions.

Yeager, Daniel B., A Radical Community of Aid: A Rejoinder to Opponents of Affirmative Duties to Help Strangers, 71 Washington University Law Quarterly 1 (1993). Reprinted with permission.

CRIMINAL LAW AND ITS PROCESSES

CASES AND MATERIALS

chapter 1

Institutions and Processes

A. THE STRUCTURE OF THE CRIMINAL JUSTICE SYSTEM

NOTES[1]

1. A general view. The criminal justice system is society's primary mechanism for enforcing standards of conduct designed to protect the safety and security of individuals and the community. Yet to speak of a criminal justice "system" is something of a misnomer. To be sure, the various agencies and institutions of criminal justice are highly interdependent, and efforts to address problems in one of them are likely to fail if they do not take into account the repercussions of reform on all the others. But the agencies of criminal justice are not part of a single, coherent organization. Their relationships with one another often are haphazard and uncoordinated.

Police, prosecutors, courts, and correctional agencies inevitably interact. The results of police effort—suspects arrested—are passed on to prosecutors for the filing of charges, those charged move into the judicial system for adjudication, and those convicted and sentenced become the responsibility of the probation services, jails, and prisons. Yet each of these steps in the process is managed by an official who is, to a considerable degree, independent of the others, and the officials are responsible to different groups of constituents. There are some 40,000 independent police departments in the country, roughly one for every city and town in the nation. The chief of police is typically appointed by a mayor, who in turn is elected by the voters of the *municipality*. But the chief prosecutor typically is not appointed by or responsible to the mayor. The prosecutor is usually an independent elected official; she may or may not represent the same political party as the mayor. Either

---

1. Except as otherwise noted, the material in these Notes is drawn from U.S. Dept. of Justice, Bureau of Justice Statistics, Sourcebook of Criminal Justice Statistics, http://www.albany.edu/sourcebook/; id., Crime in the United States—2009 (2010); and President's Commission on Law Enforcement and the Administration of Justice, The Challenge of Crime in a Free Society 7-12, 91-107, 127-137, 141-150 (1967).

way, she may be a political rival, and in most instances, she is elected by the voters of the *county*, a constituency that may be larger (as in the Chicago area) or smaller (as in New York City) than the constituency that elects the mayor. Judges are often elected on a countywide basis, but sometimes they are appointed by the governor of the *state*. The agencies responsible for punishment and corrections are similarly fractured. Probation services and jails are typically run and paid for by the county, but prisons and parole systems are run and paid for by the state.

In practice, criminal justice authority is even more dispersed and decentralized than this oversimplified picture suggests. State governments have their own police forces (state troopers), many cities have independent police agencies with specialized missions (transit police, housing police), and most cities and states have independent prosecuting authorities with specialized mandates (a city department for municipal code enforcement, a state attorney general's office).

Alongside all of this, and entirely independent of it, is the powerful engine of *federal* law enforcement. The federal process (again, it would be an exaggeration to call it a "system") has its own complement of prosecutors (U.S. Attorneys appointed by the President and centrally supervised, to a degree, by the Department of Justice), independent judges (appointed for life terms by the President, on the advice and consent of the Senate), and correctional authorities (the U.S. Probation Service, responsible to the courts, and the Federal Bureau of Prisons, within the Department of Justice). For its police force, the federal government of course has the FBI, responsible to the Department of Justice, but that is not all: Also of great importance are the Drug Enforcement Administration (DEA), also in the Department of Justice; the Bureau of Alcohol, Tobacco and Firearms (ATF) in the Treasury Department; the bureaus of Customs and Border Protection (CBP) and Immigration and Customs Enforcement (ICE) in the Department of Homeland Security; and the Enforcement Division of the Securities and Exchange Commission (SEC) for certain white-collar offenses—to name only a few.

The criminal justice system, in short, is extremely *decentralized*. Many view the uncoordinated, overlapping, and conflicting responsibilities of its various agencies as inefficient and even irrational. Others view the same chaotic arrangement as a valuable mechanism for preventing the accumulation and centralization of power, with its accompanying dangers of abuse. Either way, extreme decentralization is and will remain a dominant fact of life in American criminal justice. As a Presidential Commission stated in 1967:[2]

> What most significantly distinguishes the system of one country from that of another is the extent and the form of the protections it offers individuals in the process of determining guilt and imposing punishment. Our system of justice deliberately sacrifices much in efficiency and even in effectiveness in order to preserve local autonomy and to protect the individual.

---

2. President's Commission, supra note 1, at 12.

Three other features of American criminal justice deserve particular mention. First, the agencies of criminal justice must deal with what is, by any measure, a *high volume of cases*. As a result, although the mission of the criminal process is to deliver carefully individualized justice, in practice "the process is in fact one of mass production."[3] Second, the agencies of criminal justice face a *chronic shortage of resources and personnel*. The interaction of these two factors, heavy volume and restricted resources, multiplies the pressures for a mass-production approach and mandates a high degree of selectivity in choosing the individuals who will be arrested, charged, convicted, and sentenced at the highest available levels.

Finally, that selection process operates through the exercise of broad, largely unguided and largely uncontrolled *discretion*. Within police departments, decisions about what crimes to target and which individuals to arrest are often left to the personal judgment of the police officer on the beat. Within the prosecutor's office, charging decisions are often left to the personal judgment of the assistant district attorney assigned to the case, subject to guidance and review that is extensive in some offices but virtually nonexistent in others. The result can be wide variation in the criminal justice treatment of similarly situated offenders and outcomes determined by many considerations extraneous to the formal criteria of the law on the books. We examine the phenomenon of discretion in some detail in Chapter 10, infra.

2. The police. To an important extent, crimes are defined, in practice, by the police officer on the beat. Because officers cannot possibly arrest all the offenders they encounter, they must decide which scuffles warrant an arrest for assault. They must decide when a juvenile responsible for vandalism should be arrested rather than merely warned or taken home to his parents. Sometimes the police chief or precinct captain sets guidelines. More often, the decision is made ad hoc by the individual officer. It may or may not be the same as the decisions made in similar circumstances by other officers or even by the same officer at other times.

3. Prosecutors. The decision whether there is sufficient evidence to send a case to trial is initially made by the prosecutor. Although that judgment must be approved by a judge at a preliminary hearing or by a grand jury, these steps are largely formalities, because the level of proof required at those stages is low. The grand jury and the preliminary-hearing judge almost always ratify the prosecutor's decision. As a result, the prosecutor wields enormous power, deciding whether to press or drop a case, whether to file the highest possible charges or something less, and whether to reduce the charges after they are filed.

Yet many prosecutors serve only part-time, while conducting a private law practice on the side. And whether full-time or part-time, prosecutors generally are elected on a partisan political basis and serve for relatively short terms.

---

3. Geoffrey C. Hazard, Jr., Criminal Justice System: Overview, in 2 Encyclopedia of Crime and Justice 450, 454 (S.H. Kadish ed., 1983).

Often the position serves as a stepping-stone to higher political office. Only the federal government and four states (Alaska, Connecticut, Delaware, and New Jersey) choose their chief prosecutors by appointment. The system of choosing chief prosecutors by popular election (rather than by professional training and advancement) is a distinctively American practice, virtually unknown elsewhere in the world.

Large cities always have a chief prosecutor employed full-time and a large staff of full-time assistants, but 25 percent of American jurisdictions do not have a full-time chief prosecutor, and 30 percent of the chief prosecutors have no full-time assistant prosecutors.[4]

4. Defense counsel. Only about 20 percent of criminal defendants have the means to hire their own lawyers, so the kind of defense representation commonly seen in civil litigation is the exception on the criminal side. Five distinct criminal-defense systems are in use—two for defendants who can afford to retain counsel and three for those who cannot.

(a) Non-indigent defendants. In the approach most analogous to representation in major tort and contract suits, a defendant of substantial means retains a highly experienced attorney (or team of attorneys), agreeing to compensate them on an hourly basis or paying up front a substantial retainer (often in the range of $100,000 or more). This approach is often used in white-collar and political-corruption cases, but overall it is the rare exception, even for the minority of defendants who can afford to retain counsel at all.

Far more common for these non-indigent defendants is a second system, in which a person with limited financial resources retains an attorney by paying in advance a modest fee (a few hundred or a few thousand dollars) that will constitute the lawyer's sole compensation. Because rules of court typically prevent a retained attorney from withdrawing from a case once an appearance is entered, the lawyer's compensation under this approach remains identical, regardless of whether the defendant quickly accepts a guilty plea offer, prefers to negotiate at length, or seeks to present an elaborate defense at trial. Attorneys who defend cases under this arrangement must manage their ethical obligation to provide vigorous representation along with their personal need to avoid strategies that require large amounts of uncompensated time.

(b) Indigent defendants. All three systems in common use for indigent defendants share one common characteristic: All of them deny the defendant any say in choosing his or her counsel. Under each system a judge, court administrator, or some other official makes the choice, and the indigent defendant must either accept the lawyer who has been selected or agree to proceed without professional assistance.[5] One common approach is the

---

4. See U.S. Dept. of Justice, Bureau of Justice Statistics, Prosecutors in State Courts, 2005 (June 2006), p. 2.

5. See Stephen J. Schulhofer & David Friedman, Rethinking Indigent Defense: Promoting Effective Representation through Consumer Sovereignty and Freedom of Choice for all Criminal Defendants, 31 Am. Crim. L. Rev. 73 (1993).

appointed counsel system: A judge or court official selects defense counsel from a list of attorneys in private practice. The system of conscripting these lawyers to serve "pro bono," without compensation, still exists in a few jurisdictions but is now rare. Instead, appointed attorneys typically are compensated at a fixed hourly rate up to a predetermined maximum. The maximum usually is higher for felonies than for misdemeanors, but it usually is not higher for complex cases that go to trial than for simple cases that plead out quickly. In a second approach, the *contract system*, a lawyer or group of lawyers in private practice agree that over the course of a year, in return for a substantial retainer paid by the government, they will represent a specified number of indigent criminal defendants along with their own paying clients. Again, the attorney's compensation for the indigent defense side of her work remains independent of the time and effort spent on the representation. Finally, in the *defender system*, often used in the larger cities, an agency funded by the city, county, or state (sometimes with partial support from private sources) represents most or all criminal defendants in the jurisdiction. Its staff attorneys are paid an annual salary and usually serve full-time. As a result, they are not under personal financial pressure to control the time spent on individual cases, and many defender offices are organized to permit a team of attorneys, social workers, and investigators to work intensively on felony jury trials and other high-stakes cases. Many defender offices, however, are characterized by high caseloads and strong pressures for staff attorneys to budget their time carefully.

   5. *Judges.* The mechanism for selecting judges varies from jurisdiction to jurisdiction, and some states use different methods of selection for appellate judges than for lower court judges. In 21 states, judges are chosen by popular election. In 29 states, judges are initially appointed either by the governor or the legislature, but in some of these states they must run for election after serving their first term. Thus, in the great majority of states, judges must stand for election at some point. In some states a nonpartisan screening committee identifies well-qualified candidates, but that safeguard of competence and quality is not in widespread use, nor is it always effective in jurisdictions where it exists. Political party influence and, more recently, expensive television advertising are widely used in the effort to achieve electoral success. Among Western democracies, the United States is virtually unique in selecting its judges predominantly by popular election.[6]

   Congestion, delay, and hasty decisions when a case is finally ready for disposition are especially common in the lower criminal courts where misdemeanors and "petty offenses" are handled. These courts process the overwhelming majority of offenses and offenders, yet they are chronically understaffed. In many jurisdictions, judges in the lower courts must handle a hundred cases or more in a single day. Observers report that speed becomes more important than care, and casual out-of-court bargains are often

---

6. See Craig M. Bradley, Criminal Procedure: A Worldwide Study (2d ed. 2007).

substituted for adjudication.[7] In 2008, American courts achieved an average of 991 criminal case dispositions per judge. Federal judges have, on average, only 115 criminal cases per year, but the average number of felony case filings per judge in a single year (1995) was 487 in Los Angeles, 516 in San Francisco, and 776 in Denver.

6. Corrections. Although it remains customary to identify the agency responsible for a state's prison system as the "Department of Corrections," incarceration no longer aims primarily to "correct" (i.e., rehabilitate) offenders. Punishment itself and incapacitation have become the system's principal purposes. There are now more than 2.1 million prisoners in federal and state custody at any given time, and these account for only 30 percent of the offenders under supervision; more than 4.8 million offenders are on probation or parole.

The population subject to criminal justice supervision has grown at a striking rate, and each year new records are set. At year-end 2009, 1 of every 32 American adults was subject to some form of criminal justice system control, including over 4.2 million offenders on probation (a 37 percent increase since 1995) and 819,000 offenders on parole (a 21 percent increase since 1995).

The growth in incarceration has been especially dramatic. At year-end 2009, there were over 1.5 million offenders in state or federal prisons (a 41 percent increase since 1995) and 760,000 inmates in local jails (a 50 percent increase since 1995). Compared to the figures for 1980, there have been increases of 272 percent in parole, 276 percent in probation, 317 percent in jail populations, and 377 percent in prison populations. The United States now imprisons more people per capita than any industrialized country, including Russia.[8] Some observers believe that America's high rate of imprisonment is a consequence of our greater volume of serious crime and the more extensive reach of our criminal law; others argue that the phenomenon is primarily a result of the prevalence of increasingly high arrest rates, more punitive attitudes in American culture, and more aggressive policies in the enforcement of our drug laws.[9]

Increases in incarceration were especially steep during the 1980s and early 1990s; the rate of increase in the correctional population has slowed in the past decade. Nonetheless, the trend has been steadily in the upward direction, despite the fact that crime rates have not increased substantially since the 1970s. The rate of violent crime remained roughly constant during the 1980s, while the rate of property crime actually declined; crime rates for both types of offenses then declined steeply throughout the 1990s and

---

7. For a vivid account, see Steve Bogira, Courtroom 302 (2005).

8. See The Sentencing Project, New Incarceration Figures: Growth in Population Continues (2006), p. 1.

9. See John Pfaff, The Empirics of Prison Growth: A Critical Review and Path Forward, 98 J. Crim. L. & Criminology 547 (2008); James P. Lynch, A Comparison of Prison Use in England, Canada, and West Germany, 79 J. Crim. L. & Criminology, 180 (1999).

stabilized in the early 2000s at "the lowest levels recorded since the [Justice Department] survey's inception in 1973."[10]

Women are incarcerated at a far lower rate than are men. At year-end 2009, there were 68 female prison inmates per 100,000 women in the United States, compared to approximately 954 male prison inmates per 100,000 males in the United States.

The precipitous growth of the corrections system has had a particularly severe impact on young black males. Studies in the District of Columbia suggest that at any one time, 42 percent of the city's black males aged 18 to 35 are subject to some form of criminal justice system control (incarceration, probation, parole, or bond for release pending disposition of criminal charges).[11] For Baltimore, the corresponding figure is 56 percent.[12] For an inner-city black male, the lifetime risk of arrest and incarceration may approach 90 percent.[13] Nationally, nearly one in three African-American males aged 20-29 is under some form of criminal justice supervision.[14] In the age group 25-29, one in ten black males was in prison or jail in 2009, and in that year black males had a 32 percent chance of serving time in prison at some point in their lives.[15] Much of the recent increase in these numbers appears to be attributable to patterns of enforcement in the "war on drugs,"[16] and to the persistence of disturbing evidence that "African Americans and Hispanics routinely receive . . . harsher sentences than whites for crimes of equivalent severity."[17]

One result of the emphasis on incapacitation is that there is little interest in, or resources for, creative programs to treat or educate offenders. This is true not only of prison inmates but also of offenders on probation and parole. While probationers and parolees need varying degrees of assistance and supervision, most experts agree that an average of no more than 35 cases per officer is necessary to give convicted offenders sufficient attention and support. Yet

---

10. U.S. Dept. of Justice, Bureau of Justice Statistics, Criminal Victimization—2004 (Sept. 2005), p. 1. Preliminary data for 2005 suggest a possible shift in this trend. Although the crime rate for property offenses continued to decline, dropping by 1.6 percent, the crime rate for violent offenses rose by 2.5 percent in 2005. FBI, Preliminary Annual Uniform Crime Report—2005 (June 12, 2006).

11. See Jerome G. Miller, Hobbling a Generation: Young African American Males in D.C.'s Criminal Justice System (Natl. Center on Institutions & Alternatives 1992); Mark Mauer, Young Black Men and the Criminal Justice System: A Growing National Problem 8 (The Sentencing Project 1990).

12. Jerome G. Miller, Hobbling a Generation: Young African American Males in the Criminal Justice System of America's Cities: Baltimore, Maryland (Natl. Center on Institutions & Alternatives 1992).

13. Miller, supra, footnote 12.

14. Young Black Americans and the Criminal Justice System: Five Years Later (The Sentencing Project, 1995), available at http://www.sentencingproject.org/pdfs/9070smy.pdf.

15. See http://sentencingproject.org/doc/publications/publications/inc_factsAboutPrisons_Dec 2010.pdf.

16. See, e.g., Michael Tonry, Malign Neglect (1995); Joseph E. Kennedy, Drug Wars in Black and White, 66 Law & Contemp. Probs. 153 (2003).

17. Sharon L. Davies, Study Habits: Probing Modern Attempts to Assess Minority Offender Disproportionality, 66 Law & Contemp. Probs. 17, 29 (2003).

probation supervision caseloads now average about 117 offenders per officer.[18]

In addition to these obstacles to successful rehabilitation, convicted offenders typically encounter difficulty obtaining housing and lawful employment when they re-enter free society. Even if charges do not lead to imprisonment, the encounter with the criminal justice system can have devastating consequences. This problem has always existed to some extent, but it is becoming increasingly common and severe, because statutory restrictions on obtaining occupational licenses, educational assistance, and other public benefits and necessities have proliferated. Criminologists find, moreover, that "[t]he ubiquity of criminal-background checks and the efficiency of information technology . . . have meant that millions of Americans—even those who served probation or parole but were never incarcerated—continue to pay a price long after the crime." Alfred Blumstein & Kiminori Nakamura, Paying a Price, Long After the Crime, N.Y. Times, Jan. 9, 2012. And these collateral consequences of conviction have a disproportionate and especially severe impact on offenders of color. See Michael Pinard, Collateral Consequences of Criminal Convictions: Confronting Issues of Race and Dignity, 85 N.Y.U. L. Rev. 457 (2010).

B. CRIMINAL JUSTICE PROCEDURES

NOTES

1. Overview. A common impression of the criminal justice process is that when a crime is committed, a policeman finds the perpetrator, if he can, arrests him, and brings him promptly before a magistrate. If the offense is minor, the magistrate disposes of it on the spot. If the offense is serious, the magistrate retains the case for further action and releases the defendant on bail. Next, again according to the theory, the file goes to a prosecutor, who charges the defendant with a specific offense. The charge is reviewed at a preliminary hearing, where a judge determines whether there is a prima facie case sufficient to hold the defendant for trial, and in some jurisdictions, if the offense is a felony, the charges must be presented to a grand jury, which determines whether to issue an indictment. If the defendant pleads "not guilty," the case goes to trial, and witnesses called by the opposing attorneys describe the facts to a jury. If the jury finds the defendant guilty, the judge sentences him to probation, jail (a local facility for sentences under one year), or prison (for offenders serving longer terms).

---

18. See U.S. Dept. of Justice, Bureau of Justice Statistics, Characteristics of State Parole Supervising Agencies, 2006 (Aug. 2008), p. 1; Joan Petersilia, Community Corrections: Probation, Parole, and Prisoner Reentry, in Crime and Public Policy (James Q. Wilson & Joan Petersilia eds., 2011).

Some cases do proceed in that fashion, especially when they involve acts of violence or thefts of large amounts of money. But not all major cases follow this route. And in any event, the great majority of criminal offenses are far less serious—petty thefts, disorderly conduct, simple assaults, and the like. These relatively minor cases and many of the more serious ones are disposed of in informal and sometimes haphazard fashion.

2. *The initial stages of a case. (a) Investigation.* Unless an arrest has been made at the scene, police must attempt to identify the perpetrator, and in all cases they must assemble sufficient evidence to prove guilt beyond a reasonable doubt. Most large police departments have a corps of detectives who question victims, suspects, and witnesses; seek physical evidence at the crime scene; and undertake other investigative work. Often, however, the crime simply is not solvable. In most cases, personal identification by a victim or witness is the only clue to the perpetrator's identity. FBI statistics for 2009 indicate that of the violent crimes (murder, aggravated assault, forcible rape, and robbery) reported or otherwise known to the police, 47 percent were cleared by an arrest. Of the serious property crimes (burglary, motor vehicle theft, and other larceny-theft), only 19 percent of offenses known to the police were cleared by an arrest. For cities with a population over 1 million, only 39 percent of violent offenses and 13 percent of serious property offenses were cleared.

(b) Dismissal and diversion. In roughly half of the cases initiated by an arrest, the case is eventually dismissed at an early stage, either by the police, a prosecutor, or a magistrate. Some suspects avoid prosecution because they are not guilty, or cannot be proved guilty, either because they did not commit the acts in question or because they have a legally acceptable explanation for committing them. Often, however, offenders who could be convicted are released simply because police or prosecutors are too busy to pursue their cases. In other instances, police or prosecutors decline to proceed because an offender appears to have mental, emotional, or social problems that can be better dealt with by official agencies, private organizations, or individuals outside the criminal justice process. First offenders are often dealt with in this way, as are those who commit minor offenses such as shoplifting (if restitution has been made), statutory rape (when both parties are young), and automobile theft (when committed by teenagers solely for the purpose of joyriding).

In many jurisdictions, these dismissals sometimes have a more formal character. The defendant may be placed in a "pretrial diversion" program that requires him to meet certain conditions (such as attending a drug or alcohol treatment program or an anger management class) and to avoid rearrest for a designated period, usually a year. Defendants who complete such a program successfully then qualify to have all charges formally dismissed; those who fail the program have their cases reopened.

(c) Pretrial release. Most arrestees brought into a magistrate's court are released (or convicted and sentenced) within 24 hours of their arrest. The

remainder may wait weeks or months for the disposition of their cases, depending on the prosecutor's workload, the complexity of the case, and the calendar of the judge assigned to hear it. Usually, the magistrate who conducts this initial proceeding decides whether to release the defendants pending further proceedings. Traditionally, the device most often used to free an untried defendant and at the same time assure his or her appearance for trial was money bail. In this system, still in use in many areas, the court fixes the amount of a bond to be posted in cash or by a secured pledge; defendants able to post the required amount win their release and recover the sum upon appearance for trial. Defendants unable to raise the required amount usually attempt to secure the services of a bail-bond agency, which posts the necessary bond in return for a fixed fee, typically 10 percent of the total bail. In this system the bondsman's obligations are satisfied upon the defendant's appearance, but the 10 percent charge has to be paid by the defendant in any event.

The money bail system is unsatisfactory in many respects. It results in confinement of large numbers of untried defendants, solely on account of inability to raise the required amounts. And in many localities, the relationships between bail-bond agencies and court officials have been a source of malfeasance and corruption.

During the 1960s and 1970s, bail-reform projects were initiated in numerous cities around the country. The principal aims of these projects were to ascertain the kinds of community ties that would make defendants safe candidates for release without financial guarantees, to establish procedures for expeditiously collecting the information necessary to identify these defendants, and to develop a better system of financial guarantees for defendants who could not qualify for release on any other basis. Pretrial release projects are now operational in more than 100 cities. They help the local magistrates to identify defendants who can be released without money bail and often follow up with the defendant to help insure that he or she returns for any scheduled appearances. When money bail is used, many jurisdictions now follow a "10 percent plan," under which the defendant is permitted to post directly with the court 10 percent of the face amount of the bail bond, and most or all of this sum is refundable when the defendant appears for trial. These reforms led to dramatic increases in the proportion of defendants released rather than detained for trial.[19] Nevertheless, traditional money bail survives in many localities as the primary avenue of pretrial release.

The Bail Reform Act of 1984, 18 U.S.C. §§1341-1350, expressly authorizes preventive detention prior to trial in federal criminal prosecutions, on a finding that "no condition or conditions [of release] will reasonably assure the appearance of the [defendant] as required and the safety of any other person

---

19. For example, from 1962 to 1971, the percentage of defendants who were detained throughout the period prior to trial dropped from 52 percent to 33 percent in felony cases and from 21 percent to only 12 percent in major misdemeanor cases. See W. Thomas, Bail Reform in America (1976).

and the community." §3142 (e). The Supreme Court upheld the constitutionality of the preventive detention provisions in United States v. Salerno, 481 U.S. 739 (1987). Partly as a result, pretrial detention in the federal courts has been rising sharply since the 1990s. In 1996, 34 percent of federal defendants were detained prior to trial, but for cases filed during 2002, 72 percent of the defendants were detained until their trials.[20] And at least one study suggests that blacks and Hispanics are much more likely to be detained than white defendants facing similar charges.[21] Detention rates in state court remain significant, but have not increased substantially since the reforms of the 1970s; in 2006, 42 percent of the felony defendants in large urban counties were detained prior to trial. Again, there are disturbing indications that minority defendants must meet higher bail and are more likely to be detained than similarly situated whites.[22]

3. *The guilty plea.* Most convictions—more than 90 percent in most jurisdictions—are not the result of adjudications at trial but of guilty pleas, often obtained by negotiation over the charge or the sentence.[23] A plea negotiation can involve lengthy conferences in which the relevant facts and applicable legal defenses are explored in detail. More often, however, the guilty plea discussion involves little more than a hurried conversation in a courthouse hallway or even a prosecutor's quick "take it or leave it" offer to defense counsel. In some courts there are no explicit negotiations at all, but most defendants plead guilty nonetheless, usually in the expectation that their plea will win them some leniency from the sentencing judge. The guilty plea, a crucially important feature of the American criminal justice system, is considered briefly in Section C, The Process for Determining Guilt, infra, and explored in more detail in Chapter 10, Discretion, infra.

4. *The trial.* Cases decided at trial are a small fraction of the total. In one study, 96 percent of the cases filed were resolved by guilty plea, dismissal, or pretrial diversion; only 4 percent of the defendants went to trial, and only 1 percent were acquitted.[24] But the exceptional, fully adjudicated cases establish standards that influence much of what happens in matters that never reach the trial stage. The legal rules that define crimes and defenses, the effectiveness of prosecutors, the attitudes of judges, and the conviction propensities of juries all have an impact (*how much* of an impact is an important,

---

20. U.S. Dept. of Justice, Bureau of Justice Statistics, Federal Justice Statistics, 2008—Statistical Tables (Nov. 2010), p. 14.

21. Report of the Working Committees to the Second Circuit Task Force on Gender, Racial and Ethnic Fairness in the Courts, 1997 Ann. Surv. Am. L. 124, 318 (1997).

22. Ian Ayres & Joel Waldfogel, A Market Test for Race Discrimination in Bail Setting, 46 Stan. L. Rev. 987 (1994).

23. Guilty pleas accounted for 94 percent of felony convictions in state courts in 2006, U.S. Dept. of Justice Bureau of Justice Statistics, Felony Convictions in State Courts, 2006 (Dec. 2009), and 96 percent of convictions in federal courts in 2008. U.S. Dept. of Justice Bureau of Justice Statistics, Federal Justice Statistics, 2008—Statistical Tables (Nov. 2010), at 18.

24. Daniel Givelber, Lost Innocence: Speculation and Data About the Acquitted, 42 Am. Crim. L. Rev. 1167, 1172 (2005).

much debated question) on decisions whether to arrest, charge, dismiss, divert before trial, and bargain over a plea.

5. *Sentencing.* Although the adjudication of guilt in contested cases is an elaborately formal procedure, the determination of punishment for convicted offenders is always much less formal, and it can even be exceedingly informal. We examine the sentencing process in depth in Chapter 10, infra.

6. *The flow of cases through the criminal justice system.* The chart presented on the following page[25] sets forth in graphic form the flow of cases through the agencies of criminal justice. It dramatically illustrates the filtering process that winnows out the vast majority of cases prior to trial.

C. THE PROCESS FOR DETERMINING GUILT

1. An Overview of Pleas and Trials

NOTE ON GUILTY PLEAS

The vast majority of criminal convictions are the result of guilty pleas entered without any formal factfinding. Does the guilty plea system produce results different from those that would occur at trial? To be more specific, does it convict defendants who are in fact innocent (*and* would be acquitted) or convict defendants who committed the offense but could not be found guilty beyond a reasonable doubt at trial? Does the plea negotiation process produce convictions for offenses significantly different from the crimes a defendant may actually have committed? For the many observers who are inclined to give affirmative answers to these questions, the entire body of substantive criminal law may seem a supreme irrelevance; convictions obtained by guilty pleas are seen as the outcome of hurried horse-trading rather than the thoughtful application of complex legal principles to the known facts. What is the practical significance of substantive law in a world dominated by plea bargaining? Consider the following comments:

Arnold Enker, Perspectives on Plea Bargaining, in President's Commission on Law Enforcement and the Administration of Justice, Task Force Report: The Courts 113-114 (1967): [C]oncern over the possibility that a negotiated plea can result in an erroneous judgment of conviction assumes a frame of reference by which the accuracy of the judgment is to be evaluated. It assumes an objective truth existing in a realm of objective historical fact which it is the sole function of our process to discover. Some, but by no means all, criminal cases fit this image. For example, this is a relatively accurate description of the

---

25. The chart is based on one that appears in President's Commission, supra note 1, at 8.

A General View of the Criminal Justice System

This chart seeks to present a simple yet comprehensive view of the movement of cases through the criminal justice system. Procedures in individual jurisdictions may vary from the pattern shown here. The differing weights of line indicate the relative volumes of cases disposed of at various points in the system, but this is only suggestive since no nationwide data of this sort exists.

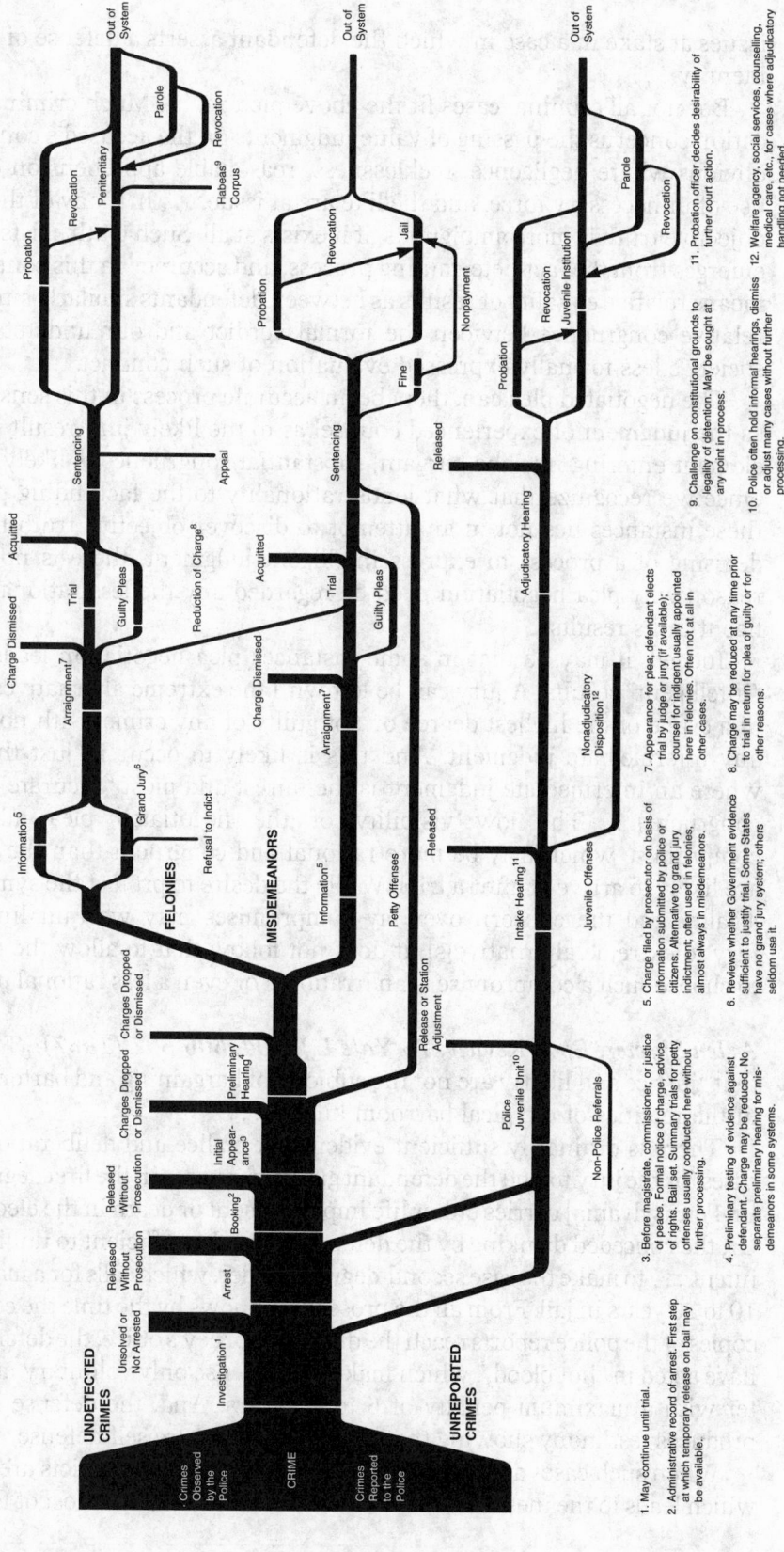

1. May continue until trial.

2. Administrative record of arrest. First step at which temporary release on bail may be available.

3. Before magistrate, commissioner, or justice of peace. Formal notice of charge, advice of rights. Bail set. Summary trials for petty offenses usually conducted here without further processing.

4. Preliminary testing of evidence against defendant. Charge may be reduced. No separate preliminary hearing for misdemeanors in some systems.

5. Charge filed by prosecutor on basis of information submitted by police or citizens. Alternative to grand jury indictment; often used in felonies, almost always in misdemeanors.

6. Reviews whether Government evidence sufficient to justify trial. Some States have no grand jury system; others seldom use it.

7. Appearance for plea; defendant elects trial by judge or jury (if available); counsel for indigent usually appointed here in felonies. Often not at all in other cases.

8. Charge may be reduced at any time prior to trial in return for plea of guilty or for other reasons.

9. Challenge on constitutional grounds to legality of detention. May be sought at any point in process.

10. Police often hold informal hearings, dismiss or adjust many cases without further processing.

11. Probation officer decides desirability of further court action.

12. Welfare agency, social services, counselling, medical care, etc., for cases where adjudicatory handling not needed.

13

issues at stake in a case in which the defendant asserts a defense of mistaken identity. . . .

But not all criminal cases fit the above picture. . . . Much criminal adjudication concerns the passing of value judgments on the accused's conduct as is obvious where negligence, recklessness, reasonable apprehension of attack, use of unnecessary force, and the like are at issue. . . . In many of these cases, objective truth is more ambiguous, if it exists at all. Such truth exists only as it emerges from the fact-determining process, and accuracy in this context really means relative equality of results as between defendants similarly situated and relative congruence between the formal verdict and our understanding of society's less formally expressed evaluation of such conduct.

The negotiated plea can, then, be an accurate process in this sense. So long as the judgment of experienced counsel as to the likely jury result is the key element entering into the bargain, substantial congruence is likely to result. Once we recognize that what lends rationality to the factfinding process in these instances lies not in an attempt to discover objective truth but in the devising of a process to express intelligent judgment, there is no inherent reason why plea negotiation need be regarded any the less rational or intelligent in its results.

Indeed, it may be that in some instances plea negotiation leads to more "intelligent" results. A jury can be left with the extreme alternatives of guilty of a crime of the highest degree or not guilty of any crime, with no room for any intermediate judgment. And this is likely to occur in just those cases where an intermediate judgment is the fairest and most "accurate" (or most congruent). . . . The low visibility of the negotiated plea allows this compromise which may be more rational and congruent than the result we are likely to arrive at after a trial. While the desire to protect the symbolism of legality and the concern over lay compromises may warrant limiting the jury to extreme alternative[s], it does not follow that to allow the defendant to choose such a compromise is an irrational or even a less rational procedure.

Arlen Specter, Book Review, 76 Yale L.J. 604, 606-607 (1967): The dictum that "justice and liberty are not the subjects of bargaining and barter" does not fit the realities of a typical barroom killing. . . .

There is ordinarily sufficient evidence of malice and deliberation in such cases for the jury to find the defendant guilty of murder in the first degree, which [in Pennsylvania] carries either life imprisonment or death in the electric chair. Or, the conceded drinking by the defendant may be sufficient to nullify specific intent . . . to make the case second-degree murder, which calls for a maximum of 10 to 20 years in jail. From all the prosecutor knows by the time the cold carbon copies of the police reports reach the district attorney's office, the defendant may have acted in "hot blood," which makes the offense only voluntary manslaughter with a maximum penalty of 6 to 12 years. And, the defense invariably produces testimony showing that the killing was pure self-defense.

When such cases are submitted to juries, a variety of verdicts are returned, which leads to the inescapable conclusion of variable guilt. Most of those trials result in convictions for second-degree murder or voluntary manslaughter. The judges generally impose sentences with a minimum range of 5 to 8 years and a maximum of 10 to 20 years. That distilled experience enables the assistant district attorney and the defense lawyer to bargain on the middle ground of what experience has shown to be "justice" without the defense running the risk of the occasional first-degree conviction ... and without the Commonwealth tying up a jury room for 3 to 5 days and running the risk of acquittal.

Albert W. Alschuler, The Prosecutor's Role in Plea Bargaining, 36 U. Chi. L. Rev. 50, 71-79 (1968): [District Attorney Specter's] argument seems to rest on the notion that when a man has seen one barroom killing, he has seen them all. [Yet] Specter's argument is a forceful one. In the homicide area particularly, ... the distinctions drawn by the criminal code ... sometimes prove too fine for workable, everyday application.

... If the perspective of these practitioners is sound, the best solution to the defects they perceive in the trial system does not lie in a shift from trial procedures to off-stage compromises. It lies instead in a simplification of the criminal code to reflect "everyday reality." [But] it seems doubtful that plea negotiation can eliminate the irrationalities of the criminal code without substituting more serious irrationalities of its own. ... Most barroom killings seem to end in bargained pleas to voluntary manslaughter; but some end in bargained pleas to second-degree murder; some end in bargained pleas to various categories of felonious assault; and I know of one barroom shooting that was resolved by a guilty plea to the crime of involuntary manslaughter, which, under the circumstances, seemed to be the last crime in the code of which the defendant might be guilty. It is therefore not clear that plea negotiation leads to greater uniformity of result than trial by jury.

Juries, of course, have biases, but the rules of evidence attempt to direct their attention to relevant issues. There are no rules of evidence in plea negotiation; individual prosecutors may be influenced not only by a desire to smooth out the irrationalities of the criminal code but by thoroughly improper considerations that no serious reformer of the penal code would suggest. ... Juries may react differently to the circumstances of indistinguishable crimes, but at least they react to the circumstances of the crimes. A jury is unlikely to seek conviction for the sake of conviction, to respond to a defense attorney's tactical pressures, to penalize a defendant because he has taken an inordinate share of the court's and the prosecutor's time, to do favors for particular defense attorneys in the hope of future cooperation, or to attempt to please victims and policemen for political reasons.

Stephanos Bibas, Plea Bargaining Outside the Shadow of Trial, 117 Harv. L. Rev. 2463, 2464-2468 (2004): The conventional wisdom is that litigants bargain toward settlement in the shadow of expected trial outcomes. [T]he classic shadow-of-trial model predicts that the likelihood of conviction at trial and the likely post-trial sentence largely determine plea bargains. ...

The shadow-of-trial model is, however, far too simplistic. . . . First, there are many structural impediments that distort bargaining in various cases. Poor lawyering, agency costs [the difficulty a client faces in trying to monitor the performance of her agent, the lawyer] and lawyers' self-interest are prime examples, as are bail rules and pretrial detention. . . . Second, the shadow-of-trial model assumes that the actors are fundamentally rational. Recent scholarship on negotiation and behavioral law and economics, however, undercuts this strong assumption of rationality. Instead, overconfidence, self-serving biases, . . . denial mechanisms, . . . and risk preferences all skew bargains.

[As a result,] many plea bargains diverge from the shadows of trials. By "the shadows of trials," I mean the influence exerted by the strength of the evidence and the expected punishment after trial. Structural forces and psychological biases sometimes inefficiently prevent mutually beneficial bargains or induce harmful ones. [Some] defendants plead when they would otherwise go to trial, or go to trial (and usually receive heavier sentences) when they would otherwise plead. Furthermore, some defendants' plea bargains diverge from trial shadows much more than others'. . . . Rather than basing sentences on the need for deterrence, retribution, incapacitation, or rehabilitation, plea bargaining effectively bases sentences in part on wealth, sex, age, education, intelligence, and confidence. Though trials allocate punishment imperfectly, plea bargaining adds another layer of distortions that warp the fair allocation of punishment.

NOTES

1. *Conflicts of interest.* What sorts of "lawyers' self-interest" could skew the bargaining process in the ways that Professor Bibas describes? Can you think of personal motivations that might (consciously or subconsciously) lead a defense attorney to advise her client to accept an unduly severe plea offer? Can you think of personal motivations that might lead a prosecutor to offer an overly lenient plea offer? Would it ever be in a defense attorney's self-interest to recommend *rejection* of a favorable plea agreement?

2. *Agency costs.* Where potential conflicts of interest exist, monitoring is essential; there must be some way to assure that attorneys act in the best interests of their clients—the accused in the case of the defense attorney and the general public in the case of the prosecutor. What factors make it difficult for some (or all) defendants to determine whether their attorney's advice is influenced by the attorney's personal interests? What factors make it difficult for the general public to determine whether the prosecutor's actions are influenced by her personal interests? For further discussion of the problems of attorney self-interest and agency costs, see Stephen J. Schulhofer, Criminal Justice Discretion as a Regulatory System, 17 J. Legal Stud. 43 (1988).

3. *Implications for substantive criminal law.* Despite the distortions described by Alschuler and Bibas, there undoubtedly remains a degree of

truth in the picture painted by Enker: At least to some extent, the substantive law and the expected outcome of a trial remain important elements (though not the only elements) in determining the outcome of plea negotiation. At this early point in the study of criminal law, it is premature to discuss plea bargaining in greater detail or to investigate possibilities for reform. We defer those issues to Chapter 10, where we consider the ways in which the modern administrative state uses prosecutorial discretion, plea bargaining, and sentencing practices to determine culpability and impose punishment outside the framework of the formal criminal trial.

For present purposes, our concern is to set the stage for the study of substantive criminal law by taking realistic account of the extent to which its principles actually matter in a world dominated by plea bargaining. On that question, there can be no doubt that criminal law matters, though it is not the only thing that matters. And we can expect the role of the substantive law to grow when cases are handled by the most sophisticated attorneys and when they know the doctrines of criminal law well enough to invoke them effectively in the course of bargaining.

NOTE ON FORMAL TRIAL PROCEDURE

Section A of this chapter describes the organization of the criminal justice system and typical pretrial procedures. To introduce our examination of the trial stage itself, the present note briefly summarizes the typical course of a formal criminal trial. Naturally, the procedure followed in some jurisdictions or in particular cases may differ in points of detail from that set out in this preliminary overview.

A formal trial typically begins with the selection of the jury. A panel of prospective jurors (called a *venire*) enters the courtroom, and the judge describes the nature of the case and the identity of the parties so that any prospective jurors who are personally involved may be excused. Prospective jurors are then questioned individually by the judge or by opposing counsel to determine possible bias. On the basis of this questioning (called *voir dire*) prospective jurors may be excused *for cause*, and both prosecution and defense may remove a certain number of the panel, without showing cause, by exercising *peremptory challenges*. When the requisite number of acceptable jurors (usually 12) has been obtained by this procedure, the panel is sworn.

Now the presentation of the case begins. Usually the indictment is read to the jury; the prosecutor then makes an opening statement outlining the facts she plans to prove. Defense counsel also may make an opening statement. Claims made in these statements do not constitute *evidence*; they serve only to help the jury understand the testimony about to be presented. In many jurisdictions, motions relating to the scope or validity of the indictment and motions to suppress evidence must be made prior to trial. In others, such motions can be made at the outset of the trial. If the judge grants a motion to dismiss the indictment, the case will terminate at this point. Otherwise the trial goes forward, although motions may be made or renewed as the trial proceeds.

Next the prosecution calls its witnesses. Their testimony often evokes objections from counsel, and the judge must decide the bounds of permissible testimony under complex rules of evidence. We examine some of these rules in the sections to follow. When the prosecution has completed the presentation of its evidence, the defense may choose to stand on the *presumption of innocence* and move for a *directed verdict* or *judgment of acquittal* on the ground that the charges have not been proved beyond a reasonable doubt. If such a motion is not made, or if the motion is made and denied, the defense may decide to offer its own evidence (through the defendant or other witnesses). The prosecution then will have an opportunity to present further evidence in rebuttal. When both sides have finished presenting their evidence, counsel may make closing arguments to the jury. Ordinarily the prosecution's closing argument is presented first (because it bears the burden of proof), and the prosecutor is usually allowed an opportunity for rebuttal after the closing argument of the defense.

At this point the work of the opposing parties has been completed. The judge now intercedes with her most important contribution—the *instructions to the jury*. Ordinarily, judicial comment on the evidence tends to be cautious and limited. Formal instructions on the law, however, are always given, and they are typically quite detailed. The instructions serve both as a guide for the jury's deliberations and as a focal point for challenges on appeal in the event of a conviction. Usually the instructions cover responsibilities of the jurors (for example, how to elect a foreperson, when to refrain from discussing the case with other jurors or outsiders), matters related to the relevance of particular kinds of testimony, and, above all, detailed explanations of the substantive criminal law applicable to the case, including the facts necessary to establish the offense and definitions of legal concepts that the jury is called on to apply.

The jury at last retires to deliberate. Its verdict of guilty or not guilty on each charge must be reached by a substantial majority (and usually by unanimity). After a verdict of guilty and the imposition of sentence (usually by the judge), the trial terminates. There may of course be an appeal. If it finds trial errors, the reviewing court may reverse the conviction and order another trial, since American double jeopardy principles generally do not bar the retrial of a defendant who has successfully appealed her conviction.[26] A verdict of not guilty is not subject to review of any kind, even when flagrant errors prejudicial to the prosecution occurred at trial.[27] When the jury is unable to agree by the requisite majority on a verdict of either guilty or not guilty (a hung jury case), a *mistrial* is declared, and the defendant then may be retried at the prosecutor's discretion.

---

26. Burks v. United States, 437 U.S. 1 (1978). The English practice is somewhat different. In that country, when a reviewing court finds prejudicial error, the conviction is "quashed," and ordinarily no retrial is permitted. Criminal Appeal Act, ch. 19, §2(2)-(3). But the English courts have discretion to order a new trial when "the interests of justice so require." Id. §7.

27. To avoid this difficulty many states provide for rulings prior to the start of trial on significant issues of law and permit the prosecutor to appeal an adverse ruling at that point. For discussion of prosecution appeals, see James A. Strazzella, The Relationship of Double Jeopardy to Prosecution Appeals, 73 Notre Dame L. Rev. 1 (1997).

Such, in rough outline, is the procedure by which guilt must be established when a criminal case is fully litigated through the formal trial stage. Further treatment of trial procedure lies beyond the province of this book. Nevertheless, a book devoted primarily to the substantive law should provide an introduction to the central features of the process of proof, in order to illuminate the context in which criminal law is applied and the ways in which the procedural system shapes the substantive content of the criminal law. The remaining sections of this chapter undertake such an exploration.

2. The Presentation of Evidence

INTRODUCTORY NOTES

1. The order of proof. At trial the evidence is presented in a formally prescribed order. The prosecution first calls witnesses in an effort to prove the elements of the offense charged. As we have seen, page 18 supra, the case may terminate at this point if the prosecution fails to sustain its burden of proof. If not, the defense may then call witnesses to refute the prosecution's *case-in-chief* or to establish some *affirmative defense.* The prosecution has an opportunity to recall witnesses or to call new witnesses for purposes of *rebuttal,* that is, to refute evidence offered by the defense. The defense in turn is afforded a chance to answer by *rejoinder* any matters introduced in the prosecutor's rebuttal.

Within these stages the examination of each witness follows a similar pattern. The witness is first questioned by the party that called the witness (*direct examination*), and afterward the opposing party has an opportunity to question that witness (*cross-examination*). Further questioning by the first party (*re-direct*) and by the opposing side (*re-cross*) may follow.

2. Relevance. The rules governing the admissibility of evidence are extremely complex. For present purposes, it will be useful to begin by focusing on one obvious but deceptively simple requirement, the rule of relevancy. Irrelevant evidence is *never* admissible. The converse cannot be stated so categorically. Relevant evidence is *generally* admissible, but there are many exceptions to this principle. Before turning to the exceptions, we must first be clear about the meaning of *relevancy.*

Evidence is considered relevant for purposes of the rules of evidence only if it is both *probative* and *material*, and these are precise terms of art. Evidence is probative only if it tends to establish the proposition for which it is offered or—to be precise—if the proposition is more likely to be true given the evidence than it would be without the evidence. Thus, if the proposition to be proved is that H was the person who killed his wife W, evidence of a motive (that is, that H stood to inherit a substantial estate on W's death) is probative. Of course, the existence of the motive does not, by itself, make it probable that H is the killer, but H is more likely to be the killer if he had a motive than if he did not; this greater likelihood is all that is required to establish probative value.

Probative value alone is often thought of as synonymous with relevancy. But relevancy for purposes of the rules of evidence requires in addition that the proposition that the evidence tends to prove be one that will affect the outcome of the case under applicable law. So, for example, evidence in a homicide prosecution that the defendant acted in self-defense is material, because under the substantive law self-defense is a defense. But evidence that the deceased consented to be killed is not material, because under the substantive law consent by the victim is not a defense to a homicide charge. Thus, evidence may be excluded as irrelevant for one of two distinct reasons— either because the evidence does not tend to establish the proposition in question or because that proposition is not material to the outcome of the case. The materiality requirement means that the first prerequisite for determining the relevancy and hence the admissibility of evidence is a command of the substantive law of crimes.

We may sum up what we have so far said about relevancy by quoting the formulation used in the Federal Rules of Evidence:

RULE 401

"Relevant evidence" means evidence having any tendency to make the existence of any fact that is of consequence to the determination of the action more probable or less probable than it would be without the evidence.

RULE 402

All relevant evidence is admissible, except as otherwise provided. . . . Evidence which is not relevant is not admissible.

3. *Privilege.* Under what circumstances is relevant evidence *not* admissible? The law of evidence embodies dozens of distinct rules requiring the exclusion of relevant evidence. For example, the various rules relating to *privilege* give individuals the right to withhold certain kinds of testimony, often in order to protect particular interests of a witness or specially important relationships with others.

One of the most important privileges is the privilege against self-incrimination. The Fifth Amendment provides: "[N]or shall [any person] be compelled in any criminal case to be a witness against himself." The Supreme Court has construed this provision to imply that the government cannot require a criminal defendant to take the witness stand, cannot invite a jury to draw adverse inferences from a defendant's refusal to testify, and cannot in any other way compel the defendant to disclose potentially incriminating facts about the case. These principles are of great significance for the substantive criminal law. They not only make the prosecutor's task more difficult than it otherwise would be, but they pose an especially difficult barrier when the defendant's own frame of mind is an essential part of what the prosecutor must prove. The effect of the privilege against self-incrimination is to place largely beyond the government's reach the best (and sometimes the only) source of information about these elusive state-of-mind facts. As a result, substantive criminal law must constantly consider whether the government should be obliged to prove state-of-mind facts, and if so, what kinds of evidence will satisfy that obligation.

4. Other exclusionary rules: prejudice. Like the rules of privilege, many other rules of evidence operate to exclude relevant evidence. One of the best known is the rule barring the use of evidence obtained through an illegal search. Indeed, criminal lawyers often refer to this prohibition as *the* exclusionary rule, and it is a major topic of study in criminal procedure. We will consider some of the other important exclusionary rules in connection with the substantive crimes for which they have the greatest significance.[28] The balance of the present section is devoted to exploring one open-ended rule— the rule that evidence must be excluded whenever its probative value is outweighed by its *prejudicial effect.*

The term *prejudicial effect* has a technical meaning. To pursue the example previously mentioned, suppose that in *H*'s murder prosecution, testimony is offered that shortly before the discovery of *W*'s bullet-ridden body, *H* was seen running from the scene carrying a smoking revolver. This testimony will undoubtedly be harmful to *H*'s chances for acquittal, but it will not be prejudicial in the technical sense, because its harmfulness flows solely from its legitimate probative value. Evidence is considered prejudicial only when it is likely to affect the result in some *improper* way. Thus, prejudice is involved if the jury is likely to overestimate the probative value of the evidence or if the evidence will arouse undue hostility toward one of the parties.

The exclusionary rule relating to prejudicial effect is of pervasive importance in the substantive criminal law, and we will encounter it repeatedly in the chapters that follow. The principle of weighing probative value against prejudicial effect is particularly central to developing doctrines in such areas as rape-shield laws; the adequacy of victim provocation in homicide; battered spouse evidence; and testimony concerning intoxication, diminished capacity, and the insanity defense. As a foundation for the study of such topics throughout this book, the present section considers the problem of prejudicial effect in depth, in a context of recurring importance for criminal prosecutions: the rules concerning evidence of other crimes.

The next case illustrates the principle of probative value and prejudicial effect, and their relationship to basic conceptions of criminal responsibility.

PEOPLE v. ZACKOWITZ

New York Court of Appeals
254 N.Y. 192, 172 N.E. 466 (1930)

[Defendant was convicted of first-degree murder and sentenced to death.]

CARDOZO, C.J. On November 10, 1929, shortly after midnight, the defendant in Kings county shot Frank Coppola and killed him without justification or excuse. A crime is admitted. What is doubtful is the degree only.

---

28. Special restrictions intended to protect the privacy of a witness are examined in connection with the materials on rape, pages 410-418 infra.

Four young men, of whom Coppola was one, were at work repairing an automobile in a Brooklyn street. A woman, the defendant's wife, walked by on the opposite side. One of the men spoke to her insultingly, or so at least she understood him. The defendant, who had dropped behind to buy a newspaper, came up to find his wife in tears. He was told she had been insulted, though she did not then repeat the words. Enraged, he stepped across the street and upbraided the offenders with words of coarse profanity. He informed them, so the survivors testify, that "if they did not get out of there in five minutes, he would come back and bump them all off." Rejoining his wife, he walked with her to their apartment house located close at hand. He was heated with liquor which he had been drinking at a dance. Within the apartment he induced her to tell him what the insulting words had been. A youth had asked her to lie with him, and had offered her two dollars. With rage aroused again, the defendant went back to the scene of the insult and found the four young men still working at the car. In a statement to the police, he said that he had armed himself at the apartment with a twenty-five calibre automatic pistol. In his testimony at the trial he said that this pistol had been in his pocket all the evening. Words and blows followed, and then a shot. The defendant kicked Coppola in the stomach. There is evidence that Coppola went for him with a wrench. The pistol came from the pocket, and from the pistol a single shot, which did its deadly work. . . .

At the trial the vital question was the defendant's state of mind at the moment of the homicide. Did he shoot with a deliberate and premeditated design to kill? Was he so inflamed by drink or by anger or by both combined that, though he knew the nature of his act, he was the prey to sudden impulse, the fury of the fleeting moment?[a] If he went forth from his apartment with a preconceived design to kill, how is it that he failed to shoot at once? How [can one] reconcile such a design with the drawing of the pistol later in the heat and rage of an affray? These and like questions the jurors were to ask themselves and answer before measuring the defendant's guilt. Answers consistent with guilt in its highest grade can reasonably be made. Even so, the line between impulse and deliberation is too narrow and elusive to make the answers wholly clear. The sphygmograph records with graphic certainty the fluctuations of the pulse. There is no instrument yet invented that records with equal certainty the fluctuations of the mind. . . . With only the rough and ready tests supplied by their experience of life, the jurors were to look into the workings of another's mind, and discover its capacities and disabilities, its urges and inhibitions, in moments of intense excitement. Delicate enough and subtle is the inquiry, even in the most favorable conditions, with every warping influence excluded. There must be no blurring of the issues by evidence illegally admitted and carrying with it in its admission an appeal to prejudice and passion.

---

a. Under New York law, a deliberate and premeditated killing would be first-degree murder, while a killing in "the fury of the fleeting moment" would be second-degree murder. At the time of the *Zackowitz* decision the former offense was punishable by death and the latter by imprisonment from a minimum of 20 years to a maximum of life. N.Y. Penal Law §§1045, 1048 (Penal Code of 1909, as amended 1928). For current penalty provisions in New York and other representative states, see pages 421-426 infra.—EDS.

Evidence charged with that appeal was, we think, admitted here. . . . Almost at the opening of the trial the People began the endeavor to load the defendant down with the burden of an evil character. He was to be put before the jury as a man of murderous disposition. To that end they were allowed to prove that at the time of the encounter and at that of his arrest he had in his apartment, kept there in a radio box, three pistols and a teargas gun. There was no claim that he had brought these weapons out at the time of the affray, no claim that with any of them he had discharged the fatal shot. He could not have done so, for they were all of different calibre. The end to be served by laying the weapons before the jury was something very different. The end was to bring persuasion that here was a man of vicious and dangerous propensities, who because of those propensities was more likely to kill with deliberate and premeditated design than a man of irreproachable life and amiable manners. Indeed, this is the very ground on which the introduction of the evidence is now explained and defended. The District Attorney tells us in his brief that the possession of the weapons characterized the defendant as "a desperate type of criminal," a "person criminally inclined." [Yet t]he weapons were . . . left in his apartment where they were incapable of harm. In such circumstances, ownership of the weapons, if it has any relevance at all, has relevance only as indicating a general disposition to make use of them thereafter, and a general disposition to make use of them thereafter is without relevance except as indicating a "desperate type of criminal," a criminal affected with a murderous propensity. . . .

If a murderous propensity may be proved against a defendant as one of the tokens of his guilt, a rule of criminal evidence, long believed to be of fundamental importance for the protection of the innocent, must be first declared away. [C]haracter is never an issue in a criminal prosecution unless the defendant chooses to make it one. In a very real sense a defendant starts his life afresh when he stands before a jury, a prisoner at the bar. There has been a homicide in a public place. The killer admits the killing, but urges self-defense and sudden impulse. Inflexibly the law has set its face against the endeavor to fasten guilt upon him by proof of character or experience predisposing to an act of crime. . . . The principle back of the exclusion is one, not of logic, but of policy. There may be cogency in the argument that a quarrelsome defendant is more likely to start a quarrel than one of milder type, a man of dangerous mode of life more likely than a shy recluse. The law is not blind to this, but equally it is not blind to the peril to the innocent if character is accepted as probative of crime. "The natural and inevitable tendency of the tribunal—whether judge or jury—is to give excessive weight to the vicious record of crime thus exhibited, and either to allow it to bear too strongly on the present charge, or to take the proof of it as justifying a condemnation irrespective of guilt of the present charge" (Wigmore, Evidence, vol. 1, §194, and cases cited).

A different question would be here if . . . the defendant had been shown to have gone forth from the apartment with all the weapons on his person. To be armed from head to foot at the very moment of an encounter may be a circumstance worthy to be considered, like acts of preparation generally, as a proof of preconceived design. There can be no such implication from the ownership of weapons which one leaves behind at home.

The endeavor was to generate an atmosphere of professional criminality. It was an endeavor the more unfair in that, apart from the suspicion attaching to the possession of these weapons, there is nothing to mark the defendant as a man of evil life. . . . If his own testimony be true, he had gathered these weapons together as curios, a collection that interested and amused him. Perhaps his explanation of their ownership is false. There is nothing stronger than mere suspicion to guide us to an answer. Whether the explanation be false or true, he should not have been driven by the People to the necessity of offering it. Brought to answer a specific charge, and to defend himself against it, he was placed in a position where he had to defend himself against another, more general and sweeping. He was made to answer to the charge, pervasive and poisonous even if insidious and covert, that he was a man of murderous heart, of criminal disposition. . . .

The judgment of conviction should be reversed, and a new trial ordered.

NOTES ON ZACKOWITZ

1. On the facts of *Zackowitz,*we may assume that the killing was intentional. The principal issue at trial was whether the killing was "deliberate" (that is, whether the intent to kill was formulated before the shot, making the crime first-degree murder) or whether the killing was instead "impulsive" (that is, whether the intent to kill was formulated during the final scuffle, making the crime second-degree murder). Does the defendant's possession of the weapons have some bearing on this issue? Recall that very slight probative value is usually sufficient to render evidence admissible; for example, evidence that Zackowitz stood to inherit money from the victim would undoubtedly be admissible as tending to show a motive for a deliberate killing. Does the evidence of weapons possession have at least that much probative value?

2. If the weapons evidence was relevant, as Judge (later Justice) Cardozo seems to assume, are there convincing reasons for excluding it? Judge Cardozo stresses that the issue in the case was a "delicate" and "subtle" one. Under these circumstances was it not particularly important for the jury to have access to as much relevant evidence as possible? In which case will the trier of fact be better able to evaluate what actually happened: When it knows about the weapons, knows the defendant's explanation for them and has a chance to judge the credibility of that explanation, or when—as *Zackowitz* requires—all of this information is withheld?

NOTES ON "OTHER-CRIMES" EVIDENCE
UNDER CURRENT LAW

1. The general rule and its foundations. Subject to certain exceptions to be explored below, the basic principle invoked by the majority in *Zackowitz* appears to enjoy universal acceptance: Other crimes (and indeed any other kind of evidence designed to show "bad character") may not be introduced to show that the accused had an evil disposition and thus was more likely to have committed the offense charged.

Rules 403 and 404(b) of the Federal Rules of Evidence illustrate one rigorous statement of these principles:

RULE 403 . . .

Although relevant, evidence may be excluded if its probative value is substantially outweighed by the danger of unfair prejudice, confusion of the issues, or misleading the jury, or by considerations of undue delay, waste of time, or needless presentation of cumulative evidence.

RULE 404 . . .

(b) Other crimes, wrongs, or acts. Evidence of other crimes, wrongs, or acts is not admissible to prove the character of a person in order to show action in conformity therewith. It may, however, be admissible for other purposes, such as proof of motive, opportunity, intent, preparation, plan, knowledge, identity, or absence of mistake or accident. . . .

What is the justification for these principles? McCormick states that such evidence "is not irrelevant, but in the setting of jury trial the danger of prejudice outweighs the probative value." C. McCormick, Evidence §190, at 447 (2d ed. 1972). See also Michelson v. United States, 335 U.S. 469, 475-476 (1948): "The inquiry is not rejected because character is irrelevant; on the contrary it is said to weigh too much with the jury and to so overpersuade them as to prejudge one with a bad general record and deny him a fair opportunity to defend against a particular charge." Undoubtedly, this statement holds true in a very wide range of contexts. But there can be situations in which the danger of prejudice is arguably insufficient to justify the exclusion. Are there more basic reasons for restricting the admissibility of other-crimes evidence?

Consider how the criminal process would be affected if the prosecution were free to support its case by proving previous instances of criminal conduct by the accused. The defendant, who of course is contesting the charges of the present indictment, may deny having committed the other crimes as well. In particular, if the prosecution has not already obtained a formal conviction for the other crimes, the entire focus of the trial could be diverted by the dispute about whether the other crimes were in fact committed.

Even if the defendant admits to committing other crimes or the other crimes are easily proved by a record of prior convictions, the defendant may feel called upon to explain the background of the other offenses or to claim extenuating circumstances. The vice here is not simply that time and attention may be diverted from the main issue in the case. It is also that a defendant should not be forever obliged to explain prior transgressions in order to dispel suspicions of further misconduct. Thus, a person who has suffered conviction and sentence is said to have "paid his debt to society"; the slate should be wiped clean. Cardozo alludes to these concerns when he states: "In a very real sense a defendant starts his life afresh when he stands before a jury, a prisoner at the bar. . . . Whether the explanation [for Zack-owitz's possession of the weapons] be true or false, he should not have been driven by the People to the necessity of offering it."

Whether or not a defendant has already "paid his debt" for the prior offense, basic assumptions about criminal responsibility are tested when the focus of the trial becomes centered on the defendant's general character rather than on his behavior in a discrete situation. To be sure, a trial designed to determine a defendant's responsibility for particular events often must explore many circumstances of his life, but ultimately the events themselves are at issue, the concrete behavior precisely specified in the charges. The criminal trial usually is not viewed as a vehicle for passing judgment on the whole person. Again, Cardozo alludes to this principle: "Brought to answer a specific charge, [the defendant] had to defend himself against another, more general and sweeping[,] . . . pervasive and poisonous even if insidious and covert, that he was a man of murderous heart, or criminal disposition." Consider Gerard E. Lynch, RICO: The Crime of Being a Criminal, Parts III & IV, 87 Colum. L. Rev. 920, 934-936 (1987):

> [T]he model of crime based on specific incidents or acts [is] associated with a particular conception of the individual as a moral actor. . . . The individual is implicitly conceived not only as free in principle to act in accordance with or in violation of defined norms, but also as free at any given moment to make choices at odds with any consistent character that may be deduced from his prior acts. To infer that a defendant committed the particular offense for which he is being tried from the fact that he has previously committed other crimes of a generally similar nature—or, worse still, other crimes of an entirely different nature—is not only unfair, but inconsistent with a fundamental supposition that criminal behavior is punishable because it represents a free choice at a particular moment in time to commit an immoral act.

Questions: To what extent are the values described fundamental to a just system of criminal law? Are they, for example, more important than the most accurate possible determination of the truth? Should they apply with as much force in proceedings to determine sentence (or the *degree* of the offense in *Zackowitz*) as they do when the issue is guilt versus innocence?[29] Consider the extent to which these values in fact *are* respected, or flouted, by the doctrines of criminal law examined in the remainder of this section and throughout this book.

2. *Exceptions to the rule.* Despite the concerns mentioned by the court in *Zackowitz*, the rule against admitting other-crimes evidence is subject to a number of "exceptions." For example, evidence that the defendant had previously stolen the pistol with which the victim was shot ordinarily will be admissible—not to show the defendant's disposition to crime but to help *identify* him as the killer. Similarly, evidence that the defendant had

---

29. For exploration of the question whether punishment should be tailored to the character of the offender rather than the seriousness of the offense, see Chapter 2 infra.

previously committed a robbery witnessed by the victim ordinarily will be admissible—not to show propensity but to show his *motive* for this particular killing. See, e.g., White v. Commonwealth, 178 S.W.3d 470 (Ky. 2005).

Technically speaking, these situations do not involve exceptions to the rule of exclusion because, properly stated, that rule renders other-crimes evidence inadmissible only when offered "to prove the character of a person in order to show action in conformity therewith." Fed. R. Evid. 404(b). In other words, the rule itself does not bar the use of other-crimes evidence for some purpose *other than* that of suggesting that he acted in conformity with a bad character.

When evidence of other crimes is not offered to prove propensity, and therefore is not barred by Rule 404(b), the evidence nonetheless may run afoul of some other prohibition. In particular, evidence offered to prove identity or other nonpropensity matters will be barred by Rule 403 if its prejudicial effect substantially outweighs its probative value. Evidence, even when relevant, must be excluded when it "tends to subordinate reason to emotion in the factfinding process." United States v. Queen, 132 F.3d 991, 997 (4th Cir. 1997). When other-crimes evidence is both highly relevant and highly inflammatory, courts face a dilemma; in such cases, the Supreme Court has held, judges must consider using factual stipulations or other alternative methods for conveying the essential facts to the jury in less prejudicial fashion. Old Chief v. United States, 519 U.S. 172 (1997).

It is not always easy to tell whether other-crimes evidence links the defendant to the crime in some legitimate way or whether it simply suggests a criminal propensity. The problem generates a large volume of litigation. For helpful discussion, see Richard Uviller, Evidence of Character to Prove Conduct: Illusion, Illogic and Injustice in the Courtroom, 130 U. Pa. L. Rev. 845 (1982).

3. *Sex offenses.* The Violent Crime Control and Law Enforcement Act of 1994 amended the Federal Rules of Evidence by adding the following provision (Fed. R. Evid. 413(a)):

> In a criminal case in which the defendant is accused of an offense of sexual assault, evidence of the defendant's commission of another offense or offenses of sexual assault is admissible, and may be considered for its bearing on any matter to which it is relevant.

An analogous provision (Fed. R. Evid. 414(a)) rendered the defendant's commission of child molestation admissible in a prosecution for other acts of child molestation. Evidence of prior sex crimes can be admitted under Rules 413 and 414 only when the evidence also passes the Rule 403 requirement that its prejudicial effect not outweigh its probative value. United States v. Loughry, 2011 U.S. App. LEXIS 20599 (7th Cir. 2011). With this safeguard in place, the admission of evidence of prior sex crimes does not amount to an unconstitutional denial of due process. People v. Falsetta, 986 P.2d 182 (Cal. 1999); Enjady v. United States, 134 F.3d 1427 (10th Cir. 1998). Nonetheless, some courts treat Rules 413 and 414 as "provid[ing] a presumption in favor of . . . admission" for prior sexual offenses and rarely hold such evidence to be barred under Rule 403. E.g., United States v. Merz, 396 Fed. Appx. 838, 843 (3d Cir. 2010). Some have admitted evidence of prior sexual offenses even when those offenses were committed several decades before the incident in question. E.g., United States v. Benally, 500 F.3d 1085 (10th Cir. 2007). See Aviva Orenstein, Deviance, Due Process, and the False Promise of Federal Rule of Evidence 403, 90 Cornell L. Rev. 1487, 1519-1521 (2005).

What is the justification for treating prior sexual acts differently from other evidence of bad character or criminal propensity? Can an exception to the rule of exclusion be justified on the ground that sexual misconduct has greater value than other misconduct in predicting future behavior? Or should the rule of exclusion be applied even *more* strictly, on the ground that evidence of prior sexual misconduct has especially strong prejudicial effects?

For in-depth examination of the issues, see Katharine K. Baker, Once a Rapist? Motivational Evidence and Relevancy in Rape Law, 110 Harv. L. Rev. 563 (1997). Professor Baker charges that "Rule 413's proponents rely on antiquated notions of rapists as rare, depraved psychopaths who have some sort of perverse psychological need for sex." The empirical evidence, she argues, indicates that convicted rapists are much less likely to repeat their crimes than are convicted larcenists and burglars. Professor Baker concludes that Rule 413 is misguided because it "relies on outmoded and demonstrably false stereotypes of who rapes, what rape is, and why rape might be different from other crimes." Id. at 565, 578, 589.

In accord with Professor Baker's analysis, the Judicial Conference of the United States, the policy-making body of the federal judiciary chaired by Chief Justice William Rehnquist, sharply criticized the new rules and urged Congress to repeal them. The Judicial Conference concluded that "the new rules, which are not supported by empirical evidence, could diminish significantly the protections that have safeguarded persons accused in criminal cases," and noted that the rules posed a "danger of convicting a criminal defendant for past, as opposed to charged, behavior or for being a bad person." The Judicial Conference also noted that its conclusions about the undesirability of Rules 413 and 414 reflected a "highly unusual unanimity" of the judges, lawyers, and academics who serve on its advisory committees. See 56 Crim. L. Rptr. 2139-2140 (Feb. 15, 1995). Nonetheless, Congress has declined to modify or repeal the rules.

Several states have adopted special rules, modeled on Federal Rule 413, for admitting evidence of prior sex crimes, on the theory that a defendant's "lustful disposition" is especially probative in sex-offense prosecutions. In most states, however, the usual rule excluding evidence of prior misconduct continues to apply in rape and child abuse trials, just as it does in other prosecutions, and in some states, legislative changes similar to Rules 413 and 414 have been held to violate the state constitution. E.g., State v. Gresham, 2012 Wash. LEXIS 1 (Wash., Jan. 5, 2012); State v. Cox, 781 N.W.2d 757 (Iowa 2010). See David P. Bryden & Roger C. Park, "Other Crimes" Evidence in Sex Offense Cases, 78 Minn. L. Rev. 529 (1994); Sara Sun Beale, Prior Similar Acts in Prosecutions for Rape and Child Sex Abuse, 4 Crim. L.F. 307 (1993).

4. The impeachment exception. In all of the situations so far discussed, the question has been whether the prosecution can use evidence of other crimes as part of its case-in-chief. Even when the other-crimes evidence is clearly inadmissible for this purpose, if the accused chooses to testify in his own defense, then the prosecution generally will be permitted to ask about the other crimes in its cross-examination of the accused. The prosecution will also be permitted to introduce other-crimes evidence in its rebuttal for purposes of impeaching the defendant's testimony. Many states hold that such evidence is always admissible automatically, regardless of whether its probative value outweighs its prejudicial effect. E.g., State v. Harrington, 800 N.W.2d 46 (Iowa 2011). In theory, the other-crimes evidence may not be used to provide affirmative support for the prosecution's case. It may be considered only for purposes of judging the credibility of the defendant's testimony, and the jury will be so instructed.

The rationale of the impeachment exception appears to be that a person convicted of crime may be more likely to give false testimony than a citizen with a "clean" record. Whatever the soundness of this rationale when the previous misconduct involves perjury or similar crimes of dishonesty, its invocation in the case of other crimes can border on the absurd. In a prosecution for burglary, previous burglary convictions are clearly inadmissible for the purpose of showing the defendant's disposition to commit this crime, but if the defendant claims to have been elsewhere at the time, the burglary convictions will generally be held admissible to show a possibility that the defendant may be disposed to perjury!

The impeachment exception is premised on the assumption that the jury will consider the other crimes *only* for the limited purpose of judging credibility and will not treat the other crimes as affirmative evidence of guilt. Is this a plausible assumption? Lawyers and social scientists have studied the question but have not reached definitive conclusions. The Note that follows explores the effectiveness of cautionary instructions and collects some of the available findings. The problem immediately at hand is to understand how the rules concerning other-crimes evidence actually function, but questions about the effectiveness of jury instructions are central to understanding the actual impact of all the elaborately crafted rules of criminal law and evidence that the jury is called upon to apply.

NOTE ON THE EFFECTIVENESS OF JURY INSTRUCTIONS

When other-crimes evidence has been introduced for impeachment purposes, a typical instruction to the jury might read as follows (1 E. Devitt & C. Blackmar, Federal Jury Practice and Instructions §11.12 (4th ed. 1992)):

> Evidence of a defendant's previous conviction of a crime may be considered by the jury only insofar as it may affect the credibility of the defendant as a witness and must never be considered as any evidence of [his][her] guilt of the crime for which the defendant is now on trial.

Such an instruction calls on the jury to perform an intellectual task that is bound to run counter to the jury's natural inclinations. Indeed the rule generally excluding other-crimes evidence is premised on the assumption that such evidence *is* relevant to guilt and is very difficult for the jury to keep in perspective once it becomes known. Thus jurors may be strongly tempted to disregard the instruction, even if they are able to grasp the subtle distinction it asks them to draw. The problem arises over and over in administering the complex rules that ostensibly govern the criminal process. Yet just as the jury creates the need for many of these rules, the nature of the jury raises doubts about whether subtle or counterintuitive instructions actually affect the outcome of the case.

Experienced judges have expressed sharply divergent views about the effectiveness of jury instructions. In Spencer v. Texas, 385 U.S. 554, 565 (1967), the Supreme Court expressed its faith in "the ability of juries to approach their task responsibly and to sort out discrete issues given to them under proper instructions." Others have been more skeptical. Justice Robert H. Jackson warned: "The naive assumption that prejudicial effects can be overcome by instructions to the jury . . . all practicing lawyers know to be unmitigated fiction." Krulewitch v. United States, 336 U.S. 440, 453 (1949) (concurring opinion). In Dunn v. United States, 307 F.2d 883, 886 (5th Cir. 1962), the court was equally pessimistic:

> [O]ne cannot unring a bell; after the thrust of the saber it is difficult to say forget the wound; and finally, if you throw a skunk into the jury box, you can't instruct the jury not to smell it.

The empirical evidence is mixed. A study of pretrial publicity found that volunteer "jurors" exposed to a sensational newspaper account of the case were much more likely to convict, but among jurors instructed to disregard the newspaper accounts, the difference in conviction rates disappeared.[30] In contrast, researchers found that exposure to a legally inadmissible confession significantly increased the likelihood of a guilty verdict when other evidence was weak and that instructions to disregard the confession had no significant effect on the likelihood of conviction.[31] Studies focusing on the impact of juror exposure to a defendant's record of prior convictions often find that evidence of previous similar offenses substantially increases the likelihood of conviction and that cautionary instructions remove little or none of the prejudicial effect.[32]

To the extent that cautionary instructions fail to eradicate prejudicial effects, the result could be due, in part, to jurors' inability to *understand* the subtle distinctions that such instructions sometimes require. Several studies have produced disturbing evidence that jurors often do not grasp the judge's

---

30. Rita James Simon, The Effects of Newspapers on the Verdicts of Potential Jurors, in R. Simon, The Sociology of Law 617-627 (1968).

31. See Saul M. Kassin & Lawrence S. Wrightsman, Coerced Confessions, Judicial Instruction and Mock Juror Verdicts, 11 J. Applied Soc. Psych. 489 (1981).

32. See Joel D. Lieberman & Bruce D. Sales, What Social Science Teaches Us About the Jury Instruction Process, 3 Psychol. Pub. Pol'y & L. 589, 601-602 (1997).

explanations of legal concepts. *One study found that the average juror understands less than half of the judge's instructions on the law.*[33]

QUESTIONS ON JURY INSTRUCTIONS

Whatever the available evidence may suggest about the usefulness of jury instructions, there clearly remain substantial doubts about whether instructions are as effective in practice as they are assumed to be in theory. What are the implications of this situation? Granted that jury instructions function imperfectly (at best), what is the alternative?

One pragmatic approach has been to work on improving the wording of instructions, so that their meaning is more clearly explained to the jury.[34] Beyond this, when a judge tells a jury to disregard evidence, should she explain *why* the law considers the evidence misleading? The standard cautionary instructions tend to be rather perfunctory. For ways to convey a more forceful message, see Albert W. Alschuler, Courtroom Misconduct by Prosecutors and Trial Judges, 50 Tex. L. Rev. 629, 652-654 (1972).

Can ameliorative reforms cure the difficulties of overly cumbersome jury instructions, or is the basic problem more fundamental? Note that jury instructions are necessary in the first place only because we want citizens without special training to participate and at the same time, we want their decisions to conform to law. Do these partially inconsistent desires require a system that is simply too complex to function properly? This problem can be reconsidered in connection with the materials on other countries' approaches to lay participation. See page 55 infra.

3. *Proof Beyond a Reasonable Doubt*

IN RE WINSHIP

Supreme Court of the United States
397 U.S. 358 (1970)

[The defendant, a juvenile, was charged with committing acts that, if done by an adult, would have constituted larceny. The juvenile court found by a preponderance of the evidence that the defendant had committed the acts as charged, and it ordered him confined for one and a half years at a "training school." In one part of its opinion, the Supreme Court held that the judge in a juvenile delinquency proceeding cannot apply a lower standard of proof than that applicable in a criminal trial. The Court accordingly had to decide

---

33. Alan Reifman, Spencer Grusick & Phoebe C. Ellsworth, Real Jurors' Understanding of the Law in Real Cases, 16 Law & Hum. Behav. 539 (1992).

34. William E. Schwartzer, Communicating with Juries: Problems and Remedies, 69 Calif. L. Rev. 731 (1981). See also Lawrence J. Severance, Edith Greene & Elizabeth F. Loftus, Toward Criminal Jury Instructions that Jurors Can Understand, 75 J. Crim. L. & Criminolgy 198 (1984).

whether the preponderance-of-the-evidence standard was constitutionally permissible in a criminal case.]

JUSTICE BRENNAN delivered the opinion of the Court. . . .

The requirement that guilt of a criminal charge be established by proof beyond a reasonable doubt dates at least from our early years as a Nation. . . . The reasonable-doubt standard . . . is a prime instrument for reducing the risk of convictions resting on factual error. The standard provides concrete substance for the presumption of innocence—that bedrock "axiomatic and elementary" principle whose "enforcement lies at the foundation of the administration of our criminal law." . . .

The accused during a criminal prosecution has at stake interests of immense importance, both because of the possibility that he may lose his liberty upon conviction and because of the certainty that he would be stigmatized by the conviction. Accordingly, a society that values the good name and freedom of every individual should not condemn a man for commission of a crime when there is reasonable doubt about his guilt. . . .

Moreover, use of the reasonable-doubt standard is indispensable to command the respect and confidence of the community in applications of the criminal law. It is critical that the moral force of the criminal law not be diluted by a standard of proof that leaves people in doubt whether innocent men are being condemned. It is also important in our free society that every individual going about his ordinary affairs have confidence that his government cannot adjudge him guilty of a criminal offense without convincing a proper factfinder of his guilt with utmost certainty.

[W]e explicitly hold that the Due Process Clause protects the accused against conviction except upon proof beyond a reasonable doubt of every fact necessary to constitute the crime with which he is charged.

JUSTICE HARLAN, concurring. . . .

If . . . the standard of proof for a criminal trial were a preponderance of the evidence rather than proof beyond a reasonable doubt, there would be a smaller risk of factual errors that result in freeing guilty persons, but a far greater risk of factual errors that result in convicting the innocent. Because the standard of proof affects the comparative frequency of these two types of erroneous outcomes, the choice of the standard to be applied in a particular kind of litigation should, in a rational world, reflect an assessment of the comparative social disutility of each.

When one makes such an assessment, the reason for different standards of proof in civil as opposed to criminal litigation becomes apparent. In a civil suit between two private parties for money damages, for example, we view it as no more serious in general for there to be an erroneous verdict in the defendant's favor than for there to be an erroneous verdict in the plaintiff's favor. . . .

In a criminal case, on the other hand, we do not view the social disutility of convicting an innocent man as equivalent to the disutility of acquitting someone who is guilty. . . . In this context, I view the requirement of proof beyond a reasonable doubt in a criminal case as bottomed on a fundamental value determination of our society that it is far worse to convict an innocent man than to let a guilty man go free.

NOTES

1. *The basis of the reasonable-doubt requirement.* Is it clear, as Justice Harlan argues, that the "social disutility" of convicting an innocent person is always far worse than that of releasing a guilty person? William Blackstone went even further, asserting the often-repeated view that it is "better that ten guilty persons escape, than that one innocent suffer." 4 William Blackstone, Commentaries on the Laws of England *352 (1765). Other judges and commentators have approved even higher ratios, such as one hundred to one or even more. See Alexander Volokh, *n* Guilty Men, 146 U. Pa. L. Rev. 173, 187-191 (1997). But how can we really be sure that it is less "costly" to release ten (or one hundred) suspected serial killers who are guilty than to convict one suspected serial killer who is innocent?

Although the reasonable-doubt requirement appears to enjoy broad support, some skeptics wonder where Blackstone and Justice Harlan can get the information necessary to calculate and compare these kinds of social costs. If the cost comparisons are arbitrary and indeterminate, does it follow that the reasonable-doubt requirement is not justified after all? Or does the reasonable-doubt requirement rest on a different principle? Regardless of any alleged balance of societal gains and losses, doesn't every individual enjoy a fundamental right not to suffer punishment in the absence of reliable proof of fault?

2. *How burden-of-proof problems arise.* Problems relating to the reasonable-doubt standard normally arise first at the close of the prosecution's case. If the judge decides that the evidence raises a reasonable doubt about guilt *as a matter of law* (an elusive concept explored in the next Note), the judge must direct a verdict for the defendant. The same problem of assessing the sufficiency of the evidence may be presented to the judge again at the close of all the evidence (when the defendant may again move for a directed verdict); it will be a central concern of the jurors in their deliberations; and it may arise again on appeal (when the defendant may seek reversal on the basis of insufficient evidence).

3. *Reasonable doubt "as a matter of law."* Courts often have difficulty determining whether the evidence is insufficient as a matter of law. In a sense the judges must give the defendant the *benefit of the doubt.* If there is a reasonable doubt, then a guilty verdict would seem improper. On the other hand, before taking a case away from the jury (or reversing a jury's verdict), judges must resolve all evidentiary doubts against the proponent of the motion; in this sense the courts must give the *prosecution* the benefit of the doubt on the question whether its evidence does prove guilt beyond a reasonable doubt. The following comment from the opinion in Curley v. United States, 160 F.2d 229, 232-233 (D.C. Cir. 1947), helps clarify this elusive

problem and explains the test that judges apply to determine evidentiary sufficiency:

> [It is sometimes said] that unless the evidence excludes the hypothesis of innocence, the judge must direct a verdict . . . [and] that if the evidence is such that a reasonable mind might fairly conclude either guilt or innocence, a verdict of guilt must be reversed on appeal. But obviously neither of those translations is the law. Logically the ultimate premise of that thesis is that if a reasonable mind might have a reasonable doubt, there is, therefore, a reasonable doubt. That is not true. . . .
>
> The functions of the jury include the determination of the credibility of witnesses, the weighing of the evidence, and the drawing of justifiable inferences of fact from proven facts. It is the function of the judge to deny the jury any opportunity to operate beyond its province: The jury may not be permitted to conjecture merely, or to conclude upon pure speculation or from passion, prejudice or sympathy. The critical point in this boundary is the existence or non-existence of a reasonable doubt as to guilt. If the evidence is such that reasonable jurymen must necessarily have such a doubt, the judge must require acquittal, because no other result is permissible within the fixed bounds of jury consideration. But if a reasonable mind might fairly have a reasonable doubt or might fairly not have one, the case is for the jury, and the decision is for the jurors to make. . . .
>
> The true rule, therefore, is that a trial judge, in passing upon a motion for directed verdict of acquittal, must determine whether upon the evidence, giving full play to the right of the jury to determine credibility, weigh the evidence, and draw justifiable inferences of fact, a reasonable mind might fairly conclude guilt beyond a reasonable doubt. . . . If he concludes that either of the two results, a reasonable doubt or no reasonable doubt, is fairly possible, he must let the jury decide the matter.

4. *Explaining reasonable doubt.* The problem of evidentiary sufficiency arises not only for judges but for the jury, and the instructions accordingly must tell the jury how it should evaluate the evidence. Empirical studies confirm that jurors convict more readily when instructed under a more-likely-than-not standard than when instructed under the reasonable-doubt standard,[35] and courts must protect the jury against any instruction that might dilute the latter standard. Accordingly, a conviction must be reversed for error in explaining the reasonable-doubt standard to the jury, even when the appellate court does not find the evidence insufficient as a matter of law.

(a) In McCullough v. State, 657 P.2d 1157 (Nev. 1983), the trial judge had explained degrees of proof to the jury in terms of "a scale of zero to ten." He placed the preliminary hearing standard of probable cause at one and the burden of persuasion in civil trials at just over five. He then described beyond

---

35. See Irwin A. Horowitz & Laird C. Kirkpatrick, A Concept in Search of a Definition: The Effects of Reasonable Doubt Instructions on Certainty of Guilt Standards and Jury Verdicts, 20 Law & Hum. Behav. 655 (1996). For exploration of the impact of jury instructions generally, see pages 29-31 supra.

a reasonable doubt as "seven and a half, if you had to put it on a scale." The Nevada Supreme Court reversed, stating (id. at 1159): "The concept of reasonable doubt is inherently qualitative. Any attempt to quantify it may impermissibly lower the prosecution's burden of proof, and is likely to confuse rather than clarify."

(b) Courts often get into trouble when attempting to explain "reasonable doubt" in qualitative terms. In Cage v. Louisiana, 498 U.S. 39 (1990), the trial judge in a first-degree murder prosecution had instructed the jury that "a reasonable doubt [must be] founded upon a real tangible substantial basis and not upon mere caprice and conjecture. It must be such doubt as would give rise to a grave uncertainty. . . . A reasonable doubt is not a mere possible doubt. It is an actual substantial doubt. . . . What is required is not an absolute or mathematical certainty, but a moral certainty." The Supreme Court reversed the conviction, holding that the references to "grave uncertainty," "substantial doubt," and "moral certainty" improperly diluted the *Winship* standard.

(c) A traditionally accepted definition of reasonable doubt was the following, which was required by Cal. Penal Code §1096 (1994):

> Reasonable doubt is . . . not a mere possible doubt; because everything relating to human affairs, and depending on moral evidence, is open to some possible or imaginary doubt. It is that state of the case which, after the entire comparison and consideration of all the evidence, leaves the minds of the jurors in that condition that they cannot say they feel an abiding conviction, to a moral certainty, of the truth of the charge.

This language was drawn verbatim from an 1850 jury instruction given by Massachusetts Chief Justice Lemuel Shaw. See Commonwealth v. Webster, 59 Mass. 295, 320 (1850). But what is the meaning, to a modern juror, of "moral evidence" and "moral certainty"? Does the instruction meet the requirements of *Winship* and *Cage v. Louisiana*?

In Sandoval v. California, 511 U.S. 1 (1994), the Court distinguished *Cage* and upheld the constitutionality of the California instruction. The court conceded that "the phrase 'moral evidence' is not a mainstay of the modern lexicon," and that "moral certainty is ambiguous" but concluded that the instruction as a whole gave sufficient content to the reasonable-doubt requirement. Several concurring justices agreed that use of the nineteenth-century phrases was not unconstitutional, but they urged states to choose more comprehensible modern language. California responded the following year by deleting the "moral certainty" language; the current statute describes reasonable doubt as a situation in which jurors "cannot say they feel an abiding conviction of the truth of the charge." Cal. Penal Code §1096 (2011). But in some states the "moral certainty" language is still used. E.g., 7 Tenn. Prac. Pattern Jury Instr. T.P.I.-Crim 2.03 (2006), explaining that "[a]bsolute certainty of guilt is not demanded . . . , but moral certainty is required, and this certainty is required as to every element of proof necessary to constitute the offense." Recent studies indicate that among various formulations, jurors told that they must be "firmly convinced" were most likely to differentiate between strong and weak cases, acquitting in the latter. But even when given the "firmly convinced" language, "more than one-third of the [mock] juries voted to convict when the prosecution's evidence did not even satisfy a preponderance of the evidence standard." See Stoltie v. California, 501 F. Supp. 2d 1252, 1261 (C.D. Cal. 2007). Many experts believe "[c]olloquial words that describe subjective certainty will likely be more effective in explaining to the jury the truly high standard of proof and the presumption of innocence." Id. at 1262. But to date, courts have not required more emphatic explanations of this sort.

(d) Because reasonable doubt is difficult to explain correctly, several courts consider it preferable to give the jury no explanation at all. In United States v. Walton, 207 F.3d 694 (4th Cir. 2000), a jury that had received no explanation of reasonable doubt sent the judge a note asking him to define it. After the judge refused, the jury convicted. The Fourth Circuit affirmed, stating that trying to explain things will "confuse rather than clarify." Is this an appropriate solution to the problem?

a. Allocating the Burden of Proof

INTRODUCTORY NOTE

An important aspect of the overall sufficiency of the evidence is the burden of proof on particular subsidiary issues in the case. Even though the prosecution must prove guilt beyond a reasonable doubt, the state is sometimes permitted to allocate the burden of persuasion on certain subsidiary issues to the defense.

The Supreme Court considered one such effort to subdivide the burden of proof in Mullaney v. Wilbur, 421 U.S. 684 (1975). *Mullaney* involved Maine's complex scheme of homicide statutes. The state treated intentional homicide as a single "offense," but separate provisions specified separate punishments, depending on whether the homicide was classified as murder or manslaughter. Murder was defined as a killing with "malice aforethought," and malice aforethought was defined as a state of mind consisting of, among other things, an intent to kill "without a considerable provocation." A killing *with* provocation was classified as manslaughter and was subject to a lower punishment. At the defendant's trial, the jury was instructed that any intentional killing would involve "malice aforethought" and would therefore constitute murder, unless the defendant could rebut malice aforethought by proving, by a preponderance of the evidence, that he had acted "in the heat of passion, on sudden provocation."

The Supreme Court held that the defendant's due process rights were violated by Maine's decision to place upon him the burden of proving provocation. Because provocation negated the "malice aforethought" required to convict him of murder, the approach used in Maine had violated the *Winship* requirement that the state prove "beyond a reasonable doubt every fact necessary to constitute the crime charged."

Mullaney, however, left room for argument about the crucial question of *why* the absence of provocation was a necessary fact. Was it because provocation was inherently important in determining the degree of culpability and punishment? Or was it because the absence of provocation had been included in the statutory definition of what murder was? The Supreme Court soon faced a case requiring it to choose between these two approaches.

PATTERSON v. NEW YORK

Supreme Court of the United States
432 U.S. 197 (1977)

JUSTICE WHITE delivered the opinion of the Court. . . .

After a brief and unstable marriage, the appellant, Gordon Patterson, Jr., became estranged from his wife, Roberta. Roberta resumed an association with John Northrup, a neighbor to whom she had been engaged prior to her marriage to appellant. On December 27, 1970, Patterson borrowed a rifle from an acquaintance and went to the residence of his father-in-law. There, he observed his wife through a window in a state of semiundress in the presence of John Northrup. He entered the house and killed Northrup by shooting him in the head.

Patterson was charged with second-degree murder. In New York there are two elements of this crime: (1) "intent to cause the death of another person"; and (2) "caus[ing] the death of such person or of a third person." Malice aforethought is not an element of the crime. In addition, the State permits a person accused of murder to raise an affirmative defense that he "acted under the influence of extreme emotional disturbance for which there was a reasonable explanation or excuse."[a]

New York also recognizes the crime of manslaughter. A person is guilty of manslaughter if he intentionally kills another person "under circumstances which do not constitute murder because he acts under the influence of extreme emotional disturbance." Appellant confessed before trial to killing Northrup, but at trial he raised the defense of extreme emotional disturbance.

The jury was . . . instructed, consistently with New York law, that the defendant had the burden of proving his affirmative defense by a preponderance of the evidence. The jury was told that if it found beyond a reasonable doubt that appellant had intentionally killed Northrup but that appellant had demonstrated by a preponderance of the evidence that he had acted under the influence of extreme emotional disturbance, it had to find appellant guilty of manslaughter instead of murder. The jury found appellant guilty of murder. [The New York Court of Appeals affirmed, rejecting Patterson's argument

---

a. The relevant provisions of the New York Penal Code may be found at pages 424-426 infra.—EDS.

that the statutory scheme had improperly shifted to him the burden of proof on the crucial question of extreme emotional disturbance.]

In determining whether New York's allocation to the defendant of proving the mitigating circumstances of severe emotional disturbance is consistent with due process, it is . . . relevant to note that this defense is a considerably expanded version of the common-law defense of heat of passion on sudden provocation and that at common law the burden of proving the latter, as well as other affirmative defenses—indeed, "all . . . circumstances of justification, excuse or alleviation"—rested on the defendant. 4 W. Blackstone, Commentaries *201. This was the rule when the Fifth Amendment was adopted, and it was the American rule when the Fourteenth Amendment was ratified.

In 1895 the common-law view was abandoned with respect to the insanity defense in federal prosecutions. Davis v. United States, 160 U.S. 469 (1895). This ruling had wide impact on the practice in the federal courts with respect to the burden of proving various affirmative defenses, and the prosecution in a majority of jurisdictions in this country sooner or later came to shoulder the burden of proving the sanity of the accused and of disproving the facts constituting other affirmative defenses, including provocation. Davis was not a constitutional ruling, however, as Leland v. Oregon, [343 U.S. 790 (1952)], made clear.

At issue in Leland v. Oregon was the constitutionality under the Due Process Clause of the Oregon rule that the defense of insanity must be proved by the defendant beyond a reasonable doubt. Noting that Davis "obviously establish[ed] no constitutional doctrine," the Court refused to strike down the Oregon scheme, saying that the burden of proving all elements of the crime beyond reasonable doubt, including the elements of premeditation and deliberation, was placed on the State under Oregon procedures and remained there throughout the trial. To convict, the jury was required to find each element of the crime beyond a reasonable doubt, based on all the evidence, including the evidence going to the issue of insanity. Only then was the jury "to consider separately the issue of legal sanity per se. . . ." This practice did not offend the Due Process Clause even though among the 20 States then placing the burden of proving his insanity on the defendant, Oregon was alone in requiring him to convince the jury beyond a reasonable doubt. . . .

We cannot conclude that Patterson's conviction under the New York law deprived him of due process of law. . . . The death, the intent to kill, and causation are the facts that the State is required to prove beyond a reasonable doubt if a person is to be convicted of murder. No further facts are either presumed or inferred in order to constitute the crime. . . . It seems to us that the State satisfied the mandate of Winship [page 31 supra,] that it prove beyond a reasonable doubt "every fact necessary to constitute the crime with which [Patterson was] charged."

Even if we were to hold that a State must prove sanity to convict once that fact is put in issue, it would not necessarily follow that a State must prove beyond a reasonable doubt every fact, the existence or nonexistence of which it is willing to recognize as an exculpatory or mitigating circumstance affecting the degree of culpability or the severity of the punishment. Here, in revising its criminal code, New York provided the affirmative defense of extreme emotional disturbance, a substantially expanded version of the older heat-of-passion concept; but it was willing to do so only if the facts making out the defense were established by the defendant with sufficient certainty. The State was itself unwilling to undertake to establish the absence of those facts beyond a reasonable doubt, perhaps fearing that proof would be too difficult and that too many persons deserving treatment as murderers would escape that punishment if the evidence need merely raise a reasonable doubt about the defendant's emotional state. . . . The Due Process Clause, as we see it, does not put New York to the choice of abandoning such defenses or undertaking to disprove their existence in order to convict of a crime which otherwise is within its constitutional powers to sanction by substantial punishment. . . .

This view may seem to permit state legislatures to reallocate burdens of proof by labeling as affirmative defenses at least some elements of the crimes now defined in their statutes. But there are obviously constitutional limits beyond which the States may not go in this regard. "[I]t is not within the province of a legislature to declare an individual guilty or presumptively guilty of a crime." McFarland v. American Sugar Rfg. Co., 241 U.S. 79, 86 (1916). The legislature cannot "validly command that the finding of an indictment, or mere proof of the identity of the accused, should create a presumption of the existence of all the facts essential to guilt." Tot v. United States, 319 U.S. 463, 469 (1943). . . .

It is urged that Mullaney v. Wilbur necessarily invalidates Patterson's conviction. . . . *Mullaney*'s holding, it is argued, is that the State may not permit the blameworthiness of an act or the severity of punishment authorized for its commission to depend on the presence or absence of an identified fact without assuming the burden of proving the presence or absence of that fact, as the case may be, beyond a reasonable doubt. In our view, the *Mullaney* holding should not be so broadly read. . . . The Maine Supreme Judicial Court made it clear that . . . malice, in the sense of the absence of provocation, was part of the definition of that crime. Yet malice, i.e., lack of provocation, was presumed and could be rebutted by the defendant only by proving by a preponderance of the evidence that he acted with heat of passion upon sudden provocation. . . .

As we have explained, nothing was presumed or implied against Patterson. . . . The judgment of the New York Court of Appeals is affirmed.

JUSTICE POWELL, with whom JUSTICE BRENNAN and JUSTICE MARSHALL join, dissenting. . . .

Mullaney held invalid Maine's requirement that the defendant prove heat of passion. The Court today, without disavowing the unanimous holding of *Mullaney*, approves New York's requirement that the defendant prove extreme emotional disturbance. The Court manages to run a constitutional boundary line through the barely visible space that separates Maine's law from New York's. It does so on the basis of distinctions in language that are formalistic rather than substantive. . . . The test the Court today establishes allows a legislature to shift, virtually at will, the burden of persuasion with respect to any factor in a criminal case, so long as it is careful not to mention the nonexistence of that factor in the statutory language that defines the crime. . . .

With all respect, this type of constitutional adjudication is indefensibly formalistic. . . . What *Winship* and *Mullaney* had sought to teach about the limits a free society places on its procedures to safeguard the liberty of its citizens becomes a rather simplistic lesson in statutory draftsmanship. Nothing in the Court's opinion prevents a legislature from applying this new learning to many of the classical elements of the crimes it punishes. . . .[8]

The Court understandably . . . issues a warning that "there are obviously constitutional limits beyond which the States may not go in this regard." . . . But if the State is careful to conform to the drafting formulas articulated today, the constitutional limits are anything but "obvious." This decision simply leaves us without a conceptual framework for distinguishing abuses from legitimate legislative adjustments of the burden of persuasion in criminal cases.

It is unnecessary for the Court to retreat to a formalistic test for applying *Winship*. . . . The Due Process Clause requires that the prosecutor bear the burden of persuasion beyond a reasonable doubt only if the factor at issue makes a substantial difference in punishment and stigma. The requirement of course applies a fortiori if the factor makes the difference between guilt and innocence. But a substantial difference in punishment alone is not enough. It also must be shown that in the Anglo-American legal tradition the factor in question historically has held that level of importance. If either branch of the test is not met, then the legislature retains its traditional authority over matters of proof. . . .

I hardly need add that New York's provisions allocating the burden of persuasion as to "extreme emotional disturbance" are unconstitutional when judged by these standards. "Extreme emotional disturbance" is, as the Court of Appeals recognized, the direct descendant of the "heat of passion" factor considered at length in *Mullaney*. . . . The presence or absence of extreme emotional disturbance makes a critical difference in punishment and stigma, and throughout our history the resolution of this issue in fact, although expressed in somewhat different terms, has distinguished manslaughter from murder. . . . New ameliorative affirmative defenses, about which the Court expresses concern, generally remain undisturbed by the

---

8. For example, a state statute could pass muster under the only solid standard that appears in the Court's opinion if it defined murder as mere physical contact between the defendant and the victim leading to the victim's death, but then set up an affirmative defense leaving it to the defendant to prove that he acted without culpable mens rea. The State, in other words, could be relieved altogether of responsibility for proving *anything* regarding the defendant's state of mind, provided only that the face of the statute meets the Court's drafting formulas. . . .

holdings in *Winship* and *Mullaney*—and need not be disturbed by a sound holding reversing Patterson's conviction.

NOTES AND QUESTIONS

1. *The burden of production versus the burden of persuasion.* Rules allocating the burden of proof deal with two distinct problems. The first concerns allocating the burden of coming forward with enough evidence to put a certain fact in issue. This is commonly referred to as the burden of *production.* The second problem concerns allocating the burden of convincing the trier of fact. This is commonly referred to as the burden of *persuasion.* With respect to most facts relevant to guilt, the prosecution bears *both* burdens. That is, the prosecution must introduce enough evidence not only to put the facts in issue but also to persuade the trier of fact beyond a reasonable doubt. In some instances state law may require the defense to bear both burdens. But note that an intermediate position is possible: State law might allocate the burden of *production* to the defense but the burden of *persuasion* to the prosecution. For example, the state might provide that a defendant seeking acquittal on grounds of duress must introduce some evidence of duress, but that once this is done, the prosecution must prove the absence of duress beyond a reasonable doubt. In this situation it is sometimes said (confusingly) that the defendant bears the initial burden of proof and that, once duress is at issue, the burden *shifts* to the prosecution. Or it may be said that absence of duress is *presumed,* but that when evidence of duress is introduced the presumption is *rebutted* or simply *disappears.* All these expressions are equivalent to the more straightforward statement that the defendant bears the burden of production and the prosecution the burden of persuasion.

When the defendant bears the burden of production on an issue, the issue is commonly referred to as an *affirmative defense.* In some states, when an issue is designated an affirmative defense, the defendant must bear the burdens of both production and persuasion, but it is common practice to treat burdens of production and persuasion as separate issues. Thus, the defendant may bear the burden of persuasion on *some* affirmative defenses, but with respect to others he may bear *only* the burden of production.

When the defendant bears the burden of production, how much evidence is necessary to satisfy that burden so that the prosecution will be required to disprove the claim beyond a reasonable doubt? Most courts require that the evidence be sufficient to raise at least a reasonable doubt on the matter. See Frazier v. Weatherholtz, 572 F.2d 994 (4th Cir. 1978). When the defense produces evidence sufficient to satisfy the threshold requirements, it becomes necessary to determine which party must bear the burden of persuading the trier of fact.

2. *Allocating the burden of persuasion: the basis of* **Patterson.** Are states free to allocate the burden of persuasion however they choose, or does the reasoning of *Patterson* suggest some limits? Consider the following problems.

(a) Liberalizing and nonliberalizing changes in the law. In *Patterson* the affirmative defense involved "a substantially expanded version of the older heat-of-passion concept," and the Court stressed the need for permitting the states flexibility in this situation. But what if, after *Patterson*, a state shifts to the defendant a burden of persuasion previously imposed on the prosecution and does not enlarge the scope of the defense? Should it matter whether the traditional defense might otherwise have been restricted or repealed?

(b) Gratuitous defenses. The *Patterson* majority assumed that New York could eliminate the "extreme emotional disturbance" defense altogether, a point conceded by Justice Lewis Powell's dissent. If this is so, how can there be any serious challenge to the constitutionality of recognizing the defense only in diluted form, that is, when the defendant can prove it? Several commentators argue that "the greater power should include the lesser."[36] Under this analysis, states would be free to reallocate burdens of persuasion relating to any fact that is not a constitutionally mandated prerequisite to just punishment. But conversely, states would be required to prove a fact beyond a reasonable doubt if punishment would be impermissible (or excessive, violating Eighth Amendment proportionality requirements) as applied to conduct not involving that fact. See, e.g., Ronald Allen, The Restoration of *In re Winship:* A Comment on Burdens of Persuasion in Criminal Cases after *Patterson v. New York*, 76 Mich. L. Rev. 30 (1977). Consider the following comment:

John C. Jeffries Jr. & Paul B. Stephan, Defenses, Presumptions and Burdens of Proof in the Criminal Law, 88 Yale L.J. 1325, 1345-1347 (1979): Implementing the presumption of innocence—whether on an actual or a symbolic level—requires that *something* be proved beyond a reasonable doubt. It does not, however, speak to the question of *what* that something must be. [When] the state considers a gratuitous defense, that is, one that it may grant or deny as it sees fit, a constitutional insistence on proof beyond a reasonable doubt no longer makes sense. Such a rule would purport to preserve individual liberty and the societal sense of commitment to it by forcing the government *either* to disprove the defense beyond a reasonable doubt *or* to eliminate the defense altogether. The latter solution results in an extension of penal liability despite the presence of mitigating or exculpatory facts. It is difficult to see this result as constitutionally compelled and harder still to believe that it flows from a general policy, whether actual or symbolic, in favor of individual liberty. . . .

The trouble lies in trying to define justice in exclusively procedural terms. *Winship*'s insistence on the reasonable doubt standard is thought to express a preference for letting the guilty go free rather than risking conviction of the innocent. This value choice, however, cannot be implemented by a purely procedural concern with burden of proof. Guilt and innocence are substantive

---

36. The originator of the greater-includes-the-lesser argument in this context is generally thought to be Justice Holmes, who advanced it in his opinion for the Court in Ferry v. Ramsey, 277 U.S. 88 (1928).

concepts. Their content depends on the choice of facts determinative of liability. If this choice is remitted to unconstrained legislative discretion, no rule of constitutional procedure can restrain the potential for injustice. . . .

For scholarship critical of *Patterson*'s "greater includes the lesser" approach, see Scott E. Sundby, The Reasonable Doubt Rule and the Meaning of Innocence, 40 Hastings L.J. 457 (1989); Donald A. Dripps, The Constitutional Status of the Reasonable Doubt Rule, 75 Calif. L. Rev. 1665 (1987). Both authors argue that the Due Process Clause should be construed to require proof beyond a reasonable doubt for any fact that makes a significant difference in the authorized range of punishment. Compare Luis E. Chiesa, When an Offense Is Not an Offense: Rethinking the Supreme Court's Reasonable Doubt Jurisprudence, 44 Creighton L. Rev. 647 (2011), arguing that *Winship* should not be read to require the prosecution to disprove excuse defenses beyond a reasonable doubt.

(c) Nongratuitous defenses. In *Patterson* the affirmative defense was "gratuitous," in the sense that the state could have eliminated the defense completely. Should the state's freedom to shift the burden of proof extend to defenses that are *not* gratuitous? Consider, for example, the insanity defense. There is a long-standing debate (see pages 984-985 infra) over the question whether some form of an insanity defense is constitutionally mandated. Yet in Rivera v. Delaware, 429 U.S. 877 (1976), the Court summarily dismissed a challenge to a Delaware law that required the defendant to bear the burden of proving insanity. Should *Rivera* be read as holding, by implication, that states are free to eliminate the insanity defense completely? If not, what is the justification for permitting states to avoid the reasonable-doubt requirement and to "dilute" a defense that may be constitutionally mandated?

In connection with these questions, consider Martin v. Ohio, 480 U.S. 228 (1987). The defendant, a battering victim, shot her husband in what she claimed was an act of self-defense. She was charged with aggravated murder, which is defined under Ohio law as a killing "purposely, and with prior calculation and design." Ohio law also provides that self-defense is a complete defense when "the defendant was not at fault in creating the situation giving rise to the argument; [and] had an honest belief that she was in imminent danger of death or great bodily harm and that her only means of escape from such danger was in the use of such force. . . ." At trial, the jury was instructed that the prosecution had to prove beyond a reasonable doubt all the elements of aggravated murder, but that the defendant was required to prove her self-defense claim by a preponderance of the evidence. The defendant's aggravated murder conviction was upheld by the Supreme Court. Writing for the majority, Justice Byron White said (id. at 233-235):

> The State did not exceed its authority in defining the crime of murder as purposely causing the death of another with prior calculation or design. It did not seek to shift to Martin the burden of proving any of those elements, and the jury's verdict reflects that none of her self-defense evidence raised a

reasonable doubt about the state's proof that she purposefully killed with prior calculation and design. . . .

Justice Powell, writing for the four dissenters, argued that the defense claim of imminently necessary self-defense was inherently inconsistent with the prosecution claim of killing "by prior calculation and design." As a result, he argued, the instruction requiring the defendant to prove self-defense was in direct conflict with the instruction requiring the prosecution to prove aggravated murder beyond a reasonable doubt. As to this point, the majority asserted (id. at 235) that "the instructions were sufficiently clear to convey to the jury that the state's burden of proving prior calculation did not shift."

Note that no member of the Court challenged Justice White's assertion, supra, that "[t]he State did not exceed its authority in defining the crime of murder as purposely causing the death of another. . . ." Is this so clear? Could a state constitutionally abolish the defense of self-defense altogether? Could the state condemn as a murderer, and sentence to long-term imprisonment, a person who kills when such an act is the only available means to avoid an unlawful threat of imminent death?

3. Sentencing enhancements. Legislatures often define a crime and then specify that the punishment to be imposed will depend on certain characteristics of the offense committed (such as whether the offense involved a firearm or a given quantity of drugs). Usually the judge determines at a sentencing hearing whether such circumstances exist and then imposes sentence accordingly. The procedure at the sentencing hearing is relatively informal, and the judge is not required to find beyond a reasonable doubt every fact she considers in fixing the sentence. Thus, McMillan v. Pennsylvania, 477 U.S. 79 (1986), involved a state statute imposing a mandatory minimum sentence of five years' imprisonment on anyone convicted of certain felonies if the judge found at sentencing by a preponderance of the evidence that he had possessed a firearm during the commission of the offense. The Court held that this provision did not violate the constitutional requirement of proof beyond a reasonable doubt because the fact in question—possession of a weapon—did not increase the maximum sentence that the judge was authorized to impose, and accordingly the judge *could have* imposed the same five-year sentence whether or not the defendant had possessed a firearm.

Clearly, this technique affords an easy way to ease the burden of compliance with the requirement of proof beyond a reasonable doubt—facts that dictate a large increase in punishment can be established merely by a preponderance of the evidence. But this technique is available only when the facts at issue are merely "sentencing factors," rather than elements of a separate offense. For facts of the latter sort, as *Mullaney* holds, nothing less than proof beyond a reasonable doubt will suffice. A technical question of statutory structure therefore takes on great importance—when is a fact that enhances the sentence merely a sentencing factor and when is it an element of a separate, aggravated offense?

In a landmark decision, Apprendi v. New Jersey, 530 U.S. 466 (2000), the Supreme Court made clear that the states do not have unlimited discretion to characterize facts as mere sentencing considerations rather than elements of the offense. *Apprendi* involved a "hate-crimes" statute that provided for doubling the maximum punishment applicable to any offense if the sentencing judge found by a preponderance of the evidence that the offense was committed with "a purpose to intimidate an individual or group of individuals because of race, color, gender, handicap, religion, sexual orientation, or ethnicity." (Id. at 469.) The Court held this scheme unconstitutional, ruling that any fact (other than prior criminal record) that increases the maximum penalty applicable to an offense is an "element" of the offense, which therefore must be proved beyond a reasonable doubt. And the Court has held the *Apprendi* principle applicable not only to facts that increase a *statutory* maximum but also to facts that increase the maximum punishment authorized under sentencing guidelines. Blakely v. Washington, 542 U.S. 296 (2004); United States v. Booker, 543 U.S. 220 (2005).

In contrast, however, facts that affect the choice of sentence within an authorized range continue to be treated merely as "sentencing factors," and such facts do not have to be proved beyond a reasonable doubt. Legislatures therefore can give themselves considerable flexibility simply by setting a very high maximum sentence for an offense. They can then authorize or even require judges to impose a *lower* sentence if certain facts are proved by a mere preponderance. Similarly, as in *McMillan*, legislatures can require judges to impose a severe mandatory *minimum* sentence whenever the prosecution proves certain facts by a mere preponderance at the sentencing hearing. Although this approach to statutory drafting seems to dilute the reasonable-doubt requirement in almost the same way that the New Jersey hate-crimes statute did in *Apprendi*, the Court has explicitly reaffirmed the *McMillan* holding that the reasonable-doubt requirement does not apply to facts that trigger a mandatory minimum. Harris v. United States, 536 U.S. 545 (2002).

This distinction between facts that are offense "elements" and those that are mere "sentencing factors" has important implications not only for the reasonable-doubt principle but also for the right to jury trial and for the dynamics of the sentencing process. We explore those implications below at page 71 with respect to jury trial, and at pages 1187-1189 with respect to sentencing.

4. *How should a jurisdiction exercise its discretion?* Even where *Patterson* leaves a jurisdiction free to impose a burden of persuasion on the defendant, the decision does not imply that the state must do so or should do so. Legislatures (or courts, when statutes do not control) must decide what is desirable with respect to each defense of this kind. The Supreme Court held, for example, that in a federal prosecution for illegally receiving a firearm, a defendant who claims duress must bear the burden of proving that defense by a preponderance of the evidence. Dixon v. United States, 548 U.S. 1 (2006).

In contrast, the New Hampshire Supreme Court has held that once a defendant presents some evidence supporting the partial defense of provocation, the state must prove the absence of provocation beyond a reasonable doubt. State v. Soto, 2011 N.H. LEXIS 169 (Nov. 22, 2011). Burden-of-proof questions therefore must be reconsidered in light of problems associated with particular substantive law doctrines.

b. Presumptions

As the preceding section shows, the prosecution's burden of proof often can be eased by defining an offense in such a way that the burden of proving certain facts can be assigned to the defense. Another device that can ease the prosecutor's burden is the *presumption*. The presumption can come into play even when the state has not exercised (or cannot exercise) the *Patterson* option of reallocating the burden of proof. Suppose, for example, that murder is defined as an *intentional* killing. The state might hesitate to redefine murder as including all killing (with lack of intent relevant only as an affirmative defense). Can the state instead choose to retain intent as a required element of murder, but then provide that the existence of the necessary intent will be *presumed* from some other fact (for example, from the use of a deadly weapon)? The question assumes great practical importance because intent is a required element of so many criminal offenses, but there is often no direct evidence of what was going on in the defendant's mind. Rather than give a straightforward answer to the question, the Supreme Court has held that it is sometimes—but not always—permissible to presume the existence of an essential fact (like intent) from proof of some other fact. The Court has said that a *mandatory* presumption—one that the jury is required to accept in the absence of defense rebuttal—is constitutionally acceptable only if, over the universe of all cases in general, the presumed relationship holds true beyond a reasonable doubt. In contrast, in order for the prosecution to rely on a *permissive* inference—one that the jury may choose to accept or reject even in the absence of any defense rebuttal—all that is required is that the relationship be "more likely than not" to hold true under the circumstances of the particular case. County Court v. Allen, 442 U.S. 140 (1979).

Consider the application of this standard to one of the criminal law's most commonly invoked presumptions—the presumption that a "person of sound mind and discretion is presumed to intend the natural and probable consequences of his acts." After *County Court*, is reliance on this presumption constitutionally permissible? For example, if the defendant, a person of sound mind, shoots at the victim, hitting him in the chest and killing him, is it permissible to presume that the defendant intended to kill? The issue was presented in Francis v. Franklin, 471 U.S. 307 (1985). The case involved an escaped convict (Franklin) who shot a 72-year-old man in the course of an attempt to steal the man's car. The trial judge told the jury that Franklin was "presumed to intend the natural and probable consequences of his acts, but the presumption may be rebutted." Franklin was convicted of murder and sentenced to death. The Supreme Court held the jury instruction unconstitutional and reversed the conviction. Do you see why?

4. The Role of the Jury

DUNCAN v. LOUISIANA

Supreme Court of the United States
391 U.S. 145 (1968)

JUSTICE WHITE delivered the opinion of the Court.

Appellant, Gary Duncan, was convicted of simple battery in the Twenty-fifth Judicial District Court of Louisiana. Under Louisiana law simple battery is a misdemeanor, punishable by two years' imprisonment and a $300 fine.[a]

Appellant sought trial by jury, but because the Louisiana Constitution grants jury trials only in cases in which capital punishment or imprisonment at hard labor may be imposed, the trial judge denied the request. Appellant was convicted and sentenced to serve 60 days in the parish prison and pay a fine of $150. Appellant sought review in the Supreme Court of Louisiana, asserting that the denial of jury trial violated rights guaranteed to him by the United States Constitution. The Supreme Court [of Louisiana denied review.] We noted probable jurisdiction. . . .

While driving on Highway 23 in Plaquemines Parish on October 19, 1966, [appellant] saw two younger cousins engaged in a conversation by the side of the road with four white boys. Knowing his cousins, Negroes who had recently transferred to a formerly all-white high school, had reported the occurrence of racial incidents at the school, Duncan stopped the car, got out, and approached the six boys. . . . The testimony was in dispute on many points, but the witnesses agreed that appellant and the white boys spoke to each other, that appellant encouraged his cousins to break off the encounter and enter his car, and that appellant was about to enter the car himself for the purpose of driving away with his cousins. The whites testified that just before getting in the car appellant slapped Herman Landry, one of the white boys, on the elbow. The Negroes testified that appellant had not slapped Landry, but had merely touched him. The trial judge concluded that the State had proved beyond a reasonable doubt that Duncan had committed simple battery, and found him guilty.

[Despite the clear language of the Sixth Amendment ("In all criminal prosecutions, the accused shall enjoy the right to a speedy and public trial, by an impartial jury. . . . "), the jury trial issue before the Court in *Duncan* was not completely straightforward, because in Barron v. Mayor of Baltimore, 32 U.S. (7 Pet.) 243 (1833), the Court had held that the first eight amendments to the

---

a. The applicable Louisiana statute provided that "Simple battery is a battery, without the consent of the victim, committed without a dangerous weapon." La. Rev. Stat. §14:35 (1950). As traditionally understood, a battery includes any "offensive touching"; neither pain nor physical injury is required. See Wayne R. LaFave, Criminal Law 816 (4th ed. 2003).—EDS

Constitution apply only to the federal government and are not directly binding on the states. The principal limitation on criminal procedure in state prosecutions is the clause of the Fourteenth Amendment providing that "[no] State [shall] deprive any person of life, liberty, or property without due process of law." The Court had interpreted "due process" in this context to forbid only those procedures that violate *fundamental fairness.* Thus the precise issue before the Court in *Duncan* was whether denying a criminal defendant the opportunity to be tried by jury was *fundamentally unfair.*]

. . . Because we believe that trial by jury in criminal cases is fundamental to the American scheme of justice, we hold that the Fourteenth Amendment guarantees a right of jury trial in all criminal cases which—were they to be tried in a federal court—would come within the Sixth Amendment's guarantee. Since we consider the appeal before us to be such a case, we hold that the Constitution was violated when appellant's demand for jury trial was refused.

The history of trial by jury in criminal cases has been frequently told. It is sufficient for present purposes to say that by the time our Constitution was written, jury trial in criminal cases had been in existence in England for several centuries and carried impressive credentials traced by many to the Magna Carta. Its preservation and proper operation as a protection against arbitrary rule were among the major objectives of the revolutionary settlement which was expressed in the Declaration and Bill of Rights of 1689. . . .

The guarantees of jury trial in the Federal and State Constitutions reflect a profound judgment about the way in which law should be enforced and justice administered. A right to jury trial is granted to criminal defendants in order to prevent oppression by the Government. Those who wrote our constitutions knew from history and experience that it was necessary to protect against unfounded criminal charges brought to eliminate enemies and against judges too responsive to the voice of higher authority. The framers of the constitutions strove to create an independent judiciary but insisted upon further protection against arbitrary action. Providing an accused with the right to be tried by a jury of his peers gave him an inestimable safeguard against the corrupt or overzealous prosecutor and against the compliant, biased, or eccentric judge. If the defendant preferred the common-sense judgment of a jury to the more tutored but perhaps less sympathetic reaction of the single judge, he was to have it. Beyond this, the jury trial provisions in the Federal and State Constitutions reflect a fundamental decision about the exercise of official power—a reluctance to entrust plenary powers over the life and liberty of the citizen to one judge or to a group of judges. . . . The deep commitment of the Nation to the right of jury trial in serious criminal cases as a defense against arbitrary law enforcement qualifies for protection under the Due Process Clause of the Fourteenth Amendment, and must therefore be respected by the States. . . .

We are aware of the long debate, especially in this century, among those who write about the administration of justice, as to the wisdom of permitting untrained laymen to determine the facts in civil and criminal proceedings.

[M]ost of the controversy has centered on the jury in civil cases. [A]t the heart of the dispute have been express or implicit assertions that juries are incapable of adequately understanding evidence or determining issues of fact and that they are . . . little better than a roll of dice. Yet, the most recent and exhaustive study of the jury in criminal cases concluded that juries do understand the evidence and come to sound conclusions in most of the cases presented to them and that when juries differ with the result at which the judge would have arrived, it is usually because they are serving some of the very purposes for which they were created and for which they are now employed.[26] The State of Louisiana urges that holding that the Fourteenth Amendment assures a right to jury trial will cast doubt on the integrity of every trial conducted without a jury. . . . We would not assert, however, that every criminal trial—or any particular trial—held before a judge alone is unfair or that a defendant may never be as fairly treated by a judge as he would be by a jury. Thus we hold no constitutional doubts about the practices, common in both federal and state courts, of accepting waivers of jury trial and prosecuting petty crimes without extending a right to jury trial. However, the fact is that in most places more trials for serious crimes are to juries than to a court alone; a great many defendants prefer the judgment of a jury to that of a court. Even where defendants are satisfied with bench trials, the right to a jury trial very likely serves its intended purpose of making judicial or prosecutorial unfairness less likely.

Louisiana's final contention is that even if it must grant jury trials in serious criminal cases, the conviction before us is valid and constitutional because here the petitioner was tried for simple battery and was sentenced to only 60 days in the parish prison. We are not persuaded. It is doubtless true that there is a category of petty crimes or offenses which is not subject to the Sixth Amendment jury trial provision and should not be subject to the Fourteenth Amendment jury trial requirement here applied to the States. . . .

We need not, however, settle in this case the exact location of the line between petty offenses and serious crimes. It is sufficient for our purpose to hold that a crime punishable by two years in prison is, based on past and contemporary standards in this country, a serious crime and not a petty offense. Consequently, appellant was entitled to a jury trial and it was error to deny it. . . .

Reversed and remanded.

JUSTICE HARLAN, with whom JUSTICE STEWART joins, dissenting. . . .

[There] is a wide range of views on the desirability of trial by jury, and on the ways to make it most effective when it is used; there is also considerable variation from State to State in local conditions such as the size of the criminal caseload, the ease or difficulty of summoning jurors, and other trial conditions

---

26. Kalven & Zeisel, [The American Jury (1966)].

bearing on fairness. We have before us, therefore, an almost perfect example of a situation in which the celebrated dictum of Mr. Justice Brandeis should be invoked. It is, he said, "one of the happy incidents of the federal system that a single courageous state may, if its citizens choose, serve as a laboratory. . . ." New State Ice Co. v. Liebmann, 285 U.S. 262, 280, 311 (dissenting opinion). This Court, other courts, and the political process are available to correct any experiments in criminal procedure that prove fundamentally unfair to defendants.

NOTES

1. **Duncan** *in context.* Justice White mentions, early in his opinion, that Duncan's cousins had recently transferred to a previously all-white high school where "racial incidents" had been reported. That description of the circumstances was a colossal, and no-doubt deliberate, understatement. The previous year, the U.S. attorney general had declared Plaquemines Parish one of the nine most discriminatory counties in the nation, and in 1966, at the time of incident, the parish was in the midst of a ferocious school desegregation battle, pitting Justice Department attorneys, civil rights lawyers, and the federal courts against Leander H. Perez, Sr., a political figure and ardent segregationist (known locally as "the Bonaparte of the Bayou") who had ruled the parish with an iron fist for decades. Perez had hand-picked all judges and other officials in the parish, and he tolerated no opposition. Many civil rights activists who dared to enter the parish were arrested as "outside agitators." When the civil rights lawyer who had taken Duncan's case appeared at the courthouse to file a motion needed for the appeal to the U.S. Supreme Court, the Plaquemines sheriff arrested him on a charge of practicing law without a license and confiscated the briefcase that contained all of Duncan's appeal papers. For a fascinating, in-depth description of this background, see Nancy J. King, *Duncan v. Louisiana*: How Bigotry in the Bayou Led to Federal Regulation of State Juries, in Criminal Procedure Stories (C. Steiker ed., 2006).

Why didn't the Court make more of these local circumstances? The political situation in Plaquemines Parish seems to afford a perfect opportunity to make vivid the value of the jury as a check on official power. Would an emphasis on these facts have made the Court's opinion more persuasive? Or would such an emphasis detract from the Court's effort to establish a more general principle—that the jury should be considered an important safeguard against abuse even in a well-functioning democracy?

2. *The scope of the right to jury trial.* Justice Felix Frankfurter once wrote that "[n]o changes or chances can alter the content of the verbal symbol of 'jury'—a body of twelve men who must reach a unanimous conclusion if the verdict is to go against the defendant." Rochin v. California, 342 U.S. 165, 170 (1952). Except for the limitation to males, which had passed away long before Justice Frankfurter reiterated it, this statement expressed a nearly universal view about what was meant by a jury. Nevertheless, in Williams v. Florida, 399 U.S. 78, 86 (1970), the Court said that the decision to fix the size of the jury at 12 "appears to have been a historical accident, unrelated to the great purposes that gave rise to the jury" and held that a 6-member jury satisfied the constitutional requirement.[37] In Apodaca v. Oregon, 406 U.S. 404 (1972), the Court held that unanimity was not required in state criminal trials, so long as a substantial majority of the jury supports the verdict. The Court in that case upheld guilty verdicts obtained by 11–1 and 10–2 votes, without ruling explicitly on whether a smaller majority could also be sufficiently substantial.[38]

Duncan did not resolve the question of what may be deemed a "petty offense," for which the Sixth Amendment jury trial guarantee would be inapplicable. In Baldwin v. New York, 399 U.S. 66 (1970), the Court held that no offense may be deemed petty where imprisonment for more than six months is authorized. In such cases a defendant has a constitutional right to jury trial, whether or not imprisonment is in fact likely to be imposed.

3. *The representative jury.* Contrary to popular folklore, there is no requirement that a defendant be tried by a jury of "his peers." Nor is there any requirement that the trial jury of 6 or 12 reflect the demographic character of the locality. But the Supreme Court has held that under the Sixth Amendment, the "venire"—the panel of potential jurors from which the trial jury is drawn—must reflect "a fair cross section of the community." Taylor v. Louisiana, 419 U.S. 522, 537 (1975). The Court has treated the "fair cross section" requirement as a means to ensure the *impartiality* of the jury, but has not recognized an independent Sixth Amendment right to a jury that *represents* the community in any broader sense. See Holland v. Illinois, 493 U.S. 474 (1990); Laura G. Dooley, The Dilution Effect: Federalization, Fair Cross-Sections, and the Concept of Community, 54 DePaul L. Rev. 79 (2004).

Once an appropriate venire is assembled, potential jurors who know the defendant, the victim, or a witness can be challenged "for cause" and removed from the pool. The opposing attorneys are then allowed "peremptory challenges," which permit them to remove a certain number of potential jurors without giving any reason, simply because they suspect that the potential juror may be unsympathetic to their side. In Batson v. Kentucky, 476 U.S. 79 (1986), and J.E.B. v. Alabama, 511 U.S. 127 (1994), the Supreme Court held that attorneys cannot use their peremptory challenges to deliberately exclude potential jurors on grounds of race or gender. But the requirement is often difficult to enforce because a peremptory challenge can pass muster when the attorney can offer a plausible race-neutral and gender-neutral

---

37. In Ballew v. Georgia, 435 U.S. 223 (1978), the Court held that a 5-person jury did not fulfill the constitutional jury trial requirement.

38. In Burch v. Louisiana, 441 U.S. 130 (1979), the Court held that a 5–1 vote did not satisfy constitutional requirements. Thus, where states elect to use a 6-person jury, the verdict must be unanimous. The opinions in *Apodaca* suggest that for *federal* criminal trials, a majority of the Court would continue to view unanimity as constitutionally mandated. In any event, Rule 31(a) of the Federal Rules of Criminal Procedure requires a unanimous verdict in federal prosecutions.

explanation for making it. As a result, the trial jury ultimately empanelled often will differ markedly from the character of the community as a whole, even when the venire was well balanced. For example, an experienced federal judge reported that in Boston, "the vast majority of juries in federal court . . . did not have a single African-American member." Nancy S. Gertner, 12 Angry Men (and Women) in Federal Court, 82 Chi.-Kent L. Rev. 613, 619 (2007).

4. *The effect of jury trial on the criminal justice system.* (*a*) The entire texture of the trial is influenced by the existence of the jury. Instead of addressing arguments to one law-trained person, the lawyers address themselves to 12 lay people. Lawyers are often convinced that nonlegal factors will influence the jury even when those factors are not technically "relevant," and as a result the lawyers often attempt, with some success, to find indirect ways to make the jury aware of such matters.

(*b*) Because lay people may not assess items of proof as carefully as trained lawyers, Anglo-American law includes an elaborate structure of rules providing for the exclusion of certain evidence at the trial.

(*c*) The judge is judge of the law; the jury decides questions of fact. The legal system must characterize the nature of a given question: Is it a question of law or of fact?

(*d*) Judges must formulate for jurors' use an acceptable statement of applicable legal rules, though these rules may be the most difficult imaginable. When significant errors are made in stating these rules, a conviction must be reversed and a new trial must be held.

5. *The policies served (and disserved) by jury trial.* The Court in *Duncan* summarizes the principal reasons why it regards the availability of trial by jury as an essential component of fair procedure. Is it clear that the advantages of jury trial outweigh its costs or that experimentation with different kinds of factfinding procedures should be considered intolerable? Consider the following comments:

Glanville Williams, The Proof of Guilt 271-272 (3d ed. 1963): [I]t is an understatement to describe a jury, with Herbert Spencer, as a group of twelve people of average ignorance. There is no guarantee that members of a particular jury may not be quite unusually ignorant, credulous, slow-witted, narrow-minded, biased or temperamental. The danger of this happening is not one that can be removed by some minor procedural adjustment; it is inherent in the English notion of a jury as a body chosen from the general population at random.

Dale W. Broeder, The Functions of the Jury—Facts or Fictions?, 21 U. Chi. L. Rev. 386, 413-417 (1947): From the time of the Alien and Sedition Acts, the government's attempted inroads on civil rights seem to have received the enthusiastic support of jurors. . . .

But the case against the criminal jury as a protector of individual liberty extends further than to contests between government and citizens opposed to its policies. Minority groups have often suffered at the hands of jurymen. Wholesale acquittals of lynch-law violators, convictions of Negroes on the slightest evidence, and numerous other occurrences which have now almost become a part of the jury tradition might be instanced as examples. . . .

Aside from the incidental psychological functions which the criminal jury is alleged to perform, the sole remaining virtue claimed for it lies in its ability to make allowances for the circumstances of the particular case—to dispense with a rule of law. As noted previously, however, law-dispensing is a two-edged sword, and there is no current means of ascertaining which way it more often swings. It may seriously be doubted whether entrusting the jury with law-dispensing powers is justified. While flexibility of legal administration is desirable, it would seem that the necessary exceptions to the normal rules could with better reason be fashioned by the legislature or court.

Harry Kalven & Hans Zeisel, The American Jury 7-9 (1966): The [jury] controversy centers around three large issues. First, there is a series of collateral advantages and disadvantages that are often charged against, or pointed to on behalf of, the jury as an institution. In this realm fall such positive points as that the jury provides an important civic experience for the citizen; that, because of popular participation, the jury makes tolerable the stringency of certain decisions; that, because of its transient personnel, the jury acts as a sort of lightning rod for animosity and suspicion which otherwise might center on the more permanent judge; and that the jury is a guarantor of integrity, since it is said to be more difficult to reach twelve men than one. Against such affirmative claims, serious collateral disadvantages have been urged, chiefly that the jury is expensive; . . . that jury service imposes an unfair tax and social cost on those forced to serve; and that, in general, exposure to jury duty disenchants the citizen and causes him to lose confidence in the administration of justice.

Second, there is a group of issues that touch directly on the competence of the jury. . . . On the one hand, it is urged that the judge, as a result of training, discipline, recurrent experience, and superior intelligence, will be better able to understand the law and analyze the facts than laymen, selected from a wide range of intelligence levels, who have no particular experience with matters of this sort, and who have no durable official responsibility. On the other hand, it is argued that twelve heads are inevitably better than one; that the jury as a group has wisdom and strength which need not characterize any of its individual members; that it makes up in common sense and common experience what it may lack in professional training, and that its very inexperience is an asset because it secures a fresh perception of each trial, avoiding the stereotypes said to infect the judicial eye.

The third group of issues about the jury goes to what is perhaps the most interesting point. The critics complain that the jury will not follow the law, either because it does not understand it or because it does not like it, and that thus only a very uneven and unequal administration of justice can result from reliance on the jury; indeed, it is said that the jury is likely to produce that government by man, and not by rule of law, against which Anglo-American political tradition is so steadfastly set.

This same flexibility of the jury is offered by its champions as its most endearing and most important characteristic. The jury, it is said, is a remarkable device for insuring that we are governed by the spirit of the law and not by its letter; for insuring that rigidity of any general rule of law can be shaped to justice in the particular case. One is tempted to say that what is one man's equity is another man's anarchy.

6. Defense interests versus community interests. Suppose that the defendant prefers *not* to be tried by a jury. Should the defendant's preference control, or does the community have an independent interest in jury decision making? American jurisdictions are closely divided on the issue. See Uzi Segal & Alex Stein, Ambiguity Aversion and the Criminal Process, 81 Notre Dame L. Rev. 1495, 1501-1504 (2006). Many courts permit the prosecutor to demand a jury trial, even over the defendant's objection, and some courts, as in State v. Burks, 674 N.W.2d 640 (Wis. App. 2003), permit the trial judge to insist on a jury trial even when *both* the defense and the prosecution prefer a nonjury trial.

How should these issues be resolved? The Sixth Amendment, of course, is phrased as a grant of rights *to the defendant*, but the Amendment does not give the defendant a right *to waive* the jury, i.e., to insist upon a bench trial instead. In fact, Professor Laura I. Appleman argues that in the original understanding, "the right of the jury trial . . . is all about *representation*, or the participation of the citizenry in [the] rule of law. Fairness to the defendant plays a part, . . . but the right emphasized over and over again is that belonging to the local community and to the people at large." Appleman, The Lost Meaning of the Jury Trial Right, 84 Ind. L.J. 397, 413 (2009). See also George C. Harris, The Communitarian Function of the Criminal Jury Trial and the Rights of the Accused, 74 Neb. L. Rev. 804, 805 (1995):

> [There is] a public interest in trial by jury in criminal cases that is distinct from the public's interest in a fair trial for the accused or the reliable determination of guilt and innocence. This separate public interest derives from what can be called the criminal jury's "communitarian" function. The communitarian function of public trial by jury in criminal cases can be divided into three related aspects: 1) a democratic vehicle for community participation in government in general and the criminal justice system in particular; 2) a means by which the community is educated regarding our system of justice; and 3) a ritual by which the faith of the community in the administration of justice is maintained.

Questions: Should the community's interest in jury decision making trump the defendant's perception of the procedure most likely to afford him a fair trial? If so, who (the prosecutor or the judge) should have the authority to insist upon a jury trial over the defendant's objections?

Should bench trials be eliminated altogether? Or would forcing a defendant into an unwanted jury trial undercut the perceived fairness of a criminal conviction?

7. *Lay adjudicators in other countries.* In Canada, the criminal trial jury remains a "robust" institution that continues to account for a significant proportion of criminal case dispositions. See Neil Vidmar, The Canadian Criminal Jury: Searching for a Middle Ground, 62 Law & Contemp. Probs. 141, 172 (1999). And Spain introduced criminal jury trials in 1995. But most nations, including many with strong democratic traditions (such as India, Israel, and the Netherlands) do not use jury trials in criminal cases. Even in the common-law world, jury trials have become rare, in part because governments concerned about costs and the jury's competence have steadily narrowed the range of criminal cases in which jury trial is available. See Freedom's Lamp Dims, Economist, June 23, 2005. For discussion of current practice in more than two dozen countries, see Ethan J. Leib, A Comparison of Criminal Jury Trial Rules in Democratic Countries, 5 Ohio St. J. Crim. L. 629 (2008); Symposium on the Common Law Jury, 62 Law & Contemp. Probs. 1 (1999). Do these patterns cast doubt on the importance of jury trials in the American setting? If nonjury criminal trials are fully compatible with democracy, are there other features of American culture or the American judicial system that make jury trials especially important?

8. *The behavior of the jury in the United States.* The empirical study referred to by the Court in *Duncan*, Harry Kalven & Hans Zeisel, The American Jury (1966), represents an effort to determine the extent to which juries decide cases differently from the way judges would and to determine the sources of such differences. The entire book warrants careful reading in connection with efforts to understand the impact of jury trial in American criminal cases.[39] The authors find that judges and juries disagree in roughly 25 percent of jury trial cases. In a small portion of these (2 percent of the total cases), the jury convicts when the judge would acquit; in 17 percent of all cases the jury acquits when the judge would convict; in roughly 6 percent of the cases the jury "hangs" (fails to agree on a verdict). Id. at 56-57.

The authors examine in great depth the possible reasons for judge-jury disagreement. They conclude that of the various factors apparently involved, differences in assessing the evidence in close cases played a significant role.

---

39. This groundbreaking study remains a landmark in jury trial research. For a critique of its methodology, see Michael H. Walsh, The American Jury: A Reassessment, 79 Yale L.J. 142 (1969). In more recent empirical research, the rate of judge-jury disagreement has been similar to that found in the Kalven-Zeisel study, and evidentiary strength, in combination with other factors, continues to play an important role in explaining the differences. See Theodore Eisenberg et al., Judge-Jury Agreement in Criminal Cases: A Partial Replication of Kalven and Zeisel's *The American Jury*, 2 J. Empirical Legal Stud. 171 (2005); Amy S. Farrell & Daniel James Givelber, Liberation Reconsidered: Why Judges and Juries Disagree about Guilt, 100 J. Crim. L. & Criminology 1549 (2010). For a close look at three especially important sources of judge-jury disagreement (provocation, self-defense, and insanity), see Norman J. Finkel, Commonsense Justice: Jurors' Notions of the Law (1995).

They attributed 79 percent of the disagreements to this source. The other major factors that helped account for disagreement were jury sentiments about the law (50 percent of the cases), jury sentiments about the defendant (22 percent), facts only the judge knew (5 percent), and disparity of counsel (8 percent). Id. at 111. Often there was more than one reason for disagreement in a case. In fact, the closeness of the evidence usually appeared with one of the other reasons, so that this factor apparently "liberated the jury to respond to non-evidentiary factors." Id. at 106. It thus appeared that jury sentiment about the law was one of the most significant considerations, and this factor of course lies close to the heart of the jury's function as a guarantor of lenity and equity in dispensing criminal justice. The study suggests that "in cases having a de minimus cast or a note of contributory fault or provocation . . . the jury will exercise its de facto powers to write these equities into the criminal law." Id. at 285. Other sentiments about the law that appeared to have significant impact included "impatience with the nicety of the law's boundaries hedging the privilege of self-defense" (id. at 241) and resistance to the enforcement of a few unpopular laws, primarily hunting, liquor, gambling, and drunken-driving laws. While the study provides extensive evidence of jury nullification, it also should be noted that the judge and jury *agreed* in 75 percent of the cases, that only half the disagreement cases involved jury sentiments about the law, and that these sentiments usually (78 percent of the time, id. at 113) emerged in combination with other factors, principally the closeness of the evidence. The authors thus observe that the "jury's war with the law is now a polite one" (id. at 76) and conclude (at 498):

> The jury thus represents a uniquely subtle distribution of official power, an unusual arrangement of checks and balances. It represents also an impressive way of building discretion, equity and flexibility into a legal system. Not the least of the advantages is that the jury, relieved of the burdens of creating precedent, can bend the law without breaking it.

Notice that in *Duncan* the Court, referring to Kalven and Zeisel, says that when juries differ from the judge "it is usually because they are serving some of the very purposes for which they were created." Does this mean that the jury's equity-dispensing function is constitutionally protected and that procedures designed to minimize nullification would be unconstitutional?

UNITED STATES v. DOUGHERTY

United States Court of Appeals, District of Columbia Circuit
473 F.2d 1113 (1972)

LEVENTHAL, J. Seven of the so-called "D.C. Nine" bring this joint appeal from convictions arising out of their unconsented entry into the Washington office of the Dow Chemical Company, and their destruction of certain property therein. [The defendants had disrupted Dow's operations in an attempt to publicize their opposition to the Vietnam War. They then sought to use their criminal trial as a platform to further publicize their views. They made efforts to transform the trial into a "political fray" and attempted to argue to the jury that they should be acquitted because their actions were morally justified.] . . . [A]fter a six-day trial, the seven were each convicted of two counts of malicious destruction. . . .

Appellants urge [that] the judge erroneously refused to instruct the jury of its right to acquit appellants without regard to the law and the evidence, and refused to permit appellants to argue that issue to the jury. . . .

[Appellants] say that the jury has a well-recognized prerogative to disregard the instructions of the court even as to matters of law, and that they accordingly have the legal right that the jury be informed of its power. . . .

There has evolved in the Anglo-American system an undoubted jury prerogative-in-fact, derived from its power to bring in a general verdict of not guilty in a criminal case, that is not reversible by the court. The power of the courts to punish jurors for corrupt or incorrect verdicts . . . was repudiated in 1670 when Bushell's Case, 124 Eng. Rep. 1006 (C.P. 1670), discharged the jurors who had acquitted William Penn of unlawful assembly. Juries in civil cases became subject to the control of ordering a new trial; no comparable control evolved for acquittals in criminal cases.

The pages of history shine on instances of the jury's exercise of its prerogative to disregard uncontradicted evidence and instructions of the judge. Most often commended are the 18th century acquittal of Peter Zenger of seditious libel, on the plea of Andrew Hamilton, and the 19th century acquittals in prosecutions under the fugitive slave law. The values involved drop a notch when the liberty vindicated by the verdict relates to the defendant's shooting of his wife's paramour, or purchase during Prohibition of alcoholic beverages. . . .

The existence of an unreviewable and unreversible power in the jury, to acquit in disregard of the instructions on the law given by the trial judge, has for many years co-existed with legal practice and precedent upholding instructions to the jury that they are required to follow the instructions of the court on all matters of law. . . .

The rulings [in the early cases] did not run all one way, but rather precipitated "a number of classic exchanges on the freedom and obligations of the criminal jury."[36]

This was, indeed, one of the points of clash between the contending forces staking out the direction of the government of the newly established Republic. . . . As the distrust of judges appointed and removable by the king receded, there came increasing acceptance that under a republic the protection of citizens lay not in recognizing the right of each jury to make its own law, but in following democratic processes for changing the law. . . .

---

36. M.R. Kadish and S.H. Kadish, On Justified Rule Departures by Officials, 59 Calif. L. Rev. 905, 914 (1971).

Since the jury's prerogative of lenity . . . introduces a "slack into the enforcement of law, tempering its rigor by the mollifying influence of current ethical conventions," it is only just, say appellants, that the jurors be so told. It is unjust to withhold information on the jury power of "nullification," since conscientious jurors may come, ironically, to abide by their oath as jurors to render verdicts offensive to their individual conscience, to defer to an assumption of necessity that is contrary to reality.

This so-called right of jury nullification is put forward in the name of liberty and democracy, but its explicit avowal risks the ultimate logic of anarchy. "To encourage individuals to make their own determinations as to which laws they will obey and which they will permit themselves as a matter of conscience to disobey is to invite chaos. No legal system could long survive if it gave every individual the option of disregarding with impunity any law which by his personal standard was judged morally untenable. . . ." [United States v. Moylan, 417 F.2d 1002, 1009 (4th Cir. 1969).] [T]he advocates of jury "nullification" apparently assume that the articulation of the jury's power will not extend its use or extent, or will not do so significantly or obnoxiously. Can this assumption fairly be made? . . .

The way the jury operates may be radically altered if there is alteration in the way it is told to operate. The jury knows well enough that its prerogative is not limited to the choices articulated in the formal instructions of the court. The jury gets its understanding as to the arrangements in the legal system from more than one voice. . . .

When the legal system relegates the information of the jury's prerogative to an essentially informal input, it is not being duplicitous, chargeable with chicane and intent to deceive. The limitation to informal input is, rather, a governor to avoid excess: the prerogative is reserved for the exceptional case, and the judge's instruction is retained as a generally effective constraint. We "recognize a constraint as obligatory upon us when we require not merely reason to defend our rule departures, but damn good reason."[49]

The practicalities of men, machinery and rules point up the danger of articulating discretion to depart from a rule, that the breach will be more often and casually invoked. . . . The danger of the excess rigidity that may now occasionally exist is not as great as the danger of removing the boundaries of constraint provided by the announced rules. . . .

Moreover, to compel a juror involuntarily assigned to jury duty to assume the burdens of mini-legislator or judge, as is implicit in the doctrine of nullification, is to put untoward strains on the jury system. It is one thing for a juror to know that the law condemns, but he has a factual power of lenity. To tell him expressly of a nullification prerogative, however, is to inform him, in effect, that it is he who fashions the rule that condemns. That is an overwhelming responsibility, an extreme burden for the jurors' psyche.

---

49. Kadish and Kadish, supra, note 36, 59 Calif. L. Rev. at 926. [The "damn-good-reason" position is criticized in Alan Scheflin & Jon Van Dyke, Jury Nullification: The Contours of a Controversy, 43 Law & Contemp. Probs. 51, 98-108 (1980).—Eds.]

[A] juror called upon for an involuntary public service is entitled to the protection, when he takes action that he knows is right, but also knows is unpopular, either in the community at large or in his own particular grouping, that he can fairly put it to friends and neighbors that the was merely following the instructions of the court. . . .

[W]hat is tolerable or even desirable as an informal, self-initiated exception, harbors grave dangers to the system if it is opened to expansion and intensification through incorporation in the judge's instruction. . . .

BAZELON, C.J., concurring in part and dissenting in part. . . .

[T]he Court apparently concedes—although in somewhat grudging terms—that the power of nullification is a "necessary counter to case-hardened judges and arbitrary prosecutors," and that exercise of the power may, in at least some instances, "enhance the over-all normative effect of the rule of law." We could not withhold that concession without scoffing at the rationale that underlies the right to jury trial in criminal cases, and belittling some of the most legendary episodes in our political and jurisprudential history.

The sticking point, however, is whether or not the jury should be told of its power to nullify the law in a particular case. Here, the trial judge not only denied a requested instruction on nullification, but also barred defense counsel from raising the issue in argument before the jury. The majority affirms that ruling. I see no justification for, and considerable harm in, this deliberate lack of candor.

[T]he justification for this sleight-of-hand lies in a fear that an occasionally noble doctrine will, if acknowledged, often be put to ignoble and abusive purposes—or, to borrow the Court's phrase, will "run the risk of anarchy." . . . The Court assumes that these abuses are most likely to occur if the doctrine is formally described to the jury by argument or instruction. . . . It seems substantially more plausible to me to assume that the very opposite is true. . . .

[T]he Court takes comfort in the fact that informal communication to the jury "generally convey[s] adequately enough the idea of prerogative, of freedom in an occasional case to depart from what the judge says." . . . [But if] awareness is preferable to ignorance, then I simply do not understand the justification for relying on a haphazard process of informal communication whose effectiveness is likely to depend, to a large extent, on whether or not any of the jurors are so well-educated and astute that they are able to receive the message. If the jury should know of its power to disregard the law, then the power should be explicitly described by instruction of the court or argument of counsel. . . .

NOTES AND QUESTIONS ON NULLIFICATION

1. Empirical studies have probed the impact of nullification instructions. A fundamental question underlying the nullification debate is whether jurors who nullify are reflecting the community sense of justice, or instead whether (as the *Dougherty* court feared) they may be responding to vengeful instincts and emotional biases triggered by particular characteristics of the victim or the defendant. A further question, then, is whether explicit instructions about the nullification power will exacerbate some or all of these possibilities. Empirical studies have probed these issues to some extent. One research program[40] considered the effect of instructing mock juries that "nothing would bar them from acquitting the defendant if they feel that the law . . . would produce an inequitable or unjust result." In a case involving a nurse tried for the "mercy" killing of a terminally ill cancer patient, mock juries given the nullification instruction were, predictably, less likely to convict than mock juries not given the instruction. But, unexpectedly, the instructed mock juries were *more* likely to convict in a homicide case involving a drunk driver who struck and killed a pedestrian. In deliberations, mock juries spent less time discussing the evidence and more time discussing the defendant's character when a nullification instruction had been given. Another study found that in cases where the fairness of the underlying law was a concern, jurors given negative information about the victim were less likely to acquit when given a nullification instruction, whereas negative information about the victim did not affect the likelihood of acquittal when jurors were given standard jury instructions, without reference to nullification.[41]

2. The federal courts and nearly all the states follow *Dougherty* and refuse to permit instructions informing the jury of its nullification power. See, e.g., United States v. Edwards, 101 F.3d 17 (2d Cir. 1996); State v. Hatori, 990 P.2d 115 (Haw. App. 1999).

In three states the approach rejected in *Dougherty* still survives through constitutional provisions that the jury shall be the judge of the law as well as the fact. Ga. Const. art. 1, §1, §11(a); Ind. Const. art. 1, §19; Md. Const., Decl. of Rights, art. 23. In Georgia, however, courts have tended to confine the effect of the provision, for example, by upholding a charge that the jurors are the judges of the law but are obliged to apply the court's instructions to the facts and by forbidding defense counsel to argue to the jury that it should disregard the law. See State v. Freeman, 444 S.E.2d 80 (Ga. 1994); Drummond v. State, 326 S.E.2d 787 (Ga. App. 1985). Indiana and Maryland practice is summarized in Richard St. John, Note, License to Nullify: The Democratic and Constitutional Deficiencies of Authorized Jury Lawmaking, 106 Yale L.J. 2563 (1997).

3. The *Dougherty* court appears to believe that the jury's nullification power is desirable, so long as it is not exercised too often. Compare State v. Ragland, 105 N.J. 189, 519 A.2d 1361, 1371-1372 (1986):

> [J]ury nullification . . . is absolutely inconsistent with the most important value of Western democracy, that we should live under a government of

---

40. See Irwin A. Horowitz, Jury Nullification: An Empirical Perspective, 28 N. Ill. U.L. Rev. 425, 442-444 (2008).

41. Irwin A. Horowitz et al., Chaos in the Courtroom Reconsidered: Emotional Bias and Juror Nullification, 30 Law & Hum. Behav. 163 (2006).

laws and not of men. . . . With jury nullification, [the jurors] are told, either explicitly or implicitly, that *they* are the law, . . . and that if they want to, they may convict every poor man and acquit every rich man; convict the political opponent but free the crony; put the long-haired in jail but the crew-cut on the street; imprison the black and free the white; or, even more arbitrarily, just do what they please whenever they please.

One of the biggest problems in the administration of criminal justice is the inequality of its enforcement. . . . Absolutely nowhere in the system is there some notion that someone should have the power, arbitrarily, to pick and choose who shall live and who shall die. But that is precisely what jury nullification is: the power to undo everything that is precious in our system of criminal justice, the power to act arbitrarily to convict one and acquit another where there is absolutely no apparent difference between the two. It is a power, unfortunately, that is there, that this Court cannot terminate, but a power that should be restricted as much as possible.

. . . The lengths to which we go to exclude irrelevant evidence, the expenditures made to protect defendants from juror prejudice, the energy, study, and work devoted to a particular prosecution, all of these are prodigious. Having gone through that process, admired by us both for its thoroughness and its goals, astonishing to others for its devotion to fairness and reason, it is incomprehensible that at the very end we should tell those who are to make the judgment that they may do so without regard to anything that went before and without guidance as to why they should disregard what went on before, and without the obligation of explaining why they so disregarded everything. . . .

Jury nullification is an unfortunate but unavoidable power. It should not be advertised, and, to the extent constitutionally permissible, it should be limited.

4. Other mechanisms of "arbitrary" leniency. The *Ragland* court rests part of its case against jury nullification on the ground that this power "arbitrarily, to pick and choose" defendants for unexplained leniency exists "[a]bsolutely nowhere [else] in the system." To what extent is that claim really true? At the outset of this book we noted the importance of discretion *throughout* the criminal justice system. In particular, the judgments of police and prosecutors about whether and what to charge are largely unguided and uncontrolled. See page 3, supra, and the flow chart on page 13, supra. Another important source of discretionary leniency is the power of state governors and the President to grant executive clemency, a power which is likewise unrestricted and therefore in essence "arbitrary." In *Ex parte* Garland, 71 U.S. (4 Wall) 333, 380 (1867), the Supreme Court declared that "[t]he benign prerogative of mercy reposed in [the President] cannot be fettered by any legislative restrictions." Given the phenomenon of *pervasive* discretion (which we examine in detail in Chapter 10, infra), does jury nullification really deserve special skepticism? Is unexplained leniency granted by a citizen group serving on a one-time basis more trustworthy or more problematic than unexplained leniency granted by politically accountable officials?

Professor Andrew D. Leipold considers nullification undesirable, and he challenges the *Ragland* court's premise that the nullification power is unavoidable. Professor Leipold argues that procedural doctrines protecting the nullification power (such as the rule barring prosecution appeal from unjustified acquittals) impede the truth-seeking function of the criminal process. He would restrict the de facto nullification power by authorizing prosecution appeals (a view that would require reversal of current double jeopardy case law);[42] at the same time, he would permit explicit instructions authorizing nullification in cases involving de minimis harms, and prosecution appeal from an acquittal on that ground (if made explicit by a jury's special verdict) would be barred. See Leipold, Rethinking Jury Nullification, 82 Va. L. Rev. 253 (1996).

A different view is developed in Sherman J. Clark, The Courage of Our Convictions, 97 Mich. L. Rev. 2381 (1999). Professor Clark argues that jury trials "serve as a means through which we as a community take responsibility for—own up to—inherently problematic judgments regarding the blameworthiness or culpability of our fellow citizens." Id. He suggests, accordingly, that "procedures governing the criminal jury trial [should] engender in jurors a sense of personal responsibility for the fate of the accused." Id. at 2382. He recommends that jurors be instructed in a way that stresses their responsibility for their decision and makes them aware of their nullification power, without expressly encouraging them to use it—for example, by telling the jurors (id. at 2446) that "the responsibility for this decision is entirely yours and . . . you will not be required to explain or justify your verdict except to your own conscience."

5. *Constraining jury nullification.* If jury nullification is usually or (as the *Ragland* court argues) always undesirable, how far can courts go to discourage it? In a civil suit, the judge can set aside a jury verdict for one party and enter judgment notwithstanding the verdict (often called "judgment n.o.v.") for the other side. But the Supreme Court has held that in a criminal case, a judgment n.o.v. for the prosecution violates the defendant's Sixth Amendment right to trial by jury. Connecticut v. Johnson, 460 U.S. 73, 84 (1983). Are other judicial efforts to prevent nullification similarly barred by the Sixth Amendment? Consider these situations:

(a) In People v. Fernandez, 31 Cal. Rptr. 677 (Ct. App. 1994), the jurors interrupted their deliberations to send the judge a note in which they stated their belief that the defendant had committed battery with serious bodily injury and then asked whether they nonetheless had the power to acquit on that charge and instead return a verdict of guilty on the lesser offense of assault. The trial judge simply replied, "No." The court of appeal held that this response was not error.

(b) In People v. Engelman, 92 Cal. Rptr. 2d 416 (Cal. App. 2000), the defendant was convicted of robbery after the trial judge instructed the jury: "[S]hould it occur that any juror refuses to deliberate or expresses an intention to disregard the law . . . , it is the obligation of the other jurors to immediately

---

42. E.g., United States v. Ball, 163 U.S. 662 (1896).

advise the Court of the situation." The appellate court held that the instruction was proper, rejecting the defendant's argument that the instruction would pressure jurors in the minority to acquiesce in the majority view or to abandon any intention to nullify.

(c) United States v. Thomas, 116 F.3d 606 (2d Cir. 1997), was a prosecution of several African-American defendants charged with conspiracy to distribute cocaine. During deliberations, several jurors informed the trial judge that Juror No. 5, the sole African American on the panel, was refusing to follow the judge's instructions, was calling his fellow jurors "racists," and was adamantly holding out for acquittal. The judge interrupted the deliberations and conducted interviews with each of the jurors. According to several of them, Juror No. 5 had said he thought the government's evidence was unreliable, and Juror No. 5 told the judge that he needed "substantial evidence" of guilt. But several other jurors testified that Juror No. 5 had said he favored acquittal because the defendants were black and had committed the alleged crimes out of economic necessity. The trial judge accepted the latter account and dismissed Juror No. 5 on the ground that he would not convict "no matter what the evidence was" and had "preconceived ... economic [or] social reasons [for acquittal] that are totally improper." The remaining jurors then unanimously convicted.

On appeal, the court, per Judge José Cabranes, "categorically reject[ed] the idea that jury nullification is desirable or that courts may permit it to occur when it is within their authority to prevent it." The court held that the Constitution permits removal whenever there is unambiguous evidence of a juror's refusal to follow the judge's instructions. The court reversed the convictions, however, on the narrow ground that Juror No. 5's intentions were ambiguous and that there was "some possibility" he had based his vote on his view of the evidence.

Roughly in accord with the *Thomas* standard, most of the recent decisions hold that it is error to remove an allegedly recalcitrant juror if there is any reasonable possibility that the juror is following the judge's instructions. Williams v. Cavazos, 646 F.3d 626 (9th Cir. 2010); State v. Elmore, 123 P.3d 72 (Wash. 2005). In United States v. Abbell, 271 F.3d 1286, 1302 (11th Cir. 2001), the court described this as "basically a 'beyond reasonable doubt' standard." Nonetheless, courts often find that this tough requirement has been met and accordingly uphold decisions to remove a juror who has been holding out for acquittal. In *Abbell*, supra, at 1303, one juror told the others that "she did not have to follow the law and that the court's instructions were only advisory and not binding on the jury." Although the juror insisted in subsequent deliberations that she was merely evaluating the evidence, other jurors complained that she was not, and the trial judge's decision to remove her was upheld on appeal.

(d) Merced v. McGrath, 426 F.3d 1076 (9th Cir. 2005), involved a defendant on trial for the attempted murder of a peace officer. During voir dire, one of the potential jurors stated that he believed in exercising jury

nullification "where appropriate." The state trial judge then excused the juror for cause. The Ninth Circuit held that action permissible. Do you agree?

Questions: If jury departures from the law are so unequivocally bad, why should the defendant have a constitutional right to jury trial in the first place? Was *Duncan* wrongly decided? Conversely, if the jury's equity-dispensing function is central to its constitutional role, how can it be proper for a trial judge to remove jurors who reveal their intent to exercise that function? And what effect will the existence of such a removal power have on jurors' ability to express their views candidly during deliberation? For discussion of the issues, compare Nancy S. Marder, The Myth of the Nullifying Jury, 93 Nw. U. L. Rev. 877, 947-952 (1999) (criticizing *Thomas*), with Nancy J. King, Silencing Nullification Advocacy Inside and Outside the Courtroom, 65 U. Chi. L. Rev. 433, 438-491 (1998) (supporting the *Thomas* approach).

(e) The Fully Informed Jury Association (FIJA) is a Montana-based organization supported by a politically diverse array of protest groups, including anti-abortion activists, supporters of alternative medicines, and opponents of laws regulating firearms, marijuana, motorcycle helmets, prostitution, and the right to die. See King, supra at 434; Marder, supra at 942. Through a national newsletter, Web site, and handbills distributed at courthouses, FIJA seeks to spread awareness of the nullification power and encourage its use. At many courthouses throughout the country, FIJA distributes pro-nullification literature to potential and actual jurors, and encourages them to call an 800 number to hear a recorded message describing what one juror discovered were "more rights than what was read to me by the judge."[43]

Recall that in *Dougherty*, the majority considered formal nullification instructions unnecessary, in part because "the jury gets its understanding . . . from more than one voice"; the court concluded that awareness of the nulli-fication power can best come from "informal input." Are FIJA's activities therefore legitimate and perhaps even desirable? Many judges and other court officials apparently do not think so. FIJA activists who contact jurors or engage in leafleting at the courthouse have been charged with jury tamper-ing, obstruction of justice, and contempt of court, even though FIJA's infor-mational materials are not alleged to be incorrect or misleading. An Alaska case involved an FIJA activist who approached three potential jurors and urged them to call a toll-free number to hear a recorded message about the jury's powers. He was convicted of jury tampering under a state statute that prohibits "directly or indirectly communicat[ing] with a juror . . . with intent to . . . influence the juror's vote, opinion or decision." The U.S. Court of Appeals rejected his First Amendment challenge to the conviction. Turney v. Pugh, 400 F.3d 1197, 1199 (9th Cir. 2005). More recently, federal

---

43. Turney v. State, 936 P.2d 533, 537 n.4 (Alaska 1997).

authorities filed jury tampering charges against Julian Heicklen, a 79-year-old retired university professor who allegedly stood on the plaza outside the U.S. Courthouse in Manhattan handing out brochures to passers-by (some of whom could have been potential jurors), accurately explaining the jury's power to acquit in cases where they disagree with the law. The government used an undercover agent to secretly record a conversation in which Heicklen allegedly said "I'm not telling you to find anybody not guilty. But if there is a law you think is wrong then you should do that." Prosecutors insisted that his speech was not protected by the First Amendment. Lawyers helping to defend him disagreed, but also commented that the prosecution would raise awareness of the nullification power and "surely convert more to the cause than poor Mr. Heicklen ever could on his own." See Benjamin Weiser, Prosecution Explains Jury Tampering Charge, N.Y. Times, Nov. 27, 2011.[44]

Municipalities have also responded to FIJA's efforts by enacting laws to more tightly restrict contact with potential jurors in or near the courthouse.[45] Freedom of speech principles do not prohibit reasonable restrictions on advocacy within a fixed distance from decision-making sites like courthouses or voting booths.[46] But First Amendment considerations aside, why should it be a crime to give a juror truthful information about her rights and responsibilities? If society wants to block both formal and informal sources of information about the jury's equity-dispensing role, why bother having a jury at all? For analysis of judicial efforts to silence nullification advocacy, see King, supra Note 5(d), at 492-499.

6. The "legality" principle. As we shall discuss, a traditional principle of criminal punishment—also a constitutional mandate under the requirement of "due process of law"—is that criminal punishment can be imposed only for violation of clear standards promulgated in advance of the defendant's conduct. See pages 150-186 infra. Suppose that the jurors are instructed, over the defendant's objection, that they are the judges of the law as well as the facts. Does such an instruction subject the defendant to capricious judgment and violate his right to be tried in accordance with ascertainable law? Courts have generally rejected this challenge to such instructions, but only because judges retain the power to enter a judgment of acquittal in situations where a jury "nullifies" by convicting in the absence of evidence sufficient to establish a violation of preexisting criminal law. See Isaacs v. State, 358 A.2d 273 (Md. App. 1976).

7. Race-based nullification. In Detroit, Washington, D.C., parts of New York City, and several other urban centers, observers have claimed that jury nullification is becoming more common, especially in drug prosecutions

---

44. At this writing, the charges remain pending.
45. See, e.g., Fully Informed Jury Assn. v. San Diego, 1996 U.S. App. LEXIS 4254 (9th Cir.) (upholding restrictions).
46. Burson v. Freeman, 504 U.S. 191 (1992).

involving African-American defendants. See Marder, supra Note 5(d), at 899-901. Consider the following comments:

Paul Butler, Racially Based Jury Nullification: Black Power in the Criminal Justice System, 105 Yale L.J. 677 (1995): Considering the costs of law enforcement to the black community and the failure of white lawmakers to devise significant nonincarcerative responses to black antisocial conduct, it is the moral responsibility of black jurors to emancipate some guilty black outlaws. . . . I hope that the destruction of the status quo will not lead to anarchy, but rather to the implementation of certain noncriminal ways of addressing antisocial conduct. . . .

According to [some], whom I will call law enforcement enthusiasts, . . . it is in the best interest of the black community to have more, rather than less, [law enforcement]. Allowing criminals to live unfettered in the community would harm, in particular, the black poor, who are disproportionately the victims of violent crime. Indeed, the logical conclusion of the enthusiasts' argument is that African-Americans would be better off with more, not fewer, black criminals behind bars.

To my mind, the enthusiasts embrace law enforcement too uncritically: They are blind to its opportunity costs. . . . [W]hen locking up black men means that "violent criminals . . . who attack those most vulnerable" are off the streets, most people—including most law enforcement critics—would endorse the incarceration. But what about when locking up a black man has no or little net effect on public safety, when, for example, the crime with which he was charged is victimless? . . .

There is no question that jury nullification is subversive of the rule of law. . . . To borrow a phrase from the D.C. Circuit, jury nullification "betrays rather than furthers the assumptions of viable democracy. . . ." [But] "democracy," as practiced in the United States, has betrayed African-Americans far more than they could ever betray it. . . .

Because the United States is both a democracy and a pluralist society, it is important that diverse groups appear to have a voice in the laws that govern them. Allowing black people to serve on juries strengthens "public respect for our criminal justice system and the rule of law." . . . But what of the black juror who endorses racial critiques of American criminal justice? Such a person holds no "confidence in the integrity of the criminal justice system." If she is cognizant of the implicit message that the Supreme Court believes her presence sends, she might not want her presence to be the vehicle for that message. . . . In a sense, the black juror [who nullifies] engages in an act of civil disobedience, except that her choice is better than civil disobedience because it is lawful. Is the black juror's race-conscious act moral? Absolutely. It would be farcical for her to be the sole color-blind actor in the criminal process, especially when it is her blackness that advertises the system's fairness. . . .

In cases involving violent *malum in se* crimes like murder, rape, and assault, jurors should consider the case strictly on the evidence presented, and, if they have no reasonable doubt that the defendant is guilty, they should convict. For nonviolent *malum in se* crimes such as theft or perjury, nullification is an option that the juror should consider, although there should be no presumption in favor of it. A juror might vote for acquittal, for example, when a poor woman steals from Tiffany's, but not when the same woman steals from her next-door neighbor. Finally, in cases involving nonviolent, *malum prohibitum* offenses, including "victimless" crimes like narcotics offenses, there should be a presumption in favor of nullification. . . . Black people have a community that needs building, and children who need rescuing; as long as a person will not hurt anyone, the community needs him there to help. . . .

I am not encouraging anarchy. Instead, I am reminding black jurors of their privilege to serve a higher calling than law: justice. . . . I hope that there are enough of us out there, fed up with prison as the answer to black desperation and white supremacy, to cause retrial after retrial,[a] until, finally, the United States "retries" its idea of justice.

Randall L. Kennedy, Race, Crime, and the Law 301-310 (1996): [J]ury nullification is an exceedingly poor means for advancing the goal of a racially fair administration of criminal law. . . . Jury nullification as typically implemented is a low-visibility, highly ambiguous protest unlikely to focus the attention of the public clearly on social problems in need of reform. [Moreover, if] a large number of blacks clearly engage in "guerrilla warfare" as jurors, their action might call into question the right of blacks to be selected for jury service on precisely the same terms as others. Widespread adoption of Butler's proposal would likely give rise to measures designed to exclude prospective nullifiers from juries, measures that would result almost certainly in the disproportionate exclusion of blacks. . . .

Butler exudes keen sympathy for nonviolent drug offenders and similar criminals. By contrast, Butler is inattentive to the aspirations, frustrations, and fears of law-abiding people compelled by circumstances to live in close proximity to the criminals for whom he is willing to urge subversion of the legal system. Butler simply overlooks the sector of the black law-abiding population that desires more rather than less prosecution and punishment for all types of criminals. . . .

If a large number of blacks have views on the administration of criminal law that are counter to Butler's, why worry about his proposal? . . . [I]t would not take many people to wreak havoc with the jury system. The unanimity requirement renders juries uniquely susceptible to disruption by a resolute cadre of nullifiers. . . .

The most fundamental reason to oppose Professor Butler's call for racially selective jury nullification is that it is based on a sentiment that is regrettably widespread in American culture: an ultimately destructive sentiment of racial

---

a. Because this kind of nullification by a single juror would not result in an acquittal (which requires a super-majority or sometimes unanimity in support of that result), the single hold out would force a mistrial, and the prosecution would normally seek to retry the case.—Eds.

kinship that prompts individuals of a given race to care more about "their own" than people of another race. [Butler] assumes that it is proper for prospective black jurors to care more about black communities than white communities, that it is proper for black jurors to be more concerned with the fate of black defendants than white defendants, and that it is proper for black jurors to be more protective of the property (and perhaps the lives?) of black people than white people. Along that road lies moral and political disaster. The disaster includes not only increasing but, worse, legitimizing the tendency of people to privilege in racial terms "their own." Some will say that this racial privileging has already happened and is, in any event, inevitable. The situation can and will get worse, however, if Butler's plan and the thinking behind it gains adherents. His program, although animated by a desire to challenge racial injustice, would demolish the moral framework upon which an effective, attractive, and compelling alternative can and must be built.[b]

NOTES ON THE JURY'S ROLE IN SENTENCING

Because *Duncan* emphasizes that a central part of the jury's function is to afford protection against the "compliant, biased, or eccentric judge," it might seem that the constitutional right to jury trial should include not only a right to have the jury decide matters of guilt and innocence but also a right to have the jury fix the offender's punishment. In capital cases, nearly all states do give the jury this broader responsibility; we explore the jury's special role in this context in Chapter 5, pages 535-548 infra. But for other sentencing matters, only six states allow for punishment to be determined largely by the jury. In all the others, the sentencing decision is left to the judge, and this arrangement is normally not thought to violate Sixth Amendment requirements. Why not? Why should decisions about the sentence be treated differently from decisions about whether to convict? And what freedom should states have to shift factual questions from the guilt phase, where the jury must resolve them, to the sentencing phase, where the prosecution needs only to convince a single judge? Consider the Notes that follow.

1. Jury sentencing. In Arkansas, Kentucky, Missouri, Oklahoma, Texas, and Virginia, defendants who plead guilty or opt for a bench trial are sentenced by a judge, but those who elect to go to trial before a jury are sentenced by the same jury, usually in a "bifurcated" proceeding—the trial on guilt or innocence occurs first, and if the jury convicts, it then hears further evidence and retires to deliberate separately on the question of punishment. (The principal exception is Oklahoma, where first offenders are tried and sentenced in a unitary proceeding.)

---

b. For further discussion of Professor Butler's proposals, see Darryl K. Brown, Jury Nullification Within the Rule of Law, 81 Minn. L. Rev. 1149, 1185-1191 (1997); Andrew D. Leipold, The Dangers of Race-Based Jury Nullification, 44 UCLA L. Rev. 109 (1996); Marder, supra note 5(d), at 937-943.—EDS.

At the penalty phase, sentencing juries typically are not asked to direct their attention to any particular aggravating or mitigating circumstances and are not given guidelines of any sort. Instead, they are simply asked to pick any sentence within the authorized statutory range. (In contrast, in many jurisdictions guidelines and presentence reports shape the sentencing decisions of judges, as discussed in Chapter 10, infra.) As a result, jury sentencing produces enormous variation in the sentences imposed on similarly situated offenders. See Nancy J. King & Rosevelt L. Noble, Felony Jury Sentencing in Practice: A Three-State Study, 57 Vand. L. Rev. 885 (2004); Jenia Iontcheva, Jury Sentencing as Democratic Practice, 89 Va. L. Rev. 311 (2003). In addition, sentencing juries typically are afforded fewer options for leniency than are available when the sentence is fixed by the judge. For example, in several of the jury-sentencing states, judges can grant probation or a suspended sentence, but juries cannot. For this reason and others, studies suggest, defendants sentenced by a jury typically receive more severe sentences than similarly situated defendants sentenced by a judge. See Nancy J. King & Rosevelt L. Noble, Jury Sentencing in Non-Capital Cases: Comparing Severity and Variance with Judicial Sentences in Two States, 2 J. Empirical L. Studies 331 (2005).[47]

Despite these features (or perhaps because of them), state officials have shown little enthusiasm for reforms that would permit more leniency or consistency in jury sentencing, through sentencing guidelines and other devices like those now widely used to promote uniformity in sentencing by judges. Prosecutors and legislators in jury-sentencing states seem to believe that the greater severity and unpredictability of jury sentencing is an important factor in inducing guilty pleas, so that cases can be disposed of quickly and cheaply. Professor Nancy King concludes that "[T]he wild card aspect of jury sentencing helps to funnel defendants to guilty pleas and bench trials. . . . For criminal justice insiders, the unpredictability of jury sentencing is a blessing, not a curse; the more freakish, the better." Nancy J. King, How Different Is Death? Jury Sentencing in Capital and Non-Capital Cases Compared, 2 Ohio St. J. Crim. L. 195, 198 (2004). Yet courts have consistently rejected the argument that unguided jury discretion in non-capital cases violates due process. E.g., Torres v. United States, 140 F.3d 392, 397 (2d Cir. 1998).

Do these problems suggest that at the sentencing stage, the jury cannot serve as an effective equity-dispensing mechanism for the benefit of defendants? Or do they simply show that jury sentencing has not been permitted to fulfill its potential?

2. *Judicial sentencing: What is the jury permitted to know?* Does it follow from *Dougherty* that a judge not only may refuse to inform the jury of its nullification power but also may refuse to inform the jury about the severity

---

47. There is some indication, however, that jurors might be more lenient than federal judges bound by federal sentencing guidelines. See James S. Gwin, Juror Sentiment on Just Punishment: Do the Federal Sentencing Guidelines Reflect Community Values?, 4 Harv. L. & Pol'y Rev. 173 (2010).

of the sentence that a defendant faces upon conviction? The question has become increasingly important with the proliferation of mandatory minimum sentencing laws, which often dictate long terms of imprisonment for possession of small quantities of drugs, even when the defendant is a first offender. Yet nearly all courts hold that because the jury's role is solely to determine the facts relevant to guilt, the jury has no legitimate concern with the consequences of a conviction. E.g., Shannon v. United States, 512 U.S. 573 (1994); United States v. Pabon-Cruz, 391 F.3d 86, 94-95 (2d Cir. 2004). For criticism of this approach, see Michael T. Cahill, Punishment Decisions at Conviction: Recognizing the Jury as Fault-Finder, 2005 U. Chi. Legal F. 91.

One federal judge also has challenged this view. In United States v. Polizzi, 549 F. Supp. 2d 308 (E.D.N.Y. 2008), the defendant was tried on 12 counts of receiving child pornography. The jury convicted, rejecting his insanity plea despite evidence that he had suffered vicious sexual abuse as a child, had nonetheless established a home with a loving family, and had no prior criminal history. After the verdict, a poll of the jurors revealed that, had they been aware of the applicable five-year mandatory minimum sentence, they would not have convicted, because they thought the defendant should receive treatment and close supervision to prevent a recurrence, not a long prison term. Noting that a properly informed jury would likely have deadlocked or found the defendant not guilty by reason of insanity, the district judge awarded a new trial. Based on an extensive review of the history of jury trial and its importance for issues of punishment as well as guilt, the judge held that under these circumstances, the failure to inform the jury of the mandatory minimum sentence prior to its deliberations deprived the defendant of his constitutional right to jury trial, as that right had been understood at the time of the framing of the Bill of Rights. However, the Court of Appeals reversed, holding that absent unusual circumstances, it is an abuse of discretion for a trial judge to inform the jury of the sentencing consequences of its verdict. United States v. Polouizzi [a/k/a/ Polizzi], 564 F.3d 142 (2d Cir. 2009).[48] Compare United States v. Datcher, 830 F. Supp. 411, 414-418 (M.D. Tenn. 1993), where another district judge, protesting against the prevailing bar on instructions about sentencing consequences, commented:

> Argument against allowing the jury to hear information that might lead to nullification evinces a fear that the jury might actually serve its primary purpose, that is, it evinces a fear that the community might in fact think a law unjust. The government, whose duty it is to seek justice and not merely conviction, should not shy away from having a jury know the full facts and law of a case. . . .

---

48. As an example of circumstances that could warrant such an instruction, the court mentioned the situation in which comments during the trial had given jurors a *false* impression about dispositional consequences. Thus, if a witness had stated that acquittal by reason of insanity would allow the defendant to "go free," the trial judge could properly explain that civil commitment would be available to insure confinement in the event of such a verdict. See *Polouizzi*, supra, 564 F.3d at 162; see also *Shannon*, supra, 512 U.S. at 587.

Overly harsh punishments were the impetus to development of jury nullification. Institution of the jury system was meant to protect against unjust
punishment . . . , not merely unjust conviction. . . .

No instruction on jury nullification was requested by the defendant, and
none would be given if it were requested. . . . But Mr. Datcher is entitled to
have the jury perform its full oversight function, and informing the jury of
possible punishment is essential to this function. The court finds no good
reason for opposing candor.

*3. Judicial sentencing: When can factual questions be shifted from the
jury's domain to that of the judge? Duncan* protects the defendant's right
to have the jury determine, under a strict beyond-a-reasonable-doubt
standard, all facts necessary to constitute the crime charged—that is, all
"elements" of the offense. But a single judge, acting under a preponderance-
of-the-evidence standard, can determine all other facts relevant to the level of
punishment—that is, all "sentencing factors." Years of imprisonment can
therefore turn on whether the fact is characterized as an element" of the
offense or merely as a "sentencing factor." For discussion of the case law
on this issue, see page 44 Note 3, supra. Consider to what extent the "sentencing factor" option (together with the rule against informing the jury about
the sentencing consequences of a conviction (Note 2 supra) enable the legislature to defeat the jury's constitutionally protected functions identified in
Duncan—the functions of restraining overly harsh laws and preventing prosecutors from using generally reasonable laws in an oppressive manner. For
discussion, see Rachel E. Barkow, Recharging the Jury: The Criminal Jury's
Constitutional Role in an Era of Mandatory Sentencing, 152 U. Pa. L. Rev. 33
(2003).

NOTES AND QUESTIONS ON INCONSISTENT VERDICTS

1. The problem and the prevailing solution. When a prosecution involves
several separate counts, it sometimes happens that the jury's verdict on one
count will be irreconcilably in conflict with its verdict on another count.
Consider, for example, DeSacia v. State, 469 P.2d 369 (Alaska 1970). The
defendant's reckless driving forced another vehicle off the road, and both the
driver (Hogan) and passenger (Evangelista) in the other vehicle were killed.
The defendant was prosecuted on two counts of manslaughter. The jury
convicted on the count charging manslaughter of Evangelista but acquitted
on the count charging manslaughter of Hogan. Because the defendant's conduct had endangered the two victims in precisely the same way, he was in
principle guilty of manslaughter either in both cases or in neither. Should the
inconsistent verdicts nevertheless be allowed to stand?

In the *DeSacia* case, the court noted that the verdict of acquittal was final;
any relitigation of that count would violate the Double Jeopardy Clause. But
the court set aside the conviction on the other count, to assure that the conviction was not the product of jury confusion or irrationality. The court
therefore remanded for a new trial on the count relating to the death of

Evangelista. Some courts go even further. In People v. Klingenberg, 665 N.E.2d 1370 (Ill. 1996), the court not only set aside the inconsistent conviction but also held that retrial on that charge was barred. The court noted (id. at 1376) that "the jury, by its acquittal on another [charge], has rejected an essential element needed to support the conviction" and reasoned that double jeopardy principles should preclude the prosecution from attempting to establish that missing element on retrial.

Although several other American jurisdictions refuse to accept inconsistent verdicts, see, e.g., Shepherd v. State, 626 S.E.2d 96 (Ga. 2006), the federal courts and the great majority of the states permit the inconsistent conviction to stand. See Priest v. State, 879 A.2d 575 (Del. 2005); Eric L. Muller, The Hobgoblin of Little Minds? Our Foolish Law of Inconsistent Verdicts, 111 Harv. L. Rev. 771, 787-788 (1998). Which approach seems more faithful to the premises of jury trial? If the jury is expected to give voice to the rough common sense of the community, isn't the *DeSacia* court's desire for consistency out of place? Do inconsistent verdicts facilitate the exercise of the jury's leniency or do they encourage compromise *convictions* on counts about which the jury may not really be persuaded beyond a reasonable doubt? In United States v. Powell, 469 U.S. 57, 65 (1984), the Supreme Court noted:

> Inconsistent verdicts . . . present a situation where "error," in the sense that the jury has not followed the court's instructions, most certainly has occurred, but it is unclear whose ox has been gored. Given this uncertainty, and the fact that the Government is precluded from challenging the acquittal, it is hardly satisfactory to allow the defendant to receive a new trial on the conviction as a matter of course. . . . For us, the possibility that the inconsistent verdicts may favor the criminal defendant as well as the Government militates against review of such convictions at the defendant's behest.

2. Criticism of the prevailing acceptance of inconsistent verdicts. The *Powell* Court's assumptions have drawn sharp criticism. Professor Leipold notes that "[f]or every case where the jury extends mercy to a deserving defendant, there may well be another (or two, or five others) where the verdict is based on improper considerations." Andrew Leipold, Rethinking Jury Nullification, 82 Va. L. Rev. 253, 304 (1996). Professor Muller, supra note 1, at 795, argues that "by refusing to disturb inconsistent verdicts, the Court is buying a chance for [leniency] at the price of protecting jury confusion, mistake, and compromise." He concludes that fundamental trial values require courts to set aside inconsistent convictions unless the evidence supporting the conviction is so overwhelming that any jury error can be deemed harmless.

Questions: What if the prosecution seeks an instruction, in a case like *DeSacia*, that the jury must either acquit on both counts or convict on both counts? Does the result in *DeSacia* in effect require such an instruction in future cases? If so, would the defendant then be justified in claiming that the instruction improperly constrained the jury's equity-dispensing function?

In connection with these problems, consider whether it was entirely a coincidence that the *DeSacia* jury convicted for the death of Evangelista, who was a passenger, but acquitted for the death of Hogan, the other driver. As we shall see, contributory negligence ordinarily is not a defense in a criminal prosecution, see page 468 infra, but the Kalven and Zeisel study, page 55 supra, at 242-257, showed that jury nullification often occurred when contributory fault by the victim was involved. If this factor played a role in the acquittal with respect to Hogan, then wasn't the jury—to quote from *Duncan v. Louisiana*, page 49 supra—"serving some of the very purposes for which [it was] created"? Or are the dangers identified by Professor Muller (jury confusion, mistake, inappropriate compromise, and disregard of the reasonable-doubt requirement) more substantial than the risk of chilling the jury's equity-dispensing function?

chapter 2

The Justification of Punishment

INTRODUCTORY NOTE

Punishing wrongdoers for their misconduct seems self-evidently appropriate. But this straightforward idea becomes complex and controversial when we seek to apply it to actual cases, because there are many distinct reasons *why* punishment of wrongdoers may be appropriate. Although these explanations sometimes overlap or reinforce each other, often they conflict, pointing toward different legal responses. It therefore becomes essential to examine the distinct explanations for punishment in depth, in order to understand their application in real-world situations. This chapter focuses on those explanations. But before exploring them in detail, it will be useful for students first to have a concrete sense of what criminal punishment is in our society.

A. WHAT IS PUNISHMENT?

In broad outline, the principal forms of criminal punishment are familiar. Punishment may consist of a fine, probation, imprisonment or, in especially serious cases, the death penalty. Less obviously, the conviction itself is a form of punishment, carrying with it a social stigma, an impediment to future employment, a risk of enhanced punishment in the event of a future offense, as well as possible loss of voting rights, public housing access, and deportation. See Michael Pinard, Freedom in Decline: Reflections and Perspectives on Reentry and Collateral Consequences, 100 J. Crim. L. & Criminology 1213 (2010).

Courts are now actively developing "intermediate sanctions" less harsh than imprisonment but more severe than probation. These include weeks or months of home detention, mandated community service, or "intensive-supervision" probation (which often includes mandatory counseling or drug treatment).

Imprisonment, of course, represents the quintessential criminal punishment. Though not inflicted in every case, it is almost always an option that the judge has discretion to impose. And even when not imposed, imprisonment remains in the background as a possible consequence of any failure to meet conditions of a fine, probation, or intermediate sanction. The material that follows takes a close look at what imprisonment actually entails in America today.

RICHARD A. WRIGHT, PRISONS: PRISONERS, ENCYCLOPEDIA OF CRIME AND JUSTICE

1182 (J. Dressler ed., 2d ed. 2002) *

Average citizens stereotype prisons as either hell-holes filled with every imaginable evil, or country clubs (complete with swimming pools and golf courses) where inmates are sent to work on their tans. Neither of these stereotypes captures the central realities of incarceration for inmates: crushing routine and relentless boredom. . . .

The federal and most state correctional systems include an impressive array of institutions with different security level designations. Maximum security prisons [which house some 20 percent of the prison population] operate as armed fortresses, complete with steel gates, high walls (sometimes extending many feet underground to prevent escapes through tunnels), perimeter fences (topped with multiple layers of razor-sharp concertina barbed wire), gun towers, and floodlights. Some of these prisons are marvels in advanced technology, containing a complex network of electronic surveillance that includes metal detectors, concealed video cameras, and heat and touch sensors in the walls, floors, and ceilings. Correctional officers in these prisons carefully supervise and control the every move of inmates through detailed schedules and constant head counts.

Inmates in maximum security prisons have little freedom and autonomy; their lives are ruled by the same mind-numbing routines for months and years on end. These prisoners lead a depersonalized existence with little privacy: passersby can gaze into their cells to watch them eat, sleep, or use the toilet. They even shower together in large, open stalls that are closely monitored by correctional officers. In an effort to control the proliferation of drugs, weapons, and other contraband, there are frequent shakedowns (or random searches) of cellblocks in maximum security units. It is little wonder that inmates in these prisons often bitterly complain that they are displayed and managed like animals in a zoo.

While life in maximum security prisons is usually monotonous and boring, the tedium is sometimes broken by outbursts of violence. Threats, assaults, and killings are fairly commonplace in these institutions. . . . The threat of violence is real enough in maximum security prisons to produce a constant undercurrent of tension, fear, and wariness among inmates and staff; smarter prisoners in these institutions make a habit of looking over their shoulders or standing with their backs to walls whenever they venture outside their cells.

A more relaxed atmosphere prevails in most medium and minimum security prisons. Violence is much less common [and] conditions of confinement

*From Dressler (editor). Encyclopedia of Crime & Justice, 2E. © 2001 Gale, a part of Cengage Learning, Inc. Reproduced by permission. www.cengage.com/permissions.

are usually much better. . . . Inmates have greater freedom of movement and . . . are also given more privileges. . . . These prisons sometimes offer community release programs, where inmates leave the facility during the day to attend school or for work. . . .

Even within prisons, living arrangements vary considerably. Large maximum security penitentiaries usually have a least three forms of confinement: segregation units, the general population, and honor blocks. Inmates in segregation units are isolated from other prisoners, either for administrative purposes, for disciplinary infractions, or for protective custody. . . .

Those confined in segregation units have less freedom of movement and autonomy than the typical mainline inmate confined in the general population cellblocks of maximum security prisons. Unlike prisoners in segregation, those in the general population have unrestricted prison yard, gymnasium, and commissary privileges, and eat together in the prison cafeteria. . . .

[A] number of factors since the 1970s have combined to increase the pains of imprisonment experienced by most inmates. . . . The deteriorating conditions of confinement, longer prison sentences, and overcrowding together have increased the suffering that inmates experience in prison. Levels of violence, fear, and hopelessness rise in crowded cellblocks that are saturated with drugs and overrun by gang bangers. This has led to the emergence of new, indigenous prison gangs organized for self-defense and for buying and sharing drugs. [A] study of men's prisons in California found that for every gang imported into prison from the streets, another gang forms inside for protection. Some of these new prison gangs will be exported into the free world once their members are paroled.

The turmoil in modern prisons means that inmate subcultures are in a precarious state. If prison conditions worsen, the pains of imprisonment could become severe enough to breed new values and roles among inmates, fundamentally altering the criminal and conventional personalities imported from the streets. This could signal a return to the "bad old days" in corrections where convicts were irreparably damaged through prisonization, or exposure to the inmate subculture. Some commentators already sense the growing unrest and despair in the cellblocks: Victor Hassine compares the modern prison to a "runaway train" filled with prisoners only concerned about "how they are going to survive this madness."

NOTES ON PRISON CONDITIONS

1. *General violence and abuse.* A 2003 report by the Bureau of Justice Statistics[1] revealed that as of midyear 2000, out of some 1.3 million inmates in correctional facilities (excluding jails and other local and regional facilities) there were about 34,000 inmate-on-inmate assaults, and 18,000 assaults on staff. Though the number of assaults in both categories increased by about

---

1. Census of State and Federal Correctional Facilities, 2000.

30 percent over five years earlier, the rate per thousand remained roughly stable because the total inmate population had increased by a comparable amount. Data on excessive violence by guards are not provided by the Bureau. As for homicide victimization rates, they have dipped sharply from 1960 (54 per 100,000) to 1990 (8 per 100,000). By 2002, prison homicide rates had declined further, to 4 per 100,000, a rate roughly comparable to homicide victimization rates for the population at large.[2]

However, there is widespread belief that the official statistics vastly underestimate the amount of prison violence. Even the guards feel unsafe. In a vivid account, a journalist who became a prison guard reported that the New York prison where he worked was "a world of adrenaline and aggression. . . . It was an experience of living with fear—fear of inmates . . . and fear of our own capacity to [slip up]. [M]ake a mistake around the inmates and you might get hurt." Ted Conover, Newjack: Guarding Sing Sing 95 (2000). An overview of national conditions in the 2006 report of a blue-ribbon commission similarly notes:[3]

> Corrections officers told the commission about a near-constant fear of being assaulted. . . . The majority of prisons and many jails hold more people than they can deal with safely and effectively, creating a degree of disorder and tension almost certain to erupt into violence. . . . Data about deadly violence show decreasing rates nationally of homicide and suicide, but we do not have equally reliable data about the much larger universe of non-lethal violence. . . . In-depth studies suggest that actual levels of violence among prisoners are at least five times higher than what even the best administrative records capture. . . . Equally troubling, we have no national measures of non-lethal violence perpetrated by staff against prisoners, despite widespread agreement that excessive use of force happens. High rates of disease and illness among prisoners, coupled with inadequate funding for correctional health care, endanger prisoners, staff, and the public. . . . The increasing use of high-security segregation is counter-productive, often causing violence inside facilities and contributing to recidivism after release.

2. Sexual violence. Although accurate estimates of the incidence of sexual assault in prisons are difficult to obtain, even the most cautious experts acknowledge that the problem is substantial throughout the American prison system. See Mary Sigler, By the Light of Virtue: Prison Rape and the Corruption of Character, 91 Iowa L. Rev. 561, 568-570 (2006). Professors Robert Weisberg and David Mills note that "no one who knows American jails and prisons doubts that rape and sexual assault—usually perpetrated by other

---

2. Bureau of Justice Statistics, Special Report, Suicide and Homicide in State Prisons and Local Jails (Aug. 2005). These totals mask a striking variation by race. In 2002, for example, the risk of being killed was lower for whites on the outside (3.3 per 100,000) than for white inmates in prison (5 per 100,000), while for blacks, the homicide victimization rate was *ten times higher* on the outside (20.8 per 100,000) than in prison (2 per 100,000). Compare id. at 5, to Bureau of Justice Statistics, Homicide Trends by Race, http://bjs.ojp.usdoj.gov/content/homicide/tables/vracetab.cfm.

3. National Commission on Safety and Abuse in America's Prisons (2006), available at www.prisoncommission.org.

inmates but occasionally by prison staff—are facts of daily life."[4] Congress has formally endorsed this gloomy picture, finding (42 U.S.C.A. §15601 (2003)) that:

[A]t least 13 percent of the inmates in the United States have been sexually assaulted in prison. Many inmates have suffered repeated assaults. Under this estimate, nearly 200,000 inmates now incarcerated have been or will be the victims of prison rape. The total number of inmates who have been sexually assaulted in the past 20 years likely exceeds 1,000,000.

In woman's prisons, physical danger from other inmates is generally less prevalent than it is in men's prisons. But women inmates face other difficulties. In many states, prison guards often subject female prisoners under their control to rape and other forms of sexual exploitation. See Stephen J. Schulhofer, Unwanted Sex 201-205 (1998); Human Rights Watch, All Too Familiar: Sexual Abuse of Women in U.S. State Prisons (1996). In addition, because most states have only a few prisons for women, female prisoners are likely to be sent much farther from their homes and families than male prisoners are. And women's prisons typically afford more meager educational and vocational programs than men's prisons do. For a discussion of the problems, see Nicole Hahn Rafter, Partial Justice: Women, Prisons, and Social Control (2d ed. 1990).

3. Crowding. One characteristic of American prisons that is important, both as a cause of prison violence and as a serious problem in its own right, is pervasive overcrowding. A surge in prison construction during the 1990s was accompanied by a nearly equivalent surge in incarceration rates, with the result that overcrowding in state prisons declined only slightly. While experts believe that efficient prison management requires prisons to operate significantly *below* their full capacity levels, at year-end 2010, almost half of the states had inmate populations above the design capacity of their prisons, and the federal prison system was operating at 36 percent above its design capacity. See Bureau of Justice Statistics, Prisoners in 2010, at 7 (Dec. 2011).

The consequences of overcrowding include poor health care, interference with rehabilitative and educational services (which are often minimal in any event), increased idleness, constant noise, and oppressive living arrangements, all of which magnify interpersonal conflict among prisoners and create even greater impetus for inmate-on-inmate violence; such conditions also create many additional opportunities for inmates to perpetrate such violence with impunity. See Sharon Dolovich, Cruelty, Prison Conditions, and the Eighth Amendment, 84 N.Y.U. L. Rev. 881, 886-889 (2009). These impacts on inmate psychology and mental health also aggravate the likelihood of recidivism when prisoners are released. See Alan Elsner, Gates of Injustice: The

---

4. Robert Weisberg and David Mills, Violence Silence (2006), available at www.slate.com/id/2089095/.

Crisis in America's Prisons (2d ed. 2006). One prison psychiatrist, quoted in Dolovich, supra, at 887 n.20, observes:

> In crowded, noisy, unhygienic environments, human beings tend to treat each other terribly. . . . There are constant lines to use the toilets and phones, and altercations erupt when one irritable prisoner thinks another has been on the phone too long. There are rows of bunks blocking the view, so beatings and rapes can go on in one part of the dorm while officers sit at their desks in another area. The noise level is so loud that muffled screams cannot be heard. [I]s it any wonder that research clearly links prison crowding with increased rates of violence, psychiatric breakdowns, rapes, and suicides?

Courts have found overcrowded prison conditions in some states to constitute cruel and unusual punishment in violation of the Eighth Amendment.[5] The California prison system, one of the nation's largest, is also one of the most egregiously overcrowded, operating for over a decade at more than double its design capacity. In Brown v. Plata, 131 S. Ct. 1910 (2011), the Supreme Court upheld a district court order requiring the state, in the absence of new prison construction or out-of-state transfers, to release up to 46,000 inmates, in order to reduce its prison population to 137.5 percent of design capacity. The Court noted (id. at 1924):

> Prisoners are crammed into spaces neither designed nor intended to house inmates. As many as 200 prisoners may live in a gymnasium, monitored by as few as two or three correctional officers. As many as 54 prisoners may share a single toilet. . . . The consequences of overcrowding [include] a suicide rate approaching an average of one per week. . . . Because of a shortage of treatment beds, suicidal inmates may be held for prolonged periods [of up to 24 hours or more] in telephone-booth sized cages without toilets.

The remedial decree allows the state two years to achieve the mandated reductions, and in other prison reform litigation, improvements have come slowly at best, even after courts found existing conditions to constitute cruel and unusual punishment.

4. Incarceration without "imprisonment." Although imprisonment is the quintessential criminal sanction, many measures that look very much like imprisonment are not considered "punishment" at all, and are therefore subject to much less stringent constitutional safeguards. This important territory just outside the boundaries of criminal law is examined in the Note that follows.

NOTE ON CIVIL SANCTIONS

Some forms of involuntary confinement are classified as "civil" measures rather than criminal punishments. Civil commitment of the mentally ill is a

---

5. See Susanna Y. Chung, Prison Overcrowding: Standards in Determining Eighth Amendment Violations, 68 Fordham L. Rev. 2351 (2000).

prominent example. The distinction between civil and criminal measures (or between "regulation" and "punishment") has enormous practical importance. Before imposing "punishment," the government must comply with stringent safeguards, including the requirement of proof beyond a reasonable doubt. And the duration of "punishment" is limited by the perceived imperative (moral, statutory, and constitutional) of proportionality to an offender's fault. In a civil proceeding, in contrast, the burden of proof is typically lower, many other safeguards of criminal procedure do not apply, and the defendant may face loss of liberty for an indefinite period, potentially for life.

What features make a proceeding civil rather than criminal? Government cannot escape the usual criminal law restrictions simply by attaching the "civil" label to a sanction that is punitive in its purpose or effect. To determine whether a nominally civil measure is really punishment (and thus whether criminal law safeguards apply), courts must consider:[6]

> [w]hether the sanction involves an affirmative disability or restraint, whether it has historically been regarded as a punishment, whether it comes into play only on a finding of *scienter*, whether its operation will promote the traditional aims of punishment—retribution and deterrence, whether the behavior to which it applies is already a crime, whether an alternative purpose to which it may rationally be connected is assignable for it, and whether it appears excessive in relation to the alternative purpose assigned.

Involuntary commitment of the mentally ill, for the protection of themselves or others, is universally considered a civil proceeding. The person committed has a right to treatment, and he must be released when he is no longer mentally ill or dangerous. Nonetheless, such a person may, if not cured, find himself confined for life. See page 965 infra.

Other restrictions on liberty are more difficult to classify. In the early 1990s, many states enacted sexually violent predator (SVP) laws in order to permit long-term confinement of sex offenders who finish serving their criminal sentences. The typical SVP law permits indefinite commitment of persons who are not mentally ill, on the basis of a finding that they have a "mental abnormality" or "personality disorder" and are "likely to engage in predatory acts of sexual violence." SVP laws typically do not bar the provision of treatment, but many of them acknowledge that the SVP condition is difficult or impossible to treat.[7]

Can an offender be committed under such a law, after he has served his sentence, without violating the rule against double jeopardy? Can such a law be applied retroactively to a person whose sex offense was committed before the law was enacted? Can a person be adjudicated an SVP and committed indefinitely, without proof beyond a reasonable doubt that future sexual misconduct is "likely"? If the SVP proceeding is properly classified as civil, the

---

6. Kennedy v. Mendoza-Martinez, 372 U.S. 144, 168-169 (1963).
7. See Stephen J. Schulhofer, Two Systems of Social Protection: Comments on the Civil-Criminal Distinction, 7 J. Contemp. Legal Issues 69 (1996).

answer to all these questions is yes. In Kansas v. Hendricks, 521 U.S. 346 (1997), the Supreme Court upheld the "civil" classification of one such law. The Court emphasized that under the Kansas regime, inmates are not subject to punitive conditions of confinement and are entitled to immediate release whenever it is determined that they are no longer dangerous; four dissenting justices argued that the Kansas regime should nonetheless be considered criminal because treatable inmates had been afforded little or no treatment and because the committing authorities were not required to consider using less restrictive means of social protection, short of incarceration. Following the lead of the *Hendricks* majority, many state courts have upheld schemes for indefinite confinement of persons designated as sexually violent predators, even when the procedures fall short of those required in criminal prosecutions and do not require proof beyond a reasonable doubt. See, e.g., State v. Ploof, 2011 N.H. LEXIS 148 (N.H. Nov. 2, 2011).

Similar issues arise under laws that require convicted sex offenders, upon release from prison, to register with local police. Such laws, modeled on the "Megan's Law" first enacted in New Jersey, typically require the police to make such registration lists publicly available. In many instances, police must also notify schools, day care centers, and local residents of the offender's presence in the community. Should such laws be considered civil measures to which criminal law safeguards do not apply? In New Jersey, Megan's Law was upheld as a civil measure only after the state supreme court required modifications to restrict the degree of public disclosure, depending on whether the offender was found to pose a low, medium, or high risk of reoffending. See E.B. v. Verniero, 119 F.3d 107 (3d Cir. 1997). And even with this limitation, several courts hold that public disclosure is unconstitutional in the absence of a careful adversary procedure to determine the ex-offender's level of risk. E.g., State v. Williams, 952 N.E.2d 1108 (2011); Paul P. v. Farmer, 92 F. Supp. 2d 410 (D.N.J. 2000); People v. David W., 733 N.E.2d 206 (N.Y. 2000). In contrast, a Tennessee version of Megan's Law was upheld as a civil measure even though it imposed no limits on public disclosure of information about ex-offenders who had registered. Cutshall v. Sundquist, 193 F.3d 466 (6th Cir. 1999). The issues are explored in depth in Wayne A. Logan, Knowledge as Power: Criminal Registration and Community Notification Laws in America (2009).

B. PROBING THE BASIS FOR PUNISHMENT: A CLASSIC CASE

INTRODUCTORY NOTE

The next case, one of the most famous in the history of the common law, arose under circumstances that were unusual, to say the least. Nonetheless, many generations of lawyers, law students, legal scholars, and philosophers have debated—and continue to debate—the issues it poses and their implications for more commonplace problems of criminal justice. In reading the court's decision, consider whether there were good reasons to impose any punishment on these defendants. If so, what punishment was called for?

More broadly, the case also raises questions about the role of courts, about the legal method, and about the very meaning of "the law." How should a judge ascertain the correct legal principle and apply it when the facts of a case are unlike those present in prior precedents? Is a court duty-bound to enforce existing rules, even when they were established in very different circumstances? Alternatively, should judges have the right (or the obligation) to craft new rules specifically tailored to the facts before them?

Consider whether the court gives persuasive answers to these questions concerning the reasons for punishment and the proper role of the courts.

REGINA v. DUDLEY AND STEPHENS

Queen's Bench Division
14 Q.B.D. 273 (1884)

LORD COLERIDGE, C.J. The two prisoners, Thomas Dudley and Edwin Stephens, were indicted for the murder of Richard Parker on the high seas on the 25th of July in the present year. They were tried before my Brother Huddleston at Exeter on the 6th of November, and, under the direction of my learned Brother, the jury returned a special verdict, the legal effect of which has been argued before us, and on which we are now to pronounce judgment. The special verdict . . . is as follows.

> That on July 5, 1884, the prisoners, . . . with one Brooks, all able-bodied English seamen, and the deceased also an English boy, between seventeen and eighteen years of age, the crew of . . . a registered English vessel, were cast away in a storm on the high seas 1,600 miles from the Cape of Good Hope, and were compelled to put into an open boat belonging to the said [vessel]. That in this boat they had no supply of water and no supply of food, except two 1 lb. tins of turnips, and for three days they had nothing else to subsist upon. That on the fourth day they caught a small turtle, upon which they subsisted for a few days, and this was the only food they had up to the twentieth day when the act now in question was committed. That on the twelfth day the remains of the turtle were entirely consumed, and for the next eight days they had nothing to eat. That they had no fresh water, except such rain as they from time to time caught in their oilskin capes. That the boat was drifting on the ocean, and was probably more than 1,000 miles away from land. That on the eighteenth day, when they had been seven days without food and five without water, the prisoners spoke to Brooks as to what should be done if no succour came, and suggested that some one should be sacrificed to save the rest, but Brooks dissented, and the boy, to whom they were understood to refer, was not consulted. That on the 24th of July, the day before the act now in question, the prisoner Dudley proposed to Stephens and Brooks that lots should be cast who should be put to death to save the rest, but Brooks refused to consent, and it

was not put to the boy, and in point of fact there was no drawing of lots. That on the day the prisoners spoke of their families, and suggested it would be better to kill the boy that their lives should be saved, and Dudley proposed that if there was no vessel in sight by the morrow morning the boy should be killed. That next day, the 25th of July, no vessel appearing, Dudley told Brooks that he had better go and have a sleep, and made signs to Stephens and Brooks that the boy had better be killed. The prisoner Stephens agreed to the act, but Brooks dissented from it. That the boy was then lying at the bottom of the boat quite helpless and extremely weakened by famine and by drinking sea water, and unable to make any resistance, nor did he ever assent to his being killed. The prisoner Dudley offered a prayer asking forgiveness for them all if either of them should be tempted to commit a rash act, and that their souls might be saved. That Dudley, with the assent of Stephens, went to the boy, and telling him that his time was come, put a knife into his throat and killed him then and there; that the three men fed upon the body and blood of the boy for four days; that on the fourth day after the act had been committed the boat was picked up by a passing vessel, and the prisoners were rescued, still alive, but in the lowest state of prostration. . . . That if the men had not fed upon the body of the boy they would probably not have survived to be so picked up and rescued, but would within four days have died of famine. That the boy, being in a much weaker condition, was likely to have died before them. That at the time of the act in question there was no sail in sight, nor any reasonable prospect of relief. That under these circumstances there appeared to the prisoners every probability that unless they then fed or very soon fed upon the boy or one of themselves they would die of starvation. That there was no appreciable chance of saving life except by killing some one for the others to eat. That assuming any necessity to kill anybody, there was no greater necessity for killing the boy than any of the other three men. But whether upon the whole matter by the jurors found the killing of Richard Parker by Dudley and Stephens be felony and murder the jurors are ignorant, and pray the advice of the Court thereupon, and if upon the whole matter the Court shall be of opinion that the killing of Richard Parker be felony and murder, then the jurors say that Dudley and Stephens were each guilty of felony and murder as alleged in the indictment. . . .

From these facts, stated with the cold precision of a special verdict, it appears sufficiently that the prisoners were subject to terrible temptation, to sufferings which might break down the bodily power of the strongest man, and try the conscience of the best. Other details yet more harrowing, facts still more loathsome and appalling, were presented to the jury, and are to be found recorded in my learned Brother's notes. But nevertheless this is clear, that the prisoners put to death a weak and unoffending boy upon the chance of preserving their own lives by feeding upon his flesh and blood after he was killed, and with the certainty of depriving *him* of any possible chance of survival. The verdict finds in terms that "if the men had not fed upon the body of the boy they would *probably* not have survived," and that "the boy being in a much weaker condition was *likely* to have died before them." They might possibly have been picked up next day by a passing ship; they might possibly not have been picked up at all; in either case it is obvious that the

killing of the boy would have been an unnecessary and profitless act. It is
found by the verdict that the boy was incapable of resistance, and, in fact,
made none; and it is not even suggested that his death was due to any violence
on his part attempted against, or even so much as feared by, those who killed
him. . . .

[T]he real question in the case [is] whether killing under the circumstances
set forth in the verdict be or not be murder. The contention that it could be
anything else was, to the minds of us all, both new and strange, and we
stopped the Attorney General in his negative argument in order that we
might hear what could be said in support of a proposition which appeared
to us to be at once dangerous, immoral, and opposed to all legal principle and
analogy] . . . First it is said that it follows from various definitions of murder in
books of authority, which definitions imply, if they do not state, the doctrine,
that in order to save your own life you may lawfully take away the life of
another, when that other is neither attempting nor threatening yours, nor is
guilty of any illegal act whatever towards you or any one else. But if these
definitions be looked at they will not be found to sustain this contention. . . .

[T]he doctrine contended for receives no support from the great authority
of Lord Hale. . . . Lord Hale regarded the private necessity which justified, and
alone justified, the taking the life of another for the safeguard of one's own to
be what is commonly called "self-defence." [H]e thus expresses himself:—"If a
man be desperately assaulted and in peril of death, and cannot otherwise
escape unless, to satisfy his assailant's fury, he will kill an innocent person
then present, the fear and actual force will not acquit him of the crime and
punishment of murder, if he commit the fact [sic], for he ought rather to die
himself than kill an innocent; but if he cannot otherwise save his own life the
law permits him in his own defence to kill the assailant, for by the violence of
the assault, and the offence committed upon him by the assailant himself, the
law of nature, and necessity, hath made him his own protector. . . ." (Hale's
Pleas of the Crown, vol. i. 51.)

But, further still, Lord Hale in the following chapter deals with the position
asserted . . . he says, by Grotius and Puffendorf, that in a case of extreme
necessity, either of hunger or clothing; "theft is no theft, or at least not punishable as theft, as some even of our own lawyers have asserted the same."
"But," says Lord Hale, "I take it that here in England, that rule . . . is false; and
therefore, if a person, being under necessity for want of victuals or clothes,
shall upon that account clandestinely and animo furandi steal another man's
goods, it is felony, and a crime by the laws of England punishable with death."
(Hale, Pleas of the Crown, i. 54.) If, therefore, Lord Hale is clear—as he is—
that extreme necessity of hunger does not justify larceny, what would he have
said to the doctrine that it justified murder? . . .

Is there, then, any authority for the proposition which has been presented
to us? Decided cases there are none. . . . The American case cited by my
Brother Stephen in his Digest . . . in which it was decided, correctly indeed,
that sailors had no right to throw passengers overboard to save themselves, but
on the somewhat strange ground that the proper mode of determining who

was to be sacrificed was to vote upon the subject by ballot, can hardly, as my Brother Stephen says, be an authority satisfactory to a court in this country.[a] . . .

The one real authority of former time is Lord Bacon, who . . . lays down the law as follows:—"Necessity carrieth a privilege in itself. [I]f a man steals viands to satisfy his present hunger, this is no felony nor larceny. So if divers be in danger of drowning by the casting away of some boat or barge, and one of them get to some plank, . . . and another to save his life thrust him from it, whereby he is drowned, this is neither se defendendo nor by misadventure, but justifiable."[b] . . . Lord Bacon was great even as a lawyer; but it is permissible to much smaller men, relying upon principle and on the authority of others, . . . to question the soundness of his dictum. There are many conceivable states of things in which it might possibly be true, but if Lord Bacon meant to lay down the broad proposition that man may save his life by killing, if necessary, an innocent and unoffending neighbour, it certainly is not law at the present day. . . .

Now it is admitted that the deliberate killing of this unoffending and unre-sisting boy was clearly murder, unless the killing can be justified by some well-recognised excuse admitted by the law. It is further admitted that there was in this case no such excuse, unless the killing was justified by what has been called "necessity." But the temptation to the act which existed here was not what the law has ever called necessity. Nor is this to be regretted. Though law and morality are not the same, and many things may be immoral which are not necessarily illegal, yet the absolute divorce of law from morality would be of fatal consequence; and such divorce would follow if the temptation to murder in this case were to be held by law an absolute defence of it. . . . To preserve one's life is generally speaking a duty, but it may be the plainest and the highest duty to sacrifice it. War is full of instances in which it is a man's duty not to live, but to die. The duty, in case of shipwreck, of a captain to his crew, of the crew to the passengers, of soldiers to women and children impose[s] on men the moral necessity, not of the preservation, but of the sacrifice of their lives for others, from which in no country, least of all, it is

---

a. Lord Coleridge is referring to United States v. Holmes, 26 F. Cas. 360 (C.C.E.D. Pa. 1842). But that court had not suggested that the selection be made "by ballot." The relevant passage states (id. at 367):

> When . . . all sustenance is exhausted, and a sacrifice of one person is necessary to appease the hunger of others, the selection is by lot. This mode is resorted to as the fairest mode, and, in some sort, as an appeal to God, for selection of the victim. . . . In no other than this or some like way are those having equal rights put upon an equal footing, and in no other way is it possible to guard against partiality and oppression, violence and conflict.

The *Holmes* case is discussed in more detail at page 899 infra.—EDS.

b. Bacon introduced the quoted passage as follows:

> The law chargeth no man with default where the act is compulsory and not voluntary . . . : and therefore, if either there be an impossibility for a man to do otherwise, or so great a perturbation of the judgment and reason as in presumption of law man's nature cannot overcome, such necessity carrieth a privilege in itself.

Shedding, Ellis & Heath, The Works of Francis Bacon 343 (1859).—EDS.

to be hoped, in England, will men ever shrink, as indeed, they have not shrunk. It is not correct, therefore, to say that there is any absolute or unqualified necessity to preserve one's life. . . . It would be a very easy and cheap display of commonplace learning to quote from Greek and Latin authors, from Horace, from Juvenal, from Cicero, from Euripides, passage after passage, in which the duty of dying for others has been laid down in glowing and emphatic language as resulting from the principles of heathen ethics; it is enough in a Christian country to remind ourselves of the Great Example whom we profess to follow. It is not needful to point out the awful danger of admitting the principle which has been contended for. Who is to be the judge of this sort of necessity? By what measure is the comparative value of lives to be measured? Is it to be strength, or intellect, or what? It is plain that the principle leaves to him who is to profit by it to determine the necessity which will justify him in deliberately taking another's life to save his own. In this case the weakest, the youngest, the most unresisting, was chosen. Was it more necessary to kill him than one of the grown men? The answer must be "No"—

> So spake the Fiend, and with necessity
> The tyrant's plea, excused his devilish deeds.[c]

It is not suggested that in this particular case the deeds were "devilish," but it is quite plain that such a principle once admitted might be made the legal cloak for unbridled passion and atrocious crime. There is no safe path for judges to tread but to ascertain the law to the best of their ability and to declare it according to their judgment; and if in any case the law appears to be too severe on individuals, to leave it to the Sovereign to exercise that prerogative of mercy which the Constitution has intrusted to the hands fittest to dispense it.

It must not be supposed that in refusing to admit temptation to be an excuse for crime it is forgotten how terrible the temptation was; how awful the suffering; how hard in such trials to keep the judgment straight and the conduct pure. We are often compelled to set up standards we cannot reach ourselves, and to lay down rules which we could not ourselves satisfy. But a man has no right to declare temptation to be an excuse, though he might himself have yielded to it, nor allow compassion for the criminal to change or weaken in any manner the legal definition of the crime. It is therefore our duty to declare that the prisoners' act in this case was wilful murder, that the facts as stated in the verdict are no legal justification of the homicide; and to say that in our unanimous opinion the prisoners are upon this special verdict guilty of murder.[1]

The Court then proceeded to pass sentence of death upon the prisoners.[d]

---

c. The court here is quoting from John Milton, Paradise Lost.—EDS.

1. My brother Grove has furnished me with the following suggestion, too late to be embodied in the judgment but well worth preserving: "If the two accused men were justified in killing Parker, then if not rescued in time, two of the three survivors would be justified in killing the third, and of the two who remained the stronger would be justified in killing the weaker, so that three men might be justifiably killed to give the fourth a chance of surviving."—C.

d. The Crown later commuted the sentence to six months' imprisonment.—EDS.

NOTES AND QUESTIONS

For discussion of the background of *Dudley and Stephens*, see Neil Hanson, The Custom of the Sea (2000); A.W.B. Simpson, Cannibalism and the Common Law (1984). As both books report, cannibalism was an accepted fact of life at sea before the era of modern communications and rescue capabilities, because seamen occasionally found themselves stranded far from help. Through most of the nineteenth century, such cases were treated as tragedies, either celebrated or discreetly ignored; the survivors were received with sympathy or perverse fascination but were seldom considered candidates for prosecution. The "custom of the sea" (cannibalism) was so well established that Dudley talked freely about the episode with an apparently clear conscience. But British officials, concerned that the custom of the sea set a potentially bad precedent, were determined to make a test case of the incident, and the prosecution of Dudley and Stephens ensued. See also Allen D. Boyer, Crime, Cannibalism and Joseph Conrad: The Influence of *Regina v. Dudley and Stephens* on Lord Jim, 20 Loy. L.A. L. Rev. 9 (1986).

1. *Prudential concerns.* On facts like those in *Dudley and Stephens*, does punishment serve any practical purpose? Is the threat of the death penalty adequate to deter this sort of conduct? If not, should cannibalism at sea be punished by some especially painful sort of capital punishment? Conversely, what was the rationale for *reducing* the punishment, commuting the death sentence to a six months' prison term? If a severe sentence is inappropriate when a defendant faces powerful temptation to commit a prohibited act, why bother imposing any punishment at all?

Would the convictions be defensible if the "custom of the sea" was having a prejudicial impact on the British maritime industry? Would punishment on that ground be justified even if the defendants' actions were not blameworthy, or is it essential to limit punishment to those who *deserve* it? If so, *did* Dudley and Stephens deserve punishment?

The specific situation faced by Dudley and Stephens was unusual even at the time, but in a sense the underlying problem is a recurrent one for our own criminal justice system, because harmful conduct is often the product of great pressure or great temptation. Should defendants who commit crimes in such circumstances receive especially severe punishment, especially lenient punishment, or no punishment at all?

2. *The problem of desert.* Are there legitimate grounds to conclude that Dudley and Stephens did not *deserve* to be punished, despite their deliberate, carefully premeditated decision to kill Parker? Note that there are several distinct reasons why punishment may not be deserved, even when a person intentionally causes serious harm. Consider the following possibilities:

(a) *Justification.* Any reasonable legal system must provide for self-defense as a justification, and of course ours does. But should Dudley and Stephens be permitted to rely on this concept? Should a claim of self-defense fail because Parker was not threatening them? Or should self-defense be available because they sought to save their own lives? After all, it was necessary (or reasonably seemed necessary) to kill one person so that the two others had a chance of survival. In a severe storm it is desirable for a ship's captain to jettison cargo (whose owner of course has done nothing wrong) in order to keep his ship from sinking. Is it also desirable, therefore, to sacrifice one person in order to save two, rather than to let all three die? Legal doctrine governing these issues is explored in Chapter 8.B, Principles of Justification, infra, but it is worth pausing now to consider what approach makes sense in terms of the underlying purposes of punishment.

Is the problem in *Dudley and Stephens* simply that the defendants did not draw straws or use some other fair means to determine who would be sacrificed? Lord Coleridge mocks that idea and indicates that the defendants would have been guilty of murder even if the person to be sacrificed had been chosen fairly. What possible purpose would punishment serve in such a case?

(b) Excuse. The law provides a defense to certain limited classes of defendants whose actions are harmful and unjustified, when we believe they could not reasonably be expected to have done better. Children and insane people are examples. Should the same principle excuse Dudley and Stephens? Could they fairly have been expected to do better? The judges in *Dudley and Stephens*, just prior to sentencing the two defendants to death, acknowledge that they were imposing a standard of conduct that they themselves might well have been unable to reach. But how can we fairly punish an act that a law-abiding person might commit? Current law governing these issues is explored in Chapter 8.C, Principles of Excuse, infra.

3. Exploring and assessing the justifications. To pursue these issues, the next section examines the approaches that are widely accepted or commonly proposed to justify the imposition of punishment and to explain its appropriate limits.

C. WHY PUNISH?

INTRODUCTORY NOTE

Punishment is unpleasant. And unlike other potentially unpleasant experiences (paying taxes, military service in wartime), punishment is *intended* to be unpleasant. There is universal agreement, therefore, that government must have a strong justification when it deliberately seeks to inflict physical or emotional pain on an individual. And three distinct facets of punishment call for justification. The first is often called its *general justifying aim*: Why do we set up social institutions that impose punishment? Second is the question of *distribution*:—Why do we impose punishment on a particular individual? And third is the question of *degree*:—What justifies the amount of punishment imposed in a given case?

Broadly speaking, the justifications for punishment fall into two large categories, retributive and utilitarian. "[A] retributivist claims that punishment is justified because people deserve it; a utilitarian believes that justification lies in the useful purposes that punishment serves (the latter approach is sometimes referred to as 'consequentialist,' or 'instrumentalist')."[8] These are rough groupings, because precise definitions vary from one commentator to another. We will look more closely at these concepts and their implications in a moment, but for present purposes, it is sufficient to bear in mind that retributive rationales are essentially backward looking; they attribute crucial importance to the offender's behavior in the past, and in particular to the blameworthiness of that behavior. Utilitarian or "consequentialist" rationales are essentially forward looking; they seek to justify punishment on the basis of the good consequences it is expected to produce in the future, and in particular three consequences for controlling crime: deterrence (of the offender and others), incapacitation of the offender, and rehabilitation of the offender.

Debate about such justifications sometimes seems purely academic, because both retributive and utilitarian purposes often appear self-evidently sound and mutually reinforcing. Thus, when a contract killer is convicted of murder, with no extenuating circumstances, severe punishment seems appropriate for both retributive and utilitarian reasons. But even in cases of intentional killing, the justifications can sometimes be troubling or in conflict with each other. *Dudley and Stephens*, supra pages 83-87, is a rare but classic instance of this sort: Considerations of moral blame might suggest a lenient sentence, while considerations of deterrence might suggest a severe one. And tension between the objectives of punishment is by no means confined to such unusual situations; a need to choose between justifications arises almost routinely in the criminal justice system. For mentally disturbed offenders, or offenders driven to commit predatory crime because of addiction or economic need, a focus on moral blame again might suggest reducing the severity of punishment, while concern for deterrence might suggest increasing it. Both the theory of criminal law and its daily practice therefore require working with these purposes and understanding their limitations.

The present section examines the various justifications for punishment and the ways that commentators, statutes, and criminal law practitioners seek to piece them together into a coherent framework. Section C.1 considers utilitarianism. That concept's basic approach, judging social policy by its costs and benefits, is familiar. But in the context of punishment, utilitarianism often is criticized for paying insufficient attention to individual rights, and to the perceived need for a connection between punishment and the offender's *moral blame*. Section C.2 turns to retribution—the concept most often called upon to supply that connection. But retribution has its own perceived shortcomings, which Section C.2 explores. Section C.3 considers various "cousins" of retributivism—vengeance, social cohesion, and similar theories that share

---

8. Kent Greenawalt, Punishment, 4 Encyclopedia of Crime and Justice 1336 (1st ed. 1983).

the retributive focus on the past offense, but depart from classic retributivism's emphasis on moral blame as the decisive factor determining the justice of a punishment.

The supposed limitations of both utilitarian and retributive approaches prompt the search for a "mixed" theory that can incorporate their strengths without their weaknesses. Such "mixed" theories are the subject of Section C.4. Finally, to the extent that a utilitarian approach plays any role in the overall framework of just punishment, many practical issues arise when we seek to achieve the utilitarian objective of crime control in the setting of contemporary American society. Section C.5 examines the complexities of deterrence, incapacitation, and rehabilitation as crime-prevention strategies.

Following these materials on the justifications for punishment, Section D will present concrete cases that provide a basis for examining the ideas introduced in the present section and testing their implications.

1. The Utilitarian View

Jeremy Bentham, An Introduction to the Principles of Morals and Legislation, in Bentham & Mill, The Utilitarians 162, 166 (Dolphin Books, 1961): The general object which all laws have, or ought to have, in common, is to augment the total happiness of the community; and therefore, in the first place, to exclude, as far as may be, every thing that tends to subtract from that happiness: in other words, to exclude mischief.

But all punishment is mischief: all punishment in itself is evil. Upon the principle of utility, if it ought at all to be admitted, it ought only to be admitted in as far as it promises to exclude some greater evil. . . .

Jeremy Bentham, Principles of Penal Law, Pt. II, bk. 1, ch. 3, in J. Bentham's Works 396, 402 (J. Bowring ed., 1843): Pain and pleasure are the great springs of human action. When a man perceives or supposes pain to be the consequence of an act, he is acted upon in such a manner as tends, with a certain force, to withdraw him, as it were, from the commission of that act. If the apparent magnitude, or rather value of that pain be greater than the apparent magnitude or value of the pleasure or good he expects to be the consequence of the act, he will be absolutely prevented from performing it. The mischief which would have ensued from the act, if performed, will also by that means be prevented. . . .

The observation of rules of proportion between crimes and punishments has been objected to as useless, because they seem to suppose, that a spirit of calculation has place among the passions of men, who, it is said, never calculate. But dogmatic as this proposition is, it is altogether false. In matters of importance every one calculates. Each individual calculates with more or less correctness, according to the degrees of his information, and the power of the motives which actuate him, but all calculate. It would be hard to say that a madman does not calculate. Happily, the passion of cupidity, which on account of its power, its constancy, and its extent, is most formidable to society, is the passion which is most given to calculation. This, therefore, will be more successfully combated, the more carefully the law turns the balance of profit against it.

NOTES AND QUESTIONS

Jeremy Bentham, who lived from 1748 to 1832, was a leading social reformer of his day. At the time, England punished all felonies with death, and Bentham's writings were in part a reaction against those draconian sanctions. By insisting that punishment "ought only to be admitted in as far as it promises to exclude some greater evil," Bentham sought to promote "rules of proportion between crimes and punishments." But does the cost-benefit approach actually lead to proportionality? Couldn't it be "efficient" to punish all offenses by imprisonment for life?

Bentham's answer is that for trivial offenses, the cost of imprisonment would exceed the benefit in terms of the minor offenses that would be deterred. But even so, for truly serious crimes, such as robbery and rape, couldn't Bentham's approach require life imprisonment? Here the difficulty is that if robbery is subject to the highest possible punishment, the offender would suffer no additional sanction for committing additional robberies or for killing all possible witnesses. Bentham wrote, "Where two offenses are in conjunction, the greater offense ought to be subjected to severer punishment, in order that the delinquent may have a motive to stop at the lesser."[9]

Bentham's utilitarianism nonetheless can appear to support some intuitively unappealing conclusions. Consider these problems:

1. *Punishment of the innocent.* Suppose that a string of robberies has gone unsolved and police hear rumors that many people are talking about committing similar crimes, convinced that they will not get caught. From the utilitarian perspective, would the police chief be justified in seizing and framing an innocent person, in order to send a strong deterrent message that such crimes cannot be committed with impunity? If this step is unacceptable, is that because its costs would ultimately outweigh its benefits?[10] Or is there some reason to resist such a step, regardless of how all details of the cost-benefit calculus might work out?

2. *Disproportionate punishment.* Bentham gives a plausible utilitarian objection to imposing long prison sentences on those who are guilty only of a minor offense. But is it clear that the costs of doing so will always outweigh the benefits? For example, suppose that convenience stores lose millions of

---

9. Jeremy Bentham, The Theory of Legislation 201 (1975).

10. Consider Guyora Binder & Nicholas J. Smith, Framed: Utilitarianism and Punishment of the Innocent, 32 Rutgers L.J. 115, 211 (2001): "Utilitarian penology could not recommend . . . secretly framing the innocent, because a system of criminal justice could only advance its primary aim of public security if it was sufficiently transparent in design to guarantee the public that such acts would be discovered and punished."

dollars every year as a result of shoplifting, and even with security cameras, it is very difficult for them to catch individuals who walk off without paying for a candy bar. On utilitarian grounds, would it be justified to authorize a 20-year prison term for a teenager who steals a 75-cent piece of candy? To be sure, there can be many subtle, indirect costs of such a policy, and a good utilitarian must be careful to consider all such effects. If the 20-year prison term is unjustified, is that because the costs, properly measured, outweigh the benefits? Or are such elaborate cost-benefit calculations (the next excerpt calls them "the serpent-windings of utilitarianism") essentially beside the point? Is there, again, a more basic reason to reject the punishment, regardless of how its costs and benefits add up?

These and other discomforts with the utilitarian framework lead many to conclude that it cannot account for strong, unshakeable intuitions about what we know to be wrong. That conclusion prompts many to turn to retributivism as a potentially preferable grounding for our punishment practices.

2. Retribution

INTRODUCTORY NOTE

"Retributive" views (of which there are many) share an insistence that punishment must be justified by the seriousness of the offense committed, rather than by the future benefits to be obtained by punishing. But those who prefer a retributive approach often disagree about precisely what such an approach requires. One common version of retributivism holds that only the guilty may be punished; in other words, guilt is a necessary but not automatically a sufficient condition of just punishment. (This view is often called *negative retributivism*.) Another common version, however, asserts that guilt is a *sufficient* condition of just punishment; in other words, a just society *may* and indeed *must* punish the guilty. (This view is often called *positive retributivism*.) A third point of disagreement concerns the appropriate *degree* of punishment. Retributive views usually link the degree of punishment to the offender's *moral culpability*. But the term retribution is sometimes associated, perhaps inaccurately, with the rather different notion of *retaliation*— that punishment should be linked to the *harm* caused by an offense. Because that shift from blame to harm marks a fundamental change in the focus of the theory of punishment, we postpone consideration of retaliation until Section C.3.a below.

In reading the excerpts that follow, consider where the various writers stand in these debates about the nature of retributive justice. For each of them, *what* does the concept of retribution require, and more importantly, *why*?

Immanuel Kant, The Philosophy of Law (W. Hastie trans., 1887): Juridical punishment can never be administered merely as a means of promoting another good either with regard to the criminal himself or to civil society, but must in all cases be imposed only because the individual on whom it is inflicted *has committed a crime.* For one man ought never to be dealt with merely as a means subservient to the purpose of another. . . . He must first be found guilty and *punishable*, before there can be any thought of drawing from his punishment any benefit for himself or his fellow-citizens. The penal law is a categorical imperative; and woe to him who creeps through the serpent-windings of utilitarianism to discover some advantage that may discharge him from the justice of punishment, or even from the due measure of it, according to the Pharisaic maxim: "It is better that *one* man should die than that the whole people should perish." For if justice and righteousness perish, human life would no longer have any value in the world. What, then, is to be said of such a proposal as to keep a criminal alive who has been condemned to death, on his being given to understand that if he agreed to certain dangerous experiments being performed upon him, he would be allowed to survive if he came happily through them? It is argued that physicians might thus obtain new information that would be of value to the commonweal. But a court of justice would repudiate with scorn any proposal of this kind if made to it by the medical faculty; for justice would cease to be justice if it were bartered away for any consideration whatever. . . .

But what is the mode and measure of punishment which public justice takes as its principle and standard? It is just the principle of equality, by which the pointer of the scale of justice is made to incline no more to the one side than the other. It may be rendered by saying that the undeserved evil which any one commits on another is to be regarded as perpetrated on himself. Hence it may be said: "If you slander another, you slander yourself; if you steal from another, you steal from yourself; if you strike another, you strike yourself; if you kill another, you kill yourself." This is the right of retaliation (*jus talionis*); and properly understood, it is the only principle which in regulating a public court, as distinguished from mere private judgment, can definitely assign both the quality and the quantity of a just penalty. All other standards are wavering and uncertain; and on account of other considerations involved in them, they contain no principle conformable to the sentence of pure and strict justice. . . .

[W]hoever has committed murder must *die.* There is, in this case, no juridical substitute or surrogate that can be given or taken for the satisfaction of justice. There is no *likeness* or proportion between life, however painful, and death; and therefore there is no equality between the crime of murder and the retaliation of it but what is judicially accomplished by the execution of the criminal. His death, however, must be kept free from all maltreatment that would make the humanity suffering in his person loathsome or abominable. Even if a civil society resolved to dissolve itself with the consent of all its members—as might be supposed in the case of a people inhabiting an island resolving to separate and scatter themselves through the whole world—the last murderer lying in the prison ought to be executed before the resolution was carried out. This ought to be done in order that every one may realize the desert of his deeds, and that bloodguiltiness may not remain upon the people;

for otherwise they might all be regarded as participators in the murder as a public violation of justice.

Michael S. Moore, The Moral Worth of Retribution, in F. Schoeman ed., Responsibility, Character and Emotions 179 (1987): Retributivism is the view that punishment is justified by the moral culpability of those who receive it. A retributivist punishes because, and only because, the offender deserves it. Retributivism thus stands in stark contrast to utilitarian views that justify punishment of past offenses by the greater good of preventing future offenses. . . .

[Retributivism] differs from a variety of views that are often paraded as retributivist, but that in fact are not. [For example,] retributivism is sometimes identified with a particular measure of punishment such as *lex talionis*, an eye for an eye, or with a kind of punishment such as the death penalty. Yet retributivism answers a [different] question. . . . True enough, retributivists at some point have to answer the "how much" and "what type" questions for specific offenses, and they are committed to the principle that punishment should be graded in proportion to desert; but they are not committed to any particular penalty scheme. . . . It is quite possible to be a retributivist and to be against both the death penalty and *lex talionis*, the idea that crimes should be punished by like acts being done to the criminal.[a]

[Further,] retributivism is not the "view that only the guilty are to be punished." A retributivist will subscribe to such a view, but [the] distinctive aspect of retributivism is that the moral desert of an offender is a *sufficient* reason to punish him or her. . . . That future crime might also be prevented by punishment is a happy surplus for a retributivist, but no part of the justification for punishing.

. . . Retributivism is not the view that punishment of offenders satisfies the desires for vengeance of their victims. . . . A retributivist can justify punishment as deserved even if the criminal's victims are indifferent (or even opposed) to punishing the one who hurt them. Indeed, a retributivist should urge punishment on all offenders who deserve it, even if *no* victims wanted it. [Nor is p]unishment for a retributivist . . . justified by the need to prevent private violence, which is an essentially utilitarian justification. Even in the most well-mannered state, those criminals who deserve punishment should get it, according to retributivism. . . .

Retributivism is a very straightforward theory of punishment: We are justified in punishing because and only because offenders deserve it. Moral culpability ("desert") . . . gives society more than merely a right to punish culpable offenders. . . . For a retributivist, the moral culpability of an offender also gives society the *duty* to punish. Retributivism, in other words, is truly a

---

a. See, e.g., Dan Markel, State, Be Not Proud: A Retributivist Defense of the Commutation of Death Row and the Abolition of the Death Penalty, 40 Harv. C.R.-C.L. L. Rev. 407 (2005) (arguing that retributive justice, because it is committed to "modesty and dignity in modes of punishment" can support opposition to the death penalty).—EDS.

theory of justice such that, if it is true, we have an obligation to set up institutions so that retribution is achieved.

NOTE ON CRITICISMS AND DEFENSES OF RETRIBUTION

Does retributivism avoid the difficulties of the purely utilitarian approach? Are there persuasive reasons to accept the retributive view, or is it merely, as Professor H.L.A. Hart once suggested (Punishment and Responsibility 234-235 (1968)), "a mysterious piece of moral alchemy in which the combination of the two evils of moral wickedness [of the offense] and suffering [of the offender who is punished] are transmuted into good"? In thinking about whether there is a sound basis for the retributive approach, consider the materials that follow.

Herbert Morris, On Guilt and Innocence 33-34 (1976): Let us suppose that men are constituted roughly as they now are, with a rough equivalence in strength and abilities, a capacity to be injured by each other and to make judgments that such injury is undesirable, a limited strength of will, and a capacity to reason and to conform conduct to rules. Applying to the conduct of these men are a group of rules ... that prohibit violence and deception and compliance with which provides benefits for all persons. ... Making possible this mutual benefit is the assumption by individuals of a burden. The burden consists in the exercise of self-restraint by individuals over inclinations that would, if satisfied, directly interfere or create a substantial risk of interference with others in proscribed ways. If a person fails to exercise self-restraint even though he might have and gives in to such inclinations, he renounces a burden which others have voluntarily assumed and thus gains an advantage which others, who have restrained themselves, do not possess. This system, then, is one in which the rules establish a mutuality of benefit and burden and in which the benefits of noninterference are conditional upon the assumption of burdens.

Connecting punishment with the violation of these primary rules, and making public the provision for punishment, is both reasonable and just. First, it is only reasonable that those who voluntarily comply with the rules be provided some assurance that they will not be assuming burdens which others are unprepared to assume. Their disposition to comply voluntarily will diminish as they learn that others are with impunity renouncing burdens they are assuming. Second, fairness dictates that a system in which benefits and burdens are equally distributed have a mechanism designed to prevent a maldistribution in the benefits and burdens. Thus, sanctions are attached to noncompliance with the primary rules so as to induce compliance ... among those who may be disinclined to obey. In this way the likelihood of an unfair distribution is diminished.

Third, it is just to punish those who have violated the rules and caused the unfair distribution of benefits and burdens. A person who violates the rules has something others have—the benefits of the system—but by renouncing what others have assumed, the burdens of self-restraint, he has acquired an unfair advantage. Matters are not even until this advantage is in some way erased. Another way of putting it is that he owes something to others, for he has something that does not rightfully belong to him. Justice—that is punishing such individuals—restores the equilibrium of benefits and burdens by taking from the individual what he owes, that is, exacting the debt.

Jeffrie Murphy, Marxism and Retribution, 2 Phil. & Pub. Aff. 217 (1973): The retributive theory really presupposes what might be called a "gentlemen's club" picture of the relation between man and society—i.e., men are viewed as being part of a community of shared values and rules. The rules benefit all concerned and, as a kind of debt for the benefits derived, each man owes obedience to the rules. In the absence of such obedience, he deserves punishment in the sense that he owes payment for the benefits. For, as a rational man, he can see that the rules benefit everyone (himself included) and that he would have selected them in the original position of choice. . . .

But to think that [this] applies to the typical criminal, from the poorer classes, is to live in a world of social and political fantasy. [T]hey certainly would be hard-pressed to name the benefits for which they are supposed to owe obedience. If justice . . . is based on reciprocity, it is hard to see what these persons are supposed to reciprocate for. . . .

Consider one example: A man has been convicted of armed robbery. On investigation, we learn that he is an impoverished black whose whole life has been one of frustrating alienation from the prevailing socio-economic structure—no job, no transportation if he could get a job, substandard education for his children, terrible housing and inadequate health care for his whole family, condescending-tardy-inadequate welfare payments, harassment by the police but no real protection by them against the dangers in his community, and near total exclusion from the political process. Learning all this, would we still want to talk—as many do—of his suffering punishment under the rubric of "paying a debt to society"? . . . Debt for what? I do not, of course, pretend that all criminals can be so described. But I do think that this is a closer picture of the typical criminal than the picture that is presupposed in the retributive theory—i.e., the picture of an evil person who, of his own free will, intentionally acts against those just rules of society which he knows, as a rational man, benefit everyone including himself.

[I]f we are morally sensitive enough to want to be sure that we have the moral right to punish before we inflict it, then we had better first make sure that we have restructured society in such a way that criminals genuinely do correspond to the only model that will render punishment permissible—i.e., make sure that they are autonomous and that they do benefit in the requisite sense.

Jean Hampton, Correcting Harms versus Righting Wrongs: The Goal of Retribution, 39 UCLA L. Rev. 1659, 1660-1661 (1992): [A] basic difficulty with [the fair play] theory is its assumption that . . . we censure and punish . . . because [wrongdoers] are free riders. This assumption makes sense only if we believe that constraining ourselves so that we do not rape or murder or steal imposes a *cost* upon us. Yet that idea makes sense only if raping, murdering, and stealing are viewed by us as desirable and attractive. . . . However, surely this is exactly what most of us *do not* think about crime. Very few of us . . . resent murderers, muggers, or rapists because they have unfairly enjoyed benefits coveted by the rest of us. [I]t seems absurd to say that this is what is wrong with wrongdoers who murder, assault, or abuse others.

John L. Mackie, Retribution: A Test Case For Ethical Objectivity, in Joel Feinberg & Hyman Gross eds., Philosophy of Law 677 (1991): [R]*etribuo* in Latin means "I pay back." . . . Punitive retribution is the repaying of harm with harm, as reward is the repaying of benefit with benefit. We can class as an essentially retributivist approach any that sees at least some prima facie rightness in the repaying of evil with evil, especially a proportionate evil. . . . But this is a very dark saying. *Why* should it be so? . . .

Repayment: How does the criminal's suffering or deprivation pay anything to society? No doubt repaying a debt often hurts the person who pays it, but it does not follow that anything that hurts someone amounts to his repaying a debt. . . . So this account is simply incoherent. . . .

Annulment: This notion . . . seems to be that as long as a criminal goes scot-free, the crime itself still exists, still flourishes, but when the criminal is adequately punished the crime itself is somehow wiped out. It is not, therefore, by any sort of repayment or restitution that "right is restored," but just by trampling on the previously flourishing crime. But . . . there is no comprehensible way in which a penalty wipes out an otherwise still-existing crime. . . .

Fair play: Here the suggestion is that the . . . criminal has gained an unfair advantage by breaking the rules; to restore fairness this advantage must be taken away from him. Unlike our last two approaches, this one is not incoherent; it makes perfectly good sense in certain contexts. It has its clearest exemplification in the award of a penalty in football . . . when there has been a foul. . . . It is also retributivist in our basic sense of being retrospective; the justification is complete when the penalty has been imposed; fairness has then (roughly at least) been restored, irrespective of whether there are or are not any further desirable consequences. The trouble with this approach, however, is that it has little relation to most cases of punishment. Any serious attempt to apply it would lead to bizarre results. . . . Thus if a businessman has secured a contract worth $100,000, but has exceeded the speed limit in order to get to the relevant appointment on time, he should presumably be fined $100,000, whereas a fine of $1 would be enough for someone who murders a blind cripple to rob him of $1. . . . Unsuccessful attempts at murder (or anything else) should not be punished at all. . . . What is basically wrong with the fair play approach . . . is that it focuses on the advantage that may have been gained by the criminal in some sort of social competition, whereas the point of punishment surely lies not in this but in the wrongness of his act and the harm that he has done or tried to do. . . .

NOTE ON RETRIBUTION AS A CONSTRAINT

The preceding excerpts from Morris, Murphy, Hampton, and Mackie focus on *positive* retribution—the claim that a just society *must* impose punishment equivalent in severity to the seriousness of the crime. This is the most controversial form of retributivism; there has been much less discomfort with negative retribution—the claim that the seriousness of the offense sets an upper limit to permissible punishment. But what does this upper limit actually mean in practice? The notion that justice imposes a constraint on punishment is intuitively appealing, but unless that upper limit has some content, it can hardly serve as a significant constraint. So it becomes essential to know how the upper limit is fixed.

Kant, for example, insists (page 94 supra) that the amount of punishment must not be "wavering and uncertain," and he requires "equality" between crime and punishment. His analysis seems to imply an "eye for an eye" approach, but neither Kant nor other retributivists take such a formula literally. (Even capital punishment, Kant says, "must be kept free from all maltreatment that would make the humanity suffering in his person loathsome.") But how, then, can we prevent the upper limit on punishment from becoming "wavering and uncertain"?

One approach ("empirical desert") has used questionnaires to ascertain community views about deserved punishment in typical cases. Such surveys find broad agreement about the *relative* seriousness of different offenses, but little agreement about *absolute* seriousness—the *amount* of punishment warranted in a particular case.[11] In any event, are public opinion surveys (or the punishments that elected legislatures authorize) the right place to look to determine whether a particular punishment is *justified*? Professor Paul H. Robinson, who has done much of the leading work on empirical desert, also notes (The Ongoing Revolution in Punishment Theory: Doing Justice as Controlling Crime, 42 Ariz. St. L.J. 1089, 1108 (2010)) that adhering to this approach "may do injustice that is not apparent to the present community." And beyond that concern, does *any* conception of deserved punishment really set a meaningful constraint in practice? Specific constitutional doctrines relevant to a proportionality requirement are examined at pp. 186-204 and 536-557, infra. But with respect to the broader question whether "negative" retributivism delivers on its promise to limit punishment severity, consider Alice Ristroph, Desert, Democracy, and Sentencing Reform, 96 J. Crim. L. & Criminology 1293, 1293-1297 (2006):

> [I]n legal and political practice, desert has proven more illimitable than limiting. Democratic conceptions of desert are first, *elastic*: desert is hard to quantify and easy to stretch. . . . Many of the sentencing policies alleged by academics to violate "desert as a limiting principle" were (and continue to be) popularly justified in the language of desert. . . . Moreover, desert is *opaque*: it

---

11. See Paul H. Robinson, Distributive Principles of Criminal Law: Who Should Be Punished How Much? (2008).

is difficult to know or control which particular details of an offender or offense inform a decision-maker's assessment of desert. Racial bias, fear, disgust, and other arbitrary factors can shape desert assessments, but they do so under cover of a seemingly legitimate moral judgment. [T]he opacity of desert claims may enable prejudice to take effect in sentencing practices even as the moralistic tenor of desert rhetoric shields sentencing practices from meaningful scrutiny.

3. "Cousins" of Retribution

INTRODUCTORY NOTE

As we have seen, the essence of a retributive approach is its focus on the nature of the offender's crime. More specifically, classic retributivism emphasizes the blameworthiness of that crime, and views blame as a decisive concern in itself, without regard to its possible bearing on the consequences of imposing punishment. Several efforts to justify punishment are closely related to retributivism, in the sense that they too give central importance to the past offense. Indeed for that reason, some of these close relatives are often confused with retributivism or equated with it. But these theories differ in respects that are fundamental. Some of these theories—often called theories of retaliation or vengeance—focus less on the *blameworthiness* of the past offense than on the *harm* it caused. Others look to the harmfulness or blameworthiness of the past offense, but do so not because those concerns are considered sufficient in their own right but instead because that emphasis is thought to have certain beneficial *consequences*. In this section we consider these "cousins" of retributivism—first retaliation and vengeance, and then the theories of social cohesion.

a. Retaliation and Vengeance

2 James Fitzjames Stephen, A History of the Criminal Law of England 81-82 (1883 ed.): [T]he sentence of the law is to the moral sentiment of the public in relation to any offence what a seal is to hot wax. It converts into a permanent final judgment what might otherwise be a transient sentiment. The mere general suspicion or knowledge that a man has done something dishonest may never be brought to a point, and the disapprobation excited by it may in time pass away, but the fact that he has been convicted and punished as a thief stamps a mark upon him for life. In short, the infliction of punishment by law gives definite expression and a solemn ratification and justification to the hatred which is excited by the commission of the offence, and which constitutes the moral or popular as distinguished from the conscientious sanction of that part of morality which is also sanctioned by the criminal law. The criminal law thus proceeds upon the principle that it is morally right to hate criminals, and it confirms and justifies that sentiment by inflicting upon criminals punishments which express it.

QUESTIONS

Is there a moral case for tying punishment to the amount of resentment and outrage generated by a crime?[12] If it is desirable for criminal punishment to be affected by hatred, indignation, and outrage, how should we design our institutions of punishment in order to harness and reflect those emotions? Should sentences (within the legislatively authorized range) be selected by the victims of the offense, rather than by a neutral, detached judge? Alternatively, should we at least require that the judge give substantial weight to the punishment preferences of the victims? What impact would such approaches have on other goals of criminal punishment? Consider these questions in connection with the problems that follow.

PROBLEM: UNEXPECTED HARM[13]

In 2003, a catastrophic fire at a Rhode Island nightclub killed 100 people and injured more than 200. The fire was the result of a publicity stunt on the part of Daniel Biechele, the tour manager for the heavy metal band Great White. Biechele arranged for fireworks, which he ignited on stage at the club, as part of the performance. The plan went disastrously wrong when the fireworks ignited flammable soundproofing foam, setting off a maelstrom consuming the crowded wooden building. Biechele pleaded guilty to 100 counts of involuntary manslaughter pursuant to a plea agreement that authorized the judge to impose a maximum ten-year prison term. The prosecutor sought that maximum, arguing that Biechele's failure to obtain a permit for the fireworks was "not simply an unwitting and innocuous oversight, but a deliberate and intentional decision not to abide by Rhode Island law. . . . A child could have foreseen the harm" of setting off fireworks in the club jammed with people. He added, "If this isn't the case that deserves a serious sentence, what one is?" The judge, however, sentenced Biechele to serve four years in prison, leaving him eligible for parole release after serving one-third of his sentence. The judge pointed to the defendant's clean record, remorse, willingness to accept responsibility, and potential for rehabilitation. He further emphasized that the defendant never intended to harm anyone.

The sentence provoked outrage among relatives of some of the victims. One called the sentence "a joke" and said of Biechele's mother, "She'll get her son in four years, and they'll go back to being a happy family. What do we have?" Another parent, whose son was killed and daughter injured, said: "One year for every 25 people that died—it's crazy. You can do what you want in Rhode Island and get away with it." But other victims' relatives disagreed.

---

12. For helpful discussion of the issues, see Peter A. French, The Virtues of Vengeance (2001); George Fletcher, The Place of Victims in the Theory of Retribution, 3 Buff. Crim. L. Rev. 51 (1999); Michael Moore, Victims and Retribution: A Reply to Professor Fletcher, id. at 65; Jeffrie Murphy, Getting Even: The Role of the Victim, 7 Soc. Phil. & Pol'y 209 (1990).

13. Facts drawn from Pam Bulluck, Defendant in Club Fire Draws a 4-Year Sentence, N.Y. Times, May 11, 2006; Providence J., Projo.com, May 10, 2006.

A mother who lost her son said: "I think it's a fair and just reaction. He didn't set out to kill anybody. It was a horrendous accident." The father of an 18-year-old killed in the fire testified that his son would have wanted the family to accept Biechele's apology. Other relatives placed more blame on the club's owners, who had installed the highly flammable soundproofing. They were later convicted, and one of them received the same sentence as Biechele. Some relatives also blamed the fire on building inspectors for failing to issue citations for the soundproofing material.

Questions: What sentence *should* the judge have imposed? For what reasons? Retribution? Vengeance? Deterrence? Would your reaction be different if someone had succeeded in dousing the fire before it spread?

PROBLEM: VICTIM-IMPACT STATEMENTS

In state and federal sentencing proceedings, it has become common for the court to consider statements from victims and family members describing the damaging consequences of the crime. See Victoria Schwartz, The Victims' Rights Amendment, 42 Harv. J. on Legis. 525 (2005); Symposium on Crime Victim Law, Theory and Practice, 9 Lewis & Clark L. Rev. 481-668 (2005). Such statements typically detail the grief of victims and their families, physical illnesses that may have ensued, financial and emotional consequences, and the like. Sometimes such statements also recommend what the victim or family members regard as suitable punishment. The rationale for considering such statements is by no means clear. Which theory of punishment justifies the use of these statements? Consider People v. Levitt, 156 Cal. App. 3d 500, 516 (1984):

> [A] defendant's level of culpability depends . . . on circumstances over which he has control. A defendant may choose, or decline, to premeditate, to act callously, to attack a vulnerable victim, to commit a crime while on probation, or to amass a record of offenses. . . . In contrast, the fact that a victim's family is irredeemably bereaved can be attributable to no act of will of the defendant other than his commission of homicide in the first place. Such bereavement is relevant to damages in a civil action, but it has no relationship to the proper purposes of sentencing in a criminal case.

Compare Payne v. Tennessee, 501 U.S. 812 (1991). Payne had used a butcher knife to kill a young mother who had refused his sexual advances. In the same incident, Payne killed her two-year-old daughter, Lacie, and attempted to kill her three-year-old son, Nicholas. The circumstances were particularly horrifying. The state presented the testimony of Nicholas's grandmother about his reaction to the murders:

> He cries for his mom. He doesn't seem to understand why she doesn't come home. And he cries for his sister Lacie. He comes to me many times during the week and asks me, Grandmama, do you miss my Lacie. And I tell him yes. He says, I'm worried about my Lacie.

In arguing for the death penalty, the prosecutor commented on Nicholas's experience:

> Nicholas was still conscious. His eyes were open. He was able to hold his intestines in as he was carried to the ambulance. So he knew what happened to his mother and baby sister. . . . There is nothing you can do to ease the pain of any of the families involved in this case. . . . But there is something that you can do for Nicholas. . . . Somewhere down the road Nicholas is going to grow up, hopefully. . . . And he is going to know what happened to his baby sister and his mother. He is going to want to know what type of justice was done. . . . With your verdict, you will provide the answer.

The jury convicted the defendant of first-degree murder and sentenced him to death. The Supreme Court held that the victim-impact testimony and the prosecutor's arguments on that subject were relevant to the defendant's *moral blame*, which is the crucial factor in determining eligibility for the death penalty.[14] The majority opinion explained:

> [A] State may properly conclude that for the jury to assess meaningfully the defendant's moral culpability and blameworthiness, it should have before it at the sentencing phase evidence of the specific harm caused by the defendant. "[T]he State has a legitimate interest in counteracting the mitigating evidence which the defendant is entitled to put in, by reminding the sentencer that just as the murderer should be considered as an individual, so too the victim is an individual whose death represents a unique loss to society and in particular to his family."

Questions: (a) The particular details. Both the grandmother's testimony and the closing argument of the prosecutor focused on the impact of the killings on Nicholas. How was that impact relevant to Payne's blameworthiness? Would Nicholas's experience have the same relevance if he had not been present, but had heard about the attack afterwards? Would Payne be *less* deserving of capital punishment if he had succeeded in killing Nicholas instantly? If not, why was evidence of Nicholas's horrifying experience needed for the jury properly to assess Payne's blameworthiness? Justice David Souter, in a concurring opinion, responded to this challenge:

> Every defendant knows . . . that the life he will take by his homicidal behavior is that of a unique person, . . . and that the person to be killed probably has close associates . . . who will suffer harms and deprivations from the victim's death. . . . The foreseeability of the killing's consequences imbues them with direct moral relevance.

In a similar vein, courts have upheld the admissibility of testimony that a victim's aunt died of a heart attack after hearing of her nephew's killing, Young v. State, 992 P.2d 332 (Okla. Crim. App. 1998), and testimony that

---

14. See page 537 infra.

a victim's father abandoned his career after hearing of his daughter's murder, Griffith v. State, 983 S.W.2d 282 (Tex. Crim. App. 1998).

(b) Foreseeability. What is the "moral relevance" of the fact that a foreseeable consequence did or did not come about? Would the murderer in *Young* be less deserving of punishment if the victim's aunt had not died of a heart attack? Would the murderer in *Griffith* be less deserving of punishment if the victim's father had not given up his job?

Are harms that happen to result considered in sentencing because of a social interest in assessing the defendant's degree of fault, or are they considered because of a social interest in using punishment to give recompense to the victim? In the latter case, one could view the victim's satisfaction as social benefit, but many would argue that the suffering experienced by the offender should count as a social cost, especially if it involves suffering in excess of that called for by his moral blame. On what basis can we *justify* the choice to give satisfaction to a victim, at the cost of inflicting extra, arguably *undeserved* suffering on an offender? For discussion, see Paul G. Cassell, In Defense of Victim Impact Statements, 6 Ohio St. J. Crim. L. 611 (2009).

The materials in the next section, dealing with social cohesion, offer one possible answer to these questions. But note that the effort to reinforce social cohesion suggests an independent justification for punishment; it is not necessarily linked to the concept of revenge and might even be antithetical to it. In assessing the social-cohesion theories, consider whether they tend to reinforce or undermine the argument for tying punishment to desires for victim satisfaction, retaliation, or revenge.

b. Social Cohesion

H.L.A. Hart, Punishment and Responsibility 235 (1968): [Some] modern retributive theory has shifted the emphasis, from the alleged justice or intrinsic goodness of the return of suffering for moral evil done, to the value of the authoritative expression, in the form of punishment, of moral condemnation for the moral wickedness involved in the offence. This theory . . . shares with other modern retributive theories two important points of contrast with Utilitarian theories; for like [classic retributivism] it insists that the conduct to be punished must be a species of voluntary moral wrongdoing, and the severity of punishment must be proportionate to the wickedness of the offence. But this form of theory has also at least two different forms: in one of them the public expression of condemnation of the offender by punishment of his offence may be conceived as something valuable in itself; in the other it is valuable only because it tends to certain valuable results, such as the voluntary reform of the offender, his recognition of his moral error, or the maintenance, reinforcement or "vindication" of the morality of the society against which the person punished has offended. Plainly the latter version of reprobation [is a form of] Utilitarian theory, [although] the good to be achieved through punishment is less narrowly conceived than in Bentham's or in other orthodox forms of Utilitarianism.

Emile Durkheim, The Division of Labor in Society 62-63 (W.D. Halls trans., 1984): [Punishment] does not serve, or serves only very incidentally, to correct the guilty person or to scare off any possible imitators. . . . Its real function is to maintain inviolate the cohesion of society by sustaining the common consciousness in all its vigour. If that consciousness were thwarted . . . , it would necessarily lose some of its power, were an emotional reaction from the community not forthcoming to make good that loss. Thus there would result a relaxation in the bonds of social solidarity. The consciousness must therefore be conspicuously reinforced. . . . The sole means of doing so is to give voice to the unanimous aversion that the crime continues to evoke, and this by an official act, which can only mean suffering inflicted upon the wrongdoer. [T]his suffering is not a gratuitous act of cruelty. It is a sign indicating that the sentiments of the collectivity are still unchanged, that the communion of minds sharing the same beliefs remains absolute, and in this way the injury that the crime has inflicted upon society is made good. This is why it is right to maintain that the criminal should suffer in proportion to his crime, and why theories that deny to punishment any expiatory character appear, in the minds of many, to subvert the social order. In fact such theories could only be put into practice in a society from which almost every trace of the common consciousness has been expunged. . . . Thus, without being paradoxical, we may state that punishment is above all intended to have its effect upon honest people. . . . Undoubtedly, by forestalling in minds already distressed any further weakening of the collective psyche, punishment can indeed prevent such attacks from multiplying. But such a result, useful though it is, is merely a particular side-effect. In short, . . . the two opposing theories [of retribution and prevention] must be reconciled: . . . Certainly [punishment] does fulfil the function of protecting society, but this is because of its expiatory [i.e., retributive] nature. Moreover, if it must be expiatory, this is not because suffering redeems error by virtue of some mystic strength or another, but because it cannot produce its socially useful effect save on this one condition.

2 James Fitzjames Stephen, A History of the Criminal Law of England, 81-82 (1883 ed.): [The] close alliance between criminal law and moral sentiment is in all ways healthy and advantageous to the community. I think it highly desirable that criminals should be hated, [and] that the punishments inflicted upon them should be so contrived as to give expression to that hatred. . . . The doctrine that hatred and vengeance are wicked in themselves appears to me to contradict plain facts, and to be unsupported by any argument deserving of attention. . . . No doubt they are peculiarly liable to abuse, and in some states of society are commonly in excess of what is desirable, and so require restraint rather than excitement, but unqualified denunciations of them are as ill-judged as unqualified denunciations of sexual passion. The forms in which deliberate anger and righteous disapprobation are expressed, and the execution of criminal justice is the most emphatic of such forms, stand to the one set of passions in the same relation in which marriage stands to the other.

NOTE

A large literature explores what is often called the "expressive function" of criminal punishment. Some scholars treat the expressive dimension as a means to achieve socially desirable effects, such as enhanced compliance with the law. Other work in this vein bears a close affinity to classic retributivism because its proponents view the expressive dimension of punishment as worthwhile for its own sake. See especially Dan Markel, What Might Retributive Justice Be?, in Retributivism: Essays on Theory and Policy 49 (Mark D. White ed., 2011), arguing that retributive punishment is intrinsically good because it affirms the dignity of the victim and communicates respect for the offender as a responsible moral agent. See also Jean Hampton, Correcting Harms versus Righting Wrongs: The Goal of Retribution, 39 UCLA L. Rev. 1659 (1992), explaining that in an "expressive" theory of retribution, punishment serves to repudiate the offender's claim of superiority over the victim. Compare Heidi M. Hurd, Expressing Doubts About Expressivism, [2005] U. Chi Legal F. 405. Professor Hurd argues that neither crimes nor punishments have coherent "social meanings," and she questions why an attempt to communicate such meanings should be viewed as intrinsically good, regardless of its consequences.

TRANSITIONAL NOTE

We have now examined utilitarian and retributive justifications for punishment, together with several related perspectives. Although many criminal law theorists and practitioners subscribe to one of these approaches exclusively, others sense a need to combine them in some fashion. These "mixed" approaches are the subject of the next section.

4. Mixed Theories

INTRODUCTORY NOTE

As we have seen, no single approach to the justification of punishment has been able to win widespread (much less universal) support. To name just a few of the principal problems: Pure utilitarianism arguably could, under some circumstances, require punishment of the innocent or very severe punishment of those who have committed a low-level misdemeanor; pure retributivism arguably could, under some circumstances, call for punishments that, on balance, do much more harm than good—for example, requiring incarceration of an offender whose small children will be forced into foster care as a result.

One solution to this dilemma would be to permit sentencing authorities to decide, on an *ad hoc* basis, which theory to follow, according to whatever outcome the circumstances seem to warrant. But this approach leaves so much room for choice among punishments that many commentators feel it is less a theory than the complete absence of one.

A different and more rigorous solution, prominently proposed by H.L.A. Hart, stresses the need to distinguish between the *aim* of punishment, and the *limits* on its permissible use. Hart, Punishment and Responsibility 8-12 (1968). Hart argued that the aim of punishment is utilitarian—to enhance social welfare, especially by preventing crime. But we can justly pursue this aim only within retributive limits—by never punishing an innocent person and never punishing a guilty person to an extent disproportionate to his blame. Thus, utilitarian and retributive principles both play a role, but we do not simply "mix and match" them at will. Social benefit is a necessary but not a sufficient condition of just punishment, and likewise, desert is a necessary but not a sufficient condition of just punishment. As Professor Stephen P. Garvey explains (Lifting the Veil on Punishment, 7 Buff. Crim. L. Rev. 443, 450 (2004)): "Punishment's purpose is utilitarian: to reduce crime and thus protect the rights of all to be secure in their persons and property. But that purpose must be pursued within retribution's [just deserts] limits. [Thus,] a person can legitimately be punished only if he committed a crime, only in proportion to that crime, and only if doing so would produce a world with less crime." This approach bars disproportionate punishment, even if a cost-benefit calculus would arguably support it. But this approach also bars punishment that is perfectly proportionate to an offender's blame, if that punishment would not be socially beneficial under all the circumstances.

Does Hart's approach, which can be called the *classic mixed theory*, finally produce a satisfactory framework? Or does it too yield unacceptable results? This "classic" mixed theory has strong support in criminal law commentary, as well as in American statutes and precedents; it is, for example, the foundation for the Supreme Court's death penalty jurisprudence.[15] Nonetheless, important misgivings have been expressed. This section considers first an important challenge to the classic mixed theory and then turns to statutory efforts to resolve the controversies.

a. Questioning the Classic Mixed Theory

Michael S. Moore, Law and Psychiatry 238-243 (1984): There is [a] thought experiment that tests whether one truly believes the mixed theory, or is in fact a pure retributivist. . . .

---

15. Thus, in *Gregg v. Georgia*, page 537 infra, the Supreme Court stated that in order for punishment not to violate the Eighth Amendment, it "must not involve the unnecessary and wanton infliction of pain [the utilitarian requirement] [and it] must not be grossly our of proportion to the severity of the crime [the retributive constraint]."

[In *State v. Chaney*,] the defendant was . . . convicted of two counts of forcible rape and one count of robbery.[a] The defendant and a companion had picked up the prosecutrix at a downtown location in Anchorage. [They] beat her and forcibly raped her four times. [T]he victim's money was removed from her purse, and she only then was allowed to leave the vehicle after dire threats of reprisals if she attempted to report the incident. . . .

Despite this horrendous series of events, the trial judge imposed the minimum sentence on the defendant for each of the three counts and went out of his way to remark that he (the trial judge) was "sorry that the (military) regulations would not permit keeping (defendant) in the service if he wanted to stay because it seems to me that it is a better setup for everybody concerned than putting him in the penitentiary." The trial judge also mentioned that as far as he was concerned, there would be no problem for the defendant to be paroled on the very first day of his sentence, if the parole board should so decide. . . .

The thought experiment such a case begins to pose for us is as follows: Imagine . . . that after the rape but before sentencing the defendant has gotten into an accident so that his sexual desires are dampened to such an extent that he presents no further danger of rape; if money is also one of his problems, suppose further that he has inherited a great deal of money, so that he no longer needs to rob. Suppose, because of both of these facts, we are reasonably certain that he does not present a danger of either forcible assault, rape, robbery, or related crimes in the future. Since Chaney is (by hypothesis) not dangerous, he does not need to be incapacitated, specially deterred, or reformed. Suppose further that we could successfully pretend to punish Chaney, instead of actually punishing him, and that no one is at all likely to find out. Our pretending to punish him will thus serve the needs of general deterrence and maintain social cohesion, and the cost to the state will be less than if it actually did punish him. Is there anything in the mixed theory of punishment that would urge that Chaney nonetheless should really be punished? I think not, so that if one's conclusion is that Chaney and people like him nonetheless should be punished, one will have to give up the mixed theory of punishment.

NOTES AND QUESTIONS

1. Do you share Professor Moore's intuition that in the hypothetical circumstances "Chaney . . . should be punished"? If so, is that because you agree that deserved punishment *must* be imposed, regardless of its social consequences? Or do you agree only because you resist the hypothetical's assumption that we can *pretend* to punish him, without having the pretense discovered?

---

a. 477 P.2d 441 (Alaska 1970).—Eds.

2. In response to discomfort with the classic mixed theory, some recent scholarship has sought to combine the rationales for punishment in more flexible ways, so that desert alone will *sometimes* be sufficient to justify the imposition of punishment. See, e.g., Michael T. Cahill, Punishment Pluralism, in Retributivism: Essays on Theory and Policy (Mark D. White ed., 2011); Mitchell N. Berman, Punishment and Justification, 118 Ethics 258 (2008). Is the relative indeterminacy of such approaches an important drawback? Or is that flexibility a strength for a theory designed to guide social practices in a society that is itself far from uniform in its values? Although the "classic" mixed approach holds a strong position in criminal law theory and in the law itself, criminal law doctrine and practice often tend to be eclectic or (in Professor Cahill's term) "pluralistic." The next section considers the manner in which judges and legislatures actually resolve (or fail to resolve) these issues.

b. Statutory Solutions

INTRODUCTORY NOTE

Consider the following statements of the purposes of punishment and the necessary preconditions for justifiably imposing criminal sanctions. Note that some of them lean heavily in the direction of one of the competing theories, while others seem more open-ended. Try to identify the relative importance of retributive and utilitarian concerns in each of these statutory statements. Which framework best accommodates the conflicting concerns? Which of them best insures consistent treatment of similarly situated offenders? Do the statutes that fare well in terms of the first criterion also fare well in terms of the second? How *should* the governing legal principles be articulated?

Model Penal Code §1.02(2). The general purposes of the provisions governing the sentencing and treatment of offenders are: (a) to prevent the commission of offenses; (b) to promote the correction and rehabilitation of offenders; (c) to safeguard offenders against excessive, disproportionate or arbitrary punishment. . . .

New York Penal Law §1.05. The general purposes of [sentencing] are: . . . To insure the public safety by preventing the commission of offenses through the deterrent influence of the sentences authorized, the rehabilitation of those convicted, and their confinement when required in the interests of public protection.

California Penal Code §1170. The Legislature finds and declares that the purpose of imprisonment for crime is punishment. This purpose is best served by terms proportionate to the seriousness of the offense with provision for uniformity in the sentences of offenders committing the same offense under similar circumstances. [T]he elimination of disparity and the provision of uniformity of sentences can best be achieved by determinate sentences fixed by statute in proportion to the seriousness of the offense as determined by the Legislature to be imposed by the court with specified discretion.

NOTE ON A NEW MODEL PENAL CODE APPROACH

In 2007, the American Law Institute approved a tentative revision of §1.02(2), the Code's statement of the purposes that govern the sentencing of offenders. If given final approval by the Institute, the new language of §1.02(2) will read as follows:[16]

> The general purposes of the provisions on sentencing . . . are:
>
> (a) in decisions affecting the sentencing of individual offenders:
>> (i)   to render sentences in all cases within a range of severity proportionate to the gravity of offenses, the harms done to crime victims, and the blameworthiness of offenders;
>> (ii) when reasonably feasible, to achieve offender rehabilitation, general deterrence, incapacitation of dangerous offenders, restoration of crime victims and communities, and reintegration of offenders into the law-abiding community, provided these goals are pursued within the boundaries of proportionality in subsection (a)(i); and
>> (iii) to render sentences no more severe than necessary to achieve the applicable purposes in subsections (a)(i) and (a)(ii) . . . .

The Commentary explains:[17]

> [U]tilitarian goals . . . should not be allowed to produce sentences more or less severe than those deserved by offenders on moral grounds. [M]ost people's moral sensibilities . . . will orient them toward a range of permissible sanctions that are "not undeserved." . . . The proportionality limitations stated in subsection (2)(a)(i) allow generous room . . . for the consideration of utilitarian goals [in selecting a sentence within that range]. Many of these goals serve interests of public safety through crime avoidance, while others are directed toward victim reparation, offender reintegration, and the restoration of affected communities. These are compelling objectives in a humane society, and the compass given to interests of crime victims and communities goes well beyond the utilitarian palate of the original Model Penal Code.

Questions: Precisely how does the proposed new language differ from the original §1.02(2)? Would it require different sentencing results in some of the cases we have been considering, such as:

- A teenager convicted of stealing a 75-cent candy bar from a store that has lost thousands of dollars as a result of such shoplifting;
- The persons responsible for the Rhode Island nightclub fire (page 101 supra);

---

16. Model Penal Code: Sentencing, Tentative Draft No. 1, at 1 (Apr. 9, 2007).
17. Id. at 4-5, 7-8.

- The murderer who faced capital punishment in *Payne v. Tennessee* (page 102 supra);
- A first offender convicted of robbery, whose young children will be forced into foster care if a prison sentence is imposed.

Is the new wording an improvement?

TRANSITIONAL NOTE

Nearly all of the approaches to punishment that we have examined allow some role for the utilitarian crime-control purposes of deterrence, rehabilitation, and incapacitation. But deciding to focus on crime prevention, or even on a particular strategy of crime prevention (such as deterrence), does not eliminate complexities and dilemmas, because many difficulties arise when we seek to implement such an objective. The next section examines the feasibility and limitations of deterrence, incapacitation, and rehabilitation as crime-prevention strategies.

5. *The Complexities of Crime Control*

a. Deterrence

INTRODUCTORY NOTE

1. Recall that for Bentham (page 91 supra), the point of criminal punishment was to deter offenses by threatening to inflict painful consequences on those who commit them: "If the apparent magnitude, or rather value of that pain be greater than the apparent magnitude or value of the pleasure or good he expects to be the consequence of the act, he will be absolutely prevented from performing it." Like Bentham, modern scholars who favor the economic approach to law posit that potential criminals consciously or subconsciously calculate costs and benefits, even in the context of "crimes of passion." But others argue that for the most important kinds of criminal behavior, perpetrators do not calculate at all or calculate only in bizarre ways, ignoring ordinary sorts of benefits and costs (including punishment).

Few people, if any, doubt, that crime would increase, probably dramatically, if no criminal punishments were ever imposed at all. In that sense, the institution of criminal punishment surely does have a substantial deterrent effect. The debate centers around the question whether *variations* in punishment—for example, increasing its severity, either generally or for particular offenses—will lead to *variations* in the amount of crime. In other words, can we reduce crime by increasing the expected certainty or severity of the punishment? Although many empirical studies appear to show a link between expected punishment and the crime rate,[18] methodological problems make such findings fragile or difficult to interpret. Even so, why *wouldn't* increases in expected punishment reduce the amount of the targeted behavior? Isn't that relationship (as Bentham suggests) virtually inevitable, as a matter of human nature? Consider these comments:

James Q. Wilson, Thinking About Crime 117 (rev. ed. 1983): [T]he socially imposed consequences of committing a crime, unlike the market consequences of shopping around for the best price, are characterized by delay, uncertainty, and ignorance. In addition, some scholars contend that a large fraction of crime is committed by persons who are so impulsive, irrational, or abnormal that even if there were no delay, uncertainty, or ignorance attached to the consequences of criminality, we would still have a lot of crime.

Paul H. Robinson & John M. Darley, The Role of Deterrence in the Formulation of Criminal Code Rules, 91 Geo. L.J. 949, 951, 953 (2003): Lawmakers have sought to optimize the control of crime by . . . assign[ing] criminal punishments of a magnitude sufficient to deter a thinking individual from committing a crime. Although this seems initially an intuitively compelling strategy, we suggest it is a poor one. . . . If a criminal law rule is to deter violators, three prerequisites must be satisfied: The potential offender must know of the rule; he must perceive the cost of violation as greater than the perceived benefit; and he must be able and willing to bring such knowledge to bear on his conduct decision at the time of the offense. But . . . one or more of these hurdles typically block any material deterrent effect of doctrinal manipulation. The social science literature suggests that potential offenders commonly do not know the law, do not perceive an expected cost for a violation that outweighs the expected gain, and do not make rational self-interest choices.

2. *What about actors who are rational and well-informed?* Note that many crimes are committed by individuals who can and surely do (at least implicitly) calculate the potential costs and benefits of violating the law. Tax evasion, insider trading, and some sophisticated drug distribution schemes often fit that description. But many analysts suggest that even in such cases, increased punishment can sometimes induce more crime than it deters. How could this happen? One complication is the "income" effect. Severe punishments are intended to induce rational actors to shift from illegal to legal pursuits. But if severe punishment of drug dealers raises an addict's cost of buying the drugs he requires, he may have to commit more predatory crimes (robbery

---

18. For illustrative empirical studies, see Steven D. Levitt, Understanding Why Crime Fell in the 1990s, 18 J. Econ. Persp. 163 (2004); Steven D. Levitt, The Effect of Prison Population Size on Crime Rates: Evidence from Prison Overcrowding Litigation, 111 Q.J. Econ. 319 (1996); D.J. Pyle, The Economic Approach to Crime and Punishment, 6 J. Interdisc. Stud. 1, 4-8 (1995).

and burglary) in order to finance his habit.[19] Another complication, confirmed by many studies, is that very severe penalties can reduce the likelihood that significant sanctions will be imposed at all—witnesses become less willing to report crime or to cooperate in prosecution, prosecutors become reluctant to file the highest charges, and juries hesitate to convict. Thus, in practice, attempts to increase the severity of punishment sometimes have the opposite of their intended effect. For detailed exploration of these and related problems, see Neal Kumar Katyal, Deterrence's Difficulty, 95 Mich. L. Rev. 2385 (1997).

3. *Certainty versus severity.* The two plausible ways to increase the direct deterrent effect of punishment are, first, to increase the risk of conviction, and second, to increase the severity of punishment. The first alternative appears to be the more effective, but it is also the more difficult to implement. Moreover, increased enforcement does not by itself increase general deterrence. Since the effectiveness of the threat of punishment must be judged from the viewpoint of the potential criminal, increased enforcement and any resulting increase in the certainty of punishment are important only as they contribute to the *appearance* of certainty.

Increased severity of punishment has a more doubtful deterrent effect. A panel of the National Academy of Sciences concluded in 1993 that a 10 percent increase in the probability of apprehension would prevent twice as much violent crime as the same increase in the severity of punishment, partly because, as just noted, increases in severity can tend to reduce the probabilities of apprehension and conviction.[20]

4. *Moral influence.* Can the law's threat of punishment induce conformity in ways other than through cost-benefit calculations of the rational actor? Consider these observations (Paul H. Robinson & John M. Darley, The Utility of Desert, 91 Nw. U. L. Rev. 453, 468 (1997)):

> More than because of the threat of legal punishment, people obey the law (1) because they fear the disapproval of their social group if they violate the law, and (2) because they generally see themselves as moral beings who want to do the right thing as they perceive it. In social science, these two factors are referred to as (1) compliance produced by normative social influence, and (2) behavior produced by internalized moral standards and rules. . . .
>
> The evidence reviewed suggests that the influences of social group sanctions and internalized norms are the most powerful determinants of conduct, more significant than the threat of deterrent legal sanctions. But, we argue, the law is not irrelevant to the operation of these powerful forces. Criminal law . . . influences the powerful social forces of normative behavior control through its central role in the creation of shared norms. . . .
>
> The passage and subsequent failure of National Prohibition shows the law's limited ability to change norms even when the change is supported by

---

19. See Richard Posner, Economic Analysis of Law 242 (7th ed. 2007); Stephen J. Schulhofer, Solving the Drug Enforcement Dilemma: Lessons from Economics, 1994 U. Chi. Legal F. 207.

20. Albert J. Reiss, Jr. & Jeffrey A. Roth eds., Understanding and Preventing Violence: Report of the National Research Panel on the Understanding and Control of Violence 6 (1993).

a significant portion of the public. . . . The law is, rather, a vehicle by which the community debates, tests, and ultimately settles upon and expresses its norms. . . . The act of criminalization sometimes nurtures the norm, as does faithful enforcement and prosecution, and over time the community view may mature into a strong consensus. . . . We have seen the process at work recently in enhancing prohibitory norms against sexual harassment, hate speech, drunk driving, and domestic violence. It has also been at work in diluting existing norms against homosexual conduct, fornication, and adultery. . . .

Perhaps more than any other society, ours relies on the criminal law for norm-nurturing. Our greater cultural diversity means that we cannot expect a stable pre-existing consensus on the contours of condemnable conduct that is found in more homogeneous societies. . . . [W]e share no religion or other arbiter of morality that might perform this role. Our criminal law is, for us, the place we express our shared beliefs of what is truly condemnable. . . .

The criminal law also has a second effect. . . . If it has developed a reputation as a reliable statement of existing norms, people will be willing to defer to its moral authority in cases where there exists some ambiguity as to the wrongfulness of the contemplated conduct. . . .

There is evidence, largely collected and analyzed by Tyler, that people are inclined to accept the law as a source of moral authority that they themselves should take seriously. [Tom R. Tyler, Why People Obey the Law 60 (1990.] . . . Tyler reviews a number of studies that suggest that the level of commitment to obey the law is proportional to what Tyler calls the law's perceived "legitimacy." . . . [I]f one regards the law as a legitimate source of rules, if it has what we have called "moral credibility," then one should be more likely to regard the law's judgments about right and wrong actions as an appropriate input to one's own moral thinking; in turn, one should be more likely to obey the law. . . .

But the criminal law can only hope to shape moral thinking or to have people follow its rules in ambiguous cases if it has earned a reputation as an institution whose focus is morally condemnable conduct. . . . The criminal law's power in nurturing and communicating societal norms and its power to have people defer to it . . . is directly proportional to criminal law's moral credibility. If criminalization or conviction (or decriminalization or refusal to convict) is to have an effect in the norm-nurturing process, it will be because the criminal law has a reputation for criminalizing and punishing only that which deserves moral condemnation, and for decriminalizing and not punishing that which does not. . . .

Enhancing the criminal law's moral credibility requires, more than anything, that the criminal law make clear to the public that its overriding concern is doing justice. . . . The criminal law must earn a reputation for (1) punishing those who deserve it under rules perceived as just, (2) protecting from punishment those who do not deserve it, and (3) where punishment is deserved, imposing the amount of punishment deserved, no more, no less. . . .

The point is that every deviation from [desert] can incrementally undercut the criminal law's moral credibility, which in turn can undercut . . . its power to gain compliance by its moral authority. Thus, contrary to the apparent assumptions of past utilitarian debates, such deviations from desert are not cost free, and their cost must be included in the calculation when determining which distribution of liability will most effectively reduce crime.

b. Rehabilitation

MICHAEL VITIELLO, RECONSIDERING REHABILITATION

65 Tul. L. Rev. 1011, 1138-1140 (1991)

The debate between proponents of retributive justice and rehabilitation has roots dating back at least to the colonial period. In Puritan America, the law was used to advance the dominant religious beliefs and to enforce "proper standards of moral behavior." Based on the Calvinist belief in the innate depravity of human beings, the criminal law served to keep people from temptation. Punishment was not intended to save the criminal[,] because humans were inherently sinful. . . . Punishment served to keep the rest of the community from temptation. . . .

Quaker views contrasted sharply with the Puritan conception of the criminal law. Early in our history, the Quakers led a movement away from capital and corporal punishment to a system of workhouses and prisons. Viewed as grim in retrospect, that system was generally enlightened by comparison to earlier treatment of criminals. At root, it was based on an optimism about human capacity for transformation.

. . . Quakers believed that crime was the product of society, rather than a result of inherent sinfulness. But the method chosen for transformation was not "treatment." Instead, they believed that the offender could be reformed through a process of rationality. Freed from the corrupting influences and permitted to reflect on moral questions, the offender could be "restored to fellowship with God and humanity."

Around the time of the American Revolution and the adoption of the Constitution, Quaker idealism was a powerful force in penology. It led to the establishment of penitentiaries, first in Pennsylvania where Quaker influence was strongest. Modeled on monastic prisons of the Middle Ages, the penitentiary used solitary confinement, religious instruction, and hard labor to facilitate repentance.

Early prison reformers also stressed the community's responsibility for corrupting the individual. For example, one Boston clergyman inquired, "'How can it be justice to punish as a crime that which the institutions of society render unavoidable?'" Recognition that social conditions were a cause of crime did not render society incapable of punishing the offender, but it created a moral imperative to offer the offender a chance at moral transformation. Nor was the prescription mollycoddling; devices that look unabashedly punitive, like hard labor, were believed to have the beneficial effect of aiding the transformation of the offender.

Michael S. Moore, Law and Psychiatry 234-235 (1984): Rehabilitation is perhaps the most complex of the theories of punishment, because it involves two quite different ideals of rehabilitation that are usually confused. . . .

The first sort of rehabilitative ideal is one that is achieved when we make criminals safe to return to the streets. This sort of rehabilitative theory justifies punishment, not by appeal to how much better off criminals will be at the end of the process, but rather by how much better off all of us will be if "treatment" is completed because the streets will be that much safer. The second sort of rehabilitative ideal . . . seeks to rehabilitate offenders not just so they can be returned safely to the streets, but so they can lead flourishing and successful lives. Such a theory justifies punishment, not in the name of all of us, but rather in the offenders' own name; since it does so in their name, but contrary to their own expressed wishes (few offenders want to be punished), this kind of rehabilitative theory is paternalistic in character.

This paternalistic type of rehabilitative theory has no proper part to play in any theory of punishment, even in the minimal sense of constituting a prima facie justification of punishment. There are three reasons why this is so. First, such a paternalistic reform theory allocates scarce societal resources away from other, more deserving groups that want them [such as individuals with mental disabilities or the poor]. . . . Second, in any political theory according high value to liberty, paternalistic justifications are themselves to be regarded with suspicion. Criminals are not in the standard classes in society for which paternalistic state intervention is appropriate, such as [those] whose capacity for rational choice is diminished. . . . Third, such recasting of punishment in terms of "treatment" for the good of the criminal makes possible a kind of moral blindness that is dangerous in itself. As C.S. Lewis pointed out some years ago, adopting a "humanitarian" conceptualization of punishment makes it easy to inflict treatments and sentences that need bear no relation to the desert of the offender. We may do more to others "for their own good" than we ever allow ourselves to do when we see that it is really for our good that we act.

NOTE—THE RISE AND FALL OF THE MEDICAL MODEL

By the the early twentieth century, rehabilitation had taken a firm hold in the ideology (if not in the practices) of American punishment. The state agency responsible for criminal punishment came to be known as the "Department of Corrections" (a terminology that remains with us to this day). In 1949, the Supreme Court stated: "Retribution is no longer the dominant objective of the criminal law. Reformation and rehabilitation of offenders have become important goals of criminal jurisprudence." Williams v. New York, 337 U.S. 241, 248 (1949). The prevailing conception of rehabilitation, moreover, was that described by Professor Vitello—the Quaker conception that reformation could be achieved by religious instruction and hard labor.

By the 1960s, this view of rehabilitation came increasingly to be replaced by a "medical" model. As Professor Vitello notes, id. at 1016, "growing faith in psychiatry and science had strongly influenced penology. Based on a perception of the criminal as sick and in need of treatment or rehabilitation, legislatures entrusted to judges wide latitude in imposing indeterminate sentences: if the offender is ill . . . , his sentence ought to be conditioned on his cure.

Parole boards ... helped to administer indeterminate sentences by determining when the "patient" was cured."

Within a decade, however, the medical model came under attack from multiple directions. Many (especially critics on the left) saw it as paternalistic and coercive, as well as dangerously subjective, discretionary, and biased against low-income, minority defendants. There was also considerable evidence that, far from benefiting the offender, it often led to increases in the duration of penal confinement. At the same time, other observers (especially critics on the right), saw the rehabilitative approach as too costly and too lenient. A crucial point for both groups was the perception that efforts to rehabilitate offenders simply were not (and perhaps could not be) successful. By the late 1970s, rehabilitation had fallen almost totally. Since then, however, there has been a substantial resurgence of interest in rehabilitation. Many came to believe that obstacles that were decisive in the past (e.g., undue leniency, excessive discretion, disparity in the treatment of similarly situated offenders) could be addressed by procedural reform, without sacrificing rehabilitation as one among several worthy goals. Now, as in the past, a central concern remains the question whether rehabilitation can be effective.

NOTE—DOES REHABILITATION WORK?

The actual effects of rehabilitation efforts have been questioned. In an important 1974 paper (Robert Martinson, What Works?—Questions and Answers About Prison Reform, 36 Pub. Int. 22, 25 (1974)), the author concluded: "With few and isolated exceptions, the rehabilitative efforts that have been reported so far have no appreciable effect on recidivism." Martinson soon withdrew that conclusion, having found evidence that some programs do reduce recidivism for some offenders under some circumstances.[21] Subsequent research provided further support for this cautiously optimistic view.[22] Nonetheless, the conclusion that "nothing works" had become fixed in the public mind, and it has proved difficult to dislodge. Consider George Mair, What Works—Nothing or Everything?, Home Office [Great Britain], Research Bulletin #30, pp.3-5 (1991):

> Martinson—quite unintentionally—found a remarkably receptive audience from both sides of the political spectrum in the U.S.A. On the right, the period from the second half of the sixties into the seventies was seen as a time of serious disorder and instability; Vietnam, black power and youth protest were seen to threaten the traditional order. And out of all this "crime assumed new meaning and significance ... [it] became a codeword for all that was wrong with American society." The right, therefore, welcomed Martinson's attack on the rehabilitative ideal which was seen as being soft on offenders and looked forward to new, tougher methods of punishing criminals. The perspective

---

21. Robert Martinson, New Findings, New Views: A Note of Caution Regarding Sentencing Reform, 7 Hofstra L. Rev. 243 (1979).
22. See Michael Vitiello, Reconsidering Rehabilitation, 65 Tul. L. Rev. 1011 (1991).

from the left was, of course, rather different. Here, the benevolence of the state was subject to sustained questioning, a process which inevitably touched upon criminal justice. Rehabilitation and treatment became suspect; they were criticised as theoretically faulty, discriminatory and unjust, and the unfettered discretion entrusted to criminal justice professionals was attacked as leading to abuse of power and injustice. . . .

   Martinson's argument is fundamentally flawed in two ways: first, by reliance upon recidivism as the sole measure of success of a sentence; and second, by a failure to address the issue of how sentences are implemented and operate in practice. . . . If, for example, a considerable number of the [treatment programs] included in Martinson's analysis had failed to be properly implemented as planned, had been starved of resources, had used badly trained and uncommitted staff, and had been studied in the first year or so of operation, would it be any surprise that the sentences had failed? Only by studying how a sentence or treatment program has been put into practice . . . [can we] understand more clearly *why* a penal measure may be working successfully or—equally important—why it may be failing.

Controversy continues over the effectiveness of rehabilitation programs, and some researchers remain quite pessimistic.[23] Most, however, concur in Professor Vitiello's assessment (supra at 1037) that "some offenders are amenable to rehabilitation and . . . social scientists can identify those offenders by the use of objective criteria." Programs most often prove effective when they make available a variety of social and psychological services and focus primarily on high-risk offenders;[24] some successful programs have reduced recidivism by 27-90 percent.[25] For discussion of the features most often associated with effective programs, see Rachel E. Barkow, Life Without Parole and the Hope for Real Sentencing Reform 190, 199-200, in Life Without Parole (Austin Sarat & Charles J. Ogletree eds., 2012); Edward J. Letessa, What Works in Correctional Intervention, 23 S. Ill. U. L.J. 415 (1999).

Andrew von Hirsch & Lisa Maher, Should Penal Rehabilitationism Be Revived?, Crim. Just. Ethics pp. 25, 26-29 (Winter/Spring 1992): Some new advocates of penal rehabilitationism . . . stress its humaneness. . . . Treatment programs, however, seldom aim merely at social service. . . . To accomplish [their] crime-preventive aim, the intervention may well have to be more drastic. It will take more to get the drug-abusing robber to stop committing further robberies than to teach him/her a skill. . . . A proportionate sanction for [crimes of intermediate or lesser gravity] should be of no more than moderate severity. What of a rehabilitative response? That would depend on how

---

23. E.g., Steven P. Lab & John T. Whitehead, From "Nothing Works" to "The Appropriate Works," 28 Criminology 405 (1990), arguing that the great majority of rehabilitation programs have proved ineffective.

24. Daniel H. Antonowicz & Robert R. Ross, Essential Components of Successful Rehabilitation Programs for Offenders, 38 Intl. J. Offender Therapy & Comp. Criminology 97 (1994); D.A. Andrews et al., Does Correctional Treatment Work?, 28 Criminology 369 (1990).

25. Antonowicz & Ross, supra, at 102.

much intervention, and how long, is required to alter the offender's criminal propensities—and to succeed, the intervention may have to be quite substantial (as in the just-noted case of drug treatments). . . .

Some new rehabilitationists' rejection of other models, such as desert, is based on a "socially critical" perspective: how the rationale is likely to be implemented in a society characterized by race, class, and gender inequalities. Such a critique, however, cuts both ways: one also needs to consider how rehabilitationism might be implemented in such an unpropitious social setting. . . .

Treatment . . . can seldom rely on criteria relating to the blameworthiness of the conduct; whether the offender is amenable to a particular treatment depends, instead, on his/her social and personal characteristics. [O]ne is using criminal punishment, a blame-conveying response, and yet deciding the intervention on the basis of those personal and social variables that have little to do with how reprehensible the behavior is. . . . [I]t needs to be explained what role, if any, the degree of blameworthiness of the conduct should have.

One possibility would be to give proportionality a limiting role: The seriousness of the criminal conduct would set upper and lower bounds on the quantum of punishment—within which rehabilitation could be invoked to fix the sentence. . . . Here, one faces the familiar dilemma; the narrower one sets those limits, the less room there would be for treatment considerations; whereas the wider one sets the limits, the more one would need to worry about seemingly disparate or disproportionate responses.

Another possibility would be to try to dispense with notions of proportionality altogether. [But] how it is justifiable to employ punishment—a blaming institution—without regard to the blameworthiness of the conduct[?] . . . Second, the absence of significant proportionality constraints could open the way for abuses of the kind that discredited the old rehabilitation—for example, long-term, open-ended intervention against those deemed to be in special need of treatment. (One thinks of the young car thief who was confined for sixteen years at Patuxent Institution because he refused to talk to the therapists.) One might hope that we are more sophisticated now about the therapeutic value of such interventions—but is such hope enough without principled restraints upon rehabilitative responses?

The most dangerous temptation is to treat the treatment ethos as a kind of edifying fiction: If we only act as though we cared—and minister treatment to offenders as a sign of our caring—a more humane penal system will emerge. No serious inquiry is needed, on this view, about the criteria for deciding what constitutes a humane penal system or about how a renewed treatment emphasis could achieve its intended effects or lead to reasonably just outcomes. Such thinking is a recipe for failure. It is likely to cause the new treatment ethos to be rejected once its specifics (or lack of them) are subject to critical scrutiny. And it could do no more good than the old, largely hortatory treatment ethic: Create a facade of treatment behind which decision makers act as they choose.

c. Incapacitation

FRANKLIN E. ZIMRING & GORDON HAWKINS, INCAPACITATION—PENAL CONFINEMENT AND THE RESTRAINT OF CRIME

v. (1995)

Of all the justifications for the criminal punishment, the desire to incapacitate is the least complicated, the least studied, and often the most important. The major institutions of criminal punishment in the Western world—the prison and the jail—are designed and operated to restrain those under their control. All of the other objectives of incarceration are ancillary to the basic structure of the modern prison and jail: incapacitation is central.

JOHN J. DILULIO, JR., PRISONS ARE A BARGAIN, BY ANY MEASURE

N.Y. Times, Jan. 16, 1996, p. A17

Most experts . . . love to repeat, "incarceration is not the answer." If incarceration is not the answer, what, precisely, is the question? If the question is how to prevent at-risk youths from becoming stone-cold predators in the first place, then, of course, incarceration is no solution. But if the question is how to restrain known convicted criminals from murdering, raping, robbing, assaulting and stealing, then incarceration is a solution, and a highly cost-effective one. On average, it costs about $25,000 a year to keep a convicted criminal in prison. For that money, society gets four benefits: Imprisonment punishes offenders and expresses society's moral disapproval. It teaches felons and would-be felons a lesson: Do crime, do time. Prisoners get drug treatment and education. And, as the columnist Ben Wattenberg has noted, "A thug in prison can't shoot your sister."

. . . [P]risons pay big dividends even if all they deliver is relief from the murder and mayhem that incarcerated felons would be committing if free. Harvard economist Anne Piehl and I found that prisoners in New Jersey and Wisconsin committed an average of 12 crimes a year when free, excluding all drug crimes. . . . Patrick A. Langan calculated that tripling the prison population from 1975 to 1989 may have reduced "violent crime by 10 to 15 percent below what it would have been," thereby preventing a "conservatively estimated 390,000 murders, rapes, robberies and aggravated assaults in 1989 alone." . . . [T]he violent crimes committed each year will cost victims and society more than $400 billion in medical bills, lost days from work, lost quality of life—and lost life. . . . All told, research shows it costs society at least twice as much to let a prisoner loose than to lock him up. Compared with the human and financial toll of revolving-door justice, prisons are a real bargain.

Prison definitely pays, but there's one class of criminal that is an arguable exception: low-level, first-time drug offenders. Most drug felons in state prisons do not fit that description [but] it makes no sense to lock away even one drug offender whose case could be adjudicated in special drug courts and handled less expensively through intensively supervised probation featuring no-nonsense drug treatment and community service.

NOTES

1. *Estimating the benefits.* DiIulio and others argue that "it costs society at least twice as much to let a prisoner loose than to lock him up." But critics contend that these claims rest on greatly exaggerated estimates of the number of crimes that can be averted by incarcerating offenders for longer terms. Note DiIulio's claim that "prisoners in New Jersey and Wisconsin committed an *average* of 12 crimes a year when free" (emphasis added). Does this mean that extending an offender's sentence for an additional year will avert 12 crimes? Consider John J. Donohue III & Peter Seligman, Allocating Resources Among Prisons and Social Programs in the Battle against Crime, 27 J. Legal Stud. 1, 10-12 (1998):

> A common error among researchers [is] the failure to distinguish between the average number of crimes committed by the total *stock* of prisoners and the mean criminality of the group of prisoners who are poised to leave prison. . . . If there is a positive correlation between sentence length and prior record, as seems likely, then the cohort of released prisoners will tend to have lower than average [rates of offending]. Thus, the crimes prevented by keeping the current group of released prisoners incarcerated for an additional year will tend to be less than the average number of crimes committed by all prisoners—and probably dramatically so.
>
> [Studies like DiIulio's] assume that incarcerating a prisoner for an additional year will reduce crime by the number of crimes that the prisoner committed in the year prior to his incarceration. This may be plausible for some crimes but is certainly not true for others. Many crimes are committed by criminal rings or gangs; under these circumstances, the loss of one gang member will probably just lead to the recruitment of another.
>
> [M]ost criminals do not commit offenses uniformly over their entire adult lifetimes. Instead, criminal behavior is disproportionately concentrated over a much shorter period, typically in the late teens and early twenties. This fact has obvious implications for the efficacy of imprisonment as a means of controlling crime. Consider a 20-year-old who committed 40 crimes in the year prior to receiving a 10-year sentence. Simply multiplying 40 crimes/year by 10 years suggests that imprisoning this person would forestall 400 crimes over the next 10 years. But if the prisoner's criminal career would in any case have ended at age 25, the true crime reduction is only 200, and 5 years of the 10-year sentence produce no incapacitative benefit.

2. *Selective incapacitation.* If across-the-board increases in prison sentences are overinclusive and inefficient, a more cost-effective strategy might

involve efforts to target the particular offenders most likely to commit serious crimes at high rates. But consider Jacqueline Cohen, Incapacitating Criminals: Recent Research Findings, U.S. Dept. of Justice, Natl. Institute of Justice, Research in Brief (December 1983):

> Proponents [of selective incapacitation] argue that persons convicted of crimes can justly receive any lawful sentence . . . and that holding some offenders longer than others for predictive reasons raises no significant ethical problems. Moreover, proponents point out that existing sentencing is implicitly incapacitative: presumably, most judges and other officials base their decisions in part on their beliefs about an offender's future dangerousness. From this perspective, selective incapacitation policies are preferable to existing practice because predictions of future crime would no longer be ad hoc and idiosyncratic, but would be based upon the best available scientific evidence.
>
> Some critics argue against selective incapacitation in principle: punishment should be *deserved* and two persons who have committed the same offense deserve equal punishment. If selective incapacitation means that one person will be held longer than another because of predictions of future crimes, it is unjust.
>
> Other critics—including people who in principle do not object to unequal punishments—offer other objections:
>
> 1. It is *unfair* to punish people for crimes they have not yet committed, and might not commit if released.
> 2. It is unjust to incarcerate (or further incarcerate) people on the basis of predictions of future crime because those predictions are too often *wrong*. . . .
> 3. Many of the variables in prediction formulas raise other policy or ethical questions. For example, . . . the RAND formula includes employment information, . . . education and similar factors, . . . class-based variables that, in effect, discriminate against the poor.
> 4. Many prediction variables, like education, employment, and residential stability, are associated with race: some minorities are on average less well educated and less stably employed than the white majority. Building such variables into sentencing standards, while not intended to punish minorities more severely, would have that effect. . . .

3. Empirical problems of prediction. Even if ethical objections to selective incapacitation are set aside, a major difficulty lies in the inaccuracy of the judgments on which it rests. Predictions of future criminality based on intuitive clinical assessments typically have "false-positive" rates of over 60 percent; in other words, of every three individuals predicted to offend in the future, two do not. As a result, when large numbers of offenders are held for longer periods on the basis of such predictions, two-thirds of the individuals suffer unnecessary curtailment of their liberty, and of course society incurs costs of incarceration that can easily exceed the costs of the crimes prevented. An alternative approach is based on risk-assessment instruments that rely on objective risk indicators such as age, gender, mental disorder, substance abuse, and prior criminal record. These "actuarial" prediction methods have achieved much greater success, at least for smaller groups and certain types of offenders, such as the mentally ill. In some instances, such tools have had accuracy rates of over 50 percent and occasionally up to 75 percent. See Christopher Slobogin, The Civilization of the Criminal Law, 58 Vand. L. Rev. 121, 145 (2005). Nonetheless, false-positive rates remain well above 50 percent for larger groups and for more typical offenders convicted of offenses like robbery, burglary, and theft. See John Monahan, A Jurisprudence of Risk Assessment: Forecasting Harm Among Prisoners, Predators, and Patients, 92 Va. L. Rev. 391, 408-413 (2006).

4. *Taking credit for the 1990s?* From 1988 to 1998, American prison populations soared from 800,000 to 1.8 million, an increase of 125 percent. During the same period crime rates fell dramatically; in cities of more than 1 million inhabitants, for example, the homicide rate fell by 55 percent from 1991 to 1998.[26] Many attribute these crime-control successes to the incapacitation effect of the prison population boom, but many states with much smaller increases in prison population nonetheless experienced significant crime-control successes as well. As a result, many competing explanations have been offered for the drop in crime during the 1990s, including demographic trends, community policing innovations, the waning of the crack epidemic, and even the possibility that legalized abortion may have reduced the number of "unwanted" children who began reaching their crime-prone teen years during this period.[27] Efforts to sort out the impact of these diverse factors are necessarily speculative and imprecise; one careful study suggests that increases in incarceration rates in California may have produced roughly a 15 percent decrease in the volume of crime, but the reductions occurred primarily in burglaries and larcenies; no substantial incapacitation benefit was detected for homicide, robbery, and assault.[28]

5. *Cost-effective alternatives?* Three years after declaring that "prisons are a bargain," Professor DiIulio qualified his position. In a 1999 article, he insisted that increasing the incarceration rate was a justified policy in 1996 (when there were 1.6 million prisoners nationwide),[29] but with the U.S. prison and jail population then near the 2 million mark (it is now well over that figure), he argued, "the nation has 'maxed out' on the public-safety value of incarceration" and "[t]he justice system is becoming less capable of distributing sanctions and supervision rationally, especially where drug offenders are concerned." Accordingly, DiIulio maintained, "[i]t's time for policy makers to change focus, aiming for zero prison growth," and devoting more resources to drug treatment and effective supervision of offenders on probation and

---

26. U.S. Dept of Justice, Bureau of Justice Statistics, Homicide Trends in the United States: 1998 Update (Mar. 2000).

27. See John J. Donohue III & Steven Levitt, The Impact of Legalized Abortion and Crime, 116 Q.J. Econ. 379 (2001).

28. Franklin Zimring & Gordon Hawkins, Incapacitation 100-127 (1995).

29. U.S. Dept. of Justice, Bureau of Justice Statistics, Prison and Jail Inmates at Midyear 1999 (Apr. 2000), p. 2.

parole. Signaling that his changed assessment was the result of more than just a shift in the cost-benefit calculus, DiIulio concluded, "In the end, whether or not we achieve this goal [of zero prison growth] will be a profound measure not merely of how nimble we are when it comes to managing public safety cost-effectively, but also of how decent we are, despite our many differences, when it came to loving all God's children unconditionally."[30]

The soaring costs of mass incarceration have begun to generate a consensus across political lines that America's reliance on incapacitation has gone too far. For example, a group of nationally prominent conservatives has formed the organization "Right on Crime" to lobby for greater accountability and greater restraint in crime control expenditures; its statement of principles declares:[31]

> Conservatives are known for being tough on crime, but we must also be tough on criminal justice spending. That means demanding more cost-effective approaches that enhance public safety. [P]risons . . . serve a critical role by incapacitating dangerous offenders and career criminals but are not the solution for every type of offender. And in some instances, they have the unintended consequence of hardening nonviolent, low-risk offenders—making them a greater risk to the public than when they entered.

D. ASSIGNING PUNISHMENT—SENTENCING

INTRODUCTORY NOTE

Until the 1970s, the punishment decision was entrusted almost entirely to the discretion of the trial judge. Statutory limits on sentences, the prosecutor's charging power, and the releasing authority of the parole board qualified the trial judge's power, but the individual judge formally controlled the penalty. That situation still prevails in the majority of the states, but many have moved to limit the trial judge's power (1) by mandating specified punishments (particularly mandatory *minimum* sentences), (2) by establishing an administrative agency to promulgate sentencing guidelines that narrow the sentencing range within which judges can sentence, or (3) by providing for appellate review of trial-court sentencing.[32] Chapter 10, infra, explores these trends in greater detail as well as the broader question of how much discretion a sentencer should have. In this section, we examine two distinct and more general questions: (1) How long should a sentence be; and (2) What kinds of punishments are acceptable, regardless of who the decision maker may be?

---

30. John J. DiIulio, Jr., Two Million Prisoners Are Enough, Wall St. J., Mar. 12, 1999.

31. See http://www.rightoncrime.com/the-conservative-case-for-reform/statement-of-principles/.

32. See Neal B. Kauder & Brian J. Ostram, National Center for State Courts, State Sentencing Guidelines (June 2008), available at http://www.ncsconline.org/csi/PEW-Profiles-v12-online.pdf; Richard S. Frase, State Sentencing Guidelines: Diversity, Consensus, and Unresolved Policy Issues, 105 Colum. L. Rev. 1190 (2005).

1. *Sentence Length*

DIANA B. HENRIQUES & JACK HEALY, MADOFF GOES TO JAIL AFTER GUILTY PLEAS

N.Y. Times, Mar. 13, 2009

When Bernard L. Madoff entered a federal courtroom in Manhattan on Thursday to admit that he had run a vast Ponzi scheme that robbed thousands of investors of their life savings, he was as elegantly dressed as ever. . . . He admitted his guilt for the first time in public, and apologized to his victims, dozens of whom were squeezed into the courtroom benches behind him, before being handcuffed and led away to jail to await sentencing.

"I knew what I was doing was wrong, indeed criminal," he said. "When I began the Ponzi scheme, I believed it would end shortly and I would be able to extricate myself and my clients." But finding an exit "proved difficult, and ultimately impossible," he continued, stumbling slightly in his prepared remarks. "As the years went by I realized this day, and my arrest, would inevitably come." Mr. Madoff acknowledged that he had "deeply hurt many, many people," adding, "I cannot adequately express how sorry I am for what I have done."

. . . [T]he hearing made clear that Mr. Madoff is refusing to help the government build a case against anyone else. . . . The 11 counts of fraud, money laundering, perjury and theft to which Mr. Madoff, 70, pleaded guilty carry maximum terms totaling 150 years. . . .

Mr. Madoff's fraud became a global scheme that ensnared hedge funds, charities and celebrities. He enticed thousands of investors, including figures like Senator Frank Lautenberg of New Jersey, the Hall of Fame pitcher Sandy Koufax and a charity run by Elie Wiesel, the Nobel Peace Prize laureate. The fraud's collapse erased as much as $65 billion that his customers thought they had. It remains unclear how much victims will recover. A court-appointed trustee liquidating Mr. Madoff's business has so far been able to identify only about $1 billion in assets to satisfy claims.

UNITED STATES v. BERNARD L. MADOFF

United States District Court, S.D.N.Y. (June 29, 2009)[33]

CHIN, J. . . . [H]ere the guideline range is not life imprisonment, but 150 years, the maximum sentences for each of the 11 counts added together. . . . While I must give the guideline range fair and respectful consideration, I am not bound by it. . . . Instead, I must make an individualized assessment based

---

33. Available at http://www.justice.gov/usao/nys/madoff/20090629sentencingtranscript-corrected.pdf.

on all the facts and circumstances, including the factors set forth in the statute. In the end, I must impose a sentence that is reasonable.

[The court next heard from the victims, who recounted the devastation caused by their financial losses.]

[Madoff's lawyer then spoke:] "I think it's important to note . . . that Mr. Madoff stepped forward. He chose not to flee. He chose not to hide money. . . . Mr. Madoff is 71 years old, your Honor. Based upon his health . . . his family history, his life expectancy, that is why we ask for a sentence of 12 years, just short, based upon the statistics we have, of a life sentence. . . . We also said, if your Honor is inclined, . . . 15 to 20 years. So that if Mr. Madoff ever sees the light of day, in his 90s, impoverished and alone, he will have paid a terrible price. . . . [T]here is no question that this case has taken an enormous toll, not only on Mr. Madoff and his family, but to the victims to be sure. . . . We ask only, your Honor, that Mr. Madoff be given understanding and fairness, within the parameters of our legal system, and that the sentence that he be given be sufficient, but not greater than necessary."

[Madoff himself addressed the court, briefly, to apologize. He was followed by the government lawyer, who requested that Madoff be sentenced to 150 years for "carry[ing] out a fraud of unprecedented proportion over the course of more than a generation." The government rejected the defendant's proposed sentence of 12 years as "profoundly unfair. Not only would it not reflect the seriousness and the scope of the defendant's crimes, but, also, it would not promote the goals of general deterrence going forward."]

[Judge Chin then offered his analysis and sentence:] I take into account what I have read in the presentence report, the parties' sentencing submissions, and the e-mails and letters from victims. I take into account what I have heard today. I also consider the statutory factors as well as all the facts and circumstances in the case. . . .

Objectively speaking, the fraud here was staggering. It spanned more than 20 years. . . . As for the amount of monetary loss, there appears to be some disagreement. Mr. Madoff disputes that the loss amount is $65 billion or even $13 billion. . . . [T]he fraud here is unprecedented. [The sentencing guidelines offense level] is calculated by using a chart for loss amount that only goes up to $400 million. By any of these measures, the loss figure here is many times that amount. It's off the chart by many fold.

Moreover, as many of the victims have pointed out, this is not just a matter of money. The breach of trust was massive. Investors—individuals, charities, pension funds, institutional clients—were repeatedly lied to, as they were told their moneys would be invested in stocks when they were not. . . . As the victims' letters and e-mails demonstrate, as the statements today demonstrate, investors made important life decisions based on these fictitious account statements—when to retire, how to care for elderly parents, whether to buy a car or sell a house, how to save for their children's college tuition. Charitable organizations and pension funds made important decisions based on false information about fictitious accounts. . . .

It is true that Mr. Madoff used much of the money to pay back investors who asked along the way to withdraw their accounts. But large sums were also taken by him, for his personal use and the use of his family, friends, and colleagues. . . .

Mr. Madoff argues a number of mitigating factors but they are less than compelling. It is true that he essentially turned himself in and confessed to the FBI. But the fact is that with the turn in the economy, he was not able to keep up with the requests of customers to withdraw their funds, and it is apparent that he knew that he was going to be caught soon. . . . Moreover, the [trustee of the funds recovered] has advised the Court Mr. Madoff has not been helpful, and I simply do not get the sense that Mr. Madoff has done all that he could or told all that he knows. . . .

I have taken into account the sentence imposed in other financial fraud cases in this district. But, frankly, none of these other cases is comparable to this case in terms of the scope, duration and enormity of the fraud, and the degree of the betrayal.

In terms of mitigating factors in a white-collar fraud case such as this, I would expect to see letters from family and friends and colleagues. But not a single letter has been submitted attesting to Mr. Madoff's good deeds or good character or civic or charitable activities. The absence of such support is telling.

We have heard much about life expectancy analysis. Based on this analysis, Mr. Madoff has a life expectancy of 13 years, and therefore asks for a sentence of 12 years or alternatively 15 to 20 years. If [this] life expectancy analysis is correct, any sentence above 20 or 25 years would be largely, if not entirely, symbolic.

But the symbolism is important, for at least three reasons. First, retribution. One of the traditional notions of punishment is that an offender should be punished in proportion to his blameworthiness. Here, the message must be sent that Mr. Madoff's crimes were extraordinarily evil, and that this kind of irresponsible manipulation of the system is not merely a bloodless financial crime that takes place just on paper, but that is instead, as we have heard, one that takes a staggering human toil. The symbolism is important because the message must be sent that in a society governed by the rule of law, Mr. Madoff will get what he deserves, and that he will be punished according to his moral culpability.

Second, [a]nother important goal of punishment is deterrence, and the symbolism is important here because the strongest possible message must be sent to those would engage in similar conduct that they will be caught and that they will be punished to the fullest extent of the law.

Finally, symbolism is also important for the victims. . . . Mr. Madoff's very personal betrayal struck at the rich and the not-so-rich, the elderly living on retirement funds and social security, middle class folks trying to put their kids through college, and ordinary people who worked hard to save their money and who thought they were investing it safely, for themselves and their families.

I received letters, and we have heard from, for example, a retired forest worker, a corrections officer, an auto mechanic, a physical therapist, a retired New York City school secretary, who is now 66 years old and widowed, who must deal with the loss of her retirement funds. . . .

I was particularly struck by one story that I read in the letters. A man invested his family's life savings with Mr. Madoff. Tragically, he died of a heart attack just two weeks later. The widow eventually went in to see Mr. Madoff. He put his arm around her, as she describes it, and in a kindly manner told her not to worry, the money is safe with me. And so not only did the widow leave the money with him, she eventually deposited more funds with him, her 401(k), her pension funds. Now, all the money is gone. She will have to sell her home, and she will not be able to keep her promise to help her granddaughter pay for college.

A substantial sentence will not give the victims back . . . their financial security or the freedom from financial worry. But more is at stake than money. . . . The victims put their trust in Mr. Madoff. That trust was broken in a way that has left many—victims as well as others—doubting our financial institutions, our financial system, our government's ability to regulate and protect, and sadly, even themselves. . . . A substantial sentence, the knowledge that Mr. Madoff has been punished to the fullest extent of the law, may, in some small measure, help these victims in their healing process.

Mr. Madoff, please stand. It is the judgment of this Court that the defendant, Bernard L. Madoff, shall be and hereby is sentenced to a term of imprisonment of 150 years. . . .

I will not impose a fine, as whatever assets Mr. Madoff has, as whatever assets may be found, they shall be applied to restitution for the victims. . . .

NOTES

1. Reflections of Judge Denny Chin. In an interview with the *New York Times* given two years after the sentence, Judge Chin explained that one of the "struggles" in sentencing Bernard Madoff was whether to give him any hope of being released in his lifetime. "In the end, I just thought that he didn't deserve it," he said. "The benefits of giving him hope were far outweighed by all of the other considerations." Benjamin Weiser, Judge Explains 150-Year Sentence for Madoff, N.Y. Times, June 28, 2011. What were those other considerations? If retribution and symbolism are put aside, is the 150-year sentence justified on utilitarian grounds?

2. Reflections of Madoff. In the same article, Madoff questioned the judge's sentence: "Explain to me who else has received a sentence like that. . . . I mean, serial killers get a death sentence, but that's virtually what he gave me." Is Madoff's sentence proportionate to the harms caused? Should Judge Chin have contemplated how the sentence compares to sentences for other kinds of crimes, including violent crimes and homicides?

3. *Mitigating circumstances.* Judge Chin notes that white-collar offenders typically submit letters of support from people who know them, attesting to their good character and charitable contributions. See, e.g., United States v. Tomko, 562 F.3d 558, 572 (3d Cir. 2009). While the *presence* of these letters may not be sufficient for a defendant to receive a lower sentence than he otherwise would get, Judge Chin suggested that these letters have become so commonplace in white-collar cases as to become necessary. Their *absence*, in Judge Chin's words, "is telling." If individuals had submitted letters on Madoff's behalf describing his charitable works or good character, is it likely they would have made a difference in Madoff's sentence? If the answer is no, given the scope of the fraud, should Judge Chin have mentioned their absence at all?

4. *Arriving at a number.* Judge Chin further explained that "because none of the counts against Mr. Madoff carried a sentence of life imprisonment," a life sentence was not an option and a term of some years had to be selected. The term of 150 years was arrived at by stacking the maximum sentences of each count. In an article addressing the ten-year sentence of Michael Milken, another infamous white-collar offender, Stanton Wheeler made the following observations (Reflections on the Sentencing of Michael Milken, 3 Fed. Sent. R. 167 (1990)):

> Surely there is a basis in the common sense wisdom of sitting judges for sanctioning heavily those who occupy special positions of authority and responsibility and who abuse those positions by committing crimes, especially when the crimes are sophisticated and of substantial duration. The argument for stiff sentences in such cases goes both to the gravity of the offense and the importance of sending a deterrent message. Judges feel strongly about violations of trust, and about violations that have the capacity to affect the fabric of financial transactions.
>
> At the same time, there is little working out of the precise reasoning behind the numbers. Federal judges often talk about the harm caused by an offense, the blameworthiness of the offender, and the consequence the sentence is likely to have, especially the consequence for general deterrence. Words reflecting each of these concerns are found in [the judge's] remarks, but in the end we have little idea of how much of the 10 years is due to the seriousness of the offense, how much to [the defendant's] own culpability, and how much to the capacity of a long sentence to deter others.
>
> Indeed, the number 10 itself remains a mystery. Cannot one read all of [the judge's] words and come up with a different number, like 5 or 6?

5. *Questions on picking a number.* Judge Chin picked a number—150 years—that obviously cannot be satisfied in Madoff's lifetime. What is the purpose of selecting a sentence that extends beyond the defendant's life expectancy? Would the same sentence have been appropriate if Madoff were 40 years old instead of 71? Should a defendant's age and life expectancy be part of a court's calculus?

6. *An illustration.* In the next case, the appellate court lacked the authority to impose a different sentence on the defendant, but in discussing the soundness of the district court's sentencing decision, it put a spotlight on the relevant policy issues. As you read the case, consider whether you agree or disagree that the district court's sentence was appropriate.

UNITED STATES v. JACKSON

United States Court of Appeals,
7th Circuit 835 F.2d 1195 (1987)

EASTERBROOK, J. Thirty minutes after being released from prison, to which he had been sent on conviction of two bank robberies, Dwight Jackson robbed another bank. He was let out as part of a "work release program" and returned to his old line of work. Told to get a job, he decided to do a bank job. A passer-by saw a suspicious person flee the bank and noted the license plate of the car. . . . Jackson was back in prison before the sun set on the day of his release. His principal sentence—life in prison without possibility of parole—came under a statute forbidding possession of weapons by career criminals, 18 U.S.C. App. §1202. . . .

Section 1202 provided that anyone "who . . . possesses . . . any firearm and who has three previous [felony] convictions for robbery or burglary, or both, . . . shall be fined not more than $25,000 and imprisoned not less than fifteen years, and, notwithstanding any other provision of law, the court shall not suspend the sentence of, or grant a probationary sentence to, such person . . . , and such person shall not be eligible for parole with respect to the sentence imposed under this subsection." Jackson, who had been convicted of four armed bank robberies and one armed robbery, brandished his revolver and robbed the Continental Bank of Oakbrook Terrace, Illinois, on May 30, 1986, while this statute was in force. . . .

The imposition of life in prison on Jackson was permissible. The selection of a sentence within the statutory range is essentially free of appellate review. Armed bank robbery on the day of release—following earlier armed robbery convictions back to 1973—marked Jackson as a career criminal. Specific deterrence had failed. The court was entitled to consider general deterrence and incapacitation. Although life without possibility of parole is the upper end of the scale of sanctions (short of capital punishment), the statute reflects a judgment that career criminals who persist in possessing weapons should be dealt with most severely. . . . If this sentence is unduly harsh, the holder of the clemency power may supply a remedy. . . . Affirmed.

POSNER J., concurring. I join the opinion and judgment of the court; but I think the sentence Jackson received is too harsh and I think it appropriate to point this out even though he presents no ground on which we are authorized to set aside an excessively severe sentence.

Jackson is unquestionably a dangerous and hardened criminal. He has been convicted of armed robbery four times (three were bank robberies—all of the same bank!); in each robbery he was carrying a loaded gun. I do not mean to denigrate the gravity of his offenses by pointing out that he has never inflicted a physical injury; but that fact is relevant to deciding whether the sheer enormity of his conduct warrants imprisonment for the rest of his life as a matter of retributive justice. It does not. Few murderers, traitors, or rapists are punished so severely. . . . The grounds for the sentence in this case must be sought elsewhere.

One ground, the one articulated by the district judge, is the need to prevent Jackson from committing further crimes. There is little doubt that if he were released tomorrow he would commit a bank robbery, perhaps on the same day. But it is extremely unlikely that if he were released 25 or 30 years from now (he is 35 years old) he would resume his career as a bank robber. We know that criminal careers taper off with age, although with the aging of the population and the improvements in the health of the aged the fraction of crimes committed by the elderly is rising. Crimes that involve a risk of physical injury to the criminal are especially a young man's game. In 1986 more than 62 percent of all persons arrested for robbery . . . were below the age of 25, and only 3.4 percent were 60 years old or older. . . . Bank robbery in particular, I suspect, is a young man's crime. A bank robber must be willing to confront armed guards and able to make a quick getaway. To suppose that if Jackson is fortunate enough to live on in prison into his seventies or eighties it would still be necessary to detain him lest he resume his life of crime after almost a lifetime in prison is too speculative to warrant imprisoning him until he dies of old age. . . .

The remaining possibility is that this savage sentence is proper *pour encourager les autres.* Indeed, deterrence is the surest ground for punishment, since retributive norms are so unsettled and since incapacitation may, by removing one offender from the pool of offenders, simply make a career in crime more attractive to someone else. . . . Thus, even if one were sure that Jackson would be as harmless as a mouse in the last 10, or 15, or 20 years of his life, his sentence might be justified if the example of it were likely to deter other people, similarly situated, from committing such crimes. This is possible, but speculative; it was not mentioned by the district judge.

We should ask how many 35 year olds would rob a bank if they knew that if they were caught it would mean 20 years in prison with no possibility of parole (the sentence I would have given Jackson if I had been the sentencing judge), compared to the number who would do so if it would mean life in prison. Probably very few would be deterred by the incremental sentence. Bank robbery is a crime of acquisition, not of passion; the only gains are financial—and are slight (in 1986 the average "take" from a bank robbery was $2,664). The net gains, when the expected cost of punishment is figured in, must be very small indeed. Clearance rates for bank robbery are very high; of all bank robberies investigated by the FBI during 1978 and 1979 . . . , 69 percent had been cleared by arrest by 1982. Conviction rates are high (90 percent in federal prosecutions for bank robbery) and average punishments severe (more than 13 years for federal defendants). It's a losers' game at best. Persons who would go ahead and rob a bank in the face of my hypothetical 20-year sentence are unlikely to be deterred by tightening the punishment screws still further. A civilized society locks up such people until age makes them harmless but it does not keep them in prison until they die.

NOTES AND QUESTIONS

1. Postscript. In a subsequent proceeding the sentencing judge denied a motion for reduction of sentence, stating that Judge Richard Posner's concerns had not persuaded him to reconsider. The sentencing judge mentioned, among other factors, that Jackson had persisted in denying his guilt; that his prior record, in addition to seven armed robbery convictions, included an attempt to murder his army colonel in Vietnam and an assault on a sergeant; and that the possession of firearms by this "incorrigible and hostile recidivist" created a distinct possibility that severe injury or death could result from any future criminal conduct. See United States v. Jackson, 780 F. Supp. 1508 (N.D. Ill. 1991).

2. Criminal history and age. What sentence *should* be imposed on Jackson? For what purpose? How important should an offender's criminal history be in determining the sentence? Is Judge Posner right that Jackson's age should play a significant role in the length of the sentence? If so, why was Madoff's age not a bigger factor in his sentence? For a discussion of the relevance of the age of the offender to sentencing, see Dawn Miller, Sentencing Elderly Criminal Offenders, 7 NAELA J. 221 (2011).

Does Judge Posner's view suggest that an 18-year-old should receive a longer sentence than an offender who has the same criminal history and commits the same offense, but is 30 years older, based on predictions of future criminal conduct? How much should predictions about future dangerousness factor into sentencing length? For a discussion of the accuracy of such predictions, see John Monahan, A Jurisprudence of Risk Assessment, 92 Va. L. Rev. 391 (2006).

3. "Three strikes and you're out." Several states have enacted or considered legislation providing that, upon conviction of a felony (or *violent* felony) after two prior felony convictions, a defendant must be sentenced to life imprisonment without possibility of parole. What purpose is such a sentence intended to serve—in particular, is such a sentence explained by retribution or incapacitation? As to the former, are recidivists who have served their sentences for prior crimes *more culpable* than first-time offenders? For an argument that they *deserve* greater punishment, see Youngjae Lee, Recidivism as Omission: A Relational Account, 87 Tex. L. Rev. 571 (2009). For a more critical view, arguing that recidivist enhancements fail to serve the purposes of punishment, see Sarah F. Russell, Rethinking Recidivist Enhancements: The Role of Prior Drug Convictions in Federal Sentencing, 43 U.C. Davis L. Rev. 1135 (2010). Do the additional benefits of a life sentence in such cases (compared, for example, to a 15-year or 20-year sentence) justify the additional costs? See Michael Vitiello, Three Strikes: Can We Return to Rationality, 87 J. Crim. L. & Criminology 395 (1997).

4. Punishment is not just about incarceration and terms of years. Sentences may also include conditions of supervised release and probation. The next section deals with the issues surrounding what *kinds* of punishment to impose.

2. Kinds of Punishment

UNITED STATES v. GEMENTERA

United States Court of Appeals
9th Circuit 379 F.3d 596 (2004)

O'SCANNLAIN, Circuit Judge: ... Shawn Gementera pilfered letters from several mailboxes along San Francisco's Fulton Street on May 21, 2001. ... After indictment, Gementera entered a plea agreement pursuant to which he pled guilty to mail theft.

The offense was not Gementera's first encounter with the law. Though only twenty-four years old at the time, Gementera's criminal history was lengthy for a man of his relative youth, and it was growing steadily more serious. At age nineteen, he was convicted of misdemeanor criminal mischief. He was twice convicted at age twenty of driving with a suspended license. At age twenty-two, a domestic dispute led to convictions for driving with a suspended license and for failing to provide proof of financial responsibility. By twenty-four, the conviction was misdemeanor battery. Other arrests and citations listed in the Presentence Investigation Report included possession of drug paraphernalia, additional driving offenses (most of which involved driving on a license suspended for his failure to take chemical tests), and, soon after his twenty-fifth birthday, taking a vehicle without the owner's consent.

... The U.S. Sentencing Guidelines range was two to eight months incarceration; Judge Walker sentenced Gementera to the lower bound of the range, imposing two months incarceration and three years supervised release. He also imposed conditions of supervised release. One such condition required Gementera to "perform 100 hours of community service," to consist of "standing in front of a postal facility in the city and county of San Francisco with a sandwich board which in large letters declares: 'I stole mail. This is my punishment.'" Gementera later filed a motion to correct the sentence by removing the sandwich board condition. Judge Walker modified the sentence after inviting both parties to present "an alternative form or forms of public service that would better comport with the aims of the court." In lieu of the 100-hour signboard requirement, the district court imposed a four-part special condition in its stead. Three new terms, proposed jointly by counsel, mandated that the defendant observe postal patrons visiting the "lost or missing mail" window, write letters of apology to any identifiable victims of his crime, and deliver several lectures at a local school. It also included a scaled-down version of the signboard requirement:

> The defendant shall perform 1 day of 8 total hours of community service during which time he shall either (i) wear a two-sided sandwich board-style sign or (ii) carry a large two-sided sign stating, "I stole mail; this is my punishment," in front of a San Francisco postal facility identified by the probation officer. For the safety of defendant and general public, the postal facility designated shall be one that employs one or more security guards. Upon showing by defendant that this condition would likely impose upon defendant psychological harm or effect or result in unwarranted risk of harm to defendant, the public or postal employees, the probation officer may withdraw or modify this condition or apply to the court to withdraw or modify this condition.

We first address Gementera's argument that the eight-hour sandwich board condition violates the Sentencing Reform Act. See 18 U.S.C. §3583(d). The Sentencing Reform Act affords district courts broad discretion in fashioning appropriate conditions of supervised release, while mandating that such conditions serve legitimate objectives. In addition to [specified conditions] the statute explicitly authorizes the court to impose "*any other condition it considers to be appropriate.*" Such special conditions, however, [must be] "reasonably related" to "the nature and circumstances of the offense and the history and characteristics of the defendant." See 18 U.S.C. §3553(a)(1). Moreover, it must be both "reasonably related" to and "involve no greater deprivation of liberty than is reasonably necessary" to "afford adequate deterrence to criminal conduct," "protect the public from further crimes of the defendant," and "provide the defendant with needed educational or vocational training, medical care, or other correctional treatment in the most effective manner." Accordingly, the three legitimate statutory purposes of deterrence, protection of the public, and rehabilitation frame our analysis. . . .

Gementera first urges that the condition was imposed for an impermissible purpose of humiliation. See 18 U.S.C. §3553(a). He points to certain remarks of the district court at the first sentencing hearing. . . .

> [H]e needs to understand the disapproval that society has for this kind of conduct, and that's the idea behind the humiliation. And it should be humiliation of having to stand and be labeled in front of people coming and going from a post office as somebody who has stolen the mail.

According to Gementera, these remarks, among others, indicate that the district court viewed humiliation as an end in itself and the condition's purpose. Reading the record in context, however, we cannot but conclude that the district court's stated rationale aligned with permissible statutory objectives. . . .

The court expressed particular concern that the defendant did not fully understand the gravity of his offense. Mail theft is an anonymous crime and, by "bring[ing] home to defendant that his conduct has palpable significance to real people within his community," the court aimed to break the defendant of the illusion that his theft was victimless or not serious. In short, it explained:

> While humiliation may well be—indeed likely will be—a feature of defendant's experience in standing before a post office with such a sign, the humiliation or shame he experiences should serve the salutary purpose of bringing defendant in close touch with the real significance of the crime he has acknowledged committing. Such an experience should have a specific rehabilitative effect on defendant that could not be accomplished by other means, certainly not by a more extended term of imprisonment. Moreover, "[i]t will also have a deterrent effect on both this defendant and others who might not otherwise have been made aware of the real legal consequences of engaging in mail theft."

Read in its entirety, the record unambiguously establishes that the district court imposed the condition for the stated and legitimate statutory purpose of rehabilitation and, to a lesser extent, for general deterrence and for the protection of the public. . . .

Assuming the court articulated a legitimate purpose, Gementera asserts . . . that humiliation or so-called "shaming" conditions are not "reasonably related" to rehabilitation. . . .

Reflecting upon the defendant's criminal history, the court expressed concern that he did not fully understand the consequences of his continued criminality, and had not truly accepted responsibility. . . .

[T]he district court concluded that public acknowledgment of one's offense—beyond the formal yet sterile plea in a cloistered courtroom—was necessary to his rehabilitation.

It is true, of course, that much uncertainty exists as to how rehabilitation is best accomplished. Were that picture clearer, our criminal justice system would be vastly different, and substantially improved. By one estimate, two-thirds of the 640,000 state and federal inmates who will be released in 2004 will return to prison within a few years. See Bureau of Justice Statistics, Dep't of Justice, Recidivism of Prisoners Released in 1994 (2002) (finding 67.5% recidivism rate among study population of 300,000 prisoners released in 1994). The cost to humanity of our ignorance in these matters is staggering.

Gementera and amicus contend that shaming conditions cannot be rehabilitative because such conditions necessarily cause the offender to withdraw from society or otherwise inflict psychological damage, and they would erect a per se bar against such conditions. ("When it works, it redefines a person in a negative, often irreversible way" and the "psychological core" it affects cannot thereafter be rebuilt.) Though the district court had no scientific evidence before it, as Gementera complains, we do not insist upon such evidence in our deferential review. Moreover, the fact is that a vigorous, multifaceted, scholarly debate on shaming sanctions' efficacy, desirability, and underlying rationales continues within the academy. By no means is this conversation one-sided.

Criminal offenses, and the penalties that accompany them, nearly always cause shame and embarrassment. The fact that a condition causes shame or embarrassment does not automatically render a condition objectionable; rather, such feelings generally signal the defendant's acknowledgment of his wrongdoing. . . . While the district court's sandwich board condition was somewhat crude, and by itself could entail risk of social withdrawal and stigmatization, it was coupled with more socially useful provisions, including lecturing at a high school and writing apologies, that might loosely be understood to promote the offender's social reintegration. See John Braithwaite, Crime, Shame and Reintegration 55 (1989) ("The crucial distinction is between shaming that is reintegrative and shaming that is disintegrative (stigmatization). Reintegrative shaming means that expressions of community disapproval, which may range from mild rebuke to degradation ceremonies, are followed by gestures of reacceptance into the community of law-abiding citizens."). . . . In short, here we consider not a stand-alone condition intended solely to humiliate, but rather a comprehensive set of provisions that expose the defendant to social disapprobation, but that also then provide an opportunity for Gementera to repair his relationship with society—first by seeking its forgiveness and then by making, as a member of the community, an independent contribution to the moral formation of its youth.[13] These provisions, tailored to the specific needs of the offender, counsel in favor of concluding that the condition passes the threshold of being reasonably related to rehabilitation. . . .

Accordingly, we hold that the condition imposed upon Gementera reasonably related to the legitimate statutory objective of rehabilitation. In so holding, we are careful not to articulate a principle broader than that presented by the facts of this case. With care and specificity, the district court outlined a sensible logic underlying its conclusion that a set of conditions, including the signboard provision, but also including reintegrative provisions, would better promote this defendant's rehabilitation and amendment of life than would a lengthier term of incarceration. By contrast, a per se rule that the mandatory public airing of one's offense can never assist an offender to reassume his duty of obedience to the law would impose a narrow penological orthodoxy not contemplated by the Guidelines' express approval of "any other condition [the district court] considers to be appropriate." 18 U.S.C. §3583(d). . . .

HAWKINS, Circuit Judge, dissenting: . . . Although I believe that the sandwich board condition violates the Sentencing Reform Act and we should reverse the district court for that reason, I also believe that this is simply bad policy. A fair measure of a civilized society is how its institutions behave in the space between what it may have the power to do and what it should do. The shaming component of the sentence in this case fails that test. "When one shames

---

13. The dissent faults our analysis for looking beyond the signboard clause to other provisions of the four-part condition. Our purpose is not, as the dissent characterizes it, to suggest that an improper condition may be cured merely by setting it alongside proper conditions. Rather, our obligation is to assess whether an individual provision reasonably relates to the purpose of rehabilitation. Where that provision is part of an integrated rehabilitative scheme, we see no bar to looking at other aspects of the scheme in evaluating the purpose and reasonableness of the individual provision at issue. . . .

another person, the goal is to degrade the object of shame, to place him lower in the chain of being, to dehumanize him." Dan Markel, Are Shaming Punishments Beautifully Retributive? Retributivism and the Implications for the Alternative Sanctions Debate, 54 Vand. L. Rev. 2157, 2179 (2001).

To affirm the imposition of such punishments recalls a time in our history when pillories and stocks were the order of the day. . . . I would vacate the sentence and remand for re-sentencing, instructing the district court that public humiliation or shaming has no proper place in our system of justice.

NOTES

1. Other shaming conditions. The *Gementera* opinion mentions some examples and distinguishes them from the shaming penalty imposed in *Gementera* (379 F.3d at fn. 9):

> In People v. Hackler, 16 Cal. Rptr. 2d 681 (Cal. Ct. App. 1993), a California court vacated a condition requiring a defendant during his first year of probation to wear a t-shirt whenever he was outside his home. The t-shirt read, "My record plus two-six packs equal four years," and on the back, "I am on felony probation for theft." [Defendant had been convicted of shoplifting beer from a supermarket.] Noting with disapproval the trial court's stated intention of "going back to some extent to the era of stocks" and transforming the defendant into "a Hester Prim," [sic] the court held that the t-shirt could not serve the rehabilitative purpose because it would render the defendant unemployable. By contrast, Gementera's condition was sharply limited temporally (eight hours) and spatially (one post office in a large city), eliminating any risk that its effects would similarly spill over into all aspects of the defendant's life. Indeed, the district court's imposition of the condition in lieu of lengthier incarceration enables Gementera to enter the private labor market.
>
> People v. Johnson, 528 N.E.2d 1360 (Ill. 1988), involved a condition that a DWI offender publish a newspaper advertisement with apology and mug shot. Interpreting the state supervision law as intended "to aid the defendant in rehabilitation and in avoiding future violations," and for no other purpose, the court held that the publication requirement "possibly, adds public ridicule as a condition" of supervision and could inflict psychological harm that disserves the goal of rehabilitation (noting that the Illinois statute does not "refer to deterrent to others"). Relying on the fact that defendant was a young lady and a good student with no prior criminal record, had injured no one, and otherwise had no alcohol or drug problem, it found the condition impermissible, given the perceived mental health risk. By contrast, we have specifically held that mandatory public apology may be rehabilitative. Moreover, the condition specifically provided that the signboard requirement would be withdrawn if the defendant showed that the condition would inflict psychological harm.
>
> The defendant's third case, People v. Letterlough, 655 N.E.2d 146 (N.Y. 1995), also involved a probation condition imposed upon a DWI offender. If he regained driving privileges, the offender was required to affix a fluorescent

sign to his license plate, stating "CONVICTED DWI." The court imposed the condition under a catch-all provision of the New York law authorizing "any other conditions reasonably related to his [or her] rehabilitation." Under the New York statute, rehabilitation "in the sense of that word that distinguishes it from the societal goals of punishment or deterrence" was the "singular focus of the statute." Because the condition's "true design was not to advance defendant's rehabilitation, but rather to 'warn the public' of the threat presented by his presence behind the wheel," the court voided the condition. . . . In contrast to the New York scheme, the district court [in *Gementera*] made plain the rehabilitative purpose of the condition. We also note that in the federal system, unlike the New York system, rehabilitation is not the sole legitimate objective. See 18 U.S.C. §§3583(d), 3553(a).

2. Desirability of shaming conditions. Are shaming sanctions a good idea? Consider these comments:

Dan M. Kahan, What Do Alternative Sanctions Mean? 63 U. Chi. L. Rev. 591, 638 (1996): What we know about deterrence should make us confident that shaming penalties will be reasonably effective by virtue of their character as degradation ceremonies.

The consequences of shaming penalties are extremely unpleasant. Those who lose the respect of their peers often suffer a crippling diminishment of self-esteem. Moreover, criminal offenders are as likely to be shunned in the marketplace as they are in the public square, leading to serious financial hardship. . . . It stands to reason, then, that shaming penalties, which abstract disgrace from the afflictive dimension of formal sanctions, should compare favorably with imprisonment as a deterrent.

Toni M. Massaro, Shame, Culture, and American Criminal Law, 89 Mich. L. Rev. 1880, 1919-1921 (1991): The anticipated effect of public shaming is a downward change in status, coupled with symbolic and actual shunning of the offender by others. . . . The stigmatized offender thus may "drift" toward subcultures that are more accepting of her particular norm violations. [T]hen shaming not only may not promote specific deterrence or rehabilitative ends, it may defeat them.

James Gilligan, Violence 110-111 (1996): I have yet to see a serious act of violence that was not provoked by the experience of feeling shamed and humiliated, disrespected and ridiculed, and that did not represent the attempt to prevent or undo this "loss of face"—no matter how severe the punishment, even if it includes death. . . . [T]hese men mean it literally when they say they would rather kill or mutilate others, be killed or mutilated themselves, than live without pride, dignity, and self-respect. . . . The emotion of shame is the primary or ultimate cause of all violence.

James Q. Whitman, What Is Wrong with Inflicting Shame Sanctions? 107 Yale L.J. 1055, 1087-1092 (1998): [T]here are *two* aspects to what is troubling about shame sanctions: their effect on the offender and their effect on the crowd. [S]hame sanctions involve a dangerous willingness, on the part of the government, to delegate part of its enforcement power to a fickle and uncontrolled general populace. . . .

Shame sanctions, in this regard, are very different from prisons or fines. However much prisons may have declined into chaos, they are in principle controllable. However monstrous they may have become, we all agree that the state has the duty to manage them: to establish rules, to call review boards, to answer complaints in court. None of that apparatus exists to control the enforcement of shame. . . . [A] system of shaming . . . means abandoning [courts'] duty to be the imposers of *measured* punishment. . . .

[Thus,] shame sanctions lend themselves to a politics of stirring up demons. . . . We have worked, over two liberal centuries, to build an ethic of businesslike politics that denies our officials the authority to pluck on the bass strings of public psychology and that makes criminal law the province of trained and disciplined officers. Over many generations of ugly experience, we have worked to build a democratic government that acknowledges the importance of an ethic of restraint and sobriety. The new shame sanctions tend to undermine that ethic.

Dan M. Kahan, What's Really Wrong with Shaming Sanctions, 84 Tex. L. Rev. 2075, 2075-2076 (2006): The time has come for me to recant [from the position in *What Do Alternative Sanctions Really Mean?*, supra]. [T]he very persistence of the shame opponents' refusal to accept this comparative framing of the issue—what's worse, shame or imprisonment?— . . . eventually made me realize what I'd missed in my earlier argument. . . . I emphasized that punishments, to be politically acceptable, must express authoritative moral condemnation. That's true, but incomplete. Members of society also expect punishments—and essentially all laws for that matter—to affirm the core values that animate their preferred ways of life. Modes of punishments that are equivalent in their power to convey moral disapproval might still convey radically conflicting messages about the nature of the ideal society. What's really wrong with shaming penalties, I believe, is that they are deeply partisan: when society picks them, it picks sides, aligning itself with those who subscribe to norms that give pride of place to community and social differentiation rather than to individuality and equality.

Dan Markel, Wrong Turn on the Road to Alternative Sanctions: Reflections on the Future of Shaming Punishments and Restorative Justice, 85 Tex. L. Rev. 1385, 1395-1397 (2007): [T]he fact of division on shaming is not evidence that Kahan's particular side in the debate is wrong. . . . Why should the partisan disputes over shaming raise a special problem such that abandoning it altogether makes sense? . . . Nothing about shaming punishments suggests that our ordinary political institutions cannot handle [such disputes]. It could be that underlying Kahan's decision to withdraw shaming from the political marketplace is a notion that, in a pluralistic liberal democracy, recognition that a social practice is divisive, and therefore to be avoided, is one way of showing one's respect for other citizens' views. . . . But this notion is not, in the end, persuasive. While a liberal state may wish to restrict the scope of its imposed views on matters of the good, it cannot help but do so in the criminal law.

Questions: (a) Even if one worried about the force of the objections to shaming conditions, are such penalties nonetheless worthwhile if they serve to reduce the length of prison sentences judges might otherwise impose? (b) Is Dan Markel right that taking sides on questions of values is inevitable in criminal law? If so, which choice should society make with respect to shaming?

3. Other controversial conditions. Other conditions than shaming can raise controversial issues. Consider Wisconsin v. Oakley, 629 N.W.2d 200 (Wis. 2001). Defendant was convicted of intentionally refusing to support his nine children. The trial judge imposed a condition of probation that the defendant avoid having another child unless he showed that he could support that child and current children. The Wisconsin Supreme Court upheld the condition in a 4–3 decision. The majority stated:

> We conclude that in light of Oakley's ongoing victimization of his nine children and extraordinarily troubling record manifesting his disregard for the law, this anomalous condition—imposed on a convicted felon facing the far more restrictive and punitive sanction of prison—is not overly broad and is reasonably related to Oakley's rehabilitation. Simply put, because Oakley was convicted of intentionally refusing to pay child support—a felony in Wisconsin—and could have been imprisoned for six years, which would have eliminated his right to procreate altogether during those six years, this probation condition, which infringes on his right to procreate during his term of probation, is not invalid under these facts. Accordingly, we hold that the circuit court did not erroneously exercise its discretion.

The dissent concluded otherwise:

> This condition of probation subjects Oakley to imprisonment if he fathers another child without advance permission from the State. Illegitimacy and child poverty, abuse, and neglect are among our society's most serious and intractable problems. Conditioning the right to procreate upon proof of financial or other fitness may appear on the surface to be an appropriate solution in extreme cases such as this, but it is unprecedented in this country, and for good reason. The State can order non-custodial parents to financially support their children, and can criminally prosecute those who intentionally do not. The State can remove a child from a parent's custody when the child is in need of protection from parental abuse, neglect, or abandonment, and can criminally prosecute parents who mistreat their children. But I know of no authority for the proposition that the State can order that a child not be conceived or born, even to an abysmally irresponsible parent, unless the State first grants its consent.

Who has the better view?

Another area of some controversy involves restrictions on supervised release that dictate where a defendant can or cannot live. In United States v. Woods, 547 F.3d 515 (5th Cir 2008), the Fifth Circuit rejected a trial judge's condition of supervised release that the defendant not reside with anyone with whom she was not related or married. The trial court imposed the condition based on the view that the defendant's "lack of stability" in her home life contributed to her involvement in crack cocaine distribution. Id. at 519. The appeals court rejected the provision and drew a distinction between restrictions on associating with individuals with whom a defendant has a relevant criminal history, which it thought were acceptable, and the trial court's restriction, which the court thought was too broad.

Questions: What is the purpose of restricting where a defendant can live? Does the restriction at issue in *Woods* serve that goal? Is the court right to distinguish between restrictions on associations with individuals with whom the defendant had a criminal history and the restriction on living with anyone unrelated? Which is more burdensome? Which contributes more effectively to social protection? Contrast the Fifth Circuit's view with the Ninth Circuit's acceptance in United States v. Watson, 582 F.3d 974 (9th Cir. 2009), of a condition of supervised release that prohibited the defendant from entering San Francisco without approval of a probation officer. The court said the restriction gave it "some pause" but accepted it on the view that "the district court was persuaded that the only way to prevent Watson from returning to a life of further misconduct was to force him to make a new life somewhere else." Id. at 983.

4. Sex offenders. Sex offenders face many sanctions beyond their terms of incarceration. In addition to imposing residency restrictions (such as restricting offenders from living within a certain distance from schools), state and federal laws create registries containing information about convicted sex offenders for use by law enforcement and to notify the public of the identities and addresses of sex offenders. The idea behind these notification and registration requirements is that they will assist law enforcement and the public by enabling them to monitor offenders and by deterring future violations. A recent study finds that while the frequency of sex offenses decreases with registration requirements, that effect is due to a reduction in reported attacks by offenders who are known to their victims; the frequency of sex offenses committed by strangers appears to be unaffected by registration. The study also finds a reduction in the frequency of sex offenses with notification laws when registries are small, but the benefits dissipate as registries grow larger and more offenders are included within them. J.J. Prescott & Jonah E. Rockoff, Do Sex Offender Notification and Registration Laws Affect Criminal Behavior?, 54 J.L. & Econ. 161, 164-165 (2011).

Questions: What do these results suggest about how notification and registration laws should be formulated? Which offenders should be covered by the requirements? (Note that the term "sex offender" can include a variety of offenders, from child molesters to individuals who urinate in public to teenagers who engage in sexting.) Are such laws bound to afford at least *some* social protection benefits, or could they conceivably *aggravate* dangers of recidivism? (Reconsider Professor Massaro's and Professor Gilligan's concerns about shaming penalties, page 138 supra.)

Even if these laws contribute to the overall reduction of offenses, are there other reasons to doubt whether their benefits outweigh their costs? What are some of the costs to having these requirements? Recent legislation bans sex offenders from using social networking sites. Are these bans likely to serve the goals of punishment? Which ones? See Jasmine S. Wytnon (Note), Myspace, Yourspace, but Not Theirspace: The Constitutionality of Banning Sex Offenders from Social Networking Sites, 60 Duke L.J. 1859 (2011).

E. WHAT TO PUNISH?

INTRODUCTORY NOTE

Criminal punishment may be inappropriate mainly for two different reasons. The first applies when a free society should treat certain conduct as a matter of personal choice rather than seeking to prohibit it. The second applies when society has a legitimate interest in discouraging the conduct, but using the tools of the criminal law for that purpose produces more harm than good. Section E.1 below addresses the first issue, and Section E.2 deals with the second.

1. *The Domain of Personal Choice*

NOTE ON THE HARM PRINCIPLE

In the field of constitutional law, a large body of doctrine deals with identifying conduct that is protected against government interference. Religious worship and political speech are two obvious examples. The constitutional right to privacy has invalidated many prohibitions that were long embedded in Anglo-American criminal law, such as the laws criminalizing abortion (struck down in Roe v. Wade, 410 U.S. 113 (1973)) and sexual activity between same-sex consenting adults (struck down in Lawrence v. Texas, 539 U.S. 558 (2003)). Within the wide domain of conduct that government has constitutional power to regulate, however, there was at one time intense debate about whether the criminal law *should* be used to punish conduct simply on the ground that society considered it "immoral." Defending criminal laws of that sort, a British judge once wrote:[34]

> What makes a society of any sort is community of ideas, not only political ideas but also ideas about the way its members should behave and govern their lives; these latter ideas are its morals. [W]ithout shared ideas on politics, morals, and ethics no society can exist [f]or society is not something that is kept together physically; it is held by the invisible bonds of common thought. If the bonds were too far relaxed the members would drift apart. . . . Societies disintegrate from within more frequently than they are broken up by external pressures. There is disintegration when no common morality is observed . . . , so that society is justified in taking the same steps to preserve its moral code as it does to preserve its government and other essential institutions.

This view is now considered rather old-fashioned.[35] In Britain, it was largely rejected in a 1957 government report concluding that "legislation which covers acts [committed between consenting adults in private] goes beyond the proper sphere of the law's concern."[36] Instead, the prevailing principle is the one articulated by John Stuart Mill:[37]

> [T]he sole end for which mankind are warranted, individually or collectively, in interfering with the liberty of action of any of their number, is self-protection. [T]he only purpose for which power can be rightfully exercised over any member of a civilized community, against his will, is to prevent harm to others. His own good, either physical or moral, is not a sufficient warrant.

As a guide to criminalization policy, Mill's approach—the harm principle—is widely accepted today. But it has turned out to have little practical bite. As Professor Bernard Harcourt explains (The Collapse of the Harm Principle, 90 J. Crim. L. & Criminology 109, 192-193 (1999)):

> During the past two decades, the proponents of regulation and prohibition of a wide range of human activities—activities that have traditionally been associated with moral offense—have turned to the harm argument. Catharine MacKinnon has focused on the multiple harms to women and women's sexuality caused by pornography. The broken windows theory of crime prevention has emphasized how minor crimes, like prostitution and loitering, cause major crimes, neighborhood decline, and urban decay. . . . The debate on drugs has focused on the harms caused by drug use and the harms caused by the war on drugs. . . .
>
> This shift has significantly changed the structure of the debate over the legal enforcement of morality. [In the nineteenth century,] moralists could

---

34. Patrick Devlin, The Enforcement of Morals (1965).

35. A qualified recent defense of this view appears in Jeffrie G. Murphy, Legal Moralism and Retributivism Revisited, 1 Crim. L. & Phil. 5 (2007).

36. Home Office U.K., Report of the Committee on Homosexual Offences and Prostitution (Wolfenden Report) (1957).

37. John Stuart Mill, On Liberty, in Utilitarianism, Liberty and Representative Government 95-96 (Everyman's Library Edition, 1950).

argue that the immorality of the offense was sufficient to enforce a prohibition, and the proponents of the harm principle could argue that the lack of harm precluded legal enforcement. . . . Today the debate is characterized by a cacophony of competing harm arguments without any way to resolve them. . . . The original harm principle was never equipped to determine the relative importance of harms. . . .

The collapse of the harm principle . . . may help us realize that there is probably harm in most human activities and, in most cases, on both sides of the equation—on the side of the persons harmed by the purported moral offense, but also on the side of the actor whose conduct is restricted by the legal enforcement of morality.

For the reasons Professor Harcourt identifies, the challenge in criminal justice policy today is to assess the actual extent of such alleged harms, the effects in practice of attempting to use criminal sanctions to prevent them, and the potential advantages of resorting to other methods of social control. Those issues are the focus of the next section.

2. *The Optimal Tools for Regulating Harmful Conduct*

INTRODUCTORY NOTE

In a wide range of situations, use of the criminal sanction to deter misconduct may produce more harm than good. It does not follow, however, that the conduct must be left unregulated; society may attempt to discourage it in other ways. Governments can tax it or provide for civil liability. They may try to govern it through licenses or administrative rules and regulations. And finally, they may leave it to be dealt with by informal social pressure.

The following material considers the implications of choosing criminal law as the preferred means of social control. It does so by focusing on two suggestive problems: voluntary transactions that cause social harm indirectly (so-called "victimless" crimes), and aggressive conduct aimed primarily at causing emotional harm ("bullying").

PROBLEM—INDIRECT HARM AND "VICTIMLESS" CRIME

An important part of the criminal law is addressed to the behavior of adults who willingly participate in transactions that society wishes to discourage. Non-coercive prostitution is a classic example, as is the purchase of drugs for personal use. It is common to refer to such offenses as "victimless" crimes, but this terminology begs a crucial question, because in the eyes of those who support these prohibitions, the conduct is anything but victimless. Prostitution can spread AIDS and venereal disease, and can encourage the exploitation and abuse of vulnerable young men and women. Drug use allegedly makes some users more violent or draws them into predatory crime to support their habit. The extent of these indirect harms is debatable, but crimes of this sort have one characteristic that is distinctive and incontrovertible: Unlike murder, robbery, or rape, they center on a *consensual* transaction. And this feature turns out to have pervasive implications for criminal law enforcement. Consider Sanford H. Kadish, The Crisis of Overcriminalization, 394 Annals Am. Acad. Pol. & Soc. Sci. 157 (Nov. 1967):

> Prostitution has perdured in all civilizations; indeed, few institutions have proven as hardy. The inevitable conditions of social life unfailingly produce the supply to meet the ever-present demand. . . . The costs [of criminal prohibition], on the other hand, [include] diversion of police resources; encouragement of use of illegal means of police control (. . . harassment arrests to remove suspected prostitutes from the streets; and various entrapment devices, usually the only means of obtaining convictions); degradation of the image of law enforcement; discriminatory enforcement against the poor; and official corruption.
>
> To the extent that spread of venereal disease, corruption of the young, and public affront are the objects of prostitution controls, [there are many] modes of social control short of [criminalization] which would at the same time prove more effective and less costly. . . .
>
> Laws against . . . narcotics present serious problems for law enforcement. Despite arrests, prosecutions and convictions, and increasingly severe penalties, the conduct seems only to flourish. The irrepressible demand for . . . drugs, like the demand for alcohol during Prohibition days, survives the condemnation of the criminal law. . . . Nor have the laws and enforcement efforts suppressed sources of supply. . . . [I]llicit suppliers enter the market to seek the profits made available by . . . the criminal law's reduction of legitimate sources of supply, while "pusher"-addicts distribute narcotics as a means of fulfilling their own needs. Risk of conviction, even of long terms of imprisonment, appears to have little effect. Partly, this is because the immediate and compelling need of the "pusher"-addict for narcotics precludes any real attention to the distant prospect of conviction and imprisonment. For large-scale suppliers, who may not be addicts, the very process of criminalization and punishment serves to raise the stakes—while the risk becomes greater, so do the prospects of reward. . . .
>
> Our indiscriminate policy of using the criminal law against selling what people insist on buying has spawned large-scale, organized systems, often of national scope, [for] distribution of the illicit product on a continuous and thoroughly businesslike basis. Not only are these organizations especially difficult for law enforcement to deal with; they have the unpleasant quality of producing other crimes as well. . . . To enhance their effectiveness, these organized systems engage in satellite forms of crime, of which bribery and corruption of local government are the most far-reaching in their consequences. Hence the irony that, in some measure, crime is encouraged and successful modes of criminality are produced by the criminal law itself. . . .

Questions: Given the collateral costs and counterproductive side effects inherent in attempting to punish individuals who sell what others want to buy, would it make sense for the criminal law to withdraw entirely from this domain, leaving to other processes the task of discouraging voluntary transactions between consenting adults? Virtually no one advocates such a broad position, because criminal prosecution remains an essential tool for deterring many voluntary transactions that are unambiguously harmful (bribery, for example).

Controversy centers on particular criminal prohibitions for which the harms to be prevented are more speculative and for which alternative tools of social policy are available. Thus, in the case of alcohol and tobacco, heavy taxation—not criminal prohibition—is the means now used to discourage consumption. Similarly with respect to prostitution and narcotics, alternative methods of social control are potentially available, including taxation, regulation, and public health initiatives. Assessing whether in practice such alternatives actually will reduce the relevant harms, without unwanted side effects, is of course an enormous challenge, but it is an ever-present policy concern—and not just for "victimless" crime but throughout the criminal law. Consider which of the specific harms allegedly associated with prostitution or narcotics could potentially be addressed by specific alternatives to the criminal process. Can we be optimistic about their likely effectiveness? And, if so, what would be the *symbolic* effects of "decriminalizing" or "legalizing" transactions in these areas? How much should the symbolic "message" of the criminal law play a role in determining whether decriminalization should be the preferred policy?

PROBLEM—EMOTIONAL HARM AND "BULLYING"

The impact of bullying on the emotional well-being of school children and others has recently become a matter of heightened public concern. One reason may involve changing social sensitivity to emotional harm, but intensified concern also reflects the proliferation of social media, the ease and relative costlessness of electronic communication, and the potential for almost limitless dissemination of embarrassing or hurtful material online. In 2010, Tyler Clementi, a New Jersey college freshman, committed suicide after his roommate secretly recorded him having sex with another man in their dorm room and then live-streamed the video on the Internet.[38] Other suicides and emotional breakdowns have been attributed to online harassment, manipulation, or invasion of privacy. Many of these episodes have led to criminal prosecution, and nearly every state has enacted new "anti-bullying" legislation.

Most of the new laws are predominantly non-criminal in nature; they focus on mandating local schools to adopt bullying-awareness training for students and staff, as well as programs to facilitate the reporting of bullying incidents and prompt responses to them. As such, they illustrate the potential to address seriously harmful behavior through means other than the criminal process. Nonetheless, some of the new laws have a punitive dimension; New Jersey's

---

38. Lisa W. Foderaro, Private Moment Made Public, Then a Fatal Jump, N.Y. Times, Sept. 29, 2010.

law, for example, permits suspension or expulsion of students who engage in any sort of bullying, including even minor forms of teasing.[39]

Prosecutions for bullying have relied on a variety of existing criminal statutes. In the Tyler Clementi case, a New Jersey prosecutor used that state's bias-intimidation and invasion-of-privacy laws to file charges carrying two potential five-year prison terms.[40] In Missouri, a suicide apparently prompted by manipulative use of a fictitious MySpace account led to a federal prosecution for computer fraud.[41] A recent Massachusetts case, prompted by the suicide of South Hadley teenager Phoebe Prince, offers an even more vivid illustration of this criminalization strategy, because the prosecution was based almost entirely on teasing and emotional harassment, without the invasion-of-privacy or computer-fraud arguments that were available in other such prosecutions.

Phoebe Prince moved to South Hadley from Ireland in the Fall of 2009.[42] Before moving, she had been emotionally troubled and on several occasions had mutilated herself. She was an attractive teenager, popular with boys, and as a result she became the target of persistent teasing by a group of jealous girls. She also got into conflict with several girls as a result of her flirtations (or relationships) with their boyfriends. Accounts differ as to precisely who said what, and why, but there is general agreement that taunts like "whore," "stupid slut," and "Irish bitch" were repeatedly directed to her by several girls and by at least one boy she had dated; one student referred to her on a Facebook page as an "Irish slut." (The town has a large Irish-American population and many of the students allegedly responsible for these insults were themselves of Irish descent.) Reacting to the stress, Phoebe resumed cutting herself, had crying spells, and confided to friends that she was desperate. Soon thereafter, she hung herself in the stairwell outside her bedroom.

Five South Hadley students eventually pleaded guilty in adult or juvenile court to criminal charges involving either harassment or civil rights violations. They were expelled from school, and each was sentenced to a year of probation and 100 hours of community service.

One result of the tragedy was new Massachusetts legislation that strengthens both criminal and non-criminal efforts to address the problem. Mass. Session Laws, 2010, ch. 92. On the non-criminal side, the law defines "bullying" to include "written, verbal or electronic expression . . . that . . . causes physical or emotional harm to the victim . . . [or] creates a hostile environment

---

39. N.J. P.L. 2010, Ch. 122 (2010); see also Winnie Hu, Bullying Law Puts New Jersey Schools on Spot, N.Y. Times, Aug. 30, 2011.

40. The defendant declined an offer to plead guilty, and at trial, he was convicted on all charges. Kate Zernike, Jury Finds spying in Rutgers Dorm was a Hate Crime, N.Y. Times, March 16, 2012.

41. See United States v. Drew, 259 F.R.D. 449 (C.D. Cal. 2009) (overturning jury conviction on one misdemeanor count).

42. The facts in this and the following paragraph are drawn from Stacy Teicher Khadaroo, Phoebe Prince Bullies Sentenced, But How Do They Make Things Right?, Christian Sci. Monitor, May 5, 2011; Emily Bazelon, What Really Happened to Phoebe Prince?, Slate, July 20, 2010.

at school for the victim." Id. §5. It requires schools to prohibit bullying and provide clear procedures for reporting, investigating, and responding to it.

On the criminal side, the Massachusetts law significantly expands the prohibitions addressed to such behavior. Harassment statutes typically impose only light penalties and in any event include limiting requirements designed to shelter ordinary verbal conflict and legitimate communication from even mild penal sanctions. Under the MPC, for example, the offense of harassment—a petty misdemeanor—is limited to taunts "likely to provoke a violent or disorderly response," repeated communications in "offensively coarse language," or "alarming conduct serving no legitimate purpose of the actor." See MPC §250.4, Appendix. In contrast, under the new Massachusetts statute, harassment is punishable by imprisonment for up to two and a half years, and it is committed whenever someone "willfully and maliciously engages in a knowing pattern of conduct . . . which seriously alarms [a specific] person and would cause a reasonable person to suffer substantial emotional distress." Mass. Session Laws, supra, §10.

Questions: Are penal sanctions an appropriate way to address the problem of bullying? Are they overly severe in relation to the culpability of the offenders? Are non-criminal tools better suited to addressing this problem, or will they fail to convey how serious and morally unacceptable such behavior is?

There is little doubt that bullying can lead to tragic consequences. And electronic media magnify enormously the reach and permanence of insults that at one time would have been heard by only one or two people and then quickly forgotten. Of course, few of these defendants, if any, likely considered that their taunts could lead to suicide. Does that fact suggest an absence of criminal culpability? Or does it suggest even greater need to heighten awareness of the consequences of such behavior?

At her sentencing, one of Phoebe Prince's classmates said, "I am immensely ashamed of myself that I allowed my emotions to spiral into acts of unkindness."[43] Should verbal cruelty of that sort be considered a crime? Some school officials worry that the prospect of stringent sanctions for those found guilty of bullying may even deter some bullying victims from reporting their situation. From another direction, one school administrator "cautioned that an unintended consequence of the new law could be that students, or their parents, will find it easier to label minor squabbles bullying than to find ways to work out their differences. 'Kids have to learn to deal with conflict,' she said. 'What a shame if they don't know how to effectively interact with their peers when they have a disagreement.'"[44]

All things considered, does the problem of bullying warrant a criminal law response?

---

43. Quoted in Khadaroo, Phoebe Prince Bullies Sentenced, supra note 42.
44. Hu, supra note 39.

chapter 3

Defining Criminal Conduct— The Elements of Just Punishment

A. INTRODUCTION

Three foundational principles limit the imposition of punishment: legality, culpability, and proportionality. Each of these principles has a long history of recognition in common-law precedents and in state penal codes based on them. This chapter explores that common-law tradition in depth.

More recently, American criminal law has been shaped by the Model Penal Code (MPC)—a project of the American Law Institute, which is a private nonprofit association of prominent lawyers, judges, and academics. Proposals for this "model" code, drafted over a ten-year period by a large group of criminal law scholars and practitioners, culminated in a "Proposed Official Draft," which the Institute endorsed in 1962. The MPC is not, in itself, "law," and it is not legally binding anywhere. But since 1962, American courts have turned increasingly to the MPC as a basic source for the doctrines and principles that govern the imposition of criminal liability, and more than half of the states have enacted modern criminal codes that draw heavily on the MPC. The Appendix to this book reprints the principal provisions of the MPC in their entirety and, as an introduction to them, provides an overview of the origins and evolution of the MPC. See page 1191 infra.

Like the common-law tradition, the MPC gives central importance to the principles of legality, culpability, and proportionality. Its statement of guiding purposes (§1.02(1)) emphasizes that its provisions aim "to give fair warning of the nature of the conduct declared to constitute an offense" (legality), "to safeguard conduct that is without fault from condemnation as criminal" (culpability), and "to differentiate on reasonable grounds between serious and minor offenses" (proportionality). The Code expands upon the common law by implementing these principles systematically and in detail. Accordingly, along with our close examination of the common-law approach, this chapter focuses on the relevant provisions of the MPC as well.

In examining the material in this chapter, consider to what extent the system of justice in the United States is in fact faithful to the three principles identified here. And when departures from them occur, are the departures justified?

B. LEGALITY

COMMONWEALTH v. MOCHAN

Superior Court of Pennsylvania
177 Pa. Super. 454, 110 A.2d 788 (1955)

HIRT, J. [Two indictments charged that the defendant "intending the morals and manners of the good citizens of this Commonwealth ... to debauch and corrupt, and further devising and intending to harass, embarrass and vilify ... one Louise Zivkovich ... unlawfully, wickedly and maliciously did ... make numerous telephone calls to the dwelling house of the said Louise Zivkovich at all times of the day and night, in which said telephone calls and conversations resulting therefrom the said Michael Mochan did wickedly and maliciously refer to the said Louise Zivkovich as a lewd, immoral and lascivious woman of an indecent and lewd character, and other scurrilous opprobrious, filthy, disgusting and indecent language ... to the great damage, injury and oppression of the said Louise Zivkovich and other good citizens of this Commonwealth ... , and against the peace and dignity of the Commonwealth of Pennsylvania." ... Defendant was tried and convicted before a judge without a jury. He appealed on the ground that the conduct charged in the indictments, concededly not a criminal offense under any Pennsylvania statute, did not constitute a misdemeanor at common law.]

In a number of States and especially in the common law State of Pennsylvania the common law of England, as to crimes, is in force except in so far as it has been abrogated by statute. The indictments ... by their language, clearly purported to charge a common law crime not included in our Penal Code or elsewhere in our statutory law....

It is of little importance that there is no precedent in our reports which decides the precise question here involved. The test is not whether precedents can be found in the books but whether the alleged crimes could have been prosecuted and the offenders punished under the common law. In Commonwealth v. Miller, 94 Pa. Super. 499, 507, the controlling principles are thus stated: "The common law is sufficiently broad to punish as a misdemeanor, although there may be no exact precedent, any act which directly injures or tends to injure the public to such an extent as to require the state to interfere and punish the wrongdoer, as in the case of acts which injuriously affect public morality, or obstruct, or pervert public justice, or the administration of government." Cf. Com. of Penna. v. DeGrange, 97 Pa. Super. 181, in which it is said: "Whatever openly outrages decency and is injurious to public morals is a misdemeanor at common law." Any act is indictable at common law which from its nature scandalously affects the morals or health of the community....

To endeavor merely to persuade a married woman to commit adultery is not indictable. Smith v. Commonwealth, 54 Pa. 209. The present defendant's criminal intent was evidenced by a number of overt acts beyond the mere oral solicitation of adultery. The vile and disgusting suggestions of sodomy alone and the otherwise persistent lewd, immoral and filthy language used by the defendant, take these cases out of the principle of the *Smith* case. Moreover potentially at least, defendant's acts injuriously affected public morality. The operator or anyone on defendant's four-party telephone line could have listened in on the conversations, and at least two other persons in Mrs. Zivkovich's household heard some of defendant's immoral and obscene language over the telephone.

[The] charges in the body of the indictments identify the offense as a common law misdemeanor and the testimony established the guilt of the defendant.

Judgments and sentences affirmed.

WOODSIDE, J. [dissenting]: Not unmindful of the reprehensible conduct of the appellant, I nevertheless cannot agree with the majority that what he did was a crime punishable under the laws of this Commonwealth.

The majority is declaring something to be a crime which was never before known to be a crime in this Commonwealth. They have done this by the application of such general principles as "it is a crime to do anything which injures or tends to injure the public to such an extent as to require the state to interfere and punish the wrongdoer"; and "whatever openly outrages decency and is injurious to public morals is a misdemeanor." . . . Under the division of powers in our constitution it is for the legislature to determine what "injures or tends to injure the public."

One of the most important functions of a legislature is to determine what acts "require the state to interfere and punish the wrongdoer." There is no reason for the legislature to enact any criminal laws if the courts delegate to themselves the power to apply such general principles as are here applied to whatever conduct may seem to the courts to be injurious to the public.

There is no doubt that the common law is a part of the law of this Commonwealth, and we punish many acts under the common law. But after nearly two hundred years of constitutional government in which the legislature and not the courts have been charged by the people with the responsibility of deciding which acts do and which do not injure the public to the extent which requires punishment, it seems to me we are making an unwarranted invasion of the legislative field when we arrogate that responsibility to ourselves by declaring now, for the first time, that certain acts are a crime.

When the legislature invades either the judicial or the executive fields, or the executive invades either the judicial or legislative fields, the courts stand ready to stop them. But in matters of this type there is nothing to prevent our invasion of the legislative field except our own self restraint. . . . Until the legislature says that what the defendant did is a crime, I think the courts should not declare it to be such.

I would therefore reverse the lower court and discharge the appellant.

NOTES

1. The legality principle. One of the most ancient and widely repeated doctrines of the criminal law is the legality principle, often stated as *nulla poena sine lege*—no punishment without law. Does the conviction in *Mochan* violate the *nulla poena* requirement? Or is that requirement satisfied by the preexisting Pennsylvania doctrine making it a misdemeanor to commit "any act which directly injures or tends to injure the public to such an extent as to require the state to interfere and punish the wrongdoer"?

In thinking about these questions, consider what values the *nulla poena* requirement might serve. Perhaps most obvious is the need to give individuals *fair warning* as to the conduct that could subject them to prosecution. Another is the need to *control discretion* of police, prosecutors, and juries. Reflecting these concerns, the legality principle bars both *retroactivity* and *vagueness*: The *nulla poena* principle requires previously established law and that law must be announced in reasonably clear terms, so that the average person does not have to guess its meaning. The bans on retroactivity and vagueness now have constitutional status, at least under some circumstances. The constitutional issues are explored below, retroactivity in connection with *Keeler v. Superior Court*, page 163 infra, and vagueness in connection with *City of Chicago v. Morales*, page 171 infra.

Is it wise to deny courts a role in fashioning new criminal offenses retroactively? Don't the requirements of prospectivity and clarity give devious criminals an opportunity to engage in "loop-holing," finding clever ways to cheat and injure others in ways not specifically prohibited? Or is loop-holing a price we must pay for affording fair notice and controlling discretion? An unusual British decision similar to *Mochan* upheld a conviction for a new common-law offense (in this instance, "conspiracy to corrupt public morals") on the basis of conduct involving publication of a directory of prostitutes and their services (Shaw v. Director of Public Prosecutions, [1962] A.C. 220 (House of Lords)). Viscount Simonds stated:

> [T]here remains in the courts of law a residual power to enforce the supreme and fundamental purpose of the law, to conserve not only the safety and order but also the moral welfare of the State, and . . . it is their duty to guard it against attacks which may be the more insidious because they are novel and unprepared for. [G]aps [in statutory law] will always remain since no one can foresee every way in which the wickedness of man may disrupt the order of society. [I]f the common law is powerless in such an event, then we should no longer do her reverence.

2. Beyond retroactivity and vagueness: Should courts make law? Suppose that the Pennsylvania court had reversed Mochan's conviction for lack of fair warning but had held that in the future, anyone making obscene phone calls with intent to harrass or embarrass the recipient would be guilty of a misdemeanor. Suppose that the court, concerned about possible vagueness, had given specific examples of the kind of language that would be considered "obscene." If Mochan then continued to engage in similar conduct after the court's decision and if he were convicted for his subsequent behavior, would that conviction still be troublesome? Does the legality principle reflect important separation-of-powers values in addition to those protected by requiring prospectivity and clarity? Reconsider Judge Woodside's dissent.

3. *Old common-law crimes.* For centuries, the English Parliament met infrequently and legislated only sporadically. The criminal law, like the rest of the law, was left to the courts, and it developed slowly, case by case, in what we call the common-law method. As a result, crimes like murder, manslaughter, larceny, and many others were defined by the judges, with essentially no guidance from Parliament. By the time of the American Revolution, the definitions of these offenses had been largely settled through this common-law process.

After Independence, most of the new American states continued to apply the common law of England, except to the extent that it was specifically repealed by new statutes. Thus, judge-made crimes like murder, manslaughter, and larceny, often called "common law crimes," remained in force throughout the United States. As more penal laws were enacted, some states made their new legislation exclusive and abrogated all common-law crimes not recognized in new statutes. Others—like Pennsylvania at the time of *Mochan*—took the position that the common law of England remained applicable in the absence of contrary state legislation. See Note, Common Law Crimes in the United States, 47 Colum. L. Rev. 1332 (1947).

The initial round of state criminal enactments, during the nineteenth and early twentieth centuries, typically codified the common-law definitions, or sometimes simply incorporated them by implication, for example, by enacting a homicide statute that gave no definition of murder and stated merely that "all murder is punishable by death." Thus, many offenses against persons and property retained their traditional, judge-made definitions and continued to be referred to as "common law crimes," even after they acquired a hook in contemporary statutes.

Starting in the 1960s, statutes adopting the common-law definitions were replaced in most states by modern codifications inspired by the Model Penal Code. But penal codes that reflect the older pattern can still be found in perhaps as many as a third of the states. In these states, "common law crimes" of the older sort remain in force; their definitions, though initially judge-made, have long since solidified and won legislative approval. These older common-law crimes, despite their name, pose none of the problems presented in a case like *Mochan*, where judges define and punish an offense not previously recognized by statute or precedent.

4. *New common-law crimes.* Contrary to the decision in *Mochan*, nearly all American jurisdictions—including Pennsylvania—have now abolished the common-law doctrine that courts can create new crimes. See, e.g., 18 Pa. Cons. Stat. Ann. §107(b) (2011). The doctrine still survives in a few states, however. See, e.g., Fla. Stat. Ann. §775.01 (2011) ("The common law of England in relation to crimes, except so far as the same relates to the modes and degrees of

punishment, shall be of full force in this state where there is no existing provision by statute on the subject."); Mich. Const. art. III, §7 (2011); Mich. Comp. Laws Ann. 750.505 (2011); N.M. Stat. Ann. §30-1-3 (2011).

The Supreme Court has never held it unconstitutional for state judges to create new common-law crimes. To the contrary, the Court recently confirmed that judicial crime-creation is constitutionally permissible under some circumstances, as we will discuss in connection with *Rogers v. Tennessee*, page 168 infra. Nonetheless, as a matter of general criminal law principles (as distinct from the narrower requirements of constitutional law), the Court led the opposition to common-law crimes, with an early decision rejecting the authority of federal judges to create new crimes for matters prosecuted in federal courts. United States v. Hudson & Goodwin, 11 U.S. (7 Cranch) 32 (1812). Soon thereafter, in United States v. Wiltberger, 18 U.S. (5 Wheat.) 76, 95 (1820), Chief Justice John Marshall elaborated, emphasizing the "plain principle, that the power of punishment is vested in the legislative, not in the judicial department. It is the legislature, not the court, which is to define a crime, and ordain a punishment." See also United States v. Bass, 404 U.S. 336, 349 (1971): "Because of the seriousness of criminal penalties, and because criminal punishment usually represents the moral condemnation of the community, legislatures and not courts should define criminal activity."

5. *The meaning of legislation.* Because, under the prevailing view, crimes must be defined by statute, the reach of the criminal law is determined solely by statutory language. But it is left to the courts to determine what the statutory language means. How should judges go about this task? Should they approach it differently in criminal than in civil cases? How can judges make sure the crime is really defined by the legislature, not by the court? Consider these questions as you read the cases that follow.

McBOYLE v. UNITED STATES

Supreme Court of the United States
283 U.S. 25 (1931)

Mr. Justice Holmes delivered the opinion of the Court.

The petitioner was convicted of transporting from Ottawa, Illinois, to Guymon, Oklahoma, an airplane that he knew to have been stolen, and was sentenced to serve three years' imprisonment and to pay a fine of $2,000. The judgment was affirmed. . . . A writ of certiorari was granted by this Court on the question whether the National Motor Vehicle Theft Act applies to aircraft. That Act provides: "Sec. 2. That when used in this Act: (a) The term 'motor vehicle' shall include an automobile, automobile truck, automobile wagon, motor cycle, or any other self-propelled vehicle not designed for running on rails; . . . Sec. 3. That whoever shall transport or cause to be transported in interstate or foreign commerce a motor vehicle, knowing the same to have been stolen, shall be punished by a fine of not more than $5,000, or by imprisonment of not more than five years, or both."

... The question is the meaning of the word "vehicle" in the phrase "any other self-propelled vehicle not designed for running on rails." No doubt etymologically it is possible to use the word to signify a conveyance working on land, water or air, and sometimes legislation extends the use in that direction. ... But in everyday speech "vehicle" calls up the picture of a thing moving on land. ... So here, the phrase under discussion calls up the popular picture. For after including automobile truck, automobile wagon and motor cycle, the words "any other self-propelled vehicle not designed for running on rails" still indicate that a vehicle in the popular sense, that is a vehicle running on land, is the theme. It is a vehicle that runs, not something, not commonly called a vehicle, that flies. Airplanes were well-known in 1919, when this statute was passed; but it is admitted that they were not mentioned in the reports or in the debates in Congress. It is impossible to read words that so carefully enumerate the different forms of motor vehicles and have no reference of any kind to aircraft, as including airplanes under a term that usage more and more precisely confines to a different class. ...

Although it is not likely that a criminal will carefully consider the text of the law before he murders or steals, it is reasonable that a fair warning should be given to the world in language that the common world will understand, of what the law intends to do if a certain line is passed. To make the warning fair, so far as possible the line should be clear. When a rule of conduct is laid down in words that evoke in the common mind only the picture of vehicles moving on land, the statute should not be extended to aircraft, simply because it may seem to us that a similar policy applies, or upon the speculation that, if the legislature had thought of it, very likely broader words would have been used.

Judgment reversed.

UNITED STATES v. DAURAY

United States Court of Appeals, 2d Circuit
215 F.3d 257 (2000)

JACOBS, J.: Defendant-appellant Charles Dauray was arrested in possession of pictures (or photocopies of pictures) cut from one or more magazines. He was convicted following a jury trial ... of violating 18 U.S.C. §2252(a)(4)(B), which punishes the possession of (inter alia) "matter," three or more in number, "which contain any visual depiction" of minors engaging in sexually explicit conduct ... .

On May 13, 1994, an officer of the Connecticut Department of Environmental Protection approached Dauray's car in a state park and found Dauray in possession of thirteen unbound pictures of minors. The pictures were pieces of magazine pages and photocopies of those pages. [A] federal grand jury returned a one-count indictment, charging Dauray with possessing child pornography in violation of 18 U.S.C. §2252(a)(4)(B). The version of the statute then in force punished the possession of "3 or more books, magazines, periodicals, films, video tapes, or other matter" that have passed in interstate or foreign commerce and "which contain any visual depiction" [of] a minor engaged in sexually explicit conduct.

Dauray and the government stipulated at trial [that] "Dauray was aware of the contents of these visual depictions and thus he knew that genitalia of minors appear in each of them." . . . The jury found Dauray guilty. . . . The district court then considered Dauray's pretrial motion, on which the court had earlier reserved decision, to dismiss the indictment. . . . Dauray argued that each [picture] was in itself a "visual depiction" and therefore could not be "other matter which contain any visual depiction." Therefore, he reasoned, the indictment failed to charge an offense. The district court concluded that the pictures Dauray possessed were "other matter" within the plain meaning of §2252(a)(4)(B), and for the same reason denied Dauray's request to apply the rule of lenity. Dauray was sentenced [to 36 months of imprisonment]. . . .

The question presented on appeal is whether individual pictures are "other matter which contain any visual depiction" within the meaning of §2252(a)(4)(B). [W]e conclude that [the statute] can be read either to support or to defeat this indictment. We therefore apply the rule of lenity to resolve the ambiguity in Dauray's favor.

I

A. PLAIN MEANING

Our starting point in statutory interpretation is the statute's plain meaning, if it has one. Congress provided no definition of the terms "other matter" or "contain." We therefore consider the ordinary, common-sense meaning of the words. Among the several dictionary definitions of the verb "to contain," Dauray presses one, and the government emphasizes another.

(i) "To contain" means "to have within: hold." Webster's Third New International Dictionary 491 (unabridged ed. 1981). Dauray argues that a picture is not a thing that contains itself. Thus in the natural meaning of the word, a pictorial magazine "contains" pictures, but it is at best redundant to say that a picture "contains" a picture.

(ii) "To contain" also means "to consist of wholly or in part: comprise; include," and the government argues that each underlying piece of paper is "matter" (as opposed perhaps to anti-matter) that contains the picture printed on it. It is also possible, applying this latter meaning, to say that each picture, composed of paper and ink, is matter that contains its imagery.

. . . The plain meaning of another critical term—"other matter"—is also elusive. [A] pictorial magazine is "matter" that "contains" visual images. But no court that has construed §2252(a)(4)(B) has considered whether a loose photograph clipped from such a magazine is itself "matter" that "contains" a visual image. The First Circuit recently held that a single negative film strip containing three images constituted only one piece of "matter" under §2252(a)(4)(B). The court noted that "had Congress meant for the number of images to be the relevant criterion, it would have likely stated as much." The case concerned the character of singular "matter" containing multiple images, not whether each image—if loosed from the container—could itself constitute prohibited "matter."

Every other case that construes the term "other matter" has involved whether an individual computer graphics file is a "matter." Compare [United States v. Vig, 167 F.3d 443 (8th Cir. 1999)] (holding that individual files are "other matter") . . . with [United States v. Lacy, 119 F.3d 742 (9th Cir. 1997)] (holding that computer files are not "other matter," but a hard drive and a floppy disk are). These cases consider . . . whether the proper analog to a graphics file is a page in a book or a book in a library. These cases have no evident bearing on whether a single magazine (which it was no crime to possess at the time of Dauray's arrest, no matter how many pages and pictures it contained) can become prohibited material simply by detaching the staples that bind the pages. . . .

B. CANONS OF CONSTRUCTION

Because the government and Dauray each rely on a reasonable meaning of §2252(a)(4)(B), we resort to the canons of statutory interpretation to help resolve the ambiguity.

1. Lists and Other Associated Terms. Two related canons inform our analysis of the meaning of "other matter." First, the meaning of doubtful terms or phrases may be determined by reference to their relationship with other associated words or phrases (noscitur a sociis). Second, "where general words follow a specific enumeration of persons or things, the general words should be limited to persons or things similar to those specifically enumerated" (ejusdem generis). In this case, "other matter" should be construed to complete the class of items or things in the list preceding it, namely "books, magazines, periodicals, films, [or] video tapes."

Dauray argues that the listed items form a category of picture containers that can enclose within them multiple visual depictions. Because a picture taken from a magazine is not itself a picture container, like books or magazines, but is rather a thing abstracted from its container, Dauray contends that a picture in itself cannot be considered "other matter" within the meaning of the statute, and that possession of three of them is not prohibited.

But these canons equally support the government's argument. The list—at a sufficient level of generality, and completed by the catch-all "other matter"— can be read to include any physical medium or method capable of presenting visual depictions. A picture cut from a magazine, considered as paper and ink employed to exhibit images, can be said to contain an image or as many images as can be perceived in a picture or photograph, which depends on how one looks at it.

2. Statutory Structure. . . . The Protection of Children Against Sexual Exploitation Act contains four substantive subsections . . . : §2252(a)(I) prohibits the interstate transportation of child pornography; §2252(a)(2) prohibits the receipt or distribution of it; and §2252(a)(3) prohibits its sale or

possession with intent to sell. Only §2252(a)(4) specifies that the conduct forbidden involves "books, magazines, . . . or other matter which contain" the pornography. The others more simply forbid "any visual depiction" of child pornography, period. . . .

According to Dauray, the different drafting demonstrates that Congress knew how to prohibit the possession of individual pictures if it wanted to do so. [I]f Dauray had transported, distributed or sold the pictures he merely possessed, he would have violated the law unambiguously. But the government could argue: that the transport, distribution and sale of child pornography are most harmful to children, and were therefore prohibited regardless of the medium or number of visual depictions; that Congress did not want to cast so fine a net in the context of mere possession in order to assure that the accidental possessor of one piece of pornography avoids liability while the collector does not. . . . The difference between the language in §2252(a)(4) and the other subsections is therefore (according to this view) fully consistent with a congressional intent to punish the possession of three or more individual pictures. . . .

3. Statutory Amendment. A statute should be construed to be consistent with subsequent statutory amendments. In 1998, Congress amended the statute by replacing "3 or more" with "1 or more" of the same list of "books, magazines, . . . or other matter." At the same time, Congress established an affirmative defense for a defendant who could show that he possessed "less than three matters containing" child pornography and "promptly and in good faith . . . took reasonable steps to destroy" the pornography or report it to law enforcement officials without disseminating it to others.

According to the government, the list, with its catch-all of "other matter," is designed to reach even an individual photograph. That could have been accomplished without the list, however, by an amendment that simply prohibits possession of "1 or more visual depictions." Dauray argues with some force that the list is superfluous postamendment unless it serves to distinguish a "container" such as a magazine, from its contents, such as individual pictures cut from the magazine's pages. . . .

4. Avoiding Absurdity. A statute should be interpreted in a way that avoids absurd results. Whichever interpretation one accepts, the statute tends to produce absurd results. Dauray's reading would prohibit the possession of three books, each of which contains one image, but allow the possession of stacks of unbound photographs. Equally absurd, the government's reading would prohibit the possession of three individual photographs (unless they were mounted in a single album), but allow the possession of two thick illustrated tomes.

C. LEGISLATIVE HISTORY

When the plain language and canons of statutory interpretation fail to resolve statutory ambiguity, we will resort to legislative history. Unfortunately, "examination of [§2252's] legislative history . . . reveals no insight as to what Congress intended the precise scope of 'other matter' to be."

II

Due process requires that a criminal statute "give fair warning of the conduct that it makes a crime." Bouie v. City of Columbia, 378 U.S. 347 (1964). . . . The rule of lenity springs from this fair warning requirement. "In criminal prosecutions the rule of lenity requires that ambiguities in the statute be resolved in the defendant's favor." This expedient "ensures fair warning by so resolving ambiguity in a criminal statute as to apply it only to conduct clearly covered." United States v. Lanier, 520 U.S. 259, 266 (1997).

But "because the meaning of language is inherently contextual," the Supreme Court has "declined to deem a statute 'ambiguous' for purposes of lenity merely because it was possible to articulate a construction more narrow than that urged by the Government." Moskal v. United States, 498 U.S. 103, 108 (1990). "Instead, [the Court has] always reserved lenity for those situations in which a reasonable doubt persists about a statute's intended scope even after resort to 'the language and structure, legislative history, and motivating policies' of the statute." Id. It is a "doctrine of last resort."

Here, we have done what we can[, a]nd we are left with no more than a guess as to the proper meaning. . . .

The government did not show that the pictures at issue were taken from more than a single magazine. At the time of Dauray's arrest, the statute did not forbid possession of such a magazine. Nor did the statute give Dauray notice that removing several pictures from the magazine, and keeping them, would subject him to criminal penalties. This result is unconstitutionally surprising. Under these circumstances, we must apply the rule of lenity and resolve the ambiguity in Dauray's favor. [T]he judgment is hereby reversed.

KATZMANN, Circuit Judge, dissenting. . . . In Muscarello v. U.S., 524 U.S. 125 (1998), the Supreme Court stated that the "simple existence of some statutory ambiguity . . . is not sufficient to warrant application of that rule [of lenity], for most statutes are ambiguous to some degree." The Court continued: "To invoke the rule, we must conclude that there is a grievous ambiguity or uncertainty in the statute." I do not think that there is such a "grievous ambiguity or uncertainty" in the statute before us. . . . It makes sense, given the statute's purposes, that a photograph could be understood—quite naturally—to "contain" a visual depiction. . . .

NOTES

1. The rule of lenity. What, precisely, is the "rule of lenity"? In *Dauray,* the court defines it as a requirement that "[i]n criminal prosecutions . . . ambiguities in the statute [must] be resolved in the defendant's favor." Note the qualification that the rule applies only in *criminal* cases. Why don't we apply a similar "fair warning" requirement in civil cases that can result in severe negative consequences, such as the taking of a home or the revocation of a person's right to practice her profession?

Two distinct versions of the criminal law's lenity doctrine have developed. In one, the doctrine operates to block judicial speculation about the significance of context and legislative intent; it requires courts to adopt the narrowest plausible interpretation of a criminal statute. In the other version, the doctrine comes into play only as a "last resort," when all other tools of interpretation fail to clarify the statute's meaning. The first approach was more common in the past, and it still has prominent defenders. See, e.g., United States v. R.L.C., 503 U.S. 291, 307 (1992) (Scalia, J., concurring). The second approach is dominant in state and federal courts today. See United States v. Taylor, 640 F.3d 255, 260-261 (7th Cir. 2011) ("[W]hen there are two equally plausible interpretations. . . . '[T]he tie must go to the defendant.'"). But doesn't the second approach defeat the lenity doctrine's goal of ensuring fair warning? If a defendant could have determined a statute's meaning only by consulting legislative history and applying other complex tools of statutory interpretation, can we really say that he had fair warning?

The Model Penal Code, along with many state statutes, takes a third approach, in which lenity gets no special consideration at all. See MPC §1.02(3), Appendix.

In evaluating each of these approaches, consider how they apply in the following situations:

(a) McBoyle. What purpose was served by reversing McBoyle's conviction? Would conviction have subjected McBoyle to punishment without fair warning? Perhaps the Court was less concerned with fairness to McBoyle than with protecting the prerogatives of the legislature. But was there any reason to think that Congress did not want to punish actions like McBoyle's? Are the reasons for federal involvement weaker in the case of stolen airplanes than in the case of stolen automobiles?

(b) Dauray. What purpose was served by reversing Dauray's conviction? The court assumes that Dauray knew it was a crime to possess three items containing sexually explicit pictures of minors. (The problems posed when a defendant claims ignorance of the law's requirements are explored in the section on mistake of law, pages 303-329 infra. But Dauray apparently did not claim ignorance of the law's core prohibition.) As a result, there would have been no difficulty sustaining a conviction if Dauray had been found in possession of three magazines containing pictures like the ones he had clipped. Under these circumstances, can Dauray reasonably claim a lack of fair warning if instead he is convicted for possessing only the clippings?

Suppose that Dauray had carefully read the statute and thought he could avoid its prohibition by keeping only the sexually explicit clippings and discarding the rest of the magazines. In that event, would punishing him defeat his reasonable expectations and violate the requirement of fair warning? Or would it simply block an unjustified attempt to evade the law?

As in McBoyle, an additional concern may have been the court's desire to ensure that criminalization decisions be made by the legislature, not by the courts. Are there reasons to think that Congress did not want to punish conduct like Dauray's?

(c) "Using" a gun. A federal statute, 18 U.S.C. §924(c), imposes a five-year mandatory minimum sentence on anyone who "during and in relation to [a drug trafficking crime] uses or carries a firearm." John Angus Smith attempted to buy two ounces of cocaine, but instead of paying cash, he offered to trade the drugs for his MAC10 firearm. Prosecutors argued that the five-year penalty enhancement applied to anyone who "uses" a firearm in this fashion. The legislative history was silent on the subject. In Smith v. United States, 508 U.S. 223 (1993), the Court acknowledged that the statutory language "normally evokes an image of . . . use as a weapon." But the Court also saw "no reason why Congress would have [drawn] a fine metaphysical distinction between a gun's role in a drug offense as a weapon and its role as an item of barter; it creates a grave possibility of violence and death in either capacity." On that ground, the Court held that "use" should be interpreted to include use of a gun as a form of payment. Do you agree? Is the result consistent with *McBoyle*?

2. Legislative "intent." The technique of determining a statute's meaning by considering legislative history and other evidence of the legislature's apparent intent is now well accepted, especially for statutes outside the domain of criminal law. See, e.g., Wisconsin Public Intervenor v. Mortier, 501 U.S. 597, 610 n.4 (1991). But one justice continues to protest against this practice, even for ordinary civil legislation. Consider Antonin Scalia, A Matter of Interpretation 17-18, 22 (1997):

> [I]t is simply incompatible with democratic government, or indeed, even with fair government, to have the meaning of a law determined by what the lawgiver meant, rather than by what the lawgiver promulgated. . . . Men may intend what they will; but it is only the laws that they enact which bind us. [U]nder the guise or even the self-delusion of pursuing unexpressed legislative intents, common-law judges will in fact pursue their own objectives and desires, extending their lawmaking proclivities from the common law to the statutory field. [It is] not compatible with democratic theory that laws mean whatever they ought to mean, and that unelected judges decide what that is.

Questions: Is Justice Scalia's textual approach more constraining for judges than the approach he criticizes? Though he objects to reliance on legislative history, Justice Scalia maintains that textual meaning, when ambiguous, can be identified by resort to "canons of construction," such as those discussed in *Dauray.* But given the multiplicity of available canons of construction, do the canons leave judges just as much (or more) room for discretionary judgment as legislative history does? See William N. Eskridge, Jr., The New Textualism, 37 UCLA L. Rev. 621, 675-676 (1990). With respect to the *legitimacy* of resort to legislative history, consider Stephen Breyer, On the Uses of Legislative History in Interpreting Statutes, 65 S. Cal. L. Rev. 845, 847, 863, 874 (1992):

> [Law] is a human institution, serving basic human or societal needs. It is therefore properly subject to praise, or to criticism, in terms of certain pragmatic values, . . . such as helping to achieve justice by interpreting the

law in accordance with the "reasonable expectations" of those to whom it applies. . . . The "statute is the only law" argument misses the point. No one claims that legislative history is a statute, or even that, in any strong sense, it is "law." Rather, legislative history is helpful in trying to understand the meaning of the words that do make up the statute or the "law." [V]iewed in light of the judiciary's important objective of helping to maintain coherent, workable statutory law, the case for abandoning the use of legislative history has not yet been made.

3. Criminal law by analogy. The approach considered in connection with *Mochan*, supra page 150—that of allowing courts to create new common-law crimes—is in effect the opposite of the rule of lenity: The reach of the criminal law is not limited by the narrowest reading of criminal statutes, nor is it limited even by the meaning drawn from ordinary rules of interpretation. Instead, courts create new crimes, not within the ambit of any existing statute, to reach situations that are considered *analogous* to ones already covered. The doctrine of criminal law by analogy is often associated with totalitarian regimes, but as cases like *Mochan* and *Shaw*, page 152 supra, illustrate, it is not unknown to the common law. The doctrine's parameters are made clear in a 1935 decree adopted by the international free city of Danzig (now the Polish city of Gdansk).[1] The decree repealed a penal code provision stating that an act "is only punishable if the penalty applicable to it was already prescribed by a law in force before the commission of the act." In its place, the decree provided:

> Any person who commits an act . . . which is deserving of penalty according to the fundamental conceptions of a penal law and sound popular feeling, shall be punished. If there is no penal law directly covering an act, it shall be punished under the law of which the fundamental conception applies most nearly to the said act.

The decree was defended as a means to fill gaps in the penal law. Its effect, according to its supporters, was to ensure that "real justice will take the place of formal justice" and to replace the maxim *nulla poena sine lege* (no punishment without law) with a principle of *nulla crimen sine poena* (no crime without punishment).[2] Consider Hermann Mannheim, Criminal Justice and Social Reconstruction 208, 212-213 (1946):

> [P]unishment by analogy seems to constitute no essential characteristic of totalitarian legal systems. The Penal Code of Fascist Italy of 1930 prohibits it explicitly, whereas a democratic country like Denmark admits analogy. . . .
> [T]he unrestricted admission of analogy [would] be tolerable only in a perfectly homogeneous society where law and social morality have become identical. [But the] fate of civil liberty depends on the men who have to administer criminal justice much more than on this or any other legal formula.

---

1. See Advisory Opinion—Consistency of Certain Danzig Legislative Decrees with the Constitution of the Free City, Permanent Court of International Justice, A/B No. 65, at 41-53 (1935).
2. Id. at 46.

Compare United States v. Wiltberger, 18 U.S. 76, 96 (1820) (Marshall, C.J.):

> It would be dangerous, indeed, to carry the principle, that a case that is within the reason or mischief of a statute, is within its provisions, so far as to punish a crime not enumerated in the statute, because it is of equal atrocity, or of kindred character, with those which are enumerated.

4. For the suggestion that the federal courts, though purporting to follow the lenity doctrine, have largely abandoned it in practice, see Dan H. Kahan, Lenity and Federal Common Law Crimes, [1994] Sup. Ct. Rev. 345. Professor Kahan also argues that the abandonment of lenity is a good thing—that courts should seek to fashion sensible laws rather than leaving this task to Congress. He notes (id., at 351-352) that "[m]aking law takes time, [and] takes political consensus, which is difficult and time-consuming to generate." Further, the "same constraints that prevent Congress from enacting a detailed solution to a complex and controversial problem may also prevent Congress from adapting any such solution to changed circumstances." As a result, he argues (id., at 345), allowing Congress to delegate its criminal lawmaking responsibilities to the courts "is much more efficient and more effective than [requiring Congress] to make criminal law without judicial assistance."

KEELER v. SUPERIOR COURT

Supreme Court of California
2 Cal. 3d 619, 470 P.2d 617 (1970)

[Five months after obtaining a divorce, a man intercepted his ex-wife on a mountain road. She was in an advanced state of pregnancy by another man; fetal movements had already been observed by her and by her obstetrician. Her ex-husband said to her, "You sure are [pregnant]. I'm going to stomp it out of you." He shoved his knee into her abdomen and struck her. The fetus was delivered stillborn, its head fractured.]

MOSK, J. . . . An information was filed charging petitioner, in count I, with committing the crime of murder (Pen. Code, §187) in that he did "unlawfully kill a human being, to wit Baby Girl Vogt, with malice aforethought." . . . His motion to set aside the information for lack of probable cause (Pen. Code, §995) was denied, and he now seeks a writ of prohibition.[a] . . .

Penal Code section 187 provides: "Murder is the unlawful killing of a human being, with malice aforethought." The dispositive question is whether the fetus which petitioner is accused of killing was, on February 23, 1969, a "human being" within the meaning of the statute. If it was not, petitioner cannot be charged with its "murder". . . .

---

a. A writ of prohibition bars further proceedings, on the ground that the alleged conduct, even if proved, would not constitute the offense charged.—EDS.

Section 187 was enacted as part of the Penal Code of 1872. Inasmuch as the provision has not been amended since that date, we must determine the intent of the legislature at the time of its enactment. But section 187 was, in turn, taken verbatim from the first California statute defining murder, part of the Crimes and Punishments Act of 1850. . . . We begin, accordingly, by inquiring into the intent of the Legislature in 1850 when it first defined murder as the unlawful and malicious killing of a "human being." . . .

We conclude that . . . the Legislature of 1850 intended that term to have the settled common law meaning of a person who had been born alive, and did not intend the act of feticide—as distinguished from abortion—to be an offense under the laws of California. . . . We hold that in adopting the definition of murder in Penal Code section 187 the Legislature intended to exclude from its reach the act of killing an unborn fetus.

The People urge, however, that the sciences of obstetrics and pediatrics have greatly progressed since 1872, to the point where with proper medical care a normally developed fetus prematurely born at 28 weeks or more has an excellent chance of survival, i.e., is "viable"; that the common law requirement of live birth . . . is no longer in accord with scientific fact, since an unborn but viable fetus is now fully capable of independent life; and that one who unlawfully and maliciously terminates such a life should therefore be liable to prosecution for murder under section 187. We may grant the premises of this argument. . . . But we cannot join in the conclusion sought to be deduced. . . . To such a charge there are two insuperable obstacles, one "jurisdictional" and the other constitutional.

Penal Code section 6 declares in relevant part that "No act or omission" accomplished after the code has taken effect "is criminal or punishable, except as prescribed or authorized by this code, or by some of the statutes which it specifies as continuing in force . . . , or by some ordinance, municipal, county, or township regulation. . . ." This section embodies a fundamental principle of our tripartite form of government, i.e., that subject to the constitutional prohibition against cruel and unusual punishment, the power to define crimes and fix penalties is vested exclusively in the legislative branch. . . . Stated differently, there are no common law crimes in California. . . .

We recognize that the killing of an unborn but viable fetus may be deemed by some to be an offense of similar nature and gravity; but . . . to thus extend liability for murder in California is a determination solely within the province of the Legislature. . . .

The second obstacle to the proposed judicial enlargement of section 187 is the guarantee of due process of law. Assuming arguendo that we have the power to adopt the new construction of this statute as the law of California, such a ruling, by constitutional command, could operate only prospectively, and thus could not in any event reach the conduct of petitioner on February 23, 1969.

The first essential of due process is fair warning of the act which is made punishable as a crime. "That the terms of a penal statute creating a new offense must be sufficiently explicit to inform those who are subject to it what conduct on their part will render them liable to its penalties, is a well-recognized requirement, consonant alike with ordinary notions of fair play and the settled rules of law." (Connally v. General Constr. Co. (1926) 269 U.S. 385, 391.) . . .

This requirement of fair warning is reflected in the constitutional prohibition against the enactment of ex post facto laws (U.S. Const., art. I, §§9, 10; Cal. Const. art. I, §16). When a new penal statute is applied retrospectively to make punishable an act which was not criminal at the time it was performed, the defendant has been given no advance notice consistent with due process. And precisely the same effect occurs when such an act is made punishable under a preexisting statute but by means of an unforeseeable *judicial* enlargement thereof. (Bouie v. City of Columbia (1964) 378 U.S. 347.)

In *Bouie* two Negroes took seats in the restaurant section of a South Carolina drugstore; no notices were posted restricting the area to whites only. When the defendants refused to leave upon demand, they were arrested and convicted of violating a criminal trespass statute which prohibited entry on the property of another "after notice" forbidding such conduct. Prior South Carolina decisions had emphasized the necessity of proving such notice to support a conviction under the statute. The South Carolina Supreme Court nevertheless affirmed the convictions, construing the statute to prohibit not only the act of entering after notice not to do so but also the wholly different act of remaining on the property after receiving notice to leave.

The United States Supreme Court reversed the convictions, holding that the South Carolina court's ruling was "unforeseeable" and when an "unforeseeable state-court construction of a criminal statute is applied retroactively to subject a person to criminal liability for past conduct, the effect is to deprive him of due process of law in the sense of fair warning that his contemplated conduct constitutes a crime." Analogizing to the prohibition against retrospective penal legislation, the high court reasoned:

> Indeed, an unforeseeable judicial enlargement of a criminal statute, applied retroactively, operates precisely like an ex post facto law, such as Art. I, §10, of the Constitution forbids. An ex post facto law has been defined by this Court as one "that makes an action done before the passing of the law, and which was *innocent* when done, criminal; and punishes such action," or "that *aggravates* a *crime*, or makes it *greater* than it was, when committed." Calder v. Bull, 3 Dall. 386, 390. If a state legislature is barred by the Ex Post Facto Clause from passing such a law, it must follow that a State Supreme Court is barred by the Due Process Clause from achieving precisely the same result by judicial construction. The fundamental principle that "the required criminal law must have existed when the conduct in issue occurred," must apply to bar retroactive criminal prohibitions emanating from courts as well as from legislatures.

The court remarked in conclusion that "Application of this rule is particularly compelling where, as here, the petitioners' conduct cannot be deemed improper or immoral." In the case at bar the conduct with which petitioner is charged is certainly "improper" and "immoral," and it is not contended he was exercising a constitutionally favored right. But the matter is simply one of degree, and it cannot be denied that the guarantee of due process extends to violent as well as peaceful men. The issue remains, would the judicial enlargement of section 187 now proposed have been foreseeable to this petitioner? ...

Turning to the case law, we find no reported decision of the California courts which should have given petitioner notice that the killing of an unborn but viable fetus was prohibited by section 187. ... Finally, although a defendant is not bound to know the decisional law of other states, ... the cases decided in our sister states from [1947] to the present are unanimous in requiring proof that the child was born alive before a charge of homicide can be sustained. ...

We conclude that the judicial enlargement of section 187 now urged upon us by the People would not have been foreseeable to this petitioner, and hence that its adoption at this time would deny him due process of law. ...

BURKE, J., dissenting. The majority hold that "Baby Girl" Vogt, who according to medical testimony, had reached the 35th week of development, had a 96 percent chance of survival, and was "definitely" alive and viable at the time of her death, nevertheless was not a "human being" under California's homicide statutes. In my view, in so holding, the majority ignore significant common law precedents, frustrate the express intent of the Legislature, and defy reason, logic and common sense. ...

The majority opinion suggests that we are confined to common law concepts, and to the common law definition of murder or manslaughter. However, the Legislature, in Penal Code sections 187 and 192, has defined those offenses for us: homicide is the unlawful killing of a "human being." Those words need not be frozen in place as of any particular time, but must be fairly and reasonably interpreted by this court to promote justice and to carry out the evident purposes of the Legislature. ...

We commonly conceive of human existence as a spectrum stretching from birth to death. However, if this court properly might expand the definition of "human being" at one end of that spectrum, we may do so at the other end. Consider the following example: [There have been continuous] advances in the field of medicine, including new techniques for life revival, restoration and resuscitation such as artificial respiration, open heart massage, transfusions, transplants and a variety of life-restoring stimulants. ... Would this court ignore these developments and exonerate the killer of an apparently "drowned" child merely because that child would have been pronounced dead in 1648 and 1850? Obviously not. Whether a homicide occurred in that case would be determined by medical testimony regarding the capability of the child to have survived prior to the defendant's act. And that is precisely the test which this court should adopt in the instant case. ...

The majority suggest that to do so would improperly create some new offense. However, the offense of murder is no new offense. Contrary to the majority opinion, the Legislature has not "defined the crime of murder in

California to apply only to the unlawful and malicious killing of one who has been born alive." Instead, the Legislature simply used the broad term "human being" and directed the courts to construe that term according to its "fair import" with a view to effect the objects of the homicide statutes and promote justice. (Pen. Code, §4.) What justice will be promoted, what objects effectuated, by construing "human being" as excluding Baby Girl Vogt and her unfortunate successors? Was defendant's brutal act of stomping her to death any less an act of homicide than the murder of a newly born baby? No one doubts that the term "human being" would include the elderly or dying persons whose potential for life has nearly lapsed; their proximity to death is deemed immaterial. There is no sound reason for denying the viable fetus, with its unbounded potential for life, the same status.

The majority also suggest that such an interpretation of our homicide statutes would deny defendant "fair warning" that his act was punishable as a crime. Aside from the absurdity of the underlying premise that defendant consulted Coke, Blackstone or Hale before kicking Baby Girl Vogt to death, it is clear that defendant had adequate notice that his act could constitute homicide. Due process only precludes prosecution under a new statute insufficiently explicit regarding the specific conduct proscribed, or under a preexisting statute "by means of an unforeseeable *judicial* enlargement thereof." . . . The fact that the California courts have not been called upon to determine the precise question before us does not render "unforeseeable" a decision which determines that a viable fetus is a "human being" under those statutes. Can defendant really claim surprise that a 5-pound, 18-inch, 34-week-old, living, viable child is considered to be a human being? . . .

NOTES

1. The legislative response. Soon after the *Keeler* decision, the California legislature amended §187 to include the killing of "a fetus" in the definition of murder. Section 187(b) expressly excludes cases of legal abortion with the consent of the mother. The amendment differs from the approach urged in Justice Burke's dissent, in that viability is not an element of the offense; a killing can constitute murder, within the meaning of §187, whenever the fetus has progressed beyond the embryonic stage of seven to eight weeks. People v. Davis, 872 P.2d 591 (Cal. 1994). Several other states punish fetal homicide as a separate offense, with penalties generally equivalent to those applicable to murder. These statutes, even broader than California's, apply from the moment of conception. 720 Ill. Comp. Stat. Ann., §5/9-1.2 (2011); Ky. Rev. Stat. Ann., §507A.010(1)(c), 507A.020 (20011).

2. The retreat from **Bouie.** In *Bouie v. City of Columbia* (discussed in *Keeler*), the Court reasoned that that the due process restrictions on courts include the same ex post facto restrictions applicable to legislatures. That premise remained well-entrenched in the case law for more than three decades. But in Rogers v. Tennessee, 532 U.S. 451 (2001), the Supreme Court reconsidered and gave judges considerable scope to change criminal law retroactively.

Wilbert Rogers had stabbed James Bowdery with a butcher knife. Bowdery went into cardiac arrest and then a coma; he died of related complications about 15 months later. Rogers was convicted of murder, but Tennessee at the time followed the long-standing common-law rule that a homicide could be prosecuted as murder only when the victim had died within a year and a day of the defendant's acts. The Tennessee Supreme Court nonetheless sustained the murder conviction. It concluded that the original justifications for the rule were no longer applicable, announced that "we hereby abolish the common law rule," and held that its decision eliminating the year-and-a-day requirement applied to Rogers's case. The U.S. Supreme Court held that this result did not violate the Due Process or Ex Post Facto Clauses:

Rogers v. Tennessee, 532 U.S. 451 (2001): O'CONNOR, J.: [*Bouie*] concluded that "if a judicial construction of a criminal statute is 'unexpected and indefensible by reference to the law which had been expressed prior to the conduct in issue,' [the construction] must not be given retroactive effect". . . . We found that the South Carolina court's construction of the statute violated this principle because it was so clearly at odds with the statute's plain language and had no support in prior South Carolina decisions. . . .

Petitioner contends that the Ex Post Facto Clause would prohibit the retroactive application of a decision abolishing the year and a day rule if accomplished by the Tennessee Legislature. He claims that the purposes behind the Clause are so fundamental that due process should prevent the Supreme Court of Tennessee from accomplishing the same result by judicial decree. . . . To be sure, our opinion in *Bouie* does contain some expansive language that is suggestive of the broad interpretation for which petitioner argues. . . . This language, however, was dicta. Our decision in *Bouie* . . . rested on core due process concepts of notice, foreseeability, and, in particular, the right to fair warning as those concepts bear on the constitutionality of attaching criminal penalties to what previously had been innocent conduct. [N]owhere in the opinion did we go so far as to incorporate jot-for-jot the specific [ex post facto rules] into due process limitations on the retroactive application of judicial decisions.

. . . The Ex Post Facto Clause, by its own terms, does not apply to courts. Extending the Clause to courts through the rubric of due process thus would circumvent the clear constitutional text. It also would evince too little regard for the important institutional and contextual differences between legislating, on the one hand, and common law decisionmaking, on the other.

. . . In the context of common law doctrines (such as the year and a day rule), there often arises a need to clarify or even to reevaluate prior opinions as new circumstances and fact patterns present themselves. Such judicial acts, whether they be characterized as "making" or "finding" the law, are a necessary part of the judicial business in States in which the criminal law retains some of its common law elements. Strict application of ex post facto principles in that context would unduly impair the incremental and reasoned development of precedent that is the foundation of the common law system. . . . It was on account of concerns such as these that *Bouie* restricted due process limitations on the retroactive application of judicial interpretations of criminal statutes to those that are "unexpected and indefensible. . . ."

We believe this limitation . . . accords common law courts the substantial leeway they must enjoy as they engage in the daily task of . . . reevaluating and refining [criminal defenses] as may be necessary to bring the common law into conformity with logic and common sense. It also adequately respects the due process concern with fundamental fairness and protects against vindictive or arbitrary judicial lawmaking by safeguarding defendants against unjustified and unpredictable breaks with prior law. Accordingly, we conclude that judicial alteration of a common law doctrine of criminal law violates the principle of fair warning, and hence must not be given retroactive effect, only where it is "unexpected and indefensible by reference to the law which had been expressed prior to the conduct in issue."

[T]he Tennessee court's abolition of the year and a day rule was not unexpected and indefensible. The year and a day rule is widely viewed as an outdated relic of the common law. [T]he primary and most frequently cited justification for the rule is that 13th century medical science was incapable of establishing causation beyond a reasonable doubt when a great deal of time had elapsed between the injury to the victim and his death; . . . advances in medical and related science have so undermined the usefulness of the rule as to render it without question obsolete.

For this reason, the year and a day rule has been legislatively or judicially abolished in the vast majority of jurisdictions recently to have addressed the issue. [P]etitioner contends that the judicial abolition of the rule in other jurisdictions is irrelevant to whether he had fair warning that the rule in Tennessee might similarly be abolished. . . . Due process, of course, does not require a person to apprise himself of the common law of all 50 States in order to guarantee that his actions will not subject him to punishment in light of a developing trend in the law that has not yet made its way to his State. At the same time, however, the fact that a vast number of jurisdictions have "abolished a rule that has so clearly outlived its purpose" is surely relevant to whether the abolition of the rule in a particular case can be said to be unexpected and indefensible. . . . The [year-and-a-day] rule did not exist as part of Tennessee's statutory criminal code [and] had never once served as a ground of decision in any prosecution for murder in the State.

There is, in short, nothing to indicate that the Tennessee court's abolition of the rule in petitioner's case represented an exercise of the sort of unfair and arbitrary judicial action against which the Due Process Clause aims to protect. [T]he court's decision was a routine exercise of common law decisionmaking in which the court brought the law into conformity with reason and common sense. . . .

SCALIA, J., dissenting: The Court today . . . violates a principle—encapsulated in the maxim *nulla poena sine lege*—which "dates from the ancient Greeks"

and has been described as one of the most "widely held value-judgments in the entire history of human thought." J. Hall, General Principles of Criminal Law 59 (2d ed. 1960). Today's opinion produces, moreover, a curious constitution that only a judge could love. One in which . . . the elected representatives of all the people cannot retroactively make murder what was not murder when the act was committed; but in which unelected judges can do precisely that. . . . I do not believe this is the system that the Framers envisioned—or, for that matter, that any reasonable person would imagine.

[L]et us be clear that the law here was altered after the fact. . . . Though the Court spends some time questioning whether the year-and-a-day rule was ever truly established in Tennessee, the Supreme Court of Tennessee said it was, and this reasonable reading of state law by the State's highest court is binding upon us. . . .

The Court attempts to cabin *Bouie* by reading it to prohibit only " 'unexpected and indefensible' " judicial law revision. . . . *Bouie* does indeed use those quoted terms; but they have been wrenched entirely out of context. The "fair warning" to which *Bouie* and subsequent cases referred was not "fair warning that the law might be changed," but fair warning *of what constituted the crime at the time of the offense*. . . . According to *Bouie*, not just "unexpected and indefensible" retroactive changes in the common law of crimes are bad, but all retroactive changes.

. . . There is no doubt that "fair warning" of the legislature's intent to change the law does not insulate retroactive legislative criminalization. Such a statute violates the Ex Post Facto Clause, no matter that, at the time the offense was committed, the bill enacting the change was pending and assured of passage. . . . "[F]air warning" of impending change cannot insulate retroactive judicial criminalization either.

. . . According to the Court, . . . prohibiting retroactive judicial criminalization . . . would "unduly impair the incremental and reasoned development of precedent that is the foundation of the common law system." That assessment ignores the crucial difference between simply applying a law to a new set of circumstances and changing the law that has previously been applied to the very circumstances before the court. [T]he action before us here [is] a square, head on overruling of prior law. [S]uch retroactive revision of a concededly valid legal rule . . . was unheard-of at the time the original Due Process Clause was adopted. [P]roceeding in that fashion would have been regarded as contrary to the judicial traditions embraced within the concept of due process. . . .

It is not a matter, therefore, of "extending the [Ex Post Facto] Clause to courts through the rubric of due process," and thereby "circumventing the clear constitutional text." It is simply a matter of determining what due judicial process consists of—and it does not consist of retroactive creation of crimes. . . . Madison wrote that "ex-post-facto laws . . . are contrary to the first principles of the social compact, and to every principle of social legislation." The Federalist No. 44, p. 282 (C. Rossiter ed. 1961). I find it impossible to believe, as the Court does, that this strong sentiment attached only to retroactive laws passed by the legislature, and would not apply equally (or indeed with even greater force) to a court's production of the same result. . . . The injustice to the individuals affected is no less.

Even if I agreed with the Court that the Due Process Clause is violated only when there is lack of "fair warning" . . . , I would not find such fair warning here. It is not clear to me, in fact, what the Court believes the fair warning consisted of. Was it the mere fact that "the year and a day rule is widely viewed as an outdated relic of the common law"? So are many of the elements of common-law crimes, such as "breaking the close" as an element of burglary, or "asportation" as an element of larceny. Are all of these "outdated relics" subject to retroactive judicial rescission? Or perhaps the fair warning consisted of the fact that "the year and a day rule has been legislatively or judicially abolished in the vast majority of jurisdictions recently to have addressed the issue." But why not count in petitioner's favor . . . (rather than *against* him) those jurisdictions that have abolished the rule *legislatively*, and those jurisdictions that have abolished it through *prospective* rather than *retroactive* judicial rulings (together, a large majority of the abolitions)? [E]ven if it was predictable that the rule would be changed, it was not predictable that it would be changed *retroactively*. . . .

[T]he only "fair warning" relevant to the issue before us . . . is fair warning *of what the law is*. [P]etitioner had nothing that could fairly be called a "warning" that the Supreme Court of Tennessee would retroactively eliminate one of the elements of the crime of murder. . . .

NOTE

Subsequent to *Rogers*, the Wisconsin Supreme Court abrogated its common-law year-and-a-day requirement but held that the change could not apply retroactively; the court said that retroactive change "undermines stability in the law and tarnishes the image of justice." State v. Picotte, 661 N.W.2d 381, 394 (Wis. 2003). The Alabama Supreme Court held that any decision to modify that state's common-law year-and-a-day rule must be made by its legislature. Ex parte Key, 890 So. 2d 1056 (Ala. 2003). In light of these post-*Rogers* decisions, is it still reasonably foreseeable that a state court will change its year-and-a-day requirement retroactively?

CITY OF CHICAGO v. MORALES

Supreme Court of the United States
527 U.S. 41 (1999)

JUSTICE STEVENS announced the judgment of the Court and delivered the opinion of the Court with respect to Parts I, II, and V, and an opinion with respect to Parts III, IV, and VI, in which JUSTICE SOUTER and JUSTICE GINSBURG join.

In 1992, the Chicago City Council enacted the Gang Congregation Ordinance, which prohibits "criminal street gang members" from "loitering" with one another or with other persons in any public place. [In numerous cases, Illinois trial courts dismissed charges against defendants arrested under the ordinance, on the ground that the law was unconstitutionally vague. In a consolidated appeal from several of those rulings, the Illinois Supreme Court agreed with the trial courts and affirmed the dismissal of the charges against all the defendants. The U.S. Supreme Court granted review.] The question presented is whether the Supreme Court of Illinois correctly held that the ordinance violates the Due Process Clause of the Fourteenth Amendment. . . .

I . . .

The [city] council found that a continuing increase in criminal street gang activity was largely responsible for the city's rising murder rate, as well as an escalation of violent and drug related crimes. . . . Furthermore, the council stated that gang members "establish control over identifiable areas . . . by loitering in those areas and intimidating others from entering those areas; and . . . members of criminal street gangs avoid arrest by committing no offense punishable under existing laws when they know the police are present. . . ."

The ordinance creates a criminal offense punishable by a fine of up to $500, imprisonment for not more than six months, and a requirement to perform up to 120 hours of community service. Commission of the offense involves four predicates. First, the police officer must reasonably believe that at least one of the two or more persons present in a "public place" is a "criminal street gang member." Second, the persons must be "loitering," which the ordinance defines as "remaining in any one place with no apparent purpose." Third, the officer must then order "all" of the persons to disperse and remove themselves "from the area." Fourth, a person must disobey the officer's order. If any person, whether a gang member or not, disobeys the officer's order, that person is guilty of violating the ordinance. . . .[2]

---

2. The ordinance states. . . .

(a) Whenever a police officer observes a person whom he reasonably believes to be a criminal street gang member loitering in any public place with one or more other persons, he shall order all such persons to disperse and remove themselves from the area. Any person who does not promptly obey such an order is in violation of this section.

(b) It shall be an affirmative defense to an alleged violation of this section that no person who was observed loitering was in fact a member of a criminal street gang.

(c) As used in this section:

(1) "Loiter" means to remain in any one place with no apparent purpose.

(2) "Criminal street gang" means any ongoing organization, association in fact or group of three or more persons, whether formal or informal, having as one of its substantial activities the commission of one or more of the criminal acts enumerated in paragraph (3), and whose members individually or collectively engage in or have engaged in a pattern of criminal gang activity. . . .

(5) "Public place" means the public way and any other location open to the public, whether publicly or privately owned.

(e) Any person who violates this Section is subject to a fine of not less than $100 and not more than $500 for each offense, or imprisonment for not more than six months, or both. . . .

II

During the three years of its enforcement, the police issued over 89,000 dispersal orders and arrested over 42,000 people for violating the ordinance.[7]

The Illinois Supreme Court . . . held "that the gang loitering ordinance violates due process of law in that it is impermissibly vague on its face[a] and an arbitrary restriction on personal liberties." . . . We granted certiorari, and now affirm. Like the Illinois Supreme Court, we conclude that the ordinance enacted by the city of Chicago is unconstitutionally vague.

III

The basic factual predicate for the city's ordinance is not in dispute. As the city argues in its brief, "the very presence of a large collection of obviously brazen, insistent, and lawless gang members and hangers-on on the public ways intimidates residents, who become afraid even to leave their homes and go about their business. That, in turn, imperils community residents' sense of safety and security, detracts from property values, and can ultimately destabilize entire neighborhoods." . . . We have no doubt that a law that directly prohibited such intimidating conduct would be constitutional, but this ordinance broadly covers a significant amount of additional activity. Uncertainty

---

7. . . . The city believes that the ordinance resulted in a significant decline in gang-related homicides. It notes that in 1995, the last year the ordinance was enforced, the gang-related homicide rate fell by 26%. In 1996, after the ordinance had been held invalid, the gang-related homicide rate rose 11%. However, gang-related homicides fell by 19% in 1997, over a year after the suspension of the ordinance. Given the myriad factors that influence levels of violence, it is difficult to evaluate the probative value of this statistical evidence, or to reach any firm conclusion about the ordinance's efficacy. Cf. Harcourt, Reflecting on the Subject: A Critique of the Social Influence Conception of Deterrence, the Broken Windows Theory, and Order-Maintenance Policing New York Style, 97 Mich. L. Rev. 291, 296 (1998) (describing the "hotly contested debate raging among . . . experts over the causes of the decline in crime in New York City and nationally").

a. Vagueness challenges can take two forms: a challenge to a statute *on its face* and a challenge to the statute *as applied*. A facial challenge, to be successful, must demonstrate that no matter how harmful a person's conduct may be, one can never tell whether the statute covers the situation or not. An as-applied challenge, in contrast, only needs to show that the statute does not have a clear meaning in the context of a particular case. Thus, in State v. Scruggs, 905 A.2d 24 (Conn. 2006), the defendant allegedly caused severe injury to her son's mental health (and ultimately his suicide) by maintaining an extremely cluttered and unsanitary apartment. She was convicted under a statute making it a crime to willfully place one's child "in such a situation that . . . the health of such child is likely to be injured." Such a statute has a clear meaning in core situations of child abuse, such as a physical assault, and it therefore is not unconstitutional *on its face*. But the Connecticut Supreme Court held that it was unconstitutionally vague *as applied*, because it was not clear whether the statute was intended to cover what Scruggs had done.

A facial challenge is more difficult to win, but when successful, it renders the statute in question entirely invalid and unenforceable. In *Morales*, the trial courts had dismissed all charges before reaching any consideration of the facts of individual cases. Thus, in order to prevail in the U.S. Supreme Court, the defendants needed to show that the meaning of the Chicago ordinance could never be clear under any circumstances, and therefore that it was unconstitutional on its face.—Eds.

about the scope of that additional coverage provides the basis for respondents' claim that the ordinance is too vague. . . .

Vagueness may invalidate a criminal law for either of two independent reasons. First, it may fail to provide the kind of notice that will enable ordinary people to understand what conduct it prohibits; second, it may authorize and even encourage arbitrary and discriminatory enforcement. See Kolender v. Lawson, 461 U.S. at 357. Accordingly, we first consider whether the ordinance provides fair notice to the citizen and then discuss its potential for arbitrary enforcement.

IV

"It is established that a law fails to meet the requirements of the Due Process Clause if it is so vague and standardless that it leaves the public uncertain as to the conduct it prohibits. . . ." Giaccio v. Pennsylvania, 382 U.S. 399, 402-403 (1966). The Illinois Supreme Court recognized that the term "loiter" may have a common and accepted meaning, but the definition of that term in this ordinance—"to remain in any one place with no apparent purpose"—does not. It is difficult to imagine how any citizen of the city of Chicago standing in a public place with a group of people would know if he or she had an "apparent purpose." If she were talking to another person, would she have an apparent purpose? If she were frequently checking her watch and looking expectantly down the street, would she have an apparent purpose?

Since the city cannot conceivably have meant to criminalize each instance a citizen stands in public with a gang member, the vagueness that dooms this ordinance is not the product of uncertainty about the normal meaning of "loitering," but rather about what loitering is covered by the ordinance and what is not. . . .[24]

[A] number of state courts [have] upheld ordinances that criminalize loitering combined with some other overt act or evidence of criminal intent. However, state courts have uniformly invalidated laws that do not join the term "loitering" with a second specific element of the crime.

The city's principal response to this concern about adequate notice is that loiterers are not subject to sanction until after they have failed to comply with an officer's order to disperse. . . . We find this response unpersuasive for at least two reasons.

First, the purpose of the fair notice requirement is to enable the ordinary citizen to conform his or her conduct to the law. "No one may be required at peril of life, liberty or property to speculate as to the meaning of penal

---

24. One of the trial courts that invalidated the ordinance gave the following illustration: "suppose a group of gang members were playing basketball in the park, while waiting for a drug delivery. Their apparent purpose is that they are in the park to play ball. The actual purpose is that they are waiting for drugs. Under this definition of loitering, a group of people innocently sitting in a park discussing their futures would be arrested, while the 'basketball players' awaiting a drug delivery would be left alone."

statutes." Lanzetta v. New Jersey, 306 U.S. 451, 453 (1939). Although it is true that a loiterer is not subject to criminal sanctions unless he or she disobeys a dispersal order, the loitering is the conduct that the ordinance is designed to prohibit. If the loitering is in fact harmless and innocent, the dispersal order itself is an unjustified impairment of liberty. If the police are able to decide arbitrarily which members of the public they will order to disperse, then the Chicago ordinance becomes indistinguishable from the law we held invalid in Shuttlesworth v. Birmingham, 382 U.S. 87, 90 (1965).[29] Because an officer may issue an order only after prohibited conduct has already occurred, [the order] cannot retroactively give adequate warning of the boundary between the permissible and the impermissible applications of the law.

Second, the terms of the dispersal order compound the inadequacy of the notice afforded by the ordinance. It provides that the officer "shall order all such persons to disperse and remove themselves from the area." This vague phrasing raises a host of questions. After such an order issues, how long must the loiterers remain apart? How far must they move? If each loiterer walks around the block and they meet again at the same location, are they subject to arrest or merely to being ordered to disperse again? . . .

Lack of clarity in the description of the loiterer's duty to obey a dispersal order might not render the ordinance unconstitutionally vague if the definition of the forbidden conduct were clear, but it does buttress our conclusion that the entire ordinance fails to give the ordinary citizen adequate notice of what is forbidden and what is permitted. The Constitution does not permit a legislature to "set a net large enough to catch all possible offenders, and leave it to the courts to step inside and say who could be rightfully detained, and who should be set at large." United States v. Reese, 92 U.S. 214, 221 (1876). This ordinance is therefore vague "not in the sense that it requires a person to conform his conduct to an imprecise but comprehensible normative standard, but rather in the sense that no standard of conduct is specified at all." Coates v. Cincinnati, 402 U.S. 611, 614 (1971).

V

The broad sweep of the ordinance also violates " 'the requirement that a legislature establish minimal guidelines to govern law enforcement.' " Kolender v. Lawson, 461 U.S. at 358. There are no such guidelines in the ordinance. In any public place in the city of Chicago, persons who stand or sit in the company of a gang member may be ordered to disperse unless their purpose is apparent. The mandatory language in the enactment directs the police to issue an order without first making any inquiry about their possible purposes. It matters not whether the reason that a gang member and his father, for

---

29. "Literally read . . . this ordinance says that a person may stand on a public sidewalk in Birmingham only at the whim of any police officer of the city. The constitutional vice of so broad a provision needs no demonstration." 382 U.S. 87 at 90.

example, might loiter near Wrigley Field is to rob an unsuspecting fan or just to get a glimpse of Sammy Sosa leaving the ballpark; in either event, if their purpose is not apparent to a nearby police officer, she may—indeed, she "shall"—order them to disperse.

Recognizing that the ordinance does reach a substantial amount of innocent conduct, we turn, then, to its language to determine if it "necessarily entrusts lawmaking to the moment-to-moment judgment of the policeman on his beat." Kolender v. Lawson, 461 U.S. at 359. . . . The principal source of the vast discretion conferred on the police in this case is the definition of loitering as "to remain in any one place with no apparent purpose."

As the Illinois Supreme Court interprets that definition, it "provides absolute discretion to police officers to determine what activities constitute loitering." We have no authority to construe the language of a state statute more narrowly than the construction given by that State's highest court. . . .

Nevertheless, the city disputes the Illinois Supreme Court's interpretation, arguing that the text of the ordinance limits the officer's discretion. . . .

[T]he requirement that the officer reasonably believe that a group of loiterers contains a gang member does place a limit on the authority to order dispersal. That limitation would no doubt be sufficient if the ordinance only applied to loitering that had an apparently harmful purpose or effect, or possibly if it only applied to loitering by persons reasonably believed to be criminal gang members. But this ordinance . . . applies to [f]riends, relatives, teachers, counselors, or even total strangers [who] might unwittingly engage in forbidden loitering if they happen to engage in idle conversation with a gang member.

Ironically, the definition of loitering in the Chicago ordinance . . . has the perverse consequence of excluding from its coverage much of the intimidating conduct that motivated its enactment. As the city council's findings demonstrate, the most harmful gang loitering is motivated either by an apparent purpose to publicize the gang's dominance of certain territory, thereby intimidating nonmembers, or by an equally apparent purpose to conceal ongoing commerce in illegal drugs. . . . The relative importance of its application to harmless loitering is magnified by its inapplicability to loitering that has an obviously threatening or illicit purpose. . . .

VI

. . . We recognize the serious and difficult problems . . . that led to the enactment of this ordinance. "We are mindful that the preservation of liberty depends in part on the maintenance of social order." Houston v. Hill, 482 U.S. 451, 471-472 (1987). However, in this instance the city has enacted an ordinance that affords too much discretion to the police and too little notice to citizens who wish to use the public streets.

Accordingly, the judgment of the Supreme Court of Illinois is affirmed.

Justice O'Connor, with whom Justice Breyer joins, concurring: . . .

I share Justice Thomas' concern about the consequences of gang violence, and I agree that some degree of police discretion is necessary. . . . A criminal law, however, must not permit policemen, prosecutors, and juries to conduct " 'a standardless sweep . . . to pursue their personal predilections.' " *Kolender v. Lawson,* supra, at 358.

. . . Chicago's gang loitering ordinance is unconstitutionally vague because it lacks sufficient minimal standards to guide law enforcement officers. In particular, it fails to provide police with any standard by which they can judge whether an individual has an "apparent purpose." Indeed, because any person standing on the street has a general "purpose"—even if it is simply to stand—the ordinance permits police officers to choose which purposes are permissible. Under this construction the police do not have to decide that an individual is "threatening the public peace" to issue a dispersal order. [Infra, Thomas, J., dissenting]. Any police officer in Chicago is free, under the Illinois Supreme Court's construction of the ordinance, to order at his whim any person standing in a public place with a suspected gang member to disperse.

Nevertheless, there remain open to Chicago reasonable alternatives to combat the very real threat posed by gang intimidation and violence. For example, the Court properly and expressly distinguishes the ordinance from laws that require loiterers to have a "harmful purpose," from laws that target only gang members, and from laws that incorporate limits on the area and manner in which the laws may be enforced. In addition, the ordinance here is unlike a law that "directly prohibits" [the kind of behavior described in the city's brief—the] "presence of a large collection of obviously brazen, insistent, and lawless gang members and hangers-on on the public ways." . . .

[The] ordinance could have been construed more narrowly. The term "loiter" might possibly be construed . . . to mean "to remain in any one place with no apparent purpose other than to establish control over identifiable areas, to intimidate others from entering those areas, or to conceal illegal activities." Such a definition would be consistent with the Chicago City Council's findings and would avoid the vagueness problems of the ordinance as construed by the Illinois Supreme Court. [S]o would limitations that restricted the ordinance's criminal penalties to gang members or that more carefully delineated the circumstances in which those penalties would apply to nongang members. . . .

JUSTICE THOMAS, with whom THE CHIEF JUSTICE and JUSTICE SCALIA join, dissenting. . . .

[T]he ordinance does not criminalize loitering per se. Rather, it penalizes a loiterer's failure to obey a police officer's order to move along. . . . Far from according officers too much discretion, the ordinance merely enables police officers to fulfill one of their traditional functions. Police officers are not, and have never been, simply enforcers of the criminal law. They wear other hats— importantly, they have long been vested with the responsibility for preserving the public peace. . . . In their role as peace officers, the police long have had the authority and the duty to order groups of individuals who threaten the public peace to disperse. . . .

In order to perform their peace-keeping responsibilities satisfactorily, the police inevitably must exercise discretion. . . . That is not to say that the law should not provide objective guidelines for the police, but simply that it cannot rigidly constrain their every action. By directing a police officer not to issue a dispersal order unless he "observes a person whom he reasonably believes to be a criminal street gang member loitering in any public place," Chicago's ordinance strikes an appropriate balance between those two extremes. Just as we trust officers to rely on their experience and expertise in order to make spur-of-the-moment determinations about amorphous legal standards such as "probable cause" and "reasonable suspicion," so we must trust them to determine whether a group of loiterers contains individuals (in this case members of criminal street gangs) whom the city has determined threaten the public peace. . . . In sum, the Court's conclusion that the ordinance is impermissibly vague because it " 'necessarily entrusts lawmaking to the moment-to-moment judgment of the policeman on his beat,' " cannot be reconciled with common sense [and] longstanding police practice. . . .

I do not . . . overlook the possibility that a police officer, acting in bad faith, might enforce the ordinance in an arbitrary or discriminatory way. But . . . instances of arbitrary or discriminatory enforcement of the ordinance, like any other law, are best addressed when (and if) they arise. . . .

The plurality's conclusion that the ordinance "fails to give the ordinary citizen adequate notice of what is forbidden and what is permitted," is similarly untenable. There is nothing "vague" about an order to disperse.[9] [I]t is safe to assume that the vast majority of people who are ordered by the police to "disperse and remove themselves from the area" will have little difficulty understanding how to comply.

[R]espondents in this facial challenge bear the weighty burden of establishing that the statute is vague in all its applications. . . . "If any fool would know that a particular category of conduct would be within the reach of the statute, if there is an unmistakable core that a reasonable person would know is forbidden by the law, the enactment is not unconstitutional on its face." *Kolender*, 461 U.S. at 370-371 (dissenting opinion). This is certainly such a case.

[T]he ordinance does not proscribe constitutionally protected conduct— there is no fundamental right to loiter. It is also anomalous to characterize loitering as "innocent" conduct when it has been disfavored throughout American history. . . . The term "loiter" is no different from terms such as "fraud," "bribery," and "perjury." We expect people of ordinary intelligence to grasp the meaning of such legal terms despite the fact that they are arguably imprecise. . . .

---

9. . . . The logical implication of the plurality's assertion is that the police can never issue dispersal orders. For example, in the plurality's view, it is apparently unconstitutional for a police officer to ask a group of gawkers to move along in order to secure a crime scene.

The plurality underestimates the intellectual capacity of the citizens of Chicago. Persons of ordinary intelligence are perfectly capable of evaluating how outsiders perceive their conduct, and here "it is self-evident that there is a whole range of conduct that anyone with at least a semblance of common sense would know is [loitering] and that would be covered by the statute." See Smith v. Goguen, 415 U.S. 566, 584 (1974) (White, J., concurring in judgment). Members of a group standing on the corner staring blankly into space, for example, are likely well aware that passersby would conclude that they have "no apparent purpose." . . .

example of loiter thats common sense,

Today, the Court focuses extensively on the "rights" of gang members and their companions. It can safely do so—the people who will have to live with the consequences of today's opinion do not live in our neighborhoods. Rather, the people who will suffer from our lofty pronouncements are . . . people who have seen their neighborhoods literally destroyed by gangs and violence and drugs. They are good, decent people who must struggle to overcome their desperate situation, against all odds, in order to raise their families, earn a living, and remain good citizens. As one resident described, "There is only about maybe one or two percent of the people in the city causing these problems maybe, but it's keeping 98 percent of us in our houses and off the streets and afraid to shop." By focusing exclusively on the imagined "rights" of the two percent, the Court today has denied our most vulnerable citizens the very thing that Justice Stevens, elevates above all else—the "freedom of movement." And that is a shame. I respectfully dissent.

Steve Chapman, Court Upholds America's Right To Hang Out, Chi. Trib., June 13, 1999, p. 19: The Chicago City Council is famous for many things, but legal scholarship has never been its strength. When it passed an anti-gang loitering ordinance seven years ago, aldermen were confident that no such expertise was needed. Told that the law might run afoul of the Constitution, one supporter snorted, "I don't believe when the Founding Fathers were drafting the Constitution that the Latin Kings were sitting in Philadelphia."

Last week, the Supreme Court convened in Washington, where street gangs are also common, and said that the presence of the Latin Kings or the Bloods or the Crips didn't warrant a suspension of the principles established in the Bill of Rights.

It would be interesting to transport James Madison to a street corner on Chicago's Southwest Side to engage a Latin King in a discussion of where a free society should draw the line between protecting liberties and upholding public safety. Under the city ordinance, though, Madison could have found himself ordered by a police officer to terminate the conversation and leave the vicinity, or else see how he liked talking law with fellow inmates of the Cook County Jail.

Madison was never affected by the ordinance, but plenty of Chicagoans were. In the three years the law was in force, before being invalidated by the courts, police [dispersed] some 89,000 [people at] public gatherings and arrested 42,000 people who didn't move fast enough or far enough to suit the cops. Not all were gang members, since the ordinance gives police the authority to disperse a group of 10, 20, or 100 if a single person present is even suspected of belonging to a gang. [T]hough most police are decent and well-intentioned, many are not, and giving them dictatorial powers over the streets inevitably means that many law-abiding people taking part in innocent activities will be coerced, inconvenienced or even hauled off to jail.

Justice Clarence Thomas, in a dissent, excoriated the six justices who voted to overturn the ordinance. "The people who will have to live with the consequences of today's opinion do not live in our neighborhoods," he snarled. True—and Clarence Thomas, ensconced in well-to-do Fairfax County, Va., will never be ordered to leave his front sidewalk for chatting with someone who, unknown to him, is a gang member.

Thomas failed to mention that the long-suffering people who do have to live with the consequences didn't all see the law as their friend. The ordinance had the support of most white aldermen, but only six of the council's 18 black members voted for it. They knew that some white cops enforcing the law would create a new crime of "standing around while black" to go with the old one of "driving while black." . . .

Part of life in a non-totalitarian country is the freedom of people to congregate in public for idle purposes without having to ask permission from the government. The City of Chicago can attack its gang problem without trampling that right.

NOTES

1. Papachristou v. City of Jacksonville, 405 U.S. 156 (1972), has long been regarded as the leading case on the constitutionality of vagrancy-type laws. The issue in that case was the constitutionality of the following ordinance:

> Rogues and vagabonds, or dissolute persons who go about begging, common gamblers, persons who use juggling or unlawful games or plays, common drunkards, common night thieves, . . . lewd, wanton and lascivious persons, . . . persons wandering or strolling around from place to place without any lawful purpose or object, habitual loafers, disorderly persons, persons neglecting all lawful business and habitually spending their time by frequenting houses of ill fame, gaming houses, or places where alcoholic beverages are sold or served, persons able to work but habitually living upon the earnings of their wives or minor children shall be deemed vagrants and, upon conviction in the Municipal Court shall be punished as provided for Class D offenses [punishable by 90 days' imprisonment, $500 fine, or both].

Among those challenging the ordinance were four defendants (two black males and two white females) who had been stopped by Jacksonville, Florida, police while riding together in a car; they were supposedly considered suspicious for having paused near a used car lot that had been the scene of frequent thefts. Other defendants had been arrested when police who observed them walking down the street or waiting for a friend refused to accept their explanations for their behavior.

In a unanimous opinion by Justice Douglas, the Court held the ordinance unconstitutional:

The Jacksonville ordinance makes criminal activities which by modern standards are normally innocent. "Nightwalking" is one. [S]leepless people often walk at night, perhaps hopeful that sleep-inducing relaxation will result. [A] former Governor . . . commented once that "loafing" was a national virtue . . . and that it should be encouraged. It is, however, a crime in Jacksonville. "Persons able to work but habitually living upon the earnings of their wives or minor children" [might implicate] unemployed people out of the labor market, by reason of a recession. . . . Persons "neglecting all lawful business and habitually spending their time by frequenting . . . places where alcoholic beverages are sold or served" would literally embrace many members of golf clubs. . . .

Walkers and strollers and wanderers may be going to or coming from a burglary. Loafers or loiterers may be "casing" a place for a holdup. . . . The difficulty is that these activities are historically part of the amenities of life as we have known them. They are not mentioned in the Constitution or in the Bill of Rights. These unwritten amenities have been in part responsible for giving our people the feeling of independence and self-confidence, the feeling of creativity. These amenities have dignified the right of dissent and have . . . encouraged lives of high spirits rather than hushed, suffocating silence. . . .

Another aspect of the ordinance's vagueness appears when we focus, not on the lack of notice given a potential offender, but on the effect of the unfettered discretion it places in the hands of the Jacksonville police. [P]oor people, nonconformists, dissenters, idlers may be required to comport themselves according to the lifestyle deemed appropriate by the Jacksonville police and the courts. Where, as here, there are no standards governing the exercise of the discretion granted by the ordinance, the scheme permits and encourages an arbitrary and discriminatory enforcement of the law. . . . It results in a regime in which the poor and the unpopular are permitted to "stand on a public sidewalk . . . only at the whim of any police officer." Shuttlesworth v. Birmingham, 382 U.S. 87, 90. . . .

The implicit presumption in these generalized vagrancy standards—that crime is being nipped in the bud—is too extravagant to deserve extended treatment. Of course, vagrancy statutes are useful to the police. Of course, they are nets making easy the roundup of so-called undesirables. But the rule of law . . . , evenly applied to minorities as well as majorities, to the poor as well as the rich, is the great mucilage that holds society together.

The Jacksonville ordinance cannot be squared with our constitutional standards and is plainly unconstitutional.

In accord with *Papachristou*, see also Cox v. Louisiana, 379 U.S. 536, 579 (1965) (opinion of Black, J.), noting that the Constitution requires "government by clearly defined laws, [not] government by the moment-to-moment opinions of a policeman on the beat."

2. Questions. The justices voting to strike down the Chicago ordinance did not refer to *Papachristou* for support, but the dissenters did not question its continued authority; none of the *Morales* opinions cited *Papachristou* one way or the other. Why not? Under the *Papachristou* opinion, are laws aimed at nipping crime in the bud always unconstitutional if their terms permit discriminatory enforcement or an unequal impact on the poor and minorities? *Should* such laws be unconstitutional? The justices in the *Morales* majority may have been reluctant to reaffirm the broadest implications of *Papachristou*, but the dissenters may have been reluctant to question them. Why the reticence?

3. Broken windows. One theme in recent criminal justice scholarship argues that graffiti, unrepaired damage in decaying neighborhoods ("broken windows"), and "quality of life" offenses like spitting, littering, and public drinking are not trivial matters. According to this view, effective control of major crime, not to mention maintenance of decent urban environments, requires police to enforce quality-of-life laws vigorously, even though such enforcement inevitably will involve considerable discretion. See, e.g., Debra Livingston, Police Discretion and the Quality of Life in Public Spaces, 97 Colum. L. Rev. 551 (1997).

One aspect of this argument—the claimed connection between order maintenance and reduction of the most serious crimes—has been questioned. During the 1990s, crime fell dramatically in cities that practiced vigorous quality-of-life policing, but crime also fell dramatically in cities that introduced police initiatives of other sorts and in cities that simply followed traditional policing practices. See Bernard E. Harcourt, Reflecting on the Subject: A Critique of the Social Influence Conception of Deterrence, the Broken Windows Theory, and Order-Maintenance Policing New York Style, 97 Mich. L. Rev. 291 (1998). After examining the data in detail, Professor Harcourt concludes that quality-of-life enforcement and fixing "broken windows" have no significant effect on the level of serious crime.

4. Race. Supporters of quality-of-life enforcement often suggest that one of its principal dangers—the racial discrimination that was such a concern in the *Papachristou* era—presents a far different face today: Blacks themselves, it is said, bear the brunt of the inner-city crime and disorder, and at the same time, the political empowerment of urban blacks and their entry into the ranks of the urban police make racial harassment far less likely. See, e.g., Dan M. Kahan & Tracey L. Meares, The Coming Crisis of Criminal Procedure, 86 Geo. L.J. 1153, 1153-1154, 1169-1170 (1998):

> [T]he constitutional standards used to evaluate discretionary community policing . . . have outlived their utility. [T]he unmistakable premise of these doctrines was the assumption that communities could not be trusted to police their own police because of the distorting influence of racism. . . .
>
> In a world in which the coercive incidence of community policing was concentrated on a powerless and despised minority, it made perfect sense for courts to assume that communities would systematically overvalue the benefits of discretion and undervalue the costs of it. [T]hat assumption makes much less sense in settings, such as today's inner-city, in which the citizens who support

giving more discretion to the police are the same ones who are exposed to the risk that discretion will be abused. [T]he assumption that white political establishments can't be relied on to punish—and can in fact be expected to reward—law enforcers who abuse discretion to harass minorities . . . is less well founded now that law enforcers in America's big cities are accountable to political establishments that more fairly represent African-Americans. Uncompromising hostility to discretion is therefore inappropriate.

For responses to this argument, see Symposium, Boston Review, Apr./May 1999. Some who disagree with the Meares-Kahan position point to evidence that black police officers themselves are sometimes guilty of racial profiling directed against other blacks. See Jeffrey Goldberg, The Color of Suspicion, N.Y. Times Mag., June 20, 1999, p. 51. How does that happen? Should it be considered a form of racism?

Some scholars argue that political remedies rather than judicially enforceable rights are now a more effective means to protect against racial discrimination in cities where African Americans are well represented in the police force and in the electoral process. For a skeptical view, focusing on the continuing prevalence of police harassment and discrimination against black youth, see Dorothy E. Roberts, Race, Vagueness, and the Social Meaning of Order-Maintenance Policing, 89 J. Crim. L. & Criminology 775 (1999). See also Albert W. Alschuler & Stephen J. Schulhofer, Antiquated Procedures or Bedrock Rights?: A Response to Professors Meares and Kahan, 1998 U. Chi. Legal F. 215.

What about places where there is no danger of racial discrimination? In some parts of the United States, there are towns and small cities with no significant African-American population. Should such municipalities be permitted to enact ordinances like those challenged in *Morales* and *Papachristou*?

5. *The Chicago response.* In February 2000, the Chicago City Council passed a new antigang ordinance to replace the one struck down in *Morales*. The new ordinance (Chi. Municipal Code §8-4-015) again directs police officers to disperse all persons engaged in "gang loitering" in a public place, whenever they believe that one or more of those present are members of a criminal street gang. This time, the ordinance specifies that dispersal, in compliance with the order, means "remov[ing] themselves from within sight and hearing of the place at which the order was issued." It requires the police superintendent to designate particular areas within the city in which the ordinance will be enforced, and dispersal orders can be issued only when gang loitering occurs within such areas, but the location of the designated areas is not revealed to the public. The ordinance defines gang loitering as:

remaining in any one place under circumstances that would warrant a reasonable person to believe that the purpose or effect of that behavior is to enable a criminal street gang to establish control over identifiable areas, to intimidate others from entering those areas, or to conceal illegal activities.

Questions: Does the new ordinance meet the objections of Justices John Paul Stevens and Sandra Day O'Connor? Suppose that on a hot night, three teenagers hang out on a street corner, talking loudly and playing their "boomboxes." An elderly neighbor calls the police and asks them to disperse the group, saying that they are treating the corner as their private turf and that she feels intimidated from walking by in order to get to the corner store. If police reasonably believe that one of the youth is a gang member, are the teenagers subject to being dispersed under the ordinance? If the ordinance applies in this situation, should it be upheld under *Morales*?

6. Other antigang and antiloitering legislation. The Model Penal Code prohibits "loiter[ing] in a place, at a time, or in a manner not usual for law-abiding individuals under circumstances that warrant alarm for the safety of persons or property in the vicinity." See MPC §250.6, Appendix. Consider whether this provision addresses the kind of gang activity that troubled the Chicago City Council. Would it give police the authority to arrest gang members who stake out their "turf" by congregating in parks and on street corners?

Is the MPC provision constitutional after *Morales*? An ordinance in Athens, Georgia, was written in terms similar to those of the MPC. It prohibited loitering, defined as being "in a place at a time or in a manner not usual for law-abiding individuals . . . under circumstances which cause a justifiable and reasonable alarm or immediate concern that such person is involved in unlawful drug activity." Relying on *Morales*, the Georgia Supreme Court held this ordinance unconstitutionally vague. The court explained that "[t]here are no overt acts necessary to trigger criminal liability under the statute, and no specific guidelines to inform law enforcement officers of what behavior might legitimately bring the officer to believe a person was 'involved in unlawful drug activity.'" Johnson v. Athens-Clarke County, 529 S.E.2d 613 (Ga. 2000).

Ordinances reviewed in the wake of *Morales* have been upheld where they target loitering with a criminal intent or where they are limited to loitering in a specific, narrow location (such as loitering on a bridge). Thus, in State v. Stark, 802 N.W.2d 165, 171 (S.D. 2011), the court upheld a statute that prohibited registered sex offenders from loitering within designated "community safety zones" (such as areas near schools and playgrounds) "for the primary purpose of observing or contacting minors."

Even when framed in this way, antiloitering ordinances continue to raise concern about the potential for abusive enforcement. Consider Silvar v. District Court, 129 P.3d 682 (Nev. 2006), involving a county ordinance that prohibited loitering in a manner "manifesting the purpose of . . . soliciting for . . . prostitution." In an attempt to provide added clarity, the ordinance identified circumstances that could be considered in determining whether the unlawful purpose had been manifested, for example, "repeatedly beckon [ing] to . . . or engag[ing] persons passing by in conversation, or repeatedly . . .

attempt[ing] to stop motor vehicle operators by hailing, waving of arms or any other bodily gesture." Should this law pass muster under *Morales*? The Nevada Supreme Court held the ordinance unconstitutionally vague. The court viewed the ordinance as giving police officers unlimited discretion to arrest, because it did not require proof of an intent to commit prostitution and because it therefore could apply to persons strolling aimlessly or hailing a cab and to "effusive tourists celebrating a public holiday." Courts have likewise struck down ordinances that prohibit loitering "under circumstances manifesting the purpose [to sell drugs]" when "[r]epeatedly beckoning" can establish a manifested purpose, without proof of the defendant's actual intent. State v. Mello, 684 S.E.2d 477, 479 (N.C. App. 2009). For a review of *Morales*-based challenges, see Kim Strosnider, Anti-Gang Ordinances After *City of Chicago v. Morales*: The Intersection of Race, Vagueness Doctrine, and Equal Protection in the Criminal Law, 39 Am. Crim. L. Rev. 101 (2002).

7. *Vagueness and degree.* In Nash v. United States, 229 U.S. 373 (1912), the Supreme Court, in an opinion by Justice Oliver Wendell Holmes Jr., upheld a conviction for unduly obstructing trade, in violation of the Sherman Anti-Trust Act. Over the objection that the crime "contains in its definition an element of degree as to which estimates may differ, with the result that a man might find himself in prison because his honest judgment did not anticipate that of a jury," Justice Holmes replied:

> [T]he law is full of instances where a man's fate depends on his estimating rightly, that is, as the jury subsequently estimates it, some matter of degree. If his judgment is wrong, not only may he incur a fine or a short imprisonment, as here; he may incur the penalty of death. "An act causing death may be murder, manslaughter, or misadventure, according to the degree of danger attending it" by common experience in the circumstances known to the actor. . . . If a man . . . did no more than drive negligently through a street, he might get off with manslaughter or less. [And] he might be held although he himself thought that he was acting as a prudent man should. . . . [T]here is no constitutional difficulty in the way of enforcing the criminal part of the act. . . .

In United States v. Ragen, 314 U.S. 513, 523 (1941), the Court sustained a criminal conviction for willfully taking an unreasonable deduction on an income tax return, stating: "The mere fact that a penal statute is so framed as to require a jury upon occasion to determine a question of reasonableness is not sufficient to make it too vague to afford a practical guide to permissible conduct." The case law that determines when statutes are too vague is itself exceedingly vague. For a thorough discussion, see John Calvin Jeffries, Jr., Legality, Vagueness, and the Construction of Penal Statutes, 71 Va. L. Rev. 189 (1985).

8. *Problem.* Until recently, Montana had no specific speed limit on rural roads. A statute, however, made it an offense to operate a vehicle at a speed "greater than is reasonable and proper under the conditions existing at the

point of operation, taking into account the amount and character of traffic, ... grade and width of highway, ... and freedom of obstruction to the view ahead." Defendant was charged under this statute for driving at 85 miles per hour, on a clear day during daylight hours, on a dry rural road with no significant traffic in the area. The Montana Supreme Court held the statute unconstitutionally vague on its face. State v. Stanko, 974 P.2d 1132, 1137-1138 (1998):

> [The statute] impermissibly delegates the basic public policy of how fast is too fast on Montana's highways to "policemen, judges, and juries for resolution on an ad hoc and subjective basis." [Although the statute enumerates the highway conditions to be considered,] there is no specification of how these various factors are to be weighted, or whether priority should be given to some factors as opposed to others. [E]ven if law enforcement officials were qualified to make those kinds of judgments, the statute would not satisfy the requirement that a motor vehicle operator of average intelligence know what conduct is prohibited and when his or her conduct is going to be subject to criminal penalties.

Do you agree? If so, are common statutes like those mentioned by Justice Holmes—statutes that punish for manslaughter when someone kills another by driving in a grossly negligent manner—void for vagueness?

C. PROPORTIONALITY

INTRODUCTORY NOTE

The requirement that punishment be proportional to the seriousness of the offense is a core principle of punishment, both as a central limit dictated by the Eighth Amendment, and as a statutory statement of purpose in modern criminal codes. The MPC (§1.02) includes among its purposes the aim "to differentiate on reasonable grounds between serious and minor offenses," and "to safeguard offenders against excessive, disproportionate or arbitrary punishment." The New York Penal Law similarly aims (§1.05) "[t]o differentiate on reasonable grounds between serious and minor offenses and to prescribe proportionate penalties therefor." The California Penal Code declares in §1170 that "punishment" is the purpose of imprisonment for crimes, which purpose is "best served by terms proportionate to the seriousness of the offense."

What is the basis for this concern with proportionality? If we believe excessive punishment is unjust, what constitutes excessive punishment? Is there a precise kind and degree of punishment appropriate to every criminal wrong, as Immanuel Kant argued? Is the point that certain crimes cannot be punished with more than a given quantum of punishment, or is it simply that less serious crimes must be punished less severely than more serious crimes? Some believe that the aim of punishment is not justice and fairness (however defined), but a strictly utilitarian goal. If we hold this view, must we accept that any amount of punishment, no matter how severe, is justifiable if, in the circumstances, it yields a desirable balance of net benefits?

These are the principal issues addressed in the material that follows.

JEREMY BENTHAM, PRINCIPLES OF PENAL LAW

in 1 J. Bentham's Works, Pt. II, bk. 1 at 399-402
(J. Bowring ed., 1843)

Punishments may be too small or too great; and there are reasons for not making them too small, as well as not making them too great. The terms *minimum* and *maximum* may serve to mark the two extremes of this question.

[O]n the side of the first of these extremes, we may lay it down as a rule—

(I) That the value of the punishment must not be less in any case than what is sufficient to outweigh that of the profit of the offence. [If] a man, having reaped the profit of a crime, and undergone the punishment, finds the former more than equivalent to the latter, he will go on offending for ever; there is nothing to restrain him. If those, also, who behold him, reckon that the balance of gain is in favour of the delinquent, the punishment will be useless for the purposes of example. . . .

Rule III. [*When two offences come in competition, the punishment for the greater offence must be sufficient to induce a man to prefer the less.*]

Two offences may be said to be in competition, when it is in the power of an individual to commit both. When thieves break into a house, they may execute their purpose in different manners; by simply stealing, by theft accompanied with bodily injury, or murder, or incendiarism. If the punishment is the same for simple theft, as for theft and murder, you give the thieves a motive for committing murder, because this crime adds to the facility of committing the former, and the chance of impunity when it is committed.

The great inconvenience resulting from the infliction of great punishments for small offences, is, that the power of increasing them in proportion to the magnitude of the offence is thereby lost.

Rule IV. [*The punishment should be adjusted in such manner to each particular offence, that for every part of the mischief there may be a motive to restrain the offender from giving birth to it.*]

Thus, for example, in adjusting the punishment for stealing a sum of money, let the magnitude of the punishment be determined by the amount of the sum stolen. If for stealing ten shillings an offender is punished no more than for stealing five, the stealing of the remaining five of those ten shillings is an offence for which there is no punishment at all.

Rule V. [*The punishment ought in no case to be more than what is necessary to bring it into conformity with the rules here given.*] . .

What is not sufficient is easily seen, but it is not possible so exactly to distinguish in excess: an approximation only can be attained. The irregularities in the force of temptations compel the legislator to increase his punishments, till they are not merely sufficient to restrain the ordinary desires of men, but also the violence of their desires when unusually excited.

easy to fix punishment too small, not so for long punishment

[A]n error on the minimum side . . . is least likely to occur, a slight degree of attention sufficing for its escape; and when it does exist, it is at the same time clear and manifest, and easy to be remedied. An error on the maximum side, on the contrary, is that to which legislators and men in general are naturally inclined: antipathy, or a want of compassion for individuals who are represented as dangerous and vile, pushes them onward to an undue severity. It is on this side, therefore, that we should take the most precautions, as on this side there has been shown the greatest disposition to err. . . .

Rule VII. *That the value of the punishment may outweigh the profit of the offence, it must be increased in point of magnitude, in proportion as it falls short in point of certainty.*

Rule VIII. *Punishment must be further increased in point of magnitude, in proportion as it falls short in points of proximity.*

The profit of a crime is commonly more certain than its punishment; or, what amounts to the same thing, appears so to the offender. It is generally more immediate: the temptation to offend is present; the punishment is at a distance. Hence there are two circumstances which weaken the effect of punishment, its *uncertainty* and its *distance.*

Hyman Gross, A Theory of Criminal Justice 436 (1979): [T]he requirement that punishment not be disproportionately great . . . is dictated by the same principle that does not allow punishment of the innocent, for any punishment in excess of what is deserved for the criminal conduct is punishment without guilt.

H.L.A. Hart & A. Honoré, Causation in the Law 395-396 (2d ed. 1985): On a deterrent theory the rationale of the differential severity of punishments is complex. First, one crime if unchecked may cause greater harm than another, and hence on general utilitarian grounds greater severity may be used in its repression than in the repression of the less harmful crime. Secondly, the temptation to commit one sort of crime may be greater than another and hence a more severe penalty is needed to deter. Thirdly, the commission of one crime may be a sign of a more dangerous character in the criminal needing longer sentence for incapacitation or reform.

A.C. Ewing, A Study of Punishment II: Punishment as Viewed by the Philosopher, 21 Canadian B. Rev. 102, 115-116 (1943): [I]f a man is very severely punished for a comparatively slight offence, people will be liable to forget about his crime and think only of his sufferings, so that he appears a victim of cruel laws, and the whole process, instead of reaffirming the law and intensifying men's consciousness that the kind of act punished is wrong, will have the opposite effect of casting discredit on the law and making the action of the lawbreaker appear excusable or even almost heroic. These punishments are specially liable to produce an effect of this sort on their victim. He will be likely to think the penalty excessive in any case, and the great danger of punishment is that this will lead to self-pity and despair, or anger and bitterness, instead of repentance, but if he has really good grounds for complaint, this danger will be doubled. The primary object of punishment is to lead both the offender and others to realize the badness of the act punished; but, if great severity is shown, they are much more likely to realize instead the cruelty of the punishment.

H.L.A. Hart, Law, Liberty and Morality 36-37 (1963): There are many reasons why we might wish the legal graduation of the seriousness of crimes, expressed in its scale of punishments, not to conflict with common estimates of their comparative wickedness. One reason is that such a conflict is undesirable on simple utilitarian grounds: it might either confuse moral judgments or bring the law into disrepute, or both. Another reason is that principles of justice or fairness between different offenders require morally distinguishable offences to be treated differently and morally similar offences to be treated alike. These principles are still widely respected, although it is also true that there is a growing disinclination to insist on their application where this conflicts with the forward-looking aims of punishment, such as prevention or reform. But those who concede that we should attempt to adjust the severity of punishment to the moral gravity of offences are not thereby committed to the view that punishment merely for immorality is justified. For they can in perfect consistency insist on the one hand that the only justification for having a system of punishment is to prevent harm and only harmful conduct should be punished, and, on the other, agree that when the question of the quantum of punishment for such conduct is raised, we should defer to principles which make relative moral wickedness of different offenders [only] a partial determinant of the severity of punishment.

Andrew von Hirsch & Andrew Ashworth, Proportionate Sentencing: Exploring the Principles 132-135 (2005): The first account of the principle of proportionate sanctions was utilitarian. [But w]hen the proportionality principle is thus defended on grounds of [crime-preventive efficacy] and nothing more, it loses its status as an independent ethical requirement and remains subject to whatever dilutions appear to be needed in the name of crime control. . . .

[Other proponents of proportionality] have stressed the role of punishment as a reinforcement of citizens' moral inhibitions against crime. . . . The idea, ultimately, remains one of crime prevention. It involves the assertion that if sentences are made proportionate, the citizenry's moral inhibitions will better be reinforced, which in turn will enable the criminal law to carry out its crime-restraining role more successfully. [In contrast, w]e feel there is something *wrong,* not simply counterproductive . . . , about inflicting punishments that are not fairly commensurate with the gravity of offences. . . .

Punishing someone consists of inflicting a deprivation on him, because he has purportedly committed a wrong, under circumstances and in a manner that conveys disapprobation of the offender for his wrong. . . . Once one has created an institution with the condemnatory implications that punishment has, then it is a requirement of justice, not merely of efficient crime prevention, to punish offenders according to the degree of reprehensibleness of their conduct . . . [so that the allocation of sanctions] comports fairly with the degree of reprehensibleness of those acts.

EWING v. CALIFORNIA

Supreme Court of the United States
538 U.S. 11 (2003)

JUSTICE O'CONNOR announced the judgment of the Court and delivered an opinion in which THE CHIEF JUSTICE and JUSTICE KENNEDY join.

In this case, we decide whether the Eighth Amendment prohibits the State of California from sentencing a repeat felon to a prison term of 25 years to life under the State's "Three Strikes and You're Out" law.

California's three strikes law reflects a shift in the State's sentencing policies toward incapacitating and deterring repeat offenders who threaten the public safety. . . . On October 1, 1993, while [a referendum to enact such a law] was circulating, 12-year-old Polly Klaas was kidnapped from her home. . . . Her admitted killer, Richard Allen Davis, had a long criminal history that included two prior kidnapping convictions. Davis had served only half of his most recent [16-year] sentence. . . . Had Davis served his entire sentence, he would still have been in prison on the day that Polly Klaas was kidnapped.

Polly Klaas' murder galvanized support for the three strikes initiative. . . . California thus became the second State to enact a three strikes law. . . . Between 1993 and 1995, 24 States and the Federal Government enacted three strikes laws. Though the three strikes laws vary from State to State, they share a common goal of protecting the public safety by providing lengthy prison terms for habitual felons.

[Under] California's current three strikes law . . . [i]f the defendant has one prior "serious" or "violent" felony conviction, he must be sentenced to "twice the term otherwise provided as punishment for the current felony conviction." If the defendant has two or more prior "serious" or "violent" felony convictions, he must receive "an indeterminate term of life imprisonment." Defendants sentenced to life under the three strikes law become eligible for parole on a date calculated by reference to a "minimum term" which is [never less than 25 years]. . . . [C]ertain offenses [known as "wobblers"] may be classified as either felonies or misdemeanors. . . . Some crimes that would otherwise be misdemeanors become "wobblers" because of the defendant's prior record [and] prosecutors may exercise their discretion to charge a "wobbler" as either a felony or a misdemeanor. . . . California trial courts have discretion to . . . avoid imposing a three strikes sentence . . . by reducing "wobblers" to misdemeanors [or] by vacating allegations of prior "serious" or "violent" felony convictions.]

On parole from a 9-year prison term, petitioner Gary Ewing walked into the pro shop of the El Segundo Golf Course [and] walked out with three golf clubs, priced at $399 apiece, concealed in his pants leg. A shop employee, whose suspicions were aroused when he observed Ewing limp out of the pro shop, telephoned the police [who] apprehended Ewing in the parking lot.

Ewing is no stranger to the criminal justice system. In 1984, at the age of 22, he pleaded guilty to theft. [Between 1988 and September 1993, Ewing was convicted of four other theft offenses, one burglary, one battery, possession of drug paraphernalia and possession of a firearm. His sentences typically ranged from 10 to 60 days in jail, followed by probation, though he served a year in jail on one of the theft charges and six months in jail for the drug offense. Then in October and November 1993, he committed three burglaries and one robbery over a 5-week period. In one instance, when he encountered a victim, he produced a knife and absconded with the victim's money and credit cards. For these offenses, he was convicted of robbery and three counts of burglary and sentenced to 116 months.]

Only 10 months [after his release on parole in 1999], Ewing stole the golf clubs at issue in this case [and was convicted of] felony grand theft. [The trial court found] that Ewing had been convicted previously of four serious or violent felonies for the three burglaries and the robbery in [1993].

At the sentencing hearing, Ewing asked the court to reduce the conviction for grand theft . . . to a misdemeanor [and to dismiss some or all of his prior felony convictions] so as to avoid a three strikes sentence. [T]he trial judge [refused, and] Ewing was sentenced under the three strikes law to 25 years to life. The California Court of Appeal affirmed. . . . The Supreme Court of California denied Ewing's petition for review, and we granted certiorari. We now affirm.

The Eighth Amendment, which forbids cruel and unusual punishments, contains a "narrow proportionality principle" that "applies to noncapital sentences." Harmelin v. Michigan, 501 U.S. 957, 996-997 (1991) (Kennedy, J., concurring . . .).

[The Court then discussed prior Eighth Amendment cases. In Rummel v. Estelle, 445 U.S. 263 (1980), the Court upheld a life sentence with the possibility of parole for an offender who obtained $120.75 by false pretenses and whose two prior offenses were felony convictions for "fraudulent use of a credit card to obtain $80 worth of goods or services" and for "passing a forged check in the amount of $28.36." Three years later, in Solem v. Helm, 463 U.S. 277 (1983), the Court held it unconstitutional to give a life sentence without possibility of parole to a defendant who uttered a bad check for $100, his seventh nonviolent felony. In Solem, the Court explained that "three factors may be relevant to a determination of whether a sentence is so disproportionate that it violates the Eighth Amendment: (i) the gravity of the offense and the harshness of the penalty; (ii) the sentences imposed on other criminals in the same jurisdiction; and (iii) the sentences imposed for commission of the same crime in other jurisdictions."

[In *Harmelin*, the Court upheld a sentence of life without possibility of parole for a first offender convicted of possessing 672 grams of cocaine. The Court, however, could not agree on a rationale. Justice Scalia, joined by Chief Justice Rehnquist, wrote that the proportionality requirement was "an aspect of our death penalty jurisprudence, rather than a generalizable aspect of Eighth Amendment law." Justice Kennedy, joined by two other justices, accepted proportionality review for non-capital sentences. He identified four principles of proportionality review—"the primacy of the legislature, the variety of legitimate penological schemes, the nature of our federal system, and the requirement that proportionality review be guided by objective factors"—that "inform the final one: The Eighth Amendment does not require strict proportionality between crime and sentence. Rather, it forbids only extreme sentences that are 'grossly disproportionate' to the crime." By this standard, Justice Kennedy concluded that Harmelin's sentence was not "grossly disproportionate."

[In her *Ewing* opinion, Justice O'Connor concluded that "[t]he proportionality principles . . . distilled in Justice Kennedy's [*Harmelin*] concurrence guide our application of the Eighth Amendment."]

For many years, most States have had laws providing for enhanced sentencing of repeat offenders. Yet between 1993 and 1995, three strikes laws effected a sea change in criminal sentencing throughout the Nation. These laws responded to widespread public concerns about crime by targeting the class of offenders who pose the greatest threat to public safety: career criminals. . . . [L]egislatures enacting three strikes laws made a deliberate policy choice that individuals who have repeatedly engaged in serious or violent criminal behavior, and whose conduct has not been deterred by more conventional approaches to punishment, must be isolated from society in order to protect the public safety. Though three strikes laws may be relatively new, our tradition of deferring to state legislatures in making and implementing such important policy decisions is longstanding. . . .

Recidivism is a serious public safety concern in California and throughout the Nation. According to a recent report, . . . released property offenders like Ewing had higher recidivism rates than those released after committing violent, drug, or public-order offenses. Approximately 73 percent of the property offenders released in 1994 were arrested again within three years, compared to approximately 61 percent of the violent offenders, 62 percent of the public-order offenders, and 66 percent of the drug offenders.

[Deterrence] also lends some support to the three strikes law. . . . Four years after the passage of California's three strikes law, the recidivism rate of parolees returned to prison for the commission of a new crime dropped by nearly 25 percent [and] "an unintended but positive consequence of 'Three Strikes' has been [that m]ore California parolees are now leaving the state than parolees from other jurisdictions entering California. . . ."

To be sure, California's three strikes law has sparked controversy. Critics have doubted the law's wisdom, cost-efficiency, and effectiveness in reaching its goals. See, e.g., Zimring, Hawkins, & Kamin, Punishment and Democracy: Three Strikes and You're Out in California (2001); Vitiello, Three Strikes: Can We Return to Rationality? 871 Crim. L. & Criminology 395, 423 (1997). [But w]e do not sit as a "superlegislature" to second-guess these policy choices. It is enough that the State of California has a reasonable basis for believing that [its sentencing policy will further penological goals.]

Against this backdrop, we consider Ewing's claim that his three strikes sentence of 25 years to life is unconstitutionally disproportionate to his offense of "shoplifting three golf clubs." . . . Even standing alone, Ewing's theft should not be taken lightly. [And] the State's interest is not merely punishing the offense of conviction, or the "triggering" offense. [Ewing's sentence also] reflects a rational legislative judgment, entitled to deference, that offenders who have committed serious or violent felonies and who continue to commit felonies must be incapacitated. . . .

not disproportionate

JUSTICE SCALIA, concurring in the judgment. . . .

Proportionality—the notion that the punishment should fit the crime—is inherently a concept tied to the penological goal of retribution. "It becomes difficult even to speak intelligently of 'proportionality,' once deterrence and rehabilitation are given significant weight." . . . In the present case, the game is up once the plurality has acknowledged that "the Constitution does not mandate adoption of any one penological theory." . . . That acknowledgment having been made, it no longer suffices merely to assess "the gravity of the offense compared to the harshness of the penalty"; that classic description of the proportionality principle (. . . in itself quite resistant to policy-free, legal analysis) now becomes merely the "first" step of the inquiry. Having completed that step (by a discussion which, in all fairness, does not convincingly establish that 25-years-to-life is a "proportionate" punishment for stealing three golf clubs), the plurality must then add an analysis to show that "Ewing's sentence is justified by the State's public-safety interest in incapacitating and deterring recidivist felons." [W]hy that has anything to do with the principle of proportionality is a mystery. [T]he plurality reads into the Eighth Amendment . . . the unstated proposition that all punishment should reasonably pursue the multiple purposes of the criminal law. That formulation would make it clearer than ever, of course, that the plurality is not applying law but evaluating policy. . . .[a]

1st step of inquiry now

now looks at why its being done

JUSTICE BREYER, with whom JUSTICE STEVENS, JUSTICE SOUTER, and JUSTICE GINSBURG join, dissenting. . . .

---

a. Justice Thomas concurred to note that he agreed with Justice Scalia's opinion in *Harmelin* that the Eighth Amendment was adopted to outlaw certain modes of punishment (e.g., drawing and quartering) but was not intended to guarantee proportionality. In *Harmelin*, Justice Scalia noted, "While there are relatively clear historical guidelines and accepted practices that enable judges to determine which modes of punishment are 'cruel and unusual,' *proportionality* does not lend itself to such an analysis."—EDS.

[C]ourts faced with a "gross disproportionality" claim must first make "a threshold comparison of the crime committed and the sentence imposed." If a claim crosses that threshold—itself a rare occurrence—then the court should compare the sentence at issue to other sentences . . . in the same, or in other, jurisdictions. The comparative analysis will "validate" or invalidate "an initial judgment that a sentence is grossly disproportionate to a crime." [The comparative analysis looks at (a) the length of the prison term; (b) the sentence-triggering criminal conduct; and (c) the offender's criminal history.]

[C]onsider the present case. The [prior record] does not differ significantly here from that in *Solem*[, and it] would be difficult to say that the actual behavior itself here (shoplifting) differs significantly from that at issue in *Solem* (passing a bad check) or in *Rummel* (obtaining money through false pretenses). [Ewing's sentence] is considerably shorter than [the] sentence in *Solem*, which amounted, in real terms, to life in prison [but] more than twice as long as the term at issue in *Rummel*. [I]t means that Ewing himself, seriously ill when sentenced at age 38, will likely die in prison. . . . Overall, the comparison places Ewing's sentence well within the twilight zone between *Solem* and *Rummel*. . . .

I do not deny the seriousness of shoplifting, which an amicus curiae tells us costs retailers in the range of $30 billion annually. But [in terms of] "harm caused or threatened to the victim or society," . . . the sentence-triggering behavior here ranks well toward the bottom of the criminal conduct scale.

[Justice Breyer then found Ewing's sentence "extreme" under a comparative analysis:] California . . . reserves Ewing-type prison time, i.e., at least 25 real years in prison, for criminals convicted of crimes far worse than was Ewing's. [F]or the years 1945 to 1981, for example, . . . typical (non-recidivist) male first-degree murderers served between 10 and 15 real years in prison, with 90 percent of all such murderers serving less than 20 real years. [N]onrecidivists guilty of arson causing great bodily injury [serve] a maximum sentence of nine years in prison. . . .

As to other jurisdictions, . . . the federal Sentencing Guidelines [which set the punishment for federal crimes] would impose upon a recidivist, such as Ewing, a sentence that, in any ordinary case, would not exceed 18 months in prison. The Guidelines . . . reserve a Ewing-type sentence for Ewing-type recidivists who currently commit such crimes as murder; air piracy; robbery (involving the discharge of a firearm, serious bodily injury, and about $1 million); drug offenses involving more than, for example, 20 pounds of heroin; aggravated theft of more than $100 million; and other similar offenses. [There are only nine states in which] the law *might* make it legally possible to impose a sentence of 25 years or more, though that fact by itself, of course, does not mean that judges have actually done so. . . . California [and its supporting amici], despite every incentive to find [a sentence comparable to Ewing's], have come up with precisely three examples. [In one, an Alabama case involving a "life" sentence for the theft of a tractor-trailer, the offender was eligible for parole after ten years, and in the second case, the South Dakota court did not consider the constitutionality of the sentence. Only one case, from Nevada, is truly comparable]—a single instance of a similar sentence imposed outside the context of California's three strikes law, out of a prison population now approaching two million individuals. . . . Ewing's recidivist sentence is virtually unique in its harshness. . . .

One might argue that those who commit several property crimes should receive long terms of imprisonment in order to "incapacitate" them. . . . But that is not the object of this particular three strikes statute. Rather, as the plurality says, California seeks "to reduce serious and violent crime." The statute's definitions of both kinds of crime [i.e., those which can count as one of the first two "strikes"] include crimes against the person, crimes that create danger of physical harm, and drug crimes. They do not include even serious crimes against property, such as obtaining large amounts of money, say, through theft, embezzlement, or fraud. . . . Nor do the remaining criminal law objectives seem relevant. No one argues for Ewing's inclusion within the ambit of the three strikes statute on grounds of "retribution." [I]n terms of "deterrence," Ewing's 25-year term amounts to overkill. And "rehabilitation" is obviously beside the point. . . .

NOTES

1. *Determining whether a punishment is proportionate.* Should the prospect of large benefits in deterrence or incapacitation suffice to render a punishment "proportionate," or should proportionality be viewed as requiring punishment that is commensurate with culpability and the gravity of the crime for which an offender is being sentenced? What is the plurality's view in *Ewing*? On what grounds do Justices Scalia and Breyer disagree with the plurality?

A second fundamental question is whether the proportionality judgment is best made by the people, through the laws enacted by legislatures, or whether the courts must play a more robust role. Professor Youngjae Lee frames the debate between "elite" or "popular" understanding as follows (Desert and the Eighth Amendment, 11 U. Pa. J. Const. L. 101, 103-104 (2008)):

[O]ne may believe that the questions of what people deserve or do not deserve are matters of objective moral reality, and "the people," or its frequent proxy, the democratic process, may come out with a wrong answer at times. According to this view, the purpose of the Eighth Amendment is to enforce the retributivist constraint, the content of which does not change with the whims of the democratic majority. This understanding of retribution coheres well with a common image of constitutional rights in general and of the Cruel and Unusual Punishments Clause in particular, as the Clause is typically understood as playing the role of holding the excessive, and frequently irrational, punitive instincts of "the people" in check by imposing a moral constraint.

[Alternatively, one] may believe that . . . what an offender deserves is equivalent to what "the people" believe he deserves, and [that] it is a misunderstanding of desert to believe that theorists can second-guess desert determinations made by "the people." If "the people," or their democratically elected representatives, think that child molesters deserve to be punished with death, on what possible grounds can a philosopher or a judge decide that their desert judgment is "incorrect"?

If courts do second-guess the judgment of "the people," on what basis can they do so? With respect to the three-strikes law in particular, consider Michael Vitiello, California's Three Strikes and We're Out: Was Judicial Activism California's Best Hope?, 37 U.C. Davis L. Rev. 1025, 1071 (2004):

> [A]mple evidence demonstrates widespread [public] confusion about the scope of Three Strikes. Indeed, the law would not have passed but for the kid-napping and murder of Polly Klaas. Passions ran so high in favor of the law that no one seemed to notice that the Klaas family withdrew their support for the law because they found it too extreme. [I]t is exactly that kind of law, one enacted in the passion of the moment, that may trigger the need for judicial review.

Erik Luna similarly describes the three-strikes law in California as a "prime example of a moral panic." Criminal Justice and the Public Imagination, 7 Ohio St. J. Crim. L. 71, 84 (2009). Can courts effectively identify when a law is the product of "passion" or "panic" that does not deserve deference as an assessment of proportionality?

As *Ewing* illustrates, Justices Scalia and Thomas hold that the Eighth Amendment contains no proportionality requirement. John Stinneford takes issue with that claim on originalist grounds, arguing that proportionality was part of the original understanding of the Eighth Amendment. John F. Stinneford, Rethinking Proportionality Under the Cruel and Unusual Punishments Clause, 97 Va. L. Rev. 899 (2011). Ian Farrell disputes Justice Scalia's argument on philosophical grounds, disagreeing in particular with the claim that proportionality review is impossible once the Court accepts deterrence, rehabilitation, and incapacitation as legitimate goals of punishment. Ian P. Farrell, Gilbert & Sullivan and Scalia: Philosophy, Proportionality, and the Eighth Amendment, 55 Vill. L. Rev. 321 (2010). What are the relative advantages of courts and legislatures in making judgments on those pragmatic concerns?

2. Proportionality and recidivism. Lockyer v. Andrade, 538 U.S. 63 (2003), decided together with *Ewing*, was another California three-strikes case. Andrade had stolen from a Kmart on two occasions, taking videotapes worth $84.70 the first time and tapes worth $68.84 the second. Because both amounts were under $200, the offenses were classified as petty theft, normally a misdemeanor. But because Andrade had previous convictions (two misde-meanor thefts, two counts of transporting marijuana, and three counts of residential burglary), the three-strikes statute applied. As a result, for *each* of the petty thefts, he was sentenced to a term of 25 years to life, the terms to run consecutively. Justice O'Connor, writing for five members of the Court, refused to overturn the sentence.[3] Justice Souter, for the four dissenters, said (538 U.S. at 83) that "[i]f Andrade's sentence is not grossly disproportionate, the principle has no meaning."

While the sentences in *Ewing* and *Andrade* seem severe in relation to the crimes charged in those cases, both decisions involve the distinct problem of how proportionality should be affected by the *prior* criminal conduct of the offenders. Utilitarians consider longer punishments necessary because the offender was not deterred by the initial sanction. But does the enhanced punishment violate the principles of retributivism? For an argument that longer sentences are not disproportionate to culpability because an offender has a greater duty to avoid committing a new crime after being convicted the first time, see Youngjae Lee, Recidivism as Omission: A Relational Account, 87 Tex. L. Rev. 571, 610 (2009). Do you agree? Does this reasoning suffice to justify the life sentences imposed on Andrade for his two petty thefts?

GRAHAM v. FLORIDA

Supreme Court of the United States
130 S. Ct. 2011 (2010)

KENNEDY, J. delivered the opinion of the Court.

[Graham pleaded guilty to attempted robbery at the age of 16 and was sentenced to three years' probation, with the first year to be served in the county jail. Less than six months after being released, he was arrested for a home-invasion robbery with two accomplices, Bailey and Lawrence. They held two men at gunpoint and ransacked the home looking for cash. Later the same evening, the three attempted a second robbery, during which Bailey was shot. Graham drove Bailey and Lawrence to the hospital and left them there. As he drove away, a police sergeant signaled him to stop. Graham continued driving at high speed but crashed into a telephone pole, tried to flee on foot, and was apprehended. Three handguns were found in his car. The night of the robbery, he was 34 days short of his eighteenth birthday. The trial court found that Graham had violated his probation by committing the home-invasion robbery, by possessing a firearm, and by associating with persons engaged in criminal activity. It sentenced him to the maximum sentence authorized by law: life imprisonment for the home-invasion robbery and 15 years for the attempted armed robbery. Florida abolished its parole system, so the life sentence was without the possibility of parole.]

The Court's cases addressing the proportionality of sentences fall within two general classifications. The first involves challenges to the length of term-of-years sentences given all the circumstances in a particular case. The second

---

3. The case came to the Supreme Court on habeas corpus, so the proportionality issue was not presented to the Court directly. Rather, the issue was the technically more limited question whether the state court decision upholding the sentence was "unreasonable," and the Court held that it was not.

comprises cases in which the Court implements the proportionality standard by certain categorical restrictions on the death penalty.

[The latter] cases ha[ve] used categorical rules to define Eighth Amendment standards. The previous cases in this classification involved the death penalty. The classification in turn consists of two subsets, one considering the nature of the offense, the other considering the characteristics of the offender. . . .

In the cases adopting categorical rules[, the] Court first considers "objective indicia of society's standards, as expressed in legislative enactments and state practice" to determine whether there is a national consensus against the sentencing practice at issue. . . . Next, guided by "the standards elaborated by controlling precedents and by the Court's own understanding and interpretation of the Eighth Amendment's text, history, meaning, and purpose," . . . the Court must determine in the exercise of its own independent judgment whether the punishment in question violates the Constitution. . . .

The present case involves an issue the Court has not considered previously: a categorical challenge to a term-of-years sentence. This case implicates a particular type of sentence as it applies to an entire class of offenders who have committed a range of crimes. [I]n addressing the question presented, the appropriate analysis is the one used in cases that involved the categorical approach. . . .

[The Court then found life without possibility of parole (LWOP) to be a disproportionate sentence for juveniles who do not commit homicide.]

Roper [v. Simmons, 543 U.S. 551 (2005),] established that because juveniles have lessened culpability they are less deserving of the most severe punishments. . . . The Court has recognized that defendants who do not kill, intend to kill, or foresee that life will be taken are categorically less deserving of the most serious forms of punishment than are murderers. . . . It follows that, when compared to an adult murderer, a juvenile offender who did not kill or intend to kill has a twice diminished moral culpability.

As for the punishment, [i]t is true that a death sentence is "unique in its severity and irrevocability," Gregg v. Georgia, 428 U.S. 153, 187 (1976) (joint opinion of Stewart, Powell, and Stevens , JJ.); yet life without parole sentences share some characteristics with death sentences that are shared by no other sentences. [An LWOP] sentence alters the offender's life by a forfeiture that is irrevocable. It deprives the convict of the most basic liberties without giving hope of restoration, except perhaps by executive clemency—the remote possibility of which does not mitigate the harshness of the sentence. . . .

[The Court next considered the penological justifications for an LWOP sentence and concluded that] none of the goals of penal sanctions that have been recognized as legitimate—retribution, deterrence, incapacitation, and rehabilitation, see *Ewing*, 538 U.S., at 25 (plurality opinion)—provides an adequate justification.

[The Court rejected the sentence under the retributive rationale because of the lesser culpability of juveniles. Deterrence failed to support the sentence, in the Court's view, because juveniles make impetuous decisions and are less likely to take a potential punishment into account. As for incapacitation, the

Court stated that "[t]o justify life without parole on the assumption that the juvenile offender forever will be a danger to society requires the sentencer to make a judgment that the juvenile is incorrigible. The characteristics of juveniles make that judgment questionable." And, in the Court's view, "[i]ncapacitation cannot override all other considerations, lest the Eighth Amendment's rule against disproportionate sentences be a nullity." Rehabilitation failed to justify the sentence, according to the Court, because an LWOP sentence "forswears altogether the rehabilitative ideal." The Court then faced the question of whether to categorically bar LWOP for all juveniles who commit nonhomicide offenses:]

Categorical rules tend to be imperfect, but one is necessary here. [E]ven if we were to assume that some juvenile nonhomicide offenders might have "sufficient psychological maturity, and at the same time demonstrat[e] sufficient depravity," Roper, 543 U.S., at 572, to merit a life without parole sentence, it does not follow that courts taking a case-by-case proportionality approach could with sufficient accuracy distinguish the few incorrigible juvenile offenders from the many that have the capacity for change. ...

Another problem with a case-by-case approach is that it does not take account of special difficulties encountered by counsel in juvenile representation. ... Juveniles mistrust adults and have limited understandings of the criminal justice system and the roles of the institutional actors within it. They are less likely than adults to work effectively with their lawyers to aid in their defense. ... Difficulty in weighing long-term consequences; a corresponding impulsiveness; and reluctance to trust defense counsel seen as part of the adult world a rebellious youth rejects, all can lead to poor decisions by one charged with a juvenile offense. ... These factors are likely to impair the quality of a juvenile defendant's representation. ...

Finally, a categorical rule gives all juvenile nonhomicide offenders a chance to demonstrate maturity and reform. [LWOP] gives no chance for fulfillment outside prison walls, no chance for reconciliation with society, no hope. Maturity can lead to that considered reflection which is the foundation for remorse, renewal, and rehabilitation. A young person who knows that he or she has no chance to leave prison before life's end has little incentive to become a responsible individual. ...

ROBERTS, C.J., concurring in the judgment.

I agree with the Court that Terrance Graham's sentence of life without parole violates the Eighth Amendment's prohibition on "cruel and unusual punishments." Unlike the majority, however, I see no need to invent a new constitutional rule of dubious provenance in reaching that conclusion. Instead, my analysis is based on an application of this Court's precedents, in particular (1) our cases requiring "narrow proportionality" review of noncapital sentences and (2) [Roper's conclusion], that juvenile offenders are generally less culpable than adults who commit the same crimes. ...

[Although Chief Justice Roberts rejected Graham's sentence as disproportionate, he disagreed with a categorical ban in all juvenile non-homicide cases, asking:] [W]hat about Milagro Cunningham, a 17-year-old who beat and raped an 8-year-old girl before leaving her to die under 197 pounds of rock in a recycling bin in a remote landfill? . . . Or Nathan Walker and Jakaris Taylor, the Florida juveniles who together with their friends gang-raped a woman and forced her to perform oral sex on her 12-year-old son? . . . The fact that Graham cannot be sentenced to life without parole . . . says nothing whatever about these offenders, or others like them who commit nonhomicide crimes far more reprehensible than the conduct at issue here. The Court uses Graham's case as a vehicle to proclaim a new constitutional rule—applicable well beyond the particular facts of Graham's case—that a sentence of life without parole imposed on any juvenile for any nonhomicide offense is unconstitutional. This categorical conclusion is as unnecessary as it is unwise.

. . . The Court . . . argues that a case-by-case approach to proportionality review is constitutionally insufficient because courts might not be able "with sufficient accuracy [to] distinguish the few incorrigible juvenile offenders from the many that have the capacity for change."

The Court is of course correct that judges will never have perfect fore-sight—or perfect wisdom—in making sentencing decisions. But this is true when they sentence adults no less than when they sentence juveniles. It is also true when they sentence juveniles who commit murder no less than when they sentence juveniles who commit other crimes. Our system depends upon sentencing judges applying their reasoned judgment to each case that comes before them. . . .

THOMAS, J., [dissenting][a]. . . .

[Discussing the penological justifications for LWOP sentences, the dissent noted that such sentences deter and also incapacitate (by ensuring that juvenile offenders who commit crimes of violence no longer threaten their communities). Therefore, the dissent continued,] the Court's "independent judgment" and the proportionality rule itself center on retribution—the notion that a criminal sentence should be proportioned to "the personal culpability of the criminal offender."

. . . The ultimate question in this case is not whether a life-without-parole sentence 'fits' the crime at issue here or the crimes of juvenile nonhomicide offenders more generally, but to whom the Constitution assigns that decision. . . . The fact that the Court categorically prohibits life-without-parole sentences for juvenile nonhomicide offenders in the face of an overwhelming legislative majority in favor of leaving that sentencing option available under certain cases simply illustrates how far beyond any cognizable constitutional principle the Court has reached to ensure that its own sense of morality and retributive justice preempts that of the people and their representatives.

---

a. Justices Scalia and Alito joined in the portions of Justice Thomas's dissent excerpted below.—EDS.

NOTES

1. Individual versus categorical challenges. The *Graham* Court's test for whether an *individual* non-capital sentence is disproportionate comes from Justice Kennedy's concurrence in *Harmelin*. The Court must find as a threshold matter that the sentence is grossly disproportionate, and a sentence will pass that threshold inquiry so long as the state has a "reasonable basis for believing" that it will serve either deterrent, retributive, rehabilitative, or incapacitative goals. *Ewing*, 538 U.S. at 28. Until *Graham*, the Court had not struck down a single non-capital sentence as disproportionate under that inquiry. In capital cases, in contrast, the Court has held several death sentences disproportionate, partly because the test in capital cases lacks the threshold requirement of gross disproportionality. Instead, the Court turns immediately to the questions of how other jurisdictions treat the crime at issue and how the same jurisdiction treats other crimes. The Court also uses its independent judgment as to whether the gravity of the crime and the culpability of the offender merit the sentence. See page 556 infra.[4]

In *Graham*, the Supreme Court continued to reject the capital disproportionality test as a basis for challenging *individual* non-capital sentences, but for the first time it applied that test to determine the proportionality of *an entire category* of non-capital sentences. What other categories of offenders and types of punishments can be challenged successfully under this new test? Because the Court took the categorical test from its death penalty jurisprudence, capital cases may provide some guidance. For example, the Court has rejected mandatory death sentences and held discretionary death penalties for murder impermissible in the case of certain types of offenders, such as juveniles, those suffering from mental retardation, and accomplices who were not aware of the risk that their co-felons would kill. Should the Court be willing to strike down LWOP sentences in these situations as well? In that vein, the Court recently agreed to review two cases involving 14-year-olds who received mandatory LWOP sentences. Miller v. Alabama, No. 10-9646; Jackson v. Hobbs, No. 10-9647. In *Jackson*, the defendant was convicted of murder solely because he was an accomplice to a fatal robbery; he had no intent or awareness that the shop attendant would be shot by his co-felon.

Questions: What is most problematic about the LWOP sentence in *Jackson*? It is that the offender was so young? That the mandatory feature precluded the judge from considering mitigating circumstances? Is LWOP so similar to the death penalty that both of these sentences should be considered disproportionate for an offender who did not personally intend to kill?

The European Court of Human Rights recently emphasized that *mandatory* LWOP sentences merit greater scrutiny than discretionary

---

4. For further discussion of the contrast, see Rachel E. Barkow, The Court of Life and Death: The Two Tracks of Constitutional Sentencing Law and the Case for Uniformity, 107 Mich. L. Rev. 1145, 1155-1157 (2009).

LWOP sentences because they are imposed "irrespective of [the defendant's] level of culpability and irrespective of whether the sentencing court considers the sentence to be justified." Vinter and Others v. The United Kingdom (Nos. 66069/09, 130/10 and 3896/10, 17 Jan. 2012), at ¶93. But that court did not find that LWOP sentences are *per se* incompatible with the European Convention on Human Rights.

2. *Is LWOP different from other non-capital sentences?* Is LWOP unique, or should the Court be equally willing to scrutinize terms of years? For discussion of how the extinguishment of hope makes LWOP qualitatively different from other punishments, see Alice Ristroph, Hope, Imprisonment, and the Constitution, 23 Fed. Sent. Rep. 75 (2010). If the Court treats LWOP as unique, can a state avoid *Graham*-type scrutiny by imposing term-of-years sentences that exceed a natural life span (say, a sentence of 100 years)? Can a state avoid scrutiny by *authorizing* parole but rarely granting it? What if there is less than a 1 percent chance that parole will be granted? Does *Graham* give guidance for drawing these lines?

3. *Proportionality in other contexts.* The Supreme Court has enforced a proportionality requirement for fines (where the Eighth Amendment expressly prohibits "excessive[ness]") and forfeitures, United States v. Bajakajian, 524 U.S. 321 (1998), as well as punitive damages. Scrutiny of punitive damage awards has been strict. For example, in punitive-damage challenges, the Court examines proportionality issues de novo, rather than under a deferential standard of review. Cooper Industries, Inc. v. Leatherman Tool Group, Inc., 532 U.S. 424 (2001). The Court has held that states may not impose punitive damage awards to punish a defendant for harms to nonparties. Phillip Morris USA v. Williams, 549 U.S. 346, 349 (2007). And it closely scrutinizes awards, striking them down when "*a more modest punishment* for [the] reprehensible conduct *could have satisfied* the State's legitimate objectives." State Farm Mutual Automobile Insurance Co. v. Campbell, 538 U.S. 408, 419-420 (2003) (emphasis added).

Contrasting the Court's approaches to punitive damages and prison sentences, Professor Richard Frase observes (Excessive Prison Sentences, Punishment Goals, and the Eighth Amendment: "Proportionality" Relative to What?, 89 Minn. L. Rev. 571, 608-609 (2005)):

> [T]he Court [has not] required a "threshold" showing of gross disproportionality before subjecting punitive damages awards to comparative analysis. [And] in assessing punitive damages awards, the Court has added a limitation on the relevance of the defendant's "prior record": only violations of a similar nature may be considered. Thus, in at least three respects—de novo review, more frequent use of comparative analysis, and more lenient treatment of recidivists—the Court seems to be much more protective of civil defendants' bank accounts than it has been of criminal defendants' liberty.

Question: Is there a legitimate basis for more searching review of punitive damage awards than of prison terms? In *State Farm,* Justice Kennedy sought to justify the difference as follows (538 U.S. at 417-418):

[D]efendants subjected to punitive damages in civil cases have not been accorded the protections applicable in a criminal proceeding. This increases our concerns over the imprecise manner in which punitive damages systems are administered. "[P]unitive damages pose an acute danger of arbitrary deprivation of property. Jury instructions typically leave the jury with wide discretion in choosing amounts, and the presentation of evidence of a defendant's net worth creates the potential that juries will use their verdicts to express biases against big businesses,—particularly those without strong local presences." . . . Exacting appellate review ensures that an award of punitive damages is based upon an "application of law, rather than a decisionmaker's caprice."

Is this analysis persuasive? Many commentators (e.g., Frase, supra) question whether the safeguards applicable at the criminal trial on the question of guilt suffice to protect against caprice in sentencing. All things considered, is there less need for "[e]xacting appellate review" of prison sentences than of money damage awards?

4. Proportionality review in practice. Even after *Graham*, challenges to individual sentences—as opposed to challenges to entire categories of sentences—must pass the high hurdle set by *Ewing*. As a result, successful Eighth Amendment challenges continue to be rare. But, they are not unheard of. In State v. Bruce, 796 N.W.2d 397 (S.D. 2011), the court struck down a 100-year sentence for possessing child pornography. Similarly, in People v. Carmony, 127 Cal. App. 4th 1066 (2005), the court struck down a sentence of 25 years to life imposed upon a previously convicted sex offender for the "harmless technical violation" of failing to update his sex offender registration as required. State v. Davis, 79 P.3d 64 (Ariz. 2003), struck down a mandatory minimum sentence of 52 years without possibility of parole, imposed upon a 20-year-old male for four counts of having had voluntary sex with an underage teenaged girl. But State v. Berger, 134 P.3d 378 (Ariz. 2006), upheld a sentence of 200 years' imprisonment without possibility of parole (consecutive ten-year sentences on each of 20 counts) imposed on a first-time offender for possession of 20 images of child pornography that he had downloaded from the Internet. A dissenting justice observed:

Arizona's mandatory minimum 200-year sentence . . . exceeds that imposable in any other state. It is the unique combination of long mandatory minimum sentences, coupled with the requirements that each image be charged separately and that the terms be served consecutively and fully— that is, without possibility of early release—that renders Arizona's sentences extraordinarily long. Indeed, the *minimum* ten-year sentence in Arizona for possession of one image [equals or exceeds] the *maximum* sentence for possession of child pornography in [45] states. . . . Moreover, the sentence at issue is longer than that imposed in Arizona for many crimes involving serious violence. [T]he minimum sentence for possession of an image of child pornography is longer than the *presumptive* [i.e., midrange] sentence for rape or aggravated assault. [The minimum] sentence for possession of five images (fifty years) amounts as a practical matter to a life sentence without parole, more serious than the sentence imposed for virtually any crime in the state.

5. *State constitutions.* Many state constitutions contain provisions similar to the Eighth Amendment, but state courts sometimes read them as imposing more significant limits on the legislature. In People v. Bullock, 485 N.W.2d 866 (Mich. 1992), the Michigan Supreme Court overturned on state constitutional grounds the Michigan statute that the U.S. Supreme Court had upheld in *Harmelin*—a statute imposing a mandatory sentence of life without parole for possession of 650 grams of cocaine. The Michigan court emphasized the textual difference between the Eighth Amendment's prohibition of "cruel and unusual punishment" and the Michigan constitution's prohibition of "cruel *or* unusual punishment" (italics added). The court held that under the Michigan constitution, courts must apply a three-prong test, identical to that advanced in *Solem*, to determine whether a punishment is "cruel or unusual."

A number of state constitutions require that "[a]ll penalties shall be proportioned to the nature of the offense." Ind. Const. art. 1, §16; see also Me. Const. art. 1, §9; Neb. Const. art. 1, §15; N.H. Const. pt. 1, art. 18; Or. Const. art. I, §16. As Richard Frase notes, even when state constitutions are worded identically to the Eighth Amendment, "many state courts have recognized their power to interpret state constitutional law more favorably to offenders." Richard S. Frase, Limiting Excessive Prison Sentences Under Federal and State Constitutions, 11 U. Pa. J. Const. L. 39, 40 (2008). The Georgia Supreme Court, for example, applied *Harmelin* and condemned as cruel and unusual a ten-year prison sentence for a 17-year-old defendant who had consensual oral sex with a 15-year-old. Humphrey v. Wilson, 652 S.E.2d 501 (Ga. 2007). For a description of state proportionality review, see Thomas A. Balmer, Some Thoughts on Proportionality, 87 Or. L. Rev. 783 (2008). Some commentators suggest that experience with state proportionality review establishes that more robust proportionality review is readily administrable. See Julia Fong Sheketoff, Note, State Innovations in Noncapital Proportionality Doctrine, 85 N.Y.U. L. Rev. 2209 (2010).

6. *Proportionality and culpability.* The preceding material focuses on offenders who were unquestionably guilty of committing serious offenses. In all such cases, *some* punishment is unquestionably deserved; concern arises only because *a portion* of the punishment imposed arguably exceeds the offender's just deserts. That concern can arise in an even more fundamental way when circumstances suggest that the alleged offender may not be morally blameworthy at all. The next section deals in depth with this foundational issue—the constituent elements of *culpability* and the question of whether or to what extent culpability should always be a prerequisite for just punishment.

D. CULPABILITY

1. *Actus Reus—Culpable Conduct*

a. The Requirement of Voluntary Action

MARTIN v. STATE

Alabama Court of Appeals
31 Ala. App. 334, 17 So. 2d 427 (1944)

SIMPSON, J. Appellant was convicted of being drunk on a public highway, and appeals. Officers of the law arrested him at his home and took him onto the highway, where he allegedly committed the proscribed acts, viz., manifested a drunken condition by using loud and profane language.

The pertinent provisions of our statute are: "Any person who, while intoxicated or drunk, appears in any public place where one or more persons are present, . . . and manifests a drunken condition by boisterous or indecent conduct, or loud and profane discourse, shall, on conviction, be fined," etc. Code 1940, Title 14, Section 120.

Under the plain terms of this statute, a voluntary appearance is presupposed. The rule has been declared, and we think it sound, that an accusation of drunkenness in a designated public place cannot be established by proof that the accused, while in an intoxicated condition, was involuntarily and forcibly carried to that place by the arresting officer. . . .

Conviction of appellant was contrary to this announced principle and, in our view, erroneous. . . .

Reversed and rendered.

NOTES AND QUESTIONS

1. *The rationale of* **Martin**. The reversal of Martin's conviction seems intuitively fair. But what principle explains that result? Is it simply the need to respect the statutory definition of the offense? The court says that "[u]nder the plain terms of the statute, a voluntary appearance is presupposed."

Is this explanation convincing? The court's account raises two problems. First, if we focus solely on the text of the statute, where is there any hint that the appearance must be voluntary? Second, if a conviction under the circumstances of *Martin* is troubling, it would presumably remain troubling even if the statutory wording had not specifically required that the accused "appear." For example, suppose that the Alabama statute had been re-worded to provide: "Any person who, while drunk, is found in a public place is guilty of an offense." If Martin's conviction was troublesome, shouldn't it be equally troublesome under this statute as well?

2. *The actus reus requirement.* Notice that in a prosecution under the reworded statute just mentioned, a person forced to swallow alcohol and then

carried into public by the police (call him Peter Passive) would seem to meet the statutory requirements for conviction, even though he had not engaged in any conduct at all. But a conviction under those circumstances would violate the fundamental principle that criminal liability always requires an "actus reus," that is, the commission of some voluntary act that is prohibited by law. For one statutory statement of this principle, see Model Penal Code §2.01(1), Appendix. Presumably, the Alabama court's understanding of this background principle played a large role in its approach to interpreting the statute.

3. Testing the result in **Martin.** Notice that Martin, unlike Peter Passive, cannot claim that he engaged in no conduct at all. Martin presumably drank, and once in public he used loud and profane language. Is the *Martin* court in effect requiring that *all* the proscribed acts be committed voluntarily? Consider whether a requirement of that sort is really desirable. If Martin *voluntarily* used loud and profane language in public, wouldn't it be fair to punish him, regardless of how he came to be in public? How would that situation be handled under MPC §2.01(1)?

4. Contemporary applications. American courts widely acknowledge *Martin*'s status as a leading case but disagree about its application to common contemporary situations. Consider the following problems:

(a) In People v. Low, 232 P.3d 635 (Cal. 2010), the defendant was arrested for driving a stolen vehicle and taken to jail, where a search found drugs hidden in one of his socks. He was convicted not only of the stolen vehicle offense but also of "knowingly bring[ing] [a] controlled substance" into a county jail. He conceded knowing possession but invoked *Martin* to argue that since he had been taken to jail against his will, he had not *voluntarily* committed the required act of "bring[ing]" the drug into the jail. The California Supreme Court distinguished *Martin* and upheld the conviction on the ground that defendant had "a clear opportunity to avoid [the prohibited act] by voluntarily relinquishing the forbidden object . . . before entering the premises." Id. at 644. On largely identical facts, a Washington defendant was convicted of "possess[ing] a controlled substance . . . while in a county jail." The state supreme court found *Martin* controlling and reversed the drugs-in-jail conviction. State v. Eaton, 229 P.3d 704 (Wash. 2010). Responding to the state's argument that "the plain language of the statute does not contain a volitional element," the court noted that the defendant had no available choice other than to surrender evidence that would convict him of another crime, and therefore failing to read a voluntariness requirement into the statute would produce "absurd" results incompatible with the principles of criminal responsibility. Id. at 706-08. Which is the better analysis?[5]

---

5. This problem can be reconsidered in connection with the material on omissions and possession-as-an-act, pages 235-236 infra.

(b) A Los Angeles ordinance makes it an offense for any person to "sit, lie or sleep in or upon any street, sidewalk or other public way." L.A. Municipal Code §41.18(d). Thousands of homeless people living in the Los Angeles "skid row" brought suit to enjoin enforcement of the ordinance against them during nighttime hours. They proved that the city had an insufficient number of beds available to accommodate them and argued that convicting them under these circumstances would simply punish them for the "universal and unavoidable consequences of being human." The U.S. Court of Appeals agreed, holding that "the state may not criminalize 'being'; that is, the state may not punish a person for who he is, independent of anything he has done." Jones v. City of Los Angeles, 444 F.3d 1118, 1133 (9th Cir. 2006). A dissenting judge argued that the ordinance "does not punish people simply because they are homeless. It targets *conduct*—sitting, lying or sleeping on city sidewalks." Id. at 1139 (Rymer, J., dissenting).[6] Challenges to similar ordinances continue to be brought in cities across the country, and courts remain divided about whether they can be applied to the homeless.[7] Which is the better view? We consider the constitutional aspects of the issue starting at page 1009 infra. For the moment, put aside constitutional concerns and consider the issue solely in terms of ordinary criminal law principles. Would Model Penal Code §2.01(1) permit a criminal prosecution under these circumstances?

4. Which acts are voluntary? The MPC defines an "act" as a "bodily movement whether voluntary or involuntary." §1.13(2). By this definition, Martin's use of profane language certainly qualifies as an act. But does his drunkenness make that act legally "involuntary"? Should it? Consider the material that follows.

PEOPLE v. NEWTON

California District Court of Appeal
8 Cal. App. 3d 359, 87 Cal. Rptr. 394 (1970)

RATTIGAN, J. Huey P. Newton appeals from a judgment convicting him of voluntary manslaughter.

[Newton was charged with the murder of John Frey, a police officer who died of bullet wounds received in a struggle with defendant. A jury found him guilty of voluntary manslaughter.

[Frey stopped a car driven by Newton and ordered him out of the car, and an altercation ensued. From the testimony of the prosecution's witnesses, it appeared that Newton had drawn a gun, and, in the struggle for its

---

6. In subsequent proceedings, the parties settled; the Ninth Circuit then vacated its earlier opinion and dismissed the litigation as moot. Jones v. City of Los Angeles, 505F.3d 1006 (9th Cir. 2007).

7. Compare Ashbaucher v. City of Arcata, 2010 U.S. Dist. LEXIS 126590 (N.D. Cal. 2010) (upholding application to the homeless), with State v. Adams, 2010 WL 4380236 (Ala. Crim. App. 2010) (sex offender registration law cannot be applied to punish homeless sex offenders who lack a permanent address).

possession, the gun went off and wounded Heanes, another police officer. The struggle continued, and Heanes fired a shot at Newton's midsection. At some point, Newton wrested the gun away and fired several fatal shots point-blank at Frey. He then ran away. Shortly afterward, Newton appeared at a hospital emergency room, seeking treatment for a bullet wound in the abdomen.

[Newton testified that he had carried no gun. According to his account, the struggle began when Frey struck him for protesting his arrest. As he stumbled backwards, Frey drew a revolver. At this point, he felt a "sensation like . . . boiling hot soup had been spilled on my stomach," and heard an "explosion," then a "volley of shots." He remembered "crawling . . . a moving sensation," but nothing else until he found himself at the entrance of Kaiser Hospital with no knowledge of how he arrived there. He expressly testified that he was "unconscious or semiconscious" during this interval, that he was "still only semiconscious" at the hospital entrance, and that—after recalling some events at Kaiser Hospital—he later "regained consciousness" at another hospital.]

The defense called Bernard Diamond, M.D., who testified that defendant's recollections were "compatible" with the gunshot wound he had received; and that

> [a] gunshot wound which penetrates in a body cavity, the abdominal cavity or the thoracic cavity is very likely to produce a profound reflex shock reaction, that is quite different than a gunshot wound which penetrates only skin and muscle and it is not at all uncommon for a person shot in the abdomen to lose consciousness and go into this reflex shock condition for short periods of time up to half an hour or so.

Defendant asserts prejudicial error in the trial court's failure to instruct the jury on the subject of *unconsciousness* as a defense to a charge of criminal homicide. . . .

Although the evidence of the fatal affray is both conflicting and confused as to who shot whom and when, some of it supported the inference that defendant had been shot in the abdomen before he fired any shots himself. Given this sequence, defendant's testimony of his sensations when shot—supplemented to a degree, as it was, by Dr. Diamond's opinion based upon the nature of the abdominal wound—supported the further inference that defendant was in a state of unconsciousness when Officer Frey was shot.

Where not self-induced, as by voluntary intoxication or the equivalent (of which there is no evidence here . . .), unconsciousness is a complete defense to a charge of criminal homicide. (Pen. Code, §26, subd. 5; . . .) "Unconsciousness," as the term is used in the rule just cited, need not reach the physical dimensions commonly associated with the term (coma, inertia, incapability of locomotion or manual action, and so on); it can exist—and the above-stated rule can apply—where the subject physically acts in fact but is not, at the time,

conscious of acting. The statute underlying the rule makes this clear[11]. . . .
Thus, the rule has been invoked in many cases where the actor fired multiple
gunshots while inferably in a state of such "unconsciousness" . . . including
some in which the only evidence of "unconsciousness" was the actor's own
testimony that he did not recall the shooting. . . .

Where evidence of involuntary unconsciousness has been produced in a
homicide prosecution, the refusal of a requested instruction on the subject,
and its effect as a complete defense if found to have existed, is prejudicial
error. . . .

[R]eversed.

NOTES AND QUESTIONS

1. The rationale of the voluntary act requirement. The reason for excluding criminal liability in the absence of voluntary action is explained as follows
(Model Penal Code and Commentaries, Comment to §2.01 at 214-215 (1985)):

> That penal sanctions cannot be employed with justice unless these require-
> ments are satisfied seems wholly clear. It is fundamental that a civilized society
> does not punish for thoughts alone. Beyond this, the law cannot hope to deter
> involuntary movement or to stimulate action that cannot physically be per-
> formed; the sense of personal security would be undermined in a society where
> such movement or inactivity could lead to formal social condemnation of the
> sort that a conviction necessarily entails. People whose involuntary move-
> ments threaten harm to others may present a public health or safety problem,
> calling for therapy or even for custodial commitment; they do not present a
> problem of correction.

2. Distinguishing between voluntary and involuntary acts. The MPC
defines voluntariness indirectly, by simply listing examples of involuntary
acts. The examples are consistent with the general approach at common
law, but they differ from everyday usage; they do not include many types
of conduct that are often described as "involuntary" in ordinary speech—
such as an act that is the product of an "irresistible impulse." See MPC
§2.01(2). To add further confusion, the term "involuntary" does not have a
consistent meaning even within the criminal law: Many types of conduct that
are considered "involuntary" for purposes of some criminal law rules are not
considered "involuntary" for purposes of others. One example is the case of a
motorist who drives too fast, goes through a stop sign, and unintentionally
kills a pedestrian. In everyday speech and in the criminal law itself, this
offense is usually described as "involuntary manslaughter." (We explore
the offense in detail in Chapter 5, pages 464-481 infra). Yet the motorist's
actions are *not* considered "involuntary" for purposes of either the common-
law actus reus requirement or MPC §2.01(2).

---

11. Penal Code section 26 provides in pertinent part that "All persons are capable of committing
crimes except those belonging to the following classes: . . . Five—Persons who *committed the act
charged without being conscious thereof*." (Italics added.)

Question: Why should the definition of an involuntary act, for purposes of the actus reus requirement, be so much narrower than the ordinary person's understanding of what counts as an involuntary act? Consider Bratty v. Attorney-General [1963] A.C. 386, 409-410 (H.L. 1961):

> No act is punishable if it is done involuntarily: and an involuntary act in this context—some people nowadays prefer to speak of it as "automatism"—means an act which is done by the muscles without any control by the mind such as a spasm, a reflex action or a convulsion; or an act done by a person who is not conscious of what he is doing such as an act done whilst suffering from concussion or whilst sleep-walking. . . . The term "involuntary act" is, however, capable of wider connotations: and to prevent confusion it is to be observed that in the criminal law an act is not to be regarded as an involuntary act simply because the doer does not remember it. . . . Nor is an act to be regarded as an involuntary act simply because the doer could not control his impulse to do it. When a man is charged with murder, and it appears that he knew what he was doing, but he could not resist it, then his assertion "I couldn't help myself" is no defence in itself. . . . Nor is an act to be regarded as an involuntary act simply because it is unintentional or its consequences are unforeseen. When a man is charged with dangerous driving, it is no defence for him to say, however truly, "I did not mean to drive dangerously."

See also J.F. Stephen, 2 A History of the Criminal Law of England 102 (1883): "A criminal walking to execution is under compulsion if any man can be said to be so, but his motions are just as much voluntary as if he [were] going to leave his place of confinement and regain his liberty. He walks to his death because he prefers it to be being carried."

3. *Distinguishing between voluntary acts and blameworthy acts.* As the preceding comments indicate, the category of involuntary acts, for purposes of the actus reus requirement, is defined very narrowly. These involuntary acts are *never* blameworthy. But the opposite is not true. We cannot say that *voluntary* acts are *always* blameworthy, because the law and ordinary morality ordinarily impose blame only when a number of additional requirements are met in addition to voluntariness. For example, a person may act voluntarily by driving carefully to work, but may have an accident and injure someone unintentionally. Accident and mistake relate to the *effects that one has in mind* as possible results of one's voluntary actions; the normal assumption that blame entails some awareness that one's actions can cause harm is called the mens rea requirement, and we examine it in detail in Section D.2, pages 241-329 infra. Another example involves persons who choose to act in a certain way because an external threat or a mental disorder leads them to believe they have no choice; these defenses, such as duress and insanity, are called *excuses*, and we examine them in detail in Chapter 8.C, pages 921-1031 infra.

Although we are only beginning our consideration of the different categories of defenses, it is worth pausing to consider why the law might distinguish between the various reasons why a person who causes harm can avoid blame.

Professor J.G. Murphy, (Involuntary Acts and Criminal Liability, 51 Ethics 332 (1971)) points out that there are two situations in which human actions "misfire." One is where actions are done accidentally or under duress. The other is where the action misfires in a more basic way—such as in cases of convulsions, reflex movements, or somnambulism. In the first group of cases, we speak of mitigating the actor's responsibility or of excusing the act. In the second group of cases, however, we do not think of excuse but rather believe that no human action occurred at all—"talk of excuse here seems to make no more sense than would talk of excusing a rock for falling on one's head." For in-depth discussion of these issues, see Michael S. Moore, Act and Crime (1993); Douglas Husak, Rethinking the Act Requirement, 28 Cardozo L. Rev. 2437 (2007).

Another reason for distinguishing the two groups of cases is practical. Because most defenses, whatever their label, result in an acquittal, what difference does it make whether we put them into the category of actus reus, mens rea, or excuse? As we shall see when we explore various defenses in detail, the distinctions between them can have important legal consequences. One concerns the burden of proof. Since a voluntary act is a necessary element of every crime, the prosecution always bears the burden of proving that act—and its voluntary character—beyond a reasonable doubt. But, as we have seen in Chapter 1, pages 36-46 supra, the legislature has some flexibility to convert mens rea requirements from "elements" of an offense to affirmative defenses on which the prosecution need not bear the burden of proof. And the burden of proving excuses such as insanity may be, and often is, placed upon the defendant. (See page 967 infra.)

Another important practical consequence concerns the disposition of the defendant. When a defendant is acquitted on grounds of insanity, he is often subject to civil commitment or other protective or therapeutic protocols. (See page 964 infra.) In contrast, if a defendant like Newton is acquitted on the ground that his act was involuntary, he is immediately discharged without further supervision over his conduct.

Question: When a defendant is acquitted for lack of a voluntary act, is it always wise to release him without further supervision? What if, for example, a defendant is prone to spasms and seizures? Consider the problems that follow.

4. Problems. (a) Habit. The MPC treats habitual action done without thought as voluntary action. Why should this be so? Suppose, for example, that a person firmly resolves to stop saying "You know" before every sentence, but then continues to do so, in spite of her best intentions. Why is her slip-up treated as a voluntary act? Suppose that a person is driving on an interstate when his cell phone rings, and without thinking, he reaches for the phone, thus violating a traffic safety regulation and possibly causing an accident. Can his act of reaching for the phone be considered a "reflex" within the meaning of the MPC? Or will his act be considered "voluntary"? Why should a movement like this be treated as a voluntary act? See Kimberly Kessler Ferzan, Opaque Recklessness, 91 J. Crim. L. & Criminology 597, 646-647 (2001).

(b) Hypnosis. The MPC takes the position that the acts of a hypnotized subject are not voluntary. See Model Penal Code and Commentaries, Comment to §2.01 at 221 (1985):

> The widely held view that the hypnotized subject will not follow suggestions which are repugnant to him was deemed insufficient to warrant treating his conduct while hypnotized as voluntary; his dependency and helplessness are too pronounced.

Question: If habitual actions that a person cannot control are considered voluntary, why should actions under hypnosis, which the subject apparently *can* control, be considered *in*voluntary? The MPC view seems to be that habitual actions, even when unintentional, are nonetheless "a product of the effort or determination of the actor." §2.01(2)(d). Isn't that also true of actions under hypnosis? Scientific disagreement over the hypnotized subject's ability to control his own conduct, together with the difficulty of distinguishing normal from hypnotized actions, apparently have led most jurisdictions not to adopt a statutory hypnosis defense. See Paul H. Robinson et al., 2 Criminal Law Defenses §191 (2010). Is it fair to preclude a defendant from raising this defense and seeking to persuade the jury of its validity?

(c) Somnambulism [sleepwalking]

(1) The **Cogdon** *case.* Consider Norval Morris, Somnambulistic Homicide: Ghosts, Spiders, and North Koreans, 5 Res Judicatae 29, 29-30 (1951):

> Mrs. Cogdon was charged with the murder of her only child, a daughter called Pat, aged nineteen. . . . Describing the relationship between Pat and her mother, Mr. Cogdon testified: "I don't think a mother could have thought any more of her daughter. I think she absolutely adored her." On the conscious level, at least, there was no reason to doubt Mrs. Cogdon's deep attachment to her daughter.
>
> To the charge of murdering Pat, Mrs. Cogdon pleaded not guilty. Her story, though somewhat bizarre, was not seriously challenged by the Crown, and led to her acquittal. She told how, on the night before her daughter's death she had dreamt that their house was full of spiders and that these spiders were crawling all over Pat. In her sleep, Mrs. Cogdon left the bed she shared with her husband, went into Pat's room and awakened to find herself violently brushing at Pat's face, presumably to remove the spiders. . . .
>
> The morning after the spider dream she told her doctor of it. He gave her a sedative and, because of the dream and certain previous difficulties she had reported, discussed the possibility of psychiatric treatment. That evening [there] was some desultory conversation . . . about the war in Korea, and just before she put out her light Pat called out to her mother, "Mum, don't be so silly worrying about the war, it's not on our front door step yet."

Mrs. Cogdon went to sleep. She dreamt that "the war was all around the house," that the soldiers were in Pat's room, and that one soldier was on the bed attacking Pat. This was all of the dream that she could later recapture. Her first "waking" memory was of running from Pat's room, out of the house to the home of her sister who lived next door. When her sister opened the front door Mrs. Cogdon fell into her arms crying, "I think I've hurt Pattie."

In fact Mrs. Cogdon had, in her somnambulistic state, left her bed, fetched an axe from the woodheap, entered Pat's room, and struck her two accurate forceful blows on the head with the blade of the axe, thus killing her.

Mrs. Cogdon's story was supported by the evidence of her physician, a psychiatrist, and a psychologist. The burden of the evidence of all three, which was not contested by the prosecution, was that Mrs. Cogdon was suffering from a form of hysteria with an overlay of depression and that she was of a personality in which such dissociated states as fugues, amnesias, and somnambulistic acts are to be expected. They agreed that she was not psychotic and that if she had been awake at the time of the killing no defence could have been spelt out under the *M'Naughten Rules* [defining the terms of the defense of legal insanity]. They hazarded no statement as to her motives, the idea of defence of the daughter being transparently insufficient. However, the psychologist and the psychiatrist concurred in hinting that the emotional motivation lay in an acute conflict situation in her relations with her own parents; that during marital life she suffered very great sexual frustration; and that she over-compensated for her own frustration by over-protection of her daughter. Her exaggerated solicitude for her daughter was a conscious expression of her subconscious emotional hostility to her, and the dream ghosts, spiders, and Korean soldiers were projections of that aggression. . . .

At all events the jury believed Mrs. Cogdon's story. [S]he was acquitted because the act of killing itself was not, in law, regarded as her act at all.

(2) The traditional rule. The common law and the MPC are in accord with the result in *Cogdon*; on her version of the events, her act would be considered involuntary. See MPC §2.01(2)(c). But does it make sense for a person like Mrs. Cogdon to be acquitted outright and released?

(3) Recent developments. In a Canadian case similar to *Cogdon*, the accused drove several miles to the home of his in-laws and killed his mother-in-law with a fireplace iron. He won acquittal by producing convincing evidence that he had been in a state of sleep throughout the episode. The Supreme Court of Canada ruled that his defense was properly treated as one of involuntary act, rather than insanity, because the law's concern, for purposes of punishment, is with the *conscious* mind. R. v. Parks, 95 D.L.R.4th 27 (1992). In another Canadian case, a defendant was acquitted on charges of forcible rape, after a doctor specializing in sleep disorders testified that the defendant's prior history of sleepwalking, together with studies of his brain waves during sleep and other circumstances corroborated his claim to have acted involuntarily during a state of "sexsomnia." R. v. Luedecke, [2005] 35 C.R. 6th 205. Should such a defendant be subject to confinement on the ground that his sleep disorder makes him dangerous?

What if medication can control the disorder but has serious side effects that give the defendant good reasons to stop taking it? See R. v. Luedecke, 2010 ONCJ 59 (Can.).

There is now an extensive medical literature on "sleep-related violence," and a growing effort to make use of medical testimony to buttress the defense. See William Wilson et al., Violence, Sleepwalking and the Criminal Law, [2005] Crim. L. Rev. 601, 614. What should happen in cases of this sort if a defendant's evidence is strong enough to raise a reasonable doubt about whether his actions were voluntary, but not strong enough to permit the authorities to confine him in a mental hospital? (We consider related dispositional issues that arise under the *insanity defense* at pages 964-966 infra.).

(4) Problem: R.R., a 15-year-old boy, spent several nights sleeping on the sofa at the home of defendant, a 52-year-old-woman who was a family friend. On several occasions, R.R. climbed into the defendant's bed and had sexual intercourse with her. Charged with statutory rape, the defendant claimed she had been asleep throughout the encounters. In Washington, as in many states, statutory rape is a "strict liability" crime, meaning (as we shall see, pages 275-282 infra) that the state is not required to prove any "mens rea"—the mental awareness of circumstances making conduct criminal. For that reason, the trial judge ruled that the defendant had the burden to prove by a preponderance of the evidence her claim of having been asleep, and the jury convicted. The appellate court reversed, holding that "[a]lthough . . . rape of a child is a strict liability crime, the 'minimal mental element' of volition—as part of the actus reus—must be proved even for those crimes without a mens rea requirement [and thus] the State bears the burden of proving beyond a reasonable doubt that the defendant committed a volitional act." State v. Deer, 244 P.2d 965, 969 (Wash. App. 2010), rev. granted, 249 P.3d 1029 (Wash. 2011).

Questions: If social protection concerns lead a state to bar defenses based on lack of mens rea (awareness of the circumstances that make conduct criminal), would it be similarly justified to bar all defenses based on a lack of volition? In what way are lack-of-awareness defenses different from lack-of-volition defenses?

(d) Epilepsy. A person's movements during an epileptic seizure are indisputably involuntary. Can the prosecution nonetheless establish liability by pointing to earlier acts that *were* voluntary? Consider People v. Decina, 138 N.E.2d 799, 803-804 (1956):

> The indictment states essentially that defendant, *knowing* "that he was subject to epileptic attacks or other disorder rendering him likely to lose consciousness for a considerable period of time," was culpably negligent "in that he consciously undertook to and *did operate* his Buick sedan on a public highway" (emphasis supplied) and "while so doing" suffered such an attack which caused said automobile "to travel at a fast and reckless rate of speed, jumping the curb and driving over the sidewalk" causing the death

of 4 persons. In our opinion, this clearly states a violation of section 1053-a of the Penal Law. . . . ["A person who operates or drives any vehicle of any kind in a reckless or culpably negligent manner, whereby a human being is killed is guilty of criminal negligence in the operation of a vehicle resulting in death."]

Assuming the truth of the indictment, as we must on a demurrer, this defendant knew he was subject to epileptic attacks and seizures that might strike at any time. He also knew that a moving motor vehicle uncontrolled on a public highway is a highly dangerous instrumentality capable of unrestrained destruction. With this *knowledge,* and without anyone accompanying him, he deliberately took a chance by making a conscious choice of a course of action, in disregard of the consequences which he knew might follow from his conscious act, and which in this case did ensue. How can we say as a matter of law that this did not amount to culpable negligence within the meaning of section 1053-a?

To hold otherwise would be to say that a man may freely indulge himself in liquor in the same hope that it will not affect his driving, and if it later develops that ensuing intoxication causes dangerous and reckless driving resulting in death, his unconsciousness or involuntariness at that time would relieve him from prosecution under the statute. His awareness of a condition which he knows may produce such consequences as here, and his disregard of the consequences, renders him liable for culpable negligence, as the courts below have properly held. To have a sudden sleeping spell, an unexpected heart or other disabling attack, without any prior knowledge or warning thereof, is an altogether different situation.

Questions: If the prosecution can defeat the voluntary act requirement by expanding the time frame in this way, how far back in time should the prosecution be permitted to go? After all, every defendant has committed some voluntary act at some point in his life. Consider the following comments:

Mark Kelman, Interpretive Construction in the Substantive Criminal Law, 33 Stan. L. Rev. 591, 600-605 (1991): [I]f we interpret the relevant legal material as including earlier decisions . . . , we can interpret the course of the conduct that culminates in criminal harm as chosen. . . . The hidden interpretive time-framing construct becomes visible when one tries to square *Martin* with *Decina.* [Like the defendant in *Decina,*] the defendant in *Martin* . . . may have done *something* voluntarily (before the police came) that posed a risk that he would get arrested and carried into public in his drunken state . . . for instance, beating his wife. Why did the court not consider saying that the voluntary act at time one (wife beating) both posed a risk of and caused a harmful involuntary act at time two (public drunkenness) and assessing the voluntariness of the alleged criminal act with reference to the wider time-framed scenario? It cannot be that the involuntary, harmful act at time two was unforeseeable. The probability of an epileptic black-out is almost certainly far lower than the probability of ending up in public after engaging in behavior likely to draw police attention. . . . Ultimately, the *Martin* finding of voluntariness "works" not because it is "right," but because all the hard points disappear in the initial interpretive construction of the potentially relevant facts.

Michael Moore, Act and Crime 35-37 (1993): If there were a "time-framing" choice to be made in criminal cases, Kelman is right in his observation that there would be no principled way to make it. But where did Kelman get his assumption that there is such a choice to be made? [If] the court can find a voluntary act by the defendant, accompanied *at that time* by whatever culpable mens rea is required, which act in fact and proximately causes some legally prohibited state of affairs, then the defendant is prima facie liable for that legal harm. There is no "time-framing" choice here. If there is *any* point in time where the act and mens rea requirements are simultaneously satisfied, and from which the requisite causal relations exist to some legally prohibited state of affairs, then the defendant is prima facie liable. . . .

Kelman thinks that the Alabama court could justify its decision (of no voluntary act by Martin) only by a "narrow time-framing"; for a broad time-framing would reveal earlier acts by Martin that were voluntary. . . . What Kelman overlooks is that those earlier acts by Martin were not the proximate cause of being drunk in public. The police officers' intentional placing of Martin in a public place constitutes an intervening cause on anyone's reading of that notion, making Martin not a proximate cause of the legally prohibited state of affairs. In addition, had the Alabama statute required any mens rea with respect to the element of public place, as it should have, Martin's earlier acts of drinking in his home were unaccompanied by such mens rea and were thus ineligible to be the basis for his conviction for that reason too.

NOTE ON CULPABLE THOUGHTS

In the *Newton* case, page 207 supra, the defendant's physical movements killed Officer Frey, but the lack of a voluntary act (according to Newton's version of the events) signaled the complete absence of culpability. There was no mental disposition to commit any act, much less a harmful one. But suppose that a person conceives a plot to burn down a building, thinks through all the necessary details and writes them down in his diary, but is arrested before he takes any action to carry out the arson plan. (Police may, for example, have discovered the diary after arresting the defendant on an unrelated charge.) Here there is a mental disposition to take harmful action; the defendant appears to be both culpable and dangerous. Should the absence of a voluntary act nonetheless preclude liability? The law is unequivocal on this point. MPC §2.01(1) would afford a full defense, and a long-honored maxim of the criminal law states: *cogitationis poenam nemo patitur*—no one is punishable solely for his thoughts. But why should this be so? Consider the following comments:

*4 William Blackstone, Commentaries *21:* [T]o make a complete crime, cognizable by human laws, there must be both a will and an act. For though . . . a fixed design or will to do an unlawful act is almost as heinous as the commission of it, yet, as no temporal tribunal can search the heart, or fathom the intentions of the mind, otherwise than as they are demonstrated by outward actions, it therefore cannot punish for what it cannot know. For which reason in all temporal jurisdictions an overt act, or some open evidence of an intended crime, is necessary, in order to demonstrate the depravity of the will, before the man is liable to punishment.

2 James Fitzjames Stephen, A History of the Criminal Law of England 78 (1883): Sinful thoughts and dispositions of mind might be the subject of confession and of penance, but they were never punished in this country by ecclesiastical criminal proceedings. The reasons for imposing this great leading restriction upon the sphere of criminal law are obvious. If it were not so restricted it would be utterly intolerable; all mankind would be criminals, and most of their lives would be passed in trying and punishing each other for offences which could never be proved.

G. Dworkin & G. Blumenfeld, Punishments for Intentions, 75 Mind 396, 401 (1966): What would a system of laws embodying a rule providing for the punishment of intentions look like? When would punishment be administered? As soon as we find out the agent's intentions? But how do we know he will not change his mind? Furthermore, isn't the series—fantasying, wishing, desiring, wanting, intending—a continuum, making it a rather hazy matter to know just when a person is intending rather than wishing? This last objection has two aspects, the difficulty of the authorities distinguishing between fantasying, wishing, etc. and even more importantly the difficulties the individual would have in identifying the nature of his emotional and mental set. Would we not be constantly worried about the nature of our mental life? Am I only wishing my mother-in-law were dead? Perhaps I have gone further. The resultant guilt would tend to impoverish and stultify the emotional life.

Glanville Williams, Criminal Law: The General Part 2 (2d ed. 1961): Better reasons for the rule would be (1) the difficulty of distinguishing between daydream and fixed intention in the absence of behavior tending towards the crime intended, and (2) the undesirability of spreading the criminal law so wide as to cover a mental state that the accused might be too irresolute even to begin to translate into action.

Abraham Goldstein, Conspiracy to Defraud the United States, 68 Yale L.J. 405, 405-406 (1959): [T]he act requirement serves a number of closely-related objectives: it seeks to assure that the evil intent of the man branded a criminal has been expressed in a manner signifying harm to society; that there is no longer any substantial likelihood that he will be deterred by the threat of sanction; and that there has been an identifiable occurrence so that multiple prosecution and punishment may be minimized.

b. Omissions

JONES v. UNITED STATES

United States Court of Appeals, District of Columbia Circuit
308 F.2d 307 (1962)

WRIGHT, J. [Defendant was found guilty of involuntary manslaughter through failure to provide for Anthony Lee Green, which failure resulted in his death. The deceased was the ten-month-old illegitimate baby of Shirley Green. He was placed with the defendant, a family friend. Shirley Green lived in the house with defendant for some of the time, but there was conflict in the evidence as to how long. There was also conflict as to whether or not the defendant was paid for taking care of the baby. The evidence was uncontested that the defendant had ample means to provide food and medical care.] Appellant . . . takes exception to the failure of the trial court to charge that the jury must find beyond a reasonable doubt, as an element of the crime, that appellant was under a legal duty to supply food and necessities to Anthony Lee. . . . The most commonly cited statement of the rule is found in People v. Beardsley, 150 Mich. 206, 113 N.W. 1128, 1129:

> The law recognizes that under some circumstances the omission of a duty owed by one individual to another, where such omission results in the death of the one to whom the duty is owing, will make the other chargeable with manslaughter. . . . This rule of law is always based upon the proposition that the duty neglected must be a legal duty, and not a mere moral obligation. It must be a duty imposed by law or by contract, and the omission to perform the duty must be the immediate and direct cause of death. . . .

There are at least four situations in which the failure to act may constitute breach of a legal duty. One can be held criminally liable: first, where a statute imposes a duty to care for another; second, where one stands in a certain status relationship to another;[9] third, where one has assumed a contractual duty to care for another; and fourth, where one has voluntarily assumed the care of another and so secluded the helpless person as to prevent others from rendering aid.

It is the contention of the Government that either the third or the fourth ground is applicable here. However, it is obvious that in any of the four situations, there are critical issues of fact which must be passed on by the jury—specifically in this case, whether appellant had entered into a contract

---

9. 10 A.L.R. 1137 (1921) (parent to child); Territory v. Manton, 8 Mont. 95, 19 P. 387 (husband to wife); Regina v. Smith, 8 Carr. & P. 153 (Eng. 1837) (master to apprentice); United States v. Knowles, 26 Fed. Cas. 800 (No. 15,540) (ship's master to crew and passengers); cf. State v. Reitze, 86 N.J.L. 407, 92 A. 576 (innkeeper to inebriated customers).

with the mother for the care of Anthony Lee or, alternatively, whether she assumed the care of the child and secluded him from the care of his mother, his natural protector. On both of these issues, the evidence is in direct conflict, appellant insisting that the mother was actually living with appellant and Anthony Lee, and hence should have been taking care of the child herself, while Shirley Green testified she was living with her parents and was paying appellant to care for both children.

In spite of this conflict, the instructions given in the case failed even to suggest the necessity for finding a legal duty of care. The only reference to duty in the instructions was the reading of the indictment which charged, inter alia, that the [defendant] "failed to perform [her] legal duty." A finding of legal duty is the critical element of the crime charged and failure to instruct the jury concerning it was plain error. . . .

Reversed and remanded.

NOTES

1. *Jones* reflects the general Anglo-American position that unless a penal statute specifically requires a particular action to be performed, criminal liability for omission arises only when the law of torts or some other law imposes a duty to act. This is a position also taken in Model Penal Code §2.01(3) (liability for an omission only when "a duty to perform the omitted act is otherwise imposed by law").

2. Most cases where liability for homicide is imposed for a failure to act are, like the *Jones* case, cases of involuntary manslaughter. Such a case, however, might be murder if the defendant refused aid with the intention of causing death, or with full knowledge of a great risk that the decedent would die. For example, in Commonwealth v. Pestinikas, 617 A.2d 1339 (Pa. Super. Ct. 1992), the defendant permitted a 92-year-old man to die of starvation after agreeing to feed him and knowing that there was no other way for him to obtain food. The defendant was convicted of murder in the third degree.

3. The rule that there is generally no legal duty to act is inapplicable, of course, when statutory language or common-law doctrines create such a duty. But social resistance to imposing liability for omissions makes itself felt even when statutes and precedents could be readily interpreted to establish a duty to aid. Consider the material that follows.

POPE v. STATE

Maryland Court of Appeals
284 Md. 309, 396 A.2d 1054 (1979)

ORTH, J. [Joyce Lillian Pope was found guilty under the 3d and 5th counts of a nine-count indictment. The 3d count charged child abuse, presenting that "on or about April 11, 1976, . . . while having the temporary care, custody and responsibility for the supervision of Demiko Lee Norris, a minor child under the age of eighteen years, [she] did unlawfully and feloniously cause abuse to said minor child in violation of Article 27, Section 35A of the Annotated Code of Maryland. . . . " The 5th count charged misprision of felony under the common law, alleging that on the same date she "did unlawfully and willfully conceal and fail to disclose a felony to wit: the murder of Demiko Lee Norris committed by Melissa Vera Norris on April 11, 1976, having actual knowledge of the commission of the felony and the identity of the felon, with the intent to obstruct and hinder the due course of justice and to cause the felon to escape unpunished. . . . "

[Melissa Norris, a young mother with a three-month-old infant, was suffering from a serious mental illness and given to episodes of violent religious frenzy. The defendant (Mrs. Pope) took Norris and her child into her house one Friday night after church services because they had no other place to go. During the weekend Mrs. Pope fed them both and looked after the child in a variety of ways. On Sunday afternoon Melissa went into a frenzy, claiming she was God and that Satan had hidden himself in the body of her child. In Mrs. Pope's presence she savagely beat and tore at the infant. During this prolonged period Mrs. Pope did nothing to try to protect the child, to call the authorities, or to seek medical assistance. She went to church with Melissa and later brought her back to her home where she spent the night. At some point in the evening the infant died from the beating.]

[A] person may be convicted of the felony of child abuse created by §35A[a] as a principal in the first degree upon evidence legally sufficient to establish that the person

> (1) was (a) the parent of, or (b) the adoptive parent of, or (c) in loco parentis to, or (d) responsible for the supervision of a minor child under the age of eighteen years, AND
> (2) caused, by being in some manner accountable for, by act of commission or omission, abuse to the child in the form of (a) physical injury or injuries sustained by the child as the result of (i) cruel or inhumane treatment, or (ii) malicious act or acts by such person, . . .

. . . Pope's lack of any attempt to prevent the numerous acts of abuse committed by the mother over a relatively protracted period and her failure to seek medical assistance for the child, although the need therefor was

---

a. Article 27, Section 35A, insofar as it is relevant to this case, reads as follows:

> (a) Penalty. Any parent, adoptive parent or other person who has the permanent or temporary care or custody or responsibility for the supervision of a minor child under the age of eighteen years who causes abuse to such minor child shall be guilty of a felony and upon conviction shall be sentenced to not more than fifteen years in the penitentiary.
>
> (b) Definitions. Wherever used in this section, unless the context clearly indicates otherwise; . . . 7. "Abuse" shall mean any . . . physical injury or injuries sustained by a child as a result of cruel or inhumane treatment or as a result of malicious act or acts by any parent, adoptive parent or other person who has the permanent or temporary care or custody or responsibility for supervision of a minor child. . . . —Eds.

obviously compelling and urgent, could constitute a cause for the further progression and worsening of the injuries which led to the child's death. In such circumstances, Pope's omissions constituted in themselves cruel and inhumane treatment within the meaning of the statute. It follows that Pope would be guilty of child abuse *if her status brought her within the class of persons specified by the statute.* It being clear that she was neither the child's parent nor adoptive parent, and there being no evidence sufficient to support a finding that she had "the permanent or temporary care or custody" of the child so as to be in loco parentis to the child, the sole question is whether she had "responsibility for the supervision of" the child in the circumstances. If she had such responsibility the evidence was legally sufficient to find her guilty of child abuse as a principal in the first degree.

The State would have us translate compassion and concern, acts of kindness and care, performance of maternal functions, and general help and aid with respect to the child into responsibility for the supervision of the child. The crux of its argument is that although Pope was not under any obligation to assume responsibility for the supervision of the child at the outset, "once she undertook to house, feed, and care for [the mother and child], she did accept the responsibility and came within the coverage of the statute." But the mother was always present. Pope had no right to usurp the role of the mother even to the extent of responsibility for the child's supervision. . . . It would be most incongruous that acts of hospitality and kindness, made out of common decency and prompted by sincere concern for the well-being of a mother and her child, subjected the Good Samaritan to criminal prosecution for abusing the very child he sought to look after. . . .

The evidence does not show why Pope did not intervene when the mother abused the child or why she did not, at least, timely seek medical assistance, when it was obvious that the child was seriously injured. . . . But Pope's conduct, during and after the acts of abuse, must be evaluated with regard for the rule that although she may have had a strong moral obligation to help the child, she was under no legal obligation to do so unless she then had responsibility for the supervision of the child as contemplated by the child abuse statute. She may not be punished as a felon under our system of justice for failing to fulfill a moral obligation, and the short of it is that she was under no legal obligation. . . . We hold that the evidence was not sufficient in law to prove that Pope fell within that class of persons to whom the child abuse statute applies. . . .

The mental or emotional state of the mother, whereby at times she held herself out as God, does not change the result. We see no basis in the statute for an interpretation that a person "has" responsibility for the supervision of a child, if that person believes or may have reason to believe that a parent is not capable of caring for the child. There is no right to make such a subjective judgment in order to divest parents of their rights and obligations with respect to their minor children, and therefore, no obligation to do so. . . .

There is an understandable feeling of outrage at what occurred, intensified by the fact that the mother, who actually beat the child to death, was held to be not responsible for her criminal acts. But it is the law, not indignation, which governs. The law requires that Pope's conviction of the felony of child abuse be set aside as clearly erroneous due to evidentiary insufficiency. . . .

We assume, arguendo, that misprision of felony was a crime under the common law of England, and that it became the law of this State pursuant to Art. 5 of the Declaration of Rights. The question is whether it is to be deemed an indictable offense in Maryland today. . . .

We are satisfied, considering its origin, the impractical and indiscriminate width of its scope, its other obvious deficiencies, and its long non-use, that it is not now compatible with our local circumstances and situation and our general code of laws and jurisprudence. Maintenance of law and order does not demand its application, and, overall, the welfare of the inhabitants of Maryland and society as enjoyed by us today, would not be served by it. If the Legislature finds it advisable that the people be obligated under peril of criminal penalty to disclose knowledge of criminal acts, it is, of course, free to create an offense to that end, within constitutional limitations, and, hopefully, with adequate safeguards. We believe that the common law offense is not acceptable by today's standards, and we are not free to usurp the power of the General Assembly by attempting to fashion one that would be. We hold that misprision of felony is not a chargeable offense in Maryland.

NOTES

1. *Bystander indifference.* Consider Diane Kiesel, Who Saw This Happen?, 69 A.B.A. J. 1208 (1983):

> Shocking news accounts of the alleged gang rape of a woman in a Massachusetts tavern, while patrons gaped and cheered, have caused some state legislatures to consider making it a crime for witnesses to rapes and other felonies not to report them to police. . . .
>
> In May, Rhode Island enacted a law making it a misdemeanor punishable by up to one year in jail, a $500 fine or both for anyone, other than the victim, to fail to report to police a rape that takes place in his or her presence. . . .
>
> If the gang rape in March at the New Bedford, Mass., tavern happened as the witnesses said, it was unquestionably heinous and revolting. But some say the answer does not lie in laws like the one passed in Rhode Island. That measure was opposed by, surprisingly enough, the Rhode Island Rape Crisis Center, which raised questions about rape victims' privacy. The Rhode Island chapter of the American Civil Liberties Union also opposed it, citing constitutional and practical objections. Others think such statutes may be valid but ineffective. "These statutes will be no more effective than jaywalking laws," said Arthur Miller, Harvard law professor and television law commentator. "But that doesn't mean we shouldn't legislate in this area. It would give legal effect to a moral principle that we are our brother's keeper."
>
> The public outcry in the New Bedford situation recalled the uproar that followed the 1964 murder of Catherine "Kitty" Genovese in Queens, N.Y. The young bar manager was stabbed to death on the street in her middle-class neighborhood in an attack that lasted some 35 minutes. Witnesses peered through their curtains and did nothing. The assailant followed Genovese

from her parking lot toward her apartment building as she came home from work about 3:20 A.M. He started stabbing her, then fled when she screamed for help. But when her calls went unheeded, he returned to strike again. After the second assault he headed for his car and drove away while Genovese slowly crawled to her apartment doorway. Amazingly, the killer returned a third time, repeated his attack, and Genovese died. The first call to police was not made until 3:40 A.M. The man who finally called said he waited because he "didn't want to get involved."

2. How to explain bystander indifference? Consider Daniel B. Yeager, A Radical Community of Aid: A Rejoinder to Opponents of Affirmative Duties to Help Strangers, 71 Wash. U. L.Q. 1, 15 (1993):

> Why those who see others in danger so often do nothing is unclear. In the case of witnesses to crimes, danger—real or imagined—and fear of retaliation account for some failures to intervene or notify authorities. In addition, . . . a bystander's lack of opportunity for planning and rehearsal and the difficulty of quickly selecting the appropriate type of intervention might make her assistance less likely. . . .
>
> The presence of other bystanders may reduce each potential rescuer's individual sense of responsibility to the imperiled, and increase the probability of free-riding. Each is lulled into a state of "pluralistic ignorance," which induces multiple bystanders to interpret others' nonaction as a sign of no danger. [B]ecause of social inhibitions that arise in groups, people are more prone to respond to another's distress when alone than when accompanied by other witnesses.
>
> Bystanders thus face a "choice of nightmares": fail to intervene and experience the empathic distress of watching another human being suffer, the guilt of failing to live up to a minimal threshold of decency, and the shame of having that failure witnessed by others; or, intervene and risk retaliation by an assailant, the ridicule and derision of nonintervening bystanders, and the threat of being mistaken for the cause of the harm. Moreover, the victim may spurn, attack, or become completely dependent on the rescuer, while the legal system may enlist the rescuer as a witness subject to innumerable encounters with police, lawyers and judges. The nightmare then may be most easily resolved by convincing oneself that the victim is not imperiled.

3. Questions. If the factors identified by Professor Yeager help to *explain* bystander indifference, are they also sufficient to *justify* that behavior? Professor Yeager does not think so; he argues that the law should make it a criminal offense for a bystander to fail to assist a person in peril. See Yeager, supra, at 38-58. For a defense of the opposing view, see Melody J. Stewart, How Making the Failure to Assist Illegal Fails to Assist, 25 Am. J. Crim. L. 385 (1998).[8] If the criminal law should sometimes punish the failure to render assistance, what circumstances should trigger the duty to aid? Consider the following comment.

---

8. For further discussion, see Michael Menlow & Alexander McCall eds., The Duty to Rescue (1993); Theodore Y. Blumoff, On the Nature of the Action-Omission Network, 24 Ga. St. U. L. Rev. 1003 (2008); Steven J. Heyman, Foundations of the Duty to Rescue, 47 Vand. L. Rev. 673 (1994).

JOHN KLEINIG, GOOD SAMARITANISM

5 Phil. & Pub. Aff. 382 (1976)

In the Russian Criminal Code of 1845 and, since then, in almost every continental European country, the failure to be a Good Samaritan has been declared a criminal offense. The glaring exceptions to this trend have been those countries within the Anglo-American legal tradition. . . . Though the position is slowly changing in torts, the criminal law situation remains substantially the same. "The law does not compel active benevolence between man and man. It is left to one's conscience whether he shall be the Good Samaritan or not." . . . In attempting to understand the current Anglo-American position with regard to Good Samaritan legislation, it is instructive to look at some of the debate which has led to it, since it has not come about without opposition. . . .

Bentham . . . in his Introduction to the Principles of Morals and Legislation, asked the question: "In cases where the person is in danger, why should it not be made the duty of every man to save another from mischief, when it can be done without prejudicing himself . . . ?" Undoubtedly, he felt that no satisfactory answer could be given. . . .

Mill, who on matters of social policy remained close to Bentham, . . . points out that there are also "many positive acts for the benefit of others" which a person may "rightly be compelled to perform." Among these he includes

> certain acts of individual beneficence, such as saving a fellow creature's life, or interposing to protect the defenceless against ill-usage, things which whenever it is obviously a man's duty to do, he may rightfully be made responsible to society for not doing. A person may cause evil to others not only by his actions but by his inaction, and in either case he is justly accountable to them for the injury.

On Mill's view, it is our duty to render aid because, by not doing so, we *harm another*. . . .

The most influential reaction came from Lord Macaulay et al. In their *Notes on the Indian Penal Code*, . . . Macaulay criticized the proposal of an offense of homicide by omission. . . . The problem as Macaulay sees it is to draw the line between harm-producing omissions which ought to be legally proscribed, and those which ought not. He has no doubt that there are cases of each, even where the imperiled person dies. If a gaoler omits to supply a prisoner with food; if an official omits to warn travelers that the river is too high to ford; if the owner of a dog which is attacking someone omits to call it off; and death results, the person who failed to act is guilty of murder. But, if a man omits to give alms to a starving beggar; if a surgeon refuses to go from Calcutta to Meerut to perform a life-saving operation; if one traveler omits to warn others that the river is too high to ford; if a passer-by omits to call off the attacking dog; and death results, the person who failed to act is not guilty of murder. Macaulay . . . [is] prepared to grant that a rich man who lets a beggar die at his feet is morally worse than some for whom severe punishment was prescribed. "But we are unable to see where, if we make such a man legally punishable, we can draw the line." How rich is rich enough, and how much can be required? If it takes a thousand rupees to save the beggar's life, should the rich man be required to provide it? If not, where is the line to be drawn? And if the potential Good Samaritan is not a rich man, how much should he be required to give? Macaulay therefore proposes that omissions which cause or threaten harm be punishable only where they are, "on other grounds, illegal." In other words, only where there are already existing legal duties to aid should the failure to aid be indictable. . . .

What are the consequences of Good Samaritan legislation so feared by Macaulay and other opponents? On the surface it looks like a problem of legal draftsmanship. Such are the differences between men and circumstances that no workable formula for specifying those occasions on which a Samaritan ought to be legally required to render aid can be produced. . . . Livingston's criterion,[a] that aid ought to be mandatory when it can be given "without personal danger or pecuniary loss," is considered to be open to serious objection. The surgeon summoned from Calcutta to Meerut might profit financially, and the trip might present no greater dangers than staying in Bengal, but it might still be extremely inconvenient for him: "He is about to proceed to Europe immediately, or he expects some members of his family by the next ship, and wishes to be at the presidency to receive them." If he refuses to go, he is no "murderer," and a good sight better than another who, "enjoying ample wealth, should refuse to disburse an anna to save the life of another." On Livingston's criterion, the latter but not the former should go free.

About the best that could be said for this argument is that it shows the inadequacy of Livingston's criterion. . . . It does nothing to show that if Good Samaritan legislation is introduced, unreasonable sacrifices of welfare and interests will be demanded of Samaritans. As is the case with Good Samaritan provisions in those countries that already have them, the Samaritan will be required only to take reasonable steps to give or procure aid for the imperiled person. Judgments of reasonableness are not impossible of determination, and are the bread and butter of the courts. . . .

However, I think another, rather different fear underlies Macaulay's opposition to Good Samaritan legislation. [I]t is basically the fear that Good Samaritan legislation will substantially diminish freedom. In a culture steeped in individualism, nothing produces more hysteria than measures which encroach on individual liberty. "You owe me nothing; I owe you nothing. You stay out of my way, and I'll stay out of yours." That is an extreme expression, but it constitutes an important thread within the Anglo-American socio-moral fabric. . . .

The freedom to pursue one's interests is not, as Mill and Bentham clearly saw, unlimited. Where the pursuit of one's interests is a causal factor in

---

a. The reference is to the failed penal code for Louisiana drafted by Edward Livingston in 1826. See Sanford H. Kadish, Codifiers of the Criminal Law, 78 Colum. L. Rev. 1098 (1978).—Eds.

another's harm, or threatens additional harm, as in Bad Samaritanism, we have the important beginnings of a case for justifiable state interference. . . .

NOTES ON THE DUTIES OF A BYSTANDER

1. *Statutory duties to rescue.* Three American states, Minnesota, Rhode Island, and Vermont, make it a criminal offense to refuse to render aid to a person in peril. See Gabriel D. M. Ciociola, Misprision of Felony and Its Progeny, 41 Brandeis L.J. 697, 735-738 (2003). The Vermont statute (Vt. Stat. Ann. tit. 12, §519 (2011)) provides:

> A person who knows that another is exposed to grave physical harm shall, to the extent that the same can be rendered without danger or peril to himself or without interference with important duties owed to others, give reasonable assistance to the exposed person unless that assistance or care is being provided by others. [Penalty $100 fine.]

The Rhode Island statute is similar but imposes the duty only at the scene of an "emergency" and provides a penalty of up to six months' imprisonment and a $500 fine. R.I. Gen. Laws §11-56-1 (2011).

Three additional states, Florida, Hawaii, and Wisconsin, also require bystanders to be Good Samaritans, but only in more limited situations. In all three states, the duty to assist is not triggered by natural disasters but only when the person in peril is the victim of a crime. The Wisconsin and Hawaii duties to render aid extend to the victims of all violent crime, but Florida imposes a duty to assist only on persons who personally observe the commission of a sexual battery. See Ciociola, supra at 738-742. What, if anything, explains these limitations? Isn't the justification for requiring assistance *at least* as strong when the peril does not result from criminal conduct?

In all six "Good Samaritan" states, a violation of the duty to rescue is only a misdemeanor or petty misdemeanor. Even so, prosecutions are rare. See Ciociola, supra at 739. See also David A. Hyman, Rescue Without Law: An Empirical Perspective on the Duty to Rescue, 84 Tex. L. Rev. 653 (2006).

2. *Appropriate Boundaries.* Professor Ken Levy argues that a general duty to assist is justified by its potential for mitigating injury and loss of life, but that such a duty must not interfere unduly with the liberty interests of the individual. He therefore proposes that citizens not in a special relationship with the victim should have a duty to assist when (but only when) they are in close proximity to a person in grave danger and know that it will be "easy and safe" to render assistance. See Levy, Killing, Letting Die, and the Case for Mildly Punishing Bad Samaritanism, 44 Ga. L. Rev. 607, 690 (2010). The proposed duty to aid is thus narrower than that imposed by the Vermont statute, for example. Is the proposed duty *too* narrow, or is it still too broad to be widely acceptable in American jurisdictions?

3. *The European contrast.* European countries have long used the criminal law to enforce a duty to aid a person in distress. See Jacobo

Gómez-Aller, Criminal Omissions: A European Perspective, 11 New Crim. L. Rev. 419 (2008). An example is Article 323c of the German Criminal Code:

> Whoever does not render help in cases of accident, common danger or necessity although help is needed and can be provided in the circumstances without danger of serious injury to the person and without violation of other important duties, will be punished by imprisonment up to one year or by fine.

France was slower than other continental countries to recognize a general duty to rescue, but a provision similar to that of German law (art. 63(2) of the French Penal Code) was added in 1945. It carries a penalty of up to five years' imprisonment, and it has been enforced with some frequency. For example, motorists have often been prosecuted and convicted for failure to stop and assist the victims of vehicle accidents caused by others. See Edward A. Tomlinson, The French Experience with a Duty to Rescue, 20 N.Y.L. Sch. J. Intl. & Comp. L. 451 (2000).

4. *Questions on the degree of punishment.* If the *Pope* case had arisen in a "Good Samaritan" state, what penalties would Mrs. Pope face? Notice that American statutes imposing a duty to rescue are always graded as minor misdemeanors; in Vermont the offense carries a maximum penalty of a $100 fine. Could a prosecutor find any basis for imposing a more severe penalty? In a "Good Samaritan" state, could Mrs. Pope be convicted of criminal homicide? Consider State v. Martinez, 68 P.3d 606 (Haw. 2003). The defendant failed to seek medical assistance after his girlfriend severely beat her daughter, inflicting injuries that proved fatal. His duty to aid was based on the Hawaii Good Samaritan statute, and violations of that statute are classified as petty misdemeanors. Nonetheless, he was convicted of reckless manslaughter and sentenced to ten years' imprisonment, on the theory that his omission, with awareness of the danger to the child, caused her death. Should the manslaughter conviction be upheld on appeal?

5. *Misprision—the duty to report.* The common-law offense of misprision of felony, discussed in *Pope*, was abolished in England in 1967, and most American jurisdictions have likewise abolished or refused to recognize the offense. See Ciociola, supra Note 1, at 710-718. Congress enacted a misprision-of-felony statute in 1909, 18 U.S.C. §4, but this offense requires active concealment of a known felony; the mere omission of failing to report is not sufficient. United States v. Johnson, 546 F.2d 1225 (5th Cir. 1977). Only a few American states still recognize the common-law offense, see, e.g., State v. Smith, 592 S.E.2d 302 (S.C. 2004); Ciociola, supra at 710-721, but two others (South Dakota and Ohio) have re-established the offense through statutes that create a general obligation to report any known felony, and many states impose a reporting obligation on eyewitnesses to specific crimes. See Ciociola, supra at 726-734.

Additionally, all American jurisdictions require members of certain designated professions to report suspected cases of child abuse; usually the failure to do so is a misdemeanor. In recent years the duty to report in such situations has been expanded from doctors, nurses, and teachers to include clergy, optometrists, psychotherapists, and (in some jurisdictions) even attorneys. See Sandra Guerra Thompson, The White Collar Police Force: "Duty to Report" Statutes in Criminal Law Theory, 11 Wm. & Mary Bill Rts. J. 3 (2002). Building on that model, Congress and state legislatures have required individuals to report suspicions concerning a variety of other crimes, such as elder abuse, domestic violence, environmental crimes, and certain financial crimes. In many professions, the web of reporting obligations is now quite dense, with important implications for client confidentiality and the traditional conception of the individual's right to "mind his own business." See Thompson, supra.

Questions: Are there legitimate objections to imposing a general duty to report *any* felony? One concern may be that such a duty would pose an unacceptable threat to the privacy of victims, especially in the case of sexual offenses. Another concern may be the bystander's reluctance to become obliged to testify in court or fear of retaliation by the person reported. Is resistance to a reporting obligation justified if it is based not on protecting the victim's privacy but instead on preserving the bystander's autonomy right to remain uninvolved? For a discussion of these issues, see Kleinig, supra.

Should a duty to report known felonies apply to people who may be aware that drug sellers are operating in their neighborhoods? Even if drug offenses are excepted from the duty to report, will people living in high-crime neighborhoods be unfairly burdened by a general duty to report serious felonies?

NOTES ON DUTIES TRIGGERED BY SPECIAL CIRCUMSTANCES

1. Family members. As the court notes in the *Jones* case, it is well settled that a duty to aid arises "where one stands in a certain status relationship to another." But not every significant status relationship will do. Parents have a duty to aid and protect their minor children, and spouses have a similar duty to each other. But generally speaking, duties are not automatically imposed on siblings to aid each other, on parents to aid their adult children, or on adult children to aid their parents—even when the parents are elderly and unable to care for themselves.

2. De facto family members. Traditionally, the categories of spouse and parent would trigger a duty to aid only in the case of formal legal relationships. Consider People v. Beardsley, 150 Mich. 206, 113 N.W. 1128 (1907). Beardsley, who was married, apparently was having an affair with Blanche Burns, and he spent a weekend with her at his home, while his wife was out of town. At the end of the weekend, Burns took a fatal dose of morphine tablets. Beardsley failed to call a physician to help her. She died, and he was convicted of manslaughter. The court reversed the conviction because defendant owed the deceased no legal duty (113 N.W. at 1131):

> It is urged by the prosecutor that the respondent "stood towards this woman for the time being in the place of her natural guardian and protector, and as such owed her a clear legal duty which he completely failed to perform." The fact that this woman was in his house created no such legal duty as exists in law and is due from a husband towards his wife, as seems to be intimated by the prosecutor's brief. Such an inference would be very repugnant to our moral sense.

Do you agree? *Beardsley* has been widely criticized. One commentator concludes that *Beardsley* "proclaims a morality which is smug, ignorant and vindictive" (Graham Hughes, Criminal Omissions, 67 Yale L.J. 590, 624 (1958)), and courts have described its holding as "outmoded." State ex rel. Kuntz v. District Court, 995 P.2d 951, 956 (2000). See Arthur Leavens, A Causation Approach to Criminal Omissions, 78 Calif. L. Rev. 547, 561 (1988). But on facts like *Beardsley*, should the result be different today? Few contemporary courts (if any) would say that a formal marriage is always necessary to establish a familial duty. But is a de facto marriage required, or is a more casual dating relationship (like that in *Beardsley*) sufficient? If any romantic liaison will suffice, isn't a duty to aid equally justified for other personal relationships, even without a sexual dimension? Isn't the result in *Pope* even harder to defend than the result in *Beardsley*?

The cases are beginning to expand—but only slightly—the notion of who qualifies as a spouse or parent. In People v. Carroll, 93 N.Y.2d 564, 715 N.E.2d 500 (1999), a stepmother was charged with child endangerment for failing to prevent her husband from killing his daughter during a week when the daughter was temporarily visiting them. The New York Court of Appeals upheld the indictment, ruling that the stepmother owed a duty of care to her husband's children (715 N.E.2d at 500):

> [A] person who acts as the functional equivalent of a parent in a familial or household setting is . . . legally responsible for a child's care. By expanding the bounds of who is legally responsible for children beyond the realm of the traditional family and legal guardian, this standard takes into account the modern-day reality that parenting functions are not always performed by a parent.

Compare State v. Miranda, 274 Conn. 727, 878 A.2d 1118 (2005), where the Connecticut Supreme Court rejected this approach. Miranda, a live-in boyfriend, failed to protect a four-month-old child from a fatal beating inflicted by his girlfriend, the child's mother. While residing with the family, he had taken care of the child and considered himself to be her stepfather. He was convicted of first-degree assault, and in his initial appeal the Connecticut Supreme Court upheld the conviction, ruling that because he had a family-like relationship with the mother and had assumed responsibility for the welfare of her children, he was under a duty to protect the baby girl from her mother's abuse. 715 A.2d 680 (Conn. 1998). In a subsequent appeal, however, the court overruled its original decision. This time (with one of the judges who had voted to uphold the conviction now changing his vote), the court set aside the assault conviction. Writing for a plurality, the judge who changed his vote explained (878 A.2d at 1130-1131):

> [P]arental liability should [not] be extended, on a case-by-case basis, beyond the clearly established legal categories of a parent or legal guardian. . . . It will be difficult to cabin this precedent to these precise facts, and the temptation will always be there, in a case of egregious injuries—as this case is—to extend it to . . . others with regular and extended relationships with the abusing parent and the abused victim.
>
> [T]he emerging demographic trend toward nontraditional alternative family arrangements, which we cited as support in *Miranda I*, now strikes me as a counter argument. Precisely because of that trend, and the concomitant difficulty of determining in advance where it will lead and what its ultimate contours will be, the boundaries of this duty-based criminal liability will be too amorphous, and too fact-based and based on hindsight, to fit comfortably within our Penal Code. [T]he children who are the most at risk for abuse are likely to suffer the greatest harm from this amorphous criminal liability, because it will discourage well-meaning relatives, friends of the family and other members of the community from taking an active and intense interest in them, for fear of being caught in a web of criminal liability for the egregious conduct of another.
>
> Finally, I think that *Miranda I* places too much power in the hands of the state to use as a bargaining chip in plea negotiations. Precisely because its boundaries are so amorphous, it gives the state the power to threaten its use in a different but similar case, in order to extract a plea that the state might not otherwise be able to secure.

A dissenting judge responded (878 A.2d at 1154):

> [P]ersons inclined to enter relationships that involve children will [not] consciously decide against such involvement for fear of being held responsible if and when a child is abused or neglected. [A]ffording protection only to those children whose adult caregivers have chosen to have their relationships officially recognized hardly advances the public policy of protecting children from abuse.

For in-depth analysis of these issues, see Dan Markel, Jennifer M. Collins & Ethan J. Lieb, Privilege or Punish (2009), The authors criticize the law's reliance on formal categories rather than functional relationships as the basis for triggering duties of care and propose creation of a registry through which siblings, cousins, roommates, and others could opt in to reciprocal obligations of care if they wished. For a probing critique of this approach, see Michael O'Hear, Yes to Nondiscrimination, No to New Forms of Criminal Liability, 88 B.U. L. Rev. 1437 (2008).

3. *When the parent herself is a victim.* There is no doubt, of course, that a mother has a duty to protect her minor children from abuse by a third party. As a result, mothers are frequently prosecuted and convicted on child abuse or homicide charges, including murder, when their children are the victims of assault perpetrated by a male member of the household. See Jennifer M. Collins, Ethan J. Lieb & Dan Markel, Punishing Family Status, 88 B.U. L. Rev. 1327, 1329-30, 1335 (2008). Although—in theory—her duty to take protective actions is clear, culpability and the appropriate targets of criminal law enforcement become clouded when the context is infected by pervasive domestic violence. Consider Commonwealth v. Cardwell, 515 A.2d 311 (Pa. Super. 1986). Defendant Julia Cardwell lived with her daughter, Alicia, and Clyde Cardwell, who was Julia's husband and Alicia's stepfather. For four years, beginning when Alicia was about 11 years old, Clyde sexually abused Alicia. In October 1983, Alicia told her mother Julia about the assaults. Ten months later, Alicia ran away from home. Julia was convicted of child abuse for failing to take sufficient steps in the interim to protect her daughter:

> In those ten months, Julia's only actions directed at protecting her daughter consisted of writing two letters to Clyde that did little more than express her knowledge of and anger at his abuse of Alicia; applying for Alicia to transfer schools; and moving some of her and Alicia's clothing to Julia's mother's house. We note that the remedy of moving to Julia's mother's house was tragically frustrated by the destruction by fire of that house in May 1984, but the fact remains that Julia took no further steps to relieve her daughter's desperate situation in the four months that ensued from May 1984 until Alicia ran away from home in September 1984.

The court's opinion mentioned, without comment, several further details:

> Alicia testified that she and Julia were afraid of Clyde, that Clyde beat up Julia on one occasion, that he threw and broke things in the house, that he had punched a number of holes in the walls of the house, and that he carried a .357 magnum pistol, which he kept on the mantelpiece.

Nonetheless the court upheld the conviction, noting:

> The affirmative performance required . . . cannot be met simply by showing any step at all toward preventing harm, however incomplete or ineffectual. An act which will negate intent is not necessarily one which will provide a successful outcome. However, the person charged with the duty of care is required to take steps that are reasonably calculated to achieve success. Otherwise, the meaning of "duty of care" is eviscerated.

A concurring judge conceded that "Julia's real choices in view of her not unreasonable fear of her husband were limited and difficult—she could report her husband to the authorities, she could take her daughter and leave the marital home, or she could send her daughter away." The judge nonetheless concurred in affirming the conviction because Julia "unquestionably endangered her daughter's welfare by doing nothing to prevent the child's continued abuse."

Questions: How should Clyde's violence toward Julia affect the extent of her duty to prevent him from harming her child? The strict requirements for a duress defense are not met, as we shall see, infra page 924. See also Michelle S. Jacobs, Requiring Battered Women [to] Die: Murder Liability for Mothers Under Failure to Protect Statutes, 88 J. Crim. & Criminology 579 (1998). To what extent should a mother be forced to risk her own life in order to avoid criminal liability for injuries inflicted intentionally by her spouse or boyfriend? Consider Dorothy E. Roberts, Motherhood and Crime, 79 Iowa L. Rev. 95, 111-113:

> Women who fail to protect their children from violence are often victims of violence themselves. . . . Courts, however, . . . presume that a woman's obligation to her children always takes precedence over her own interest in independence and physical safety. Feminists have criticized people who ask battered women "Why didn't you leave?" because this question fails to recognize the physical, social, and legal constraints that keep women in violent homes. Courts slowly are beginning to acknowledge these constraints in self-defense cases. These impediments do not seem to matter, however, when mothers [fail to protect] abused children. Judges assume that a woman's maternal instinct to protect her children from harm overcomes any barriers to escape.

4. The duty of one who creates another person's peril. The law has long been clear that "one who by his overpowering criminal act has put another in danger of drowning has a duty to preserve her life. . . ." Jones v. State, 43 N.E.2d 1017, 1018 (Ind. 1942). The duty to act in these situations is obviously fair, but it's not so obvious why it matters. After all, if the victim drowns, the prosecution can argue simply that the defendant killed her by his initial criminal act—for example, the act of pushing her into the water. Why would it make any difference whether he had an obligation to rescue her?

The answer becomes clear if we compare the level of knowledge—and the resulting degree of blame—that attach to the initial act and to the omission. That comparison is important because the nature of an offense depends on the interaction of three elements—the actus reus (a voluntary act or culpable omission), the defendant's state of mind at the time of that actus reus, and the result caused. Suppose that Arthur, in a boisterous mood after drinking four beers, runs along a crowded fishing pier, fails to watch where he is going, and collides with Frank Fisherman, knocking him into the water. Frank yells that he can't swim and implores Arthur to throw him the nearby life preserver, but Arthur simply watches as Frank struggles and eventually drowns. Arthur's affirmative act, running heedlessly along the pier, is probably careless enough to constitute criminal negligence, and as a result, he could be convicted of involuntary manslaughter or negligent homicide. But is

[margin note: peril - exposure to injury]

he guilty of murder? That offense, as we shall see,[9] requires proof that the defendant intended to kill or *knew* that his conduct created a substantial risk of causing death. It would be difficult to prove that Arthur had that knowledge when he ran along the pier and collided with Frank. But it would be easy to prove that Arthur had that knowledge later, while he watched Frank struggle and go under. Imposing a duty to rescue (as the law does in this instance) will bring into the picture a much more culpable state of mind and will therefore markedly increase the degree of Arthur's liability in the event that Frank drowns.

5. *Problem.* Should the duty to rescue based on "creating another person's peril" be triggered when the acts that create danger are not culpable at all? Suppose that Barry, while walking slowly down the pier, accidentally bumps into a child, knocking her into the water. Barry and another bystander, Carl, then watch the child drown. On the basis of his actions alone, Barry has not committed any criminal offense. Should his innocent act, imperiling the child, give rise to a duty to rescue? Consider J.C. Smith, Liability for Omissions in Criminal Law, 14 Legal Stud. 88, 94 (1984):

> Suppose that, on leaving my office on Friday evening, I lock the storeroom door, reasonably believing the room to be empty. I then hear movement inside and realize that I have locked in a colleague and that he will be imprisoned there for the weekend unless I unlock the door and let him out. Surely my omission to do so would render me liable for false imprisonment (in criminal as well as civil law); and it should be no answer that locking the door was an entirely lawful and reasonable act. . . .
>
> I venture, therefore, to suggest a general principle: . . . Whenever the defendant's act, though without his knowledge, imperils the person, liberty or property of another, or any other interest protected by the criminal law, and the defendant becomes aware of the events creating the peril, he has a duty to take reasonable steps to prevent the peril from resulting in the harm in question.

American tort law is in accord.[10] And since a criminal-law duty to act can arise from obligations under tort and contract law, many American courts impose criminal liability as well. In Commonwealth v. Levesque, 766 N.E.2d 50 (Mass. 2002), the defendants accidentally started a fire and then, despite their awareness of the danger, failed to report it. The blaze got out of control, and six firefighters died attempting to put it out. The court upheld the defendants' conviction of involuntary manslaughter.

Questions: (a) Under the approach of cases like *Levesque*, supra, the result in the example involving the child knocked from the pier into the water is that

---

9. Pages 420-421 infra.

10. See Restatement (Second) of Torts §321, stating that a person who creates a continuing risk of physical harm to another "is under a duty to take reasonable care to prevent the risk from taking effect" and that this rule "applies even though at the time of the act the actor has no reason to believe that it will involve such a risk." In accord, see also Restatement (Third) Torts (Draft No. 4) §39.

a duty to act would be imposed on Barry (who accidentally created the peril) but not on the bystander Carl. Does this make sense? If the law is sound in allowing Carl to ignore the child's plight, why should Barry's wholly innocent act put him in a different position? And how should we analyze the liability of a third person (Dorothy) who is standing on the pier when Barry accidentally bumps into her, knocking her into the child, who as a result falls into the water? As an involuntary agent, Dorothy—or her body—caused the peril to the child. Is Dorothy, who committed no act, in the same moral (and legal) position as Carl, who also committed no act, or should she be treated like Barry, who committed a voluntary but innocent act? Recall that the law imposes no general duty to rescue. The problem, then, is to determine when the reasons for that rule (which presumably apply in the case of Carl) are no longer applicable. For a careful discussion of the issues, see Larry Alexander, Criminal Liability for Omissions, in Criminal Law Theory 121 (Stephen Shute & A.P. Simester eds., 2002).

(b) Should the duty to rescue based on "creating another person's peril" be triggered when the defendant helps a person who voluntarily *chooses* to place herself in danger? In R. v. Evans, [2009] 1 W.L.R. 1999, the defendant supplied heroin to her sister, who self-injected the drug, and then developed symptoms of overdose. Though aware of her sister's life-endangering condition, the defendant failed to summon assistance. Her conviction of manslaughter was upheld on the ground that a duty to rescue was triggered because she had "contributed to" creating the perilous situation. Id. at [31]. Is the result sound?

(c) Are the duties to rescue that arise under tort law sufficiently well defined to afford adequate notice to affected citizens, thus meeting the criminal-law "legality" principle? Or do penal prohibitions triggered by evolving tort precedent violate the constitutional void-for-vagueness doctrine? We examined the legality and vagueness doctrines in depth at pages 150-186 supra. In terms of these doctrines—or merely in terms of simple fairness—does evolving tort law provide an acceptable foundation for criminal liability? In cases like *Levesque* and *Evans*, supra, courts have not considered criminal liability unfair. Compare State v. Lisa, 945 A.2d 690, 691 (N.J. 2007). Early one evening, the defendant illegally sold a methadone tablet to his girlfriend, A.R. She then proceeded to several parties, where she drank alcohol and smoked marijuana. Around 3:00 A.M., she went to the defendant's home, drank more beer, had sex with him, and then passed out in his bedroom. When the defendant attempted to awaken her, she was unresponsive. Several friends, including one who was a nurse, urged him to call 9-1-1, but he refused, hoping she would "sleep it off." When emergency aid was finally summoned the following afternoon, A.R. was unconscious and had suffered major brain damage; she died ten days later without regaining consciousness. The defendant was charged with reckless manslaughter for failing to summon aid at a time when he knew that A.R. was in grave danger. But the trial court dismissed the indictment on the ground that he owed no duty to A.R. Affirming the dismissal, the New Jersey Supreme Court said (id. at 691):

> [T]he Restatement of Torts [does] not provide sufficient notice of a duty to which a theory of criminal omission liability may attach. [S]ufficient notice . . . cannot be found in emanations from a scholarly treatise that has never made its way into New Jersey substantive criminal law, and perhaps not into our civil law either. We fail to see how these civil common law principles [based on amorphous concepts of the Restatement, as reflected in some civil cases] could provide adequate notice to justify a criminal charge.

Do you agree?

NOTE ON POSSESSION

Is possession an omission or an act? And if it is an omission, when is there a duty to avoid or terminate the possession? These questions assume great importance as a result of the proliferation of drug-possession and firearms-possession offenses and the high priority that federal and state prosecutors continue to give to the "war on drugs."

In the simplest cases, a person buys an illegal item—a gun, for example—and puts it into his coat pocket. Here we would say that he *takes* possession; his possession is clearly an act. But suppose that Smuggler places a packet of heroin into the baggage of Respectable Traveler, hoping that Traveler will not be searched and that Smuggler can later steal Traveler's bag to retrieve the drugs. If Traveler is searched and the drugs are found, is she guilty of illegal possession? Most courts hold that she is not; they interpret possession offenses to require that the accused be aware that she has the thing she is charged with possessing, even when the statute is silent on the subject. See, e.g., Commonwealth v. Adkins, 331 S.W.2d 260 (Ky 2011); Commonwealth v. Sespedes, 810 N.E.2d 790 (Mass. 2004). The Model Penal Code likewise provides that possession can satisfy the actus reus requirement of §2.01(1) only when the accused "was aware of his control [of the thing possessed] for a sufficient period to have been able to terminate his possession." Model Penal Code §2.01(4).

Not all courts agree. State v. Bradshaw, 98 P.3d 1190 (Wash. 2004), involved a commercial truck driver who crossed the Canadian border into the state of Washington driving a large semitrailer on which someone had hidden 77 pounds of marijuana in a space between pallets of cargo. There was no evidence the driver was aware that drugs were on the truck. Nonetheless, the Washington Supreme Court upheld a conviction for possession of illegal drugs, rejecting the argument that awareness of the presence of an item is inherent in the concept of possessing it.

Questions: (1) In what sense did the truck driver commit any relevant "act"? Driving the truck, of course, is an act, but the Washington Supreme

Court did not attempt to defend liability on that basis. Its approach would support conviction even if the driver simply sat passively in the truck while (a) a smuggler hid drugs on it and then (b) a police officer, acting on a reliable informant's tip, searched and found the drugs. In what sense would the driver have committed any relevant "act" in such a case?

(2) If liability is based not on an "act" but simply on the driver's omission (his failure to get rid of the drugs), what is the justification for imposing that duty to act? Notice that in cases like *Pope* and other failure-to-rescue situations, the bystander, though well aware of a peril, is permitted to ignore it. Why should a duty be imposed when the accused had no reason to think there was any need for him to act?

(3) Suppose the truck driver, though still unaware of the presence of drugs, *should have* suspected that something was amiss? (Suppose, for example, he had noticed a suspicious person loitering near his truck and saw that a flap covering his cargo had either come loose or been untied.) If drugs are subsequently discovered, would Model Penal Code §2.01 permit a conviction for drug possession? *Should* the driver be guilty of a drug-possession offense under these circumstances?

c. Distinguishing Omissions from Acts

BARBER v. SUPERIOR COURT

California District Court of Appeal
147 Cal. App. 3d 1006, 195 Cal. Rptr. 484 (1983)

[After a preliminary hearing, the magistrate dismissed murder and conspiracy charges against two physicians. The superior court set aside the magistrate's order and reinstated the complaint. The physicians then petitioned the court of appeal for review of the decision of the superior court.]

COMPTON, A.J. . . . Deceased Clarence Herbert underwent surgery. [W]hile in the recovery room, Mr. Herbert suffered a cardio-respiratory arrest. He was revived by a team of physicians and nurses and immediately placed on life support equipment.

Within the following three days, it was determined that Mr. Herbert was in a deeply comatose state. [Tests] indicated that Mr. Herbert had suffered severe brain damage, leaving him in a vegetative state, which was likely to be permanent. At that time petitioners [his physicians] informed Mr. Herbert's family of their opinion as to his condition and chances for recovery. While there is some dispute as to the precise terminology used by the doctors, it is clear that they communicated to the family that the prognosis for recovery was extremely poor. At that point, the family convened and drafted a written request to the hospital personnel stating that they wanted "all machines taken off that are sustaining life" (sic). As a result, petitioners, either directly or as a result of orders given by them, caused the respirator and other life-sustaining equipment to be removed. Mr. Herbert continued to breathe without the equipment but showed no signs of improvement. . . . After two more days had elapsed, petitioners, after consulting with the family, ordered removal of the intravenous tubes which provided hydration and nourishment. From that point until his death, Mr. Herbert received nursing care which preserved his dignity and provided a clean and hygienic environment.

The precise issue for determination by this court is whether the evidence presented before the magistrate was sufficient to support his determination that petitioners should not be held to answer to the charges of murder, and conspiracy to commit murder. . . . "Murder is the *unlawful* killing of a human being, . . . with malice aforethought." . . .

[W]e accept the superior court judge's analysis that if petitioners unlawfully and intentionally killed Mr. Herbert, the malice could be presumed regardless of their motive.

The use of the term "unlawful" in defining a criminal homicide is generally to distinguish a criminal homicide from those homicides which society has determined to be "justifiable" or "excusable." Euthanasia, of course, is neither justifiable nor excusable in California. . . .

As a predicate to our analysis of whether the petitioners' conduct amounted to an "unlawful killing," we conclude that the cessation of "heroic" life support measures is not an affirmative act but rather a withdrawal or omission of further treatment. Even though these life support devices are, to a degree, "self-propelled," each pulsation of the respirator or each drop of fluid introduced into the patient's body by intravenous feeding devices is comparable to a manually administered injection or item of medication. Hence "disconnecting" of the mechanical devices is comparable to withholding the manually administered injection or medication. Further we view the use of an intravenous administration of nourishment and fluid, under the circumstances, as being the same as the use of the respirator or other form of life support equipment. . . .

There is no criminal liability for failure to act unless there is a legal duty to act. Thus the critical issue becomes one of determining the duties owed by a physician to a patient who has been reliably diagnosed as in a comatose state from which any meaningful recovery of cognitive brain function is exceedingly unlikely. . . .

A physician has no duty to continue treatment, once it has proved to be ineffective. Although there may be a duty to provide life-sustaining machinery in the *immediate* aftermath of a cardio-respiratory arrest, there is no duty to continue its use once it has become futile in the opinion of qualified medical personnel. . . .

Of course, the difficult determinations that must be made under these principles [are] the point at which further treatment will be of no reasonable benefit to the patient, who should have the power to make that decision and who should have the authority to direct termination of treatment. No precise guidelines as to when and how these decisions should be made can be provided by this court since this determination is essentially a medical one to be made at a time and on the basis of facts which will be unique to each case. . . .

[T]he patient's interests and desires are the key ingredients of the decision making process. . . . When the patient, however, is incapable of deciding for himself, because of his medical condition or for other reasons, there is no clear authority on the issue of who and under what procedure is to make the final decision. . . .

Under the circumstances of this case, the wife was the proper person to act as a surrogate for the patient with the authority to decide issues regarding further treatment, and would have so qualified had judicial approval been sought. There is no evidence that there was any disagreement among the wife and children. Nor was there any evidence that they were motivated in their decision by anything other than love and concern for the dignity of their husband and father. . . .

In summary we conclude that the petitioners' omission to continue treatment under the circumstances, though intentional and with knowledge that the patient would die, was not an unlawful failure to perform a legal duty. . . . The superior court erred in determining that as a matter of law the evidence required the magistrate to hold petitioners to answer.

Airedale NHS Trust v. Bland, [1993] All E.R. 821 (H.L.): [The House of Lords faced the question whether artificial feeding and antibiotic drugs may lawfully be withheld from an insensate patient with no hope of recovery, when it is known that without the treatment the patient will shortly die. The House of Lords answered the question in the affirmative. Lord Goff stated in his address:]

[T]he law draws a crucial distinction between cases in which a doctor decides not to provide, or to continue to provide, for his patient treatment or care which could or might prolong his life and those in which he decides, for example, by administering a lethal drug, actively to bring his patient's life to an end. [T]he former may be lawful, either because the doctor is giving effect to his patient's wishes by withholding the treatment or care, or even in certain circumstances in which . . . the patient is incapacitated from stating whether or not he gives his consent. But it is not lawful for a doctor to administer a drug to his patient to bring about his death, even though that course is prompted by a humanitarian desire to end his suffering, however great that suffering may be. So to act is to cross the Rubicon which runs between on the one hand the care of the living patient and on the other hand euthanasia—actively causing his death to avoid or to end his suffering. Euthanasia is not lawful at common law. It is of course well known that there are many responsible members of our society who believe that euthanasia should be made lawful; but that result could, I believe, only be achieved by legislation which expresses the democratic will that so fundamental a change should be made in our law, and can, if enacted, ensure that such legalized killing can only be carried out subject to appropriate supervision and control. It is true that the drawing of this distinction may lead to a charge of hypocrisy, because it can be asked why, if the doctor, by discontinuing treatment, is entitled in consequence to let his patient die, it should not be lawful to put him out of his misery straight away, in a more humane manner, by a lethal injection, rather than let him linger on in pain until he dies. But the law does not feel able to authorize euthanasia, even in circumstances such as these, for, once euthanasia is recognized as lawful in these circumstances, it is difficult to see any logical basis for excluding it in others.

At the heart of this distinction lies a theoretical question. Why is it that the doctor who gives his patient a lethal injection which kills him commits an unlawful act and indeed is guilty of murder, whereas a doctor who, by discontinuing life support, allows his patient to die may not act unlawfully and will not do so if he commits no breach of duty to his patient? Professor Glanville Williams has suggested (see Textbook of Criminal Law (2nd edn, 1983), p. 282) that the reason is that what the doctor does when he switches off a life support machine "is in substance not an act but an omission to struggle" and that "the omission is not a breach of duty by the doctor, because he is not obliged to continue in a hopeless case."

I agree that the doctor's conduct in discontinuing life support can properly be categorized as an omission. It is true that it may be difficult to describe what the doctor actually does as an omission, for example where he takes some positive step to bring the life support to an end. But discontinuation of life support is, for present purposes, no different from not initiating life support in the first place. In each case, the doctor is simply allowing his patient to die in the sense that he is desisting from taking a step which might, in certain circumstances, prevent his patient from dying as a result of his pre-existing condition; and as a matter of general principle an omission such as this will not be unlawful unless it constitutes a breach of duty to the patient. I also agree that the doctor's conduct is to be differentiated from that of, for example, an interloper who maliciously switches off a life support machine because, although the interloper may perform exactly the same act as the doctor who discontinues life support, his doing so constitutes interference with the life-prolonging treatment then being administered by the doctor. Accordingly, whereas the doctor, in discontinuing life support, is simply allowing his patient to die of his pre-existing condition, the interloper is actively intervening to stop the doctor from prolonging the patient's life, and such conduct cannot possibly be categorized as an omission.

The distinction appears, therefore, to be useful in the present context in that it can be invoked to explain how discontinuance of life support can be differentiated from ending a patient's life by a lethal injection. But in the end the reason for that difference is that, whereas the law considers that discontinuance of life support may be consistent with the doctor's duty to care for his patient, it does not, for reasons of policy, consider that it forms any part of his duty to give his patient a lethal injection to put him out of his agony.

NOTE

In a later chapter, we will examine the arguments in favor of allowing active euthanasia at a patient's request to qualify as an affirmative defense to a charge of homicide or assisting a suicide. See pages 914-921 infra. As we will see, only three American jurisdictions currently come close to recognizing such a defense. Yet "letting the patient die" with her consent is permissible in every American jurisdiction. Indeed, in Cruzan v. Director, Missouri Dept. of Public Health, 497 U.S. 261 (1989), the Supreme Court held that individuals have a constitutional right to refuse unwanted medical treatment. And the Court held this right available even to a person in a permanent vegetative state, provided there is clear and convincing evidence of the patient's wishes in this regard. Thus, the distinction between killing and letting die has enormous legal significance—the former is almost invariably illegal, while the latter is permissible and even constitutionally protected. But is there really a distinction, in the medical context, between an act of killing and an omission of letting die? And even if there is some distinction, does it justify the radically different legal treatment of the two? Consider these comments:

Cruzan, supra, at 296-297 (Scalia, J., concurring in the result): I readily acknowledge that the distinction between action and inaction has some bearing upon the legislative judgment of what ought to be prevented as suicide— though even there it would seem to me unreasonable to draw the line precisely between action and inaction, rather than between various forms of inaction. It would not make much sense to say that one may not kill oneself by walking into the sea, but may sit on the beach until submerged by the incoming tide; or that one may not intentionally lock oneself in a cold storage locker, but may refrain from coming indoors when the temperature drops below freezing. . . . Starving oneself to death is no different from putting a gun to one's temple as far as the common-law definition of suicide is concerned; the cause of death in both cases is the suicide's conscious decision to "pu[t] an end to his own existence." 4 Blackstone, Commentaries *189.

John Robertson, Respect for Life in Bioethical Dilemmas—The Case of Physician-Assisted Suicide, 45 Clev. St. L. Rev. 329, 333-335 (1997): [T]he central issue that remains is whether . . . the moral or social threat to respect for human life is greater from physician-assisted suicide than it is from our widely accepted current practices of nontreatment? This question is key because most opponents of physician-assisted suicide accept the patient's right to refuse life-saving medical treatment. They distinguish the two cases by citing the importance of the active/passive distinction. Opponents of physician-assisted suicide emphasize that overriding the patient's choice to refuse treatment requires a direct imposition or intrusion on the patient, while assisted suicide and active euthanasia entails a person having something done to them. Proponents of a right to physician-assisted suicide, on the other hand, claim there is no significant moral difference between the two. If causing death by foregoing or removing medical treatment is justified, then causing death by writing a lethal prescription for the patient, or even administering a lethal injection, should also be permitted. . . .

The moral distinction between killing and letting die—between actively and passively causing death—has been examined by many bioethicists, philosophers, and lawyers. Most have concluded that the distinction between active and passive, on which opponents [of physician-assisted suicide] so heavily rest, is a distinction without a significant enough moral difference to support the great weight that opponents of physician-assisted suicide have placed on it. From the perspective of the affected individual, the sought for end—the relief of suffering and demise—is the same regardless of whether the immediate cause of death is described as active or passive, killing or letting die. If a competent and informed patient knowingly consents, it does not matter morally whether the physician then withholds further treatment or writes a prescription for lethal drugs which the patient then administers to herself. . . .

The line drawn by opponents of assisted suicide between active and passive is also vulnerable to a charge of inconsistency or arbitrariness. It is difficult to know in practice why one thing is labeled active . . . and therefore not permitted, and another is labeled passive and permitted. A lethal injection is active. . . . Withdrawing treatment is said to be passive, yet many acts of withdrawal are quite active, for example, "pulling the plug" is literally an act. One cannot easily distinguish in all significant respects removing ventilators or feeding tubes from the act of writing a prescription for a drug, which the patient will later take on her own. Finally, because the interest in conserving resources exists in both cases, threats to the poor and elderly to end their life prematurely may be as great with decisions to withhold treatment as they are with asking physicians to write prescriptions for drugs that patients later use to commit suicide.

Questions: Are these critiques of the act/omission distinction convincing? If active and passive euthanasia should be treated in the same way, should both be permissible? Or should both be prohibited? For further exploration of these issues, see the materials on euthanasia as an affirmative justification, pages 911-921 infra.

2. Mens Rea—Culpable Mental States

a. Basic Conceptions

INTRODUCTORY NOTE

The criminal law does more than simply identify the harms that society seeks to prohibit by threat of punishment; it also includes an elaborate body of qualifications to these threats of punishment, based on the absence of fault. A common usage is to consider all of these qualifications and exceptions to liability as examples of the requirement of "mens rea"—a requirement often identified with the classic maxim, *actus non facit reum, nisi mens sit rea.* Or, in Blackstone's translation, "an unwarrantable act without a vicious will is no crime at all." The vicious will was the mens rea; essentially it refers to the blameworthiness entailed in choosing to commit a criminal wrong. The requirement of mens rea reflects the common sense view of justice that blame and punishment are inappropriate in the absence of choice.[11] From this perspective, a great variety of defenses to criminal liability—involuntary act, duress, legal insanity, accident, and mistake, for example—can be considered "mens rea" defenses, that is, defenses that aim to establish the absence of moral blameworthiness.

This all-encompassing usage, which treats the term "mens rea" as synonymous with moral fault, is often referred to as mens rea in its *broad* sense. But courts and commentators often use the term "mens rea" in a narrower sense. Mens rea in its *narrow* sense is a more formal and technical requirement; it refers to the kind of awareness or intention that must accompany the prohibited act, under the terms of the statute defining the offense.

Relatively few of the mental attitudes we notice in daily life are used in defining mens rea in this narrow sense. Whether the defendant acted regretfully, arrogantly, eagerly, hopefully, and so forth may be relevant for a judge considering the sentence to be imposed, but attitudes like these seldom factor into the statutory definition of a crime. Instead, almost invariably, the concern of the criminal law is limited to determining whether a defendant intended, expected, or should have expected his actions to produce particular consequences.

Consider some examples: An attempt to commit a crime consists of an act that comes close to its commission done with the *purpose* that the crime be committed. Unlawful assembly is the act of joining with a group in a public place with *intent* to commit unlawful acts. Receiving stolen goods is a crime when one receives stolen goods *knowing* they are stolen. Manslaughter is the killing of another by an act done with the *awareness* of a substantial and unjustifiable risk of doing so.

The fact that criminal liability in these instances requires mens rea in a particular *narrow* sense is obvious. That is the way these crimes are defined. But it is important to see that they are so defined because the mens rea element is crucial to the description of the conduct we want to make criminal. To revert to the examples just given, it would not make sense to punish someone for receiving stolen goods when he had no reason to know that the goods were stolen. And surely we should see nothing criminal in joining a group in a public place, apart from the intent to commit unlawful acts.

The mental element required by the definition of any crime, therefore, is of central concern. This subsection on basic concepts and terminology is designed to help identify and distinguish the various kinds of mental states that may be used in the definition of crimes. Legislatures have often left the mental element undefined or have treated it ambiguously, while courts have failed to analyze it with precision. This subsection on terminology should help

---

11. This view, of course, is only one way of looking at the problem. H.L.A. Hart has given it its clearest expression. See his Punishment and Responsibility 28 (1968).

provide a vocabulary and an analytic framework for understanding and assessing what Justice Robert H. Jackson called "the variety, disparity and confusion of [the courts'] definitions of the requisite but elusive mental element." Morissette v. United States, 342 U.S. 246, 252 (1952).

REGINA v. CUNNINGHAM

Court of Criminal Appeal
[1957] 2 Q.B. 396

BYRNE, J., read the following judgment. The appellant was convicted at Leeds Assizes upon an indictment framed under section 23 of the Offences against the Person Act, 1861, which charged that he unlawfully and maliciously caused to be taken by Sarah Wade a certain noxious thing, namely, coal gas, so as thereby to endanger the life of the said Sarah Wade.

The facts were that the appellant was engaged to be married and his prospective mother-in-law was the tenant of a house, No. 7A, Bakes Street, Bradford, which was unoccupied, but which was to be occupied by the appellant after his marriage. Mrs. Wade and her husband, an elderly couple, lived in the house next door. At one time the two houses had been one, but when the building was converted into two houses a wall had been erected to divide the cellars of the two houses, and that wall was composed of rubble loosely cemented.

On the evening of January 17, 1957, the appellant went to the cellar of No. 7A, Bakes Street, wrenched the gas meter from the gas pipes and stole it, together with its contents, and in a second indictment he was charged with the larceny of the gas meter and its contents. To that indictment he pleaded guilty and was sentenced to six months' imprisonment. In respect of that matter he does not appeal.

The facts were not really in dispute, and in a statement to a police officer the appellant said: "All right, I will tell you. I was short of money. I had been off work for three days, I got eight shillings from the gas meter. I tore it off the wall and threw it away." Although there was a stop tap within two feet of the meter the appellant did not turn off the gas, with the result that a very considerable volume of gas escaped, some of which seeped through the wall of the cellar and partially asphyxiated Mrs. Wade, who was asleep in her bedroom next door, with the result that her life was endangered.

At the close of the case for the prosecution, Mr. Brodie, who appeared for the appellant . . . , submitted that there was no case to go to the jury, but the judge, quite rightly in our opinion, rejected this submission. The appellant did not give evidence.

The act of the appellant was clearly unlawful and therefore the real question for the jury was whether it was also malicious within the meaning of section 23 of the Offences against the Person Act, 1861.

Before this court, Mr. Brodie has taken three points, all dependent upon the construction of that section. Section 23 provides:

Whosoever shall unlawfully and maliciously administer to or cause to be administered to or taken by any other person any poison or other destructive or noxious thing, so as thereby to endanger the life of such person, or so as thereby to inflict upon such person any grievous bodily harm, shall be guilty of felony. . . .

Mr. Brodie argued, first, that mens rea of some kind is necessary. Secondly, that the nature of the mens rea required is that the appellant must intend to do the particular kind of harm that was done, or, alternatively, that he must foresee that that harm may occur yet nevertheless continue recklessly to do the act. Thirdly, that the judge misdirected the jury as to the meaning of the word "maliciously." . . .

[T]he following principle was propounded by the late Professor C.S. Kenny in the first edition of his Outlines of Criminal Law published in 1902; . . .

In any statutory definition of a crime, malice must be taken not in the old vague sense of wickedness in general but as requiring either ① An actual intention to do the particular kind of harm that in fact was done; or ② recklessness as to whether such harm should occur or not (i.e., the accused has foreseen that the particular kind of harm might be done and yet has gone on to take the risk of it). It is neither limited to nor does it indeed require any ill will towards the person injured. . . .

We think that this is an accurate statement of the law. . . . In our opinion the word "maliciously" in a statutory crime postulates foresight of consequence. In his summing-up Oliver, J., directed the jury as follows:

You will observe that there is nothing there about "with intention that that person should take it." He has not got to intend that it should be taken; it is sufficient that by his unlawful and malicious act he causes it to be taken. What you have to decide here, then, is whether, when he loosed that frightful cloud of coal gas into the house which he shared with this old lady, he caused her to take it by his unlawful and malicious action. "Unlawful" does not need any definition. It is something forbidden by law. What about "malicious"? "Malicious" for this purpose means wicked—something which he has no business to do and perfectly well knows it. "Wicked" is as good a definition as any other which you would get.

The facts . . . are these. . . . [T]he prisoner quite deliberately intended to steal the money that was in the meter . . . broke the gas meter away from the supply pipes and thus released the main supply of gas at large into that house. When he did that he knew that this old lady and her husband were living next door to him. The gas meter was in a cellar. The wall which divided his cellar from the cellar next door was a kind of honeycomb wall through which gas could very well go, so that when he loosed that cloud of gas into that place he must have known perfectly well that gas would percolate all over the house. If it were part of this offense—which it is not—that he intended to poison the old lady, I should have left it to you to decide, and I should have told you that there was evidence on which you could find that he intended that, since he did an action which he must have known would result in that. As I have already told you, it is not necessary to prove that he intended to do it; it is quite enough that what he did was done unlawfully and maliciously.

With the utmost respect to the judge, we think it is incorrect to say that the word "malicious" in a statutory offence merely means wicked. We think the judge was, in effect, telling the jury that if they were satisfied that the appellant acted wickedly—and he had clearly acted wickedly in stealing the gas meter and its contents—they ought to find that he had acted maliciously in causing the gas to be taken by Mrs. Wade so as thereby to endanger her life.

In our view, it should have been left to the jury to decide whether, even if the appellant did not intend the injury to Mrs. Wade, he foresaw that the removal of the gas meter might cause injury to someone but nevertheless removed it. We are unable to say that a reasonable jury, properly directed as to the meaning of the word "maliciously" in the context of section 23, would without doubt have convicted.

In these circumstances this court has no alternative but to allow the appeal and quash the conviction.

Conviction quashed.

Regina v. Faulkner, 13 Cox Crim. Cas. 550, 555, 557 (1877): [Defendant, a sailor, went to the hold of his ship to steal some rum and lit a match in order to see better in the dark. Some of the rum caught fire and the fire spread, completely destroying the ship. He was charged with violating the Malicious Damage Act by "maliciously" setting fire to the ship. The judge instructed the jury that "although the prisoner had no actual intention of burning the vessel, still, if they found he was engaged in stealing the rum, and that the fire took place [as alleged], they ought to find him guilty." The defendant was convicted, but on appeal, the conviction was quashed. Judge Barry, in the principal opinion, explained:] A broad proposition has been contended for by the Crown, namely, that if, while a person is engaged in committing a felony, . . . he accidentally does some collateral act, which if done wilfully would be another felony either at common law or by statute, he is guilty of the latter felony. I am by no means anxious to throw any doubt upon, or limit in any way, the legal responsibility of those who engage in the commission of felony, or acts mala in se; but I am not prepared without more consideration to give my assent to so wide a proposition. [T]o constitute an offence under the Malicious Injuries to Property Act, . . . the act done must be in fact intentional and wilful, although the intention and will may (perhaps) be held to exist in, or be proved by, the fact that the accused knew that the injury would be the probable result of his unlawful act, and yet did the act reckless of such consequences. . . . The jury were, in fact, directed to give a verdict of guilty upon the simple ground that the firing of the ship, though accidental, was caused by an act done in the course of, or immediately consequent upon, a felonious operation, and no question of the prisoner's malice, constructive or otherwise, was left to the jury. . . . That direction was erroneous, [and] the conviction should be quashed.

FITZGERALD, J. I concur in opinion with my brother Barry, and for the reasons he has given, that the direction of the learned judge cannot be sustained in law, and that therefore the conviction should be quashed. Counsel for the prosecution in effect insisted that the defendant, being engaged in the commission of, or in an attempt to commit a felony, was criminally responsible for every result that was occasioned thereby, even though it was not a probable consequence of his act or such as he could have reasonably foreseen or intended. No authority has been cited for a proposition so extensive, and I am of opinion that it is not warranted by law.

NOTES ON COMMON-LAW TERMINOLOGY

1. Introduction. Traditional definitions of the common-law offenses often require proof that the defendant acted either "willfully," "intentionally," "maliciously," "corruptly," "wantonly," "recklessly," "negligently," or with "*scienter* [roughly, knowledge]." In addition, when "intent" is at issue, courts often distinguish between "general intent" and "specific intent." And these are just the most common of the mens rea terms encountered in statutes and judicial decisions.

Even with so many mens rea terms potentially in play, criminal law analysis could be manageable if each of these terms had a single, generally accepted meaning. Unfortunately, this has never been the case. Each of these terms has been given different meanings in different contexts, and some have been given different meanings by different courts, even in identical contexts. To add further confusion, some of the often-repeated definitions are merely collections of words that convey more atmosphere or emotion than concrete meaning. Having "malice," for example, is often defined as having an "abandoned and malignant heart."[12]

Under these circumstances, legal analysis in the common-law mens rea framework is inevitably imperfect; there can seldom be an authoritatively "correct" answer. In considering cases like *Cunningham*, *Faulkner*, and those that follow, the reader can escape this tangle only by focusing on concrete, practical questions: What facts, precisely, was the jury required to find in order to convict? What facts *should be* required in order to support a just conviction?

2. Malice. Notice that in *Cunningham*, the trial judge defined "malicious" as "wicked." The Court of Criminal Appeal relied on a textbook writer (Professor Kenny) for the proposition that malice refers not to wickedness but merely to "foresight of consequences." Which of these is the better view?

We can approach that question from several different perspectives. Consider first the ordinary meaning of language. Which definition is closer to the meaning of "malice" in everyday speech? Many would think that, from this

---

12. See page 422 infra.

perspective, the trial judge's definition was clearly the better one. If so, what considerations might explain the prevailing rule, reflected in both *Cunningham* and *Faulkner*, that gives malice a narrower, more technical meaning? Notice, for example, that under the everyday definition ("malicious means wicked"), the sailor in *Faulkner* would be regarded as committing the same crime as a sailor who deliberately set fire to the ship. Would that approach make sense? What happens to the boundaries between offenses in a complex criminal code if its mens rea requirements are not linked specifically to the kind of harm each offense is designed to prohibit?

The approach taken in *Cunningham* (malice means foresight of the prohibited consequence) reflects the prevailing approach at common law. Generally (though not invariably) common-law courts adopt this approach as their "default" rule—that is, the presumptively applicable standard. Absent clear indications to the contrary, courts will interpret "malice" (and other vague or ambiguous mens rea language) to require that the defendant was aware his actions posed a substantial risk of causing the prohibited harm.

Notice that we can easily imagine approaches that are either stricter or more lenient. Why not assume that "malice" requires an actual desire to cause the prohibited harm, not merely awareness that it might occur? Conversely, why not assume that "malice" requires only a careless *failure to realize* that harm might occur, rather than actual awareness of the risk?

3. Specific intent and general intent. The concepts of "specific intent" and "general intent" have been the source of endless confusion in the courts. This Note gives two examples of contexts in which these terms have been used and attempts to explain how the terms have been used. The explanations must be rough, however, because "general" and "specific" intent are often used inconsistently or misleadingly.

(a) The least mysterious and most common usage of specific intent is to identify those actions that must be done with some specified further purpose in mind. For example, burglary requires (roughly) that a person break and enter, not simply knowingly or on purpose, but with the further objective of committing a felony inside. Without proof of that further objective, there can be no conviction for burglary. It is therefore common to describe burglary as a "specific intent crime"; the description is accurate in the sense that conviction for burglary requires proof of that further ("specific") purpose to commit a felony inside the building. Similarly, assault with intent to kill requires (roughly) that a person commit a battery upon another with the specific further purpose of killing that person. Without proof of that further purpose, a case of assault with intent to kill must fail. Accordingly, it is likewise common to describe assault with intent to kill as a "specific intent crime."

May the person in the above examples be convicted of some other crime, even without proof of the specified further intention? Yes. He can be convicted of a crime that requires only a "general" intent. But what is that? "General" intent in this context usually means that the defendant can be convicted if he did what in ordinary speech we would call an intentional action. So in the first example, the actor who broke into a building would be guilty of trespass, a general intent crime; so long as he acted intentionally, in the sense that he knew the nature of the acts he performed, he would be guilty, without proof that he desired any particular further consequence. Similarly, in the second example, the actor would be guilty of simple battery, a general intent crime, regardless of whether he desired any further consequence to follow from his conduct.

(b) Another usage of specific intent is to describe a crime that requires the defendant to have actual knowledge (that is, subjective awareness) of some particular fact or circumstance. Take the crime of bigamy, which prohibits a married person from remarrying while still legally married to his or her spouse. One element of the offense relates to the defendant's *conduct* (the act of marrying) and another relates to an *attendant circumstance*—that is, a background fact (being married to another person) that is crucial for determining whether that conduct is harmful. In order to convict a defendant for bigamy, his *conduct* undoubtedly must be intentional; he must intend to be participating in a genuine marriage ceremony. A defendant who said, "I do," thinking that he was in a play, acting the part of a groom, would not intend the required conduct, and even if he were already married to another, he obviously would not be guilty of bigamy.

But when a defendant does intend the conduct (the act of marrying), must it also be shown he knew that the required attendant circumstance (the fact of still being married to another) was met at the time? This question can arise when the first spouse has been absent for several years and is assumed (perhaps incorrectly) to be dead, or when the defendant has obtained a divorce decree and assumes (perhaps incorrectly) that the decree is legally effective. Should the offense of bigamy require proof that the defendant *knew* his first wife was still alive or that his first marriage was still legally in effect? It's quite clear in bigamy that the *conduct* element must be committed intentionally; no one would suggest otherwise. But with respect to the *attendant circumstance* element, different answers are possible. If a particular jurisdiction does not require proof that the defendant knew he was still married to another, we would say that bigamy is a general intent crime. In this context, in other words, a "general intent" crime is one for which the awareness of the attendant circumstance need not be proved; some lesser mental state—perhaps recklessness or negligence—will suffice. In contrast, if a jurisdiction requires proof that the defendant knew he was still legally married to another, then we would say that bigamy is a "specific intent" crime; in that state, bigamy would not only require proof of an intent to engage in specified conduct but would also require proof of actual awareness of the specified attendant circumstances.

In the discussion so far, it has been possible to give clear meaning to the terms "specific" and "general" intent, because we have focused on an offense—bigamy—that has only one conduct element and one attendant circumstance element. But most offenses require proof of many elements. Burglary, for example, traditionally is defined as the (1) breaking and entering

(2) of a dwelling place (3) of another person (4) in the nighttime (5) with intent to commit a felony inside. Burglary is customarily labeled a specific intent crime, because it requires proof of specified conduct committed with some further intent. But in this case there are three attendant circumstance elements, and a defendant might be unaware of any or all of them. He might think he was entering a building not used as a dwelling, he might think the building was his own home, or he might not realize that it was nighttime. As to any or all of these, a jurisdiction might decide to permit conviction without proof that the defendant was aware of the specified facts. Courts and legislatures need to consider whether they *should* permit conviction without proof that the defendant was aware of particular attendant circumstances, and we will examine that question, in different contexts, throughout this chapter. But whatever the best answer to that question for various elements of various crimes, it is clearly a question of policy that turns on the particulars of specific offenses. Courts could not wisely answer it—and virtually none do—by simply invoking the observation that "burglary is a specific intent crime."

4. *Proving awareness and intent.* Most forms of mens rea involve a defendant's internal thoughts and perceptions. A prosecutor can prove a defendant's acts (through eyewitnesses, for example), but how can she prove what was in the defendant's mind when he was acting? Unless the defendant admits the crucial mental facts, the prosecutor must prove mens rea indirectly, through so-called circumstantial evidence. The difficulty of proving what was in the defendant's mind, and proving it beyond a reasonable doubt, is one reason why prosecutors may argue that certain mental facts should not have to be proved at all.

When an offense does include awareness or intent as one of its elements, the process of proving it is often facilitated by resort to various kinds of presumptions. For example, it is often said that a person is presumed to intend the natural and probable consequences of his acts; if Arthur aims a pistol at Barry's head and fires six times, it is reasonable to assume that Arthur intended to kill Barry. But a presumption of this sort becomes troublesome if, for example, Arthur fired only once, without making obvious efforts to aim. To assume that Arthur must have intended to kill in that situation would dilute the requirement of proof beyond a reasonable doubt and shift to the defendant the burden of explaining his actions. For that reason, the Supreme Court has imposed strict limits on the use of mandatory presumptions—those the jury is *required* to draw in the absence of contrary evidence.

We explored at pages 46-47, supra, the standard for determining when a mandatory presumption is constitutionally permissible. In a nutshell, presumptions are constitutional only when we can have confidence that over all criminal cases in general, the presumed fact will always be present when the fact used to trigger that presumption is present. In Francis v. Franklin, 471 U.S. 307, 312 (1985), the Supreme Court applied this test to the old and then widely used presumption that "[a] person of sound mind and discretion is presumed to intend the natural and probable consequences of his acts." Because this presumption does not hold true in all cases, the Court held the use of this traditional presumption unconstitutional.

In contrast, the Constitution allows more flexibility in the use of *permissive inferences*, in which the judge informs the jury about a factual conclusion that it is permitted but not required to draw. Permissive inferences are allowed whenever the conclusion is "more likely than not" to be true under the circumstances of the particular case. Thus, in Barnes v. United States, 412 U.S. 837 (1973), the Supreme Court upheld the use of an inference commonly used to help establish knowledge—the inference that "[p]ossession of recently stolen property, if not satisfactorily explained, is ordinarily a circumstance from which [the jury may infer] that the person in possession knew that the property had been stolen."

5. Negligence. Another response to the difficulty of establishing internal thoughts and perceptions is to eliminate any requirement of proving that sort of mens rea and instead only to require proof that the defendant was *negligent*. That form of culpability is particularly important in homicide cases, where cases attempting to define "negligence" have developed a distinctive body of doctrine, which we examine at pages 464-481 infra. But "negligence" is also designated as the required form of mens rea for some crimes outside the homicide context. Like other traditional common-law terms, it lacks precision, and courts often disagree about what it means. Some interpret it to require nothing more than ordinary carelessness. E.g., United States v. Ortiz, 427 F.3d 1278 (10th Cir. 2005). Others hold that negligence requires a "gross" departure from normal standards of care. E.g., State v. Chavez, 211 P.3d 891 (N.M. 2009). Consider the following cases.

State v. Hazelwood, 946 P.2d 875 (Alaska 1997): [Defendant, the captain of the oil tanker *Exxon Valdez*, ran his ship aground on a reef, with the result that 11 million gallons of oil spilled into the ecologically sensitive waters of Prince William Sound. He was prosecuted under an Alaska statute that made it an offense for any person to "discharge, cause to be discharged, or permit the discharge of petroleum . . . upon the waters or land of the state except . . . as the department may by regulation permit." When committed "negligently," the offense was designated a misdemeanor, punishable by up to 90 days' imprisonment.

[At trial, Hazelwood urged that the statute should be interpreted to require proof of "criminal negligence," that is, "something more than the slight degree of negligence necessary to support a civil action for damages[;] negligence of a degree so gross as to be deserving of punishment." The trial judge rejected that view and instructed the jury that "[a] person acts 'negligently' . . . when the person fails to perceive an unjustifiable risk that the result will occur; the risk must be of such a nature and degree that the failure to perceive it constitutes a deviation from the standard of care that a reasonable person would observe in the situation." The jury convicted, and the defendant was sentenced to 90 days in jail and a $1,000 fine, both suspended on condition that Hazelwood

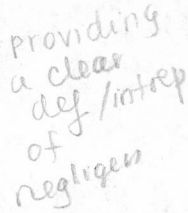

providing a clear def/interp of negligen

complete one year of probation, perform 1,000 hours of community work, and pay $50,000 in restitution.

[The intermediate appellate court, noting that "we are faced with interpreting the penalty statute's ambiguous and undefined use of the term 'negligently,'" upheld the defendant's position and ruled that the trial judge's definition of negligence was erroneous. The Alaska Supreme Court reversed and reinstated the conviction:]

RABINOWITZ, J. . . . The difference between criminal and civil negligence although not major is distinct. Under both standards, a person acts "negligently" when he fails to perceive a substantial and unjustifiable risk that a particular result will occur. [But c]riminal negligence requires a greater risk. This standard is met only when the risk is "of such a nature and degree that the failure to perceive it constitutes a gross deviation from the standard of care that a reasonable person would observe in the situation." In essence, then, the criminal negligence standard requires the jury to find negligence so gross as to merit not just damages but also punishment. It does not spill over into recklessness; there is still no requirement that the defendant actually be aware of the risk of harm. However, criminal negligence does require a more culpable mental state than simple, ordinary negligence. . . .

An appropriate place to begin an explanation for objective fault crimes is with the objections of those who would abolish them altogether. In Jerome Hall, Negligent Behavior Should Be Excluded from Penal Liability, 63 Colo. L. Rev. 632 (1963), Professor Hall, . . . contends crimes that are not based on subjective awareness of wrongdoing [cannot deter because they are addressed to those who] "have not in the least thought of their duty, their dangerous behavior, or any sanction." The difficulty with this thesis is that it assumes legal regulations can operate only through the offender's conscious reason. . . . Even when an offender does not of his own accord realize that his conduct is wrongful, he can in many cases be made to take care. Coercion that causes the offender to pay attention can serve important social aims. . . .

The fulcrum for deciding what level of intent is the absolute minimum for a particular offense is a question of when an expectation of individual conformity is reasonable. . . . Negligence, rather than gross negligence, [is sufficient to provide] assurance that criminal penalties will be imposed only when the conduct at issue is something society can reasonably expect to deter. Partisans of the criminal negligence approach have expressed the concern that an ordinary negligence standard gives the criminal proceeding an unseemly resemblance to tort law. . . . This fear of tort standards is unfounded. . . . We are not persuaded that the simple or ordinary civil negligence standard is inadequate to protect Hazelwood's interests. . . .

The [trial court's] adoption of an ordinary negligence standard was not erroneous.

COMPTON, C.J., dissenting. . . . In my view, notions of fundamental fairness . . . require a showing of something more than "failure to act reasonably" before a defendant may be subjected to imprisonment. . . . Civil negligence provides an acceptable standard of fault for allocating any burden which neglectful conduct creates. [But] a punishment of imprisonment is sufficiently severe that it should not [ordinarily] be imposed . . . for conduct which involves only civil negligence [or] for any deviation whatsoever from "reasonableness." . . .

It is well established that "mere negligence is insufficient to justify an award of punitive damages." It is difficult to accept the proposition that an action which cannot form the basis for a punitive civil award fairly can be sanctioned with imprisonment. . . . I would affirm the decision of the court of appeals.

Santillanes v. New Mexico, 115 N.M. 215, 849 P.2d 358 (1993): [Defendant cut his seven-year-old nephew's neck with a knife during an altercation and was convicted of child abuse under a statute defining that offense as including "negligently . . . causing . . . a child to be . . . placed in a situation that may endanger the child's life or health. . . . " The trial court gave the jury a standard definition of negligence sufficient to support civil liability: "An act, to be 'negligence,' must be one which a reasonably prudent person would foresee as involving an unreasonable risk of injury to himself or to another and which such a person, in the exercise of ordinary care, would not do." The Supreme Court found this instruction erroneous:] [W]hen moral condemnation and social opprobrium attach to the conviction of a crime, the crime should typically reflect a mental state warranting such contempt. . . . We construe the intended scope of the statute as aiming to punish conduct that is morally culpable. . . . We interpret the mens rea element of negligence in the child abuse statute, therefore, to require a showing of criminal negligence instead of ordinary civil negligence.

NOTE ON THE MODEL PENAL CODE REFORMS

Responding to the problems posed by common-law mens rea terminology, the MPC proposed a fresh approach that has proved extremely influential. The Code's mens rea framework has been adopted explicitly in more than half of American jurisdictions, and it often influences judicial interpretation in the remaining jurisdictions as well. The older framework for mens rea analysis survives, however, and indeed it remains dominant in a number of jurisdictions. Common-law terms are used in many state penal codes and in the increasingly significant field of federal criminal law. The requirement of a "willful" mens rea, for example, persists in many important federal crimes. One recent study finds that "courts, legislatures, and scholars [continue to use] meaningless mens rea terms such as 'willful'; to employ the simplistic but ineffective distinction between specific- and general-intent crimes; [and] to fail to see that mens rea questions are element-specific." Michael L. Seigel, Bringing Coherence to Mens Rea Analysis for Securities-Related Offenses,

2006 Wis. L. Rev. 1563, 1564. It is therefore important to emphasize that this older approach remains very much in play, despite the success of the more modern MPC framework, which we now examine,

The MPC attempts to mitigate the difficulties of mens rea analysis through three distinct tools—manageable categories, precise definitions, and convenient default rules. First, the Code eliminates the use of general intent, specific intent, and other ambiguous common-law terms, replacing the ten-plus varieties of common-law mens rea with just four mental states—purpose, knowledge, recklessness, and negligence. Second, the Code provides a relatively clear, rigorous definition for each of its four mens rea terms. Third, the Code provides rules of interpretation (default rules) to enable courts to determine the required mental state sensibly and predictably when the statutory language concerning mens rea is silent, ambiguous, or contradictory.

Because they are technical and rigorously precise, the MPC provisions are not an easy read, but mastering them is an essential prerequisite for the successful study and practice of contemporary criminal law in any American jurisdiction. As the first step in the process of acquiring that mastery, the student should at this point turn to the Appendix and read with great care the MPC provisions that embody its three mens rea reforms, specifically:

- §2.02(1), which reduces the many common-law mens rea terms to four manageable categories;
- §§2.02(2)(a)-(d), which provide precise definitions for each of the four mental states used in the MPC framework; and
- §§2.02(3)-(4), which provide specific default rules to govern statutory interpretation.

The significance of these provisions and their underlying rationale is explained in the following excerpt, which likewise should be examined with care.

MODEL PENAL CODE AND COMMENTARIES
Comment to §2.02, at 229-241 (1985)

Defendant has to have some sort of awareness

1. *Objective.* This section expresses the Code's basic requirement that unless some element of mental culpability is proved with respect to each material element of the offense, no valid criminal conviction may be obtained. . . .

The section further attempts the extremely difficult task of articulating the kinds of culpability that may be required for the establishment of liability. It delineates four levels of culpability: purpose, knowledge, recklessness and negligence. It requires that one of these levels of culpability must be proved with respect to each "material element" of the offense, which may involve (1) the nature of the forbidden conduct, (2) the attendant circumstances, or

(3) the result of conduct.[1] The question of which level of culpability suffices to establish liability must be addressed separately with respect to each material element, and will be resolved either by the particular definition of the offense or the general provision of this section.

The purpose of articulating these distinctions in detail is to . . . dispel the obscurity with which the culpability requirement is often treated. . . . The Model Code's approach is based upon the view that clear analysis requires that the question of the kind of culpability required to establish the commission of the offense be faced separately with respect to each material element of the crime. The Code provision on rape will afford an illustration. Under Section 213.1(1), a purpose to effect the sexual relation is clearly required. But other circumstances are also made relevant by the definition of the offense. The victim['s] consent to sexual relations would, of course, preclude the crime. Must the defendant's purpose have encompassed the [fact that] she opposed his will? [This is an] entirely different [question]. Recklessness may be sufficient for [this circumstance] of the offense, although purpose is required with respect to the sexual result that is an element of the offense. . . . Failure to face the question of culpability separately with respect to each of these ingredients of the offense results in obvious confusion. . . .

2. *Purpose and Knowledge.* In defining the kinds of culpability, the Code draws a narrow distinction between acting purposely and knowingly, one of the elements of ambiguity in legal usage of the term "intent." Knowledge that the requisite external circumstances exist is a common element in both conceptions.[a] But action is not purposive with respect to the nature or result of the actor's conduct unless it was his conscious object to perform an action of that nature or to cause such a result. It is meaningful to think of the actor's attitude as different if he is simply aware that his conduct is of the required nature or that the prohibited result is practically certain to follow from his conduct.

It is true, of course, that this distinction is inconsequential for most purposes of liability: acting knowingly is ordinarily sufficient. But there are areas where the discrimination is required and is made under traditional law, which uses the awkward concept of "specific intent." [I]n attempts, complicity and conspiracy, [for example,] a true purpose to effect the criminal result is requisite for liability. . . .

---

1. Section 1.13(9) defines an "element of an offense" to include conduct, attendant circumstances or results that are included in the description of the offense, that negative an excuse or justification for an offense, or that negative a defense under the statute of limitations or establish jurisdiction or venue. Section 1.13(10) defines the concept of "material element" to include all elements except those that relate exclusively to statutes of limitation, jurisdiction, venue, and the like. The "material elements" of offenses are thus those characteristics (conduct, circumstances, result) of the actor's behavior that, when combined with the appropriate level of culpability, will constitute the offense.

a. Is this an accurate summary of the MPC definitions of "purposely" and "knowingly" in §§2.02(a) & (b)? Note that a person can act knowingly only when he is actually aware that particular circumstances exist and that his conduct will cause any required result. §2.02(b)(i) & (ii). But a person can act purposely even when he thinks that required circumstances or results are unlikely, provided that he "hopes that they exist" or will be caused by his conduct. §2.02(a)(i) & (ii). For exploration of this issue, see page 257, Note 4, infra.—Eds.

3. *Recklessness.* An important discrimination is drawn between acting either purposely or knowingly and acting recklessly. As the Code uses the term, recklessness involves conscious risk creation. It resembles acting knowingly in that a state of awareness is involved, but the awareness is of risk, that is of a probability less than substantial certainty; the matter is contingent from the actor's point of view. Whether the risk relates to the nature of the actor's conduct, or to the existence of the requisite attendant circumstances, or to the result that may ensue, is immaterial; the concept is the same, and is thus defined to apply to any material element.

The risk of which the actor is aware must of course be substantial in order for the recklessness judgment to be made. The risk must also be unjustifiable. Even substantial risks, it is clear, may be created without recklessness when the actor is seeking to serve a proper purpose, as when a surgeon performs an operation that he knows is very likely to be fatal but reasonably thinks to be necessary because the patient has no other, safer chance. Some principle must, therefore, be articulated to indicate the nature of the final judgment to be made after everything has been weighed. Describing the risk as "substantial" and "unjustifiable" is useful but not sufficient, for these are terms of degree, and the acceptability of a risk in a given case depends on a great many variables. Some standard is needed for determining how substantial and how unjustifiable the risk must be in order to warrant a finding of culpability. There is no way to state this value judgment that does not beg the question in the last analysis; the point is that the jury must evaluate the actor's conduct and determine whether it should be condemned. . . .

4. *Negligence.* The fourth kind of culpability is negligence. It is distinguished from purposeful, knowing or reckless action in that it does not involve a state of awareness. A person acts negligently under this subsection when he inadvertently creates a substantial and unjustifiable risk of which he ought to be aware. He is liable if given the nature and degree of the risk, his failure to perceive it is, considering the nature and purpose of the actor's conduct and the circumstances known to him, a gross deviation from the care that would be exercised by a reasonable person in his situation. As in the case of recklessness, both the substantiality of the risk and the elements of justification in the situation form the relevant standards of judgment. And again it is quite impossible to avoid tautological articulation of the final question. . . . The jury must find fault, and must find that it was substantial and unjustified; that is the heart of what can be said in legislative terms. . . .

5. *Offense Silent as to Culpability.* Subsection (3) provides that unless the kind of culpability sufficient to establish a material element of an offense has been prescribed by law, it is established if a person acted purposely, knowingly or recklessly with respect thereto. This accepts as the basic norm what usually is regarded as the common law position. More importantly, it represents the most convenient norm for drafting purposes. When purpose or knowledge is required, it is conventional to be explicit. And since negligence is an exceptional basis of liability, it should be excluded as a basis unless explicitly prescribed. . . .

6. *Ambiguous Culpability Requirements.* Subsection (4) seeks to assist in the resolution of a common ambiguity in penal legislation, the statement of a particular culpability requirement . . . in such a way that it is unclear whether the requirement applies to all the elements of the offense or only to the elements that it immediately introduces. . . .

The Code proceeds in the view that if a particular kind of culpability has been articulated at all by the legislature as sufficient with respect to any element of the offense, the assumption is that it was meant to apply to all material elements. Hence this construction is required, unless a "contrary purpose clearly appears." When a distinction is intended, as it often is, proper drafting ought to make it clear.

[For example, f]alse imprisonment is defined by section 212.3 of the Model Code to include one who "knowingly restrains another unlawfully so as to interfere substantially with his liberty." Plainly, . . . the actor must, in order to be convicted under this section, know that he is restraining his victim. The question whether "knowingly" also qualifies the unlawful character of the restraint is not clearly answered by the definition of the offense, but is answered in the affirmative by the subsection under discussion.

NOTES ON APPLYING THE MPC APPROACH

1. The basic framework. In order to determine the mens rea required for conviction in any situation, the MPC analysis involves two steps. First, we must determine the "material elements" of an offense. The criteria for making this determination are found in MPC §1.13(9), which defines an "element," and in §1.13(10), which specifies when an element is "material." Second, we must determine which type of mens rea (purpose, knowledge, recklessness, or negligence) is required with respect to each material element. This determination is governed in the first instance by the terms of the offense itself, and then, in the event those terms are ambiguous, by the default rules of MPC §2.02(3) and §2.02(4).

2. Exercises. Four illustrative state crimes are set forth below. To become familiar with mens rea analysis, consider how the required mens rea would be identified by a court applying MPC principles. What are the "material elements" of each offense? Does the statute itself make clear the state of mind specifically required with respect to a particular material element? If not, what level of mens rea is required by the applicable MPC default rule?

Consider those questions, step by step, with respect to the following statutes.

Burglary (N.Y. Penal Law §140.25) (2011): A person is guilty of burglary in the second degree when he knowingly enters or remains unlawfully in a building with intent to commit a crime therein, and when . . . [t]he building is a dwelling.

Burglary (Cal. Penal Code §§459-460) (2011): Every person who enters any house, room, apartment . . . or other building . . . with intent to commit grand or petit larceny or any felony is guilty of burglary.

. . . Every burglary of an inhabited dwelling house . . . is burglary of the first degree.

. . . All other kinds of burglary are burglary of the second degree.

Destruction of Property (D.C. Code Ann. §22-303) (2011): Whoever maliciously injures or breaks or destroys, or attempts to injure or break or destroy, by fire or otherwise, any public or private property, whether real or personal, not his or her own, of the value of $1000 or more, shall be fined not more than $5,000 or shall be imprisoned for not more than 10 years, or both. . . .

Destruction of Property (N.Y. Penal Law §145.10) (2011): A person is guilty of criminal mischief in the second degree when with intent to damage property of another person, and having no right to do so nor any reasonable ground to believe that he has such right, he damages property of another person in an amount exceeding one thousand five hundred dollars.

3. *Distinguishing between purpose and motive.* Does an actor's motive differ from the MPC concept of his "purpose"? Consider Glanville Williams, The Mental Element in Crime 10, 14 (1965). The author defines intention in terms of desiring a consequence: "A consequence is intended when it is desired to follow as the result of the actor's conduct." He then cautions:

> [T]he consequence need not be desired as an end in itself; it may be desired as a means to another end. . . . There may be a series of ends, each a link in a chain of purpose. Every link in the chain, when it happens, is an intended consequence of the original act. Suppose that a burglar is arrested when breaking into premises. It would obviously be no defence for him to say that his sole intention was to provide a nurse for his sick daughter, and for that purpose to take money from the premises, but that he had no desire or intention to deprive anyone of anything. Such an argument would be fatuous. He intended (1) to steal money (2) in order to help his daughter. These are two intentions, and the one does not displace the other. English lawyers call the first an "intent" and the second a "motive"; this is because the first (the intent to steal) enters into the definition of burglary and is legally relevant, while the second (the motive of helping the daughter) is legally irrelevant, except perhaps in relation to sentence. Although the verbal distinction between "intention" and "motive" is convenient, it must be realized that the remoter intention called motive is still an intention.

If motive is irrelevant to criminal liability, why should it be regarded as relevant to sentencing? For a comprehensive analysis, see Elaine M. Chiu, The Challenge of Motive in the Criminal Law, 8 Buff. Crim. L. Rev. 653 (2005).

4. *Distinguishing between a purpose and a wish.* Suppose that a person gives an airline ticket to a hated aunt, hoping that the plane will crash and kill

her. If the crash occurs, causing the aunt's death, has the nephew killed her purposely? Would the answer depend on whether:

a. the defendant knew that the chances of the plane's crashing were exceedingly remote, but he liked to take long shots; or

b. the defendant believed the plane would crash because his astrologer predicted it would; or

c. the defendant believed it would crash because he knew that a group of terrorists had targeted it.

5. *Distinguishing recklessness from negligence.* The MPC distinguishes two kinds of culpable unintentional actions, those that are reckless and those that are negligent. Negligence is less culpable because the actor acts only inadvertently; the actor should have been aware of the danger, but was not. The fault is inattentiveness. Recklessness is more culpable because the actor was aware of the danger but acted anyway. The fault is choosing to run the risk.

So the crucial factor distinguishing these levels of culpability is awareness. But awareness of precisely what? The MPC requires for reckless conduct that the person "consciously disregards a substantial and unjustifiable risk" that some circumstance exists or that some result will follow from his conduct. Does this mean that the actor must be aware (1) that there is a risk, (2) that the risk is substantial, *and* (3) that the risk is unjustifiable? Or does it mean only that the actor must be aware that there is some risk, which the jury finds to be substantial and unjustifiable? Or could it mean that the actor must be aware that there is a substantial risk, which the jury finds to be unjustifiable?

Grammatically, the MPC appears to require conscious awareness as to all three of the crucial factors. But is this interpretation tenable in practice? Consider State v. Muniz, 2011 WL 96320 (Ariz. App. 2011). The defendant fired a .22 caliber rifle at a backyard chair in a neighbor's yard where several children were playing. His friends urged him not to shoot because he might miss and hit one of the kids, but Muniz, confident of his marksmanship, fired anyway. He hit one of the children in the head, inflicting severe physical and cognitive injuries. He was convicted of endangerment of a minor and aggravated assault, both requiring proof of recklessness. The defendant was clearly negligent, but was he reckless? Consider Glanville Williams, The Unresolved Problem of Recklessness, 8 Legal Stud. 74, 77 (1988):

> [The subjective] theory [of recklessness] has to deal with the awkward customer who undertook a course of conduct that he knew would involve serious risks if performed by someone not highly skilled, but thought that he himself possessed sufficient skill to eliminate danger. [T]ake *Shimmen's* case [84 Cr. App. R. 7 (1986)]. The defendant, who held a green belt and yellow belt in the Korean art of self-defence, was demonstrating his skill to his friends. To do this, he made as if to strike a plate-glass window with his foot; however, his kick broke the window. A Divisional Court held that he was guilty of criminal damage by recklessness, since he "was aware of the kind of

risk which would attend his act if he did not take adequate precautions," even though he believed he had taken enough precautions to eliminate or minimise risk. . . .

On subjective principles the court was wrong in saying that a person who believes he has taken enough precautions to eliminate risk is to be held guilty of recklessness merely because he perceived a risk before taking the precautions. If Shimmen thought he had eliminated risk, he was not subjectively reckless, but the court might have remitted the case to the magistrates with an instruction to decide whether [Shimmen] thought he had eliminated or merely mitigated the risk. This was a case where the defendant needed to be cross-examined. "Would you have kicked with such force towards your girl friend's or wife's or your baby's head, relying on your ability to stop within an inch of it? No? Then you knew that there was some risk of your boot travelling further than you intended." A person may be convinced of his own skill, and yet know that on rare (perhaps very rare) occasions it may fail him. In the case at bar, the victim, the owner of the window, did not agree to the demonstration of skill. [T]he actor has no right to impose any foreseen risk on him, beyond those associated with the ordinary business of life. He could be given a hot time in the witness-box if he says that in his opinion there was literally no risk.

Question: Would this basis for finding recklessness in the *Shimmen* case be possible under the MPC's definition of recklessness? For careful analysis of the alternative ways of interpreting the MPC concept of recklessness, see Kenneth W. Simons, Should the Model Penal Code's Mens Rea Provisions Be Amended?, 1 Ohio St. J. Crim. L. 179 (2003); David Trieman, Recklessness and the Model Penal Code, 9 Am. J. Crim. L. 283, 361-371 (1981).

A more common problem is illustrated by a case arising from the death of Morgan Pena, a two-year-old child killed by a driver who was distracted while using his cell phone. See Kimberly Kessler Ferzan, Opaque Recklessness, 91 J. Crim. L. & Criminology 597, 600 (2001). The driver surely recognized that there was some risk involved in driving while attempting to dial a number on his phone, and he may not have considered himself exceptionally skillful. But the driver nonetheless apparently failed to appreciate the full extent of the danger his conduct created. He was cited for careless driving and running a stop sign, but he was not charged with a more serious offense because the police determined that he was not reckless. Is the outcome defensible? Conduct of this sort, which Professor Ferzan labels "opaque recklessness" (awareness of some risk but failure to appreciate how substantial it was), is probably a regular feature of dangerous behavior, and it arguably lies somewhere between the MPC notions of recklessness and negligence. Do actors of this sort lack the level of culpable awareness that should be required for criminal punishment? Or, as Professor Ferzan argues, is their culpability too serious to escape criminal sanctions? See Ferzan, supra, at 627-641; Larry Alexander, Insufficient Concern: A Unified Conception of Criminal Culpability, 88 Calif. L. Rev. 931 (2000); Kenneth W. Simons, Rethinking Mental States, 72 B.U. L. Rev. 463 (1992).

b. Distinguishing Recklessness from Knowledge

INTRODUCTORY NOTE

Is there a significant difference between being aware that a legally troublesome circumstance *probably* exists and *knowing* that it exists? What if the only reason a defendant doesn't *know* the truth is that he chooses to look the other way? Consider the material that follows.

UNITED STATES v. JEWELL

United States Court of Appeals, 9th Circuit
532 F.2d 697 (1976)

BROWNING, J. [A]ppellant entered the United States driving an automobile in which 110 pounds of marijuana . . . had been concealed in a secret compartment. [He] testified that he did not know the marijuana was present. There was circumstantial evidence from which the jury could infer that appellant [did know], and that his contrary testimony was false. On the other hand there was evidence from which the jury could conclude that . . . although appellant knew of the presence of the secret compartment and had knowledge of facts indicating that it contained marijuana, he deliberately avoided positive knowledge of the presence of the contraband to avoid responsibility in the event of discovery. If the jury concluded the latter was indeed the situation, and if positive knowledge is required to convict, the jury would have no choice consistent with its oath but to find appellant not guilty even though he deliberately contrived his lack of positive knowledge.

[The jury convicted after being instructed that the prosecution could establish knowledge by proving beyond a reasonable doubt that] "if the defendant was not actually aware that there was marijuana in the vehicle . . . his ignorance in that regard was solely and entirely a result of his having made a conscious purpose to disregard the nature of that which was in the vehicle, with a conscious purpose to avoid learning the truth."

The legal premise of these instructions is firmly supported by leading commentators here and in England. . . . [7] The substantive justification for the rule is that deliberate ignorance and positive knowledge are equally culpable. The textual justification is that in common understanding one "knows"

---

7. [See G. Williams, Criminal Law: The General Part, §57 (2d ed. 1961)] at 159. . . . :

The rule that wilful blindness is equivalent to knowledge is essential, and is found throughout the criminal law. It is, at the same time, an unstable rule, because judges are apt to forget its very limited scope. A court can properly find wilful blindness only where it can almost be said that the defendant actually knew. He suspected the fact; he realised its probability; but he refrained from obtaining the final confirmation because he wanted in the event to be able to deny knowledge. This, and this alone, is wilful blindness. It requires in effect a finding that the defendant intended to cheat the administration of justice. Any wider definition would make the doctrine of wilful blindness indistinguishable from the civil doctrine of negligence in not obtaining knowledge.

[handwritten margin note: I acted w/ the possibility that she had weed in the CAR (PREVENTIVE)]

facts of which he is less than absolutely certain. To act "knowingly," therefore, is not necessarily to act only with positive knowledge, but also to act with an awareness of the high probability of the existence of the fact in question. When such awareness is present, "positive" knowledge is not required.

This is the analysis adopted in the Model Penal Code. Section 2.02(7) states:

> When knowledge of the existence of a particular fact is an element of an offense, such knowledge is established if a person is aware of a high probability of its existence, unless he actually believes that it does not exist.

. . . Appellant's narrow interpretation of "knowingly" is inconsistent with the Drug Control Act's general purpose to deal more effectively "with the growing menace of drug abuse in the United States." Holding that this term introduces a requirement of positive knowledge would make deliberate ignorance a defense. It cannot be doubted that those who traffic in drugs would make the most of it. . . .

It is no answer to say that in such cases the fact finder may infer positive knowledge. It is probable that many who performed the transportation function, essential to the drug traffic, can truthfully testify that they have no *positive* knowledge of the load they carry. Under appellant's interpretation of the statute, such persons will be convicted only if the fact finder errs in evaluating the credibility of the witness or deliberately disregards the law. . . .

It is worth emphasizing that the required state of mind differs from positive knowledge only so far as necessary to encompass a calculated effort to avoid the sanctions of the statute while violating its substance. . . . In the language of the instruction in this case, the government must prove, "beyond a reasonable doubt, that if the defendant was not actually aware . . . his ignorance in that regard was *solely* and *entirely* a result of . . . a conscious purpose to avoid learning the truth." . . .

[A]ffirmed.

KENNEDY, J., dissenting. . . . In light of the Model Penal Code's definition, the "conscious purpose" jury instruction is defective in three respects. First, it fails to mention the requirement that Jewell have been aware of a high probability that a controlled substance was in the car. It is not culpable to form "a conscious purpose to avoid learning the truth" unless one is aware of facts indicating a high probability of that truth. To illustrate, a child given a gift-wrapped package by his mother while on vacation in Mexico may form a conscious purpose to take it home without learning what is inside; yet his state of mind is totally innocent unless he is aware of a high probability that the package contains a controlled substance.

[Second, the instruction] did not alert the jury that Jewell could not be convicted if he "actually believed" there was no controlled substance in the car. The failure to emphasize, as does the Model Penal Code, that subjective belief is the determinative factor, may allow a jury to convict on an objective theory of knowledge—that a reasonable man should have inspected the car and would have discovered what was hidden inside. . . . Third, the jury instruction clearly states that Jewell could have been convicted even if . . . "not actually aware" that the car contained a controlled substance. [T]rue ignorance, no matter how unreasonable, cannot provide a basis for criminal liability when the statute requires knowledge. A proper jury instruction based on the Model Penal Code would be presented as a way of defining knowledge, and not as an alternative to it. . . .

NOTES

1. In both federal and state cases, willful blindness or "ostrich" instructions are often used to help establish "knowledge"—not only in drug prosecutions but also in cases involving mail fraud, money laundering, environmental pollution, and a variety of other common-law and regulatory offenses. See United States v. Alston-Graves, 435 F.3d 331, 338 n.2 (D.C. Cir. 2006); Williamson v. State, 685 S.E.2d 784 (Ga. App. 2009).

2. With respect to federal prosecutions, the Supreme Court recently addressed the problem of willful blindness in Global-Tech Appliances, Inc. v. SEB S.A., 131 S. Ct. 2060 (2011). This was a civil suit requiring proof of a knowing patent infringement, but the Court discussed the issue in terms that apply to civil and criminal cases generally. Justice Samuel Alito, writing for eight Justices, said (id. at 2070-2071):

> Given the long history of willful blindness [in criminal law], we can see no reason why the doctrine should not apply in civil lawsuits. . . . While the Courts of Appeals articulate the doctrine of willful blindness in slightly different ways, all appear to agree on two basic requirements: (1) the defendant must subjectively believe that there is a high probability that a fact exists and (2) the defendant must take deliberate actions to avoid learning of that fact. We think these requirements give willful blindness an appropriately limited scope that surpasses recklessness and negligence. [A] willfully blind defendant is one who takes deliberate actions to avoid confirming a high probability of wrongdoing. . . . By contrast, a reckless defendant is one who merely knows of a substantial and unjustified risk of such wrongdoing, see ALI, Model Penal Code §2.02(2)(c) (1985), and a negligent defendant is one who should have known of a similar risk but, in fact, did not, see §2.02(2)(d).

Justice Kennedy, dissenting, reiterated the concerns he had expressed as a court of appeals judge in *Jewell* (id. at 2072-2073):

> Willful blindness is not knowledge; and judges should not broaden a legislative proscription by analogy. . . . One can believe that there is a "high probability" that acts might infringe a patent but nonetheless conclude they do not infringe. The [person] who believes a device is noninfringing cannot be said to know otherwise.
>
> The Court justifies its substitution of willful blindness for the statutory knowledge requirement . . . by citing the "traditional rationale" that willfully blind defendants "are just as culpable as those who have actual knowledge." But the moral question is a difficult one. Is it true that the lawyer who knowingly suborns perjury is no more culpable than the lawyer who avoids learning

that his client, a criminal defendant, lies when he testifies that he was not the shooter? See Hellman, Willfully Blind for Good Reason, 3 Crim. L. & Philosophy 301, 305-308 (2009); Luban, Contrived Ignorance, 87 Geo. L.J. 957 (1999). The answer is not obvious. Perhaps the culpability of willful blindness depends on a person's reasons for remaining blind. Or perhaps only the person's justification for his conduct is relevant. *E.g.*, [L. Alexander & K. Ferzan, Crime and Culpability: A Theory of Criminal Law (2009)] at 23-68. This is a question of morality and of policy best left to the political branches. . . .

3. *Recklessness plus what?* Exactly what is the extra element needed to convert mere recklessness into the state of mind sufficient to meet a knowledge requirement? In *Global-Tech*, the Supreme Court says a defendant "must take deliberate actions to avoid learning [the truth]." Note that this prerequisite is not expressly required under Model Penal Code §2.02(7). Should it be? Consider the following problems:

(a) Acts versus omissions. Did Jewell "take deliberate actions" to avoid learning the truth? Note that in order to actually "know" what he was transporting, Jewell apparently would have had to dismantle the secret compartment in which the drugs were hidden. If so, his liability resulted not from "shutting his eyes" but rather from his failure to actively investigate. Under the *Global-Tech* standard, should Jewell's conviction have been reversed?

Many willful blindness cases state that a defendant must "purposely contrive" to avoid learning the truth,[13] without making clear whether a mere failure to make inquiry is sufficient to meet the requirement. If the Supreme Court meant to require *affirmative acts* to avoid knowledge, is that requirement too stringent? See Alan C. Michaels, Acceptance: The Missing Mental State, 71 S. Cal. L. Rev. 953 (1998); Robin Charlow, Willful Ignorance and Criminal Culpability, 70 Tex. L. Rev. 1351 (1992).

Compare United States v. Giovannetti, 919 F.2d 1223 (7th Cir. 1990). Defendant Janis was convicted of aiding and abetting a gambling operation by renting his house to some gamblers, "knowing" that the lessees would use it for gambling. There was no direct evidence of Janis's knowledge, but knowing that his lessees were professional gamblers, he made no inquiries about their intended use of the house. The court (per Posner, J.) reversed the conviction, holding that it was error to give an "ostrich" instruction under these circumstances (id. at 1228-1229):

> [Notice] just what it is that real ostriches do (or at least are popularly supposed to do). They do not just fail to follow through on their suspicions of bad things. They are not merely *careless* birds. They bury their heads in the sand so that they will not see or hear bad things. They *deliberately* avoid acquiring unpleasant knowledge. The ostrich instruction is designed for cases in which there is evidence that the defendant, knowing or strongly suspecting that he is involved in shady dealings, takes steps to make sure that he does not acquire full or exact knowledge of the nature and extent of those dealings. . . .

---

13. E.g., United States v. Pacific Hide & Fur Depot, Inc., 768 F.2d 1096, 1098-99 (9th Cir. 1985).

For example,
he normally
say inspects prop every run.
If he decides not
to one sunday
came we truly
see a
tree with party!
Gambling
ner must
is willfull
Blindness.

The government points out that the rented house ... was a short way down a side street from the thoroughfare on which Janis commuted to work daily. It would have been easy for him to drive by the house from time to time to see what was doing, and if he had done so he might have discovered its use [for gambling]. He did not do so. But this is not the active avoidance with which the ostrich doctrine is concerned. ... Janis failed to display curiosity, but he did nothing to prevent the truth from being communicated to him. He did not *act* to avoid learning the truth.

[T]he deliberate effort to avoid guilty knowledge ... can be a mental, as well as a physical, effort—a cutting off of one's normal curiosity by an effort of will. There is no evidence of either sort of effort here.

Questions: Is the decision analytically sound? If so, does the result suggest that defendants like Janis should not be convicted, or does it suggest that the statutory mens rea requirement should be relaxed? Why might it be sound to require affirmative efforts to avoid guilty knowledge? Cf. Deborah Hellman, Prosecuting Doctors for Trusting Patients, 16 Geo. Mason L. Rev. 3 (2009).

(b) Motive. In United States v. Heredia, 483 F.3d 913 (9th Cir. 2007), the defendant was caught driving her mother from Nogales, Mexico, to Tucson, Arizona, with 349 pounds of marijuana in the trunk of the car, which she had borrowed from an aunt. Charged with knowing possession of a controlled substance, she admitted that she had noticed a "detergent" smell in the car and did not believe her aunt's explanation for it (that "fabric softener" had spilled in the vehicle). She testified that she suspected there might be drugs in the car, because her mother was visibly nervous during the trip. But she claimed that her suspicions were not aroused until she had passed the last freeway exit before the checkpoint, by which time it was too dangerous to pull over and investigate. The judge instructed the jury that they could find the defendant guilty if she was aware of a high probability that drugs were in the vehicle and "deliberately avoided learning the truth." The court of appeals upheld the conviction, stating (483 F.3d at 918-920):

" '[K]nowingly' in criminal statutes ... includes the state of mind of one who does not possess positive knowledge only because he consciously avoided it." ... [O]ur cases have not been consistent [on w]hether the jury must be instructed that defendant's motive in deliberately failing to learn the truth [must be] to give himself a defense in case he should be charged with the crime. ... Heredia argues that the motive prong is necessary to avoid punishing individuals who fail to investigate because circumstances render it unsafe or impractical to do so. She claims that ... her suspicions did not arise until she was driving on an open highway where it would have been too dangerous to pull over. She thus claims that she had a motive *other* than avoiding criminal culpability. ...

We believe, however, that the second prong of the instruction, the requirement that defendant have *deliberately* avoided learning the truth, provides sufficient protections for defendants in these situations. ... A decision influenced by coercion, exigent circumstances or lack of meaningful choice is, perforce, not deliberate. A defendant who fails to investigate for these reasons has not deliberately chosen to avoid learning the truth.

Judge Kleinfeld, concurring on other grounds, objected (id. at 928-929):

> The majority converts the statutory element that the possession be "knowing" into something much less—a requirement that the defendant be suspicious and deliberately avoid investigating. The imposition on people who intend no crime of a duty to investigate has no statutory basis. The majority says that its [approach would] protect defendants who cannot investigate because of "coercion, exigent circumstances or lack of meaningful choice." . . . The majority seems to mean that if someone can investigate, they must. A criminal duty to investigate the wrongdoing of others to avoid wrongdoing of one's own is a novelty in the criminal law.
>
> . . . The government has not conscripted the citizenry as investigators, and the statute does not impose that unpleasant and sometimes risky obligation on people. Shall someone who thinks his mother is carrying a stash of marijuana in her suitcase be obligated, when he helps her with it, to rummage through her things? Should Heredia have carried tools with her, so that (if her story was true) she could open the trunk for which she had no key? Shall all of us who give a ride to [a] child's friend search her purse or his backpack? . . .
>
> A *Jewell* instruction ought to require (1) a belief that drugs are present, (2) avoidance of confirmation of the belief, and (3) wilfulness in that avoidance—that is, choosing not to confirm the belief in order to "be able to deny knowledge if apprehended."

4. Consider the distinction drawn by David Luban between what he calls the ostrich and the fox, in Contrived Ignorance, 87 Geo. L.J. 957, 962 (1999):

> The focus in a willful ignorance case is on whether the actor deliberately avoided guilty knowledge. The inquiry is about whatever steps the actor took to ward off knowledge prior to the misdeed. [The fox.] The focus in the Model Penal Code, by contrast, is on how certain the actor is about a fact. The inquiry is about the actor's subjective state at the moment of the misdeed. [The ostrich.] These are completely different issues. An actor can be aware of the high probability of a fact whether or not she took steps to avoid knowing it, and an actor can screen herself from knowledge of facts regardless of whether their probability is high or low. . . . Douglas Husak and Craig Callender illustrate the latter with a nice pair of examples [Willful Ignorance, Knowledge, and the "Equal Culpability" Thesis, [1994] Wis. L. Rev. 29, 37-38]. Suppose that a dope distributor tells each of his three couriers never to look in the suitcase he gives to each one, adding that it isn't necessary for them to know what the suitcases contain. If the suitcases contain dope, the case is plainly one of willful ignorance. But now suppose that the distributor adds that two of the three suitcases contain nothing but clothing, that he is truthful, and that the distributors know he is truthful. If the couriers deliver the suitcases without looking inside and without asking any questions, the case seems indistinguishable from the first case. It is still willful ignorance. But in the second case, the courier with dope in his suitcase lacks awareness of the high probability that it contains dope. Indeed, he knows that the probability

is one-third. He may even believe that his suitcase contains nothing but clothes. Thus, in the language of the Model Penal Code §2.02(7), he not only lacks awareness of a high probability of the fact's existence, "he actually believes that it does not exist."

c. Mistake of Fact

REGINA v. PRINCE

Court of Crown Cases Reserved
L.R. 2 Cr. Cas. Res. 154 (1875)

[Defendant was convicted of taking an unmarried girl under 16 years of age out of the possession and against the will of her father in violation of 24 & 25 Vict., c. 100, §55, providing:

> Whosoever shall unlawfully take or cause to be taken any unmarried girl, being under the age of sixteen years, out of the possession and against the will of her father or mother, or of any person having the lawful care or charge of her, shall be guilty of a misdemeanor. . . .

The jury found that the girl, Annie Phillips, was 14 at the time, but that she had told the defendant she was 18, that the defendant honestly believed that statement, and that his belief was reasonable. On appeal, the Court for Crown Cases Reserved upheld the conviction.]

BRAMWELL, B. [Finding that to sustain the defendant's position it would be necessary to read into the statute language requiring the prosecution to prove that the accused believed the girl he had taken was over the age of 16, the opinion continues:] These words are not there, and the question is, whether we are bound to construe the statute as though they were, on account of the rule that the mens rea is necessary to make an act a crime. I am of opinion that we are not, . . . and for the following reasons: The act forbidden is wrong in itself, if without lawful cause; I do not say illegal, but wrong. [W]hat the statute contemplates, and what I say is wrong, is the taking of a female of such tender years that she is properly called a *girl*, can be said to be in another's *possession*, and in that other's *care or charge*. No argument is necessary to prove this; it is enough to state the case. The legislature has enacted that if anyone does this wrong act, he does it at the risk of her turning out to be under sixteen. This opinion gives full scope to the doctrine of the mens rea. If the taker believed he had the father's consent, though wrongly, he would have no mens rea; so if he did not know she was in anyone's possession, nor in the care or charge of anyone. In those cases he would not know he was doing the *act* forbidden by the statute—an act which, if he knew she was in possession and in care or charge of anyone, he would know was a crime or not, according as she was under sixteen or not. He would not know he was doing an act wrong in itself, whatever was his intention, if done without lawful cause. The same principle applies in other cases. A man was held liable for assaulting a police officer in the execution of his duty, though he did not know he was a police officer. Why? Because the act was wrong in itself. So, also, in the case of burglary, could a person charged claim an acquittal on the ground that he believed it was past six when he entered, or in housebreaking, that he did not know the place broken into was a house? It seems to me impossible to say that where a person takes a girl out of her father's possession, not knowing whether she is or is not under sixteen, that he is not guilty; and equally impossible when he believes, but erroneously, that she is old enough for him to do a wrong act with safety. I think the conviction should be affirmed.

BRETT, J., [dissenting]. [I]f the facts had been as the prisoner, according to the findings of the jury, believed them to be, and had reasonable ground for believing them to be, he would have done no act which has ever been a criminal offence in England; he would have done no act in respect of which any civil action could have ever been maintained against him; he would have done no act for which, if done in the absence of the father, and done with the continuing consent of the girl, the father could have had any legal remedy. . . . Upon all the cases I think it is proved that there can be no conviction for crime in England in the absence of a criminal mind or mens rea. Then comes the question, what is the true meaning of the phrase. I do not doubt that it exists where the prisoner knowingly does acts which would constitute a crime if the result were as he anticipated, but in which the result may not improbably end by bringing the offence within a more serious class of crime. As if a man strikes with a dangerous weapon, with intent to do grievous bodily harm, and kills, the result makes the crime murder. The prisoner has run the risk. So, if a prisoner do the prohibited acts, without caring to consider what the truth is as to facts—as if a prisoner were to abduct a girl under sixteen without caring to consider whether she was in truth under sixteen—he runs the risk. So if he without abduction defiles a girl who is in fact under ten years old, with a belief that she is between ten and twelve. If the facts were as he believed he would be committing the lesser crime. Then he runs the risk of his crime resulting in the greater crime. It is clear that ignorance of the law does not excuse. It seems to me to follow that the maxim as to mens rea applies whenever the facts which are present in the prisoner's mind, and which he has reasonable ground to believe, and does believe to be the facts, would, if true, make his acts no criminal offence at all. I come to the conclusion that a mistake of facts, on reasonable grounds, to the extent that if the facts were as believed the acts of the prisoner would make him guilty of no criminal offence at all, is an excuse and that such excuse is implied in every criminal charge and every criminal enactment in England.

NOTES AND QUESTIONS ON MISTAKES OF FACT

1. The rationale of Prince. In *Prince*, the defendant claimed to have made a mistake in an especially sensitive area: The offense implicitly targeted sexual conduct, and the alleged mistake related to Annie Phillips's age. We might therefore think that the result rests on a narrow ground—that a mistake, even when reasonable, should not be a defense when it relates to the age of a minor in a sexual offense. Is the court's opinion limited in that way, or is its analysis relevant to mistakes of fact more generally? Notice that near the end of its opinion the court states that "[t]he same principle" that precludes a defense for Prince also applies to mistakes of fact in offenses like burglary and assaulting a police officer. What is that principle? *Prince* has long been considered a landmark in common-law mens rea analysis. But there is continuing dispute about whether its rationale is sound, and about where that rationale applies. Under the *Prince* approach, what are the circumstances under which a mistake of fact can or cannot be raised as a defense?

2. *The "moral-wrong" principle.* The court in *Prince* insists that "[our] opinion gives full scope to the doctrine of mens rea." But if the defendant made a reasonable mistake, how can it be said that he had any mens rea? Consider Peter Brett, An Inquiry into Criminal Guilt 149 (1963):

> [The opinion] of Bramwell, B. is to my mind clearly in accord with principle. It reflects the view that we learn our duties, not by studying the statute book, but by living in a community. A defense of mistake rests ultimately on the defendant's being able to say that he has observed the community ethic, and this Prince could not do.

But Professor Brett is an exception. Most of the academic commentary has been highly critical of *Prince.* See, e.g., George Fletcher, Rethinking Criminal Law 727 (1978). Consider Graham Hughes's response to Peter Brett in Criminal Responsibility, 16 Stan. L. Rev. 470, 480-481 (1964):

> [T]his appears as an appallingly dangerous position which comes close to giving the jury a discretion to create new crimes. In *Prince* what the accused was doing that he knew to be wrong was presumably to take away a young girl from the possession of her parents without their consent. Let us vary the position slightly and assume that the charge is one of unlawful sexual intercourse with a girl under sixteen. The accused reasonably believed that the girl was over sixteen. Should he be convicted because he knew that he was fornicating and because fornication is wrong according to the community ethic? In the first place this assumes that there is a clear community judgment about the wrongfulness of fornication, which is not so. . . . The truth is that there are many community ethics. . . . Even though ethical attitudes owe much to culture and environment, there is enough room for individual divergence to make Professor Brett's approach a slippery one.
>
> But the more serious objection is that there seems no reason why the community ethic concerning some conduct, even though clear, should be relevant to a determination of whether other conduct is criminal. . . . If fornication is not a crime in itself, as it is not in England, why should it become one when the defendant makes a reasonable mistake about the age of his partner?

3. *The "acoustic separation" approach.* Professor Meir Dan-Cohen offers a different interpretation of *Prince.* In Decision Rules and Conduct Rules: On Acoustic Separation in Criminal Law, 97 Harv. L. Rev. 625, 655 (1984), he uses *Prince* as an example of how sometimes the same criminal statute may be

taken as speaking to two audiences: the general public, to which it directs a conduct rule, and legal officials, to whom it directs a decision rule. The age limitation in *Prince*, Professor Dan-Cohen argues, was part of the decision rule addressed to the court, a bright line to limit judicial discretion. The statute's conduct rule was an enactment of the moral norm against taking girls from their parents. It was as though Parliament had enacted two statutes: One, addressed to the public, said don't take young girls from their parents; the other, addressed to officials, said don't prosecute or convict unless the girl is under 16. Professor Dan-Cohen defends the distinction between decision rules and conduct rules as follows:

> [C]oncerns other than reinforcement of community morality motivate decision rules. Primary among such concerns is the need to shape, control, and constrain the power wielded by decisionmakers. To attain this aim, the rules governing official decisionmaking must be characterized by a greater degree of precision and determinacy than can normally be expected of the community's moral precepts. Accordingly, whereas a conduct rule may be fully coextensive with the relevant moral precept, the corresponding decision rule need not be. Instead, the decision rule should define, as clearly and precisely as possible, a range of punishable conduct that is unquestionably within the bounds of the community's relevant moral norm.

Questions: How can we tell whether the statute's age limitation is merely a decision rule, as Professor Dan-Cohen claims? From the distance of more than a century, it is hard to be sure what Parliament and the *Prince* court were thinking. But notice the statement of Judge Brett in dissent: "If the facts had been as [Prince] believed them to be, . . . he would have done no act which has ever been a criminal offense in England." If Parliament had really wanted to make it a crime to take any young girl away from her parents, why wouldn't it have said so?

Consider the implications of Professor Dan-Cohen's approach for the *nulla poena* (legality) principle examined in Section B, pages 150-186 supra. Even if he is correct about what the relevant conduct rule was in this instance, is it a good idea to give courts the authority to decide which elements of a statutory offense establish the moral norm to which citizens must adhere?

4. The "lesser-crime" principle. Judge Brett, while dissenting in *Prince*, nonetheless had no doubt that when a defendant knowingly commits a crime, "he runs the risk of his crime resulting in the greater crime." In that situation, Judge Brett agreed, the defendant cannot raise a mistake of fact as a defense. This "lesser-crime" principle is narrower than the majority's "moral-wrong" approach. But why should a mens rea for one crime justify a conviction for a different, more serious crime? Recall the *Cunningham* case, supra page 243, where the court held that a defendant who was guilty of stealing a gas meter could not be convicted of the more serious offense of endangering Mrs. Wade, unless it was proved that he was aware of that danger. Is Judge Brett's approach consistent with *Cunningham*?

Consider a variation on *Prince*. Suppose that the defendant had no interest in Annie Phillips but only wanted to steal her father's horse and carriage, which he drove away without realizing that the girl was asleep in the back seat. Under the lesser-crime principle, would he be guilty of violating the statute applied in *Prince*, or should he be allowed to present a mistake-of-fact defense? If it makes sense to allow the defendant's claim of mistake in cases like *Cunningham* and in the situation where Prince steals the horse and carriage, why shouldn't mistake be a defense to a housebreaking charge, when the defendant reasonably believed the building he entered was not being used as a house?

5. *The Model Penal Code approach.* As in its approach to mens rea issues generally, the MPC sets aside much of the traditional common law framework. In its place the Code aims for both analytic clarity and a substantive focus on subjective culpability. With respect to the first aim, the Code emphasizes that the mens rea elements of an offense and the rules governing mistake are logically connected and cannot be addressed as separate issues. Thus, claims about mistake must be resolved by determining whether the mistake negates the mens rea required for the crime in question. With respect to the second aim, we have already seen (page 255 supra) that the Code disfavors criminal liability in the absence of subjective fault (at least recklessness). The MPC provisions dealing with mistake carry forward this preference for subjective culpability in addressing the "lesser-crime" issue considered in Note 4 above. For these situations (for example, where a person knowingly breaks into a building but is not aware of the aggravating fact that the building is a residence), the MPC presumes that, in general, aggravating circumstances should trigger more severe penalties only when the defendant was subjectively aware of those circumstances. The precise statutory formulation of these principles appears in §§2.02(3), 2.04(1), and 2.04(2), which should be read carefully at this point. The thinking behind these provisions is explained as follows:

MODEL PENAL CODE AND COMMENTARIES

Comment to §2.04, at 269-274 (1985)

[T]he significance of ignorance . . . of fact . . . , or a mistake as to such matters, is determined by the mental state required for the commission of the offense involved. Thus ignorance or mistake is a defense when it negates the existence of a state of mind that is essential to the commission of an offense, or when it establishes a state of mind that constitutes a defense under a rule of law relating to defenses. In other words, ignorance or mistake has only evidential import; it is significant whenever it is logically relevant . . .

The critical legislative decisions, therefore, relate to the establishment of the culpability for specific offenses as they are defined in the criminal code. [If] no culpability level is explicitly stated in the definition of the offense, purpose, knowledge or recklessness is required by Section 2.02(3) as to each material element. . . .

To put the matter as this subsection does is not to say anything that would not otherwise be true, even if no provision on the subject were made. As Glanville Williams has summarized the matter, . . . "the law could be stated equally well without reference to mistake. . . . It is impossible to assert that a crime requiring intention or recklessness can be committed although the accused laboured under a mistake negating the requisite intention or recklessness. Such an assertion carries its own refutation." This obvious point has, however, sometimes been overlooked in general formulations purporting to require that mistake be reasonable if it is to exculpate, without regard to the mode of culpability required to commit the crime. . . . There is no justification . . . for requiring that ignorance or mistake be reasonable if the crime or the element of the crime involved requires acting purposely or knowingly. . . . Generalizations about mistake of fact . . . or about honest and reasonable mistakes as relevant to general and specific intent crimes, tend to obscure rather than clarify that simple point. . . .

Subsection (2) is addressed to a limited problem that may produce distortion in the law, namely where the defendant claims mistake but where the criminal offense still would have occurred had the situation been as the defendant believed it to be. If the defense were denied altogether, an actor culpable in respect to one offense could be convicted of a much more serious offense. On the other hand, the defendant should not go free, for on either view—the facts as they occurred or as the defendant believed them to be—a criminal offense was committed. . . .

The doctrine that when one intends a lesser crime he may be convicted of a graver offense committed inadvertently leads to anomalous results if it is generally applied in penal law; and while the principle obtains to some extent in homicide, its generality has rightly been denied.

[The solution] embraced in section 2.04(2), is to deny the defense in certain circumstances, but to limit the classification of the offense and the available dispositions of the defendant to those that would have been available upon conviction of the lesser offense. . . . The important point . . . is that the effective measure of the defendant's liability should be his culpability, not the actual consequences of his conduct.

NOTE ON CURRENT LAW

In many states, the MPC's mistake proposals have had a major influence on legislative revision or on case law. But elsewhere, the contrasting approach to mens rea analysis reflected in the *Prince* case continues to dominate. The "moral-wrong" and "lesser-crime" principles remain especially important in offenses involving minors, sexual behavior, and/or drugs.

In State v. Benniefield, 678 N.W.2d 42 (Minn. 2004), the defendant was convicted of possessing drugs within 300 feet of a school. The court held that the prosecution must prove the defendant knew he was in possession of drugs, but that the defendant could be convicted of the more serious school-zone offense without any proof that he knew or should have known he was near a school. Absent statutory language to the contrary, this is the prevailing approach, but it remains controversial. In United States v. Cordoba-Hincapie, 825 F. Supp. 485 (E.D.N.Y. 1993), the court held that denying a defense for a mistake about the seriousness of the offense committed violates the requirement that punishment be calibrated to the degree of culpability. And consider Stephen F. Smith, Proportional Mens Rea, 46 Am. Crim. L. Rev. 127, 128 (2009):

> Creating implied mens rea requirements, where necessary to ensure proportional punishment, is not a judicial usurpation of the legislative function. Rather, it is to take seriously the role that courts play, under both constitutional and substantive criminal law, to ensure that punishment "fits" the crime. Moreover, proportional mens rea would represent a needed counterweight to prosecutorial behavior whereas current doctrine does not. [M]ens rea doctrine aimed only at protecting moral blamelessness from punishment will largely be redundant of prosecutorial discretion. Proportionality of punishment, however, is a concern that [many prosecutors] routinely ignore. Judicial mens rea selection, therefore, has a substantial contribution to make to the achievement of proportionality of punishment.

Sexual offenses involving minors raise similar issues, in a context where traditional, pre-Model Penal Code precedent was especially resistant to mistake-of-fact defenses. Should courts continue to follow the *Prince* approach in this context today? Consider the material that follows.

PEOPLE v. OLSEN

Supreme Court of California
36 Cal. 3d 638, 685 P.2d 52 (1984)

BIRD, C.J. Is a reasonable mistake as to the victim's age a defense to a charge of lewd or lascivious conduct with a child under the age of 14 years (Pen. Code, §288, subd. (a)[1])?

In early June 1981, Shawn M. was 13 years and 10 months old. At that time, her parents were entertaining out-of-town guests. Since one of the visitors was using Shawn's bedroom, Shawn suggested that she sleep in her family's camper trailer which was parked in the driveway in front of the house. Shawn's parents agreed to this arrangement on the condition that she keep the windows shut and door locked. . . .

---

1. Section 288, subdivision (a) provides in relevant part:

   Any person who shall willfully and lewdly commit any lewd or lascivious act . . . upon or with the body, or any part or member thereof, of a child under the age of 14 years, with the intent of arousing, appealing to, or gratifying the lust or passions or sexual desires of such person or of such child, shall be guilty of a felony and shall be imprisoned in the state prison for a term of three, six, or eight years. . . .

At trial, Shawn testified to the following events. On her third night in the trailer, she locked the door as instructed by her parents. She then fell asleep, but was . . . awakened by the sound of barking dogs and by Garcia, who had a knife by her side and his hand over her mouth.[2] Garcia called to appellant to come in, and appellant entered the trailer. Garcia told Shawn to let appellant "make love" to her, or he—Garcia—would stab her. . . . Appellant proceeded to have sexual intercourse with Shawn. . . . While appellant was still [doing so], her father entered the trailer. Mr. M. grabbed appellant as he was trying to leave, and Garcia stabbed Mr. M. in order to free appellant.

Shawn testified that she knew Garcia "pretty well." . . . She also testified that she was very good friends "off and on" with appellant and that during one three-month period she spent almost every day at appellant's house. At the time of the incident, however, Shawn considered Garcia her boyfriend.[3] Finally, Shawn admitted that she told both Garcia and appellant that she was over 16 years old. She also conceded that she looked as if she were over 16.

Garcia testified to quite a different set of events. . . . On . . . the day before the offense Shawn invited him to spend the night in the trailer with her so that they could have sex. He and Shawn engaged in sexual intercourse about four times that evening. Shawn invited Garcia to come back the following night at midnight.

The next night, after two unsuccessful attempts to enter the trailer, Garcia and appellant were told by Shawn to return at midnight. . . . Shawn, wearing only a pair of panties, opened the door and invited them in. She told them . . . that she wanted "to make love" with appellant first. When Mr. M. entered the trailer, appellant was on top of Shawn. Garcia denied threatening Shawn with a knife, . . . breaking into the trailer or forcing her to have sex with them.[5]

At the conclusion of the trial, the court found Garcia and appellant guilty of violating section 288, subdivision (a).[7] In reaching its decision, the court rejected defense counsel's argument that a good faith belief as to the age of the victim was a defense to the section 288 charge. Appellant was sentenced to the lower term of three years in state prison. This appeal followed. . . .

Twenty years ago, this court in People v. Hernandez[, 393 P.2d 673 (1964),] overruled established precedent, and held that an accused's good

---

2. Although Shawn testified she locked the trailer door, she failed to explain how Garcia entered the trailer. A subsequent examination of the trailer revealed that there were no signs of a forced entry.

3. Shawn admitted that she had engaged in sexual intercourse before the night of June 3d, but denied having any such prior experience with either Garcia or the appellant. However, she did admit having had sexual relations, short of intercourse, with both of them in the past.

5. Appellant's sister corroborated Shawn's testimony that Shawn made daily visits to the Olsen home during a three-month period. She testified that during these visits Shawn and appellant would go into the latter's bedroom and close the door. On one occasion appellant's sister saw the two in bed together. [Four other witnesses described similar episodes involving Shawn and either appellant or other boys.]

7. Garcia was also found guilty of assault with a deadly weapon with infliction of great bodily injury [in the assault on Mr. M.]. Both Garcia and appellant were found not guilty of burglary, forcible rape, and lewd or lascivious acts upon a child under the age of 14 by use of force. . . .

faith, reasonable belief that a victim was 18 years or more of age was a defense to a charge of statutory rape. . . .

One Court of Appeal has declined to apply *Hernandez* in an analogous context. In People v. Lopez (1969) 77 Cal. Rptr. 59, the court refused to recognize a reasonable mistake of age defense to a charge of offering or furnishing marijuana to a minor. The court noted that the act of furnishing marijuana is criminal regardless of the age of the recipient and that furnishing marijuana to a minor simply yields a greater punishment than when the substance is furnished to an adult. "[A] mistake of fact relating only to the gravity of an offense will not shield a deliberate offender from the full consequences of the wrong actually committed." (Ibid.)

. . . There exists a strong public policy to protect children of tender years. [S]ection 288 was enacted for that very purpose. Furthermore, even the *Hernandez* court recognized this important policy when it made clear that it did not contemplate applying the mistake of age defense in cases where the victim is of "tender years." . . .

This conclusion is supported by the Legislature's enactment of section 1203.066. Subdivision (a)(3) of that statute renders certain individuals convicted of lewd or lascivious conduct who "honestly and reasonably believed the victim was 14 years old or older" eligible for probation. The Legislature's enactment of section 1203.066, subdivision (a)(3) . . . strongly indicates that the Legislature did not intend such a defense to a section 288 charge. To recognize such a defense would render section 1203.066, subdivision (a)(3) a nullity, since the question of probation for individuals who had entertained an honest and reasonable belief in the victim's age would never arise. . . .

The Legislature has also determined that persons who commit sexual offenses on children under the age of 14 should be punished more severely than those who commit such offenses on children under the age of 18. . . .

It is significant that a violation of section 288 carries a much harsher penalty than does unlawful sexual intercourse (§261.5), the crime involved in *Hernandez*. Section 261.5 carries a maximum punishment of one year in the county jail or three years in state prison, while section 288 carries a maximum penalty of eight years in state prison. The different penalties for these two offenses further supports the view that there exists a strong public policy to protect children under 14. . . . The legislative purpose of section 288 would not be served by recognizing a defense of reasonable mistake of age. . . . Accordingly, the judgment of conviction is affirmed.

GRODIN, J., concurring and dissenting. I agree that the enactment of Penal Code section 1203.066, which renders eligible for probation persons convicted of lewd or lascivious conduct who "honestly and reasonably believed the victim was 14 years old or older" is persuasive evidence that in the eyes of the Legislature such a belief is not a defense to the crime.[1] What troubles me is

---

1. I do not agree that legislative intent to eliminate good faith mistake of fact as a defense can be inferred from the imposition of relatively higher penalties for that crime. On the contrary, as this

the notion that a person who acted with such belief, and is not otherwise shown to be guilty of any criminal conduct,[2] may not only be convicted but be sentenced to prison notwithstanding his eligibility for probation when it appears that his belief did not accord with reality. To me, that smacks of cruel or unusual punishment.

. . . I recognize . . . that our legal system includes certain "strict liability" crimes, but generally these are confined to the so-called "regulatory" or "public welfare" offenses. . . . (Morissette v. United States (1952) 342 U.S. 246). Moreover, with respect to such crimes, . . . "*penalties commonly are relatively small, and conviction does no grave damage to an offender's reputation.*" (Id., at p. 256, emphasis added.)

Even in the regulatory context, "judicial and academic acceptance of liability without fault has not been enthusiastic." (Jeffries & Stephen, Defenses, Presumptions, and Burden of Proof in the Criminal Law (1979) 88 Yale L.J. 1325, 1373.) And "with respect to traditional crimes, it is a widely accepted normative principle that conviction should not be had without proof of fault. At least when the offense carries serious sanctions and the stigma of official condemnation, liability should be reserved for persons whose blameworthiness has been established" (Id., at 1373-1374.)

. . . No doubt the standard of what is reasonable must be set relatively high in order to accomplish the legislative objective of protecting persons under 14 years of age. . . . Perhaps it is not enough that a person "looks" to be more than 14; perhaps there is a duty of reasonable inquiry besides. At some point, however, the belief becomes reasonable by any legitimate standard, so that one would say the defendant is acting in a way which is no different from the way our society would expect a reasonable, careful, and law-abiding citizen to act.

At that point, it seems to me, the imposition of criminal sanctions, particularly imprisonment, simply cannot be tolerated in a civilized society. . . .

QUESTIONS ON OLSEN

What "moral wrongs" or "lesser crimes" did Olsen commit? In California, as in many states, the criminality of sexual behavior turns on three factors: the age of the victim, whether force was used, and whether the sexual contact included intercourse. Under the California Penal Code, *forcible* sexual contact is always criminal, regardless of the victim's age and the nature of the sexual contact. For *consensual* behavior, intercourse is criminal whenever the victim is under 18, but sexual contact short of intercourse is criminal only when the victim is under 14. According to Shawn's version of the events, of course,

---

court has stated in connection with the crime of bigamy: "The severe penalty imposed . . . and the fact that it has been regarded . . . as a crime involving moral turpitude, make it extremely unlikely that the Legislature meant to include the morally innocent to make sure the guilty did not escape." (People v. Vogel (1956) 299 P.2d 850.)

2. The People suggest that defendant was at least guilty of "sexual intercourse accomplished with a female not the wife of the perpetrator, where the female is under the age of 18 years." Defendant was neither charged nor convicted of that offense, however, and it is by no means clear from the record that he had sexual intercourse with the victim.

Olsen's conduct clearly met the requirements for forcible rape. But the trial judge acquitted Olsen of all the charges involving the alleged use of force. The judge found beyond a reasonable doubt only the facts necessary to convict for consensual misconduct under §288(a). See page 273 and footnote 7, supra.

In upholding the conviction on that charge, the California Supreme Court relied on the "lesser-crime" principle, quoting from California cases like *People v. Lopez*, page 274 supra. But was that principle really applicable on the facts of *Olsen*? According to the trial judge's version of the events, did Olsen's mistake relate only to the *gravity* of the offense? What was the lesser crime, if any, that Olsen *knew* (or should have known) he was committing?

An alternative basis for upholding Olsen's conviction might be the controversial "moral wrong" theory. But again, was that principle really applicable on the facts of *Olsen*? What were the sexual acts Olsen *knew* (or should have known) he was committing? In what sense were those acts morally wrong?

B (A MINOR) v. DIRECTOR OF PUBLIC PROSECUTIONS

House of Lords
[2000] 1 All E.R. 833

[B, a 15-year-old boy, repeatedly asked a 13-year-old girl to perform oral sex. The girl refused, and B was subsequently charged with inciting a child under the age of 14 to commit an act of gross indecency, contrary to §1(1) of the Indecency with Children Act 1960.[a] At trial, it was accepted that B had honestly believed that the girl was over 14 years old, but the trial justices ruled that his mistake could not constitute a defense. As a result, B changed his plea from not guilty to guilty, preserving his right to appellate review. On appeal, one of the principal questions before the House of Lords was whether the holding of *Regina v. Prince* governed in this case, and if so, whether the English courts should continue to adhere to it.]

LORD NICHOLLS: . . . As habitually happens with statutory offences, . . . Parliament defined the prohibited conduct solely in terms of the proscribed physical acts. Section 1(1) says nothing about the mental element. . . . In these circumstances the starting point for a court is the established common law presumption that a mental element, traditionally labelled mens rea, is an essential ingredient unless Parliament has indicated a contrary intention either expressly or by necessary implication. . . .

The existence of the presumption is beyond dispute, but in one respect the traditional formulation of the presumption calls for re-examination. [T]he

---

a. Section 1(1) provides as follows:

> Any person who commits an act of gross indecency with or towards a child under the age of fourteen, or who incites a child under that age to such an act with him or another, shall be liable on conviction on indictment to imprisonment for a term not exceeding ten years. . . . —EDS.

presumption is expressed traditionally to the effect that an honest mistake by a defendant does not avail him unless the mistake was made on reasonable grounds. ... The "reasonable belief" school of thought held unchallenged sway for many years. But over the last quarter of a century there have been several important cases where ... the courts have placed new, or renewed, emphasis on the subjective nature of the mental element in criminal offences. The courts have rejected the reasonable belief approach and preferred the honest belief approach. ... [See] R. v. Williams, [1987] 3 All ER 411, 415:

> The reasonableness or unreasonableness of the defendant's belief is material to the question of whether the belief was held by the defendant at all. If the belief was in fact held, its unreasonableness, so far as guilt or innocence is concerned, is neither here nor there. It is irrelevant.

Considered as a matter of principle, the honest belief approach must be preferable. ... To the extent that an overriding objective limit ("on reasonable grounds") is introduced, the subjective element is displaced. ... When that occurs the defendant's "fault" lies exclusively in falling short of an objective standard. His crime lies in his negligence. A statute may so provide expressly or by necessary implication. But this can have no place in a common law principle, of general application, which is concerned with the need for a mental element as an essential ingredient of a criminal offence.

[A]n age-related ingredient of a statutory offence stands on no different footing from any other ingredient. If a man genuinely believes that the girl with whom he is committing a grossly indecent act is over 14, he is not intending to commit such an act with a girl under 14. Whether such an intention is an essential ingredient of the offence depends upon a proper construction of [the] Act. ...

In §1(1) of the 1960 Act Parliament ... created an entirely new criminal offence, in simple unadorned language. The offence so created is a serious offence. The more serious the offence, the greater is the weight to be attached to the presumption [requiring proof of mens rea], because the more severe is the punishment and the graver the stigma which accompany a conviction. Under §1 conviction originally attracted a punishment of up to two years' imprisonment. This has since been increased to a maximum of ten years' imprisonment. ... The conduct may be depraved by any acceptable standard, or it may be relatively innocuous behaviour in private between two young people. These factors reinforce, rather than negative, the application of the presumption in this case. ...

The purpose of the section is, of course, to protect children. ... This factor in itself does not assist greatly. ... There is no general agreement that strict liability is necessary to the enforcement of the law protecting children in sexual matters. ... Is there here a compellingly clear implication that Parliament should be taken to have intended that the ordinary common law requirement of a mental element should be excluded in respect of the age ingredient of this new offence? ... I cannot find, either in the statutory context or otherwise, any indication of sufficient cogency to displace the application of the common law presumption. In my view the necessary mental element regarding the age ingredient in §1 of the 1960 Act is the absence of a genuine belief by the accused that the victim was 14 years of age or above. The burden of proof of this rests upon the prosecution in the usual way. If Parliament considers that the position should be otherwise regarding this serious social problem, Parliament must itself confront the difficulties and express its will in clear terms. I would allow this appeal.

I add a final observation. [W]ithout expressing a view on the correctness of the actual [decision in *R. v. Prince*], I must observe that some of the reasoning in *R. v. Prince* is at variance with the common law presumption regarding mens rea as discussed above. To that extent, the reasoning must be regarded as unsound. . . . *R. v. Prince*, and later decisions based on it, must now be read in the light of [the present decision] on the nature and weight of the common law presumption.

LORD STEYN: [O]ne can be confident that the reasoning of Bramwell, B. [in *R. v. Prince*], if tested in a modern court, would not be upheld. . . . In any event, I would reject the contention that there is a special rule of construction in respect of age-based sexual offences. . . . *R. v. Prince* is out of line with the modern trend in criminal law which is that a defendant should be judged on the facts as he believes them to be. . . .

[Appeal allowed.]

Garnett v. State, 332 Md. 571, 632 A.2d 797 (1993): Raymond [Garnett] is a young retarded man. At the time of the incident in question he was 20 years old. He has an I.Q. of 52. [He] read on the third-grade level, did arithmetic on the 5th-grade level, and interacted with others socially . . . at the level of someone 11 or 12 years of age.

[A] friend introduced Raymond to Erica Frazier, then aged 13; the two subsequently talked occasionally by telephone. On February 28, 1991, Raymond . . . approached the girl's house at about nine o'clock in the evening. Erica opened her bedroom window . . . ; he testified that "she just told me to get a ladder and climb up her window." The two talked, and later engaged in sexual intercourse. Raymond left at about 4:30 A.M. the following morning. On November 19, 1991, Erica gave birth to a baby, of which Raymond is the biological father.

[Raymond was charged with second-degree rape under Md. Code, art. 27, §463.[a]] At trial, the defense twice proffered evidence to the effect that Erica

---

a. "(a) . . . A person is guilty of rape in the second degree if the person engages in vaginal intercourse with another person:

"(1) By force or threat of force against the will and without the consent of the other person; or . . .

"(3) Who is under 14 years of age and the person performing the act is at least four years older than the victim.

"(b) Penalty. Any person violating the provisions of this section is guilty of a felony and upon conviction is subject to imprisonment for a period of not more than 20 years."—EDS.

herself and her friends had previously told Raymond that she was 16 years old, and that he had acted with that belief. The trial court excluded such evidence as immaterial, explaining [that] "It is in the Court's opinion a strict liability offense." The court found Raymond guilty. It sentenced him to a term of five years in prison, suspended the sentence and imposed five years of probation, and ordered that he pay restitution to Erica and the Frazier family. . . .

Raymond asserts that the events of this case were inconsistent with the criminal sexual exploitation of a minor by an adult. . . . With an I.Q. of 52, Raymond functioned at approximately the same level as the 13-year-old Erica. . . . The precise legal issue here rests on Raymond's unsuccessful efforts to introduce into evidence testimony that Erica and her friends had told him she was 16 years old, the age of consent to sexual relations, and that he believed them. Thus the trial court did not permit him to raise a defense of reasonable mistake. . . .

Statutory rape laws are often justified on the "lesser legal wrong" theory or the "moral wrong" theory; by such reasoning, the defendant acting without mens rea nonetheless deserves punishment for having committed a lesser crime, fornication, or for having violated moral teachings that prohibit sex outside of marriage. [But] Maryland has no law against fornication. . . . Moreover, the criminalization of an act, performed without a guilty mind, deemed immoral by some members of the community rests uneasily on subjective and shifting norms. "[D]etermining precisely what the 'community ethic' actually is [is] not an easy task in a heterogeneous society in which our public pronouncements about morality often are not synonymous with our private conduct." LaFave & Scott, [Criminal Law (2d ed. 1986)] at 411. . . .

We think it sufficiently clear, however, that Maryland's second degree rape statute . . . makes no allowance for a mistake-of-age defense. The plain language of §463 . . . and the legislative history of its creation lead to this conclusion. . . . This interpretation is consistent with the traditional view of statutory rape as a strict liability crime designed to protect young persons from the dangers of sexual exploitation by adults, loss of chastity, physical injury, and, in the case of girls, pregnancy. The majority of states retain statutes which impose strict liability for sexual acts with underage complainants. [E]ven among those states providing for a mistake-of-age defense in some instances, the defense often is not available where the sex partner is 14 years old or less; the complaining witness in the instant case was only 13. . . . Any new provision introducing an element of mens rea . . . should properly result from an act of the Legislature itself, rather than judicial fiat. Until then, defendants in extraordinary cases, like Raymond, will rely upon the tempering discretion of the trial court at sentencing.[b]

---

b. For criticism of the strict liability approach in the particular context of a statutory-rape defendant who suffers from mental retardation, see Elizabeth Nevins-Saunders, Incomprehensible Crimes: Defendants with Mental Retardation Charged with Statutory Rape, 85 N.Y.U. L. Rev. 1067 (2010).—EDS.

BELL, J., dissenting: . . . To hold, as a matter of law, that section 463(a)(3) does not require the State to prove that a defendant possessed the necessary mental state . . . or that the defendant may not litigate that issue in defense, "offends a principle of justice so rooted in the traditions of conscience of our people as to be ranked as fundamental." . . . So interpreted, section 463(a)(3) not only destroys absolutely the concept of fault, but it renders meaningless, in the statutory rape context, the presumption of innocence and the right to due process.

NOTE ON STATUTORY RAPE

In statutory rape prosecutions, the traditional insistence on imposing strict liability for mistakes about age is beginning to erode. Either by statute or judicial decision, more than 20 states now permit the defense of mistake at least under some circumstances—typically when the relevant age of consent is greater than 14 or when the two parties are close in age. But even in those situations, nearly all the states that allow the defense do so only when the mistake is reasonable, and more than half the states, like Maryland, do not permit a mistake defense under any circumstances. Thus, the *Prince* case, though now repudiated in England, continues to exert a powerful influence on American law.

The Model Penal Code generally allows a defense for honest mistake, whether reasonable or not, but it provides for strict liability when criminality in a sexual offense turns on a child's being below the age of ten. And when criminality turns on a critical age greater than ten, the MPC treats mistake as an affirmative defense on which the defendant must carry the burden of proving that the mistake was reasonable. See §213.6(1). The various American statutory rape provisions are analyzed comprehensively in Catherine Carpenter, On Statutory Rape, Strict Liability, and the Public Welfare Offense Model, 53 Am. U. L. Rev. 313, 385-391 (2003). See also Annot., 46 A.L.R.5th 499 (2005).

One American court, in accord with Judge Bell's reasoning in *Garnett*, supra, has held strict liability in statutory rape to be unconstitutional. See State v. Guest, 583 P.2d 836 (Alaska 1978). But for the time being, that remains an isolated holding. Virtually all American courts, even when they express discomfort with strict liability in statutory rape, continue to uphold its constitutionality. See, e.g., State v. Jadowski, 680 N.W.2d 810 (Wis. 2004); Owens v. State, 724 A.2d 43 (Md. 1999). In *Owens*, the court said (id. at 53, 55) that "[t]he state's overwhelming interest in protecting children from these risks outweighs any interest that the individual may have in engaging in sexual relations with children near the age of consent" and that "by disallowing a mistake-of-age defense, the state avoids the risk that the inevitably emotional statutory rape trial will focus unjustifiably on the child's appearance and level of maturity."

This approach predominates even though the punishment for statutory rape can be severe. In Maryland, the offense carries a penalty of up to 20 years' imprisonment.[14] In Wisconsin, sexual intercourse or sexual contact with a minor under the age of 16 is punishable by imprisonment for up to 40 years, and if the minor is under 13, the maximum sentence rises to 60 years' imprisonment.[15] In Georgia, statutory rape of a minor under the age of 16 carries a maximum sentence of 20 years, with a mandatory minimum of imprisonment for at least one year if the perpetrator is 19 or 20 years of age, and a mandatory minimum of at least ten years if the perpetrator is 21 or older.[16]

Two developments may prompt reconsideration of strict liability:

(1) One is the increasing importance of mandatory sentencing laws. In particular, the ability of sentencing courts to mitigate the harsh impact of a statutory rape conviction, when the defendant is morally innocent, has been undercut by the proliferation of laws requiring registration and community notification for sex offenders. As Professor Carpenter notes, supra at 376:

> Whether it carries significant prison time or minimal jail time, conviction of statutory rape in most jurisdictions bears the public equivalent of the "scarlet letter"—the requirement that sex offenders, after serving their sentences, must register with law enforcement officials. Further, in most states, [statutes] require officials to notify members of the community of the offender's location. Whatever the underlying basis for the statutory rape conviction—intentional exploitation of a young child, or strict liability in the face of a reasonable mistake—all who are convicted in the vast majority of jurisdictions are subject to sexual offender registration laws. . . .

Questions: Is it fair—or even rational—to include individuals like Olsen and Garnett on a registry of supposedly dangerous sex offenders? But if statutory rape defendants who lack mens rea can be sentenced to prison (recall that Olsen received a three-year prison term), why should it be considered worse—and impermissible—to subject them to mandatory registration and notification laws?

(2) The second development is Lawrence v. Texas, 539 U.S. 558 (2003), the decision holding it unconstitutional for a state to punish private sexual activity by consenting adults, whether married or not. Why would this decision affect the merits of strict liability for sexual activity when one of the parties is *not* an adult? Note how *Lawrence* changes mens rea analysis within the *Prince* framework. If the acts the defendant *intended* to commit (fornication) cannot be made illegal, what is the "lesser crime"? If those acts are constitutionally protected, as a valuable aspect of individual liberty and autonomy, how can they be regarded as a "moral wrong"? For careful development of the argument that strict liability becomes unconstitutional when

---

14. Md. Crim. Code Ann. §3-304(b) (2010).
15. Wis. Stat. §§939.50(3), 948.02 (2010).
16. Ga. Code Ann. §16-6-3(b) (2010).

the state has no power to punish the underlying activity (i.e., the acts the defendant is aware of committing), see Alan C. Michaels, Constitutional Innocence, 112 Harv. L. Rev. 829 (1999). The implications of this principle in the wake of *Lawrence* are closely examined in Carpenter, supra, at 364-367.

d. Strict Liability

INTRODUCTORY NOTE

In the treatment of mistake of fact in the preceding section we encountered cases of strict liability, that is, cases where liability was imposed without any demonstrated culpability, not even negligence, with respect to at least one of the material elements of the offense. In all such cases that we have considered so far, however, there was—and courts considered it essential that there was—at least some sort of mens rea—that is, some sort of legal or moral fault. In this section, we consider a more extreme form of strict liability, one in which the defendant neither knew nor had any reason to know that anything about his behavior was legally or even morally wrong. We will examine the main problems posed by this form of strict liability—how and why it came to be relied on by legislators as a regulatory device; the role of courts in affecting the extent of strict liability through their authority to interpret statutes; what the virtues and vices of strict liability are; and how far it can be squared with the requirements of just punishment.

United States v. Balint, 258 U.S. 250 (1922): [Defendants were indicted for violating the Narcotic Act of 1914 by selling derivatives of opium and coca leaves without the order form required by the Act.[a] The crime was punishable by up to five years in prison. Defendants argued that the indictment was defective for failing to charge that they knew they were selling prohibited drugs. The Supreme Court held that proof of such knowledge was not required by the statute, stating:]

While the general rule at common law was that the scienter was a necessary element in the indictment and proof of every crime, and this was followed in regard to statutory crimes even where the statutory definition did not in terms include it, there has been a modification of this view in respect to prosecutions under statutes the purpose of which would be obstructed by such a requirement. It is a question of legislative intent to be construed by the court. [I]n the prohibition or punishment of particular acts, the State may in the maintenance of a public policy provide "that he who shall do them shall do them at his peril and will not be heard to plead in defense good faith or ignorance." Many instances of this are to be found in regulatory measures in the exercise of what is called the police power where the emphasis of the

---

a. "[I]t shall be unlawful for any person to sell, barter, exchange, or give away any of the aforesaid drugs except in pursuance of a written order of the person to whom such article is sold, bartered, exchanged, or given, on a form [issued] for that purpose by the Commissioner of Internal Revenue. . . ."—EDS.

statute is evidently upon achievement of some social betterment rather than the punishment of the crimes as in cases of mala in se. . . . [The Act's] manifest purpose is to require every person dealing in drugs to ascertain at his peril whether that which he sells comes within the inhibition of the statute, and if he sells the inhibited drug in ignorance of its character, to penalize him. Congress weighed the possible injustice of subjecting an innocent seller to a penalty against the evil of exposing innocent purchasers to danger from the drug, and concluded that the latter was the result preferably to be avoided. Doubtless considerations as to the opportunity of the seller to find out the fact and the difficulty of proof of knowledge contributed to this conclusion.

United States v. Dotterweich, 320 U.S. 277 (1943): [Buffalo Pharmacal Company was a corporation that bought drugs from manufacturers, repackaged them, and shipped them to physicians and others under its own labels, which contained the manufacturers' descriptions of the products. On two occasions the manufacturers' labels, and hence the corporation's labels, were in error, and as a consequence the corporation and Dotterweich, its president and general manager, were prosecuted for shipping misbranded or adulterated products in interstate commerce in violation of the Federal Food, Drug and Cosmetic Act.[b] The jury, remarkably, acquitted the corporation but convicted Dotterweich, who was sentenced to a fine and probation for 60 days, although under the statute he could have been sentenced to imprisonment for a year. The Supreme Court affirmed the conviction, holding that the statute required no mens rea at all with respect to whether those charged knew or should have known the shipment was mislabeled. Justice Felix Frankfurter, writing for the Court, observed:]

The Food and Drugs Act of 1906 was an exertion by Congress of its power to keep impure and adulterated food and drugs out of the channels of commerce. By the Act of 1938, Congress extended the range of its control over illicit and noxious articles and stiffened the penalties for disobedience. The purposes of this legislation thus touch phases of the lives and health of people which, in the circumstances of modern industrialism, are largely beyond self-protection. Regard for these purposes should infuse construction of the legislation if it is to be treated as a working instrument of government and not merely as a collection of English words. The prosecution to which Dotterweich was subjected is based on a now familiar type of legislation whereby penalties serve as effective means of regulation. Such legislation dispenses with the conventional requirement for criminal conduct—awareness of some wrongdoing. In the interest of the larger good it puts the burden of acting at hazard upon a person otherwise innocent but standing in responsible relation to a public danger. United States v. Balint, 258 U.S. 250. . . .

---

b. Section 301 of the Act prohibits the "Introduction or delivery for introduction into interstate commerce of any . . . drug . . . that is adulterated or misbranded."—EDS.

Hardship there doubtless may be under a statute which thus penalizes the transaction though consciousness of wrongdoing be totally wanting. Balancing relative hardships, Congress has preferred to place it upon those who have at least the opportunity of informing themselves of the existence of conditions imposed for the protection of consumers before sharing in illicit commerce, rather than to throw the hazard on the innocent public who are wholly helpless.

MORISSETTE v. UNITED STATES

Supreme Court of the United States
342 U.S. 246 (1952)

Justice Jackson delivered the opinion of the Court.

[Morissette, a junk dealer, openly entered an Air Force practice bombing range and took spent bomb casings that had been lying about for years exposed to the weather and rusting away. He flattened them out and sold them at a city junk market at a profit of $84. He was indicted and convicted of violating 18 U.S.C. §641, which made it a crime to "knowingly convert" government property.[a] The defendant admittedly knew that what he had taken were Air Force bomb casings, and there was therefore no question that the defendant had "knowingly convert[ed]" to his own use property that previously did not belong to him. His defense was that he honestly believed that the casings had been abandoned by the Air Force and that he was therefore violating no one's rights in taking them. The trial judge rejected Morissette's defense and instructed the jury that "[t]he question on intent is whether or not he intended to take the property." The court of appeals affirmed, ruling that the statute created several separate offenses, including stealing and knowing conversion. While the crime of stealing traditionally has required an intent to take another's property, in violation of the owner's rights, the court of appeals held that knowing conversion did not include an element of intent to violate the rights of another, because no such intent was expressly required by the statute. In other words, the court of appeals assumed that Congress meant the term "knowingly convert" to carry its conventional tort law meaning—simply an intentional exercise of dominion over property that is not one's own. The Supreme Court reversed, concluding that the defendant must be proven to have had knowledge of the facts that made the conversion wrongful, that is, that the property had not been abandoned by its owner.]

The contention that an injury can amount to a crime only when inflicted by intention is no provincial or transient notion. It is as universal and

---

a. "Whoever embezzles, steals, purloins, or knowingly converts to his use or the use of another, or without authority, sells, conveys or disposes of any record, voucher, money, or thing of value of the United States . . . shall be fined not more than $10,000 or imprisoned not more than ten years, or both; but if the value of such property does not exceed the sum of $100, he shall be fined not more than $1,000 or imprisoned not more than one year, or both."—Eds.

persistent in mature systems of law as belief in freedom of the human will and a consequent ability and duty of the normal individual to choose between good and evil. A relation between some mental element and punishment for a harmful act is almost as instinctive as the child's familiar exculpatory "But I didn't mean to," and has afforded the rational basis for a tardy and unfinished substitution of deterrence and reformation in place of retaliation and vengeance as the motivation for public prosecution. . . .

Crime, as a compound concept, generally constituted only from concurrence of an evil-meaning mind with an evil-doing hand, was congenial to an intense individualism and took deep and early root in American soil. As the states codified the common law of crimes, even if their enactments were silent on the subject, their courts assumed that the omission did not signify disapproval of the principle but merely recognized that intent was so inherent in the idea of the offense that it required no statutory affirmation. . . .

However, the *Balint* and *Behrman*[b] offenses belong to a category of another character, with very different antecedents and origins. The crimes there involved depend on no mental element but consist only of forbidden acts or omissions. This, while not expressed by the Court, is made clear from examination of a century-old but accelerating tendency, discernible both here and in England, to call into existence new duties and crimes which disregard any ingredient of intent. The industrial revolution multiplied the number of workmen exposed to injury from increasingly powerful and complex mechanisms, driven by freshly discovered sources of energy, requiring higher precautions by employers. Traffic of velocities, volumes and varieties unheard of, came to subject the wayfarer to intolerable casualty risks if owners and drivers were not to observe new cares and uniformities of conduct. Congestion of cities and crowding of quarters called for health and welfare regulations undreamed of in simpler times. Wide distribution of goods became an instrument of wide distribution of harm when those who dispersed food, drink, drugs, and even securities, did not comply with reasonable standards of quality, integrity, disclosure and care. Such dangers have engendered increasingly numerous and detailed regulations which heighten the duties of those in control of particular industries, trades, properties or activities that affect public health, safety or welfare.[20]

While many of these duties are sanctioned by a more strict civil liability, lawmakers, whether wisely or not, have sought to make such regulations more effective by invoking criminal sanctions to be applied by the familiar technique of criminal prosecutions and convictions. This has confronted the

---

b. United States v. Behrman, 258 U.S. 280 (1922), a companion case to *Balint*, was another prosecution for a narcotics offense.—Eds.

20. Sayre, Public Welfare Offenses, 33 Col. L. Rev. 55, 73, 84 (1933), cites and classifies a large number of cases and concludes that they fall roughly into subdivisions of (1) illegal sales of intoxicating liquor, (2) sales of impure or adulterated food or drugs, (3) sales of misbranded articles, (4) violations of antinarcotic Acts, (5) criminal nuisances, (6) violations of traffic regulations, (7) violations of motor-vehicle laws, and (8) violations of general police regulations, passed for the safety, health or well-being of the community.

courts with a multitude of prosecutions, based on statutes or administrative regulations, for what have been aptly called "public welfare offenses." . . . Many of these offenses . . . are in the nature of neglect where the law requires care, or inaction where it imposes a duty. Many violations of such regulations result in no direct or immediate injury to person or property but merely create the danger or probability of it which the law seeks to minimize. [T]heir occurrence impairs the efficiency of controls deemed essential to the social order as presently constituted. In this respect, whatever the intent of the violator, the injury is the same, and the consequences are injurious or not according to fortuity. Hence, legislation applicable to such offenses, as a matter of policy, does not specify intent as a necessary element. The accused, if he does not will the violation, usually is in a position to prevent it with no more care than society might reasonably expect and no more exertion than it might reasonably exact from one who assumed his responsibilities. Also, penalties commonly are relatively small, and conviction does no grave damage to an offender's reputation. Under such considerations, courts have turned to construing statutes and regulations which make no mention of intent as dispensing with it and holding that the guilty act alone makes out the crime.[c] This has not, however, been without expressions of misgiving. . . .

After the turn of the Century . . . New York enacted numerous and novel regulations of tenement houses, sanctioned by money penalties. Landlords contended that a guilty intent was essential to establish a violation. Judge Cardozo wrote the answer:

> The defendant asks us to test the meaning of this statute by standards applicable to statutes that govern infamous crimes. The analogy, however, is deceptive. The element of conscious wrongdoing, the guilty mind accompanying the guilty act, is associated with a concept of crimes that are punished as infamous. Even there, it is not an invariable element. But in the prosecution of minor offenses there is a wider range of practice and of power. Prosecutions for petty penalties have always constituted in our law a class by themselves. That is true, though the prosecution is criminal in form.

Tenement House Dept. v. McDevitt, 109 N.E. 88, 90, (1915). . . .

---

c. But see Henry M. Hart, The Aims of the Criminal Law, 23 Law & Contemp. Probs. 401, 431 n.70 (1958):

> "In relation to offenses of a traditional type, the Court's opinion seems to be saying, we must be much slower to dispense with a basis for genuine blameworthiness in criminal intent than in relation to modern regulatory offenses. But it is precisely in the area of traditional crimes that the nature of the act itself commonly gives some warning that there may be a problem about its propriety and so affords, without more, at least some slight basis of condemnation for doing it. Thus, Morissette knew perfectly well that he was taking property which, at least up to the moment of caption, did not belong to him.
> "In the area of regulatory crimes, on the other hand, the moral quality of the act is often neutral; and on occasion, the offense may consist not of any act at all, but simply of an intrinsically innocent omission, so that there is no basis for moral condemnation whatever."—EDS.

Thus, for diverse but reconcilable reasons, state courts converged on the same result, discontinuing inquiry into intent in a limited class of offenses against such statutory regulations. . . .

Before long, similar questions growing out of federal legislation reached this Court. Its judgments were in harmony with this consensus of state judicial opinion, the existence of which may have led the Court to overlook the need for full exposition of their rationale in the context of federal law. . . .

Neither this Court nor, so far as we are aware, any other has undertaken to delineate a precise line or set forth comprehensive criteria for distinguishing between crimes that require a mental element and crimes that do not. We attempt no closed definition, for the law on the subject is neither settled nor static. The conclusion reached in the *Balint* and *Behrman* Cases has our approval and adherence for the circumstances to which it was there applied. A quite different question here is whether we will expand the doctrine of crimes without intent to include those charged here.

Stealing, larceny, and its variants and equivalents, were among the earliest offenses known to the law that existed before legislation; they are invasions of rights of property which stir a sense of insecurity in the whole community and arouse public demand for retribution, the penalty is high and, when a sufficient amount is involved, the infamy is that of a felony, which, says Maitland, is " . . . as bad a word as you can give to man or thing." State courts of last resort, on whom fall the heaviest burden of interpreting criminal law in this country, have consistently retained the requirement of intent in larceny-type offenses. . . .

Congress, therefore, omitted any express prescription of criminal intent from the enactment before us in the light of an unbroken course of judicial decision in all constituent states of the Union holding intent inherent in this class of offense, even when not expressed in a statute. Congressional silence as to mental elements in an Act merely adopting into federal statutory law a concept of crime already so well defined in common law and statutory interpretation by the states may warrant quite contrary inferences than the same silence in creating an offense new to general law, for whose definition the courts have no guidance except the Act. Because the offenses before this Court in the *Balint* and *Behrman* Cases were of this latter class, we cannot accept them as authority for eliminating intent from offenses incorporated from the common law. . . .

The Government asks us by a feat of construction radically to change the weights and balances in the scales of justice. The purpose and obvious effect of doing away with the requirement of a guilty intent is to ease the prosecution's path to conviction, to strip the defendant of such benefit as he derived at common law from innocence of evil purpose, and to circumscribe the freedom heretofore allowed juries. Such a manifest impairment of the immunities of the individual should not be extended to common-law crimes on judicial initiative. . . .

We hold that the mere omission from §641 of any mention of intent will not be construed as eliminating that element from the crimes denounced. . . .

Of course, the jury, considering Morissette's awareness that these casings were on government property, his failure to seek any permission for their removal and his self-interest as a witness, might have disbelieved his profession of innocent intent and concluded that his assertion of a belief that the casings were abandoned was an after-thought. Had the jury convicted on proper instructions it would be the end of the matter. But juries are not bound by what seems inescapable logic to judges. They might have concluded that the heaps of spent casings left in the hinterland to rust away presented an appearance of unwanted and abandoned junk, and that lack of any conscious deprivation of property or intentional injury was indicated by Morissette's good character, the openness of the taking, crushing and transporting of the casings, and the candor with which it was all admitted. They might have refused to brand Morissette as a thief. Had they done so, that too would have been the end of the matter.

Reversed.

STAPLES v. UNITED STATES

Supreme Court of the United States
511 U.S. 600 (1994)

JUSTICE THOMAS delivered the opinion of the Court.

[Defendant was charged with violating the National Firearms Act, which makes possession of an unregistered firearm punishable by up to ten years in prison. The rifle found in his possession met the Act's definition of a firearm—a weapon capable of automatically firing more than one shot with a single pull of the trigger. The rifle originally had a metal piece that precluded automatic firing, but at some time it had been filed down. Defendant testified that the rifle never fired automatically in his possession and that he didn't know it was capable of doing so. He sought an instruction that the government had to prove that he "knew that the gun would fire fully automatically." This was refused, and the jury convicted. On appeal, the Tenth Circuit court of appeals affirmed his conviction, and the Supreme Court granted certiorari.]

Whether or not §5861(d) requires proof that a defendant knew of the characteristics of his weapon that made it a "firearm" under the Act is a question of statutory construction. . . . Section 5861(d) is silent concerning the mens rea required for a violation. It states simply that "[i]t shall be unlawful for any person . . . to receive or possess a firearm which is not registered to him in the National Firearms Registration and Transfer Record." Nevertheless, silence on this point by itself does not necessarily suggest that Congress intended to dispense with a conventional mens rea element, which would require that the defendant know the facts that make his conduct illegal. . . . On the contrary, we must construe the statute in light of the background rules of the common law, in which the requirement of some mens rea for a crime is firmly embedded. . . .

Relying on the strength of the traditional rule, we have stated that offenses that require no mens rea generally are disfavored, and have suggested that some indication of congressional intent, express or implied, is required to dispense with mens rea as an element of a crime.

. . . The Government argues that Congress intended the Act to regulate and restrict the circulation of dangerous weapons. Consequently, in the Government's view, this case fits in a line of precedent concerning what we have termed "public welfare" or "regulatory" offenses, in which we have understood Congress to impose a form of strict criminal liability through statutes that do not require the defendant to know the facts that make his conduct illegal. In construing such statutes, we have inferred from silence that Congress did not intend to require proof of mens rea to establish an offense. . . .

Typically, our cases recognizing such offenses involve statutes that regulate potentially harmful or injurious items. . . . In such situations, we have reasoned that as long as a defendant knows that he is dealing with a dangerous device of a character that places him "in responsible relation to a public danger," [United States v.] Dotterweich, [320 U.S. 277] at 281, he should be alerted to the probability of strict regulation, and we have assumed that in such cases Congress intended to place the burden on the defendant to "ascertain at his peril whether [his conduct] comes within the inhibition of the statute." [United States v.] Balint, [258 U.S. 250] at 254.

[T]he Government argues that §5861(d) defines precisely the sort of regulatory offense described in *Balint*. In this view, all guns, whether or not they are statutory "firearms," are dangerous devices that put gun owners on notice that they must determine at their hazard whether their weapons come within the scope of the Act.

[T]he Government seeks support for its position from our decision in the United States v. Freed, 401 U.S. 601 (1971), which involved a prosecution for possession of unregistered grenades under §5861(d). The defendant knew that the items in his possession were grenades, and we concluded that §5861(d) did not require the Government to prove the defendant also knew that the grenades were unregistered.

[O]ur analysis in *Freed* likening the Act to the public welfare statute in *Balint* rested entirely on the assumption that the defendant knew that he was dealing with hand grenades—that is, that he knew he possessed a particularly dangerous type of weapon (one within the statutory definition of a "firearm"), possession of which was not entirely "innocent" in and of itself. . . .

In glossing over the distinction between grenades and guns, the Government ignores the particular care we have taken to avoid construing a statute to dispense with mens rea where doing so would "criminalize a broad range of apparently innocent conduct." Liparota [v. United States], 471 U.S. [419] at 426 (1985).

[T]here is a long tradition of widespread lawful gun ownership by private individuals in this country. Such a tradition did not apply to the possession of hand grenades in *Freed* or to the selling of dangerous drugs that we considered in *Balint.* . . . Roughly 50 per cent of American homes contain at least one firearm of some sort, and in the vast majority of States, buying a shotgun or rifle is a simple transaction that would not alert a person to regulation any more than would buying a car. . . .

We concur in the Fifth Circuit's conclusion [in an earlier case] on this point: ["It is unthinkable to us that Congress intended to subject such law-abiding, well-intentioned citizens to a possible ten-year term of imprisonment if . . . what they genuinely and reasonably believed was a conventional semiautomatic [weapon] turns out to have worn down into or been secretly modified to be a fully automatic weapon."] As we noted in *Morissette,* the "purpose and obvious effect of doing away with the requirement of a guilty intent is to ease the prosecution's path to conviction." We are reluctant to impute that purpose to Congress where, as here, it would mean easing the path to convicting persons whose conduct would not even alert them to the probability of strict regulation in the form of a statute such as §5861(d).

The potentially harsh penalty attached to violation of §5861(d)—up to 10 years' imprisonment—confirms our reading of the Act. . . . [P]unishing a violation as a felony is simply incompatible with the theory of the public welfare offense. In this view, absent a clear statement from Congress that mens rea is not required, we should not apply the public welfare offense rationale to interpret any statute defining a felony offense as dispensing with mens rea.

[Reversed and remanded.]

Justice Ginsburg, with whom Justice O'Connor joins, concurring in the judgment. . . .

The question before us is not whether knowledge of possession is required, but what level of knowledge suffices: (1) knowledge simply of possession of the object; (2) knowledge, in addition, that the object is a dangerous weapon; (3) knowledge, beyond dangerousness, of the characteristics that render the object subject to regulation, for example, awareness that the weapon is a machine gun. . . .

The Nation's legislators chose to place under a registration requirement only a very limited class of firearms, those they considered especially dangerous. The generally "dangerous" character of all guns, the Court therefore observes, did not suffice to give individuals in Staples' situation cause to inquire about the need for registration. Only the third reading . . . suits the purpose of the mens rea requirement—to shield people against punishment for apparently innocent activity. . . .

For these reasons, I conclude that conviction under §5861(d) requires proof that the defendant knew he possessed not simply a gun, but a machine gun. . . . I therefore concur in the Court's judgment.

PROBLEM

United States v. X-Citement Video, Inc., 513 U.S. 64 (1994), involved a conviction of defendant for violating the Protection of Children Against Sexual Exploitation Act of 1977, which provided:

> Any person who . . .
> (1) knowingly transports or ships in interstate or foreign commerce by any means including by computer or mails, any visual depiction, if . . .
> (A) the producing of such visual depiction involves the use of a minor engaging in sexually explicit conduct; and
> (B) such visual depiction is of such conduct;
> (2) knowingly receives, or distributes, any visual depiction that has been mailed, or has been shipped in interstate or foreign commerce, if . . .
> (A) the producing of such visual depiction involves the use of a minor engaging in sexually explicit conduct; and
> (B) such visual depiction is of such conduct; . . . shall be punished [by up to ten years' imprisonment].

Should a conviction under this statute require proof that the defendant knew that the person shown in the visual depiction was a minor, or only that he knew that the thing he shipped or received was a "visual depiction"? In other words, how far down the sentence does the word "knowingly" travel?

In an opinion by Chief Justice Rehnquist, the Court acknowledged that under "the most natural grammatical reading, . . . the term 'knowingly' would modify only the surrounding verbs [and] would not modify the elements of the minority of the performers, or the sexually explicit nature of the material." But, the Court continued, "we do not think this is the end of the matter, both because of anomalies which result from this construction, and because of the [presumption] that some form of scienter is to be implied in a criminal statute even if not expressed. . . . *Morissette*, reinforced by *Staples*, instructs that the presumption in favor of a scienter requirement should apply to each of the statutory elements that criminalize otherwise innocent conduct." (id. at 68-69, 72). The Court therefore held that the statute must be construed to require proof, not just that the defendant had shipped or received something he knew to be a visual depiction, but also that he knew that the depiction involved a minor engaged in sexually explicit acts. Justice Stevens, concurring, wrote (id. at 79-80) that "to give the statute its most grammatically correct reading . . . would be ridiculous."

Justice Scalia was not persuaded, and he did not think that the Court's result followed from cases like *Morissette* and *Staples*. He asserted first that interpreting the statute so that "knowingly" modified only the surrounding verbs was not simply the "most natural grammatical reading [but] *the only grammatical reading*," and he argued that the presumption in favor of a scienter requirement had never been applied "*when the plain text of the statute says otherwise*" (id. at 81) (emphasis in original).

Which is the better view? Which approach is more faithful to the principles underlying *Morissette* and *Staples*? Which approach better captures the proper role of courts in statutory interpretation? See Eric A. Johnson, Does Criminal Law Matter? Thoughts on *Dean v. United States* and *Flores-Figueroa v. United States*, 8 Ohio St. L.J. 123 (2010).

STATE v. GUMINGA

Supreme Court of Minnesota
395 N.W.2d 344 (1986)

YETKA, J. [In the course of an undercover operation, two investigators entered Lindee's Restaurant with a 17-year-old woman. All three ordered alcoholic beverages. The minor had never been in Lindee's before, and the waitress did not ask her age or request identification.] When the waitress returned with their orders, the minor paid for all the drinks. After confirming that the drink contained alcohol, the officers arrested the waitress for serving intoxicating liquor to a minor in violation of Minn. Stat. §340.73 (1984). The owner of Lindee's, defendant George Joseph Guminga, was subsequently charged with violation of section 340.73 pursuant to Minn. Stat. §340.941 (1984), which imposes vicarious criminal liability on an employer whose employee serves intoxicating liquor to a minor. The state does not contend that Guminga was aware of or ratified the waitress's actions.

Guminga moved to dismiss the charges on the ground that section 340.941 violates the due process clauses of the federal and state constitutions. . . . After holding a hearing on August 28, 1985, the court denied the motion to dismiss. . . .

The certified question of law before this court is as follows:

> Whether Minn. Stat. §340.941, on its face, violates the defendant's right to due process of law under the Fourteenth Amendment to the United States Constitution and analogous provisions of the Constitution of the State of Minnesota.

We find that the statute in question does violate the due process clauses of the Minnesota and the United States Constitutions and thus answer the question in the affirmative. . . .

Minn. Stat. §340.73 (1984) provides criminal penalties [gross misdemeanor] for any person selling intoxicating liquor to a minor. . . . Minn. Stat. §340.941 (1984) imposes vicarious criminal liability on the employer for an employee's violation of section 340.73. . . . Under Minn. Stat. §609.03 (1984), a defendant who commits a gross misdemeanor may be sentenced to "imprisonment for not more than one year or to payment of a fine of not more than $3,000 or both." In addition, a defendant convicted under section 340.941 may, at the discretion of the licensing authority, have its license suspended, revoked or be unable to obtain a new license. . . .

Since this is not an appeal from a conviction, we do not yet know whether, if found guilty, Guminga would be subjected to imprisonment, a suspended sentence, or a fine. Even if there is no prison sentence imposed, under the new sentencing guidelines, a gross misdemeanor conviction will affect his criminal history score were he to be convicted of a felony in the future. ...

We find that criminal penalties based on vicarious liability under Minn. Stat. §340.941 are a violation of substantive due process and that only civil penalties would be constitutional. A due process analysis of a statute involves a balancing of the public interest protected against the intrusion on personal liberty while taking into account any alternative means by which to achieve the same end. ... Section 340.941 serves the public interest by providing additional deterrence to violation of the liquor laws. The private interests affected, however, include liberty, damage to reputation and other future disabilities arising from criminal prosecution for an act which Guminga did not commit or ratify. Not only could Guminga be given a prison sentence or a suspended sentence, but, in the more likely event that he receives only a fine, his liberty could be affected by a longer presumptive sentence in a possible future felony conviction. Such an intrusion on personal liberty is not justified by the public interest protected, especially when there are alternative means by which to achieve the same end, such as civil fines or license suspension, which do not entail the legal and social ramifications of a criminal conviction. See Model Penal Code §1.04 comment (b)(1985).[3] ...

The dissent argues that vicarious liability is necessary as a deterrent so that an owner will impress upon employees that they should not sell to minors. However, it does not distinguish between an employer who vigorously lectures his employees and one who does not. According to the dissent, each would be equally guilty. We believe it is a deterrent enough that the employee who sells to the minor can be charged under the statute and that the business is subject to fines or suspension or revocation of license. ...

We find that, in Minnesota, no one can be convicted of a crime punishable by imprisonment for an act he did not commit, did not have knowledge of, or give expressed or implied consent to the commission thereof.

The certified question is thus answered in the affirmative. ...

KELLEY, J. (dissenting): [I]mposition of vicarious liability and the threat of a short jail, not prison, sentence is reasonably related to the legislative purpose:

---

3. We agree with the reasoning of the Georgia Supreme Court in Davis v. City of Peachtree City, 251 Ga. 219, 304 S.E.2d 701 (1983). *Davis* involved the criminal conviction of the president of a chain of convenience stores whose employee had sold liquor to a minor. The defendant was prosecuted under a city ordinance holding licensees responsible for the acts of their employees and received a $300 fine and a 60-day suspended sentence. The Georgia Supreme Court reversed the conviction: ...

> Although some commentators and courts have found that vicarious criminal liability does not violate due process in misdemeanor cases which involve as punishment only a slight fine and not imprisonment, we decline to so hold. The damage done to an individual's good name and the peril imposed on an individual's future are sufficient reasons to shift the balance in favor of the individual. The imposition of such a burden on an employer "cannot rest on so frail a reed as whether his employee will commit a mistake in judgment," but instead can be justified only by the appropriate prosecuting officials proving some sort of culpability or knowledge by the employer.

enforcement of laws prohibiting liquor sales to minors. Without the deterrent of possible personal criminal responsibility and a sentence, the legislature could have rationally concluded that liquor establishment owners will be less likely to impress upon employees the need to require identification of age before serving liquor. Limiting punishment to a fine allows bar owners to view their liability for violations as nothing more than an expense of doing business. The gravity of the problems associated with minors who consume alcoholic beverages justifies the importance by the legislature of harsher punishment on those who help contribute to those problems. The state has the right to impose limited criminal vicarious liability on bar proprietors as a reasonable exchange for the state-granted privilege of a liquor license. . . .

NOTES ON VICARIOUS LIABILITY

1. Vicarious liability of employers. As we shall see in Chapter 7.C, infra, corporations and other organizations are routinely held criminally liable for crimes committed by their employees within the scope of their employment. This type of *entity liability*, though controversial, is qualitatively different and far less problematic than the attempt (illustrated by *Guminga*) to impose criminal liability on the employer *as an individual*. When possible sanctions are limited to fines, courts generally uphold convictions of individuals for the illegal conduct of their employees, even without proof of employer fault. See Annot., 89 A.L.R.3d 1256 §§15-18 (2005). But as *Guminga* indicates, there is disagreement about offenses that carry a sanction of imprisonment. Compare *Guminga* with State v. Beaudry, 123 Wis. 2d 40, 365 N.W.2d 593 (1985). The defendant and her husband were sole shareholders of a corporation with a license to sell alcohol at the Village Green Tavern. The defendant was the designated agent for the corporate licensee. One night the tavern manager violated the terms of the license by remaining open past closing time, against the instructions of the absent owners, for the sole purpose of entertaining his own friends. Nonetheless, the defendant was convicted on the basis of vicarious liability. The court upheld the conviction, even though the statute authorized a 90-day jail sentence, on the ground that the penalty imposed was solely a $200 fine.

2. Vicarious liability of parents. A number of jurisdictions seek to hold parents vicariously liable for crimes committed by their minor children. Is vicarious criminal liability more problematic in the case of a parent than in the case of an employer? If not, should vicarious liability be permitted in both situations or in neither? State v. Akers, 400 A.2d 38 (N.H. 1979) involved a statute imposing criminal liability on parents of minor children who drive off-highway vehicles on public highways. No evidence of parental culpability was required. The court struck down the statute, stating (id. at 40):

> Without passing upon the validity of statutes that might seek to impose vicarious criminal liability on the part of an employer for acts of his employees, we

have no hesitancy in holding that any attempt to impose such liability on parents simply because they occupy the status of parents, without more, offends the due process clause of our State constitution.

Questions: On what principle can the court condemn vicarious parental liability "without passing upon" vicarious employer liability? What is the distinction between the two situations?

Other parental responsibility laws have been enacted throughout the country. See Jennifer M. Collins, Ethan J. Lieb & Dan Markel, Punishing Family Status, 88 B.U. L. Rev. 1327, 1338-1343 (2008). One of the broadest, in Oregon, imposes misdemeanor liability on the parents of any juvenile who violates a curfew law or commits any crime. Ore. Rev. Stat. Ann. 163.577(1) (2011). The statute requires no showing that the parent knew about the violation or contributed to it. The policy justification for such statutes is ostensibly straightforward: controlling juvenile crime by giving parents a strong incentive to exercise oversight. Are there countervailing concerns? One scholar, after examining police and prosecutorial practices in Oregon, concludes that such laws can lead to overly restrictive parenting and are likely to be "enforced disproportionately against poor, single parents." Leslie Joan Harris, An Empirical Study of Parental Responsibility Laws, 2006 Utah L. Rev. 5, 11.

Apart from policy concerns, do such statutes violate basic principles of constitutional law and just punishment? Consider City of Maple Heights v. Ephraim, 898 N.E.2d 974 (Ohio App. 2008). A juvenile was involved in "fighting" and a variety of offenses resulting from his flight to evade arrest. His mother was then charged with violating a municipal ordinance that imposes criminal penalties on the parent of any minor who commits any felony or misdemeanor. The appellate court stuck down the ordinance, stating (id. at 981):

> Strict liability may . . . be imposed when the harm does not consist of a wrongful act, but of a failure to act at all. . . . In such cases the omission to act constitutes the actus reus. Vicarious liability, however, imputes the acts of one person to another. [Such liability] "is a substantial departure from the ordinary rule that a principal is not answerable criminally for the acts of his agent without the principal's authorization, consent or knowledge . . ." [because] guilt must be individual. . . .

Most parental responsibility laws are technically less problematic because they impose liability for "contributing to delinquency" or "failure to supervise." This framework means that the parent is not convicted for the child's delinquent act as such but rather for the parents' own actus reus—the omission of failing to supervise. Nonetheless, in practice these laws often treat failure to supervise as a matter that is established automatically by the child's commission of a delinquent act. Is there a moral or constitutional problem here? See James Herbie Difonzi, Parental Responsibility for Juvenile Crime, 80 Or. L. Rev. 1 (2001).

NOTES ON THE INVOLUNTARY ACT DEFENSE
TO A STRICT LIABILITY CRIME

If vicarious liability offends a basic principle of criminal responsibility, should a similar objection apply when liability is based on an *omission*, such as an alleged failure to supervise? What if liability is based on an allegedly *involuntary* act? Consider these problems:

1. In State v. Baker, 571 P.2d 65 (Kan. 1977), a defendant convicted of speeding sought to introduce evidence that the cruise control on his car had become stuck in the "accelerate' position, that he had unsuccessfully tried to deactivate it, and that subsequent examination confirmed that the device was defective. Upholding the conviction, the court ruled that the evidence was properly excluded. Mens rea was unnecessary (speeding was a strict liability offense), and with respect to the defendant's argument that he had not committed a voluntary act, the court responded (id. at 67-69):

> [I]f defendant were able to establish that his act of speeding was the result of an unforeseen occurrence or circumstance, which was not caused by him and which he could not prevent, ... such would constitute a valid defense. ... But, ... a malfunction of a device attached to the motor vehicle operated by the defendant over which he had or should have had absolute control ... does not suggest that the operation of the motor vehicle on the day of his arrest was anything but a voluntary act on his part, nor that anyone other than himself activated the cruise control. [U]nexpected brake failure ... differ[s] significantly from the malfunction of a cruise control device to which the driver has voluntarily delegated partial control of that automobile. [D]efendant assumed the full operation of his motor vehicle and when he did so and activated the cruise control attached to that automobile, he clearly was the agent in causing the act of speeding. ...

Questions: What is the difference between brakes that fail and a cruise control device that fails? Should a driver have an involuntary act defense in both situations? In neither?

Suppose that a child, in a show of affection, grabs the driver's arm long enough to make the car swerve into the opposing lane of traffic, in violation of the traffic laws. Does the driver have an involuntary act defense, because he didn't choose to steer the car into the opposing lane, or is he ineligible for such a defense because he was voluntarily driving?

2. In Barnfather v. London Borough, [2003] EWHC 418 (admin), a mother was convicted of a crime, for failing to assure that her 13-year-old child attended school regularly. The court held that the statute imposed strict liability and denied her the opportunity to prove that she had been doing her best to ensure that her child attended school. Is the result sound? Did the court eliminate only the mens rea, or did it also eliminate the normal requirement of a voluntary act?

3. Why should the absence of a voluntary act be a defense to a strict liability offense? See M. Budd & J. Lynch, Voluntariness, Causation and Strict Liability, [1978] Crim. L. Rev. 74, 75 n.6:

> It is strange . . . for the law to acquit those in a state of automatism of offences of strict liability but to convict those acting voluntarily. . . . It must certainly be wrong for the law to treat differently those who are both equally free of moral blame and whose conviction would be equally relevant to advancing the purposes of strict liability.

For discussion of this question, see Douglas Husak & Brian P. McLaughlin, Time Frames, Voluntary Acts, and Strict Liability, 12 Law & Phil. 95 (1993); Larry Alexander, Reconsidering the Relationship Among Voluntary Acts, Strict Liability, and Negligence in Criminal Law, in Ellen Frankel Paul, Fred D. Miller Jr. & Jeffrey Paul eds., Crime, Culpability, and Remedy 84 (1990).

REGINA v. CITY OF SAULT STE. MARIE

Supreme Court of Canada
85 D.L.R.3d 161 (1978)

DICKSON, J. . . . Various arguments are advanced in justification of absolute liability in public welfare offences. Two predominate. Firstly, it is argued that the protection of social interests requires a high standard of care and attention on the part of those who follow certain pursuits and such persons are more likely to be stimulated to maintain those standards if they know that ignorance or mistake will not excuse them. The removal of any possible loophole acts, it is said, is an incentive to take precautionary measures beyond what would otherwise be taken. . . . The second main argument is one based on administrative efficiency. Having regard to both the difficulty of proving mental culpability and the number of petty cases which daily come before the Courts, proof of fault is just too great a burden in time and money to place upon the prosecution. . . . In short, absolute liability, it is contended, is the most efficient and effective way of ensuring compliance with minor regulatory legislation and the social ends to be achieved are of such importance as to override the unfortunate by-product of punishing those who may be free of moral turpitude. In further justification, it is urged that slight penalties are usually imposed and that conviction for breach of a public welfare offence does not carry the stigma associated with conviction for a criminal offense.

Arguments of greater force are advanced against absolute liability. The most telling is that it violates fundamental principles of penal liability. It also rests upon assumptions which have not been, and cannot be, empirically established. There is no evidence that a higher standard of care results from absolute liability. If a person is already taking every reasonable precautionary measure, is he likely to take additional measures, knowing that however much care he takes, it will not serve as a defence in the event of breach? If he has exercised care and skill, will conviction have a deterrent effect upon him or others? Will the injustice of conviction lead to cynicism and disrespect for the law, on his part and on the part of others? . . . The argument that no stigma attaches does not withstand analysis, for the accused will have suffered loss of time, legal costs, exposure to the processes of the criminal law at trial and, however one may downplay it, the opprobrium of conviction. It is not sufficient to say that the public interest is engaged. . . . In serious crimes, the public interest is [also] involved and [nevertheless] mens rea must be proven. . . .

The unfortunate tendency in many past cases has been to see the choice as between two stark alternatives: (i) full mens rea; or (ii) absolute liability. . . . There [is], however, . . . a middle position, fulfilling the goals of public welfare offences while still not punishing the entirely blameless. [This approach] holds that where an offence does not require full mens rea, it is nevertheless a good defence for the defendant to prove that he was not negligent. [That] doctrine proceeds on the assumption that the defendant could have avoided the prima facie offence through the exercise of reasonable care and he is given the opportunity of establishing, if he can, that he did in fact exercise such care. . . . This burden falls upon the defendant as he is the only one who will generally have the means of proof. This would not seem unfair as the alternative is absolute liability which denies an accused any defence whatsoever. While the prosecution must prove beyond a reasonable doubt that the defendant committed the prohibited act, the defendant must only establish on the balance of probabilities that he has a defence of reasonable care.

I conclude . . . that there are compelling grounds for the recognition of three categories of offences rather than the traditional two:

1. Offences in which mens rea, consisting of some positive state of mind such as intent, knowledge, or recklessness, must be proved by the prosecution. . . .

2. Offences in which there is no necessity for the prosecution to prove the existence of mens rea; the doing of the prohibited act prima facie imports the offence, leaving it open to the accused to avoid liability by proving that he took all reasonable care. . . .

3. Offences of absolute liability where it is not open to the accused to exculpate himself by showing that he was free of fault.

Offences which are criminal in the true sense fall in the first category. Public welfare offences would, prima facie, be in the second category. . . . An offence of this type would fall in the first category only if such words as "wilfully," "with intent," "knowingly," or "intentionally" are contained in the statutory provision creating the offence. . . . Offences of absolute liability would be those in respect of which the Legislature had made it clear that guilt would follow proof merely of the proscribed act. The over-all regulatory pattern adopted by the Legislature, the subject-matter of the legislation, the importance of the penalty, and the precision of the language used will be primary considerations in determining whether the offence falls into the third category.

NOTES

1. In a subsequent decision, the Canadian Supreme Court held absolute liability unconstitutional, finding that imprisonment for an absolute liability offense is a deprivation of liberty not "in accordance with the precepts of fundamental justice" guaranteed by Section 7 of the Canadian Charter of Rights and Freedoms. Reference Re Section 94(2) of the Motor Vehicle Act, 23 C.C.C.3d 289 (1985). Its reasons were essentially those it had given in *Sault Ste. Marie.*

The Canadian court was obliged to confront the qualification in Section 1 of the Charter that makes the protected freedoms subject to "such reasonable limits prescribed by law as can be demonstrably justified in a free and democratic society." It ruled that administrative expediency could justify imprisonment for absolute liability "only in cases arising out of exceptional conditions, such as natural disasters, the outbreak of war, epidemics and the like." (Id. at 313.) The court continues to reaffirm its view that offenses involving imprisonment require the prosecution to prove mens rea, and that public welfare offenses not involving imprisonment presumptively fall into the middle category (where the accused is permitted to raise due care as an affirmative defense) unless a legislative intent to preclude such a defense is clearly expressed. City of Lévis v. Tétreault, 2006 S.C.C. 12.

2. The middle approach discussed in *Sault Ste. Marie* has been taken up by at least one American court. United States v. United States District Court (Kantor), 858 F.2d 534 (9th Cir. 1988). See Laurie L. Levenson, Good Faith Defenses: Reshaping Strict Liability Crimes, 78 Cornell L. Rev. 401 (1993), for a proposal to extend to all strict liability offenses an affirmative defense of absence of blameworthy conduct.

3. In 2002, Florida amended its drug control statutes to provide that "knowledge of the illicit nature of a controlled substance is not an element of any offense under this chapter"; lack of such knowledge was made an affirmative defense on which the defendant would bear the burden of proof. Fla. Stat. §893.101 (2002). As a result, a defendant convicted of delivering a container that proved to hold cocaine would face a sentence (depending on his criminal history) of either 15 years, 30 years, or life imprisonment, regardless of whether the prosecution could prove that he knew or should have known the nature of the contents. After Shelton was convicted under this statute and sentenced to 18 years in prison, a federal court held the statute unconstitutional. Shelton v. Sec'y, Dept. of Corrections, 2011 U.S. Dist. LEXIS 86898 (M.D. Fla. 2011). The court said (id. at *24, *30-31, *39):

> No strict liability statute carrying penalties of [this] magnitude . . . has ever been upheld under federal law. . . . Where laws proscribe conduct that is neither inherently dangerous nor likely to be regulated, the Supreme Court has consistently either invalidated them or construed them to require proof of *mens rea* in order to avoid criminalizing "a broad range of apparently innocent conduct." . . .

> To state the obvious, there is a long tradition throughout human existence of lawful delivery and transfer of containers that might contain substances . . . : carrying luggage on and off of public transportation; carrying bags in and out of stores and buildings; carrying book bags and purses in schools and places of business . . . —the list extends *ad infinitum.* Under Florida's statute, that conduct is rendered immediately criminal if it turns out that the substance is a controlled substance, without regard to the deliverer's knowledge or intent.

In response to the argument that the statute's constitutionality was saved by allowing a defendant to raise lack of knowledge as an affirmative defense, the court stated (id. at *43-*49):

> [T]he State . . . cannot shift the burden of proof to a Defendant on an essential element of an offense. [To do so would] dispense with the fundamental precept underlying the American system of justice—the "presumption of innocence." . . . Florida's statute is not a "drug dealer beware" statute but a "citizen beware statute." Consider the student in whose book bag a classmate hastily stashes his drugs to avoid imminent detection. The bag is then given to another for safekeeping. Caught in the act, the hapless victim is guilty based upon the only two elements of the statute: delivery . . . and the illicit nature of the substance. [At trial] he is presumed guilty because he is in fact guilty of the two elements. He must then prove his innocence. . . .
>
> Because [the statute] imposes harsh penalties, gravely besmirches an individual's reputation, and regulates and punishes otherwise innocuous conduct without proof of knowledge or other criminal intent, . . . it violates the due process clause and . . . is unconstitutional on its face.

NOTES ON THE ACADEMIC DEBATE

The great majority of academic writing has opposed absolute liability.[17] In recent years, however, some academics have defended it.[18] For perspectives on the issues, see A.P. Simester ed., Appraising Strict Liability (2005). Consider the following comments:

Arthur Goodhart, Possession of Drugs and Absolute Liability, 84 L.Q. Rev. 382, 385-386 (1968): [T]here are certain offences that have a serious effect on the public interest but which it is difficult to prove under the usual procedure. [There is a] long-established saying that "it is better that ten guilty men should escape than that one innocent man should be convicted." . . . On the other hand . . . in certain circumstances . . . the future harm that the ten guilty men who have been acquitted may do, either by repeating their own offences or by encouraging others by showing how easy it is to avoid conviction, far

---

17. E.g., Herbert Packer, The Limits of the Criminal Sanction 121-131 (1968); Henry M. Hart, The Aims of the Criminal Law, 23 Law & Contemp. Probs. 401, 422-425 (1958).

18. E.g., James Brady, Strict Liability Offenses: A Justification, 8 Crim. L. Bull. 217 (1972); Steven Nemerson, Criminal Liability Without Fault: A Philosophical Perspective, 75 Colum. L. Rev. 1517 (1975). Cf. Kenneth W. Simons, When Is Strict Criminal Liability Just? 87 J. Crim. L. & Criminology 1075 (1997).

exceeds any injury that the innocent man can suffer by his conviction. The question then becomes: Is it better that ten young persons should be tempted to become drug addicts than that one innocent man should be convicted of being in possession of unauthorized drugs?

Mark Kelman, Strict Liability: An Unorthodox View, in Encyclopedia of Crime and Justice 1512, 1516-1517 (1983)*: H.L.A. Hart's argument that the defendant convicted of a strict-liability offense "could not have helped" committing the crime depends on the use of a rationally indefensible narrow time frame in focusing on the defendant's conduct. [I]f one looks only at the precise *moment* at which harm is consummated, the strictly liable actor may seem powerless to avoid criminality, but it is invariably the case that the actor could have avoided liability by taking earlier steps which were hardly impossible. . . .

It is . . . only by constructing the underlying material in the strict-liability situations with a very narrow time frame that the distinction between liability predicated on negligence, and strict liability, maintains its practical import in many critical situations.

An example is the familiar problem of "reasonable" (non-negligent) mistakes as to the victim's age in the statutory rape setting. Is one's view of a "reasonable" belief to be ascertained solely by reference to perceptions available to the defendant during the purportedly illegal seduction (she "*looked*" sixteen or "she told me she was sixteen"), or does one require that some checks prior to seduction be taken, such as checking birth certificates or asking parents? Of course, if one is hostile to statutory rape laws in general, it is perfectly reasonable to negate them by defining negligent perceptions in terms of the girl's physical appearance—that is, in terms of judgments which can be made at the narrow time-framed moment of the allegedly criminal incident. But it is hardly conceivable that a defendant ought to attract serious sympathy as someone unable to avoid crime when he has certainly had the opportunity to check on the legal appropriateness of his companion as an object of sexual desire.[a]

Phillip Johnson, Strict Liability: The Prevalent View, in Encyclopedia of Crime and Justice 1518, 1520-1521 (1983)*: The objection to strict liability is not that it punishes people who are literally helpless to avoid committing the act, because it is obvious that they could have avoided any possibility of liability by not going into business in the first place. The point is that selling meat or managing a factory is a productive activity which the law means to

---

* From Dressler (editor). Encyclopedia of Crime & Justice, 2E. © 2001 Gale, a part of Cengage Learning, Inc. Reproduced by permission. www.cengage.com/permissions.

a. Does this argument imply that there is no practical difference between a strict liability standard with a narrow time frame and a negligence standard with an expanded time frame? Will the precautions that an actor failed to take at earlier points in time necessarily involve "a gross deviation from the standard of care that a reasonable person would observe" (MPC §2.02(2)(d))? Note that by using a broad time frame, Professor Kelman is able to argue, in effect, that the defendant in his example *was* negligent. But will the defendant have the same opportunity to respond to such an argument if the applicable standard is strict liability rather than negligence? Will the jury's role be the same?—EDS.

encourage, not discourage, and we should not punish people who have taken all reasonable steps to comply with the law. Where strict liability is present in the traditional criminal law, as in the felony-murder doctrine or in the rule that mistake of age is no defense to statutory rape, the defendant's underlying conduct (robbery or fornication) is deemed wrongful or socially undesirable in itself. Unless we regard business activity as similarly inherently wrongful, holding business managers up to strict liability is unjustifiable even though they have voluntarily assumed their positions of employment.

Stephen J. Schulhofer, Harm and Punishment: A Critique of Emphasis on the Results of Conduct in the Criminal Law, 122 U. Pa. L. Rev. 1497, 1586-1587 (1974): [Some argue that strict liability can reduce injuries because those who fear liability can avoid activities subject to this stringent form of regulation. Although those] who continue to engage in the activity may be those who believe they can be careful enough, . . . there is no guarantee that these will be the ones who are in fact the most careful. [T]hose who are most confident of their ability to avoid causing harm may be just the ones who are most likely to be . . . careless.[290] Thus, the strict liability crime may exclude a few accident-prone people [but may] fail to select out most of those about whom the law should be most concerned. At the same time, . . . those who are careful and make provision for risks may be the most likely to take the sensible precaution of not engaging in this activity at all. [Thus], the dynamic effect [of strict liability] could be to increase the total harm caused by increasing the proportion of those engaged in the activity who are relatively careless.

Douglas Husak, Strict Liability, Justice, and Proportionality, in A.P. Simester ed., Appraising Strict Liability 81, 100 (2005): [T]he injustice [of strict liability] is a function of the severity of the punishment imposed . . . and is not due to the existence of the strict liability . . . statute itself. Moreover, the very same objections may apply to statutes that do *not* impose formal strict liability, so the repeal of [strict liability] offenses provides no assurance that the injustice will be reduced. No one needs to resort to formal strict liability in order to inflict draconian punishments that disregard principles of proportionality.

Model Penal Code and Commentaries, Comment to §2.05 at 282-283 (1985): This section makes a frontal attack on absolute or strict liability in the penal law, whenever . . . a sentence of probation or imprisonment may be imposed. The method used is not to abrogate strict liability completely, but to provide that when conviction rests upon that basis the grade of the offense is reduced to a violation, which is not a "crime" and under Sections 1.04(5) and 6.02(4) may result in no sentence other than a fine, or a fine and forfeiture or other authorized civil penalty.

---

290. This confidence may be one reason why such people are dangerous; if they were concerned about the danger, they would not be inadvertent so often. . . .

This position is affirmed not only with respect to offenses defined by the penal code; it is superimposed on the entire corpus of the law so far as penal sanctions are involved. Since most strict liability offenses involve special regulatory legislation, normally found in titles of a code other than the criminal title, this superimposition is essential if the principle of no criminality, probation or imprisonment for strict liability offenses is to be made effective.

... It has been argued, and the argument undoubtedly will be repeated, that strict liability is necessary for enforcement in a number of the areas where it obtains. But if practical enforcement precludes litigation of the culpability of alleged deviation from legal requirements, the enforcers cannot rightly demand the use of penal sanctions for the purpose. Crime does and should mean condemnation and no court should have to pass that judgment unless it can declare that the defendant's act was culpable. This is too fundamental to be compromised. The law goes far enough if it permits the imposition of a monetary penalty in cases where strict liability has been imposed.

e. Mistake of Law

INTRODUCTORY NOTE

One legal doctrine that is especially familiar to non-lawyers is the rule that "ignorance of the law is no excuse." Yet, as we shall see, this supposedly well-known "rule" turns out to be murky, misleading, and sometimes simply false. Several distinct problems are presented. First, mistakes of law sometimes arise because a person is aware of a law but misinterprets its meaning; in other instances, the individual does not know that any such law exists at all. Second, misinterpretation or complete ignorance may relate to the criminal prohibition itself, or it may concern some part of the vast corpus of laws that determine contractual duties, ownership rights in property, regulatory obligations, and so forth. Third, a mistake about the law can arise in the same way as a mistake of fact; when (and *why*) should a mistake of law (even a highly reasonable one) be considered irrelevant if good-faith mistakes of fact normally excuse even when they are highly *un*reasonable. Finally, if a mistake of law is of the type that normally does not excuse, can the defendant nonetheless claim a defense when his misinterpretation is based on an *official* document or *official* advice that turns out to be incorrect?

The case that follows appears to present a single question, but in fact it involves most of the distinct problems just mentioned. The defendant placed his hopes primarily on the last and most limited type of argument—that his mistake (though *normally* irrelevant) should nonetheless excuse because the state penal code recognized a narrow defense for mistakes resulting from reliance on an official source. Before focusing on that issue, however, it will be worth pausing to consider whether the defendant should have a valid excuse even in the absence of this special penal code provision. In light of the principles of culpability considered up to this point, shouldn't the defendant's mistake give him a mens rea defense even without this particular type of reliance? And if not, then consider whether the special statutory defense should change the result.

PEOPLE v. MARRERO

New York Court of Appeals
69 N.Y.2d 382, 507 N.E.2d 1068 (1987)

[Defendant, a corrections officer at a federal prison in Connecticut, was arrested in a Manhattan social club for unlicensed possession of a loaded .38 caliber pistol, in violation of N.Y. Penal Law §265.02.[a] When arrested, he protested that as a federal corrections officer, he was not subject to §265.02. The statutory framework was complex. Section 265.02 made it a crime for any person to possess a loaded firearm, subject to exemptions stated in §265.20. That provision exempted "peace officers as defined in . . . section 1.20 of the criminal procedure law [CPL]," and CPL §1.20, referring in turn to a definition in CPL §2.10, defined "peace officer" to include "correction officers of any state correction facility or of any penal correctional institution." Marrero was nonetheless charged with violating §265.02. His pretrial motion to dismiss the indictment was granted on the ground that he was a peace officer within the meaning of the statutes. The Appellate Division reinstated the indictment, holding, by a 3–2 vote, that the defendant was not a "peace officer" within the meaning of CPL §§1.20, 2.10. He was then convicted at a trial where the judge refused to instruct the jury to acquit if it found that Marrero reasonably believed he qualified for the statutory exemption. The defendant appealed.]

BELLACOSA, J. . . . The central issue is whether defendant's personal misreading or misunderstanding of a statute may excuse criminal conduct in the circumstances of this case.

The common-law rule on mistake of law was clearly articulated in *Gardner v. People*, (62 N.Y. 299). In *Gardner*, the defendants misread a statute and mistakenly believed that their conduct was legal. The court insisted, however, that the "mistake of law" did not relieve the defendants of criminal liability. . . . This is to be contrasted with People v. Weiss, 276 N.Y. 384, 12 N.E.2d 514 [1938,] where, in a kidnapping case, the trial court precluded testimony that the defendants acted with the honest belief that seizing and confining the [victim] was done with "authority of law." We held it was error to exclude such testimony since a good-faith belief in the legality of the conduct would negate an express and necessary element of the crime of kidnapping, i.e., intent, without authority of law, to confine or imprison another.[b]

---

a. At the time of Marrero's offense, this provision read as follows: "A person is guilty of criminal possession of a weapon in the third degree [a class D felony] when . . . [h]e possesses any loaded firearm. . . ." N.Y. Penal Law §265.02 (McKinney 1983).—EDS.

b. In *Weiss*, the defendants were charged with kidnapping a person suspected of murdering the Lindbergh child. Under the statutory definition, kidnapping was committed when a person "willfully . . . [s]eizes, confines, inveigles, or kidnaps another, with intent to cause him, without authority

[T]he instant case, of course, falls within the *Gardner* rationale because the weapons possession statute violated by this defendant imposes liability independent of one's intent [to violate the law].

The desirability of the *Gardner*-type outcome . . . is underscored by Justice Holmes' statement: "It is no doubt true that there are many cases in which the criminal could not have known that he was breaking the law, but to admit the excuse at all would be to encourage ignorance where the lawmaker has determined to make men know and obey, and justice to the individual is rightly outweighed by the larger interests on the other side of the scales" (Holmes, The Common Law, at 48 [1881]).

The revisors of New York's Penal Law intended no fundamental departure from this common-law rule in Penal Law §15.20, which provides in pertinent part:

> 2. A person is not relieved of criminal liability for conduct because he engaged in such conduct under a mistaken belief that it does not, as a matter of law, constitute an offense, unless such mistaken belief is founded upon an official statement of the law contained in (a) a statute or other enactment . . . (d) an interpretation of the statute or law relating to the offense, officially made or issued by a public servant, agency, or body legally charged or empowered with the responsibility or privilege of administering, enforcing or interpreting such statute or law.

The defendant claims as a first prong of his defense that he is entitled to raise the defense of mistake of law under section 15.20(2)(a) because his mistaken belief that his conduct was legal was founded upon an official statement of the law contained in the statute itself. Defendant argues that his mistaken interpretation of the statute was reasonable in view of the alleged ambiguous wording of the peace officer exemption statute, and that his "reasonable" interpretation of an "official statement" is enough to satisfy the requirements of subdivision (2)(a). . . .

The prosecution . . . counters defendant's argument by asserting that one cannot claim the protection of mistake of law under section 15.20(2)(a) simply by misconstruing the meaning of a statute but must instead establish that the statute relied on actually permitted the conduct in question and was only later found to be erroneous. To buttress that argument, the People analogize New York's official statement defense to the approach taken by the Model Penal Code (MPC). Section 2.04 of the MPC provides:

> (3) A belief that conduct does not legally constitute an offense is a defense to a prosecution for that offense based upon such conduct when . . . (b) he acts in reasonable reliance upon an official statement of the law, *afterward*

---

of law, to be confined or imprisoned, . . . against his will." The defendants were precluded from introducing testimony to show that they believed that a law enforcement officer had authorized them to seize the murder suspect. The Court of Appeals reversed their conviction, on the ground that such belief would show that defendants lacked the required intent to confine the victim "without authority of law."—Eds.

determined to be invalid or erroneous, contained in (i) a statute or other enactment (emphasis added).[c]

Although the drafters of the New York statute did not adopt the precise language of the Model Penal Code provision with the emphasized clause, it is evident and has long been believed that the Legislature intended the New York statute to be similarly construed. . . .

It was early recognized that the "official statement" mistake of law defense was a statutory protection against prosecution based on reliance on a statute that did *in fact* authorize certain conduct. . . . While providing a narrow escape hatch, the idea was simultaneously to encourage the public to read and rely on official statements of the law, not to have individuals conveniently and personally question the validity and interpretation of the law and act on that basis. If later the statute was invalidated, one who mistakenly acted in reliance on the authorizing statute would be relieved of criminal liability. That makes sense and is fair. To go further does not make sense and would create a legal chaos. . . . [In the case before us, the underlying statute never *in fact* authorized the defendant's conduct; the defendant only thought [it did].]

[W]hile our construction of Penal Law §15.20 provides for narrow application of the mistake of law defense, it does not, as the dissenters contend, "rule out *any* defense based on mistake of law." To the contrary, mistake of law is a viable exemption in those instances where an individual . . . relies on the validity of [a] law and, later, it is determined that there was a *mistake in the law itself.* [W]here the government has affirmatively, albeit unintentionally, misled an individual as to what may or may not be legally permissible conduct, the individual should not be punished as a result. [However,] where, as here, the government is not responsible for the error (for there is none except in the defendant's own mind), mistake of law should not be available as an excuse. . . . Any broader view fosters lawlessness.

. . . If defendant's argument were accepted, the exception would swallow the rule. Mistakes about the law would be encouraged, rather than respect for and adherence to law. There would be an infinite number of mistake of law defenses which could be devised from a good-faith, perhaps reasonable but mistaken, interpretation of criminal statutes, many of which are concededly complex. Even more troublesome are the opportunities for wrongminded individuals to contrive in bad faith solely to get an exculpatory notion before the jury. These are . . . the realistic and practical consequences were the dissenters' views to prevail. Our . . . statutory scheme . . . was not designed to allow false and diversionary stratagems. . . . This would not serve the ends

---

c. An example may clarify the kind of situation this provision contemplates. Suppose that a state anti-pollution law exempts nonprofit corporations. Relying on that provision, a nonprofit corporation dumps water in a way that would violate the statute were it not for the exemption. In a prosecution of the corporation, the trial court finds the exemption invalid on some ground (perhaps because it conflicts with federal legislation). The corporation would have a defense under this MPC provision.—EDS.

of justice but rather would serve game playing and evasion from properly imposed criminal responsibility.

[A]ffirmed.

HANCOCK, J. (dissenting). . . . The basic difference which divides the court may be simply put. Suppose the case of a man who has committed an act which is criminal not because it is inherently wrong or immoral but solely because it violates a criminal statute. He has committed the act in complete good faith under the mistaken but entirely reasonable assumption that the act does not constitute an offense because it is permitted by the wording of the statute. Does the law require that this man be punished? The majority says that it does and holds that (1) Penal Law §15.02(2)(a) must be construed so that the man is precluded from offering a defense based on his mistake of law and (2) such construction is compelled by prevailing considerations of public policy and criminal jurisprudence. We take issue with the majority on both propositions.

There can be no question that under the view that the purpose of the criminal justice system is to punish blameworthiness or "choosing freely to do wrong"[1] our supposed man who has acted innocently and without any intent to do wrong should not be punished. . . . Since he has not knowingly committed a wrong there can be no reason for society to exact retribution. Because the man is law-abiding and would not have acted but for his mistaken assumption as to the law, there is no need for punishment to deter him from further unlawful conduct. Traditionally, however, under the ancient rule of Anglo-American common law that ignorance or mistake of law is no excuse, our supposed man would be punished.

The maxim "*ignorantia legis neminem excusat*" finds its roots in Medieval law. . . . Various justifications have been offered for the rule, but all are frankly pragmatic and utilitarian—preferring the interests of society (e.g., in deterring criminal conduct, fostering orderly judicial administration, and preserving the primacy of the rule of law) to the interest of the individual in being free from punishment except for intentionally engaging in conduct which he knows is criminal.

Today there is widespread criticism of the common-law rule mandating categorical preclusion of the mistake of law defense. The utilitarian arguments for retaining the rule have been drawn into serious question but the fundamental objection is that it is simply wrong to punish someone who, in good-faith reliance on the wording of a statute, believed that what he was doing was lawful. . . . This basic objection to the maxim "*ignorantia legis neminem excusat*" may have had less force in ancient times when most crimes consisted of acts which by their very nature were recognized as evil. In modern times, however, with the profusion of legislation making otherwise

---

1. "Historically, our substantive criminal law is based upon a theory of punishing the vicious will. It postulates a free agent confronted with a choice between doing right and doing wrong and choosing freely to do wrong" (Pound, Introduction to Sayre, Cases on Criminal Law [1927], quoted in Morissette v. United States, 342 U.S. 246, 250, n.4).

lawful conduct criminal (*malum prohibitum*), the "common law fiction that every man is presumed to know the law has become indefensible in fact or logic."

With this background we proceed to a discussion of our disagreement with the majority's construction of Penal Law §15.20(2)(a). . . .

It is difficult to imagine a case more squarely within the wording of Penal Law §15.20(2)(a) or one more fitted to what appears clearly to be the intended purpose of the statute than the one before us. . . .

Defendant's mistaken belief that, as a Federal corrections officer, he could legally carry a loaded weapon without a license was based on the express exemption from criminal liability under Penal Law §265.02 accorded . . . to "peace officers" . . . and on his reading of the statutory definition for "peace officer" . . . as meaning a correction officer "of *any* penal correctional institution" (emphasis added), including an institution not operated by New York State. Thus, he concluded erroneously that, as a corrections officer in a Federal prison, he was a "peace officer" and, as such, exempt by the express terms of Penal Law §265.20(a)(1)(a). [This mistaken belief, based in good faith on the statute defining "peace officer" is, defendant contends, the precise sort of "mistaken belief . . . founded upon an official statement of the law contained in . . . a statute or other enactment" which gives rise to a mistake of law defense under Penal Law §15.20(2)(a).] He points out, of course, that when he acted in reliance on his belief he had no way of foreseeing that a court would eventually resolve the question of the statute's meaning against him and rule that his belief had been mistaken, as three of the five-member panel at the Appellate Division ultimately did in the first appeal.

The majority, however, has accepted the People's argument that to have a defense under Penal Law §15.20(2)(a) "a defendant must show that the statute *permitted his conduct*, not merely that he believed it did." . . .

Nothing in the statutory language suggests the interpretation urged by the People and adopted by the majority. . . . It is self-evident that in enacting Penal Law §15.20(2) as part of the revision and modernization of the Penal Law the Legislature intended to effect a needed reform by abolishing what had long been considered the unjust archaic common-law rule totally prohibiting mistake of law as a defense. . . .

The majority construes the statute, however, so as to rule out *any* defense based on mistake of law. In so doing, it defeats the only possible purpose for the statute's enactment and resurrects the very rule which the Legislature rejected in enacting Penal Law §15.20(2)(a) as part of its modernization and reform of the Penal Law. . . .

Instead, the majority bases its decision on an analogous provision in the Model Penal Code and concludes that despite its totally different wording and meaning Penal Law §15.20(2)(a) should be read as if it were Model Penal Code §2.04(3)(b)(i). But New York in revising the Penal Law did not adopt the Model Penal Code. As in New Jersey, which generally adopted the Model

Penal Code but added one section which is substantially more liberal,[10] New York followed parts of the Model Penal Code provisions and rejected others. . . .

Thus, the precise phrase in the Model Penal Code limiting the defense under section 2.04(3)(b)(i) to reliance on a statute "afterward determined to be invalid or erroneous" which, if present, would support the majority's narrow construction of the New York statute, is omitted from Penal Law §15.20(2)(a). How the Legislature can be assumed to have enacted the very language which it has specifically rejected is not explained. . . .

not contained in the actual law

letting him have a defense because could open the floodgates

NOTES ON THE RATIONALE OF IGNORANTIA LEGIS

1. What would have been the result in *Marrero* if the defendant did have a handgun permit, the permit had expired, and he claimed a good-faith mistake about what its expiration date was (perhaps because he misread the date printed on it)? Offenses like the one at issue in *Marrero* are often strict liability misdemeanors. If so, a mistake about the expiration date of the permit would not afford a defense, even though this error would only involve a mistake of *fact*.

So in *Marrero*, is the key to the result not the kind of mistake made but simply the fact that the statute involved was treated as a strict liability offense? If so, then the result might have been different—and Marrero's claim of mistake about qualifying as a "peace officer" would have been allowed—if the statute had prohibited "*knowing* possession of an unlicensed handgun." Yet that conclusion is hard to reconcile with the court's references to the "common law rule on mistake of *law*" (emphasis added) and its concern that "[i]f the defendant's argument were accepted, the exception would swallow the rule. Mistakes about the law would be encouraged. . . ." Those passages suggest that Marrero's claim of mistake about the legal meaning of the term "peace officer" was not allowed as a defense, even though a mistake about the relevant facts (such as the expiration date of a permit) would be. But why should mistakes of law be treated differently from mistakes of fact?

2. The traditional explanation for the rule against allowing even reasonable mistakes of law to be a defense is that given by Justice Holmes, quoted in the *Marrero* decision: "to admit the excuse at all would be to encourage ignorance where the lawmaker has determined to make men know and obey." Professor Dru Stevenson suggests a more complex

---

10. In addition to permitting defenses based on ignorance of the law and reasonable reliance on official statements afterward determined to be invalid or erroneous, the New Jersey statute provides a defense, under the following broad provision, when: "(3) The actor otherwise diligently pursues all means available to ascertain the meaning and application of the offense to his conduct and honestly and in good faith concludes his conduct is not an offense in circumstances in which a law-abiding and prudent person would also so conclude" (N.J. Stat. Ann. §2C:2-4[c][3]).

explanation: Mistake-of-law doctrine presumes that everyone knows the law, not to "guarant[ee] that the law is adequately communicated to the citizenry," but instead to create "limited uncertainty about the law," because uncertainty can deter harmful behavior by promoting "caution and restraint." Stevenson, Toward a New Theory of Notice and Deterrence, 26 Cardozo L. Rev. 1535, 1539 (2005).

Deterrence explanations of this sort are challenged in Dan M. Kahan, Ignorance of the Law *Is* an Excuse—But Only for the Virtuous, 96 Mich. L. Rev. 127 (1997). Professor Kahan argues that a defense for *reasonable* mistake of law would punish *unjustified* ignorance of the law while providing a strong incentive for people to maximize their understanding of relevant legal rules. A more plausible explanation for the ignorance-of-law rule, he suggests, is "that individuals are and should be aware of society's morality and that morality furnishes a better guide for action than does law itself. Thus, far from trying to maximize the incentive that presumptively bad men have to know the law, the doctrine seeks to obscure the law so that citizens are more likely to behave like good ones." Id. at 153. Therefore, he argues, courts need to make "context-specific judgments about which actors have characters good enough to be excused for their mistakes of law," id. at 152, in order to distinguish them from loopholers who seek to exploit the uncertainties of the law, such as "designer drug manufacturers and other strategically inquisitive wrongdoers." Consider Crain v. State, 153 S.W. 155 (Tex. Crim. App. 1913). The defendant was aware that state law prohibited his taking a gun to a private home, but he expected to meet someone there to whom he wanted to transfer the weapon, so he disassembled the gun, carrying the cylinder in one pocket and the rest of the gun in another. When charged with illegal possession of a firearm, he claimed that he did not think it was unlawful to carry disassembled parts of a weapon. If reasonable mistake of law is exculpatory, would Crain have a good defense? *Should* Crain have a good defense?

Professor Kahan argues that Marrero was denied a mistake-of-law defense, not because of a firm doctrinal rule against it, but rather because Marrero had "decided to be strategic, availing himself of . . . a largely fortuitous gap in the law," and because Marrero's "bad character" was signaled by facts not mentioned in the court's opinion, such as his having "menacingly reached for his weapon when the police approached him in the Manhattan club." (Id. at 141.)

Questions: *(a)* Suppose that the New York Court of Appeals faced another case at the same time as Marrero's, involving a federal correctional officer of exceptionally good character who had made the same mistake and had been charged with the same offense. Would that court (and should that court) allow the "good" officer to present to his jury the same mistake defense that it had ruled unavailable to Marrero?

(b) Is it a good idea to give judges or juries the authority to determine whether the defendant in a particular case has a good enough character to deserve a mistake-of-law defense? If so, what evidence should be admissible on the issue?

NOTES ON SCOPE OF THE IGNORANTIA LEGIS DOCTRINE

Despite the familiarity of the "rule" that "ignorance of the law is no excuse," courts have consistently ruled that ignorance of the law *can* be an excuse in many circumstances. Consider these situations:

1. *Damage to property.* In Regina v. Smith (David), [1974] 2 Q.B. 354, the defendant, in preparing to leave his rented apartment, damaged some wall panels and floor boards in order to retrieve stereo wiring he earlier had installed, with the landlord's permission, behind wall panels and floor boards of his own construction. He was charged with violating the Criminal Damage Act, which read: "A person who without lawful excuse destroys or damages any property belonging to another intending to destroy or damage any such property or being reckless as to whether any such property would be destroyed or damaged, shall be guilty of an offence." His defense, in his own words, was: "Look, how can I be done in for smashing my own property. I put the flooring and that in, so if I want to pull it down it's a matter for me." He was convicted under an instruction that told the jury that "belief by the defendant . . . that he had the right to do what he did is not a lawful excuse within the meaning of the Act . . . because in law he had no right to do what he did." On appeal, the prosecution argued that "the mental element in the offence relates only to causing damage or to destroying property, [so] that if in fact the property damaged or destroyed is shown to be another's property the offence is committed although the defendant did not intend or foresee damage to another person's property." The court of appeal reversed, finding the jury instruction erroneous:

> Construing the language of section 1(1) we have no doubt that the actus reus is "destroying or damaging any property belonging to another." It is not possible to exclude the words "belonging to another" which describes the "property." Applying the ordinary principles of mens rea, the intention and recklessness and the absence of lawful excuse required to constitute the offence have reference to property belonging to another. It follows that in our judgment no offence is committed under this section if a person destroys or causes damage to property belonging to another if he does so in the honest though mistaken belief that the property is his own, and provided that the belief is honestly held it is irrelevant to consider whether or not it is a justifiable belief.

2. *Theft.* In State v. Varszegi, 635 A.2d 816 (Conn. App. 1993), the defendant was a landlord whose commercial tenant had missed several payments for a rented office space. In the belief that he was acting pursuant to the lease's default clause, he came to the office on a weekend, picked the lock, and removed two computers. On the following Monday, the tenant noticed that the equipment was missing and called the police, who warned the defendant that he had no right to confiscate the property and that he should return it.

Nonetheless, the defendant proceeded to sell the equipment. He was convicted of theft, but the appellate court reversed, stating (id. at 818):

> "A person commits larceny when, with intent to deprive another of property . . . , he wrongfully takes, obtains or withholds such property from an owner. . . . A defendant who acts under the subjective belief that he has a lawful claim on property lacks the required felonious intent to steal. Such a defendant need not show his mistaken claim of right was reasonable, . . . so long as he can establish his claim was made in good faith."

3. Compare the two preceding cases, *Varszegi* and the *David Smith* case, to *Marrero*. In *Marrero*, a seemingly reasonable mistake of law is *not* a defense, but in the first two, a mistake of law can be a defense even if it is *un*reasonable! In these two situations (and many others) ignorance of law *is* an excuse. The MPC sets forth a similar pair of seemingly contradictory rules. Section 2.04(1) provides:

> Ignorance or mistake as to a matter of fact or *law* is a defense if [it] negatives the purpose, belief, recklessness or negligence required to establish a material element of the offense. [Emphasis added.]

Yet section 2.02(9) provides:

> Neither knowledge nor recklessness or negligence as to whether conduct constitutes an offense or as to the existence, meaning or application of the law determining the elements of an offense is an element of such offense, unless the definition of the offense or the Code so provides.

How should these two provisions be reconciled? Taken together, do they afford a defense for Marrero, for David Smith, for both, or for neither? Intuition cannot be a very helpful guide here; it is necessary to apply the two MPC provisions carefully, step by step, to each of the two cases. The background principle involved, and the separate domains of the two provisions, are explained in Model Penal Code and Commentaries, Comment to §2.02 at 250 (1985):

> [T]he general principle that ignorance or mistake of law is no excuse is greatly overstated; it has no application, for example, when the circumstances made material by the definition of the offense include a legal element. Thus it is immaterial in theft, when claim of right is adduced in defense, that the claim involves a legal judgment as to the right of property. Claim of right is a defense because the property must belong to someone else for the theft to occur and the defendant must have culpable awareness of that fact. Insofar as this point is involved, there is no need to state a special principle; the legal element involved is simply an aspect of the attendant circumstances, with respect to which knowledge, recklessness or negligence, as the case may be, is required for culpability. . . . The law involved is not the law defining the offense; it is some other legal rule that characterizes the attendant circumstances that are material to the offense.
>
> The proper arena for the principle that ignorance or mistake of law does not afford an excuse is thus with respect to the particular law that sets forth the

definition of the crime in question. It is knowledge of *that* law that is normally not a part of the crime, and it is ignorance or mistake as to *that* law that is denied defensive significance by this subsection of the Code and by the traditional common law approach to the issue.

On the foregoing analysis, how should the following cases be decided?

(*a*) The defendant was a single woman who traveled with Leo Shuffelt from Vermont to Reno, Nevada, where Shuffelt instituted divorce proceedings against his wife, who was neither a Nevada resident nor present in Nevada. The Nevada judge entered a divorce decree, following which he married the defendant and Shuffelt. Upon return to Vermont, the defendant was prosecuted under a Vermont statute, commonly known as the *Blanket Act,* which provided: "A man with another man's wife, or a woman with another woman's husband, found in bed together, under circumstances affording presumption of an illicit intention, shall each be imprisoned in the state prison not more than three years or fined not more than $1,000." The defendant requested an instruction to the jury that an honest belief in the validity of the Nevada divorce and of her subsequent marriage to Shuffelt would be a defense to the prosecution. Is she entitled to this instruction? Would she be if she had requested an instruction that a *reasonable* belief would be a defense? See State v. Woods, 107 Vt. 354, 179 A. 1 (1935).

(*b*) A physician, attending a patient whom he knows to be brain dead, takes steps to stop his heart, preliminary to removing it for a transplant. He believes the legislature in his jurisdiction has enacted a brain death statute. It hasn't, and the common-law definition of death (cessation of heart functions) is in effect. Can the physician be convicted of *intentionally* killing his patient? On the one hand, ignorance of the law is no excuse. On the other hand, how can a person be found to have intentionally killed a person he believed already dead?

CHEEK v. UNITED STATES

Supreme Court of the United States
498 U.S. 192 (1991)

[Cheek, a pilot for American Airlines, was convicted of willfully failing to file federal income tax returns for a number of years, in violation of 26 U.S.C. §7201, which provides that any person is guilty of a felony "who willfully attempts in any manner to evade or defeat any tax imposed by this title or the payment thereof." His defense was that based on information he received from a group opposing the institution of taxation, he sincerely believed that under the tax laws he owed no taxes, including taxes on his wages, and that if he did, these laws were unconstitutional.

[During its deliberations, the jury sent out a note saying that it could not reach a verdict because "[w]e are divided on the issue as to if Mr. Cheek

honestly & reasonably believed that he was not required to pay income tax."
Thereupon the trial judge further instructed the jury that "[a]n honest but
unreasonable belief is not a defense and does not negate willfulness," and that
"[a]dvice or research resulting in the conclusion that wages of a privately
employed person are not income or that the tax laws are unconstitutional
is not objectively reasonable and cannot serve as the basis for a good faith
misunderstanding of the law defense." The judge also instructed the jury that
"[p]ersistent refusal to acknowledge the law does not constitute a good faith
misunderstanding of the law."

[Cheek appealed his convictions, charging the trial judge with error in
instructing that only an objectively reasonable misunderstanding of the law
negates the statutory willfulness requirement. The court of appeals affirmed,
and the Supreme Court granted certiorari.]

JUSTICE WHITE delivered the opinion of the Court.

The general rule that ignorance of the law or a mistake of law is no defense
to criminal prosecution is deeply rooted in the American legal system. Based
on the notion that the law is definite and knowable, the common law presumed that every person knew the law. . . .

The proliferation of statutes and regulations has sometimes made it difficult for the average citizen to know and comprehend the extent of the duties
and obligations imposed by the tax laws. Congress has accordingly softened
the impact of the common-law presumption by making specific intent to violate the law an element of certain federal criminal tax offenses . . . [thus] carving out an exception to the traditional rule. This special treatment of criminal
tax offenses is largely due to the complexity of the tax laws. [T]he standard for
the statutory willfulness requirement is the "voluntary, intentional violation
of a known legal duty."

Cheek . . . challenges the ruling that . . . a good-faith belief that one is not
violating the law, if it is to negate willfulness, must be objectively reasonable.
We agree that the Court of Appeals and the District Court erred in this respect.

. . . We deal first with the case where the issue is whether the defendant
knew of the duty purportedly imposed by the provision of the statute or
regulation he is accused of violating, a case in which there is no claim that
the provision at issue is invalid. In such a case, if the Government proves
actual knowledge of the pertinent legal duty, the prosecution, without more,
has satisfied the knowledge component of the willfulness requirement. But
carrying this burden requires negating a defendant's claim of ignorance of
the law or a claim that because of a misunderstanding of the law, he had a
good-faith belief that he was not violating any of the provisions of the tax
laws. . . . In the end, the issue is whether, based on all the evidence, the Government has proved that the defendant was aware of the duty at issue, which
cannot be true if the jury credits a good-faith misunderstanding and belief
submission, whether or not the claimed belief or misunderstanding is objectively reasonable.

In this case, if Cheek asserted that he truly believed that the Internal Revenue Code did not purport to treat wages as income, and the jury believed him, the Government would not have carried its burden to prove willfulness, however unreasonable a court might deem such a belief. . . . Of course, the more unreasonable the asserted beliefs or misunderstandings are, the more likely the jury will consider them to be nothing more than simple disagreement with known legal duties . . . and will find that the Government has carried its burden of providing knowledge.

Cheek [also asserted] that he should be acquitted because he believed in good faith that the income tax law is unconstitutional as applied to him and thus could not legally impose any duty upon him of which he should have been aware. Such a submission is unsound, not because Cheek's constitutional arguments are . . . frivolous, which they surely are, but because . . . the willfulness requirement in the criminal provisions of the Internal Revenue Code . . . require proof of knowledge of the law. This was because in "our complex tax system, uncertainty often arises even among taxpayers who earnestly wish to follow the law" and " 'it is not the purpose of the law to penalize frank difference of opinion or innocent errors made despite the exercise of reasonable care.' " United States v. Bishop, 412 US. 346, 360-361 (1973).

Claims that some of the provisions of the tax code are unconstitutional are submissions of a different order. They do not arise from innocent mistakes caused by the complexity of the Internal Revenue Code. Rather, they reveal full knowledge of the provisions at issue and a studied conclusion, however wrong, that those provisions are invalid and unenforceable. Thus in this case, Cheek paid his taxes for years, but after attending various seminars and based on his own study, he concluded that the income tax laws could not constitutionally require him to pay a tax.

We do not believe that Congress contemplated that such a taxpayer . . . could ignore the duties imposed upon him by the Internal Revenue Code and refuse to utilize the mechanisms provided by Congress to present his claims of invalidity to the courts and to abide by their decisions. There is no doubt that Cheek, from year to year, was free to pay the tax that the law purported to require, file for a refund and, if denied, present his claims of invalidity, constitutional or otherwise, to the courts. [I]n some years, [Cheek did not do so,] and when he did was unwilling to accept the outcome. . . . Of course, Cheek was free in this very case to present his claims of invalidity and have them adjudicated, but like defendants in criminal cases in other contexts, who "willfully" refuse to comply with the duties placed upon them by the law, he must take the risk of being wrong.

[It] was therefore not error in this case for the District Judge to instruct the jury not to consider Cheek's claims that the tax laws were unconstitutional. However, it was error for the court to instruct the jury that petitioner's asserted beliefs that wages are not income and that he was not a taxpayer within the meaning of the Internal Revenue Code should not be considered by the jury in determining whether Cheek had acted willfully.

[On retrial, defendant was convicted on an instruction allowing the jury to consider "whether the defendant's stated belief about the tax statute was reasonable as a factor in deciding whether he held that belief in good faith." United States v. Cheek, 3 F.3d 1057 (7th Cir. 1993).]

NOTE ON "WILLFULLY" AND "KNOWINGLY"

The starting place for the analysis in *Cheek* is an essentially self-evident point—the rule, also stated in Model Penal Code §2.02(9), that a mistake about the existence or meaning of the law defining the offense is a defense if that law itself allows that defense. But how does a court decide *whether* that law allows the defense? Does the presence of mens rea language like "knowledge" or "willfulness" determine the answer? Note that in *Cheek,* the court interpreted the word "willfully" to mean the defendant must be aware of some legal conclusions (that wages are "income") but not others (that the income tax statute is constitutionally valid). In other cases involving the interpretation of federal statutes, the Court has sometimes held that "knowledge" or "willfulness" requires either (1) awareness of the specific statute at issue, or (2) just a more general awareness that the acts committed are unlawful, or (3) even less—merely awareness of what acts were committed (i.e., awareness only of the *facts*). The statutory language itself seldom signals which of these meanings was intended. Surveying an extensive body of case law, Professor Sharon L. Davies finds that courts have construed a dozen or more federal criminal laws to require knowledge of illegality. Davies, The Jurisprudence of Ignorance: An Evolving Theory of Excusable Ignorance, 48 Duke L.J. 341, 344-347 (1998). Nonetheless, in many instances, courts continue to interpret "knowledge" or "willfulness" as requiring only an awareness of the facts. What circumstances determine whether knowledge of the law is or should be required? Consider the following cases:

United States v. International Minerals & Chemical Corp., 402 U.S. 558 (1971): A statute made it a crime for a person to "knowingly violat[e]" a regulation of the Interstate Commerce Commission regarding the transportation of corrosive liquids. Does that mean the prosecution must prove that defendant knew of the existence and meaning of the applicable regulation, or only that the actions the defendant knowingly committed violated that regulation? The Court held the latter.

Liparota v. United States, 471 U.S. 419 (1985): Here the Court reached the opposite conclusion. A statute governing food stamp fraud provided that "whoever knowingly uses, transfers, acquires, alters, or possesses coupons or authorization cards in any manner not authorized by [the statute] or the regulations [of the Department of Agriculture]" is subject to fine and imprisonment. Does this mean that the prosecution must prove the defendant knew of the existence and meaning of the relevant regulation, or only that he was aware of doing the acts that violated the regulation? This time the Court held for the former interpretation, influenced by the concern that "to interpret the statute otherwise would be to criminalize a broad range of apparently innocent conduct." The Court continued:

> §2024(b)(1) declares . . . that "[c]oupons issued to eligible households shall be used by them only to purchase food in retail food stores which have been approved for participation in the food stamp program *at prices prevailing in such stores.*" (emphasis added). This seems to be the *only* authorized use. A strict reading of the statute with no knowledge-of-illegality requirement would thus render criminal a food stamp recipient who, for example, used stamps to purchase food from a store that, unknown to him, charged higher than normal prices to food stamp program participants.

United States v. Ansaldi, 372 F.3d 118 (2d Cir. 2004): The defendant was charged with selling the chemical compound GBL, which is listed as a controlled substance because when metabolized by the human body, it is converted into GHB, the so-called date rape drug. Under the statute in question, 21 U.S.C. §841(a), it is unlawful to "knowingly or intentionally . . . distribute . . . a controlled substance." Defendant knew he was distributing GBL but claimed not to know that GBL is a controlled substance. The court recognized that knowledge of the law is required for conviction of tax evasion but stated, without elaboration, that the drug distribution statute is different: "Knowledge of, or intent to violate, the law is simply not an element of this offense." Id. at 128.

United States v. Overholt, 307 F.3d 1231 (10th Cir. 2002): Defendant was charged with "willfully" violating the Safe Drinking Water Act (SDWA) by unlawfully disposing of contaminated waste water. At trial, the jury was instructed that it must find that the defendant knew he was doing something unlawful, but the judge refused to instruct that the jury must find (as in *Liparota,* supra) that the defendant was aware of the specific law he was violating. The court of appeals upheld the conviction, finding the case to be governed not by *Liparota* and *Cheek* but by *International Minerals* (id. at 1246):

> [W]hen addressing laws like the SDWA [which regulate noxious materials], the Supreme Court has been particularly resistant to requiring proof of knowledge of the law. [See] *United States v. Int'l Minerals & Chem. Corp.* [Defendant] is correct when he asserts that environmental regulations are now the most complex of federal regulations, exceeding even tax regulations. But we strongly doubt that as the federal government has sought to protect the environment by imposing more and more restrictions on those handling dangerous chemicals, Congress has intended to reduce the burden on such persons to inform themselves of what the law requires. In short, we have no reason to believe that the word willful in [the SDWA] requires proof of knowledge of the regulation allegedly violated.

For discussion of these issues, see John S. Wiley, Not Guilty by Reason of Blamelessness: Culpability in Federal Criminal Interpretation, 85 Va. L. Rev.

1021 (1999); Davies, supra; and Michael Vitiello, Does Culpability Matter?: Statutory Construction Under 42 U.S.C. §6928, 6 Tul. Envtl. L.J. 187 (1993).

NOTES ON OFFICIAL RELIANCE

1. The traditional view. Because the reasonableness of a defendant's mistake of penal law ordinarily is irrelevant, courts traditionally refused to consider the defense even when the mistake was based on the assurances of a public official or the decision of a court. Consider Hopkins v. State, 193 Md. 489, 69 A.2d 456 (1950). The defendant was convicted of violating a statute making it unlawful to erect or maintain any sign intended to aid in the solicitation of performance of marriages. He had erected signs that read: "Rev. W.F. Hopkins" and "W.F. Hopkins, Notary Public, Information." On appeal he argued that the trial judge erred in excluding testimony offered to show that the State's Attorney advised him before he erected the signs that they would not violate the law. The Maryland Supreme Court affirmed his conviction, stating:

> It is generally held that the advice of counsel, even though followed in good faith, furnishes no excuse to a person for violating the law and cannot be relied upon as a defense in a criminal action. . . . Moreover, advice given by a public official, even a State's Attorney, that a contemplated act is not criminal will not excuse an offender if, as a matter of law, the act performed did amount to a violation of the law. . . . These rules are founded upon the maxim that ignorance of the law will not excuse its violation. If an accused could be exempted from punishment for crime by reason of the advice of counsel, such advice would become paramount to the law. . . .
>
> In the case at bar defendant did not claim that the State's Attorney misled him regarding any facts of the case, but only that the State's Attorney advised him as to the law based upon the facts. Defendant was aware of the penal statute enacted by the Legislature. He knew what he wanted to do, and he did the thing he intended to do. He claims merely that he was given advice regarding his legal rights. . . . If the right of a person to erect a sign of a certain type and size depends upon the construction and application of a penal statute, and the right is somewhat doubtful, he erects the sign at his peril. In other words, a person who commits an act which the law declared to be criminal cannot be excused from punishment upon the theory that he misconstrued or misapplied the law.

2. The MPC approach. Reflecting a widespread view that decisions like *Hopkins* are unfair, and indeed pointless, the Code adopts a limited defense for situations in which a defendant reasonably believes that his conduct does not constitute an offense. See §2.04(3), Appendix. The Commentaries explain (Model Penal Code and Commentaries, Comment to §2.04 at 274-275 (1985)):

> All of the categories dealt with in the formulation involve, for the most part, situations where the act charged is consistent with the entire law-abidingness of the actor, where the possibility of collusion is minimal, and where a judicial determination of the reasonableness of the belief in legality should not present

substantial difficulty. It is hard, therefore, to see how any purpose can be served by a conviction. It should be added that in the area of regulatory offenses, where the defense would normally apply, penal sanctions are appropriate in general only for deliberate evasion or defiance. When less than this is involved, lesser sanctions should suffice, for these typically are situations where a single violation works no major public or private injury; it is persistent violations that must be brought to book. And obviously the defense afforded by this section would normally be available to a defendant only once; after a warning he can hardly have a reasonable basis for belief in the legality of his behavior.

The MPC's official reliance defense is widely accepted. See, e.g., United States v. Levin, 973 F.2d 463, 468 (6th Cir. 1992); Commonwealth v. Twitchell, 416 Mass. 114, 617 N.E.2d 609 (1993); Annot., 89 A.L.R.4th 1026 (1991).

3. Due process limitations. Under the label "entrapment by estoppel," the Supreme Court has held it a violation of due process to convict a defendant for conduct that governmental representatives, in their official capacity, had earlier stated was lawful. The doctrine was first recognized in Raley v. Ohio, 360 U.S. 423 (1959). Defendants invoked their privilege against self-incrimination before an Ohio governmental commission after the commission instructed them that they were permitted to do so. This, apparently, was bad advice, however, since an Ohio statute granted automatic immunity in such situations, thereby depriving them of any privilege to refuse to answer. They were then convicted of contempt for refusing to answer the commission's questions. The Supreme Court found this to violate due process, stating that to affirm the convictions in these circumstances "would be to sanction the most indefensible sort of entrapment by the State—convicting a citizen for exercising a privilege which the State clearly had told him was available to him" (id. at 438).

For discussion, see John T. Parry, Culpability, Mistake, and Official Interpretations of Law, 25 Am. J. Crim. L. 1 (1997); Sean Connelly, Bad Advice: The Entrapment by Estoppel Doctrine in the Criminal Law, 48 U. Miami L. Rev. 627 (1994).

4. The reasonableness requirement. Under MPC §2.04(3)(b), the reliance defense is available only when the defendant "acts in *reasonable* reliance upon an official statement of the law, afterward determined to be invalid or erroneous." (emphasis added). Why would it ever be unreasonable to rely on an official statement of the law not yet determined to be erroneous at the time when the defendant acts? Consider United States v. Albertini, 830 F.2d 985 (1987). The defendant was convicted of trespass for engaging in a protest demonstration on a naval base. On appeal, the Ninth Circuit (in *Albertini I*) set aside the conviction on the ground that his conduct was protected by the First Amendment. The government then filed a petition for certiorari, seeking review by the Supreme Court. At that point, but before the Supreme Court decided whether to review the case, Albertini engaged in a second protest demonstration. After the second demonstration, the Supreme Court granted review and reversed the Ninth Circuit, on the ground that the protest at a military installation was not protected by the First Amendment. The conviction in *Albertini I* was therefore reinstated, but the government also decided to prosecute Albertini for the second demonstration, which had occurred before the Supreme Court's decision to review *Albertini I*. In *Albertini II*, he was convicted for participating in the second demonstration and of course no longer had a First Amendment defense. The court of appeals nonetheless reversed the conviction in *Albertini II*, this time on the ground that he had a due process right to rely on the previous Ninth Circuit decision ruling that his conduct was lawful:

> If the due process clause is to mean anything, it should mean that a person who holds the latest controlling court opinion declaring his activities constitutionally protected should be able to depend on that ruling to protect like activities from criminal conviction until that opinion is reversed, or at least until the Supreme Court has granted certiorari. . . . To hold otherwise would sanction a kind of "entrapment" by the government—convicting Albertini for acts that the government has told him are protected by the first amendment. . . .

Do you agree? What if most commentators had criticized the result in *Albertini I* and predicted that the Supreme Court would reverse it? If there were contrary authority in other circuit courts, would it then become unreasonable for citizens living in the Ninth Circuit to rely on that court's interpretation of the law? Some might argue that even in that situation, a citizen should still have the right to rely on the "latest controlling court opinion" in his jurisdiction. But the Supreme Court rejected that view. In United States v. Rodgers, 466 U.S. 475, 484 (1984), the Court said that "the existence of conflicting cases from other Courts of Appeals made review of that issue by this Court and against the position of the respondent reasonably foreseeable."[19] Accordingly, in a case presenting a similar issue concerning the foreseeability of a Supreme Court decision issued after a defendant's alleged offense, the Ninth Circuit overruled *Albertini II* and applied the subsequent Supreme Court decision "retroactively." It then upheld the conviction of a person whose conduct had been declared lawful under Ninth Circuit precedent in effect at the time he acted. United States v. Qualls, 172 F.3d 1136, 1138 (9th Cir. 1999). In dissent, Judge Hawkins, describing the result as "unfortunate and unfair," observed (id. at 1139-1140):

> *Rodgers* has the effect of requiring that a citizen look not to the established law of the circuit in which he resides, but to the law of the circuit taking the most expansive view of conduct prohibited by a statute, . . . until that point in time when the Supreme Court resolves any interpretative disagreement among the circuits. This can have the effect of restraining for years conduct that the Court may ultimately decide was always perfectly legal.

---

19. *Rodgers* was decided three years before *Albertini II*, but apparently none of the parties in the latter case had called the Ninth Circuit's attention to *Rodgers*.

For discussion of these issues, see Trevor W. Morrison, Fair Warning and Retroactive Judicial Expansion of Federal Criminal Statutes, 74 S. Cal. L. Rev. 455 (2001).

LAMBERT v. CALIFORNIA

Supreme Court of the United States
355 U.S. 225 (1957)

JUSTICE DOUGLAS delivered the opinion of the Court.

Section 52.38(a) of the Los Angeles Municipal Code defines "convicted person" as follows:

> Any person who, subsequent to January 1, 1921, has been or hereafter is convicted of an offense punishable as a felony in the State of California, or who has been or who is hereafter convicted of any offense in any place other than the State of California, which offense, if committed in the State of California, would have been punishable as a felony.

Section 52.39 provides that it shall be unlawful for "any convicted person" to be or remain in Los Angeles for a period of more than five days without registering; it requires any person having a place of abode outside the city to register if he comes into the city on five occasions or more during a 30-day period; and it prescribes the information to be furnished the Chief of Police on registering.

Section 52.43(b) makes the failure to register a continuing offense, each day's failure constituting a separate offense.

Appellant, arrested on suspicion of another offense, was charged with a violation of this registration law. . . . The case was tried to a jury which found appellant guilty. The court fined her $250 and placed her on probation for three years. . . .

The registration provision, carrying criminal penalties, applies if a person has been convicted "of an offense punishable as a felony in the State of California" or, in case he has been convicted in another State if the offense "would have been punishable as a felony" had it been committed in California. No element of willfulness is by terms included in the ordinance nor read into it by the California court as a condition necessary for a conviction.

We must assume that appellant had no actual knowledge of the requirement that she register under this ordinance, as she offered proof of this defense which was refused. The question is whether a registration act of this character violates Due Process where it is applied to a person who has no actual knowledge of his duty to register, and where no showing is made of the probability of such knowledge.

. . . There is wide latitude on the lawmakers to declare an offense and to exclude elements of knowledge and diligence from its definition. . . . But we deal here with conduct that is wholly passive—mere failure to register. It is unlike the commission of acts, or the failure to act under circumstances that should alert the doer to the consequences of his deed. Cf. . . . United States v. Balint, 258 U.S. 250; United States v. Dotterweich, 320 U.S. 277, 284. The rule that "ignorance of the law will not excuse" . . . is deep in our law, as is the principle that of all the powers of local government, the police power is "one of the least limitable." . . . On the other hand, Due Process places some limits on its exercise. Engrained in our concept of Due Process is the requirement of notice. Notice is sometimes essential so that the citizen has the chance to defend charges. Notice is required before property interests are disturbed, before assessments are made, before penalties are assessed. Notice is required in a myriad of situations where a penalty or forfeiture might be suffered for mere failure to act. Recent cases illustrating the point . . . involved only property interests in civil litigation. But the principle is equally appropriate where a person, wholly passive and unaware of any wrongdoing, is brought to the bar of justice for condemnation in a criminal case.

Registration laws are common and their range is wide. . . . Many such laws are akin to licensing statutes in that they pertain to the regulation of business activities. But the present ordinance is entirely different. Violation of its provisions is unaccompanied by any activity whatever, mere presence in the city being the test. Moreover, circumstances which might move one to inquire as to the necessity of registration are completely lacking. At most the ordinance is but a law enforcement technique designed for the convenience of law enforcement agencies through which a list of the names and addresses of felons then residing in a given community is compiled. The disclosure is merely a compilation of former convictions already publicly recorded in the jurisdiction where obtained. Nevertheless, this registrant on first becoming aware of her duty to register was given no opportunity to comply with the law and avoid its penalty, even though her default was entirely innocent. She could but suffer the consequences of the ordinance, namely, conviction with the imposition of heavy criminal penalties thereunder. We believe that actual knowledge of the duty to register or proof of the probability of such knowledge and subsequent failure to comply are necessary before a conviction under the ordinance can stand. . . . Its severity lies in the absence of an opportunity either to avoid the consequences of the law or to defend any prosecution brought under it. Where a person did not know of the duty to register and where there was no proof of the probability of such knowledge, he may not be convicted consistently with Due Process. Were it otherwise, the evil would be as great as it is when the law is written in print too fine to read or in a language foreign to the community.

Reversed. . . .

JUSTICE FRANKFURTER, whom JUSTICE HARLAN and JUSTICE WHITTAKER join, dissenting.

The present laws of the United States and of the forty-eight States are thick with provisions that command that some things not be done and others be done, although persons convicted under such provisions may have had no awareness of what the law required or that what they did was wrongdoing.

The body of decisions sustaining such legislation, including innumerable registration laws, is almost as voluminous as the legislation itself. The matter is summarized in United States v. Balint, 258 U.S. 250, 252: "Many instances of this are to be found in regulatory measures in the exercise of what is called the police power where the emphasis of the statute is evidently upon achievement of some social betterment rather than the punishment of the crimes as in cases of mala in se."

Surely there can hardly be a difference as a matter of fairness, of hardship, or of justice, if one may invoke it, between the case of a person wholly innocent of wrongdoing, in the sense that he was not remotely conscious of violating any law, who is imprisoned for five years for conduct relating to narcotics, and the case of another person who is placed on probation for three years on condition that she pay $250, for failure, as a local resident, convicted under local law of a felony, to register under a law passed as an exercise of the State's "police power."

[W]hat the Court here does is to draw a constitutional line between a State's requirement of doing and not-doing. What is this but a return to Year Book distinctions between feasance and nonfeasance—a distinction that may have significance in the evolution of common law notions of liability, but is inadmissible as a line between constitutionality and unconstitutionality. . . .

If the generalization that underlies, and alone can justify, this decision were to be given its relevant scope, a whole volume of the United States Reports would be required to document in detail the legislation in this country that would fall or be impaired. I abstain from entering upon a consideration of such legislation, and adjudications upon it, because I feel confident that the present decision will turn out to be an isolated deviation from the strong current of precedents—a derelict on the waters of the law. Accordingly, I content myself with dissenting.

NOTES AND QUESTIONS

1. *Questions.* What precisely, in Justice Frankfurter's view, is the "generalization that underlies, and alone can justify" the decision in *Lambert*? Would it invalidate all strict liability legislation, as he seems to imply? Would it invalidate the traditional rule that even reasonable mistake of law is not a defense? Could the generalization be confined to cases of omissions? Consider, for example, an ordinance that prohibited "convicted persons" from accepting employment as babysitters in the city of Los Angeles.

2. *Problem.* Bryant was convicted of a sex offense in South Carolina. At the time of his conviction, the sentencing judge informed him of South Carolina's sex offender registration law, but the judge did not comply with a federal requirement that Bryant also be advised of his obligation to register as a sex offender in any other state to which he might move. Later, Bryant

moved to North Carolina and was convicted of a crime when authorities discovered that he had failed to register there. The intermediate appellate court held that under *Lambert*, Bryant's conviction violated due process. The North Carolina Supreme Court reversed. First, that court held, *Lambert* was distinguishable, because the Los Angeles registration statute was a general law enforcement device rather than a public safety measure. Second, the court said, because all states now have some sort of sex offender registration regime, the case was "overflowing with circumstances" that should have moved Bryant to inquire about the need to register. State v. Bryant, 614 S.E.2d 479, 488 (N.C. 2005). Is the result consistent with the reasoning of *Lambert*? If not, which is the better approach?

3. Entrapment by omission? As we saw above, it is considered a violation of due process to convict a defendant who reasonably relies on an official assurance that his conduct is lawful. See *Raley v. Ohio*, page 319 supra. Should a similar principle afford a defense when a defendant reasonably relies on the failure of a government official to alert him that his conduct will be unlawful?

State v. Leavitt, 27 P.3d 622 (Wash. Ct. App. 2001), involved a man who had been convicted of a misdemeanor domestic violence offense. The sentencing judge failed to comply with a state law requiring that defendants convicted in such cases be notified that they can no longer possess a firearm. Instead, the judge told Leavitt that he could not possess a firearm during the one-year probation imposed for the misdemeanor. That statement was not false, but it was misleading because Leavitt was also barred from possessing a firearm after the one-year period. Leavitt took his guns to his brother for safekeeping during the year, but after the expiration of his probation, Leavitt got into trouble again, police found guns in his car, and he was convicted of unlawful possession. The Washington court noted that knowledge of illegality was not an element of the firearm-possession offense. Nonetheless, the court reversed the conviction because the "combined actions and inactions of the predicate-sentencing court [in the domestic violence case] misled Leavitt reasonably to understand that his firearm possession restriction was limited to one year. [I]t would be a denial of due process to require Leavitt to speculate about additional firearm-possession restrictions beyond his one-year probation where the sentencing court did not inform him otherwise." Id. at 628.

Is the result sound? In a similar case, the Seventh Circuit reached the opposite result. Wilson's wife obtained an order of protection against him. In a hearing that lasted only ten minutes, Wilson and his wife discussed child support and visitation, and the state judge explained the terms of the order of protection. State law allowed the judge to require Wilson to give up his firearms as part of the order, but the judge did not do so, apparently because Wilson had not used any weapons to threaten his wife. Nonetheless, a federal statute (not mentioned by the state judge) automatically made firearms possession unlawful under such circumstances. Wilson was convicted of the federal offense and sentenced to 41 months in prison. In United States v.

Wilson, 159 F.3d 280, 289 (7th Cir. 1998), the court of appeals affirmed, stating simply that "a 'knowing' violation of the statute only requires proof of knowledge by the defendant of the facts that constitute the offense." In dissent, Chief Judge Richard Posner observed (id. at 293-296):

> Congress created, and the Department of Justice sprang, a trap on Carlton Wilson as a result of which he will serve more than three years in federal prison for an act (actually an omission to act) that he could not have suspected was a crime or even a civil wrong. We can release him from the trap by interpreting the statute under which he was convicted to require the government to prove that the violator knew that he was committing a crime. This is the standard device by which the courts avoid having to explore the outer boundaries of the constitutional requirement of fair notice of potential criminal liability.
>
> [This law] is not the kind of law that a lay person would intuit existed. . . . Yet the Department of Justice took no steps to publicize the existence of the law until long after Wilson violated it. . . .
>
> The federal criminal code contains thousands of separate prohibitions, many ridiculously obscure, such as the one against using the coat of arms of Switzerland in advertising, or using "Johnny Horizon" as a trade name without the authorization of the Department of the Interior. The prohibition [at issue here] is one of the most obscure. A person . . . knows or should know that if he is convicted of a felony he will have to get rid of [his] gun; if he doesn't know, the judge or the probation service will tell him. But should he be made subject to a restraining order telling him to keep away from his ex-wife, . . . it will not occur to him that he must give up the gun unless the judge issuing the order tells him. The judge didn't tell Wilson; so far as appears, the judge was unaware of the law. Wilson's lawyer didn't tell him either—Wilson didn't have a lawyer. . . . The fact that the restraining order contained no reference to guns may have lulled him into thinking that, as long as he complied with the order and stayed away from his wife, he could carry on as before. . . .
>
> We want people to familiarize themselves with the laws bearing on their activities. But a reasonable opportunity doesn't mean being able to go to the local law library and read Title 18. . . . If none of the conditions that make it reasonable to dispense with proof of knowledge of the law is present, then to intone "ignorance of the law is no defense" is to condone a violation of fundamental principles for the sake of a modest economy in the administration of criminal justice.
>
> Actually a false economy. The purpose of criminal laws is to bring about compliance with desired norms of behavior. . . . This purpose is ill served by keeping the law a secret, which has been the practical upshot of the Department of Justice's failure . . . either to enforce the law vigorously or to notify the relevant state officials of the law's existence. . . . The [Supreme] Court voided Lambert's conviction. We should do the same for Wilson's conviction.

Question: Would Wilson have a defense under MPC §2.04(3)(a)?

CALIFORNIA JOINT LEGISLATIVE COMMITTEE FOR REVISION OF THE PENAL CODE, PENAL CODE REVISION PROJECT

(Tent. Draft No. 2, 1968)

SECTION 500. IGNORANCE OR MISTAKE . . .

(2) A person's belief that his conduct does not constitute a crime is a defense only if it is reasonable and,

(a) if the person's mistaken belief is due to his ignorance of the existence of the law defining the crime, he exercised all the care which, in the circumstances, a law-abiding and prudent person would exercise to ascertain the law; or

(b) if the person's mistaken belief is due to his misconception of the meaning or application of the law defining the crime to his conduct,

(i) he acts in reasonable reliance upon an official statement of the law, afterward determined to be invalid or erroneous, contained in a statute, judicial decision, administrative order or grant of permission, or an official interpretation of the public officer or body charged by law with the responsibility for interpreting, administering or enforcing the law defining the crime; or,

[(ii) he otherwise diligently pursues all means available to ascertain the meaning and application of the crime to his conduct and honestly and in good faith concludes his conduct is not a crime in circumstances in which a law-abiding and prudent person would also so conclude].

Comments (64-67) . . .

[We] think exculpation should be made out in all cases where a law-abiding and prudent person would not have learned of the law's existence. One such case is Lambert v. California, 355 U.S. 225 (1957). . . . Certainly there would not be many cases of this kind. Where the prohibition reaches plainly wrongful conduct, the conduct itself alerts the law-abiding and prudent person to the need for inquiry if there is any doubt. And even in the mala prohibita crimes the circumstances would normally suggest inquiry—engaging in such closely regulated activities as liquor selling, food merchandising, apartment renting, etc. [But] where this is not the case only a blind and brutal law would insist on punishment. Subsection (2)(b) is addressed to the situation where the defendant (still reasonably), although aware of the existence of the crime, was mistaken as to its meaning or its applicability to conduct. Subsection (i), dealing with situations of reliance on official and responsible interpretations . . . imports no innovation in present law. Subsection (ii), however, does, insofar as it generalizes the essential quality of the unfairness in holding defendants who are misled by official reliance; i.e., they did all that could be done to learn the nature of the prohibition and in concluding that it was lawful reacted no differently than would any law-abiding and prudent person. The subsection is placed in brackets because some of the Reporters believe it may go too far for reasons that will be stated shortly. The case to be made in favor of this subsection is as follows:

The central point is that it is plainly unjust to hold a defendant criminally liable where a jury is prepared to conclude that the conditions of this subsection are met. A case which illustrates this is Long v. State, 44 Del. 262, 65 A.2d 489 (1949). The court reversed a conviction of bigamy because the court below excluded evidence offered by the defendant to show his reasonable belief that his Arkansas divorce legally severed his prior marriage relationship. [T]he court dealt with the defense as though it were a defense of misconception of the law defining the offense and allowed the defense on the ground that the defendant "before engaging in the conduct made a bona fide, diligent effort, adopting a course and resorting to sources and means at least as appropriate as any afforded under our legal system, to ascertain and abide by the law, and . . . acted in good faith reliance upon the results of such effort." We agree with the Delaware court that in such circumstances the practical difficulties commonly invoked to deny the defense of mistake of law are inapposite. It cannot be said to "encourage ignorance" of the law where the defense requires a showing of diligent and exhaustive effort to comprehend the law. And difficulties of proof are not here substantial since the defendant is required to show affirmative acts of inquiry addressed to an objective standard. . . .

On the other hand some feel that this provision is subject to abuse. It opens up a new and potentially time-consuming defense in many cases. Further, the defense can be too easily fabricated out of disingenuous advice obtained from lawyers ready to lend themselves to a scheme of evasion through venality or partisanship in their client's cause. Finally, it is believed that the potential injustice is adequately guarded against by the use of the prosecutor's discretion not to prosecute in cases in which the accused acted in good faith, and his conduct was not harmful.

NOTE

The California proposal, §2(b)(ii), was adopted in New Jersey. See N.J. Stat. Ann. tit. 2C, §2-4(c)(3). Where statutory language does not govern the issue of mistake of law after due diligence and reliance on unofficial legal advice, nearly all courts hold that such a defense is not available. E.g., United States v. Ragsdale, 426 F.3d 765 (5th Cir. 2005). But the Delaware Supreme Court continues to endorse it. See Bryson v. State, 840 A.2d 631 (Del. 2003). Fears about potential abuse of the defense apparently have not materialized in New Jersey and Delaware. Are the practical concerns sufficient to justify the prevalent view that the defense is too easily manipulated?

For arguments favoring substantial expansion of the mistake-of-law defense, see Douglas Husak & Andrew von Hirsch, Culpability and Mistake of Law, in Action and Value in Criminal Law 157-174 (John Gardner, Jeremy Horder, & Stephen Shute eds., 1993); to the contrary, see Sharon Davies, The Jurisprudence of Willfullness, 48 Duke L.J. 341 (1998).

PROBLEM: THE "CULTURAL DEFENSE"

Should the law afford an excuse for foreigners who violate the law by actions acceptable in their native cultures? An English court faced this issue in Rex. v. Esop, 7 C. & P. 456 (1836). A sailor who was a native of Baghdad was convicted for sodomy committed aboard an East India ship while it was docked in London harbor. The court sustained the conviction over the defendant's objection that sodomy was not a crime in his native land. A number of incidents reported in the press raise questions about the propriety of applying the traditional *ignorantia legis* rule in such situations. Examples are described in Doriane Lambelet Coleman, Individualizing Justice Through Multiculturalism: The Liberals' Dilemma, 96 Colum. L. Rev. 1093, 1093 (1996):

> In California, a Japanese-American mother drowns her two young children in the ocean at Santa Monica and then attempts to kill herself; rescuers save her before she drowns. The children's recovered bodies bear deep bruises where they struggled as their mother held them under the water. The mother later explains that in Japan, where she is from, her actions would be understood as the time-honored, customary practice of parent-child suicide. She spends only one year in jail—the year she is on trial.
>
> In New York, a Chinese-American woman is bludgeoned to death by her husband. Charged with murder, her husband explains that his conduct comports with a Chinese custom that allows husbands to dispel their shame in this way when their wives have been unfaithful. He is acquitted of murder charges.
>
> Back in California, a young Laotian-American woman is abducted from her place of work at Fresno State University and forced to have sexual intercourse against her will. Her Hmong immigrant assailant explains that, among his tribe, such behavior is not only accepted, but expected—it is the customary way to choose a bride. He is sentenced to 120 days in jail, and his victim receives $900 in reparations.
>
> A Somali immigrant living in Georgia allegedly cuts off her two-year-old niece's clitoris, partially botching the job. The child was cut in accordance with the time-honored tradition of female circumcision; this custom attempts to ensure that girls and women remain chaste for their husbands. The State charges the woman with child abuse, but is unable to convict her.

The argument in favor of a defense in these cases is that it "will advance two desirable ends consistent with the broader goals of liberal society and the criminal law: (1) the achievement of individualized justice for the defendant; and (2) a commitment to cultural pluralism." James J. Sing, Culture as Sameness: Toward a Synthetic View of Provocation and Culture in the Criminal Law, 108 Yale L.J. 1845, 1847 (1999). Professor Coleman, however, points to a dilemma (96 Colum. L. Rev. at 1094-1096):

> Allowing sensitivity to a defendant's culture to inform the application of laws to that individual [furthers] the idea that the defendant should get as much individualized (subjective) justice as possible. [But what] happens to the victims—almost always minority women and children—when multiculturalism and individualized justice are advanced by dispositive cultural evidence? The answer, both in theory and in practice, is stark: They are denied the protection of the criminal laws because their assailants generally go free, either immediately or within a relatively brief period of time. [W]hen cultural

evidence is permitted to excuse otherwise criminal conduct, the system effectively is choosing to adopt a different, discriminatory standard of criminality
for immigrant defendants, and hence, a different and discriminatory level of
protection for victims who are members of the culture in question. . . . Thus,
the use of cultural defenses is anathema to another fundamental goal of the
progressive agenda, namely the expansion of legal protections for some of the
least powerful members of American society: women and children.

There is a lively debate about these issues. Professor Elaine Chiu notes that
the criminal justice system already acknowledges the relevance of culture as a
mitigating or exonerating factor, but it relies almost exclusively on the discretion of judges and prosecutors to achieve justice in such situations; she condemns the arbitrariness of that approach and proposes greater reliance on a
formal doctrinal defense. See Elaine M. Chiu, Culture as Justification, Not
Excuse, 43 Am. Crim. L. Rev. 1317 (2006). For an analysis supporting a
defense, together with a comprehensive review of the contexts in which cultural issues arise, see Alison Dundes Renteln, The Cultural Defense (2004).
For a contrary view, see Eliot M. Held & Reid Griffith Fontaine, On the
Boundaries of Culture as an Affirmative Defense, 51 Ariz. L. Rev. 237
(2009). The conflict between feminism and multiculturalism in this context
is explored in Holly Maguigan, Cultural Evidence and Male Violence: Are
Feminist and Multicultural Reformers on a Collision Course in Criminal
Courts?, 70 N.Y.U. L. Rev. 36 (1995).

The cultural defense may also involve using the defendant's distinctive
culture to rebut the existence of a required mens rea. See, e.g., People v. Wu,
286 Cal. Rptr. 869 (Cal. App. 1991) (premeditation, provocation); People v.
Rhines, 182 Cal. Rptr. 478 (Cal. App. 1982) (mistake as to consent in rape
prosecution). For further discussion, see Martin P. Golding, The Cultural
Defense, 15 Ratio Juris 146 (2002); Nancy S. Kim, The Cultural Defense
and the Problem of Cultural Preemption: A Framework for Analysis, 27
N.M. L. Rev. 101 (1997).

chapter 4

Rape

Few areas of criminal law have attracted as much attention and controversy over the past three decades as the law of rape. Widespread criticism that rape law was unfair to women led to extensive changes in the definition of rape, in the rules of evidence and procedure affecting rape trials, and in the processing of rape complaints.

Is rape law now in accord with prevailing attitudes about the expression of consent in sexual contacts? What are those attitudes (and are they the same for women as for men)? Has the focus on male sexual abuse of women obscured or overshadowed the prevalence and gravity of same-sex sexual violence and the sexual victimization of men? If prevailing attitudes remain unfair to victims of sexual offenses, should the criminal law move beyond them?

Issues analogous to these rarely present any difficulty in connection with crimes like homicide, burglary, robbery, and theft. But in connection with rape, these questions are difficult to answer and acutely controversial. An understanding of the legal issues therefore requires attention to the nature of the targeted behavior, the kinds of harm it inflicts, and the social dynamics underlying it. We begin by considering several contrasting perspectives on the social and behavioral aspects of rape. We then examine the legal doctrines relevant to actus reus, mens rea, and problems of proof.

A. PERSPECTIVES

MARGARET T. GORDON & STEPHANIE RIGER, THE FEMALE FEAR: THE SOCIAL COST OF RAPE

2, 26-28, 32-36 (1991)

Most women experience fear of rape as a nagging, gnawing sense that something awful could happen, an angst that keeps them from doing things they want or need to do, or from doing them at the time or in the way they might otherwise do. Women's fear of rape is a sense that one must always be on guard, vigilant and alert, a feeling that causes a woman to tighten with anxiety if someone is walking too closely behind her, especially at night. . . . It is worse than fear of other crimes because women know they are held responsible for avoiding rape, and should they be victimized, they know they are likely to be blamed. . . .

While stranger rapes may constitute people's image of what is typical, acquaintance rapes or nonstranger rapes . . . account for 55 to 60 percent of rapes reported to police. . . .

But the words "nonstranger" or "acquaintance" cover a wide range of types of relationships. [One] type of acquaintance rape is referred to as date rape; this occurs when the victim initially is willing to be in the company of a man who then becomes violent toward her. For several reasons, many of these rapes are not reported. [D]ate-rape victims often feel they won't be believed or will be perceived as having "asked for it"—by the police, the courts, and everyone else and, therefore, there is no point in reporting it. . . .

Many campus rapes seem to involve the use of excessive amounts of alcohol by one or both persons involved. One victim of campus rape blamed herself because she was drunk. When a faculty member reminded her that it is a crime to rape, but not a crime to get drunk, the coed decided to file charges. Experts in this field say, "Clearly, among college students, sexual aggression is rare among strangers and common among acquaintances." . . .

[R]esearchers argue that . . . [p]eople are conditioned to accept sexual roles in which male aggression is an acceptable part of our modern courtship culture. According to this line of reasoning, campus rapists are ordinary males operating in an ordinary social context, not even knowing they are doing something wrong, let alone against the law.

NOTES

1. The frequency of rape. Attempts to understand the frequency of rape are important but controversial.

(a) Among female victims, under-reporting of sexual assault has long been a pervasive problem, and acquaintance rapes are especially likely to go unreported. According to one study, even when the assailant is a stranger, 54 percent of completed rapes are not reported to the police; the percentage rises to 61 percent in the case of rapes by an acquaintance and to 77 percent for rapes by a current or former husband or boyfriend.[1]

The reported official figures have been misleading for another reason, because FBI statistics compiled through the end of 2011 counted only *forcible* rape, defined as vaginal penetration by physical force. The definition thus excluded several offenses now considered rape in many states—not only the sexual assault of a man (which we discuss in Note 1(b) below), but also forcible anal penetration of a woman, and nonconsensual sex not

---

1. Callie Marie Rennison, Rape and Sexual Assault: Reporting to Police and Medical Attention, 1992-2000 at 3 (U.S. Dept. of Justice, Bureau of Justice Statistics, 2002).

involving physical force, such as the sexual abuse of people who cannot resist because they are drugged or heavily intoxicated. In early 2012, the Justice Department announced that in compiling national statistics, it will henceforth define as rape "[t]he penetration, no matter how slight, of the vagina or anus with any body part or object, or oral penetration by a sex organ of another person, without the consent of the victim."[2] Note that this definition is used *solely for statistical purposes*; the FBI's new terminology makes no change in the legal definition of rape, which continues to vary widely among the states. In addition, the FBI expects that it will take several years for the law enforcement agencies that submit data for national reports to take the broader new definition into account.

Though many rapes are not reported even to survey interviewers, the Justice Department's surveys are nonetheless revealing. Recent ones show significant drops in victimization rates over the past two decades.[3] Many criminologists and women's advocates believe that progress has been made and that "there has clearly been a decline over the last 10 to 20 years."[4] But small sample sizes and persistent under-reporting make the figures difficult to interpret. One of the most comprehensive efforts, the Justice Department's 1998 National Violence Against Women Survey (NVAW), found an annual rape victimization rate of 870 per 100,000 women aged 18 or older, equivalent to 876,000 completed and attempted rapes for this age group alone. Fifteen percent of the adult women had experienced one or more completed rapes in their lifetimes, and another 3 percent had been victims of attempted rape.

For college women, victimization rates appear to be especially high. A 1999 national survey for the Justice Department found that 2.8 percent of college women had experienced a completed or attempted rape during the preceding six months, suggesting an annual victimization rate of roughly 4,900 per 100,000 college women. As a result, the research team concluded, "[o]ver the course of a college career—which now lasts an average of 5 years—the percentage of completed or attempted rape victimization among women in higher educational institutions might climb to between one-fifth and one-quarter."[5] A 2007 study found similar numbers: 14 percent of undergraduate women had been victims of one or more sexual assaults since entering college.[6] At one large Midwestern university, 12 percent of the women undergraduates had been victims of completed or attempted sexual intercourse

2. http://www.fbi.gov/news/pressrel/press-releases/attorney-general-eric-holder-announces-revisions-to-the-uniform-crime-reports-definition-of-rape.

3. See Jennifer L. Truman & Michael R. Rand, National Crime Victimization Survey—2009 at 1. 2 (U.S. Dept. of Justice, Bureau of Justice Statistics, 2010).

4. See David A. Farenthold, Statistics Show Drop in U.S. Rape Cases, Wash. Post, June 19, 2006 (quoting Kim Gandy, president of the National Organization for Women).

5. Bonnie S. Fisher, Francis T. Cullen & Michael G. Turner, The Sexual Victimization of College Women, 10 (Natl. Instit. of Justice 2000). Compare Timothy C. Hart, Violent Victimization of College Students 2 (Bureau of Justice Statistics 2003), reporting that for female college students, the annual rate of victimization for rape and sexual assault over the period 1995-2000 was 620 per 100,000.

6. Christopher P. Krebs et al., The Campus Sexual Assault (CSA) Study at vii (2007).

during the preceding seven months; use of physical force and threats was infrequent, but in more than half the cases the other person "just did it before you had a chance to protest," and in 26 percent of the cases the other person "ignored your protests."[7]

Figures like these have stirred considerable controversy. One critic notes that 73 percent of the women counted as rape victims in one major study did not label their own experience as "rape," and 42 percent of them subsequently dated and had sex again with their supposed attackers. See Neil Gilbert, The Phantom Epidemic of Sexual Assault, 103 Pub. Int. 54, 60, 63 (Spring 1991). That argument raises important questions about the evolving social conception of what rape is. Does the apparent anomaly that Gilbert emphasized— that rape seemed to occur more frequently in the eyes of researchers than it did in the eyes of the college women themselves—simply reflect the tendency of the college women to accept the now-obsolete assumption that coercion on a date cannot be "rape"? Even today, when date-rape sensitivity discussions are common on college campuses, one-third to one-half of the college women who describe an incident of physically coerced sex still do not label the encounter as rape.[8] Some researchers argue that such behavior on the part of victims—the tendency to blame themselves when their date turns violent and to deny that the experience was rape—is itself a confirmation of the seriousness and prevalence of sexual abuse. See Robin Warshaw, I Never Called It Rape (1988).

(b) *Male victims.* Victimization rates are roughly five to six times higher for women than for men, but sexual abuse of men is by no means rare. Victimization rates are particularly high in prisons. Male inmates are often targeted regardless of their sexual orientation. Gay and transgender men can face particularly acute risks of abuse, but administrative efforts to mitigate that problem have sometimes caused more harm than good. See Russell K. Robinson, Masculinity as Prison: Sexual Identity, Race, and Incarceration, 99 Calif. L. Rev. 1309 (2011).

In a recent Justice Department survey, 4.5 percent of prison inmates reported sexual assault during the previous year, and 13 percent had been sexually victimized (often many times) during their time in custody.[9] To address the difficulties of tracking and preventing sexual abuse in prison, Congress created a Prison Rape Elimination Commission, which in turn has recommended procedures to facilitate victim reporting and to permit

---

7. Laurel Crown & Linda J. Roberts, Against Their Will: Young Women's Nonagentic Sexual Experiences, 24 J. Soc. & Pers. Relationships 385, 392, 396 (2007).

8. Heather Littleton et al., Sexual Assault Victims' Acknowledgment Status and Revictimization Risk, 33 Psychol. Women Q. 34, 34 (2009) (finding that "a majority" of college rape victims did not label their experience as rape); Bonnie S. Fisher et al., Acknowledging Sexual Victimization as Rape: Results from a National-Level Study, 20 Just. Q. 535, 538, 560 (2003) (half to two-thirds labeled their experience rape).

9. Allen J. Beck & Paige M. Harrison, Sexual Violence in State and Federal Prisons—2007 (Bureau of Justice Statistics 2008).

successful monitoring and punishing of these offenses.[10] As yet, however, implementation of the recommendations has been limited.[11] Just as "date rape" was long ignored in our culture or dismissed as something different from "real rape," public opinion has been slow to acknowledge prison sexual abuse as a serious crime rather than an acceptable facet of a convicted offender's punishment. See Alice Ristroph, Sexual Punishments, 15 Colum. J. Gender & L. 139 (2006); Mary Sigler, Just Deserts, Prison Rape, and the Pleasing Fiction of Guideline Sentencing, 38 Ariz. St. L.J. 561 (2006).

Sexual victimization of men outside of prison has ranked even lower in public awareness and concern. Yet the NVAW survey found that 3 percent of adult men had been victims of completed or attempted rape in their lifetimes.[12] Under-reporting is endemic, partly because male victims and their advocates confront pervasive disbelief or indifference on the part of authorities and the wider public. For in-depth discussion of the issues, see I. Bennett Capers, Real Rape Too, 99 Calif. L. Rev. 1259 (2011).

(c) To keep these problems in perspective, it is essential to stress that even the estimates at the "low" end represent an enormous amount of abuse. But the debate over the prevalence of rape remains important for understanding the nature of the task that criminal law confronts: Is the law addressing serious but infrequent, aberrational behavior? Or should the law condemn (and does it already condemn) a type of conduct that is commonplace among ordinary, otherwise law-abiding people?

2. The alpha-male: the frequency (and acceptability) of sexually aggressive behavior. Writing in the 1980s, Elizabeth A. Stanko argued that the law and culture of the time were far too tolerant of sexual abuse of women (Intimate Intrusions 9 (1985)):

> To be a woman—in most societies, in most eras—is to experience physical and/or sexual terrorism at the hands of men. Our everyday behaviour reflects our precautions, the measures we take to protect ourselves. We are wary of going out at night, even in our own neighbourhoods. We are warned by men and other women not to trust strangers. But somehow they forget to warn us about men we know: our fathers, our acquaintances, our co-workers, our lovers, our teachers. Many men familiar to us also terrorize our everyday lives in our homes, our schools, our workplaces.

Is this an accurate perception? Even in the 1980s, many men clearly did not think so. Professor Robin West wrote (The Difference in Women's Hedonic Lives, 3 Wis. Women's L.J. 81, 95 (1987)), "[T]he claim that women's lives are

---

10. See Jamie Fellner, Ensuring Progress: Accountability Standards Recommended by the National Prison Rape Elimination Commission, 30 Pace L. Rev. 1625 (2010).

11. See Anthony C. Thompson, What Happens Behind Locked Doors: The Difficulty of Addressing and Eliminating Rape in Prison, 33 New Eng. J. on Crim. & Civ. Confinement 119 (2009).

12. Patricia Tjaden & Nancy Thoennes, Extent, Nature and Consequences of Rape Victimization: Findings from the National Violence Against Women Survey 7-8 (Natl. Institute of Justice 2006).

ruled by fear is heard by these men as wildly implausible. They see no evidence in their own lives to support it." On the other hand, Professor Menachem Amir's study, Patterns in Forcible Rape (1971), reported (p. 130) "general assumptions . . . that there are constant pressures for sexual gratification and experience among all males and that some aggression is an expected part of the male role in sexual encounters." From that perspective, some male aggressiveness may have been present, but not noticed as aberrant, in situations ranging from marriage through dates, jobs, and even encounters between strangers.

Of course, American culture and the law have changed considerably since those days. But beneath the surface, traditional assumptions about sex roles may persist. Professor Andrew E. Taslitz finds (Willfully Blinded: On Date Rape and Self-Deception, 28 Harv. J.L. & Gender 381, 405-406 (2005)) that "changes in popular culture and in officially stated norms [have] at best had only a modest impact, if any, on the unconscious social norms actually at work in rape cases." Many share Professor Ann J. Cahill's concern (Rethinking Rape 1 (2001)) that "[t]he threat of rape . . . constitutes a persistent and pervasive element in women's lives." Others, of course, continue to find this kind of claim exaggerated or hard to understand.

Against this background, controversies about the prevalence of sexual abuse and law's adequacy in preventing it turn in part on what kind of conduct is considered aggressive, and they also turn on perceptions about the extent to which aggression is expected and acceptable (and to whom).

3. What precisely is the nature of the harm in rape? Many think of rape as a crime of violence. On this view the offense appears as a species of aggravated assault, and some argue that the essential harm to a rape victim is similar to that experienced in any severe beating. Men who view the offense in these terms often see the threat of rape faced by women as not fundamentally different from the threat of non-sexual assault to which men are often exposed. In contrast, many feminists suggest that the important harm in rape is not violence but unwanted sexual intrusion. Taking this view of the essential harm, feminists argue that men often have difficulty understanding when women feel raped and more generally what women fear about male behavior. Feminist law reformers assert that these "male" attitudes lead to inappropriate conceptions about the amount of force necessary to constitute rape. Consider Catharine A. MacKinnon, Feminism Unmodified 86-87 (1987):

> The point of view of men up to this time, called objective, has been to distinguish sharply between rape on the one hand and intercourse on the other; sexual harassment on the one hand and normal, ordinary sexual initiation on the other. . . . What women experience does not so clearly distinguish the normal, everyday things from those abuses from which they have been defined by distinction. . . . What we are saying is that sexuality in exactly these normal forms often *does* violate us.

Other concerns also have been suggested:

> Intercourse with an unconscious woman is prohibited not because the act is violent (though it does have violent aspects) but more fundamentally because taking advantage of a woman's incapacitation in this manner violates, without any conceivable justification, her right to control access to her own body. Once it is recognized that these features (rather than implicit violence) are essential to existing criminal prohibitions, sexual autonomy emerges as an independent value.[13]
>
> [E]very person [has a] right to control the boundaries of his or her own sexual experience. . . . Sexual autonomy [requires] an internal capacity to make reasonably mature and rational choices and an external freedom from impermissible pressures and constraints. [A] third dimension is equally important. The core concept of the person . . . implies a physical boundary. . . . Even without making threats that restrict the exercise of free choice, an individual violates a woman's autonomy when he engages in sexual conduct without ensuring that he has her valid consent.[14]

4. One reason that controversy about rape law continues is that underlying attitudes about sexual relationships have become highly controversial and are themselves in a state of flux. Criminal law always reflects, responds to, and acts upon the culture of the community. Nowhere have these interactions become more vivid, and more problematic, than in the law of rape. Professor Susan Estrich, who has written of her experience as a rape victim, offers this perspective on the issues (Teaching Rape Law, 102 Yale L.J. 509, 514-515 (1992)):

> I know many students, and even a few professors, who believe that . . . if [the woman] didn't consent fully and voluntarily, it is rape, no matter what she said or did, or what he did or did not realize. . . . And that's what they want to hear in class. This kind of orthodoxy is not only bad educationally but, in the case of rape, it also misses the point. Society is not so orthodox in its views. There is a debate going on in the courthouses and prosecutors' offices, and around coffee machines and dinner tables . . . about when women should be believed, and what counts as consent. There's a debate going on in America as to what is reasonable when it comes to sex. . . . To silence that debate in the classroom is to remove the classroom from reality, and to make ourselves irrelevant. It may be hard for some students, but ultimately the only way to change things—and that's usually the goal of those who find the discussions most difficult—is to confront the issues squarely. . . .

---

13. Stephen J. Schulhofer, Taking Sexual Autonomy Seriously: Rape Law and Beyond, 11 Law & Phil. 35, 68 (1992).

14. Stephen J. Schulhofer, Unwanted Sex 15, 111 (1998).

B. STATUTORY FRAMEWORKS

INTRODUCTORY NOTE

In the eighteenth century, William Blackstone defined rape as "carnal knowledge of a woman forcibly and against her will."[15] Until the 1950s, most American statutes preserved Blackstone's definition, with only minor verbal differences. This uniformity began to erode with a wave of reforms initiated in the 1960s and 1970s. Along with changes to procedures and rules of evidence (considered in Section E below), the reforms addressed such substantive issues as the gender-specific character of the crime (traditionally, only a woman could be raped), the labeling of the offense as "rape," the degree of force and/or resistance required, the need to differentiate between degrees of the offense, and the traditional exemption for men who forcibly raped their wives.

The upshot is enormous diversity in state approaches today. Many states still adhere closely to traditional conceptions; in Maryland, for example, rape is defined, as in Blackstone's day, as "vaginal intercourse . . . by force, or the threat of force, without the consent of the other."[16] In other jurisdictions, statutory provisions make a sharp break with the past or combine new features with vestiges of the older concepts. To illustrate these variations, we present the 1950 California provision, which was typical of the rape statutes of its time, the 1962 Model Penal Code proposal, and three contrasting regimes currently in effect—those of California, New York, and Wisconsin.

For an initial overview, we suggest that students note how statutory regimes have changed over time and how states now differ in the way they label, grade, and punish the offense. In addition, it is especially important to note the variations in the kinds of facts required to obtain a conviction. In what ways is the legal definition of rape or sexual assault in these jurisdictions broader or narrower than the definition used by the FBI (page 332, Note 1(a) supra) for statistical purposes? We also suggest returning to these distinct regimes to consider which of them affords the best framework for resolving the concrete problems posed in the cases that will follow.

CALIFORNIA PENAL CODE, TITLE 9 (1950)

SECTION 261. RAPE

Rape [punishable by imprisonment for up to fifty years] is an act of sexual intercourse accomplished with a female not the wife of the perpetrator . . . :

(1) Where the female is under the age of eighteen years;

(2) Where she is incapable, through . . . unsoundness of mind . . . of giving consent;

---

15. William Blackstone, 4 Commentaries on the Laws of England 210 (1765).
16. Md. Code, Criminal Law §§3-303(a)(1), 3-304(a)(1)(2010).

(3) Where she resists but her resistance is overcome by force or violence;

(4) Where she is prevented from resisting by threats of great and immediate bodily harm, ... or by any intoxicating [or] narcotic ... substance, administered by or with the privity of the accused.

(5) Where she is at the time unconscious of the nature of the act, and this is known to the accused. ...

(6) Where she submits under the belief that the person committing the act is the victim's spouse, and this belief is induced by any artifice, pretense, or concealment practiced by the accused, with intent to induce such belief.

MODEL PENAL CODE PROPOSED OFFICIAL DRAFT (1962)

SECTION 213.1.
[See Appendix].

CALIFORNIA PENAL CODE, TITLE 9 (2011)

SECTION 261. RAPE DEFINED

(a) Rape [punishable by imprisonment for three, six, or eight years[a]] is an act of sexual intercourse accomplished with a person not the spouse of the perpetrator ... :

(1) Where a person is incapable, because of a mental disorder or developmental or physical disability, of giving legal consent, and this is known or reasonably should be known to the person committing the act. ...

(2) Where it is accomplished against a person's will by means of force, violence, duress, menace, or fear of immediate and unlawful bodily injury on the person or another.

(3) Where a person is prevented from resisting by any intoxicating or anesthetic substance, ... and this condition was known, or reasonably should have been known by the accused.

(4) Where a person is at the time unconscious of the nature of the act, and this is known to the accused. ...

(5) Where a person submits under the belief that the person committing the act is the victim's spouse, and this belief is induced by any artifice, pretense, or concealment practiced by the accused, with intent to induce the belief.

(6) Where the act is accomplished against the victim's will by threatening to retaliate in the future against the victim or any other person, and there is a reasonable possibility that the perpetrator will execute the threat. "[T]hreatening to retaliate" means a threat to kidnap or falsely imprison, or to inflict extreme pain, serious bodily injury, or death. ...

(b) "[D]uress" means a direct or implied threat of force, violence, danger, or retribution sufficient to coerce a reasonable person of ordinary

---

a. California law authorizes additional years of imprisonment for rape in violation of this section when the victim is a minor or when the perpetrator has a record of prior similar offenses. The punishment increases to life imprisonment in cases involving severe aggravating circumstances (e.g., kidnapping, torture, or use of a deadly weapon). Cal. Penal Code §§667.6, 667.61.—EDS.

susceptibilities [to] acquiesce in an act to which one otherwise would not have submitted. . . .

(c) "[M]enace" means any threat, declaration, or act which shows an intention to inflict an injury upon another.

SECTION 261.5. UNLAWFUL SEXUAL INTERCOURSE WITH A PERSON UNDER 18 . . .

Unlawful sexual intercourse is an act of sexual intercourse accomplished with a person [under 18 years of age] who is not the spouse of the perpetrator. . . . [Imprisonment for up to four years when the minor is more than three years younger than the perpetrator.[b]]

SECTION 261.6. "CONSENT." . . .

In prosecutions under Section 261 [or] 262 . . . in which consent is at issue, "consent" shall be defined to mean positive cooperation in act or attitude pursuant to an exercise of free will. The person must act freely and voluntarily and have knowledge of the nature of the act or transaction involved. . . .

SECTION 262. RAPE OF A SPOUSE. . . .

Rape of a person who is the spouse of the perpetrator [punishable as provided under §261] is an act of sexual intercourse accomplished under any of the . . . circumstances [specified in §261(2), (3), (4), or (6)].

NEW YORK PENAL LAW (2011)

SECTION 130.00. SEX OFFENSES; DEFINITIONS OF TERMS. . . .

8. "Forcible compulsion" means to compel by either: (a) use of physical force; or (b) a threat, express or implied, which places a person in fear of immediate death or physical injury to himself, herself or another person, or in fear that he, she or another person will immediately be kidnapped.

SECTION 130.05. SEX OFFENSES; LACK OF CONSENT

1. Whether or not specifically stated, it is an element of every offense defined in this article that the sexual act was committed without consent of the victim.

2. Lack of consent results from: (a) Forcible compulsion; or (b) Incapacity to consent; or . . . (d) Where the offense charged is rape in the third degree as defined in subdivision three of section 130.25, . . . circumstances under which, at the time of the act of intercourse, . . . the victim clearly expressed that he or she did not consent to engage in such act, and a reasonable person in the actor's situation would have understood such person's words and acts as an expression of lack of consent to such act under all the circumstances.

3. A person is deemed incapable of consent when he or she is: (a) less than seventeen years old; or (b) mentally disabled; . . . or (d) physically helpless; or (e) committed to the care and custody of [a state agency] . . . and the actor is an

---

b. The offense drops to a misdemeanor, with a one-year maximum sentence, when the minor is not more than three years younger than the perpetrator. –EDS.

employee, not married to such person, who knows or reasonably should know that such person is committed to the care and custody of such [agency]; or . . . (h) a client or patient and the actor is a health care provider . . . charged with rape in the third degree as defined in section 130.25, . . . and the act of sexual conduct occurs during a treatment session [or] consultation. . . .

SECTION 130.20. SEXUAL MISCONDUCT

[S]exual intercourse with another person without such person's consent . . . is a class A misdemeanor [one-year maximum]. . . .

SECTION 130.25. RAPE IN THE THIRD DEGREE

A person is guilty of rape in the third degree [four-year maximum] when:

1. He or she engages in sexual intercourse with another person who is incapable of consent by reason of some factor other than being less than seventeen years old;

2. Being twenty-one years old or more, he or she engages in sexual intercourse with another person less than seventeen years old; or

3. He or she engages in sexual intercourse with another person without such person's consent where such lack of consent is by reason of some factor other than incapacity to consent. . . .

SECTION 130.30. RAPE IN THE SECOND DEGREE

A person is guilty of rape in the second degree [seven-year maximum] when . . . he or she engages in sexual intercourse with another person who is . . . mentally disabled [or less than fifteen years old and is more than four years younger than the perpetrator]. . . .

SECTION 130.35. RAPE IN THE FIRST DEGREE

A person is guilty of rape in the first degree [25-year maximum] when he or she engages in sexual intercourse with another person [b]y forcible compulsion; or [when the other person is] physically helpless; or [less than] thirteen years old. . . .

WISCONSIN STATUTES (2011)

SECTION 940.225. SEXUAL ASSAULT

(1) First degree sexual assault . . . a Class B felony [60-year maximum] [is committed whenever any person has] sexual contact or sexual intercourse with another person without consent of that person and causes pregnancy or great bodily harm to that person [or uses or threatens to use] a dangerous weapon. . . .

(2) Second degree sexual assault . . . a Class C felony [40-year maximum] [is committed whenever any person has sexual contact or sexual intercourse]:

    (a) . . . with another person without consent of that person by use or threat of force or violence.

    (b) . . . with another person without consent of that person and causes injury, illness, . . . or mental anguish requiring psychiatric care for the victim.

(c) ... with a person who suffers from a mental illness or deficiency which renders that person temporarily or permanently incapable of appraising the person's conduct, and the defendant knows of such condition.

(cm) ... with a person who is under the influence of an intoxicant to a degree which renders that person incapable of giving consent if the defendant has actual knowledge that the person is incapable of giving consent and the defendant has the purpose to have sexual contact or sexual intercourse with the person while the person is incapable of giving consent.

(d) ... with a person who the defendant knows is unconscious. ...

(3) Third degree sexual assault. Whoever has sexual intercourse with a person without the consent of that person is guilty of a Class G felony [ten-year maximum]. ...

(4) Consent ... means words or overt actions by a person who is competent to give informed consent indicating a freely given agreement to have sexual intercourse or sexual contact. ...

SECTION 948.02. SEXUAL ASSAULT OF A CHILD

... Whoever has sexual contact or sexual intercourse with a person who has not attained the age of 16 years is guilty of a Class C felony [40-year maximum]^c. ...

C. ACTUS REUS

1. Force and Resistance

INTRODUCTORY NOTE

Whatever may be the threshold of unacceptable behavior as a matter of social decency or the codes of conduct applicable on college campuses, proof of *force* was—and still is—an essential prerequisite for a criminal conviction of rape in most American jurisdictions. The next example was considered a "close case" on that issue in 1981. As you read the court's decision, consider whether the case should still be considered a "close" one today. And if you think a contemporary court would more readily uphold the conviction, consider which aspects of the defendant's conduct are necessary to support that conclusion. Would the case remain a close one, even today, if the state had failed to prove any of the details of the defendant's alleged conduct?

---

c. The offense rises to a Class B felony, with a 40-year maximum, if the act involves intercourse with a child under 12 years of age or if the act is committed by use of threat of force or violence. The offense is a Class A felony, punishable by life imprisonment, if the victim is under 13 and suffers great bodily harm. Under §948.09, the offense drops to a Class A misdemeanor, with a nine-month maximum, if the victim is at least 16 but less than 18 years of age.—EDS.

STATE v. RUSK

Court of Appeals of Maryland
289 Md. 230, 424 A.2d 720 (1981)

MURPHY, C.J. Edward Rusk was found guilty by a jury . . . of second degree rape in violation of Maryland Code Art. 27, §463(a)(1), which provides in pertinent part:

> A person is guilty of rape in the second degree if the person engages in vaginal intercourse with another person [b]y force or threat of force against the will and without the consent of the other person. . . .[a]

On appeal, the Court of Special Appeals, sitting en banc, . . . concluded by an 8–5 majority that [there was] insufficient evidence of Rusk's guilt . . . to permit the case to go to the jury. We granted certiorari to consider whether the Court of Special Appeals properly applied the [law].

At the trial, the 21-year-old prosecuting witness, Pat, testified that . . . she met a girl friend, Terry, and agreed to drive in their respective cars to Fells Point to have a few drinks. . . . They went to a bar where . . . Rusk approached and said "hello" to Terry. [Terry] said "Hi, Eddie." Rusk then began talking with Pat and during their conversation both of them acknowledged being separated from their respective spouses and having a child. Pat told Rusk that she had to go home [and] Rusk requested a ride to his apartment. Although Pat did not know Rusk, she thought that Terry knew him [and] agreed to give him a ride. Pat cautioned Rusk on the way to the car that "I'm just giving a ride home, you know, as a friend, not anything to be, you know, thought of other than a ride." . . .

After a twenty-minute drive, they arrived at Rusk's apartment. . . . Pat testified that she was totally unfamiliar with the neighborhood. She parked the car at the curb . . . but left the engine running. Rusk asked Pat to come in, but [n]otwithstanding her repeated refusals, Pat testified that Rusk reached over and turned off the ignition to her car and took her car keys. He got out of the car, walked over to her side, opened the door and said, "Now, will you come up?" Pat explained her subsequent actions:

> At that point, because I was scared, because he had my car keys. I didn't know what to do. I was someplace I didn't even know where I was. . . . I didn't know whether to run. I really didn't think at that point, what to do.
>
> Now, I know that I should have blown the horn. I should have run. There were a million things I could have done. I was scared, at that point, and I didn't do any of them.

---

a. The Maryland statute, currently codified at Md. Code, Criminal Law §§3-303, 3-304 (2010), provides that second-degree rape is punishable by imprisonment for a period not to exceed 20 years. First-degree rape includes intercourse by force or threat of force where the defendant uses a deadly weapon, inflicts or threatens "suffocation, strangulation, disfigurement, serious physical injury, or kidnapping," or is aided by one or more other persons. First-degree rape is punishable by a maximum of life imprisonment.—EDS.

Pat testified that at this moment she feared that Rusk would rape her. She said: "[I]t was the way he looked at me, and said 'Come on up, come on up'; and when he took the keys, I knew that was wrong."

It was then about 1 A.M. Pat accompanied Rusk across the street into a totally dark house. . . . Rusk unlocked the door to his one-room apartment, and turned on the light. . . . She sat in a chair beside the bed. . . . After Rusk talked for a few minutes, he left the room for about one to five minutes. [Pat] made no noise and did not attempt to leave. She said that she did not notice a telephone in the room. When Rusk returned, he turned off the light and sat down on the bed. Pat . . . told him that she wanted to go home. . . . She said, "Now, [that] I came up, can I go?" Rusk, who was still in possession of her car keys, said he wanted her to stay.

Rusk then asked Pat to get on the bed with him. He pulled her by the arms to the bed and began to undress her. . . . Pat removed the rest of her clothing, and then removed Rusk's pants because "he asked me to do it." After they were both undressed Rusk started kissing Pat as she was lying on her back. Pat explained what happened next:

> I was still begging him to please let, you know, let me leave. I said, "you can get a lot of other girls down there, for what you want," and he just kept saying, "no"; and then I was really scared, because I can't describe, you know, what was said. It was more the look in his eyes; and I said, at that point—I didn't know what to say; and I said, "If I do what you want, will you let me go without killing me?" Because I didn't know, at that point, what he was going to do; and I started to cry; and when I did, he put his hands on my throat, and started lightly to choke me; and I said, "If I do what you want, will you let me go?" And he said, yes, and at that time, I proceeded to do what he wanted me to.

Pat testified that Rusk made her perform oral sex and then vaginal intercourse.

Immediately after the intercourse, Pat asked if she could leave. She testified that Rusk said, "Yes," after which she got up and got dressed and Rusk returned her car keys. She said that Rusk then

> walked me to my car, and asked if he could see me again; and I said, "Yes"; and he asked me for my telephone number; and I said, "No, I'll see you down Fells Point sometime," just so I could leave.

Pat testified that she "had no intention of meeting him again." She asked him for directions out of the neighborhood and left.

. . . As she sat in her car reflecting on the incident, Pat said she began to

> wonder what would happen if I hadn't of done what he wanted me to do. So I thought the right thing to do was to go report it, and I went from there to Hillendale to find a police car.

She reported the incident to the police at about 3:15 A.M. . . .

[Rusk and two of his friends testified that they had gone together to a bar to "tr[y] to pick up some ladies," and the friends testified that later in the evening they had seen Rusk walking arm-in-arm with a woman who was "hanging all over him." One of the friends was fairly certain that the woman was Pat.]

According to Rusk, when they arrived in front of his apartment Pat parked the car and turned the engine off. They sat for several minutes "petting each other." . . . Rusk testified that Pat came willingly to his room and that at no time did he make threatening facial expressions. . . . Rusk explained that after the intercourse, Pat "got uptight."

> Well, she started to cry. She said that—she said, "You guys are all alike," she says, "just out for," you know, "one thing." . . . And she said, that she just wanted to leave; and I said, "Well, okay"; and she walked out to the car. I walked out to the car. She got in the car and left.

Rusk denied placing his hands on Pat's throat or attempting to strangle her. He also denied using force or threats of force to get Pat to have intercourse with him.

In reversing Rusk's second-degree rape conviction, the Court of Special Appeals [noted that]:

> Force is an essential element of the crime [of rape] and to justify a conviction, the evidence must warrant a conclusion either that the victim resisted and her resistance was overcome by force or that she was prevented from resisting by threats to her safety. . . .
>
> In all of the victim's testimony we have been unable to see any resistance on her part to the sex acts and certainly can we see no fear as would overcome her attempt to resist or escape. . . . Possession of the keys by the accused may have deterred her vehicular escape but hardly a departure seeking help in the rooming house or in the street. We must say that "the way he looked" fails utterly to support the fear required. . . .

[D]ue process requirements mandate that a criminal conviction not be obtained if the evidence does not reasonably support a finding of guilt beyond a reasonable doubt. However, . . . the reviewing court does not ask itself whether *it* believes that the evidence established guilt beyond a reasonable doubt; rather, the applicable standard is "whether, after viewing the evidence in the light most favorable to the prosecution, *any* rational trier of fact could have found the essential elements of the crime beyond a reasonable doubt."

[L]ack of consent is generally established through proof of resistance or by proof that the victim failed to resist because of fear. The degree of fear necessary to obviate the need to prove resistance, and thereby establish lack of consent, . . . "includes, but is not necessarily limited to, a fear of death or serious bodily harm, or a fear so extreme as to preclude resistance, or a fear which would well nigh render her mind incapable of continuing to resist, or a fear that so overpowers her that she does not dare resist."

[While] the victim's fear [must] be genuine, [the] majority of jurisdictions have required that the victim's fear be reasonably grounded in order to obviate the need for either proof of actual force on the part of the assailant or physical resistance on the part of the victim. We think that, generally, this is the correct standard. . . .

We think the reversal of Rusk's conviction by the Court of Special Appeals was in error [because that court] substituted [its] own view of the evidence (and the inferences that may fairly be drawn from it) for that of the judge and jury. [T]he reasonableness of Pat's apprehension of fear was plainly a question of fact for the jury to determine. . . . Quite obviously, the jury disbelieved Rusk and believed Pat's testimony. From her testimony, the jury could have reasonably concluded that the taking of her car keys was intended by Rusk to immobilize her alone, late at night, in a neighborhood with which she was not familiar; . . . that Pat was afraid that Rusk would kill her unless she submitted; that she began to cry and Rusk then put his hands on her throat and began "lightly to choke" her; that Pat asked him if he would let her go without killing her if she complied with his demands; that Rusk gave an affirmative response, after which she finally submitted.

Just where persuasion ends and force begins in cases like the present is essentially a factual issue. . . . Considering all of the evidence in the case, with particular focus upon the actual force applied by Rusk to Pat's neck, we conclude that the jury could rationally find that the essential elements of second-degree rape had been established and that Rusk was guilty of that offense beyond a reasonable doubt.[b] . . .

COLE, J., dissenting. [The majority] concludes that ". . . the reasonableness of Pat's apprehension of fear was plainly a question of fact for the jury to determine." In so concluding, the majority has skipped over the crucial issue. It seems to me that whether the prosecutrix's fear is reasonable becomes a question only after the court determines that the defendant's conduct under the circumstances was reasonably calculated to give rise to a fear on her part to the extent that she was unable to resist. . . .

While courts no longer require a female to resist to the utmost or to resist where resistance would be foolhardy, they do require her acquiescence in the act of intercourse to stem from fear generated by something of substance. She may not simply say, "I was really scared," and thereby transform consent or mere unwillingness into submission by force. . . . She must follow the natural instinct of every proud female to resist, by more than mere words, the violation of her person by a stranger or an unwelcomed friend. She must make it plain that she regards such sexual acts as abhorrent and repugnant to her natural sense of pride. She must resist unless the defendant has objectively manifested his intent to use physical force to accomplish his purpose. The law regards rape as a crime of violence. The majority today attenuates this proposition. It declares the innocence of an at best distraught young woman. It does not demonstrate the defendant's guilt of the crime of rape.

. . . The majority suggests that "from her testimony the jury could have reasonably concluded that the taking of her keys was intended by Rusk to

---

immobilize her alone, late at night, in a neighborhood with which she was unfamiliar. . . ." But on what facts does the majority so conclude? There is no evidence descriptive of the tone of his voice; her testimony indicates only the bare statement quoted above. . . .

She also testified that she was afraid of "the way he looked". . . . But what can the majority conclude from [a] "look" that remained undescribed? There is no evidence whatsoever to suggest that this was anything other than a pattern of conduct consistent with the ordinary seduction of a female acquaintance who at first suggests her disinclination. . . .

The majority further suggests that the jury could infer the defendant's affirmative response [to her question "If I do what you want, will you let me go without killing me?"]. The facts belie such inference since by the prosecutrix's own testimony the defendant made *no* response. *He said nothing!*

She then testified that she started to cry and he "started lightly to choke" her, whatever that means. Obviously, the choking was not of any persuasive significance. During this "choking" she was able to talk. She said "If I do what you want will you let me go?" It was at this point that the defendant said yes.

I find it incredible for the majority to conclude that on these facts, without more, a woman was *forced* to commit oral sex upon the defendant and then to engage in vaginal intercourse. [T]here are no acts or conduct on the part of the defendant to suggest . . . that he made any objective, identifiable threats to her which would give rise to this woman's failure to flee, summon help, scream, or make physical resistance. . . . In my judgment the State failed to prove the essential element of force beyond a reasonable doubt. . . .

Elizabeth A. Stanko, Intimate Intrusions, 9-11 (1985): [E]xplanations of [male violence] centre around the naturalness or unnaturalness of male aggression in relation to women's behaviour. . . . The sexual advance by a male professor toward a young female student, . . . the wolf whistle on the street, . . . the man's brushing up against a female secretary's body in the xerox room (and on and on) are, most people accept, natural expressions of maleness. These expressions are assumed to be non-threatening to women, even, some would say, flattering. The vicious rape, the brutal murder of a woman [are] the aberrant examples of maleness. . . . In the abstract we easily draw lines between those aberrant (thus harmful) and those typical (thus unharmful) types of male behaviour. . . .

What becomes lost, though, in this commonsensical separation between "aberrant" and "typical" male behaviour is a woman-defined understanding of what is threatening. . . . Often, women themselves are confused—sometimes defining male behaviour as typical, other times as aberrant—but nonetheless feel[ing] threatened by some displays of either. . . . Essentially, the categories *typical* and *aberrant* are not useful for understanding women's feelings about, and thus women's experiences of male intimidation and violence. Confusing though they may be, women's experiences point to a potential for violence in many of women's ordinary encounters with men.

NOTES ON RUSK

1. Consider Susan Estrich, Rape, 95 Yale L.J. 1087, 1114-1115 (1986): "The [*Rusk* court's] emphasis on the light choking/heavy caresses is, perhaps, understandable. . . . As it happens, however, that force was not applied until the two were already undressed and in bed. Whatever it was—choking or caressing—was a response to the woman's crying as the moment of intercourse approached. It was not, it seems fairly clear, the only force that produced that moment."

2. For a probing examination of the background of the *Rusk* prosecution, its impact on the parties, and its contemporary significance, see Jeannie Suk, "The Look in His Eyes": The Story of *State v. Rusk* and Rape Reform, in Criminal Law Stories (Robert Weisberg & Donna Coker eds., 2011).

State v. DiPetrillo, 922 A.2d 124 (R.I. 2007): [The victim was a 19-year-old employee in the 30-year-old defendant's business. One night, after asking her to work late, he called her over to his desk. He then] grabbed her by the wrist, pulled her onto his lap, and began kissing her. According to Jane, she initially . . . kissed him back. But then she protested, telling DiPetrillo "we can't do this". . . . [He then] physically moved her from his lap onto the seat of the chair. With his hands placed on each of the chair's arms, he stood over her and continued kissing her; he also put his hand under her shirt and touched her breast.

At trial, Jane testified that at this point she was in fear, tried to avoid the kissing by moving her face away, and repeatedly told defendant to "stop it; he was my boss, we couldn't do this." She also tried to stop him from touching her breast by telling him several times "no, we ha[ve] to stop" and then pushing his hand away. This resistance was unavailing. DiPetrillo continued his assault by pulling Jane's pants and underwear down to her knees and then digitally penetrating her vagina with one of [his] fingers. . . . Scared and in shock, Jane again told DiPetrillo "we have to stop;" she stood up, restored her clothing, and [was eventually able] to walk away. . . . The defendant then said, "we shouldn't tell anybody about what happened."

[Defendant was charged with first-degree sexual assault (Rhode Island's statutory equivalent of rape), requiring proof of sexual penetration by "force or coercion" and second-degree sexual assault, requiring proof of sexual contact by "force or coercion." After a bench trial, the court found defendant guilty on both counts.]

The trial justice . . . found that the evidence satisfied two distinct categories of force and coercion:

> [A]ll of the ingredients were present on the evening of March 20th for the defendant to overbear the will of this diminutive and attractive young girl, either by the very authority that he represented, or by a modicum of physical force. As it turned out, . . . both of those circumstances occurred. [A]part from

a single kiss at the outset, she did not want the defendant to continue his advances. [She] kept telling . . . him it was wrong. . . . She pushed at his chest and tried, to no avail, to push away from his grasp. [S]he described how the defendant hovered over her as she sat trapped and fearful in his chair, with both of his hands on each arm of the chair. [A]ll of the relevant hallmarks of force or coercion . . . , both physical as well as psychological, were part and parcel of the defendant's misconduct. . . .

Generally speaking, force or coercion means overcoming the victim of sexual assault through the application of physical force or violence, against her will, and without her consent. It also includes compelling the victim to submit by threatening to use force or violence. . . . Force or coercion may also consist of the imposition of psychological pressure upon a person who, under all of the circumstances, is vulnerable and susceptible to such pressure.

The defendant asserts that when the trial justice defined the elements of first- and second-degree sexual assault, he interpreted the element of "force or coercion"[3] . . . by reference to improper or inapplicable standards. Specifically, DiPetrillo argues that the trial justice "conflated the 'force or coercion' standard" adopted by the General Assembly with other theories, such as: "the non-consent standard; the psychological-coercion-of-susceptible-victim standard; and the disagreeable sexual encounter standard."

[I]n State v. Burke, 522 A.2d 725 (R.I. 1987), . . . the defendant, a uniformed and armed police officer, was convicted of two counts of first-degree sexual assault upon an alcoholic victim whom he had picked up in his police cruiser while she was hitchhiking. Although the defendant in Burke never orally threatened the victim with violence if she did not submit to his command to perform oral sex upon him, we nonetheless agreed that the defendant coerced the victim to submit "by threatening to use force or violence on [her] and [that] the victim reasonably believe[d] that the accused ha[d] the present ability to execute those threats." . . . However, we also noted that the factual situation in Burke was unusual in that "the sexual assault crime involve[d] a person in a position of authority who is armed, speaks in terms of peremptory command," and "that the victim did not consent to the sexual activity and reasonably believed that resistance would be useless." . . .

DiPetrillo now argues that . . . the Burke analysis of psychological-pressure-on-a-vulnerable-victim should [not] apply to the facts in his case. . . . We agree. [W]e are not willing to extend the Burke analysis of

---

3. General Laws 1956 §11-37-1 states in pertinent part: . . .

   (2) "Force or coercion" means when the accused does any of the following:

      (i) Uses or threatens to use a weapon, or any article used or fashioned in a manner to lead the victim to reasonably believe it to be a weapon.

      (ii) Overcomes the victim through the application of physical force or physical violence.

      (iii) Coerces the victim to submit by threatening to use force or violence on the victim and the victim reasonably believes that the accused has the present ability to execute these threats.

implied threats to the facts in this case, in which the implied threat arose solely in the context of an employment relationship.

[W]e are not convinced that the trial justice's finding of guilt based on physical force . . . can constitute a separate and independent finding of guilt beyond a reasonable doubt. The trial justice's finding that "all of the ingredients were present" in order "for the defendant to overbear the will" of this victim, "either by the very authority that he represented, or by a modicum of physical force" and his conclusion that all of the "relevant hallmarks of force or coercion . . . both physical as well as psychological, were part and parcel of the defendant's misconduct," gives us pause. [W]e are left with uncertainty about whether defendant was convicted based on a finding of force and coercion by physical force. . . .

We therefore vacate the judgment and remand this case to the trial justice with directions to . . . determine whether the state has established, beyond a reasonable doubt, that defendant is guilty of the crimes charged in the indictment, based solely on physical force as set forth in §11-37-1(2)(ii).

FLAHERTY, J., dissenting. [T]he only fair reading of the trial justice's decision is that he found that the complaining witness (Jane) was overborne by a combination of psychological pressure arising from DiPetrillo's authority over her as an employee and the application of some minimal physical force. [The trial justice] found that the evidence of physical force . . . amounted to only a "modicum," and that Jane was ultimately overcome by the entirety of the misconduct and not by either of the individual elements that comprised it. [T]here was no finding that the amount of physical force present in the record—i.e. a modicum[16]—could have, by itself, overcome the complaining witness. . . . [18] [It is] apparent that, putting those psychological considerations aside, . . . the state failed to prove, and the trial justice did not find, that the element of force or coercion was satisfied beyond a reasonable doubt. . . .

There is little doubt . . . that Craig DiPetrillo's actions on the night in question were boorish to the extreme, and that he may be a cad and a louse. But because the state failed to prove that all the elements of the crimes charged were satisfied beyond a reasonable doubt, I would vacate his conviction and order the entry of a judgment of acquittal.

NOTES ON DiPETRILLO

1. *Economic and psychological pressure?* Sexual interactions in the workplace (both mutually desired and otherwise) can be quite problematic, but they are also common. Company policies may limit the scope of permissible behavior, and sexual harassment laws may provide for civil liability under some

---

16. The dictionary definition of the word modicum is "a moderate or small amount." Random House Unabridged Dictionary 1236 (2d ed. 1993).

18. . . . [E]ven though defendant was the employer of the complainant and he was physically imposing as compared to her, he was neither a police officer, nor was he armed. . . .

circumstances. But most workplaces do not categorically prohibit all sexual advances, and sexual relationships between employees (including those between a supervisor and a subordinate) are often permitted, *provided* that they are consensual. Thus, employees like Jane often face pressure to acquiesce in the sexual advances of a boss or supervisor. Workers in that situation sometimes say "OK" or even "yes." There may appear to be consent (of a sort), but the consent arguably is tainted rather than authentic. There is continuing disagreement in the law about whether a defendant who obtains submission in that manner should be guilty of rape or sexual assault, and we will consider that question in a moment (at page 382 infra).

But notice that the *DiPetrillo* case did not necessarily turn on this controversial issue, because Jane *did not* acquiesce or submit. In spite of the incentives for her to accommodate her employer's wishes, she made plain that she would not cooperate. Under those circumstances, why is there doubt about DiPetrillo's guilt? Was the problem for the prosecution the fact that Jane did not flee more quickly or resist more forcefully? If so, should the employment relationship (or their relative ages and sizes) affect the significance of any perceived lack of resistance on her part? In what way is the evidence unclear with respect to any element of the offense under Rhode Island law?

2. Force or coercion? Notice that the Rhode Island Supreme Court interprets its statute to require that the element of "force or coercion" must be "based solely on physical force." Is this approach justified? And even if it is, don't the trial judge's findings indicate that DiPetrillo *did* use physical force? Apparently, the concern for both the majority and the dissent was that the physical force he used was not especially powerful, and that a mere "modicum" of physical force might not suffice for conviction. Is this further gloss on the "force or coercion" requirement justified?

3. Comparing Rusk *and* DiPetrillo. As we saw above, the *Rusk* court, ruling in 1981, might not have upheld the conviction in the absence of the evidence of "light" choking. If so, would that result—reversal of the conviction in the absence of choking evidence—be different today? How would the Rhode Island court rule on such facts? Under statutes like those of Maryland and Rhode Island, how much have the requirements for a rape conviction changed in the past three decades?

NOTES ON FORCE AND RESISTANCE

1. The force requirement. Traditionally, perpetrating intercourse without consent was not necessarily a crime. The absence of consent was sufficient to trigger criminal liability only under special circumstances—when the victim was below a given age ("statutory" rape), unconscious, or mentally incompetent. See, e.g., Cal. Penal Code §261 (1950), page 338 supra; Deborah W. Denno, Sexuality, Rape, and Mental Retardation, 1997 U. Ill. L. Rev. 315. A growing number of American jurisdictions, departing from this traditional view, now criminalize all instances of nonconsensual intercourse. Yet this approach, which we explore at pages 363-375 infra, remains in the minority. As Professor Michelle J. Anderson notes (Negotiating Sex, 78 S. Cal. L. Rev. 101, 103 (2005)), "the vast majority of states . . . still overwhelmingly require both the defendant's force and the victim's nonconsent before an act of sexual penetration becomes a felony." Thus, for example, the force-based Maryland statute, which controlled in *Rusk*, remains in effect today. And for the majority of courts, the required force "does not mean the force inherent in all sexual penetration . . . but physical compulsion, or a threat of physical compulsion, that causes the victim to submit to the sexual penetration against his or her will." People v. Denbo, 868 N.E.2d 347, 355 (Ill. App. 2007). See, e.g., Commonwealth v. Lopez, 745 N.E.2d 961, 965 (Mass. 2001):

> We have construed the [statutory] element, "by force and against his will," as truly encompassing two separate elements each of which must independently be satisfied. Therefore, the Commonwealth must demonstrate beyond a reasonable doubt that the defendant committed sexual intercourse (1) by means of physical force; nonphysical, constructive force [such as a police officer's threat to arrest the victim]; or threats of bodily harm, either explicit or implicit; and (2) at the time of penetration, there was no consent.

2. The resistance requirement. (a) Current law. In some states, resistance is included among the formal statutory elements, but more often resistance has been read into the statutes as a requirement somehow implicit in the elements of force or non-consent. Only one American state retains the old requirement that the victim resist "to the utmost,"[17] but several require "earnest resistance,"[18] and in roughly half the states, contemporary statutes or court decisions still require at least "reasonable resistance." See, e.g., Mo. Rev. Stat. §566.30 (2011), requiring "physical force that overcomes reasonable resistance"; Hull v. State, 687 So. 2d 708, 723 (Miss. 1996), holding that a rape victim must use "all reasonable physical resistance available to her under the circumstances." In the remaining states, resistance is no longer formally required, but courts continue to consider resistance (or its absence) as highly probative on the question whether the victim consented. See Michelle J. Anderson, Reviving Resistance in Rape Law, 1998 U. Ill. L. Rev. 953 (1999). Moreover, recent research finds that even when potential jurors declare themselves opposed to a resistance requirement and are "well versed in the socially 'appropriate' attitudes to be voiced at [an] abstract level,"[19] nonetheless in deliberations the same individuals argue strongly for acquittal based on the complainant's lack of clear physical resistance.

---

17. La. Rev. Stat. Ann. §14:42A(1) (2011), specifying that aggravated rape is committed "[w]hen the victim resists the act to the utmost, but whose resistance is overcome by force." In contrast, the Louisiana offense of "forcible rape" requires only reasonable resistance, §14.42:1, and there is no resistance requirement for the lesser offense of "simple rape." §14.43.

18. E.g., Ala. Code §13A-6-60(8) (2011); W. Va. Code §61-8B-1(1)(a) (2011).

19. Louise Ellison & Vanessa E. Munro, A Stranger in the Bushes, or an Elephant in the Room?: Critical Reflections Upon Received Rape Myth Wisdom in the Context of a Mock Jury Study, 13 New Crim. L. Rev. 781, 799 (2010).

(b) Policy concerns. California's statutory resistance requirement was repealed in 1980. Compare Cal. Penal Code §261(3) (1950) with Cal. Penal Code §261(a)(2)(2005), pages 338-340 supra. The concerns that led to the repeal are summarized in People v. Barnes, 721 P.2d 110, 117-120 (Cal. 1986):

> The requirement that a woman resist her attacker appears to have been grounded in the basic distrust with which courts and commentators traditionally viewed a woman's testimony regarding sexual assault. . . . [T]he requirement of resistance insured against wrongful conviction based solely on testimony the law considered to be inherently suspect. . . .
>
> Recently, however, the entire concept of resistance to sexual assault has been called into question. It has been suggested that while the presence of resistance may well be probative on the issue of force or nonconsent, its absence may not. For example, some studies have demonstrated that while some women respond to sexual assault with active resistance, others "freeze." . . . The "frozen fright" response resembles cooperative behavior. Indeed, as [one psychologist] notes, the "victim may smile, even initiate acts, and may appear relaxed and calm." Subjectively, however, she may be in a state of terror. [L]ack of physical resistance may reflect a "profound primal terror" rather than consent.
>
> [T]he law does not expect . . . that in defending oneself or one's property from [robbery, kidnapping and assault], a person must risk injury or death by displaying resistance in the face of attack. The amendment of §261(a)(2) acknowledges that previous [assumptions], which singled out the credibility of rape complaints as suspect, have no place in a modern system of jurisprudence.

Compare David P. Bryden, Redefining Rape, 3 Buff. Crim. L. Rev. 317, 375-376 (2000):

> Citizens need to know, approximately, the boundary between lawful and unlawful conduct. This is especially true of a serious crime like rape. Physical force marks the well-known bright line between seduction and rape. . . . Courts could say, of course, that the man is guilty if the woman did not consent *and he knew it.* This would create a bright line of sorts, but the question would remain: When is he supposed to know it? Without an answer to that question, the line between lawful and unlawful behavior would be obscure and subject to the vagaries of aberrant juries.

See also Anderson, supra, 1998 U. Ill. L. Rev. at 977-990. Professor Anderson agrees that victim resistance should not be an essential prerequisite to a rape conviction, but she notes that "[w]omen's fear that resisting rape risks serious injury or death is wildly exaggerated." She explains:

> Despite popular mythology, a woman's physical resistance to a sexual aggressor decreases her chance of being raped and does not increase her risk for serious bodily injury or death. The conclusion of the 1977 Department of Justice study of reported rapes—that women who resist are more likely to suffer serious injury—was flatly contradicted two years later by a 1979 Department of Justice study. . . . [O]f the women who fought back, more than 80 percent avoided being raped. Of the women who did not fight back,

only 33 percent avoided being raped. [S]erious injury requiring medical attention and hospital treatment correlated positively with rape completion, and rape victims were injured more seriously than were victims of attempted rape. Therefore, according to the 1979 Department of Justice study, a . . . passive woman [would] increase both her risk that the rape would be completed and her risk of serious injury requiring medical attention. . . .

Resisting a rapist, [moreover], is associated with less self-blame, shorter recovery times, and obtaining treatment after the rape. One study concluded that "one of the most important functions of physical resistance is to keep women from feeling depressed even if they have been raped." Resistance, then, appears to be potentially psychologically beneficial, even when ultimately unsuccessful in deterring the rapist.

(c) All courts recognize at least some occasions when resistance is unnecessary—for example, when a victim is thrown to the ground by a stranger pointing a gun at her head. In such a situation the fear aroused by the defendant's conduct could overpower the victim and prevent her from resisting. Thus, the question whether the victim offered "reasonable" resistance is in effect displaced by the question whether the victim "reasonably" feared serious bodily harm—so that the "reasonable" amount of resistance, under the circumstances, was no resistance at all. See Merzbacher v. State, 697 A.2d 432, 442 (Md. 1997).

Questions: Do statutes like California's solve the problem of resistance? What result if the *Rusk* case had been tried in California? What would be the result in *Rusk* under Model Penal Code §213.1?

3. The requirement of a "reasonable" apprehension. In *Rusk*, all the judges accepted the rule that the victim's fear must be reasonably grounded; they divided only over the question whether a jury could properly find that it was, on the facts. But why should the absence of resistance have to be explained by fears that are objectively "reasonable"? One obvious concern is to assure that the defendant realizes the woman is submitting out of fear rather than desire. But suppose the defendant *knows* that the victim is genuinely afraid. Suppose that he subtly but deliberately reinforces those fears. (Reconsider the facts of *Rusk*.) Shouldn't a conviction be proper regardless of the "reasonableness" of the fears?[20] Conversely, suppose that the victim's fears are reasonable but that the defendant is totally unaware of them. Shouldn't a conviction be *improper*, regardless of whether the fears are "reasonable"? Or is it appropriate to require defendants to know when their conduct arouses fear of bodily harm and to make sure to dispel any apprehension on the part of their partners?

---

20. Though most courts insist that the victim's fear must be objectively reasonable, at least one has held that a conviction can nonetheless be sustained, when "the victim's fear [is] unreasonable, [if] the perpetrator knew of the victim's subjective fear and took advantage of it." People v. Iniguez, 872 P.2d 1183, 1188 (Cal. 1994).

NOTES ON COERCION AND DURESS

Should the notion of "force" be expanded, so that it can be satisfied not only by physical force and threats to inflict bodily harm but also by other forms of coercion? These Notes examine several dimensions of the problem.

1. Implicit threats. In State v. Alston, 310 N.C. 399, 312 S.E.2d 470 (1984), the defendant and his victim had lived together for six months. After Alston repeatedly struck the victim, she moved out and ended their relationship. A month later, Alston encountered her at her school, said he was going to "fix" her face to show he "was not playing," and told her that he had a "right" to have sex with her one more time. He led her to the house of one of his friends, and when she told him she did not want to have sex, he pulled her up from a chair, took off her clothes, pushed her legs apart, and penetrated her. Alston was convicted of rape, but the North Carolina Supreme Court reversed. The court conceded that the evidence of non-consent was "unequivocal," but held that the evidence did not establish the element of "force." Do you agree? Consider these comments:

Susan Estrich, Real Rape 61-62, 65, 69 (1987): *Alston* reflects the adoption of the most traditional male notion of a fight as the working definition of "force." In a fight you hit your assailant with your fists or your elbows or your knees. In a fight the person attacked fights back. In these terms there was no fight in *Alston.* ... To say that there is no "force" in this situation, as the North Carolina court did, is to create a gulf between power and force and to define the latter strictly in schoolboy terms. [This] version of a reasonable person is one who does not scare easily, one who does not feel vulnerable, one who is not passive, one who fights back, not cries. The reasonable woman, it seems, is not a schoolboy "sissy"; she is a real man.

[Thus,] the force standard ... effectively guarantees men freedom to intimidate women and exploit their weakness and passivity, so long as they don't "fight" with them. And it makes clear that the responsibility and blame for such seductions should be placed squarely on the woman.

Vivian Berger, Not So Simple Rape, 7 Crim. Just. Ethics 69, 75-76 (1988): [N]o bright line exists to [mark] the border separating justified use of rape law to safeguard female personhood and choice ... from abuse of this law to "defend" women who abdicate self and will entirely. Because overprotection risks enfeebling instead of empowering women, the tension between reformist goals ... seems to me to make cases like *Alston* a close call, not a springboard for moral outrage.

2. Nonphysical threats. Consider the following cases:

State v. Thompson, 792 P.2d 1103 (Mont. 1990): [Defendant, a high school principal, allegedly forced one of his students to submit to sexual intercourse by threatening to prevent her from graduating from high school. The court affirmed the dismissal of sexual assault charges.] Section 45-5-503, MCA, states the following:

> A person who knowingly has sexual intercourse without consent with a person of the opposite sex commits the offense of sexual intercourse without consent. . . .

The phrase "without consent"[,] . . . defined in §45-5-501, [means:]

> the victim is compelled to submit by force or by threat of imminent death, bodily injury, or kidnapping to be inflicted on anyone; . . .

The District Court in its order [dismissing the charges] defined force as follows:

> The word "force" is used in its ordinary and normal connotation: physical compulsion, the use or immediate threat of bodily harm, injury.

. . . [T]he State argues the fear and apprehension of Jane Doe show Thompson used force against her. We agree with the State that Thompson intimidated Jane Doe; however, we cannot stretch the definition of force to include intimidation, fear, or apprehension. Rather, we adopt the District Court's definition of force. . . .

The alleged facts, if true, show disgusting acts of taking advantage of a young person by an adult who occupied a position of authority over the young person. If we could rewrite the statutes to define the alleged acts here as sexual intercourse without consent, we would willingly do so. The business of courts, however, is to interpret statutes, not to rewrite them, nor to insert words not put there by the legislature. With a good deal of reluctance, and with strong condemnation of the alleged acts, we affirm the District Court.

Commonwealth v. Mlinarich, 498 A.2d 395 (Pa. Super. 1985), affirmed by an equally divided court, 542 A.2d 1335 (Pa. 1988): [The victim was a 14-year-old girl who had been committed to a juvenile detention home after stealing from her brother. Subsequently defendant agreed to assume custody for her, and she was placed in defendant's home. The victim submitted to defendant's sexual advances after he threatened to send her back to the detention home if she refused. He was convicted of corrupting the morals of a minor and of committing rape "by threat of forcible compulsion. . . ." 18 Pa. C.S. §3121(2). The Superior Court reversed the rape conviction:] Our task in this case is made more difficult because the victim of appellant's sexual advances was a fourteen-year-old child. The definition which we adopt, however, will know no age limitation. It is with a view to general application, therefore, that we attempt to define the parameters of the legislative proscription against sexual intercourse by forcible compulsion or threat of forcible compulsion.

The term "force" and its derivative, "forcible," when used to define the crime of rape, have historically been understood by the courts and legal scholars to mean physical force or violence. . . .

To define "forcible compulsion" so as to permit a conviction for rape whenever sexual intercourse is induced by "any threat" or by "physical, moral or intellectual means or by the exigencies of the circumstances" will undoubtedly have unfortunate consequences. If a man takes a destitute widow into his home and provides support for her and her family, such a definition of forcible compulsion will convict him of attempted rape if he threatens to withdraw his support and compel her to leave unless she engages in sexual intercourse. Similarly, a person may be guilty of rape if he or she extorts sexual favors from another person upon threat of discharging the other or his or her spouse from a position of employment, or upon threat of foreclosing the mortgage on the home of the other's parents, . . . or upon threat of disclosing the other's adultery. [S]uch an interpretation of forcible compulsion will place in the hands of jurors almost unlimited discretion to determine which acts, threats or promises will transform sexual intercourse into rape. Without intending to condone any of the foregoing, reprehensible acts, our use of them serves to illustrate the intolerable uncertainty which a wholly elastic definition of rape will create. . . .

We hold that rape, as defined by the legislature . . . requires actual physical compulsion or violence or a threat of physical compulsion or violence sufficient to prevent resistance by a person of reasonable resolution. . . .

[SPAETH, J., dissenting, wrote:] It is frequently said that the words of a statute are to be "given their plain meaning," or are to be "understood according to their common and approved usage." These maxims, however, will not yield the meaning of the phrase, "threat of forcible compulsion," for "force" has more than one plain, or common and approved, meaning. Webster's Third New International Dictionary (1968) provides eleven definitions of "force," some of these being subdivided. . . .

As one considers the range and tone of these several definitions it becomes evident that appellant's threat . . . might, or might not, have been a "threat of forcible compulsion." It was *not* such a threat if "forcible" is to be considered as limited to meaning "to do violence to"; it *might* have been such a threat if "forcible" is to be construed as meaning "to constrain or compel by physical, moral, or intellectual means or by the exigencies of the circumstances," or as meaning "to press, impose, or thrust urgently, importunately, inexorably." . . .

Our problem, therefore, is not to choose *the* "plain meaning" of the phrase, "threat of forcible compulsion," but, rather, to decide *which of several* plain meanings the legislature had in mind. . . .

I have no hesitancy in concluding that the legislature did *not* mean force in the limited sense of "to do violence to," and *did* mean force in the more general sense of "to constrain or compel by physical, moral, or intellectual means or by the exigencies of the circumstances." Only this conclusion is consistent with the legislature's manifested agreement with the Model Penal Code that a "fresh approach" should be taken, and the focus of inquiry shifted away from the victim's consent to the actor's force.

. . . I believe that the jury was entitled to find that the complainant was compelled to submit to appellant's demands by the exigencies of her circumstances, and, further, that in submitting, she acted as a person of reasonable resolution.

3. *Solutions to the problem of nonphysical threats.* (a) Consider the following observations (Comment, Towards a Consent Standard in the Law of Rape, 43 U. Chi. L. Rev. 613, 644-645 (1976)):

> Although the force element has traditionally furthered the policy of physical protection, as well as serving an evidentiary function, . . . freedom of sexual choice rather than physical protection is the primary value served by criminalization of rape. Furthermore, a woman's decision to submit to physical force may be less agonizing than her decision to have intercourse with a person who holds economic or emotional power over her and her family. Although one can argue that a man who obtains intercourse through threats of nonphysical harm should be punished less severely than a violent rapist, the growing legal appreciation of the reality of mental injury and the power of economic duress suggests that he nonetheless should be punished. [T]he freedom of sexual choice which is to be protected by rape law can be as effectively negated by nonphysical as by physical coercion.

(b) MPC §213.1(2) permits a conviction for "gross sexual imposition" in cases where submission is compelled by threat of force or "by any threat that would prevent resistance by a woman of ordinary resolution." Reconsider State v. Thompson, Note 2 supra. Would the principal's threat in that case "prevent resistance by a woman of ordinary resolution"? Are the requirements for conviction under §213.1(2) too stringent?

Conversely, as applied to the hypothetical posed by the *Mlinarich* court (the destitute widow who submits to sexual intercourse with a man who threatens to stop supporting her) does MPC §213.1(2) extend criminal liability too far? Note that the MPC offense of "gross sexual imposition" requires two distinct findings. First, the defendant's proposal must "prevent resistance by a woman of ordinary resolution." Can we say, in the case of the destitute widow, that it would? Second, *even if it would*, the defendant still would not be guilty under the Code unless he has made a "threat." Is the proposition to the destitute widow a threat or just an offer? The choice of labels may seem arbitrary, but it has large implications for the scope of criminal liability. And perhaps surprisingly, the Code's drafters did not intend to cover all inducements that would cause a woman of ordinary resolution to submit. See Model Penal Code and Commentaries §213.1, at 314 (1980):

> [S]ubmission [must result] from coercion rather than bargain. [I]f a wealthy man were to threaten to withdraw financial support from his unemployed girlfriend, it is at least arguable [that this] "would prevent resistance by a woman of ordinary resolution." The reason why this case is excluded from liability . . . is not the gravity of the harm threatened—it may be quite substantial—but its essential character as part of a process of a bargain. He is not guilty of compulsion overwhelming the will of his victim but only of offering her an unattractive choice to avoid some unwanted alternative.

The upshot of this framework is that the criminal liability of the man who "threatens to withdraw his support [from a destitute widow] unless she engages in sexual intercourse" depends on whether the situation involves coercion or bargaining. Which is it?

(c) Several states use an approach similar to that of §213.1(2) by extending the offense of rape or sexual assault to situations in which consent is obtained by "duress" (Cal. Penal Code §261(a)(2), page 339 supra), "coercion,"[21] "extortion,"[22] or using a "position of authority."[23] Are these concepts broad enough to permit conviction in the *Thompson* case or in the case of the destitute widow? Are they *too* broad?

(d) In 1995, the Pennsylvania legislature adopted a statute defining the "forcible compulsion" required for a rape conviction as "[c]ompulsion by use of physical, intellectual, moral, emotional or psychological force, either express or implied." Pa. Stat. §3101. Does a defendant commit rape in Pennsylvania if he uses *psychological* pressure, for example, if "the victim had an adolescent crush on the Defendant and the Defendant was aware of her feelings for him" and obtained her consent by taking advantage of those feelings? See Commonwealth v. Meadows, 553 A.2d 1006, 1013 (Pa. Super. 1989) (upholding conviction on this basis). Do you agree? For discussion of *Meadows*, see Stephen J. Schulhofer, Unwanted Sex 91-93, 121-124 (1998).

4. Problem. In State v. Lovely, 480 A.2d 847 (N.H. 1984), the manager of a liquor store (Lovely), hired a drifter to work at the store, began paying the rent on the man's apartment, and invited the man to move into Lovely's home, where they began a sexual relationship. When the drifter tried to break off the affair, Lovely pressured him to submit to further sexual acts by threatening to stop paying the man's rent, to kick him out of Lovely's home, and to get him fired from his liquor store job. The New Hampshire statute made it a felony to coerce submission to sexual penetration "by threatening to retaliate against the victim." Lovely's conviction was upheld; the court ruled that the trial judge had properly allowed the jury to consider, as impermissible retaliation, not only Lovely's threat to get the man fired but also his threats to stop paying the man's rent and to evict the man from Lovely's home.[24] Does this mean that a man who asks the destitute widow to move out of his apartment, because she is no longer willing to continue their affair, is guilty of a felony in New Hampshire or Pennsylvania? Should he be? Consider these viewpoints.

---

21. E.g., N.J. Stat. §§2C:14-1 (j), 2 (c) (1), defining coercion to include threatening to "[a]ccuse anyone of an offense," "[e]xpose any secret which would tend to subject any person to hatred, contempt or ridicule"; or "[p]erform any other act which would not in itself substantially benefit the actor but which is calculated to substantially harm another person. . . ."

22. Del. Code, tit. 11, §776.

23. Wyo. Stat. §6-2-303(a)(vi).

24. Compare the narrow definition of "retaliate" in Cal. Penal Code §261(a)(6), page 339, supra.

(a) Schulhofer, supra Note 3(d), at 163-164:

Sex is not a permissible condition of ordinary employment. But sexual fulfill-ment *is* a legitimate and valued goal of marriage and other ongoing, intimate relationships. [A wealthy man's] implicit "threat" ("I won't support you unless we have a sexual relationship") expresses one of the choices he is—and should be—entitled to make in shaping his personal relationships. And his "threat" takes from the woman nothing that she is—or should be—entitled to claim. . . .

The coercion problem seems different when a man who is attracted to [a destitute] mother . . . threatens to terminate a current relationship and throw the mother and her children out onto the street unless she meets his sexual needs. The mother may reasonably feel that she has no real choice but to submit to his demands.

As always, however, conclusions about coercion [should] turn not on the degree of pressure but on the legitimacy of the proposal itself. When [a film] producer gives the fashion model a chance to star in a movie, on condition that she sleep with him, the pressure may be slight, but it is clearly illegitimate. When a man offers the desperate woman a chance to have food and a decent home, the pressure is intense, but it might *not* be illegitimate. We have to know whether the man's "threat" to withhold his assistance will violate the mother's rights. If . . . the relationship has been short-lived and without mutual com-mitments, existing laws would not obligate the man to support her.

If we hope to safeguard sexual autonomy in a realistic way, we cannot ignore the impact of legal rules that leave the desperate mother vulnerable in this way. . . . An obligation of financial support could certainly be imposed upon [the man] even in the absence of marriage. . . .

There are limits, however, to how far in this direction the law can sensibly develop. . . . A central component of [sexual autonomy] is the freedom to seek intimacy with persons of our own choosing. . . . Equally important, in the case of relationships short of marriage or its equivalent, is the freedom to move on—to live independently or to seek a new partner—when existing ties become a source of unacceptable emotional and sexual stress.

A legal system that obliged a man to support a former sexual partner, in the absence of the mutual commitments of a long-term relationship, would impose an enormous burden on these components of freedom. . . . Efforts to use financial leverage in personal relationships ("Do it tonight or pack your bags") surely deserve criticism. . . . But they should not inevitably violate legal rights.

(b) Martha Chamallas, Consent, Equality, and the Legal Control of Sexual Conduct, 61 S. Cal. L. Rev. 777, 826 (1988):

The refusal to regard economically coerced sex as rape allows men to continue to use their economic superiority to gain sexual advantages, provided that they use only their own resources (not their employer's) and target only those women who show some willingness to tie sex to financial gain. From the target's standpoint, however, the economic pressure may feel the same regardless of whether it is her employer or her lover who threatens economic harm if sex is denied them.

(c) David P. Bryden, Redefining Rape, 3 Buff. Crim. L. Rev. 317, 445 (2000):

Of course, men often "use their economic superiority to gain sexual advantages," but women often use their sexual superiority to gain economic advantages. So who is the extortionist?

5. *Sex trafficking.* Until recently, the traditional refusal to consider psychological and financial pressures as impermissible coercion applied even to the use of these methods to control vulnerable women who are pressured to work as prostitutes. A federal statute enacted after the Civil War makes it a crime to "knowingly and willfully [hold] to involuntary servitude . . . any other person." 18 U.S.C. §1584. But *involuntary* servitude was not defined. In a 1988 case, defendants accused of forcing mentally retarded individuals to work in oppressive conditions were convicted of violating §1584 on the basis of purely psychological coercion. The Supreme Court reversed, holding that the statute extended only to physical or legal compulsion. United States v. Kozminski, 487 U.S. 931 (1988). Congress responded by expressly overturning *Kozminski.* Finding that "[t]raffickers primarily target women and girls, who are disproportionately affected by poverty, the lack of access to education, chronic unemployment, discrimination, and the lack of economic opportunities in countries of origin," Congress enacted the Trafficking Victims Protection Act (TVPA) of 2000, 18 U.S.C. §1591. As amended in 2008, the statute provides that:

(a) Whoever knowingly . . . entices, harbors, . . . or maintains by any means a person; . . . knowing, or in reckless disregard of the fact, that means of force, threats of force, fraud, coercion described in subsection (e)(2), or any combination of such means will be used to cause the person to engage in a commercial sex act, or that the person has not attained the age of 18 years and will be caused to engage in a commercial sex act, shall be punished . . . [by] imprisonment for any term of years not less than 15 or for life[a]. . . .

(e) (2) The term "coercion" means . . . any scheme, plan, or pattern intended to cause a person to believe that failure to perform an act would result in serious harm to or physical restraint against any person. . . .

(e) (4) The term "serious harm" means any harm, whether physical or nonphysical, including psychological, financial, or reputational harm, that is sufficiently serious, under all the surrounding circumstances, to compel a reasonable person of the same background and in the same circumstances to perform or to continue performing commercial sexual activity in order to avoid incurring that harm.

Congress stated that the broad definition of serious harm was intended to:[25]

streamline the jury's consideration in cases involving coercion and . . . more fully capture the imbalance of power between trafficker and victim. [S]erious

---

a. The authorized punishment drops to "imprisonment for not less than 10 years or for life" if no force, fraud, or coercion is used and the victim is over 14 but under 18. 18 U.S.C. §1591(b)(2).—Eds.

25. William Wilberforce Trafficking Victims Protection Reauthorization Act of 2008, 154 Cong. Rec. H10888, H10904.

harm may refer to nonviolent and psychological coercion, including but not limited to isolation, denial of sleep and punishments, or preying on mental illness, infirmity, drug use or addictions (whether pre-existing or developed by the trafficker).

Since 2000, 45 states have passed anti-trafficking statutes modeled to some degree on the TVPA.[26] Under N.Y. Penal Law §230.34 (2011), "sex trafficking" is a class B felony, punishable by up to 25 years' imprisonment. Such statutes now reach conduct that would have been difficult or impossible to prosecute under the *Kozminski* standard. Consider United States v. Monsalve, 342 F. App'x 451 (11th Cir. 2009), where the defendant's conviction and 20-year sentence rested in part on these facts (id. at 456-458):

> Victims 1 and 2 came to the United States thinking they would be waitresses. After arriving in the United States illegally, they were told they owed Monsalve a $16,000 smuggling fee and that they must repay him by working as prostitutes. They had their identification documents taken from them, spoke no English, and depended on Monsalve and his associates for food, water, shelter, and clothing. Melchor, one of Monsalve's managers, threatened Victims 1 and 2 that he could have them deported if they [refused to cooperate].

Questions: Consider whether the TVPA's broad definition of coercion should apply only to those who organize commercial prostitution or whether it should be extended further:

(a) Patronizing a prostitute is a crime in almost all jurisdictions, but it is typically graded as a misdemeanor.[27] Should the "John" who patronizes an adult prostitute be guilty of a coercive sex offense? Has he violated §1591? What if he knows (or should know) that the prostitute is an undocumented immigrant who speaks little English and is probably working under the orders of a person like Monsalve?

(b) What about acute social and economic pressures that are brought to bear in settings other than conventional prostitution? Should the man who takes a destitute widow into his home and supports her and her family (on condition that she have sex with him) be guilty of committing an offense similar to §1591?

For detailed analysis of the "intricate power dynamics that characterize many human-trafficking cases," see Kathleen Kim, The Coercion of Trafficked Workers, 96 Iowa L. Rev. 409, 415 (2011).

6. For other efforts to identify the boundaries of illegitimate coercion, see Alan Wertheimer, Consent to Sexual Relations (2003); Donald A. Dripps, Beyond Rape: An Essay on the Difference Between the Presence of Force and the Absence of Consent, 92 Colum. L. Rev. 1780 (1992); Robin L. West, Legitimating the Illegitimate: A Comment on *Beyond Rape*, 93

---

26. See U.S. Dep't of State, Trafficking in Persons Report (2011); Polaris Project: National Human Trafficking Resource Center, available at http://www.polarisproject.org/state-map.

27. E.g., N.Y. Penal Law §230.06 (2011) (one-year maximum when person patronized is not a minor).

Colum. L. Rev. 1442 (1993). See also the proposed Model Statute, §202(c), pages 402-403 infra.

2. Eliminating the Force Requirement

Even in the absence of expressed or implied threats, the act of intercourse itself almost always involves some physical force. Should this kind of force meet the force requirement for a rape conviction? Why not simply eliminate the force requirement altogether? Consider the material that follows.

STATE IN THE INTEREST OF M.T.S.

New Jersey Supreme Court
129 N.J. 422, 609 A.2d 1266 (1992)

HANDLER, J. Under New Jersey law a person who commits an act of sexual penetration using physical force or coercion is guilty of second-degree sexual assault. The sexual assault statute does not define the words "physical force." The question posed by this appeal is whether the element of "physical force" is met simply by an act of non-consensual penetration involving no more force than necessary to accomplish that result.

[M.T.S.], a seventeen-year-old boy, engaged in consensual kissing and heavy petting with a fifteen-year-old girl and thereafter engaged in actual sexual penetration of the girl to which she had not consented. There was no evidence or suggestion that the juvenile used any unusual or extra force or threats to accomplish the act of penetration.

The trial court determined that the juvenile was delinquent for committing a sexual assault. The Appellate Division reversed, . . . concluding that non-consensual penetration does not constitute sexual assault unless it is accompanied by some level of force more than that necessary to accomplish the penetration. We granted the State's petition for certification. . . .

C.G. was living with her mother [and] several other people, including M.T.S. and his girlfriend. [M.T.S.] slept downstairs on a couch. C.G. had her own room on the second floor. . . . At trial, C.G. and M.T.S. offered very different accounts [of the incident]. The trial court did not credit fully either teenager's testimony.

C.G. stated that . . . M.T.S. had told her three or four times that he "was going to make a surprise visit up in [her] bedroom." [C.G. said she considered the comments a joke because M.T.S. frequently teased her. She testified that she awoke that night at approximately 1:30 A.M. and saw M.T.S., fully clothed, standing in her doorway. According to C.G., M.T.S. said "he was going to tease [her] a little bit." C.G. testified that she "didn't think anything of it"; she used the bathroom and returned to bed, falling into a "heavy" sleep within fifteen minutes. The next event C.G. claimed to recall was waking up with M.T.S. on top of her, her underpants and shorts removed.] She said "his penis was into

[her] vagina." As soon as C.G. realized what had happened, she said, she immediately slapped M.T.S. once in the face, then "told him to get off [her], and get out." She did not scream or cry out. She testified that M.T.S. complied in less than one minute after being struck. . . .

C.G. said that after M.T.S. left the room, she "fell asleep crying." . . . She explained that she did not immediately tell her mother or anyone else in the house of the events of that morning because she was "scared and in shock." . . . By her own account, C.G. was not otherwise harmed by M.T.S.

[At about 7:00 A.M., C.G. went downstairs and told her mother about the encounter and said that they would have to "get [M.T.S.] out of the house." C.G. and her mother then filed a complaint with the police.]

According to M.T.S., he and C.G. had been good friends for a long time. [He] testified that during the three days preceding the incident they had been "kissing and necking" and had discussed having sexual intercourse. . . . He said C.G. repeatedly had encouraged him to "make a surprise visit up in her room."

M.T.S. testified that at [1:15 A.M.], he entered C.G.'s bedroom as she was walking to the bathroom. He said C.G. soon returned from the bathroom, and the two began "kissing and all," eventually moving to the bed. Once they were in bed, he said, they undressed each other and . . . proceeded to engage in sexual intercourse. According to M.T.S., [he] "did it [thrust] three times, and then the fourth time . . . , that's when [she] pulled [him] off of her." M.T.S. said that as C.G. pushed him off, she said "stop, get off," and he "hopped off right away." [He] asked C.G. what was wrong; she replied with a back-hand to his face. He recalled asking C.G. what was wrong a second time, and her replying, "how can you take advantage of me or something like that." M.T.S. said that he proceeded to get dressed and told C.G. to calm down, but that she then told him to get away from her and began to cry. Before leaving the room, he told C.G., "I'm leaving. . . . I'm going with my real girlfriend, . . . stay out of my life . . . don't tell anybody about this . . . it would just screw everything up." He then walked downstairs and went to sleep.

. . . M.T.S. was charged with conduct that if engaged in by an adult would constitute second-degree sexual assault. [T]he court concluded that the victim had consented to a session of kissing and heavy petting with M.T.S. [and had not] been sleeping at the time of penetration, but nevertheless found that she had not consented to the actual sexual act. Accordingly, the court concluded that the State had proven second-degree sexual assault beyond a reasonable doubt. On appeal, following the imposition of suspended sentences on the [sexual assault] charges,[a] the Appellate Division . . . reversed the juvenile's adjudication of delinquency. . . .

---

a. In the case of an adult sexual assault offender, the New Jersey sentencing system ordinarily would not permit suspension of the minimum five-year term of imprisonment in the absence of "extraordinary and unanticipated" circumstances. See State v. Johnson, 118 N.J. 10, 570 A.2d 395, 396 (1990).—EDS.

N.J.S.A. 2C:14-2c(1) defines "sexual assault" as the commission "of sexual penetration" "with another person" with the use of "physical force or coercion."[1] [B]oth the act of "sexual penetration" and the use of "physical force or coercion" are separate and distinct elements of the offense. . . .

The State would read "physical force" to entail any amount of sexual touching brought about involuntarily. A showing of sexual penetration coupled with a lack of consent would satisfy the elements of the statute. The Public Defender urges an interpretation of "physical force" to mean force "used to overcome lack of consent." That definition equates force with violence and leads to the conclusion that sexual assault requires the application of some amount of force in addition to the act of penetration. . . .

Under traditional rape law, in order to prove that a rape had occurred, the State had to show both that force had been used and that the penetration had been against the woman's will. [A] woman who was above the age of consent had actively and affirmatively to withdraw that consent for the intercourse to be against her will. . . . Critics of rape law agreed that the focus of the crime should be shifted from the victim's behavior to the defendant's conduct, and particularly to its forceful and assaultive, rather than sexual, character. [T]he reform goal was not so much to purge the entire concept of consent from the law as to eliminate the burden that had been placed on victims to prove they had not consented.

Similarly, [t]raditional interpretations of force were strongly criticized for failing to acknowledge that force may be understood simply as the invasion of "bodily integrity." Susan Estrich, Rape, 95 Yale L.J. 1087, 1105 (1986).

[The] Model Penal Code (MPC) proposed provisions did not present a break from traditional rape law. They would have established two principal sexual offenses: aggravated rape . . . and [gross sexual imposition], defined as sexual intercourse . . . to which [the female] was compelled to submit by any threat that would prevent resistance by a woman of ordinary resolution. The comments to the MPC [state] that the words "compels to submit" require more than "a token initial resistance." MPC, §213.1, comments at 306 (revised commentary 1980).

The Legislature did not endorse the Model Penal Code approach to rape. Rather, it passed a fundamentally different proposal in 1978. . . . The new statutory provisions covering rape were formulated by a coalition of feminist

---

1. The sexual assault statute, N.J.S.A.:2C:14-2c(1), reads as follows:

An actor is guilty of sexual assault if he commits an act of sexual penetration with another person under any one of the following circumstances:

(1) The actor *uses physical force or coercion,* but the victim does not sustain severe personal injury; . . .

(5) The victim is at least 13 but less than 16 years old and the actor is at least 4 years older than the victim.

Sexual assault is a crime of the second degree [punishable by a minimum of 5 and a maximum of 10 years' imprisonment.]

[When committed with a weapon or when "severe personal injury" is sustained, the offense is aggravated sexual assault, a crime of the first degree, punishable by a minimum of 10 and a maximum of 20 years' imprisonment.—EDS.]

groups assisted by the National Organization of Women (NOW) National Task Force on Rape. The stated intent of the drafters . . . had been to remove all features found to be contrary to the interests of rape victims. . . .

The reform statute defines sexual assault as penetration accomplished by the use of "physical force" or "coercion," but it does not define either "physical force" or "coercion." . . . The task of defining "physical force" therefore was left to the courts. . . .

The Legislature's concept of sexual assault and the role of force was significantly colored by its understanding of the law of assault and battery. . . . Any "unauthorized touching of another [is] a battery." Perna v. Pirozzi, 92 N.J. 446, 462 (1983). . . . Thus, just as any unauthorized touching is a crime under traditional laws of assault and battery, . . . so is any unauthorized sexual penetration a crime under the reformed law of sexual assault. . . . Under the new law, the victim no longer is required to resist and therefore need not have said or done anything in order for the sexual penetration to be unlawful. . . . [A]n interpretation of the statutory crime of sexual assault to require physical force in addition to that entailed in an act of involuntary or unwanted sexual penetration would be fundamentally inconsistent with the legislative purpose to eliminate any consideration of whether the victim resisted or expressed non-consent.

We note that the contrary interpretation of force—that the element of force need be extrinsic to the sexual act—would not only reintroduce a resistance requirement into the sexual assault law, but also would immunize many acts of criminal sexual contact short of penetration. . . . That the Legislature would have wanted to decriminalize unauthorized sexual intrusions on the bodily integrity of a victim by requiring a showing of force in addition to that entailed in the sexual contact itself is hardly possible.

. . . We conclude, therefore, that any act of sexual penetration engaged in by the defendant without the affirmative and freely given permission of the victim to the specific act of penetration constitutes the offense of sexual assault. . . . The definition of "physical force" is satisfied under N.J.S.A. 2C:14-2c(1) if the defendant applies any amount of force against another person in the absence of what a reasonable person would believe to be affirmative and freely given permission to the act of sexual penetration. [The requirement] of "physical force" [is] neither inadvertent nor redundant. [It] acts to qualify the nature and character of the "sexual penetration." Sexual penetration accomplished through the use of force is unauthorized sexual penetration. . . .

Although it is possible to imagine a set of rules in which persons must demonstrate affirmatively that sexual contact is unwanted or not permitted, such a regime would be inconsistent with modern principles of personal autonomy. The Legislature recast the law of rape as sexual assault to bring that area of law in line with the expectation of privacy and bodily control that long has characterized most of our private and public law. . . . Each person has the right not only to decide whether to engage in sexual contact with another, but also to control the circumstances and character of that contact.

[P]ermission to the specific act of sexual penetration ... can be indicated either through words or through actions that, when viewed in the light of all the surrounding circumstances, would demonstrate to a reasonable person affirmative and freely given authorization for the specific act of sexual penetration. The role of the factfinder is not to decide whether reasonable people may engage in acts of penetration without the permission of others. The Legislature answered that question when it enacted the reformed sexual assault statute: reasonable people do not engage in acts of penetration without permission, and it is unlawful to do so. The role of the factfinder is ... only [to decide] whether the defendant's belief that the alleged victim had freely given affirmative permission was reasonable.

[T]he law places no burden on the alleged victim to have expressed non-consent or to have denied permission, and no inquiry is made into what he or she thought or desired or why he or she did not resist or protest. ... Under the reformed statute, a person's failure to protest or resist cannot be considered or used as justification for bodily invasion.

We acknowledge that cases such as this are inherently fact sensitive and depend on the reasoned judgment and common sense of judges and juries. The trial court concluded that the victim had not expressed consent to the act of intercourse, either through her words or actions. We conclude that the record provides reasonable support for the trial court's disposition. Accordingly, we reverse the judgment of the Appellate Division and reinstate the disposition of juvenile delinquency for the commission of second-degree sexual assault.

NOTES

1. *Statutory interpretation.* Professor David P. Bryden comments (Redefining Rape, 3 Buff. Crim. L. Rev. 317, 397 (2000)): "As a matter of statutory interpretation, *M.T.S.* is easy to criticize. If all sex is forcible, then why did the statute require force in addition to penetration?"

The *M.T.S.* court notes that those who worked to revise New Jersey law wanted "the focus of the crime [to] be shifted from the victim's behavior to the defendant's conduct, and particularly to its forceful and assaultive, rather than sexual, character." Is the court's interpretation of the statute consistent with that goal? Or does it shift the focus of the crime *away from* the assaultive character of the defendant's conduct and back to the nature of the *victim's* behavior? The court seems to suggest that the reformer's real concern was not so much to shift attention away from the victim's behavior as it was to change the kind of victim behavior that was important—not resistance indicating *non*-consent but affirmative behavior indicating *authorization*. Did the statute, as written, accomplish that shift? How should sexual assault offenses be defined (and graded) in order to achieve that goal most effectively?

2. *Legislative developments.* Although force or threat of physical force remains a prerequisite to conviction in most jurisdictions, several states have made intercourse without consent criminal in the absence of force. Professor

Michelle Anderson finds (All-American Rape, 79 St. John's L. Rev. 625, 629-633 (2005)) that only 14 states punish nonconsensual intercourse as a felony in the absence of force; an additional 8 states treat such conduct as a misdemeanor, and in the remaining states, such conduct is not punishable at all. Consider how the grading structures described below differ from each other and from New Jersey's statute, as interpreted in *M.T.S.* Which approach is preferable?

(a) Under Wis. Stat. §940.225 (pages 341-342 supra), first-degree and second-degree sexual assault include intercourse without consent by "use or threat of force or violence." Third-degree sexual assault is defined as "sexual intercourse with a person without the consent of that person," and consent is defined as "words or actions by a person who is competent to give informed consent indicating a freely given agreement to have sexual intercourse." The third-degree offense is punishable by up to ten years' imprisonment.

(b) In Florida, nonconsensual penetration committed by a threat of force likely to cause serious injury is a first-degree felony punishable by up to 30 years' imprisonment. Nonconsensual penetration committed without using such force is a second-degree felony, punishable by up to 15 years' imprisonment.[28] The preamble to the statute, enacted in 1992 (Fla. Ch. 92-135), states that conviction of the second-degree felony does not "require any force or violence beyond the force and violence that is inherent in the accomplishment of 'penetration.'"

3. For development of the argument that sexual offense statutes should distinguish more sharply between crimes involving violence and those based on the absence of consent, and should fashion distinct levels of punishment appropriate to these distinct forms of misconduct, see Meredith J. Duncan, Sex Crimes and Sexual Miscues: The Need for a Clearer Line Between Forcible Rape and Nonconsensual Sex, 42 Wake Forest L. Rev. 1087 (2007).

4. "Law in action." Even in jurisdictions that have abolished the force requirement in theory, prosecutors in practice often refuse to go forward in the absence of evidence of physical force or resistance. See Stephen J. Schulhofer, Unwanted Sex 90, 97 (1998). That pattern may reassure those who believe that the *M.T.S.* decision goes too far, but it frustrates those who consider nonconsensual intercourse a serious crime. And American law affords the victim no legal right to challenge a prosecutor's decision not to proceed.[29] The next Note and the next principal case provide an opportunity to examine the force requirement and the issues of acquaintance rape against the background of this important institutional reality. The material permits us to consider the substantive problem of how to define rape along side the institutional problem of the prosecutor's role and its implications.

---

28. Fla. Stat. §794.011 (4) (b), (5). The statute states (§794.011 (1) (a)): "'Consent' means intelligent, knowing, and voluntary consent and does not include coerced submission."

29. For exploration of the charging discretion of American prosecutors, see pages 1113-1132 infra.

NOTE ON DEVELOPMENTS ABROAD

The issues discussed in *M.T.S.* have become prominent concerns throughout the world. They were always present in ordinary prosecutions in national courts. More recently, they have been addressed in international tribunals, reflecting a now-widespread view that rape and other acts of violence against women violate fundamental human rights. See Rape and Sexual Violence: Human Rights Law and Standards in the International Criminal Court (Amnesty International, 2011). International human rights law is a complex topic far outside the scope of an introductory criminal law course. Nonetheless, developments in this area can shed light on issues confronting American courts and policy makers. And occasionally the relationship is more direct. An example is Lawrence v. Texas, 539 U.S. 558 (2003), where the Supreme Court relied upon a judgment of the European Court of Human Rights (ECHR) in deciding to overrule U.S. precedent and grant constitutional protection to consenting sexual relations between same-sex adults.

For these reasons, it is increasingly useful for American lawyers to have some exposure to legal principles now evolving around the world, and especially so in connection with the law of rape. The next case, which also arose in the ECHR, touches directly on many concerns of this chapter. Our present interest is not with the European human rights system but rather with problems that are common to criminal law in any jurisdiction. And the European court must inevitably concentrate on these general, widely shared concerns, since its judgments govern diverse cultures and legal systems, from the common law of Britain to the civil law of Germany, from Western nations like France to former Soviet-bloc nations like Hungary, and from Catholic Spain to Muslim Turkey. In examining *M.C. v. Bulgaria*, the ECHR case that follows, consider how that court approaches the following questions, which are present in rape law everywhere:

First, how should rape be defined? Should physical force or resistance be required? Should the law of rape protect only the interest against brutal physical attack or also the victim's interest in being free of other pressures and constraints?

Second, to what extent do governments bear an affirmative obligation to protect those interests effectively? What should be the prosecutor's role in deciding whether a defendant should face trial? Does adequate protection require criminal sanctions rather than or in addition to other remedies?

M.C. v. BULGARIA

European Court of Human Rights
[2003] ECHR 39272/98

[PER CURIAM]. . . . The applicant is a Bulgarian national who . . . alleged that she had been raped by two men . . . , when she had been fourteen years and ten months old.[a] [The ensuing investigation was terminated when prosecutors found insufficient proof that she had been compelled to have sex. M.C. then filed a complaint against the Bulgarian government under the European Convention on Human Rights.[b]]

[T]he applicant . . . had been waiting to enter a disco bar . . . when three men [P., A., and V.A.] arrived. . . . The applicant knew P. [and A., who] invited the applicant to go with him and his friends to a disco bar in a small town 17 km away. According to the applicant, she agreed on condition that she would be back home before 11 P.M. [The group went to the bar, and] late in the evening the group left and headed back. . . . A. suggested stopping for a swim at a nearby reservoir. According to the applicant, they went there despite her objections. [When the others went swimming, M.C. remained in the car.] Soon afterwards P. came back and sat in the front seat next to the applicant.

[M.C. told the police that P. had started kissing her, and that she tried to push him away. P. then moved the car-seat to a horizontal position and forced her to have sexual intercourse. M.C. stated that she] had been scared and . . . had not had the strength to resist violently or to scream. . . . "It was my first time and it hurt a lot. I felt sick and I wanted to throw up. I started crying." [P. claimed that M.C. had fully consented.]

[A]t around 3 A.M. the group went to a neighbouring town, where V.A.'s relatives had a house. . . . The applicant stated to the police that she had felt helpless and in need of protection. As A. was the brother of a classmate of hers, she had expected such protection from him and had followed him . . . into a room on the ground floor of the house. There was one bed in the room and the applicant sat on it. . . . The applicant maintained that at that point A. had sat next to her . . . and forced her to have sex with him. The applicant had not had the strength to resist violently. She had only begged the man to stop. . . . A. [testified] that he had had sex with [M.C.] with her full consent. . . .

[Later that morning, M.C. returned home. She] and her mother went directly to the local hospital. . . . The medical examiner found that the hymen had been freshly torn. He also noted on the applicant's neck [an abrasion and] bruises. . . .

[T]he District Prosecutor opened criminal proceedings [and] referred the case to an investigator. [The investigator proposed terminating] the proceedings [and] the District Prosecutor [agreed, finding] that the use of force or threats had not been established beyond reasonable doubt. . . . The applicant lodged consecutive appeals with the Regional Prosecutor's Office and the

---

a. At the time of the incident, the alleged perpetrators, P. and A., were 21 and 20 years old, respectively.—EDS.

b. The European court cannot reverse the decision of a national court or compel a member government to act. But when it upholds a complaint, it can award damages, and the Committee of Ministers of the Council of Europe exercises oversight to insure that member states bring their legislation and practices into compliance with the court's judgments. See European Civil Liberties and the European Convention on Human Rights (Conor A. Gearty ed., 1997).—EDS.

Chief Public Prosecutor's Office. [Each of these offices dismissed the appeals and issued written decisions stating]:

> There can be no criminal act under [the Criminal Code] unless the applicant was coerced . . . by means of physical force or threats. This presupposes resistance, but there is no evidence of resistance. . . . P. and A. could be held criminally responsible only if they understood that they were having sexual intercourse without the applicant's consent and if they used force or made threats precisely with the aim of having sexual intercourse against the applicant's will. There is insufficient evidence to establish [those elements]. . . .

[Under the Bulgarian Criminal Code, in cases involving a woman over the age of 14 and not physically incapacitated,] Article 152 §1 . . . defines rape as "sexual intercourse with a woman . . . who was compelled by means of force or threats." [The offense is punishable by two to eight years' imprisonment.] In one case the [Bulgaria] Supreme Court stated that "force" was to be understood not only as direct violence but could also consist of placing the victim in such a situation where she could see no other solution than to submit against her will. . . .

Relevant Comparative and International Law and Practice

[The court here discussed the rape statutes of a number of European countries. Although several defined rape to include any intercourse without consent, most of the statutes required proof of "force," "violence," or even "immediate danger to life or limb."]

The Committee of Ministers [of the Council of Europe] recommends that member States adopt and implement, in the manner most appropriate to each country's national circumstances, a series of measures to combat violence against women. [M]ember States should, inter alia, "penalise any sexual act committed against non-consenting persons, even if they do not show signs of resistance; . . . penalise any abuse of the position of a perpetrator, and in particular of an adult vis-à-vis a child."

The International Criminal Tribunal for the former Yugoslavia [has discussed the definition of] rape under international criminal law. . . . In [*Prosecutor v. Kunarac*,] a Muslim girl in an occupied area was [raped] by armed soldiers [and then] brought to a room where she herself initiated sexual contact with the accused Mr. Kunarac, the commanding officer[, having] been told . . . that she should satisfy [him] sexually or risk her life. . . . The Trial Chamber [found that Kunarac] could not have been "confused" by the behaviour of the victim, given the . . . wartime situation and the specifically delicate situation of the Muslim girls in the region. [The] Chamber made the following observations on the elements of rape under international law:

> The basic principle which is truly common to [the reviewed] legal systems is that serious violations of sexual *autonomy* are to be penalised. Sexual autonomy is violated wherever the person subjected to the act has not freely agreed to it. [T]he absence of genuine and freely given consent or voluntary

participation may be *evidenced* by the presence of the various factors specified in other jurisdictions—such as force, [but c]oercion, force, or threat of force [are] not to be interpreted narrowly . . .

[T]he actus reus of the crime of rape in international law is constituted by . . . sexual penetration . . . where [it] occurs without . . . consent given voluntarily, as a result of the victim's free will, assessed in the context of the surrounding circumstances. The mens rea is the intention to effect this sexual penetration, and the knowledge that it occurs without the consent of the victim.

[On appeal], the Appeals Chamber stated:

The Appellants' bald assertion that nothing short of continuous resistance provides adequate notice to the perpetrator that his attentions are unwanted is wrong on the law and absurd on the facts. . . . Force or threat of force provides clear evidence of non-consent, but force is not an element *per se* of rape. . . . A narrow focus on force or threat of force could permit perpetrators to evade liability . . . by taking advantage of coercive circumstances without relying on physical force . . .

Alleged Violations of Articles 3, 8 and 13 of the Convention

The relevant Convention provisions read:

Article 3: "No one shall be subjected to torture or to inhuman or degrading treatment or punishment."
    Article 8 §1: "Everyone has the right to respect for his private . . . life. . . ."
    Article 13: "Everyone whose rights and freedoms as set forth in [the] Convention are violated shall have an effective remedy before a national authority. . . ."

The applicant [argued that local law] and practice required proof of physical resistance by the victim and thus left unpunished certain acts of rape. [She argued that prosecutorial] practice was not based on written instructions but on institutional tradition and culture. . . . She further stated that by setting at 14 the age of consent for sexual intercourse and at the same time limiting the prosecution of rape to cases of violent resistance . . . , the authorities had left children insufficiently protected against rape.

[T]he Government argued [that] after a careful and impartial investigation, the authorities had not found [the allegations of rape] established to the level of proof necessary to secure a criminal conviction. . . . On the other hand, it was open to the applicant to submit a civil action for damages against the alleged perpetrators. She would be required to prove the unlawfulness of the perpetrators' acts but no proof of mens rea would be necessary. . . .

[A detailed country-by-country analysis submitted to the court stated that rape is now understood as] an offence against women's autonomy and its essential element [is] lack of consent. [It is] not necessary to establish that the accused [has] overcome the victim's physical resistance[,][although in some countries, the U.K., for example,] the reality is that prosecution is unlikely to proceed . . . in the absence of threats.

[In the United States, in an increasing number of states,] non-consensual intercourse without extrinsic force (force extrinsic to that required to effect penetration) is expressly criminalised by statute. [Here the court cited and quoted from *In re M.T.S.*, 609 A.2d 1266 (N.J. 1992).] Increasingly, courts in the United States are taking into account relevant social-science data indicating that . . . some women become frozen with fear at the onset of a sexual attack and thus cannot resist. [Similarly,] lack of consent [is] the defining element of rape and sexual abuse in [Australia, Canada, and South Africa].

[T]he Convention . . . requires States to take measures designed to ensure that individuals within their jurisdiction are not subjected to ill-treatment, including ill-treatment administered by private individuals. Positive obligations on the State are inherent in the right to effective respect for private life under Article 8. . . . While the choice of the means to secure compliance with Article 8 . . . is in principle within the State's margin of appreciation [i.e., the area of permissible choices to which the European court must defer], effective deterrence against grave acts such as rape . . . requires efficient criminal-law provisions. . . . States have a positive obligation . . . to enact criminal-law provisions effectively punishing rape and to apply them in practice through effective investigation and prosecution. . . .

In most European countries influenced by the continental legal tradition the definition of rape contains references to the use of violence or threats of violence. . . . It is significant, however, that in case-law and legal theory lack of consent, not force, is seen as the constituent element of the offence. [T]he prosecution of non-consensual sexual acts [even in the absence of force] is sought in practice by means of interpretation of the relevant statutory terms . . . and through a context-sensitive assessment of the evidence. . . .

[There is] a universal trend towards regarding lack of consent as the essential element of rape and sexual abuse [and] the evolution of societies towards effective equality and respect for each individual's sexual autonomy. In the light of the above, . . . the Convention must be seen as requiring the penalisation and effective prosecution of any non-consensual sexual act, including in the absence of physical resistance by the victim. . . .

Turning to the particular facts of the applicant's case, . . . the prosecutors gave reasoned decisions, explaining their position in some detail. [The] authorities faced a difficult task, as they were confronted with two conflicting versions of the events. [N]onetheless, . . . the presence of two irreconcilable versions of the facts obviously called for a context-sensitive assessment of the credibility of the statements. . . . Little was done, however, to test the credibility of the version of the events proposed by P. and A. [even though] some of their statements called for caution, such as the assertion that the applicant, 14 years old at the time, had started caressing A. minutes after having had sex for the first time in her life with another man. [Thus,] the authorities failed to explore the available possibilities for establishing all the surrounding circumstances.

[T]he reason for that failure was, apparently, . . . that since what was alleged to have occurred was a "date rape," in the absence of "direct" proof of rape, such as traces of violence and resistance or calls for help, [the prosecutors] could not infer proof of lack of consent [and] that in any event, in the absence of proof of resistance, it could not be concluded that the perpetrators had understood that the applicant had not consented. The prosecutors forwent the possibility of proving the perpetrators' mens rea by assessing all the surrounding circumstances, such as evidence that they had deliberately misled the applicant in order to take her to a deserted area, thus creating an environment of coercion. [Their failure] to investigate sufficiently . . . was the result of them putting undue emphasis on "direct" proof . . . , practically elevating "resistance" to the status of the defining element of the offence. [Their] approach . . . fell short of the requirements inherent in the States' positive obligations . . . to establish and apply effectively a criminal-law system punishing all forms of rape and sexual abuse.

As regards the Government's argument that the national legal system provided for the possibility of a civil action for damages against the perpetrators, . . . effective protection against rape and sexual abuse requires measures of a criminal-law nature.

The Court thus finds that in the present case there has been a violation of the respondent State's positive obligations under both Articles 3 and 8 of the Convention. . . .

[The court awarded the applicant damages, to be paid by the Bulgarian government, for "psychological trauma resulting at least partly from the shortcomings in the authorities' approach."]

NOTES AND QUESTIONS

1. "Forcible" intercourse? In most American states, the defendants in *M.C.* would be guilty of statutory rape—all but three states set the age of consent at 16 or older.[30] But if the complainant had been 16, and if the case had arisen in America, would the evidence in *M.C.* suffice to sustain a conviction for forcible rape (assuming that the jurisdiction followed the approach reflected in cases like *Rusk*, page 343 supra)? What circumstances could be invoked to support a finding of "force"?

2. Nonconsensual intercourse? Under the *M.T.S.* approach it seems clear that the victim's testimony, if believed, would be sufficient to support a conviction. Would it, therefore, be inappropriate for an American prosecutor to decline to pursue the case? Or could there be legitimate reasons for an American prosecutor to decide not to proceed?

The *M.C.* court acknowledges that regardless of the legal standard technically applicable, prosecutors in practice typically refuse to go forward in the absence of evidence of physical force or resistance. As we have noted (page

---

30. Sharon Elstein & Noy Davis, Sexual Relationships Between Adult Males and Young Teen Girls 19 (Am. Bar Assn. 1997); U.S. Dept. of Justice, Office for Victims of Crime, State Legislators' Handbook for Statutory Rape Issues 8-10 (Feb. 2000).

368 supra), American law gives the victim no legal right to challenge such a decision. If an American prosecutor chose to drop the charges in a case like M.C.'s, what remedies *should be* available to her?

3. Policy concerns. If prosecutors and juries continue to look for physical force, is that a reason to retain it as a formal requirement, or does that fact reinforce the need for the law to "send a message" that nonphysical coercion is also unacceptable? Are there other reasons to resist extending the criminal law in the manner suggested by the courts in the *M.C.* and *M.T.S.* cases? Consider the next excerpt, in which Professor David Bryden argues that requiring proof of force, in addition to non-consent, serves legitimate functions.

David P. Bryden, Redefining Rape, 3 Buff. Crim. L. Rev. 317, 376-387 (2000): [The force requirement] has reduced the danger of erroneous convictions by requiring objective evidence of the victim's nonconsent and the perpetrator's intention to have nonconsensual intercourse. [Numerous criminal law rules are cast as substantive requirements, though in reality they merely serve a corroborative function, such as the requirement of a "substantial step" in the law of attempt (pages 617-636 infra).] The common thread running through all these corroborative rules is not so much distrust of crime victims as distrust of the abilities of jurors to resolve certain types of issues.

[I]f the [force requirement] is abolished, the physical act of rape will not necessarily differ from ordinary sex. . . . Claims of mistake will be more plausible, and courts may [have to] become more receptive to those claims.

[The force requirement also serves the] Rubicon Function. . . . Sometimes, at least, one does not truly know one's intentions until the time comes to cross the Rubicon. . . . Ambivalence, sudden decisions, and changes of mind are all extremely common. . . . In some cases, even an omniscient factfinder could not describe the woman's subjective state of mind as either consent or nonconsent. Even if the law does not prescribe it, the fact finder must rely on some sort of external standard.

An external standard is also valuable in ascertaining the man's intentions. [A claim of consent is] usually implausible, if a man claimed that his acquaintance had given him his wallet full of cash, identification, and credit cards. In contrast, the mere act of intercourse is as consistent with consensual as with nonconsensual sex. . . . In short, the difficulties of drawing a boundary between consensual and nonconsensual events, and of ascertaining whether the defendant deliberately or negligently crossed that boundary, are far greater in the context of sex with an acquaintance than in such fields as transfers of property, stranger rapes, and nonsexual assaults.

Yet [t]o say that a rule has important theoretical virtues is not to say that those virtues necessarily outweigh its costs. . . . Inevitably, the [force requirement] permits some unwanted sexual encounters. . . . The moral, in short, is not that the [force requirement] is necessarily the best possible rule, but that the problem is considerably more complex than most critics of [that requirement] have recognized.

... e of Consent

...DUCTORY NOTE

...nceptual ambiguities of "consent." Traditional rape statutes have ... both force and non-consent. Under the approach reflected in ...ent becomes even more important, because it is the only fact (apart from mens rea) that separates legitimate sexual intercourse from a criminal offense. But what is "consent"? The seemingly simple concept has many distinct meanings in ordinary usage and in law. Most fundamentally, is consent a *state of mind* (something a person *feels*, like willingness)? Or is it an *action* (something a person *does*, like giving authorization)? Statutes and case law sometimes use one meaning rather than the other, and one common formula, found in the *Rusk* statute, page 343 supra, emphasizes both, prohibiting intercourse by force "against the will and without the consent of the other person." Sometimes the usage in statutes and cases is unclear or internally inconsistent. For rigorous analysis of the concept of consent, see Peter Westen, The Logic of Consent (2003); Alan Wertheimer, Consent to Sexual Relations (2003); Kenneth W. Simons, The Conceptual Structure of Consent in Criminal Law, 9 Buff. Crim. L. Rev. 577 (2006).

2. The range of possible answers. Traditional law avoided having to choose between the two most basic alternatives (consent as a state of mind versus consent as an action) by requiring non-consent in both senses; the evidence had to establish both subjective unwillingness and external acts refusing consent. Physical resistance was essential, and verbal protests were considered insufficient because "a woman may desire sexual intercourse, [but] it is customary for her to say 'no, no, no' (although meaning 'yes, yes, yes') and to expect the male to be the aggressor.... It is always difficult in rape cases to determine whether the female really meant 'no.'"[31]

This view has few defenders today. But if physical resistance is not necessary to signal non-consent, what should the prosecution have to prove? Possible conceptions of non-consent might include:

1. verbal resistance (saying "no") *plus* other behavior that makes unwillingness clear (a totality of circumstances approach);
2. verbal resistance alone ("no" always means no);
3. verbal resistance *or* passivity, silence or ambivalence (anything other than affirmative permission by words or conduct); or
4. all words and actions other than express verbal permission (everything other than saying "yes").

The Wisconsin statute, page 342 supra, and the *M.T.S.* court opt for the third approach: Only affirmative permission can count as consent. Should the

---

31. Ralph Slovenko, A Panoramic View, in Sexual Behavior and the Law 5, 51 (R. Slovenko ed., 1965).

law now be prepared to go further? Should it require *verbal* permission, in order to protect women from men whose wishful thinking leads them to misinterpret "body language"?

Alternatively, does the third approach (that of Wisconsin and *M.T.S.*) go *too far*? If a woman doesn't say no, does it make sense to treat her silence or failure to object as proof of unwillingness? Does it violate contemporary mores, or patronize women, to treat intercourse as a felony even when a woman *did not* say "no"? Many courts and contemporary statutes continue to presume consent in the absence of some affirmative expression of unwillingness. And some of these jurisdictions remain committed to the first approach—a verbal "no" does not necessarily mean non-consent. Note the following examples:

(*a*) Neb. Rev. Stat. §28-318 (8) (2011): "Without consent means . . . the victim expressed a lack of consent through words [or] conduct. . . . The victim need only resist, either verbally or physically, so as to make the victim's refusal to consent genuine and real and so as to reasonably make known to the actor the victim's refusal to consent." See State v. Gangahar, 609 N.W.2d 690, 693, 695 (Neb. App. 2000):

> [Hatfield was an undercover police officer investigating charges that the defendant, a hotel manager, sexually harassed his employees. When she arrived at the hotel posing as a job applicant, defendant took her to a hotel room, and she chose to sit on the edge of the bed, where the defendant attempted to kiss and fondle her.]
>
> Hatfield [repeatedly] pulled away and told him to stop. Gangahar then put his right leg over Hatfield's left leg and rolled on top of her. She then pushed him away and got up. . . .
>
> [Defendant was convicted of sexual assault short of intercourse. The Nebraska court of appeals reversed:] [A] jury could have concluded that Hatfield's conduct was not sufficient to make her refusal of consent reasonably known to Gangahar. [W]hile Hatfield said "no," the statute allows Gangahar to argue that given all of her actions or inaction, "no did not really mean no." [R]eversible error occurred because the jury was not instructed to consider whether Hatfield's refusal of consent was genuine, was real, and would be known as such to a reasonable person in Gangahar's position.

(*b*) N.Y. Penal Law §130.05(2)(d)(2006), page 340 supra (enacted as part of rape reform legislation in 2001): "Lack of consent results from . . . circumstances under which . . . the victim clearly expressed that he or she did not consent to engage in such act, and a reasonable person in the actor's situation would have understood such person's words and acts as an expression of lack of consent to such act under all the circumstances."

3. Which approach to defining consent is most appropriate? Consider these views:

Vivian Berger, Rape Law Reform at the Millennium, 3 Buff. Crim. L. Rev. 513, 522 (2000): [Professor Berger argues that a verbal "no" should suffice to establish non-consent. But, she continues,] the jury has to believe that she *did* say "no." . . . Women should not be *over* protected.

Stephen J. Schulhofer, Taking Sexual Autonomy Seriously, 11 Law & Phil. 35, 74-75 (1992): Consider this parable. A hospitalized athlete, suffering from chronic knee problems, consults a surgeon, who recommends an operation. The athlete is not sure. If the operation is successful, he will enjoy a long, fulfilling career with his team. But there are imponderables. The operation carries a risk of a burdensome infection that can be hard to cure. The procedure may not produce the expected benefits. In any event, it is sure to be stressful in the short run. The athlete hesitates. There are clear advantages, clear disadvantages, and lots of uncertainties. What to do? Maybe he should postpone this big step for a while, see how things go without it. The surgeon is encouraging: "Try it. You'll like it." Still the athlete is unsure.

Now our surgeon becomes impatient. . . . The athlete's hesitation is becoming tiresome and annoying. So the surgeon signals an anesthesiologist to ready the drugs that will flow through an intravenous tube already in place. One last time the surgeon (a sensitive, modern male) reminds the athlete, "You don't have to go ahead with this. If you really want me to stop, just say so." But the athlete, his brain still clouded with doubts, fears, hopes, and uncertainties, says nothing. So the surgeon starts the anesthesia and just *does it*.

Consent? Of course not. But why not? The athlete was not compelled to submit. Nobody forced him. . . . If he really objected, all he had to do was say so!

There are, to be sure, important contextual differences between surgery and sexual intimacy. But even allowing for those differences, it would not be implausible to find "consent" by the patient, provided we could get ourselves to think of illegal surgery as an offense requiring "forcible compulsion," and to think of "nonconsent" in this context as revulsion, aversion, or a clearly crystallized negative attitude.

We do not see matters this way because we are not thinking about a crime of violence. We are thinking about an offense against the patient's autonomy. . . . Nonconsent is simply anything that is not . . . an affirmative, crystallized expression of willingness. To treat the athlete as a victim is not, of course, to patronize him. It is merely to recognize an obvious violation of the physical autonomy of his person.[a]

Douglas N. Husak & George C. Thomas III, Date Rape, Social Convention and Reasonable Mistakes, 11 Law & Phil. 95, 113-123 (1992): [Those who] claim that "no means no" . . . seldom provide any empirical support for [the claim]. [T]his common-sense notion turns out to be empirically questionable. [M]ost of the women in the Perper and Weis study described what

---

a. For criticism of the suggested parallels between consent to surgery and consent to sex, see David P. Bryden, Redefining Rape, 3 Buff. Crim. L. Rev. 317, 402-407 (2000).—EDS.

the researchers called an "incomplete rejection" strategy ... for example, permitting the man to hug and kiss her but not responding "in a really warm way."

[S]urely (common sense suggests that) under normal circumstances a woman who is faced with imminent sexual intercourse against her will should have no difficulty delivering an explicit, unambiguous "no." If so, virtually all incomplete rejection strategies would eventually escalate into blunt, explicit rejections. . . . Again, however, reality is more complex than ideology. . . . A single physical rejection (for example, *F* removes *M*'s hand from her leg) following hours of intense foreplay obviously presents a very different picture of nonconsent than repeated physical and verbal rejections, delivered in an emotional and frightened manner. At some point along this spectrum, it is no longer reasonable for *M* to think that *F* has consented. The reason . . . is not that the word "no" has a magic, transcendental quality. Rather, [t]he social convention is that a certain pattern of linguistic and nonlinguistic behavior could not reasonably be understood to mean anything other than no.[b]

George C. Thomas III & David Edelman, Consent to Have Sex: Empirical Evidence About "No," 61 U. Pitt. L. Rev. 579, 581 (2000): [After comparing the results of older and more recent surveys, the authors note that the assumption in dating situations that "no" may not mean no is "significantly less visible" than it was in the early 1990s. Nonetheless,] stereotypical conventions persist that women say "no" when they mean maybe or not now.

Michelle J. Anderson, Negotiating Sex, 78 S. Cal. L. Rev. 101, 105 (2005): [Reforms requiring affirmative permission, by words *or conduct*, do not go far enough. That approach] relies on a man's ability to infer actual willingness from a woman's body language. Yet study after study indicates that men consistently misinterpret women's nonverbal behavior. They impute erotic innuendo and sexual intent where there is none. Any theory that relies on a man's ability to intuit a woman's actual willingness allows him to construct consent out of stereotype and hopeful imagination.

Moreover, [an approach that infers consent from conduct] assumes that consent to sexual petting implies consent to sexual penetration. [But p]eople often engage in petting instead of penetration in order to minimize the potential health consequences associated with penetration. Even if someone actively engages in "passionate kissing, hugging, and sexual touching," it would therefore not be . . . "sensible to infer actual willingness" to penetration [merely because of the absence of] a verbal objection. If two people are engaged

---

b. Compare Stephen J. Schulhofer, The Feminist Challenge in Criminal Law, 143 U. Pa. L. Rev. 2151, 2174 (1995): "It can hardly be fatal to the feminist position . . . to discover that women who say 'no' do not always mean the same thing. . . . As with any default rule, the legal proposition that 'no' means no does not claim infallible accuracy; to the contrary, the absence of empirical consensus is its raison d'etre. It presupposes ambiguity and seeks to allocate the risk of the inevitable misunderstandings."—Eds.

in petting and one escalates the situation, mental dissociation and frozen fright can occur, paralyzing the victim's ability to resist or say "no."[a]

4. For forceful criticism of arguments for requiring affirmative permission, see Dan Subotnik, "Hands Off": Sex, Feminism, Affirmative Consent, and the Law of Foreplay, 16 S. Cal. Rev. L. & Soc. Justice 249 (2007). Among other points, Professor Subotnik argues that requiring verbal consent is probably unrealistic for most people and that rules designed to insure greater clarity in communication can be undesirable because "the speed of the roller coaster is central to the experience" and because "talking may damage romantic relationships." (Id. at 294). Do you agree? If there is intense disagreement on such an issue, is it inappropriate for the criminal law to take a stand? Or do the interests affected justify stringent criminal law safeguards? Reconsider the data (page 334, Note 1(a), supra) on the incidence of unwanted sexual intercourse when the perpetrator "just did it before you had a chance to protest" or "ignored your protests."

NOTES ON DEFECTIVE CONSENT

When is consent "freely given" within the meaning of *M.T.S.* and the Wisconsin statute (page 342 supra)? When is it "voluntary" within the meaning of the Florida statute (page 368, footnote 28, supra)? When does a person lack the *capacity* to give valid consent? Consider the following issues.

1. Maturity. With respect to youth, statutes always draw a bright line, setting a specific age of consent. This form of rape ("statutory rape") reflects a combination of concerns, including not only the young person's capacity to make a mature decision, but also (1) the social goal of deterring teen pregnancy and (2) the risk of implicit coercion, especially when one party is older than the other. See Michelle Oberman, Girls in the Master's House, 50 DePaul L. Rev. 799 (2002).

Mental retardation, another ground for invalidating consent, is more difficult to define. The MPC imposes liability when the defendant knows that the person consenting to sex "suffers from a mental disease or defect which renders her incapable of appraising the nature of her conduct." §213.2(b). How can we set a standard that protects vulnerable victims from exploitation, without making it illegal for them ever to have fulfilling sexual relationships? See Deborah W. Denno, Sexuality, Rape, and Mental Retardation, 1997 U. Ill. L. Rev. 315.

2. Incapacity—drugs and alcohol. All states impose liability for rape when a defendant has intercourse with a person who was completely

---

a. Professor Anderson goes on to argue: "Not only must rape law abolish the force and resistance requirements, it must also abolish the nonconsent requirement. . . . In its place, the law . . . would require only what conscientious and humane partners already have: a communicative exchange, before penetration occurs, about whether they want to engage in sexual intercourse." Id. at 106.—Eds.

unconscious. And similarly, nearly all states impose liability when the defendant has intercourse with a person who—though not completely unconscious—was severely incapacitated by drugs or alcohol he gave her without her knowledge. But many rape statutes do not impose liability if the victim was in an incapacitated condition short of complete unconsciousness, and if *someone other than the defendant* had secretly drugged the victim. Why should that last fact afford a defense when, as is typically the case, the defendant is well aware that the victim is severely intoxicated? The MPC is especially restrictive, imposing liability in these situations only when (1) the defendant has administered an intoxicant, (2) without the victim's knowledge, and (3) "for the purpose of preventing resistance." See §213.1(1)(b).

The barriers to liability are even higher when the defendant has intercourse with a conscious (perhaps just barely conscious) person who is incapacitated as a result of alcohol she herself knowingly chose to consume. Yet heavy drinking, in combination with immaturity and inexperience with both sex and alcohol, is a major factor in sexual overreaching and sexual abuse, on college campuses and elsewhere. See Karen M. Kramer, Rule by Myth: The Social and Legal Dynamics Governing Alcohol-Related Acquaintance Rapes, 47 Stan. L. Rev. 115 (1994). One analysis found that "in student populations, up to 81% of incidents can involve drinking on the part of the victim." Sharon Cowan, The Trouble with Drink: Intoxication, (In)capacity, and the Evaporation of Consent to Sex, 41 Akron. L. Rev. 899, 904-905 (2008). In State v. Haddock, 664 S.E.2d 339 (N.C. App. 2008), the victim, after drinking heavily during a New Year's Eve celebration, accompanied the defendant to his apartment and collapsed on his bed, where he then had intercourse with her. He was convicted of rape under a statute prohibiting intercourse with a person "who, due to any act committed upon the victim is rendered substantially incapable of either appraising the nature of his or her conduct , or of resisting the act." Id. at 345. The court held that the statute was not "intended for the protection of . . . alleged victims who have voluntarily ingested intoxicating substances through their own actions." Id. at 346. Because the incapacity was not caused by acts of the defendant himself, the court reversed the conviction. About two-thirds of the states impose a similar restriction. See Patricia J. Falk, Rape by Drugs: A Statutory Overview and Proposals for Reform, 44 Ariz. L. Rev. 131, 173 (2002).

Is the idea behind this restriction that the victim's willingness to drink should be equated with consent to have sex? Or that her willingness to drink should forfeit her right to protection against *nonconsensual* sex?

Several states have addressed the risks of abuse in these situations, by providing that intoxication—even when voluntary—can negate consent. See Falk, supra. But how should incapacity be defined in this context? One approach is to let the jury reach its own judgment about how much intoxication is too much. In Massachusetts the test is simply whether "the complainant was so impaired as to be incapable of consenting." Commonwealth v. Bache, 880 N.E.2d 736, 743 n.14 (Mass. 2008). The Kansas courts reason that "[l]ay persons are familiar with the effects of alcohol. If the jury concluded [the victim] was drunk enough to be unable to consent to sex, we should give great deference to that finding." State v. Smith, 178 P.3d 672, 877 (Kan. App. 2008). Is that the best any court can do, or is it unduly (and impermissibly) vague? Alternatively, should incapacity be defined by a bright line, such as the level of intoxication sufficient to render a person too drunk to drive (usually a blood-alcohol level of 0.1 or 0.08)? Consider these alternatives:

(a) In People v. Giardino, 82 Cal. App. 4th 454, 462-463 (2000), the 16-year-old victim drank several glasses of bourbon, became "tipsy," and then actively participated in numerous acts of intercourse and oral sex. Because of error in the jury instructions, the defendant's rape conviction was reversed and sent back for retrial. The court held that intoxication could invalidate consent even when it was not physically incapacitating. Rather, the court said, the focus should be on "the effect of the intoxicants on the victim's powers of judgment rather than on the victim's powers of resistance." The court suggested two ways to formulate the test for the jury on retrial—whether alcohol rendered the victim "unable to make a reasonable judgment as to the nature or harmfulness of the conduct," or, more simply, whether the victim "would not have engaged in intercourse with [the defendant] had she not been under the influence of the [intoxicants]." In a subsequent decision, the court explained that "even a poor judgment is a reasonable judgment so long as the woman is able to understand and weigh the physical nature of the act, its moral character, and probable consequences." People v. Smith, 191 Cal. App. 4th 199, 205 (2010). Is this standard appropriate or too broad?

(b) In State v. Al-Hamdani, 2001 WL 1645773 (Wash. App. 2001), the defendant was convicted on the basis of an expert's testimony that a blood-alcohol level of 0.15 was sufficient to render the victim incapable of meaningful consent because individuals in that condition cannot "appreciate the consequences of their actions." Is that the right standard? And should a blood-alcohol level of 0.15 be considered sufficient to meet it?

(c) Professor Christine Chambers Goodman argues that the best way to address the problem is to demand explicit consent and to "raise the level of explicitness required to constitute effective consent with the number of drinks or level of intoxication of the parties." Goodman, Protecting the Party Girl: A New Approach for Evaluating Intoxicated Consent, 2009 BYU L. Rev. 57, 58 (2009). She adds that "[a]lcohol, like fear, can have an impact on a woman's ability to resist," and therefore "silence never should be adequate to constitute consent when either of the parties has consumed alcohol." Id. at 60.

2. Pressure and threats. Suppose that a woman sleeps with her supervisor because he promises, in return for sex, not to veto a promotion for which she has been recommended. Is this a case of voluntary consent or a case of criminal sexual assault? Does it matter whether her company has a grievance procedure for sexual harassment? Should the result be different if she sleeps with him because he promises, in return for sex, to help her get a promotion that will otherwise go to someone else?

Recall the case of the destitute widow who submits to sexual intercourse with a man who will otherwise kick her and her children out of his house and refuse to continue supporting them. In New Jersey, Wisconsin, and Florida, is that a case of voluntary consent or a case of criminal sexual assault?

3. *Authority and trust.* Is a patient in psychotherapy capable of giving valid consent to the sexual advances of the psychiatrist who is treating her? Such relationships violate medical ethics, and in the majority of states they are criminalized as a form of sexual assault. But some types of mental health professionals and marriage counselors are not governed by similar rules of professional ethics, and in many states such sexual relationships are not illegal. Should they be? Is it justified to assume that an adult patient being treated for anxiety or depression is inherently incapable of giving valid consent?

Should the criminal law prohibit, as potentially or inherently coercive, any sexual relationship between a job supervisor and his subordinate? Consider this observation:[32]

> [S]exual autonomy is two sided, consisting of both the freedom from unwanted sex and the freedom to have a wanted intimate relationship with another person who is also willing. Indeed, the need for intimacy is fundamental. . . . Were that not the case, the protection of sexual autonomy would be a simple matter, for we could simply prohibit all sexual encounters in the absence of a fully informed, freely chosen agreement between parties who are in every sense social and economic equals. But a rule of that sort, vigorously protecting . . . our negative sexual autonomy (the freedom from unwanted sex), would have a devastating impact on our positive sexual autonomy (the freedom to pursue a sexual relationship that is mutually desired).

Outside the context of psychiatrist-patient relationships, criminal law generally does not invalidate consent in adult relationships, even when they are strongly influenced by authority or trust. See Stephen J. Schulhofer, Unwanted Sex 168-253 (1998); Patricia J. Falk, Rape by Fraud and Rape by Coercion, 64 Brook. L. Rev. 39, 89-132 (1998). Are there areas in which that approach is no longer justifiable? For example, should the law prohibit, on grounds of coerced or inauthentic consent, a sexual relationship between a divorce lawyer and his client? Or between a teacher and his student? For a detailed proposal to prohibit abuse of power in sexual relationships on the job and in academic settings, see Michal Buchhandler-Raphael, Criminalizing Coerced Submission in the Workplace and in the Academy, 19 Colum. J. Gender & L. 409 (2010).

---

32. Stephen J. Schulhofer, Rape-Law Reform circa June 2002, 989 Annals N.Y. Acad. Sci. 276, 277 (2003).

4. Deception

PEOPLE v. EVANS

Supreme Court, New York County, Trial Term
85 Misc. 2d 1088, 379 N.Y.S.2d 912 (1975)

GREENFIELD, J. The question presented in this case is whether the sexual conquest by a predatory male of a resisting female constitutes rape or seduction. [A] jury has been waived [and] the Court first makes the following findings of fact:

The defendant, a bachelor of approximately thirty-seven years of age, aptly described in the testimony as "glib," on July 15, 1974, met an incoming plane at LaGuardia Airport, from which disembarked L.E.P., of Charlotte, North Carolina, a twenty-year-old petite, attractive second-year student at Wellesley College, an unworldly girl, evidently unacquainted with New York City and the sophisticated city ways, a girl who proved to be, as indicated by the testimony, incredibly gullible, trusting and naive. [The] defendant struck up a conversation with her, posing as a psychologist doing a magazine article and using a name that was not his, inducing Miss P. to answer questions for an interview.

[T]he defendant invited Miss P. to accompany him by automobile to Manhattan, her destination being Grand Central Station. [Then the] defendant and a girl named Bridget took Miss P. to [a singles' bar], which the defendant explained was for the purpose of conducting a sociological experiment in which he would observe her reactions and the reactions of males towards her.... After several hours there, ... she was induced to come up to an apartment ... which the defendant explained was used as one of his five offices or apartments. ...

She had been there for one to two hours when the defendant made his move and pulled her on to the opened sofa-bed in the living room ... and attempted to disrobe her. [U]ltimately she was able to ward off these advances and to get herself dressed again. At that point, the defendant's tactics ... changed.

First, he informed her of his disappointment that she had failed the test, that this was all part of his psychological experiment, that, in fact, this was a way in which he was trying to reach her innermost consciousness. [Then,] he took steps to cause doubt and fear to arise in [her] mind. He said, "Look where you are. You are in the apartment of a strange man. How do you know that I am really who I say I am? How do you know that I am really a psychologist?" Then, he went on and said, "I could kill you. I could rape you. I could hurt you physically."

Miss P. testified that at that point she became extremely frightened, that she realized, indeed, how vulnerable she was. ... Then there was ... an abrupt switch in which the defendant attempted to play on the sympathy of Miss P. by telling her a story about his lost love, how Miss P. had reminded him of her, and the hurt that he had sustained when she had driven her car off a cliff. Obviously, Miss P.'s sympathy was engaged, and at that time acting instinctively, she took a step forward and reached out for him and put her hand on his shoulders, and then he grabbed her and said, "You're mine, you are mine." There thereupon followed an act of sexual intercourse, an act of oral-genital contact; a half-hour later a second act of sexual intercourse, and then, before she left, about seven o'clock that morning, an additional act. . . .

The testimony indicates that during these various sexual acts Miss P., in fact, offered little resistance. . . . There was no torn clothing, there were no scratches [or] bruises. Finally, at approximately seven A.M. Miss P. dressed and left the apartment. . . .

The question is whether having had sexual intercourse by the . . . means described constitutes rape in the first degree. The essential element of rape in the first degree is forcible compulsion. The prevailing view in this country is that there can be no rape which is achieved by fraud, or trick, or stratagem. Provided there is actual consent, the nature of the act being understood, it is not rape, absent a statute, no matter how despicable the fraud, even if a woman has intercourse with a man impersonating her husband . . . or even if a doctor persuades her that sexual intercourse is necessary for her treatment and return to good health. . . .

It should be noted that seduction, while not considered to be a criminal act at common law, has been made a criminal offense by statute in some jurisdictions. In seduction, unlike rape, the consent of the woman, implied or explicit, has been procured, by artifice, deception, flattery, fraud or promise. The declared public policy of this state looks with disfavor on actions for seduction since the civil action was abolished more than forty years ago[;] there are no presently existing penal sanctions against seduction. The law recognizes that there are some crimes [such as larceny] where trickery and deceit do constitute the basis for a criminal charge. . . . But of course, for a larceny there has to be a taking of property of value. I do not mean to imply that a woman's right to her body is not a thing of value, but it is not property in the sense which is defined by the law.

It is clear [that] P. was intimidated; that she was confused; that she had been drowned in a torrent of words and perhaps was terrified. But it is like-wise clear . . . that the defendant did not resort to actual physical force. . . .

So the question here is . . . whether threats uttered by the defendant had paralyzed her capacity to resist and had, in fact, undermined her will. [. . . He said, ". . . I could kill you. I could rape you. I could hurt you physically." Those words, as uttered, are susceptible to two possible and diverse interpretations. The first would be in essence that—you had better do what I say, for you are helpless and I have the power to use ultimate force should you resist. That clearly would be a threat which would induce fear and overcome resistance. The second possible meaning of those words is, in effect, that—you are a foolish girl. . . . You put yourself in the hands of a stranger, and you are vulnerable and defenseless. The possibility would exist of physical harm to you were you being confronted by someone other than the person who uttered this statement.

Of course, it is entirely possible that Miss P. . . . construed [the statement] as a threat, even though it may not have been intended as such by the person who uttered those words. The question arises as to which is the controlling state of mind—that of a person who hears the words and interprets them as a threat, or [that] of the person who utters such words. It appears to the Court that the controlling state of mind must be that of the speaker. [T]his being a criminal trial, it is basic that the criminal intent of the defendant must be shown beyond a reasonable doubt. . . . And so, if he utters words which are taken as a threat by the person who hears them, but are not intended as a threat by the person who utters them, there would be no basis for finding the necessary criminal intent to establish culpability under the law. . . . Since the Court, therefore, can find neither forcible compulsion nor threat beyond a reasonable doubt, the defendant is found not guilty on the charges of rape, sodomy and unlawful imprisonment.

Now, acquittal on these charges does not imply that the Court condones the conduct of the defendant. The testimony in the case reveals that the defendant was a predator, and that naive and gullible girls like . . . P. were his natural prey. He posed. He lied. . . . He used psychological techniques to achieve vulnerability and sympathy, and the erosion of resistance. A young and inexperienced girl like . . . P. was then unable to withstand the practiced onslaught. . . . The Court finds his conduct, if not criminal, to be reprehensible. [Nevertheless,] the Court must conclude that the defendant's conduct towards Miss P. cannot be adjudged criminal so as to subject him to the penalty of imprisonment for up to twenty-five years. . . .

Boro v. Superior Court, 163 Cal. App. 3d 1224, 210 Cal. Rptr. 122 (1985): Ms. R., the rape victim, . . . received a telephone call from a person who identified himself as "Dr. Stevens" and said that he worked at Peninsula Hospital.

"Dr. Stevens" told Ms. R. that he had the results of her blood test and that she had contracted a dangerous, highly infectious and perhaps fatal disease. . . .

"Dr. Stevens" further explained that there were only two ways to treat the disease. The first was a painful surgical procedure—graphically described—costing $9,000, and requiring her uninsured hospitalization for six weeks. A second alternative, "Dr. Stevens" explained, was to have sexual intercourse with an anonymous donor who had been injected with a serum which would cure the disease. The latter, nonsurgical procedure would only cost $4,500. When the victim replied that she lacked sufficient funds the "doctor" suggested that $1,000 would suffice as a down payment. The victim thereupon agreed to the nonsurgical alternative and consented to intercourse with the mysterious donor, believing "it was the only choice I had."

. . . Ms. R. . . . went to her bank, withdrew $1,000 and, as instructed, checked into [a] hotel. . . .[a] About a half hour later the defendant "donor" arrived at her room [and] had sexual intercourse with her. At the time of penetration, it was Ms. R.'s belief that she would die unless she consented

---

a. Ms. R. was a relatively recent immigrant, and Dr. Stevens apparently had made a practice of targeting such people for his deceptive scheme.—EDS.

to sexual intercourse with the defendant: as she testified, "My life felt threatened, and for that reason and that reason alone did I do it."

[Defendant was charged with rape "accomplished by means of force or fear of immediate and unlawful bodily injury," Penal Code §261(2), and with rape "[w]here a person is at the time unconscious of the nature of the act and this is known to the accused," Penal Code §261(4). Conviction of either charge would carry a penalty of three, six, or eight years in prison. A pretrial motion to dismiss the former charge was granted by the lower court. Defendant challenged the lower court's failure to set aside the latter charge.[b]]

The People's position is [that] "at the time of the intercourse Ms. R., the victim, was 'unconscious of the nature of the act': because of [petitioner's] misrepresentation she believed it was in the nature of a medical treatment and not a simple, ordinary act of sexual intercourse." Petitioner, on the other hand, stresses that the victim was plainly aware of the *nature* of the act in which she voluntarily engaged, so that her motivation in doing so (since it did not fall within the proscription of section 261, subdivision (2)) is irrelevant.

[A]s a leading authority has written, "if deception causes a misunderstanding as to the fact itself (fraud in the factum) there is no legally recognized consent because what happened is not that for which consent was given; whereas consent induced by fraud is as effective as any other consent, so far as direct and immediate legal consequences are concerned, if the deception relates not to the thing done but merely to some collateral matter (fraud in the inducement)." (Perkins & Boyce, Criminal Law (3d ed. 1982) p. 1079.) . . .

Another relatively common situation in the literature . . . is the fraudulent obtaining of intercourse by impersonating a spouse. . . . Some courts have taken the position that such a misdeed is fraud in the inducement on the theory that the woman consents to exactly what is done (sexual intercourse) and hence there is no rape; other courts, with better reason it would seem, hold such a misdeed to be rape on the theory that it involves fraud in the factum since the woman's consent is to an innocent act of marital intercourse while what is actually perpetrated upon her is an act of adultery. . . .

In California, of course, we have by statute adopted the majority view that such fraud is in the factum, not the inducement, and have thus held it to vitiate consent. [See Cal. Penal Code §261(a)(5), page 339 supra.]

[T]he Legislature well understood how to draft a statute to encompass fraud in the factum (§261, subd. (5)) and how to specify certain fraud in the inducement as vitiating consent.[4] [A] concurring opinion in Mathews [v. Superior Court, 119 Cal. App. 3d 309 (1981),] specifically decried the lack of a California statutory prohibition against fraudulently induced consent to sexual relations in [other] circumstances. . . .

---

b. The defendant was also charged with attempted grand theft and burglary (entry into the hotel room with intent to commit theft). These charges were not challenged on appeal.—EDS.

4. Prior to its repeal [in] 1984, section 268 provided that: "Every person who, under promise of marriage, seduces and has sexual intercourse with an unmarried female of previous chaste character, is punishable by imprisonment in the state prison. . . ."

The People, however, direct our attention to Penal Code section 261.6, which in their opinion has changed the rule that fraud in the inducement does not vitiate consent. That provision reads as follows: "In prosecutions under sections 261, 286, 288a or 289, in which consent is at issue, 'consent' shall be defined to mean positive cooperation in act or attitude pursuant to an act of free will. The person must act freely and voluntarily and have knowledge of the nature of the act or transaction involved." . . . If the Legislature at that time had desired to correct the apparent oversight decried in *Mathews*, supra,[5]—it could certainly have done so. But the Attorney General's strained reading of section 261.6 would render section 261, subdivision (5) meaningless surplusage. . . .

To so conclude is not to vitiate the heartless cruelty of petitioner's scheme, but to say that it comprised crimes of a different order than a violation of section 261, subdivision (4). Let a peremptory writ of prohibition issue. . . .

HOLMDAHL, J. [S]ection 261.6, defining "consent" applies in this case. It is apparent from the abundance of appropriate adjectives and adverbs in the statute that the Legislature intended to the point of redundancy to limit "consent" to that which is found to have been truly free and voluntary, truly unrestricted and knowledgeable. [W]hile the Legislature in section 261.6 did not expressly repeal the legalisms distinguishing "fraud in the factum" and "fraud in the inducement," its intention certainly was to restrict "consent" to cases of true, good faith consent, obtained without substantial fraud or deceit.

I believe there is a sufficient basis for prosecution of petitioner pursuant to section 261, subd. (4). . . .

NOTES ON DECEPTION

1. In 2002, almost 20 years after the *Boro* decision, California amended the provision at issue, §261(a)(4), to specify that a victim will be considered "unconscious of the nature of the act" when she was "not aware . . . of the essential characteristics of the act due to the perpetrator's fraudulent representation that the sexual penetration served a professional purpose when it served no professional purpose." Why did the legislature adopt such a narrow view of the circumstances under which it should be criminal to obtain consent to intercourse by misrepresentation?

2. How should *Evans* and *Boro* be decided under the *M.T.S.* standard, which permits a conviction for sexual assault any time there is intercourse in the absence of "affirmative and freely given permission"? Should use of any deceptive inducement suffice to make the actor guilty of rape?

3. A person who knowingly uses false material representations to obtain tangible personal property is universally held guilty of a criminal offense,

---

5. It is not difficult to conceive of reasons why the Legislature may have consciously wished to leave the matter where it lies. Thus, as a matter of degree, where consent to intercourse is obtained by promises of travel, fame, celebrity and the like—ought the liar and seducer to be chargeable as a rapist? Where is the line to be drawn?

usually theft or fraud. See, e.g., MPC §223.3, Appendix. Similarly, such a person would be liable for damages in a civil suit. Yet there is generally neither civil nor criminal liability when the false representations are used to obtain sex. Why the distinction? For discussion, see Russell L. Christopher & Kathryn H. Christopher, Adult Impersonation: Rape by Fraud as a Defense to Statutory Rape, 101 Nw. U. L. Rev. 75 (2007); Stephen J. Schulhofer, Unwanted Sex 152-159 (1998); Patricia J. Falk, Rape by Fraud and Rape by Coercion, 64 Brook. L. Rev. 39 (1998).

D. MENS REA

COMMONWEALTH v. SHERRY

Supreme Judicial Court of Massachusetts
386 Mass. 682, 437 N.E. 2d 224 (1982)

[Three codefendants were charged with rape and kidnapping. The jury acquitted on the kidnapping charge and convicted of rape. Each defendant was sentenced to a prison term of not less than three nor more than five years. The judge stipulated that only the first six months of the sentence was to be served, with the balance of the sentence suspended. Defendants appealed.]

LIACOS, J. . . . The victim, a registered nurse, and the defendants, all doctors, were employed at the same hospital in Boston. The defendant Sherry, whom the victim knew professionally, with another doctor was a host at a party in Boston for some of the hospital staff. . . . The victim was not acquainted with the defendants Hussain and Lefkowitz prior to this evening.

According to the victim's testimony, she had a conversation with Hussain at the party, during which he made sexual advances toward her. Later in the evening, Hussain and Sherry pushed her and Lefkowitz into a bathroom together, shut the door, and turned off the light. They did not open the door until Lefkowitz asked them to leave her in peace. At various times, the victim had danced with both Hussain and Sherry.

Some time later, as the victim was walking from one room to the next, Hussain and Sherry grabbed her by the arms and pulled her out of the apartment as Lefkowitz said, "We're going to go up to Rockport." The victim verbally protested but did not physically resist the men because she said she thought that they were just "horsing around" and that they would eventually leave her alone.[3] She further testified that once outside, Hussain carried her

---

3. The victim testified that she was not physically restrained as they rode down an elevator with an unknown fifth person, or as they walked through the lobby of the apartment building where other persons were present.

over his shoulder to Sherry's car and held her in the front seat as the four drove to Rockport. En route, she engaged in superficial conversation with the defendants. She testified that she was not in fear at this time. When they arrived at Lefkowitz's home in Rockport, she asked to be taken home. Instead, Hussain carried her into the house.

Once in the house, the victim and two of the men smoked some marihuana, and all of them toured the house. Lefkowitz invited them into a bedroom to view an antique bureau, and, once inside, the three men began to disrobe. The victim was frightened. She verbally protested, but the three men proceeded to undress her and ... attempted intercourse. She told them to stop.[a] At the suggestion of one of the defendants, two of the defendants left the room temporarily. Each defendant separately had intercourse with the victim in the bedroom. The victim testified that she felt physically numbed and could not fight; she felt humiliated and disgusted. . . .

Some time later, Lefkowitz told the victim that they were returning to Boston because Hussain was on call at the hospital. On their way back, the group stopped to view a beach, to eat breakfast, and to get gasoline. The victim was taken back to where she had left her car the prior evening, and she then drove herself to [her] apartment. . . .

The defendants testified to a similar sequence of events, although the details of the episode varied significantly. According to their testimony, Lefkowitz invited Sherry to accompany him from the party to a home that his parents owned in Rockport. The victim was present when this invitation was extended and inquired as to whether she could go along. As the three were leaving, Sherry extended an invitation to Hussain. At no time on the way out of the apartment, in the elevator, lobby, or parking lot did the victim indicate her unwillingness to accompany the defendants.

Upon arrival in Rockport, the victim wandered into the bedroom where she inquired about the antique bureau. She sat down on the bed and kicked off her shoes, whereupon Sherry entered the room, dressed only in his underwear. Sherry helped the victim get undressed, and she proceeded to have intercourse with all three men separately and in turn. Each defendant testified that the victim consented to the acts of intercourse. . . .

The evidence was sufficient to permit the jury to find that the defendants had sexual intercourse with the victim by force and against her will. The victim is not required to use physical force to resist; any resistance is enough when it demonstrates that her lack of consent is "honest and real." The jury could well consider the entire sequence of events and acts of all three defendants as it affected the victim's ability to resist. . . .

The defendants ... contend that because the judge failed to give two instructions exactly as requested, the judge's jury charge, considered as a

---

a. The victim testified that when she asked the defendants why they were behaving in this manner, one of them replied, "Stop playing games."—Eds.

whole, was inadequate and the cause of prejudicial error. The requested instructions in their entirety are set out in the margin.[8] . . .

[The trial judge refused to give the requested instructions. He stated that the jury "should look at the acts of the defendants, [the victim's] responses to [those] acts, whatever words were used, examining the entire atmosphere, and not look at [the case] from the point of view of the defendant's perceptions. . . . I don't think that's the law."]

To the extent the defendants, at least as to the first requested instruction, appear to have been seeking to raise a defense of good faith mistake on the issue of consent, the defendants' requested instruction would have required the jury to "find beyond a reasonable doubt that the accused had *actual knowledge* of [the victim's] lack of consent" (emphasis added). The defendants, on appeal, argue that mistake of fact negating criminal intent is a defense to the crime of rape. . . . We need not reach the issue whether a reasonable and honest mistake to the fact of consent would be a defense, for even if we assume it to be so, the defendants did not request a jury instruction based on a reasonable good faith mistake of fact. We are aware of no American court of last resort that recognizes mistake of fact, without consideration of its reasonableness[,] as a defense; nor do the defendants cite such authority. There was no error.

[In a companion case arising out of the same facts,[b] Justice Brown of the Appeals Court of Massachusetts commented as follows:] It is time to put to rest the societal myth that when a man is about to engage in sexual intercourse with a "nice" woman "a little force is always necessary." [W]hen a woman says "no" to someone[,] any implication other than a manifestation of non-consent that might arise in that person's psyche is legally irrelevant, and thus no defense. Any further action is unwarranted and the person proceeds at his peril. In effect, he assumes the risk. In 1985, I find no social utility in establishing a rule defining non-consensual intercourse on the basis of the subjective (and quite likely wishful) view of the more aggressive player in the sexual encounter.

COMMONWEALTH v. FISCHER

Superior Court of Pennsylvania
721 A.2d 1111 (1998)

BECK, J.: . . . Appellant, an eighteen-year-old college freshman, was charged with involuntary deviate sexual intercourse (IDSI), . . . and related offenses

---

8. "Unless you find beyond a reasonable doubt that [the victim] clearly expressed her lack of consent, or was so overcome by force or threats of bodily injury that she was incapable of consenting, and unless you find beyond a reasonable doubt that the accused had actual knowledge of [the victim's] lack of consent, then you must find them not guilty."

"If you find that [the victim] had a reasonable opportunity to resist being taken to Rockport, Massachusetts, from the apartment . . . , and had a reasonable opportunity to avoid or resist the circumstances that took place in the bedroom at Rockport, but chose not to avail herself of those opportunities, then you must weigh her failure to take such reasonable opportunities on the credibility of her claim that she was kidnapped and raped."

b. Commonwealth v. Lefkowitz, 20 Mass. App. 513, 481 N.E.2d 277, 232 (1985).—EDS.

in connection with an incident that occurred in a Lafayette College campus dormitory. The victim was another freshman student. . . .

At trial, both the victim and appellant testified that a couple of hours prior to the incident at issue, the two went to appellant's dorm room and engaged in intimate contact. The victim testified that the couple's conduct was limited to kissing and fondling. Appellant, on the other hand, testified that during this initial encounter, he and the victim engaged in "rough sex" which culminated in the victim performing fellatio on him. According to appellant, the victim acted aggressively at this first rendezvous by holding appellant's arms above his head, biting his chest, stating "You know you want me," and initiating oral sex.

After the encounter, the students separated and went to the dining hall with their respective friends. They met up again later and once more found themselves in appellant's dorm room. While their accounts of what occurred at the first meeting contained significant differences, their versions of events at the second meeting were grossly divergent. The victim testified that appellant locked the door, pushed her onto the bed, straddled her, held her wrists above her head and forced his penis into her mouth. She struggled with appellant throughout the entire encounter. . . . She also . . . repeatedly stated that she did not want to engage in sex, but her pleas went unheeded. According to the victim, appellant [said] "I know you want it," . . . and "Nobody will know where you are." When the victim attempted to leave, appellant blocked her path. Only after striking him in the groin with her knee was the victim able to escape.

Appellant characterized the second meeting in a far different light. He stated that as he led the victim into his room, she told him it would have to be "a quick one." . . . Thereafter, according to appellant, he began to engage in the same type of behavior the victim had exhibited in their previous encounter. Appellant admitted that he held the young woman's arms above her head, straddled her and placed his penis at her mouth. . . . When she [said] "no," appellant answered "No means yes." After another verbal exchange that included the victim's statement that she had to leave, appellant again insisted that "she wanted it." This time she answered "No, I honestly don't." Upon hearing this, appellant no longer sought to engage in oral sex and removed himself from her body. However, as the two lay side by side on the bed, they continued to kiss and fondle one another. . . . According to appellant, the victim enjoyed the contact and responded positively to his actions. At some point, however, she stood up and informed appellant that she had to leave. When appellant again attempted to touch her, this time on the thigh, she told him she was "getting pissed" [and] abruptly left the room.

At trial, . . . [m]edical personnel testified to treating the victim on the night in question. Many of the victim's friends and classmates described her as nervous, shaken and upset after the incident.

Defense counsel argued throughout the trial and in closing that appellant, relying on his previous encounter with the victim, did not believe his actions were taken without her consent. . . . In light of his limited experience and the victim's initially aggressive behavior, argued counsel, appellant's beliefs were reasonable. Further . . . as soon as appellant realized that the victim truly did not wish to engage in oral sex a second time, appellant stopped seeking same. As a result, appellant's actions could not be deemed forcible compulsion.

The jury returned a verdict of guilty on virtually all counts. Appellant was sentenced to two to five years in prison. On direct appeal, he retained new counsel who has raised a single issue [—] that trial counsel provided ineffective assistance in failing to request a jury charge on the defense of mistake of fact. Specifically, appellant claims that counsel should have asked the court to instruct the jurors that if they found appellant reasonably, though mistakenly, believed that the victim was consenting to his sexual advances, they could find him not guilty. . . .

Counsel cannot be deemed ineffective for failing to pursue a baseless claim. Further, the quality of counsel's stewardship is based on the state of the law as it existed at time of trial; counsel is not ineffective if he fails to predict future developments or changes in the law.

The Commonwealth relies . . . on an opinion by a panel of this court. Commonwealth v. Williams, 439 A.2d 765 (Pa. Super. 1982), concerned the rape and assault of a Temple University student. The facts established that the victim accepted a ride from the appellant on a snowy evening in Philadelphia. Instead of taking the young woman to the bus station, appellant drove her to a dark area, threatened to kill her and informed her that he wanted sex. The victim told Williams to "go ahead" because she did not wish to be hurt.

[Appellant there] argued, among other things, that the trial court erred in refusing to instruct the jury "that if the defendant reasonably believed that the prosecutrix had consented to his sexual advances that this would constitute a defense. . . ." This court rejected Williams's claim and held:

> . . . When one individual uses force or the threat of force to have sexual relations with a person not his spouse and without the person's consent he has committed the crime of rape. *If the element of the defendant's belief as to the victim's state of mind is to be established as a defense to the crime of rape then it should be done by our legislature which has the power to define crimes and offenses. We refuse to create such a defense.*

Id. (emphasis supplied.) The Commonwealth insists that under *Williams*, appellant was not entitled to the instruction he now claims trial counsel should have requested.

In response, appellant makes two arguments. First, he argues that the "stranger rape" facts of *Williams* were far different from those of this case, making the case inapplicable. Second, he maintains that the law with respect to rape and sexual assault has changed significantly over the last decade, along with our understanding of the crime and its permutations, making a mistake of fact instruction in a date rape case a necessity for a fair trial. . . .

Although the rape and IDSI laws have always required the element of "forcible compulsion," that term was not initially defined. [In 1995,] the legislature amended the sexual assault law by adding a definition for forcible compulsion:

> "Forcible Compulsion." Compulsion by use of physical, intellectual, moral, emotional or psychological force, either express or implied. . . .

It is this broader definition, argues appellant in this case, that prompts the necessity for a mistake of fact jury instruction. . . . According to appellant: "The language of the present statute inextricably links the issues of consent with mens rea. To ask a jury to consider whether the defendant used 'intellectual or moral' force, while denying the instruction as to how to consider the defendant's mental state at the time of alleged encounter is patently unfair to the accused."

Appellant's argument is bolstered by the fact that the concept of "mistake of fact" has long been a fixture in the criminal law. The concept is codified in Pennsylvania and provides [18 Pa.C.S.A. §304]:

> Ignorance or mistake as to a matter of fact, for which there is reasonable explanation or excuse, is a defense if . . . the ignorance or mistake negatives the intent, knowledge, belief, recklessness, or negligence required to establish a material element of the offense; or the law provides that the state of mind established by such ignorance or mistake constitutes a defense.

. . . Courts in other jurisdictions have likewise held that jury instructions regarding the defendant's reasonable belief as to consent are proper.

Although the logic of these other cases is persuasive, we are unable to adopt the principles enunciated in them because of the binding precedent with which we are faced, namely, *Williams.* In an effort to avoid application of *Williams,* appellant directs our attention to the Subcommittee Notes of the Pennsylvania Criminal Suggested Standard Jury Instructions. The possible conflict between *Williams* and §304 (Mistake of Fact) was not lost on the Subcommittee. . . .

> In the opinion of the Subcommittee there may be cases, especially now that . . . the definition of force [includes] psychological, moral and intellectual force, where a defendant might non-recklessly or even reasonably, but wrongly, believe that his words and conduct do not constitute force or the threat of force and that a non-resisting female is consenting. An example might be "date rape" resulting from mutual misunderstanding. The boy does not intend or suspect the intimidating potential of his vigorous wooing. The girl, misjudging the boys' character, believes he will become violent if thwarted; she feigns willingness, even some pleasure. In our opinion the defendant in such a case ought not to be convicted of rape.

. . . We agree with the Subcommittee that the rule in *Williams* is inappropriate in the type of date rape case described above. Changing codes of sexual conduct, particularly those exhibited on college campuses, may require that we give greater weight to what is occurring beneath the overt actions of young men and women. Recognition of those changes, in the form of specified jury instructions, strikes us an appropriate course of action.

Despite appellant's excellent presentation of the issues, there remain two distinct problems precluding relief in this case. First [t]his case . . . is not one of the "new" varieties of sexual assault contemplated by the amended statute. . . . This is a case of a young woman alleging physical force. . . . We are keenly aware of the differences between *Williams* and this case. Most notable is the fact that Williams and his victim never met before the incident in question. Here, appellant and the victim not only knew one another, but had engaged in intimate contact just hours before the incident in question. It is clear, however, that the *Williams* court's basis for denying the jury instruction was its conclusion that the law did not require it and, further, that the judiciary had no authority to grant it. . . .

In any event, distinguishing *Williams* on the basis of the parties' previous contacts . . . is not enough to allow appellant the relief he seeks. Even if we . . . are persuaded by appellant's arguments chronicling the history of sexual assault law . . . , we face a second barrier. Because this appeal raises ineffective assistance of counsel, we are required to find that appellant's trial lawyer made a mistake. That mistake is the failure to ask the trial court for an instruction that the *Williams* case held is unwarranted. In other words, we would have to find that counsel's failure to argue for a change in the law constituted ineffectiveness. This, of course, is not possible. . . . The relief appellant seeks represents a significant departure from the current state of the law. Despite its compelling nature, it cannot be the basis for an ineffective assistance of counsel claim.

Judgment of sentence affirmed.

NOTE ON THE FISCHER CASE

Fischer was sentenced to two to five years in prison. Though reportedly a model prisoner, teaching English and math to fellow prisoners, he was denied parole (consistent with normal Pennsylvania practice with regard to sex offenders) and served the full five-year term. At a meeting of the Pennsylvania Bar Association, Judge Phyllis Beck, the author of the *Fischer* opinion, commented that she found the case the most difficult and personally distressing of any she had decided that year.[33]

NOTES ON MISTAKE AS TO CONSENT

1. *Strict liability?* Note that the defendants in *Sherry* did not seek acquittal on the ground that their alleged mistake was both honest and reasonable. In a subsequent acquaintance rape case, Commonwealth v. Simcock, 575 N.E.2d 1137, 1142-1143 (Mass. App. 1991), the trial judge not only refused a defense request for instructions on reasonable mistake but also told the jury that "a belief that the victim consented would not be a defense even if reasonable."

---

33. Interview with Jonathan L. Swichar, Esq., appellate counsel for Fischer, Nov. 25, 2001.

The appellate court affirmed the rape conviction, stating that the result was "in harmony with the analogous rule that a defendant in a statutory rape case is not entitled to an instruction that a reasonable mistake as to the victim's age is a defense."

Questions: Is the analogy flawed? Or is the court right in suggesting that defendants should be held strictly accountable for the existence of consent by their sexual partners?

In Commonwealth v. Lopez, 745 N.E.2d 961 (Mass. 2001), the Massachusetts court defended its refusal to allow a mistake of fact defense on the issue of consent; the court reasoned that the prosecution is in any event required to prove that the defendant used force and that subjective culpability is therefore inherent in his actions. The argument poses two sets of questions:

(a) As a factual matter, is it true that subjective culpability is inherent in actions involving the use of "force"? In cases where a jury finds the element of force to be met by evidence of implicitly threatening behavior, is it inevitable that the defendant will have *realized* that the victim perceived his actions as threatening?

(b) If courts feel that a finding of culpability is important, and if they are relying on the element of "force" to ensure that culpability is present, will they resist efforts to expand the concept of what counts as force? If so, is it desirable to define the offense in such a way that the mens rea element is easy to establish, while the actus reus element of force remains difficult to establish? Compare the approach of the European Court of Human Rights in *M.C. v. Bulgaria*: The court held that European states must extend their definitions of force to encompass subtly coercive circumstances, but it also assumed that a conviction of rape requires proof of the defendant's *awareness* that the victim felt coerced. See page 372 supra. Is this solution less protective of victims than the *Lopez* strict-liability approach?

The weight of American authority now runs strongly against strict liability on the consent issue, but a few states appear to have joined Massachusetts and Pennsylvania in opting for this approach. See, e.g., State v. Reed, 479 A.2d 1291 (Me. 1984).

2. Recklessness or only negligence? Most of the American cases permit a mistake defense, but only when the defendant's error as to consent is honest and reasonable. See, e.g., State v. Oliver, 627 A.2d 144 (N.J. 1993); State v. Smith, 554 A.2d 713 (Conn. 1989). In England, in contrast, the House of Lords ruled that the prosecution must prove that the defendant either knew consent was absent or was willing to proceed "willy-nilly, not caring whether the victim consents or no." See Regina v. Morgan, [1976] A.C. 182:

> Once one has accepted, what seems to me abundantly clear, that the prohibited act in rape is non-consensual sexual intercourse, and that the guilty state of mind is an intention to commit it, it seems to me to follow as a matter of inexorable logic that . . . honest belief . . . negatives intent, [and that] the

reasonableness or otherwise of that belief can only be evidence for or against the view that the belief and therefore the intent was actually held. . . . Any other view . . . can only have the effect of saying that a man intends something which he does not. . . .

Alaska is one of the few American jurisdictions to require proof of reck-lessness. See Hess v. State, 20 P.3d 1121, 1124 (Alaska 2001). In its leading decision on the issue, the court reasoned as follows (Reynolds v. State, 664 P.2d 621, 624-625 (Alaska Ct. App. 1983)):

[R]ecent cases have substantially diluted the requirement of "resistance to the utmost," increasing the risk that a jury might convict a defendant under cir-cumstances where lack of consent was ambiguous. To counteract this risk, some courts . . . have held that the defendant is entitled to an instruction on reasonable mistake of fact. . . .

Alaska has dispensed with any requirement that the victim resist at all. . . . Thus, the legislature has substantially enhanced the risk of conviction in ambiguous circumstances. . . . We are satisfied, however, that the legisla-ture counteracted this risk . . . by shifting the focus of the jury's attention from the victim's resistance or actions to the defendant's understanding of the total-ity of the circumstances. . . . No specific mental state is mentioned in AS 11.41.-410(a)(1) governing the surrounding circumstances of "consent." Therefore, the state must prove that the defendant acted "recklessly" regarding his putative victim's lack of consent.[a] This requirement serves to protect the defendant against conviction for first-degree sexual assault where the circum-stances regarding consent are ambiguous. . . .

3. Correspondence or mismatch between culpability and punishment? An offender convicted of rape, even under a strict liability or negligence standard, generally faces a substantial minimum term of imprisonment, as well as mandatory sex offender registration, prohibitions on residing near schools or parks, and identification on publicly available Web sites, often with a des-ignation as a "sexually violent predator." See Michael Vitiello, Punishing Sex Offenders: When Good Intentions Go Bad, 40 Ariz. St. L.J. 651, 667-674 (2008). How should the proliferation of these largely mandatory sanctions affect the status of judicial precedent accepting strict liability or negligence as a sufficient mens rea on the issue of consent?

4. Victim consent in other crimes. Although victim consent is not a defense to homicide and other offenses involving serious bodily injury, consent in other situations can deprive conduct of its criminal character. See MPC §2.11, Appendix. Sexual contact is but one of these situations in which liability may turn on the consequences of a mistake about consent. Consider State v. Kelly, 338 S.E.2d 405 (W. Va. 1985). The defendant, a construction contractor, removed oak fireplace mantels from two unoccupied

---

a. The court based this conclusion on an Alaska statute providing, as does MPC §2.02(3), that when a penal prohibition is silent as to the required culpability, then the state must prove reckless-ness with respect to any specified circumstances or results.—Eds.

houses and sold the mantels to an antique dealer. Evidence suggested that the defendant had broken into the houses and torn locks off the front doors to gain access. He testified that a man named Bradley had called, met him at the houses, and discussed tearing them down or salvaging their contents. After the defendant sold the mantels, he paid the $140 proceeds to Bradley and received $40 for his efforts. He also testified that a neighbor told him that Bradley and his wife owned the houses. In fact, the houses were owned by Bradley's estranged wife, who had not consented to removal of the mantels. The defendant was convicted of larceny. The appellate court reversed:

> [O]ne who takes property in good faith . . . , honestly believing he . . . has a right to take it, is not guilty of larceny, even though he is mistaken in such belief, since in such case the felonious intent is lacking. [As] summarized in W. LaFave & A. Scott, Handbook on Criminal Law 638 (1972) . . . : "[H]e lacks the intent to steal required for larceny, even though his mistaken but honest belief was unreasonable. . . ." In this case [the evidence] does not establish beyond a reasonable doubt that the defendant acted with criminal intent because he believed that he had proper authority to remove the mantels.

Questions: If knowledge of the owner's non-consent is required for a larceny conviction, why shouldn't knowledge of the woman's non-consent be required for a rape conviction? Does the requirement of some subjective awareness of wrongdoing flow from the essential character of conviction for any serious crime? Or does the need for that requirement depend on the particular kind of harm caused by failing to assure consent? Consider Andrew E. Taslitz, Willfully Blinded: On Date Rape and Self-Deception, 28 Harv. J.L. & Gender 381, 387-388 (2005): "Rape is different from other crimes in a way that justifies severe potential penalties even when liability is based solely upon negligent conduct [because] male self-deception about whether a woman has consented . . . is morally worse than ordinary forms of criminal negligence." Do you agree?

5. *The practical effect of a negligence standard.* Does the mistake-of-fact standard matter? Consider this comment:[34]

> Given the [*Sherry*] victim's isolation in an unfamiliar setting, her intimidation by three naked men, and her explicit protests, there could not possibly have been (from the feminist perspective) a reasonable mistake. For the same reasons, however, one would have to say that these defendants actually *knew* that the victim was not consenting. At the very least, they were all aware that she *might* not be consenting. . . . In other words, . . . these defendants were *subjectively* culpable and would be convicted whether or not we insist on a negligence standard.
>
> [But there] is one perspective from which these defendants might have made an honest mistake. That is the perspective that "no" does not really mean "no," that women . . . just want to feign some initial reluctance. . . . But

---

34. Stephen J. Schulhofer, The Gender Question in Criminal Law, 7 Soc. Phil. & Pol. 105, 132-133 (1990).

if you hold this view of consent (and of women) . . . you might even conclude that the victim really *did* consent—that the doctors made no mistake at all. Once one accepts this alternative (hopefully outmoded) conception of what consent means, the defendants could conceivably be acquitted even if they were tried under a strict liability standard.

The point here is not that choice of the mens rea standard can never make a difference. Certainly, conviction becomes progressively easier as we move toward the strict liability approach. But we are working at the fringes of the problem. The [argument for a negligence standard] begs the most important question, or sweeps it under the rug of jury findings about reasonableness. This is really not a debate about mens rea standards. Rather, it is (or ought to be) a debate about what we mean by the construct that we call "consent." . . . The debate about mistake of fact standards diverts attention from the question of what it is that you have to be mistaken about. Rather than requiring that the mistake be reasonable, and then leaving the jurors to their own conceptions of what is "reasonable" and what is "consent," we need to spell out what the concept of consent means.

6. *Limiting the reasonable mistake defense.* Tyson v. State, 619 N.E.2d 276 (Ind. App. 1993), involved the prosecution of heavyweight boxing champion Mike Tyson for the rape of D.W., a woman who had agreed to accompany him to his hotel room at 2 A.M. Tyson testified that D.W. had responded positively to his kissing her in the limousine on the way to his hotel; that "we had both made it clear earlier that day what was going to happen"; and that D.W. cooperated in the act of intercourse. D.W. testified that when Tyson made sexual advances in the room, she was terrified, repeatedly objected, and "tried to fight him" without success. The trial court refused to instruct the jury that a reasonable mistake as to consent would be a defense. Tyson was convicted of rape, and the court of appeals affirmed (id. at 295):

> Tyson's description is a plain assertion of actual consent. . . . There is no recitation of equivocal conduct by D.W. which reasonably could have led Tyson to believe that D.W. only appeared to consent to the charged sexual conduct; no gray area exists from which Tyson can logically argue that he misunderstood D.W.'s actions. According to Tyson, he exerted no force and D.W. offered no resistance; instead, she was an active and equal participant in the conduct. While this testimony would negate an element of the crime—that Tyson forcibly engaged in sexual conduct with D.W.—and challenges D.W.'s credibility, it does not support the giving of a mistake of fact instruction.

Questions: Is this approach sound? In cases involving this type of "swearing contest," it seems obvious that once the jury finds one party to be telling the truth and the other party to be lying, there is no possibility for a reasonable mistake. But is it inevitable that one of the two competing stories must be completely true? What if the jury believes that *both* parties are exaggerating? See Rosanna Cavallaro, A Big Mistake: Eroding the Defense of Mistake of Fact About Consent in Rape, 86 J. Crim. L. & Criminology 815 (1996).

7. *Applying a reasonableness standard.* What factors should determine whether a man's mistake about consent was "reasonable"? Consider Robin D. Weiner, Shifting the Communication Burden: A Meaningful Consent Standard in Rape, 6 Harv. Women's L.J. 143, 147-149 (1983):

> [A] gender gap in sexual communications exists. . . . Because both men and women are socialized to accept coercive sexuality as the norm in sexual behavior, men often see extreme forms of this aggressive behavior as seduction, rather than rape. . . . Miscommunication of this sort may create a situation where [a] woman may believe she has communicated her unwillingness to have sex—and other women would agree, thus making it a "reasonable" female expression. Her male partner might still believe she is willing—and other men would agree with his interpretation, thus making it a "reasonable" male interpretation. The woman, who believes that she *has* conveyed her lack of consent, may interpret the man's persistence as an indication that he does not care if she objects and plans to have sex despite her lack of consent. She may then feel frightened by the man's persistence, and may submit against her will.

For an analysis of the cultural attitudes that influence conceptions of "consent" in sexual interaction, see Douglas N. Husak & George C. Thomas III, Rapes Without Rapists: Consent and Reasonable Mistake, 11 Phil. Issues 86 (2001); Lynne Henderson, Getting to Know: Honoring Women in Law and in Fact, 2 Tex. J. Women & L. 41 (1993).

8. *Questions:* How should law respond to the "gender gap"? Should notions of reasonableness be left to evolve in response to changing social mores? Or should legislatures and courts set specific standards, for example, by specifying that "no means no"? In one survey of women undergraduates, 39 percent reported that they had sometimes said no when they "meant 'yes,'" and 61 percent of the sexually experienced women in the survey said that they had sometimes done so.[35] These findings do not, however, prove that "no" usually means "yes." To the contrary, 61 percent of the women reported that they had never engaged in such "token" resistance, and "over three fourths of the women who had engaged in token resistance reported doing so five or fewer times. Thus, when a woman says no, chances are that she means it."[36] Nonetheless, among the many women who sometimes meant yes, 90 percent said that "fear of appearing promiscuous" was an important reason for their

---

35. Charlene L. Muehlenhard & Lisa C. Hollabaugh, Do Women Sometimes Say No When They Mean Yes?, 54 J. Personality & Soc. Psych. 872, 874-878 (1988). Specifically, the women were asked about three situations: how often they had said no, meaning no; how often they had said no, meaning "maybe"; and how often they had been in a situation where "you indicated that you didn't want to [engage in sexual intercourse], although you had every intention to and were willing to. . . . In other words, you indicated 'no' and you meant 'yes.'" This frequently cited study was confined to women at a single university in Texas and is now more than 20 years old. But more recent surveys at colleges, universities, and law schools across the United States report similar findings, with no regional differences. See Stephen J. Schulhofer, Unwanted Sex 260 (1998); George C. Thomas III & David Edelman, Consent to Have Sex: Empirical Evidence About "No," 61 U. Pitt. L. Rev. 579 (2000).

36. Muehlenhard & Hollabaugh, supra, at 878.

behavior, and about 75 percent said they also wanted their dates to wait or "talk me into it." Some said they told their dates no because they "want[ed] him to be more physically aggressive." The authors of the study pointed out that this pattern of communication, though rational for some women, can teach men to disregard women's refusals and thereby increase the incidence of rape.

Do findings of this sort confirm the view that "no" doesn't necessarily mean "no"? Or do such findings suggest an even greater need for legal standards to guarantee that "no" *will be treated as* "no"? Compare the following viewpoints:

Douglas N. Husak & George C. Thomas III, Date Rape, Social Convention and Reasonable Mistakes, 11 Law & Phil. 95, 123, 125 (1992): The social convention wcs[a] provides the vehicle through which *M* [a man] interprets the words or actions of *F* [a woman]. [T]here is little empirical evidence that the social convention wcs is consistent with the [no-means-no] claims of some rape law reformers. Instead, the evidence suggests a convention wcs that might produce somewhat frequent mistakes of fact about a woman's consent. If so, and if the reformers succeed in restricting or eliminating the mistake-of-fact defense, some men will be convicted of rape even though they had reason to believe that consent had been given.

Some might welcome this result. [O]ne might believe that it is more important to seek to change the social convention or to send a symbolic message than to do justice in an individual case. But if one believes that the criminal law should seek to apply the just result in particular cases, men whose belief in consent is consistent with the social convention seem unlikely candidates for convictions of a serious felony. For this reason, legislatures should proceed slowly when removing some of the common law barriers to rape convictions.

Catharine A. MacKinnon, Feminism, Marxism, Method, and the State: Toward a Feminist Jurisprudence, 8 Signs 635, 652-654 (1983): [M]en are systematically conditioned not even to notice what women want. They may have not a glimmer of women's indifference or revulsion. . . . Men's pervasive belief that women fabricate rape charges after consenting to sex makes sense in this light. To them, the accusations *are* false because, to them, the facts describe sex. To interpret such events as rapes distorts their experience. . . .

But the deeper problem is the rape law's assumption that a single, objective state of affairs existed, one which merely needs to be determined by evidence, when many (maybe even most) rapes involve honest men and violated women. When the reality is split—a woman is raped but not by a rapist?—the law tends to conclude that a rape *did not happen.* To attempt to solve this by adopting the standard of reasonable belief without asking, on a substantive social basis, to whom the belief is reasonable and why . . . is one-sided: male-sided.

---

a. The authors use the term "wcs" to designate the social conventions that women use to express consent to have sex.—EDS.

E. A STATUTORY SOLUTION?

Are the problems raised in the preceding sections best addressed by public discussion and education? Instead (or in addition), should we empower courts and juries to apply flexible standards of reasonableness in order to punish sexual overreaching? Or is it possible and desirable to adopt specific statutory criteria to mark the boundary between permissible and unlawful behavior? Consider the advantages and shortcomings of the following attempt to articulate specific statutory standards.

PROPOSED MODEL STATUTE[a]

SECTION 201. SEXUAL ASSAULT

(a) An actor is guilty of sexual assault, a felony of the second degree, if he uses physical force or a threat of physical force to compel another person to submit to an act of sexual penetration.

(b) An actor is guilty of sexual assault, a felony of the second degree, if he commits an act of sexual penetration with another person, when he knows that the victim is less than thirteen years old.

(c) An actor is guilty of aggravated sexual assault, a felony of the first degree, if he violates subsection (a) of this section while using a weapon or if he violates subsection (a) of this section and causes serious bodily harm to the victim.

SECTION 202. SEXUAL ABUSE

(a) An actor is guilty of sexual abuse, a felony of the third degree, if he commits an act of sexual penetration with another person, when he knows that he does not have the consent of the other person.

(b) Consent, for purposes of this section, means that at the time of the act of sexual penetration there are actual words or conduct indicating affirmative, freely given permission to the act of sexual penetration.

(c) Consent is not freely given, for purposes of this section, whenever:

(1) the victim is physically helpless, mentally defective, or mentally incapacitated; or

(2) the victim is at least thirteen years old but less than sixteen years old and the actor is at least four years older than the victim; or

(3) the victim is at least sixteen years old but less than eighteen years old and the actor is a parent, foster parent, guardian, or other person with supervisory or disciplinary authority over the victim; or

(4) the victim is on probation or parole, or is detained in a hospital, prison, or other custodial institution, and the actor has supervisory or disciplinary authority over the victim; or

---

a. Adapted from Stephen J. Schulhofer, Unwanted Sex 283-284 (1998).—EDS.

(5) the actor obtains the victim's consent by threatening to:

(i) inflict bodily injury on a person other than the victim or commit any other criminal offense; or

(ii) accuse anyone of a criminal offense; or

(iii) expose any secret tending to subject any person to hatred, contempt, or ridicule, or to impair the credit or business repute of any person; or

(iv) take or withhold action as an official or cause an official to take or withhold action; or

(v) violate any other right of the victim or inflict any other harm that would not benefit the actor; or

(6) the actor is engaged in providing professional treatment, assessment, or counseling of a mental or emotional illness, symptom, or condition of the victim over a period concurrent with or substantially contemporaneous with the time when the act of sexual penetration occurs; or

(7) the actor obtains the victim's consent by representing that the act of sexual penetration is for purposes of medical treatment; or

(8) the actor obtains the victim's consent by leading the victim to believe that he is a person with whom the victim has been sexually intimate, or by representing that the victim is in danger of physical injury or illness.

SECTION 203. CULPABILITY

(a) Recklessness. Whenever knowledge of a fact is required to convict an actor of violating any provision of sections 201 or 202, the requirement of knowledge can be met by proof that, at the time of his conduct, the actor was consciously aware of a substantial and unjustifiable risk that the fact in question existed.

(b) Criminal Negligence. If the actor was not consciously aware of such a risk, he can nonetheless be convicted of violating the provision in question, provided that the prosecution proves that his failure to appreciate that risk involved a gross deviation from the standard of care that a reasonable person would observe in the actor's situation. If an actor is convicted of violating Article 201 on the basis of criminal negligence, the offense shall be graded as a felony of the third degree. If an actor is convicted of violating Article 202 on the basis of criminal negligence, the offense shall be graded as a felony of the fourth degree.

NOTE ON REFORM

Most empirical studies find that reform efforts have had little impact on rape reporting, processing of complaints, and conviction rates. See Richard Klein, An Analysis of Thirty-Five Years of Rape Reform, 41 Akron L. Rev. 981, 1030-1032 (2008). A detailed study of one of the nation's most ambitious reforms found a Michigan statute relatively unsuccessful in extending the criminal prohibition to conduct previously thought to be permissible or "borderline"; one law enforcement official dismissed the law's expanded coverage as "messing with the folkways."[37] Another report analyzed data from six jurisdictions with widely differing approaches to reform, from the far-reaching Michigan effort to relatively minor reforms in Texas and Georgia.[38] The study found only small improvements in Michigan and virtually none in the other jurisdictions.[39] Researchers attributed these disappointing results to the wide discretion exercised by criminal justice officials, who "continue[d] to use the informal norms developed in the courtroom work group to guide the processing of cases."[40] And there is considerable evidence that even when prosecutions are brought, juries still seem guided by traditional assumptions about the importance of physical force and resistance.[41]

Do these findings suggest that legislative reform is bound to prove futile? One researcher observes that "passage of the reforms sent an important symbolic message regarding the seriousness of rape cases," and that "[i]n the long run this symbolic message may be more important than the instrumental change that was anticipated."[42] But if cultural change is the key to improving case outcomes, what is the best way to achieve it? And should *criminal* law be an instrument for producing such change? Professor Aya Gruber argues (Rape, Feminism, and the War on Crime, 84 Wash. L. Rev. 581 (2009)) that because of criminal law's harsh sanctions, reform efforts should reject the punitive approach and focus on changing social attitudes. Many reformers urge greater attention to sex education and rape awareness programs. See Carol Withey, Rape and Sexual Assault Education, 13 New Crim. L. Rev. 802 (2010); Michelle J. Anderson, Sex Education and Rape, 17 Mich. J. Gender & L. 83 (2010). Others caution that such programs are "not necessarily effective and can reinforce stereotypes and actually do harm." Gruber, supra, at 658 n.428. From a contrasting perspective, Professor Donald Dripps proposes a way to make criminal law more effective, despite "the gap between elite and popular opinion": Cases involving nonconsensual sex but no physical force would be prosecuted in "a special sex-crimes court" where non-jury trials would be constitutionally permissible because the court would not have authority to impose more than a six-month sentence. See Dripps, After Rape Law: Will the Turn to Consent Normalize the Prosecution of Sexual Assault, 41 Akron L. Rev. 957, 976-979 (2008). Is it appropriate to

---

37. Jeanne C. Marsh, Alison Geist & Nathan Caplan, Rape and the Limits of Law Reform 25-26, 42-49, 107 (1982).

38. Cassia Spohn & Julia Horney, Rape Law Reform (1992).

39. Id. at 86, 160, 173. The finding that Michigan conviction rates (as a percentage of indictments) remained constant can nonetheless be viewed as a modest victory for the reform effort: Reporting rates had increased somewhat, more cases were coming into the system, and more were being indicted. The constant rate of conviction as a percentage of indictments suggests the possibility that the new law facilitated conviction in grey-area cases that might not have been prosecuted before. See id. at 104.

40. Id. at 173.

41. See Stephen J. Schulhofer, Unwanted Sex 97 (1998); Andrew E. Taslitz, Willfully Blinded: On Date Rape and Self-Deception, 28 Harv. J.L. & Gender 381, 405-406 (2005).

42. Cassia C. Spohn, The Rape Reform Movement: The Traditional Common Law and Rape Law Reforms, 39 Jurimetrics 119, 129-130 (1999).

use criminal punishment in this way, as a means to alter social norms that are prevalent in the community (or in substantial segments of it)?

The pitfalls of criminal prosecution have led reformers to explore a variety of other remedies, including protective orders against the offender, protection of the victim's employment and educational rights when a sexual assault has occurred at school or work, college grievance procedures in cases that arise on campus, victim compensation funds, tort suits against offenders, and suits against third parties such as employers and hotel owners. These options offer promising possibilities for some victims but pose many problems of their own. For examination of the alternative remedies, see Susan H. Vickers ed., Beyond the Criminal Justice System: Our Nation's Response to Rape (Victim Rights Law Center 2003).

F. THE MARITAL EXEMPTION

1 Matthew Hale, The History of the Pleas of the Crown 629 (S. Emlyn ed. 1778): [T]he husband cannot be guilty of a rape committed by himself upon his lawful wife, for by their mutual matrimonial consent and contract the wife hath given up herself in this kind unto her husband, which she cannot retract.

People v. Liberta, 64 N.Y.2d 152, 474 N.E.2d 567 (1984): [After Liberta began beating his wife, she obtained an order of protection requiring him to move out of their home. Nonetheless, during a visit with his son, when his wife was present, he threatened to kill her and forced her to have sexual intercourse. At the time, the New York statute applied only to rape of a female "not married" to the perpetrator, but it treated couples living apart under court order as "not married." Liberta accordingly was subject to the statute, and he was convicted of rape. On appeal, he challenged the constitutionality of the statutory distinctions between different categories of married couples. The court of appeals affirmed his conviction on the ground that *all* distinctions based on marital status were irrational and that a marital exemption could not constitutionally be applied under any circumstances, even for married couples living together.] [T]here is no rational basis for distinguishing between marital rape and nonmarital rape. . . . Lord Hale's notion of an irrevocable implied consent . . . is untenable. Rape is not simply a sexual act to which one party does not consent. Rather, it is a degrading, violent act which violates the bodily integrity of the victim and frequently causes severe, long-lasting physical and psychic harm. To ever imply consent to such an act is irrational and absurd. [A] marriage license should not be viewed as a license for a husband to forcibly rape his wife with impunity. . . . If a husband feels "aggrieved" by his wife's refusal to engage in sexual intercourse, he should seek relief in the courts governing domestic relations, not in "violent or forceful self-help."

The other traditional justifications for the marital exemption were the common-law doctrines that a woman was the property of her husband and that the legal existence of the woman was "incorporated and consolidated into that of the husband" (1 Blackstone's Commentaries (1966 ed.), p. 430). Both these doctrines, of course, have long been rejected in this State. Indeed, "[n]owhere in the common-law world—[or] in any modern society—is a woman regarded as chattel or demeaned by denial of a separate legal identity and the dignity associated with recognition as a whole human being" (Trammel v. United States, 445 U.S. 40, 52).

Because the traditional justifications for the marital exemption no longer have any validity, other arguments have been advanced in its defense. [I]t is not tenable to argue that elimination of the marital exemption would disrupt marriages because it would discourage reconciliation. [I]f the marriage has already reached the point where intercourse is accomplished by violent assault it is doubtful that there is anything left to reconcile. . . .

The final argument in defense of the marital exemption is that marital rape is not as serious an offense as other rape and is thus adequately dealt with by the possibility of prosecution under criminal statutes, such as assault statutes, which provide for less severe punishment. The fact that rape statutes exist, however, is a recognition that the harm caused by a forcible rape is different, and more severe, than the harm caused by an ordinary assault.

NOTES

1. *The prevalence of marital rape.* Although once assumed to be extremely rare, marital rape is now thought to occur with disturbing frequency. Reliable statistics are difficult to obtain for any form of rape, but one study based on interviews with a random sample of nearly 1,000 women found that 14 percent of the women who had been married were the victims of at least one completed or attempted rape by their husbands. See Diana E. H. Russell, Rape in Marriage 57 (2d ed. 1990).

2. *The Model Penal Code view.* The MPC, drafted in the 1950s, chose to preserve the marital exemption. Consider the following effort to justify that position (Model Penal Code and Commentaries, Comment to §213.1, at 344-346 (1980)):

> Retaining the spousal exclusion avoids [an] unwarranted intrusion of the penal law into the life of the family. [T]he law already authorizes a penalty for assault. . . . The issue is whether the still more drastic sanctions of rape should apply. The answer depends on whether the injury caused by forcible intercourse by a husband is equivalent to that inflicted by someone else. The gravity of the crime of forcible rape derives not merely from its violent character but also from its achievement of a particularly degrading kind of unwanted intimacy. Where the attacker stands in an ongoing relation of sexual intimacy, that evil, as distinct from the force used to compel submission, may well be thought qualitatively different.

The notion that the harm of marital rape is less serious than that of stranger rape is criticized in Russell, supra, at 190-191, 198-199:

[W]ife rape can be as terrifying and life-threatening to the victim as stranger rape. In addition, it often evokes a powerful sense of betrayal, deep disillusionment, and total isolation. . . . When a woman has been raped by her husband she cannot seek comfort and safety at home. She can decide to leave the marriage or to live with what happened. Either choice can be devastating. [S]taying usually means being raped again, often repeatedly. . . . A vicious cycle is set in motion that can lead a wife to suicide or madness.

3. *Legislative developments*. Recent statutory reforms have substantially eroded the marital rape exemption. Roughly half the states have abolished the exemption entirely or retained it only to the extent of exempting husbands from prosecution for statutory rape (i.e., the situation in which intercourse is consensual but the wife is under the legally prescribed age of consent). Nonetheless, nearly half the states retain qualified versions of the marital rape exemption—for example, by prescribing lower punishment for marital rape, or by permitting prosecution only when the husband has used the most serious forms of force. See Jill Elaine Hasday, Protecting Them from Themselves: The Persistence of Mutual Benefits Arguments for Sex and Race Inequality, 84 N.Y.U. L. Rev. 1464, 1471 (2009); Michelle J. Anderson, Marital Immunity, Intimate Relationships, and Improper Inferences: A New Law on Sexual Offenses by Intimates, 54 Hastings L.J. 1465 (2003). And regardless of the statutory framework, reporting rates are even lower than for other rapes (see page 332, Note 1(a), supra), "prosecution remains infrequent, and conviction rates are low." Emily J. Sack, Is Domestic Violence a Crime?," 24 St. Johns J. Legal Comment. 535, 557 (2010).

4. *Judicial approaches*. When state statutes do not explicitly require that the rape victim be "a female not his wife," courts have some flexibility in determining whether the common law marital exemption should remain a part of contemporary law. Although defendants have argued that such a change in previously settled understandings should come only from the legislature, several courts have held that a marital exemption should no longer be read into their statutes. See, e.g., State v. Smith, 426 A.2d 38 (N.J. 1981). England likewise abolished the marital exemption by judicial decision. R. v. R., [1991] 4 All E.R. 481.

A narrower approach is taken in Weishaupt v. Commonwealth, 315 S.E.2d 847 (Va. 1984). The court there abolished the marital exemption only for cases in which the wife had "conduct[ed] herself in a manner that establishes a de facto end to the marriage." (In *Weishaupt* the parties had been separated for 11 months at the time of the offense.) Does *Weishaupt* provide a workable compromise approach? If not, is a simple "living apart" test preferable? Or is preservation of the marital exemption under any conditions fundamentally unsound?

G. PROBLEMS OF PROOF

The preceding sections suggest some of the ways in which concerns about unfounded accusations of rape influenced the law relating to the required actus reus and mens rea. The same concerns have also influenced the law of evidence, especially in three areas: requirements of corroboration, jury instructions relating to the complainant's credibility, and rules relating to cross examination. The present section examines these three areas, the first two briefly (their interest is now largely historical) and the third, which presents problems of continuing difficulty, in some detail.

NOTES ON CORROBORATION

1. The traditional concerns. At one time, most American jurisdictions imposed special corroboration requirements as a prerequisite for a rape conviction. The MPC, drafted in the 1950s and approved by the American Law Institute in 1962, does likewise. See §213.6(5), Appendix. In United States v. Wiley, 492 F.2d 547 (D.C. Cir. 1974), Judge Bazelon, concurring, explained the "tangled web" of rationales for this approach (id. at 552-555):

> The most common [concern] is that false charges of rape are more prevalent than false charges of other crimes. . . . It is contended that a woman may fabricate a rape accusation because, having consented to intercourse she is ashamed and bitter, or because she is pregnant and feels pressured to create a false explanation, or because she hates the man she accuses or wishes to blackmail him. . . . There are, however, countervailing reasons not to report a rape. One said to be a victim of rape may be stigmatized by society, there may be humiliating publicity, and the necessity of facing the insinuations of defense counsel may be a deterrent. . . . One result of all of these obstacles is that rape is one of the most under-reported of all crimes. . . .
>
> In addition to the problem of false charges, the corroboration requirement is justified on the theory that rape is a charge unusually difficult to defend against. In 1680 Lord Chief Justice Hale wrote . . . that rape "is an accusation easily to be made and hard to be proved, and harder to be defended by the party accused, tho never so innocent." . . . Juries are said to be unusually sympathetic to a woman wronged, thus weakening the presumption of innocence. [But w]hat studies are available suggest that . . . juries may be more skeptical of rape accusations than is often supposed. . . .
>
> Still another basis for the corroboration requirement lies in "the sorry history of racism in America." There has been an enormous danger of injustice when a black man accused of raping a white woman is tried before a white jury. [Today, however, juries] are more integrated than in the past and racial prejudice may be at a somewhat lower level. Numerous rape victims are black and their interests, as well as those of white women, may have been slighted by the concern for black defendants.

2. The issue of false charges. Although the treatment of rape victims has improved since the time when Judge Bazelon addressed the issue in *Wiley*, rape remains the most underreported of the major crimes. See page 332, Note 1(a), supra. For this and other reasons, many scholars believe that concerns about false charges are wildly exaggerated. They argue that there is no more reason to impose heightened requirements of proof in prosecutions for rape than in prosecutions for any other offense. See Susan Brownmiller, Against Our Will: Men, Women and Rape 386-387 (1975). Others, however, suggest that while rape might be underreported by some potential complainants, it is over-reported by others. Professor Alan Dershowitz points to FBI statistics indicating that police classify 8.4 percent of reported rapes as "unfounded," and he argues that the "[number of] false rape reports each year . . . is dramatically higher than the number of false reports of other serious crimes," namely 3.8 percent for burglary, 3.5 percent for robbery, and 1.6 percent for assault.[43]

Question: Does the 8.4 percent figure show that false reports are more common for rape or that undue police skepticism is more common for rape? For review of the issues, see David P. Bryden & Sonja Lengnick, Rape in the Criminal Justice System, 87 J. Crim. L. & Criminology 1194, 1295-1315 (1997).

3. *Current law.* No American state now requires corroboration in all forcible rape cases. See Annot., 31 A.L.R.4th 120 (2011). Texas, one of the few states to preserve some form of the old rule, still requires corroboration in cases involving an adult victim who reports the offense more than a year after it occurred. See Tex. Code Crim. Proc. §38.07 (2011). In support of the current consensus against requiring corroboration, see United States v. Sheppard, 569 F.2d 114, 118-119 (D.C. Cir. 1977):

> The corroboration requirement . . . foreclose[s] jury consideration of cases in which a highly credible complainant prosecutes charges, on the basis of her testimony alone, against a defendant whose account of the events is clearly less credible. . . . Elimination of the corroboration requirement, however, hardly leaves defendants unprotected against unjust convictions. . . . Where the motivation of the complainant in bringing the charge is an issue, . . . the defense attorney is free to emphasize to the jury the dangers of falsification, and the judge should instruct the jury as to those dangers. . . .

NOTES ON SPECIAL JURY INSTRUCTIONS

1. Many American jurisdictions long required that the jury in every rape prosecution must be given an instruction like the following (from Cal. Jury Instructions—Criminal No. 10.22 (3d ed. 1970)):

> A charge such as that made against the defendant in this case is one which is easily made and, once made, difficult to defend against, even if the person accused is innocent. Therefore, the law requires that you examine the testimony of the female person named in the information with caution.

---

43. Alan Dershowitz, The Abuse Excuse 275 (1994).

The instruction, based on the remarks of Sir Matthew Hale previously quoted (page 408, Note 1, supra), has fallen into disfavor for essentially the same reasons that brought the corroboration requirement under attack. Several jurisdictions now bar the instruction, either by statute (e.g., Pa. Stat. Ann. tit. 18, §3106) or by judicial decision (e.g., People v. Rincon-Pineda, 538 P.2d 247 (Cal. 1975)).

2. *The Model Penal Code.* The MPC requires a special instruction warning the jury in a sex offense prosecution to evaluate the complainant's testimony "with special care." See §213.6(5), Appendix. Like the MPC provision requiring corroboration, the jury-instruction rule reflects American law as it stood in the 1950s, and the developments described in Note 1 above have rendered it largely obsolete. See Deborah W. Denno, Why the Model Penal Code's Sexual Offense Provisions Should Be Pulled and Replaced, 1 Ohio St. J. Crim. L. 207 (2003).

NOTES ON CROSS-EXAMINATION AND SHIELD LAWS

1. *The crucial issue of credibility.* Consider Susan Estrich, Palm Beach Stories, 11 Law & Phil. 5, 14 (1992):

> [B]ecause it is all but impossible these days to argue successfully that no means yes, or that . . . stupidity as to consent should serve as a defense, men charged with rape . . . have few options but to argue the incredibility of the woman victim. And the argument has appeal, I think, because many people, including many prosecutors and judges, remain ambivalent about the expansion of rape liability: unwilling to continue to afford men the privilege of aggression, but also chary with their sympathy for women who should know better. So the old myths of the lying woman are reasserted, now that the rules of liability will no longer protect male defendants.
>
> Thus, we face a new stage in the changing realities of rape law. . . . Today's debate, on the radio, in the newspaper, and in the courtroom, is about when women should be believed—and about what we need to know about the woman before we can decide whether to believe her.

2. *The importance of shield laws.* Until the late 1970s, a common defense tactic in rape prosecutions was to claim consent and to support that claim by offering evidence of the complainant's "loose" reputation, provocative clothing, or prior sexual experiences; the theory was that such evidence tended to make the claim of consent more plausible. In the words of an infamous early decision, jurors allegedly would "more readily infer assent in the practised [*sic*] Messalina, in loose attire, than in the reserved and virtuous Lucretia." People v. Abbot, 19 Wend. 192 (N.Y. 1838). Of course, the notion that a woman was *likely* to have consented to sex with a stranger, just because she was wearing "loose attire," was far-fetched, even by the social standards of the nineteenth century. But the test for the admissibility of evidence does not require that the evidence make the legally crucial fact (such as consent in a rape case) likely to be true. Instead, background circumstances (such as the complainant's prior sexual experience) are deemed to have probative value, and hence to be presumptively admissible, whenever the crucial fact (such as consent) is *more* likely to be true when those circumstances are present than when they are not. See pages 19-20 supra. By this standard, does evidence of prior sexual activity have at least *some* probative value? For example, if the complaining witness has often consented to sexual intercourse with men shortly after meeting them in a bar, wouldn't that fact make it a little bit more likely that she consented to intercourse with the defendant shortly after meeting him in a bar?

Given the very slender increase in probabilities that is considered sufficient to make evidence technically relevant, the most persuasive objection to admitting evidence of a complainant's prior sexual history usually is not that such evidence completely lacks probative value. Rather, the principal justification for exclusion is that any probative value is outweighed by prejudicial effect. (See pages 21-28 supra.) In the present context two kinds of prejudicial effect are important. First, such evidence can impair the truth-finding function at trial because its value may be *over* estimated or because it may lead to confusion of the issues. Second, the very process of airing such evidence can be painful to the victim, aggravating the injury of the original offense and deterring other victims from seeking prosecution. Many rape victims once reported feeling that they had been raped twice—first by their assailant and then a second time in the courtroom. See Vivian D. Berger, Man's Trial, Woman's Tribulation: Rape Cases in the Courtroom, 77 Colum. L. Rev. 1 (1977).

3. Current law. Responding to such concerns, nearly all American jurisdictions have enacted "rape shield laws" to limit the admissibility of evidence bearing on a rape complainant's prior sexual behavior. For discussion of the issues posed by these statutes, see Michelle J. Anderson, From Chastity Requirement to Sexuality License: Sexual Consent and a New Rape Shield Law, 70 Geo. Wash. L. Rev. 51 (2002); Berger, supra. Some of the statutes admit evidence of sexual history only when it involves prior incidents with the defendant. Others identify various exceptions to the rule of exclusion. Some states provide a catch-all exception for any evidence that has probative value greater than its prejudicial effect. Finally, a few states simply provide a procedure for pretrial hearings while leaving the ultimate decision to the trial judge's discretion. See Harriett R. Galvin, Shielding Rape Victims in the State and Federal Courts: A Proposal for the Second Decade, 70 Minn. L. Rev. 763 (1986).

Rape shield statutes aim to protect victim-witnesses from serious abuses in the trial process, and some observers believe that even the most restrictive statutes do not go far enough in this regard. For example, Professor Michelle J. Anderson criticizes the exception (in virtually all rape shield statutes) for prior sexual conduct between the complainant and the defendant; she argues that evidence of such interactions should be excluded in the absence of certain unusual circumstances. See Anderson, Diminishing the Legal Impact of Negative Social Attitudes Toward Acquaintance Rape Victims,

13 New Crim. L. Rev. 644, 659-662 (2010). But would the exclusion of such evidence interfere with the defendant's right to a fair trial? Do the narrower exclusionary rules mandated by existing law do so? Consider the cases that follow.

STATE v. DeLAWDER

Maryland Court of Special Appeals
28 Md. App. 212, 344 A.2d 446 (1975)

ORTH, C.J. . . . DeLawder was found guilty by a jury . . . of carnal knowledge of a female under the age of 14 years. A 15 year sentence was imposed. The judgment was affirmed on direct appeal. [DeLawder then sought postconviction relief.] . . .

In affirming the judgment on direct appeal, we held that the trial court did not err in [barring] questions attempting to show that the prosecuting witness had sexual intercourse with other men on other occasions. The general rule is that because consent is not an issue in a carnal knowledge prosecution, evidence that the prosecutrix had prior intercourse with men other than the accused, or that her reputation for chastity was bad is immaterial when offered as an excuse or justification, and so is inadmissible for that reason. . . . The trial judge correctly applied these rules. . . .

As *Davis* [v. Alaska, 415 U.S. 308 (1974)] was decided subsequent to our decision, we must determine whether it affects the validity of DeLawder's conviction. In *Davis*, the Supreme Court of the United States reviewed the reach of the Confrontation Clause of the Sixth Amendment to the federal Constitution. . . . "Confrontation means more than being allowed to confront the witness physically. '[A] primary interest secured by [the confrontation clause] is the right of cross-examination.'" "Cross-examination," the Court observed, "is the principal means by which the believability of a witness and the truth of his testimony are tested. . . ." A witness may be discredited . . . by means of cross-examination directed toward revealing possible biases, prejudices, or ulterior motives of the witness. . . . The Supreme Court has recognized "that the exposure of a witness's motivation in testifying is a proper and important function of the constitutionally protected right of cross-examination." . . .

Davis was convicted of burglary and grand larceny . . . at a trial in which the court [prohibited] the questioning of Richard Green, a key prosecution witness, concerning Green's adjudication as a juvenile delinquent relating to a burglary and his probation status at the time of the events as to which he was to testify. The motion was granted in reliance on a state rule and statute which preserved the confidentiality of juvenile adjudications of delinquency. . . . The defense made clear that it did not intend to use Green's juvenile record to impeach his credibility generally, but only as necessary to examine him for any possible bias and prejudice. "Not only might Green have made a hasty and faulty identification of [Davis] to shift suspicion away from himself . . . , but Green might have been subject to undue pressure from the police and made his identification under fear of possible probation revocation." The trial court rejected even this limited use of Green's adjudication, but defense counsel did his best to expose Green's [possible bias]. Green, however, made a flat denial to questions whether he was upset by the fact that the [stolen] safe was found on his property [and] whether he felt the authorities might suspect him, . . .

The Alaska Supreme Court . . . affirmed the conviction on the grounds that [this cross-examination] was adequate to develop the issue of bias. . . . The [U.S.] Supreme Court did not accept this. It said: "On the basis of the limited cross-examination that was permitted, the jury might well have thought that defense counsel was engaged in a speculative and baseless line of attack on the credibility of an apparently blameless witness. [T]o make any such inquiry effective, defense counsel should have been permitted to expose to the jury the facts from which jurors, as the sole triers of fact and credibility, could appropriately draw inferences relating to the reliability of the witness." It held that disallowance of the defense's attempt to show bias . . . by cross-examination concerning the witness's juvenile record violated Davis's Sixth and Fourteenth Amendment rights.[2] . . .

DeLawder's counsel made clear . . . that the defense strategy would be to discredit the prosecuting witness [by] proving that . . . she thought she was pregnant by someone else and claimed that DeLawder raped her because she was afraid to tell her mother she voluntarily had sexual intercourse with others. To show that she thought she was pregnant at the time of the alleged encounter with DeLawder, it would be necessary to establish that she had engaged in prior acts of sexual intercourse. . . .

We cannot speculate . . . as to whether the jury . . . would have accepted this line of reasoning had counsel been permitted to present it fully. But [it] seems clear to us, in the light of *Davis,* that defense counsel should have been permitted to expose to the jury the facts from which jurors, as the sole triers of fact and credibility, could appropriately draw inferences relating to the reliability of the witness. By being prevented from so doing DeLawder was denied the right of effective cross-examination. . . . We conclude, as the Court concluded in *Davis,* that the desirability that the prosecutrix fulfill her public duty to testify free from embarrassment and with her reputation unblemished must fall before the right of an accused to seek out the truth in the process of defending himself. . . .

NOTES

1. A number of courts have held restrictive rape shield statutes unconstitutional when they bar evidence of relevant sexual history. E.g.,

---

2. The Court did not challenge the State's interest [in preserving] the anonymity of a juvenile offender [but held that this interest] "is outweighed by petitioner's right to probe into the influence of possible bias."

Commonwealth v. Spiewak, 617 A.2d 696 (Pa. Super. 1992). Some courts have avoided striking down their rape shield statutes by reading in a "catch-all" exception for evidence needed to preserve the defendant's right to a fair trial. E.g., Neeley v. Commonwealth, 437 S.E.2d 721 (Va. App. 1993).

2. Though rape shield statutes have proved more porous than reformers initially expected, they have nonetheless had a major impact on trial administration. Empirical studies uniformly report that victims are better treated in the judicial process and that efforts to limit the admissibility of sexual history evidence are largely successful.[44]

3. *Problems.* *(a)* In Commonwealth v. Harris, 825 N.E.2d 58 (Mass. 2005), a rape defendant argued that the complainant had consented to an act of prostitution and then accused him of rape as retribution for his failure to pay her full fee. The defendant sought to impeach her testimony by offering evidence that she had a prior conviction for prostitution. The state's rape shield statute bars "[e]vidence of specific instances of a victim's sexual conduct" with persons other than the defendant. Mass. Gen. Laws, ch. 233, §21B. But another statute authorizes the admission of a witness's prior conviction for purposes of impeaching the witness's credibility. Id. §21. Which of the two conflicting rules should prevail? The Massachusetts Supreme Judicial Court held that the statute permitting impeachment use of prior convictions controlled and that the evidence of the complainant's sexual history was admissible. Apart from the question of statutory interpretation, what is the best way to handle this problem? Does the prejudicial impact of casting the complainant as a prostitute outweigh the possible relevance of her prior conviction? Or does excluding the evidence unfairly impede the defendant's ability to present a possibly truthful defense?

(b) In Neeley v. Commonwealth, 437 S.E.2d 721 (Va. App. 1993), the complainant, a 14-year-old white female, alleged that defendant, a young African-American male who lived nearby, climbed through her bedroom window in the middle of the night and forcibly raped her. Defendant denied entering the house that evening. The prosecution introduced expert testimony that a hair fragment found in the complainant's cervix, though not positively identifiable as defendant's, was "characteristic of hair from a person of African-American descent." The defendant offered to prove that shortly before the alleged rape, the complainant had had sexual intercourse with her boyfriend and that the boyfriend was also African-American. A provision of the state's rape shield law permitted the use of sexual history evidence when "offered to provide an alternative explanation for physical evidence of the offense charged which is introduced by the prosecution, limited to evidence

---

44. See Cassia Spohn & Julia Horney, Rape Law Reform: Grassroots Revolution and Its Impact 129 (1992).

designed to explain the presence of semen, pregnancy, disease, or physical injury to the complaining witness's intimate parts. . . ." Because the defendant's evidence was offered to explain the presence of a hair sample rather than semen, it did not meet the terms of this or any other statutory exception, and the trial court excluded it. On appeal, should the ruling be upheld? Or, as applied to these facts, is the statutory exclusion unconstitutional?

(c) The defendant was charged with forcing his former girlfriend to have sex simultaneously with himself and one of his friends. He claimed consent, and in an effort to make the defense credible, he sought to introduce evidence that on previous occasions she had willingly engaged in sexual acts involving multiple partners or offered to do so. Is that evidence unduly prejudicial? Or would excluding it deny the defendant the opportunity for a fair trial on his defense of consent? See Gagne v. Booker, 606 F.3d 278 (6th Cir. 2010).

4. Prior behavior of the defendant. In Chapter 1, we considered the principle that evidence of a defendant's prior misconduct is not admissible to prove a propensity to engage in similar conduct. And as we saw there, most jurisdictions apply the prior-misconduct rule just as strictly in rape trials as in other kinds of prosecutions. See page 27-28, Note 3, supra.

Is the willingness of courts to admit evidence of some prior sexual acts by a rape complainant inconsistent with the rule that precludes reference to prior misconduct by the defendant? In one highly publicized prosecution, William Kennedy Smith was charged with committing a sexual assault upon a woman who had accompanied him back to his family's vacation home, after drinking and dancing with him at a bar. The case turned on the credibility of the woman's testimony that Smith ignored her protests and forced her to submit. Prior to trial, three other women came forward to allege that Smith had sexually assaulted them. The trial judge excluded this evidence, and Smith was acquitted. See N.Y. Times, Dec. 13, 1992, at B14. Was the ruling correct? If not, should the judge admit evidence of the prior sexual conduct of *both* Smith and his accuser? Consider Susan Estrich, Teaching Rape Law, 102 Yale L.J. 509, 519 (1992):

> One [approach] is to say that we need symmetry: exclude all the evidence about both of them. That's the approach the judge followed in the William Kennedy Smith case. On the surface, it is neat and appealing. The only problem is that it's a false symmetry. . . . [E]vidence that a man has abused other women is much more probative of rape than evidence that a woman has had consensual sex with other men is probative of consent. [T]he mere fact that a woman has had lovers tells us almost nothing about whether she consented on the particular occasion that she is charging as rape. But won't we all look at a defendant differently if three other women have also come forward to say they were abused? The danger with such evidence is not that it proves so little, but that it may prove too much. Symmetry won't get you out of this hole. . . .

GOVERNMENT OF THE VIRGIN ISLANDS v. SCUITO

United States Court of Appeals, 3d Circuit
623 F.2d 869 (1980)

ADAMS, J. In this appeal from a conviction for forcible rape, the defendant Louis Scuito asserts . . . [that the] trial judge abused or failed to exercise his discretion in denying the defendant's motion for a psychiatric examination of the complainant. . . .

The complainant worked as a waitress at the Drunken Shrimp restaurant, where the defendant was a frequent patron. When the complainant worked late on the night of July 9, 1978, the owner of the restaurant arranged for Scuito to give the complainant a ride to her apartment. It is undisputed that Scuito took a detour down a beach road, where the two had sexual intercourse, after which he took the complainant home. The crucial issue at trial was solely whether she consented.

According to the complainant, Scuito turned down the beach road to relieve himself, and then continued to a turnaround, stopped the jeep, and began kissing her. She expressed lack of interest, but the defendant then told her he had a knife and would throw her into the ocean if she did not cooperate. She testified that she did not actually see the knife in the dark, but felt "something metal" cut into her neck, after which she ceased resistance and attempted to calm him and avoid harm by cooperating. At trial there was medical and other testimony of a cut on the side of the complainant's neck where she said the knife was held. After taking off her clothes, the defendant raped and sodomized her. During the course of the assault she prayed and recited her "mantra."[2] Upon being dropped off at home, she kissed the defendant on the forehead because, she testified, "I was praying for him" and "it was just kind of like an end to the prayer."

Scuito testified that he casually knew the complainant and her sister and had previously driven them home from the restaurant. He said that on the night of July 9, when he gave the complainant a ride to her apartment, she seemed "a little spaced, not all there." While riding home, she offered him marijuana and he drove off the main road to smoke it with her. He later "came on to her," he said. Although initially she protested, he eventually changed her mind without using or threatening any physical force.

[Defendant's first trial ended in a mistrial after the prosecutor referred to inadmissible evidence that Scuito had previously raped another young woman.] Scuito moved before the second trial for a psychiatric examination of the complainant. In a supporting affidavit, his attorney made the following specific representations:

> [1] I have been informed by any number of persons in the community that the said complainant appears to be often, if not almost constantly, in a "spaced out" or trancelike state; I have personally observed this; I have been further

---

2. A mantra has been defined as "[a] sound aid used while meditating. Each meditator has his own personal mantra which is never to be revealed to any other person." Malnak v. Yogi, 592 F.2d 197, 198 (3d Cir. 1979). . . .

informed by persons in the community that the said complainant is addicted to, and does continually use, controlled substances, and that she is frequently in altered states of consciousness therefrom; and I have further observed and been told of the said complainant's habit of dressing and being seen publicly in see-through top garments which seem indicative of socially aberrant behavior;

[2] Further, my observation of the said complainant at the first trial herein showed, in my opinion, a rather strange and mysterious countenance on her part, and her testimony appeared strange, not only from the standpoint of her account of not reporting the alleged crimes until the next day, but particularly from her admitted interest and devotion to a certain book, written by a guru devotee of Timothy Leary which contains passages of religious-like worship of LSD and other mind-altering drugs; [and]

[3] That the foregoing observations are highly indicative of a personality which fantasizes to extremes and which indulges in and seeks altered states of consciousness. . . .

Defendant does not press the extreme position, espoused by Wigmore, that a psychiatric examination of a complainant should be required in all sexual offense prosecutions. Rather, defendant agrees with the Government that the decision to order an examination is "entrusted to the sound discretion of the trial judge in light of the particular facts." . . .

This discretion is not, of course, unbounded, for there are countervailing considerations weighing heavily against ordering a psychiatric examination of a complainant. . . . "[A] psychiatric examination may seriously impinge on a witness' right to privacy; the trauma that attends the role of complainant to sex offense charges is sharply increased by the indignity of a psychiatric examination; the examination itself could serve as a tool of harassment; and the impact of all these considerations may well deter the victim of such a crime from lodging any complaint at all." United States v. Benn, 476 F.2d at 1131. . . .

Fed. R. Evid. 412 is specifically addressed to evidence of a rape victim's prior sexual conduct,[a] whereas defendant's motion was not an attempt to introduce such evidence, but an effort to obtain an expert opinion regarding the complainant's general ability to perceive reality and separate fact from fantasy. Because the rule does not directly apply to his motion, the defendant argues that the court either abused or did not exercise its discretion in denying the motion. The judge's ruling, however, was not based on the letter but on the spirit of Rule 412 [and] nothing alleged in defense counsel's affidavit indicates that he abused his discretion. To the extent admissible, and we express no opinion on that matter, evidence that the complainant was thought by members of the community to indulge in drugs leading to "altered states of consciousness" or to dress in a manner "indicative of socially aberrant behavior" could be introduced by direct rather than expert testimony. If, however, such

---

a. Rule 412 excludes "(1) evidence offered to prove that any alleged victim engaged in other sexual behavior; and (2) evidence offered to prove any alleged victim's sexual predisposition." Rule 412 would not literally apply to the kind of "mental stability" evidence at issue in *Scuito.*—EDS.

matters are not relevant or otherwise admissible, there is no justification for letting them into the trial by allowing an expert to give his opinion regarding them. . . .

The judgment of the trial court will be affirmed.

NOTES AND QUESTIONS

1. Is the disfavoring of expert testimony in *Scuito* justified in terms of the truth-seeking function of the trial or only in terms of the desire to protect the complainant from degrading psychological tests? If the latter explanation is the more satisfactory, is the result in *Scuito* consistent with *Davis v. Alaska*?

2. Do you think the court's view of the case (or yours) is influenced by awareness of the inadmissible evidence that Scuito had previously raped another woman? *Should* that fact be relevant?

3. In Abbott v. State, 138 P.3d 462 (Nev. 2006), the defendant was accused of abusing a nine-year-old child. Because the child had made false allegations of child abuse in the past, he sought an order requiring the child to undergo an independent psychological evaluation. The Nevada Supreme Court held that the defendant had established a "compelling need" for such an examination and that without it, the defendant would be deprived of a meaningful opportunity to argue that the child was not a truthful witness. Is *Abbott* consistent with *Scuito*? If not, which is the better approach? Does the *Abbott* standard expose sex abuse victims to excessive trauma and risk of harassment? Or is that approach necessary to guarantee sex-abuse defendants a fair trial?

chapter 5

Homicide

A. INTRODUCTION

One may ask two kinds of questions about any category of crime. The first is a question of criminality: What distinguishes criminal from non-criminal behavior? The second is a question of grading: What factors warrant greater or lesser punishment when behavior qualifies as criminal? In the preceding chapter on rape, we dealt primarily with the first question. In this chapter, we deal primarily with the second. The distinction between criminal and non-criminal homicide usually turns on such issues as causation, self-defense, insanity, etc. We will deal separately with these issues in later chapters, because they arise for many different kinds of crimes. The principal focus of the present chapter is on the severity of punishment authorized for homicides that are criminal.

Conventional public thinking about criminal law understandably concentrates on the threshold question of guilt versus innocence. The severity of the sentence is obviously important too, but we are less accustomed to thinking of this issue as one governed by rigorous legal analysis. Yet the stakes in determining the *degree* of punishment are always high, and nowhere more so than when a victim has died. Homicide that seems a product of mere carelessness or extraordinary provocation is often punished by no more than a fine or a few months in jail; at the other extreme, some defendants who kill incur the death penalty or imprisonment for life with no possibility for parole. A society under the rule of law must have clear, objective ways for choosing between these dramatically different alternatives (and the many that fall in between).

Legislative grading is accomplished by dividing homicidal conduct into crimes of different names (murder and manslaughter) and by dividing the same crime into different degrees (first-degree and second-degree murder). Following the historical and statutory materials in this introductory section, Section B considers the grading of intended killings and Section C examines the grading of unintended killings. Section C also considers the distinction between involuntary manslaughter and wrongful killings that are not subject to criminal punishment at all. With that last exception, however, the behavior in this chapter is always a crime of some sort; the central concern is to

[Handwritten margin notes: "How MUCH punishment can be imposed." "TWO prob • substantive problem • institut prob"]

determine how much punishment can be imposed. And in addressing that issue, the law has traditionally been preoccupied with two distinct problems. The first, and most obvious, is a *substantive* problem—which facts determine whether punishment will be more severe. The second problem, though less obvious, is often equally important for lawyers; this is the *institutional* problem—which decision-making institution (for example, trial judge or jury) has authority to make the controlling assessment of these facts.

REPORT OF THE ROYAL COMMISSION ON CAPITAL PUNISHMENT, 1945-1953

25-28 (1953)

Basic Principles of the Law of Murder in England,

72. Homicide is the killing of a human being by a human being. Unlawful homicide may be murder, manslaughter, suicide or infanticide. Murder and manslaughter are felonies at common law and are not defined by statute. The traditional definition or description of murder ... is in common practice often ... briefly defined as "unlawful killing with 'malice aforethought' "; while manslaughter is defined as "unlawful killing without 'malice aforethought.' " ...

74. The meaning of "malice aforethought," which is the distinguishing criterion of murder, is certainly not beyond the range of controversy. The first thing that must be said about it is that neither of the two words is used in its ordinary sense: the phrase "malice aforethought" is now a highly technical term of art. "It is now only an arbitrary symbol. For the 'malice' may have in it nothing really malicious; and need never be really 'aforethought,' except in the sense that every desire must necessarily come before—though perhaps only an instant before—the act which is desired. The word 'aforethought,' in the definition, has thus become either false or else superfluous. The word 'malice' is neither; but it is apt to be misleading, for it is not employed in its original (and its popular) meaning." "Malice aforethought" is simply a comprehensive name for a number of different mental attitudes which have been variously defined at different stages in the development of the law, the presence of any one of which in the accused has been held by the courts to render a homicide particularly heinous and therefore to make it murder. ...

75. We must now consider how "malice aforethought" came to be the distinctive element of murder and to bear such a meaning as is given to it at the present time. ... It is sufficient to say here that "murder" originally meant a "secret killing" and only gradually, from the fourteenth century onwards, came to be the name of the worst form of homicide characterised by "malice prepense" or "malice aforethought." ... It seems clear that at this period and for sometime afterwards "malice prepense" or "malice aforethought" was understood to mean a deliberate, premeditated intent to kill formed some time beforehand, and that no killing "on a sudden," even without provocation or on slight provocation, was considered to be murder. In effect the law regarded unlawful killings as being of only two kinds—killing with malice

aforethought and killing on a sudden quarrel. Experience showed, however, that this view was much too simple and the definitions founded upon it inadequate. There were many kinds of killing which should clearly be considered unlawful but which did not fall into either of these categories, and many such cases seemed to deserve the extreme penalty although the offender had no premeditated desire to kill his victim. During the last four centuries the meaning to be given to the term "malice aforethought" has been affected by the changes in the conception of mens rea as a necessary ingredient in criminal liability at common law for all crimes. The courts and the writers of legal textbooks have responded to this change by giving to "malice aforethought" a wider and more technical meaning. As Stephen put it, "the loose term 'malice' was used, and then when a particular state of mind came under their notice, the Judges called it 'malice' or not, according to their view of the propriety of hanging particular people. That is, in two words, the history of the definition of murder." There can be no doubt that the term now covers, and has for long covered, all the most heinous forms of homicide, as well as some cases—those of "constructive murder"—whose inclusion in the category of murder has often been criticised.

76. Thus the following propositions are commonly accepted:

(i) It is murder if one person kills another with intent to do so, without provocation or on slight provocation, although there is no premeditation in the ordinary sense of the word.

(ii) It is murder if one person is killed by an act intended to kill another.

(iii) It is murder if a person is killed by an act intended to kill, although not intended to kill any particular individual, as if a man throws a bomb into a crowd of people.

(iv) It is murder if death results from an act which is intended to do no more than cause grievous bodily harm. An early example may be found in the case of Grey, where a blacksmith, who had had words with an apprentice, struck him on the head with an iron bar and killed him. It was held that it "is all one as if he had run him through with a sword" and he was found guilty of murder.

(v) It is murder if one person kills another by an intentional act which he knows to be likely to kill or to cause grievous bodily harm, although he may not intend to kill or to cause grievous bodily harm and may either be recklessly indifferent as to the results of his act or may even desire that no harm should be caused by it.

CALIFORNIA PENAL CODE (2011)

SECTION 187. MURDER DEFINED

(a) Murder is the unlawful killing of a human being, or a fetus,[a] with malice aforethought. . . .

---

a. Except where done in the course of a legal abortion or by a physician pursuant to a medical judgment or where consented to by the mother. Section 187(b). The language was added following

Section 188. Malice Defined

Such malice may be express or implied. It is expressed when there is manifested a deliberate intention unlawfully to take away the life of a fellow creature. It is implied, when no considerable provocation appears, or when the circumstances attending the killing show an abandoned and malignant heart. . . .

Section 189. Degrees of Murder

All murder which is perpetrated by means of a destructive device or explosive, a weapon of mass destruction, knowing use of ammunition designed primarily to penetrate metal or armor, poison, lying in wait, torture, or by any other kind of willful, deliberate, and premeditated killing, or which is committed in the perpetration of, or attempt to perpetrate, arson, rape, carjacking, robbery, burglary, mayhem, kidnapping, train wrecking, or any act punishable under Section 206, 286, 288, 288a, or 289 [prohibiting various forcible sexual acts and certain sexual acts with minors], or any murder which is perpetrated by means of discharging a firearm from a motor vehicle, intentionally at another person outside of the vehicle with intent to inflict death, is murder of the first degree [punishable by death or imprisonment for life without possibility of parole where special enumerated circumstances exist, or imprisonment for 25 years to life]. All other kinds of murders are of the second degree [punishable by imprisonment for 15 years to life]. . . .

To prove the killing was "deliberate and premeditated," it shall not be necessary to prove the defendant maturely and meaningfully reflected upon the gravity of his or her act.

Section 192. Manslaughter

Manslaughter is the unlawful killing of a human being without malice. It is of three kinds:

(a) Voluntary—upon a sudden quarrel or heat of passion. [Punishable by imprisonment for three, six, or 11 years.]

(b) Involuntary—in the commission of an unlawful act, not amounting to felony; or in the commission of a lawful act which might produce death, in an unlawful manner, or without due caution and circumspection. This subdivision shall not apply to acts committed in the driving of a vehicle. [Punishable by imprisonment for two, three, or four years.]

(c) Vehicular—

(1) . . . driving a vehicle in the commission of an unlawful act, not amounting to felony, and with gross negligence; or driving a vehicle in the commission of a lawful act which might produce death, in an unlawful manner, and with gross negligence. [Punishable by up to one year in county jail or imprisonment for two, four, or six years.]

Keeler v. Superior Court, page 163 supra, 1970 Cal. Laws ch. 1311, §1. In People v. Davis, 872 P.2d 591 (Cal. 1994), the court held that viability is not an element of the offense of fetal murder; the killing of a fetus can constitute murder, within the meaning of §187(a), as long as the state can show that the fetus has progressed beyond the embryonic stage of seven to eight weeks.—Eds.

(2) Driving a vehicle in the commission of an unlawful act, not amounting to felony, but without gross negligence; or driving a vehicle in the commission of a lawful act which might produce death, in an unlawful manner, but without gross negligence. [Punishable by a county jail term not to exceed one year.] . . .

This section shall not be construed as making any homicide in the driving of a vehicle punishable that is not a proximate result of the commission of an unlawful act, not amounting to felony, or of the commission of a lawful act which might produce death, in an unlawful manner.

"Gross negligence," as used in this section, shall not be construed as prohibiting or precluding a charge of murder under Section 188 upon facts exhibiting wantonness and a conscious disregard for life to support a finding of implied malice, or upon facts showing malice, consistent with the holding of the California Supreme Court in People v. Watson, 30 Cal. 3d 290.[b]

PENNSYLVANIA CONSOLIDATED STATUTES, TITLE 18 (2010)

SECTION 2501. CRIMINAL HOMICIDE

(a) OFFENSE DEFINED.—A person is guilty of criminal homicide if he intentionally, knowingly, recklessly or negligently causes the death of another human being.

(b) CLASSIFICATION.—Criminal homicide shall be classified as murder, voluntary manslaughter, or involuntary manslaughter.

SECTION 2502. MURDER

(a) MURDER OF THE FIRST DEGREE.—A criminal homicide constitutes murder of the first degree when it is committed by an intentional killing. [Punishable by death or life imprisonment.]

(b) MURDER OF THE SECOND DEGREE.—A criminal homicide constitutes murder of the second degree when it is committed while defendant was engaged as a principal or an accomplice in the perpetration of a felony. [Punishable by life imprisonment.]

(c) MURDER OF THE THIRD DEGREE.—All other kinds of murder shall be murder of the third degree. Murder of the third degree is a felony of the first degree. [Punishable by maximum of 20 years.]

(d) DEFINITIONS.—As used in this section the following words and phrases shall have the meanings given to them in this subsection: . . .

"Intentional killing." Killing by means of poison, or by lying in wait, or by any other kind of willful, deliberate and premeditated killing.

thought about it & meant it

---

b. The court held that the statutory provisions defining murder are not preempted by the more specific provisions applicable to vehicular homicides, because greater culpability is required for the former. Thus, second-degree murder may be charged when the facts surrounding a vehicular homicide support a finding of implied malice; vehicular manslaughter would be the appropriate charge when the facts demonstrate only gross negligence.—EDS.

"Perpetration of a felony." The act of the defendant in engaging in or being an accomplice in the commission of, or an attempt to commit, or flight after committing, or attempting to commit robbery, rape, or deviate sexual intercourse by force or threat of force, arson, burglary or kidnapping. . . .

SECTION 2503. VOLUNTARY MANSLAUGHTER

(a) GENERAL RULE.—A person who kills an individual without lawful justification commits voluntary manslaughter if at the time of the killing he is acting under a sudden and intense passion resulting from serious provocation by:

(1) the individual killed; or

(2) another whom the actor endeavors to kill, but he negligently or accidentally causes the death of the individual killed.

(b) UNREASONABLE BELIEF KILLING JUSTIFIABLE.—A person who intentionally or knowingly kills an individual commits voluntary manslaughter if at the time of the killing he believes the circumstances to be such that, if they existed, would justify the killing under Chapter 5 of this title, but his belief is unreasonable.

(c) GRADING.—Voluntary manslaughter is a felony of the first degree. [20-year maximum.]

SECTION 2504. INVOLUNTARY MANSLAUGHTER

(a) GENERAL RULE.—A person is guilty of involuntary manslaughter when as a direct result of the doing of an unlawful act in a reckless or grossly negligent manner, or the doing of a lawful act in a reckless or grossly negligent manner, he causes the death of another person.

(b) GRADING.—Involuntary manslaughter is a misdemeanor of the first degree. . . . [Five-year maximum.]

SECTION 2505. CAUSING OR AIDING SUICIDE

(a) CAUSING SUICIDE AS CRIMINAL HOMICIDE.—A person may be convicted of criminal homicide for causing another to commit suicide only if he intentionally causes such suicide by force, duress, or deception.

(b) AIDING OR SOLICITING SUICIDE AS AN INDEPENDENT OFFENSE.—A person who intentionally aids or solicits another to commit suicide is guilty of a felony of the second degree if his conduct causes such suicide or an attempted suicide, and otherwise of a misdemeanor of the second degree. [Two-year maximum.]

NEW YORK PENAL LAW (2011)

SECTION 125.00. HOMICIDE DEFINED

Homicide means conduct which causes the death of a person . . . under circumstances constituting murder, manslaughter in the first degree, manslaughter in the second degree, [or] criminally negligent homicide. . . .

Section 125.10. Criminally Negligent Homicide

A person is guilty of criminally negligent homicide when, with criminal negligence,[a] he causes the death of another person.

Criminally negligent homicide is a class E felony. [Four-year maximum.]

Section 125.15. Manslaughter in the Second Degree

A person is guilty of manslaughter in the second degree when:

1. He recklessly[b] causes the death of another person; or . . .

3. He intentionally[c] causes or aids another person to commit suicide.

Manslaughter in the second degree is a class C felony. [15-year maximum.]

Section 125.20. Manslaughter in the First Degree

A person is guilty of manslaughter in the first degree when:

1. With intent to cause serious physical injury to another person, he causes the death of such person or of a third person; or

2. With intent to cause the death of another person, he causes the death of such person or of a third person under circumstances which do not constitute murder because he acts under the influence of extreme emotional disturbance, as defined in paragraph (a) of subdivision one of section 125.25. . . .

Manslaughter in the first degree is a class B felony. [25-year maximum.]

Section 125.25. Murder in the Second Degree

A person is guilty of murder in the second degree when:

1. With intent to cause the death of another person, he causes the death of such person or of a third person; except that in any prosecution under this subdivision, it is an affirmative defense that:

(a) The defendant acted under the influence of extreme emotional disturbance for which there was a reasonable explanation or excuse, the reasonableness of which is to be determined from the viewpoint of a person in the defendant's situation under the circumstances as the defendant believed them to be. . . . ; or

(b) The defendant's conduct consisted of causing or aiding, without the use of duress or deception, another person to commit suicide. . . . ; or

2. Under circumstances evincing a depraved indifference to human life, he recklessly engages in conduct which creates a grave risk of death to another person, and thereby causes the death of another person; or

3. Acting either alone or with one or more other persons, he commits or attempts to commit robbery, burglary, kidnapping, arson, rape in the first degree, criminal sexual act in the first degree, sexual abuse in the first degree, aggravated sexual abuse, escape in the first degree, or escape in the second degree, and, in the course of and in furtherance of such crime or of immediate flight therefrom, he, or another participant, if there be any, causes the death

---

a. Defined similarly to Model Penal Code §2.02(2)(d).—Eds.
b. Defined similarly to Model Penal Code §2.02(2)(c).—Eds.
c. Defined similarly to "purposely" in Model Penal Code §2.02(2)(a).—Eds.

of a person other than one of the participants; except that in any prosecution under this subdivision, in which the defendant was not the only participant in the underlying crime, it is an affirmative defense that the defendant:

(a) Did not commit the homicidal act or in any way solicit, request, command, importune, cause or aid the commission thereof; and

(b) Was not armed with a deadly weapon, or any instrument, article or substance readily capable of causing death or serious physical injury and of a sort not ordinarily carried in public places by law-abiding persons; and

(c) Had no reasonable ground to believe that any other participant was armed with such a weapon, instrument, article or substance; and

(d) Had no reasonable ground to believe that any other participant intended to engage in conduct likely to result in death or serious physical injury. . . .

Murder in the second degree is a class A-I felony. [Punishable by from 15 years to life imprisonment.]

Section 125.27. Murder in the First Degree

[Under this section, intentional killings that would be second-degree murder under §125.25(1) are raised to first-degree murder in special circumstances, such as when the victim is a police officer or an employee of a state or local correctional institution, or when the crime is committed while a defendant is in custody serving a life sentence. First-degree murder is punishable by death, but at this writing New York no longer has a valid regime for imposing capital punishment.][d]

MODEL PENAL CODE

Section 210.1 to 210.4

[See Appendix for text of this section.]

THE PENAL CODE OF SWEDEN[a]

Section 1

A person who takes the life of another shall be sentenced for murder to imprisonment for ten years or for life.

Section 2

If, in view of the circumstances that led to the act or for other reasons, the crime mentioned in Section 1 is considered to be less grave, imprisonment for manslaughter shall be imposed for at least six and at most ten years. . . .

---

d. The New York Court of Appeals invalidated its capital punishment statute, People v. LaValle, 3 N.Y.3d 88, 817 N.E.2d 341 (2004), and to date legislative attempts to enact another have failed.—Eds.

a. National Council for Crime Prevention (Sweden), The Swedish Penal Code 1999, ch. 3, §§1-7 (1999) (unofficial translation published by the Ministry of Justice).—Eds.

Section 7

A person who through carelessness causes the death of another shall be sentenced for causing another's death to imprisonment for at most two years or, if the crime is less grave, to pay a fine.

If the crime is gross, imprisonment shall be imposed for at least six months and at most four years.

If the act was committed by driving a motor vehicle, special consideration shall be given, in assessing whether the crime is gross, to whether the sentenced person was under the influence of alcohol or other substance.

B. LEGISLATIVE GRADING OF INTENDED KILLINGS

1. *The Premeditation-Deliberation Formula*

INTRODUCTORY NOTE

Model Penal Code and Commentaries, Comment to §210.2 at 16 (1980): Prior to the recodification effort begun by the Model Penal Code, most American jurisdictions maintained a law of murder built around ... common-law [concepts]. The most significant departure was the division of murder into degrees, a change initiated by the Pennsylvania legislation of 1794. That statute provided that "all murder, which shall be perpetrated by means of poison, or by lying in wait, or by any other kind of willful, deliberate and premeditated killing, or which shall be committed in the perpetration, or attempt to perpetrate any arson, rape, robbery or burglary shall be deemed murder in the first degree; and all other kinds of murder shall be deemed murder in the second degree." The thrust of this reform was to confine the death penalty, which was then mandatory on conviction of any common-law murder, to homicides judged particularly heinous. Other states followed the Pennsylvania practice until at one time the vast majority of American jurisdictions differentiated degrees of murder and the term "first-degree murder" passed into common parlance.

COMMONWEALTH v. CARROLL

Supreme Court of Pennsylvania
412 Pa. 525, 194 A.2d 911 (1963)

Bell, C.J. The defendant, Carroll, pleaded guilty generally to an indictment charging him with the murder of his wife, and was tried by a judge without a jury. . . . The Court found him guilty of first-degree murder and sentenced him to life imprisonment. [D]efendant took this appeal. The only questions involved are thus stated by the appellant:

> [1] Does not the evidence sustain a conviction no higher than murder in the second degree?

[2] Does not the evidence of defendant's good character, together with the testimony of medical experts, including the psychiatrist for the Behavior Clinic of Allegheny County, that the homicide was not premeditated or intentional, require the Court below to fix the degree of guilt of defendant no higher than murder in the second degree?

facts

The defendant married the deceased in 1955, when he was serving in the Army in California. Subsequently he was stationed in Alabama, and later in Greenland. During the latter tour of duty, defendant's wife and two children lived with his parents in New Jersey. Because this arrangement proved incompatible, defendant returned to the United States on emergency leave in order to move his family to their own quarters. On his wife's insistence, defendant was forced first to secure a "compassionate transfer" back to the States, and subsequently to resign from the Army in July of 1960, by which time he had attained the rank of Chief Warrant Officer. Defendant was a hard worker, earned a substantial salary and bore a very good reputation among his neighbors.

In 1958, decedent-wife suffered a fractured skull while attempting to leave defendant's car in the course of an argument. Allegedly this contributed to her mental disorder which was later diagnosed as a schizoid personality type. In 1959 she underwent psychiatric treatment at the Mental Hygiene Clinic in Aberdeen, Maryland. She complained of nervousness and told the examining doctor "I feel like hurting my children." This sentiment sometimes took the form of sadistic "discipline" toward their very young children. Nevertheless, upon her discharge from the Clinic, the doctors considered her much improved. With this background we come to the immediate events of the crime.

In January, 1962, defendant was selected to attend an electronics school in Winston-Salem, North Carolina, for nine days. His wife greeted this news with violent argument. Immediately prior to his departure for Winston-Salem, at the suggestion and request of his wife, he put a loaded .22 calibre pistol on the window sill at the head of their common bed, so that she would feel safe. On the evening of January 16, 1962, defendant returned home and told his wife that he had been temporarily assigned to teach at a school in Chambersburg, which would necessitate his absence from home four nights out of seven for a ten week period. A violent and protracted argument ensued at the dinner table and continued until four o'clock in the morning.

Defendant's own statement after his arrest details the final moments before the crime:

We went into the bedroom a little before 3 o'clock on Wednesday morning where we continued to argue in short bursts. Generally she laid with her back to me facing the wall in bed and would just talk over her shoulder to me. I became angry and more angry especially what she was saying about my kids and myself, and sometime between 3 and 4 o'clock in the morning I remembered the gun on the window sill over my head. I think she had dozed off. I reached up and grabbed the pistol and brought it down and shot her twice in the back of the head.[2]

Defendant's testimony at the trial elaborated this theme. He started to think about the children:

> seeing my older son's feet what happened to them. I could see the bruises on him and Michael's chin was split open, four stitches. I didn't know what to do. I wanted to help my boys. Sometime in there she said something in there, she called me some kind of name. I kept thinking of this. During this time I either thought or felt—I thought of the gun, just thought of the gun. I am not sure whether I felt my hand move toward the gun—I saw my hand move, the next thing—the only thing I can recollect after that is right after the shots or right during the shots. I saw the gun in my hand just pointed at my wife's head. She was still lying on her back—I mean her side. I could smell the gunpowder and I could hear something—it sounded like running water. I didn't know what it was at first, didn't realize what I'd done at first. Then I smelled it. I smelled blood before. . . .
>
> Q. At the time you shot her, Donald, were you fully aware and intend to do what you did?
> A. I don't know positively. All I remember hearing was two shots and feeling myself go cold all of a sudden.

Shortly thereafter defendant wrapped his wife's body in a blanket, spread and sheets, tied them on with a piece of plastic clothesline and took her down to the cellar. He tried to clean up as well as he could. That night he took his wife's body, wrapped in a blanket with a rug over it to a desolate place near a trash dump. He then took the children to his parents' home in Magnolia, New Jersey. He was arrested the next Monday in Chambersburg where he had gone to his teaching assignment.

Although defendant's brief is voluminous, the narrow and only questions which he raises on this appeal are as hereinbefore quoted. Both are embodied in his contention that the crime amounted only to second-degree murder and that his conviction should therefore be reduced to second degree or that a new trial should be granted. . . .

[The court then reviewed the Pennsylvania murder statute, which at the time divided murder into two degrees, in accordance with the formula adopted in 1794. That formula, still in effect for Pennsylvania in 1963 and followed in many states to this day, is quoted above in the excerpt immediately preceding *Carroll*.[a] Then, as now, first-degree murder included killings by poison, lying in wait, "or any other kind of willful, deliberate and premeditated killing."]

The specific intent to kill which is necessary to constitute in a nonfelony murder, murder in the first degree, may be found from a defendant's words or conduct or from the attendant circumstances together with all reasonable

---

2. When pressed on cross-examination defendant approximated that five minutes elapsed between his wife's last remark and the shooting.

a. A further refinement adopted in Pennsylvania in 1976 produced three degrees of murder: See the current statute at page 423 supra.—EDS.

inferences therefrom, and may be inferred from the intentional use of a deadly weapon on a vital part of the body of another human being. . . .

If we consider only the evidence which is favorable to the Commonwealth, it is without the slightest doubt sufficient in law to prove first degree. However, even if we believe all of defendant's statements and testimony, there is no doubt that this killing constituted murder in the first degree. Defendant first urges that there was insufficient time for premeditation in the light of his good reputation. This is based on an isolated and oft repeated statement in Commonwealth v. Drum, 58 Pa. 9, 16, that "'no time is too short for a wicked man to frame in his mind the scheme of murder.'" Defendant argues that, conversely, a long time is necessary to find premeditation in a "good man." We find no merit in defendant's analogy or contention. As Chief Justice Maxey appropriately and correctly said in Commonwealth v. Earnest, 342 Pa. 544, 549-550, 21 A.2d 38, 40: "Whether the intention to kill and the killing, that is, the premeditation and the fatal act, were within a brief space of time or a long space of time is immaterial if the killing was in fact intentional, wilful, deliberate and premeditated." . . .

Defendant further contends that the time and place of the crime, the enormous difficulty of removing and concealing the body, and the obvious lack of an escape plan, militate against and make a finding of premeditation legally impossible. This is a "jury argument"; it is clear as crystal that such circumstances do not negate premeditation. This contention of defendant is likewise clearly devoid of merit.

Defendant's most earnestly pressed contention is that the psychiatrist's opinion of what defendant's state of mind must have been and was at the time of the crime, clearly establishes not only the lack but also the legal impossibility of premeditation. Dr. Davis, a psychiatrist . . . , testified that defendant was

> for a number of years . . . passively going along with a situation which he [was] not controlling and he [was] not making any decisions, and finally a decision [was] forced on him. . . . He had left the military to take this assignment, and he was averaging about nine thousand a year; he had a good job. He knew that if he didn't accept this teaching assignment in all probability he would be dismissed from the Government service, and at his age and his special training he didn't know whether he would be able to find employment. More critical to that was the fact that at this point, as we understand it, his wife issued an ultimatum that if he went and gave this training course she would leave him. . . . He was so dependent upon her he didn't want her to leave. He couldn't make up his mind what to do. He was trapped. . . .

The doctor then gave his opinion that "rage," "desperation," and "panic" produced

> an impulsive automatic reflex type of homicide, . . . as opposed to an intentional premeditated type of homicide, . . . Our feeling was that if this gun had fallen to the floor he wouldn't have been able to pick it up and consummate that homicide. And I think if he had to load the gun he wouldn't have done it. This is a matter of opinion, but this is our opinion about it.

There are three answers to this contention. First, . . . neither a judge nor a jury has to believe all or any part of the testimony of the defendant or of any witness. Secondly, the opinion of the psychiatrists was based to a large extent upon statements made to them by the defendant, which need not be believed and which are in some instances opposed by the facts themselves. Thirdly, a psychiatrist's opinion of a defendant's impulse or lack of intent or state of mind is, in this class of case, entitled to very little weight, and this is especially so when defendant's own actions, or his testimony or confession, or the facts themselves, belie the opinion. . . .

Defendant's own statement after his arrest, upon which his counsel so strongly relies, as well as his testimony at his trial, clearly convict him of first-degree murder. . . . From his own statements and from his own testimony, it is clear that, terribly provoked by his allegedly nagging, belligerent and sadistic wife, defendant remembered the gun, deliberately took it down, and deliberately fired two shots into the head of his sleeping wife. There is no doubt that this was a willful, deliberate and premeditated murder.

While defendant makes no contention that he was insane at the commission of the murder or at any time, what this Court said in Commonwealth v. Tyrrell, 174 A.2d 852, 856-857, is equally appropriate here:

> Defendant's psychiatrist did not testify that the defendant was insane. What he did say was that because defendant's wife frequently picked on him and just before the killing insulted or goaded him, defendant had an emotional impulse to kill her which he could not resist. . . . [S]ociety would be almost completely unprotected from criminals if the law permitted a blind or irresistible impulse or inability to control one's self, to excuse or justify a murder or to reduce it from first degree to second degree. In the times in which we are living, nearly every normal adult human being has moments or hours or days or longer periods when he or she is depressed and disturbed with resultant emotional upset feelings and so-called blind impulses; and the young especially have many uncontrolled emotions every day which are euphemistically called irresistible impulses. The Courts of Justice should not abdicate their function and duty of determining criminal responsibility to the psychiatrist. In such event, the test will differ not only with each psychiatrist but also with the prevailing psychiatric winds of the moment. . . .

Just as the Courts cannot abdicate to the psychiatrists the task of determining criminal responsibility in law, so also they cannot remit to psychiatrists the right to determine the intent or the state of mind of an accused at the time of the commission of a homicide. . . .

Judgment and sentence affirmed.

NOTES

1. Many courts follow the *Carroll* approach by suggesting that some premeditation is required, and simultaneously holding that "no time is too short" for the necessary premeditation to occur. See State v. Berhanu, 724 N.W.2d 181, 186 (S.D. 2006); Annot., 18 A.L.R.4th 961 (2010).

Consider Young v. State, 428 So. 2d 155, 158 (Ala. Crim. App. 1982). Defendant and his brother were playing cards with several friends when an argument and then a scuffle broke out. Defendant fired several shots, and two of the men were hit; each died from a single .22 caliber shot to the chest. The court upheld defendant's conviction on two counts of first-degree murder. Stressing that "[no] appreciable space of time between the formation of the intention to kill and the act of killing" was required, the court said that "[p]remeditation and deliberation may be formed while the killer is 'pressing the trigger that fired the fatal shot.'"

Question: Given decisions like *Carroll* and *Young*, what is the difference between a premeditated intention to kill and an intention to kill without premeditation?

2. Later Pennsylvania decisions clarify *Carroll*, by holding that "the requirement of premeditation and deliberation is met whenever there is a conscious purpose to bring about death. . . . We can find no reason where there is a conscious intent to bring about death to differentiate between the degree of culpability on the basis of the elaborateness of the design to kill." Commonwealth v. O'Searo, 352 A.2d 30, 37-38 (1976).

3. In an attempt to resolve difficulties in defining the premeditation element of first-degree murder, the Arizona legislature amended its statute as follows, A.R.S Sec.13-1101(1):

> [p]remeditation means that the defendant acts with either the intention or the knowledge that he will kill another human being, when such intention or knowledge precedes the killing by any length of time to permit reflection. Proof of actual reflection is not required, but an act is not done with premeditation if it is the instant effect of a sudden quarrel or heat of passion.

If "proof of actual reflection is not required," then what distinguishes intentional killings that are first-degree murders from those that are second-degree? In State v. Thompson, 204 Ariz. 241, 65 P.3d 420 (2003), the Arizona Supreme Court could find no difference. It therefore concluded that the statute was unconstitutional because arbitrary and capricious, in violation of due process. To save its constitutionality the court interpreted the statute to require proof of actual reflection.

STATE v. GUTHRIE

Supreme Court of Appeals of West Virginia
194 W. Va. 657, 461 S.E.2d 163 (1995)

CLECKLEY, J.: The defendant, Dale Edward Guthrie, appeals the . . . jury verdict finding him guilty of first-degree murder [defined to include "any willful, deliberate and premeditated killing"]. [He] was sentenced to serve a life sentence with a recommendation of mercy. . . .

It is ... undisputed that on the evening of February 12, 1993, the defendant removed a knife from his pocket and stabbed his co-worker, Steven Todd Farley, in the neck and killed him. The two men worked together as dishwashers at Danny's Rib House in Nitro and got along well together before this incident. On the night of the killing, the victim [and other employees] were joking around while working in the kitchen of the restaurant. The victim was poking fun at the defendant who appeared to be in a bad mood. He told the defendant to "lighten up" and snapped him with a dishtowel several times. Apparently, the victim had no idea he was upsetting the defendant very much. The dishtowel flipped the defendant on the nose and he became enraged.

The defendant removed his gloves and started toward the victim. Mr. Farley, still teasing, said: "Ooo, he's taking his gloves off." The defendant then pulled a knife from his pocket and stabbed the victim in the neck. He also stabbed Mr. Farley in the arm as he fell to the floor. Mr. Farley looked up and cried: "Man, I was just kidding around." The defendant responded: "Well, man, you should have never hit me in my face." ...

It is ... undisputed that the defendant suffers from a host of psychiatric problems. He experiences up to two panic attacks daily and had received treatment for them ... for more than a year preceding the killing. He suffers from chronic depression (dysthymic disorder), an obsession with his nose (body dysmorphic disorder), and borderline personality disorder. The defendant's father shed some light on his nose fixation. He stated that dozens of times a day the defendant stared in the mirror and turned his head back and forth to look at his nose. ... The defendant repeatedly asked for assurances that his nose was not too big. This obsession began when he was approximately seventeen years old. The defendant was twenty-nine years old at the time of trial.

The defendant testified he suffered a panic attack immediately preceding the stabbing. He described the attack as "intense"; he felt a lot of pressure and his heart beat rapidly. [He] could not understand why Mr. Farley was picking on him because he had never done that before. Even at trial, the defendant did not comprehend his utter overreaction to the situation. In hindsight, the defendant believed the better decision would have been to punch out on his time card and quit over the incident. However, all the witnesses related that the defendant was in no way attacked, as he perceived it, but that Mr. Farley was playing around. The defendant could not bring himself to tell the other workers to leave him alone or inform them about his panic attacks. ...

The principal question before us ... is whether our instructions on murder [are] wrong and confusing. ... [T]he defendant argues [that] the instructions were ... improper because the terms wilful, deliberate, and premeditated were equated with a mere intent to kill. ...

State's Instruction No. 8, ... stated:

> The Court instructs the jury that to constitute a willful, deliberate and premeditated killing, it is not necessary that the intention to kill should exist for

any particular length of time prior to the actual killing; it is only necessary that such intention should have come into existence for the first time at the time of such killing, or at any time previously.

State's Instruction No. 10 stated: ". . . in order to constitute a 'premeditated' murder an intent to kill need exist only for an instant." State's Instruction No. 12 stated: . . . "[W]hat is meant by the language willful, deliberate and premeditated is that the killing be intentional." State's Instruction Nos. 10 and 12 are commonly referred to as *Schrader* instructions.

The linchpin of the problems that flow from these instructions is the failure adequately to inform the jury of the difference between first- and second-degree murder. Of particular concern is the lack of guidance to the jury as to what constitutes premeditation and the manner in which the instructions confuse premeditation with the intent to kill. . . .

[W]ithin the parameters of our current homicide statutes [we believe that] the *Schrader* definition of premeditation and deliberation is confusing, if not meaningless. To allow the State to prove premeditation and deliberation by only showing that the intention came "into existence for the first time at the time of such killing" completely eliminates the distinction between the two degrees of murder. Hence, we feel compelled in this case to attempt to make the dichotomy meaningful by making some modifications to our homicide common law.

Premeditation and deliberation should be defined in a . . . way to give juries both guidance and reasonable discretion. Although premeditation and deliberation are not measured by any particular period of time, there must be some period between the formation of the intent to kill and the actual killing, which indicates. . . . an opportunity for some reflection on the intention to kill after it is formed. The accused must kill purposely after contemplating the intent to kill. Although an elaborate plan or scheme to take life is not required, our *Schrader* instruction's notion of instantaneous premeditation and momentary deliberation is not satisfactory for proof of first-degree murder. In Bullock v. United States, 122 F.2d 213, 214 (1941), the court discussed the need to have some appreciable time elapse between the intent to kill and the killing:

> To speak of premeditation and deliberation which are instantaneous or which take no appreciable time, is a contradiction in terms. . . . Statutes like ours, which distinguish deliberate and premeditated murder from other murder, reflect a belief that one who meditates an intent to kill and then deliberately executes it is more dangerous, more culpable or less capable of reformation than one who kills on sudden impulse; or that the prospect of the death penalty is more likely to deter men from deliberate than from impulsive murder. The deliberate killer is guilty of first degree murder; the impulsive killer is not.

Thus, there must be some evidence that the defendant considered and weighed his decision to kill in order for the State to establish premeditation and deliberation under our first-degree murder statute. . . . Any other intentional killing, by its spontaneous and nonreflective nature, is second-degree murder. . . .

[Reversed and remanded for a new trial.]

NOTES ON PREMEDITATION

The *Carroll* and *Guthrie* approaches exemplify the split in American jurisdictions on the meaning of premeditation. See Matthew A. Pauley, Murder by Premeditation, 36 Am. Crim. L. Rev. 145 (1999). The *Carroll* approach in effect equates "premediation" with any intent to kill. Thus, in the case of intentional killings, the *Carroll* approach eliminates any distinction between first- and second-degree murder.

But is the *Guthrie* court correct in concluding that this approach "*completely eliminates* the distinction between the two degrees of murder"? Is there any kind of *unintentional* killing that could demonstrate "malice" and thus qualify for a second-degree but not a first-degree conviction? Note that common-law courts traditionally have considered a wide range of circumstances sufficient to establish "malice aforethought." (See the summary of the Royal Commission on Capital Punishment, pages 420-421 supra.) In Pennsylvania, are all of these murder situations eligible for designation as *first-degree*? If not—that is, if the *Carroll* approach does preserve some distinction between first- and second-degree murder—is there any other reason to reject its interpretation of "premeditation"?

While the *Guthrie* approach distinguishes between mere intent to kill and intent *plus* premeditation, it raises two troublesome issues: What kind of evidence is sufficient to establish this more substantial sort of premeditation? And how useful is this sort of premeditation as a basis for distinguishing the worst forms of murder?

1. Proof of premeditation. Jurisdictions that interpret "premeditation" to require actual reflection have to consider what kind of evidence is sufficient to support this finding, particularly when the accused has made no statements indicating that the killing was the result of a preconceived plan. In a leading decision relied on in many jurisdictions, the California Supreme Court (People v. Anderson, 447 P.2d 942 (Cal. 1968)) explained that evidence sufficient to sustain a finding of premeditation generally falls into three basic categories: (1) facts regarding the defendant's behavior prior to the killing which might indicate a design to take life ("planning" activity); (2) facts about the defendant's prior relationship with the victim which might indicate a reason to kill ("motive"); and (3) evidence that "the *manner* of killing was so particular and exacting that the defendant must have intentionally killed according to a 'preconceived design.'" The court added that "this court sustains verdicts of first degree murder typically when there is evidence of all three types and otherwise requires at least extremely strong evidence of (1) or evidence of (2) in conjunction with either (1) or 3)."

Although the *Guthrie* court reversed the defendant's conviction because of the erroneous instruction, it found the evidence adequate to permit a properly instructed jury to find premeditation under the *Anderson* standard. Do you agree? Are the *Anderson* tests met on the facts of *Guthrie*? Could they be met in the *Carroll* case?

In subsequent decisions, the California Supreme Court has backed away from its view that a finding of premeditation requires particular types of evidence. Instead, the California court now maintains that no specific combination of these classes of evidence is essential and that other types of evidence may also suffice. People v. Solomon, 234 P.3d 501, 517 (Cal. 2010).[1] Other jurisdictions continue to approve *Anderson*'s suggestion that premeditation requires evidence falling in all three categories or in the specified combinations of (1), (2), and (3). See, e.g., Mattern v. State, 151 P.3d 1116, 1129-30 (Wyo. 2007).

2. *Identifying the worst murders.*

(a) The *Anderson* case referred to in the previous note involved the brutal murder of a ten-year-old girl. The victim's brother and mother had returned home one afternoon to find blood on the living room couch. The defendant (who was also living in the house) claimed first that he had cut himself and later that the victim had cut herself. Both claims proved false when the child's nude body was discovered in another room. Police later found the defendant's blood-spotted clothing and a knife. The victim's blood-stained clothes were scattered throughout the house, and there was blood in almost every room except the kitchen, which appeared to have been mopped. Over 60 wounds, extending over the victim's entire body, were found. Several of the wounds were post-mortem. The California Supreme Court reversed the first-degree murder conviction, finding this evidence insufficient to show premeditation: There was no evidence that defendant planned the killing; nothing in his prior relationship with the victim revealed a motive; and the court said that the manner of killing (by multiple random knife wounds) suggested an explosion of violence rather than a preconceived design to kill.

Questions: How do you explain the court's conclusion? If the result seems unacceptable, is that because the evidence did prove actual premeditation, or because actual premeditation is not an appropriate requirement for identifying the most serious homicides?

(b) Consider State v. Forrest, 321 N.C. 186, 362 S.E.2d 252 (N.C. 1987). The defendant took a pistol with him on a visit to his hospitalized, terminally ill father and, sobbing with emotion, killed his father with a single shot to the head. He was convicted of first-degree murder and sentenced to life imprisonment. The North Carolina Supreme Court upheld the conviction.

Questions: Is Forrest more deserving of severe punishment than Guthrie or Anderson? If not, does the court's decision to uphold his conviction indicate a flaw in its assessment of the evidence of premeditation or a flaw in the concept of premeditation itself?

Consider Samuel H. Pillsbury, Judging Evil: Rethinking the Law of Murder and Manslaughter 104-105 (1998). Commenting on the California court's

---

1. See Suzanne Mounts, Premeditation and Deliberation in California: Returning to a Distinction Without a Difference, 36 U.S.F. L. Rev. 261 (2002).

decision to reverse Anderson's first-degree murder conviction, Professor Pillsbuty observes:

> As a matter of statutory interpretation, the *Anderson* decision is defensible. Premeditation does seem to involve coolness and calculation, and proof of those was weak at trial. [But] even if we assume the killing was unplanned and impassioned, there were significant aggravating circumstances. . . . The butchering of a child for reasons of sexual frustration and rage . . . ranks high on any intuitive scale of wrongdoing, and may explain why many appellate courts have been so reluctant to take premeditation seriously—it leads to decisions like *Anderson.* In particular, the case leads us to doubt whether an impassioned decision to kill is necessarily less culpable than a dispassionate one. [D]epending on motivation, an unplanned killing may present a more culpable offense than a reflective killing by a brooding, self-doubting, self-reflective offender. *Anderson* suggests that what premeditation misses is the moral importance of the motive for the homicide.

(c) Following the lead of the Model Penal Code, some states have rejected premeditation as the basis for identifying murders that deserve the greatest punishment. See, e.g., the New York provisions, page 424 supra. The rationale of this approach is set out in Model Penal Code and Commentaries, Comment to §210.6, at 127-128 (1980):

> [T]he case for a mitigated sentence on conviction of murder does not depend on a distinction between impulse and deliberation. Prior reflection may reveal the uncertainties of a tortured conscience rather than exceptional depravity. The very fact of a long internal struggle may be evidence that the homicidal impulse was deeply aberrational and far more the product of extraordinary circumstances than a true reflection of the actor's normal character. [M]ost mercy killings are the consequence of long and careful deliberation, but they are not especially appropriate cases for imposition of capital punishment. . . . It also seems clear, moreover, that some purely impulsive murders will present no extenuating circumstances. The suddenness of the killing may simply reveal callousness so complete and depravity so extreme that no hesitation is required.

2. Mitigation to Manslaughter

a. The Concept of Provocation

GIROUARD v. STATE

Court of Appeals of Maryland
321 Md. 532, 583 A.2d 718 (1991)

COLE, J. In this case we are asked to reconsider whether the types of provocation sufficient to mitigate the crime of murder to manslaughter should be limited to the categories we have heretofore recognized, or whether the sufficiency of the provocation should be decided by the factfinder on a case-by-case basis. Specifically, we must determine whether words alone are provocation adequate to justify a conviction of manslaughter rather than one of second-degree murder.

The Petitioner, Steven S. Girouard, and the deceased, Joyce M. Girouard, had been married for about two months on October 28, 1987, the night of Joyce's death. Both parties . . . were in the army. The . . . marriage was often tense and strained, and there was some evidence that after marrying Steven, Joyce had resumed a relationship with her old boyfriend, Wayne.

On the night of Joyce's death [an angry argument developed, and Joyce taunted Steven] by saying, "I never did want to marry you and you are a lousy fuck and you remind me of my dad" [who had apparently abused her as a child]. The barrage of insults continued with her telling Steven that she wanted a divorce. . . . She also told him she had seen his commanding officer and filed charges against him for abuse. She then asked Steven, "What are you going to do?" Receiving no response, she continued her verbal attack. She added that she had filed charges against him in the Judge Advocate General's Office (JAG) and that he would probably be court martialed. . . .

After pausing for a moment, Joyce [again] asked what Steven was going to do. What he did was lunge at her with the kitchen knife he had hidden behind the pillow and stab her 19 times. Realizing what he had done, he dropped the knife and went to the bathroom to shower off Joyce's blood. Feeling like he wanted to die, Steven . . . slit his own wrists, . . . but when he realized that he would not die from his self-inflicted wounds, he . . . called the police, telling the dispatcher that he had just murdered his wife.

When the police arrived they found Steven wandering around outside his apartment building. Steven was despondent and tearful and seemed detached, according to police officers who had been at the scene. He was unconcerned about his own wounds, talking only about how much he loved his wife and how he could not believe what he had done. Joyce Girouard was pronounced dead at the scene.

[In a bench trial without a jury,] Steven Girouard was convicted . . . of second-degree murder and was sentenced to 22 years of incarceration, 10 of which were suspended. . . .

Petitioner relies primarily on out of state cases to provide support for his argument that the provocation to mitigate murder to manslaughter should not be limited only to the traditional circumstances of: extreme assault or battery upon the defendant; mutual combat; defendant's illegal arrest; injury or serious abuse of a close relative of the defendant's; or the sudden discovery of a spouse's adultery. Petitioner argues that manslaughter is a catchall for homicides which are criminal but that lack the malice essential for a conviction of murder. [He] argues . . . that the categories of provocation adequate to mitigate should be broadened to include factual situations such as this one. The State counters by stating that [w]ords spoken by the victim, no matter how abusive or taunting, fall into a category society should not accept as adequate provocation. . . .

For provocation to be "adequate," it must be "calculated to inflame the passion of a reasonable man and tend to cause him to act for the moment from passion rather than reason." The issue we must resolve, then, is whether the taunting words uttered by Joyce were enough to inflame the passion of a *reasonable* man so that that man would be sufficiently infuriated so as to strike out in hot-blooded blind passion to kill her. Although we agree with the trial judge that there was needless provocation by Joyce, we also agree with him that the provocation was not adequate to mitigate second-degree murder to voluntary manslaughter.

[W]ords can constitute adequate provocation if they are accompanied by conduct indicating a present intention and ability to cause the defendant bodily harm. Clearly, no such conduct was exhibited by Joyce in this case. While Joyce did step on Steven's back and pull his hair, he could not reasonably have feared bodily harm at her hands. . . . Joyce was about 5'1" tall and weighed 115 pounds, while he was 6'2" tall, weighing over 200 pounds. Joyce simply did not have the size or strength to cause Steven to fear for his bodily safety. . . .

Other jurisdictions overwhelmingly agree with our cases and hold that words alone are not adequate provocation. Thus, . . . the provocation in this case was not enough to cause a reasonable man to stab his provoker 19 times. Although a psychologist testified to Steven's mental problems and his need for acceptance and love, . . . "there must be not simply provocation in psychological fact, but one of certain fairly well-defined classes of provocation recognized as being adequate as a matter of law." The standard is one of reasonableness; it does not and should not focus on the peculiar frailties of mind of the Petitioner. That standard of reasonableness has not been met here. We cannot in good conscience countenance holding that a verbal domestic argument ending in the death of one spouse can result in a conviction of manslaughter. [S]ocial necessity dictates our holding. Domestic arguments easily escalate into furious fights. We perceive no reason for a holding in favor of those who find the easiest way to end a domestic dispute is by killing the offending spouse.

We will leave to another day the possibility of expansion of the categories of adequate provocation to mitigate murder to manslaughter. The facts of this case do not warrant the broadening of the categories recognized thus far.

[Affirmed.]

MAHER v. PEOPLE

Supreme Court of Michigan
10 Mich. 212, 81 Am. Dec. 781 (1862)

CHRISTIANCY, J. The prisoner was charged with an assault with intent to kill and murder one Patrick Hunt. [The prosecution's evidence was that defendant entered a saloon in an agitated manner, approached Hunt, said something unintelligible to him, and shot him, inflicting a non-fatal wound "in and through the left ear." Maher offered evidence to show an adulterous intercourse between his wife and Hunt less than an hour before the assault. He had followed his wife and Hunt as they entered the woods together, and when they left a half hour later, he followed Hunt to the saloon; just before he entered the saloon a friend told him that Hunt and his wife had had intercourse in the woods the day before. The trial court ruled this evidence inadmissible and convicted Maher of assault with intent to murder.]

Was the evidence properly rejected? This is the main question in the case, and its decision must depend upon the question whether the proposed evidence would have tended to reduce the killing—had death ensued—from murder to manslaughter. . . . If the homicide—in case death had ensued—would have been but manslaughter, then defendant could not be guilty of the assault with intent to murder, but only of a simple assault and battery. The question therefore involves essentially the same principles as where evidence is offered for a similar purpose in a prosecution for murder. . . .

[W]ithin the principle of all the recognized definitions [of malice aforethought], the homicide must, in all ordinary cases, have been committed with some degree of coolness and deliberation or, at least, under circumstances in which ordinary men . . . would not be liable to have their reason clouded or obscured by passion; and the act must be prompted by, or the circumstances indicate that it sprung from, a wicked, depraved or malignant mind. . . .

But if the act of killing, though intentional, be committed under the influence of passion or in heat of blood, produced by an adequate or reasonable provocation, and before a reasonable time has elapsed for the blood to cool and reason to resume its habitual control, and is the result of the temporary excitement, by which the control of reason was disturbed, rather than of any wickedness of heart or cruelty or recklessness of disposition: then the law, out of indulgence to the frailty of human nature, or rather, in recognition of the laws upon which human nature is constituted, very properly regards the offense as of a less heinous character than murder, and gives it the designation of manslaughter.

To what extent the passions must be aroused and the dominion of reason disturbed to reduce the offense from murder to manslaughter, the cases are by no means agreed. . . .

The principle involved . . . would seem to suggest as the true general rule that reason should, at the time of the act, be disturbed or obscured by passion to an extent which might render ordinary men, of fair average disposition, liable to act rashly or without due deliberation or reflection, and from passion, rather than judgment.

To the question, what shall be considered in law a reasonable or adequate provocation for such state of mind, so as to give to a homicide, committed under its influence, the character of manslaughter? On principle, the answer, as a general rule, must be, anything the natural tendency of which would be to produce such a state of mind in ordinary men, and which the jury are satisfied did produce it in the case before them—not such a provocation as must, by the laws of the human mind, produce such an effect with the certainty that physical effects follow from physical causes; for then the individual could hardly be held morally accountable. Nor, on the other hand, must the provocation, in every case, be held sufficient or reasonable, because such a state of excitement has followed from it; for then, by habitual and long continued indulgence of evil passions, a bad man might acquire a claim to mitigation which would not be available to better men, and on account of that very wickedness of heart which, in itself, constitutes an aggravation both in morals and in law.

In determining whether the provocation is sufficient or reasonable, ordinary human nature, or the average of men recognized as men of fair average mind and disposition, should be taken as the standard. . . .

It is doubtless, in one sense, the province of the court to define what, in law, will constitute a reasonable or adequate provocation, but not, I think, in ordinary cases, to determine whether the provocation proved in the particular case is sufficient or reasonable. This is essentially a question of fact, and to be decided with reference to the peculiar facts of each particular case. . . . [J]urors from the mode of their selection, coming from the various classes and occupations of society, and conversant with the practical affairs of life, are, in my opinion, much better qualified to judge of the sufficiency and tendency of a given provocation and much more likely to fix, with some degree of accuracy, the standard of what constitutes the average of ordinary human nature, than the judge whose habits and course of life give him much less experience of the workings of passion in the actual conflicts of life.

The judge, it is true, must, to some extent, assume to decide upon the sufficiency of the alleged provocation, when the question arises upon the admission of testimony, and when it is so clear as to admit of no reasonable doubt upon any theory, that the alleged provocation could not have had any tendency to produce such state of mind, in ordinary men, he may properly exclude the evidence; but, if the alleged provocation be such as to admit of any reasonable doubt, whether it might not have had such tendency, it is much safer, I think, and more in accordance with principle, to let the evidence go to the jury under the proper instructions. . . . The law can not with justice assume by the light of past decision, to catalogue all the various facts and combinations of facts which shall be held to constitute reasonable or adequate provocation. Scarcely two past cases can be found which are identical in all their circumstances; and there is no reason to hope for greater uniformity in future. Provocations will be given without reference to any previous model, and the passions they excite will not consult the precedents.

The same principles which govern, as to the extent to which the passions must be excited and reason disturbed, apply with equal force . . . to the question of cooling time. This, like the provocation itself, must depend upon the nature of man and the laws of the human mind, as well as upon the nature and circumstances of the provocation. . . . I am aware there are many cases in which it has been held a question of law, but I can see no principle on which such a rule can rest. The court should, I think, define to the jury the principles upon which the question is to be decided, and leave them to determine whether the time was reasonable under all the circumstances of the particular case. . . .

△'s evidence of "provocation" (hot passion) should have been admitted to allow the jury to decide on a reasonable basis therefore manslaughter should be considered vs. assault w/ intent to kill Murder 1

Based on the Circumstances act was committed in hot passion to equating provocation = Manslaughter

It remains only to apply these principles to the present case. The proposed evidence, in connection with what had already been given, would have tended strongly to show the commission of adultery by Hunt with the prisoner's wife, within half an hour before the assault; that the prisoner saw them going to the woods together, under circumstances calculated strongly to impress upon his mind the belief of the adulterous purpose; that he followed after them to the woods; that Hunt and the prisoner's wife were, not long after, seen coming from the woods, and that the prisoner followed them, and went in hot pursuit after Hunt to the saloon, and was informed by a friend on the way that they had committed adultery the day before in the woods. I can not resist the conviction that this would have been sufficient evidence of provocation to go to the jury, and from which, when taken in connection with the excitement and "great perspiration" exhibited on entering the saloon, the hasty manner in which he approached and fired the pistol at Hunt, it would have been competent for the jury to find that the act was committed in consequence of the passion excited by the provocation, and in a state of mind which, within the principle already explained, would have given to the homicide had death ensued, the character of manslaughter only. . . .

The judgment should be reversed and a new trial granted.

MANNING, J. I differ from my brethren in this case. I think the evidence was properly excluded. To make that manslaughter which would otherwise be murder, the provocation—I am not speaking of its sufficiency, but of the provocation itself—must be given in the presence of the person committing the homicide. . . . Any other rule in an offense so grave as taking the life of a fellow-being, in the heat of passion, I fear would be more humane to the perpetrator than wise in its effects on society. More especially since the abolition of the death penalty for murder, and the division of the crime into murder in the first and second degree there is not now the same reason, namely, the severity of the punishment, for relaxing the rules of law in favor of a party committing homicide as before. It would, it seems to me, be extremely mischievous to let passion engendered by suspicion, or by something one has heard, enter into and determine the nature of a crime committed while under its influence. The innocent as well as the guilty, or those who had not as well as those who had given provocation, might be the sufferers. If it be said that in such cases the giving of the provocation must be proved or it would go for nothing; the answer is, that the law will not, and should not permit the lives of the innocent to be exposed with the guilty in this way, as it would do did it not require the cause of the provocation to occur in the presence of the person committing the homicide.

NOTES

the Girouard approach →

1. The *Girouard* and *Maher* cases present contrasting approaches to provocation. The former, reflecting the predominant common-law position, maintains that only a few specific circumstances (e.g., battery, sudden mutual

combat) can serve as legally adequate provocation. And jurisdictions that follow this categorical approach rarely consider insulting words to be sufficient. Annot., 2 A.L.R.3d 1292 (2005). But the prevailing view that words cannot suffice has been softened in many jurisdictions to allow an exception when the words provoke, not simply because they are insulting, but because they disclose facts that could be sufficient if the defendant had observed them directly. The *Maher* approach, in contrast, holds that provoking circumstances need not conform to any pre-established categories and that it is normally a question for the jury to decide whether the facts as a whole demonstrate sufficient provocation. Although this remains the minority view, several American jurisdictions follow this approach. See, e.g., People v. Le, 69 Cal. Rptr. 3d 831 (Ct. App. 2007). For a review and assessment of American law, see Victoria Nourse, Passion's Progress: Modern Law Reform and the Provocation Defense, 106 Yale L.J. 1331 (1999).

Maher approach of leaving "provocation" to the jury is the minority approach.

2. Rationale of the provocation defense. A variety of rationales for the mitigating effect of provocation have been offered. They are critically reviewed in Stephen P. Garvey, Passion's Puzzle, 90 Iowa L. Rev. 1677 (2005). The two most common rationales are grounded in the notion of either partial justification or partial excuse. Professor Vera Bergelson explains the distinction (Justification or Excuse? Exploring the Meaning of Provocation, 42 Tex. Tech L. Rev. 307, 307 (2009)):

> Justifications focus on the wrongfulness of an act; excuses focus on the culpability of the actor. [W]hen we say that a perpetrator is excused, we wholly condemn what he did and forgive him merely because of his reduced volitional or cognitive capacity. When we say that the perpetrator is justified, even in part, we treat him as a fully responsible agent and acknowledge that what he did was right or at least not entirely wrong. . . .

Which of these concepts best explains the law's willingness to mitigate punishment in the classic instances of provocation cited in *Girouard* ("serious abuse of a close relative . . . or the sudden discovery of a spouse's adultery")? Are defendants in those situations partially *justified* in responding with lethal force? Or are their actions entirely wrong but partially *excusable* because they lacked their usual ability to exercise self control? Consider these efforts to explain the basis of the provocation defense:

(a) Provocation as partial excuse. The *Maher* opinion states one classic argument for the provocation doctrine—a concession to the frailty of human nature. See also the observations of Judge Robert Boochever, concurring in United States v. Roston, 986 F.2d 1287, 1294 (9th Cir. 1993):

> [Some observers speak as if] the provocation must be such as would "arouse a reasonable and ordinary person to kill someone." I cannot envision such a provocation that would not constitute [a complete] justification for the crime. "[A] reasonable person does not kill even when provoked. . . ." Model Penal Code §210.3 cmt. 5(a), at 56 (1980). The Model Criminal Jury Instructions for the Ninth Circuit set forth what appears to me to be a more appropriate

standard: "Provocation, in order to be adequate, must be such as might naturally cause a reasonable person in the passion of the moment to lose self-control and act on impulse and without reflection." This standard does not imply that reasonable people kill, but rather focuses on the degree of passion sufficient to reduce the actor's ability to control his actions.

Professor Samuel H. Pillsbury clarifies this crucial point (Misunderstanding Provocation, 43 U. Mich. J.L. Reform 143, 145-146 (2009)):

> Law students often, and courts on occasion, speak about provocation as requiring a judgment that the defendant did as the reasonable person would do in the situation. [H]owever, this is clearly incorrect. [The adequately provoked defendant] has committed a serious crime. No matter how we define the reasonable person, the adjective describes a law-abiding individual. We do not expect a law-abiding person to commit a felony, let alone a serious crime of homicidal violence. [A] finding of provocation does not represent a judgment that the defendant's conduct was in any sense morally acceptable.

See also Jerome Michael & Herbert Wechsler, A Rationale of the Law of Homicide, 37 Colum. L. Rev. 1261, 1281-1282 (1937):

> Provocation . . . must be estimated by the probability that [the provocative] circumstances would affect most men in like fashion. . . . Other things being equal, the greater the provocation, measured in that way, the more ground there is for attributing the intensity of the actor's passions and his lack of self-control on the homicidal occasion to the extraordinary character of the situation in which he was placed rather than to any extraordinary deficiency in his own character. While it is true, it is also beside the point, that most men do not kill on even the gravest provocation; the point is that the more strongly they would be moved to kill by circumstances of the sort which provoked the actor to the homicidal act, and the more difficulty they would experience in resisting the impulse to which he yielded, the less does his succumbing serve to differentiate his character from theirs. But the slighter the provocation, the more basis there is for ascribing the actor's act to an extraordinary susceptibility to intense passion, to an unusual deficiency in those other desires which counteract in most men the desires which impel them to homicidal acts, or to an extraordinary weakness of reason, and consequent inability to bring such desires into play.

(b) Provocation as partial justification. Others argue that the provocation defense rests in part on notions of justification. Consider A.J. Ashworth, The Doctrine of Provocation, 35 Cambridge L.J. 292, 307-308 (1976):

> The term partial justification [is closely related to] the moral notion that the punishment of wrongdoers is justifiable. This is not to argue that it is ever morally right to kill a person who does wrong. Rather, the claim implicit in partial justification is that an individual is to some extent morally justified in making a punitive return against someone who intentionally causes him serious offence, and that this serves to differentiate someone who is provoked to lose his self-control and kill from the unprovoked killer. Whereas the paradigmatic case of murder might be an attack on an innocent victim, the paradigm of

provocation generally involves moral wrongs by both parties. [T]he complicity of the victim cannot and should not be ignored, for the blameworthiness of his conduct has a strong bearing on the court's judgment of the seriousness of the provocation and the reasonableness of the accused's failure to control himself.

(c) Both or neither? Does it matter which explanation for the defense we choose? Some argue that the underlying rationale of the provocation defense does not have practical consequences. See, e.g., Gabriel J. Chin, Unjustified: The Practical Irrelevance of the Justification/Excuse Distinction, 43 U. Mich. J.L. Reform 79 (2009). Professor Bergelson notes (supra at 309) that "[a]s a product of historical tradition, political compromise, and changing cultural norms, the law often combines elements of more than one rationale." But she also cautions (id., at 308) that "[k]nowing whether . . . the defendant was right or wrong in what he did and whether society can fairly expect others in his situation to behave differently is essential for society's collective sense of justice and for people's ability to make personal decisions." If so, then should we treat the defendant who kills in response to serious abuse of a close relative as partially justified or partially excused? Test your answers by applying them to a few simple variations on this classic scenario:

(1) Suppose the defendant kills Paul two days after learning that Paul had seriously abused the defendant's child. Paul's wrong does not diminish with the passage of time; yet the traditional common-law approach always denies a provocation defense in this situation.[2] If provocation is a partial justification, why should it become unavailable after "cooling time" has elapsed?

(2) Conversely, suppose that immediately after learning of Paul's serious abuse, the defendant shoots at him but misses; the bullets ricochet and kill an innocent bystander. The defendant's loss of self control and the reasons for it are the same regardless of the identity of the person hit by his shots; yet common-law courts often deny a provocation defense in this situation.[3] If the defense is based on an excusable loss of self-control, shouldn't it remain available regardless of whether the person killed was the actual provoker or someone innocent of wrongdoing?

(3) In State v. Pittman, 647 S.E.2d 144 (S.C. 2007), a 12-year old boy was living with his grandfather Joe Frank, when Frank, as a punishment, hit him across the back and buttocks five or six times with a paddle. Sent to his room, the boy grabbed a shotgun, waited ten minutes in his room, and then shot and killed his grandfather. Tried as an adult, the boy was convicted of murder, after the trial judge refused to instruct the jury on the provocation defense. The state supreme court affirmed. Although noting that "an overt threatening act or a physical encounter may constitute sufficient legal provocation," the court held that rule

---

2. See page 450, Note 6, infra.
3. See page 451, Note 1, infra.

inapplicable because "Appellant's guardian . . . was legally entitled to paddle him," and therefore "we decline to hold that a child has sufficient legal provocation to use deadly force against a guardian who disciplines through corporal punishment." Id. at 168. Is the decision sound? On what principle?

3. Should the provocation defense be abolished? *(a) The policy arguments.* Consider:

Stephen J. Morse, Undiminished Confusion in Diminished Capacity, 75 J. Crim. L. & Criminology 1, 33-343 (1984): I would abolish [the provocation defense] and convict all intentional killers of murder. Reasonable people do not kill no matter how much they are provoked, and even enraged people generally retain the capacity to control homicidal or any other kind of aggressive or antisocial desires. We cheapen both life and our conception of responsibility by maintaining the provocation/passion mitigation. This may seem harsh and contrary to the supposedly humanitarian reforms of the evolving criminal law. But this . . . interpretation of criminal law history is morally mistaken. It is humanitarian only if one focuses sympathetically on perpetrators and not on their victims, and views the former as mostly helpless objects of their overwhelming emotions and irrationality. This sympathy is misplaced, however, and is disrespectful to the perpetrator. As virtually every human being knows because we all have been enraged, it is easy not to kill, even when one is enraged.

Emily L. Miller (Comment), (Wo)manslaughter: Voluntary Manslaughter, Gender, and the Model Penal Code, 50 Emory L.J. 665, 692 (2000): [J]uries cannot be expected to enforce a standard of reasonableness which adequately protects a woman's life. Social science indicates that both aggressors and juries view the world through lenses of cultural construction: masculine violence is simply an inevitable fact of life. . . . Instead of reinforcing cultural values that condone masculine violence, the law must take a normative stand.

[S]uch a normative stand may come with costs. In the absence of the doctrine of voluntary manslaughter, killers would be tried for murder. Juries may be reluctant to reach the conclusion of murder where the aggressor was angry and upset; more acquittals may result. This possible consequence of abolition should not be ignored and has led some advocates of women's rights to support retention of the doctrine.

[B]ecause what is reasonable cannot be determined without reference to value systems biased in favor of men, the only truly egalitarian approach is abolition. The value of human life must trump the law's sympathy for the defendant's response. By virtue of its brutal discrimination against women under both common law and MPC, the defense of voluntary manslaughter no longer has a place in American penal law.

Law Commission (U.K.), Report No. 290, Partial Defences to Murder 38-39 (2004): Powerful arguments can be advanced for and against the abolition of provocation as a defense. . . . The debate has generated interesting discussion about the moral qualities of the emotions of anger and fear. One school of thought holds that anger cannot ethically afford any ground for mitigating the gravity of deliberately violent action, or at any rate violent action which threatens life. . . . Nevertheless, a killing in anger produced by serious wrong-doing is ethically less wicked, and therefore deserving of a lesser punishment, than say, a killing out of greed, lust, jealousy or for political reasons. . . . There is a distinction in moral blameworthiness between overreaction to grave provocation and unprovoked use of violence. . . .

We favour as the moral basis for retaining a defense of provocation that the defendant had legitimate ground to feel seriously wronged by the person at whom his or her conduct was aimed, and this lessens the moral culpability of the defendant reacting to that outrage in the way that he or she did. It is the justification of the sense of outrage which provides a partial excuse for their responsible conduct.[a]

(b) Recent reforms. In a move that is rare among common-law jurisdictions, three Australian states recently abolished the provocation defense; defendants who kill in response to reasonable provocation are therefore subject to conviction for murder. For a careful description and assessment of these reforms, see Carolyn B. Ramsey, Provoking Change: Comparative Insights on Feminist Homicide Law Reform, 100 J. Crim. L. & Criminology 33 (2010).

Questions: If a jurisdiction abolishes the provocation defense, what punishment should be imposed on defendants convicted of murder? Should provoked defendants face the same punishment as defendants who kill in cold blood, or should judges be authorized to extend some form of leniency when the killing is the result of "reasonable" provocation? If the latter, has the provocation defense been *abolished* or merely *moved* to a different place in the criminal process? If provocation should he taken into account in some fashion, where and how is this best accomplished?

Consider People v. Nesler, 941 P.2d 87 (Cal. 1997). The defendant confronted a man who had sexually abused her son, and in a burst of anger, she shot and killed him. She was convicted of manslaughter. Should murder be the only appropriate charge for a defendant like Nesler? How should her sentence be determined and by whom?

4. Sexual infidelity as provocation. (a) Why has the law traditionally regarded sexual infidelity as adequate provocation? What does it share with the other categories that the common law allowed—for example, serious

---

a. Endorsing this approach, Parliament in 2009 modified the standard for mitigation to require that a defendant show that his loss of control was the result of "a justifiable sense of being seriously wronged." Coroners and Justice Act 2009, c. 25, Part 2, ch. 1 §55(4)(b).—EDS.

physical assault, mutual combat, and illegal arrest? For discussion of the cultural presuppositions of voluntary manslaughter doctrine, see Donna K. Coker, Heat of Passion and Wife Killing: Men Who Batter/Men Who Kill, 2 S. Cal. Rev. L. & Women's Stud. 71 (1992). Note that women seldom kill their unfaithful male partners. Does this fact have a bearing on the reasonableness of a husband's loss of self-control in response to unfaithfulness by his wife?

Although the *Girouard* court mentions "sudden discovery of a spouse's adultery" as an allowable form of provocation in Maryland, this rule prompted a public outcry in 1994 when Keith Peacock killed his unfaithful wife, was convicted of manslaughter, and was sentenced only to an 18-month term in a work-release program. In response, Maryland amended its law to provide that "discovery of one's spouse engaged in sexual intercourse with another person does not constitute legally adequate provocation for the purpose of mitigating a killing from the crime of murder to voluntary manslaughter."[4] The British Parliament enacted a similar provision in 2009.[5] But few other common-law jurisdictions have taken this step.

Questions: Should the sudden, unexpected discovery of a spouse's adultery provide the basis for a provocation defense? If not, is that because adultery is (usually) not illegal? Is it because sexual infidelity does not constitute a significant wrong or a significant harm to the deceived spouse? Professor Susan D. Rozelle argues that the provocation defense should be restricted to "defendants who were legally entitled to use some amount of force when they killed," and accordingly that sudden discovery of a spouse's adultery should never suffice. Controlling Passion: Adultery and the Provocation Defense, 37 Rutgers L.J. 197, 200 (2005). But Professor Rozelle acknowledges that under this approach, an enraged husband who kills his wife's rapist (in circumstances not sufficient to establish a privilege to use defensive force) would be guilty of murder. Is that an acceptable result?

How should the issue be analyzed if provocation is viewed not as a partial justification but rather as a partial excuse? Is a provocation defense inappropriate because an emotionally healthy individual would not become exceptionally upset, would not lose their normal capacity for self-control, upon unexpectedly discovering a spouse's infidelity? Or is a provocation defense inappropriate because society must condemn and forcefully deter the response of the deceived spouse, *even if* his (or her) loss of self-control is understandable? To what extent should the policy decision be shaped by the fact that defendants who invoke this defense are overwhelmingly male, and that the victims of such killings are overwhelmingly female? For probing discussion of the issues, see Samuel H. Pillsbury, Judging Evil: Rethinking the Law of Murder and Manslaughter (1998); Carolyn B. Ramsey, Provoking Change:

---

4. Md. Code, art. 27, §387A (1997), currently codified at Md. Code §2-207(b) (2010).
5. Coroners and Justice Act 2009, supra, §55(6)(c).

Comparative Insights on Feminist Homicide Law Reform, 100 J. Crim. L. & Criminology 33 (2010); Coker, supra.

(b) Courts that permit sexual infidelity to qualify for a heat-of-passion defense often interpret the boundaries of this category narrowly. In State v. Simonovich, 688 S.E.2d 67, 72 (N.C. App. 2010), the defendant killed his wife in a rage after she admitted to past acts of adultery and taunted him, stating that she intended to continue having sex with other men. The court held that the defendant was not entitled to voluntary manslaughter instructions, because he had not discovered his wife "in the very act of intercourse." In Dennis v. State, 661 A.2d 175 (Md. Ct. Spec. App. 1995), the defendant, after observing his wife, her dress raised, in a sexual embrace with another man, burst into the room and fatally shot the other man. The court held it proper to instruct the jury that the circumstances could qualify as legally adequate provocation only if the defendant had seen sexual intercourse, not other sorts of sexual contact. State v. Turner, 708 So. 2d 232 (Ala. Crim. App. 1997), was an unusual case in which an enraged woman shot and killed a sexually unfaithful man. But the court held that voluntary manslaughter instructions were not required because the defendant and her victim, who had lived together for many years, were not legally married.

Questions: Does the absence of a formal marriage affect the emotional significance of sexual infidelity when the parties are living together in a long-standing relationship? Does the relevancy of a formal marriage depend on whether provocation is a partial justification or a partial excuse?

5. *Homosexual advances as provocative acts.* Trial judges sometimes allow defendants to raise a provocation defense when they have killed in response to an unwelcome, though nonviolent, homosexual advance. Several appellate courts, however, have ruled provocation claims of this sort to be insufficient as a matter of law, e.g., People v. Garcia, 651 N.E.2d 100 (Ill. 1995); Commonwealth v. Pierce, 642 N.E.2d 579 (Mass. 1994).

Questions: Why should a proposal to engage in *consensual* sexual activity, whether from a member of the same or the opposite sex, ever be sufficient provocation to reduce an intentional killing from murder to manslaughter? Joshua Dressler argues that there can sometimes be valid, nonhomophobic reasons to permit a provocation defense in such cases because "ordinary, fallible human beings might become so upset that their out of control reaction deserves mitigated punishment." Dressler, When "Heterosexual" Men Kill "Homosexual" Men: Reflections on Provocation Law, Sexual Advances, and the "Reasonable Man" Standard, 85 J. Crim. Law & Criminology 726 (1995). To what extent can the defendant's anger or indignation in such cases be disentangled from feelings of homophobia? Compare Robert B. Mison, Comment, Homophobia in Manslaughter: The Homosexual Advance as Insufficient Provocation, 80 Calif. L. Rev. 133 (1992) (opposing this view and emphasizing that such a defense is likely to exploit bias against gays and to imply that their lives are less worthy of protection).

Professor Cynthia Lee takes a third position. In The Gay Panic Defense, 42 U.C. Davis L. Rev. 471, 471 (2008), Professor Lee recognizes that such a defense "promote[s] negative stereotypes about gay men" and "seek[s] to capitalize on unconscious bias in favor of heterosexuality." Nonetheless, Professor Lee argues, "gay panic" arguments should not be banned in homicide cases; instead, she suggests, the best way for a prosecutor to undermine explicit or implicit arguments of this sort is to permit them to be aired and then to counter them directly. Do you agree? What are the likely advantages and obstacles to implementing her suggestion in the courtroom?

6. *Cooling time.* The common-law view is that a significant lapse of time between the provocation and the act of killing renders the provocation inadequate "as a matter of law" and therefore deprives the defendant of the right to an instruction on voluntary manslaughter. In United States v. Bordeaux, 980 F.2d 534 (8th Cir. 1992), defendant was told, during the course of an all-day drinking party, that Shelby White Bear, also at the party, had raped defendant's mother 20 years earlier. Later, about midday, defendant's mother confirmed the report. Sometime during the early evening, defendant and some friends severely beat White Bear and left him lying in a bedroom. Defendant returned to the bedroom shortly afterward, saw White Bear lying on the floor bleeding, and slashed his throat. He then told a friend that he had killed White Bear because of the rape and said he would do it again because "[h]e deserved it." The court of appeals upheld the trial judge's refusal to instruct the jury on voluntary manslaughter and affirmed the conviction of murder. The court said that because the revelation of the rape had occurred much earlier in the day, and because the fatal act was committed "well after" the beating of White Bear had ended, there was "no rational basis for the jury to find that Bordeaux killed White Bear in the heat of passion. . . ."

The cooling-time limitation can sometimes be surmounted by arguing that an event immediately preceding the homicide rekindled an earlier provocation. But many courts refuse to take note of "rekindling." Consider State v. Gounagias, 88 Wash. 304, 153 P. 9 (1915). The deceased had committed an act of sodomy upon the defendant and then bragged to others about it. Those who heard of the episode repeatedly ridiculed the defendant, and after two weeks he finally lost control and killed the man who had assaulted him. The defendant argued that the cumulative effect of the taunts, reminding him of the previous provocation, led to a sudden heat of passion. But the court held that the legally sufficient provoking event had occurred two weeks before the killing and that the interval constituted adequate cooling time as a matter of law. Many modern courts are similarly unwilling to allow "rekindling" of prior provocation. In Commonwealth v. LeClair, 708 N.E.2d 107 (Mass. 1999), a man had for several weeks suspected his wife of infidelity and upon suddenly confirming his suspicions, he strangled her in a rage. The court held that his prior suspicions provided adequate cooling time, and therefore no manslaughter instructions were required. Some courts, however, permit the jury to make the judgment whether sufficient cooling time has elapsed. Thus, in People v. Berry, 556 P.2d 777 (Cal. 1976), the provoked defendant waited for his victim in her apartment for 20 hours before killing her. The court held that the defendant was nevertheless entitled to a manslaughter instruction, because the jury could find that the defendant's heat of passion resulted from a long-smoldering prior course of provocative conduct by the victim, the passage of time serving to aggravate rather than cool defendant's agitation.

NOTE ON NONPROVOKING VICTIMS AND PROVOKING DEFENDANTS

1. *Victims other than the provoker.* Sometimes the defendant kills someone other than her provoker. How should the following cases be handled?

(a) *Derivative provocation.* Three friends, Nathan, Matt, and Talia, are having a drink at the local bar when suddenly the conversation becomes acrimonious. Nathan sics his little dog, Osa, on Matt, and while Matt is struggling with the dog and screaming with fear and anger, Nathan cruelly tells Matt the lie that Osa has never had a rabies inoculation. Talia thinks it's all very funny and laughs uproariously. Matt becomes enraged and shoots both Nathan and Talia dead. Assuming Matt is entitled to a voluntary manslaughter instruction in a prosecution for the murder of Nathan (query: Would he be?), is he also entitled to such an instruction in a prosecution for the murder of Talia?

(b) *Misdirected reaction.* In State v. Mauricio, 117 N.J. 402, 568 A.2d 879 (1990), a bouncer forcefully ejected the defendant from a bar. He slammed defendant against a wall and then kicked and pushed him down the stairs, making him hit his head sharply on the floor. Expecting the bar to close shortly (it was 2:30 A.M.), defendant waited outside for the bouncer to emerge. About five minutes later, a patron who had not been involved in the fight left the bar. Defendant mistook the patron for the bouncer, followed him, and shot him dead. The New Jersey Supreme Court reversed a murder conviction, holding that the trial judge had erred in refusing to give voluntary manslaughter instructions. Several states would reach the same result by statute. See, e.g., Pa. Stat. §2503(a)(2), page 424 supra. Are these results sound if the provocation defense is designed to afford mitigation for partially justified killings? Or do these results suggest that provocation must be viewed as a partial excuse? Compare Tex. Pen. Code §19.04, requiring the provocation be given "by the individual killed or another acting with the person killed."

(c) *Violence aimed at non-provoking victims.* Suppose that the person killed is not associated with the provoker and is not the accidental victim of anger directed against the provoker. Should a justifiably enraged defendant be able to claim mitigation to manslaughter when the person he intends to kill is an innocent bystander? In Rex v. Scriva, [1951] Vict. L.R. 298, a father observed an automobile driver knock down and severely injure his daughter. When the father, brandishing a knife, went after the driver, a bystander attempted to restrain him, and the father then fatally stabbed the bystander. In People v. Spurlin, 156 Cal. App. 3d 119, 202 Cal. Rptr. 663 (1984), the defendant killed his wife after an intense argument over their respective sexual escapades, and still in a rage, killed his sleeping nine-year-old son.

In both *Scriva* and *Spurlin*, the courts held that a provocation defense was unavailable on the charges of murdering the non-provoking victims.[6] Are these holdings sound? If a defendant claiming provocation must show that the killing was partially *justified* by the victim's wrongful conduct, then *Scriva* and *Spurlin* are obviously correct. But courts often permit a provocation defense when the defendant's loss of control is merely *excusable*. Are the decisions in *Scriva* and *Spurlin* appropriate on the ground that a loss of self-control is understandable *only* when it prompts violence directed against the actual or perceived provoker? Compare R.S. O'Regan, Indirect Provocation and Misdirected Retaliation, [1968] Crim. L. Rev. 319, 323: "Once an accused loses his self-control it is unreal to insist that his retaliatory acts be directed only against his provoker. When his reason has been dethroned a man cannot be expected . . . 'to guide his anger with judgment.'" For a detailed analysis that probes the psychological dynamics of provocation and concurs in this view, see Reid Griffith Fontaine, Adequate (Non)Provocation and Heat of Passion as Excuse Not Justification, 43 U. Mich. J.L. Reform 27 (2009).

2. Defendants who elicit provocation. In Regina v. Johnson, [1989] 2 All E.R. 839, defendant had threatened and insulted Roberts; Roberts responded by pouring beer over the defendant's head, pinning him to a wall, and then punching him. Defendant drew a knife and fatally stabbed Roberts. The trial judge refused to instruct the jury on provocation, ruling that it was "difficult to see how a man who excites provocative conduct can in turn rely on it as provocation in the criminal law." The appellate court reversed, stating, "[W]e find it impossible to accept that the mere fact that a defendant caused a reaction in others, which in turn led him to lose his self-control, should result in the issue of provocation being kept outside a jury's consideration." Some American statutes preclude the defense in these circumstances. E.g., Or. Rev. Stat. §163.135(1) (1995). Which is the better response to this issue?

---

6. Compare State v. Stewart, 624 N.W.2d 585, 589-90 (Minn. 2001). On facts similar to those in *Spurlin*, the court stated that the defendant would have been entitled to a verdict of manslaughter in the killing of his infant son, if the jury had been persuaded that he had acted in an emotionally aroused state. But the *Stewart* court reached that conclusion under a statute that, like the Model Penal Code (see pages 453-458 infra), permits mitigation on broader grounds than those accepted under traditional common-law tests.

b. The Model Penal Code Approach

PEOPLE v. CASASSA

New York Court of Appeals
49 N.Y.2d 668, 404 N.E.2d 1310 (1980)

JASEN, J. . . . On February 28, 1977, Victoria Lo Consolo was brutally murdered. Defendant Victor Casassa and Miss Lo Consolo . . . met in August, 1976, as a result of their residence in the same apartment complex. . . . The two apparently dated casually . . . until November, 1976, when Miss Lo Consolo informed defendant that she was not "falling in love" with him. Defendant claims that Miss Lo Consolo's candid statement of her feelings "devastated him."

Miss Lo Consolo's rejection of defendant's advances also precipitated a bizarre series of actions on the part of defendant which, he asserts, demonstrate the existence of extreme emotional disturbance upon which he predicates his affirmative defense. Defendant, aware that Miss Lo Consolo maintained social relationships with others, broke into the apartment below Miss Lo Consolo's on several occasions to eavesdrop. These eavesdropping sessions allegedly caused him to be under great emotional stress. Thereafter, on one occasion, he broke into Miss Lo Consolo's apartment while she was out . . . , disrobed and lay for a time in Miss Lo Consolo's bed. During this break-in, defendant was armed with a knife which, he later told police, he carried "because he knew that he was either going to hurt Victoria or Victoria was going to cause him to commit suicide."

Defendant's final visit to his victim's apartment occurred on February 28, 1977. Defendant brought several bottles of wine and liquor with him to offer as a gift. Upon Miss Lo Consolo's rejection of this offering, defendant produced a steak knife which he had brought with him, stabbed Miss Lo Consolo several times in the throat, dragged her body to the bathroom and submerged it in a bathtub full of water to "make sure she was dead." . . .

Defendant [was charged with second-degree murder. He] waived a jury and proceeded to trial before the County Court. . . . The defendant did not contest the underlying facts of the crime. Instead, the sole issue presented to the trial court was whether the defendant, at the time of the killing, had acted under the influence of "extreme emotional disturbance." The defense presented only one witness, a psychiatrist, who testified, in essence, that the defendant had become obsessed with Miss Lo Consolo and that the course which their relationship had taken, combined with several personality attributes peculiar to defendant, caused him to be under the influence of extreme emotional disturbance at the time of the killing.

In rebuttal, the People produced . . . a psychiatrist who testified that although the defendant was emotionally disturbed, he was not under the influence of "extreme emotional disturbance" within the meaning . . . of the Penal Law, because his disturbed state was not the product of external factors but rather was "a stress he created from within himself, dealing mostly with a fantasy, a refusal to accept the reality of the situation."

The trial court . . . considered the appropriate test to be whether in the totality of the circumstances the finder of fact could understand how a person might have his reason overcome. Concluding that the test was not to be applied solely from the viewpoint of defendant, the court found that defendant's emotional reaction at the time of the commission of the crime was so peculiar to him that it could not be considered reasonable so as to reduce the conviction to manslaughter in the first degree. Accordingly, the trial court found defendant guilty of the crime of murder in the second degree. . . . On this appeal defendant contends that the trial court erred in failing to afford him the benefit of the affirmative defense of "extreme emotional disturbance." . . .

Section 125.25(1)(a) of the Penal Law provides that it is an affirmative defense to the crime of murder in the second degree where "[t]he defendant acted under the influence of extreme emotional disturbance for which there was a reasonable explanation or excuse." . . . In enacting [this provision], the Legislature adopted the language of the manslaughter provisions of the Model Penal Code. The only substantial distinction between the New York statute and the Model Penal Code is the designation by the Legislature of "extreme emotional disturbance" as an "affirmative defense," thus placing the burden of proof on this issue upon defendant. . . .

The "extreme emotional disturbance" defense is an outgrowth of the "heat of passion" doctrine [but] the new formulation is significantly broader in scope than the "heat of passion" doctrine which it replaced.

For example, the "heat of passion" doctrine required that a defendant's action be undertaken as a response to some provocation which prevented him from reflecting upon his actions. Moreover, such reaction had to be immediate. The existence of a "cooling off" period completely negated any mitigating effect which the provocation might otherwise have had. In *Patterson* [39 N.Y.2d 288], however, this court recognized that "[a]n action influenced by an extreme emotional disturbance is not one that is necessarily so spontaneously undertaken. Rather, it may be that a significant mental trauma has affected a defendant's mind for a substantial period of time, simmering in the unknowing subconscious and then inexplicably coming to the fore." This distinction between the past and present law of mitigation, enunciated in *Patterson*, was expressly adopted by the trial court and properly applied in this case.

The thrust of defendant's claim, however, concerns a question arising out of another perceived distinction between "heat of passion" and "extreme emotional disturbance" . . . , to wit: whether, assuming that the defense is applicable to a broader range of circumstances, the standard by which the reasonableness of defendant's emotional reaction is to be tested must be an entirely subjective one. Defendant [claims] that the reasonableness of his "explanation or excuse" should be determined solely with reference to his own subjective viewpoint. [This argument] is misplaced. . . .

Consideration of the Comments to the Model Penal Code, from which the New York statute was drawn, are instructive. The defense of "extreme emotional disturbance" has two principal components—(1) the particular defendant must have "acted under the influence of extreme emotional disturbance," and (2) there must have been "a reasonable explanation or excuse" for such extreme emotional disturbance, "the reasonableness of which is to be determined from the viewpoint of a person in the defendant's situation under the circumstances as the defendant believed them to be." The first requirement is wholly subjective—i.e., it involves a determination that the particular defendant did in fact act under extreme emotional disturbance, that the claimed explanation as to the cause of his action is not contrived or sham.

The second component is more difficult to describe—i.e., whether there was a reasonable explanation or excuse for the emotional disturbance. It was designed to sweep away "the rigid rules that have developed with respect to the sufficiency of particular types of provocation, such as the rule that words alone can never be enough. . . . The ultimate test, however, is objective; there must be 'reasonable' explanation or excuse for the actor's disturbance." In light of these comments and the necessity of articulating the defense in terms comprehensible to jurors, we conclude that the determination whether there was reasonable explanation or excuse for a particular emotional disturbance should be made by viewing the subjective, internal situation in which the defendant found himself and the external circumstances as he perceived them at the time, however inaccurate that perception may have been, and assessing from that standpoint whether the explanation or excuse for his emotional disturbance was reasonable, so as to entitle him to a reduction of the crime charged from murder in the second degree to manslaughter in the first degree.[2] We recognize that even such a description of the defense provides no precise guidelines and necessarily leaves room for the exercise of judgmental evaluation by the jury. This, however, appears to have been the intent of the draftsmen. "The purpose was explicitly to give full scope to what amounts to a plea in mitigation based upon a mental or emotional trauma of significant dimensions, with the jury asked to show whatever empathy it can." (Wechsler, Codification of Criminal Law in the United States: The Model Penal Code, 68 Col. L. Rev. 1425, 1446.)

By suggesting a standard of evaluation which contains both subjective and objective elements, we believe that the drafters of the code adequately achieved their dual goals of broadening the "heat of passion" doctrine to apply to a wider range of circumstances while retaining some element of objectivity in the process. The result of their draftsmanship is a statute which offers the defendant a fair opportunity to seek mitigation without requiring that the trier of fact find mitigation in each case where an emotional disturbance is shown—or as the drafters put it, to offer "room for argument as to the reasonableness of the explanations or excuses offered." . . .

---

2. We emphasize that this test is to be applied to determine whether defendant's emotional disturbance, and not the act of killing, was supported by a reasonable explanation or excuse.

We conclude that the trial court, in this case, properly applied the statute. The court apparently accepted, as a factual matter, that defendant killed Miss Lo Consolo while under the influence of "extreme emotional disturbance," a threshold question which must be answered in the affirmative before any test of reasonableness is required. The court, however, also recognized that in exercising its function as trier of fact, it must make a further inquiry into the reasonableness of that disturbance. In this regard, the court considered each of the mitigating factors put forward by defendant, including his claimed mental disability, but found that the excuse offered by defendant was so peculiar to him that it was unworthy of mitigation. The court obviously made a sincere effort to understand defendant's "situation" and "the circumstances as defendant believed them to be," but concluded that the murder in this case was the result of defendant's malevolence rather than an understandable human response deserving of mercy. We cannot say, as a matter of law, that the court erred in so concluding. . . .

In our opinion, this statute would not require that the jury or the court as trier of fact find mitigation on any particular set of facts, but, rather, allows the finder of fact the opportunity to do so, such opportunity being conditional only upon a finding of extreme emotional disturbance in the first instance. . . .

[Affirmed.]

NOTES ON THE MODEL PENAL CODE

1. Influence of the MPC. Of the 34 jurisdictions that revised their criminal codes in the post-MPC era, five adopted its provocation proposals almost whole (Arizona, Arkansas, Connecticut, Kentucky, and New York). At least a dozen other states adopted some of the Code's features, usually the "extreme emotional disturbance" (EED) formulation, but with significant alterations, for example, requiring a provocative act and rejecting the "actor's situation" language in favor of a more general "reasonableness" standard. See Law Commission Working Paper, Partial Defences to Murder, Appendix F: The Model Penal Code's Provocation Proposal and Its Reception in the State Legislatures (Law Comm. No. 290) (2010). Altogether, roughly 20 states now employ some version of the EED test. See Caroline Forell, Homicide and the Unreasonable Man, 72 Geo. Wash. L. Rev. 597, 603 (2004).

2. Distinctive features of the MPC formula. What was the "provocation" in the *Casassa* case? Under the MPC standard, does emotional disturbance require manslaughter instructions even when the disturbance is not attributable to any provocative behavior at all? Consider State v. White, 251 P.2d 820 (Utah 2011). After a troubled marriage, Brenda and Jon White divorced. Brenda won ownership of their house in the divorce settlement but had difficulty meeting the mortgage payments, in part because Jon allegedly failed to provide child support and other financial assistance. After mounting stress because of the financial difficulties and other problems, Brenda one day drove to Jon's place of work, and when he emerged into the parking lot, she drove toward him at high speed, striking him twice with her vehicle and nearly killing him. In a prosecution for attempted murder, she argued for an EED defense on the ground that mounting anger and grief had caused her to lose control of her emotions. An intermediate appellate court held that the defense was properly denied because "defendant's loss of control [must] be in reaction to a highly provocative triggering event . . . contemporaneous with the defendant's loss of self-control." The Utah Supreme Court reversed, holding that an EED defense may be based on "a significant mental trauma [that] has affected the defendant's mind for a substantial period of time, simmering in the unknowing subconscious and then inexplicably coming to the fore." Id. at 823, 827. Is this the correct interpretation of the MPC standard? If so, is the standard itself too broad?

In State v. Elliot, 177 Conn. 1, 411 A.2d 3 (1979), the defendant had for years suffered from an overwhelming fear of his brother. One day, for no apparent reason, he appeared at his brother's house and killed him. The defendant was convicted of murder, but the Connecticut Supreme Court reversed, holding that under Connecticut's statute (based on the MPC), instructions on extreme emotional disturbance were required. The Court said:

> [T]he defense does not require a provoking or triggering event. [T]o establish the "heat of passion" defense a defendant had to prove that the "hot blood" had not had time to "cool off" at the time of the killing. A homicide influenced by an extreme emotional disturbance, in contrast, is not one which is necessarily committed in the "hot blood" stage, but rather one that was brought about by a significant mental trauma that caused the defendant to brood for a long period of time and then react violently, seemingly without provocation.

Question: If the traditional provocation formula and the EED test produce different results in cases like *White* and *Elliot*, which approach is preferable?

For a study of developments in MPC jurisdictions, see Victoria Nourse, Passion's Progress: Modern Law Reform and the Provocation Defense, 106 Yale L.J. 1331 (1997). Professor Nourse concludes that the EED test aggravates the provocation defense's unfairness to women by greatly expanding the kinds of frictions in intimate settings that may suffice to reduce a killing from murder to manslaughter. A particularly frequent and disturbing scenario is the "separation killing," one that occurs when a man reacts violently to his domestic partner's decision to move out or file for divorce. Professor Nourse found that trial courts frequently permitted defendants in such cases to present an EED claim to the jury, and that no appellate court had held "separation" to be an insufficient basis for such a claim under the EED test. Id. at 1333.

These examples arguably suggest that the EED test is too broad, permitting inappropriate mitigation where the traditional common-law approach justifiably precludes it. But are there situations in which the common-law test is too narrow, precluding *appropriate* mitigation where the EED test would allow it? Consider Boyle v. State, 363 Ark. 356 (2005), where a distraught defendant shot and killed his partner, because she suffered from severe physical ailments and lived in extreme pain. Does Boyle have a claim for mitigation to manslaughter under either the EED or common-law tests? *Should* Boyle have a claim for mitigation to manslaughter?

3. Roles of judge and jury. In People v. Walker, 473 N.Y.S.2d 460 (1984), the defendant, a drug dealer, received a $4,500 consignment of marijuana from his supplier, William Edmunds. He failed to pay Edmunds and claimed that he had been robbed of the marijuana. In spite of the defendant's plea for additional consignments, Edmunds refused to supply him. One evening, the defendant encountered Edmunds in a restaurant. A witness heard an angry argument between the two. Edmunds demanded his money, the defendant responded that he did not have any, and Edmunds then asked how he could afford to eat in the restaurant. The defendant replied that Edmunds should give him money, to which Edmunds responded, "The only dough you're going to get is the dough in that bread." The defendant was then heard to say, "Take your damn hand out of my plate," after which he rose, gun in hand, and fired several shots in rapid succession, killing Edmunds.

At Walker's trial on murder charges, the judge refused to instruct the jury on an extreme emotional disturbance defense. Was this error? The appellate court affirmed, but a dissenting judge commented:

> From the evidence presented at the trial the jury could reasonably have found that the defendant killed the deceased in a burst of anger, that a smoldering sense of grievance had been ignited by insulting and contemptuous words and actions. . . .
>
> Once it is determined that there was "evidence of extreme emotional disturbance," the controlling rule is clear . . . : "it is for the trier of fact to decide, in light of all the circumstances of the case, whether there exists a reasonable explanation or excuse for the actor's mental condition." (Model Penal Code and Commentaries, §210.3, p. 61.) . . .
>
> This is not a sympathetic case. The plight of a narcotics dealer cut off from his source of supply, and then subjected to insulting and contemptuous words and actions by his former supplier, is not likely to evoke widespread feelings of acute compassion. Nevertheless, it is clear that the controlling statutory sections were carefully designed to permit the essential judgment on the kind of issue presented here to be made by jurors on the basis of all the circumstances, and not by the trial judge as a matter of law.

c. The Reasonable Person Requirement

NOTES

The common-law and MPC approaches both require an objective element—not every defendant who flies off the handle and kills is a candidate for the provocation defense. The loss of self-control must in some sense be "reasonable." What should that mean? Consider the following:

1. The MPC solution. As the *Casassa* opinion points out, the MPC test is whether the defendant acted "under the influence of extreme emotional disturbance for which there is reasonable explanation or excuse." The Code then directs that the determination of the reasonableness of the explanation or excuse shall be made "from the viewpoint of a person in the actor's situation under the circumstances as he believes them to be." In explaining this formulation, the Reporter's Comments state (Model Penal Code and Commentaries, Comment to §210.3, at 62-63 (1980)):

> The word "situation" is designedly ambiguous. On the one hand, it is clear that personal handicaps and some external circumstances must be taken into account. Thus, blindness, shock from traumatic injury, and extreme grief are all easily read into the term "situation" . . . for it would be morally obtuse to appraise a crime for mitigation of punishment without reference to these factors. On the other hand, it is equally plain that idiosyncratic moral values are not part of the actor's situation. An assassin who kills a political leader because he believes it is right to do so cannot ask that he be judged by the standard of a reasonable extremist. Any other result would undermine the normative message of the criminal law. In between these two extremes, however, there are matters neither as clearly distinct from individual blameworthiness as blindness . . . nor as integral a part of moral depravity as a belief in the rightness of killing. . . . The proper role of such factors cannot be resolved satisfactorily by abstract definition. . . . The Model Code endorses a formulation that affords sufficient flexibility to differentiate in particular cases between those special aspects of the actor's situation that should be deemed material for purpose of grading and those that should be ignored. There thus will be room for interpretation of the word "situation," and that is precisely the flexibility desired. . . . In the end, the question is whether the actor's loss of self-control can be understood in terms that arouse sympathy in the ordinary citizen. Section 210.3 faces this issue squarely and leaves the ultimate judgment to the ordinary citizen in the function of a juror assigned to resolve the specific case.

2. *Problems.* Consider how the common-law and MPC reasonableness standards would deal with the following special circumstances:

(a) Culture. Should the defendant's nationality and cultural background be taken into account? Suppose that the defendant recently emigrated from a country where the provoking circumstances (e.g., marital infidelity or a particular insult) are regarded as far more serious than they are in the United States. Suppose that ordinary people in the immigrant's country are far more likely to respond violently to such circumstances. Should the defendant's response be assessed from the perspective of the reasonable person of his cultural background? Or is it more appropriate to hold such a defendant to the standards of self-control that our society expects Americans to exercise?

In The Queen v. Zhang, [2011] N.I.C.A. 25 (N. Ire. Ct. App.), the defendant had been brought up in China, spoke no English, and lived within the Chinese community in Dublin. When his girlfriend admitted that she had been working as a prostitute, he killed her in a rage. An expert witness for the defense testified that in light of his upbringing and "the concept of face" as understood in Chinese society, her admission was "tantamount to throwing down a gauntlet, challenging his manhood," and that its effect on a person of his background would be quite different from the effect of such an admission on others in Northern

Ireland. The trial judge initially permitted the jury to hear this testimony but ultimately told the jury that the expert's testimony was not relevant to the question whether "an ordinary man of ordinary self-control would have done what the appellant did." The court of appeal upheld this instruction and affirmed a conviction for murder. Is this the appropriate standard for assessing whether the circumstances warrant some mitigation in the appropriate degree of punishment? Consider the views of an Australian justice, dissenting in Masciantonio v. R., 129 Austr. L.R. 575 (High Court Australia, 1995):

> Without incorporating [the general characteristics of an ordinary person of the same age, race, culture, and background as the accused on the self-control issue] the law of provocation is likely to result in discrimination and injustice. In a multicultural society such as Australia, invocation [of the reasonable-man standard] in cases heard by juries of predominately Anglo-Saxon-Celtic origin almost certainly results in the accused being judged by the standard of self-control attributed to a middle class Australian of Anglo-Saxon-Celtic heritage. . . . If it is objected that [incorporating the characteristics of an ordinary person of the same cultural background as the accused] will result in one law of provocation for one class of persons and another law for a different class, I would answer that that must be the natural consequence of true equality before the law in a multicultural society when the criterion of criminal liability is made to depend upon objective standards of personhood.

Questions: Does the suggested approach—incorporating the characteristics of an ordinary person of the same cultural background as the accused—eliminate discrimination against members of the ethnic minority, or is this approach itself discriminatory? Does it advantage or disadvantage members of that ethnic minority? Compare the problem of cultural background as a factor in administering the mistake-of-law defense. See supra, page 327.

(b) *Battered women.* In State v. McClain, 248 N.J. Super. 409, 591 A.2d 652 (1991), defendant shot and killed the man with whom she had lived for nine years in a troubled relationship. Though the man had not physically assaulted her for several years (there had been two beating incidents, several years apart, earlier in the relationship), a psychologist testified that the defendant suffered from battered woman syndrome because a series of psychological humiliations had triggered a mental "breakdown" and led to the killing. The court held that evidence relating to the defendant's status as a battered woman was "irrelevant on the question of whether the victim's conduct was adequately provocative because that inquiry requires application of the 'reasonable person' test." In accord, see J.C.S., Comment on *R. v. Thornton,* [1996] Crim. L. R. 597, 598:

> The concept of an ordinary person suffering from a personality disorder and battered woman syndrome is a difficult one. It could be . . . put to the jury in some such form as: "If you think that she may in fact have lost her self-control, you must not convict of murder unless you are sure that a woman, suffering from this personality disorder and from battered woman syndrome but

otherwise an ordinary woman, exercising such restraint as could reasonably be expected of a woman in that condition, would not have lost her self-control and done what the accused did." But this seems substantially to abandon the notion of the reasonable or ordinary person.

For criticism of this approach, see Lawrence S. Lustberg & John V. Jacobi, The Battered Woman as a Reasonable Person: A Critique of the Appellate Division Decision in *State v. McClain*, 22 Seton Hall L. Rev. 365 (1992). See also State v. Felton, 110 Wis. 2d 485, 329 N.W.2d 161, 172-173 (1983): "It is proper in applying the objective test . . . to consider how other persons similarly situated with respect to that type, or that history, of provocation would react. [T]he objective test may be satisfied by considering the situation of the ordinary person who is a battered spouse."

Questions: Should a defendant's situation include the fact that she has been battered, the fact that she suffers from battered woman syndrome, both, or neither? The problem of battered woman syndrome is explored at greater length in Chapter 8, infra.

(c) Mental disorder. In State v. Klimas, 288 N.W.2d 157 (Wis. Ct. App. 1979), the defendant, after months of intense conflict with his wife, shot and killed her. He claimed to be distraught over the disintegration of his marriage, his wife's relationship with another man, and her efforts to obtain a divorce. He sought to introduce psychiatric testimony to the effect that he had been suffering severe depression, that events on the day preceding the killing had "overwhelmed" him, and that although not legally insane, he was "a desperate man overwhelmed by a psychotic depressive illness." The defendant apparently sought to have his conduct assessed from the perspective of a person in that emotional situation. The trial judge ruled the psychiatric evidence irrelevant and therefore inadmissible. In another case the court held inadmissible the proffered evidence that the defendant was a traumatized Vietnam veteran who had just "snapped" when he heard the sound of an approaching helicopter. People v. Steele, 27 Cal. 4th 1220, 47 P.3d 225 (2002). Are these rulings sound? On what principle?

3. **Partial** *individualization?* In D.P.P. v. Camplin, [1978] A.C. 705, a 15-year-old murder defendant had killed an older man in response to sexual abuse and taunting. The trial judge instructed the jury that in applying the reasonableness standard, they had to consider whether "the provocation was sufficient to make a reasonable man in like circumstances act as the defendant did. Not a reasonable boy, as [counsel for Camplin] would have it, . . . ; it is an objective test—a reasonable man." The House of Lords held these instructions erroneous. It ruled that in considering the *gravity* of the provoking words or actions, the reasonable man should be assumed to share "such of the accused's characteristics as they think would affect the gravity of the provocation to him." However, in considering the *self-control* to be exercised, the jury was to apply the standard of a "person having the power of self-control to be expected of an ordinary person of the age and sex of the accused," without regard to any other special characteristics of the defendant.

The case for considering personal characteristics of the defendant in determining the *gravity* of the provocation was explained in one of the *Camplin* opinions as follows: "[The] expression . . . 'Your character is as crooked as your back' would have a different connotation to a hunchback . . . and to a man with a back like a ramrod." The case for not considering personal characteristics in determining the required level of *self-control* is likewise readily explicable: The law could not allow an exceptionally angry or aggressive person to exercise less self-control than everyone else. But why should the expected degree of self-control be individualized for "the age and sex of the accused"?

(a) With respect to age, the House of Lords said that "to require old heads on young shoulders is inconsistent with the law's compassion [for] human infirmity." If that point is well taken, shouldn't it apply to other unchosen and immutable characteristics, like cultural upbringing (reconsider *The Queen v. Zhang*, page 459 supra) or a life-long history of having a short temper?

(b) With respect to gender, the *Camplin* opinions gave no explanation for mandating an individualized standard of self-control. What is the justification for that feature of the decision? And justified or not, what does it mean? Is the required degree of self-control higher for women than for men, or vice versa? Does our society expect men and women to abide by different standards of self-control? And if so, should the law endorse those expectations?

(c) These difficulties aside, is it *feasible* to distinguish between personal characteristics relevant to gravity and those relevant to self-control? In Regina v. Smith (Morgan), [2001] 1 A.C. 146, a clinically depressed alcoholic stabbed and killed a friend who had stolen from him. Under the *Camplin* approach, the trial judge was required to instruct the jury that it should first consider the defendant's depression and alcoholism in judging the seriousness of the provocation, and then ask how a person with ordinary powers of self-control would have reacted. The "reasonable" person, in other words, was a clinically depressed alcoholic with ordinary powers of self-control. Faced with that prospect, the House of Lords altered course. Noting that the *Camplin* formula produced "glazed looks" in jurors' eyes, the House of Lords held that the jury should simply be left to decide whether in all the circumstances "there was some characteristic of the accused . . . which it would be unjust not to take into account." Is this a satisfactory way to preserve an objective but suitably individualized standard. *Smith (Morgan)* was sharply criticized for inviting "an evaluative free-for-all in which anything that induces sympathy by the same token helps to excuse [and] little more than lip-service is paid to the all-important objective (impersonal) standard of the reasonable person." John Gardner & Timothy Macklen, Compassion Without Respect? Nine Fallacies in *R. Smith*, [2001] Crim. L. Rev. 623, 635.

(d) Responding to such criticism, a subsequent English decision rejected *Smith (Morgan)* and returned to the *Camplin* distinction, under which the

defendant's personal characteristics must be considered in assessing the gravity of the provocation but cannot be considered (except with respect to age and gender) in assessing the expected degree of self-control. Attorney-general for Jersey v. Holley [2005] 2 A.C. 580.[7] Four years later, Parliament amended the relevant legislation and largely endorsed the *Camplin* distinction as well. The new statute permits a provocation defense only when a defendant *D* can show that his loss of control was the result of "a justifiable sense of being seriously wronged."[8] The necessary loss of control is established if "a person of *D*'s sex and age, with a normal degree of tolerance and self-restraint and in [all of *D*'s circumstances other than those whose only relevance to *D*'s conduct is that they bear on *D*'s general capacity for tolerance or self-restraint], might have reacted in the same or in a similar way to *D*."[9]

4. Problem. In Regina v. Morhall, [1996] 1 A.C. 90, a drug addict, taunted about his addiction, killed the person who had been mocking him. Consider how the relevance of his drug addiction should be explained to the jury charged with deciding whether his actions qualify for mitigation. What instructions would be appropriate under the new British legislation quoted above? What instructions would be appropriate under the MPC? Which approach provides a better framework for grading the severity of punishment in such a case?

C. LEGISLATIVE GRADING OF UNINTENDED KILLINGS

1. The Creation of Homicidal Risk

Unintended killings present questions of both criminalization and grading. Section C.1.a deals with the criteria for establishing criminal, as opposed to solely civil, liability for unintended homicide. Section C.1.b deals with the question whether criminal liability for unintended homicide should rest on a subjective or objective standard. Section C.1.c considers the special circumstances that may make an unintended killing murder.

---

7. *Holley*, a decision of the Privy Council, technically did not bind the House of Lords, which had jurisdiction over appeals from a different group of courts. But *Holley* was widely believed to reflect the views of the House of Lords since many of the same judges served on both courts. Since the date of these decisions, the British court system has been reorganized, and the appellate jurisdiction of the House of Lords has been assumed by a new court of last resort, the Supreme Court of the United Kingdom.

8. Coroners and Justice Act 2009, c. 25, Part 2, ch. 1 §55(4)(b).

9. Id. §54(1)(c), (3).

a. Distinguishing Civil and Criminal Liability

COMMONWEALTH v. WELANSKY

Massachusetts Supreme Judicial Court
316 Mass. 383, 55 N.E.2d 902 (1944)

LUMMUS, J. On November 28, 1942, and for about nine years before that day, a corporation named New Cocoanut Grove, Inc., maintained and operated a "night club" in Boston. . . . The corporation, its officers and employees, and its business, were completely dominated by the defendant Barnett Welansky. . . .

The defendant was accustomed to spend his evenings at the night club, inspecting the premises and superintending the business. On November 16, 1942, he became suddenly ill, and was carried to a hospital, where [he] remained until discharged on December 11, 1942. . . . There is no evidence of any act, omission or condition at the night club on November 28, 1942 (apart from the lighting of a match hereinafter described), that was not within the usual and regular practice during the time before the defendant was taken ill. . . .

The physical arrangement of the night club on November 28, 1942, as well as on November 16, 1942, when the defendant last had personal knowledge of it, was as follows. [The only entrance to the club was through a single revolving door. Various rooms were connected by narrow passageways and corridors to one another and to a various exits. Three emergency exits were in obscure locations, poorly marked and accessible only to knowledgeable employees. The court observed that an emergency escape "would be difficult for a patron not thoroughly familiar with parts of the premises not ordinarily open to him." Two other emergency exits were marked by "Exit" lights and equipped with panic bars, but one of the two was blocked by a screen and dining tables; the other was regularly kept locked, and the court noted that "if that door should be left so that it could be opened by means of the panic bar, a patron might leave through that door without paying his bill."]

A little after ten o'clock on the evening of Saturday, November 28, 1942, the night club was well filled with a crowd of patrons. It was during the busiest season of the year. An important football game in the afternoon had attracted many visitors to Boston. [T]here were from two hundred fifty to four hundred persons in the Melody Lounge, from four hundred to five hundred in the main dining room and the Caricature Bar, and two hundred fifty in the Cocktail Lounge. . . .

A bartender in the Melody Lounge noticed that an electric light bulb which was in or near the cocoanut husks of an artificial palm tree in the corner had been turned off and that the corner was dark. He directed a sixteen-year-old bar boy who was waiting on customers at the tables to cause the bulb to be lighted. [The bar boy lit a match to see the bulb, turned the bulb in its socket to light it, and blew out the match. The flame of the match ignited a palm tree, which in turn ignited a low cloth ceiling nearby.] The fire spread with great rapidity. . . . The crowd were panic stricken, and rushed and pushed in every direction through the night club, screaming, and overturning tables and chairs in their attempts to escape.

The door at the head of the Melody Lounge stairway was not opened until firemen broke it down from outside [and found it locked], so that the panic bar could not operate. . . . The head waiter and another waiter tried to get open the panic doors from the main dining room to Shawmut Street, and succeeded after some difficulty. The other two doors to Shawmut Street were locked, and were opened by force from outside by firemen and others. . . . A considerable number of patrons escaped through the Broadway door, but many died just inside that door. Some employees, and a great number of patrons, died in the fire.

[Defendant was charged with numerous counts of involuntary manslaughter based on overcrowding, installation of flammable decorations, absence of fire doors, and failure to maintain proper means of egress. He was found guilty and sentenced to a term of not less than 12 years and not more than 15 years, the first day of the term to be in solitary confinement and the residue at hard labor.]

The Commonwealth disclaimed any contention that the defendant intentionally killed or injured the persons named in the indictments as victims. It based its case on involuntary manslaughter through wanton or reckless conduct. The judge instructed the jury correctly with respect to the nature of such conduct.

Usually wanton or reckless conduct consists of an affirmative act, like driving an automobile or discharging a firearm, in disregard of probable harmful consequences to another. But where as in the present case there is a duty of care for the safety of business visitors invited to premises which the defendant controls, wanton or reckless conduct may consist of intentional failure to take such care in disregard of the probable harmful consequences to them or of their right to care.

To define wanton or reckless conduct so as to distinguish it clearly from negligence and gross negligence is not easy. Sometimes the word "wilful" is prefaced to the words "wanton" and "reckless" in expressing the concept. That only blurs it. Wilful means intentional. In the phrase "wilful, wanton or reckless conduct," if "wilful" modifies "conduct" it introduces something different from wanton or reckless conduct, even though the legal result is the same. Wilfully causing harm is a wrong, but a different wrong from wantonly or recklessly causing harm. If "wilful" modifies "wanton or reckless conduct" its use is accurate. What must be intended is the conduct, not the resulting harm. The words "wanton" and "reckless" are practically synonymous in this connection, although the word "wanton" may contain a suggestion of arrogance or insolence or heartlessness that is lacking in the word "reckless." But intentional conduct to which either word applies is followed by the same legal consequences as though both words applied. . . .

The judge charged the jury correctly when he said, "To constitute wanton or reckless conduct, as distinguished from mere negligence, grave danger to others must have been apparent and the defendant must have chosen to run the risk rather than alter his conduct so as to avoid the act or omission which caused the harm. If the grave danger was in fact realized by the defendant, his subsequent voluntary act or omission which caused the harm amounts to wanton or reckless conduct, no matter whether the ordinary man would have realized the gravity of the danger or not. But even if a particular defendant is so stupid (or) so heedless . . . that in fact he did not realize the grave danger, he cannot escape the imputation of wanton or reckless conduct in his dangerous act or omission, if an ordinary normal man under the same circumstances would have realized the gravity of the danger. A man may be reckless within the meaning of the law although he himself thought he was careful."

The essence of wanton or reckless conduct is intentional conduct, by way either of commission or of omission where there is a duty to act, which conduct involves a high degree of likelihood that substantial harm will result to another. Wanton or reckless conduct amounts to what has been variously described as indifference to or disregard of probable consequences to that other. . . .

The words "wanton" and "reckless" are thus not merely rhetorical, vituperative expressions used instead of negligent or grossly negligent. They express a difference in the degree of risk and in the voluntary taking of risk so marked, as compared with negligence, as to amount substantially and in the eyes of the law to a difference in kind. . . .

Notwithstanding language used commonly in earlier cases, and occasionally in later ones, it is now clear in this Commonwealth that at common law conduct does not become criminal until it passes the borders of negligence and gross negligence and enters into the domain of wanton or reckless conduct. There is in Massachusetts at common law no such thing as "criminal negligence." . . .

To convict the defendant of manslaughter, the Commonwealth was not required to prove that he caused the fire by some wanton or reckless conduct. Fire in a place of public resort is an ever present danger. It was enough to prove that death resulted from his wanton or reckless disregard of the safety of patrons in the event of fire from any cause.

[A]ffirmed.

NOTES AND QUESTIONS

1. The traditional tests. Does *Welansky* offer a reasonably clear statement of the difference between the ordinary negligence that suffices for civil tort liability and the more culpable kind required for criminal liability? What are the distinctive features of actions that "[pass] the borders of negligence and gross negligence and [enter] into the domain of wanton and reckless conduct"? How is "wanton and reckless conduct" in Massachusetts different from ordinary civil negligence? The court states that wanton and reckless conduct requires "a high degree of likelihood" of injury to another. Was there such a likelihood in *Welansky*? What was the statistical likelihood that a raging fire would break out at a time when the club was filled to capacity? What does "likelihood" mean? Consider the following explanations:

Rex v. Bateman, 19 Crim. App. 8, 11-12 (1925): "In explaining to juries the test which they should apply to determine whether the negligence, in the particular case, amounted or did not amount to a crime, judges have used many epithets such as 'culpable,' 'gross,' 'wicked,' 'clear,' 'complete.' But whatever epithet be used and whether an epithet be used or not, in order to establish criminal liability the facts must be such that, in the opinion of the jury, the negligence of the accused went beyond a mere matter of compensation between subjects and showed such disregard for the life and safety of others as to amount to a crime against the State and conduct deserving punishment."

State v. Barnett, 63 S.E.2d 57, 58-59 (S.C. 1951): "The degree of negligence necessary to establish criminal liability has perplexed the courts of England and America for centuries. . . . In the early development of the criminal law in England it was held that ordinary negligence, that is, the failure to exercise due care, was sufficient. Later it was found that this rule was too harsh. A noted English authority observed that an accident brought about by an act of ordinary negligence 'may be the lot of even the wisest and the best of mankind.' The English courts finally concluded that more carelessness was required to create criminal liability than civil but they found it difficult to determine 'how much more.'[In the United States] it is now generally held that the negligence of the accused must be 'culpable,' 'gross,' or 'reckless,' that is, the conduct of the accused must be such a departure from what would be the conduct of an ordinarily prudent or careful man under the same circumstances as to be incompatible with a proper regard for human life, or conduct amounting to an indifference to consequences. In perhaps a majority of the states, the offense of involuntary manslaughter is now defined by statute. Although variously worded, these statutes, with a few exceptions, have been construed as requiring gross negligence or recklessness."

Jerome Hall, General Principles of Criminal Law 124 (2d ed. 1960): "[Judicial opinions defining criminal negligence] run in terms of 'wanton and wilful negligence,' 'gross negligence,' and more illuminating yet, 'that degree of negligence that is more than the negligence required to impose tort liability.' The apex of this infelicity is 'wilful, wanton negligence,' which suggest a triple contradiction—'negligence' implying inadvertence; 'wilful,' intention; and 'wanton,' recklessness."

  2. Problem. Cal. Penal Code §192(b) defines involuntary manslaughter (in cases not involving vehicular homicide) to include deaths that result from an act committed "without due caution and circumspection." See page 422 supra. Under the appropriate principles of statutory interpretation, should this language be construed to require gross negligence or to impose criminal liability for ordinary civil negligence? See People v. Penny, 285 P.2d 926, 937 (Cal. 1955); People v. Gilbert, 2004 WL 2416533, at *2 (Cal. Ct. App. 2004).

3. *Contributory negligence.* Notwithstanding the ambiguity of the line between civil and criminal negligence, one difference is clear. In civil cases, the deceased's contributory negligence is a complete defense, except in jurisdictions that have adopted comparative negligence. In criminal cases, however, the deceased's contributory negligence or other misconduct has never afforded a defense. In Dickerson v. State, 441 So. 2d 536 (Miss. 1983), the defendant drove his car into another car and killed its drunken driver, who had stopped the car with its lights off in the middle of the road. Commenting on the import of this evidence, the court observed (id. at 538):

> Contributory negligence is not a defense to manslaughter. All that the state must prove with respect to the victim is that he was prior to the incident a live human being. The homicide laws of this State protect all living beings within the jurisdiction, sinners as well as saints, drunks as well as deacons.

Note, however, that although contributory negligence does not itself afford a defense as it usually would in a civil case, it may bear on the whether the defendant's conduct was a proximate cause of the death. See the material on causation in Chapter 6, infra.

4. *The MPC alternative.* The MPC creates two crimes, manslaughter (§210.3) and a lesser crime, negligent homicide (§210.4), distinguished by whether the defendant was aware of the unwarranted risk he was creating. A killing is manslaughter if the actor was "reckless," that is, if he "consciously disregarded a substantial and unjustifiable risk that his conduct would cause the death of another"; and if the risk was "of such a nature and degree that, considering the nature and purpose of his conduct and the circumstances known to him, its disregard involves a gross deviation from the standard of conduct that a law-abiding person would observe in the actor's situation." By contrast, a killing is negligent homicide when a person *should have been* aware of such a risk.

Questions: The MPC distinction between unintentional killings that are criminal and those that are not (found in its definition of negligent homicide) is designed to avoid the epithets typical in earlier formulations and thereby to give greater guidance to the jury. Does it succeed? Are juries apt to reach better and more consistent conclusions if they are asked to decide according to the MPC standard than if they are asked whether conduct was "culpable and gross"? Could the MPC drafters have done a better job?

A number of modern statutory revisions have followed the MPC. The following case illustrates the MPC formula in action.

PEOPLE v. HALL

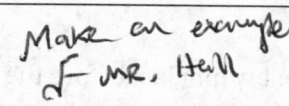

Supreme Court of Colorado
999 P.2d 207 (2000)

BENDER, J.: While skiing on Vail mountain, Hall flew off of a knoll and collided with Allen Cobb, who was traversing the slope below Hall. Cobb sustained traumatic brain injuries and died as a result of the collision. The People charged Hall with felony reckless manslaughter.

At a preliminary hearing to determine whether there was probable cause for the felony count, the county court found that Hall's conduct "did not rise to the level of dangerousness" required under Colorado law to uphold a conviction for manslaughter, and the court dismissed the charges. [Colorado statutes followed the MPC definitions of manslaughter and negligent homicide.] On appeal, [t]he district court determined that in order for Hall's conduct to have been reckless, it must have been "at least more likely than not" that death would result. Because the court found that "skiing too fast for the conditions" is not "likely" to cause another person's death, the court concluded that Hall's conduct did not constitute a "substantial and unjustifiable" risk of death. Thus, the district court affirmed the finding of no probable cause.

The charge of reckless manslaughter requires that a person "recklessly cause the death of another person."§18-3-104(1)(a). For his conduct to be reckless, the actor must have consciously disregarded a substantial and unjustifiable risk that death could result from his actions. See §18-1-501(8)....

The district court's conclusion that Hall's conduct did not represent a substantial and unjustifiable risk of death rested on an erroneous construction of recklessness, [finding] that for the risk to be "substantial" it must "be at least more likely than not that death would result." [A] risk of death that has less than a fifty percent chance of occurring may nonetheless be a substantial risk depending on the circumstances of the particular case. Because this case was dismissed at the preliminary hearing, we must consider the facts in the light most favorable to the prosecution and we must draw all inferences against the defendant....

We first ask whether the prosecution presented sufficient evidence to show that Hall's conduct created a substantial and unjustifiable risk of death. Like other activities that generally do not involve a substantial risk of death, such as driving a car ... "skiing too fast for the conditions" is not widely considered behavior that constitutes a high degree of risk. However, we hold that the specific facts in this case support a reasonable inference that Hall created a substantial and unjustifiable risk that he would cause another's death.

Several ... eyewitnesses all said that Hall was travelling too fast for the conditions.... All the witnesses said Hall ... was skiing straight down the fall line. Hall was back on his skis, with his ski tips in the air and his arms out to his sides to maintain balance. [A witness, himself a ski instructor,] said that Hall was bounced around by the moguls on the slope rather than skiing in control and managing the bumps. Hall admitted ... that he first saw Cobb when he was airborne and that he was unable to stop when he saw people below him just before the collision. Hence, in addition to finding that Hall was skiing at a very high rate of speed, a reasonably prudent person could have concluded that Hall was unable to anticipate or avoid a potential collision with a skier on the trail below him.

While skiing ordinarily carries a very low risk of death to other skiers, a reasonable person could have concluded that Hall's excessive speed, lack of control, and improper technique for skiing bumps significantly increased both the likelihood that a collision would occur and the extent of the injuries that might result from such a collision, including the possibility of death, in the event that a person like Cobb unwittingly crossed Hall's downhill path. [Another experienced witness] testified that he was aware of only two other deaths from skier collisions on Vail mountain in the past eleven years, but a reasonable person could have determined that Hall's conduct was precisely the type of skiing that risked this rare result.

We next ask whether a reasonable person could have concluded that Hall's creation of a substantial risk of death was unjustified. To the extent that Hall's extremely fast and unsafe skiing created a risk of death, Hall was serving no direct interest other than his own enjoyment. Although the sport often involves high speeds and even moments where a skier is temporarily out of control, a reasonable person could determine that the enjoyment of skiing does not justify skiing at the speeds and with the lack of control Hall exhibited. Thus, a reasonable person could have found that Hall's creation of a substantial risk was unjustifiable.

In addition to our conclusion that a reasonable person could have entertained the belief that Hall's conduct created a substantial and unjustifiable risk, we must ask whether Hall's conduct constituted a "gross deviation" from the standard of care that a reasonable law-abiding person (in this case, a reasonable, law-abiding, trained ski racer and resort employee) would have observed in the circumstances, [as opposed to the kind of deviation from the reasonable standard of care that results in civil liability for ordinary negligence.[12] . . .]

[T]he nature of the sport involves moments of high speeds and temporary losses of control. However, the General Assembly [enacted a statute, Colo. Rev. Stat. Section 33-104-109(2), imposing] upon a skier the duty to avoid collisions with any person or object below him. Although this statute may not form the basis of criminal liability, it establishes the minimum standard of care for uphill skiers and, for the purposes of civil negligence suits, creates a rebuttable presumption that the skier is at fault whenever he collides with skiers on the slope below him. A violation of a skier's duty in an extreme fashion, such as here, may be evidence of conduct that constitutes a "gross deviation" from

---

12. We note that both criminal negligence and recklessness require that the actor's conduct involve a "gross deviation" from the standard of care that a reasonable person would exercise under the circumstances in each case. Thus, the same risk will suffice for either criminally negligent or reckless conduct. However, the standards are sufficiently distinct to justify unequal penalties because in the case of reckless conduct *the actor must be aware of the risk* he creates, while criminally negligent conduct requires only that he failed to perceive the risk.

the standard of care imposed by statute for civil negligence. Hall admitted . . . that as he flew off a knoll, he saw people below him but was unable to stop; Hall was travelling so fast and with so little control that he could not possibly have respected his obligation to avoid skiers below him on the slope. Additionally, Hall skied in this manner for some time over a considerable distance, demonstrating that his high speeds and lack of control were not the type of momentary lapse of control or inherent danger associated with skiing. . . .

[W]e next ask whether a reasonably prudent person could have entertained the belief that Hall consciously disregarded that risk. Hall is a trained ski racer who had been coached about skiing in control and skiing safely. Further, he was an employee of a ski area and had a great deal of skiing experience. Hall's knowledge and training could give rise to the reasonable inference that he was aware of the possibility that by skiing so fast and out of control he might collide with and kill another skier unless he regained control and slowed down. . . .

Thus, interpreting the facts presented in the light most favorable to the prosecution, we hold that a reasonably prudent and cautious person could have entertained the belief that Hall consciously disregarded a substantial and unjustifiable risk that by skiing exceptionally fast and out of control he might collide with and kill another person on the slope.

Obviously, this opinion does not address whether Hall is ultimately guilty of any crime. Rather, we hold only that the People presented sufficient evidence to establish probable cause that Hall committed reckless manslaughter, and the court should have bound Hall's case over for trial.

Should have went to trial

NOTES

1. The outcome in Hall. In a subsequent trial, a jury composed entirely of skiers and snowboarders rejected the charge of reckless manslaughter and convicted only of the lesser offense of negligent homicide, which carried a sentence of up to three years' imprisonment.[10] Hall was sentenced to a 90-day jail term. See Editorial, Skier Penalty Warranted, Denv. Post, Feb. 6, 2001, at B10. A juror, who identified herself as one of the last holdouts, said the jurors agreed that "going fast is not a gross deviation, . . . and being out-of-control is not a gross deviation," but said she was convinced to vote for conviction because "the gross deviation was that a beginner skier [was] hit from behind by . . . one who is employed on the mountain and therefore has a mandate . . . , more than anybody else, to protect the people on the mountain." See Steve Lipsher, Ski Verdict Tough, Juror Says Hall's Ability Decided Matter, Denv. Post, Nov. 20, 2000, at B1. For a close analysis of the issues in *Hall* and other recent prosecutions for deaths that occur in the course of risky recreational

---

10. Colo. Rev. Stat. §§18-3-105; 18-1.3-401(V)(A) (2011).

activities, see Carolyn B. Ramsey, Homicide on Holiday: Prosecutorial Discretion, Popular Culture, and the Boundaries of the Criminal Law, 54 Hastings L.J. 1641 (2003).

2. *Awareness.* The argument for imposing a lower punishment when the actor was *not aware* of creating an unjustified risk is that she is less culpable than the person who does have this awareness. But should it matter *why* the defendant lacks this awareness? For example, compare two defendants: Skier *A* loses control because he doesn't (but should) realize that conditions are icy, while skier *B* knows that conditions are icy but skis anyway and loses control because he incorrectly thinks he is a hot-shot skier. Or suppose that skier *B* knows that the danger is substantial but figures that taking risks is part of the good life and hence justifiable. If the reasons for unawareness matter, how should the definitions of recklessness and negligence be changed to take account of them?

b. Objectivity and Individualization in the Concept of Criminal Negligence

INTRODUCTORY NOTE

One may ask two major questions about the offense of negligent homicide: its justification and its definition.

(a) Justification. Are the MPC and most American jurisdictions right to punish inadvertent (negligent) killing? Is it ever justified to convict a person of a homicidal crime when she did not realize that her actions were dangerous?

(b) Definition. Even if punishment for negligence can sometimes be justified, how should the jury determine whether a defendant *was* negligent? The standard, in principle, is that of the reasonable man or woman in the circumstances. But what circumstances should be considered? Do they include the competence and capabilities of the particular defendant? Or should the law apply a single invariant standard for all, regardless of a particular defendant's ability to meet that standard?

The following case provides a setting for examining both problems—justification and definition.

STATE v. WILLIAMS

Washington Court of Appeals
4 Wash. App. 908, 484 P.2d 1167 (1971)

HOROWITZ, C.J. Defendants, husband and wife, were charged by information filed October 3, 1968, with the crime of manslaughter for negligently failing to supply their 17-month child with necessary medical attention, as a result of which he died on September 12, 1968. Upon entry of findings, conclusions and judgment of guilty, sentences were imposed on April 22, 1969.[a] Defendants appeal.

The defendant husband, Walter Williams, is a 24-year-old full-blooded Shoshon[e] Indian with a sixth-grade education. His sole occupation is that of laborer. The defendant wife, Bernice Williams, is a 20-year-old part Indian with an 11th grade education. At the time of the marriage, the wife had two children, the younger of whom was a 14-month-old son. Both parents worked and the children were cared for by the 85-year-old mother of the defendant husband. The defendant husband assumed parental responsibility with the defendant wife to provide clothing, care and medical attention for the child. Both defendants possessed a great deal of love and affection for the defendant wife's young son.

The court expressly found:

> That both defendants were aware that William Joseph Tabafunda was ill during the period September 1, 1968, to September 12, 1968. The defendants were ignorant. They did not realize how sick the baby was. They thought that the baby had a toothache and no layman regards a toothache as dangerous to life. They loved the baby and gave it aspirin in hopes of improving its condition. They did not take the baby to a doctor because of fear that the Welfare Department would take the baby away from them. They knew that medical help was available because of previous experience. They had no excuse that the law will recognize for not taking the baby to a doctor.
>
> The defendants Walter L. Williams and Bernice J. Williams were negligent in not seeking medical attention for William Joseph Tabafunda.
>
> That as a proximate result of this negligence, William Joseph Tabafunda died.

From these and other findings, the [trial] court concluded that the defendants were each guilty of the crime of manslaughter as charged. . . .

[The court of appeals held that both defendants were under a legal duty to obtain medical assistance for the child.] On the question of the quality or seriousness of breach of the duty, at common law, in the case of involuntary manslaughter, the breach had to amount to more than mere ordinary or simple negligence—gross negligence was essential. . . . Under [Washington] statutes [however] the crime is deemed committed even though the death of the victim is the proximate result of only simple or ordinary negligence. . . .

The concept of simple or ordinary negligence describes a failure to exercise the "ordinary caution" necessary to make out the defense of excusable homicide. Ordinary caution is the kind of caution that a man of reasonable prudence would exercise under the same or similar conditions. If, therefore, the conduct of a defendant, regardless of his ignorance, good intentions and good faith, fails to measure up to the conduct required of a man of reasonable prudence, he is guilty of ordinary negligence because of his failure to use

---

a. Defendants each received suspended sentences of three years' imprisonment. Paul Robinson, Would You Convict? Seventeen Cases That Challenged the Law 142 (1999).—Eds.

"ordinary caution." . . . If such negligence proximately causes the death of the victim, the defendant, as pointed out above, is guilty of statutory manslaughter. . . .

The remaining issue of proximate cause requires consideration of the question of when the duty to furnish medical care became activated. If the duty to furnish such care was not activated until after it was too late to save the life of the child, failure to furnish medical care could not be said to have proximately caused the child's death. Timeliness in the furnishing of medical care also must be considered in terms of "ordinary caution." [T]he duty as formulated in People v. Pierson, 176 N.Y. 201, 68 N.E. 243 (1903) . . . properly defines the duty contemplated by our manslaughter statutes. . . . The court there said: "We quite agree that the Code does not contemplate the necessity of calling a physician for every trifling complaint with which the child may be afflicted, which in most instances may be overcome by the ordinary household nursing by members of the family; that a reasonable amount of discretion is vested in parents, charged with the duty of maintaining and bringing up infant children; and that the standard is at what time would an ordinarily prudent person, solicitous for the welfare of his child and anxious to promote its recovery, deem it necessary to call in the services of a physician."

It remains to apply the law discussed to the facts of the instant case.

Defendants . . . contended below and on appeal that they are not guilty of the crime charged. Because of the serious nature of the charge against the parent and step-parent of a well-loved child, and out of our concern for the protection of the constitutional rights of the defendants, we have made an independent examination of the evidence to determine whether it substantially supports the court's express finding on proximate cause and its implied finding that the duty to furnish medical care became activated in time to prevent death of the child. . . .

Dr. Gale Wilson, the autopsy surgeon and chief pathologist for the King County Coroner, testified that the child died because an abscessed tooth had been allowed to develop into an infection of the mouth and cheeks, eventually becoming gangrenous. . . . Dr. Wilson testified that in his opinion the infection had lasted for approximately 2 weeks, and that the odor generally associated with gangrene would have been present for approximately 10 days before death. He also expressed the opinion that had medical care been first obtained in the last week before the baby's death, such care would have been obtained too late to have saved the baby's life. Accordingly, the baby's apparent condition between September 1 and September 5, 1968 became the critical period for the purpose of determining whether in the exercise of ordinary caution defendants should have provided medical care for the minor child.

The testimony concerning the child's apparent condition during the critical period is not crystal clear, but is sufficient to warrant the following statement of the matter. The defendant husband testified that he noticed the baby was sick about 2 weeks before the baby died. The defendant wife testified that she noticed the baby was ill about a week and a half or 2 weeks before the baby died. The evidence showed that in the critical period the baby was fussy; that he could not keep his food down; and that a cheek started swelling up. The swelling went up and down, but did not disappear. In that same period, the cheek turned "a bluish color like." The defendants, not realizing that the baby was as ill as it was or that the baby was in danger of dying, attempted to provide some relief to the baby by giving the baby aspirin during the critical period and continued to do so until the night before the baby died. The defendants thought the swelling would go down and were waiting for it to do so; and defendant husband testified, that from what he had heard, neither doctors nor dentists pull out a tooth "when it's all swollen up like that." There was an additional explanation for not calling a doctor given by each defendant. Defendant husband testified that "the way the cheek looked, . . . and that stuff on his hair, they would think we were neglecting him and take him away from us and not give him back." Defendant wife testified that the defendants were "waiting for the swelling to go down," and also that they were afraid to take the child to a doctor for fear that the doctor would report them to the welfare department, who, in turn, would take the child away. "It's just that I was so scared of losing him." They testified that they had heard that the defendant husband's cousin lost a child that way. The evidence showed that the defendants did not understand the significance or seriousness of the baby's symptoms. However, there is no evidence that the defendants were physically or financially unable to obtain a doctor, or that they did not know an available doctor, or that the symptoms did not continue to be a matter of concern during the critical period. Indeed, the evidence shows that in April 1968 defendant husband had taken the child to a doctor for medical attention.

In our opinion, there is sufficient evidence from which the court could find, as it necessarily did, that applying the standard of ordinary caution, i.e., the caution exercisable by a man of reasonable prudence under the same or similar conditions, defendants were sufficiently put on notice concerning the symptoms of the baby's illness and lack of improvement in the baby's apparent condition in the period from September 1 to September 5, 1968 to have required them to have obtained medical care for the child. The failure so to do in this case is ordinary or simple negligence, and such negligence is sufficient to support a conviction of statutory manslaughter.

The judgment is affirmed.

NOTES AND QUESTIONS

1. The manslaughter statutes involved in *Williams* were repealed in 1975. The current statutes create two degrees of manslaughter: recklessly causing death and causing death by criminal negligence. See Wash. Rev. Code §§9A.32.060, 9A.32.070 (2011). In accord with generally prevailing law, Washington no longer imposes manslaughter liability in cases involving ordinary negligence. See State v. Norman, 808 P.2d 1159, 1162 (Wash. App. 1991).

Questions: Would the *Williams* court have reached a different result under the statute in effect today? On the court's view of the facts, wasn't the couple's departure from ordinary standards of care so substantial that it would qualify as *criminal* negligence?

2. Many will find the conviction of the Williams couple unjust and, perhaps, pointless. Why were the defendants punished?

(a) Note that the court calls attention to the race of the defendants. In what respect, if any, did their race have a bearing on the issues in the case?

(b) Were the defendants punished only because of their ignorance and limited education? If the conviction seems unjust, is this because they were not aware of the danger to their child? If so, does it follow that punishment for negligence (where there is no awareness of the risk) is always unjust?

(c) Alternatively, was the Williams couple punished because they *were* aware of the danger and chose not to seek help, out of fear that the Welfare Department would take the baby away from them? If so, should this be viewed as a case of unjustifiably "taking the law into their own hands." Or was it a *justified* response to their perception that state authorities were too quick to charge members of their community with child neglect? For a perceptive analysis of this aspect of *Williams*, see Samuel H. Pillsbury, Judging Evil 181-184 (1998).

3. In thinking about the preceding questions, consider the materials in the Note that follows.

NOTES ON THE OBJECTIVE STANDARD

1. Support for punishment in the absence of subjective awareness.

(a) Justice Oliver Wendell Holmes, Jr. defended an objective standard in Commonwealth v. Pierce, 138 Mass. 165 (1884). Pierce, a physician, had been convicted of manslaughter on evidence that:

> being called to attend a sick woman, [he] caused her, with her consent, to be kept in flannels saturated with kerosene for three days, more or less, by reason of which she died. There was evidence that he had made similar applications with favorable results in other cases, but that in one the effect had been to blister and burn the flesh as in the present case.

The trial court had refused to instruct the jury that a finding of recklessness was required for conviction. Justice Holmes formulated the issue as follows (id. at 175-176):

> [R]ecklessness in a moral sense means a certain state of consciousness with reference to the consequences of one's acts. No matter whether defined as indifference to what those consequences may be, or as a failure to consider their nature or probability as fully as the party might and ought to have done, it is understood to depend on the actual condition of the individual's mind with

regard to consequences, as distinguished from mere knowledge of present or past facts or circumstances from which some one or everybody else might be led to anticipate or apprehend them if the supposed act were done. We have to determine whether recklessness in this sense was necessary to make the defendant guilty of felonious homicide, or whether his acts are to be judged by the external standard of what would be morally reckless, under the circumstances known to him, in a man of reasonable prudence. More specifically, the questions . . . are whether an actual good intent and the expectation of good results are an absolute justification of acts, however foolhardy they may be if judged by the external standard supposed, and whether the defendant's ignorance of the tendencies of kerosene administered as it was will excuse the administration of it.

After reviewing the objective standards applicable in civil cases, Holmes concluded:

If this is the rule adopted in regard to the redistribution of losses, which sound policy allows to rest where they fall in the absence of a clear reason to the contrary, there would seem to be at least equal reason for adopting it in the criminal law, which has for its immediate object and task to establish a general standard, or at least general negative limits, of conduct for the community, in the interest of the safety of all.

(*b*) While Justice Holmes justifies punishment for inadvertent negligence on the basis of its assumed public safety benefits, Professor Stephen P. Garvey argues (What's Wrong with Involuntary Manslaughter?, 85 Tex. L. Rev. 333, 337-338 (2006)) that punishment for inadvertent negligence is *fair*, under the principles of retributive justice, because of the actor's "culpable failure to exercise . . . control over desires that influence the formation and awareness of one's beliefs."

(*c*) In support of retaining negligence as a basis of criminal liability, Model Penal Code and Commentaries, Comment to §2.02 at 243-244 (1980), states:

When people have knowledge that conviction and sentence, not to speak of punishment, may follow conduct that inadvertently creates improper risk, they are supplied with an additional motive to take care before acting, to use their faculties and draw on their experience in gauging the potentialities of contemplated conduct. To some extent, at least, this motive may promote awareness and thus be effective as a measure of control. Moreover, moral defect can properly be imputed to instances where the defendant acts out of insensitivity to the interests of other people, and not merely out of an intellectual failure to grasp them.

(*d*) Samuel H. Pillsbury, Crimes of Indifference, 49 Rutgers L. Rev. 105, 106, 150-151 (1996):

The key to culpability for failure to perceive is why the person failed to perceive. Assume two cases in which a driver runs a red light and fatally injures a pedestrian in the cross-walk. One case involves a father rushing his severely injured child to the hospital. Another involves a teenager showing off for his friends. Assume that in both cases the driver saw neither the light nor the pedestrian. Culpability should depend on the drivers' reasons for perceptive failure, not on the failure itself. The father's lack of perception may be attributed to his overriding and morally worthy desire to help his child. . . . The teenager placed a higher value on winning the admiration of friends than on attending to the risks of fast driving. [His] conduct demonstrates an attitude of indifference toward others, a morally culpable state to which society should forcefully respond by conviction and punishment. . . .

Individuals deserve punishment for all acts displaying serious disregard for the moral worth of other human beings. Such acts involve many different levels of awareness. . . . In all cases we should judge the actor's choices: what she has chosen to care about and perceive, and what she has chosen not to care about and perceive. These choices give the individual's conduct a distinct moral meaning.

2. Criticism of the objective standard. (a) Larry Alexander & Kimberly Kessler Ferzan, Crime and Culpability 71 (2009):

An injunction to notice, remember, and be fully informed about anything that bears on risks to others is an injunction no human being can comply with, so violating this injunction reflects no moral defect. Even those most concerned with the well-being of others will violate this injunction constantly.

(b) Glanville Williams, Criminal Law: The General Part 122-123 (2d ed. 1961):

With the best will in the world, we all of us at some times in our lives make negligent mistakes. It is hard to see how justice (as distinct from some utilitarian reason) requires mistakes to be punished.

[T]he deterrent theory . . . finds itself in some difficulty when applied to negligence. At best the deterrent effect of the legal sanction is a matter of faith rather than of proved scientific fact; but there is no department in which this faith is less firmly grounded than that of negligence. Hardly any motorist but does not firmly believe that if he is involved in an accident it will be the other fellow's fault. It may seem, therefore, that the threat of punishment for negligence must pass him by, because he does not realize that it is addressed to him. Even if a person admits that he occasionally makes a negligent mistake, how, in the nature of things, can punishment for inadvertence serve to deter?

3. Individualizing the objective standard. Professor H.L.A. Hart has argued that the problem with the so-called objective approach is not that it sets an objective standard but that the standard is applied without regard to the ability of the defendant to comply with it. He notes there is a crucial difference between objective standards that are "invariant" and those that are "individualized" (Punishment and Responsibility 153-154 (1968)):

The expression "objective" and its partner "subjective" are unhappy because, as far as negligence is concerned, they obscure the real issue. . . . For, when negligence is made criminally punishable, this itself leaves open the question:

whether, before we punish, both or only the first of the following two questions must be answered affirmatively:

(i) Did the accused fail to take those precautions which any reasonable man with normal capacities would in the circumstances have taken?

(ii) Could the accused, given his mental and physical capacities, have taken those precautions?

. . . It may well be that, even if the "standard of care" is pitched very low so that individuals are held liable only if they fail to take very elementary precautions against harm, there will still be some unfortunate individuals who, through lack of intelligence, powers of concentration or memory, or through clumsiness, could not attain even this low standard. If our conditions of liability are invariant and not flexible, i.e., if they are not adjusted to the capacities of the accused, then some individuals will be held liable for negligence though they could not have helped their failure to comply with the standard. In such cases, indeed, criminal responsibility will be made independent of any "subjective element," since the accused could not have conformed to the required standard. But this result [has] nothing to do with negligence being taken as a basis for criminal liability. . . . "Absolute liability" results, not from the admission of the principle that one who has been grossly negligent is criminally responsible for the consequent harm even if "he had no idea in his mind of harm to anyone," but from the refusal in the application of this principle to consider the capacities of an individual who has fallen below the standard of care.

The present German law adopts an approach similar to Hart's. As expressed in a leading 1922 case, The Case of the Gable-Wall (Giebelmauer), 56 RGSt 343, 349 (1922), "A harm caused by defendants can be said to be caused by negligence only when it is established that they disregarded the care which they were obliged to exercise and of which they were capable under the circumstances and according to their personal knowledge and abilities. . . ." For discussion of this approach, see Tatjana Hoernle, Social Expectations in the Criminal Law: The "Reasonable Person" in a Comparative Perspective, 11 New Crim. L. Rev. 1 (2008).

Questions: This approach would seem to make legal guilt and moral blameworthiness more nearly the same, but is it workable? How could we know whether a defendant lacked the capacity to be aware of a danger, except in cases of demonstrable mental abnormality? And must the incapacity be total, or is it sufficient that his capacity is limited? And if the latter, then *how* limited? Consider the Williams couple. Were they unable to be aware of the degree of danger, or was it just that they were in fact unaware this time? One should consider these kinds of questions again when confronting the defense of diminished capacity generally, infra page 998.

4. The MPC on individualization. In contrast to the German approach, the MPC definition of negligence rejects a fully individualized standard. However, some elements of an individualized standard are invited by its reference to "the care that would be exercised by a reasonable person *in [the actor's] situation."* (Italics added). Model Penal Code and Commentaries, Comment to §2.02 at 242 (1985) states:

> There is an inevitable ambiguity in "situation." If the actor were blind or if he had just suffered a blow or experienced a heart attack, these would certainly be facts to be considered in a judgment involving criminal liability, as they would be under traditional law. But the heredity, intelligence or temperament of the actor would not be held material in judging negligence, and could not be without depriving the criterion of all its objectivity. The Code is not intended to displace discriminations of this kind, but rather to leave the issue to the courts.

Recall that the MPC took a similar approach in its test for provocation, where the objectivity of the standard is qualified by the sentence (§210.3): "The reasonableness of such explanation or excuse shall be determined from the viewpoint of a person *in the actor's situation* under the circumstances as he believes them to be." [Italics added.]

Question: How would the *Williams* case be decided under the Code?

5. *The case law on individualization.* Although the MPC leaves to the courts the problem of determining the appropriate degree of individualization, the courts remain ambivalent or in conflict. In State v. Everhart, 291 N.C. 700, 231 S.E.2d 604 (1977), the defendant, a young girl with an IQ of 72, gave birth in her own bedroom and, thinking that the baby had been born dead, wrapped it from head to foot in a blanket. The baby smothered to death. The court reversed a conviction for involuntary manslaughter, holding that because of the defendant's low IQ and the admittedly accidental nature of the death, the state had not proved culpable negligence. Compare State v. Patterson, 131 Conn. App. 65 (2011). The defendant withheld water from a two-year-old boy in her care in order to prevent him from wetting his bed. After four days of this mistreatment, the child stopped breathing and died as a result of severe dehydration. The defense argued that the defendant, who had an IQ of 61 (placing her in the bottom one-half of 1 percent of the population), "was cognitively unable to perceive the risks created by her actions." The appellate court nonetheless upheld her conviction for criminally negligent homicide, stating that "[e]ven if . . . the defendant was incapable of perceiving the risk of death . . . , we cannot consider the defendant's diminished mental capacity in the context of criminally negligent homicide because we employ an objective standard."

Question: What purpose (retributive, utilitarian, or otherwise) does conviction serve in such a case?

PROBLEM

In Walker v. Superior Court, 763 P.2d 852 (Cal. 1988), the defendant's four-year-old daughter fell ill with flu-like symptoms, and four days later she developed a stiff neck. In accord with the tenets of her religion, the defendant, a member of the Church of Christ Scientist, elected to treat her daughter with prayer rather than medicine.[11] An "accredited Christian Scientist prayer practitioner" was summoned to supervise the child's treatment. Over a 17-day period, the child's condition worsened. She lost weight, grew disoriented, and eventually died of meningitis.

Questions: Is the mother guilty of involuntary manslaughter? Are the arguments for conviction stronger or weaker than those in the *Williams* case?

Many states provide that parents who treat a child only with prayer cannot be prosecuted for child neglect. But that exemption typically is inapplicable when the child's condition is life-threatening, and advocacy groups estimate that in the past 25 years, roughly 300 children have died after medical care was withheld on religious grounds.[12] Under current law, the First Amendment right to free exercise of religion affords no constitutional defense to a prosecution for child endangerment or involuntary manslaughter in such cases.[13]

How should the mother's religious beliefs be treated in the *Walker* case, in considering whether her conduct *was* criminally negligent? Given the special deference owed to religious conviction in our society, should those beliefs count among the justifications that must be weighed against the degree of the risk? Is the mother's religion part of her "situation," so that the proper standard would be to consider the actions expected of a reasonable member of her church? In *Walker*, the court sustained the manslaughter indictment, holding (763 P.2d at 868) that "criminal negligence must be evaluated objectively" and that the controlling question was whether "a reasonable person in defendant's position would have been aware of the risk involved." Would this be the proper approach under the MPC? For discussion of the issues, see Edward Smith, Note, The Criminalization of Belief: When Free Exercise Isn't, 42 Hastings L.J. 1491 (1991).

---

11. The court explained (763 P.2d at 855 n.1):

> Members of the Church "believe that disease is a physical manifestation of errors of the mind." The use of medicine is believed to perpetuate such error and is therefore discouraged. Nonetheless, "the Church sets up no abstract criteria for determining what diseases or injuries should be treated by prayer or other methods but, rather, leaves such questions to individual decision in concrete instances. . . . If some turn in what they think is an urgent time of need to medical treatment for themselves or their children, they are *not*—contrary to some recent charges—stigmatized by their church." (Talbot, The Position of the Christian Science Church 26 New Eng. J. Med. 1641, 1642 (1983); italics in original.)

12. See Dirk Johnson, Trials for Parents Who Choose Faith Over Medicine, N.Y. Times, Jan. 21, 2009.

13. See Prince v. Massachusetts, 321 U.S. 158, 170 (1944): "Parents may be free to become martyrs themselves. But it does not follow they are free, in identical circumstances, to make martyrs of their children before they (the children) have reached the age of full and legal discretion when they can make that choice for themselves."

c. Distinguishing Murder from Manslaughter

COMMONWEALTH v. MALONE

Supreme Court of Pennsylvania
354 Pa. 180, 47 A.2d 445 (1946)

MAXEY, C.J. This is an appeal from the judgment and sentence under a conviction of murder in the second degree.[a] William H. Long, age 13 years, was killed by a shot from a 32-caliber revolver held against his right side by the defendant, then aged 17 years. These youths were on friendly terms at the time of the homicide. The defendant and his mother while his father and brother were in the U.S. Armed Forces, were residing in Lancaster, Pa., with the family of William H. Long, whose son was the victim of the shooting.

On the evening of February 26th, 1945, when the defendant went to a moving picture theater, he carried in the pocket of his raincoat a revolver which he had obtained at the home of his uncle on the preceding day. In the afternoon preceding the shooting, the decedent procured a cartridge from his father's room and he and the defendant placed it in the revolver.

After leaving the theater, the defendant went to a dairy store and there met the decedent. Both youths sat in the rear of the store ten minutes, during which period the defendant took the gun out of his pocket and loaded the chamber to the right of the firing pin and then closed the gun. A few minutes later, both youths sat on stools in front of the lunch counter and ate some food. The defendant suggested to the decedent that they play "Russian Poker."[1] Long replied, "I don't care; go ahead." The defendant then placed the revolver against the right side of Long and pulled the trigger three times. The third pull resulted in a fatal wound to Long. The latter jumped off the stool and cried: "Oh! Oh! Oh!" and Malone said: "Did I hit you, Billy? Gee, Kid, I'm sorry." Long died from the wounds two days later.

The defendant testified that the gun chamber he loaded was the first one to the right of the firing chamber and that when he pulled the trigger he did not "expect to have the gun go off." He declared he had no intention of harming Long, who was his friend and companion. The defendant was indicted for murder, tried and found guilty of murder in the second degree and sentenced to a term in the penitentiary for a period not less than five years and not exceeding ten years. A new trial was refused and after sentence was imposed, an appeal was taken.

---

a. The Pennsylvania homicide statute in effect at the time divided murder into two degrees, in accordance with the formula adopted in 1794. After classifying certain especially heinous murders as murders of the first degree, the statute provided simply that "[a]ll other kinds of murder shall be murder in the second degree." Comparable statutory language continues to define second-degree murder in many jurisdictions and what is now called "third-degree murder" in Pennsylvania. See 18 Pa. Stat. Ann. §2502(c), reproduced at page 423 supra.—EDS.

1. It has been explained that "Russian Poker" is a game in which the participants, in turn, place a single cartridge in one of the five chambers of a revolver cylinder, give the latter a quick twirl, place a muzzle of the gun against the temple and pull the trigger, leaving it to chance whether or not death results to the trigger puller.

Appellant . . . contends that the facts did not justify a conviction for any form of homicide except involuntary manslaughter. This contention we overrule. A specific intent to take life is, under our law, an essential ingredient of murder in the first degree. At common law, the "grand criterion" which "distinguished murder from other killing" was malice on the part of the killer and this malice was not necessarily "malevolent to the deceased particularly" but "any evil design in general; the dictate of a wicked, depraved and malignant heart"; 4 Blackstone 199. . . .

When an individual commits an act of gross recklessness for which he must reasonably anticipate that death to another is likely to result, he exhibits that "wickedness of disposition, hardness of heart, cruelty, recklessness of consequences, and a mind regardless of social duty" which proved that there was at that time in him "the state or frame of mind termed malice." This court has declared that if a driver "wantonly, recklessly, and in disregard of consequences" hurls "his car against another, or into a crowd" and death results from that act "he ought . . . to face the same consequences that would be meted out to him if he had accomplished death by wantonly and wickedly firing a gun": Com. v. Mayberry, 290 Pa. 195, 199, 138 A. 686, 688, citing cases from four jurisdictions. . . .

The killing of William H. Long by this defendant resulted from an act intentionally done by the latter, in reckless and wanton disregard of the consequences which were at least sixty percent certain from his thrice attempted discharge of a gun known to contain one bullet and aimed at a vital part of Long's body. This killing was, therefore, murder, for malice in the sense of a wicked disposition is evidenced by the intentional doing of an uncalled-for act in callous disregard of its likely harmful effects on others. The fact that there was no motive for this homicide does not exculpate the accused. In a trial for murder proof of motive is always relevant but never necessary. All the assignments of error are overruled and the judgment is affirmed.

NOTES

1. *The facts in* Malone. In concluding that there was a 60 percent chance of the gun's discharging, the court apparently assumed that the defendant twirled the revolver cylinder once before beginning to pull the trigger (see footnote 1 of the opinion), contrary to the implication of the defendant's testimony that he loaded the chamber to the right of the firing pin and fired without spinning the cylinder. On the court's assumption, pulling the trigger of a five-chambered gun three consecutive times creates roughly a three-out-of-five chance of the gun's discharging.[14] Some, however, might want to argue that the relevant risk is that of the gun's discharging on the third pull, which is

---

14. More technically, some might argue that if Malone had decided from the outset to pull the trigger three times, the odds of a discharge on any of those three pulls (if the gun had not fired on a previous pull) is higher than 60 percent, but the legal analysis is not affected by whether the probability of a discharge is 60 percent or instead somewhat higher.

one out of three. Which is the appropriate way to characterize the defendant's course of conduct? Would the choice affect the defendant's liability? Suppose the gun discharged on the first pull, when the chance of that happening would have been only one out of five? Would the defendant still be guilty of murder?

If, in fact, the defendant did just what he testified he did—loaded the chamber to the right of the firing pin and then fired without twirling the chamber—how is it that the gun discharged? The gun may have misfired in some fashion. Or conceivably there was more than one bullet in the gun. (Recall the testimony about how the gun was handled during the afternoon preceding the shooting.) If the court had accepted the defendant's version of the facts, would the result have been different?

2. *Definitions of unintentional murder.* Common-law formulations of the circumstances under which an unintentional killing constituted murder rather than manslaughter have been incorporated into many American statutes either directly or by reference to such common-law terms as "malice." The formulas have tended to rely primarily on colorful epithets—"the dictate of a wicked, depraved and malignant heart"; or "an abandoned and malignant heart." The *Malone* case is an example of circumstances in which the criteria have been held satisfied. Other classic examples are throwing a heavy object down upon a busy street, shooting into an occupied building, and beating a person to death. Some states have tried to give these terms an interpretation more meaningful to juries. For example, in People v. Dellinger, 49 Cal. 3d 1212, 1215, 783 P.2d 2001 (1989), the court defined malice to be implied "when the killing results from an intentional act, the natural consequences of which act was deliberately performed by a person who knows that his conduct endangers the life of another and who acts with conscious disregard for life."

Many state statutes now use formulas inspired instead by the Model Penal Code. The Code treats an unintended killing as murder when it is committed recklessly (as defined in §2.02(2)(c)) and "under circumstances manifesting extreme indifference to the value of human life." (§210.2) The Commentary explains (Model Penal Code and Commentaries, Comment to §210.2 at 21-22 (1980)):

> Under the Model Code, [the first] judgment must be made in terms of whether the actor's conscious disregard of the risk, given the circumstances of the case, so far departs from acceptable behavior that it constitutes a "gross deviation from the standard of conduct that a law-abiding person would observe in the actor's situation." Ordinary recklessness in this sense is made sufficient for a conviction of manslaughter under Section 210.3 (1)(a). In a prosecution for murder, however, the Code calls for the further judgment whether the actor's conscious disregard of the risk, under the circumstances, manifests extreme indifference to the value of human life. The significance of purpose or knowledge as a standard of culpability is that, cases of provocation or other mitigation apart, purposeful or knowing homicide demonstrates precisely such indifference to the value of human life. Whether recklessness is so extreme that it demonstrates similar indifference is not a question, it is submitted, that can be further clarified. It must be left directly to the trier of fact under

instructions which make it clear that recklessness that can fairly be assimilated to purpose or knowledge should be treated as murder and that less extreme recklessness should be punished as manslaughter.

Insofar as Subsection (1)(b) includes within the murder category cases of homicide caused by extreme recklessness, though without purpose to kill, it reflects both the common law and much pre-existing statutory treatment usually cast in terms of conduct evidencing a "depraved heart regardless of human life" or some similar words.

3. Distinguishing manslaughter from unintentional murder. The common law and statutes derived from it distinguished between manslaughter and unintentional murder based on how wicked and depraved the killing seemed to be. That approach, of course, remits the issue to subjective judgment calls of the judge or jury. The MPC formula, requiring recklessness—"in circumstances manifesting extreme indifference to the value of human life"— omits the vituperative common-law language, but does it make the call less subjective? Several scholars have tried to do better. See Alan C. Michaels, Defining Unintended Murder, 85 Colum. L. Rev. 786 (1985); Kyron Huigens, Homicide in Aretaic Terms, 6 Buff. L. Rev. 97 (2002).

Courts applying the MPC approach have had a hard time with these issues. The New York murder statute roughly follows the MPC language, only substituting "depraved indifference" for "extreme indifference." The New York Court of Appeals has held that "depraved indifference" requires a finding of "utter depravity, uncommon brutality and inhuman cruelty." People v. Taylor, 939 N.E.2d 1206, 1209 (N.Y. 2010). Consider how this standard should be applied to these cases:

(a) In *Taylor*, supra, after the defendant and his female neighbor had smoked crack together, she attacked him, and he hit her on the head to defend himself. Later, he covered her head with a tightly knotted plastic bag (allegedly to stop the blood from spreading) and carried her to the roof of his building, where she was found dead the next morning. The court of appeals, stressing that "the People did not establish 'torture or a brutal, prolonged' course of conduct," held that the evidence was legally insufficient to establish the depravity required to establish second-degree murder rather than manslaughter. Id. Do you agree?

(b) In People v. Prindle, 944 N.E.2d 1130 (N.Y. 2011), the defendant, after stealing a snowplow blade, led pursuing police officers on a high-speed chase through the streets of Rochester, N.Y., running five red lights and repeatedly driving into the lanes of oncoming traffic before colliding with another vehicle and killing its driver. Dividing 4–3, the court set aside a conviction for depraved indifference murder, finding the evidence sufficient only to establish reckless manslaughter. The dissenting judges insisted that the defendant's conduct was " 'so deficient in a moral sense of concern, so devoid of regard of the live or lives of others . . . ' as to render defendant as culpable as one whose conscious objective was to kill." Id. at 1134.

4. Murder by omission. We have seen that the death of an infant through its parents' neglect may constitute manslaughter. *State v. Williams*, page 472 supra. May such neglect constitute murder? A California court upheld a second-degree murder conviction of a father for his conscious and callous failure to feed his child resulting in death through malnutrition and dehydration. The evidence showed that the father was aware during the last two weeks of the baby's life that it was starving to death, that he did not remember anyone's having fed the baby in that period, and that he himself did nothing to feed the baby, because he "just didn't care." The court stated: "The omission of a duty is in law the equivalent of an act and when death results, the standard for determination of the degree of homicide is identical." People v. Burden, 72 Cal. App. 3d 603, 616 (1977). In accord, see Simpkins v. State, 596 A.2d 655 (Md. App. 1991).

UNITED STATES v. FLEMING

United States Court of Appeals, 4th Circuit
739 F.2d 945 (1984)

WINTER, C.J.: [Defendant was convicted of second-degree murder in the death of Margaret Haley. At about 3:00 P.M., he was driving southbound on the George Washington Memorial Parkway, a park within federal jurisdiction, at speeds between 70 and 100 miles per hour (m.p.h.), in zones where the speed limit was 45 m.p.h. Several times he drove into the northbound lanes in order to avoid traffic congestion in the southbound lanes. Northbound traffic had to move out of his way in order to avoid a head-on collision. Approximately six miles from where his car was first observed traveling at excessive speed, Fleming lost control and struck the car driven by Mrs. Haley that was coming in the opposite direction. His car was estimated to be traveling 70 to 80 m.p.h. at the moment of impact, in a zone where the speed limit was 30 m.p.h. Mrs. Haley received multiple severe injuries and died before she could be extricated from her car.]

Fleming was pulled from the wreckage of his car and transported to a Washington hospital for treatment. His blood alcohol level was there tested at .315 percent. [He] was indicted by a grand jury on a charge of second-degree murder, . . . tried before a jury and convicted.

Defendant maintains that the facts of the case cannot support a verdict of murder. Particularly, defendant contends that the facts are inadequate to establish the existence of malice aforethought, and thus that he should have been convicted of manslaughter at most.

Malice aforethought, as provided in 18 U.S.C. §1111(a),[a] is the distinguishing characteristic which, when present, makes a homicide murder rather than

---

a. 18 U.S.C. §1111 (a) provides: "Murder is the unlawful killing of a human being with malice aforethought. Every murder perpetrated by poison, lying in wait, or any other kind of willful, deliberate, malicious, and premeditated killing; or committed in the perpetration of [designated felonies] is murder in the first degree. Any other murder is murder in the second degree."—EDS.

manslaughter. . . . Proof of the existence of malice . . . may be established by evidence of conduct which is "reckless and wanton and a gross deviation from a reasonable standard of care, of such a nature that a jury is warranted in inferring that defendant was aware of a serious risk of death or serious bodily harm." To support a conviction for murder, the government need only have proved that defendant intended to operate his car in the manner in which he did with a heart that was without regard for the life and safety of others.[3]

We conclude that the evidence regarding defendant's conduct was adequate to sustain a finding by the jury that defendant acted with malice aforethought. . . .

The difference between malice, which will support conviction for murder, and gross negligence, which will permit of conviction only for manslaughter, is one of degree rather than kind. In the present case, . . . the facts show a deviation from established standards of regard for life and the safety of others that is markedly different in degree from that found in most vehicular homicides. In the average drunk driving homicide, there is no proof that the driver has acted while intoxicated with the purpose of wantonly and intentionally putting the lives of others in danger. Rather, his driving abilities were so impaired that he recklessly put others in danger simply by being on the road and attempting to do the things that any driver would do. In the present case, however, . . . defendant drove in a manner that could be taken to indicate depraved disregard of human life, particularly in light of the fact that because he was drunk his reckless behavior was all the more dangerous. . . .

Affirmed.

NOTES AND QUESTIONS

1. Murder by drunk driving. In accord with *Fleming*, the great majority of American courts hold that egregiously dangerous driving can support a conviction of murder. See David Luria, Death on the Highway: Reckless Driving as Murder, 67 Or. L. Rev. 799 (1988). Usually the theory is that the defendant had an actual awareness of a great risk of fatal harm. See, e.g., Pears v. State, 672 P.2d 903 (Alaska Ct. App. 1983). Despite warnings by two police officers and by a companion that he was too drunk to drive, the defendant returned to his truck and drove at high speed through several stop signs and red lights until he collided with a car at an intersection. Two people in the car were killed. The appellate court affirmed a murder conviction,

---

3. We note that, even assuming that subjective awareness of the risk is required to establish murder where the killing resulted from reckless conduct, an exception to the requirement of subjective awareness of risk is made where lack of such awareness is attributable solely to voluntary drunkenness. See, e.g., Model Penal Code §2.08(2) ("When recklessness establishes an element of the offense, if the actor, due to self-induced intoxication, is unaware of a risk of which he would have been aware head he been sober, such unawareness is immaterial.") Defendant's state of voluntary intoxication thus would not have been relevant to whether the jury could have inferred from the circumstances of the crime that he was aware of the risk created by his conduct.

holding that the statutory requirement of "extreme indifference to the value of human life" was satisfied because the warnings Pears had received made him "abundantly aware of the dangerous nature of his driving . . ." (672 P.2d at 910), and his actions therefore were not merely inadvertent.

Compare People v. Watson, 637 P.2d 279 (Cal. 1981), where again a drunk driver was convicted of murder. Here the court found sufficient evidence of an actual awareness of the danger merely because the defendant "had driven his car to the establishment where he had been drinking, and he must have known that he would have to drive it later. It also may be presumed that defendant was aware of the hazards of driving while intoxicated." 637 P.2d at 285-286. A dissent observed (id. at 288):

> The act of speeding through a green light at 55 or 60 miles per hour in a 35-mile-per-hour zone was dangerous, but was not an act likely to result in the death of another. It was 1 o'clock in the morning. The person whose car respondent nearly collided with testified that he saw no other cars around. . . .
>
> The fact that respondent was under the influence of alcohol made his driving more dangerous. . . . No one holds a brief for this type of activity. However, [d]eath or injury is not the probable result of driving while under the influence of alcohol. "Thousands, perhaps hundreds of thousands, of Californians each week reach home without accident despite their driving intoxicated." [T]he majority's reasoning [could] be used to establish second-degree murder in every case in which a person drives a car to a bar, a friend's home, or a party, drinks alcohol so that he is under its influence, drives away and is involved in a fatal accident.

Questions: Nearly everyone knows (is "consciously aware") that the risks of a serious collision are greater when driving while intoxicated than when driving in the same way while sober. Should that mean that whenever a drunk driver causes a fatal accident, he should be guilty of murder? If not, should the kind of egregiously bad driving illustrated by Fleming be necessary, or does that sort of requirement set the bar too high? See James Jacobs, Drunk Driving: An American Dilemma 87-88 (1989); Douglas Husak, Is Drunk Driving a Serious Offense? 23 Phil. & Pub. Aff. 52 (1994).

2. The Model Penal Code and inadvertent murder. Under §210.2(1)(b), murder requires proof that the defendant acted "recklessly under circumstances manifesting extreme indifference to the value of human life." According to the official Comment (Model Penal Code and Commentaries, Comment to §210.2 at 27-28 (1980)):

> The Model Penal Code provision makes clear that inadvertent risk creation, however extravagant and unjustified, cannot be punished as murder. . . . This result is consistent with the general conception of the Model Code that serious felony sanctions should be grounded securely in the subjective culpability of the actor. To the extent that inadvertent risk creation, or negligence, should be recognized as a form of criminal homicide, that question should be faced separately from the offense of murder. . . . At least it seems clear that negligent

homicide should not be assimilated to the most serious forms of criminal homicide catalogued under the offense of murder.

Despite this strong position, the Model Penal Code provides in §2.08(2) (as we saw in footnote 3 of the *Fleming* case) that recklessness *need not* be shown if the defendant was unaware of the risk because of voluntary intoxication. This approach appears inconsistent with the quoted commentary, since it makes negligence (in drinking before driving) a sufficient mens rea for murder. Knowledge that drinking impairs driving ability is widely disseminated, of course. All the same, some drivers believe that they can drive safely while drunk. These people are of course grossly negligent, but are they reckless under the Code's definition of that term? And even if they are, have they "manifest[ed] extreme indifference to the value of human life"?

Consider State v. Dufield, 549 A.2d 1205 (N.H. 1988). The defendant was convicted of reckless murder of a woman on whom he had inflicted brutal injuries in the course of a drunken sexual orgy. The New Hampshire reckless murder statute used the same language as the MPC, and also excluded voluntary intoxication as a basis for claiming a lack of awareness. On appeal, the defendant argued that even though his intoxication was immaterial on the issue of recklessness, it was relevant to the extreme indifference required for murder. Hence, he argued, the trial court erred in refusing to recognize his defense. Justice David Souter, then a state judge writing for the New Hampshire Supreme Court, outlined the possible lines of statutory interpretation (549 A.2d at 1206-1207):

> If, on the one hand, proof of "circumstances manifesting extreme indifference" required evidence from which a finder of fact would be able to infer a subjective state of indifference, . . . then the defendant might plausibly argue that voluntary intoxication would be relevant to proof of that mental state. On this view, "indifference" would be regarded as an element of an offense comparable to a knowing or purposeful state of mind, which must be shown to have occurred with specific reference to the times and facts to which it relates.
>
> On the other hand, it could be that the function of proving the existence of "circumstances manifesting extreme indifference" is to establish, not a subjective state of mind, but a degree of divergence from the norm of acceptable behavior even greater than the "gross deviation" from the law-abiding norm, by which reckless conduct is defined. On this view, the words in question would describe a way of objectively measuring such a deviation, in which case any voluntary intoxication that might have blinded a defendant to the risks of such extreme deviant behavior would be [irrelevant].

The court chose the latter interpretation and affirmed the conviction. Do you agree? Is the holding consistent with the rationale of the "extreme indifference" requirement, as explained in the MPC Commentary, page 488 supra?

3. *Intent to inflict great bodily harm.* Evidence that a defendant intended to inflict serious injury obviously provides some indication that he recklessly created a risk of death. Such evidence undoubtedly can be considered in deciding whether the defendant did harbor that sort of recklessness. But the common law went further, by giving such facts independent substantive significance. The malice required for murder was established by the defendant's intent to inflict great bodily harm. This intent-to-inflict-grievous-harm formula is followed in many American jurisdictions. See Wayne R. LaFave, Criminal Law 737 (4th ed. 2003). In some states, the doctrine survives as a consequence of statutes retaining the common-law definition of murder (that is, a killing with "malice aforethought"). In a few states, homicide statutes adopt the "great bodily harm" formula explicitly, for example, 720 Ill. Comp. Ann. Stat. §5/9-1(a) (2011).

What is the justification for treating an intent to inflict grievous harm as independently sufficient to support a murder conviction when death happens to result? The MPC omitted the doctrine on the ground that recklessness manifesting extreme indifference to the value of human life captures all the nonintentional homicides that should be elevated to murder. Comment to §210.2 at 28 (1980). Does it?

2. The Felony-Murder Rule

a. The Basic Doctrine

REGINA v. SERNÉ

Central Criminal Court
16 Cox Crim. Cas. 311 (1887)

The prisoners Leon Serné and John Henry Goldfinch were indicted for the murder of a boy, Sjaak Serné, the son of the prisoner Leon Serné, it being alleged that they wilfully set on fire a house and shop, No. 274 Strand, London, by which act the death of the boy had been caused.

It appeared that the prisoner Serné with his wife, two daughters, and two sons were living at the house in question; and that Serné, at the time he was living there, in Midsummer, 1887, was in a state of pecuniary embarrassment, and had put into the premises furniture and other goods of but very little value, which at the time of the fire were not of greater value than £30. It also appeared that previously to the fire the prisoner Serné had insured the life of the boy Sjaak Serné, who was imbecile, and on the first day of September, 1887, had insured his stock at 274 Strand, for £500, his furniture for £100, and his rent for another £100; and that on the 17th of the same month the premises were burnt down.

Evidence was given on behalf of the prosecution that fires were seen breaking out in several parts of the premises at the same time, soon after the prisoners had been seen in the shop together, two fires being in the lower part of the house and two above, on the floor whence escape could be made on the roof of the adjoining house, and in which part were the prisoners, and the wife, and two daughters of Serné, who escaped. That on the premises were a quantity of tissue transparencies for advertising purposes, which were of a most inflammable character; and that on the site of one of the fires was found a great quantity of these transparencies close to other inflammable materials. That the prisoner Serné, his wife and daughters, were rescued from the roof of the adjoining house, the other prisoner being rescued from a window in the front of the house, but that the boys were burnt to death, the body of the one being found on the floor near the window from which the prisoner Serné, his wife, and daughters had escaped, the body of the other being found at the basement of the premises.

STEPHEN, J. Gentlemen, it is now my duty to direct your attention to the law and the facts into which you have to inquire. The two prisoners are indicted for the wilful murder of the boy Sjaak Serné, a lad of about fourteen years of age; . . . The definition of murder is unlawful homicide with malice afore-thought, and the words malice aforethought are technical. You must not, therefore, construe them or suppose that they can be construed by ordinary rules of language. The words have to be construed according to a long series of decided cases, which have given them meanings different from those which might be supposed. One of those meanings is, the killing of another person by an act done with an intent to commit a felony. Another meaning is, an act done with the knowledge that the act will probably cause the death of some person. Now it is such an act as the last which is alleged to have been done in this case; and if you think that either or both of these men in the dock killed this boy, either by an act done with intent to commit a felony, that is to say, the setting of the house on fire in order to cheat the insurance company, or by conduct which to their knowledge was likely to cause death and was therefore emi-nently dangerous in itself—in either of these cases the prisoners are guilty of wilful murder in the plain meaning of the word.

I will say a word or two upon one part of this definition, because it is capable of being applied very harshly in certain cases, and also because, though I take the law as I find it, I very much doubt whether the definition which I have given, although it is the common definition, is not somewhat too wide. Now when it is said that murder means killing a man by an act done in the commission of a felony, the mere words cover a case like this, that is to say, a case where a man gives another a push with an intention of stealing his watch, and the person so pushed, having a weak heart or some other internal disorder, dies. To take another very old illustration, it was said that if a man shot a fowl with intent to steal it and accidentally killed a man, he was to be accounted guilty of murder, because the act was done in the commission of a felony.[a] I very much doubt, however, whether that is really the law, or

---

a. Edward Coke, Institutes 56 (1644): "If the act be unlawful it is murder. As if *A* meaning to steale a deer in the park of *B*, shooteth at the deer, and by the glance of the arrow killeth a boy that is hidden in a bush; this is murder, for that the act was unlawful, although *A* had no intent to hurt the boy, nor knew not of him. But if *B* the owner of the park has shot at his own deer, and without any ill intent had killed the boy by the glance of his arrow, this had been homicide by misadventure, and no felony. So if one shoot at any wild fowle upon a tree, and the arrow killeth any reasonable creature afar off, without any evill intent in him, this is per infortunium: for it was not unlawful to shoot at the wilde fowle: but if he had shot at a cock or hen, or any tame fowle of another mans, and the arrow by mischance had killed a man, this had been murder, for the act was unlawfull."—EDS.

whether the Court for the Consideration of Crown Cases Reserved would hold it to be so.

The present case, however, is not such as I have cited, nor anything like them. In my opinion the definition of the law which makes it murder to kill by an act done in the commission of a felony might and ought to be narrowed, while that part of the law under which the Crown in this case claim to have proved a case of murder is maintained. I think that, instead of saying that any act done with intent to commit a felony and which causes death amounts to murder, it would be reasonable to say that any act known to be dangerous to life and likely in itself to cause death, done for the purpose of committing a felony which causes death, should be murder. As an illustration of this, suppose that a man, intending to commit a rape upon a woman, but without the least wish to kill her, squeezed her by the throat to overpower her, and in so doing killed her, that would be murder. I think that every one would say in a case like that, that when a person began doing wicked acts for his own base purposes, he risked his own life as well as that of others. That kind of crime does not differ in any serious degree from one committed by using a deadly weapon, such as a bludgeon, a pistol, or a knife. If a man once begins attacking the human body in such a way, he must take the consequences if he goes further than he intended when he began. That I take to be the true meaning of the law in the subject.

In the present case, gentlemen, you have a man sleeping in a house with his wife, his two daughters, his two sons, and a servant, and you are asked to believe that this man, with all these people under his protection, deliberately set fire to the house in three or four different places and thereby burnt two of them to death. It is alleged that he arranged matters in such a way that any person of the most common intelligence must have known perfectly well that he was placing all those people in deadly risk. It appears to me that if that were really done, it matters very little indeed whether the prisoners hoped the people would escape or whether they did not. If a person chose, for some wicked purpose of his own to sink a boat at sea, and thereby caused the deaths of the occupants, it matters nothing whether at the time of committing the act he hoped that the people would be picked up by a passing vessel. He is as much guilty of murder if the people are drowned, as if he had flung every person into the water with his own hand. Therefore, gentlemen, if Serné and Goldfinch set fire to this house when the family were in it, and if the boys were by that act stifled or burnt to death, then the prisoners are as much guilty of murder as if they had stabbed the children. I will also add, for my own part, that I think, in so saying, the law of England lays down a rule of broad, plain common-sense. . . .

There was a case tried in this court which you will no doubt remember, and which will illustrate my meaning. [A] man named Barrett was charged with causing the death of several persons by an explosion which was intended to release one or two men from custody; and I am sure that no one can say truly that Barrett was not justly hanged. With regard to the facts in the present case, the very horror of the crime, if crime it was, the abomination of it, is a reason for your taking the most extreme care in the case, and for not imputing to the prisoners anything which is not clearly proved. God forbid that I should, by what I say, produce on your minds, even in the smallest degree any feeling against the prisoners. You must see, gentlemen, that the evidence leaves no reasonable doubt upon your minds; but you will fail in the performance of your duty if, being satisfied with the evidence, you do not convict one or both the prisoners of wilful murder, and it is wilful murder of which they are accused.

[Verdict, not guilty.]

People v. Stamp, 2 Cal. App. 3d 203, 82 Cal. Rptr. 598 (1969): [Defendant burglarized the business premises of one Carl Honeyman and robbed him at gunpoint. During the robbery, Honeyman had been led from his office by the elbow and required to lie on the floor for about ten minutes, until the defendant had fled. Shortly thereafter, Honeyman began suffering chest pains, collapsed, and died of a heart attack. He was described as "an obese 60-year-old man, with a history of heart disease, who was under a great deal of pressure due to the intensely competitive nature of his business. Additionally, he did not take good care of his heart." Doctors testified that "[t]he fright induced by the robbery was too much of a shock to Honeyman's system." Defendant's conviction of first-degree murder was upheld. The court stated:] The [felony-murder] doctrine is not limited to those deaths which are foreseeable. Rather a felon is held strictly liable for all killings committed by him or his accomplices in the course of the felony. As long as the homicide is the direct causal result of the robbery the felony-murder rule applies whether or not the death was a natural or probable consequence of the robbery. So long as a victim's predisposing physical condition, regardless of its cause, is not the only substantial factor bringing about his death, that condition and the robber's ignorance of it, in no way destroys the robber's criminal responsibility for the death. So long as life is shortened as a result of the felonious act it does not matter that the victim might have died soon anyway. In this respect, the robber takes his victim as he finds him.

NOTES ON THE SCOPE OF THE FELONY-MURDER RULE

1. Strict liability? Is the result in *Stamp* consistent with Judge Stephen's understanding of the felony-murder rule, as he explains it in *Serné*? Judge Stephen presented a hypothetical very similar to the facts of *Stamp*: One man pushes another, intending to steal his watch, and the man who was pushed then dies of a heart attack. Judge Stephen assumed that the felony-murder rule did not apply to purely accidental killings, and that the English courts of his day therefore would not find felony murder on such facts.

Unlike Judge Stephen, some early English commentators stated that the felony-murder rule did apply in this situation. See, for example, the hypothetical in Edward Coke's Institutes, footnote a, supra page 491. But one close examination of the history concludes that every common-law felony-murder case required at least some element of fault for the killing, in addition to the fault involved in committing the accompanying felony. See Guyora Binder, The Origin of American Felony-Murder Rules, 57 Stan. L. Rev. 59 (2004).

In the United States, in any event, that qualification was lost, and courts adopted a broad, unqualified felony-murder rule, believing that it was part of the English common law at the time of American independence. Thus, the *Stamp* case illustrates the view generally accepted in American courts—that the felony-murder rule imposes *strict liablilty* for killings that result from the commission of a felony, regardless of whether the felons knew or should have known that their conduct was endangering life.

2. Sentencing consequences. Whatever its reach, the original common-law felony-murder rule seldom made much practical difference, because very few criminal offenses were considered felonies, and all felonies were punishable by death, even when no victim of the offense had been killed. The principal use of the felony-murder rule was to permit capital punishment when death resulted from an unsuccessful *attempt* to commit a felony, because the unsuccessful attempt by itself was only a misdemeanor at common law. See Model Penal Code and Commentaries, Comment to §210.2, pp. 30-32 (1980). Today, of course, legislatures have enacted a long list of statutory felonies, many of them nonviolent. And even for the most serious felonies, authorized sanctions generally are much lower than those applicable to murder. Transposed into the modern context, therefore, the felony-murder rule can produce a dramatic increase in the applicable punishment.

3. The causation requirement. Although the traditional felony-murder rule eliminates the mens rea requirement of murder, it does not dispense with the actus reus and causation requirements. Hence, it must be shown, as in all murder cases, that the defendant's conduct "caused" a person's death. As we shall see when we reach the material on causation, starting at page 571 infra, a common formulation of this requirement is that (1) "but for" the felony, the death would not have occurred, and (2) the result must have been the natural and probable consequence of the defendant's action, or that it must have been foreseeable. Underlying the second prong of this formula is the perception that the result must be fairly attributable to the defendant's action, rather than to mere coincidence or to the intervening action of another.

For example, in King v. Commonwealth, 368 S.E.2d 704 (Va. Ct. App. 1988), defendant King and his copilot were transporting 500 pounds of marijuana in a light plane when they became lost in fog and crashed into a mountainside. King survived the crash, but his copilot did not, and as a result King was convicted of felony murder. The appellate court reversed, holding that the drug-distribution crime was not the proximate cause of the death. Although the "but for" requirement was met (the crash would not have occurred but for the commission of the felony), the crash was not a *foreseeable* result of the felony because it was not made more likely by the fact that the plane's cargo was contraband. The court noted that, in contrast, a finding of proximate causation might have been possible if the crash had resulted from flying the plane at low altitude to avoid detection.

NOTES ON THE RATIONALE OF THE FELONY-MURDER RULE

We have previously examined the proposition sometimes asserted that the mens rea of a lesser offense may substitute for the mens rea of a greater offense. Reconsider *People v. Olsen*, page 272 supra. That proposition is now rejected in England and in many American jurisdictions. Yet precisely that proposition serves as the basis of liability in felony murder. Does it have any greater justification in homicidal offenses than in other crimes? If the law is sound in requiring a particular mens rea to establish murder, is it, by definition, unsound to require less solely because the actor is guilty of another crime? The offense accompanying the killing has its own punishment. In what sense does that offense also make a crime of an otherwise noncriminal killing or justify more severe punishment for a killing that would otherwise deserve a lower sentence?

Professor Guyora Binder argues (The Culpability of Felony Murder, 83 Notre Dame L. Rev. 965, 967 (2008)) that a person who negligently kills in the course of committing another felony can justifiably be punished for murder, not just negligent homicide, because "the felon's additional depraved purpose aggravates his culpability for causing death carelessly." A related argument is developed in Kenneth W. Simons, When Is Strict Criminal Liability Just?, 87 J. Crim. L. & Criminology 1075, 1121-1125 (1997):

> [L]et us assume [an armed robber] recklessly caused death. So his punishment for felony murder can be at least as severe as the combined punishment that retributive principles permit for the felony and for reckless homicide. But can the punishment be more? I believe that it can, insofar as knowingly creating a risk of death in the context of another criminal act is more culpable behavior than knowingly creating a risk of death in the context of an innocent or less culpable act. . . .
>
> Now consider a . . . case [where] the foreseeability of death resulting from a particular felony is just below the threshold that we require for negligent homicide. For example, consider an unarmed bank robbery in which the risk of death (from a guard or police officer) is real but not sufficient to surpass that threshold. Should we conclude that the bank robber has displayed no culpability as to the risk of death . . . ?
>
> [That conclusion would rest] on too narrow a conception of negligence. . . . To express genuine differentials in retributive blame, we should take a more subtle, holistic view of negligence. . . . [T]he unarmed bank robber . . . can properly be found negligent as to the risk of death even if the foreseeable risk of harm is less than would be required to find him negligent had he been engaged in an innocent or less culpable activity.

In assessing Professor Simon's argument, note that creating a substantial risk of death may or may not be culpable, depending on whether the risk can be *justified*; and the desire to commit a felony obviously cannot justify taking such a risk. Does the wrongness of the accompanying felony aggravate the culpability of the risky action in some additional way?

Consider, in addition, the following observations concerning the felony-murder rule:

1. People v. Washington, 62 Cal. 2d 777, 402 P.2d 130, 133 (1965): The purpose of the felony-murder rule is to deter felons from killing negligently or accidentally by holding them strictly responsible for killings they commit.

2. T.B. Macaulay, A Penal Code Prepared by the Indian Law Commissioners, Note M, 64-65 (1838): It will be admitted that, when an act is in itself innocent, to punish the person who does it because bad consequences which no human wisdom could have foreseen have followed from it would be in the highest degree barbarous and absurd. [T]o pronounce [that person] guilty of one offence because a misfortune befell him while he was committing another offence . . . is surely to confound all the boundaries of crime. . . .

[That] is a course which evidently adds nothing to the security of human life. No man can so conduct himself as to make it absolutely certain that he shall not be so unfortunate as to cause the death of a fellow creature. The utmost that he can do is to abstain from everything which is at all likely to cause death. No fear of punishment can make him do more than this. . . . The only good effect which such punishment can produce will be to deter people from committing any of those offences which turn into murders what are in themselves mere accidents. It is in fact an addition to the punishment of those offences, and it is an addition in the very worst way. For example, hundreds of persons in some great cities are in the habit of picking pockets. They know that they are guilty of a great offence. But it has never occurred to one of them, nor would it occur to any rational man, that they are guilty of an offence which endangers life. Unhappily one of these hundreds attempts to take the purse of a gentleman who has a loaded pistol in his pocket. The thief touches the trigger: the pistol goes off: the gentleman is shot dead. To treat the case of this pick-pocket differently from that of the numerous pick-pockets who steal under exactly the same circumstances, with exactly the same intentions, with no less risk of causing death, with no greater care to avoid causing death,—to send them to the house of correction as thieves, and him to the gallows as a murderer,—appears to us an unreasonable course. If the punishment for stealing from a person be too light, let it be increased, and let the increase fall alike on all the offenders. Surely the worst mode of increasing the punishment of an offence is to provide that, besides the ordinary punishment, every offender shall run an exceedingly small risk of being hanged. The more nearly the amount of punishment can be reduced to a certainty the better. But if chance is to be admitted there are better ways of admitting it. It would be a less capricious, and therefore a more salutary course, to provide that every fiftieth or every hundredth thief selected by lot should be hanged, than to provide that every thief should be hanged who, while engaged in stealing, should meet with an unforeseen misfortune such as might have befallen the most virtuous man while performing the most virtuous action.

3. George P. Fletcher, Reflections on Felony-Murder, 12 Sw. U. L. Rev. 413, 427 (1981): [One] unrefined mode of thought behind the [felony-murder] rule begins not with the deadly outcome, but with the felonious background. That someone engages in a felony lowers the threshold of moral responsibility for the resulting death. If there is a principle behind this way of thinking, it is that a wrongdoer must run the risk that things will turn out worse than she expects. The same principle has motivated common law courts and legislatures to reject the claim of mistake in cases of abducting infants, statutory rape, and assaulting a police officer. If the act is wrong, even as the defendant conceives the facts to be, then she presumably has no grounds for complaining if the facts turn out to be worse than she expects. . . .

[This mode of thought violates] a basic principle of just punishment. Punishment must be proportional to wrongdoing. When the felony-murder rule converts an accidental death into first-degree murder, then punishment is rendered disproportionate to the wrong for which the offender is personally responsible. [T]he principle that the wrongdoer must run the risk explicitly obscures the question of actual responsibility for the harmful result.

4. James J. Tomkovicz, The Endurance of the Felony-Murder Rule, 51 Wash. & Lee L. Rev. 1429, 1448-1449 (1994): The primary justification offered for the contemporary felony-murder rule is deterrence. . . . One deterrent argument holds that the threat of a murder conviction for any killing in furtherance of a felony, even an accidental killing, might well induce a felon to forego committing the felony itself. . . . Another argument . . . maintains that the rule is aimed at discouraging certain conduct during the felony, not the felony itself. The goal is to encourage greater care in the performance of felonious acts. . . . Still another view suggests that felons who might kill intentionally in order to complete their felonies successfully will be discouraged . . . because of their awareness that the chance of constructing a defense that would eliminate or mitigate liability is virtually nonexistent and that, therefore, their likely fate is a murder conviction. . . .

The problem with the modern felony-murder doctrine is not only that it seeks practical goals by prescribing severe punishments without proof of fault, but that it does so on the basis of unproven and highly questionable assumptions. . . . The number of killings during felonies is relatively low. The subset of such killings that are nonculpable—thus not already subject to the threat of a substantial sanction—is undoubtedly considerably smaller. . . . Moreover, some who are aware of and even sensitive to the threatened sanction will probably still kill negligently or accidentally.

Admittedly, it would be difficult, if not impossible, to prove that the felony-murder rule does not annually save a considerable number of lives. Nonetheless, in a world in which the evidence is uncertain (or nonexistent) and in which it seems unlikely that felons actually hear the rule's deterrent message in the ways that courts presume that they do, common sense would suggest putting the burden of proof upon those who contend that deterrent gains are sufficient to outweigh the infringement of our fundamental philosophy of fault and punishment. . . . Without a credible foundation in established facts, deterrence is not a real justification, but is instead a poor excuse for our infidelity [to fundamental principles of culpability].

5. Model Penal Code and Commentaries, Comment to §210.2 at 37-39 (1980): [The American Law Institute recommended eliminating the felony-murder rule. However, it provided that for the purpose of establishing murder by an act "committed recklessly under circumstances manifesting extreme indifference to the value of human life," the fact that the actor is "engaged, or is an accomplice in the commission of, or an attempt to commit, or flight after committing or attempting to commit robbery, rape or deviate sexual intercourse by force or threat of force, arson, burglary, kidnapping or felonious escape" creates a rebuttable presumption (defined in §1.12(5)) that the required indifference and recklessness existed.

[In support of this proposal, the Comment states:] Principled argument in favor of the felony-murder doctrine is hard to find. The defense reduces to the explanation that Holmes gave for finding the law "intelligible as it stands":

> [I]f experience shows, or is deemed by the law-maker to show, that somehow or other deaths which the evidence makes accidental happen disproportionately often in connection with other felonies, or with resistance to officers, or if on any other ground of policy it is deemed desirable to make special efforts for the prevention of such deaths, the law-maker may consistently treat acts which, under the known circumstances, are felonious, or constitute resistance to officers, as having a sufficiently dangerous tendency to be put under a special ban. The law may, therefore, throw on the actor the peril, not only of the consequences foreseen by him, but also of consequences which, although not predicted by common experience, the legislator apprehends.[95]

The answer to such arguments is twofold. First, there is no basis in experience for thinking that homicides which the evidence makes accidental occur with disproportionate frequency in connection with specified felonies.[a]

---

95. O. Holmes, The Common Law 49 (1881).

a. In a footnote at this point the MPC Comment reports on a Philadelphia study showing that, out of 6,432 robberies, just 38 were fatal; out of 1,113 rapes, just 4 were fatal; and out of 27,669 burglaries, just one was fatal. Although the relatively low numbers arguably understate the fatality risk from these felonies, another objection to this argument accepts the validity of the data but draws a different conclusion. Professor Kevin Cole observes (Killings During Crime, 28 Am. Crim. L. Rev. 73, 105 (1990)):

> [O]nly about 0.6 percent of all armed robberies end in death. But just because this rate is lower than we might have thought does not mean that robberies are safe relative to the normal range of human activities. . . . If the average robbery takes an hour (probably an [over]estimate), that means one homicide occurs every 166 hours of robbery. If everyday activities were as dangerous as robbery, and if the average person is awake 16 hours a day, then the average person would kill one person every eleven days.

—EDS.

Second, it remains indefensible in principle to use the sanctions that the law employs to deal with murder unless there is at least a finding that the actor's conduct manifested an extreme indifference to the value of human life. The fact that the actor was engaged in a crime of the kind that is included in the usual first-degree felony-murder enumeration or was an accomplice in such crime, as has been observed, will frequently justify such a finding. Indeed, the probability that such a finding will be justified seems high enough to warrant the presumption of extreme indifference that Subsection (1)(b) creates. But liability depends, as plainly it should, upon the crucial finding. The result may not differ often under such a formulation from that which would be reached under some form of the felony-murder rule. But what is more important is that a conviction on this basis rests solidly upon principle.

NOTES ON THE MISDEMEANOR-MANSLAUGHTER RULE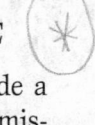

1. The basic doctrine. Just as a felony resulting in death can provide a basis for a murder conviction without proof of malice, in many states a misdemeanor resulting in death can provide a basis for an involuntary manslaughter conviction without proof of recklessness or negligence. The misdemeanor-manslaughter rule, also known as the unlawful-act doctrine, was reflected in the traditional common-law definition of involuntary manslaughter. The language of Cal. Penal Code §192(b), drawn from William Blackstone's formulation, is typical: Involuntary manslaughter is a killing "in the commission of an unlawful act, not amounting to a felony; or in the commission of a lawful act which might produce death, in an unlawful manner, or without due caution and circumspection."

In states that retain the traditional common-law formula, the prosecution thus has two theories available to establish involuntary manslaughter. Under the first theory, if a defendant, after driving through a red light, has killed a pedestrian, the prosecution can argue for involuntary manslaughter on the basis that the defendant's conduct amounted to criminal negligence under the circumstances. See page 464 supra. Under the second theory, however, in states that recognize the unlawful-act doctrine, the prosecution need only show that the defendant's unlawful act caused the death; proof of criminal negligence becomes unnecessary. See State v. Hupf, 101 A.2d 355 (Del. 1953).

2. Limitations on the unlawful-act doctrine. In states that retain the unlawful-act doctrine, some of its harshest effects have been moderated by a variety of limitations. Most of these limitations are similar to the ones that apply to the felony-murder rule.

(a) Proximate cause. In Commonwealth v. Williams, 133 Pa. Super. 104, 1 A.2d 812 (1938), the defendant had been convicted of manslaughter by vehicle on the basis of his unlawful act of failing to renew his driver's license. The court reversed, holding that the expiration of the license had no causal connection to the accident, which had resulted from the carelessness of another driver.

(b) Regulatory offenses. Some courts restrict the unlawful-act doctrine to malum in se as opposed to malum prohibitum misdemeanors. E.g., People v. Holtschlag, 684 N.W.2d 730, 740 (Mich. 2004).

(c) Dangerousness. Another approach is to limit the doctrine to misdemeanors that rise to the level of criminal negligence (State v. Green, 647 S.W.2d 736, 746 (W. Va. 2007)), or to violations that "evince a marked disregard for the safety of others" (State v. Lingman, 91 P.2d 457 (Utah 1939)).

NOTES ON STATUTORY REFORM

England abolished all versions of the felony-murder rule by statute in 1957 (Homicide Act of 1957, 5 & 6 Eliz. 2, ch. 11, §1):

> Where a person kills another in the course or furtherance of some other offence, the killing shall not amount to murder unless done with the same malice aforethought (express or implied) as is required for a killing to amount to murder when not done in the course or furtherance of another offence.

A few American legislatures have followed suit,[15] but the great majority have retained some version of the felony-murder rule, even in the face of heavy academic and judicial criticism of it. See James J. Tomkovicz, The Endurance of the Felony-Murder Rule, 51 Wash. & Lee L. Rev. 1429, 1431 (1994). While the influence of the MPC in other areas has been great, it has had little success with its modest proposal to replace the felony-murder rule with a rebuttable presumption. However, statutes over the years have qualified the severity of the common-law rule in a variety of ways.

1. Limiting the list of eligible felonies. Some states have designated particular felonies (such as rape, arson, burglary, kidnapping, and robbery) as the only felonies on which a felony-murder conviction may be obtained. Other felonies serve only as the possible basis of a manslaughter conviction (E.g., Ind. Code §35-42-1-4) or cannot by themselves serve as the basis for conviction of any form of culpable homicide (N.Y. Pen. Law §125.25(3), page 425 supra).

2. Grading of felony murder. In states that still permit a wide range of felonies to trigger the felony-murder rule, a few particularly dangerous felonies—such as arson, rape, robbery, and burglary—are designated as the only felonies on which a first-degree felony-murder conviction can be obtained. Where this approach is followed (see, e.g., Cal. Pen. Code §189, page 422 supra), a killing in the course of a nondesignated felony still triggers the felony-murder rule, but the offense becomes murder in the second degree.

---

15. E.g., Haw. Rev. Stat. §707-701 (2011); Ky. Rev. Stat. §507.020 (2011).

3. Requiring a homicidal mens rea. Another approach is to provide that a killing in the course of the felony can constitute murder only when it is otherwise culpable—for example, providing that the defendant must "recklessly" cause the death (Del. Code Ann. tit. 11, §636).

4. Permitting affirmative defenses. Some states, like New York, allow an affirmative defense when a co-felon caused the death and the defendant himself was not armed and had no reason to believe that co-felon was likely to kill. N.Y. Pen. Law §125.25 (3), supra page 426.

Question: To what extent do these various qualifications meet the criticisms of the felony-murder rule made by Macaulay, Tomcovicz, and the Model Penal Code, supra? For an analysis suggesting that a carefully drafted felony-murder statute can avoid the principal criticisms leveled against the traditional rule, see David Crump, Reconsidering the Felony Murder Rule in Light of Modern Criticisms, 32 Harv. J.L. & Pub. Pol'y 1155 (2009).

NOTES ON JUDICIAL REFORM

1. Abolition. One state supreme court has abolished the felony-murder rule. In People v. Aaron, 409 Mich. 672, 299 N.W.2d 304 (1980), the statute did not explicitly codify the felony-murder rule but provided that any murder in the course of designated felonies would be murder of the first degree. Since the statute did not define murder, the court felt free to employ its common-law authority to reject the precedents recognizing the felony-murder theory as a route to establishing malice and treated the statute as simply raising what is otherwise murder (because malice has been proved) to first-degree murder when occurring in the commission of an enumerated felony. "We believe that it is no longer acceptable to equate the intent to commit a felony with the intent to kill, intent to do great bodily harm, or wanton and willful disregard of the likelihood [of] death or great bodily harm. Today we exercise our role in the development of the common law by abrogating the common-law felony-murder rule."

Question: Is this an appropriate exercise of judicial authority?

2. Statutory interpretation. In People v. Dillon, 668 P.2d 697 (Cal. 1983), the California Supreme Court decided not to follow *Aaron*, even though the wording of California's statute is identical to Michigan's and even though both statutes were based on the same 1794 Pennsylvania model. The court concluded that subsequent reenactments by the California legislature demonstrated an intent to codify the felony-murder rule. But *Aaron* has influenced judicial interpretation of homicide statutes in several other states. In State v. Ortega, 817 P.2d 1196 (N.M. 1991), a case of homicide in the course of a kidnapping and robbery, the court read into New Mexico's first-degree felony-murder statute a requirement that the state prove intent to kill or conscious disregard for life. Similarly, in Commonwealth v. Matchett, 436

N.E.2d 400 (Mass. 1982), the court held that, before prosecutors can invoke that state's second-degree felony-murder rule for nonenumerated felonies, the jury must find that the defendant demonstrated a conscious disregard for the risk to human life.

3. *Constitutional issues.* If the felony-murder rule is required by statute, then to what extent is its application to nonintentional killings unconstitutional? In *Dillon*, supra, the court read California's felony-murder statute as imposing first-degree murder liability for a wide range of robbery killings— from accidental to premeditated homicides—and held that in order to comply with the constitutional prohibition on cruel and unusual punishment, the sentencing court would have to consider whether the first-degree penalty, life imprisonment, was disproportionate to the culpability of the defendant in the particular case. Nelson E. Roth and Scott E. Sundby argue (The Felony-Murder Rule: A Doctrine at Constitutional Crossroads, 70 Cornell L. Rev. 446 (1985)) that courts should hold the felony-murder rule unconstitutional because it either conclusively presumes malice (thus violating the requirement of proof beyond a reasonable doubt) or eliminates malice (thus violating the Eighth Amendment requirement that severe punishments be proportional to culpability). In The Queen v. Vaillancourt, [1987] S.C.R. 636, the Canadian Supreme Court held that the felony-murder provisions of that country's Criminal Code permit conviction in the absence of mens rea and therefore violate the Canadian Charter of Rights and Freedoms, in particular §7 (requiring respect for "principles of fundamental justice") and §11(d) (guaranteeing the presumption of innocence).

What do you mean by dangerously

4. The major limitations on the felony-murder rule that we now consider derive from three judicial improvisations: the inherently dangerous felony limitation, the merger doctrine, and restrictions on liability for killings not in furtherance of the felonious objective.

b. The "Inherently Dangerous Felony" Limitation

PEOPLE v. PHILLIPS

Supreme Court of California
64 Cal. 2d 574, 414 P.2d 353 (1966)

TOBRINER J. [Deceased was an eight-year-old child with a fast-growing cancer of the eye. At a medical center, her parents were advised to consent to immediate removal of the eye as the only means of saving or prolonging her life. However, defendant, a doctor of chiropractics, induced them not to do so by representing that he could cure her without surgery by treatment designed "to build up her resistance." Defendant charged the parents $700 for his treatment and medicine. The child died in about six months. At the conclusion of the defendant's trial on charges of murdering the child, the judge instructed the jury that it could convict of second-degree murder if it found that defendant committed the felony of grand theft (theft by deception) and that the child died as a proximate result. Upon conviction, the defendant appealed, and the Supreme Court reversed, finding the instruction on felony murder to be erroneous. Previous California cases had ruled that the felony-murder rule could be triggered only by felonies inherently dangerous to life, and the court ruled that the felony of grand theft did not meet this requirement.]

We have . . . recognized that the felony-murder doctrine expresses a highly artificial concept that deserves no extension beyond its required application. [But the prosecution, a]dmitting that grand theft is not inherently dangerous to life . . . asks us to encompass the entire course of defendant's conduct so that we may incorporate such elements as would make his crime inherently dangerous. In so framing the definition of a given felony for the purpose of assessing its inherent peril to life the prosecution would abandon the statutory definition of the felony as such and substitute the factual elements of defendant's actual conduct. In the present case the Attorney General would characterize that conduct as "grand theft medical fraud," and this newly created "felony," he urges, clearly involves danger to human life and supports an application of the felony-murder rule.

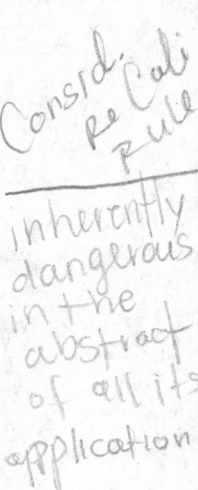

To fragmentize the "course of conduct" of defendant so that the felony-murder rule applies if any segment of that conduct may be considered dangerous to life would widen the rule beyond calculation. It would then apply not only to the commission of specific felonies, which are themselves dangerous to life, but to the perpetration of any felony during which defendant may have acted in such a manner as to endanger life. The proposed approach would entail the rejection of our holding in *Williams* [63 Cal. 2d 452, that the elements of the felony in the abstract, not as committed, determine its inherent dangerousness.] [O]nce the Legislature's own definition is discarded, the number or nature of the contextual elements which could be incorporated into an expanded felony terminology would be limitless. We have been, and remain, unwilling to embark on such an uncharted sea of felony murder.

The felony-murder instruction should not, then, have been given; its rendition, further, worked prejudice upon defendant. It withdrew from the jury the issue of malice, permitting a conviction upon the bare showing that Linda's death proximately resulted from conduct of defendant amounting to grand theft. The instruction as rendered did not require the jury to find either express malice or the implied malice which is manifested in an "intent with conscious disregard for life to commit acts likely to kill." (People v. Washington, 62 Cal. 2d 777, 780.)

[Reversed.[a]]

---

a. On remand, the defendant was again convicted of second-degree murder. This time the prosecution's theory was that malice was established by the defendant's conscious disregard of the risk to the child's life.—EDS.

NOTES ON INHERENT DANGER "IN THE ABSTRACT"

1. In People v. Henderson, 19 Cal. 3d 86 (1977), the California Supreme Court reversed a second-degree felony-murder conviction based on the felony of "false imprisonment . . . effected by violence, menace, fraud or deceit." Defendant held a gun to the head of a hostage. When the hostage ducked and attempted to deflect the barrel of the gun, it went off and killed a bystander. The court found that false imprisonment does not necessarily involve the danger to life required for felony-murder because the statutory elements—violence, menace, fraud, or deceit—do not all involve life-endangering conduct. Violence and menace may endanger life, but the other independently sufficient elements do not. Therefore, viewing the offense in the abstract, it is not inherently dangerous to life. The prosecution argued that the matter would not differ in substance if the legislature had created two separate false imprisonment felonies, one by violence or menace, the other by fraud or deceit. The court disagreed (19 Cal. 3d at 95):

> The Legislature has not evinced a particular concern for violent as opposed to nonviolent acts of false imprisonment by separate statutory treatment, proscription, or punishment. Accordingly, we cannot conclude that the cause of deterring homicide during the commission of false imprisonment is better served by imputing malice to one who kills in the course of committing false imprisonment rather than allowing the jury to determine directly the question of the presence of malice aforethought.

2. Although the "abstract" approach sets a high bar for holding an offense inherently dangerous, California courts have found the requirement satisfied for many felonies, including arson of a motor vehicle, shooting at an inhabited dwelling, poisoning with intent to injure, and manufacturing methamphetamine. See People v. Howard, 34 Cal. 4th 1129, 1136 (2005).

3. In *Howard*, supra, the defendant, after being stopped for a traffic violation, attempted to flee and led pursuing officers on a high-speed chase, running several red lights and stop signs, at speeds up to 90 miles per hour. After running an additional red light, he collided with another car, killing the driver. He was convicted of felony-murder, based on the predicate felony of "attempt[ing] to elude a pursuing peace officer [while] driv[ing] in a willful or wanton disregard for the safety of persons or property." Cal. Veh. Code §2800.2.

Is this felony inherently dangerous to life when analyzed in the abstract? In a 1993 decision, a California appellate court held that it was, but in an unrelated development the legislature later amended §2880.2 to more clearly define "willful or wanton disregard for the safety persons or property"; the 1996 amendment specified that this requirement could be met if the fleeing driver committed three or more violations of the traffic code. Is §2800.2 *still* inherently dangerous? A majority of the California Supreme Court held that it was not, because "willful and wanton disregard" could now consist of such conduct as driving with a suspended license or making a right turn without signaling. In dissent, Justice Baxter argued that traffic infractions committed while attempting to elude the police are inherently dangerous in all circumstances. In a third opinion, Justice Brown acknowledged that §2800.2 violations must be considered inherently dangerous (because a fleeing motorist inevitably endangers pursuing officers), but she nonetheless concurred in reversal of Howard's conviction; she argued that because the second-degree felony-murder doctrine is "irredeemably arbitrary," she would "abrogate the rule entirely." 34 Cal. 4th at 1140.

Questions: Which of the three approaches is the most sound? How *should* the *Howard* case be decided?

4. Problem. Consider People v. Burroughs, 35 Cal. 3d 824, 678 P.2d 894 (1984). Lee Swatsenbarg was diagnosed as having terminal leukemia. He sought treatment from Burroughs, who instructed him to "drink lemonade, salt water, and herb tea, but consume nothing more for the ensuing 30 days." Burroughs also bathed Swatsenbarg in tinted lights and gave him massages, for an additional fee per session. Within two weeks, Swatsenbarg's condition began to deteriorate. Shortly thereafter, he died from a massive hemorrhage brought on by Bourroughs's massages. Because the *Phillips* decision precluded reliance on grand theft as a predicate felony, prosecutors sought a felony-murder conviction by using the predicate offense of felonious unlicensed practice of medicine, defined as willfully practicing "any system or mode of treating the sick [without a valid license] under circumstances or conditions which cause or create a risk of great bodily harm, serious physical or mentaol illness, or death." Burroughs had clearly committed this offense, and he was also convicted of felony-murder, with this offense as the predicate felony. Should the offense qualify as inherently dangerous under the California test?

HINES v. STATE

Supreme Court of Georgia
276 Ga. 491, 578 S.E.2d 868 (2003)

FLETCHER, C.J. While hunting, Robert Lee Hines mistook his friend Steven Wood for a turkey and shot him dead. A jury convicted Hines of felony murder based on the underlying crime of possession of a firearm by a convicted felon. [T]he evidence at trial showed that, late in the afternoon of April 8, 2001, Hines and some of his friends and relatives went turkey hunting. They split into two groups, with Hines and his friend Randy Stoker hunting together in one area, and the victim, the victim's wife, and Hines's son hunting in a different area, approximately one-fourth mile away. As the sky was growing dark, Hines heard a turkey gobble, "saw it fan out and shot." Hines's shot went through heavy foliage and hit the victim approximately eighty feet away. Immediately thereafter, the victim's wife screamed, "You shot Wood." Hines and his son went for help, but the victim died before help could arrive.

... Hines contends that a convicted felon's possession of a firearm while turkey hunting cannot be one of the inherently dangerous felonies required to support a conviction of felony murder. A felony is "inherently dangerous" when it is "dangerous per se" or "by its circumstances create[s] a foreseeable risk of death." Hulme v. State, 273 Ga. 676, 678 (2001). Depending on the facts, possession of a firearm by a convicted felon can be an inherently dangerous felony. . . .

In Ford v. State, 262 Ga. 602 (1992), the defendant was a convicted felon who was unloading a handgun when it accidentally discharged, went through the floor, and killed an occupant of the apartment below. A jury convicted Ford for felony murder based on his felonious possession of a firearm. This court reversed, finding that, because no evidence showed the defendant knew there was an apartment below him or that the victim was present, his possession of a firearm could not support a conviction of felony murder.

In contrast to *Ford*, Hines intentionally fired his shotgun intending to hit his target. He had been drinking before he went hunting, and there was evidence that he had been drinking while hunting. He knew that other hunters were in the area and was unaware of their exact location. He also knew that other people visited the area in which he was hunting. He took an unsafe shot at dusk, through heavy foliage, at a target eighty feet away that he had not positively identified as a turkey. Under these circumstances, we conclude that Hines's violation of the prohibition of a firearm created a foreseeable risk of death. Hines's violation of the prohibition against convicted felons possessing firearms was an inherently dangerous felony that could support a felony-murder conviction. . . .

Judgment affirmed.

SEARS, P.J., dissenting. . . . In *Ford* . . . we did not specify how to determine whether a particular felony, whether by its nature or as it was committed, was inherently dangerous to human life. Because of the severe punishments that accompany a conviction of murder . . . I conclude that for purposes of our felony-murder doctrine, a felony is inherently dangerous per se or as committed if it carries "a high probability that [a human] death will result." People v. Patterson, 778 P.2d 549, 558 (Cal. 1989). This standard will ensure that our felony-murder rule is not inappropriately expanded by "reducing the seriousness of the act which a defendant must commit in order to be charged with murder." Id.

. . . The fact that Hines was hunting, a dangerous sport; the fact that he had been drinking . . . ; the fact that he was hunting at dusk; and the fact that he fired a shot when he knew other hunters were in the general area . . . may establish that Hines was negligent, but do not establish that his acts created a high probability that death to a human being would result, or that he had a "life-threatening state of mind." . . . Even though Hines may not, as stated by the majority, have positively identified his target as a turkey, he had to make a split-second decision regarding his target and concluded, based on hearing a gobble and seeing something "fan out," that the object was a turkey. I cannot conclude that, under these circumstances, the failure of the hunter to identify his target beyond doubt carried a high probability that a human being would be killed or that he acted with a "life-threatening state of mind." The death in this case is clearly a tragic accident. . . . But the sanction of life in prison for murder should be reserved for cases in which the defendant's moral failings warrant such punishment. Here, the application of the felony-murder statute to Hines's actions punishes him more severely than his culpability merits. [He] will be serving the same punishment—life in prison—as an arsonist convicted of felony murder who firebombed an apartment that he knew was occupied, causing the death of two young children, and the same punishment as an armed robber convicted of felony murder who entered a store with a firearm and shot and killed a store employee. This result is unwarranted and unnecessary, as Hines could be prosecuted and convicted of an appropriate lesser crime, such as involuntary manslaughter or the misuse of a firearm while hunting.

. . . Hunting is a time-honored recreational activity encouraged by the State of Georgia and enjoyed by many of our State's citizens. No doubt a number of hunters have probably engaged in negligent hunting practices similar to those in this case. Although I do not condone such careless practices, neither can I agree with subjecting so many hunters to the possibility of spending life in prison when they do not fastidiously follow proper hunting procedures and accidentally shoot a fellow hunter.

NOTES ON INHERENT DANGER "AS COMMITTED"

1. *The degree of danger.* Only a few American jurisdictions follow the California approach of limiting the felony-murder rule to felonies that are dangerous "in the abstract." See Fisher v. State, 786 A.2d 706, 730-733 (Md. 2001); Annot. 50 A.L.R.3d 397 (2005). Instead, most will permit a felony (even a nonviolent felony like theft) to qualify if it is committed in a dangerous way. But *how* dangerous does the felony have to be? What likelihood of death does the *Hines* majority consider sufficient? What likelihood is sufficient for the dissenting judge? Should inherent danger to life mean that serious bodily harm is *likely*, that it is *possible*, or only that such harm is not completely unforeseeable?

2. *Who decides?* The *Hines* majority declares: "*[W]e* conclude that Hines's violation . . . created a foreseeable risk of death," and the dissent states: "*I* conclude that [the] circumstances . . . were not inherently dangerous." (emphasis added.) Thus, although the justices differ about the dangerousness of the circumstances, they agree that the appellate justices themselves must make that assessment. But if dangerousness under all the circumstances is required for conviction, how can this factual determination be taken away from the jury? Some courts hold that "[t]he proper procedure is to present the facts and circumstances of the particular case to the trier of fact and for the trier of fact to determine if a felony is inherently dangerous in the manner and the circumstances in which it was committed." People v. Stewart, 663 A.2d

912, 920 (R.I. 1995). Is this a more principled approach? Or does it, by requiring the prosecution to litigate dangerousness in each case, defeat a major purpose of the felony-murder rule?

When the dangerousness determination is left to the jury, is there any practical difference between second-degree murder on a felony-murder theory and second-degree murder on a theory of ordinary malice—i.e., recklessly endangering life? Consider the facts of *Stewart*, supra. Stewart, the mother of a two-month-old infant, went on a crack binge for two to three days, and during this period she failed to feed the little boy, who died from dehydration. The prosecution did not claim that Stewart intentionally withheld care but only that she had neglected her son because in her intoxicated state she had forgotten to feed him. Instead of alleging murder on a theory of conscious recklessness, the prosecution argued that Stewart was guilty of felonious child neglect and that this felony, inherently dangerous to life under the circumstances, was the cause of the infant's death. The Rhode Island Supreme Court upheld a second-degree felony-murder conviction obtained on this basis.

Question: If the felony-murder theory had been unavailable, could Stewart be convicted of second-degree murder on the basis of ordinary malice? What difficulties would be presented?[16]

3. Evaluating the "abstract" and "as committed" approaches. In light of the difficulties indicated in the preceding notes, is the "as committed" approach a sensible way to manage the felony-murder rule? Would it be better to abandon the inherent-danger requirement entirely, so that *any* felony resulting in death could support a murder conviction? If not, how can courts limit the reach of the rule and preserve the legislative preference for maintaining discrete degrees of homicide, while also honoring the legislative preference for denying that calibration of culpability for those who commit (certain) felonies?

c. The Merger Doctrine

PEOPLE v. BURTON

Supreme Court of California
6 Cal. 3d 375, 491 P.2d 793 (1971)

SULLIVAN, Justice.

[Defendant killed a person in the course of committing an armed robbery. The jury found the defendant guilty of first-degree felony murder, and

---

16. In some jurisdictions, the element of conscious awareness required for "recklessness" is modified when a defendant is voluntarily intoxicated. See page 943 infra. Where this rule can be invoked in a murder prosecution, a jury determining the element of malice would in effect have to find a mental state amounting to criminal negligence rather than conscious recklessness. How does this factual determination differ from the factual determination that *Stewart* requires for murder on a felony-murder theory—namely, whether the underlying felony was inherently dangerous in the manner committed?

defendant appealed. Defendant contends] that it was error, in the circumstances of this case, to instruct the jury on first-degree felony murder, because the underlying felony was armed robbery. He claims that armed robbery is an offense included in fact within the offense of murder and, therefore, under the rule announced in People v. Ireland, 70 Cal. 2d 522, as applied in People v. Wilson (1969) 1 Cal. 3d 431, such offense cannot support a felony-murder instruction. . . .

[In *Ireland* the defendant, having shot and killed his wife, claimed that alcohol, prescribed medications, and cumulative emotional pressure established diminished capacity sufficient to preclude the malice required for murder.] The judge instructed the jury on the felony-murder rule, utilizing assault with a deadly weapon as the supporting felony. The effect of such instruction [was] to substantially eviscerate the defense of diminished capacity to negative malice, since malice was imputed. The net effect of this imputation would be to hold that all intentional killings accomplished by means of a deadly weapon . . . could never be mitigated to manslaughter, since all such killings included in fact an assault with a deadly weapon. We held that such effect was impermissible: "This kind of bootstrapping finds support neither in logic nor in law. We therefore hold that a second degree felony-murder instruction may not properly be given when it is based upon a felony which is an integral part of the homicide and which the evidence produced by the prosecution shows to be an offense included in fact within the offense charged."

In *Wilson* the underlying felony which supported the felony-murder instruction was burglary—specifically entry coupled with the intent to commit assault with a deadly weapon. [The defendant, intending to assault his estranged wife, entered her home, then entered the bathroom where she had taken refuge. He then shot and killed her.] Since in *Ireland* we had held that assault with a deadly weapon could not support an instruction on second-degree felony murder, in *Wilson* we were faced with the question whether it could support first-degree felony murder because coupled with an entry. We concluded there was no meaningful distinction between assaults with deadly weapons indoors and outdoors, saying: "Where the intended felony of the burglar is an assault with a deadly weapon, the likelihood of homicide from the lethal weapon is not significantly increased by the site of the assault. Furthermore, the burglary statute in this state includes within its definition numerous structures other than dwellings as to which there can be no conceivable basis for distinguishing between an assault with a deadly weapon outdoors and a burglary in which the felonious intent is solely to assault with a deadly weapon." Thus, even though burglary is one of the felonies specifically enumerated in Penal Code section 189, we excluded burglary from the operation of the felony-murder rule in those cases where the intended felony was assault with a deadly weapon for the reasons stated in *Ireland.*

Defendant contends that the language and reasoning of *Ireland* and *Wilson* compel us to hold that armed robbery is included in fact within murder and, therefore, cannot support a felony-murder instruction. He argues that armed robbery includes as a necessary element assault with a deadly weapon by the following chain of reasoning: robbery "is the felonious taking of personal property in the possession of another, from his person or immediate presence, and against his will, accomplished by means of force or fear" (Pen. Code, §211); thus robbery is assault (force or fear directed against a person) coupled with larceny, which when accomplished by means of a deadly weapon necessarily includes in fact assault with a deadly weapon; any charge of murder with respect to a killing arising out of armed robbery then necessarily includes in fact assault with a deadly weapon and cannot support a felony-murder instruction.

The net effect of defendant's argument would be to eliminate the application of the felony-murder rule to all unlawful killings which were committed by means of a deadly weapon, since in each case the homicide would include in fact assault with a deadly weapon, even if the homicide resulted from the commission of one of the six felonies (arson, rape, mayhem, robbery, burglary or lewd and lascivious acts upon the body of a child) enumerated in section 189 of the Penal Code. . . . [W]e reject this interpretation of that language and its consequent assertion that the felony-murder rule has been abolished in all homicides accomplished by means of a deadly weapon as unwarranted both in logic and in principle.

We conclude that there is a very significant difference between deaths resulting from assaults with a deadly weapon, where the purpose of the conduct was the very assault which resulted in death, and deaths resulting from conduct for an independent felonious purpose, such as robbery or rape, which happened to be accomplished by a deadly weapon. . . . Our inquiry cannot stop with the fact that death resulted from the use of a deadly weapon and, therefore, technically included an assault with a deadly weapon, but must extend to an investigation of the purpose of the conduct. In both *Ireland* and *Wilson* the purpose of the conduct which eventually resulted in a homicide was . . . the infliction of bodily injury. . . . The desired infliction of bodily injury was in each case not satisfied short of death. Thus, there was a single course of conduct with a single purpose.

However, in the case of armed robbery, as well as the other felonies enumerated in section 189 of the Penal Code, there is an independent felonious purpose, namely in the case of robbery to acquire money or property belonging to another. Once a person has embarked upon a course of conduct for one of the enumerated felonious purposes, he comes directly within a clear legislative warning—if a death results from his commission of that felony it will be first-degree murder, regardless of the circumstances. . . . "The purpose of the felony-murder rule is to deter felons from killing negligently or accidentally by holding them strictly responsible for killings they commit." The Legislature has said in effect that this deterrent purpose outweighs the normal legislative policy of examining the individual state of mind of each person causing an unlawful killing . . . and calibrating our treatment of the person accordingly. Once a person perpetrates or attempts to perpetrate one of the enumerated felonies, then in the judgment of the Legislature, he is no longer entitled to such fine judicial calibration, but will be deemed guilty of first-degree murder for any homicide committed in the course thereof.

Wilson, when properly understood, does not eliminate this rule as urged by defendant, but merely excludes from its effect one small area of conduct, which would be irrationally included, due to the unusual nature of burglary.... In the normal case, burglary [is] undertaken with an independent felonious purpose, namely to acquire the property of another. In such instances the felony-murder rule would apply..., even if the burglary were accomplished with a deadly weapon. However, in *Wilson* the entry was coupled with the intent to commit assault with a deadly weapon, the defendant in that case bursting through the bathroom door intending to do violent injury upon the body of his wife. We were there presented with the exact situation we faced in *Ireland*, namely a single purpose, a single course of conduct, except that in *Wilson* the single course of conduct happened to include an entry, and thus technically became burglary.... We merely excluded from the first-degree felony-murder rule the special circumstances of *Wilson* where the entry was with the intent to commit assault with a deadly weapon....

Defendant in this case by embarking upon the venture of armed robbery brought himself within the class of persons who the Legislature has concluded must avoid causing death or bear the consequences of first-degree murder. The trial judge quite correctly instructed on felony murder based on homicides directly resulting from the commission of armed robbery.

[Reversed on other grounds.]

NOTES ON THE MERGER DOCTRINE

Although a few jurisdictions permit felonious assault to serve as a predicate felony that automatically converts a resulting death into murder,[17] the great majority acknowledge the need for some "merger" doctrine, in order to insure that the felony-murder rule does not obliterate grading distinctions the legislature itself seems to have desired. See, e.g., State v. Heemstra, 721 N.W.2d 549 (Iowa 2006). But courts have had difficulty determining which felonies should merge. To keep the issues in focus, the following Notes center on the law of a single jurisdiction (California), but comparable questions inevitably arise in any jurisdiction that recognizes some sort of merger doctrine.

1. Enumerated felonies and first-degree felony murder. Two tests commonly used to determine merger are (i) whether the felony is "included in fact" in the homicide and (ii) whether the felony is "independent" of the homicide. As *Burton* indicates, the first test would require merger in all robbery cases, a result plainly in conflict with the legislative intent in enumerating this crime as a basis for felony murder. The "independent purpose" test

---

17. See, e.g., Barnett v. State, 263 P.3d 959 (Okla. Crim. App. 2011); State v. Stallman, 289 S.W.3d 776 (Mo. App. 2009).

avoids this result and requires merger only in relatively uncommon situations like *Wilson*, where the only objective of the burglary was to commit an assault. But the *Wilson* holding produces anomalies of its own. Consider these problems:

(a) Indoors vs. outdoors. Most jurisdictions reject the *Wilson* holding and permit burglary to support a conviction for first-degree felony murder, even when the defendant's only objective was to assault the victim. E.g., People v. Miller, 297 N.E.2d 85 (N.Y. 1973). These courts generally support their conclusion by arguing that assaults committed indoors are more dangerous than those committed outside. Is that claim convincing? And even if it is, why is dangerousness relevant to the merger question? Consider two crimes committed outdoors. In the first, the defendant sees a well-dressed person on the street, pushes him to the ground, and steals his wallet. In the second, the defendant, after being insulted and beaten by a person he encounters in the street, shoots him in anger, intending to kill. Which crime is more dangerous to human life? Which can be invoked as a basis for a felony-murder conviction if the victim dies?

(b) Non-assaultive and non-independent purposes. Under *Wilson*, a defendant who enters a home intending to steal a TV is guilty of first-degree murder if the homeowner dies as an accidental result of the burglary, but a defendant who enters the home and kills the homeowner intentionally might not be guilty of first-degree murder. Does this make sense? If so, what should be the result if the defendant enters a home intending to kill one person but accidentally kills someone else? Should the merger rule apply, so that his mental state would have to be assessed under all the circumstances, or should he be guilty of first-degree murder automatically under the felony-murder rule? Is this situation a felony murder, because the defendant had a purpose independent of the homicide he actually committed, or is it "anomalous to place the person who intends to attack one person and in the course of the assault kills another inadvertently . . . in a worse position than the person who from the outset intended to attack both persons and killed one or both"?[18]

Consider People v. Farley, 46 Cal. 4th 1053 (2009). The defendant became so obsessed with Laura Black, a fellow employee, that he was fired, but he continued to stalk and harass her. One day he entered her place of work armed with a semiautomatic weapon and began firing, killing seven people and wounding (but not killing) four others, including Black. Under California precedent, if Farley's sole intent had been to assault just one of the workers—Black—he would be guilty of seven counts of first-degree felony murder. But if Farley had intended to assault *all 11* workers, he would be permitted to raise mitigating mens rea defenses. The California Supreme Court moved to eliminate this anomaly, but not by permitting merger in both scenarios. Instead, the court overruled *Wilson* and held that burglary

---

18. People v. Sears, 2 Cal. 3d 180, 189 (1970) (opinion of Peters, C.J.).

and other enumerated felonies would *never* merge. The court concluded that "there is no room for interpretation when the Legislature has defined first degree felony murder to include any killing 'committed in the perpetration of, or attempt to perpetrate, . . . burglary.' [T]he power to define crimes lies exclusively with the Legislature." 46 Cal. 4th, at 1119.

Questions: Is *Farley* sound? Given the absence of legislative history indicating the legislature's intentions with respect to a fact situation like *Wilson*, is the court's reliance on statutory wording persuasive? Does *Farley* eliminate the dilemmas of first-degree felony murder, or does it produce new anomalies that the legislature itself might not have intended?

2. Non-enumerated felonies and second-degree felony murder. In People v. Mattison, 4 Cal. 3d 177 (1971), the defendant had supplied methyl alcohol to a fellow prison inmate, who died from ingesting it. Applying the independent-purpose test, the court found merger inappropriate and upheld a conviction for second-degree felony murder, based on the offense of furnishing the drug. In People v. Robertson, 34 Cal. 4th 156 (2004), the defendant shot and killed a person he believed was trying to steal hubcaps from his car. In defense he claimed he had not intended to kill but was only trying to scare the victim. The court again found merger inappropriate and upheld a second-degree felony-murder conviction, based this time on the felony of discharging a firearm in a grossly negligent manner (Cal. Pen. Code §246.3). The court held that the independent purpose necessary for felony murder was established by the defendant's *defense*—that he was merely trying to frighten away the thief. But three dissenting justices expressed concern over the irony that what might be an accidental killing or involuntary manslaughter became murder because the defendant denied having an intent to kill. Justice Brown's dissent noted that the merger rule "was intended to avoid elevating every felonious assault that ends in death to second-degree murder, a result that would usurp most of the law of homicide." She then observed:

> This [explanation for the merger rule] begins with a nonsequitur from which it never recovers. The merger doctrine applied in this fashion actually ensures the Legislature's careful calibration of culpability will be ignored in precisely those cases where the absence of malice is a critical issue. Thus, in cases involving intentional assaults—where there will likely be evidence of premeditation and malice—the People must prove every element of the crime. In cases where evidence of malice is likely to be absent or highly equivocal, the second-degree felony-murder rule makes proof of malice unnecessary and imposes murder liability for what might otherwise be manslaughter. It takes no genius to discern that a rule that relieves the People of the need to prove malice because the defendant asserts he did not harbor any is problematic. . . . The problem is: second-degree felony murder . . . is incompatible with the idea of careful gradations of liability.

The California Supreme Court was forced to revisit these second-degree felony-murder issues once more in the case that follows.

PEOPLE v. CHUN

Supreme Court of California
45 Cal. 4th 1172; 203 P.3d 425 (2009)

CHIN, J. In this murder case, the trial court instructed the jury on second degree felony murder with shooting at an occupied vehicle under Penal Code section 246 the underlying felony.

[On September 13, 2003, Judy Onesavanh, Sophal Ouch, and Bounthavy Onethavong] were driving to the store . . . in a blue Mitsubishi that Onesavanh's father owned. Onesavanh's brother, George, also drives the car. The police consider George to be highly ranked in the Asian Boys street gang (Asian Boys). That evening Ouch was driving, with Onesavanh in the front passenger seat and Onethavong behind Ouch. While they were stopped . . . at a traffic light, a blue Honda with tinted windows pulled up beside them. [G]unfire erupted from the Honda, hitting all three occupants of the Mitsubishi. Onethavong was killed. . . . Onesavanh was hit in the back and seriously wounded. Ouch was shot in the cheek and suffered a fractured jaw.

Ouch and Onesavanh identified the Honda's driver as . . . Rathana Chan, a member of the Tiny Rascals Gangsters (Tiny Rascals), a [rival] criminal street gang. . . . Chan was never found. . . . Two months after the shooting, [defendant] was arrested and subsequently . . . admitted he was in the backseat of the Honda at the time [of the shooting. He] also admitted he fired a .38-caliber firearm. He said he did not point the gun at anyone; he just wanted to scare them.

Defendant . . . was charged with murder . . . , two counts of attempted murder, [and] shooting into an occupied vehicle. . . . The court also instructed the jury on second degree felony murder based on shooting at an occupied motor vehicle (§246). . . . The jury found defendant guilty of second degree murder [but] acquitted defendant of both counts of attempted murder. . . .

To avoid the anomaly of putting a person who merely intends to frighten the victim in a worse legal position than the person who actually intended to shoot at the victim, . . . we need to reconsider our holdings in *Robertson* [supra page 513]. . . . When the underlying felony is assaultive in nature, such as a violation of section 246 or 246.3 [discharging a firearm in a grossly negligent manner], we now conclude that the felony merges with the homicide and cannot be the basis of a felony-murder instruction. An "assaultive" felony is one that involves a threat of immediate violent injury. . . . In determining whether a crime merges, the court looks to its elements and not the facts of the case. Accordingly, if the elements of the crime have an assaultive aspect, the crime merges with the underlying homicide even if the elements also include conduct that is not assaultive. For example, in People v. Smith, [35 Cal. 3d 798 (1984)], the court noted that child abuse under section 273a "includes both active and passive conduct, i.e., child abuse by direct assault and child endangering by extreme neglect." Looking to the facts before it, the court decided the offense was "of the assaultive variety," and therefore merged. . . . It reserved the question whether the nonassaultive variety would merge. . . . Under the approach we now adopt, both varieties would merge. . . . This approach both avoids the necessity of consulting facts that might be disputed and extends the protection of the merger doctrine to the potentially less culpable defendant whose conduct is not assaultive. . . .

We do not have to decide at this point exactly what felonies are assaultive in nature, . . . and which are inherently collateral to the resulting homicide and do not merge. But shooting at an occupied vehicle under section 246 is assaultive in nature and hence cannot serve as the underlying felony for purposes of the felony-murder rule. . . .

We overrule *People v. Robertson*. . . . This conclusion means the trial court erred in this case in instructing the jury on the second degree felony-murder rule. [The court went on to hold that this error was harmless because no reasonable juror could have found that defendant participated in the shooting without also concluding that he harbored implied malice.]

MORENO, J. . . . The majority's reformulation of the merger doctrine is an improvement, but it does not correct the basic flaw in the felony-murder rule; that it is largely unnecessary and, in those unusual instances in which it would produce a different result, may be unfair. . . . Only in those rare cases in which it is not clear that the defendant acted in conscious disregard of life will the second degree felony-murder rule make a difference, but those are precisely the rare cases in which the rule might result in injustice. I would eliminate the second degree felony-murder rule and rely instead upon the wisdom of juries to recognize those situations in which a defendant commits second degree murder by killing the victim during the commission of a felony that is inherently dangerous to life.

QUESTIONS

Has California now solved the merger problem? How should other jurisdictions deal with it? Where the felony-murder rule is grounded in statute, how should courts preserve consistency and fairness in felony-murder cases, while also respecting the legislative intent to impose more severe punishment when death results from commission of a felony? How should a legislature shape its homicide grading provisions to ensure just punishment in such cases?

d. Killings Not "In Furtherance" of the Felony

INTRODUCTORY NOTE

The felony-murder rule applies only when the act of killing is done in furtherance of the felony. In the materials considered so far, this condition has been easily met. In this section we deal with three situations where this requirement makes felony-murder liability less clear—situations where the lethal act arguably occurs *after commission* of the felony, where the lethal act arguably is *unrelated* to the felony, and where the lethal act is committed by someone *resisting* the felony.

1. Lethal acts after commission of the felony. Suppose that a burglar causes a fatal accident while making his getaway or shortly thereafter. If his actions are considered necessary to successfully complete his crime, they would be "in furtherance" of the felony, and he would be guilty of first-degree murder. But if the accident occurred after his getaway was complete, he might be guilty only of involuntary manslaughter or of no crime at all.

Consider People v. Gillis, 474 Mich. 105, 712 N.W.2d 419 (2006). When a homeowner detected the defendant trying to break in, the defendant abandoned his attempt and drove away. Ten to 15 minutes later, about ten miles from the home, a trooper spotted a car matching the homeowner's description and tried to stop it. The defendant sped away and collided with another vehicle, killing two of its occupants. Did these deaths occur in the perpetration of the burglary? Was Gillis still escaping from the commission of that offense, or—having already escaped—was he merely attempting to flee from the officer who pulled him over? The Michigan Supreme Court, by a 3–2 majority, ruled that Gillis was fleeing *from the burglary* and hence was guilty of first-degree murder. Do you agree? Suppose Gillis had stopped for a hamburger before resuming his drive. Would a fatal accident at this point make him guilty of first-degree murder?

For other situations presenting these issues, see Annot., 58 A.L.R.3d 851 (2009).

2. Lethal acts unrelated to the felony. Suppose that felon A, after entering a building to commit arson, sees an elderly tenant, decides to rob him, and in the process accidentally kills him. The "in furtherance" requirement does not seem to matter here because A is guilty of felony murder, regardless of whether his act furthers the original arson plan; his predicate felony of robbery is sufficient by itself to establish felony murder. But the "in furtherance" requirement becomes important when A has a confederate (felon B) who planned the arson with him. If the robbery by A is unrelated to the arson that B helped plan, then B is not guilty of either the robbery or the resulting homicide. But if the robbery somehow furthers the arson plan, B could be guilty of murder.

The latter conclusion, of course, assumes that B can be held responsible for the acts of his co-felon A. We have not examined that issue in the preceding material, because all the felony-murder cases considered up to this point have focused on the liability of a single perpetrator. As we have seen, that person's liability for his own actions can increase dramatically when the felony-murder rule applies. But the common situation involving multiple confederates introduces an additional complication, because the felony-murder rule sometimes increases the liability of all co-felons, while in other situations it may apply only to the one who is most directly responsible for the killing.

Analyzing these situations requires an understanding of the laws of complicity and conspiracy, which govern the liability of one person for the criminal conduct of another. We examine this subject in depth in Chapter 7 infra, but for present purposes it is sufficient to keep in mind the core principle—a person is liable for the criminal acts of another when he intentionally aids or encourages those acts, or (under some circumstances) when those acts are reasonably foreseeable in furtherance of a common objective of the participants. Roughly speaking, therefore, we may say that in cases involving several co-felons, the "in furtherance" requirement does double duty: It determines when felon *A* is subject to the felony-murder rule for his own lethal actions, and it determines when those lethal actions can trigger felony-murder liability for his confederates.

Consider People v. Cabaltero, 87 P.2d 364 (Cal. App. 1939). A lookout during a robbery panicked at the approach of a car and fired shots at the occupants. The leader of the group, angered by his co-felon's stupidity, shot and killed him. The leader can, of course, be convicted of murder. Can the other members of the group be convicted of murder as well? The court upheld first-degree felony-murder convictions of all the participants, on the ground that the shooting helped ensure the success of the ongoing robbery. Do you agree? What arguments could the defense make to support the contrary result? See Case Note, 13 So. Cal. L. Rev. 149 (1939-1940).

3. Lethal acts by persons resisting the felony. The most difficult of the "in-furtherance" problems, and the one that has produced the greatest volume of litigation, concerns the responsibility of felons for deaths resulting from the actions of police officers and private citizens who try to thwart the attempted crime. Consider the material that follows.

STATE v. CANOLA

Supreme Court of New Jersey
73 N.J. 206, 374 A.2d 20 (1977)

CONFORD, J. [The owner of a jewelry store], in an attempt to resist an armed robbery, engaged in a physical skirmish with one of the four robbers. A second conspirator, called upon for assistance, began shooting, and the store owner returned the gunfire. Both the owner and the felon, one Lloredo, were fatally shot in the exchange, the latter by the firearm of the owner.

Defendant and two others were indicted on two counts of murder [and] one count of robbery.... The murder counts were based on the deaths, respectively, of the robbery victim and the cofelon. After trial on the murder counts defendant was found guilty on both and was sentenced to concurrent terms of life imprisonment. [The Appellate Division upheld both convictions The supreme court granted a petition for certification addressed to homicide of the co-felon.]

Conventional formulations of the felony-murder rule would not seem to encompass liability in this case. [T]he early formulations ... were concerned solely with situations where the felon or a confederate did the actual killing. [The traditional view is that], at least in theory, the doctrine of felony murder does not extend to a killing, although growing out of the commission of the felony, if directly attributable to the act of one other than the defendant or those associated with him in the unlawful enterprise.... This rule is sometimes rationalized on the "agency" theory of felony murder.[2] [The] contrary view, ... would attach liability under the felony-murder rule for any death proximately resulting from the unlawful activity—even the death of a cofelon—notwithstanding the killing was by one resisting the crime....

At one time the proximate cause theory was espoused by the Pennsylvania Supreme Court.... Commonwealth v. Almeida, 68 A.2d 595 (Pa. 1949)..., involving the killing of a policeman shot by other police attempting to apprehend robbers[.] [T]he question later arose whether [that theory] should be applied to an effort to inculpate a defendant for the killing of his cofelon at the hands of the victim of the crime. Commonwealth v. Redline, 137 A.2d 472 (Pa. 1958). The court there held against liability[, concluding] that "in order to convict for felony-murder, the killing must have been done by the defendant or by an accomplice or confederate or by one acting in furtherance of the felonious undertaking." The court refused, however, actually to overrule the *Almeida* decision, thereby creating a distinction ... between the situation in which the victim was an innocent party and the killing therefore merely "excusable" and that in which the deceased was a felon and the killing thus "justifiable." Twelve years later the Pennsylvania court did overrule *Almeida* in a case involving *Almeida*'s companion, Smith. (Commonwealth ex rel. Smith v. Myers, 261 A.2d 550 (Pa. 1970).) The court noted, inter alia, the harsh criticism leveled against the common-law felony rule, its doubtful deterrent effect, the failure of the cases cited in *Almeida* to support the conclusions reached therein, the inappropriateness of tort proximate-cause principles to homicide prosecution, and the "will-of-the-wisp" distinction drawn by the *Almeida* court between justifiable and excusable homicides....

To be distinguished from the situation before us here ... are the so-called "shield" cases.... Taylor v. State, 55 S.W. 961 (Tex. Cr. App. 1900), and Keaton v. State, 57 S.W. 1125 (Tex. Cr. App. 1900). In attempting to escape after robbing a train, defendants thrust the brakeman in front of them as a shield, as a result of which he was fatally shot by law officers. The court had no difficulty in finding defendants guilty of murder. The court in *Taylor* noted ... that a person could not be held liable for homicide unless the act is either actually or constructively committed by him, but indicated it was inapplicable to a case where defendants forced deceased to occupy a place of danger in order that they might carry out the crime. In *Keaton*, the court said defendant would be responsible for the "reasonable, natural and probable result of his act" of placing deceased in danger of his life. The conduct of

---

2. The classic statement of the theory is found in ... Commonwealth v. Campbell, 89 Mass. (7 Allen) 541, 544 (Sup. Jud. Ct. 1863), as follows: "No person can be held guilty of homicide unless the act is either actually or constructively his, and it cannot be his act in either sense unless committed by his own hand or by someone acting in concert with him or in furtherance of a common object or purpose."

the defendants in cases such as these is said to reflect "express malice," justifying a murder conviction. . . .

Most modern progressive thought in criminal jurisprudence favors restriction rather than expansion of the felony-murder rule. . . . It has frequently been observed that although the rule was logical at its inception, when all felonies were punishable by death, its survival to modern times when other felonies are not thought to be as blameworthy as premeditated killings is discordant with rational and enlightened views of criminal culpability and liability. [I]t appears to us regressive to extend the application of the felony-murder rule . . . to lethal acts of third persons not in furtherance of the felonious scheme. The language of [our] statute does not compel it,[a] and . . . is entirely compatible with the traditional limitations of the rule. Tort concepts of foreseeability and proximate cause have shallow relevance to culpability for murder in the first degree. Gradations of criminal liability should accord with [the] degree of moral culpability for the actor's conduct. . . .

The judgment of the Appellate Division is modified so as to strike the conviction and sentencing of defendant for murder of the cofelon Lloredo.

SULLIVAN, J. (concurring in result only). The practical result of the majority holding is that even though some innocent person or a police officer be killed during the commission of an armed robbery, the felon would bear no criminal responsibility of any kind for that killing as long as it was not at the hand of the felon or a confederate. The legislative intent, as I see it, is otherwise. . . . The only exception I would recognize would be the death of a cofelon, which could be classified as a justifiable homicide and not within the purview of the statute. . . .

NOTES

1. *Who does the killing?* Under the agency theory, the identity of the actual killer becomes a central issue; only if the act of killing is done by a co-felon or someone acting in concert with a co-felon will the felony-murder rule apply. Under the proximate-cause theory, in contrast, the central issue is whether the killing (regardless of who did it) is within the foreseeable risk in committing the felony.

Although a substantial majority of American jurisdictions adhere to the agency theory,[19] a number of states have adopted the proximate cause approach.[20] Complicating the picture are statutory revisions that arguably

---

a. That statute, in effect at the time of the *Canola* decision, provided as follows: "If any person, in committing or attempting to commit an arson, burglary, kidnapping, rape, robbery, sodomy or any unlawful act against the peace of this state, of which the probable consequences may be bloodshed, kills another, *or if the death of anyone ensues from the committing or attempting to commit any such crime act; . . . then such person so killing is guilty of murder.*" (Emphasis added.)—EDS.

19. See Comer v. State, 977 A.2d 334, 341 (Del. 2009); Annot., 89 A.L.R.4th 683 (2010).

20. See, e.g., People v. Hudson, 856 N.E.2d 1078 (Ill. 2006). For a survey of this aspect of felony-murder law, see Michelle S. Simon, Whose Crime Is It Anyway?: Liability for the Lethal Acts of Nonparticipants in the Felony, 72 U. Det. Mercy L. Rev. 223, 260 (1994).

introduce proximate-cause concepts. For example, New York Penal Law §125.25, page 425 supra, provides that a person is guilty of murder if, "in the course of and in furtherance of [designated felonies,] he, or another participant ... causes the death of a person other than one of the participants." Several other states follow the New York model. See, e.g., Conn. Gen. Stat. §53A-54(c); Or. Rev. Stat. §163.115.

Questions: Does the New York statute's "in-furtherance" requirement signify the adoption of the agency approach, or does the "he ... causes" language require adoption of the proximate-cause theory? The New York Court of Appeals chose the latter interpretation and upheld a felony-murder conviction where a policeman was fatally shot by a fellow officer in the course of a gun battle with several armed robbers. See People v. Hernandez, 624 N.E.2d 661 (N.Y. 1993). Do you agree with that reading of the statute?

In New Jersey, the legislature responded to *Canola* by adopting a new statute modeled closely on that of New York. Under N.J. Stat. §2C:11-3a(3), a person is now guilty of murder whenever he commits or attempts to commit a designated felony, and "in the course of and in furtherance of [the crime] ... any person *causes the death* of any person other than one of the participants" (emphasis added). The New Jersey statute, like that of New York, affords an affirmative defense for felons who can show that they had no reason to anticipate the use of deadly force. N.J. Stat. §2C:11-3a(3)(a)-(d). The New Jersey Supreme Court held that this statute was intended to adopt the position that Justice Sullivan had advanced in his *Canola* concurrence: a proximate-cause approach, coupled with an exception precluding liability when the victim is a co-felon. See State v. Martin, 573 A.2d 1359 (N.J. 1990). Thus, although the *Canola* decision remains influential in guiding judicial interpretation outside New Jersey, the decision has been superseded by legislation in its home state.

What accounts for the tendency of some legislatures to expand the felony-murder rule by adopting the proximate-cause approach? Professor Leonard Birdsong argues that this broader approach "would better serve to deter felons who might kill while also reaffirming the sanctity of human life, even the life of co-felons who may be killed." Birdsong, The Felony Murder Doctrine Revisited, 33 Ohio N.U. L. Rev. 497, 499 (2007). See also People v. Hernandez, supra, 624 N.E.2d at 665-666:

> Advocates of the agency theory suggest that no culpable party has the requisite mens rea when a nonparticipant is the shooter. We disagree. . . . Whether the death is an immediate result or an attenuated one, the necessary mens rea is present if the causal act is part of the felonious conduct. No more persuasive is the argument that the proximate cause view will extend criminal liability unreasonably. First, New York law is clear that felony murder . . . is limited to those deaths caused by one of the felons in furtherance of their crime. More than civil tort liability must be established; criminal liability will adhere only

when the felons' acts are a sufficiently direct cause of the death.[a] ... Second, the New York felony-murder statute spells out the affirmative defense available to the accomplice who does not cause the death. ... In short, our established [rules] provide adequate boundaries to felony-murder liability.

2. *Implied malice.* Where a killing by a non-felon occurs during a highly dangerous felony, are the felons liable for "implied malice" or "depraved heart murder" without resort to the felony-murder doctrine, on the ground that the felonious actions were taken with a conscious disregard for life? The MPC apparently supports this view. The Commentary to its causation provision, §2.03, provides the following example: "[I]f one of the participants in a robbery shoots at a policeman with intent to kill and provokes a return of fire by that officer that kills a bystander ... the robber who initiates the gunfire could be charged with purposeful murder." Model Penal Code and Commentaries, Part I, at 263 (1985). Some courts have reached the same conclusion, e.g., Commonwealth v. Gaynor, 648 A.2d 295, 298 (Pa. 1994); People v. Gilbert, 408 P.2d 365, 373 (Cal. 1966). California has adopted the agency view of killings by non-felons, and accordingly the felony-murder theory is not available to convict felon A of murder when the victim of an armed robbery kills his co-felon B. But in *Gilbert*, supra, the court explained that in some circumstances, the surviving felons can be held for murder without relying on the felony-murder rule (id. at 373):

> When the defendant or his accomplice, with a conscious disregard for life, intentionally commits an act that is likely to cause death, and his victim or a police officer kills in reasonable response to such act, ... the killing is attributable, not merely to the commission of a felony, but to the intentional act of the defendant or his accomplice committed with conscious disregard for life. Thus, the victim's self-defensive killing or the police officer's killing in the performance of his duty cannot be considered an independent intervening cause for which the defendant is not liable, for it is a reasonable response to the dilemma thrust upon the victim or the policeman by the intentional act of the defendant or his accomplice.

Questions: (a) Procedurally, what difference (if any) is there between the results obtainable under this theory and those obtainable under a felony-murder theory? Was the court inconsistent in rejecting the proximate-cause theory for felony murder but adopting it for implied-malice murder?

(b) What facts should be sufficient to convict for murder on the implied-malice theory, without resort to the felony-murder rule? Presumably, a robber who opens fire on his victim would exhibit conscious disregard for life, and the victim's decision to shoot back would be "a reasonable response to the dilemma thrust upon the victim." Should a court reach the same result if

---

a. When the actions of another person constitute lawful, defensive force, they are not regarded as supervening or unforeseeable under the law of causation, and therefore the felon's acts can be considered the proximate cause of deaths that result from this defensive force. See infra page 592.—EDS.

the robber simply points his gun at the victim, without actually firing? See Taylor v. Superior Ct., 477 P.2d 131 (Cal. 1970). What if the robber simply says "your money or your life" without displaying a weapon at all?

3. Who is killed? A number of felony-murder statutes specifically exclude killings of participants in the felony. E.g., Colo. Rev. Stat. §18-3-101; N.Y. Pen. Law §125.25(3). Some courts adopt this position even in the absence of specific statutory language requiring it. See Annot., 89 A.L.R.4th 683 (2010). What is the appeal of this distinction? Consider these possibilities:

(a) Justifiable homicide? Suppose the felon is justifiably killed by a police officer. Is that a reason for not applying the felony-murder rule to the surviving felon? The following argument was advanced in the *Redline* case, discussed in *Canola*:

> [O]ne of the robbers . . . while resisting apprehension . . . was shot and killed by a policeman in the performance of his duty. Thus, the homicide was justifiable and, obviously, could not be availed of, on any rational legal theory, to support a charge of murder. How can anyone, no matter how much of an outlaw he may be, have a criminal charge lodged against him for the consequences of the lawful conduct of another person?

How cogent is the reasoning? Suppose two felons are holed up in a house and engaged in a gun battle with police officers surrounding the house. Felon *A* tells felon *B* to run out the back door where, he says, the coast is clear. He says this because he wants felon *B* dead and he knows that the police have the back door well covered. As felon *B* dashes out, gun in hand, he is shot dead by police. Is it self-evident that felon *A* is not criminally liable for the police officer's killing of felon *B*?

(b) Protecting the innocent? Another argument for the exemption of the death of felons was stated as follows (State v. Williams, 254 So. 2d 548, 550-551 (Fla. App. 1971)):

> [T]he statute is primarily designed to protect the innocent public; and it would be incongruous to reach a conclusion having the effect of placing the perpetrators themselves beneath its mantle. . . . This does not mean to say, however, that co-conspirators acting in furtherance of their conspiracy . . . can kill or murder each other with impunity. . . . Certainly, one conspirator may be guilty of the murder of a co-conspirator if the facts support premeditated murder or a lesser degree of unlawful homicide. But this is quite apart from the felony-murder concept with which we are here concerned.

Compare State v. Perez, 382 So. 2d 731 (Fla. App. 1980), overruling *Williams* on the ground that Florida's felony-murder statute does not expressly limit the rule to "innocent" victims. But as a matter of policy, *should* a felony-murder rule be so limited? Consider United States v. Martinez, 16 F.3d 202 (7th Cir. 1994). Martinez, along with Mahn and Mares, planned to bomb several adult bookstores whose owners had refused to pay them "protection" money. Mares built six pipe bombs that could be detonated by remote-control electronic devices. He and Mahn then drove through downtown Chicago, placed one of the bombs and headed for a second destination along one of Chicago's main streets, "traversing an area dense with electro-magnetic signals" (id. at 208). One of their bombs exploded, killing Mares. The court held that Martinez and Mahn could be sentenced for felony murder, on the basis of the death of their co-felon. Judge Richard Posner wrote for the court (id. at 207):

> The lives of criminals are not completely worthless, so their deaths should not be considered nonevents for sentencing purposes. [W]e add that liability for felony murder in a case such as the present serves the practical function of deterring felons from using lethal weaponry, more broadly from committing the kind of felony in which someone is likely to be shot or run down or otherwise injured (and hence possibly killed), by punishing them severely should death result—to anyone.

D. THE DEATH PENALTY

The preceding materials suggest the variety of homicidal behavior and the importance of classifying such behavior in degrees of seriousness by reference to the dangerousness of the conduct and the moral turpitude of the offender. What penalty should be authorized for the most serious homicidal offenses? Are there situations in which capital punishment is an appropriate or even a necessary response to a criminal offense? In this section we explore the case for and against the death penalty, in terms of principles applicable to criminal punishments generally and in terms of the special requirements of constitutional law flowing from the Eighth Amendment prohibition of "cruel and unusual punishments." Of course, the two perspectives are closely intertwined. We believe it preferable to put constitutional problems to one side, for a moment, and to consider first the factors that might motivate a state legislator or a concerned citizen to support or oppose capital punishment as a policy matter.

1. The Current Context[21]

In 1977, capital punishment resumed in the United States under the modern death penalty regime, and by the end of 2010, approximately 1,250 executions had taken place. In 1977, only one execution took place; in 1999, when the

---

21. Except as otherwise noted, all statistics in this section are drawn from U.S. Dept. of Justice, Bureau of Justice Statistics, Capital Punishment Statistics, http://bjs.ojp.usdoj.gov/index.cfm; Death Penalty Information Center, Facts About the Death Penalty, Jan. 17, 2012, available at http://www.deathpenaltyinfo.org/documents/FactSheet.pdf; and NAACP Legal Defense and Education Fund, Criminal Justice Project, Death Row U.S.A. Spring, 2006, available at http://naacpldf.org/files/publications/DRUSA_Spring_2006.pdf.

rate of executions reached its peak, 98 people were executed, an average of two per week. This rate dropped off significantly in the following years: 43 people were executed in 2011. The rate of death sentencing has similarly declined. Beginning at a rate of 137 sentences per year in 1977, capital sentences peaked at 317 in 1996. Rates declined unevenly thereafter, but have declined steadily since 2003 and reached their lowest point in 2010, when 104 inmates were sentenced to death.

As of April 2011, approximately 3,222 people were on death row awaiting execution in 35 states and in the federal system. Before the death penalty for juveniles was declared unconstitutional in 2005 by the Supreme Court,[22] approximately 2 percent of people on death row had been 17 or younger at the time of their offenses. Inmates on death row today range from those still in their teens to some over 80. Women are a very small minority, comprising less than 2 percent of inmates. In terms of race and ethnicity, approximately 44 percent of death row inmates are white, 42 percent are black, and 12 percent (including all races) are of Hispanic origin. Native Americans and Asians each comprise about 1 percent. Approximately one-third of those on death row have no prior felony convictions, though about 9 percent have a prior homicide conviction. The 52 inmates executed in 2009 spent an average of 14 years on death row, the longest average period since the reintroduction of the death penalty.

Capital punishment is expensive, with the administration of the death penalty costing substantially more than non-capital prosecution, including the costs of incarceration.[23] Kansas offers an example of how these costs accrue: A capital case in that state requires investigation costs that are three times greater than what is required in a comparable homicide case in which the death penalty is not sought. Trial costs are 16 times greater, and appeals costs are 21 times greater.[24] One study concluded that the death penalty costs the state of North Carolina $2.16 million per execution more than a system imposing a maximum sentence of life imprisonment.[25]

In spite of its cost, the death penalty enjoys substantial public support, at least in the abstract. The polling question "Are you in favor of the death penalty for persons convicted of murder?" almost always generates a national majority in support. Public support for capital punishment ranged from a low point of 42 percent in favor in 1966 to a peak of 80 percent in favor in 1994. In the wake of media attention to the conviction and capital sentencing of innocent people, support for the death penalty now holds stable at around 66 percent.[26] However, when the question is framed as a choice between

---

22. Roper v. Simmons, 543 U.S. 551 (2005), is discussed at pages 554-555 infra.

23. Richard Dieter, Testimony before the New York State Assembly, Standing Committees on Codes, Judiciary, and Corrections: "Cost of the Death Penalty and Related Issues" (Jan. 25, 2005).

24. Summary of the Kansas Death Penalty Cost Report by DPIC, http://www.deathpenaltyinfo.org/node/1080.

25. P. Cook, The Costs of Processing Murder Cases in North Carolina, Duke University (May 1993).

26. Gallup, In U.S., Two-Thirds Continue to Support Death Penalty (Oct. 13, 2009), available at http://www.deathpenaltyinfo.org/documents/GallupPoll1009.pdf.

capital punishment and life imprisonment without the possibility of parole, Americans are roughly evenly divided between the two options.[27]

Opinion polls find little regional variation in public support for capital punishment, but states differ widely in the extent to which that support is translated into criminal justice policy. Sixteen states (and the District of Columbia) do not authorize the death penalty under any circumstances, many others produce very few death sentences, and five death-penalty states have had no executions in the modern era. In contrast, just five states— Florida, Missouri, Oklahoma, Texas, and Virginia—accounted for about two-thirds of all executions during the 1977-2009 period, and a single state, Texas, carried out more than one-third of the executions. Perhaps more surprisingly, several states issue many death sentences but carry out few actual executions: California has the largest death row population in the nation (approximately 670) but has performed only 13 executions since 1976.[28]

In recent years, a number of states have begun to turn away from the death penalty. Since 2004, four states have abolished the death penalty, either by legislative repeal or court decision. Two other states have imposed temporary moratoria since 2000, and in about a dozen more, lawmakers have introduced bills proposing a moratorium or repeal.[29] There is an important difference between repeal and moratorium movements, however. Many states have suspended executions with an eye to preventing the execution of innocent people; they hope to reform the death penalty rather than abolish it. Toward this same end, many non-moratorium states have undertaken reviews of their capital punishment procedures. For example, Virginia initiated an audit of crime-lab errors, and Texas created a commission to look into the adequacy of criminal justice procedures in light of advances in DNA and other forensic technology.

These developments underscore that the law governing the death penalty is far from stable. Punishment rules and practices have changed dramatically over time and from place to place. What factors shape (and should shape) a citizen's views on this fundamental question? And when, in a democracy, is it appropriate for elected officials and criminal justice professionals to support conceptions of appropriate punishment different from those preferred by the public at large? What accounts for this variation?

27. The Gallup Poll, Two in Three Favor Death Penalty for Convicted Murderers: Public Divided over Death Penalty or Life Imprisonment as Better Punishment (June 1, 2006), http://www.gallup.com/poll/23167/two-three-favor-death-penalty-convicted-murderers.aspx.

28. See Carol S. Steiker & Jordan M. Steiker, A Tale of Two Nations: Implementation of the Death Penalty in "Executing" vs. "Symbolic" States in the United States, 84 Tex. L. Rev. 1869 (2006); U.S. Dept. of Justice, Bureau of Justice Statistics, Capital Punishment Statistics, http://bjs.ojp.usdoj.gov/index.cfm.

29. American Bar Association, Death Penalty Moratorium Implementation Project, Frequently Asked Questions, http://www.americanbar.org/groups/individual_rights/projects/death_penalty_moratorium_implementation_project/frequently_asked_questions.html.

2. Policy Considerations

The central considerations in public debates about the death penalty are related to the animating principles of criminal law more generally. In Chapter 2 we examined a variety of materials bearing on the justification of criminal punishments. One concern throughout that chapter was to identify the extent to which punishment serves various utilitarian goals. Another was to consider whether wrongdoing itself justifies punishment of wrongdoers—regardless of the social utility or disutility of doing so—and whether punishment of wrongdoers is not merely morally permissible but rather morally required. These issues, explored in Chapter 2 with reference to punishment in general, can provide a framework for examining the justification of the ultimate punishment of death.

a. Deterrence

There has been intense debate for decades about whether the death penalty deters (or, more precisely, whether it deters more effectively than life imprisonment). The debate takes three tracks. One is theoretical, using deterrence principles to generate predictions about the effect of capital punishment. Another track is empirical, applying sophisticated methods to data in an attempt to measure the deterrent effect. The third track focuses on the burden of proof: If deterrence effects remain unclear, does that uncertainty argue for or against the death penalty?

(1) *At the theoretical level*, the argument for a deterrent effect from capital punishment derives from both its severity and its salience. As long as most potential murderers believe that execution is a worse fate than life imprisonment, the more severe sanction should—all else equal—decrease the homicide rate. Moreover, even infrequent application of an especially severe sanction should have this effect, given that people tend to overestimate the likelihood of particularly feared or "salient" harms.[30] But from another perspective, theory undermines the case for a deterrent effect. The certainty and speed of imposing a sanction play key roles in generating deterrence,[31] and the death penalty is anything but speedy and sure. There are approximately 15,000-20,000 murders each year in the United States. But the national execution rate is in the range of 50-100 each year, and an average of ten years elapses between sentencing and execution. Furthermore, the mental impairments that many capital defendants suffer and the impulsive nature of many capital crimes work against the assumption of rational calculation that deterrence theory must maintain. Deterrence theory can even be used to predict that capital punishment will *increase* the murder rate, because state executions may

---

30. See Cass R. Sunstein & Adrian Vermeule, Is Capital Punishment Morally Required? Acts, Omissions, and Life-Life Tradeoffs, 58 Stan. L. Rev. 703, 714 (2005).

31. See Hugo Bedau, The Courts, the Constitution, and Capital Punishment 56 (1977) (noting that deterrent efficacy is determined not only by the severity of a punishment, but also by "the facility, celerity, and reliability with which the punishment can be inflicted").

have a "brutalization effect"[32] by encouraging the use of violence to deal with problems. Thus, theory tells us that the death penalty will deter murder, have no effect on murder, or increase the number of murders. Some economists have urged that only empirical analysis can sort among these three options.[33]

(2) *Empirical analysis* initially resulted in a stalemate;[34] for decades, the consensus view was that there was no reliable evidence that capital punishment deterred homicide, but also no reliable evidence that it failed to do so. Recently, economists have continued the attempt to isolate the effect of capital punishment. Although some of the new studies support the "no effect" and "brutalization" claims, most find significant deterrent effects.[35]

Critics of these claims for a deterrent effect emphasize three problems. The first is *aggregation*: the overwhelming influence of one or two outlier states (particularly Texas) or outlier years. See Richard Berk, New Claims About Executions and General Deterrence: Déjà Vu All Over Again?, 2 J. Empirical Legal Stud. 303, 327 (2005).

Second, critics contend that the new deterrence studies fail to account sufficiently for *hard-to-quantify social and institutional factors*, such as the performance of the criminal justice system overall (including the clearance rates for violent crimes) and the deterrent effects of life without parole sentences.[36] John Donahue and Justin Wolfers note that although one might intuitively think the death penalty deters, the real question is how much deterrence it produces beyond that resulting from the threat of imprisonment alone, because the death penalty "can only have a possible useful effect on a very small number of individuals—those that would *not* be deterred by the prospect of life without possibility of parole but *would* be deterred by the presence of the death penalty." John J. Donahue, III & Justin Wolfers, Estimating the Impact of the Death Penalty on Murder, 11 Am. L. & Econ. Rev. 249, 296 (2009).

Third, critics argue that the new deterrence studies lack *robustness*—small changes in research design or in the time periods and places included can result in enormous changes in the conclusions. See Ethan Cohen-Cole et al., Model

---

32. See William Bowers & Glenn Pierce, Deterrence or Brutalization? What Is the Effect of Executions? 26 Crime & Delinquency 453 (1980).

33. John J. Donohue & Justin Wolfers, Uses and Abuses of Empirical Evidence in the Death Penalty Debate, 58 Stan. L. Rev. 791, 796 (2005).

34. See Thorsten Sellin, "Homicides in Retentionist and Abolitionist States," in Capital Punishment at 138 (Thorsten Sellin ed., 1967) (analyzing homicide rates over time in contiguous states with different capital punishment policies and finding no deterrent effect); Isaac Ehrlich, The Deterrent Effect of Capital Punishment: A Question of Life and Death, 65 Am. Econ. Rev. 397 (1975) (employing regression analysis and finding a substantial deterrent effect); Lawrence R. Klein et al., The Deterrent Effect of Capital Punishment, in Deterrence and Incapacitation: Estimating the Effects of Criminal Sanctions on Crime Rates 336-360 (Alfred Blumstein et al. eds., 1978) (rejecting Erhlich's results).

35. See Robert Weisberg, The Death Penalty Meets Social Science: Deterrence and Jury Behavior Under New Scrutiny, 1 Ann. Rev. L. & Soc. Sci. 151, 157 (2005).

36. Jeffrey Fagan, Testimony to the New York Standing Committee on Codes, Assembly Standing Committee on Judiciary, and Assembly Standing Committee on Correction, Hearings on the Future of Capital Punishment in New York: Deterrence and the Death Penalty: A Critical Review of the New Evidence 7-10 (Jan. 21, 2005).

Uncertainty and the Deterrent Effect of Capital Punishment, 11 Am. L. & Econ. Rev. 335 (2009); Jeffrey Fagan, Death and Deterrence Redux: Science, Alchemy and Causal Reasoning on Capital Punishment, 4 Ohio St. J. Crim. L. 255 (2006); John J. Donohue & Justin Wolfers, Uses and Abuses of Empirical Evidence in the Death Penalty Debate, 58 Stan. L. Rev. 791, 796 (2005).[37]

(3) These complex critiques raise the *burden-of-proof* question: How sure do we need to be of the death penalty's deterrent effect in order to justify capital punishment? Philosophy professor Louis Pojman phrases the argument this way: "To bet against capital punishment is to bet against the innocent and for the murderer."[38] Do you agree? If we cannot show that the death penalty deters murders, should we nonetheless execute convicted murderers in the hope that it might?

Even more fundamentally, is deterrence (or the lack thereof) the main source of support or opposition to the death penalty? For an argument that deterrence does not matter to supporters or opponents of capital punishment, see Dan M. Kahan, The Secret Ambition of Deterrence, 113 Harv. L. Rev. 413, 437-439 (1999). Many of those opposed to the death penalty say they would reject it as immoral or unfair even if it were known to deter. Conversely, proponents of the death penalty often consider it a morally appropriate response to certain crimes, whether or not it deters. Is it justifiable to set aside the deterrence issue in this way? If the death penalty has no net deterrent effect (or if it actually encourages some murders), would it be wrong to inflict capital punishment without any prospect of a crime-control benefit? Conversely, if the death penalty really deters, would it be wrong to forgo the opportunity to use capital punishment to save innocent lives? Professors Cass Sunstein and Adrian Vermeule contend that if capital punishment were known to deter, then the government would be obligated to employ it to save innocent lives. In their view, opponents of capital punishment are mistaken to distinguish between the government's responsibility for capital punishment and its responsibility for inadequately deterred private murder: Both kinds of killings result from choices by the state. The government saves and loses lives no matter which path it pursues:

> The only interesting or even meaningful question government ever faces is not whether to act, but what action should be taken—what mix of criminal justice policies government ought to pursue. The policy mix that does not include capital punishment is not an "omission" or a "failure to act" in any meaningful sense. If a government chooses that mix, it is allocating a certain set of rights to both murderers and their victims; the latter are certainly given a right to be free from murder, but the right is limited by the terms of the anticipated punishment. . . .

---

37. One recent study found that approximately 88 percent of criminologists do not believe that the death penalty has a deterrent effect beyond long-term imprisonment. Michael L. Radelet & Traci L. Lacock, Do Executions Lower Homicide Rates?: The Views of Leading Criminologists, 99 J. Crim. L. & Criminology 489, 501 (2009).

38. Louis P. Pojman, Why the Death Penalty Is Morally Permissible, in Debating the Death Penalty 66 (Hugo Bedau & Paul Cassell eds., 2004).

[Assuming that capital punishment were known to deter, the] legal regime whose package of crime-control instruments happens not to include capital punishment [is] a policy that inevitably and predictably opts for more murders rather than fewer.[39]

One critic responds that inadequately deterred private murders are not the moral equivalent of executions, because the government itself does not intend to kill the innocent murder victims and is not purporting to punish them.[40] Consider also the logical implications of Sunstein and Vermeule's argument. If net lives would be saved by executing someone for drunk driving, would such an execution be morally required? What if it would save net lives to execute the drunk driver's children?[41]

Whatever the import of the empirical studies, psychological research indicates that people's positions on the death penalty are resistant to change, even in the face of contradictory evidence. Dan Kahan and Donald Braman claim that individuals view empirical information through the lens of their preexisting cultural beliefs; such "cultural cognition" explains why people often do not alter their views when confronted with inconsistent empirical information, but rather choose to reject the empirical findings instead.[42] In doing so, they may be responding to other values and commitments. What commitments, moral or otherwise, might be at work? For a probing analysis of American death penalty practices in light of America's commitment to democracy and federalism, see David Garland, Peculiar Institution: America's Death Penalty in an Age of Abolition (2010).

b. Retribution

Recall the justification for punishment given by Immanuel Kant in Chapter 2, pages 93-95 supra. In his framework, the deterrent value of the sanction makes no difference to the justification of any punishment, even the ultimate one:

> Even if a civil society resolved to dissolve itself with the consent of all its members—as might be supposed in the case of a people inhabiting an island resolving to separate and scatter themselves through the whole world—the last murderer in prison ought to be executed before the resolution was carried out.[43]

Why is it morally required—or even morally permissible—to execute a murderer whose death would no longer serve any purpose?

---

39. Sunstein & Vermeule, supra note 30, at 722-723.
40. Carol S. Steiker, No, Capital Punishment Is Not Morally Required: Deterrence, Deontology, and the Death Penalty, 58 Stan. L. Rev. 751, 755 (2005).
41. See id. at 775-782.
42. See Dan M. Kahan & Donald Braman, Cultural Cognition and Public Policy, 24 Yale L. & Pol'y Rev. 149 (2006).
43. Immanuel Kant, The Philosophy of Law 198 (W. Hastie trans., 1887).

One retributivist answer is that punishment is required even when it will not benefit society because only punishment can restore equality among persons. Under this view, as explained by Herbert Morris and critiqued by John Mackie, pages 96-97, 98 supra, an offender asserts superiority and gains an unfair advantage through wrongdoing that can be repudiated only through proportional punishment.

The death penalty also serves a powerful expressive function. "Through the imposition of just punishment, civilized society expresses its sense of revulsion toward those who, by violating its laws, have not only harmed individuals but also weakened the bonds that hold communities together." Paul G. Cassell, In Defense of the Death Penalty, in Debating the Death Penalty 183, 198 (Hugo Bedau & Paul Cassell eds., 2004). "The death penalty reminds us . . . that we are responsible for what we do, so that dire consequences for immoral acts are eminently appropriate." Louis P. Lojman, Why the Death Penalty is Morally Permissible, in Debating the Death Penalty, supra, at 58. David Garland observes that "[t]o announce a capital sentence is to make a distinct and powerful statement, signaling the heinous nature of the crime and the evil nature of the criminal. It is to mark the murderer as among the worst of the worst. . . . " Garland, supra, at 291.

Others posit that there are utilitarian reasons to respect the deep-rooted desire for retribution that people feel when horrific crimes occur. Paul Robinson and John Darley assert that "[t]he criminal law's power in nurturing and communicating societal norms and its power to have people defer to it . . . is directly proportional to criminal law's moral credibility." Paul H. Robinson & John M. Darley, The Utility of Desert, 91 Nw. U. L. Rev. 453, 477 (1997). This argument suggests that, if a large majority of the population believes that justice requires the death penalty, the law should reflect that view to maintain legitimacy and compliance and to avoid having people take the law into their own hands.

Do these accounts of retributivism require that punishment mirror the crime committed—the biblical principle of lex talionis or "an eye for an eye"? Or can the imposition of lesser or different punishments adequately respect the equality of victims, express revulsion at the crime, and therefore maintain the criminal law's legitimacy? Kant maintained that only the lex talionis could provide a standard sufficiently certain and unwavering, see supra 94. But many who endorse retributivism interpret it to require simply that punishment be proportional to the offense rather than an exact mirror of it.[44] After all, as Blackstone noted long ago, the lex talionis is often either impossible to apply or impossibly extreme: "[T]here are very many crimes, that will in no shape admit of [lex talionis] penalties, without manifest absurdity

---

44. See, e.g., Andrew von Hirsch, Doing Justice: The Choice of Punishments (1976). For an application of this approach to the issue of capital punishment, see David McCord, Imagining a Retributivist Alternative to Capital Punishment, 50 Fla. L. Rev. 1 (1998).

and wickedness. Theft cannot be punished by theft, defamation by defamation, forgery by forgery, adultery by adultery, and the like."[45]

In fact, our justice system does not torture torturers as punishment for their crimes. Why not? The question is not as silly as it might first appear. Some criminal acts may be so dreadful that a simple execution would not come close to mirroring the harm inflicted by the perpetrator. What arguments are there, either within or outside of retributivism, for such limitations on punishment? Moreover, the death penalty itself is now carried out in a manner that is designed to make it as painless as possible through lethal injection. Justice Stevens has observed that "by requiring that an execution be relatively painless, we necessarily protect the inmate from enduring any punishment that is comparable to the suffering inflicted on his victim." Baze v. Rees, 533 U.S. 35, 80-81 (2008) (Stevens, J., concurring in the judgment).[46]

One retributivist argument against extreme punishments emphasizes the requirement that punishment be fully deserved. Under this view, the poverty, discrimination, and other societal deprivation suffered by many murderers mitigate their responsibility and thus preclude the most severe penalty. The criminal law recognizes that some situations or mental impairments negate the ability to make rational choices, and it accordingly provides full or partial defenses from criminal liability in such circumstances. See Chapter 8, infra, pages 921-1031. Should disabilities that fall just short of a full or partial defense nonetheless serve to preclude the most severe punishments? If murderers who have suffered from social deprivation or psychological impairment do not deserve the death penalty, what do they deserve? For discussion of these arguments, see Carol S. Steiker, The Death Penalty and Deontology 444-452, in The Oxford Handbook of Philosophy of Criminal Law (John Deigh & David Dolinko eds., 2011).

c. Error

The retributivist requirement that punishment be deserved is most clearly flouted when those who are executed deserve no punishment at all. The possibility of executing the innocent has become more than a mere hypothetical in recent years. A 2009 investigative report makes a powerful case that Texas executed an innocent man when it put to death Cameron Todd Willingham on the basis of faulty forensic evidence. David Grann, Trial by Fire: Did Texas Execute an Innocent Man?, New Yorker, Sept. 7, 2009. Illinois provides another source of concern.[47] Thirteen Illinois death row inmates who had been convicted and sentenced to death in the post-1976 era were exonerated, some only days or hours before their scheduled executions. Republican

---

45. 4 William Blackstone, Commentaries *13 (1769).

46. For constitutional arguments that some methods of execution may, because of their painfulness, violate the Eighth Amendment's proscription of "cruel and unusual punishment," see Deborah W. Denno, Getting to Death: Are Executions Constitutional?, 82 Iowa L. Rev. 319 (1997).

47. See Franklin Zimring, The No-Win 1990s, in The Contradictions of Capital Punishment 166 (2004).

Governor George Ryan, a former supporter of the death penalty, responded first by declaring a moratorium on executions in the state and ultimately by granting clemency to the entire death row population of 171 inmates. "Until I can be sure that everyone sentenced to death in Illinois is truly guilty," said Ryan, "until I can be sure with moral certainty that no innocent man or woman is facing lethal injection, no man or woman will meet that fate."[48] Was Governor Ryan's decision to grant clemency justified even in cases in which there appeared to be no doubt about the offender's guilt?

The scope of the innocence problem remains a matter of great debate. Compare Hugo A. Bedau & Michael L. Radelet, Miscarriages of Justice in Potentially Capital Cases, 40 Stan. L. Rev. 21 (1987) (contending that 350 innocent people were wrongfully convicted of capital or potentially capital crimes since 1900, 23 of whom were executed), with Stephen J. Markman & Paul G. Cassell, Protecting the Innocent: A Response to the Bedau-Radelet Study, 41 Stan. L. Rev. 121, 121 (1988) (calling the study "severely flawed" and maintaining that the risk of executing the innocent is "too small to be a significant factor in the debate over the death penalty"). The advent of DNA evidence has allowed more certainty in some cases: Of the more than 135 death row inmates who have been released since 1973 as a result of evidence suggesting their innocence, 17 were exonerated through DNA evidence.[49]

Concerns about the risk of executing the innocent no doubt played a role in the decline of public support for capital punishment in the late 1990s. See supra pages 524-525. Such concerns also have led to a variety of governmental responses—from Governor Ryan's mass clemencies, to the creation of law reform commissions to correct deficiencies in the criminal justice process, to the passage of federal "innocence protection" legislation,[50] and to the proliferation of "innocence projects," which use public and private funding to investigate convicted inmates' claims of innocence.

Will more widespread use of DNA testing substantially reduce the risk of error? Some observers are not optimistic; they suggest that forensic evidence is not available in most cases and that the outcome of these cases will still be affected by the factors that led to false convictions before the availability of DNA testing—faulty eyewitness identifications, perjured testimony, planted evidence, jailhouse informants who falsely claim that the cellmate confessed to them, and so on. Brandon Garrett, Convicting the Innocent: Where Criminal Prosecutions Go Wrong (2011), documents the pervasiveness of such practices. Garrett studied the trials of 250 people exonerated by DNA evidence and found non-DNA related flaws to be so common that he

---

48. Governor George Ryan, Speech, Commutation of 167 Death Sentences in Illinois, Jan. 11, 2003, available at http://www.ocadp.org/educate/ryan_speech_commutations.htm.

49. Death Penalty Information Center, Innocence and the Death Penalty, http://www.death-penaltyinfo.org/innocence-list-those-freed-death-row (last visited Aug. 10, 2011).

50. For example, the Innocence Protection Act of 2004, Title IV of the Justice for All Act, Pub. Law 108-405, created a DNA testing program for federal prisoners, a grant program to help states pay for DNA testing for state prisoners, and a grant program to improve the quality of prosecution and defense representation in state capital cases.

concluded that the 250 may be "just the tip of the iceberg." Id. at 11. For instance, in many of the cases Garrett studied, police had fed details of the crime to defendants during extensive interrogations, often coupled with abuse or threats. As a result, a high proportion of the exonerees confessed and included in their confession details of the crime that only the perpetrator could have known. Id. at 23-27, 38-39. Is Garrett correct that those exonerated by DNA evidence likely represent only the tip of the iceberg? What rate of wrongful convictions would be acceptable?

A risk of error is inherent in any human endeavor. Is this risk less acceptable in capital cases than in ordinary criminal cases? Many seem to think so, but why? Obviously, it is not possible to correct a wrongful execution after the fact, but is it really possible to "correct" a lengthy term of imprisonment? Are mistakes more likely in capital cases than in ordinary cases? On the one hand, capital cases receive more resources at trial and on appeal, which ought to promote greater accuracy. On the other hand, ineffective assistance of counsel in capital trials is far from uncommon, so the impact of trial resources should not be overstated. David R. Dow, The Autobiography of an Execution (2010). Moreover, the most aggravated murders generate intense pressure to "solve" the case quickly and produce a conviction, which can lead to dubious police investigatory practices, such as reliance on coercive interrogations that generate false statements. The same pressures may lead prosecutors to offer unreliable evidence, such as testimony from jailhouse informants, and to suppress potentially exculpatory information. See Samuel R. Gross, The Risks of Death: Why Erroneous Convictions Are Common in Capital Cases, 44 Buff. L. Rev. 469 (1996).

For some supporters of capital punishment, the risk of error does not call the practice into question. Consider Ernest van den Haag, Punishing Criminals 219-220 (1975):

> Many social policies have intended effects that are statistically certain, irrevocable, unjust, and deadly. Automobile traffic unintentionally kills innocent victims; so does surgery (and most medicines); so does the death penalty. These activities are justified, nevertheless, because benefits (including justice) are felt to outweigh the statistical certainty of unintentionally killing innocents.

Are these analogies convincing? If the benefits of the death penalty are less certain than the benefits of these other activities, does that suggest that society should tolerate less error? Does the fact that the death penalty involves intentional killing distinguish it from fatalities that occur in traffic accidents and surgery?

Some abolitionists also criticize the focus on the innocence issue. They argue that execution of the innocent is a less significant difficulty than the endemic problems of disproportionate punishment of the "guilty" and the arbitrary and discriminatory treatment of offenders. See Carol S. Steiker & Jordan M. Steiker, The Seduction of Innocence: The Attraction and Limitations of the Focus on Innocence in Capital Punishment Law and Advocacy, 95

J. Crim. L. & Criminology 587 (2005). Steiker and Steiker argue that disproportionate punishment of the guilty is just as wrong (and much more frequent) than capital sentences imposed on the innocent. Do you agree?

d. Bias

Racial bias has a long history in American law enforcement in general and in
the administration of capital punishment in particular, with roots in the frequent use of harsh criminal sanctions to control slaves prior to the Civil War.
See Randall Kennedy, Race, Crime and the Law (1997); Stuart Banner, The
Death Penalty: An American History (2003); David Garland, Peculiar Institution: America's Death Penalty in an Age of Abolition (2010). Today, blacks
remain substantially over-represented on death row relative to their numbers
in the population, see page 524 supra, but there is controversy over the causes
of that disparity. Some of it can be explained by differences in rates of offending and the kinds of offenses committed. But evidence suggests that, even after
those differences are accounted for, the death penalty is more likely when the
defendant is black and the victim is white. We examine this evidence in depth
at pages 557-568 infra, in connection with the constitutional limits on capital
punishment.

  Constitutional challenges aside, what bearing should evidence of racial bias
have on the wisdom or morality of the death penalty? What about other kinds
of inequality? It is clear that poor defendants get much worse legal representation than wealthy defendants, and this disparity—though not the product of
intentional discrimination—leads to disproportionate numbers of poor people
on death row. See Stephen B. Bright, Counsel for the Poor: The Death
Sentence Not for the Worst Crime but for the Worst Lawyer, 103 Yale L.J.
1835 (1994). One view, pungently expressed by Ernest van den Haag, Refut-
ing Reiman and Nathanson, in Punishment and the Death Penalty: The
Current Debate 207, 214 (Robert M. Baird & Stuart E. Rosenbaum eds.,
1995) is that "unequal justice [punishing some guilty offenders according to
desert, even if others get away] is the only justice we have, and certainly better
than equal injustice—giving no murderer the punishment his crimes
deserves."

  Critics of this view maintain that racial bias and economic inequality
should make us question whether we can be sure that those who get the
death penalty actually "deserve" it. Moreover, even if we could be sure of
desert, some question whether unequal justice can be called justice at all.
Consider Stephen Nathanson, Does It Matter If the Death Penalty Is Arbitrarily Administered?, in Punishment and the Death Penalty, supra, at 161,
167-168:

> [Suppose] I tell my class that anyone who plagiarizes will fail the course. Three
> students plagiarize papers, but only one receives a failing grade. The other two,
> in describing their motivation, win my sympathy, and I give them passing
> grades. . . . Suppose further that I am regularly more lenient with attractive
> female students than with others. Or suppose that it is only redheads or

wealthy students whom I fail. . . . In these instances, I think the plagiarizers who are punished have grounds for complaint, even though they were, by the announced standards, clearly guilty and deserving of punishment.

What "grounds for complaint" do the plagiarizers who are punished have? What remedy would be just under the circumstances? What if Nathanson was more punitive towards female students, who have a history of being excluded from institutions of higher education? How much should a history of bias— and particularly racial bias—matter in the death penalty context? Do concerns about racial bias and inequality demand special attention in *death penalty* cases, or are these problems no different—and perhaps even less significant, given the fewer numbers of defendants involved—than inequalities in punishment throughout the criminal justice system in general? Reconsider these questions in relation to *McCleskey v. Kemp*, infra page 557.

3. *Constitutional Limitations*

INTRODUCTORY NOTE

Until the middle of the twentieth century, opponents of the death penalty had largely devoted their efforts to legislative reform, as it was widely assumed that the Constitution left the question of capital punishment—like nearly all other questions of criminal justice—to the states and the political branches of the federal government. During the 1950s and 1960s, however, when the Supreme Court shined a constitutional spotlight on issues of racial justice and the rights of criminal defendants, abolitionists launched a concentrated assault on the constitutionality of capital punishment.[51] Recall that at common law all murder was punishable by death. Gradually, the scope of capital punishment was narrowed, first by the division of murder into two degrees, so that only the more serious was subject to mandatory capital punishment, and then by the introduction of discretion in sentencing even for the highest category of criminal homicides. By the beginning of the twentieth century, 23 American jurisdictions made capital punishment discretionary in first-degree murder cases, and by 1962, all the remaining jurisdictions had adopted this approach.[52]

Litigation challenging this punishment scheme focused on two issues:

1. Procedural due process. All the states committed the death penalty decision to the discretion of the judge or jury, but none provided any standards to guide the exercise of that discretion. The reliance on unguided discretion was prevalent in sentencing decisions generally, but many thought that when a choice between life and death was to be made, due process required some

---

51. The development of a detailed strategy for litigation against the death penalty is recounted in Michael Meltsner, Cruel and Unusual: The Supreme Court and Capital Punishment (1973).

52. The history is detailed in Model Penal Code and Commentaries, Comment to §210.6 at 120-132 (1980).

explicit criteria of decision. The Court rejected that view in McGautha v. California, 402 U.S. 183, 207-208 (1971), holding that "committing to the untrammeled discretion of the jury the power to pronounce life or death is [not] offensive to anything in the Constitution." The Court reasoned that:

> To identify before the fact those characteristics of criminal homicides and their perpetrators which call for the death penalty, and to express these characteristics in language which can be fairly understood and applied by the sentencing authority, appear to be tasks which are beyond present human ability. . . . The States are entitled to assume that jurors confronted with the truly awesome responsibility of decreeing death for a fellow human will act with due regard for the consequences of their decision and will consider a variety of factors. . . .

McGautha proved to be less significant than it seemed, however, because the same concerns about unguided discretion soon surfaced in attacks based on the Eighth Amendment's Cruel and Unusual Punishment Clause.

2. *Cruel and unusual punishment.* Only a year after *McGautha*, a 5–4 majority of the Court held in Furman v. Georgia, 408 U.S. 238 (1972), that capital punishment, as then administered, violated the Eighth Amendment's prohibition of "cruel and unusual punishments." The Court's holding was stated in a brief per curiam opinion that made no attempt to set forth the majority's reasoning. Each of the nine justices filed a separate concurring or dissenting opinion explaining his own approach to the Eighth Amendment issue, with none of the five justices in the majority joining any of the others' opinions. Only Justices Brennan and Marshall concluded that all capital punishment was unconstitutional. Justice Brennan argued that capital punishment did not comport with human dignity, while Justice Marshall maintained that average citizens, if fully informed of the death penalty's excessiveness in relation to its penological purposes, would reject it as morally unacceptable. The other three concurring justices put their objections to capital punishment on narrower grounds. Justice Douglas stressed the potential for discriminatory administration of the death penalty. Justice White noted that the extreme infrequency of imposition of the death penalty in the years preceding *Furman* rendered the penalty incapable of promoting its social or public purposes. In perhaps the most famous passage of the voluminous *Furman* opinions (id. at 309-310), Justice Stewart emphasized not only the infrequency, but also the randomness of the penalty's imposition:

> These death sentences are cruel and unusual in the same way that being struck by lightning is cruel and unusual. [I]f any basis can be discerned for the selection of these few to be sentenced to die, it is the constitutionally impermissible basis of race. But racial discrimination has not been proved, and I put it to one side. I simply conclude that the Eighth and Fourteenth Amendments cannot tolerate the infliction of a sentence of death under legal systems that permit this unique penalty to be so wantonly and so freakishly imposed.

The Chief Justice and Justices Blackmun, Powell, and Rehnquist dissented. The dissenters stressed the long tradition and continued acceptance of capital punishment and argued that the majority's position involved an unwarranted intrusion into the legislative process.

Because a clear majority of the Justices had neither rejected capital punishment outright nor indicated under what conditions it might be preserved, *Furman* created considerable confusion for states that desired to retain the death penalty. Two alternatives appeared plausible to address the concerns raised in *Furman* about the arbitrary or discriminatory application of the death penalty: (1) enacting legislation to make capital punishment mandatory in certain cases; or (2) establishing guidelines to determine who would be subjected to capital punishment. By 1976, at least 35 states and the U.S. Congress had enacted new capital punishment legislation; half of these jurisdictions had adopted provisions for a mandatory death penalty, while the remainder opted for schemes under which the sentencing authority would be required to consider specified aggravating and mitigating circumstances.[53] The Court soon confronted challenges to the new legislation, granting certiorari to hear challenges to new death penalty statutes from Georgia, Florida, Texas, North Carolina, and Louisiana.

GREGG v. GEORGIA

Supreme Court of the United States
428 U.S. 153 (1976)

[Gregg was convicted by a jury on two counts of armed robbery and two counts of murder. After the guilty verdicts, a penalty hearing was held before the same jury, under guidelines enacted in response to the *Furman* decision. The jury imposed the death sentence on each count. The Georgia Supreme Court set aside the death sentences for armed robbery, on the ground that capital punishment had rarely been imposed for that crime, but the court affirmed the convictions on all counts and upheld the death sentences on the murder counts. The U.S. Supreme Court granted certiorari.]

JUSTICE STEWART, JUSTICE POWELL, and JUSTICE STEVENS announced the judgment of the Court and filed an opinion delivered by JUSTICE STEWART. . . .

We address initially the basic contention that the punishment of death for the crime of murder is, under all circumstances, "cruel and unusual" in violation of the Eighth and Fourteenth Amendments of the Constitution. . . . We now hold that the punishment of death does not invariably violate the Constitution. . . .

It is clear from the . . . precedents that the Eighth Amendment has not been regarded as a static concept. As Chief Justice Warren said, in an oft-quoted phrase, "[t]he Amendment must draw its meaning from the evolving standards of decency that mark the progress of a maturing society." Trop v. Dulles,

---

53. For details concerning these enactments, see Samuel R. Gross, The Romance of Revenge: Capital Punishment in America, 13 Stud. L. Pol. & Soc'y 17, 84-92 (1993); Model Penal Code and Commentaries, Comment to §210.6 at 156-157 & nn.144-148 (1980).

356 U.S. 86, 101 (1958). Thus, an assessment of contemporary values concerning the infliction of a challenged sanction is relevant to the application of the Eighth Amendment. . . .

But our cases also make clear that public perceptions of standards of decency with respect to criminal sanctions are not conclusive. A penalty also must accord with "the dignity of man," which is the "basic concept underlying the Eighth Amendment." Trop v. Dulles, supra, 356 U.S., at 100. This means, at least, that the punishment not be "excessive." [T]he inquiry into "excessiveness" has two aspects. First, the punishment must not involve the unnecessary and wanton infliction of pain. Second, the punishment must not be grossly out of proportion to the severity of the crime.

Of course, the requirements of the Eighth Amendment must be applied with an awareness of the limited role to be played by the courts. [W]hile we have an obligation to insure that constitutional bounds are not overreached, we may not act as judges as we might as legislators. . . .

Therefore, in assessing a punishment selected by a democratically elected legislature against the constitutional measure, we presume its validity. We may not require the legislature to select the least severe penalty possible so long as the penalty selected is not cruelly inhumane or disproportionate to the crime involved.

. . . We now consider specifically whether the sentence of death for the crime of murder is a per se violation of the Eighth and Fourteenth Amendments to the Constitution. We note first that history and precedent strongly support a negative answer to this question. It is apparent from the text of the Constitution itself that the existence of capital punishment was accepted by the Framers. . . . For nearly two centuries, this Court, repeatedly and often expressly, has recognized that capital punishment is not invalid per se. . . .

Four years ago, the petitioners in *Furman* and its companion cases predicated their argument primarily upon the asserted proposition that standards of decency had evolved to the point where capital punishment no longer could be tolerated. . . . The petitioners in the capital cases before the Court today renew the "standards of decency" argument, but developments during the four years since *Furman* have undercut substantially the assumptions upon which their argument rested. Despite the continuing debate, dating back to the 19th century, over the morality and utility of capital punishment, it is now evident that a large proportion of American society continues to regard it as an appropriate and necessary criminal sanction. . . . The legislatures of at least 35 States have enacted new statutes that provide for the death penalty for at least some crimes that result in the death of another person. [T]he relative infrequency of jury verdicts imposing the death sentence does not indicate rejection of capital punishment per se. Rather, the reluctance of juries in many cases to impose the sentence may well reflect the humane feeling that this most irrevocable of sanctions should be reserved for a small number of extreme cases. . . .

As we have seen, however, the Eighth Amendment demands more than that a challenged punishment be acceptable to contemporary society. The

Court also must ask whether it comports with the basic concept of human dignity at the core of the Amendment. Although we cannot "invalidate a category of penalties because we deem less severe penalties adequate to serve the ends of penology," the sanction imposed cannot be so totally without penological justification that it results in the gratuitous infliction of suffering.

The death penalty is said to serve two principal social purposes: retribution and deterrence of capital crimes by prospective offenders.

In part, capital punishment is an expression of society's moral outrage at particularly offensive conduct. This function may be unappealing to many, but it is essential in an ordered society that asks its citizens to rely on legal processes rather than self-help to vindicate their wrongs. "The instinct for retribution is part of the nature of man, and channeling that instinct in the administration of criminal justice serves an important purpose in promoting the stability of a society governed by law. When people begin to believe that organized society is unwilling or unable to impose upon criminal offenders the punishment they 'deserve,' then there are sown the seeds of anarchy—of self-help, vigilante justice, and lynch law." Furman v. Georgia, 408 U.S., at 308 (Stewart, J., concurring). . . .

Statistical attempts to evaluate the worth of the death penalty as a deterrent to crimes by potential offenders have occasioned a great deal of debate. The results simply have been inconclusive. . . . The value of capital punishment as a deterrent of crime is a complex factual issue the resolution of which properly rests with the legislatures, which can evaluate the results of statistical studies in terms of their own local conditions and with a flexibility of approach that is not available to the courts. . . .

Finally, we must consider whether the punishment of death is disproportionate in relation to the crime for which it is imposed. There is no question that death as a punishment is unique in its severity and irrevocability. . . . But we are concerned here only with the imposition of capital punishment for the crime of murder, and when a life has been taken deliberately by the offender, we cannot say that the punishment is invariably disproportionate to the crime. It is an extreme sanction, suitable to the most extreme of crimes.

We hold that the death penalty is not a form of punishment that may never be imposed, . . . regardless of the procedure followed in reaching the decision to impose it. . . . Because of the uniqueness of the death penalty, *Furman* held that it could not be imposed under sentencing procedures that created a substantial risk that it would be inflicted in an arbitrary and capricious manner. . . .

Jury sentencing has been considered desirable in capital cases in order "to maintain a link between contemporary community values and the penal system—a link without which the determination of punishment could hardly reflect 'the evolving standards of decency that mark the progress of a maturing society.'" But it creates special problems. Much of the information that is relevant to the sentencing decision may have no relevance to the question of guilt, or may even be extremely prejudicial to a fair determination of that question. This problem, however, is scarcely insurmountable. Those who have studied the question suggest that a bifurcated procedure—one in which the question of sentence is not considered until the determination of guilt has been made—is . . . likely to ensure elimination of the constitutional deficiencies in *Furman.*

But the provision of relevant information under fair procedural rules is not alone sufficient to guarantee that the information will be properly used. . . . Since the members of a jury will have had little, if any, previous experience in sentencing, they are unlikely to be skilled in dealing with the information they are given. . . . It seems clear, however, that the problem will be alleviated if the jury is given guidance regarding the factors about the crime and the defendant that the State, representing organized society, deems particularly relevant to the sentencing decision. . . .

While some have suggested that standards to guide a capital jury's sentencing deliberations are impossible to formulate, the fact is that such standards have been developed. [The Court here referred to the MPC proposals. See §210.6, Appendix.] While such standards are by necessity somewhat general, they do provide guidance to the sentencing authority and thereby reduce the likelihood that it will impose a sentence that fairly can be called capricious or arbitrary. . . .

In summary, the concerns expressed in *Furman* that the penalty of death not be imposed in an arbitrary or capricious manner can be met by a carefully drafted statute that ensures that the sentencing authority is given adequate information and guidance. As a general proposition these concerns are best met by a system that provides for a bifurcated proceeding at which the sentencing authority is apprised of the information relevant to the imposition of sentence and provided with standards to guide its use of the information. . . .

We now turn to consideration of the constitutionality of Georgia's capital-sentencing procedures. In the wake of *Furman,* Georgia amended its capital punishment statute, but chose not to narrow the scope of its murder provisions. Thus, now as before *Furman,* in Georgia "[a] person commits murder when he unlawfully and with malice aforethought, either express or implied, causes the death of another human being." Ga. Code Ann. §26-1101(a) (1972). All persons convicted of murder "shall be punished by death or by imprisonment for life." §26-1101(c) (1972).

Georgia did act, however, to narrow the class of murderers subject to capital punishment by specifying 10 statutory aggravating circumstances, one of which must be found by the jury to exist beyond a reasonable doubt before a death sentence can ever be imposed.[48] In addition, the jury is authorized to consider any other appropriate aggravating or mitigating

---

48. The text of the statute enumerating the various aggravating circumstances is [as follows:

(1) The offense of murder, rape, armed robbery, or kidnapping was committed by a person with a prior record of conviction for a capital felony, or the offense of murder was committed by a person who has a substantial history of serious assaultive criminal convictions.

(2) The offense of murder, rape, armed robbery, or kidnapping was committed while the offender was engaged in the commission of another capital felony, or

circumstances. The jury is not required to find any mitigating circumstance in order to make a recommendation of mercy that is binding on the trial court, but it must find a *statutory* aggravating circumstance before recommending a sentence of death. . . .

On their face these procedures seem to satisfy the concerns of *Furman*. No longer should there be "no meaningful basis for distinguishing the few cases in which [the death penalty] is imposed from the many cases in which it is not."

The petitioner contends, however, that the changes in the Georgia sentencing procedures are only cosmetic, that the arbitrariness and capriciousness condemned by *Furman* continue to exist. . . . First, the petitioner focuses on the opportunities for discretionary action that are inherent in the processing of any murder case under Georgia law. He notes that the state prosecutor has unfettered authority to select those persons whom he wishes to prosecute for a capital offense and to plea bargain with them. Further, at the trial the jury may choose to convict a defendant of a lesser included offense rather than find him guilty of a crime punishable by death, even if the evidence would support a capital verdict. And finally, a defendant who is convicted and sentenced to die may have his sentence commuted by the Governor of the State and the Georgia Board of Pardons and Paroles.

The existence of these discretionary stages is not determinative of the issues before us. At each of these stages an actor in the criminal justice system makes a decision which may remove a defendant from consideration as a candidate for the death penalty. *Furman*, in contrast, dealt with the decision to impose the death sentence on a specific individual who had been convicted of a capital offense. Nothing in any of our cases suggests that the decision to afford an individual defendant mercy violates the Constitution. *Furman* held only that, in order to minimize the risk that the death penalty would be

---

aggravated battery, or the offense of murder was committed while the offender was engaged in the commission of burglary or arson in the first degree.

(3) The offender by his act of murder, armed robbery, or kidnapping knowingly created a great risk of death to more than one person in a public place by means of a weapon or device which would normally be hazardous to the lives of more than one person.

(4) The offender committed the offense of murder for himself or another, for the purpose of receiving money or any other thing of monetary value.

(5) The murder of a judicial officer, former judicial officer, district attorney or solicitor or former district attorney or solicitor during or because of the exercise of his official duty.

(6) The offender caused or directed another to commit murder or committed murder as an agent or employee of another person.

(7) The offense of murder, rape, armed robbery, or kidnapping was outrageously or wantonly vile, horrible or inhuman in that it involved torture, depravity of mind, or an aggravated battery to the victim.

(8) The offense of murder was committed against any peace officer, corrections employee or fireman while engaged in the performance of his official duties.

(9) The offense of murder was committed by a person in, or who has escaped from, the lawful custody of a peace officer or place of lawful confinement.

(10) The murder was committed for the purpose of avoiding, interfering with, or preventing a lawful arrest or custody in a place of lawful confinement, of himself or another.]

imposed on a capriciously selected group of offenders, the decision to impose it had to be guided by standards so that the sentencing authority would focus on the particularized circumstances of the crime and the defendant. . . .

For the reasons expressed in this opinion, we hold that the statutory system under which Gregg was sentenced to death does not violate the Constitution. Accordingly, the judgment of the Georgia Supreme Court is affirmed. . . .

[The concurring opinion of Justice White, joined by the Chief Justice and Justice Rehnquist, the concurring opinion of Justice Blackmun, and the dissenting opinion of Justice Brennan are omitted.]

JUSTICE MARSHALL, dissenting. . . .

[I]f the constitutionality of the death penalty turns, as I have urged, on the opinion of an *informed* citizenry, then even the enactment of new death statutes cannot be viewed as conclusive. In *Furman*, I observed that the American people are largely unaware of the information critical to a judgment on the morality of the death penalty, and concluded that if they were better informed they would consider it shocking, unjust, and unacceptable. . . .

The two purposes that sustain the death penalty as nonexcessive in the Court's view are general deterrence and retribution. . . . The evidence I reviewed in *Furman* remains convincing, in my view, that "capital punishment is not necessary as a deterrent to crime in our society."

. . . The other principal purpose said to be served by the death penalty is retribution. . . . As my Brother Brennan stated in *Furman*, "[t]here is no evidence whatever that utilization of imprisonment rather than death encourages private blood feuds and other disorders." It simply defies belief to suggest that the death penalty is necessary to prevent the American people from taking the law into their own hands. . . .

The . . . contentions that society's expression of moral outrage through the imposition of the death penalty pre-empts the citizenry from taking the law into its own hands and reinforces moral values are not retributive in the purest sense. They are essentially utilitarian in that they portray the death penalty as valuable because of its beneficial results. These justifications for the death penalty are inadequate because the penalty is . . . not necessary to the accomplishment of those results.

There remains for consideration, however, . . . the purely retributive justification for the death penalty that . . . the taking of the murderer's life is itself morally good. . . . The mere fact that the community demands the murderer's life in return for the evil he has done cannot sustain the death penalty, for as [the plurality] remind[s] us, "the Eighth Amendment demands more than that a challenged punishment be acceptable to contemporary society." To be sustained under the Eighth Amendment, the death penalty must "compor[t] with the basic concept of human dignity at the core of the Amendment." . . . Under these standards, the taking of life "because the wrongdoer deserves it" surely must fall, for such a punishment has as its very basis the total denial of the wrongdoer's dignity and worth. . . .

NOTES

1. The provisional nature of the 1976 decisions. The Supreme Court did not attempt to catalog the essential elements of a constitutional death penalty statute in *Gregg* or its quartet of accompanying cases. In *Gregg*, the Court explained that "each distinct system must be examined on an individual basis." In Proffitt v. Florida, 428 U.S. 242 (1976), the Court upheld Florida's new capital scheme, which (like Georgia's) required the weighing of aggravating and mitigating factors prior to the imposition of the death penalty, but placed ultimate responsibility for sentencing with the trial judge rather than the jury. In Jurek v. Texas, 428 U.S. 262 (1976), the Court upheld the Texas system, which limited capital punishment to a subset of five categories of murders[54] and required the jury to answer three yes-or-no questions during the sentencing phase.[55] If the jury answered "yes" to all three questions, then the judge was required to impose a death sentence. The Court reasoned that the five categories of murders were equivalent to aggravating circumstances and noted that Texas courts had read the second question put to the jury—the probability of the defendant's future dangerousness—as permitting the defense to place before the jury whatever mitigating circumstances might exist. The three statutory schemes from Georgia, Florida, and Texas that passed constitutional muster in 1976 came to be known as "guided discretion" statutes, in that they neither mandated the imposition of capital punishment upon conviction of a given offense nor left the decision to the standardless discretion of the sentencer. In Woodson v. North Carolina, 428 U.S. 280 (1976), and Roberts v. Louisiana, 428 U.S. 325 (1976), the Court struck down statutes that mandated the automatic imposition of a capital sentence upon conviction of certain categories of murders.

These five opinions, issued on the same day, marked a beginning rather than an end to the Supreme Court's constitutional regulation of capital punishment. Since then, the Court has continued to demarcate the constitutional contours of capital trials, sometimes revising its holdings and reasoning in the 1976 cases.

2. Requiring individualized capital sentencing. In *Woodson* and *Roberts*, the Court rejected mandatory capital sentencing, despite its obvious appeal as a response to concerns about excessive sentencing discretion. A plurality of the Justices held that mandatory death sentences were inconsistent with contemporary standards of decency. Moreover, the plurality expressed the concern that any mandatory capital sentencing scheme would fail to guide

---

54. The categories were murder of a peace officer or firefighter, intentional murder in the course of specified felonies, murder committed for remuneration, murder committed while escaping from prison, or murder of a prison employee by an inmate.

55. The three questions were (1) whether the conduct was done deliberately and with a reasonable expectation of causing death; (2) whether there was a probability that the defendant would pose a continuing threat to society through future criminal acts of violence; and (3) if raised by the evidence, whether the defendant's conduct was an unreasonable response to provocation by the deceased.

juries effectively, because past experience with mandatory statutes suggested that juries would simply refuse to convict of capital murder when they felt that death was an inappropriate punishment. Thus, the plurality observed, the "mandatory statutes enacted in response to *Furman* have simply papered over the problem of unguided and unchecked jury discretion." *Woodson*, 428 U.S. at 302.

Question: Can the same point be made about the statute upheld in *Gregg*?

Most importantly for future cases, the *Woodson* plurality (id. at 303-304) emphasized that the fundamental respect for individual dignity underlying the Eighth Amendment requires

> the particularized consideration of relevant aspects of the character and record of each convicted defendant [and the circumstances of the offense] before the imposition upon him of a sentence of death. . . . A process that [fails to provide such consideration] . . . treats all persons convicted of a designated offense not as uniquely individual human beings, but as members of a faceless, undifferentiated mass to be subjected to the blind infliction of the penalty of death.

The Court later struck down an exceptionally narrow mandatory statute that required a death sentence only for murder committed by a defendant serving a sentence of life imprisonment without possibility of parole. Sumner v. Shuman, 483 U.S. 66 (1987). The Court noted that prior conviction of an offense carrying a life sentence provided insufficient information about the seriousness of the present killing, the defendant's leadership role in its commission, or mitigating circumstances that might fall short of a complete defense. The Court also noted that a mandatory capital sentence was not essential for deterrence because life prisoners who kill could still face the death penalty under a regime of guided discretion.

The Court's reasons for rejecting wholly mandatory statutes led to challenges to capital statutes that limited the kinds of information that a sentencer could consider in mitigation. Sandra Lockett was a young woman who participated in the robbery of a pawnshop. She had stayed in the car while her brother and two other men entered the shop and shot the pawnbroker after an unexpected struggle. Rejecting a plea offer to voluntary manslaughter and aggravated robbery, Lockett went to trial for capital murder and was sentenced to death. The sentencing judge was permitted to consider neither her youth, minor role in the offense, lack of serious criminal record, nor her good prospects for rehabilitation. Ohio's capital statute specified that once any of seven aggravating circumstances was found, the death penalty must be imposed unless the judge found that (1) the victim had induced or facilitated the offense, (2) it was unlikely that the defendant would have committed the offense but for the fact that he or she was under duress, coercion, or strong provocation, or (3) the offense was primarily the product of the defendant's psychosis or mental deficiency. The Court struck down this statute by a 7-1 vote but was widely split in its reasoning. The four-member plurality, led by Chief Justice Burger, found the narrow range of permissible mitigating circumstances to be a fatal flaw. "[T]he sentencer, in all but the rarest kind of capital case, [must] not be precluded from considering *as a mitigating factor*, any aspect of a defendant's character or record and any of the circumstances of the offense that the defendant proffers as a basis for a sentence less than death." Lockett v. Ohio, 438 U.S. 586, 604 (1978).

Cases subsequent to *Lockett* extended this principle. In Eddings v. Oklahoma, 455 U.S. 104 (1982), the defense offered in mitigation the fact that the defendant, who was 16 years old at the time of the offense, had a history of beatings by a harsh father and serious emotional disturbance. The Oklahoma statute permitted consideration of "any mitigating circumstances," but the sentencing judge ruled that while the defendant's youth was relevant in mitigation, the troubled family background and emotional disturbance were not relevant as a matter of law. The Court held that the evidence of Eddings's background could not be ruled irrelevant and that the sentencer must give some consideration to it. The Court said that "a consistency produced by ignoring individual differences is a false consistency." 455 U.S. at 112. In Skipper v. South Carolina, 476 U.S. 1 (1986), the Court held it impermissible to exclude evidence regarding the defendant's good behavior in jail while awaiting trial, despite the dissent's argument that such evidence had little probative value given the special incentives for good behavior under the circumstances.

The *Woodson-Lockett* line of cases eventually led to a partial invalidation of both the Florida and the Texas statutes that had been upheld in 1976. In Hitchcock v. Dugger, 481 U.S. 393 (1987), the Court held that Florida's statute was deficient because it, like the Ohio statute invalidated in *Lockett*, precluded the sentencer from considering mitigating factors not specified in the statute. In Penry v. Lynaugh, 492 U.S. 302 (1989), the Court held that the Texas statute violated the requirement of individualized sentencing because it precluded adequate consideration of Penry's particular mitigating evidence—which concerned his mental retardation and abused childhood. The only place for consideration of such evidence in the Texas scheme was in relation to the question whether "the defendant would pose a continuing threat to society through future criminal acts of violence." See page 543, footnote 55 supra. On *that* question, Penry's evidence was far more likely to be considered aggravating than mitigating. The Court ruled that because the Texas scheme prevented the jury from considering Penry's mental retardation and abused background as *mitigating* factors, it precluded a "reasoned moral response to the defendant's background, character, and crime." Id. at 328.

3. The central tension in the Supreme Court's Eighth Amendment jurisprudence. The Court's approach to mitigating evidence seems to flow naturally from its 1976 decision in *Woodson*, but it is in obvious tension with the *Furman* and *Gregg* goals of confining and structuring the sentencing decision. Can the two principles be harmonized? A majority of the Court has always assumed so, but two Justices have given up, with markedly different results.

Justice Scalia, concurring in Walton v. Arizona, 497 U.S. 639 (1990), lamented that *Woodson* and *Lockett* "completely exploded whatever coherence the notion of 'guided discretion' once had." Id. at 661. And he refused any attempt to reconcile the commands of individualization and guided discretion: "To acknowledge that 'there perhaps is an inherent tension' between [the *Woodson-Lockett*] line of cases and the line stemming from *Furman* . . . is rather like saying that there was perhaps an inherent tension between the Allies and the Axis Powers in World War II." Id. at 664. He concluded that the only possible response was to jettison the requirement of individualized sentencing, because it bore no relation to the text of the Eighth Amendment. "*Woodson* and *Lockett* . . . have some claim to my adherence because of the doctrine of stare decisis. [But s]tare decisis cannot command the impossible. Since I cannot possibly be guided by what seem to me incompatible principles, I must reject the one that is plainly in error. . . . Accordingly, I will not, in this case or in the future, vote to uphold an Eighth Amendment claim that the sentencer's discretion has been unlawfully restricted." Id. at 672-673.

Justice Blackmun, dissenting from the Court's denial of certiorari in Callins v. Collins, 510 U.S. 1141 (1994), agreed with Justice Scalia that the tension between the commands of individualized sentencing and guided sentencing was constitutionally intolerable, but he reached a different conclusion about how to handle the conflict (id. at 1144-1153):

> Experience has taught us that the constitutional goal of eliminating arbitrariness and discrimination from the administration of death can never be achieved without compromising an equally essential component of fundamental fairness—individualized sentencing.
>
> It is tempting, when faced with conflicting constitutional commands, to sacrifice one for the other or to assume that an acceptable balance between them already has been struck. In the context of the death penalty, however, such jurisprudential maneuvers are wholly inappropriate. The death penalty must be imposed "fairly, and with reasonable consistency, or not at all." Eddings v. Oklahoma, 455 U.S. 104, 112 (1982). . . .
>
> From this day forward, I no longer shall tinker with the machinery of death. For more than 20 years I have endeavored—indeed, I have struggled—along with a majority of this Court, to develop procedural and substantive rules that would lend more than the mere appearance of fairness to the death penalty endeavor. Rather than continue to coddle the Court's delusion that the desired level of fairness has been achieved, . . . I feel morally and intellectually obligated simply to concede that the death penalty experiment has failed. . . .
>
> The theory underlying . . . *Lockett* is that an appropriate balance can be struck between the *Furman* promise of consistency and the *Lockett* requirement of individualized sentencing. . . . While one might hope that providing the sentencer with as much relevant mitigating evidence as possible will lead to more rational and consistent sentences, experience has taught otherwise. It seems that the decision whether a human being should live or die is so inherently subjective—rife with all of life's understandings, experiences, prejudices, and passions—that it inevitably defies the rationality and consistency required by the Constitution.

Are Justices Scalia and Blackmun right that there is no possible reconciliation of *Furman* and *Lockett*? For one close consideration of the tension and an attempt to resolve it, see Scott E. Sunby, The *Lockett* Paradox: Reconciling Guided Discretion and Unguided Mitigation in Capital Sentencing, 38 UCLA L. Rev. 1147 (1991). Professor Sunby argues (id. at 1207) that death penalty administration does not pose an "all-or-nothing [choice] between discretion or no discretion," and that the Court can continue to seek a middle ground between the position of Justice Scalia (which entails overruling *Lockett*) and that of Justice Blackmun (which entails overruling *Gregg*).

4. Other concerns. Justice Stevens, a necessary fifth vote to reinstate the death penalty in *Gregg* and the companion cases, changed his views about the death penalty before leaving the bench, but he did not rely on the tension between *Gregg* and *Lockett*. Instead, he pointed to his concerns that death-qualified juries are biased in favor of convictions, that the risk of error in capital cases is greater because of the disturbing facts, that application of the death penalty is discriminatory, and that the sentence is irrevocable. These factors led him to conclude that the death penalty does not survive a cost-benefit analysis. Baze v. Rees, 553 U.S. 35, 84-86 (2008) (Stevens, J., concurring in the judgment). If Justice Stevens is correct that these factors exist, are they—either alone or in combination—sufficient to strike down the death penalty? Justice Scalia sharply disagreed with Justice Stevens. He argued that Justice Stevens had failed to prove why the death penalty in particular was problematic, because disturbing facts and discriminatory sentencing are not limited to death penalty cases. Similarly, he argued, any analysis that found fault with death-qualifying juries must necessarily extend to the whole system of challenges for cause and peremptory strikes. Regardless, Justice Scalia concluded, parsing the social benefits and costs of the death penalty is beyond the scope of the Court's authority and is best left to legislatures. Id. at 87-93 (Scalia, J., concurring in the judgment).

Questions: Is Justice Stevens wrong to single out the death penalty as more deserving of abolition than, say, life without parole or other non-capital sentences? If capital cases were proven to be administered more fairly than non-capital cases, do you think Justice Stevens would have reverted to favoring the death penalty? Should he?

5. Is death different? The Court has rejected challenges to mandatory sentences in non-capital cases, including mandatory sentences of life without the possibility of parole. Harmelin v. Michigan, 501 U.S. 957 (1991). See page 192 supra. The Court also made clear in *Lockett* that, in contrast to capital cases, "legislatures remain free to decide how much discretion in sentencing should be reposed in the judge or jury in noncapital cases." 438 U.S. at 603 (plurality opinion). Are there good reasons to treat capital cases differently from non-capital cases as a constitutional matter? For discussion, see Rachel E. Barkow, The Court of Life and Death: The Two Tracks of Constitutional Sentencing Law and the Case for Uniformity, 107 Mich. L. Rev. 1145 (2009); Carol S. Steiker & Jordan M. Steiker, Opening a Window or Building a Wall?

The Effect of Death Penalty Law and Advocacy on Criminal Justice More Broadly, 11 U. Pa. J. Const. L. 155 (2008).

ATKINS v. VIRGINIA

Supreme Court of the United States
536 U.S. 304 (2002)

JUSTICE STEVENS delivered the opinion of the Court.

Those mentally retarded persons who meet the law's requirements for criminal responsibility should be tried and punished when they commit crimes. Because of their disabilities in areas of reasoning, judgment, and control of their impulses, however, they do not act with the level of moral culpability that characterizes the most serious adult criminal conduct. Moreover, their impairments can jeopardize the reliability and fairness of capital proceedings against mentally retarded defendants. Presumably for these reasons, in the 13 years since we decided Penry v. Lynaugh, 492 U.S. 302 (1989) [upholding the constitutionality of capital punishment for mentally retarded offenders], the American public, legislators, scholars, and judges have deliberated over the question whether the death penalty should ever be imposed on a mentally retarded criminal. The consensus reflected in those deliberations informs our answer to the question presented by this case: whether such executions are "cruel and unusual punishments" prohibited by the Eighth Amendment to the Federal Constitution.

I

Petitioner, Daryl Renard Atkins, was convicted of abduction, armed robbery, and capital murder, and sentenced to death. At approximately midnight on August 16, 1996, Atkins and William Jones, armed with a semiautomatic handgun, abducted Eric Nesbitt, robbed him of the money on his person, drove him to an automated teller machine in his pickup truck where cameras recorded their withdrawal of additional cash, then took him to an isolated location where he was shot eight times and killed. . . .

In the penalty phase, the defense relied on one witness, Dr. Evan Nelson, a forensic psychologist who had evaluated Atkins before trial and concluded that he was "mildly mentally retarded." His conclusion was based on interviews with people who knew Atkins, a review of school and court records, and the administration of a standard intelligence test which indicated that Atkins had a full scale IQ of 59.[5]

The jury sentenced Atkins to death. . . .

---

5. . . . The mean score of the test is 100, which means that a person receiving a score of 100 is considered to have an average level of cognitive functioning. It is estimated that between 1 and 3 percent of the population has an IQ between 70 and 75 or lower, which is typically considered the cutoff IQ score for the intellectual function prong of the mental retardation definition.

II

The Eighth Amendment succinctly prohibits "[e]xcessive" sanctions. . . .

A claim that punishment is excessive is judged not by the standards that prevailed in 1685 when Lord Jeffreys presided over the "Bloody Assizes" or when the Bill of Rights was adopted, but rather by those that currently prevail.

Proportionality review under those evolving standards should be informed by "'objective factors to the maximum possible extent.'" . . . We have pinpointed that the "clearest and most reliable objective evidence of contemporary values is the legislation enacted by the country's legislatures." Relying in part on such legislative evidence, we have held that death is an impermissibly excessive punishment for the rape of an adult woman, Coker v. Georgia, 433 U.S. 584, 593-596 (1977), or for a defendant who neither took life, attempted to take life, nor intended to take life, Enmund v. Florida, 458 U.S. 782, 789-793 (1982). . . .

We also acknowledged in *Coker* that the objective evidence, though of great importance, did not "wholly determine" the controversy, "for the Constitution contemplates that in the end our own judgment will be brought to bear on the question of the acceptability of the death penalty under the Eighth Amendment."

III

. . . In [1986], the public reaction to the execution of a mentally retarded murderer in Georgia apparently led to the enactment of the first state statute prohibiting such executions. In 1988, when Congress enacted legislation reinstating the federal death penalty, it expressly provided that a "sentence of death shall not be carried out upon a person who is mentally retarded." In 1989, Maryland enacted a similar prohibition. . . .

Much has changed since then. . . . In 1990, Kentucky and Tennessee enacted statutes similar to those in Georgia and Maryland, as did New Mexico in 1991, and Arkansas, Colorado, Washington, Indiana, and Kansas in 1993 and 1994. In 1995, when New York reinstated its death penalty, it emulated the Federal Government by expressly exempting the mentally retarded. Nebraska followed suit in 1998. . . . [I]n 2000 and 2001 six more States— South Dakota, Arizona, Connecticut, Florida, Missouri, and North Carolina—joined the procession. The Texas Legislature unanimously adopted a similar bill, and bills have passed at least one house in other States, including Virginia and Nevada.

It is not so much the number of these States that is significant, but the consistency of the direction of change. . . . Moreover, even in those States that allow the execution of mentally retarded offenders, the practice is uncommon. . . . Only five states have executed offenders possessing a known IQ less than 70 since we decided *Penry*. The practice, therefore, has become truly unusual, and it is fair to say that a national consensus has developed against it.[21]

IV

This consensus unquestionably reflects widespread judgment about the relative culpability of mentally retarded offenders. . . . Additionally, it suggests that some characteristics of mental retardation undermine the strength of the procedural protections that our capital jurisprudence steadfastly guards. . . .

Our death penalty jurisprudence provides two reasons consistent with the legislative consensus that the mentally retarded should be categorically excluded from execution. First, there is a serious question as to whether either justification that we have recognized as a basis for the death penalty applies to mentally retarded offenders. Gregg v. Georgia, 428 U.S. 153, 183 (1976) identified "retribution and deterrence of capital crimes by prospective offenders" as the social purposes served by the death penalty. . . .

With respect to retribution . . . the severity of the appropriate punishment necessarily depends on the culpability of the offender. Since *Gregg*, our jurisprudence has consistently confined the imposition of the death penalty to a narrow category of the most serious crimes. . . . If the culpability of the average murderer is insufficient to justify the most extreme sanction available to the State, the lesser culpability of the mentally retarded offender surely does not merit that form of retribution. . . .

With respect to deterrence . . . the same cognitive and behavioral impairments that make these defendants less morally culpable—for example, the diminished ability to understand and process information, to learn from experience, to engage in logical reasoning, or to control impulses— . . . also make it less likely that they can process the information of the possibility of execution as a penalty and, as a result, control their conduct based upon that information. . . .

The reduced capacity of mentally retarded offenders provides a second justification for a categorical rule making such offenders ineligible for the

---

21. [T]his legislative judgment reflects a much broader social and professional consensus. For example, several organizations with germane expertise have adopted official positions opposing the imposition of the death penalty upon a mentally retarded offender, [citing *amicus* briefs for the American Psychological Association and the American Association of Mental Retardation]. In addition, representatives of widely diverse religious communities in the United States, reflecting Christian, Jewish, Muslim, and Buddhist traditions, have filed an *amicus curiae* brief explaining that even though their views about the death penalty differ, they all "share a conviction that the execution of persons with mental retardation cannot be morally justified." Moreover, within the world community, the imposition of the death penalty for crimes committed by mentally retarded offenders is overwhelmingly disapproved, [citing *amicus* brief for the European Union]. Finally, polling data shows a widespread consensus among Americans, even those who support the death penalty, that executing the mentally retarded is wrong. Although these factors are by no means dispositive, their consistency with the legislative evidence lends further support to our conclusion that there is a consensus among those who have addressed the issue.

death penalty. The risk "that the death penalty will be imposed in spite of factors which may call for a less severe penalty," Lockett v. Ohio, 438 U.S. 586, 605 (1978), is enhanced, not only by the possibility of false confessions, but also by the lesser ability of mentally retarded defendants to make a persuasive showing of mitigation. . . . Mentally retarded defendants may be less able to give meaningful assistance to their counsel and are typically poor witnesses, and their demeanor may create an unwarranted impression of lack of remorse for their crimes. As *Penry* demonstrated, moreover, reliance on mental retardation as a mitigating factor can be a two-edged sword that may enhance the likelihood that the aggravating factor of future dangerousness will be found by the jury. Mentally retarded defendants in the aggregate face a special risk of wrongful execution.

Our independent evaluation of the issue reveals no reason to disagree with the judgment of "the legislatures that have recently addressed the matter" and concluded that death is not a suitable punishment for a mentally retarded criminal. . . . [W]e therefore conclude that such punishment is excessive and that the Constitution "places a substantive restriction on the State's power to take the life" of a mentally retarded offender. . . .

JUSTICE SCALIA, with whom the CHIEF JUSTICE and JUSTICE THOMAS join, dissenting.

Today's decision is the pinnacle of our Eighth Amendment death-is-different jurisprudence. Not only does it, like all of that jurisprudence, find no support in the text or history of the Eighth Amendment; it does not even have support in current social attitudes regarding the conditions that render an otherwise just death penalty inappropriate. Seldom has an opinion of this Court rested so obviously upon nothing but the personal views of its Members. . . .

The Court . . . miraculously extracts a "national consensus" forbidding execution of the mentally retarded, from the fact that 18 States—less than *half* (47%) of the 38 States that permit capital punishment (for whom the issue exists)—have very recently enacted legislation barring execution of the mentally retarded. . . . Our prior cases have generally required a much higher degree of agreement before finding a punishment cruel and unusual on "evolving standards" grounds. In *Coker*, we proscribed the death penalty for rape of an adult woman after finding that only one jurisdiction, Georgia, authorized such a punishment. In *Enmund*, we invalidated the death penalty for mere participation in a robbery in which an accomplice took a life, a punishment not permitted in 28 of the death penalty States (78%). . . .

The Court attempts to bolster its embarrassingly feeble evidence of "consensus" with the following: "It is not so much the number of these States that is significant, but the *consistency* of the direction of change." (emphasis added). But in what other direction *could we possibly* see change? Given that 14 years ago all the death penalty statutes included the mentally retarded, any change (except precipitate undoing of what had just been done) was *bound to be* in the one direction the Court finds significant enough to overcome the lack of real consensus. . . .

Even less compelling (if possible) is the Court's argument that evidence of "national consensus" is to be found in the infrequency with which retarded persons are executed in States that do not bar their execution. . . . *If* execution of the mentally retarded is "uncommon"; and if it is not a sufficient explanation of this that the retarded constitute a tiny fraction of society (1% to 3%); then surely the explanation is that mental retardation is a constitutionally mandated mitigating factor at sentencing, *Penry.* For that reason, even if there were uniform national sentiment in *favor* of executing the retarded in appropriate cases, one would still expect execution of the mentally retarded to be "uncommon." . . .

But the Prize for the Court's Most Feeble Effort to fabricate "national consensus" must go to its appeal (deservedly relegated to a footnote) to the views of assorted professional and religious organizations, members of the so-called "world community," and respondents to opinion polls. . . . [T]he views of professional and religious organizations and the results of opinion polls are irrelevant. Equally irrelevant are the practices of the "world community," whose notions of justice are (thankfully) not always those of our people. . . .

Beyond the empty talk of a "national consensus," the Court gives us a brief glimpse of what really underlies today's decision: pretension to a power confined *neither* by the moral sentiments originally enshrined in the Eighth Amendment (its original meaning) nor even by the current moral sentiments of the American people. " '[T]he Constitution,' the Court says, 'contemplates that in the end *our own judgment* will be brought to bear on the question of the acceptability of the death penalty under the Eighth Amendment.' " . . . The arrogance of this assumption of power takes one's breath away. And it explains, of course, why the Court can be so cavalier about the evidence of consensus. . . .

The Court gives two reasons why the death penalty is an excessive punishment for all mentally retarded offenders. First, the "diminished capacities" of the mentally retarded raise a "serious question" whether their execution contributes to the "social purposes" of the death penalty, viz., retribution and deterrence. (The Court conveniently ignores a third "social purpose" of the death penalty—"incapacitation of dangerous criminals and the consequent prevention of crimes that they may otherwise commit in the future," Gregg v. Georgia, 428 U.S. 153, 183, n.28 (1976) (joint opinion of Stewart, Powell, and Stevens, JJ.). But never mind; its discussion of even the other two does not bear analysis.) Retribution is not advanced, the argument goes, because the mentally retarded are *no more culpable* than the average murderer, whom we have already held lacks sufficient culpability to warrant the death penalty. . . .

[W]hat scientific analysis can possibly show that a mildly retarded individual who commits an exquisite torture-killing is "no more culpable" than the "average" murderer in a holdup-gone-wrong or a domestic dispute? . . . Surely culpability, and deservedness of the most severe retribution, depends not merely (if at all) upon the mental capacity of the criminal (above the level where he is able to distinguish right from wrong) but also upon the depravity of the crime—which is precisely why this sort of question has traditionally been thought answerable not by a categorical rule of the sort the Court today imposes upon all trials, but rather by the sentencer's weighing of the circumstances (both degree of retardation and depravity of crime) in the particular case. . . .

As for the other social purpose of the death penalty that the Court discusses, deterrence: That is not advanced, the Court tells us, because the mentally retarded are "less likely" than their non-retarded counterparts to "process the information of the possibility of execution as a penalty and . . . control their conduct based upon that information." . . . [T]he Court does not say that *all* mentally retarded individuals cannot "process the information of the possibility of execution as a penalty and . . . control their conduct based upon that information"; it merely asserts that they are "less likely" to be able to do so. But surely the deterrent effect of a penalty is adequately vindicated if it successfully deters many, but not all, of the target class. . . .

Today's opinion adds one more to the long list of substantive and procedural requirements impeding imposition of the death penalty imposed under this Court's assumed power to invent a death-is-different jurisprudence. . . . There is something to be said for popular abolition of the death penalty; there is nothing to be said for its incremental abolition by this Court.

NOTES

1. Applying **Atkins.** The *Atkins* Court did not mandate procedures for determining whether a capital defendant is mentally retarded. States have varied in their definitions of mental retardation, their allocations of decision-making authority between judge and jury, and their burdens of proof. Pennsylvania, for example, requires a capital defendant to prove his mental retardation by a preponderance of the evidence. See Commonwealth v. Sanchez, 2011 WL 6412518 (Pa. 2011). In Georgia a capital defendant must prove mental retardation beyond a reasonable doubt. See Stripling v. State, 711 S.E.2d 665 (Ga. 2011).

Question: Is that latter requirement compatible with the constitutional principles recognized in *Atkins*? See Carol S. Steiker & Jordan M. Steiker, *Atkins v. Virginia*: Lessons from Substance and Procedure in the Constitutional Regulation of Capital Punishment, 57 DePaul L. Rev. 721, 724-731 (2008).

*2. Pre-*Atkins *proportionality cases.* In proportionality decisions prior to *Atkins*, the Court had ruled the death penalty unconstitutional for rape of an adult woman, Coker v. Georgia, 433 U.S. 584 (1977), and for felony murder attributed to a defendant "who does not himself kill, attempt to kill, or intend that a killing take place or that lethal force will be employed," Enmund v. Florida, 458 U.S. 782, 797 (1982). The force of *Enmund* was limited, however, in Tison v. Arizona, 481 U.S. 137 (1987). *Tison* concluded that a felony murder could sometimes be punished by death, even when the defendant did not himself kill or intend to kill, because "major participation in the felony committed, combined with reckless indifference to human life, is sufficient to satisfy the *Enmund* culpability requirement." Id. at 158.

While the Court was willing to demarcate *offenses* to which the death penalty was constitutionally inapplicable, it was less sympathetic, prior to *Atkins,* to claims that certain kinds of *offenders* could not be executed. The same year that the Court initially condoned execution for mentally retarded offenders in *Penry,* it also allowed the execution of defendants older than 15 but younger than 18 at the time of their offenses. Stanford v. Kentucky, 492 U.S. 361 (1989). When the Court overruled *Penry* in *Atkins,* many predicted— correctly, it turned out—that *Stanford* would no longer survive.

**3. *Post*-Atkins *proportionality cases. (a)* Three years after *Atkins,* the Court overruled *Stanford,* holding that the death penalty is a disproportionate punishment for defendants who were juveniles at the time of their offenses. Roper v. Simmons, 543 U.S. 551 (2005). The Court relied on the methodology of *Atkins* to find a new societal consensus against the execution of juvenile offenders. The Court found objective indicia of a national consensus in the rejection of the juvenile death penalty in a substantial number of states, the infrequency of its use where it remained on the books, and the consistency in the trend toward abolition of the practice.

The Court also relied upon common knowledge (what "any parent knows") and "scientific and sociological studies" to establish that "juvenile offenders cannot, with reliability, be classified among the worst offenders." Id. at 569. The Court noted "the comparative immaturity and irresponsibility of juveniles," that juveniles "are more vulnerable or susceptible to negative influences and outside pressures," and that the personality traits of juveniles are "more transitory, less fixed." Id. at 569-570. The Court concluded that "[o]nce the diminished culpability of juveniles is recognized, it is evident that the penological justifications for the death penalty [retribution and deterrence] apply to them with lesser force than to adults." Id. at 571.

Finally, the Court discussed, in detail, international law and practice, a factor its *Atkins* opinion had mentioned only briefly. See supra footnote 21. The Court stressed that "the United States is the only country in the world that continues to give official sanction to the juvenile death penalty," (id. at 575) that international human rights covenants had repudiated the juvenile death penalty, and that the United Kingdom in particular had long rejected it. The Court concluded, "It does not lessen our fidelity to the Constitution or our pride in its origins to acknowledge that the express affirmation of certain fundamental rights by other nations and peoples simply underscores the centrality of those same rights within our own heritage of freedom." Id. at 578.

Three dissenters, in an opinion by Justice Scalia, rejected both the outcome and the methodology of the *Simmons* majority: "The Court reaches this implausible result by purporting to advert, not to the original meaning of the Eighth Amendment, but to 'the evolving standards of decency' of our national society . . . [which it determines by reference to] the subjective views of five Members of this Court and like-minded foreigners." Id. at 608.

Justice O'Connor dissented on a narrower ground. She accepted the Court's "evolving standards" methodology but argued that no new societal consensus had emerged on the propriety of the juvenile death penalty.

Questions: Is the proportionality analysis performed by the Court in *Simmons* and *Atkins* persuasive? Do other Eighth Amendment principles, such as the requirements to guide discretion and assure consideration of mitigating evidence, preclude the execution of juveniles? See Carol Steiker & Jordan Steiker, Defending Categorical Exemptions to the Death Penalty: Reflections on the ABA's Resolutions Concerning the Execution of Juveniles and Persons with Mental Retardation 61 Law & Contemp. Probs. 89 (1998).

(b) In Kennedy v. Louisiana, 554 U.S. 407 (2008), the Court overturned a statute authorizing the death penalty for the rape of a child under the age of 12. The Court followed the blueprint of *Simmons* and *Atkins.* The Court also found it significant that child rape occurs more often than first-degree murder; thus to allow the death penalty for child rape could not "be reconciled with our evolving standards of decency and the necessity to constrain the use of the death penalty." Id. at 439.

Questions: Why is the high incidence of child sex offenses an argument *against* the death penalty? Why shouldn't states be permitted to use aggravating factors to reduce the number of child rape cases that would qualify for death? The Court's view was that jurors could not be trusted to balance aggravating factors against mitigating factors in this context because the crime "in many cases will overwhelm a decent person's judgment." Id. at 439. Is that prediction realistic? If so, does it cast doubt on the jury's ability to balance these factors in any capital murder case?

4. Methodological questions. (a) Societal consensus? In both *Atkins* and *Simmons,* the Justices disagreed on how to evaluate the indicia of an emerging societal consensus. In considering whether legislative change has led to a new consensus narrowing the permissible scope for the death penalty, how should the Court count states that have abolished the death penalty entirely? How should the Court count states that have called for a moratorium on executions? Should we count the federal government as one jurisdiction out of 51? Justice Thomas has argued that a federal law permitting a punishment in a given circumstance should automatically refute any claim that there is a consensus against that punishment, no matter the tally in the states. Graham v. Florida, 130 S. Ct. 2011, 2049 (2010) (Thomas, J., dissenting). For a critique of this argument, see Rachel E. Barkow, Categorizing *Graham*, 23 Fed. Sent'g Rep. 49, 52 (2010).

Should the Court consider indicia of societal consensus other than domestic legislation? Does statistical evidence of decreasing executions indicate societal rejection of the death penalty? See Kennedy v. Louisiana, 554 U.S. 407, 433-434 (2008). Is the Court justified in considering foreign law and international human rights conventions? See Youngjae Lee, International

Consensus as Persuasive Authority in the Eighth Amendment, 156 U. Pa. L. Rev. 63 (2007).

(b) *The Court's independent judgment.* In *Atkins* and *Simmons*, the Court portrayed proportionality analysis as a two-step process: first, determination of the national consensus, and then the Court's own assessment of penological justifications. Where should that assessment fit into the analysis? If society has not reached a consensus against the death penalty in a given category of cases, but the Court nonetheless concludes that sound penological justifications are lacking, why should the Court's own analysis control? Conversely, if there is an overwhelming societal consensus against executing mentally retarded or juvenile offenders, should the Court's "own judgment" that there are good penological reasons for that practice suffice to render it permissible in the one state that dissents from the otherwise uniform national and international view?

5. *Future applications.* Are there other *categories of defendants* who should be exempted from the death penalty? What about those with serious mental illness who do not meet the legal standard for a complete defense of insanity? See Bruce J. Winick, The Supreme Court's Evolving Death Penalty Jurisprudence: Severe Mental Illness as the Next Frontier, 50 B.C. L. Rev. 785 (2009); Christopher Slobogin, What *Atkins* Could Mean for People with Mental Illness, 33 N.M. L. Rev. 293 (2003). Note that serious mental illness can be considered an aggravating factor from the perspective of a person's future dangerousness. From the perspective of retribution (or deterrence), how would you analyze the creation of a categorical exemption for offenders who have serious mental illness?

Are there *crimes* other than murder for which death can be a proportionate punishment? In *Kennedy*, the Court reserved judgment on whether "offenses against the State"—a list that included, according to the Court, "treason, espionage, terrorism and drug kingpin activity"—would merit the death penalty even when they did not involve the taking of life. 554 U.S. at 437.

How should questions of "consensus" and penological justification be assessed for each of these crime and offender categories? Instead of adopting categorical exclusions, does it make more sense to place a cap on the number of capital cases prosecutors can bring, thereby forcing them to choose the worst cases? See Adam M. Gershowitz, Imposing a Cap on Capital Punishment, 72 Mo. L. Rev. 73 (2007).

6. *The relevance of the risk of wrongful conviction.* The recent spate of DNA and other exonerations of those on death row has led to a heightened concern about the rate of wrongful convictions in capital cases, see supra pages 531-535. Can such concerns rise to the level of constitutional infirmities? The Court in *Atkins* supported its case for exempting mentally retarded defendants from the death penalty on the ground that they face a higher likelihood of wrongful conviction. Could a similar rationale help justify eliminating the death penalty for mentally ill defendants who also may have

trouble providing meaningful assistance to counsel? One federal district court invalidated the Federal Death Penalty Act under the Fifth Amendment's Due Process Clause, holding that "the unacceptably high rate at which innocent persons are convicted of capital crimes, when coupled with the frequently prolonged delays before such errors are detected (and then often only fortuitously or by application of newly-developed techniques), compels the conclusion that execution . . . , by cutting off the opportunity for exoneration, denies due process and, indeed, is tantamount to foreseeable, state-sponsored murder of innocent human beings." United States v. Quinones, 205 F. Supp. 2d 256, 268 (S.D.N.Y. 2002) (Rakoff, J.). The Second Circuit reversed 313 F.3d 49, 52 (2d Cir. 2002):

> [T]o the extent the defendants' arguments rely upon the Eighth Amendment, their argument is foreclosed by the Supreme Court's decision in *Gregg v. Georgia*. With respect to the defendants' Fifth Amendment due process claim, we observe that the language of the Due Process Clause itself recognizes the possibility of capital punishment. Moreover, . . . [the Supreme Court has held that] there is no fundamental right to a continued opportunity for exoneration throughout the course of one's natural life.

Questions: Was the Second Circuit right that *Gregg* forecloses arguments based on high rates of wrongful conviction? Or does *Gregg* leave room for future claims based on empirical evidence? What is the force of the Second Circuit's observation that "the language of the Due Process Clause itself recognizes the possibility of capital punishment"? Note that the language of the Fifth Amendment includes not only a reference to capital punishment in the Due Process Clause ("[n]o person shall . . . be deprived of life . . . without due process of law") but also a reference to severe corporal punishment in the Double Jeopardy Clause ("nor shall any person be subject for the same offence to be twice put in jeopardy of life or limb"). Is it obvious that these references establish the constitutionality of amputation (or other severe bodily injury) as a form of punishment? If not, then is it plausible to read the Constitution's Due Process, Equal Protection, and Cruel and Unusual Punishments Clauses as limiting the circumstances in which government is permitted to subject offenders to loss of life or limb?

McCLESKEY v. KEMP

Supreme Court of the United States
481 U.S. 279 (1987)

JUSTICE POWELL delivered the opinion of the Court.

This case presents the question whether a complex statistical study that indicates a risk that racial considerations enter into capital sentencing determinations proves that petitioner McCleskey's capital sentence is unconstitutional under the Eighth or Fourteenth Amendment.

I

McCleskey, a black man, was convicted of two counts of armed robbery and one count of murder in the Superior Court of Fulton County, Georgia, on October 12, 1978. McCleskey's convictions arose out of the robbery of a furniture store and the killing of a white police officer during the course of the robbery. The evidence at trial indicated that McCleskey and three accomplices planned and carried out the robbery. All four were armed. . . . During the course of the robbery, a police officer, answering a silent alarm, entered the store through the front door. [Two shots] struck the officer. One hit him in the face and killed him. At trial, the State introduced evidence that at least one of the bullets that struck the officer was fired [by McCleskey].

The jury convicted McCleskey of murder [and] found two aggravating circumstances to exist beyond a reasonable doubt: the murder was committed during the course of an armed robbery, and the murder was committed upon a peace officer engaged in the performance of his duties. . . . McCleskey offered no mitigating evidence. The jury recommended that he be sentenced to death. . . . The court followed the jury's recommendation and sentenced McCleskey to death. [T]he Supreme Court of Georgia affirmed. . . .

[After state court challenges, McCleskey filed a petition for a writ of habeas corpus.] His petition raised 18 claims, one of which was that the Georgia capital sentencing process is administered in a racially discriminatory manner in violation of the Eighth and Fourteenth Amendments to the United States Constitution. In support of his claim, McCleskey proffered a statistical study performed by Professors David C. Baldus, George Woodworth, and Charles Pulaski (the Baldus study) that purports to show a disparity in the imposition of the death sentence in Georgia based on the race of the murder victim and, to a lesser extent, the race of the defendant. The Baldus study is actually two sophisticated statistical studies that examine over 2,000 murder cases that occurred in Georgia during the 1970s. The raw numbers collected by Professor Baldus indicate that defendants charged with killing white persons received the death penalty in 11% of the cases, but defendants charged with killing blacks received the death penalty in only 1% of the cases. The raw numbers also indicate a reverse racial disparity according to the race of the defendant: 4% of the black defendants received the death penalty, as opposed to 7% of the white defendants.

Baldus also divided the cases according to the combination of the race of the defendant and the race of the victim. He found that the death penalty was assessed in 22% of the cases involving black defendants and white victims; 8% of the cases involving white defendants and white victims; 1% of the cases involving black defendants and black victims; and 3% of the cases involving white defendants and black victims. . . .

Baldus subjected his data to an extensive analysis, taking account of 230 variables that could have explained the disparities on nonracial grounds. One of his models concludes that, even after taking account of 39 nonracial variables, defendants charged with killing white victims were 4.3 times as likely to receive a death sentence as defendants charged with killing blacks. [T]he Baldus study indicates that black defendants, such as McCleskey, who kill white victims have the greatest likelihood of receiving the death penalty.[5]

The District Court . . . found that the methodology of the Baldus study was flawed in several respects. . . . Accordingly, the Court dismissed the petition. The Court of Appeals affirmed. . . .

II

McCleskey's first claim is that the Georgia capital punishment statute violates the Equal Protection Clause of the Fourteenth Amendment.[7] . . . As a black defendant who killed a white victim, McCleskey claims that the Baldus study demonstrates that he was discriminated against because of his race and because of the race of his victim. . . .

Our analysis begins with the basic principle that a defendant who alleges an equal protection violation has the burden of proving "the existence of purposeful discrimination." [T]o prevail under the Equal Protection Clause, McCleskey must prove that the decision-makers in *his* case acted with discriminatory purpose. He offers no evidence specific to his own case that would support an inference that racial considerations played a part in his sentence. Instead, he relies solely on the Baldus study. . . . McCleskey's claim that these statistics are sufficient proof of discrimination, without regard to the facts of a particular case, would extend to all capital cases in Georgia, at least where the victim was white and the defendant is black.

. . . McCleskey challenges decisions at the heart of the State's criminal justice system. . . . Because discretion is essential to the criminal justice process, we would demand exceptionally clear proof before we would infer that the discretion had been abused. . . . Accordingly, we hold that the Baldus study is clearly insufficient to support an inference that any of the decision-makers in McCleskey's case acted with discriminatory purpose.

McCleskey also suggests that the Baldus study proves that the State as a whole has acted with a discriminatory purpose. He appears to argue that the State has violated the Equal Protection Clause by adopting the capital

---

5. Baldus's 230-year variable model divided cases into eight different ranges, according to the estimated aggravation level of the offense. Baldus argued in his testimony to the District Court that the effects of racial bias were more striking in the mid-range cases. "[W]hen the cases become tremendously aggravated so that everybody would agree that if we're going to have a death sentence, these are the cases that should get it, the race effects go away. It's only in the mid-range of cases where the decision makers have a real choice as to what to do. If there's room for the exercise of discretion, then the [racial] factors begin to play a role." Under this model, Baldus found that 14.4% of the black-victim mid-range cases received the death penalty, and 34.4% of the white-victim cases received the death penalty. According to Baldus, the facts of McCleskey's case placed it within the mid-range.

7. Although the District Court rejected the findings of the Baldus study as flawed, the Court of Appeals assumed that the study is valid and reached the constitutional issues. Accordingly, those issues are before us. As did the Court of Appeals, we assume the study is valid statistically without reviewing the factual findings of the District Court. . . .

punishment statute and allowing it to remain in force despite its allegedly discriminatory application. But " '[d]iscriminatory purpose' . . . implies more than intent as volition or intent as awareness of consequences. It implies that the decisionmaker, in this case a state legislature, selected or reaffirmed a particular course of action at least in part 'because of,' not merely 'in spite of,' its adverse effects upon an identifiable group." For this claim to prevail, McCleskey would have to prove that the Georgia Legislature enacted or maintained the death penalty statute *because of* an anticipated racially discriminatory effect. In Gregg v. Georgia, 428 U.S. 153 (1976), this Court found that the Georgia capital sentencing system could operate in a fair and neutral manner. There was no evidence then, and there is none now, that the Georgia Legislature enacted the capital punishment statute to further a racially discriminatory purpose. . . .

IV

. . . McCleskey also argues that the Baldus study demonstrates that the Georgia capital sentencing system violates the Eighth Amendment. . . .

To evaluate McCleskey's challenge, we must examine exactly what the Baldus study may show. Even Professor Baldus does not contend that his statistics prove that race enters into any capital sentencing decisions or that race was a factor in McCleskey's particular case.[29] . . . There is, of course, some risk of racial prejudice influencing a jury's decision in a criminal case. . . . The question "is at what point that risk becomes constitutionally unacceptable."

McCleskey's argument that the Constitution condemns the discretion allowed decisionmakers in the Georgia capital sentencing system is antithetical to the fundamental role of discretion in our criminal justice system. Discretion in the criminal justice system offers substantial benefits to the criminal defendant. Not only can a jury decline to impose the death sentence, it can decline to convict, or choose to convict of a lesser offense. . . . Similarly, . . . a prosecutor can decline to charge, offer a plea bargain, or decline to seek a death sentence in any particular case. Of course, "the power to be lenient [also] is the power to discriminate," K. Davis, Discretionary Justice 170 (1973), but a capital-punishment system that did not allow for discretionary acts of leniency "would be totally alien to our notions of criminal justice." Gregg v. Georgia, 428 U.S., at 200, n.50.

---

29. According to Professor Baldus: "McCleskey's case falls in [a] grey area where . . . you would find the greatest likelihood that some inappropriate consideration may have come to bear on the decision. In an analysis of this type, obviously one cannot say that we can say to a moral certainty what it was that influenced the decision. We can't do that."

[*Questions:* Is the Court saying that in order to "prove" a proposition for purposes of constitutional litigation, a party must establish that proposition "to a moral certainty"? Is this the proper burden of persuasion?—EDS.]

... The discrepancy indicated by the Baldus study is "a far cry from the major systemic defects identified in *Furman*."[36] Where the discretion that is fundamental to our criminal process is involved, we decline to assume that what is unexplained is invidious. In light of the safeguards designed to minimize racial bias in the process, the fundamental value of jury trial in our criminal justice system, and the benefits that discretion provides to criminal defendants, we hold that the Baldus study does not demonstrate a constitutionally significant risk of racial bias affecting the Georgia capital-sentencing process.[37]

V

Two additional concerns inform our decision in this case. First, McCleskey's claim, taken to its logical conclusion, throws into serious question the principles that underlie our entire criminal justice system. The Eighth Amendment is not limited in application to capital punishment, but applies to all penalties. Thus, if we accepted McCleskey's claim that racial bias has impermissibly tainted the capital sentencing decision, we could soon be faced with similar claims as to other types of penalty. Moreover, the claim that his sentence rests on the irrelevant factor of race easily could be extended to apply to claims based on unexplained discrepancies that correlate to membership in other minority groups, and even to gender. ... Also, there is no logical reason that such a claim need be limited to racial or sexual bias. If arbitrary and capricious punishment is the touchstone under the Eighth Amendment, such a claim could—at least in theory—be based upon any arbitrary variable, such as the defendant's facial characteristics, or the physical attractiveness of the defendant or the victim,[44] that some statistical study indicates may be influential in jury decisionmaking. As these examples illustrate, there is no limiting principle to the type of challenge brought by McCleskey. ...

Second, McCleskey's arguments are best presented to the legislative bodies. ... Legislatures also are better qualified to weigh and "evaluate the results of statistical studies in terms of their own local conditions and with a flexibility of approach that is not available to the courts," Gregg v. Georgia, supra. ... Despite McCleskey's wide ranging arguments that basically

---

36. The Baldus study in fact confirms that the Georgia system results in a reasonable level of proportionality among the class of murderers eligible for the death penalty. As Professor Baldus confirmed, the system sorts out cases where the sentence of death is highly likely and highly unlikely, leaving a mid-range of cases where the imposition of the death penalty in any particular case is less predictable.

37. ... The dissent repeatedly emphasizes the need for "a uniquely high degree of rationality in imposing the death penalty." [Yet,] no suggestion is made as to how greater "rationality" could be achieved under any type of statute that authorizes capital punishment. [T]he dissent's call for greater rationality is no less than a claim that a capital-punishment system cannot be administered in accord with the Constitution. ...

44. Some studies indicate that physically attractive defendants receive greater leniency in sentencing than unattractive defendants, and that offenders whose victims are physically attractive receive harsher sentences than defendants with less attractive victims.

challenge the validity of capital punishment in our multi-racial society, the only question before us is whether in his case the law of Georgia was properly applied. We agree with the District Court and the Court of Appeals for the Eleventh Circuit that this was carefully and correctly done in this case.

Accordingly, we affirm. . . .

JUSTICE BRENNAN, [with whom JUSTICES MARSHALL, BLACKMUN, and STEVENS join], dissenting. . . .

It is important to emphasize at the outset that the Court's observation that McCleskey cannot prove the influence of race on any particular sentencing decision is irrelevant in evaluating his Eighth Amendment claim. Since Furman v. Georgia, 408 U.S. 238 (1972), the Court has been concerned with the *risk* of the imposition of an arbitrary sentence, rather than the proven fact of one. . . . As Justice O'Connor observed in Caldwell v. Mississippi, 472 U.S. 320, 343 (1985), a death sentence must be struck down when the circumstances under which it has been imposed "creat[e] an unacceptable *risk* that 'the death penalty [may have been] meted out arbitrarily or capriciously' or through 'whim or mistake'" (emphasis added). This emphasis on risk . . . reflects the fact that concern for arbitrariness focuses on the rationality of the system as a whole, and that a system that features a significant probability that sentencing decisions are influenced by impermissible considerations cannot be regarded as rational. . . . McCleskey's claim does differ, however, in one respect from these earlier cases: it is the first to base a challenge not on speculation about how a system *might* operate, but on empirical documentation on how it *does* operate. . . .

The Baldus study . . . distinguishes between those cases in which (1) the jury exercises virtually no discretion because the strength or weakness of aggravating factors usually suggests that only one outcome is appropriate; and (2) cases reflecting an "intermediate" level of aggravation, in which the jury has considerable discretion in choosing a sentence. McCleskey's case falls into the intermediate range. In such cases, . . . just under 59 percent —almost 6 in 10—defendants comparable to McCleskey would not have received the death penalty if their victims had been black. . . .

The statistical evidence in this case . . . relentlessly documents the risk that McCleskey's sentence was influenced by racial considerations. This evidence shows that there is a better than even chance in Georgia that race will influence the decision to impose the death penalty: a majority of defendants in white-victim crimes would not have been sentenced to die if their victims had been black. . . . In determining the guilt of a defendant, a state must prove its case beyond a reasonable doubt. . . . Surely, we should not be willing to take a person's life if the chance that his death sentence was irrationally imposed is *more* likely than not. . . .

McCleskey's claim is not a fanciful product of mere statistical artifice. For many years, Georgia operated openly and formally precisely the type of dual system the evidence shows is still effectively in place. . . . By the time of the Civil War, a dual system of crime and punishment was well established in

Georgia. The state criminal code contained separate sections for "Slaves and Free Persons of Color" and for all other persons. [Justice Brennan here cited numerous instances in which the Georgia Penal Code had provided more severe punishments for crimes committed by blacks and for crimes (especially rape) committed against white victims.]

. . . Citation of past practices does not justify the automatic condemnation of current ones. But it would be unrealistic to ignore the influence of history in assessing the plausible implications of McCleskey's evidence.

. . . The Court . . . declines to find McCleskey's evidence sufficient in view of "the safeguards designed to minimize racial bias in the [capital sentencing] process." In Gregg v. Georgia, 428 U.S., at 226, the Court rejected a facial challenge to the Georgia capital sentencing statute, describing such a challenge as based on "simply an assertion of lack of faith" that the system could operate in a fair manner. Justice White observed that the claim that prosecutors might act in an arbitrary fashion was "unsupported by any facts." . . . *Gregg* bestowed no permanent approval on the Georgia system. It simply held that the State's statutory safeguards were assumed sufficient to channel discretion without evidence otherwise. . . .

The Court next states [its] fear that recognition of McCleskey's claim would open the door to widespread challenges to all aspects of criminal sentencing. [T]o reject McCleskey's powerful evidence on this basis is to ignore both the qualitatively different character of the death penalty and the particular repugnance of racial discrimination. . . .

Finally, the Court justifies its rejection of McCleskey's claim by cautioning against usurpation of the legislatures' role in devising and monitoring criminal punishment. . . . Those whom we would banish from society or from the human community itself often speak in too faint a voice to be heard above society's demand for punishment. It is the particular role of courts to hear these voices, for the Constitution declares that the majoritarian chorus may not alone dictate the conditions of social life.

[I]t has been scarcely a generation since this Court's first decision striking down racial segregation, and barely two decades since the legislative prohibition of racial discrimination in major domains of national life. These have been honorable steps, but we cannot pretend that in three decades we have completely escaped the grip of an historical legacy spanning centuries. Warren McCleskey's evidence confronts us with the subtle and persistent influence of the past. His message is a disturbing one to a society that has formally repudiated racism, and a frustrating one to a Nation accustomed to regarding its destiny as the product of its own will. Nonetheless, we ignore him at our peril, for we remain imprisoned by the past as long as we deny its influence in the present. . . .

JUSTICE BLACKMUN, [with whom JUSTICES MARSHALL, BRENNAN, and STEVENS join], dissenting. . . .

The Court today seems to give a new meaning to our recognition that death is different. Rather than requiring "a correspondingly greater degree of scrutiny of the capital sentencing determination," California v. Ramos, 463 U.S.

992, 998-999 (1983), the Court relies on the very fact that this is a case involving capital punishment to apply a *lesser* standard of scrutiny under the Equal Protection Clause. . . .

A criminal defendant alleging an equal protection violation must prove the existence of purposeful discrimination. He may establish a prima facie case of purposeful discrimination "by showing that the totality of the relevant facts gives rise to an inference of discriminatory purpose." Batson v. Kentucky, 106 S. Ct., at 1721. Once the defendant establishes a prima facie case, the burden shifts to the prosecution to rebut that case. "The State cannot meet his burden on mere general assertions that its officials did not discriminate or that they properly performed their official duties." Ibid. The State must demonstrate that the challenged effect was due to " 'permissible racially neutral selection criteria.' " Ibid. . . .

McCleskey . . . demonstrated that it was more likely than not that the fact that the victim he was charged with killing was white determined that he received a sentence of death—20 out of every 34 defendants in McCleskey's midrange category would not have been sentenced to be executed if their victims had been black. [T]he race of the victim is more important in explaining the imposition of a death sentence than is the factor whether the defendant was a prime mover in the homicide.[9] Similarly, the race-of-victim factor is nearly as crucial as the statutory aggravating circumstance whether the defendant had a prior record of a conviction for a capital crime.[10] . . . In sum, McCleskey has demonstrated a clear pattern of differential treatment according to race that is "unexplainable on grounds other than race."

The Court's explanations for its failure to apply this well-established equal protection analysis to this case are not persuasive. . . . I do not believe acceptance of McCleskey's claim would eliminate capital punishment in Georgia. [I]n extremely aggravated murders the risk of discriminatory enforcement of the death penalty is minimized. . . . Moreover, the establishment of guidelines for Assistant District Attorneys as to the appropriate basis for exercising their discretion at the various steps in the prosecution of a case would provide at least a measure of consistency. The Court's emphasis on the procedural safeguards in the system ignores the fact that there are none whatsoever during the crucial process leading up to trial. As Justice White stated for the plurality in Turner v. Murray, I find "the risk that racial prejudice may have infected petitioner's capital sentencing unacceptable in light of the ease with which that risk could have been minimized." 106 S. Ct., at 1688. I dissent.

Justice Stevens, with whom Justice Blackmun joins, dissenting.

. . . This sort of disparity is constitutionally intolerable. It flagrantly violates the Court's prior "insistence that capital punishment be imposed fairly,

---

9. A defendant's chances of receiving a death sentence increase by a factor of 4.3 if the victim is white, but only by 2.3 if the defendant was the prime mover behind the homicide.

10. A prior record of a conviction for murder, armed robbery, rape, or kidnapping with bodily injury increases the chances of a defendant's receiving a death sentence by a factor of 4.9.

and with reasonable consistency, or not at all." Eddings v. Oklahoma, 455 U.S. 104, 112 (1982).

The Court's decision appears to be based on a fear that the acceptance of McCleskey's claim would sound the death knell for capital punishment in Georgia. If society were indeed forced to choose between a racially discriminatory death penalty (one that provides heightened protection against murder "for whites only") and no death penalty at all, the choice mandated by the Constitution would be plain. But the Court's fear is unfounded. One of the lessons of the Baldus study is that there exist certain categories of extremely serious crimes for which prosecutors consistently seek, and juries consistently impose, the death penalty without regard to the race of the victim or the race of the offender. If Georgia were to narrow the class of death-eligible defendants to those categories, the danger of arbitrary and discriminatory imposition of the death penalty would be significantly decreased, if not eradicated. ... [S]uch a restructuring of the sentencing scheme is surely not too high a price to pay. ...

NOTES

1. *Scholarly treatment of* **McCleskey.** For helpful discussions of the issues posed by *McCleskey*, see David C. Baldus, George G. Woodworth & Charles A. Pulaski, Equal Justice and the Death Penalty (1990); Welsh S. White, The Death Penalty in the Eighties, 113-139 (1987); Randall Kennedy, *McCleskey v. Kemp*: Race, Capital Punishment, and the Supreme Court, 101 Harv. L. Rev. 1388 (1988); Samuel R. Gross, Race and Death: The Judicial Evaluation of Evidence of Discrimination in Capital Sentencing, 18 U.C. Davis L. Rev. 1275 (1985).

2. *The nature of the racial discrimination.* (a) The race of defendants and victims. In the period before *Furman* and the Court's regulation of the death penalty, there was widespread evidence that black defendants were disproportionately targeted for capital punishment. Between 1930 and 1967, 54 percent of those executed were black, and of the 455 men executed for rape in that period, 90 percent were black. In the post-*Furman*, post-*Gregg* period, in contrast, 56 percent of those executed were white. Charles Lane, The Death Penalty and Racism, The American Interest, Nov-Dec. 2010.

A noteworthy feature of the Baldus study and subsequent research is that the race of the defendant, standing alone, does not appear to be a driving force in whether prosecutors seek a capital sentence. See, e.g., Isaac Unah, Choosing Those Who Will Die: The Effect of Race, Gender, and Law in Prosecutorial Decision To Seek the Death Penalty in Durham County, North Carolina, 15 Mich. J. Race & L. 135 (2009). Empirical studies find large effects based on the race of the victim, as cases involving white victims are far more likely to lead to capital charges. But within the category of cases with white victims, the Baldus study found that after controlling for relevant variables, black defendants were 10 percent more likely to receive a death sentence than white defendants.

(b) Local demographics. One possible explanation of racial disparity is that local prosecutors might not seek the death penalty as often in black-on-black homicides because those crimes typically take place in localities with large black populations. Survey data show that blacks are the one demographic group in the United States that largely opposes the death penalty. Lane, supra. Thus, in jurisdictions with large black populations, prosecutors' charging decisions may reflect what they believe to be the community sentiment about capital punishment. Theodore Eisenberg's study of county-level data in five states found that capital sentences for black-on-black homicides decreased as the percentage of blacks in a county's population increased. Eisenberg thus concluded that "minority community skepticism about the justness of the death penalty is a contributing factor to low death sentence rates" when murder victims are black. Theodore Eisenberg, Death Sentence Rates and County Demographics: An Empirical Study, 90 Cornell L. Rev. 347, 370 (2005).

Questions: If imposition of the death penalty varies based on community support, does that negate claims that it is "infected" with racial bias? Is prosecutorial bias distinguishable from community bias? As elected officials, do prosecutors have a responsibility to respond to their electorates' preferences?

(c) Predicting the jury's attitude. Prosecutors also may be anticipating how the victim-offender racial configuration may affect what a prospective jury is likely to do, especially when that jury (in any community) has a significant proportion of white members. For example, one study found that the death penalty is three times more likely in a black defendant/white victim case that has five or more white male jurors than in one that has fewer such jurors. See William J. Bowers et al., Death Sentencing in Black and White, 3 U. Pa. J. Const. L. 171 (2001). The study also found a life sentence to be "twice as likely for a defendant who draws a black male juror than for the one who fails to do so." Id.

Another source of disparity comes from the process of "death qualifying" juries. In capital cases, jurors can be struck for cause if they oppose capital punishment in all cases. As a result, death-qualified juries are more likely to be male, white, and politically conservative. Brooke Butler, The Role of Death Qualification in Capital Trials Involving Juvenile Defendants, 37 J. Applied Soc. Psychol. 549 (2007). This factor in turn may lead to juries that are more prone to implicit racial biases. See Justin D. Levinson et al., Guilty by Implicit Racial Bias: The Guilty/Not Guilty Implicit Association Test, 8 Ohio St. J. Crim. L. 187 (2010).

Questions: Should the process of death qualification be eliminated on these grounds? What other mechanisms can ensure that juries are free from racial bias without eliminating death qualification? Imagine you are a defense attorney questioning prospective jurors during voir dire. What types of questions would you ask if you were seeking to uncover implicit racial bias? How effective are the questions likely to be in rooting out bias?

(d) Electoral politics. In three death penalty states—Alabama, Delaware, and Florida—judges are permitted to override a jury sentence and make the final decision on whether a defendant will get the death penalty. A recent

report found that in Alabama, 92 percent of judge overrides consisted of judges overruling jury verdicts of life to impose the death penalty, and that judge overrides account for 21 percent of the state's death row. Equal Justice Initiative, The Death Penalty in Alabama 4 (2011). Additionally, while only 35 percent of murders in Alabama involved white victims, 75 percent of the life-to-death overrides involved white victims. Id. at 18. The report also found that judges frequently tout their willingness to impose the death penalty during judicial campaigns as evidence of their tough-on-crime mentality, with some judges airing campaign commercials that remind voters of their performance in specific cases. Id. at 14-15. What is the penological justification for permitting a judge to override a jury's verdict in a capital case?

(e) Other local influences. A recent study in Georgia found that prosecutors in counties with the fewest murder cases sought death about twice as often as prosecutors in counties with the highest volume of murder cases. Bill Rankin et al., A Matter of Life or Death, Atlanta J. Const., Sept. 22, 2007. But if one justification for the death penalty is deterrence, wouldn't we expect to see the opposite pattern? Why would communities with fewer murder cases be more likely to support the death penalty?

Question: If the factors discussed explain the disparities, does that lessen the cause for concern or heighten it?

3. Post-*McCleskey* *legislative initiatives.* Critics of the result in *McCleskey* have sought to overturn the decision by enacting national legislation requiring states to demonstrate that their enforcement of the death penalty is racially neutral. A provision to this effect was passed by the U.S. House of Representatives as part of the Crime Control Act of 1994, but the House-Senate conference committee deleted it from the bill. See N.Y. Times, July 29, 1994, at A1, A9.

In 1998, Kentucky became the first state to allow capital defendants to challenge their prosecutions using statistical evidence of racial discrimination. The Kentucky Racial Justice Act (KRJA), Ky. Rev. Stat. Ann. §§532.300-.309, requires capital defendants to raise challenges to the prosecutor's charging decision prior to trial. The Act allows for the consideration of statistical evidence of discrimination in capital charging practices but also requires a defendant to "state with particularity how the evidence supports a claim that racial considerations played a significant part in the decision to seek a death sentence in his or her case." The defendant bears the burden of establishing by "clear and convincing evidence" that race was "the basis" of the prosecutor's decision to seek the death penalty. As of 2011, there were no reported reversals of capital convictions based on violations of the KRJA, though there is some reason to believe that the act may have influenced the charging and plea-bargaining behavior of prosecutors. See Alex Lesman, Note, State Responses to the Specter of Racial Discrimination in Capital Proceedings: The Kentucky Racial Justice Act and the New Jersey Supreme Court's Proportionality Review Project, 13 J.L. & Pol'y 359 (2005).

North Carolina's Racial Justice Act, N.C. Gen. Stat. §§15A-2010 to -2012, passed in 2009, allows defendants to use statistical evidence of racial discrimination to challenge not only charging decisions, but also the use of race in jury selection and the jury's decision to impose the death penalty. See Seth Kotch & Robert P. Mosteller, The Racial Justice Act and The Long Struggle with Race and the Death Penalty in North Carolina, 88 N.C. L. Rev. 2031, n.381 (2010). Once a defendant produces statistically significant evidence of a pattern of racial discrimination, the burden shifts to the government to prove by a preponderance of the evidence that there was a nonracial explanation for the defendant's sentence. If a defendant prevails with statistical evidence, the death sentence is vacated and the defendant is resentenced to life without parole. Is the North Carolina statute more likely to be effective in reducing racial disparities than the Kentucky law? How *should* a statute be structured in order to minimize racial bias without imposing unmanageable litigation burdens in every capital case?

4. *The Model Penal Code.* In October 2009, the American Law Institute (ALI) withdrew §210.6, the death penalty provision of the MPC, "in light of the current intractable institutional and structural obstacles to ensuring a minimally adequate system for administering capital punishment."[56] While the ALI refused to formally endorse or oppose the continued use of the death penalty, Carol Steiker and Jordan Steiker have noted the significance of the ALI action:

> The ALI's decision to withdraw the MPC capital provisions—and to decline to investigate further reform—reflects skepticism about the capacity of sentencing instructions to ensure accurate, evenhanded capital decision making. The past ten years have seen similar expressions of skepticism from lawmakers and judges confronted with concrete evidence about the administration of the American death penalty. But even though the skepticism is not new, it likely carries distinctive weight when voiced by the very body that invested its labor and prestige in the effort to craft such instructions.[57]

5. *Assessing the constitutional doctrines.* Consider Carol S. Steiker & Jordan M. Steiker, Sober Second Thoughts: Reflections on Two Decades of Constitutional Regulation of Capital Punishment, 109 Harv. L. Rev. 355, 357-360, 433-436 (1995):

> Virtually no one thinks that the constitutional regulation of capital punishment has been a success. [S]ome critics claim that the Court's work has burdened the administration of capital punishment with an overly complex . . . body of constitutional law that . . . "obstructs, delays, and defeats" the administration of capital punishment. [A] different set of critics claims that the Supreme Court has in fact turned its back on regulating the death penalty

---

56. Message from Lance Liebman, Dir., Am. Law Inst. (Oct. 23, 2009), http://www.ali.org/_news/10232009.htm.

57. Carol S. Steiker & Jordan M. Steiker, No More Tinkering: The American Law Institute and The Death Penalty Provisions of the Model Penal Code, 89 Tex. L. Rev. 353 (2010).

and no longer even attempts to meet the concerns about the arbitrary and discriminatory imposition of death that animated . . . *Furman.*

[W]e conclude that both sets of criticisms of the Court's work are substantially correct: the death penalty is, perversely, both over- and under-regulated.

[There is] a substantial hidden cost of the Court's chosen path . . . , which creates an impression of enormous regulatory effort but achieves negligible regulatory effects. [P]owerful evidence suggests that death penalty law makes actors within the criminal justice system more comfortable with their roles by inducing an exaggerated belief in the essential rationality and fairness of the system. [T]he Court's focus on controlling the discretion of capital sentencers creates a false aura of rationality, even science, around the necessarily moral task of deciding life or death [and] has diluted judges' and jurors' sense of ultimate responsibility for imposing the death penalty.

[T]he public's impression [is] that any death sentences that are imposed and finally upheld are the product of a rigorous—indeed, too rigorous—system of constraints. . . . The Supreme Court's death penalty law, by creating an impression of enormous regulatory effort while achieving negligible regulatory effects, effectively obscures the true nature of our capital sentencing system, in which the pre-*Furman* world of unreviewable sentencer discretion lives on, with much the same consequences in terms of arbitrary and discriminatory sentencing patterns.

Some are more optimistic about the efficacy of the Supreme Court's death penalty jurisprudence. Consider David McCord, Judging the Effectiveness of the Supreme Court's Death Penalty Jurisprudence According to the Court's Own Goals: Mild Success or Major Disaster? 24 Fla. St. U. L. Rev. 545, 593 (1997):

The best available evidence shows that the Court's regulatory death penalty jurisprudence has been successful in decreasing overinclusion, which is the primary vice that the Court has seen in death penalty systems for the last quarter of a century. One can argue that the Court was wrong to focus (or focus so exclusively) on minimizing overinclusion. . . . [But] the populations of death rows since 1972 very likely comprise a more carefully selected and "worse" collection of malefactors than before 1972. This is not an insignificant achievement. So, while death penalty opponents rue the Court's failure to regulate death more severely, I doubt that there is one experienced capital defense lawyer in this country who would rather return to the pre-*Furman* era. Perhaps not even many prosecutors would want to return to the days before *Furman*, when such an unguided power of life and death rested in their hands.

chapter 6

The Significance of Resulting Harm

A. CAUSATION

Where a crime is defined without regard to any result of the defendant's conduct (for example, an attempt), there is no need to face the issue of causation. But where a particular result is a necessary element of the crime charged, a perplexing problem sometimes arises as to whether the defendant's act or culpable omission *caused* the result. And procedurally, this problem falls to the prosecution, which must prove that causal link (like any other required element) beyond a reasonable doubt.

Homicide cases are the most fertile source of causation problems. When the actor kills the very person he meant to kill, in precisely the way he intended, no causation difficulty arises. Nor is there difficulty in the case of unintended killings when the death occurs in precisely the way that the defendant's risky conduct made likely. But when the intended death occurs in a way not intended or the unintended death occurs in an unlikely way, the law must distinguish variations (between the actual result and the result intended or risked) that preclude liability from variations that do not preclude liability. The following hypotheticals suggest the scope of the problem.

1. Accused places poison by the bedside of his sick wife intending that she drink it. During the night, she dies of a heart attack without having consumed the drink.
2. Same as above, except that the wife sips the poison and is repelled by the taste; to wash it away, she goes to the bathroom for water, slips, and injures herself fatally.
3. Accused attempts to shoot her husband, but she misses. In response, he decides to flee to his brother's home and boards a train to get there but then is killed in a train wreck.
4. Accused shoots at deceased intending to kill him. The bullet misses but deceased dies of fright.
5. While thoroughly intoxicated, accused No. 1 drives his car containing sleeping children at a speed greatly in excess of the speed limit. He crashes into the rear of a truck stalled in the middle of the road around

a bend, the truck's driver, accused No. 2, having failed to leave his lights on or otherwise give warning to approaching cars. The children of accused No. 1 are killed in the crash.

6. Accused administers a vicious blow to victim's head with a blackjack. The victim is taken to a hospital for treatment where (a) due to negligent medical treatment of the wound he dies of meningitis, (b) he dies of scarlet fever communicated by a nurse, (c) he is mortally wounded by a knife-wielding maniac, (d) he is decapitated by a maniac, (e) he deliberately takes a fatal dose of sleeping pills to end his misery, or (f) he is seized with an attack of appendicitis from which he dies.

7. Accused No. 1 throws a live hand grenade into the room of accused No. 2 intending to kill him. The latter seizes it and throws it out his window where it falls to the crowded street below, exploding and killing several persons.

8. Accused and deceased engage in an armed robbery. Deceased is killed in an exchange of bullets with the police.

1. Foreseeability and Coincidence

PEOPLE v. ACOSTA

Court of Appeal of California, 4th District
284 Cal. Rptr. 117 (1991)

WALLIN, J. Vincent William Acosta appeals his conviction on three counts of second degree murder . . . contending: (1) there was insufficient evidence his conduct was the proximate cause of the deaths; (2) there was insufficient evidence of malice. . . . At 10 P.M. on March 10, 1987, Officers Salceda and Francis . . . saw Acosta in [a] stolen Nissan Pulsar parked on the street. The officers approached Acosta and identified themselves. Acosta inched the Pulsar forward, then accelerated rapidly. He led Salceda, Francis and officers from other agencies on a 48-mile chase along numerous surface streets and freeways throughout Orange County. The chase ended near Acosta's residence in Anaheim.

During the chase, Acosta engaged in some of the most egregious driving tactics imaginable. He ran stop signs and red lights, and drove on the wrong side of streets, causing oncoming traffic to scatter or swerve to avoid colliding with him. . . .

Police helicopters from Anaheim, Costa Mesa, Huntington Beach, and Newport Beach assisted in the chase by tracking Acosta. During the early part of the pursuit, the Costa Mesa and Newport Beach craft were used, pinpointing Acosta's location with their high beam spotlights. The Costa Mesa helicopter was leading the pursuit, in front of and below the Newport Beach helicopter. As they flew into Newport Beach, the pilots agreed the Newport Beach craft should take the lead. . . .

At the direction of the Costa Mesa pilot, the Newport Beach helicopter moved forward and descended while the Costa Mesa helicopter banked to the right. Shortly after commencing this procedure, the Costa Mesa helicopter, having terminated radio communication, came up under the Newport Beach helicopter from the right rear and collided with it. Both helicopters fell to the ground. Three occupants in the Costa Mesa helicopter died as a result of the crash.

Menzies Turner, a retired Federal Aviation Administration (FAA) investigator, testified as an expert and concluded the accident occurred because the Costa Mesa helicopter, the faster of the two aircraft, made a 360-degree turn and closed too rapidly on the Newport Beach helicopter. He opined the Costa Mesa helicopter's pilot violated an FAA regulation prohibiting careless and reckless operation of an aircraft by failing to properly clear the area, not maintaining communication with the Newport Beach helicopter, failing to keep the other aircraft in view at all times, and not changing his altitude. He also testified the Costa Mesa pilot violated another FAA regulation prohibiting operation of one aircraft so close to another as to create a collision hazard.

Turner could not think of any reason for the Costa Mesa helicopter's erratic movement. The maneuver was not a difficult one, and was not affected by the ground activity at the time. He had never heard of a midair collision between two police helicopters involved in tracking a ground pursuit, and had never investigated a midair collision involving helicopters.[3] . . .

Acosta claims there was insufficient evidence . . . that he proximately caused the deaths of the victims. [He] argues that although a collision between ground vehicles was a foreseeable result of his conduct, one between airborne helicopters was not, noting his expert had never heard of a similar incident. He also contends the Costa Mesa helicopter pilot's violation of FAA regulations was a superseding cause. Because the deaths here were unusual, to say the least, the issue deserves special scrutiny. . . .

"Proximate cause" is the term historically used[6] to separate those results for which an actor will be held responsible from those not carrying such responsibility. The term is, in a sense, artificial, serving matters of policy surrounding tort and criminal law and based partly on expediency and partly on concerns of fairness and justice. Because such concerns are sometimes more a matter of "common sense" than pure logic, the line of demarcation is flexible, and attempts to lay down uniform tests which apply evenly in all situations have failed. That does not mean general guidelines and approaches to analysis cannot be constructed.

The threshold question in examining causation is whether the defendant's act was an "actual cause" of the victim's injury. It is a sine qua non test: But for the defendant's act would the injury have occurred? Unless an act is an actual cause of the injury, it will not be considered a proximate cause.

---

3. Our research yielded no published civil or criminal case nationwide which involved a two-helicopter collision.

6. The American Law Institute has urged the use of "legal cause" instead. Although there is some merit to its arguments, I abide with the traditional term, "proximate cause."

[The court then reviewed the various tests used by courts to determine "proximate" cause and concluded that in this case, the issue was whether the death of the helicopter pilots was foreseeable.]

Prosser and Keeton, in an in-depth discussion of the dynamics of foresight, conclude that although it is desirable to exclude extremely remarkable and unusual results from the purview of proximate cause, it is virtually impossible to express a logical verbal formula which will produce uniform results. (Prosser & Keeton, [Torts] 300 [(5th ed. 1984)].) I agree. The standard should be simply stated, exclude extraordinary results, and allow the trier of fact to determine the issue on the particular facts of the case using "the common sense of the common man as to common things." As with other ultimate issues, appellate courts must review that determination, giving due deference to the trier of fact. The "highly extraordinary result" standard serves that purpose. It is consistent with the definition of foreseeability used in California. It does not involve the defendant's state of mind, but focuses upon the objective conditions present when he acts.[19] ...

Here, but for Acosta's conduct of fleeing the police, the helicopters would never have been in position for the crash. ...

The result was not highly extraordinary. Although a two-helicopter collision was unknown to expert witness Turner and no reported cases describe one, it was "a possible consequence which reasonably might have been contemplated." Given the emotional dynamics of any police pursuit, there is an "appreciable probability" that one of the pursuers, in the heat of the chase, may act negligently or recklessly to catch the quarry. That no pursuits have ever before resulted in a helicopter crash or midair collision is more a comment on police flying skill and technology than upon the innate probabilities involved. ... Given these circumstances, a finding of proximate cause is appropriate. ...

[On the other issue in the case, whether there was sufficient evidence of malice, the court found in the negative because there was not enough evidence to show that Acosta consciously disregarded the risk to the helicopter pilots: "In the absence of more evidence, no reasonable juror could find a conscious disregard for a risk which is barely objectively cognizable."]

The judgment is reversed. ...

CROSBY, J., ... Whether the defendant may be held criminally culpable for the tragic deaths in this case is the key issue before us. Justice Wallin says yes, but not for murder. ... I disagree ... because the law does not assign blame to an otherwise blameworthy actor when neither the intervening negligent conduct nor the risk of harm was foreseeable.

Or, as Justice Cardozo put it,

We are told that one who drives at reckless speed through a crowded city street is guilty of a negligent act and, therefore, of a wrongful one irrespective of the

---

19. The Model Penal Code takes a similar approach, focusing on whether the result is "too remote or accidental in its occurrence to have a [just] bearing on the actor's liability or on the gravity of his offense." (Model Pen. Code, §2.03(2)(b).) ...

A DUTY

consequences. Negligent the act is, and wrongful in the sense that it is unsocial, but wrongful and unsocial in relation to other travelers, only because the eye of vigilance perceives the risk of damage. . . . [R]isk imports relation; it is risk to another or to others within the range of apprehension.

(Palsgraf v. Long Island R. Co. (1928) 248 N.Y. 339.) The occupants of these helicopters were surely not "within the range of apprehension" of a fleeing criminal on the ground.

To be sure, defendant represented a threat to everyone traveling the same roads and would have been responsible for any injury directly or indirectly caused by his actions in those environs; but to extend that responsibility to persons in the air, whose role was merely to observe his movements, a simple enough task in far speedier helicopters, defies common sense. . . . They were not in the zone of danger in this case by any stretch of the imagination, and the manner and circumstances of the collision could hardly have reasonably been foreseen. . . . Although less remote than a dispatcher suffering a coronary, perhaps, this was a "highly extraordinary result" by any measure and, properly viewed, beyond the long arm of the criminal law. . . .

NOTES AND QUESTIONS

1. People v. Brady, 29 Cal. Rptr. 3d 286 (Ct. App. 2005), involved the mid-air collision of two firefighting planes that were attempting to extinguish a fire in a remote wooded area. Defendant had recklessly started the fire, which quickly spread to his clandestine methamphetamine lab nearby, setting off an intense blaze. When fire control aircraft arrived on the scene, one pilot deviated from the customary flight pattern, approached from the wrong direction, and crashed into another plane, killing himself and the other pilot. Defendant was convicted of causing both deaths. The appellate court upheld the jury's finding that the deaths were reasonably foreseeable, in part because—given the location of the fire—an effort to control it was bound to require a number of aircraft flying at low altitude. Was there a comparable degree of foreseeability in *Acosta*? If not, was the helicopter crash in the latter case nonetheless *sufficiently* foreseeable to justify holding Acosta accountable for it?

2. Acosta was not guilty of murder, the court holds, because he didn't have the required mens rea; it couldn't be found that he "consciously disregarded a risk which was barely objectively cognizable." Would the court have reached the same conclusion if Acosta had collided with and killed another driver on the ground? If not, what practical difference is there between the conclusions reached by the majority and the dissent? *Yes*

3. If Acosta was not guilty of murder, what crime *did* he commit? Is the "barely objectively cognizable" risk to the helicopter pilots sufficient to make Acosta guilty of criminally negligent homicide? Why should the low likelihood of the harm that actually occurred be relevant in determining whether Acosta acted with a culpable mens rea?

NOTE ON "FACTUAL CAUSE"

In conventional formulations, the causation requirement has two components: The defendant's wrongful act must be both the *factual* cause and the *proximate* cause of the relevant harm. Factual cause, sometimes called the "but-for" or "*sine qua non*" requirement, simply means that the harm would not have occurred in the absence of the defendant's act. Proximate cause means that the act, in addition to being a but-for cause, must bear a sufficiently close relationship to the resulting harm. The great majority of causation problems present only the second set of issues. Note, for example, the eight hypotheticals presented at the outset of this section, pages 571-572 supra. Nearly all of them easily meet the factual cause requirement. (Which of them does not?) Similarly in *Acosta*, only the second set of issues is debatable; there is no doubt that, as the court states, "but for Acosta's conduct . . . , the helicopters would never have been in position for the crash."

By comparison to the elusive concept of proximate cause, factual causation seems a relatively uncontroversial requirement. Suppose, for example, that one of the pilots pursuing Acosta had a heart attack and died, not because of the stress of the events but solely because of a blood clot that would have produced fatal results at that moment no matter what the pilot was doing. In such a case, there is no reason to hold Acosta responsible for the death, and indeed statutes and case law typically treat factual causation as an invariable prerequisite to liability. See, e.g., MPC §2.03(1)(a).

Would it ever make sense to treat conduct as a legal cause even though it is not a factual cause? Consider State v. Montoya, 61 P.3d 793 (N.M. 2002). A private bodyguard shot and severely wounded Lowery. Montoya, one of the shooter's associates, then drove the victim to a secluded location and left him there to die. Montoya was convicted of murder on the theory that he had caused the death by preventing Lowery from getting help. The testimony, however, established only that immediate medical attention "could have" saved Lowery's life. Should the conviction be upheld on appeal? Recall that since a necessary element of a murder case is proof that the defendant's conduct caused death, the prosecution had to prove *beyond a reasonable doubt* that, but for Montoya's actions, Lowery would have survived. The evidence was clearly insufficient to support that conclusion, and the appellate court reversed the conviction. But does it make sense for Montoya—who *wanted* Lowery to die—to escape a murder conviction simply by showing that his victim *might* have died anyway?

In State v. Muro, 695 N.W.2d 425 (Neb. 2005), the defendant came home to discover that her husband had beaten their daughter, fracturing her skull. Muro waited four hours before summoning medical attention, and the daughter died later that night. The Nebraska Supreme Court held that because the state had proved "only the *possibility* of survival with earlier treatment," it had failed to prove but-for causation beyond a reasonable doubt. Id. at 432. Note the clash between the requirements of mens rea and those of causation. If early treatment would have given the child a 90 percent chance of survival, the mother's failure to summon help would show a high level of culpability—extreme recklessness or negligence. But the same probability (a 90 percent chance of survival) would defeat any effort to prove causation, because of the 10 percent chance that the child would have died just as quickly anyway. For criticism of courts' insistence on proof of but-for causation in cases where the defendant deprives the victim of a *chance* of survival, see Eric A. Johnson, Criminal Liability for Loss of a Chance, 91 Iowa L. Rev. 59 (2005).

PEOPLE v. ARZON

Supreme Court, New York County
92 Misc. 2d 739, 401 N.Y.S.2d 156 (1978)

MILONAS, J. The defendant was indicted on September 28, 1977 for two counts of murder in the second degree and arson in the third degree after he allegedly intentionally set fire to a couch, thus causing a serious fire on the fifth floor of an abandoned building at 358 East 8th Street in New York County. The New York City Fire Department, in responding to the conflagration, arrived to find the rear portion of the fifth and sixth floors burning. The firemen attempted to bring the situation under control, but making no progress and there being no additional assistance available, they decided to withdraw from the building. At that point, they were suddenly enveloped by a dense smoke, which was later discovered to have arisen from another independent fire that had broken out on the second floor.

Although this fire was also determined to have originated in arson, there is virtually no evidence implicating the defendant in its responsibility. However, the combination of the thick smoke and the fifth floor fire made evacuation from the premises extremely hazardous, and, in the process, Fireman Martin Celic sustained injuries from which he subsequently died. Accordingly, the defendant was accused [in the first count] of murder in the second degree for having, "Under circumstances evincing a depraved indifference to human life, recklessly engaged in conduct which created a grave risk of death to another person," thereby causing the death of Martin Celic, and [alternatively, in the second count] with felony murder. The third charge of the indictment, arson, is not at issue for purposes of the instant application.

It is the defendant's contention that the evidence before the grand jury is insufficient to support the first two counts. He argues that . . . murder requires a causal link between the underlying crime and the death, a connection which, in the defendant's view, is here lacking.

[In] People v. Kibbe, 321 N.E.2d 773 (N.Y. 1974), the Court of Appeals affirmed the [murder] conviction of defendants who had abandoned their helplessly intoxicated robbery victim by the side of a dark road in subfreezing temperature, one-half mile from the nearest structure, without shoes or eyeglasses, with his trousers at his ankles, his shirt pulled up and his outer clothing removed. The court held that while the deceased was actually killed by a passing truck, the defendants' conduct was a sufficiently direct cause of

the Defense

the ensuing death to warrant criminal liability and that "it is not necessary that the ultimate harm be intended by the actor. It will suffice if it can be said beyond a reasonable doubt, as indeed it can here be said, that the ultimate harm is something which should have been foreseen as being reasonably related to the acts of the accused."

Clearly, an obscure or merely probable connection between the defendant's conduct and another person's death is not enough to support a charge of homicide. People v. Stewart, [358 N.E.2d 487 (N.Y.1976)]. In *Stewart*, the victim had been operated upon for a stab wound in the stomach inflicted by the defendant. Afterwards, the surgeon performed an entirely unrelated hernia procedure on him, and he died. According to the court, "the prosecutor must, at least, prove that the defendant's conduct was an actual cause of death, in the sense that it forged a link in the chain of causes which actually brought about the death. . . ." In this instance, the possibility that death resulted from a factor not attributable to the defendant could not be ruled out beyond a reasonable doubt, since the patient would, in all likelihood, have survived except for the hernia operation. . . .

[T]he defendant's conduct need not be the sole and exclusive factor in the victim's death. In the standard established by *People v. Kibbe*, supra, and *People v. Stewart*, supra, an individual is criminally liable if his conduct was a sufficiently direct cause of the death, and the ultimate harm is something which should have been foreseen as being reasonably related to his acts. It is irrelevant that, in this instance, the fire which had erupted on the second floor intervened, thus contributing to the conditions that culminated in the death of Fireman Celic. In *Kibbe*, the victim was killed when he was struck by a truck. This did not relieve the defendants in that case from criminal responsibility for his murder, as it does not absolve the defendant here. Certainly, it was foreseeable that firemen would respond to the situation, thus exposing them, along with the persons already present in the vicinity, to a life-threatening danger. The fire set by the defendant was an indispensable link in the chain of events that resulted in the death. It continued to burn out of control, greatly adding to the problem of evacuating the building by blocking off one of the access routes. At the very least, the defendant's act, as was the case in *Kibbe*, placed the deceased in a position where he was particularly vulnerable to the separate and independent force, in this instance, the fire on the second floor.

Consequently, the defendant's motion to dismiss the [murder counts] of the indictment is denied.

People v. Warner-Lambert Co., 51 N.Y.2d 295, 414 N.E.2d 660 (1980): [Defendant corporation and several of its officers and employees were indicted for second-degree manslaughter (N.Y. Penal Law §125.15, page 425 supra) and criminally negligent homicide (N.Y. Penal Law §125.10, page 425 supra). Several of the corporation's employees were killed (and many more injured) in a massive explosion at one of its chewing-gum factories. Evidence before the grand jury showed that the corporation used two potentially explosive substances in its manufacturing process, magnesium stearate (MS) and liquid nitrogen; that defendants had been warned by their insurance carrier that the high concentrations of MS dust, combined with other conditions, created an explosion hazard; and that these hazards were not eliminated by the time of the accident. On the issue of what triggered the explosion there was apparently no hard proof, only speculations by experts that it could have been caused by mechanical sparking in the machines or by the liquid nitrogen dripping onto a concentration of MS and igniting under the impact of a moving metal part. The court held that the evidence before the grand jury was not legally sufficient to establish the foreseeability of the immediate, triggering cause of the explosion and therefore dismissed the indictment. The court stated:]

It has been the position of the People that but-for causation is all that is required for the imposition of criminal liability. Thus, it is their submission, reduced to its simplest form, that there was evidence of a foreseeable and indeed foreseen risk of explosion of MS dust and that in consequence of defendants' failure to remove the dust a fatal explosion occurred. The chain of physical events by which the explosion was set off, i.e., its particular cause, is to them a matter of total indifference. [T]he People contended that liability could be imposed if the cause of the explosion were the lighting of a match by an uninvited intruder or the striking of a bolt of lightning. In effect they would hold defendants to the status of guarantors until the ambient dust was removed. It thus appears that the People would invoke an expanded application of proximate cause principles lifted from the civil law of torts.

We have rejected the application of any such sweeping theory of culpability under our criminal law, however. . . . [In *People v. Kibbe* (discussed in the *Arzon* case, supra)] the critical issue was whether the defendants should be held criminally liable for murder when the particular cause of death was vehicular impact rather than freezing. Under the theory now advanced by the People it would have been irrelevant that death had been the consequence of one particular chain of causation rather than another; it would have been enough that the defendants exposed their victim to the risk of death and that he died. That, of course, was not the analysis of culpability that we adopted. [W]e held that . . . "we subscribe to the requirement that the defendants' actions must be a *sufficiently direct cause* of the ensuing death before there can be any imposition of criminal liability, and recognize, of course, that this standard is greater than that required to serve as a basis for tort liability." Thus, we were concerned for the nature of the chain of particularized events which in fact led to the victim's death; it was not enough that death had occurred as the result of the defendants' abandonment of their helpless victim. To analogize the factual situation in the case now before us to that in *Kibbe* it might be hypothesized that the abandoned victim in *Kibbe* instead of being either frozen to death or killed when struck by a passing motor vehicle was killed when struck by an airplane making an emergency landing on the highway or when hit by a stray bullet from a hunter's rifle—occasions of death not reasonably to have been foreseen when the defendants abandoned their victim.

NOTES ON FORESEEABILITY

1. Statutory standards. Most state codes include no explicit rules for determining causation. In these jurisdictions, the courts are left to decide the question on the basis of evolving common-law principles. MPC §2.03 seeks to articulate an appropriate standard, and roughly a dozen states have adopted causation provisions based on it. See Model Penal Code and Commentaries, Comment to §2.03, at 264-265 (1985). Does the MPC standard narrow or clarify the issues? What result would it produce in *Acosta*, *Arzon*, and *Warner-Lambert*?

2. The specific causal mechanism. Is *Warner-Lambert* sound in requiring that the defendant foresee the specific triggering cause of an explosion? In recent decisions, the New York courts have limited the "specific-causal-mechanism" requirement to contexts that involve "a commercial or manufacturing process," and have held it inapplicable where fires have led to fatalities in residential or other settings. See People v. Rios, 907 N.Y.S.2d 440, at *8 n.9 (Sup. Ct. 2010). But if the specific-causal-mechanism requirement is sound in principle, shouldn't it apply in residential situations as well? If we can't determine how a fire started, should the person responsible for a hazardous condition be held liable anyway, because it is plausible to assume that the fatal spark was produced in some ordinary way? Or should that person escape liability, because the prosecution has not proved beyond a reasonable doubt that the fatal spark was *not* produced in some bizarre, unforeseeable way?

In defense of the foreseeability test, Professor Lawrence Crocker argues that "the key concept [in proximate cause analysis] is probability—probability as it would be understood by ordinary persons antecedent to the event, with no special access to information about the facts of the event."[1] Does this approach help clarify the problem? What result does it suggest for *Acosta*? For *Warner-Lambert*?

Criticizing the foreseeability test, Professor Michael Moore argues that the concept of foreseeability is inherently arbitrary and manipulable, because of what he calls "the multiple-description problem," namely that "there are many equally accurate ways to describe any particular [harm-causing event]," and thus conclusions about foreseeability inevitably depend on the level of generality at which we choose to describe what occurred.[2] If Professor Moore is right, how *should* causation issues be decided? Why should it ever matter whether culpable conduct did or did not "cause" a subsequent outcome?

3. Vulnerability of the victim. In *People v. Stamp*, page 493 supra, a robbery victim who suffered from coronary disease died of a heart attack triggered by fright experienced during the offense. The court held the defendant guilty

---

1. Crocker, A Retributive Theory of Causation, [1994] J. Contemp. Legal Issues 65, 100.
2. Moore, Foreseeing Harm Opaquely, In Action and Value in Criminal Law 125, 126-127 (S. Shute et al. eds., 1993).

of felony-murder, stating that liability was "not limited to those deaths which are foreseeable. [T]he robber takes his victim as he finds him." *Yet* if death results from an unusual disease unforeseeably contracted by the victim *after* an assault, the defendant presumably is relieved of liability. This remains true even when the victim would not have contracted the disease, but for the situation created by the injuries.

Questions: Why should the result be different when the disease producing death was contracted by the victim *before* the defendant's assault? Why should it be the case that the defendant always "takes his victim as he finds him"?

Consider State v. Lane, 444 S.E.2d 233 (N.C. Ct. App. 1994). Lane argued with Linton and punched him once in the face. Linton, who was extremely drunk, fell to the street. A city rescue squad arrived on the scene but concluded that Linton had not suffered any serious injury. He died two days later from brain swelling caused by the punch. A medical examiner testified that because Linton was a chronic alcoholic, he was especially susceptible to incurring such an injury from any blow to the head. At trial, Lane was convicted of misdemeanor-manslaughter under the unlawful-act doctrine. What result on appeal? Is it unfair to apply the vulnerable-victim rule against Lane when the victim himself is responsible for his preexisting condition? Or is it inappropriate to permit conclusions about causation to turn on the perceived blameworthiness of the victim?

4. *Is medical malpractice foreseeable? (a)* Consider the following efforts to summarize the applicable principle:

1 M. Hale, Pleas of the Crown 428: [If a] wound or hurt be not mortal, but with ill applications by the party, or those about him, of unwholesome salves or medicines the party dies, if it can clearly appear, that this medicine, and not the wound, was the cause of his death, it seems it is not homicide, but then that must appear clearly and certainly to be so.

But if a man receives a wound, which is not in itself mortal, but either for want of helpful applications, or neglect thereof, it turns to a gangrene, or a fever, and that gangrene or fever be the immediate cause of his death, yet, this is murder or manslaughter in him that gave the stroke or wound, for that wound, tho it were not the immediate cause of his death, yet, if it were the mediate cause thereof, and the fever or gangrene was the immediate cause of his death, yet the wound was the cause of the gangrene or fever, and so consequently is causa causati.

Regina v. Cheshire, [1991] 3 All E.R. 670: [I]f at the time of death the original wound is still an operating cause and a substantial cause, then the death can properly be said to be the result of the wound, albeit that some other cause of death is also operating. Only if it can be said that the original wounding is merely the setting in which another cause operates can it be said that the death does not result from the wound.

(b) Many courts find the initial assailant liable for the victim's death even when significant medical error contributes to the result. But courts disagree about the extent to which subsequent medical mistakes affect the initial assailant's liability. Consider the following cases:

State v. Shabazz, 719 A.2d 440, 444-445 (1998): [The defendant allegedly stabbed the victim in the abdomen, lung, and liver. The victim was taken to Yale–New Haven Hospital, where he underwent surgery, followed by a period in the postoperative recovery room. Thereafter he was placed in a regular hospital room. He died the following morning, due to heavy bleeding that resulted from the liver surgery. The trial judge barred the defense from introducing the testimony of two medical experts who would have testified that the hospital had been grossly negligent (1) by giving the victim an anticoagulant drug after surgery, when the medical objective at that point was to encourage rather than prevent clotting of the blood; and (2) by transferring the victim to a regular room, rather than placing him in the intensive care unit, where his vital signs could have been closely monitored. The appellate court held that the defense testimony was properly excluded:] [T]here was no evidence from which the jury rationally could have inferred that the hospital's gross negligence was the sole cause of the victim's death. Both [defense experts] acknowledged that the stab wounds . . . would have been fatal in the absence of any medical treatment. At the most, the purported gross negligence would have been a contributing factor, not the sole cause. . . . We see no sound reason of policy why a defendant who has committed a homicidal act should escape criminal liability simply because the hospital . . . contributed to the death. [G]ross negligence may permit the defendant to escape liability [only] when it was the sole cause of the death. . . .

United States v. Main, 113 F.3d 1046 (9th Cir. 1997): [Fleeing a traffic stop at high speed, defendant's truck veered off the road and collided with an obstacle. Defendant was thrown clear, but his passenger was trapped inside the wreckage. The pursuing officer reached the scene and noticed that the passenger was still breathing. The officer decided not to move him, because of fear that head or neck injuries might be aggravated by movement. When another officer arrived seven minutes later, the passenger was dead, apparently because he had been left in a position in which he could not breathe properly. Defendant argued that the first officer's failure to move the victim or summon assistance more promptly was an intervening cause. The trial judge refused to instruct the jury that it could find that the defendant's actions were not the proximate cause of death, and defendant was convicted of involuntary manslaughter. The court of appeals reversed:] It will be said that a failure to get prompt medical attention is not an unlikely hazard for the victim of an automobile accident. Agreed. But that judgment remains a judgment [for] the jury. When the jury is not told that it must find that the victim's death was within the risk created by the defendant's conduct, an element of the crime has been erroneously withdrawn from the jury.

(c) Is the result in *Main* reconcilable with the result in *Shabazz*? When *should* subsequent treatment errors relieve the initial wrongdoer of liability for the ultimate harm?

NOTE ON OMISSIONS AS CAUSES

Suppose that an intruder pushes a small child into a pool; the child's babysitter deliberately refuses to come to its aid, and the child then drowns. The babysitter clearly had a duty to save the child, but can we say that the babysitter *caused* the child to drown? It is sometimes argued that only the intruder, not the babysitter, can be considered the cause of the child's death. See Michael Moore, Act and Crime 78 et seq. (1993).

Is the argument convincing? A result rarely has only one but-for cause. A number of conditions may be necessary for an event to occur (in the case of a fire—wood, paper, a breeze, the striking of a match). The babysitter's omission is a necessary condition in the same sense: But for the sitter's failure to aid, the child would not have died. Does it follow that every passer-by who failed to rescue the child also must be considered the cause of its death? One solution is to say that omissions by the passers-by are indeed necessary conditions, and thus causes—but nonculpable causes—of the result, because they have *no duty* to aid the child. Whatever we think of these conceptual difficulties, courts are uniformly willing to treat an omission as the legal cause of a result in situations where there is a duty to act. See, e.g., *Jones v. United States*, page 218 supra.

NOTE ON THE RATIONALE OF THE CAUSATION REQUIREMENT

In evaluating any causation standard that might be proposed, consider two questions. First, *what difference will it make*, in terms of whether the defendant's conduct is punishable at all or in terms of the severity of the punishment, if the defendant's conduct is held to be the "cause" of the result? This question should be asked with respect to each of the cases and hypotheticals in this chapter. Second, what is the *reason* for that difference in liability or in the severity of punishment? One answer, of course, is simply statutory—a person cannot be convicted of murder unless he or she has caused a death. But what is *the rationale* for treating conduct that "causes" death differently from identical conduct that does not? In other words, why should the result of conduct ever make a difference? Consider Meir Dan-Cohen, Causation, in 1 Encyclopedia of Crime and Justice 165-166 (1983):

> [T]here is considerable difficulty in establishing the relevance of the occurrence of actual harm to criminal liability or severity of punishment. . . . That the actual death of the victim is somehow relevant to determining the accused's criminal liability is nonetheless a widely shared and deeply entrenched intuition. . . . The legal concept of causation may . . . be seen as a corollary of

this intuition. Although the intuition itself resists rationalization by reference to the goals of the criminal law, . . . it is hard to deny both the pervasiveness of that underlying sentiment and the influence it actually exerts on the criminal law, even in the absence of compelling rational arguments to support it. . . . Posed in connection with the retributive goal of punishment, the question of causation (namely, "Is there a causal relation between *A's* conduct and *B's* death?") amounts to asking whether punishing *A* is necessary to satisfy the retributive urge aroused by the fact of *B's* death.

[Yet t]he statement that *A* caused *B's* death may, in ordinary speech, be as much a conclusory statement, based on the prior tacit judgment that *A* deserves to be punished for *B's* death, as it is an independent statement of fact. . . . Put differently, in ordinary usage the concepts of causation and blame or deserts often reverse the idealized roles usually assigned to them in moral and legal theory. [O]ne would expect the conclusion that *A* should be punished for *B's* death to be based, in part, on the judgment that *A* caused *B's* death. In fact, the conclusion that *A* deserves to be punished may be directly and intuitively generated by the retributive urge, preceding and merely rationalized by the finding of a sufficient causal relationship between *A's* acts and *B's* death.

Compare Michael S. Moore, Causation and Responsibility, 16 Soc. Phil. & Pol. 1, 4-5 (1999). Rejecting as inadequate any policy-based approach to defining "cause" for legal purposes, he writes:

[L]egal liability tracks moral responsibility. . . . If the point of criminal law were [the] utilitarian point of deterring crime, then a [functional definition] of legal cause perhaps could be justified; such a functional definition would take into account the incentive effects of various liability rules. But the function of criminal law is not utilitarian; it is retributive. . . . This requires that its liability rules track closely the moral criteria for blameworthiness. One of those criteria is causation of morally prohibited states of affairs. Thus, again, "cause" as used in criminal law must mean what it means in morality, and what it means in morality is to name a relation that is natural and *not* of the law's creation.[3]

NOTES ON TRANSFERRED INTENT

1. Defendant shoots at Lucky, intending to kill him. The bullet misses but strikes and kills Unlucky, perhaps because the bullet ricocheted in an odd way. Is Defendant guilty of murdering Unlucky, regardless of how unforeseeable that killing may have been? The answer in all jurisdictions is yes. The conceptual justification is the doctrine of transferred intent, according to which Defendant's intent to kill Lucky is "transferred" to his action that killed Unlucky.

Does this approach make sense? Isn't it a pure fiction to say that Defendant intended to kill Unlucky, when in fact he killed Unlucky by accident? Absent

---

3. For further exploration of the justification for imposing a lower punishment when harm is not "proximately caused" (or when harm does not eventuate at all), see the materials that consider this issue in connection with the grading of attempts, pages 607-610 infra.

the notion of "transferring" his intent, we might say that Defendant is guilty of the attempted murder of Lucky and (perhaps) the involuntary manslaughter of Unlucky—if the required level of criminal negligence could be shown. Why should we punish Defendant much more severely than other would-be murderers whose attempts miscarry?

Consider Justice Stanley Mosk, concurring in People v. Scott, 14 Cal. 4th 544, 556 (1996):

> [O]ne cannot reasonably distinguish between A, who unlawfully kills B unlawfully intending to kill B, and X, who unlawfully kills Y unlawfully intending to kill Z. Both A and X harbor the same blameworthy mental state, an unlawful intent to kill. Both A and X cause the same blameworthy result, an unlawful killing.

The MPC would likewise convict the defendant of murder in these scenarios; §2.03(2)(a) provides that where the crime requires that a defendant intentionally cause a particular result (e.g., killing someone), that element of the crime is satisfied if the defendant accidentally inflicts that injury on one person while intentionally trying to injure another.

Is there a principled justification for this approach? Consider these situations:

(a) Doris shoots at her enemy, intending to kill him, then hops in her car and speeds away. Her enemy recovers from his wounds, but a pedestrian hit by Doris's speeding car is accidentally killed. Did Doris *murder* the pedestrian? Is there a logically relevant difference between this situation and the case above in which Defendant's shot accidentally killed Unlucky?

(b) Suppose that when Doris shoots at her enemy, intending to kill him, the bullet hits him, passes through his body, goes through the floor, and kills a tenant in the apartment below. If Doris's enemy dies, is the doctrine of transferred intent still available, so that Doris is guilty of murdering her enemy *and* the tenant? Or is her intent "used up," so that in the case of the tenant she is guilty only of involuntary manslaughter? The cases are divided.[4] Which is the better view? Is there any good reason to hold Doris responsible for *two* murders? But if Doris has *not* intentionally killed the tenant, why should that conclusion change in the event that her enemy luckily recovers from his wounds?

For useful criticism of the transferred-intent doctrine, see Douglas Husak, Transferred Intent, 10 Notre Dame J.L. Ethics & Pub. Pol'y 65 (1996).

2. The problem of transferred intent is not confined to homicidal crimes. In State v. Contua-Ramirez, 718 P.2d 1030 (Ariz. App. 1986), the defendant, attempting to strike his wife, accidentally hit their baby, whom she was holding in her arms. He was convicted of *intentionally* injuring the child.

---

4. Compare State v. Rodrigues-Gonzales, 790 P.2d 287 (Ariz. Ct. App. 1990) (finding defendant guilty of multiple murders), with People v. Birreuta, 208 Cal. Rptr. 635 (Ct. App. 1984) (only one murder).

Intentional assault upon an adult was a class 1 misdemeanor, but intentional injury of a child was a class 4 felony. The court held that the defendant was properly convicted of the more serious offense. Is this sound?

2. Subsequent Human Actions

a. Subsequent Actions Intended to Produce the Result

PEOPLE v. CAMPBELL

Court of Appeals of Michigan
124 Mich. App. 333, 335 N.W.2d 27 (1983)

HOEHN, J. [Campbell and Basnaw were drinking heavily. Campbell, who was angry with Basnaw for having had sex with Campbell's wife, encouraged Basnaw to kill himself. When Basnaw said he had no weapon, Campbell offered to sell Basnaw his own gun, for any price. Eventually, he gave Basnaw his gun with five shells and left. Shortly thereafter, Basnaw shot and killed himself. Charged with murder, Campbell moved to dismiss the information, on the ground that a homicide charge cannot be based on the act of providing a weapon to a person who subsequently uses it to commit suicide. The circuit court denied the motion and the court of appeals granted leave to appeal.]

The prosecutor argues that inciting to suicide, coupled with the overt act of furnishing a gun to an intoxicated person, in a state of depression, falls within the prohibition, "or other wilful, deliberate and premeditated killing." There exists no statutory definition of the term "murder." That crime is defined in the common law. "Homicide is the killing of one human being by another." . . . The term suicide excludes by definition a homicide. Simply put, the defendant here did not kill another person.

A second ground militates against requiring the defendant to stand trial for murder. Defendant had no present intention to kill. He provided the weapon and departed. Defendant hoped Basnaw would kill himself but hope alone is not the degree of intention requisite to a charge of murder. . . .

While we find the conduct of the defendant morally reprehensible, we do not find it to be criminal under the present state of the law. The remedy for this situation is in the Legislature.

The trial court is reversed and the case is remanded with instructions to quash the information and warrant and discharge the defendant.

PEOPLE v. KEVORKIAN

Supreme Court of Michigan
447 Mich. 436, 527 N.W.2d 714 (1994)

CAVANAGH, C.J., and BRICKLEY and GRIFFIN, J.J. [Defendant Kevorkian allegedly assisted in the deaths of Sherry Miller and Marjorie Wantz on October 23,

1991, roughly a year before Michigan enacted a statute that prohibited giving assistance in a suicide. He was indicted on two counts of murder. The circuit judge dismissed the charges, concluding that assisting in suicide does not fall within the crime of murder. On appeal, the court of appeals concluded that the circuit court erred in quashing the information. Kevorkian appealed that ruling to the Michigan Supreme Court.]

Each woman was said to be suffering from a condition that caused her great pain or was severely disabling. Each separately had sought defendant Kevorkian's assistance in ending her life. The women and several friends and relatives met the defendant at a cabin in Oakland County on October 23, 1991.

According to the testimony presented at the defendant's preliminary examination, the plan was to use his "suicide machine." The device consisted of a board to which one's arm is strapped to prevent movement, a needle to be inserted into a blood vessel and attached to IV tubing, and containers of various chemicals that are to be released through the needle into the bloodstream. Strings are tied to two of the fingers of the person who intends to die. The strings are attached to clips on the IV tubing that control the flow of the chemicals. [T]he person raises that hand, releasing . . . anesthesia rapidly. When the person falls asleep, the hand drops, pulling the other string, which [allows] potassium chloride to flow into the body in concentrations sufficient to cause death.

The defendant tried several times, without success, to insert the suicide-machine needle into Ms. Miller's arm and hand. He then left the cabin, returning several hours later with a cylinder of carbon monoxide gas and a mask apparatus. He attached a screw driver to the cylinder, and showed Ms. Miller how to use the tool as a lever to open the gas valve. The defendant then turned his attention to Ms. Wantz. He was successful in inserting the suicide-machine needle into her arm. The defendant explained to Ms. Wantz how to activate the device. . . . The device was activated, and Ms. Wantz died.

The defendant then placed the mask apparatus on Ms. Miller. The only witness at the preliminary examination who was present at the time said that Ms. Miller opened the gas valve by pulling on the screw driver. The cause of her death was determined to be carbon-monoxide poisoning. . . .

The Court of Appeals majority [in reinstating the murder charges] relied principally on People v. Roberts, 178 N.W. 690 (1920). . . . In *Roberts*, the defendant's wife was suffering from advanced multiple sclerosis and in great pain. She previously had attempted suicide and, according to the defendant's statements at the plea proceeding, requested that he provide her with poison. He agreed, and placed a glass of poison within her reach. She drank the mixture and died. The defendant was charged with murder. He pleaded guilty, and the trial court determined the crime to be murder in the first degree.

The defendant [argued on appeal] that because suicide is not a crime in Michigan, and his wife thus committed no offense, he committed none in acting as an accessory before the fact. The Court rejected that argument, explaining:

[D]efendant is not charged with [being an accessory to the offense of suicide]. He is charged with murder. [W]hen defendant mixed the paris green with water and placed it within reach of his wife to enable her to put an end . . . to her life, he was guilty of murder by means of poison within the meaning of the statute, even though she requested him to do so.

[D]efendant Kevorkian [argues] that the discussion of this issue in *Roberts* was dicta because the defendant in that case had pleaded guilty of murder, and thus the controlling authority was People v. Campbell, 335 N.W.2d 27 (1983). . . . We must [therefore] determine whether *Roberts* remains viable.

Minority → [F]ew jurisdictions, if any, have retained the early common-law view that assisting in a suicide is murder. The modern statutory scheme in the majority *Majority →* of states treats assisted suicide as a separate crime, with penalties less onerous than those for murder.

Recent decisions draw a distinction between active participation in a suicide and involvement in the events leading up to the suicide, such as providing the means. [I]n State v. Sexson, 869 P.2d 301 (N.M. App. 1994), the defendant was charged with first-degree murder in connection with the fatal shooting of his wife. . . . It was not disputed that there was a suicide agreement between the two. . . . The defendant claimed simply to have held the rifle in position while the decedent pulled the trigger, and that he had failed to then kill himself because he "freaked out." . . . The appellate court rejected the defendant's argument that he could not be prosecuted under the more general murder statute because of the specific assisted suicide statute . . . :

> It is well accepted that "aiding," in the context of determining whether one is criminally liable for their involvement in the suicide of another, is intended to mean providing the means to commit suicide, not actively performing the act which results in death. . . . [Sexson's] action transcends merely providing Victim a means to kill herself and becomes active participation in the death of another.

[This] distinction [is] consistent with the overwhelming trend of modern authority. [A] conviction of murder is proper if a defendant participates in the final overt act that causes death, such as firing a gun or pushing the plunger on a hypodermic needle [but not] where a defendant is involved merely "in the events leading up to the commission of the final overt act, such as furnishing the means. . . ."

[W]e would overrule *Roberts* to the extent that it can be read to support the view that the common-law definition of murder encompasses the act of intentionally providing the means by which a person commits suicide. Only where there is probable cause to believe that death was the direct and natural result of a defendant's act can the defendant be properly bound over on a charge of murder.[70]

---

70. However, there may be circumstances where one who recklessly or negligently provides the means by which another commits suicide could be found guilty of a lesser offense, such as involuntary manslaughter. There are a number of cases in which providing a gun to a person known to the defendant to be intoxicated and despondent or agitated has constituted sufficient recklessness to support such a conviction. . . .

[T]he lower courts did not have the benefit of the analysis set forth in this opinion for evaluating the degree of participation by defendant Kevorkian in the events leading to the deaths of Ms. Wantz and Ms. Miller. Accordingly, we remand this matter to the circuit court for reconsideration of the defendant's motion to quash in light of the principles discussed in this opinion.

BOYLE, J. (concurring in part and dissenting in part). . . . I disagree with the conclusion that one who provides the means for suicides and participates in the acts leading up to death may not be charged with murder as long as the final act is that of the decedent. . . . Absent standards established to distinguish between those who are in fact terminally ill or suffering in agony and rationally wish to die and those who are not, there is no principled vehicle in the judicial arsenal to protect against abuse. . . .

The lead opinion [distinguishes] between acts of participation that are merely "the events leading up to" the deaths of the decedents and "the final overt act that causes death." . . . Such a "test"[is] an invitation to [let results turn on whether] the defendant intended to kill [for] impure reasons. . . . To the extent that this Court reduces culpability for those who actively participate in acts that produce death, we do so at the risk of the most vulnerable members of our society—the elderly, the ill, the chronically depressed, those suffering from a panoply of stressful situations. . . .

[T]he cases cited [by the lead opinion] do not support [its] conclusion that if the defendant did not participate "in the act that . . . directly cause[s] death," he cannot be bound over on a charge of murder. Sexson did not pull the trigger, he held up the gun. . . . Likewise, defendant Kevorkian did not pull the trigger for Ms. Miller, but he assisted Ms. Miller in completing the act. In Ms. Wantz's case, his involvement was even more direct. . . . There is no principled method by which the Court can amend the common-law definition of murder. . . .

NOTES ON ASSISTED SUICIDE

1. Subsequent Kevorkian cases. Kevorkian allegedly continued to help others commit suicide after the enactment of Michigan's assisted-suicide statute, and accordingly he was charged under the new statute as well. Meanwhile, in an effort to help another patient, he personally injected lethal drugs into a 52-year-old man suffering from Lou Gehrig's disease. He also made a videotape of his actions, gave the tape to CBS News (which aired it on prime-time television), and dared prosecutors to file charges against him. They did so, and in March 1999, Kevorkian was convicted of murder, not assisted suicide, because he himself had administered the fatal injection. He was sentenced to a term of 10 to 25 years in prison. He served eight years and was paroled in 2007, after assuring officials that he would never again participate in another person's efforts to end his or her life.[5]

---

5. See Ellen Piligian & Monica Davey, Kevorkian Is Released from Prison, N.Y. Times, June 1, 2007.

2. Current law. The *Campbell* and *Kevorkian* cases reflect generally prevailing American law: One who successfully urges or assists another to commit suicide is not guilty of murder, at least so long as the deceased was mentally responsible and was not forced or deceived. Most states also reject the possibility of a manslaughter or negligent homicide conviction, provided again that the deceased's actions were fully voluntary.[6] In accord, MPC §210.5(1) permits convicting a person of criminal homicide for causing another to take his life, but "only if he purposely causes such suicide by force, duress or deception."

Most states that follow this approach do not permit defendants like Campbell and Kevorkian to act with impunity, however. A majority of the states now have statutes that define a separate offense for assisting a suicide. Many are similar to MPC §210.5(2), which makes the offense a felony (punishable at the same level as manslaughter).

Under this statutory scheme, what should be the result on the facts of People v. Minor, 898 N.Y.S.2d 440 (Sup. Ct. 2010)? Seeking to commit suicide, the decedent, sitting in the driver's seat of his car, convinced the defendant to hold a knife against the steering wheel while the decedent repeatedly lunged into the knife, causing fatal wounds. Did the defendant murder the decedent or merely assist him in committing suicide?

Statutes that punish those who merely assist another to commit suicide are highly controversial. Many argue that there should be a constitutional right, statutory right, or criminal-law justification defense for doctors who help terminally ill patients or others in extreme pain to commit suicide. In Washington v. Glucksberg, 521 U.S. 702 (1997), the Supreme Court held that individuals who wish to commit suicide have no constitutional right to obtain assistance in doing so. But jurisdictions remain free to permit such assistance by statute; the Netherlands and at least one American state (Oregon) have done so. That aspect of the subject is explored in detail in the material on justifications, Chapter 8.A, infra.

3. An exception for reckless or negligent aid? In footnote 70 of its opinion, the *Kevorkian* court draws an important distinction: One who intentionally provides another person with the means to commit suicide cannot be convicted of murder, but the court suggests that one who *recklessly or negligently* makes such means available to a person who is "intoxicated and despondent or agitated" can sometimes be convicted of a lesser degree of homicide, such as involuntary manslaughter. What is the logic of this position? The court's footnote focuses on whether the person providing aid has a sufficiently reckless mens rea, but isn't this the wrong question? If the decedent is sufficiently rational for his actions to constitute a superseding cause, how can the defendant be convicted of causing any homicide at all?

Perhaps the court meant to imply that intoxication or despondency can render the suicide victim's act insufficiently voluntary to constitute a

---

6. E.g., City of Akron v. Head, 657 N.E.2d 1389 (Ohio Mun. 1995).

superseding cause. But recall the *Campbell* case, where the defendant was not considered responsible for Basnaw's suicide, even though Basnaw was heavily intoxicated when the defendant, knowing this, gave him a gun and encouraged him to use it. At what point does a suicide victim's intoxication or despondency become sufficient to render the person who helps him guilty of homicide?

NOTES ON INTERVENING HUMAN ACTION

1. Foreseeability vs. autonomy. It is plain that Basnaw's suicide was a readily foreseeable result of Campbell's actions. Likewise, the death of Kevorkian's patients was readily foreseeable. Indeed, both Campbell and Kevorkian wanted their actions to have precisely the effects that they did have. If the applicable doctrine is the foreseeability test reflected in cases like *Acosta*, page 572 supra, and *Arzon*, page 577 supra, Campbell and Kevorkian would surely be seen as causing the death of others. Why doesn't the foreseeability test of causation apply in cases like theirs?

A leading explanation points to a strain in our culture that treats human action as differing from physical events.[7] We tend to regard a person's acts as the product of his or her choice, not as events governed by physical laws. This view (roughly, the hypothesis of free will and the rejection of determinism) is of course hotly contested in philosophical literature. But whether accurate or not, the assumption of free will reflects the way most people in our culture respond to human action, and it reflects, most importantly, the premise on which notions of blame in the criminal law ultimately rest. Naturally, the rules of causation in the law tend to embody the same premise.

As a result, the law of causation treats *physical events* that follow from a person's actions as caused by him or her, but it ordinarily does not treat *human* action that follows from an initial actor's conduct as caused by that actor, even when the subsequent human action is entirely foreseeable.[8] The results that follow from the second person's actions are caused by him or her alone. As it is sometimes put, there has been a *novus actus interveniens*—a later action by another person that displaces the relevance of prior conduct and provides a new foundation for causal responsibility. As Glanville Williams explains:[9]

> The legal attitude, in general, rests on what is known to philosophers as the principle of autonomy, which enters deeply into our traditional moral

---

7. See Sanford H. Kadish, Blame and Punishment: Essays in the Criminal Law 140-145 (1987).

8. The MPC terminology partly reflects and partly departs from this causal conception. It provides that one who assists a voluntary suicide ordinarily cannot be convicted of homicide (§210.5(1)), but it also creates a separate offense for a person who aids or encourages a suicide, with felony penalties applicable when "his conduct *causes* such suicide" to occur. (§210.5(2)). The latter provision appears to presuppose that one can "cause" the entirely voluntary suicide of another person. (When a suicide is not fully voluntary, a person who causes it can be prosecuted for homicide under §210.5(1).)

9. *Finis* for *Novus Actus?*, 48 Cambridge L.J. 391, 392 (1989).

perceptions, reinforced by language. . . . The autonomy doctrine, expressing itself through its corollary, the doctrine of *novus actus interveniens*, teaches that the individual's will is the autonomous (self-regulating) prime cause of behavior.

This conception of human action creates the need for special rules to govern the responsibility of one person for the acts of another. The law of causation is not available to ground the responsibility of the first actor, so other doctrines must be created to hold responsible those who instigate or help another to commit a crime. These other doctrines, principally those of complicity and conspiracy, are explored in Chapter 7, infra.

2. Qualifications and exceptions. Not all subsequent human actions are treated as outside of causal law—only those that have been chosen freely.[10] Involuntary acts (e.g., a spasm in person *B* produced by drugs that person *A* administered) are of course caused by the prior actor *A*. Similarly, if *A* asks *B* to use a cell phone to call a certain number, and *B* does so, not knowing that the call will trigger an explosion, *A* caused *B*'s act (and thus caused the explosion) because *B* acted without knowledge of the relevant circumstances. See MPC §2.06(2)(a). Other acts that we view as *caused* by a prior actor are those "constrained" by compulsion of duty, by duress, or by a momentary emergency precipitated by the prior actor. Examples would include the firefighter who enters a burning building (*Arzon*, supra page 577), the helicopter pilot who participates in a police chase (*Acosta*, supra page 572), or the police officer who kills in the performance of his duty, "for it is a reasonable response to the dilemma thrust upon the victim or the policeman by the intentional act of the defendant."[11] These limitations mean that it becomes crucial to determine whether subsequent actions *were* constrained by the first actor, rather than freely chosen by the second. Consider the material that follows.

STEPHENSON v. STATE

Supreme Court of Indiana
205 Ind. 141, 179 N.E. 633 (1932)

[Defendant was the Grand Dragon of the Ku Klux Klan in southern Indiana and exercised considerable local power. With the aid of several associates, he abducted the deceased, a woman he had known socially for several months, and in the ensuing days subjected her to various forms of sexual assault, including the infliction of bite wounds. In an effort to commit suicide, the woman seized a chance to secretly buy and take six tablets of bichloride of mercury. She became violently ill. Defendant had her drink a bottle of milk and offered to take her to a hospital, but she refused. Defendant then drove her home. On the way, deceased's pain grew worse, and she screamed for a doctor.

---

10. H.L.A. Hart & Tony Honoré, Causation in the Law (2d ed. 1985).
11. People v. Gilbert, 408 P.2d 365, 374 (Cal. 1965).

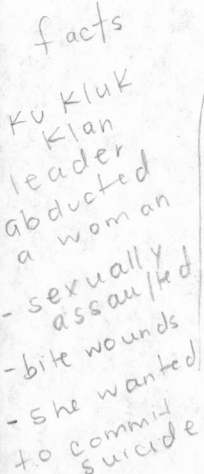

Defendant, however, did not stop until he reached his home. Soon thereafter she was taken to her parents. They summoned a doctor, who treated her, and in the ensuing ten days, all her wounds healed normally except one, which became infected. She grew worse and died, although the infected wound had healed at the time of her death. The medical cause of death was a combination of shock, loss of food and rest, action of the poison and the infection, and lack of early treatment, probably none of which, individually, would have been sufficient to produce death.

[The indictment charged defendant with murder arising from the following: that on March 16 he kidnapped the deceased, detained her on a railroad train en route to Chicago, struck, bit, and grievously wounded her with intent to rape in a drawing room on the train, and forced her to get off at Hammond and to occupy a hotel bed with him; that on March 17 deceased, "distracted with the pain and shame so inflicted upon her," swallowed poison; that defendant neither administered an antidote nor called for medical help although able to do so; that the same day he forced her into a car and drove her back to Indianapolis where he kept her in his garage without administering an antidote or calling for medical help until March 18; and that she died on April 14 "from the effects of her wounds inflicted as aforesaid and said poison taken as aforesaid."

[The jury found defendant guilty of murder, and the state supreme court affirmed.]

PER CURIAM. [Appellant] argues that the evidence does not show appellant guilty of murder. He points out . . . that, after they reached the hotel, Madge Oberholtzer left the hotel and purchased a hat and the poison, and voluntarily returned to his room, and at the time she took the poison she was in an adjoining room to him, and that she swallowed the poison without his knowledge, and at a time when he was not present. From these facts he contends that she took her life by committing suicide; that her own act in taking poison was [the act of] an intervening responsible agent which broke the causal connection between his acts and the death; that . . . the taking of the poison was the proximate cause of death. . . .

In the case of State v. Preslar, [48 N.C. 421 (1856)], the defendant in the nighttime fought with his wife, and she left to go in the house of her father. When she reached a point about two hundred yards from her father's home, she, for some reason, did not want to go in the house till morning, laid down on a bed cover, which she had wrapped around her, till daylight. The weather was cold and the next morning she could not walk, but made herself known. She afterwards died. The court held that the wife without necessity exposed herself, and the defendant was not guilty. . . . But we do not believe that the rule stated in the above case is controlling here. . . .

In Rex v. Valade (Que.), 26 Can. Cr. Cas. 233, where the accused induced a young girl under the age of consent to go along with him to a secluded apartment, and there had criminal sexual intercourse with her, following which she jumped from a window to the street to get away from him, and was killed by the fall, the accused was held guilty of murder. Bishop in his work on Criminal Law, vol. 2 (9th Ed.), page 484, says: "When suicide follows a wound inflicted by the defendant his act is homicidal, if deceased was rendered irresponsible by the wound and as a natural result of it."

We do not understand that by the rule laid down by Bishop, supra, that the wound which renders the deceased mentally irresponsible is necessarily limited to a physical wound. We should think the same rule would apply if a defendant engaged in the commission of a felony such as rape or attempted rape, and inflicts upon his victim both physical and mental injuries, the natural and probable result of which would render the deceased mentally irresponsible and suicide followed, we think he would be guilty of murder. In the case at bar, appellant is charged with having caused the death of Madge Oberholtzer while engaged in the crime of attempted rape. The evidence shows that. . . . appellant's control and dominion over the deceased was absolute and complete [both on the train and subsequently at the hotel]. The evidence further shows that the deceased asked for money with which to purchase a hat, and it was supplied her by "Shorty," at the direction of appellant, and that she did leave the room and was taken by Shorty to a shop and purchased a hat and then, at her request, to a drug store where she purchased the bichloride of mercury tablets, and then she was taken back to the room in the hotel, where about 10 o'clock A.M. she swallowed the poison.

Appellant argues that the deceased was a free agent on this trip to purchase a hat, etc., and that she voluntarily returned to the room in the hotel. This was a question for the jury, and the evidence would justify them in reaching a contrary conclusion. Appellant's chauffeur accompanied her on this trip, and the deceased had, before she left appellant's home in Indianapolis, attempted to get away, and also made two unsuccessful attempts to use the telephone to call help. She was justified in concluding that any attempt she might make, while purchasing a hat or while in the drug store to escape or secure assistance, would be no more successful in Hammond than it was in Indianapolis. We think the evidence shows that the deceased was at all times from the time she was entrapped by the appellant at his home on the evening of March 15th till she returned to her home two days later, in the custody and absolute control of appellant. Neither do we think the fact that the deceased took the poison some four hours after they left the drawing-room on the train or after the crime of attempted rape had been committed necessarily prevents it from being a part of the attempted rape. . . . At the very moment Madge Oberholtzer swallowed the poison she was subject to the passion, desire, and will of appellant. She knew not what moment she would be subjected to the same demands that she was while in the drawing-room on the train. . . . The same forces, the same impulses, that would impel her to shoot herself during the actual attack or throw herself out of the car window after the attack had ceased, [were] pressing and overwhelming her at the time she swallowed the poison. The evidence shows that she was so weak that she staggered as she left the elevator to go to the room in the hotel, and was assisted by appellant and Gentry; that she was very ill, so much that she could not eat,

Appellant says "free agent"

Accompanied by chauffeur.

all of which was the direct and proximate result of the treatment accorded to her by appellant. . . .

To say that there is no causal connection between the acts of appellant and the death of Madge Oberholtzer, and that the treatment accorded her by appellant had no causal connection with the death of Madge Oberholtzer would be a travesty on justice. The whole criminal program was so closely connected that we think it should be treated as one transaction, and should be governed by the same principles of law as was applied in the case of . . . Valade, supra. We therefore conclude that the evidence was sufficient and justified the jury in finding that appellant . . . rendered the deceased distracted and mentally irresponsible, and that such was the natural and probable consequence of such unlawful and criminal treatment, and that the appellant was guilty of murder [as charged].

Comment on Stephenson, *31 Mich. L. Rev. 659, 668-674 (1933):* At the outset it is clear that homicide cannot be committed by the defendant unless the intervening actor who strikes the fatal blow has been rendered irresponsible by defendant's unlawful act. This act may provide another with the opportunity, the instrument, or the motive for striking, but if it leaves him sane, the courts will not look behind the last responsible, self-determining actor. . . . Suppose a man commits suicide after losing all his money to a criminal swindler; is the swindler guilty of homicide? . . . Our common law, whatever may be said of divine law, does not hold him responsible for the death.

A new element enters the situation when the intervening actor is insane. . . . Where a policeman was grappling with a lunatic to arrest him, and defendant by freeing his hand enabled the lunatic to shoot the policeman, defendant was held guilty of homicide. From this case we may derive the principle that an insane intervening actor will not break the causal connection between defendant's act and the death.

We have been assuming, however, that the intervening actor is already insane at the time of defendant's act. The facts of Stephenson v. State put a further strain on the causal connection. To convict of homicide there, it was necessary to prove, not only that deceased was irresponsible when she took the poison, but also that defendant's unlawful acts caused her irresponsibility. For such a conviction no square precedent is to be found. Indeed the cases reveal, if anything, a marked reluctance to permit proof of any purely mental link in the causal chain. . . .

It is true that certain psychological phenomena have been admitted to proof when they have been induced by physical violence. The mentally paralyzing effect of fear and the mentally unbalancing effect of pain and fever are sufficiently familiar to the average man so that he can pass a sound judgment upon their causal relation. . . . Where a dangerous wound has been inflicted, which unseats the mind of deceased through pain or fever and so causes him to kill himself, the courts are . . . ready to hold defendant for homicide.

These last cases come nearest to supporting the majority opinion in Stephenson v. State, but they are not squarely in point. The prosecution did not seriously contend, nor did the court think, that deceased was rendered irresponsible by the physical injuries, the bruises and bites, inflicted by defendant. It was rather the shame and humiliation of having been raped. . . .

We have noted above that all prior unlawful actors in the causal chain are insulated from liability if the person who strikes the fatal blow is a responsible, self-determining actor. [H]owever, [if] a man who takes his own life or another's is [insane,] . . . criminal liability for the death may then be cast on the next previous actor. So also the actual killer's responsibility will be destroyed if he acts innocently in ignorance of fact, or in necessary self-defense, or instinctively as a result of fear, or in pursuance of public duty. [B]ecause the reaction is natural and instinctive, the law holds for homicide the previous actor who unlawfully created the situation. . . .

It is difficult to fit *Stephenson v. State* into this picture of liability. True, the law justifies the taking of life when necessary to prevent the commission of rape. And had deceased been helpless in the manual grasp of defendant at the time of her suicidal act, or had a third-party defender, bursting upon the scene, shot her to death through faulty aim, then defendant might have been liable for her death within the principles developed above. But [the] predominant motive for her suicide, clearly, was not to escape further assault but to escape the shame of what had already been done to her. The case represents a new and doubtful departure in so far as it suggests that the unlawful infliction of shame and disgrace may lead so naturally to suicide as to amount to a killing by him who inflicted it.

NOTES ON SUBSEQUENT VICTIM BEHAVIOR

1. Variations on **Stephenson.** The *Stephenson* court emphasizes that until the victim returned to her home in Indianapolis, she "was at all times . . . in the custody and absolute control of the appellant." Is the court implying that the result would be different if (as defendant claimed) Madge Oberholtzer had been a "free agent" at the time she bought and consumed the poison? Would the court reach a different result if she had taken the poison after she returned home to Indianapolis? Why should the last situation be treated differently from *Stephenson* itself?

One possible answer might be that the victim's suicidal act in the last situation would no longer be foreseeable. But isn't such an act at least as foreseeable as the collision of the helicopters in *Acosta*? Another possible answer is that the two situations are not significantly different—that Stephenson should be held liable in both or in neither. With respect to those possibilities, consider the cases that follow.

2. In February 1993, Jose Alonso Garcia was indicted for sexually assaulting a 79-year-old woman. When the woman died of congestive heart failure a month after the attack, he was also indicted for first-degree felony murder.

Prosecutors argued that the woman died because Garcia "destroyed her will to live," and pointed to testimony that the deceased cried daily after the incident and ceased talking about her future. Prosecutors analogized this case to one where a victim collapses of a heart attack during or shortly after the crime. A rape prosecutor from New York expressed doubts about this theory: "I think they'll have a huge causation problem. I mean, how many of my victims, down the road, either commit suicide or die of drug or alcohol abuse because of rape?" Wall St. J., Aug. 23, 1993, at B4.

3. In an automobile collision caused by the defendant's negligent driving, Carol Suprenant suffered severe injuries and was kept alive for several days by a ventilator that allowed her to breathe. But as her breathing difficulties and other discomfort increased, she demanded to be taken off the ventilator, even though she understood that without it "her death was probable . . . and that conversely, her injuries were potentially survivable if she remained on the ventilator." See Commonwealth v. Carlson, 849 N.E.2d 790, 793 (Mass. 2006). The doctors complied with her wishes, and she died a few hours later. Defendant was convicted of negligent homicide. What should be the result on appeal? Did the defendant cause Suprenant's death, or did she voluntarily choose to end her own life?

4. In Regina v. Blaue, [1975] 3 All E.R. 446, defendant had stabbed a girl. With proper treatment and a blood transfusion, her wounds would not have proved fatal. But as a Jehovah's Witness, she refused a transfusion and died. In a situation like that in the previous Note, many would argue that Ms. Suprenant's response, in refusing treatment, was not voluntary, because that treatment could only prolong her pain and discomfort. But in *Blaue* the treatment apparently would have restored the stabbing victim to health. Consider whether that fact should make a difference. Do the religious beliefs of the stabbing victim make the blood transfusion unacceptable in a way that is comparable to the unacceptability of indefinite life support to Ms. Suprenant? Or should we consider the *Blaue* victim's decision an autonomous choice? Does the stabbing victim's religious commitment make *Blaue* a preexisting-condition case (thus liability for homicide) or an intervening-actor case (thus no liability for homicide)?

NOTES ON SUBSEQUENT ACTS OF THIRD PARTIES

1. Consider the story of Uriah the Hittite, as told in the Bible, 2 Samuel 11, 12. Uriah was a captain in King David's army. David ordered his general to place Uriah in the "forefront of the hardest fighting, and then draw back from him, that he may be struck down and die." David's motive was to be rid of Uriah so he could marry Uriah's wife, Bathsheba. The plan worked: Uriah was killed in battle with the Ammonites, and David married Bathsheba. The judgment of the Lord upon King David: "You have struck down Uriah the Hittite with a sword, the man himself you murdered by the sword of the

Ammonites." Would it be proper for a court to so hold under American law? If so, would King David's liability depend on the prosecution's ability to prove that he had ordered his own troops to draw back, leaving Uriah exposed? What should be the result if King David had ordered his army to fight in the usual way but had nonetheless selected Uriah to lead the troops from the most dangerous position because he hoped that Uriah would be killed? Consider Glanville Williams, *Finis* for *Novus Actus?*, 48 Cambridge L.J. 391 (1989):

> A distinguished writer recently raised the question whether a general who orders his troops to battle intentionally kills those of his men who fall in action. He was considering this as a problem [of] intention. There may be some argument on intentionality, but none on the subject of killing. Obviously, it is the enemy, not the general, who kills the men. The reason why the general cannot be said to kill them is . . . not because he does not expect the deaths of many of them to follow from obedience to his command; and not because he is justified in issuing the command; it is simply that he has not committed or helped the act of killing, or influenced anybody to do the deed.
>
> A person is primarily responsible for what he himself does. He is not responsible, not blameworthy, for what other people do. The fact that his own conduct, rightful or wrongful, provided the background for a subsequent voluntary and wrong act by another does not make him responsible for it. What he does may be a but-for cause of the injurious act, but he did not do it. . . . Only the later actor, the doer of the act that intervenes between the first act and the result, the final wielder of human autonomy in the matter, bears responsibility (along with his accomplices) for the result that ensues.

Questions: How cogent is this analysis? Recall an analogous problem considered in connection with felony murder, page 522 supra: Felons *A* and *B*, holed up in a house, are fighting off the police. Felon *A* tells felon *B* to run out the back door where, he says, the coast is clear. He says that, though he knows police have the door well covered, because he wants *B* dead. Felon *B* dashes out the back door and is shot dead by police. The police, of course, are duty-bound to shoot, so their actions are not fully "voluntary." But the same must be said of the enemy soldiers who killed the opposing troops in Williams's example. Is it "[obvious that] it is the enemy, not the general, who kills the men"?

2. In Bailey v. Commonwealth, 329 S.E.2d 37 (Va. 1985), an appeal from a conviction of involuntary manslaughter, the court summarized the facts as follows:

> Bailey and Murdock lived about two miles apart. [Murdock] was "legally blind," with vision of only 3/200 in the right eye and 2/200 in the left. Bailey knew [this and] also knew that Murdock owned a handgun and had boasted "about how he would use it and shoot it and scare people off with it." Bailey knew further that Murdock was easily agitated and that he became especially angry if anyone disparaged his war hero, General George S. Patton.

come & Back

[On the evening in question, Bailey knew that Murdock was intoxicated. During a heated conversation by two-way radio,] Bailey implied that General Patton and Murdock himself were homosexuals [and] demanded that Murdock arm himself . . . and wait on his front porch for Bailey to come and injure or kill him. Murdock responded by saying he would be waiting on his front porch, and he told Bailey to "kiss [his] mother or [his] wife and children goodbye because [he would] never go back home."

Bailey then made two anonymous telephone calls to the Roanoke City Police Department. In the first, Bailey reported "a man . . . out on the porch [at Murdock's address] waving a gun around." A police car was dispatched to the address, but the officers reported they did not "see anything."

Bailey called Murdock back on the radio and chided him for not "going out on the porch." More epithets and threats were exchanged. Bailey told Murdock he was "going to come up there in a blue and white car" [both Bailey and the police drove blue and white cars] and demanded that Murdock "step out there on the . . . porch" with his gun "in [his] hands" because he, Bailey, would "be there in just a minute."

Involuntary Manslaughter?

Bailey telephoned the police again. This time, Bailey . . . told the dispatcher that Murdock had "a gun on the porch" [and] had "threatened to shoot up the neighborhood." . . . Bailey insisted that the police "come out here and straighten this man out." . . .

Three uniformed police officers . . . were dispatched to Murdock's home. None of the officers knew that Murdock was intoxicated or that he was in an agitated state of mind. Only Officer Beavers knew that Murdock's eyesight was bad, and he did not know "exactly how bad it was." When the officers arrived, [they] observed Murdock come out of his house with "something shiny in his hand." . . .

Officer Chambers approached Murdock . . . and told him to "[l]eave the gun alone and walk down the stairs away from it." Murdock "just sat there." When Chambers repeated his command, Murdock cursed him. Murdock then reached for the gun, stood up, advanced in Chambers' direction, and opened fire. Chambers retreated and was not struck.

All three officers returned fire, and Murdock was struck. Lying wounded on the porch, he said several times, "I didn't know you was the police." He died from [the gunshot wounds.] In the investigation which followed, Bailey stated that he was "the hoss that caused the loss."

Questions: Was he? How would you analyze the liability of Bailey? Did he kill Murdock?

b. Subsequent Actions That Recklessly Risk the Result

INTRODUCTORY NOTES

1. The distinction between intentional and reckless choices by the subsequent actor. As the preceding section indicates, the voluntary-intervening-actor doctrine means that the first actor in a sequence of events usually cannot be considered responsible for subsequent human action when the subsequent action is entirely voluntary. As a result, if the subsequent action causes harm,

voluntary-Intervening actor doctrine

. . . what happens after by voluntary human action . . .

the first actor cannot be said to have "caused" it, even when that harm was a perfectly foreseeable consequence of the first actor's conduct. In all the situations of this kind that we have seen so far, the subsequent actor *intended* to cause the harm in question. However, in many common situations (drag races are one recurring example), the subsequent actor—though arguably reckless—did not intend to cause that harm. Should this difference in the second actor's intent affect the liability of the first actor? The material in this section is addressed to that problem.

2. *The exception for* involuntary *choices by the subsequent actor.* As in the cases involving subsequent actions *intended* to cause harm, the voluntary-intervening-actor doctrine in the setting of reckless subsequent conduct can be invoked only when that subsequent action reflects a fully voluntary choice. Courts therefore have no hesitation in holding that a subsequent actor's risky choices do not negate the liability of the first actor, when those choices are the result of a predicament created by the first actor. Consider these examples:

(a) *People v. Kern, 545 N.Y.S.2d 4 (App. Div. 1989).* [This case arose from the infamous "Howard Beach incident," in which a group of white teenagers assaulted several black men who were walking in the neighborhood after their car had broken down. The teenagers chased the men, while wielding bats, screaming racial epithets, and threatening to kill them. One of the men, Griffith, tried to escape by running across a highway; he was struck by a car and killed. The defendants were convicted of second-degree manslaughter and appealed, arguing that there was insufficient evidence of causation. Upholding the convictions, the court stated:] [U]nder these circumstances, the defendants' actions were a "sufficiently direct cause" of Griffith's ensuing death so as to warrant the imposition of criminal liability. . . . [T]he only reasonable alternative left open to Griffith while being persistently chased and threatened by the defendants and their friends, several of whom were carrying weapons, was to seek safety by crossing the parkway where he unfortunately met his death. Clearly, on the basis of these facts, it cannot be said that the defendants' despicable conduct was not a sufficiently direct cause of Griffith's death. The defendants will not be heard to complain that, in desperately fleeing their murderous assault, Griffith chose the wrong escape route.

(b) In People v. Matos, 83 N.Y.2d 509 (1994), the defendant, running from the scene of an armed robbery he had just committed, climbed a ladder to the roof of a building and fled in the dark across the Manhattan rooftops. The police officer chasing him fell down an air shaft and plunged 25 feet to his death. The New York Court of Appeals upheld a conviction for felony murder on the ground that the officer's risky pursuit was in the performance of his duty and that his death was a foreseeable result of the defendant's crime and subsequent flight.

3. *The underlying policy puzzle when the subsequent actor makes a purely* **voluntary** *choice.* In principle, it might seem that the voluntary-intervening-actor doctrine should apply in exactly the same way, regardless of whether the

subsequent conduct is intentional or merely reckless. After all, so long as the second actor is making an entirely voluntary choice, we cannot easily say that this choice was in any sense "caused" by the first actor. Nonetheless, as we shall see, judicial intuitions often seem to change in situations where the subsequent actor was merely reckless or negligent. In thinking through the cases that follow, consider whether there is good reason to apply the voluntary-intervening-actor doctrine *only* in situations in which the subsequent acts are intended to cause harm.

COMMONWEALTH v. ROOT

Supreme Court of Pennsylvania
403 Pa. 571, 170 A.2d 310 (1961)

JONES, C.J. The appellant was found guilty of involuntary manslaughter for the death of his competitor in the course of an automobile race between them on a highway. . . . [*facts*]

The testimony . . . discloses that, on the night of the fatal accident, the defendant accepted the deceased's challenge to engage in an automobile race; that the racing took place on a rural 3-lane highway; that the night was clear and dry, and traffic light; that the speed limit on the highway was 50 miles per hour; that, immediately prior to the accident, the two automobiles were being operated at varying speeds of from 70 to 90 miles per hour; that the accident occurred in a no-passing zone on the approach to a bridge where the highway narrowed to two directionally opposite lanes; that, at the time of the accident, the defendant was in the lead and was proceeding in his right hand lane of travel; that the deceased, in an attempt to pass the defendant's automobile, when a truck was closely approaching from the opposite direction, swerved his car to the left, crossed the highway's white dividing line and drove his automobile on the wrong side of the highway head-on into the oncoming truck with resultant fatal effect to himself.

This evidence would of course amply support a conviction of the defendant for speeding, reckless driving and, perhaps, other violations of The Vehicle Code. [But] unlawful or reckless conduct is only one ingredient of the crime of involuntary manslaughter. Another essential and distinctly separate element of the crime is that the unlawful or reckless conduct charged to the defendant was the *direct* cause of the death in issue. The first ingredient is obviously present in this case but, just as plainly, the second is not. [*2 essential ingredients for involuntary manslaughter*]

While precedent is to be found for application of the tort law concept of "proximate cause" in fixing responsibility for criminal homicide, the want of any rational basis for its use in determining criminal liability can no longer be properly disregarded. When proximate cause was first borrowed from the field of tort law and applied to homicide prosecutions in Pennsylvania, the concept connoted a much more direct causal relation in producing the alleged culpable result than it does today. Proximate cause, as an essential element of a tort founded in negligence, has undergone in recent times, and is still undergoing, a marked extension. More specifically, this area of civil law has been progressively liberalized in favor of claims for damages for personal injuries to which careless conduct of others can in some way be associated. To persist in applying the tort liability concept of proximate cause to prosecutions for criminal homicide after the marked expansion of *civil* liability of defendants in tort actions for negligence would be to extend possible *criminal* liability to persons chargeable with unlawful or reckless conduct in circumstances not generally considered to present the likelihood of a resultant death. . . .

Here, the action of the deceased driver in recklessly and suicidally swerving his car to the left lane of a 2-lane highway into the path of an oncoming truck was not forced upon him by any act of the defendant; it was done by the deceased and by him alone, who thus directly brought about his own demise. . . .

Legal theory which makes guilt or innocence of criminal homicide depend upon such accidental and fortuitous circumstances as are now embraced by modern tort law's encompassing concept of proximate cause is too harsh to be just. . . .

In the case now before us, the deceased was aware of the dangerous condition created by the defendant's reckless conduct in driving his automobile at an excessive rate of speed along the highway but, despite such knowledge, he recklessly chose to swerve his car to the left and into the path of an oncoming truck, thereby bringing about the head-on collision which caused his own death. [T]he defendant's reckless conduct was not a sufficiently direct cause of the competing driver's death to make him criminally liable therefor.

[Reversed.]

EAGEN, J., dissenting. . . . If the defendant did not engage in the unlawful race and so operate his automobile in such a reckless manner, this accident would never have occurred. He helped create the dangerous event. He was a vital part of it. The victim's acts were a natural reaction to the stimulus of the situation. The race, the attempt to pass the other car and forge ahead, the reckless speed, all of these factors the defendant himself helped create. . . . That the victim's response was normal under the circumstances, that his reaction should have been expected and was clearly foreseeable, is to me beyond argument. That the defendant's recklessness was a substantial factor is obvious. All of this, in my opinion, makes his unlawful conduct a direct cause of the resulting collision. . . .

PROBLEMS

1. In a highly publicized auto accident, Princess Diana and a friend were killed, along with the driver of their car, when he crashed into the pillar of a tunnel in Paris. See N.Y. Times, Sept. 6, 1997, at A1. Evidence suggested that "paparazzi" were pursuing her car at high speed in order to take pictures of her with her companion. Her driver, who was heavily intoxicated, apparently accelerated to evade the paparazzi and then lost control of the car. The attempt to take her picture in public was not illegal, but in the course of their chase, the paparazzi apparently reached speeds that were dangerous and possibly unlawful. French authorities considered holding some of the photographers responsible for the crash, but ultimately decided not to charge any of them.[12] What would be the result under American law? If the accident had occurred in an American city, could the paparazzi be convicted of manslaughter for the deaths of Diana and her companion? For the death of her driver? Is this situation controlled by *Root* or by cases like *Kern* and *Matos*, discussed in the Introductory Note, supra?

2. Perez-Cervantez stabbed Thomas in the back and side. Thomas was treated at a hospital and released in stable condition. After his release, he resumed his prior consumption of cocaine. The drug raised his blood pressure and caused his internal wounds to bleed again; within a week he died from internal bleeding. Is Perez-Cervantez responsible for Thomas' death? As we have seen, Note 3, page 580 supra, when a defendant's act proves fatal because of an unforeseeable but preexisting condition of the victim, the defendant can be held responsible for homicide, under the doctrine that "he takes his victim as he finds him." Is Perez-Cervantez therefore guilty of homicide? Or is he not responsible, because Thomas's act of taking cocaine after his release from the hospital constitutes an intervening cause? Should the answer depend on whether Thomas's preexisting condition was simply prior experience with cocaine, or whether instead he was *addicted*, so that his actions after the offense could be considered "involuntary"? See State v. Perez-Cervantez, 952 P.2d 204 (Wash. Ct. App. 1998).

Recall that in *State v. Lane*, page 581 supra, the defendant was found guilty of manslaughter after he punched a drunk, who then died from brain swelling attributable to the impact of the punch on a brain affected by chronic alcoholism. Thus, the upshot of the vulnerable-victim and intervening-actor doctrines seems to be that Lane is liable, because his victim's substance abuse occurred before the illegal blow, but that Perez-Cervantez is not liable because his victim's substance abuse occurred, in part, after the illegal blow. Does this difference in results make sense? Is there any sound policy reason for treating the two cases differently?

STATE v. McFADDEN

Supreme Court of Iowa
320 N.W.2d 608 (1982)

ALLBEE, J. This case stems from a drag race between defendant Michael Dwayne McFadden and another driver, Matthew Sulgrove. . . . Sulgrove

---

12. Wash. Post, Aug. 18, 1999, at C1.

lost control of his automobile and swerved into a lane of oncoming traffic, where he struck a lawfully operated northbound vehicle. This third vehicle contained a six-year-old passenger, Faith Ellis, who was killed in the collision along with Sulgrove. Defendant's automobile did not physically contact either of the two colliding vehicles.

Defendant was charged with two counts of involuntary manslaughter. . . . Having waived a jury, defendant was tried to the court and convicted and sentenced on both counts. In this appeal, . . . defendant's main contention is that proof of the causation element . . . was lacking.

[In the deaths of both Ellis and Sulgrove, the trial court found the defendant guilty under two distinct theories. One was that he had aided and abetted Sulgrove in Sulgrove's commission of involuntary manslaughter and was therefore vicariously responsible for Sulgrove's crimes. This kind of vicarious liability and the aiding-and-abetting doctrine are examined beginning at page 680 infra. The trial court's other theory was] that defendant himself committed the crime of involuntary manslaughter by recklessly engaging in a drag race so as to proximately cause the Sulgrove-Ellis collision.

. . . Although a vicarious liability theory may be sufficient to convict defendant for the death of Faith Ellis, the same is not true with regard to the death of Sulgrove. This is because the involuntary manslaughter statute requires proof that the perpetrator caused the death of "another person." Obviously, Sulgrove could not have committed involuntary manslaughter with respect to his own death. Therefore, a theory under which defendant is only vicariously liable for Sulgrove's crime would be inadequate to convict defendant for Sulgrove's death. We turn, then, to consideration of the [other] theory of liability, i.e., that defendant's reckless commission of the public offense of drag racing was a proximate cause of the Sulgrove and Ellis deaths. . . .

Defendant asserts that because Sulgrove was a competitor in the drag race, he assumed the risk of his own death, and therefore defendant could not be convicted or sentenced for that death. . . . [We disagree.] "The acts and omissions of two or more persons may work concurrently as the efficient cause of an injury and in such case each of the participating acts or omissions is regarded in law as a proximate cause." [Commonwealth v. Peak, 12 Pa. D. & C. 379, 382 (1961)].

Next, defendant contends [that the] trial court erred in applying the civil standard of proximate cause in a criminal prosecution, rather than adopting the more stringent standard of "direct causal connection" used by the Pennsylvania court in Commonwealth v. Root, 170 A.2d 310, 314 (Pa. 1961). In Root, the court held that "the tort liability concept of proximate cause has no proper place in prosecutions for criminal homicide and more direct causal connection is required for conviction." . . . We had occasion to consider a similar standard-of-causation issue in State v. Marti, 290 N.W.2d 570, 584-585 (Iowa 1980). [W]e said in Marti that we were "unwilling to hold as a blanket rule of law that instructions used in civil trials regarding proximate cause are inappropriate for criminal trials." [D]efendant has suggested no specific policy differences, nor can we think of any, that would justify a different standard of proximate causation under our involuntary manslaughter statute than under our tort law. The *Root* court opined that "[l]egal theory which makes guilt or innocence of criminal homicide depend upon such accidental and fortuitous circumstances as are now embraced by modern tort law's encompassing concept of proximate cause is too harsh to be just." We do not agree. . . . We believe the foreseeability requirement, coupled with the requirement of recklessness . . . will prevent the possibility of harsh or unjust results in involuntary manslaughter cases. . . .

Accordingly, we hold that trial court did not err in applying ordinary proximate cause principles to determine whether the causation element . . . had been met, and in declining to adopt the more stringent "direct causal connection" standard of *Root*.   *Holding.*

[Convictions affirmed.]

COMMONWEALTH v. ATENCIO

Supreme Judicial Court of Massachusetts
345 Mass. 627, 189 N.E.2d 323 (1963)

WILKINS, C.J. Each defendant has been convicted upon an indictment for manslaughter in the death of Stewart E. Britch. . . .   *facts*

On Sunday, October 22, 1961, the deceased, his brother Ronald, and the defendants spent the day drinking wine in the deceased's room in a rooming house in Boston. At some time in the afternoon, with reference to nothing specific so far as the record discloses, Marshall said, "I will settle this," went out, and in a few minutes returned clicking a gun, from which he removed one bullet. Early in the evening Ronald left, and the conversation turned to "Russian roulette."   *"Russian roulette"*

[T]he "game" was played. The deceased and Atencio were seated on a bed, and Marshall was seated on a couch. First, Marshall examined the gun, saw that it contained one cartridge, and after spinning it on his arm, pointed it at his head, and pulled the trigger. Nothing happened. He handed the gun to Atencio, who repeated the process, again without result. Atencio passed the gun to the deceased, who spun it, put it to his head, then pulled the trigger. The cartridge exploded, and he fell over dead. . . . [Stewart]

We are of opinion that the defendants could properly have been found guilty of manslaughter. This is not a civil action against the defendants by the personal representatives of Stewart Britch. In such a case his voluntary act, we assume, would be a bar. Here the Commonwealth had an interest that the deceased should not be killed by the wanton or reckless conduct of himself and others. . . . Such conduct could be found in the concerted action and cooperation of the defendants in helping to bring about the deceased's foolish act. . . .

The defendants argue as if it should have been ruled, as matter of law, that there were three "games" of solitaire and not one "game" of "Russian roulette."

That the defendants participated could be found to be a cause and not a mere condition of Stewart Britch's death. It is not correct to say that his act could not be found to have been caused by anything which Marshall and Atencio did, nor that he would have died when the gun went off in his hand no matter whether they had done the same. The testimony does not require a ruling that when the deceased took the gun from Atencio it was an independent or intervening act not standing in any relation to the defendants' acts which would render what he did imputable to them. . . . There could be found to be mutual encouragement in a joint enterprise. In the abstract, there may have been no duty on the defendants to prevent the deceased from playing. But there was a duty on their part not to cooperate or join with him in the "game." Nor, if the facts presented such a case, would we have to agree that if the deceased, and not the defendants, had played first that they could not have been found guilty of manslaughter. The defendants were much more than merely present at a crime. It would not be necessary that the defendants force the deceased to play or suggest that he play.

We are referred in both briefs to cases of manslaughter arising out of automobiles racing upon the public highway. . . .

Whatever may be thought of those . . . decisions, there is a very real distinction between drag racing and "Russian roulette." In the former much is left to the skill, or lack of it, on the competitor. In "Russian roulette" it is a matter of luck as to the location of the one bullet, and except for a misfire (of which there was evidence in the case at bar) the outcome is a certainty if the chamber under the hammer happens to be the one containing the bullet. . . .

The judgments on the indictments for manslaughter are affirmed. . . .

NOTES AND QUESTIONS

1. *The drug provider.* Suppose that Lydia gives Gus a gun at Gus's request, knowing or even hoping that he will kill himself. As we have seen, if Gus uses the gun to intentionally kill himself, Lydia cannot be held for killing him; at most she might be guilty of assisting a suicide. See *People v. Campbell*, page 586 supra. But suppose that Lydia provides Gus with cocaine or heroin, not expecting or hoping that he will kill himself with it, but just to indulge his desire to get high. If Gus dies of a drug overdose, can Lydia be held responsible for killing Gus? Courts often ignore or reject the intervening-act doctrine in this setting (just as the courts did in the *McFadden* and *Atencio* cases); they are typically willing to hold the drug supplier responsible for the foreseeable, though freely chosen, acts of his purchaser. E.g., People v. Galle, 573 N.E.2d 569 (N.Y. 1991). How can we account for the paradox that if Lydia only intends to help Gus enjoy the drug, she can be held liable for killing him, but if she intends for Gus to die, she cannot be?

2. *Statutory formulations.* MPC §2.03 holds an actor responsible for a result when his action is a but-for antecedent, if it involves the same kind of harm he intended or risked, so long as it is "not too remote or accidental in

its occurrence to have a [just] bearing on the actor's liability or on the gravity of his offense." In Causation in the Law 398 (2d ed. 1985), H.L.A. Hart and Tony Honoré criticize this formulation:

> [it] does not provide *specifically* for those cases where . . . another human action . . . is involved in the production of the proscribed harm. These are treated merely as one kind of case where harm may or may not be "too accidental" in its manner or occurrence. This is surely a weakness in a scheme which is designed to reproduce . . . the convictions of common sense that, even if harm would not have occurred without the act of accused, it is still necessary to distinguish, for purposes of punishment, one manner of upshot from another. For whatever else may be vague or disputable about common sense in regard to causation and responsibility, it is surely clear that the primary case where it is reluctant to treat a person as having caused harm which would not have occurred without his act is that where another voluntary human action has intervened.

Is this criticism persuasive? Would it be an improvement to provide, as several states have, that the result must be "not . . . too dependent on another's volitional conduct to have a bearing on the defendant's liability"? See Haw. Rev. Stat. §§702-215(2) (2011); N.J. Stat. Ann. tit. §2C2-3 (2011).

B. ATTEMPT

1. Introduction

Statutory definitions of the crime of attempt are usually minimal. Consider some representative examples: "A person is guilty of an attempt to commit a crime when, with intent to commit a crime, he engages in conduct which tends to effect the commission of such crime" (N.Y. Penal Law §110.00 (2011)); "Every person who attempts to commit any crime, but fails, or is prevented or intercepted in its perpetration shall be punished . . ." (Cal. Penal Code §664) (2011)); "A person commits the offense of attempt when, with intent to commit a specific offense, he or she does any act which constitutes a substantial step toward the commission of that offense" (720 Ill. Comp. Stat. §5/8-4(a) (2010)).

At common law, attempts were misdemeanors. Today the usual punishment for attempt is a reduced factor of the punishment for the completed crime. In California (Cal. Penal Code §664 (2011)), attempt carries a maximum term of not more than one-half of the maximum term authorized for the completed offense. Under New York Penal Law, which uses punishment classification of offenses, the sentence for an attempt is one classification below that for the completed crime (§110.05 (2011)), except for certain offenses, notably drug offenses, where the punishment is the same. Since the MPC proposals, however, a substantial minority of states have departed from the predominant scheme by making the punishment the same for the attempt as for the crime attempted, except for crimes punishable by death or life imprisonment. See, e.g., Conn. Gen. Stat. Ann. §53a-51 (2011); 720 Ill. Comp. Stat. §5/8-4(c) (2010)).

What is the justification for the traditional approach of punishing attempt less severely than the completed crime? The relationship of harm to the proper degree of punishment is a pervasive problem in criminal law. The issue is implicit in several topics we have already considered. Thus, all the cases on causation in effect require us to consider the reasons why conduct that causes harm should ever be treated differently from identical conduct that does not. A similar issue is implicit in the Chapter 5 materials dealing with homicidal risk creation. An actor whose recklessness or criminal negligence creates a substantial risk of death can be convicted of manslaughter and sometimes even of murder, provided that death actually results. But what crime has the actor committed if the person he endangers suffers only nonlethal injuries or escapes with no injuries at all? Because such an actor is not "attempting" to kill anyone, he normally cannot be convicted of any form of attempted homicide. (We explore this point in connection with the mens rea of attempt at page 611 infra.) Absent some statutory risk-creation offense (such as MPC §211.2), such an actor may have committed no crime at all. But even if there is a criminal offense that applies to his conduct, its penalties will be far lower than those applicable under homicide statutes when a death occurs. The law of attempts poses the same issue in its starkest form. The actor who intentionally seeks to cause a harm (the death of another person, for example) is traditionally punished much less severely if his attempt proves unsuccessful. Is it justified to attribute importance in punishment to the actual result of a defendant's conduct? Consider the following comments.

James Fitzjames Stephen, A History Of The Criminal Law (Vol. 3) 311 (1883): If two persons are guilty of the very same act of negligence, and if one of them causes thereby a railway accident, involving the death and mutilation of many persons, whereas the other does no injury to anyone, it seems to me that it would be rather pedantic than rational to say that each had committed the same offence, and should be subjected to the same punishment. In one sense, each has committed an offence, but the one has had the *bad luck* to cause a horrible misfortune, and to attract public attention to it, and the other the good *fortune* to do no harm. Both certainly deserve punishment, but it gratifies a natural public feeling to choose out for punishment the one who actually has caused great harm, and the effect in the way of preventing a repetition of the offence is much the same as if both were punished.

H.L.A. Hart, The Morality of the Criminal Law 52-53 (1965): [Professor Hart, after quoting the above extract from Stephen, observes:] This doctrine allocating to "public feeling" so important a place in the determination of punishment reflects the element of populism which, as we have seen, is often prominent in English judicial conceptions of the morality of punishment. But it conflicts with important principles of justice as between different offenders which would prima facie preclude treating two persons, guilty of "the very same act" of negligence, differently because of a fortuitous difference in the outcome of these acts. No doubt there is often an inclination to treat punishment like compensation and measure it by the outcome alone. There may even be at times a public demand that this should be done. And no doubt if the machinery of justice were nullified or could not proceed unless the demand were gratified we might have to gratify it and hope to educate people out of this misassimilation of the principles of punishment to those of compensation. But there seems no good reason for adopting this misassimilation as a principle or to stigmatise as pedantic the refusal to recognise that the difference made by "bad fortune" and "good luck" to the outcome of the very same acts justifies punishing the one and not the other.

Stephen J. Morse, Reason, Results, and Criminal Responsibility, [2004] U. Ill. L. Rev. 363, 385: [C]riminal blame and punishment . . . are the most stigmatizing and afflictive impositions of state power. . . . Whether or to what degree people should be branded as criminals and imprisoned, or even put to death, should not be a matter of a lottery.

Joel Feinberg, Equal Punishment for Failed Attempts, 37 Ariz. L. Rev. 117, 131 (1995): The principle of proportionality . . . does not decree that the severity of the punishment be proportionate to the offender's good or bad luck, but rather to his good or bad deserts, or blameworthiness.

Aya Gruber, A Distributive Theory of Criminal Law, 52 Wm. & Mary l. Rev. 1, 38 (2010): [T]he remedial requirements attendant to actual victimhood simply do not exist when the attempter has not produced harm . . . and a different judicial response is warranted.

Stephen J. Schulhofer, Attempt, in 1 Encyclopedia of Crime and Justice 97 (1983): [T]he most plausible explanation for more lenient treatment of attempts is that the community's resentment and demand for punishment are not aroused to the same degree when serious harm has been averted. This explanation, however, raises further questions. Can severe punishment (in the case of completed crime, for example) be justified simply by reference to the fact that society "demands" or at least desires this? To what extent should the structure of penalties serve to express intuitive societal judgments that cannot be rationalized in terms of such instrumental goals as deterrence, isolation, rehabilitation, and even retribution—that is, condemnation reflecting the moral culpability of the act? Conversely, to what extent should the criminal justice system see its mission as one not of expressing the intuitive social demand for punishment, but rather as one of restraining that demand and of protecting *from* punishment the offender who, rationally speaking, deserves a less severe penalty?

Model Penal Code §5.05(1): Except as otherwise provided in this Section, attempt, solicitation and conspiracy are crimes of the same grade and degree as the most serious offense which is attempted or solicited or is an object of the conspiracy. An attempt, solicitation or conspiracy to commit a [capital crime or a] felony of the first degree is a felony of the second degree. [Under §6.06, a felony of the first degree is punishable by imprisonment for a term whose minimum is between one and ten years and whose maximum is life. A felony of the second degree is punishable by imprisonment for a term whose minimum is between one and three years and whose maximum is ten years.]

Model Penal Code and Commentaries, Comment to §5.05 at 490 (1985): The theory of this grading system may be stated simply. To the extent that sentencing depends upon the antisocial disposition of the actor and the demonstrated need for a corrective sanction, there is likely to be little difference in the gravity of the required measures depending on the consummation or the failure of the plan. It is only when and insofar as the severity of sentence is designed for general deterrent purposes that a distinction on this ground is likely to have reasonable force. It is doubtful, however, that the threat of punishment for the inchoate crime can add significantly to the net deterrent efficacy of the sanction threatened for the substantive offense that is the actor's object, which he, by hypothesis, ignores. Hence, there is a basis for economizing in use of the heaviest and most afflictive sanctions by removing them from the inchoate crimes.

NOTE

For further exploration of these issues, see Sanford H. Kadish, The Criminal Law and the Luck of the Draw, 84 J. Crim. L. & Criminology 679 (1994); Stephen J. Schulhofer, Harm and Punishment: A Critique of Emphasis on the Results of Conduct in the Criminal Law, 122 U. Pa. L. Rev. 1497 (1974). Supporting lighter punishment for unsuccessful attempts, Professor Theodore Y. Blumoff maintains (A Jurisprudence for Punishing Attempts Asymmetrically, 6 Buff. Crim. L. Rev. 951, 958, 973 (2003)) that "most criminals [have] been 'profoundly disadvantaged by unjust social institutions,'" and "often have suffered from bad luck which we can hardly imagine"; thus, he argues, less severe punishment for attempts that miscarry does not really reward good luck but instead serves as a partial "counterweight" to the overall bad luck of the offender's social circumstances. For another defense of lesser punishment when the harm does not occur, see Michael Moore, The Independent Moral Significance of Wrongdoing, 1 J. Contemp. Legal Issues 1 (1994); for a critique of Professor Moore's argument, see Kimberly D. Kessler, The Role of Luck in the Criminal Law, 142 U. Pa. L. Rev. 2183 (1994).

2. Mens Rea

SMALLWOOD v. STATE

Court of Appeals, Maryland
343 Md. 97, 680 A.2d 512 (1996)

MURPHY, Chief Judge. [Smallwood was convicted in a non-jury trial of three counts of assault with intent to murder his rape victims, based on evidence that despite his awareness that he was HIV positive and that he had been warned by a social worker of the need to practice "safe sex," he did not use a condom in any of his attacks.]

Smallwood argues that the fact that he engaged in unprotected sexual intercourse, even though he knew that he carried HIV, is insufficient to infer an intent to kill. The most that can reasonably be inferred, Smallwood contends, is that he is guilty of recklessly endangering his victims by exposing them to the risk that they would become infected themselves. The State disagrees, arguing that the facts of this case are sufficient to infer an intent to kill. The State likens Smallwood's HIV-positive status to a deadly weapon and argues that engaging in unprotected sex when one is knowingly infected with HIV is equivalent to firing a loaded firearm at that person.

In Faya v. Almaraz, 329 Md. 435, 438-440 (1993), . . . we described HIV as a retrovirus that attacks the human immune system, weakening it, and ultimately destroying the body's capacity to ward off disease. We also noted that:

> [t]he virus may reside latently in the body for periods as long as ten years or more, during which time the infected person will manifest no symptoms of illness and function normally. . . . Medical studies have indicated that most people who carry the virus will progress to AIDS. . . .

In this case, we must determine what legal inferences may be drawn when an individual infected with the HIV virus knowingly exposes another to the risk of HIV infection, and the resulting risk of death by AIDS.

As we have previously stated, "[t]he required intent in the crimes of assault with intent to murder and attempted murder is the specific intent to murder, i.e., the specific intent to kill under circumstances that would not legally justify or excuse the killing or mitigate it to manslaughter." State v. Earp, 319 Md. 156, 167 (1990). [Smallwood] was properly found guilty of attempted murder and assault with intent to murder only if there was sufficient evidence from which the trier of fact could reasonably have concluded that Smallwood possessed a specific intent to kill at the time he assaulted each of the three women. . . .

An intent to kill may be proved by circumstantial evidence. . . . Therefore, the trier of fact may infer the existence of the required intent from surrounding circumstances such as "the accused's acts, conduct and words." State v. Raines, 326 Md. 582, 591 (1992). As we have repeatedly stated, "under the proper circumstances, an intent to kill may be inferred from the use of a deadly

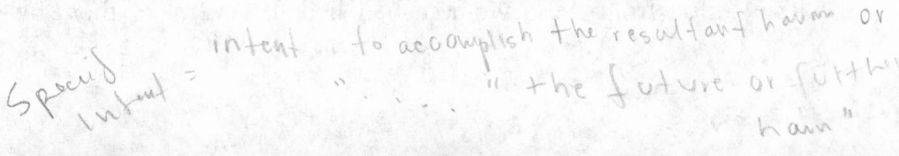

weapon directed at a vital part of the human body." *Raines*, supra. [T]here we upheld the use of such an inference. In that case, Raines and a friend were traveling on a highway when the defendant fired a pistol into the driver's side window of a tractor trailer in an adjacent lane. The shot killed the driver of the tractor trailer, and Raines was convicted of first-degree murder. The evidence in the case showed that Raines shot at the driver's window of the truck, knowing that the truck driver was immediately behind the window. We concluded that "Raines's actions in directing the gun at the window, and therefore at the driver's head on the other side of the window, permitted an inference that Raines shot the gun with the intent to kill."

The State argues that our analysis in *Raines* rested upon two elements: (1) Raines knew that his weapon was deadly, and (2) Raines knew that he was firing it at someone's head. The State argues that Smallwood similarly knew that HIV infection ultimately leads to death, and that he knew that he would be exposing his victims to the risk of HIV transmission by engaging in unprotected sex with them. Therefore, the State argues, a permissible inference can be drawn that Smallwood intended to kill each of his three victims. The State's analysis, however, ignores several factors.

First, we must consider the magnitude of the risk to which the victim is knowingly exposed. The inference drawn in *Raines*, supra, rests upon the rule that "[i]t is permissible to infer that 'one intends the natural and probable consequences of his act.'" . . . When a deadly weapon has been fired at a vital part of a victim's body, the risk of killing the victim is so high that it becomes reasonable to assume that the defendant intended the victim to die as a natural and probable consequence of the defendant's actions.

. . . While the risk to which Smallwood exposed his victims when he forced them to engage in unprotected sexual activity must not be minimized, the State has presented no evidence from which it can reasonably be concluded that death by AIDS is a probable result of Smallwood's actions to the same extent that death is the probable result of firing a deadly weapon at a vital part of someone's body. Without such evidence, it cannot fairly be concluded that death by AIDS was sufficiently probable to support an inference that Smallwood intended to kill his victims in the absence of other evidence indicative of an intent to kill.

In this case, we find no additional evidence from which to infer an intent to kill. Smallwood's actions are wholly explained by an intent to commit rape and armed robbery, the crimes for which he has already pled guilty. . . .

The cases cited by the State demonstrate the sort of additional evidence needed to support an inference that Smallwood intended to kill his victims. The defendants in these cases have either made explicit statements demonstrating an intent to infect their victims or have taken specific actions demonstrating such an intent and tending to exclude other possible intents. In State v. Hinkhouse, 912 P.2d 921 (Or. App. 1996), for example, the defendant engaged in unprotected sex with a number of women while knowing that he was HIV positive. The defendant had also actively concealed his HIV-positive status from these women, had lied to several of them by stating that he was not HIV-positive, and had refused the women's requests that he wear condoms. There was also evidence that he had told at least one of his sexual partners that "if he were [HIV-]positive, he would spread the virus to other people." ... The Oregon Court of Appeals found this evidence to be sufficient to demonstrate an intent to kill. ... In State v. Caine, 652 So. 2d 611 (La. App. 1995), a conviction for attempted second-degree murder was upheld where the defendant had jabbed a used syringe into a victim's arm while shouting "I'll give you AIDS." ...

In contrast with these cases, the State in this case would allow the trier of fact to infer an intent to kill based solely upon the fact that Smallwood exposed his victims to the risk that they might contract HIV. Without evidence showing that such a result is sufficiently probable to support this inference, we conclude that Smallwood's convictions for attempted murder and assault with intent to murder must be reversed.[a]

NOTES AND QUESTIONS

1. The intent requirement. Both the common law and most American statutory formulations agree with the holding in the principal case that an attempt requires a purpose (or "specific intent") to produce the proscribed result, even when recklessness or some lesser mens rea would suffice for conviction of the completed offense. See, e.g., People v. Beck, 24 Cal. Rptr. 3d 228, 230 (2005) ("[E]very attempt requires specific intent to commit the target crime even if the completed crime does not require specific intent."); People v. Campbell, 532 N.E.2d 86 (N.Y. 1988); MPC §5.01(1)(b). In Jones v. State, 689 N.E.2d 722 (Ind. 1997), defendant shot at a house full of people, wounding several and killing one. He was convicted of murder of the person he killed but acquitted of attempted murder of those he wounded. The court rejected defendant's claim that this was an inconsistent verdict. Attempted murder requires a specific intent to kill, but it is sufficient for murder that defendant engages in conduct knowing of a high probability that in doing so he will kill someone.

2. Why specific intent? Why should an attempt conviction require a "specific intent" or "purpose" if the defendant, though he lacked "purpose," had the mental state sufficient for conviction of the substantive offense? Consider three possible explanations. One is linguistic: To attempt something is to try to accomplish it, and one cannot be said to try if one does not intend to succeed. Another explanation is moral: One who intends to commit a criminal harm does a greater moral wrong than one who does so recklessly or negligently. The third is utilitarian: As Justice Oliver Wendell Holmes, Jr. put it in

a. In response to the problems of an attempted murder prosecution in the context of HIV transmission, many states have passed legislation making it a criminal offense for persons who are HIV-positive to engage in unprotected sex, or to do so without disclosing their HIV status to their partner. For a critical analysis of the problems of criminalization in this context, see Margo Kaplan, Rethinking HIV-Exposure Crimes, 87 Ind. L.J. (forthcoming 2012).—Eds.

The Common Law 68 (1881): "The importance of the intent is not to show that the act was wicked but that it was likely to be followed by hurtful consequences."

Does Justice Holmes's explanation for the intent requirement apply in a case like Thacker v. Commonwealth, 114 S.E. 504 (Va. 1922)? A drunk, angered by the refusal of a woman who was camping in a tent to admit him, walked down the road, turned, and shot at the light shining through the canvas. If the bullet had accidentally killed the woman, the defendant could be convicted of murder. But in *Thacker*, the bullet fortunately missed the woman. The court held that defendant, lacking intent to kill, could not be convicted of attempted murder. But why do we need the bullet to hit the woman to be assured that the action "was likely to be followed by hurtful consequences"? Moreover, if the defendant is not guilty of attempt, for what crime (if any) could he be convicted? Do the penalties provided for an offense such as MPC §211.2 (reckless endangerment) afford adequate punishment for a case of this kind? Consider another observation of Justice Holmes in The Common Law at 66:

> It may be true in the region of attempts, as elsewhere, the law began with cases of actual intent, as those cases are the most obvious ones. But it cannot stop with them, unless it attaches more importance to the etymological meaning of the word attempt than to the general principles of punishment.

Consider People v. Thomas, 729 P.2d 972 (Colo. 1986). The defendant fired three shots at a man he believed to be a fleeing rapist. Two of the shots struck the man. The defendant claimed that one of the shots had been fired accidentally and that the other two were warning shots. At trial, he was convicted of attempted reckless manslaughter under Colo. Rev. Stat. §18-2-101(1), which provides:

> A person commits criminal attempt if, acting with the kind of culpability otherwise required for commission of an offense, he engages in conduct constituting a substantial step toward the commission of the offense.

Noting that the statute differed from MPC §5.01, the Colorado Supreme Court upheld a conviction for attempted reckless manslaughter, but the court declined to rest that result solely on the language of the attempt statute. Instead, the court reasoned that the traditional requirement of intent served to identify cases where conduct was likely to produce harmful consequences. The court found that the necessary potential for future harm is present not only in cases of intentional conduct but also when the defendant knows that the prohibited result is practically certain to occur or when he recklessly disregards a substantial risk.[13]

---

13. As indicated in Note 1, supra, nearly all American jurisdictions reject this view. For two exceptions, upholding convictions for attempted murder based on recklessness, see Reilly v. State, 55 P.3d 1259 (Wyo. 2002); Brown v. State, 790 So. 2d 389 (Fla. 2001).

Question: Under the court's approach, is the crime of attempted negligent homicide committed every time that a Colorado motorist substantially exceeds the speed limit or drives while intoxicated? *Should* such conduct be punishable as an attempt? For an argument in favor of creating an offense of attempted homicide on the basis of recklessness—and careful analysis of the difficulties of relying solely on an offense like MPC §211.2 (reckless endangerment) as a gap-filler—see Michael T. Cahill, Attempt, Reckless Homicide, and the Design of the Criminal Law, 78 U. Colo. L. Rev. 879 (2007).

3. *Attempted felony-murder?* Suppose that two felons fire at a guard in the course of their escape from a bank holdup. The guard is wounded but survives. The evidence suggests that the felons intended to frighten the guard but did not intend to kill him. Can the robbers be convicted of attempted felony-murder on the ground that they had a specific intent to commit the felony? Most states that have considered the issue have rejected the concept of attempted felony-murder. See, e.g., State v. Gray, 654 So. 2d 552 (Fla. 1995). Arkansas is a rare exception. See White v. State, 585 S.W.2d 952 (Ark. 1979). Why this virtual unanimity? After all, a robber can be held for felony-murder when his wounded victim dies, so shouldn't he be held for attempted felony-murder if his wounded victim survives? Note the implications of that view: A robber is guilty of felony-murder if his victim dies from a heart attack, so should it follow that a robber is guilty of attempted felony-murder if his victim has a *nonfatal* heart attack? Should every robber and burglar be guilty of attempted felony-murder, even if shots are never fired and none of the victims suffers any physical injury?

[handwritten: Majority]

4. *Attempted manslaughter?* Where, as in nearly all jurisdictions, an attempt requires specific intent, there clearly can be no crime of attempted involuntary manslaughter: The attempt charge requires proof of intent to kill, and the essence of involuntary manslaughter is unintentional killing, so such a charge is a contradiction in terms. See State v. Holbron, 904 P.2d 912 (Haw. 1995). But can there be a crime of attempted *voluntary* manslaughter? Suppose that a defendant, acting under extreme provocation, shoots at his provoker, trying to kill him. Is he attempting to commit murder or manslaughter? In *Holbron*, supra, the court stated (id. at 922) that "the overwhelming weight of the case law" recognizes the offense of attempted voluntary manslaughter. See, e.g., State v. Mitchell, 894 So. 2d 1240 (La. 2005).

5. *Meaning of specific intent.* While the specific intent requirement is broadly accepted, its meaning in practice is not always clear. When a harmful result has not materialized, what precisely is the difference between intent, knowledge, and recklessness? For example, in the *Smallwood* case, page 611 supra, how much additional evidence would have been required to support an inference that Smallwood intended to kill? The court discussed several cases as examples. In *Hinkhouse*, the defendant, like Smallwood, knew he had HIV, both men failed to use condoms, and both failed to disclose their HIV status to their sexual partners. But Smallwood did not affirmatively misrepresent his HIV status (instead he secured his victims' submission by force), while Hinkhouse *lied* to his otherwise consenting sexual partners. Why should that difference make Hinkhouse (but not Smallwood) guilty of attempted murder? Taking account of his deliberate deception, was Hinkhouse's mens rea (with respect to the risk of killing his partners) one of intention, knowledge, or mere recklessness?

Another difference between the cases may have been important: Hinkhouse told one of his partners that he believed intercourse by an HIV-positive person "would" transmit the virus. But does that additional fact, strictly speaking, establish an *intent* to kill or only *knowledge*? Under MPC §2.02(2)(a)(i), a person is deemed to act purposely with respect to a harmful result only when it is his "*conscious object* . . . to cause such a result" (emphasis added). Does this requirement mean that Hinkhouse could not be convicted of attempted murder under the Code? Consider this hypothetical: Defendant, in order to destroy a competitor's experimental aircraft, plants a bomb on the plane and sets it to explode in midair, having no particular wish to injure the test pilot but knowing that if the bomb goes off as intended, the pilot will be killed. The bomb fails to explode. May the defendant be convicted of attempted murder? Does she have a "purpose" or "specific intent" to kill? Note the solution to this problem in MPC §5.01(1)(b): The required mens rea is satisfied if the defendant acts "with the purpose of causing or with the belief that [his conduct] will cause" the prohibited result.

6. Attendant circumstances. Does the specific intent requirement extend to attendant circumstances that are necessary elements of the crime attempted? Consider the following:

(a) In Regina v. Khan, [1990] 1 W.L.R. 813, the defendant was charged with attempted rape. The judge instructed the jury that the completed offense of rape requires proof that the defendant had intercourse and either knew that the woman did not consent or "was reckless as to whether [she] was consenting or not." The judge then explained that "the principles relevant to consent apply in exactly the same way in attempted rape." Defendant was convicted of attempted rape. The court of appeal affirmed, stating:

> [T]he intent of the defendant is precisely the same in rape and in attempted rape and the mens rea is identical, namely, an intention to have intercourse plus a knowledge of or recklessness as to the woman's absence of consent. . . . We believe this to be a desirable result which in the instant case did not require the jury to be burdened with different directions as to the accused's state of mind, dependent upon whether the individual achieved or failed to achieve sexual intercourse.

(b) In Commonwealth v. Dunne, 474 N.E.2d 538 (Mass. 1985), the defendant was convicted of assault with intent to commit statutory rape, an offense that the court referred to as "attempted statutory rape." The statutory

age of consent was 16, and the victim was 15 years and 4 months old on the date of the offense. There was no allegation that the defendant knew (or should have known) that the victim was underage. Affirming the conviction, the court said:

> [In Massachusetts,] in a prosecution for statutory rape "it is immaterial that the defendant reasonably believed that the victim was sixteen years of age or older." This is the rule in most jurisdictions. Similarly, in a prosecution for an assault with intent to commit statutory rape, this court has held that whether or not the defendant is aware of the victim's age is irrelevant. . . . Indeed, it would be incongruous for us to posit one rule for the completed act and another for the attempt.

Are these cases sound? How can a person be convicted of attempting (trying) to do what he is unaware of doing?

(c) How the text of the MPC (§5.01) would handle these cases is less than clear, but the commentary states explicitly that §5.01(1)(c) is meant to reach the same conclusion as these cases. Model Penal Code and Commentaries, Comments to §5.01 at 301-304 (1985):

> Under the formulation in Subsection (1)(c), the proffered defense would not succeed in either case. In the statutory rape example, the actor must have a purpose to engage in sexual intercourse with a female in order to be charged with the attempt, and must engage in a substantial step in a course of conduct planned to culminate in his commission of that act. With respect to the age of the victim, however, it is sufficient if he acts "with the kind of culpability otherwise required for the commission of the crime," which in the case supposed is none at all. Since, therefore, mistake as to age is irrelevant with respect to the substantive offense, it is likewise irrelevant with respect to the attempt.

Question: Is this a persuasive reading of Subsection (1)(c)?

(d) For a probing analysis of the issues involved in considering the mens rea as to attendant circumstances required for attempt, see Larry Alexander & Kimberley D. Kessler, Mens Rea and Inchoate Crimes, 87 J. Crim. L. & Criminology 1139, 1157 (1997). Concerning the difficulties of distinguishing circumstances from conduct or consequences, see R.A. Duff, The Circumstances of an Attempt, 50 Cambridge L.J. 104-111 (1991).

3. *Preparation versus Attempt*

King v. Barker [1924] N.Z.L.R. 865: That the common law has recognized the distinction between acts of attempt and acts of preparation—between acts which are, and acts which are not, too remote to constitute a criminal attempt—is undoubted. . . . If, however, we proceed to inquire as to the precise nature of the distinction thus recognised and indicated, we find that the common law authorities are almost as silent as the Crimes Act itself. . . . The rule . . . suggested [by Baron Parke] in R. v. Eagleton [169 E.R. 826 (1855)] was that in order to constitute a criminal attempt, as opposed to mere preparation, the accused must have taken the last step which he was able to take along the road of his criminal intent. He must have done all that he intended to do and was able to do for the purpose of effectuating his criminal purpose. When he has stopped short of this, whether because he has repented, or because he has been prevented, or because the time or occasion for going further has not arrived, or for any other reason, he still has a locus penitentiae[a] and still remains within the region of innocent preparation. . . . On this principle the act of firing a pistol at a man would be attempted murder, although the bullet missed him. So would the act of pulling the trigger, although the pistol missed fire. But the prior and preliminary acts of procuring and loading the pistol, and of going with it to look for his enemy, and of lying in wait for him, and even of presenting the pistol at him, would not constitute criminal attempts, none of these being the proximate and final step towards the fulfillment of his criminal purpose. . . .

Subsequent authorities make it clear that the [*Eagleton*] test is not the true one. [I]n R. v. White, [1910] 2 K.B. 124 it was held that the first administration of poison in a case of intended slow poisoning by repeated doses amounted in itself to attempted murder. It is said by the Court: "The completion [or attempted completion] of one of a series of acts intended by a man to result in killing is an attempt to murder, even though the completed act would not, unless followed by other acts, result in killing." It might be the beginning of an attempt but would none the less be an attempt.

Although the [*Eagleton*] test has been rejected, no definite substitute for it has been formulated. All that can be definitely gathered from the authorities is that to constitute a criminal attempt, the first step along the way of criminal intent is not necessarily sufficient and the final step is not necessarily required. The dividing line between preparation and attempt is to be found somewhere between these two extremes; but as to the method by which it is to be determined the authorities give no clear guidance.

PEOPLE v. RIZZO

Court of Appeals of New York
246 N.Y. 334, 158 N.E. 888 (1927)

CRANE. J. The police of the city of New York did excellent work in this case by preventing the commission of a serious crime. It is a great satisfaction to realize that we have such wide-awake guardians of our peace. Whether or not the steps which the defendant had taken up to the time of his arrest amounted to the commission of a crime, as defined by our law, is, however, another matter. He has been convicted of an attempt to commit the crime of

---

a. An opportunity to repent, change one's mind.—EDS.

robbery in the first degree, and sentenced to state's prison. There is no doubt that he had the intention to commit robbery, if he got the chance. An examination, however, of the facts is necessary to determine whether his acts were in preparation to commit the crime if the opportunity offered, or constituted a crime in itself, known to our law as an attempt to commit robbery in the first degree. Charles Rizzo, the defendant, appellant, with three others, . . . on January 14th planned to rob one Charles Rao of a pay roll valued at about $1,200 which he was to carry from the bank for the United Lathing Company. These defendants, two of whom had firearms, started out in an automobile, looking for Rao or the man who had the pay roll on that day. Rizzo claimed to be able to identify the man, and was to point him out to the others, who were to do the actual holding up. The four rode about in their car looking for Rao. They went to the bank from which he was supposed to get the money and to various buildings being constructed by the United Lathing Company. At last they came to One Hundred and Eightieth street and Morris Park avenue. By this time they were watched and followed by two police officers. As Rizzo jumped out of the car and ran into the building, all four were arrested. The defendant was taken out from the building in which he was hiding. Neither Rao nor a man named Previti, who was also supposed to carry a pay roll, were at the place at the time of the arrest. The defendants had not found or seen the man they intended to rob. . . . The four men intended to rob the pay roll man, whoever he was. They were looking for him, but they had not seen or discovered him up to the time they were arrested.

Does this constitute the crime of an attempt to commit robbery . . . ? The Penal Law prescribes, "An act, done with intent to commit a crime, and tending but failing to effect its commission, is an attempt to commit that crime." The word "tending" is very indefinite. It is perfectly evident that there will arise differences of opinion as to whether an act in a given case is one tending to commit a crime. "Tending" means to exert activity in a particular direction. Any act in preparation to commit a crime may be said to have a tendency towards its accomplishment. The procuring of the automobile, searching the streets looking for the desired victim, were in reality acts tending toward the commission of the proposed crime. The law, however, has recognized that many acts in the way of preparation are too remote to constitute the crime of attempt. The line has been drawn between those acts which are remote and those which are proximate and near to the consummation. The law must be practical, and therefore considers those acts only as tending to the commission of the crime which are so near to its accomplishment that in all reasonable probability the crime itself would have been committed, but for timely interference. The cases which have been before the courts express this idea in different language, but the idea remains the same. The act or acts must come or advance very near to the accomplishment of the intended crime. [As said by Justice Holmes, dissenting in Hyde v. United States, 225 U.S. 347, 387 (1912):] "There must be dangerous proximity to success." . . .

How shall we apply this rule of immediate nearness to this case? The defendants were looking for the pay roll man to rob him of his money. . . . To constitute the crime of robbery, the money must have been taken from Rao by

means of force or violence, or through fear. . . . Did the acts above described come dangerously near to the taking of Rao's property? Did the acts come so near the commission of robbery that there was reasonable likelihood of its accomplishment but for the interference? Rao was not found; the defendants were still looking for him; no attempt to rob him could be made, at least until he came in sight; he was not in the building at One Hundred and Eightieth street and Morris Park avenue. There was no man there with the pay roll for the United Lathing Company whom these defendants could rob. Apparently no money had been drawn from the bank for the pay roll by anybody at the time of the arrest. In a word, these defendants had planned to commit a crime, and were looking around the city for an opportunity to commit it, but the opportunity fortunately never came. Men would not be guilty of an attempt at burglary if they had planned to break into a building and were arrested while they were hunting about the streets for the building not knowing where it was. Neither would a man be guilty of an attempt to commit murder if he armed himself and started out to find the person whom he had planned to kill but could not find him. So here these defendants were not guilty of an attempt to commit robbery . . . when they had not found or reached the presence of the person they intended to rob.

Holding
(c)

NOTES

1. The dangerous proximity test. The New York attempt statute now requires that the defendant engage in conduct "which tends to effect the commission" of the crime. N.Y. Pen. Law §110.00 (2011). The court of appeals has held that this language makes no change in the law, which continues to be as stated in *Rizzo.* People v. Acosta, 609 N.E.2d 518, 521 (N.Y. 1993).

Many jurisdictions continue to apply the *Rizzo* court's dangerous-proximity approach. Consider Commonwealth v. Bell, 917 N.E.2d 740 (Mass. 2009). An undercover police officer posing as a prostitute met the defendant in a parking lot and agreed that for $200, she would take him to a nearby park, one mile away, where she would allow him to have sexual intercourse with her (fictitious) four-year-old child. After telling the defendant to follow her in his car, she drove out of the parking lot, with the defendant close behind. As he turned out of the lot, he was arrested and subsequently convicted of two offenses: soliciting an act of prostitution and attempted rape. The Massachusetts Supreme Judicial Court upheld his solicitation conviction but reversed the conviction for attempted rape because "he had yet to see a child and did not know the exact location of the child. He had yet to follow [the officer] to any type of house or park, and he had not yet paid for the child." Id. at 748. Relying on Justice Holmes's formulation of the proximity requirement (quoted in the *Rizzo* decision), the court explained: "[W]e look to the actions left to be taken, or the 'distance or gap between the defendant's actions and the (unachieved) goal of the consummated crime—the distance must be relatively short, the gap narrow, if the defendant is to be held guilty of a criminal attempt.'" Id.

2. *Proximity evaluated.* Are the results in *Rizzo* and *Bell* justifiable? What are their implications for effective law enforcement? Consider Glanville Williams, Police Control of Intending Criminals, [1955] Crim. L. Rev. 66, 69:

> In a rational system of justice the police would be given every encouragement to intervene early where a suspect is clearly bent on crime. Yet in England, if the police come on the scene too early they may find that they can do nothing with the intending offender except admonish him. This is largely because of the rule that an attempt, to be indictable, must be sufficiently "proximate" to the crime intended. . . . One is led to ask whether there is any real need for the requirement of proximity in the law of attempt. Quite apart from this requirement, it must be proved beyond reasonable doubt that the accused intended to commit the crime . . . and that he did some act towards committing it. If only a remote act of preparation is alleged against him, that will weigh with the court in deciding whether he had the firm criminal intention alleged against him. If, however, the court finds that this intention existed, is there any reason why the would-be criminal should not be dealt with by the police and by the criminal courts?

NOTE ON THE INTERACTION BETWEEN PROXIMITY AND ABANDONMENT

One reason for judicial reluctance to move the threshold of criminality to an earlier point in time has been the desire to preserve for the defendant a "locus penitentiae"—an opportunity to repent, to change one's mind. It is important to see how that opportunity is lost once the defendant crosses the threshold of criminality. First, a defendant may be arrested before she has the chance to take the steps remaining to complete the crime. Such a defendant will be liable for attempt even though we cannot be sure she would have taken those steps. Second, a defendant may be arrested after she has fully abandoned the criminal plan. Here the defendant could be held liable for committing an attempt (by crossing the threshold of criminality), even though she later did everything in her power to prevent any actual harm.

Should defendant's abandoning her criminal purpose defeat liability for attempt? If inchoate crimes are to be treated like other offenses, the answer would have to be no: Remorse and restitution may affect the sentence, but they cannot erase liability once the elements necessary for conviction are complete. See Alec Walen, Criminalizing Statements of Terrorist Intent, 101 J. Crim. L. & Criminology 803 (2011). Applying this reasoning, the law traditionally denied any defense of abandonment, and many courts continue to adhere to that view. See, e.g., United States v Young, 613 F.3d 735 (8th Cir. 2010) ("[A] defendant cannot abandon an attempt once it has been completed"); State v. Robins, 646 N.W.2d 287, 295 (Wis. 2002) ("There is no . . . defense of voluntary abandonment once an attempt is completed"). To minimize the resulting potential for unfairness, many courts therefore insist that the threshold of criminality be placed very close to the last act, even when this approach means freeing some defendants who almost certainly would *not* have repented. Recall the facts of *Rizzo* and *Bell.*

A way to avoid this dilemma is to recognize abandonment (sometimes called renunciation) as a complete defense. A number of states have done so, either by statute or judicial decision. A typical requirement is that the abandonment occur "under circumstances manifesting a voluntary and complete renunciation of [the] criminal purpose." N.Y. Penal Code §40.10(3) (2011). MPC §5.01(4) is similar. For the definition of when the renunciation is considered "voluntary" and "complete," see §5.01(4). Most of the recently revised codes adopt a renunciation defense substantially similar to that of the MPC. See Daniel G. Moriarty, Extending the Defense of Renunciation, 62 Temp. L. Rev. 1, 7-11 (1989).

Consider these cases: (*a*) In People v. Johnston, 448 N.Y.S.2d 902, 902-903 (App. Div. 1982), defendant entered a gas station, pulled a gun, and demanded money. When the station attendant produced only $50 and said that this was all the cash available, defendant departed, stating, "I was just kidding, forget it ever happened." The court denied a renunciation defense, but several commentators favor a defense in these circumstances. See, e.g., George P. Fletcher, Rethinking Criminal Law 191-192 (1978). Which is the better view?

(*b*) In People v. McNeal, 393 N.W.2d 907 (Mich. App. 1986), defendant accosted a girl who had been waiting at a bus stop and forced her at knife point to accompany him to a house, with the intent to rape her. After an extended conversation in which the girl pleaded with him to let her go, defendant released the girl, saying that he was sorry and would never engage in such behavior again. The court affirmed a conviction for attempted sexual assault, upholding a finding that because of the victim's "unexpected resistance," the defendant's renunciation was not voluntary. On similar facts, the court in Ross v. State, 601 So. 2d 872, 875 (Miss. 1992), found abandonment as a matter of law and reversed a conviction for attempted rape, stating: "[Defendant] did not fail in his attack. No one prevented him from completing it. [The victim] did not sound an alarm. She successfully persuaded Ross, of his own free will, to abandon his attempt."

McQUIRTER v. STATE

Alabama Court of Appeals
36 Ala. App. 707, 63 So. 2d 388 (1953)

Price J. Appellant, a Negro man, was found guilty of an attempt to commit an assault with intent to rape, under an indictment charging an assault with intent to rape. The jury assessed a fine of $500.

About 8:00 o'clock on the night of June 29, 1951, Mrs. Ted Allen, a white woman, with her two children and a neighbor's little girl, were drinking Coca-Cola at the "Tiny Diner" in Atmore. When they started in the direction of Mrs. Allen's home she noticed appellant sitting in the cab of a parked truck.

As she passed the truck appellant said something unintelligible, opened the truck door and placed his foot on the running board.

Mrs. Allen testified appellant followed her down the street and when she reached Suell Lufkin's house she stopped. As she turned into the Lufkin house appellant was within two or three feet of her. She waited ten minutes for appellant to pass. When she proceeded on her way, appellant came toward her from behind a telephone pole. She told the children to run to Mr. Simmons' house and tell him to come and meet her. When appellant saw Mr. Simmons he turned and went back down the street to the intersection and leaned on a stop sign just across the street from Mrs. Allen's home. Mrs. Allen watched him at the sign from Mr. Simmons' porch for about thirty minutes, after which time he came back down the street and appellant went on home. . . .

Mr. W.E. Strickland, Chief of Police of Atmore, testified that appellant stated in the Atmore jail he didn't know what was the matter with him; that he was drinking a little; that he and his partner had been to Pensacola; that his partner went to the "Front" to see a colored woman; that he didn't have any money and he sat in the truck and made up his mind he was going to get the first woman that came by and that this was the first woman that came by. He said he got out of the truck, came around the gas tank and watched the lady and when she started off he started off behind her; that he was going to carry her in the cotton patch and if she hollered he was going to kill her. He testified appellant made the same statement in the Brewton jail. . . .

Appellant, as a witness in his own behalf, testified he and Bill Page, another Negro, carried a load of junk-iron from Monroeville to Pensacola; on their way back to Monroeville they stopped in Atmore. They parked the truck near the "Tiny Diner" and rode to the "Front," the colored section, in a cab. Appellant came back to the truck around 8:00 o'clock and sat in the truck cab for about thirty minutes. He decided to go back to the "Front" to look for Bill Page. As he started up the street he saw prosecutrix and her children. He turned around and waited until he decided they had gone, then he walked up the street toward the "Front." When he reached the intersection at the street telegraph pole he decided he didn't want to go to the "Front" and sat around there a few minutes, then went on to the "Front" and stayed about 25 to 30 minutes, and came back to the truck.

He denied that he followed Mrs. Allen or made any gesture toward molesting her or the children. He denied making the statements testified to by the officers. . . . Appellant insists the trial court erred in refusing the general affirmative charge and in denying the motion for a new trial on the ground the verdict was contrary to the evidence. . . .

Under the authorities in this state, to justify a conviction for an attempt to commit an assault with intent to rape the jury must be satisfied beyond a reasonable doubt that defendant intended to have sexual intercourse with prosecutrix against her will, by force or by putting her in fear. Intent is a question to be determined by the jury from the facts and circumstances adduced on the trial, and if there is evidence from which it may be inferred that at the time of the attempt defendant intended to gratify his lustful desires against the resistance of the female a jury question is presented. In determining the question of intention the jury may consider social conditions and customs founded upon racial differences, such as that the prosecutrix was a white woman and defendant was a Negro man.

After considering the evidence in this case we are of the opinion it was sufficient to warrant the submission of the question of defendant's guilt to the jury, and was ample to sustain the judgment of conviction. . . .

Affirmed.

NOTES AND QUESTIONS

1. McQuirter and race. What is troublesome about the conviction in this case? The context of racial bigotry certainly is—black man, white woman, small town in the South in the 1950s. Consider I. Bennett Capers, The Unintentional Rapist, 87 Wash. U. L. Rev. 1345, 1385 (2010):

> When I first read *McQuirter*, what troubled me as much as McQuirter's conviction was the appellate court's ruling that, "In determining the question of intention the jury may consider social conditions and customs founded upon racial differences, such as that the prosecutrix was a white woman and the defendant was a negro man." Now, ... I appreciate the court's honesty, though faced with the court's instruction, I might have applied the instruction differently. The court suggested that McQuirter's intent was inferable from racial mores. But would not the mores of the time have supported a finding of the absence of intent? Is it really likely that McQuirter, alone in the white part of town in Alabama in 1951, and observing Mrs. Ted Allen walking along a residential street with two children, intended to assault her, let alone rape her? With neighbors on either side of the street? With Suell Lufkin's house right there and with Mr. Simmons watching him? With Mrs. Allen watching him from Mrs. Simmons's porch? In the state . . . that had a history of lynching black men, and where two black men had been lynched just the year before? But then again, . . . perhaps the "social conditions and customs" that allowed the jury to infer guilt trumped the "social conditions and customs" that suggested the absence of intent.

2. McQuirter and confessions. Whatever weight the jury may have given to the "social conditions," notice that the only *direct* evidence of culpable intent came from the sheriff's testimony about what the defendant said in jail. Reliance on confessions allegedly given in police custody continues to be common in criminal cases, even though defendants often deny making such statements or claim that they were coerced. Our system leaves the trier of fact to sort out the relative credibility of the police (who may have a strong incentive to exaggerate the incriminating character of the defendant's statements) and the defendant (who inevitably has a strong incentive to understate or deny the incriminating character of any statements he may have made.) Under these circumstances, even if the context involved no racial element, wouldn't the conviction still be troublesome? Recall the earlier criticism of the dangerous-proximity test. Does a case like *McQuirter* redeem that test?

3. The equivocality test. Another approach that would foreclose conviction in a case like *McQuirter* is the equivocality test. Unlike the dangerous proximity test for determining what acts suffice for attempt (once intent is proven), the equivocality test looks not to how far the defendant has gone but to how clearly his acts bespeak his intent. The principle was formulated as follows in The King v. Barker, [1924] N.Z.L.R. 865, 874-875:

> An act done with intent to commit a crime is not a criminal attempt unless it is . . . in itself sufficient evidence of the criminal intent with which it is done. A criminal attempt is an act which shows criminal intent on the face of it. The case must be one in which *Res ipsa loquitur.* An act, on the other hand, which is in its own nature and on the face of it innocent is not a criminal attempt. It cannot be brought within the scope of criminal attempt by evidence aliunde [e.g., admission or confession] as to the criminal purpose with which it is done. . . . The law does not punish men for their guilty intentions or resolutions in themselves. Nor does it commonly punish them even for the expression, declaration, or confession of such intentions or resolutions. That a man's unfulfilled criminal purposes should be punishable they must be manifested not by his words merely, or by acts which are in themselves of innocent or ambiguous significance, but by overt acts which are sufficient in themselves to declare and proclaim the guilty purpose with which they are done. . . . The reason for thus holding a man innocent who does an act with intent to commit a crime is the danger involved in the admission of evidence upon which he may be punished for acts which in themselves and in appearance are perfectly innocent.
>
> . . . To buy a box of matches with intent to use them in burning a haystack is not an attempt to commit arson, for it is in itself and in appearance an innocent act, there being many other reasons than arson for buying matches. . . . But he who takes matches to a haystack and there lights one of them and blows it out on finding that he is observed, has done an act which speaks for itself, and he is guilty of criminal attempt accordingly. . . . The purchaser of matches would not be guilty of attempted arson even if he declared to the vendor or to any other person the guilty purpose with which he bought them. Such evidence is relevant for the purpose of satisfying the jury that the requisite criminal intent existed, but it is not relevant in determining the prior question of law whether the act charged amounts in law to an attempt or is too remote for that purpose.

When formulated that strictly, the test has few adherents, but it has influenced several American formulations. In People v. Miller, 2 Cal. 2d 527, 531-532 (1935), the defendant, who had threatened to kill Jeans, entered a field where Jeans and the local constable were planting hops. The defendant was carrying a rifle, and he walked straight toward them. He stopped once to load his rifle, but at no time did he lift it to take aim. Jeans fled, and the constable disarmed the defendant. A conviction of attempted murder was reversed. The court stated:

> The reason for requiring evidence of a direct act, however slight, toward consummation of the intended crime, is . . . that in the majority of cases up to that

time the conduct of the defendant, consisting merely of acts of preparation, has never ceased to be equivocal; and this is necessarily so, irrespective of his declared intent. It is that quality of being equivocal that must be lacking before the act becomes one which may be said to be a commencement of the commission of the crime, or an overt act, or before any fragment of the crime itself has been committed, and this is so for the reason that, so long as the equivocal quality remains, no one can say with certainty what the intent of the defendant is. . . . In the present case, up to the moment the gun was taken from defendant, no one could say with certainty whether defendant had come into the field to carry out his threat to kill Jeans or merely to demand his arrest by the constable.

See also Wis. Stat. §939.32(3)(2011):

An attempt to commit a crime requires that the actor have an intent to perform acts and attain a result which, if accomplished, would constitute such crime and that he does acts toward the commission of the crime which demonstrate unequivocally, under all the circumstances, that he formed that intent and would commit the crime except for the intervention of another person or some other extraneous factor.

The test is criticized in Glanville Williams, Criminal Law: The General Part 630 (2d ed. 1961):

D goes up to a haystack, fills his pipe, and lights a match. The act of lighting the match, even to a suspicious-minded person, is ambiguous. It may indicate only that D is going to light his pipe; but perhaps, on the other hand, the pipe is only a "blind" and D is really bent on setting fire to the stack. We do not know. Therefore, on the equivocality test, the act is not proximate. But suppose that as a matter of actual fact D, after his arrest, confesses to the guilty intent, and suppose that that confession is believed. We are now certain of the intent and the only question is as to proximity. It becomes clear that the act satisfies all the requirements for a criminal attempt. Since it is practically the last act that D intended to do in order to commit the crime (the very last being setting the match to the stack), it is almost necessarily proximate. That the act is ambiguous, which in itself might have created a doubt as to the mens rea, no longer matters, for the mens rea has been proved by the confession.

NOTE ON SUBSTANTIVE CRIMES OF PREPARATION

There are many inchoate substantive crimes that do not require resort to the law of attempt with its various restrictions. Several come from the common law. These include the crimes of solicitation (or incitement) and conspiracy, both of which we deal with later in this book. Two other important common-law crimes that consist solely of preparatory behavior are burglary and assault.

1. Burglary. Common-law burglary was defined as breaking and entering a dwelling of another at night with the intent to commit some felony inside. Under the common law of attempt, a person apprehended while breaking into a dwelling with intent to commit a felony would not be guilty of attempt because he would not have arrived at the scene of his projected felony. The development of the offense of burglary provided a partial solution to this problem. Today, cases and statutes have gradually enlarged the offense. Some burglary statutes still apply only to entries at night but no longer require a physical "breaking"; the entry can simply be without permission or under false pretenses. See, e.g., Wagner v. State, 864 A.2d 1037, 1055-1056 (Md. Spec. App. 2005). Other statutes extend the offense to include any entry, in day as well as at night, into any structure, with intent to commit any crime. For example, in People v. Salemme, 3 Cal. Rptr. 2d 398 (Ct. App. 1992), the court held that the defendant had committed burglary when he entered a person's home with the intent to perpetrate a fraudulent sale of securities.

2. Assault. Assault is sometimes defined as the infliction of harm upon another (a battery), see MPC §2.11(1)(a), but more often as an attempt to commit a battery. See, e.g., Cal. Penal Code §240(2011): "An assault is an unlawful attempt, coupled with a present ability, to commit a violent injury on the person of another." Note that the crime of assault is typically defined more narrowly than the tort of assault. A person who deliberately places another in fear of a battery, but does not actually intend to carry out the attack, normally would not be guilty of assault under traditional criminal law definitions, although she might be liable for damages in tort. Some modern statutes extend the definition of assault to cover such conduct under some circumstances. See MPC §211.1(1)(c).

3. Modern statutes. The law today contains many instances of merely preparatory behavior defined as substantive crimes. As the court in State v. Young, 271 A.2d 569 (N.J. 1970), observed, in holding within the police power of the state a law forbidding entry into school buildings with the intent to disrupt classes:

> There are a host of statutes, federal and State, which condemn acts, themselves innocent, if done with a forbidden intent. . . . There is nothing necessarily wrong in teaching or demonstrating the use, application or making of a firearm or explosive . . . , but 18 U.S.C.A. §231(a)(1) makes it a crime to do so "intending that the same will be unlawfully employed for use in, or in furtherance of, a civil disorder which may in any way or degree obstruct, delay, or adversely affect commerce." . . . There are a number of statutes which make possession criminal if there is an intent to do some hostile act. [For example, laws] relating to possession of burglar tools [and] weapons and explosives. [T]he many statutes we recounted above have the common feature of punishing an act only because of the evil purpose it pursues, without regard to whether the act would constitute an attempt to commit the offense the statutes seek to head off, and even though the act, absent such purpose, may be one protected by the Constitution.

4. Policing measures. Other approaches that avoid the restrictions of the law of attempt include measures for dealing with persons who engage in suspicious activity not amounting to an attempt to commit a crime. One approach is procedural, allowing police to stop and detain a suspect in circumstances short of those sufficient under the Fourth Amendment to justify an arrest. See Terry v.

Ohio, 392 U.S. 1 (1968). The other approach is substantive, for example, making it a crime to loiter in circumstances giving rise to apprehension that a crime may be afoot. See *City of Chicago v. Morales*, supra page 171.

5. Stalking. Anti-stalking statutes criminalize harassing conduct that serves to terrorize and torment another, or which may serve as a prelude to a violent attack. These statutes were the product of a wave of widely reported incidents of persons, primarily women, suffering continued harassment and sometimes violent injury, perpetrated by "obsessed fans, divorced or separated spouses, ex-lovers, rejected suitors, neighbors, coworkers, classmates, gang members, former employees, [or] disgruntled defendants, as well as complete strangers."[14] One news report noted:[15]

> For more than a month, a young woman in Stratford, N.J., was hounded by a man she had briefly dated. He followed her to work and to the hairdresser. He left repeated messages on her answering machine. She talked to the police several times and filed a harassment complaint, but there was little the police could do except ask the man to stop. "Our hands were tied," said Jay Wilkins, a detective in the Stratford Police Department. "We were in the position of waiting for a crime to happen."

In 1990, California became the first state to enact an anti-stalking law; since then virtually all states have followed.[16] There is general agreement that legislation of this kind is desirable. The chief difficulty has been drafting a law that criminalizes the targeted misconduct without sweeping in constitutionally protected activity, like speech, and without using terms of excessive vagueness. The California law, Cal. Penal Code §646.9 (2011), makes stalking a crime subject to a maximum of one year in prison and defines stalking as:

> [a]ny person who willfully, maliciously, and repeatedly follows or willfully and maliciously harasses another person and who makes a credible threat with the intent to place that person in reasonable fear for his or her safety, or the safety of his or her immediate family, . . .

The term "harasses" is defined as:

> a knowing and willful course of conduct directed at a specific person that seriously alarms, annoys, torments, or terrorizes the person, and which serves no legitimate purpose. This course of conduct must be such as would cause a reasonable person to suffer substantial emotional distress, and must actually cause substantial emotional distress to the person.

"Credible threat" is defined to mean:

> a verbal or written threat . . . or a threat implied by a pattern of conduct . . . made with the intent to place the person that is the target of the threat in

---

14. Kathleen G. McAnaney et al., Note, From Imprudence to Crime: Anti-Stalking Laws, 68 Notre Dame L. Rev. 819, 821-823 (1993).

15. Tamar Lewin, New Laws Address Old Problem, N.Y. Times, Feb. 8, 1993, at A1.

16. See Matthew J. Gilligan, Note, Stalking the Stalker: Developing New Laws to Thwart Those Who Terrorize Others, 27 Ga. L. Rev. 285 (1992).

reasonable fear for his or her safety . . . and made with the apparent ability to carry out the threat. . . . It is not necessary to prove that the defendant had the intent to actually carry out the threat.

Question: Do anti-stalking laws cast the net of criminal punishment too widely, or is their reach so limited that the problem of stalking remains unsolved? Consider the following issues:

(a) Overbroad? Are statutes like California's too vague to give adequate notice of what is prohibited and to confine the discretion of prosecutors and judges?[17] Most courts have rejected constitutional challenges, finding that the crucial element of harassment (conduct that "alarms, annoys [or] torments") is not overly vague when statutes define those terms by an objective standard (for example, requiring conduct that "would cause a reasonable person to suffer substantial emotional distress"). See, e.g., State v. Bernhardt, 338 S.W.2d 830 (Mo. App. 2011); People v. Ewing, 76 Cal. App. 4th 199 (1999). The Kansas Supreme Court found its anti-stalking statute unconstitutionally vague because that statute, unlike its California counterpart, made liability depend on the personal sensibilities of the particular victim. After the legislature amended the statute to require proof that the conduct would cause "a reasonable person" to suffer emotional distress, the Kansas Supreme Court rejected a new vagueness challenge and upheld the statute. State v. Rucker, 987 P.2d 1080 (Kan. 1999).

(b) Underinclusive? As limited by the requirements of harassment and a "credible threat," both defined objectively, is the California statute too narrow to deal effectively with the problem of stalking? Consider "cyber-stalking." In a number of cases, would-be lovers and estranged spouses have resorted to e-mail and Internet Web postings as a way to harass and frighten their victims, and the ease and reach of e-communication exponentially expands the frequency and potential impact of stalking behavior. E-mail messages containing threats of rape or assault would easily meet the requirements of traditional stalking statutes, and nearly all states have amended their laws to make explicit that they apply to the transmission of threats electronically. See Ashley N.B. Beagle, Modern Stalking Laws: A Survey of State Anti-Stalking Statutes, 14 Chap. L. Rev. 457, 482 (2011). Nonetheless, existing regimes are often unable to reach many common forms of this behavior. See Naomi Harlin Goodno, Cyberstalking, a New Crime, 72 Mo. L. Rev. 125 (2007) For example, endlessly repeated sexual proposals or requests for dates may not involve express or implied threats.

Another concern is the emerging problem of "stalking apps"—software secretly implanted in a victim's cell phone and then used to permit GPS tracking of the victim's location 24 hours a day. The Fourth Amendment prohibits GPS tracking by the government (at least when the tracking device is attached

---

17. For examination of U.S. Supreme Court doctrine governing the constitutional prohibition of vagueness, see *City of Chicago v. Morales* and the Notes following, page 171 supra.

to a person's car without his or her consent). United States v. Jones, 2012 U.S. LEXIS 1063 (U.S., Jan. 23, 2012). But the Constitution would not prohibit such conduct by private parties, and current statutes do not necessarily make such conduct a crime, absent the extra elements required under anti-stalking statutes.[18] But since "stalking apps" are clandestine, the victim is typically unaware of the stalker's attention, and the statutory requirements of "threat" or "harassment" may be missing until the stalker attempts some other offense. Another hard-to-reach form of cyber-stalking was illustrated in a recent case where a man deluged his former girlfriend with messages filled with obscenities and demands for attention; local authorities concluded that the conduct did not qualify as stalking.[19] Does such conduct amount to "stalking" under a statute like California's? If not, should some other law be crafted to cover it— and if so, how?

In a New York case, the defendant approached a young woman in his neighborhood, offered her a Valentine's Day gift, repeatedly asked her for dates, and often followed her, even after she emphatically told him to leave her alone. Would such conduct constitute stalking in California? If not, should stalking laws be amended to cover it? In the New York case, a stalking conviction was upheld under a statute that, unlike California's, does not require a "credible threat" to the victim's safety but instead extends to any course of conduct that "causes material harm to the victim's mental or emotional health," after the defendant has been "clearly told to stop." See People v. Stuart, 100 N.Y.2d 412, 426 (2003). Is this an appropriate way to address the problem, or does it extend criminal liability too widely? Would it criminalize the actions of a tenant who persists in calling and e-mailing her landlord because the leaky faucet in her apartment has not been repaired?

Another way to reach conduct like that of the New York defendant is the offense of harassment, defined in MPC §250.4 and classified as a petty misdemeanor. Does the New York case qualify as harassment under the MPC?

(c) Problem. On the evidence presented in the McQuirter case, would it be possible to convict the defendant of "stalking," as defined in California? If so, should that be considered troublesome or reassuring? Consider another observation of Professor I. Bennett Capers, supra, 87 Wash. U. L. Rev. at 1393:

> In these interactions, where the black male is perceived as a sexual threat, it is the black male whose individuality . . . is denied. It is the black male who becomes a projection of someone else's fears. It is the black man who is reduced . . . to a dangerous body. [I] wonder who was in greater fear: Mrs. Ted Allen, surrounded by three children, on her own street securely on the white

---

18. See Alexei Alexis, Bipartisan Senate Group Urges FTC, DOJ to Investigate, Prosecute "Stalking Apps," 90 Crim. L. Rep. 169 (Nov. 2, 2011).

19. See Mary L. Boland, Taking Aim at the High-Tech Stalker, Criminal Justice (ABA Criminal Justice Section), pp. 40, 42 (Spring 2005).

side of town, with Suell Lufkin's house nearby, with Mr. Simmons at her side . . . ? Or was it McQuirter, a black man alone on the white side of town in 1950s Alabama . . . ?[a]

UNITED STATES v. JACKSON

United States Court of Appeals, 2d Circuit
560 F.2d 112 (1977)

FREDERICK VAN PELT BRYAN, J.: Robert Jackson, William Scott, and Martin Allen appeal from judgments of conviction entered . . . after a trial before Chief Judge Jacob Mishler without a jury.

Count one of the indictment alleged that between June 11 and June 21, 1976, the appellants conspired to commit an armed robbery of the Manufacturers Hanover Trust. . . . Counts two and three each charged appellants with an attempted robbery of the branch on June 14 and on June 21, 1976, respectively. . . . Chief Judge Mishler filed a memorandum of decision finding each defendant guilty on all . . . counts.

Appellants' principal contention is that the court below erred in finding them guilty on counts two and three. While they concede that the evidence supported the conspiracy convictions on count one, they assert that, as a matter of law, their conduct never crossed the elusive line which separates "mere preparation" from "attempt."[b] The Government's evidence at trial consisted largely of the testimony of Vanessa Hodges, an unindicted co-conspirator, and of various FBI agents who surveilled the Manufacturers Hanover branch on June 21, 1976.

[On June 11, 1976, Hodges recruited Allen to rob the Manufacturers Hanover branch. Allen agreed, proposed the date of June 14, and told her he had guns and a car. On June 14, Allen arrived with a confederate, Jackson, in a car containing a sawed-off shotgun, shells, materials intended as masks, and handcuffs to bind the bank manager. After picking up another confederate, Scott, they drove to the bank, where Allen entered to check the surveillance cameras, while Jackson installed a false cardboard license plate on the car. Scott then entered the bank too, but returned with the news that the tellers

---

a. For arguments in support of anti-stalking statutes, see Marion Buckley, Stalking Laws— Problem or Solution? 9 Wis. Women's L.J. 23 (1994). For another critical view, suggesting that statutes like that of California violate constitutional prohibitions against vagueness and overbreadth, see Robert P. Faulkner & Douglas H. Hsiao, And Where You Go I'll Follow: The Constitutionality of Antistalking Laws and Proposed Model Legislation, 31 Harv. J. on Legis. 1 (1994).—EDS.

b. Since the defendants conceded the validity of their conspiracy convictions, why did it matter whether they could also be convicted of attempt? The answer is that the federal conspiracy statute, 18 U.S.C. §371, carries a maximum sentence of five years' imprisonment, while 18 U.S.C. §2113(a) provides that attempted bank robbery is punishable by a maximum of 20 years' imprisonment. In the present case, defendant Jackson received a two-year sentence on the conspiracy count and a suspended sentence on the other counts; Scott received a five-year sentence on the conspiracy count and concurrent seven-year terms on the attempt counts; Allen received a five-year sentence on the conspiracy count and concurrent ten-year terms on the attempt counts.—EDS.

were separating the weekend deposits and many patrons were still there. They then rescheduled the robbery for June 21.

[On June 18, Hodges was arrested on an unrelated offense and decided to cooperate with the police. She told FBI agents of the robbery planned for June 21, and early on that date FBI agents took surveillance positions around the bank. They saw a brown Lincoln with a New York license on the front and a cardboard facsimile of a license plate on the rear. It stopped near the bank and was occupied by three men fitting the description Hodges had provided. One of the men got out, stood for a while in front of the bank, and returned to the car. The Lincoln drove up and down the streets near the bank and then stopped for several minutes a few blocks away. When it returned and parked near the bank, agents noticed that its front license plate was now missing. After parking for 30 minutes, the car began moving in the direction of the bank.]

At some point near the bank . . . , the appellants detected the presence of the surveillance agents. The Lincoln . . . was overtaken by FBI agents who ordered the appellants out of the car and arrested them. The agents then observed a black and red plaid suitcase in the rear of the car [and in it they found] two loaded sawed-off shotguns, a toy nickel-plated revolver, a pair of handcuffs, and masks. A New York license plate was seen lying on the front floor of the car. . . .

Chief Judge Mishler concluded that the evidence against Jackson, Scott, and Allen was "overwhelming" on [the conspiracy count]. In contrast, he characterized the question of whether the defendants had attempted a bank robbery as charged in counts two and three or were merely engaged in preparations as "a close one." After canvassing the authorities . . . Chief Judge Mishler applied the following two-tiered inquiry formulated in United States v. Mandujano, 499 F.2d 370, 376 (5th Cir. 1974):

First, the defendant must have been acting with the kind of culpability otherwise required for the commission of the crime which he is charged with attempting. . . . Second, the defendant must have engaged in conduct which constitutes a substantial step toward commission of the crime. A substantial step must be conduct strongly corroborative of the firmness of the defendant's criminal intent.

He concluded that on June 14 and again on June 21, the defendants took substantial steps, strongly corroborative of the firmness of their criminal intent, toward commission of the crime of bank robbery and found the defendants guilty on each of the two attempt counts. These appeals followed.

[T]here is no comprehensive statutory definition of attempt in federal law. [Our court has] selected the two-tiered inquiry of United States v. Mandujano, supra, as stating the proper test for determining whether . . . conduct constituted an attempt. [That] analysis "conforms closely to the sensible definition of an attempt proffered by the American Law Institute's Model Penal Code [§5.01]."

The draftsmen of the Model Penal Code recognized the difficulty of arriving at a general standard for distinguishing acts of preparation from acts constituting an attempt. . . . The formulation upon which the draftsmen ulti-mately agreed required, in addition to criminal purpose, that an act be a substantial step in a course of conduct designed to accomplish a criminal result, and that it be strongly corroborative of criminal purpose in order for it to constitute such a substantial step. The following differences between this test and previous approaches to the preparation-attempt problem were noted:

> First, this formulation shifts the emphasis from what remains to be done—the chief concern of the proximity tests—to what the actor *has already done.* The fact that further major steps must be taken before the crime can be completed does not preclude a finding that the steps already undertaken are substantial. It is expected, in the normal case, that this approach will broaden the scope of attempt liability.
>
> Second, although it is intended that the requirement of a substantial step will result in the imposition of attempt liability only in those instances in which some firmness of criminal purpose is shown, no finding is required as to whether the actor would probably have desisted prior to completing the crime. . . .
>
> Finally, the requirement of proving a substantial step generally will prove less of a hurdle for the prosecution than the *res ipsa loquitur* approach, which requires that the actor's conduct must itself manifest the criminal purpose. . . .

Model Penal Code §5.01, Comment at 47 (Tent. Draft No. 10, 1960).

The draftsmen concluded that, in addition to assuring firmness of criminal design, the requirement of a substantial step would preclude attempt liability, with its accompanying harsh penalties, for relatively remote preparatory acts. At the same time, however, by not requiring a "last proximate act" or one of its various analogues it would permit the apprehension of dangerous persons at an earlier stage than the other approaches without immunizing them from attempt liability. . . .

Chief Judge Mishler [concluded that on both June 14 and June 21,] these men were seriously dedicated to the commission of a crime, had passed beyond the stage of preparation, and would have assaulted the bank had they not been dissuaded by certain external factors, *viz.*, the breaking up of the weekend deposits and crowd of patrons in the bank on June 14 and the detection of the FBI surveillance on June 21.

We cannot say that these conclusions . . . were erroneous. On two separate occasions, appellants reconnoitered the place contemplated for the commission of the crime and possessed the paraphernalia . . . —loaded sawed-off shotguns, extra shells, a toy revolver, hand-cuffs, and masks—which was specially designed for such unlawful use and which could serve no lawful purpose under the circumstances. Under the Model Penal Code formulation, either type of conduct, standing alone, was sufficient as a matter of law to constitute a "substantial step" if it strongly corroborated their criminal purpose. Here both types of conduct coincided on both June 14 and June 21, along with numerous other elements strongly corroborative of the firmness of appellants' criminal intent. [We] thus affirm the convictions for attempted bank robbery on counts two and three.

NOTE ON STATUTORY REFORM

The Model Penal Code draws on elements of both the proximity and the equivocality tests. Its approach has proved influential with many jurisdictions. Altogether, roughly half the states and two-thirds of the federal circuits now use a "substantial step" test comparable to that of the MPC. See Robert Batey, Book Review (Paul Robinson's Criminal Law), 73 Notre Dame L. Rev. 781, 794 (1998). Some states have adopted the Code's substantial step formula without the requirement that the actor's conduct strongly corroborate the intent. E.g., Ga. Code §16-4-1 (2011); 720 Ill. Comp. Stat. §5/8-4 (2010). Several of the statutes include significant variations on the MPC approach. Colo. Rev. Stat., §18-2-101 (2011) defines a "substantial step" as one which is "strongly corroborative of the firmness of the actor's purpose."

Question: What is the intention behind this change in wording?

PROBLEMS

1. In United States v. Harper, 33 F.3d 1143 (9th Cir. 1994), the defendants were found in a car parked in a parking lot adjacent to a branch of the Bank of America. Under a bush six feet from their car, police discovered two handguns, and in the car they found a stun gun, surgical gloves, and ammunition for the two hand guns. An ATM camera showed that one of the defendants, Harper, had used a stolen ATM card to withdraw $20 from the ATM, but had not removed the cash. As Harper knew, this created a "bill trap," causing the ATM to shut down and summon technicians to repair it, their response time being between 45 and 90 minutes. The prosecution obtained a conviction for conspiracy and attempted bank robbery, the latter on the theory that Harper had deliberately set the "bill trap" in order to rob the technicians of the money in the machine when they arrived to repair it. The court of appeals affirmed the conspiracy conviction but reversed the attempt conviction, stating:

> True, Harper had [caused] a bill trap that would eventually bring service personnel to the ATM. That act, however, is equivocal in itself. The robbery was in the future and . . . the defendants never made a move toward the victims or the Bank to accomplish the criminal portion of their intended mission. They had not taken a step of "such substantiality that, unless frustrated, the crime would have occurred." Their situation is therefore distinguishable from that of the defendant in United States v. Moore, 921 F.2d 207 (9th Cir. 1990). . . . In *Moore*, the defendant was apprehended "walking toward the bank, wearing a ski mask, and carrying gloves, pillowcases and a concealed, loaded gun." These actions were a true commitment toward the robbery, which would be in progress the moment the would-be robber entered the bank. . . . That stage of the crime had not been reached by [the defendants]; their actual embarkation on the robbery lay as much as 90 minutes away from the time when Harper left money in the ATM, and that time had not expired when they were apprehended. . . .

When criminal intent is clear, identifying the point at which the defendants' activities ripen into an attempt is not an analytically satisfying enterprise. There is, however, a substantial difference between causing a bill trap, which will result in the appearance of potential victims, and moving toward such victims with gun and mask, as in [*Moore*]. Making an appointment with a potential victim is not of itself such a commitment to an intended crime as to constitute an attempt, even though it may make a later attempt possible. Little more happened here. . . . Accordingly, we reverse the appellants' convictions for attempted bank robbery.

Question: Would the MPC produce the same result?

United States v. Joyce, 693 F.2d 838 (8th Cir. 1982): [Government informant Gebbie called Joyce and informed him that cocaine] was available for purchase in St. Louis. Joyce indicated that he had twenty-two thousand dollars and would be in St. Louis the following day, October 21, 1980. Gebbie and Joyce agreed that twenty-two thousand dollars would be more than sufficient to purchase a pound of cocaine.

On October 21, 1980, Joyce flew from Oklahoma City [to St. Louis], where he met Gebbie and undercover officer Robert Jones, who was posing as a cocaine seller. Jones and Gebbie took Joyce to a [hotel] room. . . . Jones told Joyce that the cocaine was not in the hotel room, but could be easily obtained by Jones if Joyce was interested in dealing rather than merely talking. After Joyce professed his interest in dealing, Jones recited prices for various quantities of cocaine and Joyce said that he could "handle" a pound of cocaine for twenty thousand dollars. Officer Jones then went to his office and obtained the cocaine.

When officer Jones returned to the hotel room, he handed Joyce a duct-tape wrapped plastic package said to contain a kilogram of cocaine. Without unwrapping the tape, Joyce immediately returned the package, stating that he could not see the cocaine. Jones then unwrapped about half of the tape covering the plastic package and handed the package back to Joyce. Joyce again returned the package to Jones and asked Jones to open up the package so that Joyce could examine the cocaine more closely. Jones answered that he would only open the plastic package if and when Joyce showed the money that he intended to use to purchase the cocaine.[a] Joyce then replied that he would not produce his money until Jones first opened up the plastic package. After Jones persisted in asking Joyce to produce his money, Joyce again refused, stating that he would not deal with officer Jones no matter how good the cocaine was. Realizing that Joyce was not going to show his money or purchase the cocaine, Jones told Joyce to leave and Joyce left, with no apparent intention of returning at a later time to purchase any cocaine.

---

a. Elsewhere in its opinion, the court explained that "Jones was acting in compliance with DEA guidelines which prohibit illegal drugs from going into the physical possession of persons under investigation."—EDS.

As Joyce left the hotel, he was arrested by DEA agents. A search warrant was thereafter obtained and used to search Joyce's luggage revealing twenty-two thousand dollars in cash.

[Joyce was convicted of attempting to purchase cocaine with intent to distribute, but the Eighth Circuit, applying the MPC test, reversed:]

Whatever intention Joyce had to procure cocaine was abandoned prior to the commission of a necessary and substantial step to effectuate the purchase. . . . While Joyce professed a desire to purchase cocaine during his preliminary discussions with Jones, Joyce never attempted to carry through with that desire by producing the money necessary to purchase and hence ultimately possess the cocaine. And, although Jones gave Joyce the sealed and wrapped package said to contain a kilogram of cocaine, Joyce did not open the package but immediately returned [it]. Thus, all we have here is a preliminary discussion regarding the purchase of cocaine which broke down. . . .

We also find unpersuasive the government's claim that Joyce would have purchased the cocaine had it not been for Jones's refusal to open the package of cocaine. We simply fail to see why Joyce's motive for refusing to commit a "substantial step" toward possession of the cocaine is particularly relevant. Joyce's motive for refusing to purchase the cocaine here is no different than had he refused to purchase because he disagreed with Jones as to the price for which the cocaine was offered. And, while we may agree with the government's suggestion that Joyce, who was presumably "street-wise," may have been tipped off that Jones was a DEA undercover agent when Jones refused to open the package, we fail to see how an increased awareness of the risk of apprehension converts what would otherwise be "mere preparation" into an attempt.

Question: Is the result sound? Compare People v. Acosta, 609 N.E.2d 518, 521 (N.Y. 1993):

> A person who orders illegal narcotics from a supplier, admits a courier into his or her home and examines the quality of the goods has unquestionably passed beyond mere preparation and come "very near" to possessing those drugs. Indeed, the only remaining step between the attempt and the completed crime is the person's acceptance of the proffered merchandise, an act entirely within his or her control.

2. Note that under MPC §5.01(1)(c), the actus reus of attempt can include "an act or omission constituting a substantial step. . . . " How (or when) can *an omission* constitute a substantial step? Suppose that one evening a nursing home attendant who has a duty to care for an elderly patient deliberately chooses not to bring the patient her medicine because the attendant can no longer tolerate the patient's complaints and wants to see the patient dead. A few hours later, another attendant discovers the patient in distress because of the missed medications but manages to rectify the situation. Has the first attendant taken "a substantial step" sufficient to make him guilty of attempted murder? See Michael T. Cahill, Attempt by Omission, 94 Iowa L. Rev. 1208 (2009).

4. Solicitation

STATE v. DAVIS

Supreme Court of Missouri
319 Mo. 1222, 6 S.W.2d 609 (1928)

DAVIS, C. [Defendant was convicted of attempted murder in the first degree on the following facts. He and Alberdina Lourie planned to have the latter's husband, Edmon Lourie, killed in order to collect the insurance and live together. He sought the help of Earl Leverton in obtaining an ex-convict to do the job, but Leverton disclosed the plot to Dill, a police officer, who decided to pose as the ex-convict. Defendant paid Dill $600 to carry out plans he had devised for killing Lourie. After several conferences and one aborted plan, a scheme was arranged whereby Dill was to appear at the Lourie home, kill Edmon, and feign a robbery by "mussing up" Alberdina and taking her jewels. At the appointed hour Dill appeared at the Lourie home but at this point revealed his identity. He then proceeded to defendant's home where he made an arrest.]

The sufficiency of the evidence to sustain the conviction is raised. . . .

[T]he great weight of authority warrants the assertion that mere solicitation, unaccompanied by an act moving directly toward the commission of the intended crime, is not an overt act constituting an element of the crime of attempt. [T]he state contends that the arrangement of a plan for the accomplishment of the murder of Lourie and the selecting and hiring of the means or instrumentality by which the murder was to be consummated were demonstrated. We take it that the state means by the foregoing declarations that overt acts were shown. To that we do not agree. The evidence goes no further than developing a verbal arrangement with Dill, the selection of Dill as the one to kill Lourie, the delivery of a certain drawing and two photographs of Lourie to Dill, and the payment of a portion of the agreed consideration. These things were mere acts of preparation, failing to lead directly or proximately to the consummation of the intended crime. . . .

The employment of Dill as agent to murder Lourie was not tantamount to an attempt. Dill not only had no intention of carrying out the expressed purpose of defendant, but was guilty of no act directly or indirectly moving toward the consummation of the intended crime. He did nothing more than listen to the plans and solicitations of defendant without intending to act upon them. It was not shown that Dill committed an act that could be construed as an attempt. . . .

It follows from what we have said that the judgment must be reversed, and the defendant discharged. It is so ordered.

United States v. Church, 29 M.J. 679 (A.C.M.R. 1989): [Appellant] was found guilty of the attempted premeditated murder of his wife [and sentenced] to a dishonorable discharge, confinement for ten years, [and] forfeiture of all pay and allowances. . . . [On appeal] defense counsel conceded that the appellant is guilty of soliciting another to commit murder, but argued forcefully that he was not guilty of attempted murder because no act beyond mere preparation was proven.[3] To resolve this matter, it will be necessary to review the evidence of record in some detail.

[Appellant, an airman stationed in North Dakota, had separated from his wife after two years of marriage. The wife won custody of their son and moved with the child to Michigan. Appellant hoped to regain custody of his son but realized that he was unlikely to succeed in doing so through the courts. At that point he began talking about finding a "hit man" to kill his wife. Eventually some of appellant's associates began to take him seriously, and they reported the matter to the Office of Special Investigations (OSI). Shortly thereafter, an undercover OSI agent was presented as a "hit man."

[In a motel room meeting, appellant provided the agent with a partial payment, expense money for the round trip flight to Michigan, street maps of Mrs. Church's neighborhood, photographs of Mrs. Church and their son, and descriptions of all the people in the house, including where they slept and what their work schedules were. Appellant also approved use of the weapon the agent presented, a .22-caliber pistol with silencer, and he expressed a preference for where on the victim he wanted the shots placed. The job was to be done while appellant was conspicuously on duty in North Dakota. Unbeknownst to appellant, the entire conversation was videotaped. Several days later, appellant was notified through command channels that his wife had been murdered. Appellant put on "a Class A act" of grief. That same day, he was notified by the undercover agent to meet him at the North Dakota motel. Appellant arrived, expressed satisfaction with the job done, paid the agent, and identified his wife's "body" from a staged photograph. This meeting also was videotaped. Appellant was then arrested.]

In various factual situations involving "contracting out" for crimes, [many courts have] held that the evidence only established mere acts of preparation not leading directly or proximately to consummation of the intended crime. . . . Typical [is *State v. Davis*, supra]. . . .

Not all authority favors the defense position. A few state courts have upheld attempt convictions in cases involving crimes for hire. . . . We are not convinced [that] a factual situation such as that present in the *Davis* [case] [should] not constitute an attempt to commit a crime. . . . The appellant's conduct in obtaining the services of Nicholas Karnezis [the purported "hit man"] to murder his wife, his detailed participation in planning the intended crime, up to advising the agent exactly how he wanted his wife shot, and his payment of the agreed upon consideration, . . . constitutes "a substantial step toward commission of the crime," and establishes the requisite overt act amounting to more than mere preparation. We can envision

---

3. Among other punishments, confinement for 20 years is authorized for attempted murder, whereas the period of confinement authorized for soliciting another to commit murder is 5 years. . . .

nothing else the appellant could possibly have done to effect what he believed would be his wife's murder, short of committing the act himself (which is precisely what he did not want to do). As characterized by appellate government counsel during oral argument, the appellant armed a missile (Nick) and fired it off, fully believing it was aimed directly at his intended victim.

NOTE

On review of the decision in *Church*, the U.S. Court of Military Appeals noted (32 M.J. 70, 70-71 n.1, 74 n.7 (1991)):

The real stake in this appeal is the sentence. [See footnote 3 of the lower court's opinion.] Of course, if the facts stood as appellant believed and hoped them to be, he would be guilty as a principal to premeditated murder—and conspiracy as well. Under those circumstances, the *minimum* term he could have received would have been confinement for life. Fortuitously for all concerned, appellant's efforts were frustrated by law enforcement personnel. Thus, murder is not applicable because the intended victim is not dead. Conspiracy is also arguably not available because the *agent* did not actually agree to kill Mrs. Church. . . .

These vast distinctions in punishment ceilings among solicitations, attempts, and completed offenses . . . reflect the traditional view that the punishment should be commensurate with the *resulting harm*, irrespective of the badness of the actor or the seriousness of the threat. The modern approach, on the other hand, . . . is to make the punishment levels generally the same or nearly the same for solicitations, attempts, and completed offenses—based upon the badness of the actor, not upon the fortuitousness of the results. See, e.g., [MPC] §5.05; §2X1.1, Federal Sentencing Guidelines. Narrowing these vast discrepancies in punishment ceilings would lessen the premium put on factfinder hair-splitting as the evidence proceeds down the continuum of solicitation, conspiratorial agreement, [attempt], etc. It would also remove the illogical consequence that the punishment for soliciting premeditated murder can be no greater than that for soliciting the making of a check of $101 without sufficient funds.

Affirming the conviction, the court held:

It is clear that appellant did everything he thought not only necessary but possible to make the enterprise successful. . . . Looking to his conduct only, we agree the evidence was sufficient for a rational factfinder to find, beyond a reasonable doubt, that his actions exceeded mere preparation.

NOTES ON SOLICITATION

1. Solicitation as an attempt. Near the end of its opinion in *Davis*, the court states: "It was not shown that Dill committed an act that could be construed as an attempt." What difference would it have made if Dill *had* gone further? Would the prosecution's difficulties have been solved if Dill had been instructed to play the scene to the hilt, for example, by aiming his pistol at the husband's chest? Since Dill was only a feigned participant, traditional common-law doctrines would not permit him to be treated as Davis's *accomplice,* and therefore Davis could not be held accountable for the steps taken by Dill, no matter how far those steps went. Davis's liability would have to rest on *his own* actions. See *State v. Hayes,* page 693 infra.

Courts differ over the question whether the solicitation itself constitutes an attempt by the person making it. In accord with *Church,* many courts hold that a solicitation can constitute a punishable attempt if it represents a "substantial step" under the circumstances. See Ashford v. Commonwealth., 626 S.E.2d 464 (Va. App. 2006); United States v. May, 625 F.2d 186, 194 (8th Cir. 1980). But many states adhere to the view that "no matter what acts the solicitor commits, he cannot be guilty of an attempt because it is not his purpose to commit the offense personally." Model Penal Code and Commentaries, Comment to §5.02 at 369 (1985).

2. *Solicitation as an independent crime.* At common law, inciting or soliciting another to commit a crime was a crime itself, independent of any other offense that either party might commit. For a long time, American codes by and large did not contain provisions incorporating this offense, but rather made criminal the solicitation of particular crimes. However, a substantial number of states now have general solicitation statutes. They are usually patterned after MPC §5.02. The commentary defends that formulation as follows (Model Penal Code and Commentaries, Comment to §5.02 at 365-366, 375-378 (1985)):

> It has been argued [that the solicitor's] conduct is not dangerous because the resisting will of an independent moral agent is interposed between the solicitor and the commission of the crime that is his object. By the same token it is urged that the solicitor, manifesting his reluctance to commit the crime himself, is not a significant menace. The opposing view is that a solicitation is, if anything, more dangerous than a direct attempt, because it may give rise to the special hazard of cooperation among criminals. Solicitation may, indeed, be thought of as an attempt to conspire. . . .
>
> There should be no doubt on this issue. Purposeful solicitation presents dangers calling for preventive intervention and is sufficiently indicative of a disposition towards criminal activity to call for liability. Moreover, the fortuity that the person solicited does not agree to commit or attempt to commit the incited crime plainly should not relieve the solicitor of liability, when otherwise he would be a conspirator or an accomplice.

3. *Free speech.* Suppose the speaker at a political rally harshly attacks the party in power and says, "These bums deserve to die." Is the speaker guilty of solicitation to commit murder? Consider whether a prosecutor could satisfy the requirements for conviction under MPC §5.02. Less dramatically, suppose that a speaker urges members of his church to provide shelter and employment to illegal immigrants who are fleeing from persecution abroad but are unable to qualify for political asylum in the United States. Is the speaker guilty of solicitation to violate the immigration laws?

Solicitation of crime may in some circumstances be protected speech under the First Amendment. For a sustained discussion of this and related issues see

Kent Greenawalt, Speech, Crime, and the Uses of Language (1989). On the line between punishable and protected speech, see Rice v. Paladin Enterprises, 128 F.3d 233 (4th Cir. 1997), where the publisher of a how-to-do-it murder manual was held civilly liable for the murder of three people committed by a person who had used the manual.

5. *Impossibility*

PEOPLE v. JAFFE

New York Court of Appeals
185 N.Y. 497, 78 N.E. 169 (1906)

BARTLETT, J. The indictment charged that the defendant on the 6th day of October, 1902, in the county of New York, feloniously received 20 yards of cloth, of the value of 25 cents a yard, belonging to the copartnership of J.W. Goddard & Son, knowing that the said property had been feloniously stolen, taken, and carried away from the owners. It was found under section 550 of the Penal Code, which provides that a person who buys or receives any stolen property knowing the same to have been stolen is guilty of criminally receiving such property. The defendant was convicted of an attempt to commit the crime charged in the indictment. The proof clearly showed, and the district attorney conceded upon the trial, that the goods which the defendant attempted to purchase on October 6, 1902, had lost their character as stolen goods at the time when they were offered to the defendant and when he sought to buy them. In fact the property had been restored to the owners and was wholly within their control and was offered to the defendant by their authority and through their agency. The question presented by this appeal, therefore, is whether upon an indictment for receiving goods, knowing them to have been stolen, the defendant may be convicted of an attempt to commit the crime where it appears without dispute that the property which he sought to receive was not in fact stolen property.

The conviction was sustained by the Appellate Division chiefly upon the authority of the numerous cases in which it has been held that one may be convicted of an attempt to commit a crime notwithstanding the existence of facts unknown to him which would have rendered the complete perpetration of the crime itself impossible. Notably among these are what may be called the "Pickpocket Cases," where, in prosecutions for attempts to commit larceny from the person by pocketpicking, it is held not to be necessary to allege or prove that there was anything in the pocket which could be the subject of larceny. Much reliance was also placed in the opinion of the learned Appellate Division upon the case of People v. Gardner, 144 N.Y. 119, 38 N.E. 1003, where a conviction of an attempt to commit the crime of extortion was upheld, although the woman from whom the defendant sought to obtain money by a threat to accuse her of a crime was not induced to pay the money by fear, but was acting at the time as a decoy for the police, and hence could not have been subjected to the influence of fear.

In passing upon the question here presented for our determination, it is important to bear in mind precisely what it was that the defendant attempted to do. He simply made an effort to purchase certain specific pieces of cloth. He believed the cloth to be stolen property, but it was not such in fact. The purchase, therefore, if it had been completely effected, could not constitute the crime of receiving stolen property, knowing it to be stolen, since there could be no such thing as knowledge on the part of the defendant of a non-existent fact, although there might be a belief on his part that the fact existed. . . .

The crucial distinction between the case before us and the pickpocket cases, and others involving the same principle, lies not in the possibility or impossibility of the commission of the crime, but in the fact that, in the present case, the act, which it was doubtless the intent of the defendant to commit, would not have been a crime if it had been consummated. If he had actually paid for the goods which he desired to buy and received them into his possession, he would have committed no offense under section 550 of the Penal Code, because [it is] an essential element of the crime that the accused shall have known the property to have been stolen. . . . No man can know that to be so which is not so in truth and in fact. He may believe it to be so but belief is not enough under this statute. In the present case . . . the goods which the defendant intended to purchase had lost their character as stolen goods at the time of the proposed transaction. Hence, no matter what was the motive of the defendant, and no matter what he supposed, he could do no act which was intrinsically adapted to the then present successful perpetration of the crime denounced by this section of the Penal Code, because neither he nor any one in the world could know that the property was stolen property inasmuch as it was not, in fact, stolen property. In the pickpocket cases the immediate act which the defendant had in contemplation was an act which, if it could have been carried out, would have been criminal, whereas in the present case the immediate act which the defendant had in contemplation (to wit, the purchase of the goods which were brought to his place for sale) could not have been criminal under the statute even if the purchase had been completed. . . .

If all which an accused person intends to do would, if done, constitute no crime, it cannot be a crime to attempt to do with the same purpose a part of the thing intended. The crime of which the defendant was convicted necessarily consists of three elements: First, the act; second, the intent; and third, the knowledge of an existing condition. There was proof tending to establish two of these elements, the first and second, but none to establish the existence of the third. . . . The defendant could not know that the property possessed the character of stolen property when it had not in fact been acquired by theft. . . . A particular belief cannot make that a crime which is not so in the absence of such belief. Take, for example, the case of a young man who attempts to vote, and succeeds in casting his vote under the belief that he is but 20 years of age, when he is in fact over 21 and a qualified voter. His intent to commit a crime, and his belief that he was committing a crime, would not make him guilty of any offense under these circumstances, although the moral turpitude of the transaction, on his part, would be just as great as it would if he were in fact under age. So also, in the case of a prosecution under the statute of this state, which makes it rape in the second degree for a man to perpetrate an act of sexual intercourse with a female not his wife under the age of 18 years. There could be no conviction if it was established upon the trial that the female was in fact over the age of 18 years, although the defendant believed her to be younger and intended to commit the crime. No matter how reprehensible would be his act in morals, it would not be the act forbidden by this particular statute. "If what a man contemplates doing would not be in law a crime, he could not be said, in point of law, to intend to commit the crime. If he thinks his act will be a crime, this is a mere mistake of his understanding where the law holds it not to be such, his real intent being to do a particular thing. If the thing is not a crime, he does not intend to commit one whatever he may erroneously suppose." 1 Bishop's Crim. Law (7th Ed.) §742.

The judgment of the Appellate Division and of the Court of General Sessions must be reversed, and the defendant discharged upon this indictment. . . .

PEOPLE v. DLUGASH

New York Court of Appeals
41 N.Y.2d 725, 363 N.E.2d 1155 (1977)

JASEN, J. . . . The 1967 revision of the Penal Law approached the impossibility defense to the inchoate crime of attempt in a novel fashion. The statute provides that, if a person engaged in conduct which would otherwise constitute an attempt to commit a crime,

> it is no defense to a prosecution for such attempt that the crime charged to have been attempted was, under the attendant circumstances, factually or legally impossible of commission, if such crime could have been committed had the attendant circumstances been as such person believed them to be.

(Penal Law, §110.10.) This appeal presents to us, for the first time, a case involving the application of the modern statute. We hold that, under the proof presented by the People at trial, defendant Melvin Dlugash may be held for attempted murder [of Michael Geller], though the target of the attempt may have already been slain, by the hand of another [Bush], when Dlugash made his felonious attempt. . . .

Defendant stated [to police] that, on the night of December 21, 1973, he, Bush and Geller had been out drinking. Bush had been staying at Geller's apartment and, during the course of the evening, Geller several times demanded that Bush pay $100 towards the rent on the apartment. According to defendant, Bush rejected these demands, telling Geller that "you better shut up or you're going to get a bullet." All three returned to Geller's apartment at approximately midnight, took seats in the bedroom, and continued to drink until sometime between 3:00 and 3:30 in the morning. When Geller again pressed his demand for rent money, Bush drew his .38 caliber pistol, aimed it at Geller and fired three times. Geller fell to the floor. After the passage of a few minutes, perhaps two, perhaps as much as five, defendant walked over to the fallen Geller, drew his .25 caliber pistol, and fired approximately five shots in the victim's head and face. Defendant contended that, by the time he fired the shots, "it looked like Mike Geller was already dead." . . .

After [Officer] Carrasquillo had taken the bulk of the statement, he asked the defendant why he would do such a thing. According to Carrasquillo, the defendant said, "gee, I really don't know." Carrasquillo repeated the question 10 minutes later, but received the same response. After a while, Carrasquillo asked the question for a third time and defendant replied, "well, gee, I guess it must have been because I was afraid of Joe Bush."

[A]t the trial . . . the prosecution sought to establish that Geller was still alive at the time defendant shot at him. Both physicians testified that each of the two chest wounds, for which defendant alleged Bush to be responsible, would have caused death without prompt medical attention. Moreover, the victim would have remained alive until such time as his chest cavity became fully filled with blood. Depending on the circumstances, it might take 5 to 10 minutes for the chest cavity to fill. Neither prosecution witness could state, with medical certainty, that the victim was still alive when, perhaps five minutes after the initial chest wounds were inflicted, the defendant fired at the victim's head.

The defense produced but a single witness, the former Chief Medical Examiner of New York City. This expert said that, in his view, Geller might have died of the chest wounds "very rapidly" since, in addition to the bleeding, a large bullet going through a lung and the heart would have other adverse medical effects. . . .

The trial court declined to charge the jury, as requested by the prosecution, that defendant could be guilty of murder on the theory that he had aided and abetted the killing of Geller by Bush. Instead, the court submitted only two theories to the jury: that defendant had either intentionally murdered Geller or had attempted to murder Geller. The jury found the defendant guilty of murder. . . .

On appeal, the Appellate Division . . . ruled that "the People failed to prove beyond a reasonable doubt that Geller had been alive at the time he was shot by defendant; defendant's conviction of murder thus cannot stand." . . . Further, the court held that the judgment could not be modified to reflect a conviction for attempted murder because "the uncontradicted evidence is that the defendant, at the time that he fired the five shots into the body of the decedent, believed him to be dead." . . .

To sustain a homicide conviction, it must be established, beyond a reasonable doubt, that the defendant caused the death of another person. [A]ll three medical expert witnesses testified that they could not, with any degree of medical certainty, state whether the victim had been alive at the time . . . shots were fired by the defendant. Thus, the People failed to prove beyond a reasonable doubt that the victim had been alive at the time he was shot by the defendant. Whatever else it may be, it is not murder to shoot a dead body. . . .

[W]e must now decide whether, under the evidence presented, the defendant may be held for attempted murder. . . .

The most intriguing attempt cases are those where the attempt to commit a crime was unsuccessful due to mistakes of fact or law on the part of the would-be criminal. A general rule developed in most American jurisdictions that legal impossibility is a good defense but factual impossibility is not. . . . Thus, for example, it was held that defendants who shot at a stuffed deer did not attempt to take a deer out of season, even though they believed the dummy to be a live animal. The court stated that there was no criminal attempt because it was no crime to "take" a stuffed deer, and it is no crime to attempt to do that which is legal. (State v. Guffey, 262 S.W.2d 152 [Mo. Ct. App.]; see, also, State v. Taylor, 345 Mo. 325, 133 S.W.2d 336 [no liability for attempt to bribe a juror where person bribed was not, in fact, a juror].) These cases are illustrative of legal impossibility. . . .

On the other hand, factual impossibility was no defense. For example, a man was held liable for attempted murder when he shot into the room in which his target usually slept and, fortuitously, the target was sleeping elsewhere in the house that night. Although one bullet struck the target's customary pillow, attainment of the criminal objective was factually impossible. . . .

The New York cases can be parsed out along similar lines. One of the leading cases on legal impossibility is People v. Jaffe, 185 N.Y. 497, in which we held that there was no liability for the attempted receipt of stolen property when the property received by the defendant in the belief that it was stolen was, in fact, under the control of the true owner. . . . Factual impossibility, however, was no defense. Thus, a man could be held for attempted grand larceny when he picked an empty pocket. . . .

As can be seen from even this abbreviated discussion, the distinction between "factual" and "legal" impossibility was a nice one indeed and the courts tended to place a greater value on legal form than on any substantive danger the defendant's actions posed for society. The approach of the draftsmen of the Model Penal Code was to eliminate the defense of impossibility in virtually all situations. [See §5.01(1).] Under the code provision, to constitute an attempt, it is still necessary that the result intended or desired by the actor constitute a crime. However, the code suggested a fundamental change to shift the locus of analysis to the actor's mental frame of reference and away from undue dependence upon external considerations. The basic premise of the code provision is that what was in the actor's own mind should be the standard for determining his dangerousness to society and, hence, his liability for attempted criminal conduct. . . . In the belief that neither of the two branches of the traditional impossibility arguments detracts from the offender's moral culpability . . . the Legislature substantially carried the [MPC] treatment of impossibility into the 1967 revision of the Penal Law. . . . Thus, a person is guilty of an attempt when, with intent to commit a crime, he engages in conduct which tends to effect the commission of such crime. (Penal Law, §110.00.) It is no defense that, under the attendant circumstances, the crime was factually or legally impossible of commission, "if such crime could have been committed had the attendant circumstances been as such person believed them to be." Thus, if defendant believed the victim to be alive at the time of the shooting, it is no defense to the charge of attempted murder that the victim may have been dead. . . .

Turning to the facts of the case before us, we believe that there is sufficient evidence in the record from which the jury could conclude that the defendant believed Geller to be alive at the time defendant fired shots into Geller's head. . . .

The jury convicted the defendant of murder. Necessarily, they found that defendant intended to kill a live human being. Subsumed within this finding is the conclusion that defendant acted in the belief that Geller was alive. Thus, there is no need for additional fact findings by a jury. Although it was not established beyond a reasonable doubt that Geller was, in fact, alive, such is no defense to attempted murder since a murder would have been committed "had the attendant circumstances been as [defendant] believed them to be." . . .

The Appellate Division erred in not modifying the judgment to reflect a conviction for the lesser included offense of attempted murder. . . .

NOTES ON IMPOSSIBILITY

1. Factual impossibility. When attempts misfire because of poor aim or the use of an inadequate weapon, such as an unloaded gun, courts have traditionally classified the situation as one of factual impossibility and denied a defense. In State v. Smith, 621 A.2d 493 (N.J. Super. 1993), the defendant was a county jail inmate who had tested positive for HIV, the virus that causes AIDS. During an altercation with several guards, defendant spat in one officer's face, bit his hand, and said, "[N]ow die you pig, die from what I have." At his trial for attempted murder of the officer, defendant offered evidence that it was medically impossible to transmit HIV by spitting or biting, but the court held, affirming the conviction, that such evidence was irrelevant so long as the defendant believed it possible to infect the officer and intended to kill him.

2. Legal impossibility. Prior to the enactment of statutes addressed to the issue of impossibility, courts had taken a variety of positions. All courts agreed that there was a defense of legal impossibility when, unknown to the actor, what the actor planned to do had not been made criminal. There was dispute, however, over whether "legal impossibility" could be a defense in other situations, and if so, how it was distinguished from "factual impossibility," which was not a defense.

The California Supreme Court, in a case virtually identical to *Jaffe*, reached the opposite result. People v. Rojas, 358 P.2d 921 (Cal. 1961). The California court rejected the precedent of the *Jaffe* case, quoting approvingly the following criticism of that decision in Jerome Hall, General Principles of Criminal Law 127 (1947):

> Intent is in the mind; it is not the external realities to which intention refers. The fact that defendant was mistaken regarding the external realities did not alter his intention, but simply made it impossible to effectuate it.

The MPC has had a major influence on this debate. About two-thirds of the states have revised their codes since the MPC proposals were formulated. Nearly all of them have rejected the impossibility defense entirely. See Model Penal Code and Commentaries, Comment to §5.01 at 317 (1985). Another factor driving recent resistance to the *Jaffe* view has been the perceived importance of police use of undercover officers who impersonate minors, as a way to catch adults who use the internet to arrange encounters in which they can victimize underage children. See Audrey Rogers, Protecting Children on the Internet: Mission Impossible?, 61 Baylor L. Rev. 323 (2009). Where the traditional defense of legal impossibility is recognized, the suspect in such a situation could have a defense if the intended victim turned out to be an adult. In King v. State, 921 N.E.2d 1288 (Ind. 2010), the court upheld an attempt conviction in this situation, overruling prior decisions that had permitted an impossibility defense.

Most of the federal courts of appeals now follow the MPC approach. See United States v. Yang, 281 F.3d 534, 542 (6th Cir. 2002). But a few have resisted it. The following cases illustrate two approaches that differ from that of the MPC.

United States v. Berrigan, 482 F.2d 171 (3d Cir. 1973): [Father Berrigan, an imprisoned Vietnam War resister, was convicted of an attempt to violate a federal statute making it criminal to take anything into or out of a federal prison contrary to regulations of the attorney general. The latter had promulgated a regulation prohibiting such traffic "without the knowledge and consent" of the prison warden. The conviction was based on evidence that Berrigan had smuggled letters into and out of a prison through a courier, believing that the warden was ignorant of what was going on. In fact, the warden had prior knowledge of the arrangement and had agreed to let the courier pretend cooperation in the plan. The court reversed the conviction:] Generally speaking factual impossibility is said to occur when extraneous circumstances unknown to the actor or beyond his control prevent consummation of the intended crime. The classic example is the man who puts his hand in the coat pocket of another with the intent to steal his wallet and finds the pocket empty. . . . Legal impossibility is said to occur where the intended acts, even if completed, would not amount to a crime. Thus, legal impossibility would apply to those circumstances where (1) the motive, desire and expectation is to perform an act in violation of the law; (2) there is intention to perform a physical act; (3) there is a performance of the intended physical act; and (4) the consequence resulting from the intended act does not amount to a crime.[35]

Were intent to break the law the sole criterion to be considered in determining criminal responsibility . . . we could sustain the conviction. . . . Clearly, it can be said that Father Berrigan intended to send letters to Sister McAlister. . . . Normally, of course, the exchange of letters is not a federal offense. Where one of the senders is in prison, however, the sending may or may not be a criminal offense. If the letter is sent within normal channels with the consent and knowledge of the warden it is not a criminal offense. . . . If the letter is sent without the knowledge and consent of the warden, it is a criminal offense and so is the attempt because both the intended consequence and the actual consequence are in fact criminal. Here, we are faced with a third situation where there is a motivation, desire and expectation of sending a letter without the knowledge and consent, and the intended act is performed, but unknown to the sender, the transmittal is accomplished with the knowledge and consent of the warden.

Applying the principles of the law of attempt to the instant case, the writing of the letters, and their copying and transmittal by the courier . . . constituted the *Act*. . . . What the government did not prove—and could not prove because it was a legal impossibility—was the "external, objective situation which the substantive law may require to be present," to-wit, absence of knowledge and consent of the warden. . . . Without such proof, the *Consequence* or *Result* did not constitute an offense that violated the federal statute. . . . Simply stated, attempting to do that which is not a crime is not attempting to commit a crime.[a]

United States v. Oviedo, 525 F.2d 881 (5th Cir. 1976): [An undercover agent contacted defendant and asked to buy heroin. Defendant agreed and appeared at an arranged time and place with what he claimed was heroin. The agent then performed a field test with positive result and arrested defendant. However, a later laboratory test of the substance revealed it was not in fact heroin but procaine hydrochloride (not a controlled substance), which happens to give a positive reaction to the usual field test. The prosecution therefore charged defendant with attempted distribution of heroin, and a jury convicted, apparently rejecting defendant's testimony that he knew the

---

35. Intent as used in this connection must be distinguished from motive, desire, and expectation. If *C* by reason of his hatred of *A* plans to kill him, but mistaking *B* for *A* shoots *B*, his motive desire and expectation are to kill *A* but his intent is to kill *B*. . . . If *A* takes an umbrella which he believes to belong to *B*, but which in fact is his own, he does not have the intent to steal, his intent being to take the umbrella he grasps in his hand, which is his own umbrella. . . . If a man mistakes a stump for his enemy and shoots at it, notwithstanding his desire and expectation to shoot his enemy, his intent is to shoot the object aimed at, which is the stump. Keedy, Criminal Attempts at Common Law, 102 U. of Pa. L. Rev. 464, 466-467 (1954). . . .

a. In a subsequent decision, the Third Circuit limited *Berrigan* to its facts and instead adopted an approach comparable to that of the MPC. United States v. Hsu, 155 F.3d 189 (3d Cir. 1998). *Berrigan* nonetheless illustrates an analysis that continues to have some influence and intuitive appeal.—EDS.

substance was not heroin and was only trying to "rip off" the agent. On appeal, the Fifth Circuit reversed the conviction.

[The court rejected the traditional distinction between legal and factual impossibility, saying:] These definitions are not particularly helpful here. . . . In one sense, the impossibility involved here might be deemed legal, for those *acts* which Oviedo set in motion, the transfer of the substance in his possession, were not a crime. In another sense, the impossibility is factual, for the *objective* of Oviedo, the sale of heroin, was proscribed by law, and failed only because of a circumstance unknown to Oviedo.

[However, the court also rejected an approach that would find an attempt because the objective of defendant was criminal, since "It would allow us to punish one's thoughts, desires, or motives, through indirect evidence, without reference to any objective fact." The court concluded:] We reject the notion . . . , adopted by the district court, that the conviction in the present case can be sustained since there is sufficient proof of intent, not because of any doubt as to the sufficiency of the evidence in that regard, but because of the inherent dangers such a precedent would pose in the future. . . .

When the defendant sells a substance which is actually heroin, it is reasonable to infer that he knew the physical nature of the substance, and to place on him the burden of dispelling that inference. . . . However, if we convict the defendant of attempting to sell heroin for the sale of a non-narcotic substance, we eliminate an objective element that has major evidentiary significance and we increase the risk of mistaken conclusions that the defendant believed the goods were narcotics.

Thus, we demand that in order for a defendant to be guilty of a criminal attempt, the objective acts performed, without any reliance on the accompanying mens rea, mark the defendant's conduct as criminal in nature. . . . We cannot conclude that the objective acts of Oviedo apart from any indirect evidence of intent mark his conduct as criminal in nature. Rather, those acts are consistent with a noncriminal enterprise. Therefore, we will not allow the jury's determination of Oviedo's intent to form the sole basis of a criminal offense.

THE CASE OF LADY ELDON'S FRENCH LACE

A hypothetical decision on a hypothetical state of facts, by the editors

A perennial in the crop of attempt hypotheticals was suggested by Dr. Wharton.[1] "Lady Eldon, when traveling with her husband on the Continent, bought what she supposed to be a quantity of French lace, which she hid, concealing it from Lord Eldon in one of the pockets of the coach. The package was brought to light by a customs officer at Dover. The lace turned out to be an English manufactured article, of little value, and of course, not subject to duty.

---

1. Criminal Law 304 n.9 (12th ed. 1932).

Lady Eldon had bought it at a price vastly above its value, believing it to be genuine, intending to smuggle it into England." Dr. Wharton, supra, and Professor Sayre[2] conclude that she could be found guilty of an attempt since she intended to smuggle dutiable lace into England. Professor Keedy disagrees, finding the fallacy of the argument in the failure to recognize "that the particular lace which Lady Eldon intended to bring into England was not subject to duty and therefore, although there was the wish to smuggle, there was not the intent to do so."[3]

Keedy was employing the distinction he has advanced between intent, on the one hand, and motive, desire, and expectation, on the other,[4] a distinction that served as the linchpin of the decision in *People v. Jaffe*, supra, and *United States v. Berrigan*, supra. As he sees it, what people intend to do is determined by what they do in fact, rather than by what they thought they were doing. The lace was in fact not dutiable; thus, there was no intent on the part of Lady Eldon to smuggle dutiable French lace into the country, and there could be no conviction of the crime of attempt to do so, since what she intended to do on this view was not a crime—a straightforward case of legal impossibility. Professor Perkins has advocated a similar approach.[5]

We concur with Wharton and Sayre. We submit, with respect, that Keedy and Perkins, and the courts that follow their reasoning, have been guilty of some plain silliness in supporting their position. Their conclusion that Lady Eldon must be acquitted rests on the premise that what a person intends to do is what he actually does, even if that was the furthest thing from the person's mind:

"You're eating my salad."

"Sorry, I didn't mean to; I thought it was mine."

"You might have *thought* it was yours. But in fact it was mine. So it was my salad you intended to eat. You should be ashamed!"

Surely this is an extraordinary way of describing what a person intended, quite at odds with common sense and common language. Where a circumstance is not known to the actor, there is no way consistent with straight thought that his act can be regarded as intentional as to that circumstance.

Of course, it is hardly unknown for courts to adopt strained and artificial reasoning to support a sound result. Is that the case here? Is it sound to conclude that the type of conduct engaged in by Lady Eldon should not be made criminal? Let us consider if it is.

Suppose Lady Eldon believed she had purchased an inexpensive English lace but in fact had purchased an expensive French lace. Certainly she could not be found guilty of smuggling if she got past the customs inspector or of an attempt if she failed. The reason is that the intent to smuggle French lace,

---

2. Criminal Attempts, 41 Harv. L. Rev. 821, 852 (1928).

3. Criminal Attempts at Common Law, 102 U. Pa. L. Rev. 464, 477 n.85 (1954).

4. Id. at 466-468.

5. Rollin M. Perkins, Criminal Attempt and Related Problems, 2 UCLA L. Rev. 319, 330-332 (1955).

necessary to establish either offense, does not exist. (We are assuming this is not a crime of strict liability). And it does not exist because her intent is judged by what she believed she was doing and not by what she in fact did. Now why should it make any more difference in Wharton's hypothetical that her act was objectively lawful than it does in our variation that her act was objectively unlawful? In both cases intent should be judged by the same standard—what she believed she was doing, rather than what she did in fact.

It may be argued that while an innocent mind can exculpate, a criminal mind simpliciter cannot inculpate. The reasoning might be as follows: There is no legitimate purpose to be served by punishing those who mean to act blamelessly. In contrast, a purpose could be served by punishing a person who decides to commit a crime. But it is undesirable to do so, because merely thinking evil is not a reliable indication that a person will do evil, and the criminal law may properly concern itself only with acts. See page 216 supra.

But has Lady Eldon merely *thought* to smuggle French lace? No. She has *done* everything in her power and all she thought necessary to smuggle French lace. Has she shown herself to be less eligible for the imposition of criminal sanctions because, through no fault of her own, she failed? Surely not.

Perhaps it may be argued that there is a different policy supporting exculpation in cases like Lady Eldon's—namely, that in real cases, as opposed to hypotheticals, it is too dangerous to permit juries to speculate on a defendant's intent in the absence of actions that strongly evidence that intent. One may fully agree with this point, however, without concluding that Lady Eldon should be acquitted. Of course it would be evidentiary of Lady Eldon's intent to smuggle if she had been found with dutiable French lace at the border. (But only evidentiary—after all, she might have thought it was English lace, or it might have been put with her things by her maid without her knowledge.) But why should it be held, as it was in *United States v. Oviedo*, supra, that since the lace was nondutiable in fact, a finding of intent will necessarily be suspect, regardless of the strength of the evidence? Suppose, for example, that the lace were carefully secreted in a specially tailored, concealed pocket of the coach; that a letter from Lady Eldon to her sister described her newly bought "French lace" in exquisite and appreciative detail. There would seem little danger to the innocent in allowing a jury to find an attempt to smuggle French lace on these facts. Indeed, in cases like *Jaffe* and *Berrigan*, "attempt" is charged only because of the involvement of an undercover agent, whose participation prevents completion of the intended crime. Whatever else one may say about such investigatory tactics, they do not necessarily render suspect the evidence of the defendant's intent; indeed, in practice, they usually render that evidence far *less* speculative than it otherwise would be. The proper remedy for speculative and unreliable jury findings of intent is a court alert to preclude such findings in particular cases where the evidence is insufficient.

In the end, then, the arguments in favor of Lady Eldon (and those which have been used to reverse convictions in cases like *Jaffe*, *Oviedo*, and *Berrigan*) are founded on unpersuasive policy considerations rationalized by a peculiar and Pickwickian interpretation of what it means to intend an act, one that is utterly at odds both with the common usage of our language and its usage elsewhere in the criminal law. *We conclude that the innocuous character of the action actually done (innocuous in the sense that it could not constitute a crime under the actual circumstances) will not save her from an attempt conviction if she believed that the circumstances were otherwise, and, had her belief been correct, what she set out to do would constitute a crime.* This is the principle that has found favor in virtually every serious statutory effort to deal with the problem, and in numerous decisions reached without benefit of a specific statute to tell the court that a person intends to do what he thinks he intends to do.

We must say a few words more about the final qualification to the principle just asserted; namely, that "had her belief [in the circumstances] been correct, what she set out to do would constitute a crime." The point can best be made by altering the hypothetical. Suppose the lace that Lady Eldon had purchased was in fact the expensive French lace she meant to buy. The customs officer at Dover brings it to light. He then says to Lady Eldon: "Lucky you returned to England today rather than yesterday. I just received word this morning that the government has removed French lace from the duty list." Could Lady Eldon be held for attempt to smuggle French lace in these circumstances? Certainly what she did and what she intended to do were not different simply because she acted one day later, when French lace was removed from the duty list. But there is this important difference: At the time she acted, what she intended to do (always judged, of course, from her own perspective) was not a violation of the criminal law, even though she thought it was.

It is true that Lady Eldon's action showed her to be a person who would break some law under some circumstances. But what law? The law against smuggling French lace? There no longer was such a law. The criminal laws generally? Our law does not hold that *any* antisocial attitude is sufficient to justify criminal punishment. That a person was willing to violate what she thought was the law raises the odds of her violating an actual law in the future. But as Professor Williams has pointed out, "if the legislature has not seen fit to prohibit the consummated act, a mere approach to consummation should a fortiori be guiltless. Any other view would offend against the principle of legality; in effect the law of attempt would be used to manufacture a new crime, when the legislature has left the situation outside the ambit of the law." Glanville Williams, Criminal Law: The General Part 633-634 (2d ed. 1961). Had the criminal law been changed as supposed in our variation of the Lady Eldon hypothetical, therefore, it would be just as wrong to convict her as to convict an abortionist of attempted abortion where the abortion was committed, unknown to the defendant, after the abortion law was repealed or held invalid. These are the true cases of legal impossibility.

But, it should be noted, these situations are totally different from cases like *Jaffe* and *Berrigan*, even though the courts in each case made it seem otherwise, by asserting that what the defendants intended to do could not have constituted a crime. What the abortionist intended to do (and did) could not constitute a crime because there was no such crime. What Jaffe and Berrigan intended to do (and thought they did) was indeed a crime. It is only through a perverse use of intent that we can say that Jaffe intended to receive honestly obtained property or that Berrigan intended to send out a letter the warden knew about, and that therefore they intended to do what was no crime at all.

Lady Eldon, in the actual hypothetical, in contrast to the modified hypothetical, presents no more a case of genuine legal impossibility than do *Jaffe* and *Berrigan.* She will be convicted of attempt to smuggle French lace.

Comment, 9 Hypothetical L. Rev. 1, 3-4 (1962-2012): The hypothetical *Lady Eldon* decision is a good effort, but it doesn't quite work.

First: Consider a safecracker who tries to open a safe with magic incantations. Under the *Lady Eldon* analysis, the safecracker would merely have made a mistake of fact, and he could be convicted of attempt. Or consider the case of Leroy Ivy and John Henry Ivy, two brothers who tried to use voodoo to kill a judge who had sentenced one of them to prison for robbery.[1] The brothers paid the judge's housekeeper $100 for his photo and a lock of his hair, which they planned to mail to a voodoo practitioner in Jamaica. Police officers in Tupelo, Mississippi, foiled the plot by arresting Leroy Ivy before he could send off the items needed to cast the spell. Charged with attempting to kill the judge, the brothers pleaded guilty and were sentenced to five and ten years respectively. But these defendants, like the safecracker, are more pathetic than dangerous.

The MPC, recognizing this problem, gives a court the power to dismiss a prosecution or decrease the penalty if the alleged attempt "is so inherently unlikely to result or culminate in the commission of a crime that neither such conduct nor the actor presents a public danger." Section 5.05(2). But this solution leaves the matter to the discretion of the judge; it is not a rule of law. A better approach is that developed by Professor Robbins, who proposes that a person be guilty of attempt only when "he purposely does or omits to do anything that, *under the circumstances as a reasonable person would believe them to be,*" is a substantial step in a course of conduct planned to culminate in commission of the crime.[2]

Second: The effort to deal with the so-called true legal impossibility problem is not convincing. Consider the following case. Two friends, Mr. Fact and Mr. Law, go hunting in the morning of October 15 in the fields of the state of Dakota, whose law allows hunting on that date but makes it a misdemeanor to hunt before October 1. Both men kill deer on their first day out. Mr. Fact thinks he has committed a crime because he is under the erroneous belief that the date is September 15 (when hunting is illegal). Mr. Law thinks he has

---

1. For accounts of the case, see Fred Grimm, Man Charged in Plot to Kill Judge By Hex, Miami Herald, Mar. 31, 1989, at 1, 10; R.J. Smith, Conspiracy to Commit Voodoo, Village Voice, Sept. 26, 1989, at 37-41.

2. Ira P. Robbins, Attempting the Impossible: The Emerging Consensus, 23 Harv. J. Legis. 377, 441 (1986) (emphasis added). See also N.J. Stat. Ann. §2C:5-1a(1) (2011).

committed a crime because he is under the erroneous belief that hunting is permitted only in November (as it was the previous year). Under the principle proposed by the editors to deal with Lady Eldon's case, Mr. Fact could be convicted of an attempt to hunt out of season, but Mr. Law could not be. We fail to see how any rational system of criminal law could justify convicting one and acquitting the other on the fragile and unpersuasive distinction that one made a mistake of fact, and the other made a mistake of law. If the ultimate test is the dangerousness of the actor (i.e., readiness to violate the law), as *Lady Eldon* would have it, no distinction is warranted—Mr. Law has indicated himself to be no less "dangerous" than Mr. Fact.[3]

The same point can be made with the very example that the editors use to support their *Lady Eldon* opinion—the case in which, unbeknownst to Lady Eldon, French lace has just been removed from the duty list. The editors ask, in effect, *What law* is she likely to break? Not smuggling French lace, they say, because there's no longer such a law. Correct. Not criminal laws generally, they say, because that would rest criminality on mere speculation. Correct again. But how about the law against smuggling? Has she shown herself to be less a smuggler, just because she arrived right after French lace had been removed from the duty list? The editors err in treating the case as if duties had been repealed on all goods, whereas only one item had been removed from the duty list.

Third: The opinion overlooks the strong case for retaining the defense in one class of *factual* impossibility cases. These are the cases in which the acts done by the defendant are consistent with an innocent state of mind. Take, for example, the old saw about the professor who takes his own umbrella thinking it belongs to his colleague. The act is utterly neutral. A man taking his own umbrella conveys no evidence of guilt. Of course, the matter changes if it can be proved that he believed it was his colleague's umbrella. But proof of state of mind is inherently unreliable where there are only ambiguous acts to support the inference.

Consider how the MPC deals with this very concern when it addresses itself to a different problem, i.e., drawing the line between preparation and attempt. This is typically the situation in which the actor has not yet completed all he set out to do. In §5.01, the MPC requires that his acts be "strongly

---

3. For discussion of the problems posed by this hypothetical, see Kenneth W. Simons, Mistake and Impossibility, Law and Fact, and Culpability: A Speculative Essay, 81 J. Crim. L. & Criminology 447, 467-469 (1990) and Fernand N. Dutile & Harold F. Moore, Mistake and Impossibility: Arranging a Marriage Between Two Difficult Partners, 74 Nw. U. L. Rev. 166, 166-167 (1979). The latter article disagrees with the reasoning of the Hypothetical Law Review comment on this point:

> [We argue] that Mr. Law in the Kadish and [Schulhofer] example would be acquitted, since the transaction, even as he contemplated it, was not within the statute, while Mr. Fact would not [be acquitted]. From the standpoint of symmetry, or the dangerous propensities of the defendant, there is no way to justify the result. From a "moral" standpoint they are equally culpable. [But] it is totally unclear how any system based on liability for intending to violate the law, as opposed to intending *conduct* that *is* in violation of the law, could function. . . . Such a system provides neither appropriate deterrence to crime nor proper retribution for crime.—EDS.

corroborative of the actor's criminal purpose." The primary function of this requirement is to avoid the risk of false convictions. Where the evidence of intent falls below a certain level we are not willing to allow the jury to speculate.

Now both the *Lady Eldon* opinion and the MPC are short-sighted for not seeing that the same concern may exist in the class of impossibility cases under discussion. In this respect the court in *Oviedo*, page 648 supra, and cases that have followed its lead, are on solid ground. If concern about false convictions calls for the requirement that the acts strongly corroborate the intent when the actor had to do further acts to achieve his objective, then the same concern calls for the same requirement where the actor believed he had done all he needed to do. The professor taking his own umbrella surely is such a case.

To put the suggestion in statutory form, we propose the following amendment to MPC §5.01:

> A person is guilty of an attempt to commit a crime if, acting with the kind of culpability otherwise required for commission of the crime, he: (a) purposely engages in conduct that *strongly corroborates the required culpability and* would constitute the crime if the attendant circumstances were as he believes them to be. . . .[4]

NOTE

For a rewarding effort to untangle the knots presented by the *Lady Eldon* case, see Larry Alexander, Inculpatory and Exculpatory Mistakes and the Fact/Law Distinction, 12 Law & Phil. 33, 43-70 (1993). In one of the few efforts to support a broad defense for all varieties of legal impossibility, along the lines of the *Jaffe* case, Professor John Hasnas argues that the "common law impossibility defense . . . does not go far enough. [A]ttempts, whether impossible or not, should be punished when and only when the defendant, acting with the specific intent to commit an offense known to the law, engages in conduct sufficient to cause public alarm if observed by an average citizen." See John Hasnas, Once More unto the Breach: The Inherent Liberalism of the Criminal Law and Liability for Attempting the Impossible, 54 Hastings L.J. 1, 75 (2002).

---

4. On the issues raised by this statutory proposal, see Robbins, supra at 400-412; Thomas Weigend, Why Lady Eldon Should Be Acquitted: The Social Harm in Attempting the Impossible, 27 DePaul L. Rev. 231 (1979). A related proposal has been developed by Professor Fletcher, who suggests that attempts be punishable only when two conditions are satisfied: "[T]he actor must attempt an act punishable under the law, and, further, this attempt must be dangerous on its face." George P. Fletcher, Constructing a Theory of Impossible Attempts, 5 Crim. J. Ethics 53, 67 (1986).

chapter 7

Group Criminality

A. ACCOUNTABILITY FOR THE ACTS OF OTHERS

INTRODUCTORY NOTES

1. The theory of complicity. The relationship between the doctrine of complicity and other doctrines of criminal liability is explored in the following excerpt.

Sanford H. Kadish, A Theory of Complicity, in Issues in Contemporary Legal Philosophy: The Influence of H.L.A. Hart 288 (Ruth Gavison ed., 1987): [We] regard a person's acts as the products of his choice, not of regularities of nature which require that certain happenings will occur whenever certain conditions are present. Therefore, antecedent events do not cause a person to act in the same way they cause things to happen, and neither do the antecedent acts of others. To treat the acts of others as causing a person's actions would be inconsistent with the premise on which we hold a person responsible. . . .[a] The . . . implication [of this] is that when we seek to determine the responsibility of one person for the volitional actions of another the concept of physical cause is not available to determine the answer, for whatever the relation of one person's acts to those of another, it cannot be described in terms of that sense of cause and effect appropriate to the occurrence of natural events without doing violence to our concept of a human action as freely chosen. . . .

How, then, can the law reach those whose conduct makes it appropriate to punish for the criminal actions of others—a person, for example, who persuades or helps another to commit a crime? . . . If it were not for the very special way in which we conceive of human actions, causation doctrine might serve this purpose, on the view that one who intentionally causes another to commit certain actions falls under the prohibition against committing those actions. But our conception of human actions as controlled by choice will not allow that to work. . . . Some alternative doctrine is needed,

---

a. See the material on Causation in Chapter 6, pages 571-607 supra.—EDS.

therefore, which imposes liability on the actor who is to blame for the conduct of another, but which does so upon principles that comport with our perception of human actions. This is the office of the doctrine of complicity.

2. From common law to statute. At the common law there were distinct categories of circumstances that rendered a person a participant in a course of criminal conduct. These distinctions had consequences for both procedure and punishment. The following excerpts from 4 Blackstone, Commentaries, ch. 3, *34-39, broadly describe those categories.

> A man may be *principal* in an offence in two degrees. A principal, in the first degree, is he that is the actor, or absolute perpetrator of the crime; and, in the second degree, he is who is present, aiding, and abetting the fact to be done. Which presence need not always be an actual immediate standing by, within sight or hearing of the fact; but there may be also a constructive presence, as when one commits a robbery or murder, and another keeps watch or guard at some convenient distance. . . .
>
> An *accessory* is he who is not the chief actor in the offence, nor present at its performance, but is some way concerned therein, either before or after the fact committed. . . .
>
> As to . . . who may be an accessory *before* the fact, Sir Matthew Hale defines him to be one, who being absent at the time of the crime committed, doth yet procure, counsel, or command another to commit a crime. Herein absence is necessary to make him an accessory; for if such procurer, or the like, be present, he is guilty of the crime as principal. . . .
>
> An accessory *after* the fact may be, where a person, knowing a felony to have been committed, receives, relieves, comforts, or assists the felon. . . .

Modern statutes have largely eliminated the significance of these discrete modes of criminal participation. (1) Apart from the accessory after the fact, who is still generally subject to a lesser punishment, the punishment is the same for principals and accessories. (2) It is no longer the case that accessories cannot be convicted until their principal is convicted (although, of course, it must be proved that a crime was committed). (3) It is no longer necessary in most states for a defendant to be charged *as an accomplice*; the defendant may simply be charged with the substantive crime committed by the person he or she allegedly aided or encouraged.

These changes are the result of statutes antedating the MPC. These older statutes abolish all distinctions between principals and accessories before the fact and require that all be treated as principals.

See, for example, the federal complicity statute, 18 U.S.C. §2:

> (a) Whoever commits an offense against the United States or aids, abets, counsels, commands, induces or procures its commission, is punishable as a principal.
>
> (b) Whoever willfully causes an act to be done which if directly performed by him or another would be an offense against the United States, is punishable as a principal.

Statutes of more recent vintage, influenced by the MPC (see §2.06, Appendix), typically make people who are accomplices of another person accountable for that person's conduct and define people as accomplices if they solicit that person to commit an offense or aid that person in planning or committing it. See, e.g., N.J. Stat. Ann. tit. 2C, §2C:2-6.

Note that under these statutory abrogations of the common law, complicity (variously termed "aiding and abetting" or "being an accomplice" or "being an accessory") is *not* a separate offense with its own penalty. Rather, complicity is a way of committing a substantive offense like murder or rape. In contrast, the offense of accessory after the fact is maintained in many current codes as a separate offense with its own penalty, regardless of what substantive offense is committed by the principal.

3. *Conspiracy as a doctrine of complicity.* An additional basis for holding one person liable for the crimes of another derives from the doctrine of conspiracy. In general terms, a criminal conspiracy is an agreement by two or more persons to commit a crime. Conspiracy carries its own penalty, but it sometimes has the further consequence of making each of the co-conspirators criminally responsible for the acts of fellow conspirators committed in furtherance of the criminal enterprise, whether or not those particular criminal acts were planned, so long as they were reasonably foreseeable. A co-conspirator, therefore, may be liable in some jurisdictions for the criminal acts of fellow conspirators even though he did not intend those crimes and might not be responsible under the principles of accomplice liability. This problem is explored in the Conspiracy section, in connection with *Pinkerton v. United States*, page 723 infra, and the materials following.

4. *Punishment.* Under American law, accomplices and principals are guilty of the same crime and thus subject to the same range of penalties. Of course, degrees of *culpability* are not always equal between principals and accomplices. Often, accomplices play a minor role in the offense. But sometimes it is the principal who plays the less important role. For example, in the distribution of illegal drugs, the actual seller of the drugs is the principal, even though the seller usually is a much lower-level participant than the accomplice who runs the distribution ring. American law deals with such differences in culpability through sentencing discretion or, in jurisdictions with sentencing guidelines, through specified reductions in punishment for those who played only a minor role in the offense. See, e.g., U.S. Sentencing Guidelines Manual §§3B1.1-3B1.3 (2011).

In statutes with mandatory sentencing provisions, however, there is no room to differentiate between principals and accomplices who play a minor role. Judge Posner criticized this approach in United States v. Ambrose, 740 F.2d 505, 508-509 (7th Cir. 1985), in the course of explaining why a judge should not be bound by the harsh mandatory minimum penalty provisions of the federal "drug kingpin" statute in sentencing a kingpin's aider and abettor:

> [Although the language of] 18 U.S.C. §2(a) [supra] makes clear that an aider and abettor can be punished as severely as the principal, it does not make clear that he must always be punished so severely. History is against such an interpretation. The distinction between "principal" and "aider and abettor" goes

back to the time when all felonies carried the same sanction—death. By enabling the courts to punish a class of less culpable offenders—aiders and abettors as distinct from principals—less severely, the distinction introduced a welcome element of gradation into the sentencing of felons. But as judges acquired more and more sentencing discretion, the need to distinguish between principals and aiders and abettors diminished, and since it was sometimes a difficult decision to make there was a movement to abolish it with regard to determining criminal liability. This movement culminated in 18 U.S.C. §2(a). But the purpose was not to make sure that aiders and abettors were always punished as severely as principals. Indeed, in passing the statute Congress must have realized that judges would use their sentencing discretion to proportion the severity of the sentence to the aider and abettor's fault. The history suggests that, rather than being intended to limit sentencing discretion, the abolition of the distinction between principals and aiders and abettors presupposed such discretion.

The Seventh Circuit, sitting en banc, eventually overturned its decision in *Ambrose* and held that an aider and abettor of a drug kingpin *is* subject to the statutory mandatory minimum penalty faced by the kingpin himself. United States v. Pino-Perez, 870 F.2d 1230 (7th Cir. 1989). Judge Posner again wrote the majority opinion, noting that "[t]he historic purpose of aiding and abetting liability coexists uneasily with criminal offenses that carry mandatory minimum penalties, such as the kingpin statute. . . . But simply lopping off a minimum statutory penalty for one class of violators (aiders and abettors) now strikes us . . . as exceeding the prudent bounds of judicial creativity." Id. at 1237.

Academics likewise have criticized the American approach of treating all accomplices as guilty of the same offense as their principals. The proposals for drawing lines, however, vary. For example, Joshua Dressler argues that the law should distinguish between three types of offenders: 1) those accomplices who causally contribute to the crime and play a substantial role in the offense; 2) those accomplices who causally contribute to the crime and play a minor role; and 3) those who play no causal role and provide minor assistance. He would have the first two types of offenders be treated as principals, but give the second category of offender a lesser punishment than the principal. Dressler argues those in the third category should be charged with some lesser crime, but not the same crime as the principal. Joshua Dressler, Reforming Complicity Law: Trivial Assistance As a Less Offense?, 5 Ohio St. J. Crim. L. 427, 447 (2008). Is Dressler correct that causation should be a factor? How does that square with Kadish's argument, supra page 657, that causation cannot be considered "without doing violence to our concept of a human action as freely chosen"?

Other legal systems draw different lines. For example, the German Penal Code (§25) provides different punishment for the perpetrator, the instigator, and the aider, and the law is rich in doctrine for distinguishing between these classifications of participants. See C. Roxin, Täterschaft und Tatherrschaft (1984).

1. Mens Rea

INTRODUCTORY NOTE

The problem of mens rea for complicity is complicated by the presence of two levels of mens rea: that required of the accomplice (the helper or encourager) and that required of the principal (the actual perpetrator). A true purpose, often called a specific intent, is generally required to hold a person liable as an accomplice; that is, he must actually intend his action to further the criminal *action* of the principal. We explore the meaning of this requirement and qualifications to it in Section A.1.a. We address whether this true purpose must extend to the *results* and *attendant circumstances* of the offense in Section A.1.b.

a. Mens Rea for Actions of the Principal

HICKS v. UNITED STATES

Supreme Court of the United States
150 U.S. 442 (1893)

JUSTICE SHIRAS delivered the opinion of the Court.

John Hicks, an Indian, was jointly indicted with Stand Rowe, also an Indian, for the murder of Andrew J. Colvard, a white man, by shooting him with a gun on the 13th of February, 1892. Rowe was killed by the officers in the attempt to arrest him, and Hicks was tried separately and found guilty in March, 1893. We adopt the statement of the facts in the case made in the brief for the government as correct and as sufficient for our purposes:

> It appears that on the night of the 12th of February, 1892, there was a dance at the house of Jim Rowe, in the Cherokee Nation; that Jim Rowe was a brother to Stand Rowe, who was indicted jointly with the defendant; . . . that Stand Rowe and the defendant were . . . eluding the United States marshals who were in search of them with warrants for their arrest, and were armed for the purpose of resisting arrest; they appeared at the dance, each armed with a Winchester rifle; they were both Cherokee Indians. The deceased, Andrew J. Colvard, was a white man who had married a Cherokee woman; he [was also at] the dance. . . . A good deal of whiskey was drank [sic] during the night by the persons present, and Colvard appears to have been drunk at some time during the night. Colvard spoke Cherokee fluently, and appears to have been very friendly with Stand Rowe and the defendant Hicks. . . .
>
> Some time after sunrise on the morning of the 13th [four witnesses] saw Stand Rowe, coming on horseback in a moderate walk, with his Winchester rifle lying down in front of him. . . . Stand Rowe halted within five or six feet of the main road, and the men on the porch saw Mr. Colvard and the defendant Hicks riding together down the main road from the direction of Jim Rowe's house.
>
> As Colvard and Hicks approached . . . where Stand Rowe was sitting on his horse, Stand Rowe rode out into the road and halted. Colvard then rode up

facts

to him in a lope or canter, leaving Hicks, the defendant, some 30 or 40 feet in his rear. The point where the three men were together on their horses was about 100 yards from where the four witnesses stood on the porch. The conversation between the three men on horseback was not fully heard by the four men on the porch, and all that was heard was not understood, because part of it was carried on in the Cherokee tongue; but some part of this conversation was distinctly heard and clearly understood by these witnesses; they saw Stand Rowe twice raise his rifle and aim it at Colvard, and twice he lowered it; they heard Colvard say, "I am a friend to both of you"; they saw and heard the defendant Hicks laugh aloud when Rowe directed his rifle toward Colvard; they saw Hicks take off his hat and hit his horse on the neck or shoulder with it; they heard Hicks say to Colvard, "Take off your hat and die like a man"; they saw Stand Rowe raise his rifle for the third time, point it at Colvard, fire it; . . . they saw Colvard fall from his horse; they went to where he was lying in the road and found him dead; they saw Stand Rowe and John Hicks ride off together after the shooting.

Hicks ▷ Hicks testified [and denied] that he had encouraged Rowe to shoot Colvard, and alleging that he had endeavored to persuade Rowe not to shoot. . . .

The language attributed to Hicks, and which he denied having used, cannot be said to have been entirely free from ambiguity. It was addressed not to Rowe, but to Colvard. Hicks testified that Rowe was in a dangerous mood, and that he did not know whether he would shoot Colvard or Hicks. The remark made—if made—accompanied with the gesture of taking off his own hat, may have been an utterance of desperation, occasioned by his belief that Rowe would shoot one or both of them. That Hicks and Rowe rode off together after seeing Colvard fall was used as a fact against Hicks, pointing to a conspiracy between them. Hicks testified that he did it in fear of his life; that Rowe had demanded that he should show him the road which he wished to travel. Hicks further testified, and in this he was not contradicted, that he separated from Rowe a few minutes afterwards, on the first opportunity, and that he never afterwards had any intercourse with him, nor had he been in the company of Rowe for several weeks before the night of the fatal occurrence.

[Hicks challenged the jury instruction on two grounds. First, it failed to state] that the acts or words of encouragement and abetting must have been used by the accused with the intention of encouraging and abetting Rowe. So far as the instruction goes, the words may have been used for a different purpose, and yet have had the actual effect of inciting Rowe to commit the murderous act. Hicks, indeed, testified that the expressions used by him were intended to dissuade Rowe from shooting. But the jury were left to find Hicks guilty as a principal because the effect of his words may have had the result of encouraging Rowe to shoot, regardless of Hicks' intention. In another part of the charge the learned judge did make an observation as to the question of intention in the use of the words, saying:

> If the deliberate and intentional use of words has the effect to encourage one man to kill another, he who uttered these words is presumed by the law to have intended that effect, and is responsible therefor.

This statement is itself defective in confounding the intentional use of the words with the intention as respects the effect to be produced. Hicks no doubt, *intended* to use the words he did use, but did he thereby *intend* that they were to be understood by Rowe as an encouragement to act? However this may be, we do not think this expression of the learned judge availed to cure the defect already noticed in his charge, that the mere use of certain words would suffice to warrant the jury in finding Hicks guilty, regardless of the intention with which they were used.

[Second, Hicks challenged the following] statement:

> that if Hicks was actually present at that place at the time of the firing by Stand Rowe, and he was there for the purpose of either aiding, abetting, advising, or encouraging the shooting of Andrew J. Colvard by Stand Rowe, and that, as a matter of fact, he did not do it, but was present for the purpose of aiding or abetting or advising or encouraging his shooting, but he did not do it because it was not necessary, it was done without his assistance, the law says there is a third condition where guilt is fastened to his act in that regard.

We understand this language to mean that where an accomplice is present for the purpose of aiding and abetting in a murder, but refrains from so aiding and abetting because it turned out not to be necessary for the accomplishment of the common purpose, he is equally guilty as if he had actively participated by words or acts of encouragement. Thus understood, the statement might, in some instances, be a correct instruction. Thus, if there had been evidence sufficient to show that there had been a previous conspiracy between Rowe and Hicks to waylay and kill Colvard, Hicks, if present at the time of the killing, would be guilty, even if it was found unnecessary for him to act. But the error of such an instruction, in the present case, is in the fact that there was no evidence on which to base it. The evidence . . . shows no facts from which the jury could have properly found that the encounter was the result of any previous conspiracy or arrangement. The jury might well, therefore, have thought that they were following the court's instructions, in finding the accused guilty because he was present at the time and place of the murder, although he contributed neither by word or action to the crime, and although there was no substantial evidence of any conspiracy or prior arrangement between him and Rowe. . . . The judgment of the court below is reversed and the cause remanded, with directions to set aside the verdict and award a new trial.

PROBLEM: VARIATIONS ON HICKS

Consider the responsibility of Hicks for the killing by Rowe in the following hypothetical situations.

i. Hicks hears that Rowe has set out to kill his old enemy, Colvard, and goes along to enjoy the spectacle.
ii. Same situation as in (i), except that while watching Rowe's assault on Colvard with satisfaction, Hicks shouts such words of encouragement to Rowe as "Go get him!" and "Attaboy!"

iii. Same situation as in (i), except that Hicks resolves to make certain Rowe succeeds—by helping him if necessary.

iv. Same situation as in (iii), except that Hicks tells Rowe on the way that he will help him if it seems necessary.

STATE v. GLADSTONE

Supreme Court of Washington
78 Wash. 2d 306, 474 P.2d 274 (1970)

HALE, J. A jury found defendant Bruce Gladstone guilty of aiding and abetting one Robert Kent in the unlawful sale of marijuana. . . .

Gladstone's guilt as an aider and abettor in this case rests solely on evidence of a conversation between him and one Douglas MacArthur Thompson concerning the possible purchase of marijuana from one Robert Kent. There is no other evidence to connect the accused with Kent who ultimately sold some marijuana to Thompson. . . .

[Thompson, Kent, and defendant, Gladstone, were all students at the University of Puget Sound. Thompson was hired by the Tacoma Police Department to attempt a purchase of marijuana from Gladstone. Thompson visited defendant at his home and asked to buy marijuana. Defendant replied that he did not have enough to sell him any but volunteered the name of Kent as someone who did have enough and who was willing to sell. He then gave Kent's address to Thompson and, at Thompson's request, drew a map to direct him to Kent's residence. Thompson went there and bought marijuana from Kent. There was no evidence of any communication between defendant and Kent concerning marijuana, but only, the court said, of "a possible accommodation to someone who said he wanted to buy marijuana."]

If all reasonable inferences favorable to the state are accorded the evidence, it does not, in our opinion, establish the commission of the crime charged. That vital element—a nexus between the accused and the party whom he is charged with aiding and abetting in the commission of a crime—is missing. The record contains no evidence whatever that Gladstone had any communication by word, gesture or sign, before or after he drew the map, from which it could be inferred that he counseled, encouraged, hired, commanded, induced or procured Kent to sell marijuana to Douglas Thompson as charged, or took any steps to further the commission of the crime charged. He was not charged with aiding and abetting Thompson in the purchase of marijuana, but with Kent's sale of it. . . .

[E]ven without prior agreement, arrangement or understanding, a bystander to a robbery could be guilty of aiding and abetting its commission if he came to the aid of a robber and knowingly assisted him in perpetrating the crime. But . . . there is no aiding and abetting unless one " 'in some sort associate himself with the venture, that he participate in it as in something that he wishes to bring about, that he seek by his action to make it succeed.' " Nye & Nissen v. United States, 336 U.S. 613, 619 (1949).

Gladstone's culpability, if at all, must be brought within R.C.W. 9.01.030, which makes a principal of one who aids and abets another in the commission of the crime. Although an aider and abettor need not be physically present at the commission of the crime to be held guilty as a principal, his conviction depends on proof that he did something in association or connection with the principal to accomplish the crime. Learned Hand, J., we think, hit the nail squarely when, in United States v. Peoni, 100 F.2d 401, 402 (2d Cir. 1938), he wrote that, in order to aid and abet another to commit a crime, it is necessary that a defendant "in some sort associate himself with the venture, that he participate in it as in something that he wishes to bring about, that he seek by his action to make it succeed. All the words used—even the most colorless, 'abet'—carry an implication of purposive attitude towards it." . . .

It would be a dangerous precedent indeed to hold that mere communications to the effect that another might or probably would commit a criminal offense amount to an aiding and abetting of the offense should it ultimately be committed.

There being no evidence whatever that the defendant ever communicated to Kent the idea that he would in any way aid him in the sale of any marijuana, or said anything to Kent to encourage or induce him or direct him to do so, or counseled Kent in the sale of marijuana, or did anything more than describe Kent to another person as an individual who might sell some marijuana, or would derive any benefit, consideration or reward from such a sale, there was no proof of an aiding and abetting, and the conviction should, therefore, be reversed as a matter of law. Remanded with directions to dismiss.

HAMILTON, J. (dissenting). . . . I am satisfied that the jury was fully warranted in concluding that appellant, when he affirmatively recommended Kent as a source and purveyor of marijuana, entertained the requisite conscious design and intent that his action would instigate, induce, procure or encourage perpetration of Kent's subsequent crime of selling marijuana to Thompson. . . .

NOTES AND QUESTIONS

1. *Aiding and abetting the purchase?* The court emphasizes that defendant was "not charged with aiding and abetting Thompson in the purchase of marijuana, but with Kent's sale of it." Could he have been convicted of aiding and abetting Thompson's purchase? One problem is that Thompson, the principal, might not be guilty of an offense because of his role as an agent of the police. This problem is treated infra pages 693-703. The MPC's solution is to provide for liability for *attempt* when someone aids and abets or attempts to aid and abet another who does not actually commit the crime. See MPC §206(3) & §5.01(3). But suppose that the student who sought Gladstone's help was not a police agent. Could Gladstone then be charged with aiding and abetting the student's purchase? Would Gladstone's state of mind as to the purchase by the student be any different from his state of mind as to the sale by Kent? In the case of the student purchaser, there

would be a "nexus" between Gladstone and the student. If so, would his mens rea then be sufficient to establish accomplice liability?

2. *Aiding and abetting the sale?* What kinds of actions by Gladstone might have satisfied the court that the evidence was sufficient to infer that he had the mens rea required for accomplice liability? What if, in an alternative scenario, Gladstone lived with Kent and, observing Thompson hesitate over the price Kent quoted for the sale of marijuana, had commented that it was good stuff and well worth the money? In State v. Wilson, 631 P.2d 362, 364 (Wash. 1981), the court found intent to encourage the sale under similar facts. Or, in another alternative scenario, what if Gladstone had called Kent to see if he was home and had marijuana to sell, and then remained present during the transaction? In a later case, a Washington court of appeals found accomplice liability on similar facts and distinguished *Gladstone*. The court observed that in *Gladstone*, there was "no evidence . . . from which it could be inferred that [Gladstone] counseled, encouraged, hired, commanded, induced or procured Kent to sell marijuana," whereas in the facts before it, the defendant "was present at the scene of the sale, after having personally contacted the seller." State v. McKeown, 596 P.2d 1100, 1105 (Wash. App. 1979). Are these decisions proper applications of the *Gladstone* standard? Is physical presence at the sale by itself enough to distinguish these cases from *Gladstone*, or are the critical facts the ones that suggest the association with the venture in the form of touting the product or arranging the buy personally ahead of time?

3. *The Model Penal Code's struggle with the mens rea for complicity.* Model Penal Code and Commentaries, Comment to §2.06 at 315-316 (1985), states the issue as follows:

> [Should] knowingly facilitating the commission of a crime . . . be sufficient for complicity, absent a true purpose to advance the criminal end[?] The problem, to be sure, is narrow in its focus: often, if not usually, aid rendered with guilty knowledge implies purpose since it has no other motivation. But there are many and important cases where this is the central question in determining liability. A lessor rents with knowledge that the premises will be used to establish a bordello. A vendor sells with knowledge that the subject of the sale will be used in the commission of a crime. . . . An employee puts through a shipment in the course of his employment though he knows the shipment is illegal. . . . Such cases can be multiplied indefinitely; they have given courts much difficulty when they have been brought, whether as prosecutions for conspiracy or for the substantive offense involved.

The solution originally proposed by the MPC was contained in §2.04(3)(b) (Tent. Draft No. 1 1953):

> A person is an accomplice of another person in the commission of a crime if . . . acting with knowledge that such other person was committing or had the purpose of committing the crime, he knowingly, substantially facilitated its commission.

In defense of this proposal the Commentary observed (id., Comment at 27-32):

> The draft, it is submitted, should not embrace the *Peoni* limitation [referring to Judge Hand's dictum in *United States v. Peoni*, quoted in *Gladstone*, supra]. Conduct which knowingly facilitates the commission of crimes is by hypothesis a proper object of preventive effort by the penal law, unless, of course, it is affirmatively justifiable. It is important in that effort to safeguard the innocent but the requirement of guilty knowledge adequately serves this end—knowledge both that there is a purpose to commit a crime and that one's own behavior renders aid. There are, however, infinite degrees of aid to be considered. This is the point, we think, at which distinctions should be drawn. Accordingly, when a true purpose to further the crime is lacking, the draft requires that the accessorial behavior substantially facilitate commission of the crime and that it do so to the knowledge of the actor. This qualification provides a basis for discrimination that should satisfy the common sense of justice. A vendor who supplies materials readily available upon the market arguably does not make substantial contribution to commission of the crime since the materials could have as easily been gotten elsewhere.
>
> [W]hen the only interest of the actor is his wish for freedom to forego concern about the criminal purposes of others, though he knowingly facilitates in a substantial measure the achievement of such purposes, it is an interest that, we think, is properly subordinated generally to the larger interest of preventing crime.

Note that this proposal would have required an evaluation of the degree of aid rendered by an actor to determine whether accomplice liability should lie in cases of knowing-but-not-purposeful facilitation of crime. But should we think of the degree of aid rendered as a useful way of inferring the nature of an actor's mens rea? Cf. *People v. Lauria*, infra page 713, discussing the information relevant to determining whether an actor has a sufficient mens rea of purpose or knowledge in the context of a conspiracy case.

The MPC's 1953 proposals were rejected by the American Law Institute. The Code now requires that the actor have "the purpose of promoting or facilitating" the commission of the crime. Section 2.06(3)(a).

Question: What are the inadequacies, if any, in the reporter's arguments that led to its rejection? Consider Glanville Williams, Criminal Law: The General Part 369-370 (2d ed. 1961):

> [T]he question is one of some complexity. On the one side are the policy of repressing crime, and the difficulty of distinguishing between the merchant who knowingly assists a crime and the ordinary accessory before the fact. On the other side stand the undesirability of giving too great an extension to the criminal law, and the inconvenience to legitimate trade of requiring a merchant to concern himself with the affairs of his customers. The difficulty is increased by the number of different modes in which the question may arise. The merchant may desire the crime, or he may foresee it as certain if he sells the commodity, or he may foresee it as belonging to one of many degrees of probability. The sale may be completely in the ordinary course of business, or

the order may in some way be a special one—as when a tailor makes a suit with secret pockets for poaching or smuggling. The merchant may charge the usual price or an extra price on account of the legal risk. The commodity may be appropriate only to a single crime (as with poison that is consumed only once), or may enable the purchaser to engage in a life of crime. The crime in contemplation may be a serious or a trivial one.

See also George Fletcher, Rethinking Criminal Law 676 (1978):

> From the standpoint of the supplier, the problem of refusing services to known criminals closely resembles the problem of intervening to prevent impending harm. The grocery store, the gas station, the physician, the answering service all provide routine services. Does the business-person have a duty to make an exception just because he or she knows that the purchaser is engaged in illegal activity? That question of duty corresponds to the problem of the motorist who must decide whether to stop his car and render aid to an accident victim. The assumption underlying both fields is that people are entitled to carry on their lives without deviating every time doing so might help a person in distress or hamper the execution of a criminal plan.

The case against imposing liability for knowing aid is made in R.A. Duff, "Can I Help You?" Accessorial Liability and the Intention to Assist, 10 Legal Stud. 167 (1990). Another scholar attacks the knowledge standard from the opposite direction, arguing that recklessness should be sufficient for accomplice liability. See Larry Alexander, Insufficient Concern: A Unified Conception of Criminal Culpability, 88 Cal. L. Rev. 931, 944-947 (2000). Alexander would address the issue of merchant liability by creating a safe harbor for merchants who sell at market prices. But why should merchants be treated differently from every other person who knowingly or recklessly aids a criminal offense?

4. Criminal facilitation. One response to these contending considerations is compromise: Make aid without a true purpose a separate crime with a lesser penalty than the crime aided. New York has pioneered this approach with a crime called "criminal facilitation."[1] N.Y. Penal Code §115 provides:

> A person is guilty of criminal facilitation in the second degree when, believing it probable that he is rendering aid to a person who intends to commit a crime, he engages in conduct which provides such person with means or opportunity for the commission thereof and which in fact aids such person to commit a felony. Criminal facilitation in the second degree is a class A misdemeanor.[2]

Note that the formula of liability is wider than that originally proposed by the MPC, which would have required "knowing" aid as a basis of accomplice

---

1. Several jurisdictions have followed New York's lead. Ariz. Rev. Stat. Ann. tit. 13, §13-1004; Ky. Rev. Stat. Ann. §506.080; N.D. Cent. Code §12.1-06-02.

2. Section 115.05 makes such conduct first-degree criminal facilitation when the crime committed is a class A felony (such crimes as murder, for example) and subjects it to punishment as a class C felony (maximum 15 years' imprisonment).

liability. It is enough under the New York formulation that the aider believes it "probable" that the person aided will commit a crime.

Question: Would the defendant in the *Gladstone* case be guilty of criminal facilitation under the New York statute?

5. *The seriousness of the substantive offense.* Some courts have questioned the assumption that there should be only a single mens rea standard that applies to liability for aiding and abetting. Instead, they propose that the seriousness of the offense should be considered in determining the mens rea required for complicity. In United States v. Fountain, 768 F.2d 790 (7th Cir. 1985), a prison inmate (Gometz) was convicted of aiding and abetting another inmate (Silverstein) in murdering a guard. The evidence disclosed that Silverstein, in handcuffs, was being led down the corridor by some guards. When he reached Gometz's cell he thrust his manacled hands through the bars. Gometz came close and pulled up his shirt to reveal a knife in his waistband. Somehow Silverstein got free of the handcuffs, seized the knife, and stabbed the guard with it. Judge Posner held that to convict Gometz it was not necessary to prove that it was Gometz's purpose that Silverstein should kill the guard; it was enough that he knew when he helped Silverstein obtain the knife that Silverstein would use it to attack the guards. In holding that knowledge was enough, the court borrowed the approach of a California conspiracy case (*People v. Lauria,* reported page 713 infra) that held that *purpose* was required to convict of lesser offenses, but that *knowledge* sufficed to convict of major crimes. Judge Posner stated (id. at 798):

> In *People v. Lauria*—not a federal case, but illustrative of the general point— the court, en route to holding that knowledge of the principal's purpose would not suffice for aiding and abetting of just any crime, said it would suffice for "the seller of gasoline who knew the buyer was using his product to make Molotov cocktails for terroristic use." Compare the following hypothetical cases. In the first, a shopkeeper sells dresses to a woman whom he knows to be a prostitute. . . . Little would be gained by imposing criminal liability in such a case. Prostitution, anyway a minor crime, would be but trivially deterred, since the prostitute could easily get her clothes from a shopkeeper ignorant of her occupation. In the second case, a man buys a gun from a gun dealer after telling the dealer that he wants it in order to kill his mother-in-law, and he does kill her. The dealer would be guilty of aiding and abetting the murder. This liability would help to deter—and perhaps not trivially given public regulation of the sale of guns—a most serious crime. We hold that aiding and abetting murder is established by proof beyond a reasonable doubt that the supplier of the murder weapon knew the purpose for which it would be used.

Question: Does lowering the required mens rea to knowledge only in the case of serious crimes adequately address the objections, discussed in Note 3, to the initial draft of the MPC?

There is a debate in international law about whether purpose or knowledge is the appropriate standard for aiding and abetting human rights violations. Should merchants be treated differently when they sell weapons or chemicals knowing they will be used to facilitate a war crime? For a discussion, see Doug Cassel, Corporate Aiding and Abetting of Human Rights Violations: Confusion in the Courts, 6 Nw. U. J. Int'l Hum. Rts. 304 (2008).

NOTE ON SUBSTANTIVE CRIMES OF FACILITATION

Traditional accomplice liability and liability for some lesser crime of facilitation are not the only options for responding to conduct that aids another to commit an offense. Some legislatures have passed statutes aimed at particular kinds of assistance. There is wide variation in how statutes of this type define the offenses that must be facilitated and the conduct that constitutes unlawful facilitation. In considering the following three examples, weigh the gap-filling potential of each statute against the risks that such statutes may pose, such as the risk of imposing punishment disproportionate to wrongdoing, of chilling speech and association, and of burdening legitimate business.

1. *Juvenile gun possession.* When two teenagers purchased an assault weapon and then murdered 13 people before taking their own lives at Columbine High School in Colorado in 1999, attention focused on Mark Manes, the 22-year-old computer programmer who sold the boys a TEK-DC9 assault pistol, and later sold them 100 rounds of ammunition the night before the killings. The teenage killers had made a videotape before the crime in which they thanked Manes by name: "[T]hank you to Mark. . . . Very cool. You helped us do what we needed to." But the videotape also absolved Manes and others of knowledge of the killers' plans. One boy said, "Let me tell you this much, they have no clue. So don't blame them and arrest them for what we did." The other boy added, "Yeah, you know it's not their fault. . . . We would have found someone else." Michael Janofsky, Columbine Killers, on Tape, Thanked 2 for Gun, N.Y. Times, Nov. 13, 1999, at A1.

What punishment should Manes have received? For what offense? Law enforcement officials had no reason to think that Manes knew, much less intended, that the Columbine shootings would occur. Thus, liability for the murders as an accomplice of the two boys was not an option. Yet, liability under a misdemeanor facilitation statute, such as New York's, would have resulted in only minor penalties. The statute under which Manes was convicted and sentenced to a six-year prison term (from a maximum penalty of 18 years) lies somewhere between two these options; it specifically targeted the selling of handguns to juveniles: "Any person who intentionally, knowingly, or recklessly provides a handgun with or without remuneration to any person under the age of eighteen years . . . commits [a] crime. . . ." Colo. Rev. Stat. §18-12-108.7. This statute obviated the difficulty of an accomplice prosecution by eliminating any mens rea requirement with respect to injuries the juvenile might inflict, and by requiring only recklessness as to the age of the handgun recipient. The statute also avoided the leniency of a general facilitation statute by providing for stiff felony penalties.

Questions: Does the Colorado statute provide a satisfactory solution for defendants like Manes? In cases where the defendant provides a handgun knowing that it will be used in a violent assault, is the statutory penalty severe enough? Conversely, in cases where the defendant only recklessly allows a juvenile access to an unloaded gun and no one is injured, are the statute's felony sanctions too severe?

2. *"Material support" to terrorism.* Federal legislation punishes the "knowing" provision of "material support" to "terrorists" or to "designated foreign terrorist organizations" (FTOs). 18 U.S.C. §2339A and §2339B. The legislation defines "material support" as broadly including: "any property, tangible or intangible, or service, including currency or . . . financial services, lodging, training, expert advice or assistance . . . communications equipment, . . . lethal substances, . . . personnel (1 or more individuals who may be or include oneself), and transportation, except medicine or religious materials." §2339A(b). The material support is to "terrorists" if the actor knows or intends that it will be used in carrying out one of a long list of specified federal offenses, such as damage to property, illegal use of explosives, the killing of government officials, and the destruction of aircraft. See §2339A(a). The USA PATRIOT Act of 2001 increased the maximum term of imprisonment from 10 to 15 years and provided for life imprisonment if the death of any person results from a violation.

One commentator has described this statutory scheme as follows (Norman Abrams, The Material Support Terrorism Offenses: Perspectives Derived from the (Early) Model Penal Code, 1 J. Nat'l Security L. & Pol'y 5, 18 (2005)):

> [A] trade-off was made between the mens rea required for the offenses and the actus reus or conduct required to hold the aiding person criminally liable. Thus, the statutes require that the contribution of the actor be material, and they put content into the concept of material support by defining it in terms of substantial forms of aid through the specification of listed categories. By thus "hardening up" the actus reus, the drafters made more acceptable a diluted mens rea of knowledge. . . .

Is Abrams right that the material support provisions "harden up" the actus reus of the offense?

In *Holder v. Humanitarian Law Project*, challengers to the law hoped to convince the Court to read into the statute a heightened mens rea standard based on their view that the actus reus required by the statute was not, in fact, sufficiently stringent. The challengers were citizens and humanitarian organizations that wanted to train members of designated terrorist groups in "how to use humanitarian and international law to peacefully resolve disputes" and "how to petition various representative bodies such as the United Nations for relief." 130 S. Ct. 2705, 2716 (2010). The Court concluded that these activities fit within the statutory definitions of "training" and "expert advice or assistance" because the statute defined those terms to include imparting a "specific skill" and passing on "specialized knowledge," which the Court thought covered these activities. Id. at 2720-2721. The Court rejected the argument that the material support statute should be read to require a specific intent to further the illegal ends of an FTO in order to satisfy due process. Id. at 2717. The Court concluded that Congress clearly selected knowledge of the organization's connection to terrorism as the relevant mens rea standard. That reading posed no constitutional vagueness problems, according to the Court, even when it applied to the kinds of acts at issue in the case. Id. Is the Court's reading consistent with Abrams's claim that the actus reus is sufficiently limited to justify the "diluted mens rea of knowledge"?

The Court also rejected the argument that Congress could not, consistent with the First Amendment, ban support to the legitimate activities of an FTO: "At bottom, plaintiffs simply disagree with the considered judgment of Congress and the Executive that providing material support to a designated [FTO]—even seemingly benign support—bolsters the terrorist activities of that organization. That judgment, however, is entitled to significant weight. . . ." Id. at 2728.

In light of the Court's decision, should the "material support" provisions be amended to require that the support be "substantial" or that it actually facilitate a completed terrorism offense? Without such amendments, is the statute vulnerable to the same criticism leveled at the original MPC proposal with regard to accomplice liability? Did the Court's decision do enough to avoid chilling constitutionally protected speech and association (especially of those who support religious or cultural organizations that may be designated as FTOs)? Or are these concerns mitigated by the seriousness of the crimes that must be supported and the national security context in which they occur?

3. *Money laundering.* The broadest and most widely used substantive crime of facilitation is the federal legislation against money laundering. The two main federal statutes—18 U.S.C. §1956 and §1957—were, like many state statutes against money laundering, passed as part of the war on drugs. People v. Mays, 55 Cal. Rptr. 3d 356, 363 (Ct. App. 2007). Section 1956, the most frequently used money laundering statute, makes it a crime punishable by up to 20 years' imprisonment "to conduct [any] financial transaction . . . knowing that the transaction is designed . . . to conceal or disguise the nature, the location, the source, the ownership, or the control of the proceeds of specified unlawful activity." The government is not required to prove the defendant knew the particular offense from which the proceeds were derived; it must prove only that the defendant knew they came from illegal activity of some sort.

Section 1956 shares with other targeted facilitation statutes a lowered mens rea of knowledge. What is distinctive about money laundering—and crucial to its wide use by prosecutors—is the broad range of crimes covered by the term "specified unlawful activity"; the statutory list includes all of the most common crimes and many truly obscure ones. In this way, the offenses facilitated through money laundering are not "targeted" at all. Rather, the mode of facilitation—the "financial transaction"—is targeted. Yet financial transactions are hardly a narrow category; they are defined to include any transaction involving cash or checks. Thus, §1956 potentially reaches any acceptance of ill-gotten gains by a merchant or service provider with whom a wrongdoer deals.

The second major federal money laundering statute, §1957, is in some ways even broader. It applies only to transactions involving more than $10,000, while §1956 has no minimum dollar threshold.[3] But §1957 requires knowledge only of the fact that the transaction involves money from some illegal source, without §1956's additional requirement of knowledge that the transaction is designed to "conceal or disguise" the tainted nature of the money. The less stringent mens rea of §1957 heightens the risk that ordinary citizens will face prosecution if they deal with someone who has illegal income.

Although a conviction under §1956 or §1957 requires proof that the defendant *knew* the transaction involved illegal proceeds, this requirement narrows the statute less than might appear. Consider United States v. Campbell, 977 F.2d 854 (4th Cir. 1992). Campbell, a real estate agent, arranged for a client, Lawing, to purchase a vacation home. She sensed that Lawing might be involved with illegal activity because he wanted to pay in cash and seemed somewhat secretive. The Fourth Circuit upheld her conviction under §1957, finding sufficient evidence of the required mens rea because, under the doctrine of "willful blindness" (see pages 260-266 supra), she had deliberately avoided learning where Lawing's money came from. (Some of the most troublesome convictions under a knowledge mens rea involve a willful blindness theory.) Although Campbell made no unusual profit on the transaction, all that mattered for the §1957 conviction was that she was deemed to know that Lawing was paying with money from some illegal source.

Campbell illustrates how modern legislation undercuts the traditional reluctance to impose law enforcement duties on law-abiding citizens: People carrying on normal businesses can be convicted of money laundering if they become aware of the criminal activities of their clients, or if they make a deliberate effort to look the other way. If they aren't cautious enough, they face prosecution for a serious federal felony. Samuel Buell notes the odd evolution of the money laundering statute from one designed "to deal with the elusive international heroin boss" to one that covers a situation like Campbell's where "the actor . . . gave no thought to, indeed had no interest in, structuring her activities or otherwise investing resources to evade sanctioning." As Buell notes, "[o]nly prosecutorial discretion is left to sort the heroin boss from the realtor." Samuel W. Buell, The Upside of Overbreadth, 83 N.Y.U. L. Rev. 1491, 1537 (2008). What makes legislative drafters think there should be liability in these situations that are so far afield from the "elusive international heroin boss" scenario? Is it a retributive impulse, or is it based on utilitarian needs of law enforcement? Some combination of the two?

---

3. In addition, §1957 applies to a slightly different category of transactions (those involving banks and other financial institutions rather than, as in the case of §1956, transactions by cash or check), and §1957 carries a lower maximum sentence, ten years rather than the 20-year maximum available under §1956.

There is a converse problem if people seeking to avoid liability under the money laundering statutes become overly cautious. Consider John K. Villa, A Critical View of Bank Secrecy Act Enforcement and the Money Laundering Statutes, 37 Cath. U. L. Rev. 489, 500-501 (1988):

> One who suspects a person of offering stolen goods for sale may protect himself by merely declining to purchase the suspect goods. . . . If, on the other hand, it is a crime to do any business at all with one who deals in the proceeds of illegal activity, then those who are merely suspected of crimes will find that . . . no one will risk dealing with them. The impact on the suspected individual can be severe . . . , yet there may be no means by which the suspected individual can clear himself. The social cost of imposing such a stigma on individuals—especially those who have not been convicted of, let alone charged with, any crime—should present grave civil liberties concerns even for the most ardent law-and-order legislator. . . .

b. Mens Rea for Results and Attendant Circumstances

Recall that the description of forbidden conduct in an offense often consists of more than acts: It often includes results and attendant circumstances as well. The following material discusses the mens rea required for these elements in the case of accomplice liability.

STATE v. McVAY

Supreme Court of Rhode Island
47 R.I. 292, 132 A. 436 (1926)

BARROWS, J. Heard on a certification of a question of law before trial. Three indictments for manslaughter, each containing four counts, were brought against the captain and engineer of the steamer *Mackinac*, as principals, and against Kelley, as accessory before the fact. The steamer carried several hundred passengers from Pawtucket to Newport via Narragansett Bay. The boiler producing the steam by which the vessel was propelled burst near Newport and many lives were lost. The present indictments are for causing the deaths of three persons killed by escaping steam after the explosion of the boiler. . . .

The same question is raised upon each indictment . . . :

> May a defendant be indicted and convicted of being an accessory before the fact to the crime of manslaughter arising through criminal negligence as set forth in the indictment?

. . . The charge against Kelley as accessory is that "before said felony and manslaughter was committed," he did, at Pawtucket, "feloniously and maliciously aid, assist, abet, counsel, hire, command and procure the said George W. McVay and John A. Grant [the captain and engineer, respectively], the said felony and manslaughter in manner and form aforesaid to do and commit." . . .

Because the manslaughter charge is "without malice" and "involuntary," Kelley contends that he cannot be indicted legally as an accessory before the fact. The argument is that manslaughter, being a sudden and unpremeditated crime, inadvertent and unintentional by its very nature, cannot be "maliciously" incited before the crime is committed. . . .

While every one must agree that there can be no accessory before the fact when a killing results from a sudden and unpremeditated blow, we do not think it can be broadly stated that premeditation is inconsistent with every charge of manslaughter. Manslaughter may consist, among other things, of doing an unlawful act resulting in unintentional killing, such as violation of motor vehicle laws or administration of drugs to procure an abortion. Manslaughter is likewise committed if an unintentional killing is occasioned by gross negligence in the doing of an act lawful in itself. There is no inherent reason why, prior to the commission of such a crime, one may not aid, abet, counsel, command, or procure the doing of the unlawful act or of the lawful act in a negligent manner. A premeditated act may be involved in such unlawful homicides.

[T]he present indictment for involuntary manslaughter is not self-contradictory when it charges Kelley to be an accessory before the fact. It was possible for him at Pawtucket to intentionally direct and counsel the grossly negligent act which the indictment charges resulted in the crime. Involuntary manslaughter . . . means that defendants exercised no conscious volition to take life, but their negligence was of such a character that criminal intention can be presumed. The crime was consummated when the explosion occurred. The volition of the principals was exercised when they chose negligently to create steam which the boiler could not carry. The doing of the act charged or failure to perform the duty charged was voluntary and intentional in the sense that defendants exercised a choice among courses of conduct. It is obvious that Kelley could participate and is charged with participating in procuring defendants to act in a grossly negligent manner prior to the explosion. . . . Specific duties are stated to have been laid upon the captain and engineer. Defendant is charged with full knowledge of those duties and of the fact that the boiler was unsafe. He is charged with counseling and procuring the principals at Pawtucket to disregard their duties and negligently create steam. . . . [A] jury might find that defendant Kelley, with full knowledge of the possible danger to human life, recklessly and willfully advised, counseled, and commanded the captain and engineer to take a chance by negligent action or failure to act. . . .

COMMONWEALTH v. ROEBUCK

Supreme Court of Pennsylvania
32 A.3d 613 (Pa. 2011)

SAYLOR, J. In this appeal, we consider whether it is possible, as a matter of law, to be convicted as an accomplice to third-degree murder.

[T]he victim was lured to an apartment complex, where he was ambushed, shot, and mortally wounded. Appellant participated, with others, in orchestrating the events, but he did not shoot the victim.

. . . As he did not physically perpetrate the homicide, the Commonwealth relied upon accomplice theory, [t]he matter proceeded to a bench trial, and a verdict of guilt ensued.

. . . Appellant argued that there is no rational legal theory to support accomplice liability for third-degree murder. He rested his position on the following syllogism: accomplice liability attaches only where the defendant intends to facilitate or promote an underlying offense; third-degree murder is an unintentional killing committed with malice; therefore, to adjudge a criminal defendant guilty of third-degree murder as an accomplice would be to accept that the accused intended to aid an unintentional act, which is a logical impossibility.

[The relevant Pennsylvania statute mirrors the MPC [§2.06(4)]: "When causing a particular result is an element of an offense, an accomplice in the conduct causing such result is an accomplice in the commission of that offense, if he acts with the kind of culpability, if any, with respect to that result that is sufficient for the commission of the offense." 18 Pa.C.S. §306(d).]

[The Commonwealth replies] that accomplice liability readily pertains to murder of the third degree [because] it is the shared criminal intent motivating the underlying conduct (here, designing to stage a very dangerous altercation) which establishes the requisite criminal culpability. . . . According to the Commonwealth, it is both rational and sensible to hold one who aids another in malicious conduct to account to the same degree as the principal for foreseeable consequences of the wrongful actions. . . .

[Two MPC provisions address the mens rea requirement for an accomplice:]

> (3) A person is an accomplice of another person in the commission of an offense if . . . with the purpose of promoting or facilitating the commission of the offense, he . . . aids or agrees or attempts to aid such other person in planning or committing it[.]
>
> (4) When causing a particular result is an element of an offense, an accomplice in the conduct causing such result is an accomplice in the commission of that offense if he acts with the kind of culpability, if any, with respect to that result that is sufficient for the commission of the offense.

Section 206(4) thus prescribes that an accomplice may be held legally accountable where he is an "accomplice in the conduct"—or, in other words, aids another in planning or committing the conduct with the purpose of promoting or facilitating it—and acts with recklessness (i.e., the "kind of culpability . . . sufficient for the commission of" a reckless-result offense).

[The MPC] commentary explains that the term "commission of the offense," as used in Section 2.06(3), focuses on the conduct, not the result. See id. §2.06, cmt. 6(b), at 310. . . . This diffuses any impression that an accomplice must always intend results essential to the completed crime. . . . The commentary then points to the fourth subsection as supplying the essential culpability requirement, as follows:

> One who solicits an end, or aids or agrees to aid in its achievement, is an accomplice in whatever means may be employed, insofar as they constitute or commit an offense fairly envisaged in the purposes of the association. But when a wholly different crime has been committed, thus involving conduct not within the conscious objectives of the accomplice, he is not liable for it unless the case falls within the specific terms of Subsection (4).

[Id.] at 311 (emphasis added). According to the commentary, the purport of the fourth subsection is to hold the accomplice accountable for contributing to the conduct to the degree his culpability equals what is required to support liability of a principal actor. . . .

Eakin, J., concurring: . . . As Appellant's syllogism is based on a false premise, his argument fails. Indeed, an accomplice to third degree murder does not intend to aid an unintentional murder; he intends to aid a malicious act which results in a killing. Suppose an accomplice hands a gun to the principal and says "shoot that victim—I don't care if he dies or not, but shoot him." The principal shoots the victim in the leg, but the victim dies—it is classic third degree murder, there being no proof of specific intent to kill, but a clearly malicious act regardless of the consequences. The same logic that enables a murder charge against the principal binds the accomplice as well—both committed an intentional malicious act that resulted in the death of another, and both are guilty of the murder charge that follows. . . .

NOTES AND QUESTIONS

1. *Accomplice liability based on the same mental state as the substantive offense.* We have already seen the debate over specific intent versus knowledge, supra pages 661-670, and the general rule that accomplice liability requires specific intent. But specific intent with respect to which offense elements? *McVay* and *Roebuck* make clear that there is a distinction between conduct elements and result elements. These cases recognize that for accomplice liability, the accomplice must have specific intent to further the underlying *conduct* committed by the principal, but for the *result*, he need only have the mens rea required for the result element of the substantive offense.

2. *The Model Penal Code on the mens rea required for results.* As *Roebuck* makes clear, the MPC is in accord with the analysis in *McVay*. Is the MPC's approach with respect to results consistent with its rejection of knowledge as a sufficient mens rea for accomplice liability? Why might the drafters have drawn a distinction between the mens rea one needs with respect to conduct and the mens rea one needs with respect to results?

3. *Problems.* Consider the following problems: *(a)* Passenger is in a hurry to catch a flight and asks Taxi Driver to get him to the airport on time and "do

whatever it takes." Taxi Driver drives over the speed limit and generally drives aggressively. Taxi Driver hits and kills the driver of another car after speeding through a light that turned from yellow to red as he went through. If Taxi Driver is guilty of negligent homicide, does it make sense for Passenger to avoid any criminal liability?

(*b*) Walt and Jesse are roommates. Jesse has been drinking all day and asks Walt if he can borrow Walt's car. Walt is aware that Jesse is drunk but gives him the keys to Walt's car. Jesse drives drunk and hits and kills a pedestrian. Under the principles of *McVay* and *Russell*, is Walt guilty of involuntary manslaughter or is this case distinguishable? Does Walt have the mens rea with respect to the result? Does Walt have the requisite mens rea with respect to the conduct element? What if before giving Jesse his keys, Walt asked Jesse to pick him up some pretzels at a convenience store on the way home?

4. *The Model Penal Code on the mens rea required for attendant circumstances.* The MPC takes the position that purpose is required as to "the commission of the offense," but the Code is silent on whether this requirement applies to attendant-circumstance elements of the offense. The drafters of the MPC explained in the accompanying commentary that this silence reflected a deliberate choice not to resolve the issue:

> There is deliberate ambiguity as to whether the purpose requirement extends to circumstance elements of the contemplated offense or whether, as in the case of attempts, the policy of the substantive offense on this point should control. The result, therefore, is that the actor must have a purpose with respect to the proscribed conduct, with his attitude towards the circumstances to be left to resolution by the courts. . . .

Model Penal Code and Commentaries, Comment to §206 at p. 311 n.37 (1985). How should the question of the proper mens rea for attendant circumstances in cases of accomplice liability be resolved? Consider the following problems.

(*a*) *A* is a convicted felon in a jurisdiction where it is a crime for convicted felons to possess firearms. *B* provides *A* with a firearm without knowing of *A*'s felony conviction. Should *B* be liable as an accomplice to *A*'s offense of possession? Hasn't *B* helped *A* to violate the statute? On the other hand, has *B* intended to help *A* commit a crime? One federal court has held liability improper, absent proof that *B* knew or should have known of *A*'s status as a convicted felon. United States v. Gardner, 488 F.3d 700, 714 (6th Cir. 2007). Another federal court, in contrast, holds that because *A* is strictly liable for knowing his felon status, no greater mens rea should be required for *B*. United States v. Canon, 993 F.2d 1429 (9th Cir. 1993). Are the justifications for strict liability in the case of *A* equally strong with respect to *B*? If not, is the *Gardner* court right to permit liability on the basis of negligence? If Gladstone's *knowing* assistance was insufficient for liability in the absence of purpose to aid, why should mere negligence be sufficient in the case of *B*?

(b) *B* encourages *A* to have sexual relations with a female *F*. *F* is under the age of consent, but *A* and *B* both reasonably believe that she is an adult. If the crime of statutory rape imposes strict liability, *A* is guilty of rape. Should *B* be liable as an accomplice? *B* did, after all, assist *A* in committing the rape. But did *B* intend to aid a crime? A court in Massachusetts concluded that it was appropriate to hold *B* liable without instructing the jury that it had to find that *B* had knowledge of the victim's age, at least where *B* was present at the scene and had the opportunity to make judgments about the child's age. Commonwealth v. Harris, 904 N.E.2d 478, 485 (Mass. App. Ct. 2009). But a contrary decision from North Carolina requires the jury to find that *B* had knowledge of the victim's age. State v. Bowman, 656 S.E.2d 638, 648-650 (N.C. Ct. App. 2008). Which is the better view? Are the arguments for and against strict liability for the principal perpetrator in the context of statutory rape equally relevant for the accomplice or is the case for strict liability less powerful for the latter?

5. Comparison to liability for attempt. With respect to the *result* element of crimes, we have seen that the MPC, along with the common law and most American statutes, is more demanding in prosecutions for attempt than in prosecutions for complicity. When a defendant is charged with attempt, the MPC requires that the defendant have the purpose to produce the proscribed result or the belief that his conduct will cause the result, even when recklessness or some lesser mens rea would suffice for conviction of the completed offense. Recall the *Smallwood* case, supra page 611. But when a defendant is charged with complicity in an offense, the required mens rea for resulting harm is not purpose, but only the mens rea required for the commission of the charged offense. What difference between the offense of attempt and the offense of aiding and abetting a completed crime might explain the different mens rea provisions for results? Is it that the retaliatory impulse is stronger when there is resulting harm?

When it comes to *attendant circumstances*, in contrast, the MPC is *less* demanding in cases of attempt than in cases of complicity, holding that the mens rea for attendant circumstances in cases of attempt is not purpose, but only the mens rea required for the completed crime. So in a statutory rape hypothetical like the one in Note 4(b), a person who tries but is prevented from having sex when the female is underage would be guilty of attempted statutory rape, even if he had no grounds to suspect that she was underage. Why does the MPC refuse to impose a similar, lower mens rea for attendant circumstances in cases of complicity but instead leave this decision to the courts? What might have led to the greater caution about mens rea for attendant circumstances in the context of complicity than in the context of attempt? Do the examples in Note 4 offer guidance? Consider the sweep of this approach if the MPC adopted the same mens rea for attendant circumstances in strict liability cases. In the *Dotterweich* case (supra page 283) would it mean that the defendant's wife could be held liable if she wakes him in the morning so he can get to work on time, and therefore aids him in selling what turns out to be contaminated aspirin?

PEOPLE v. RUSSELL

Court of Appeals of New York
91 N.Y.2d 280, 693 N.E.2d 193 (1998)

CHIEF JUDGE KAYE. [The three defendants battled each other in a shootout on the central mall of the Red Hook Housing Project in Brooklyn. During the course of the battle, Patrick Daly, a public school principal looking for a child who had left school, was fatally wounded by a single stray bullet. Defendants were all charged with second-degree murder. Although ballistics tests were inconclusive in determining which defendant fired the bullet that killed Daly, the theory of the prosecution was that each of them "intentionally aided" the defendant who fired the fatal shot (Penal Law §20.00). The jury convicted defendants of second-degree, depraved-indifference murder (Penal Law §125.25 [2]).]

A depraved indifference murder conviction requires proof that defendant, under circumstances evincing a depraved indifference to human life, recklessly engaged in conduct creating a grave risk of death to another person, and thereby caused the death of another person (Penal Law §125.25 [2]). . . .

Although defendants underscore that only one bullet killed Patrick Daly and it is uncertain which of them fired that bullet, the prosecution was not required to prove which defendant fired the fatal shot when the evidence was sufficient to establish that each defendant acted with the mental culpability required for the commission of depraved indifference murder, and each defendant "intentionally aided" the defendant who fired the fatal shot. Defendants urge, however, that the evidence adduced at trial did not support a finding that they—as adversaries in a deadly gun battle—shared the "community of purpose" necessary for accomplice liability. We disagree. The fact that defendants set out to injure or kill one another does not rationally preclude a finding that they intentionally aided each other to engage in the mutual combat that caused Daly's death.

People v. Abbott (445 N.Y.S.2d 344 [1981]) provides an apt illustration. That case involved two defendants—Abbott and Moon—who were engaged in a "drag race" on a residential street when Abbott lost control and smashed into another automobile, killing the driver and two passengers. Both defendants were convicted of criminally negligent homicide, but Moon asserted that he was not responsible for Abbott's actions and that his conviction should be set aside. Rejecting this argument, the court found that, although Moon did not strike the victim's car and was Abbott's adversary in a competitive race, he intentionally participated with Abbott in an inherently dangerous and unlawful activity and therefore shared Abbott's culpability. Moon's "conduct made the race possible" in the first place, as there would not have been a race had Moon not "accepted Abbott's challenge."

In the present case, the jurors were instructed: "If you find that the People have proven beyond a reasonable doubt that defendants took up each other's challenge, shared in the venture and unjustifiably, voluntarily and jointly created a zone of danger, then each is responsible for his own acts and the acts of the others ... [and] it makes no difference [whose bullet] penetrated Mr. Daly and caused his death."

[T]here was adequate proof to justify the finding that the three defendants tacitly agreed to engage in the gun battle that placed the life of any innocent bystander at grave risk and ultimately killed Daly. Indeed, unlike an unanticipated ambush or spontaneous attack that might have taken defendants by surprise, the gunfight in this case only began after defendants acknowledged and accepted each other's challenge to engage in a deadly battle on a public concourse. . . .

The evidence adduced at trial was also sufficient for the jury to determine that all three defendants acted with the mental culpability required for depraved indifference murder, and that they intentionally aided and encouraged each other to create the lethal crossfire that caused the death of Patrick Daly.

[A]ffirmed.

NOTES

1. *Being an "accomplice in the conduct."* Is it clear in *Abbott* that the concept of "accomplice in the conduct" would apply? Did participating in the race make Moon an accomplice in Abbott's conduct of crashing into the victim's car? Did Moon *want* Abbott to drive through the intersection in the manner he did? Or was he just reckless as to the possibility that Abbott would drive in that manner? And how about *Russell*? If Russell's own shots didn't kill the victim, did Russell *want* the opposing gang members to shoot back at him?

2. *Causation and complicity.* *Russell* and *Abbott* revisit the drag race problem, which we considered in the Causation section, Chapter 6.A.2.b, in connection with *Commonwealth v. Root*, supra page 601, and *State v. McFadden*, supra page 603. While those cases dealt with the liability of the defendants in terms of causation, *Russell* and *Abbott* deal with it in terms of complicity; that is, not whether the defendants personally caused the deaths, but whether they are accomplices of those who did. Which of these doctrinal approaches, causation or complicity, is the more satisfactory way to determine the criminal liability of the defendants? See Christopher Kutz, Complicity: Ethics and Law for a Collective Age 230-235 (2002).

c. The Natural and Probable Consequences Theory

The material thus far rests on the premise that liability as an accomplice for the criminal conduct of another requires that the accomplice have either specific intent to aid that conduct or, in rarer circumstances, knowledge of that conduct. There are, however, a number of cases and statutes that relax that traditional requirement. They are the subject of the material that follows.

PEOPLE v. LUPARELLO

California Court of Appeal, 4th District
187 Cal. App. 3d 410, 231 Cal. Rptr. 832 (1987)

KREMER, J. [Defendant Luparello wanted to locate Terri, his former lover who had deserted him to marry another. He thought he could discover her whereabouts from Mark Martin, a good friend of her current husband. To that end he enlisted the help of several friends, telling them that he wanted the information at any cost. His friends visited Martin but failed to get the information they sought. They returned the next evening armed with gun and sword, but without Luparello apparently, and lured Martin outside. Thereupon one of their group, waiting in a car, shot and killed Martin. Luparello was convicted of murder.]

The trial court charged the jury with several different theories by which Luparello's guilt for first degree murder could be affixed; among these were . . . aiding and abetting. On appeal . . . Luparello . . . attacks the theoretical underpinnings of . . . aiding-and-abetting liability, and specifically argues the murder here was the unplanned and unintended act of a coconspirator and therefore not chargeable to Luparello under complicity theory.

Luparello first faults [the] theor[y] for "imposing" the mens rea of the perpetrator upon him. As Luparello views it, [the] theor[y] work[s] to presume conclusively the accomplice shares the perpetrator's intent. . . . Luparello errs when he concludes the perpetrator and accomplice must "share" an identical intent to be found criminally responsible for the same crime. Technically, only the perpetrator can (and must) manifest the mens rea of the crime committed. Accomplice liability is premised on a different or, more appropriately, an equivalent mens rea. This equivalence is found in intentionally encouraging or assisting or influencing the nefarious act. . . . Thus, to be a principal to a crime . . . the aider and abettor must intend to commit the offense or to encourage or facilitate its commission. Liability is extended to reach the actual crime committed, rather than the planned or "intended" crime, on the policy [that] aiders and abettors should be responsible for the criminal harms they have naturally, probably and foreseeably put in motion. And it is precisely this policy which Luparello next challenges. . . .

The California Supreme Court [stated] in . . . People v. Croy, 710 P.2d 392 [(Cal. 1985)]:

> The requirement that the jury determine the intent with which a person tried as an aider and abettor has acted is not designed to ensure that his conduct constitutes the offense with which he is charged. His liability is vicarious. . . . [H]e is guilty not only of the offense he intended to facilitate or encourage, but also of any reasonably foreseeable offense committed by the person he aids and abets. . . .

Adopting the reasoning of the Supreme Court, we find the . . . aiding and abetting theor[y] proffered here do[es] not suffer the theoretical infirmities of which Luparello complains. In the circumstances of this case, [it] provides a sound basis to derive Luparello's criminal responsibility for first degree murder. . . .

Judgments affirmed.

WIENER, J., concurring: I concur . . . in the result reached by the majority under the compulsion of . . . *People v. Croy.* [That case] require[s] a holding that an aider and abettor or co-conspirator is liable not only for those crimes committed by a co-felon which he intended or agreed to facilitate but also for any additional crimes which are "reasonably foreseeable."[2] . . . This does not mean, however, that the announced principle is either logically consistent or theoretically sound.

. . . The major fallacy I see in the "foreseeable consequence" doctrine is not so much that it attributes an unintended act to the accomplice/co-conspirator but rather that it assesses the degree of his culpability for that act not by his own mental state but rather by the mental state of the perpetrator and/or the circumstances of the crime. . . . The assault on Mark Martin contemplated by the conspiracy involved a foreseeable risk of death or serious injury. We can assume (although there was no jury finding on the issue) that Luparello was criminally negligent in failing to appreciate the degree of risk. Under usual circumstances, a person negligently causing the death of another is guilty, at most, of involuntary manslaughter. Here, however, Luparello's liability is not based on his individual mental state but instead turns on the jury's finding that the unidentified shooter intentionally killed Martin while lying in wait. Thus, Luparello is guilty of first degree murder. If the circumstances of Luparello's participation were exactly the same but the shooter did not "lie in wait," Luparello could only be convicted of second degree murder. I am intrigued by the notion that if unknown to Luparello, the shooter ingested drugs and/or alcohol to the point where he did not in fact harbor the requisite malice, Luparello would presumably be guilty only of voluntary manslaughter. . . . I find such fortuity of result irrational. So too, apparently, do Professors LaFave and Scott in their treatise [Handbook on Criminal Law (1972) p. 516]:

> The "natural and probable consequence" rule of accomplice liability, if viewed as a broad generalization, is inconsistent with more fundamental principles of our system of criminal law. It would permit liability to be predicated upon negligence even when the crime involved requires a different state of mind. Such is not possible as to one who has personally committed a crime, and should likewise not be the case as to those who have given aid or counsel.

[T]he "foreseeable consequence" doctrine [and] the . . . felony-murder rule [are] . . . both founded on the same outmoded and logically indefensible

---

2. Henceforth I refer to this principle as the "foreseeable consequence" doctrine because that is the terminology used in *Croy.* I am concerned, however, about how a principle which was originally phrased in terms of "probable and natural consequences" was slightly modified to become the "natural and reasonable consequences" and has now been saddled with a monicker traditionally associated with theories of expanding tort liability. If we were to return to strict interpretation of the "natural and probable" standard, I would argue that liability could not be imposed here on Luparello because in no sense can it be said that Mark Martin's death was the "probable" result of a conspiracy to assault him in order to obtain information.

proposition that if a person exhibits some intent to violate the law, we need not be terribly concerned that the contemplated crime was far less serious than the crime which actually took place. . . .

The artificial imputation of stepped-up intent, inherent in both the felony-murder rule and the "foreseeable consequence" doctrine, is inconsistent with the "universal and persistent" notion that criminal punishment must be proportional to the defendant's culpable mental state. Justice Mosk's dissent in Taylor v. Superior Court, 477 P.2d 131 (Cal. [1970]) expressed it well: "Fundamental principles of criminal responsibility dictate that the defendant be subject to a greater penalty only when he has demonstrated a greater degree of culpability." The fact that the accomplice or co-conspirator intended to facilitate some less serious criminal act does not render these fundamental principles inapplicable.

Roy v. United States, 652 A.2d 1098 (D.C. Ct. App. 1995): [Peppi Miller was a paid police informant who approached defendant Roy in an attempt to make an undercover buy of a handgun. Roy told him to return later with $400, and when he did so, he was referred to Ross, who took him to another area. There Ross gave Miller the gun while Miller counted out the $400, but then Ross asked for the gun back, said he changed his mind, and robbed Miller of the $600 in his possession. To Miller's request for an explanation, he replied that he was avenging Miller's earlier stickup of one of his own group. Roy was convicted as an accomplice to Ross's armed robbery. The trial court included an instruction that it would suffice to find defendant liable if the robbery was the natural and probable consequence of the illegal attempt to sell a handgun, even if he did not intend Ross to rob Miller. At the same time, however, the judge invited a reexamination of the natural and probable consequence rule, stating:]

> The criminal law is trying . . . in these cases . . . to draw a line to serve two different policies that are . . . inconsistent with each other. On the one hand, there's clearly a policy in the criminal law not to hold people responsible for things that they did not intend to do. . . . On the other hand, there is a competing policy that says, if you put criminal conduct in motion, or you intentionally assist in the commission of a crime, then you are held responsible for the natural and probable consequences of that crime, even if they go beyond what you put in motion. . . . Somewhere between those two things, the law draws a line in what you can be held liable for, and what you can't.
>
> The natural and probable consequence doctrine of aiding and abetting . . . ought to be examined again by our Court of Appeals. . . . An early court borrowed a doctrine that was really an exception applicable in the case of the felony murder doctrine and then grafted it onto the law of aiding and abetting generally, actually borrowed it [also] from the law of conspiracy, and then grafted it onto the law of aiding and abetting as it applies to [any] offense and then repeated it so often that it became self-fulfilling without much analysis in the later cases.

[The court of appeals reversed, finding the evidence insufficient to support a conviction on the "natural and probable consequences" theory, stating:] By invoking the "natural and probable consequences" theory, the government insists that we sustain Roy's convictions of armed robbery . . . without requiring a showing that Roy intended to participate in the robbery of Miller or in any other crime of violence. Armed robbery is a felony punishable by life imprisonment; selling a handgun, on the other hand, constitutes . . . a misdemeanor of which Roy has been independently convicted. The government's application of the "natural and probable consequences" doctrine would thus dramatically expand Roy's exposure even where . . . he did not intend that a crime of violence be committed.

This court has stated that "an accessory is liable for any criminal act which in the ordinary course of things was the natural and probable consequence of the crime that he advised or commanded, although such consequence may not have been intended by him." . . . The phrase "in the ordinary course of things" refers to what may reasonably ensue from the planned events, not to what might conceivably happen, and in particular suggests the absence of intervening factors. . . . It is not enough for the prosecution to show that the accomplice knew or should have known that the principal might conceivably commit the offense which the accomplice is charged with aiding and abetting. Without inserting additional phrases or adjectives into the calculus, we think that our precedents require the government to prove a good deal more than that. A "natural and probable" consequence in the "ordinary course of things" presupposes an outcome within a reasonably predictable range. . . .

The government contends that the armed robbery of Miller was in furtherance of the common purpose because it resulted in the defendants' obtaining Miller's money—an achievement which, according to the government, was the defendant's prime design and plan in the first place. In our view, however, an exchange of a handgun for $400 is qualitatively different from an armed robbery in which Ross stole $600 and retained for himself the object which, in Roy's contemplation, was supposed to be sold. . . . The government [also] argues that Peppi Miller was a logical target of a robbery because, "given the illegal nature of the activity in which he was involved, [he] was unlikely to file a complaint with the police about the robbery." This reasoning, however, recognizes no apparent limiting principle. If we were to accept the government's position, then the robbery of any buyer or seller in a drug or unlicensed pistol sale would be viewed as the "natural and probable consequence" of that transaction, for a participant in any illegal project may well be reluctant to invoke the aid of the constabulary. . . .

Viewed in the light most favorable to the prosecution, the evidence would perhaps support a finding that Roy should have known that it was conceivable that Ross might rob Miller. The evidence was insufficient, however, to show that a robbery would follow in the "ordinary course of events," or that it was a "natural and probable consequence" of the activities in which Roy was shown to have engaged.

NOTES AND QUESTIONS

1. *State of the law.* A substantial number of jurisdictions have embraced the natural and probable consequences test used in the *Luparello* case. See

John F. Decker, The Mental State Requirement for Accomplice Liability in American Criminal Law, 60 S.C. L. Rev. 237 (2008). But the natural and probable consequences test remains controversial, and the majority of courts refuse to endorse it. Michael S. Moore, Causing, Aiding, and the Superfluity of Accomplice Liability, 156 U. Pa. L. Rev. 395, 400 n.12 (2007). For a recent example of a court rejecting the test, see State v. Lopez-Minjarez, 260 P.3d 439 (Or. 2011).

2. *Comparison to Pinkerton doctrine.* The natural and probable consequences doctrine is similar, though not identical, to the *Pinkerton* doctrine developed in conspiracy law. Under *Pinkerton*, a defendant who is guilty of conspiring to commit one offense may be convicted of other offenses that his co-conspirators commit if those additional offenses further the conspiratorial objective and are reasonably foreseeable consequences of the conspiratorial agreement. In a jurisdiction that embraces the natural and probable consequences doctrine, the *Pinkerton* doctrine does not add much because any case that could be brought under *Pinkerton* could already be brought under the natural and probable consequence theory of accomplice liability. But in the majority of jurisdictions that reject the natural and probable consequences doctrine, *Pinkerton* provides an avenue for going beyond the limits of traditional accomplice liability. Note, however, that *Pinkerton* liability is a more limited expansion of traditional accomplice liability than the natural and probable consequences doctrine because *Pinkerton* requires an agreement and imposes the additional requirement that to charge any crimes beyond the crime the conspirators conspire to commit, the prosecution must show that those additional crimes were committed to further the conspiracy. See the discussion of the *Pinkerton* case infra at pages 723-735.

Question: Could Luparello be held liable for the murder of Martin under the *Pinkerton* doctrine? Why not?

3. *Model Penal Code.* The MPC rejects the natural and probable consequences doctrine for accomplice liability. Model Penal Code and Commentaries, Comment to §2.06 at 310-313 (1985) states:

> Subsection (3)(a) requires that the actor have the purpose of promoting or facilitating the commission of the offense. . . . This does not mean, of course, that the precise means used in the commission of the crime must have been fixed or contemplated or, when they have been, that liability is limited to their employment. One who solicits an end, or aids or agrees to aid in its achievement, is an accomplice in whatever means may be employed, insofar as they constitute an offense fairly envisaged in the purposes of the association. But when a wholly different crime has been committed, thus involving conduct not within the conscious objectives of the accomplice, he is not liable for it. . . . [I]t is submitted that the liability of an accomplice ought not to be extended beyond the purposes that he shares. Probabilities have an important evidential bearing on these issues; to make them independently sufficient is to predicate the liability on negligence when, for good reason, more is normally required before liability is found.

2. *Actus Reus*

a. Encouragement

WILCOX v. JEFFERY

King's Bench Division
[1951] 1 All E.R. 464

LORD GODDARD, C.J. This is a Case stated by the metropolitan magistrate at Bow Street Magistrate's Court before whom the appellant, Herbert William Wilcox, the proprietor of a periodical called "Jazz Illustrated," was charged on an information that

> on Dec. 11, 1949, he did unlawfully aid and abet one Coleman Hawkins in contravening art. 1(4) of the Aliens Order, 1920, by failing to comply with a condition attached to a grant of leave to land, to wit, that the said Coleman Hawkins should take no employment paid or unpaid while in the United Kingdom, contrary to art. 18(2) of the Aliens Order, 1920. . . .

The case is concerned with the visit of a celebrated professor of the saxophone, a gentleman by the name of Hawkins who was a citizen of the United States. He came here at the invitation of two gentlemen of the name of Curtis and Hughes, connected with a jazz club which enlivens the neighborhood of Willesden. . . . Mr. Hawkins . . . arrived with four French musicians. When they came to the airport, among the people who were there to greet them was the appellant. He had not arranged their visit, but he knew they were coming and he was there to report the arrival of these important musicians for his magazine. So, evidently, he was regarding the visit of Mr. Hawkins as a matter which would be of interest to himself and the magazine which he was editing and selling for profit. Messrs. Curtis and Hughes arranged a concert at the Princes Theatre, London. The appellant attended that concert as a spectator. He paid for his ticket. Mr. Hawkins went on the stage and delighted the audience by playing the saxophone. The appellant did not get up and protest in the name of the musicians of England that Mr. Hawkins ought not to be here competing with them and taking the bread out of their mouths or the wind out of their instruments. It is not found that he actually applauded, but he was there having paid to go in, and, no doubt, enjoying the performance, and then, lo and behold out comes his magazine with a most laudatory description, fully illustrated, of this concert. On those facts the magistrate has found that he aided and abetted.

Reliance is placed by the prosecution on R. v. Coney ((1882), 8 Q.B.D. 534) which dealt with a prize fight. This case relates to a jazz band concert, but the particular nature of the entertainment provided, whether by fighting with bare fists or playing on saxophones, does not seem to me to make any difference to the question which we have to decide. The fact is that a man is charged with aiding and abetting an illegal act, and I can find no authority for saying that it matters what that illegal act is, provided that the aider and abettor knows the facts sufficiently well to know that they would constitute an offence in the principal. In *R. v. Coney* the prize fight took place in the neighborhood of Ascot, and four or five men were convicted of aiding and abetting the fight. The conviction was quashed on the ground that the chairman had not given a correct direction to the jury when he told them that, as the prisoners were physically present at the fight, they must be held to have aided and abetted. That direction, the court held, was wrong, it being too wide. The matter was very concisely put by Cave, J., whose judgment was fully concurred in by that great master of the criminal law, Stephen, J. Cave, J., said (8 Q.B.D. 540): "Where presence may be entirely accidental, it is not even evidence of aiding and abetting. Where presence is prima facie not accidental it is evidence, but no more than evidence, for the jury."

There was not accidental presence in this case. The appellant paid to go to the concert and he went there because he wanted to report it. He must, therefore, be held to have been present, taking part, concurring, or encouraging, whichever word you like to use for expressing this conception. It was an illegal act on the part of Hawkins to play the saxophone or any other instrument at this concert. The appellant clearly knew that it was an unlawful act for him to play. He had gone there to hear him, and his presence and his payment to go there was an encouragement. He went there to make use of the performance, because he went there, as the magistrate finds and was justified in finding, to get "copy" for his newspaper. It might have been entirely different, as I say, if he had gone there and protested, saying: "The musicians' union do not like you foreigners coming here and playing and you ought to get off the stage." If he had booed, it might have been some evidence that he was not aiding and abetting. If he had gone as a member of a claque to try to drown the noise of the saxophone, he might very likely be found not guilty of aiding and abetting. In this case it seems clear that he was there, not only to approve and encourage what was done, but to take advantage of it by getting "copy" for his paper. In those circumstances there was evidence on which the magistrate could find that the appellant aided and abetted, and for these reasons I am of opinion that the appeal fails. . . .

Appeal dismissed with costs.

QUESTIONS ON ENCOURAGEMENT AS ACTUS REUS

1. Onlookers. Would the finding of accomplice liability for Wilcox apply equally to any member of the audience who, knowing that it was illegal for Coleman Hawkins to perform in the United Kingdom, clapped politely? Does that act seem too minimal under the circumstances? Does it seem equally troubling to hold liable as accomplices those who clap, cheer, or yell encouragement during a violent assault, like a rape? In a famous Massachusetts case, on which the film *The Accused* was loosely based, six men were charged with raping a young woman on a pool table in a New Bedford tavern. Four were convicted, based on evidence that they had each committed forced sex acts on the woman, but two were acquitted in the absence of any evidence of direct

participation in the assaults, despite evidence that they had verbally encouraged the sex acts, including one man's admission that he had yelled, "Go for it!
Go for it!" while the others were raping the victim. See Two Convicted, Two
Acquitted in Barroom Gang Rape, U.P.I., Mar. 23, 1984. Should the two men
who were acquitted have been convicted as accomplices to the rapes? Should
mere presence, without clapping or cheering, be sufficient for crimes like gang
rape, dog fighting, and drag racing, that are, in many respects, motivated by a
desire to perform for an audience? Although mere presence is not enough for
accomplice liability, 48 states have outlawed the knowing and intentional
presence at a dog fight, and other states have done the same for being present
at drag races. Some argue this approach should apply to those who witness
gang rapes. Kimberley K. Allen, Note, Guilt By (More Than) Association: The
Case for Spectator Liability in Gang Rapes, 99 Geo. L.J. 837 (2011). What is
(or should be) the liability of a person who turns the corner of a side street and
sees two men raping a third person? Does the bystander have a duty to intervene or summon help? If he does not summon help but stays to watch, does he
become an accomplice to the rape?

2. Speech. Because the actus reus for accomplice liability can consist
entirely of speech, it arguably raises First Amendment concerns, which the
Wilcox case highlights. (Wilcox was, after all, a reporter there to cover the
event.) Does the requirement that the accomplice intend to facilitate criminal
conduct act as a sufficient check against prosecutors who might threaten First
Amendment interests? Eugene Volokh argues that this heightened standard
does not do much work: "[M]ost speakers of crime-facilitating speech will
know that the speech may facilitate crime, but relatively few will clearly
intend this. For many speakers, their true mental state will be hard to determine, because their words may be equally consistent with intention to facilitate crime and with mere knowledge. This means that any conclusion about
the speaker's purpose will usually just be a guess." Eugene Volokh, Crime-
Facilitating Speech, 57 Stan. L. Rev. 1095, 1185-1186 (2005). What limits, if
any, should be placed on accomplice liability to account for this concern?
Wilcox remains good law, but should accomplice liability be modified to
require more of an actus reus? Should accomplice liability require a showing
of *significant* or *substantial* aid or encouragement? Consider the materials that
follow.

b. The Materiality of the Aid

*State ex rel. Attorney General v. Tally, Judge, 102 Ala. 25, 69, 15 So. 722,
739 (1894):* [On an impeachment proceeding against Judge Tally, it was
established as follows: Ross had seduced Judge Tally's sister-in-law. Her
brothers, the Skeltons, followed Ross to the nearby town of Stevenson, in
order to kill him. Judge Tally went to the local telegraph office at Scottsboro
and while there learned that one of Ross's relatives had sent Ross a telegram
warning, "Four men on horseback with guns following. Look out." Judge Tally

then sent his own telegram to the telegraph operator at Stevenson (whom he knew), telling him not to deliver the warning telegram to Ross. The operator received both telegrams and failed to deliver the message to Ross. The Skelton brothers caught up with Ross and killed him. On these facts, the court held that the judge was an accomplice of the Skelton brothers in the killing:]

We are therefore clear to the conclusion that before Judge Tally can be found guilty of aiding and abetting the Skeltons to kill Ross, it must appear that his vigil at Scottsboro to prevent Ross from being warned of his danger was by preconcert with them, or at least known to them, whereby they would naturally be incited, encouraged and emboldened, "given confidence" to the deed, or that he aided them to kill Ross, contributed to Ross's death in point of physical fact by means of the telegram he sent to Huddleston [the telegraph operator.] . . .

The assistance given, however, need not contribute to the criminal result in the sense that but for it the result would not have ensued. It is quite sufficient if it facilitated a result that would have transpired without it. It is quite enough if the aid merely renders it easier for the principal actor to accomplish the end intended by him and the aider and abettor, though in all human probability the end would have been attained without it. If the aid in homicide can be shown to have put the deceased at a disadvantage, to have deprived him of a single chance of life, which but for it he would have had, he who furnishes such aid is guilty though it can not be known or shown that the dead man, in the absence thereof, would have availed himself of that chance. As where one counsels murder he is guilty as an accessory before the fact, though it appears to be probable that murder would have been done without his counsel, and as where one being present by concert to aid if necessary is guilty as a principal in the second degree, though had he been absent murder would have been committed, so where he who facilitates murder, even by so much as destroying a single chance of life the assailed might otherwise have had, he thereby supplements the efforts of the perpetrator, and he is guilty as principal in the second degree at common law, and is principal in the first degree under our statute, notwithstanding it may be found that in all human probability the chance would not have been availed of, and death would have resulted anyway.

PROBLEMS ON THE MATERIALITY OF THE AID OR ENCOURAGEMENT GIVEN

1. *Causation and complicity.* As *Tally* and *Wilcox* make clear, it is not necessary to establish a but-for relation between the defendant's action and the criminal conduct of another to establish accomplice liability. What is the justification for holding someone liable for a crime if it would have occurred anyway? Is it based on retributive concerns? Utilitarian arguments? Both? Consider in this respect the New Bedford gang rape case. The spectators certainly seem morally blameworthy. And even if encouragement or aid

may not be a but-for cause of criminal conduct, it makes crime more likely to occur.

2. Attempted complicity? We just noted that even a minimal possibility of actual aid or encouragement suffices for accessorial liability.

Question: Need there be *any* actual aid or encouragement at all? Consider these variations on cases we have just read.

In *Hicks*, suppose the defendant deliberately shouted encouragement to Rowe to spur him on to kill Colvard, but it is shown at the trial that Rowe was completely deaf and was, moreover, totally unaware of Hicks's presence.

In *Tally*, what would have been the result:

  a. if the telegraph operator had disregarded the judge's instructions and had tried, though in vain, to deliver the warning telegram?
  b. if the telegraph operator followed the judge's instructions and did not deliver the warning, but the pursuers never succeeded in catching up with their intended victim?
  c. if the pursuers did catch up, but were effectively resisted by their victim?

In the *Hicks* and the first *Tally* hypothetical, there is attempted encouragement or aid to the person who commits the crime, but none is in fact rendered. What should be the liability of the defendants? Under the law before the MPC, there would be no liability. See J.C. Smith, Aid, Abet, Counsel or Procure, in Reshaping the Criminal Law 132-133 (P.R. Glazebrook ed., 1978): "An attempt to counsel . . . does not amount to counselling. Advice or encouragement proffered at the scene of the crime but not communicated to the mind of the principal offender does not amount to aiding and abetting."

These difficulties are avoided by the MPC, §2.06(3), and the jurisdictions that follow its lead.[4] Defendants in the first and third of the above *Tally* hypotheticals would be accomplices because a person acting with the required mens rea is an accomplice whether the person aids or "attempts to aid" another person in planning or committing the offense. Moreover, §2.06(3)(a)(i) makes solicitation the basis for accomplice liability, and §5.02(2) provides that solicitation is established even if the actor fails to communicate with the person he solicits to commit the crime. In support of its position the Comment to the MPC observes (Model Penal Code and Commentaries, Comment to §2.06 at 314 (1985)):

> The inclusion of attempts to aid may go in part beyond present law, but attempted complicity ought to be criminal, and to distinguish it from effective complicity appears unnecessary where the crime has been committed. Where complicity is based upon agreement or solicitation, one does not ask for evidence that they were actually operative psychologically on the person who committed the offense; there ought to be no difference in the case of aid.

---

4. See, e.g., Ky. Rev. Stat. Ann. ch. 500, §502.020(1)(b) (2011); N.J. Stat. Ann. §2C:2-6(c)(1)(b) (2011); 18 Pa. Cons. Stat. Ann. §306(c)(1)(ii) (2011); Tex. Pen. Code Ann. §7.02 (2011).

Note the difficulty introduced in the second *Tally* hypothetical. Here the crime the defendant tried to aid is not committed. §2.06(3) does not cover the situation. Do you see why? How should it be dealt with? The MPC solution to this problem is sketched in the Comment to §2.06 supra, at 314 n.46:

Section 2.06(3) of the Model Code is predicated . . . on the actual commission of an offense by the person aided. Assuming the requisite culpability, one who aids, or attempts to aid, or agrees to aid, is thus liable under this section only if the principal actor actually commits an offense. . . .

Where the principal actor commits neither the completed offense nor an attempt, however, a different situation is presented. The purported accomplice in that situation would not be liable under Section 2.06 because he did not aid in the commission of a crime. His conduct designed to render aid may be criminal, however, either as an attempt (Section 5.01(3)) or, in the case of preconcert, as criminal conspiracy (Section 5.03(1)(b)). In both situations liability for the abortive effort plainly seems appropriate.

3. Complicity by omission. Can a person become an accomplice by failing to act to prevent another from committing a crime? Consistent with the general approach to determining criminal liability for omissions, the MPC provides that a person can be an accomplice if he has a legal duty to prevent the offense and he fails to do so with the purpose of promoting or facilitating the crime. §2.06(3)(a)(iii). In support of its position the commentary states (p. 320):

The policeman or the watchman who closes his eyes to a burglary fails to present an obstacle to its commission that he is obliged to interpose. If his purpose is to promote or facilitate its perpetration, a fact that normally can be proved only by preconcert with the criminals, no reason can be offered for denying his complicity. But if the dereliction is not purposeful in that respect, as when it rests upon timidity or inefficiency, it is unduly harsh to view it as participation in the crime.

Can complicity by omission be found even in the absence of preconcert? Consider People v. Stanciel, 606 N.E.2d 1201 (Ill. 1992). Violetta Burgos was charged as an accomplice to murder when her boyfriend, Stanciel, beat her three-year-old daughter to death. Burgos had violated a court order to keep Stanciel away from the child and had authorized Stanciel to discipline the child despite his past and ongoing abusive behavior. Though Burgos did not perform any of the acts that led to her daughter's death, the court ruled that her failure to protect her child from Stanciel rendered Burgos an accomplice to her daughter's murder. Most courts agree with *Stanciel* that parents can be liable under an aiding and abetting theory for a crime committed by a third party when they fail to protect their children from the abuse. People v. Rolon, 73 Cal. Rptr. 3d 358, 366 (Cal. Ct. App. 2008).

4. Omissions and mens rea. Would the result in *Stanciel* be the same under the MPC? Plainly the mother was under a legal duty, but is there enough evidence to support a finding that she acted with the purpose that Stanciel should beat the child to death? Suppose she had not authorized him to discipline the child and had stood by out of fear?

Many cases have held, in accord with *Stanciel*, that a parent can be convicted as an aider and abettor of child abuse for failing to protect a child from abuse by a third party. See generally Dorothy E. Roberts, Motherhood and Crime, 79 Iowa L. Rev. 95 (1993). How should the law address workers at child welfare agencies who fail to protect children from abusive parents? Can the worker's failure to act be the basis of criminal charges on an aiding and abetting theory? New York prosecutors believe the answer is yes, as they have recently brought the city's first-ever cases of negligent criminal homicide against child services caseworkers. Jennifer Gonnerman, The Knock at the Door, N.Y. Mag., Sept. 11, 2011.

3. The Relationship Between the Liability of the Parties

STATE v. HAYES

Supreme Court of Missouri
105 Mo. 76, 16 S.W. 514 (1891)

THOMAS, J. The defendant appeals from a sentence of five years' imprisonment in the penitentiary for burglary and larceny. [Defendant proposed to one Hill that he join him in the burglary of a general store. Hill, actually a relative of the store owners, feigned acquiescence in order to obtain the arrest of defendant and advised the store owners of the plan. On the night of the planned burglary, defendant and Hill arrived at the store together. Defendant raised the window and assisted Hill in climbing through into the building. Hill handed out a side of bacon. Shortly thereafter they were apprehended.] It will be seen the trial court told the jury in [its] instruction that defendant was guilty of burglary if he, with a felonious intent, assisted and aided Hill to enter the building, notwithstanding Hill himself may have had no such intent. In this we think the court erred. One cannot read this record without being convinced beyond a reasonable doubt that Hill did not enter the warehouse with intent to steal. . . . We may assume, then, for the sake of the argument, that Hill committed no crime in entering the wareroom. The act of Hill, however, was by the instruction of the court imputed to defendant. This act, according to the theory of the instructions, so far as Hill was concerned, was not a criminal act, but when it was imputed to defendant it became criminal because of the latter's felonious intent. This would probably be true if Hill had acted under the control and compulsion of defendant, and as his passive and submissive agent. But he was not a passive agent in this transaction. He was an active one. He acted of his own volition. He did not raise the window and enter the building with intent to commit crime, but simply to entrap defendant in the commission of crime, and have him captured.

Judge Brewer sets this idea in a very clear light in State v. Jansen, 22 Kan. 498. He says: "The act of a detective may perhaps be not imputable to the defendant, as there is a want of community of motive. The one has a criminal intent, while the other is seeking the discovery and punishment of crime." Where the owner learns that his property is to be stolen, he may employ detectives and decoys to catch the thief. And we can do no better than to quote again from Judge Brewer in the case above cited, as to the relation of the acts of detectives and the thief when a crime is alleged to have been committed by the two. He says: "Where each of the overt acts going to make up the crime charged is personally done by the defendant, and with criminal intent, his guilt is complete, no matter what motives may prompt or what acts be done by the party who is with him, and apparently assisting him. Counsel have cited and commented upon several cases in which detectives figured, and in which defendants were adjudged guiltless of the crimes charged. But this feature distinguishes them: that some act essential to the crime charged was in fact done by the detective, and not by the defendant, and, this act not being imputable to the defendant, the latter's guilt was not made out. The intent and act must combine, and all the elements of the act must exist and be imputable to the defendant."

Applying the principle here announced to the case at bar, we find that defendant did not commit every overt act that went to make up the crime. He did not enter the warehouse, either actually or constructively, and hence he did not commit the crime of burglary, no matter what his intent was, it clearly appearing that Hill was guilty of no crime. To make defendant responsible for the acts of Hill, they must have had a common motive and common design. The design and the motives of the two men were not only distinct, but dissimilar, even antagonistic. . . . The court should instruct the jury that if Hill broke into and entered the wareroom with a felonious intent, and defendant was present, aiding him with the same intent, then he is guilty; but if Hill entered the room with no design to steal, but simply to entrap defendant, and capture him in the commission of crime, and defendant did not enter the room himself, then he is not guilty of burglary and larceny as charged. He may be found guilty, however, of petit larceny, in taking and removing the bacon after it was handed to him. This overt act he did in fact commit. . . . The judgment is reversed, and the cause remanded for new trial.

Vaden v. State, 768 P.2d 1102 (Alaska 1989): [Fish and Wildlife Protection officers received a tip that Vaden, a local guide, was promoting illegal hunting practices by his customers. The officers assigned one of their undercover agents, John Snell, to pose as a hunter and to commission Vaden's services. On the hunt, Vaden piloted the aircraft and maneuvered it to facilitate Snell's shooting game from the plane with a shotgun Vaden had lent him for the purpose. Snell shot and killed four foxes. Vaden was convicted, as Snell's accomplice, of hunting in violation of Alaskan law. On appeal, the Supreme Court of Alaska affirmed the convictions, rejecting Vaden's argument that because Snell's action was justified in light of the needs of law enforcement (the "public authority justification defense"), no criminal action occurred for which he could be convicted of being an accomplice. The court reasoned that the action of Snell was not justified, but that even if it were, it would not avail Vaden, because the justification would be personal to the agent.[a] The majority also found that no entrapment had been shown and that the actions of Snell, while unlawful, were not so outrageous as to constitute a denial of due process.]

[The dissenting opinion reasoned:] The accomplice liability charges should fail on [the] ground [of] the long-standing common law rule that the act of a feigned accomplice may never be imputed to the targeted defendant for purposes of obtaining a conviction. In State v. Neely, 300 P. 561 (Mont. 1931), the Montana Supreme Court applied this principle under circumstances akin to those in the case at bar. In *Neely*, a cattle owner employed a detective, Harrington, to "get in" with suspected cattle thieves during an act of cattle rustling. Harrington associated himself with the criminal enterprise, and the crime was carried out. Harrington himself, however, committed the principal offense of purloining the cattle, while the targeted suspect merely stood watch outside the premises and offered various other forms of assistance before and after commission of the offense. The court reversed Neely's conviction as an accomplice to the crime. . . . [5] The principle enunciated in *Neely*, which has been repeated by numerous courts under a variety of factual circumstances . . . is based in sound reason. It is the general rule that one who aids and abets another in criminal activity is liable for all of the "natural and probable consequences" of his accomplice's criminal acts. Thus, the potential for abuse inherent in law enforcement methods such as those employed in the case at bar is substantial. Once an agent has succeeded in persuading an individual to take some substantial act in furtherance of his general criminal scheme, the ultimate liability of the targeted defendant, if any, will depend upon which foreseeable crimes the agent chooses to commit in order to secure convictions against his criminal "accomplice." In this case, Officer Snell shot four foxes. Vaden, as pilot of the plane from which they were shot, was charged with four separate criminal counts of taking foxes from the air out of season. Had Snell opted to shoot a fifth fox, one more count could have been added to Vaden's indictment. In my view, it is clearly inconsistent with due process principles, and manifestly unjust, that the ultimate criminal liability of a defendant

---

a. The justification referred to is that of law enforcement representatives who sometimes may break the law (not involving personal violence) in the course of enforcing it against others; for example, according to the New York Penal Law §35.05 (2009), when the conduct "is performed by a public servant in the reasonable exercise of his official powers, duties or functions."—EDS.

5. Notably, this was not a case in which the court found that the owner's consent to Harrington's taking vitiated the unlawfulness of his acts. Like the majority today, the court in *Neely* concluded that Harrington had exceeded his rightful authority in taking and butchering the cattle. 300 P. at 565. Nonetheless, the court concluded that Harrington's acts, as a feigned accomplice, could not be imputed to Neely.

should be made to depend upon the good aim and/or the good intentions of the police officer charged with securing his arrest.

NOTES AND QUESTIONS

1. Distinguishing Hayes *from* Vaden. The dissent in *Vaden* invokes the rule that acts of a feigned principal may not be imputed to the targeted defendant for the purpose of convicting him as an accomplice. This appears to be what underlay the decision to reverse the conviction of the *Hayes* case. But is the situation in the *Vaden* case distinguishable? Snell did shoot the foxes in violation of law, and Vaden did help him do so. How can it be that Snell's motive in violating the hunting laws (to secure a conviction against Vaden) could render Vaden not guilty? In the *Vaden* case there are plausible answers, turning on the public policy of discouraging unacceptable law enforcement practices. But the dissent in *Vaden* relies on a principle that is not confined to law enforcement personnel. If Snell were a private individual with a grudge against Vaden, would the dissent's argument hold up? Was Snell a "feigned" principal at all?

2. Role reversal and the importance of shared intent. Could Hill, the feigned principal, have been charged as an accomplice to Hayes if their roles in the burglary had been reversed but Hill still lacked the intent to steal the bacon? In Wilson v. People, 87 P.2d 5 (Colo. 1939), Wilson, angry at Pierce for allegedly stealing his watch, helped Pierce break into a drug store by boosting him through a transom. While Pierce was inside the store, Wilson left briefly to telephone the police and returned to receive bottles of whiskey that Pierce handed to him through the transom. When the police arrived, Wilson helped the police capture Pierce and identified Pierce as the burglar. Wilson later admitted to the police his connection to the burglary but explained that he helped Pierce only in the hopes of framing Pierce, not because Wilson had the specific intent that they commit larceny. Larceny requires the intent to permanently deprive the owner of his property, so Wilson's defense is that he never had the intent to deprive the drugstore of the whiskey bottles permanently. And if Wilson lacked the intent for larceny, he lacked the intent for burglary as well, because he did not break and enter with the intent to commit a felony. Wilson was charged and convicted of aiding in the commission of the burglary. The Colorado Supreme Court reversed Wilson's conviction holding, quoting 1 F. Wharton, Criminal Law §271 (12th ed. 1932):

> [W]hile detectives, when acting as decoys, may apparently provoke the crime, the essential element of dolus, or malicious determination to violate the law, is wanting in their case. And it is only the formal, and not the substantive, part of the crime that they provoke. They provoke, for instance, in larceny, the aspor- tation of the goods, but not the ultimate loss by the owner. They may be actuated by the most unworthy of motives, but the animus furandi in larceny is not imputable to them. . . .

Wilson thus serves as a reminder of the importance of the accomplice's mens rea in those jurisdictions that follow the traditional rule that the accomplice must have the specific intent that the crime be committed. See supra pages 661-670. What if the facts in *Wilson* were different and Wilson's goal had been to help Pierce kill the owner of the drug store in order to see Pierce do time for murder. In that situation, is it clear that Wilson could not be charged with the killing under a theory of accomplice liability?

3. *Entrapment.* In some cases involving feigned *accomplices*, the defendant may have a defense of "entrapment"—which most American jurisdictions define as government inducement of a defendant who is not "predisposed" to commit the offense—but only when the accomplice is a government agent who improperly induces the defendant's criminal activity. Routine undercover drug purchases and other "sting" operations generally do not trigger such a defense. In contrast, in Jacobson v. United States, 503 U.S. 540 (1992), the court reversed a defendant's conviction for receiving child pornography through the mail because no inference of predisposition was warranted when government agents subjected defendant to 26 months of fictitious mailings promoting child pornography, and there was no evidence that the defendant had otherwise sought or received illegal child pornography from nongovernmental sources. Why should the entrapment defense rest on whether the feigned accomplice is a government actor versus a private one?

Even if a suspect is predisposed to commit the offense (thereby negating the entrapment defense), why should a defendant's sentence depend on attendant circumstances manipulated by the government? As the dissenting opinion in *Vaden* observed, accepting law enforcement agents as principals gives them the discretion to determine the charges an accomplice faces and often the sentence as well. Law enforcement officers can engage in "sentencing entrapment"—where the government creates or induces a far greater crime than the suspect originally intends, for example, by having defendants cook powder cocaine into crack or engage in a drug transaction in a school zone, thereby exposing the defendant to a much higher sentence. Derrick Augustus Carter, To Catch the Lion, Tether the Goat: Entrapment, Conspiracy, and Sentencing Manipulation, 42 Akron L. Rev. 135, 137 (2009).

NOTES AND PROBLEMS ON THE DERIVATIVE NATURE OF ACCOMPLICE LIABILITY

The derivative nature of accomplice liability is an axiom in the doctrine of complicity: "It is hornbook law that a defendant charged with aiding and abetting the commission of a crime by another cannot be convicted in the absence of proof that the crime was actually committed." United States v. Ruffin, 613 F.2d 408, 412 (2d Cir. 1979); "There must be a guilty principal before there can be an aider and abettor." United States v. Jones, 425 F.2d 1048, 1056 (9th Cir. 1970).

It is important, however, not to confuse derivative liability with vicarious liability. Accomplice liability does not involve imposing liability on one party for the wrongs of another solely because of the relationship between the parties. Liability requires *culpability* and *conduct* by the secondary actor—intentional conduct designed to encourage or help—that makes it appropriate to blame him for what the primary actor does. The term "derivative" merely means that his liability is dependent on the principal's violating the law. What is at issue is the responsibility of the secondary party for the principal actor's violation of law. Unless the latter occurs, there can be no accomplice liability.

This axiom of accessorial liability gives rise to many problems. To a large extent these problems can be solved by making an attempt to aid a sufficient basis to convict the secondary actor for the crime of attempt *as a principal.* See Model Penal Code §5.01(3). But traditionally (and under the present law of many jurisdictions) this option has not been available, so the problems persist.

1. The nonculpable principal as innocent agent. Suppose a factual situation similar to that in *State v. Hayes,* supra page 693, but with Hayes asking a six-year-old child named Hill to go through the window and take the bacon. In this case, Hayes would be held guilty of burglary through the use of Hill, his innocent agent. This standard doctrine, the so-called innocent agent doctrine, is expressed in §2.06(2)(a) of the MPC as follows: "A person is legally accountable for the conduct of another person when . . . acting with the kind of culpability that is sufficient for the commission of the offense, he causes an innocent or irresponsible person to engage in such conduct." The drafter's comment states (Model Penal Code and Commentaries, Comment to §206 at 300 (1985)):

> Subsection (2)(a) is based upon the universally acknowledged principle that one is no less guilty of the commission of a crime because he uses the overt conduct of an innocent or irresponsible agent. He is accountable in such cases as if the conduct were his own. At common law, he was considered a principal for such behavior.

2. Limits of the innocent agent doctrine. There may be difficulties in employing an innocent agent doctrine even where the mens rea of the defendant and the innocence of the agent are established.

(a) One such case is where the statute defines the crime so that it can only be committed by designated classes of persons of which the defendant is not a member. For example, if a statute prohibits an officer or employee of a bank from entering false records of transactions, then one who is not an officer or an employee cannot commit the offense. If the outsider helps or encourages an officer who intentionally does so, the outsider can be held as an accomplice; his liability is derived from that of the culpable officer. If, however, the outsider dupes an innocent officer into doing so unknowingly, the outsider cannot be held liable as an accomplice to a crime committed by the officer, because

the officer committed no crime. The usual recourse is to apply the innocent agent concept to treat the instigator as a *principal* who has done the prohibited act himself, using the officer or employee as his instrument. But because the instigator is not an officer or employee, he cannot violate the statute. Thus, in this case, the innocent agent doctrine would not make him liable.

Federal courts have solved the difficulty by interpreting the federal aiding and abetting statute to mean that one is criminally liable as a principal for causing another to commit criminal acts where the other, even though innocent, has the capacity to commit the criminal acts and the defendant does not. See United States v. Ruffin, 613 F.2d 408 (2d Cir. 1979). The federal statute, 18 U.S.C. §2(b) reads: "Whoever willfully causes an act to be done which if directly performed by him *or another* would be an offense against the United States, is punishable as a principal." (Emphasis added.)

(b) A second situation where this difficulty can arise is rarer: It is where the nature of the action prohibited is such that it can be done only by the body of the person him- or herself and not through the instrumentality of another. For example, a sober defendant may cause an insensate and disorderly drunk to appear in a public place by physically depositing him there. But we could hardly say that the sober person has, through the instrumentality of the drunk, himself committed the criminal action of being drunk and disorderly in a public place.

Question: How would 18 U.S.C. §2(b) handle this case? How should it be handled? For a discussion of these situations, see Sanford H. Kadish, Blame and Punishment 172 (1987).

3. *The culpable-but-unconvictable principal.* Another class of cases raising questions for the traditional derivative liability doctrine is where the principal would be guilty except for a policy-based defense that makes him unconvictable. Consider, for example, Farnsworth v. Zerbst, 98 F.2d 541 (5th Cir. 1938), where the defendant conspired with and aided another in the commission of espionage, but the latter could not be convicted because of diplomatic immunity; or United States v. Azadian, 436 F.2d 81 (9th Cir. 1971), where the defendant aided a principal who had been acquitted on grounds of entrapment. As the courts held in these cases, there is no reason to grant the accomplice a defense simply because the principal has a defense—the grounds of granting the principal a defense are reasons of policy that are inapplicable to the accomplice. Yet how can convicting the accomplice be squared with the rule that makes the liability of the accomplice turn on the liability of the principal?

4. *The acquitted principal.* We have seen that in general there can be no guilty aider and abettor without a guilty principal; the situations in the above notes are distinguishable or are exceptions to that rule. What happens when the principal has been acquitted? May the accomplice who is subsequently tried raise that acquittal as a defense? In a situation of this kind where the principal had been acquitted of federal bribery charges, the United States

Supreme Court affirmed a conviction of the accomplice, stating in United States v. Standefer, 447 U.S. 10, 25-26 (1980) as follows:

> This case does no more than manifest the simple, if discomforting, reality that "different juries may reach different results under any criminal statute. That is one of the consequences we accept under our jury system." Roth v. United States, 354 U.S. 476, 492 (1957). While symmetry of results may be intellectually satisfying, it is not required. Here, [defendant] received a fair trial at which the Government bore the burden of proving beyond reasonable doubt that [the principal] violated 26 U.S.C. §7214(a)(2) and that petitioner aided and abetted him in that venture. He was entitled to no less—and to no more.

The MPC is in accord with this position. See Model Penal Code §2.06(7).

5. *When the "accomplice" is a victim.* May an accomplice have a defense even though she acts with the required mens rea? Consider the following.

(a) In The Queen v. Tyrell, [1894] 1 Q.B. 710, the court reversed a conviction of a minor for aiding, abetting, and encouraging statutory rape upon herself by an adult, stating:

> [I]t is impossible to say that the Act, which is absolutely silent about aiding or abetting, or soliciting or inciting, can have intended that the girls for whose protection it was passed should be punishable under it for the offences committed upon themselves.

The same reasoning has been applied to victims charged with conspiracy to commit an offense. See *Gebardi v. United States*, page 751 infra. For further discussion of the victim rule, see Glanville Williams, Victims and Other Exempt Parties in Crime, 10 Legal Stud. 245 (1990). Do these decisions suggest that juveniles who voluntarily take sexual images of themselves and send them to adults or other juveniles should not be prosecuted under laws that prohibit the distribution of child pornography? Prosecutors have brought charges in such cases, but some argue these prosecutions are inappropriate given the purpose of these laws. See Amy F. Kimpel, Using Laws Designed To Protect As A Weapon: Prosecuting Minors Under Child Pornography Laws, 34 N.Y.U. Rev. L. & Soc. Change 299 (2010).

(b) The Model Penal Code contains a provision, followed in a number of states, that a person is not an accomplice in an offense committed by another either if he is victim of that offense or if the offense is so defined that his conduct is inevitably incident to its commission. §2.06(6)(a), (b). The Comment on this provision states (Model Penal Code and Commentaries, Comment to §2.06 at 324-325 (1985)):

> Exclusion of the victim does not wholly meet the problems that arise. . . . Should the man who has intercourse with a prostitute be viewed as an accomplice in the act of prostitution, the purchaser an accomplice in the unlawful sale, the unmarried party to a bigamous marriage an accomplice of the bigamist, the bribe-giver an accomplice of the taker? . . . What is common to these cases, . . . is that the question is before the legislature when it defines the individual offense involved. No one can draft a prohibition of [bigamy] without awareness

that two parties to the conduct necessarily will be involved. The provision, therefore, is that the general section on complicity is inapplicable, leaving to the definition of the crime itself the selective judgment that must be made.

NOTES ON DIFFERENCES IN THE DEGREE OF CULPABILITY

1. *Lesser culpability of principal actor.* Does it follow from the derivative nature of accomplice liability that the secondary party cannot be convicted of a more serious crime than that committed by the principal actor? Consider the following situations.

(a) Regina v. Richards, [1974] Q.B. 776. The defendant, Isabelle Richards, hired two men to beat up her husband. She told them she "wanted them to beat him up bad enough to put him in the hospital for a month." The men accosted Mr. Richards and struggled with him, but he escaped without suffering any serious injuries. Mrs. Richards and the two men were tried together on charges of felonious assault, requiring proof of wounding with intent to cause grievous bodily harm, and misdemeanor assault, requiring proof of intent to cause harm, but not necessarily serious harm. The two men were acquitted on the felony charges and convicted on the misdemeanor count. Mrs. Richards, tried as their accomplice, was convicted of felonious assault. On appeal, the court reversed her felony conviction, stating:

> [The prosecution] says that here one can properly look at the actus reus, that is the physical blows struck upon Mr. Richards, and separately the intention with which the blows were struck.... We do not take that view.... There is proved on the evidence in this case one offence and one offence only, namely, the offence of unlawful wounding without the element of specific intent.... If there is only one offence committed, and that is the offence of unlawful wounding, then the person who has requested that offence to be committed, or advised that that offence be committed, cannot be guilty of a graver offence than that in fact which was committed.

Question: Was the decision correct? Commentators have disagreed. See Sanford H. Kadish, Blame and Punishment 181-186 (1987). The argument against the decision is that the blows struck by Mrs. Richards's hirelings should be treated as her own actions on the ground that she "caused" them. Therefore, she struck the blows and had the specific intent to cause grievous bodily harm when she did so. The contrary argument is that this would be true only if the hirelings were innocent agents, her unwitting instrument not knowing fully what they were doing. But since that apparently was not the case, their actions are their own and could not be said to be "caused" by Mrs. Richards, any more than any accomplice "causes" the actions of the principal. In that case, she can probably be convicted only of whatever crime they committed, or of soliciting the felonious assault. See Sanford H. Kadish, A Theory of Complicity, supra pages 657-658, and compare the result and reasoning in *State v. Hayes*, supra page 693.

(*b*) People v. McCoy, 24 P.3d 1210 (Cal. 2001). McCoy and Lakey participated in a drive-by shooting, with McCoy firing the fatal shots. Both were
convicted of murder—McCoy as a principal and Lakey as an aider and abettor.
McCoy testified at trial that he had been shot at earlier the same day at the
same intersection where the fatal shooting took place and that he armed
himself and shot only in self-defense. McCoy's conviction was overturned because the jury was not instructed properly on McCoy's defense—
that he had an unreasonable but good-faith belief in the need to use self-
defense—which, if believed by the jury, would have negated the element of
malice in murder and reduced McCoy's murder conviction to voluntary
manslaughter.

Should Lakey's conviction for aiding and abetting McCoy similarly have
been reversed? The court held that it should not, comparing Lakey to Iago in
Shakespeare's *Othello* (24 P.3d at 1216):

> [A]ssume someone, let us call him Iago, falsely tells another person, whom we
> will call Othello, that Othello's wife, Desdemona, was having an affair, hoping
> that Othello would kill her in a fit of jealousy. Othello does so without Iago's
> further involvement. In that case . . . Othello might be guilty of manslaughter,
> rather than murder, on a heat of passion theory. Othello's guilt of manslaugh
> ter, however, should not limit Iago's guilt if his own culpability were greater.
> Iago should be liable for his own acts as well as Othello's, which he induced
> and encouraged. But Iago's criminal liability, as Othello's, would be based on
> his own personal mens rea. If as our hypothetical suggests, Iago acted with
> malice, he would be guilty of murder even if Othello, who did the actual killing,
> was not.
>
> We thus conclude that when a person, with the mental state necessary for
> an aider and abettor, helps or induces another to kill, that person's guilt is
> determined by the combined acts of all the participants as well as that person's
> own mens rea. If that person's mens rea is more culpable than another's, that
> person's guilt may be greater even if the other might be deemed the actual
> perpetrator.

Professor Glanville Williams has offered the following argument for permitting the accessory to be held liable for a greater offense than the principal's in
cases like these: "In effect the primary party is an innocent agent in respect of
part of the responsibility of the secondary party."[5] He also stated: "If a person
can act through a completely innocent agent, there is no reason why he should
not act through a semi-innocent agent. It is wholly unreasonable that the partial
guilt of the agent should operate as a defence to the instigator."[6]

An alternative argument is that the actions of the principal perpetrator
(Othello in the court's example) are not fully volitional. As a result, those
actions cannot pose a barrier to our treating the actions of an instigator (such
as Iago) as the *cause* of the resulting death. See the material on Causation,

---

5. Criminal Law: The General Part 391 (2d ed. 1961).
6. Textbook on Criminal Law 374 (2d ed. 1983).

supra pages 571-607. When that is so, there is no difficulty in making the crime each party commits dependent on his own mens rea, because each is treated as a principal who has caused the death.[7] This rests on the premise that volition does not have the nature of an on/off switch, but rather exists along a spectrum. That is, the action of an intervening actor (like Othello) can be insufficiently volitional to break the causal chain, but sufficiently volitional to hold him responsible for his actions.

2. *Greater culpability of principal actor.* Does it follow from the theory of derivative liability that the instigator can be held for no lesser crime than that committed by the perpetrator? For example, suppose that an enraged Othello had hired someone else to kill Desdemona. The hired killer, presumably, would be guilty of murder. Does it follow that Othello is also guilty of murder? In Moore v. Lowe, 180 S.E. 1, 2 (W. Va. 1935), a hired killer murdered the defendant's husband at her instigation. The court held that, as an accessory to the murder, the defendant could be convicted of manslaughter. In support of its position, the court quoted 1 Wharton, Criminal Law 363-364 (12th ed. 1932):

> [T]he offense of the instigator is not necessarily of the same grade as that of the perpetrator. The instigator may act in hot blood, in which case he will be guilty only of manslaughter, while the perpetrator may act coolly, and thus be guilty of murder.

B. CONSPIRACY

INTRODUCTORY NOTES

1. *The two meanings of conspiracy.* Conspiracy has two key aspects. First, like attempt and solicitation, it is an inchoate crime that aims at preparatory conduct—the agreement to commit a crime—before it matures into the actual commission of the substantive offense. This is the stand-alone crime of conspiracy. Second, conspiracy is a form of accessory liability. It is a means by which individuals who agree to commit a crime are held liable for the actions of others in the group. [just begun]

2. *Conspiracy as an inchoate offense.* Justice Oliver Wendell Holmes offered a one-sentence summary of the stand-alone crime of conspiracy: "A conspiracy is a partnership in criminal purposes." United States v. Kissel, 218 U.S. 601, 608 (1910). Generally, conspiracy is defined as the crime of agreeing with another to commit a criminal offense. It is an inchoate offense because the conspiratorial agreement is punishable whether or not the agreed-upon offense ever occurs. But unlike attempt, the crime of conspiracy does not "merge" into the completed offense. Rather, conspiracy is generally punishable separately and in addition to the completed offense—a recognition that

---

7. Sanford H. Kadish, Blame and Punishment 1834 (1987).

the law of conspiracy is designed to not only punish preparatory activity, but also address the "special danger" posed by group criminal activity.

The traditional approach to grading is to treat the inchoate crime of conspiracy as a generic offense and to prescribe a punishment range that is unrelated to the sentence associated with whatever crime is the target of the conspiracy. For example, 18 U.S.C. §371 provides that the punishment for conspiracy is up to five years' imprisonment, regardless of the seriousness of the object offense. Under §371, an agreement to commit murder carries the same five-year maximum sentence as an agreement to commit a minor theft or embezzlement, and an agreement to commit a felony carrying a two-year maximum subjects the conspirators to a five-year sentence, while an individual who commits the object offense by himself faces only the two-year maximum. In other words, the sentence for conspiracy could be greater than the sentence for the crime that is the object of the conspiracy.

Maryland offers an example of one solution to this problem: its code provides that "[t]he punishment of a person who is convicted of conspiracy may not exceed the maximum punishment for the crime that the person conspired to commit." Rudder v. State, 956 A.2d 791, 794 (Md. Ct. Spec. App. 2008). The current federal statute addresses this issue only with respect to misdemeanors, specifying that when the object crime is a misdemeanor, punishment for the conspiracy shall not exceed the punishment authorized for the misdemeanor. Some jurisdictions have failed to take even this step, and still accept the common-law doctrine that made it a felony to conspire to commit a misdemeanor. Under Cal. Penal Code §182 (2011), a conspiracy to commit a crime against certain federal or state officials is a felony punishable by imprisonment for five, seven, or nine years; an agreement to throw a tomato at such an official would call for a *minimum* sentence of five years, though actually throwing the tomato, without a prior agreement, would be a misdemeanor assault carrying a *maximum* sentence of one year.

Though this generic approach—grading conspiracy without regard to the sentence for the object of the conspiracy—survives in a number of jurisdictions, the majority of states now reject it. Most fix the punishment for conspiracy at some term that is tied to but less than the sentence provided for the object crime. See Note, Conspiracy: Statutory Reform Since the Model Penal Code, 75 Colum. L. Rev. 1122, 1183-1188 (1975). Roughly a third of the states, following the lead of the MPC, make the punishment for conspiracy the same as that authorized for the object crime, except in the case of the most serious felonies. See Model Penal Code §5.05(1), Appendix. Recall that this is the same approach that the MPC uses in the case of attempts. But are the two offenses really comparable for grading purposes? Note that an attempt is not punishable under the Code until the defendant has taken a "substantial step" that is "strongly corroborative" of the criminal purpose. In such a case, punishment is permitted up to the level authorized for the object crime. But a conspiracy may be punishable from the moment that an agreement is made. When defendants have not taken significant steps to put their plan into action, is it appropriate to impose the same punishment authorized for successful commission of the object crime?

3. Conspiracy as a form of accessory liability. When individuals join conspiracies, they may be charged not only with the separate crime of conspiracy and the target offense (if it is completed); they may also find themselves charged with additional crimes committed by other members of the conspiracy. This is the most controversial aspect of conspiracy law.

4. Other significant consequences of a conspiracy charge. There are additional features of conspiracy charges that make conspiracy the "darling of the modern prosecutor's nursery," Harrison v. United States, 7 F.2d 259, 263 (2d Cir. 1925). These features prompted Clarence Darrow to remark that "any citizens interested in protecting human liberty" should "study the conspiracy laws of the United States." Clarence Darrow, The Story of My Life 64 (1932).

(a) Procedural consequences. Consider the following procedural advantages a conspiracy case offers the government, as discussed in Krulewitch v. United States, 336 U.S. 440 (1949):

> An accused, under the Sixth Amendment, has the right to trial "by an impartial jury of the state and district wherein the crime shall have been committed." The leverage of a conspiracy charge lifts this limitation from the prosecution and reduces its protection to a phantom, for the crime is considered so vagrant as to have been committed in any district where any one of the conspirators did any one of the acts, however innocent, intended to accomplish its object. The Government may, and often does, compel one to defend at a great distance from any place he ever did any act because some accused confederate did some trivial and by itself innocent act in the chosen district. . . .
>
> When the trial starts, the accused feels the full impact of the conspiracy strategy. Strictly, the prosecution should first establish prima facie the conspiracy and identify the conspirators, after which evidence of acts and declarations of each in the course of its execution are admissible against all. But the order of proof of so sprawling a charge is difficult for a judge to control. As a practical matter, the accused often is confronted with a hodgepodge of acts and statements by others which he may never have authorized or intended or even known about, but which help to persuade the jury of existence of the conspiracy itself. . . . The naive assumption that prejudicial effects can be overcome by instructions to the jury all practicing lawyers know to be unmitigated fiction.
>
> The trial of a conspiracy charge doubtless imposes a heavy burden on the prosecution, but it is an especially difficult situation for the defendant. . . .
>
> A co-defendant in a conspiracy trial occupies an uneasy seat. There generally will be evidence of wrongdoing by somebody. It is difficult for the individual to make his own case stand on its own merits in the minds of jurors who are ready to believe that birds of a feather are flocked together. If he is silent, he is taken to admit it and if, as often happens, co-defendants can be prodded into accusing or contradicting each other, they convict each other. . . .

(b) Spillover effects. The larger the conspiracy, the more significant are the procedural consequences and the greater is the potential for accessory liability. Conspiracy prosecutions in recent decades have grown increasingly complex. A single case involving almost two dozen defendants in a drug conspiracy with a trial lasting for more than a year is far from unusual. See, e.g., United States v.

Simpson, 2008 WL 4758588 (D. Kansas 2008). Consider Paul Marcus, Criminal Conspiracy Law: Time to Turn Back from an Ever Expanding, Ever More Troubling Area, 1 Wm. & Mary Bill Rts. J. 1, 8-11 (1992):

> [An] enormous number of cases involv[e] many defendants, complex evidentiary issues, and dozens and dozens of complicated charges. . . . It is difficult to imagine how a jury goes about sorting the testimony of hundreds of witnesses, or considering evidence it heard more than a year earlier. Indeed, how does a jury begin to apply the reasonable doubt standard when there are more than fifty counts charging more than a dozen different individuals? In today's world of conspiracy prosecution, however, such a situation—while perhaps not the norm—occurs with great frequency.

In these large conspiracy trials, defendants' primary protection against the spillover effect of evidence unrelated to their guilt is the limiting instruction given by the trial judge. These instructions generally take the form of admonitions to the jury to consider certain pieces of evidence only against some defendants and not against others. Judges typically assume that limiting instructions can cure any prejudice. See, e.g., United States v. Defreitas, 701 F. Supp. 2d 309, 316-317 (E.D.N.Y. 2010). Yet in *Krulewitch*, Justice Jackson called faith in the efficacy of such instructions "unmitigated fiction." His skepticism was echoed by the Ninth Circuit in its review of a 16-month drug conspiracy trial involving dozens of defendants, some of whom were charged with major crimes, including murder, and others of whom were charged only with relatively minor offenses (United States v. Baker, 10 F.3d 1374, 1391 (9th Cir. 1993)):

> [T]he human limitations of the jury system and the consequent risk of spillover prejudice cannot be ignored. This risk is particularly acute for comparatively peripheral defendants. . . . At oral argument in this case, the Assistant United States Attorney averred that his multiple violations of the district court's limiting instructions during closing argument were the inadvertent result of confusion. When a seasoned prosecutor is unable to keep track of nearly 200 limiting instructions given over the course of 16-month trial, our faith in a lay jury's ability to do so is stretched to the limit. Our presumption that a jury is able to follow the trial court's instructions is "rooted less in the absolute certitude that the presumption is true than in the belief that it represents a reasonable practical accommodation of the interests of the state and the defendant in the criminal justice process."

Keep in mind the consequences of a prosecution for conspiracy in assessing where the lines of culpability should be drawn.

1. *The Actus Reus of Conspiracy*

INTRODUCTORY NOTE

The substantive crime of conspiracy is typically defined as an agreement by two or more persons to commit a crime. The actus reus of the offense is thus the agreement itself. But agreements to commit crime are rarely reduced to writing, and even oral agreements are unlikely to make clear or explicit all the terms and conditions of the joint undertaking. How then can the necessary agreement be described and proved? For a representative statement of the applicable standard, consider United States v. James, 528 F.2d 999, 1011 (5th Cir. 1976):

> To establish the common plan element of a conspiracy, it is not necessary for the government to prove an express agreement between the alleged conspirators to go forth and violate law. . . . "A conspiracy is seldom born of open covenants openly arrived at. The proof, by the very nature of the crime, must be circumstantial and therefore inferential to an extent varying with the conditions under which the crime may be consummated." Direct Sales Co. v. United States, 319 U.S. 703, 714. Knowledge by a defendant of all details or phases of a conspiracy is not required. It is enough that he knows the essential nature of it. "And, it is black letter law that all participants in a conspiracy need not know each other; all that is necessary is that each know that it has a scope and that for its success it requires an organization wider than may be disclosed by his personal participation."

INTERSTATE CIRCUIT, INC. v. UNITED STATES

Supreme Court of the United States
306 U.S. 208 (1939)

JUSTICE STONE delivered the opinion of the Court.

. . . This case is here on appeal . . . from a final decree of the District Court for northern Texas restraining appellants from continuing in a combination and conspiracy condemned by the court as a violation of Section 1 of the Sherman Anti-Trust Act. . . .

[The case involved two related movie theater chains, Interstate Circuit and Texas Consolidated Theaters, which together dominated the market for exhibiting films in the cities where their theaters were located. The other members of the alleged conspiracy were eight independent corporations that distributed films to theaters; together the eight distributed 75 percent of all first-run films exhibited in the United States. Interstate and Consolidated admittedly had entered contractual agreements with each of the eight distributors, specifying the terms on which the theaters would exhibit their films, but each individual contract between the exhibitor and a distributor could not by itself constitute an unlawful conspiracy. The Sherman Act makes illegal a contract, combination, or conspiracy in restraint of commerce. 15 U.S.C. §1. Thus, in order to prove the Sherman Act violation, the Government had to establish that the eight distributors had an agreement with one another.

[The centerpiece of the Government's case was a letter written by O'Donnell, Interstate's manager, to each distributor, in which he asked compliance with two demands as a condition of Interstate's continued exhibition of that distributor's films. One demand was that the distributor agree that on subsequent runs it

2 demands

would not permit its films to be shown in theaters charging an admission price of less than 25 cents. (At the time, 1934-1935, admission tickets to see second-run films in Texas theaters sold for as little as 10 or 15 cents.) Interstate's second demand was that the distributor agree not to permit its first-run motion pictures to be shown on a double-bill with another feature film.

[The letter addressed to each distributor identified all eight distributors as addressees of the proposal, and subsequently each distributor agreed with Interstate to accept the proposed restrictions. On this basis the trial court found that the distributors had agreed and conspired *with one another* to take uniform action on the Interstate proposals and to impose the demanded restrictions, in violation of the Sherman Act.]

As is usual in cases of alleged unlawful agreements to restrain commerce, the Government is without the aid of direct testimony that the distributors entered into any agreement with each other to impose the restrictions upon subsequent-run exhibitors. In order to establish agreement it is compelled to rely on inferences drawn from the course of conduct of the alleged conspirators.

The trial court drew the inference of agreement from the nature of the proposals made on behalf of Interstate and Consolidated; from the manner in which they were made; from the substantial unanimity of action taken upon them by the distributors; and from the fact that appellants did not call as witnesses any of the superior officials who negotiated the contracts with Interstate or any official who, in the normal course of business, would have had knowledge of the existence or non-existence of such an agreement among the distributors. This conclusion is challenged by appellants because not supported by subsidiary findings or by the evidence. We think this inference of the trial court was rightly drawn from the evidence. . . .

The O'Donnell letter named on its face as addressees the eight local representatives of the distributors, and so from the beginning each of the distributors knew that the proposals were under consideration by the others. Each was aware that all were in active competition and that without substantially unanimous action with respect to the restrictions for any given territory there was risk of a substantial loss of the business and good will of the subsequent-run and independent exhibitors, but that with it there was the prospect of increased profits. There was, therefore, strong motive for concerted action, full advantage of which was taken by Interstate and Consolidated in presenting their demands to all in a single document.

There was risk, too, that without agreement diversity of action would follow. Compliance with the proposals involved a radical departure from the previous business practices of the industry and a drastic increase in admission prices of most of the subsequent-run theatres. . . .

It taxes credulity to believe that the several distributors would, in the circumstances, have accepted and put into operation with substantial unanimity such far-reaching changes in their business methods without some understanding that all were to join, and we reject as beyond the range of probability that it was the result of mere chance. . . .

While the District Court's finding of an agreement of the distributors among themselves is supported by the evidence, we think that in the circumstances of this case such agreement for the imposition of the restrictions upon subsequent-run exhibitors was not a prerequisite to an unlawful conspiracy. It was enough that, knowing that concerted action was contemplated and invited, the distributors gave their adherence to the scheme and participated in it. Each distributor was advised that the others were asked to participate; each knew that cooperation was essential to successful operation of the plan. They knew that the plan, if carried out, would result in a restraint of commerce, which, we will presently point out, was unreasonable within the meaning of the Sherman Act, and knowing it, all participated in the plan. The evidence is persuasive that each distributor early became aware that the others had joined. With that knowledge they renewed the arrangement and carried it into effect for the two successive years.

It is elementary that an unlawful conspiracy may be and often is formed without simultaneous action or agreement on the part of the conspirators. . . .

We think the conclusion is unavoidable that the conspiracy and each contract between Interstate and the distributors by which those consequences were effected are violations of the Sherman Act and that the District Court rightly enjoined the conspiracy among the distributors. Affirmed.

NOTES ON THE REQUIRED AGREEMENT

1. *Parallel action or common action? Interstate Circuit* is a landmark in the law of conspiracy, not only for antitrust cases but also for the general problem of establishing the existence of a conspiratorial relationship. How can the Court's statement that "[i]t is elementary that an unlawful conspiracy may be and often is formed without simultaneous action or agreement on the part of the conspirators" be reconciled with the definition of conspiracy? Without an agreement, what would the "conspiracy" be? Note that the evidence in *Interstate Circuit* could support an inference that the distributors actually spoke to one another and agreed to act in common. So while there might not have been an express agreement, its existence could be inferred from circumstantial evidence. Presumably, the Court meant that it was not necessary to establish this kind of express agreement. In other words, a conspiracy may exist if there is no communication and no *express* agreement, provided that there is a tacit agreement reached without communication. But then what is the difference between parallel action that occurs because of a tacit agreement (that is, a conspiracy) and parallel action that occurs without any agreement at all?

2. *Problems. (a)* During an urban riot, one teenager shouts to three of his friends, "There's great stuff in that store, and the owner's a cheat. Let's go get it!" All four run into the store and start grabbing goods. Seeing the looting, two passersby, strangers to each other, enter the store and join in the looting. Are the four teenagers guilty of conspiracy? Are the two passersby guilty of

conspiracy with each other? Are they guilty of conspiracy with the four teen-agers? Note that the answers to these questions can be important for several reasons. For example, as we shall see, a conspiracy charge could permit a substantial increase in punishment. In addition, in some jurisdictions, conspirators can be held liable for additional crimes committed by their co-conspirators that are committed in furtherance of the conspiracy.

(b) Motorist *M* loudly protests the action of an officer who stops him for a traffic violation, and a crowd gathers. When the officer attempts to make an arrest, *M* pushes the officer to the ground and various members of the crowd then assault the officer. Is *M* guilty of conspiracy? Griffin v. State, 455 S.W.2d 882 (Ark. 1970), finds a conspiracy on similar facts. Is this a correct result under the *Interstate Circuit* principle?

(c) During a party attended by members of the rival Crips and Bloods gangs, Garcia, one of the Bloods, began "talking smack" to Crips members who were present, and several of his fellow Bloods did likewise. At some point, the confrontation escalated. Garcia and others drew weapons, and shooting broke out. Several Crips were seriously injured, presumably by gun-fire from the rival gang. Garcia was seen shooting, but there was no evidence that any of the wounded were shot by him. He was convicted of conspiring with his fellow gang members to commit aggravated assault. Can common gang membership, together with parallel action (insulting their rivals, draw-ing their weapons) prove a conspiratorial agreement under the *Interstate Circuit* principle? The Ninth Circuit did not think so. Do you agree? Reversing Garcia's conviction, the court said (United States v. Garcia, 151 F.3d 1243, 1245-1246 (9th Cir. 1998)):

> An inference of an agreement is permissible only when the nature of the acts would logically require coordination and planning. [There was] nothing to suggest that the violence began in accordance with some prearrangement. The facts establish only that . . . an ongoing gang-related dispute erupted into shooting. . . . Such evidence does not establish that parties to a conspiracy "work[ed] together understandingly, with a single design for the accomplish-ment of a common purpose."
>
> [W]e are left only with gang membership as proof that Garcia conspired with fellow Bloods to shoot the [victims]. The government points to expert testimony . . . [stating] that generally gang members have a "basic agreement" to back one another up in fights, an agreement which requires no advance planning or coordination. This testimony . . . at most establishes one of the characteristics of gangs but not a specific objective of a particular gang—let alone a specific agreement on the part of its members to accomplish an illegal objective.
>
> [A]llowing a conviction on this basis would "smack . . . of guilt by associa-tion." . . . Acts of provocation such as "talking smack" or bumping into rival gang members [at most] indicates that members of a particular gang may be looking for trouble, or ready to fight. . . . The fact that gang members attend a function armed with weapons may prove that they are prepared for violence, but without other evidence it does not establish that they have made plans to

initiate it. And the fact that more than one member of the Bloods was shooting at rival[s] does not prove a prearrangement—the Crips, too, were able to pull out their guns almost immediately, suggesting that readiness for a gunfight requires no prior agreement. Such readiness may be a sad commentary on the state of mind of many of the nation's youth, but it is not indicative of a criminal conspiracy. [Otherwise, any] gang member could be held liable for any other gang member's act at any time so long as the act was predicated on "the common purpose of 'fighting the enemy.' " [A] general practice of supporting one another in fights . . . does not constitute the type of illegal objective that can form the predicate for a conspiracy charge.

NOTES ON THE OVERT ACT REQUIREMENT

Both at common law and under statutory formulations, conduct can be punishable as a conspiracy at points much farther back in the stages of preparation than the point where liability begins to attach for attempt. In some jurisdictions, the agreement alone is sufficient, without any requirement that a member of the conspiracy commit an overt act in furtherance of it. In other situations an overt act must be proved, but the act may fall well short of the kind of conduct sufficient to constitute an attempt.

1. Liability without an overt act. At common law, no "overt act" was required. Does this mean that the offense becomes purely mental? Consider Mulcahy v. The Queen, L.R. 3 E. & I. App. 306, 316-317 (H.L. Ire. 1868). Defendants were indicted for conspiracy to foment the Irish rebellion. They argued that the indictment was defective for failing to charge some overt act, such as publishing writings or procuring arms. The court rejected the argument, stating:

A conspiracy consists not merely in the intention of two or more, but in the agreement of two or more to do an unlawful act, or to do a lawful act by unlawful means. So long as such a design rests in intention only, it is not indictable. When two agree to carry it into effect, the very plot is an act in itself, and the act of each of the parties, promise against promise, actus contra actum, capable of being enforced, if lawful, punishable if for a criminal object or for the use of criminal means. And so far as proof goes, conspiracy . . . is generally a matter of inference deduced from certain criminal acts of the parties accused, done in pursuance of an apparent criminal purpose in common between them. The number and the compact give weight and cause danger, and this is more especially the case in a conspiracy like those charged in this indictment. Indeed, it seems a reduction to absurdity, that procuring a single stand of arms should be a sufficient overt act to make the disloyal design indictable, and that conspiring with a thousand men to enlist should not.

2. Statutes requiring an overt act. American conspiracy statutes have typically added an overt-act requirement. Note, for example, the wording of 18 U.S.C. §371: "If one or more persons conspire . . . to commit any offense . . . and one or more of such persons do any act to effect the object of the conspiracy. . . ." But it is not unusual for statutes to dispense with this overt-act requirement in the case of conspiracies to commit the most serious offenses. See, e.g., Model Penal Code §5.03(5), Appendix. Many statutes are silent on the subject. In Whitfield v. United States, 543 U.S. 209 (2005), the Supreme Court held that when a federal statute's text is silent, no overt-act requirement should be read into the statute, in light of the settled principle of statutory construction that, absent contrary indications, Congress intends to adopt the common-law definition of statutory terms.

When an overt act is a required element, the usual reason for requiring it is explained in Yates v. United States, 354 U.S. 298, 334 (1957): "The function of the overt act in a conspiracy prosecution is simply to manifest 'that the conspiracy is at work' . . . and is neither a project still resting solely in the minds of the conspirators nor a fully completed operation no longer in existence." Thus, even when an overt-act requirement applies, it generally can be satisfied by acts that would be considered equivocal or merely preparatory in the law of attempts. Consider, for example, United States v. Bertling, 510 F.3d 804, 810 (8th Cir. 2007), in which the court concluded that the same telephone conversation established both the agreement and the overt act, because in the first part of the conversation two brothers discussed the need to murder a potential witness, and in the remaining part of the conversation, they discussed how to find the witness: "We see no reason why these plans and arrangements cannot constitute overt acts in furtherance of the conspiracy simply because they were contained in the same phone conversation in which the conspiracy was also established." Does the latter part of the conversation establish "that the conspiracy is at work"?

By contrast, some states have required a more substantial overt act. Ohio, for example, provides that an overt act is sufficient only "when it is of a character that manifests a purpose on the part of the actor that the object of the conspiracy should be completed." Ohio Rev. Code Ann. tit. 29, §2923.01(B) (2011). Maine goes further toward bringing together the points at which liability begins for attempt and for conspiracy: The statute requires a "substantial step," which it defines as "conduct which, under the circumstances in which it occurs, is strongly corroborative of the firmness of the actor's intent to complete commission of the crime"; it further provides that "speech alone may not constitute a substantial step." Maine Rev. Stat. Ann. tit. 17-A, §151(4) (2011).

3. Justifications for the traditional approach. Unlike the Maine and Ohio statutes just mentioned, the traditional view is that any "overt act" (or sometimes the act of agreement alone) suffices to render conduct punishable as a conspiracy. But what is there about an agreement to commit a crime that justifies dispensing with the requirement of substantial preparatory conduct we use for attempts? Consider Model Penal Code and Commentaries, Comment to §5.03 at 388 (1985):

> *First:* The act of agreeing with another to commit a crime, like the act of soliciting, is concrete and unambiguous; it does not present the infinite degrees and variations possible in the general category of attempts. The danger that

truly equivocal behavior may be misinterpreted as preparation to commit a crime is minimized; purpose must be relatively firm before the commitment involved in agreement is assumed.

Second: If the agreement was to aid another to commit a crime or if it otherwise encouraged the crime's commission, complicity would be established in the commission of the substantive offense. It would be anomalous to hold that conduct that would suffice to establish criminality, if something else is done by someone else, is insufficient if the crime is never consummated. . . .

Third: [T]he act of combining with another is significant both psychologically and practically, the former because it crosses a clear threshold in arousing expectations, the latter because it increases the likelihood that the offense will be committed.

2. *The Mens Rea of Conspiracy*

PEOPLE v. LAURIA

California District Court of Appeal
251 Cal. App. 2d 471, 59 Cal. Rptr. 628 (1967)

FLEMING, J. In an investigation of call-girl activity the police focused their attention on three prostitutes actively plying their trade on call, each of whom was using Lauria's telephone answering service, presumably for business purposes.

On January 8, 1965, Stella Weeks, a policewoman, signed up for telephone service with Lauria's answering service. Mrs. Weeks, in the course of her conversation with Lauria's officer manager, hinted broadly that she was a prostitute concerned with the secrecy of her activities and their concealment from the police. She was assured that the operation of the service was discreet and "about as safe as you can get."

On February 11, Mrs. Weeks talked to Lauria on the telephone and told him her business was modeling and she had been referred to the answering service by Terry, one of the three prostitutes under investigation. She complained that because of the operation of the service she had lost two valuable customers, referred to as tricks. Lauria defended his service and said that her friends had probably lied to her about having left calls for her. But he did not respond to Mrs. Weeks' hints that she needed customers in order to make money, other than to invite her to his house for a personal visit in order to get better acquainted. In the course of his talk he said "his business was taking messages."

On February 15, Mrs. Weeks talked on the telephone to Lauria's office manager and again complained of two lost calls, which she described as a $50 and a $100 trick. On investigation the office manager could find nothing wrong, but she said she would alert the switchboard operators about slip-ups on calls.

On April 1, Lauria and the three prostitutes were arrested. Lauria complained to the police that this attention was undeserved, stating that

Hollywood Call Board had 60 to 70 prostitutes on its board while his own service had only 9 or 10, that he kept separate records for known or suspected prostitutes for the convenience of himself and the police. When asked if his records were available to police who might come to the office to investigate call girls, Lauria replied that they were whenever the police had a specific name. However, his service didn't "arbitrarily tell the police about prostitutes on our board. As long as they pay their bills we tolerate them." In a subsequent voluntary appearance before the Grand Jury Lauria testified he had always cooperated with the police. But he admitted he knew some of his customers were prostitutes, and he knew Terry was a prostitute because he had personally used her services, and he knew she was paying for 500 calls a month. . . .

To establish agreement, the People need show no more than a tacit, mutual understanding between co-conspirators to accomplish an unlawful act. . . . Here the People attempted to establish a conspiracy by showing that Lauria, well aware that his codefendants were prostitutes who received business calls from customers through his telephone answering service, continued to furnish them with such service. This approach attempts to equate knowledge of another's criminal activity with conspiracy to further such criminal activity, and poses the question of the criminal responsibility of a furnisher of goods or services who knows his product is being used to assist the operation of an illegal business. Under what circumstances does a supplier become a part of a conspiracy to further an illegal enterprise by furnishing goods or services which he knows are to be used by the buyer for criminal purposes?

The two leading cases on this point face in opposite directions. In United States v. Falcone, 311 U.S. 205, the sellers of large quantities of sugar, yeast, and cans were absolved from participation in a moonshining conspiracy among distillers who bought from them, while in Direct Sales Co. v. United States, 319 U.S. 703, a wholesaler of drugs was convicted of conspiracy to violate the federal narcotic laws by selling drugs in quantity to a codefendant physician who was supplying them to addicts. The distinction between these two cases appears primarily based on the proposition that distributors of such dangerous products as drugs are required to exercise greater discrimination in the conduct of their business than are distributors of innocuous substances like sugar and yeast.

In the earlier case, *Falcone*, the sellers' knowledge of the illegal use of the goods was insufficient by itself to make the sellers participants in a conspiracy with the distillers who bought from them. Such knowledge fell short of proof of a conspiracy, and evidence on the volume of sales was too vague to support a jury finding that respondents knew of the conspiracy [with others] from the size of the sales alone.

In the later case of *Direct Sales*, the conviction of a drug wholesaler for conspiracy to violate federal narcotic laws was affirmed on a showing that it had actively promoted the sale of morphine sulphate in quantity and had sold codefendant physician, who practiced in a small town in South Carolina, more than 300 times his normal requirements of the drug, even though it had been repeatedly warned of the dangers of unrestricted sales of the drug.

The court contrasted the restricted goods involved in *Direct Sales* with the articles of free commerce involved in *Falcone*: "All articles of commerce may be put to illegal ends," said the court. "But all do not have inherently the same susceptibility to harmful and illegal use. . . . This difference is important for two purposes. One is for making certain that the seller knows the buyer's intended illegal use. The other is to show that by the sale he intends to further, promote and cooperate in it. This intent, when given effect by overt act, is the gist of conspiracy. While it is not identical with mere knowledge that another proposes unlawful action, it is not unrelated to such knowledge. . . . The step from knowledge to intent and agreement may be taken. There is more than suspicion, more than knowledge, acquiescence, carelessness, indifference, lack of concern. There is informed and interested cooperation, stimulation, instigation. And there is also a 'stake in the venture' which, even if it may not be essential, is not irrelevant to the question of conspiracy." (319 U.S. at 710-713.)

While *Falcone* and *Direct Sales* may not be entirely consistent with each other in their full implications, they do provide us with a framework for the criminal liability of a supplier of lawful goods or services put to unlawful use. Both the element of *knowledge* of the illegal use of the goods or services and the element of *intent* to further that use must be present in order to make the supplier a participant in a criminal conspiracy.

Proof of *knowledge* is ordinarily a question of fact and requires no extended discussion in the present case. . . . Because Lauria knew in fact that some of his customers were prostitutes, it is a legitimate inference he knew they were subscribing to his answering service for illegal business purposes and were using his service to make assignations for prostitution. . . .

The more perplexing issue in the case is the sufficiency of proof of *intent* to further the criminal enterprise. . . . Direct evidence of participation, such as advice from the supplier of legal goods or services to the user of those goods or services on their use for illegal purpose, such evidence as appeared in a companion case we decide today, People v. Roy, 59 Cal. Rptr. 636, provides the simplest case.[a] . . . But in cases where direct proof of complicity is lacking, intent to further the conspiracy must be derived from the sale itself and its surrounding circumstances in order to establish the supplier's express or tacit agreement to join the conspiracy.

In the case at bench the prosecution argues that since Lauria knew his customers were using his service for illegal purposes but nevertheless continued to furnish it to them, he must have intended to assist them in carrying out their illegal activities. . . .

1. Intent may be inferred from knowledge, when the purveyor of legal goods for illegal use has acquired a stake in the venture. (United States v. Falcone, 2d

---

a. In the companion case the court upheld liability. The facts were similar, but the answering service operator actively participated in the business of prostitution by making arrangements for the sharing of customers between two supposed prostitutes who used the service.—Eds.

Cir. 109 F.2d 579, 581.[b]) For example, in Regina v. Thomas, (1957), 2 All E.R. 181, 342, a prosecution for living off the earnings of prostitution, the evidence showed that the accused, knowing the woman to be a convicted prostitute, agreed to let her have the use of his room between the hours of 9 P.M. and 2 A.M. for a charge of £3 a night. The Court of Criminal Appeal refused an appeal from the conviction, holding that when the accused rented a room at a grossly inflated rent to a prostitute for the purpose of carrying on her trade, a jury could find he was living on the earnings of prostitution.

In the present case, no proof was offered of inflated charges for the telephone answering services furnished the codefendants.

2. Intent may be inferred from knowledge, when no legitimate use for the goods or services exists. The leading California case is People v. McLaughlin, 245 P.2d 1076 (Cal. App. 1952), in which the court upheld a conviction of the suppliers of horse-racing information by wire for conspiracy to promote book-making, when it had been established that wire service information had no other use than to supply information needed by bookmakers to conduct illegal gambling operations. . . .

In Shaw v. Director of Public Prosecutions, [1962] A.C. 220, the defendant was convicted of conspiracy to corrupt public morals and of living on the earnings of prostitution, when he published a directory consisting almost entirely of advertisements of the names, addresses, and specialized talents of prostitutes. Publication of such a directory, said the court, could have no legitimate use and serve no other purpose than to advertise the professional services of the prostitutes whose advertisements appeared in the directory. The publisher could be deemed a participant in the profits from the business activities of his principal advertisers. . . .

However, there is nothing in the furnishing of telephone answering service which would necessarily imply assistance in the performance of illegal activities. Nor is any inference to be derived from the use of an answering service by women, either in any particular volume of calls, or outside normal working hours. Nightclub entertainers, registered nurses, faith healers, public stenographers, photographic models, and free lance substitute employees, provide examples of women in legitimate occupations whose employment might cause them to receive a volume of telephone calls at irregular hours.

3. Intent may be inferred from knowledge, when the volume of business with the buyer is grossly disproportionate to any legitimate demand, or when sales for illegal use amount to a high proportion of the seller's total business. In such cases an intent to participate in the illegal enterprise may be inferred from the quantity of the business done. For example, in *Direct Sales*, supra, the sale of narcotics to a rural physician in quantities 300 times greater than he would have normal use for provided potent evidence of an intent to further the

---

b. In *Falcone*, Judge Learned Hand wrote the opinion and stated: "[I]n prosecutions for conspiracy or abetting, [i]t is not enough that [a defendant] does not [forgo] a normally lawful activity, of the fruits of which he knows that others will make an unlawful use; he must in some sense promote their venture himself, make it his own, have a stake in its outcome."—EDS.

illegal activity.[c] In the same case the court also found significant the fact that the wholesaler had attracted as customers a disproportionately large group of physicians who had been convicted of violating the Harrison Act. In Shaw v. Director of Public Prosecutions, [1962] A.C. 220, almost the entire business of the directory came from prostitutes.

No evidence of any unusual volume of business with prostitutes was presented by the prosecution against Lauria.

Inflated charges, the sale of goods with no legitimate use, sales in inflated amounts, each may provide a fact of sufficient moment from which the intent of the seller to participate in the criminal enterprise may be inferred . . . because in one way or another the supplier has acquired a special interest in the operation of the illegal enterprise. His intent to participate in the crime of which he has knowledge may be inferred from the existence of his special interest.

Yet there are cases in which it cannot reasonably be said that the supplier has a stake in the venture or has acquired a special interest in the enterprise, but in which he has been held liable as a participant on the basis of knowledge alone. . . . In Regina v. Bainbridge (1959), 3 W.L.R. 656 (CCA 6), a supplier of oxygen-cutting equipment to one known to intend to use it to break into a bank was convicted as an accessory to the crime. . . . It seems apparent from these cases that a supplier who furnishes equipment which he *knows* will be used to commit a serious crime may be deemed from that knowledge alone to have intended to produce the result. . . . For instance, we think the operator of a telephone answering service with positive knowledge that his service was being used to facilitate the extortion of ransom, the distribution of heroin, or the passing of counterfeit money who continued to furnish the service with knowledge of its use, might be chargeable on knowledge alone with participation in a scheme to extort money, to distribute narcotics, or to pass counterfeit money. The same result would follow the seller of gasoline who knew the buyer was using his product to make Molotov cocktails for terroristic use.

Logically, the same reasoning could be extended to crimes of every description. Yet we do not believe an inference of intent drawn from knowledge of criminal use properly applies to the less serious crimes classified as misdemeanors. The duty to take positive action to dissociate oneself from activities helpful to violations of the criminal law is far stronger and more compelling for felonies than it is for misdemeanors or petty offenses. . . . We believe the distinction between the obligations arising from knowledge of a felony and those arising from knowledge of a misdemeanor continues to reflect basic human feelings about the duties owed by individuals to society. Heinous crime must be stamped out, and its suppression is the responsibility of all. Venial crime and crime not evil in itself present less of a danger to society, and

---

c. The court in *Direct Sales* also emphasized the quantity discounts the defendant offered to the physician.—EDS.

perhaps the benefits of their suppression through the modern equivalent of the posse, the hue and cry, the informant, and the citizen's arrest, are outweighed by the disruption to everyday life brought about by amateur law enforcement and private officiousness in relatively inconsequential delicts which do not threaten our basic security. . . .

With respect to misdemeanors, we conclude that positive knowledge of the supplier that his products or services are being used for criminal purposes does not, without more, establish an intent of the supplier to participate in the misdemeanors. With respect to felonies, we do not decide the converse, viz. that in all cases of felony knowledge of criminal use alone may justify an inference of the supplier's intent to participate in the crime. The implications of *Falcone* make the matter uncertain with respect to those felonies which are merely prohibited wrongs. . . . But decision on this point is not compelled, and we leave the matter open.

From this analysis of precedent we deduce the following rule: the intent of a supplier who knows of the criminal use to which his supplies are put to participate in the criminal activity connected with the use of his supplies may be established by (1) direct evidence that he intends to participate, or (2) through an inference that he intends to participate based on, (a) his special interest in the activity, or (b) the aggravated nature of the crime itself.

When we review Lauria's activities in the light of this analysis, we find no proof that Lauria took any direct action to further, encourage, or direct the call-girl activities of his codefendants and we find an absence of circumstances from which his special interest in their activities could be inferred. Neither excessive charges for standardized services, nor the furnishing of services without a legitimate use, nor an unusual quantity of business with call girls, are present. The offense which he is charged with furthering is a misdemeanor, a category of crime which has never been made a required subject of positive disclosure to public authority. Under these circumstances, although proof of Lauria's knowledge of the criminal activities of his patrons was sufficient to charge him with that fact, there was insufficient evidence that he intended to further their criminal activities, and hence insufficient proof of his participation in a criminal conspiracy with his codefendants to further prostitution. Since the conspiracy centered around the activities of Lauria's telephone answering service, the charges against his codefendants likewise fail for want of proof.

In absolving Lauria of complicity in a criminal conspiracy we do not wish to imply that the public authorities are without remedies to combat modern manifestations of the world's oldest profession. Licensing of telephone answering services under the police power, together with the revocation of licenses for the toleration of prostitution, is a possible civil remedy. The furnishing of telephone answering service in aid of prostitution could be made a crime. (Cf. Pen. Code, §316, which makes it a misdemeanor to let an apartment with knowledge of its use for prostitution.) Other solutions will doubtless occur to vigilant public authorities if the problem of call-girl activity needs further suppression.

The order is affirmed.

NOTES ON MENS REA

1. Purpose or knowledge in felony cases. Does the *Lauria* court's analysis imply that knowledge alone *is* a sufficient mens rea for conspiracy when the object crime is a felony? What *should be* the result when the object offense is a very serious crime? Recall that in *United States v. Fountain*, page 669 supra, the court held (relying on *Lauria*) that Gometz, who supplied a knife knowing that it would be used to kill, could be an accomplice in the murder. Should the same facts be sufficient to hold Gometz responsible for *conspiracy* to commit murder? Even if knowledge alone is considered sufficient for aiding and abetting liability, might it make sense to require more to make the supplier and his customer "partners in crime"? In this regard, recall, as we have pointed out at the beginning of this chapter, that conspiracy, unlike accomplice liability, is an inchoate offense and that it carries many broad procedural and other consequences.

The MPC solution to these problems is to require purpose for *both* conspiracy and accomplice liability. See §§2.06(3)(a); 5.03(1). For the commentary relevant to these provisions, see the MPC discussion of accomplice mens rea, set out at pages 666-667 supra. Most states likewise require purpose in conspiracy cases, even when the object crime is a serious felony. Thus, in Commonwealth v. Camerano, 677 N.E.2d 678 (Mass. App. Ct. 1997), the defendant rented land to Howell and permitted him to erect a garden enclosure in which, as Camerano surely knew, Howell was growing a large amount of marijuana. Though Camerano could have evicted Howell at any time, he allowed Howell to remain and collected $200 per month in rent, money that Howell allegedly could not have obtained from any legal source. Camerano's conviction for conspiracy to possess and distribute marijuana was nonetheless reversed, with the court noting (id. at 681) that "[i]ntent is a requisite mental state for conspiracy, not mere knowledge or acquiescence." In United States v. Scotti, 47 F.3d 1237 (2d Cir. 1995), Scotti threatened to "break Egnat's legs and burn down [his] house" unless he came up with $50,000 to pay an extortionate debt. Scotti then asked Rodriguez, a mortgage broker, to help Egnat arrange a mortgage to obtain the cash. Rodriguez did so, knowing that Egnat had been threatened and had only agreed to the transaction reluctantly. But Rodriguez's assistance, with full knowledge of the circumstances, was held insufficient to make him guilty of conspiracy to commit extortion. Was the decision correct?

2. Problems. (a) Zahm wanted to use Lawrence's house trailer as a site for manufacturing methamphetamine. The chemicals used to "cook" methamphetamine can soil or damage the work area, and there is a risk of explosion when the volatile ingredients are heated to high temperatures. Lawrence agreed to accept $1,000 for leasing the trailer to Zahm for one day. Zahm was unable to find all the necessary equipment, and the "cook" was never carried out. Is Lawrence guilty of conspiracy to manufacture methamphetamine? United States v. Blankenship, 970 F.2d 283 (7th Cir. 1992), holds that he is not. Do you agree? What arguments can be made in support of the court's conclusion?

(b) Morse owned a Beechcraft light plane that had no passenger seats, leaving more room for cargo. Though witnesses testified that the plane was worth $50,000 to $70,000, he asked two young buyers to pay $80,000 for it and then raised his price to $115,000, to be paid in cash installments. The buyers agreed, took possession of the plane, and used it to smuggle marijuana from Mexico to Texas. Is Morse guilty of conspiracy to import marijuana? In United States v. Morse, 851 F.2d 1317, 1319-1320 (11th Cir. 1988), the court held:

> The circumstantial evidence in this case adequately supports Morse's con-
> spiracy convictions. First, the plane in Florida that Morse sold to Colding
> was particularly suited for smuggling: there were no passenger seats in the
> plane, leaving more room for hauling marijuana; one witness—a customs
> agent—testified that "a Beechcraft Queen Aire happens to be one of the
> profile aircraft that is involved in narcotic smuggling." Second, Morse sold
> the plane for $115,000, almost twice its market value; he had raised the price
> from $80,000 after meeting with Cauthen and Colding. Third, all payments
> were made in cash of low denominations. Fourth, Morse sold the plane to
> Colding, a twenty-three-year old, without any contract or receipt to evidence
> the transaction. Fifth, Morse, who never had registered *his* purchase of the
> plane with the Federal Aviation Administration (FAA), sold the plane
> without providing the FAA with an aircraft registration application or bill
> of sale as required by law. Sixth, Morse was informed that the plane had
> been used to smuggle marijuana; yet he made no attempt to contact law
> enforcement officials. Seventh, when Colding failed to pay the balance of
> the agreed purchase price, Morse did not threaten to file suit to recover the
> money.

Question: Is this analysis consistent with the reasoning of *Lauria*, *Direct Sales*, and *Falcone*?

(c) Heras drove Correa, whom Heras knew to be a drug dealer, to a hotel near the airport, knowing that the purpose of the trip was for Correa to take possession of a large quantity of drugs. Is that knowledge alone sufficient to infer Heras's intent to facilitate drug distribution? While the district court thought this evidence was insufficient to infer purpose, the Second Circuit disagreed. United States v. Heras, 609 F.3d 101 (2d Cir. 2010). Which court was correct?

3. Corrupt motive. In a leading common-law precedent, People v. Powell, 63 N.Y. 88 (1875), the court held that to be criminal, a conspiracy must be animated by a "corrupt" motive or an intention to engage in conduct known to be wrongful. To understand the operation of the *Powell* doctrine, consider the following factual scenario: Suppose an election officer and a clerk agree to enter votes on the official tally sheets before the time set by law, but do so in good faith (there is no opposition candidate) and without knowing that such action is criminal. Under the *Powell* doctrine, they could not be convicted of conspiracy to enter false figures on the tally sheets. Cf. Commonwealth v. Gormley, 77 Pa. Super. 298 (1921) (citing *Powell* to require the admission of evidence of good faith and ignorance of the criminality of the act under such circumstances).

Question: Doesn't this approach in effect make mistake of law a defense in a conspiracy prosecution? The *Powell* doctrine has been widely criticized. See Model Penal Code and Commentaries, Comment to §503, at 417-418 (1985):

> The *Powell* rule . . . may be viewed as a judicial endeavor to import fair mens rea requirements into statutes creating regulatory offenses that do not rest on traditional concepts of personal fault and culpability. This should, however, be the function of the statutes defining such offenses. Section 2.04(3) specifies the limited situations when ignorance of the criminality of one's conduct is a defense in general. There is no good reason why the fortuity of concert should be used as a device for limiting criminality in this area. . . .

The *Powell* doctrine has been rejected in England, see Churchill v. Walton, [1967] 2 A.C. 224, and in most of the state codifications enacted in the wake of the MPC. See Note, Conspiracy: State Statutory Reform Since the Model Penal Code, 75 Colum. L. Rev. 1122, 1131 n.48 (1975).

4. Attendant circumstances. How should the law treat a situation where the defendant claims a mistake of *fact* as to some attendant circumstance? That is, should mistake of fact be a defense to a conspiracy charge even if it would not be a defense in a prosecution for the substantive offense? Consider the following situations:

(a) Facts that increase the gravity of the offense. Suppose that Supplier and Dealer meet with Buyer and negotiate terms for a large purchase of drugs. At Buyer's request, they agree to deliver the drugs to him at Seedy's Bar. Before the delivery is made, Supplier and Dealer are arrested. Buyer turns out to be an undercover agent, and (unknown to Dealer and Supplier) Seedy's Bar turns out to be directly across the street from a public school. State law imposes much higher penalties for drug sales that occur within 1,000 feet of a school. Can Dealer and Supplier be convicted of conspiracy to distribute drugs within 1,000 feet of a school? Consider United States v. Freed, 401 U.S. 601 (1971), supra page 289. In that case, the Supreme Court upheld an indictment charging both possession and conspiracy to possess unregistered hand grenades, despite its failure to allege that the defendant knew the grenades were unregistered. The Court treated the substantive offense of possessing unregistered hand grenades as imposing strict liability so far as the fact of registration was concerned. The Court disposed of the challenge to the conspiracy charge as follows (id. at n.14):

> We need not decide whether a criminal conspiracy to do an act "innocent in itself" and not known by the alleged conspirators to be prohibited must be actuated by some corrupt motive other than the intention to do the act which is prohibited and which is the object of the conspiracy. An agreement to acquire hand grenades is hardly an agreement innocent in itself. Therefore what we

have said of the substantive offense satisfies on these special facts the requirements for a conspiracy.

Questions: Is this holding sound? So far as the conspiracy count was concerned, was the defendant arguing only that he did not know it was a crime to possess grenades or that he did not agree to possess *unregistered* grenades? Did the Court confuse two separate defenses, namely, the defense of ignorance of the criminality of the agreement and the defense of lack of agreement to do the prohibited act?

(b) Facts essential to criminality. Suppose that, in contrast to *United States v. Freed,* supra, the alleged conspiracy involves an act "innocent in itself." For example, suppose that Alan and Mary, after spending an evening together, decide to go to a motel where they intend to have consensual sexual relations. Bill agrees to drive them there, knowing their intentions, but just before they leave, Mary's parents arrive on the scene and foil the plan. Though neither Alan nor Bill could have known it, Mary is underage. Can Alan and Bill be convicted of conspiracy to commit statutory rape?

We considered variations on this hypothetical at two earlier points above. With respect to *attempt* liability, the MPC Commentary states that a person in Alan's position would be guilty of attempted statutory rape. See page 617 supra. With respect to Bill's liability as an *accomplice,* §2.06(3)(a) appears to preclude conviction, but in this instance the Commentary argues that the Code is ambiguous and states that the issue was left for the courts to decide. See page 678 supra. With respect to the mens rea for *conspiracy,* the Commentary states likewise that the Code is ambiguous and that the issue was left to the courts. See Model Penal Code and Commentaries, Comment to §5.03 at 413 (1985). Yet §5.03(1) provides that a person is guilty of conspiracy to commit a crime only if he acts "with the purpose of promoting or facilitating its commission." How can it be said that either Alan or Bill has "the purpose of promoting or facilitating [the] commission" of the crime of statutory rape?

Apart from the question of textual interpretation, what is the sensible way to resolve this problem? Some would argue that the policies that determine the mens rea for the object crime logically govern the matter on the conspiracy charge as well. But, given the very early point at which conspiracy liability can attach, is it important to require subjective culpability? Whatever may be the right solution to this problem for complicity and attempts, how can a mens rea that is less than purpose or knowledge ever suffice for conspiracy, which—by definition—consists of an *agreement* to engage in the prohibited conduct?

The English approach acknowledges these concerns. The English Criminal Law Act, 1977, ch. 45, §1(2) states:

Where liability for any offence may be incurred without knowledge on the part of the person committing it of any particular fact or circumstance necessary for the commission of the offence, a person shall nevertheless not be guilty of conspiracy to commit that offence ... unless he and at least one other party to the agreement intend or know that that fact or circumstance shall or will exist at the time when the conduct constituting the offence is to take place.

3. *Conspiracy as a Form of Accessorial Liability*

PINKERTON v. UNITED STATES

Supreme Court of the United States
328 U.S. 640 (1946)

JUSTICE DOUGLAS delivered the opinion of the Court.

Walter and Daniel Pinkerton are brothers who live a short distance from each other on Daniel's farm. They were indicted for violations of the Internal Revenue Code. The indictment contained ten substantive counts and one conspiracy count. The jury found Walter guilty on nine of the substantive counts and on the conspiracy count. It found Daniel guilty on six of the substantive counts and on the conspiracy count. Walter was fined $500 and sentenced generally on the substantive counts to imprisonment for thirty months. On the conspiracy count he was given a two year sentence to run concurrently with the other sentence. Daniel was fined $1,000 and sentenced generally on the substantive counts to imprisonment for thirty months. On the conspiracy count he was fined $500 and given a two year sentence to run concurrently with the other sentence. The judgments of conviction were affirmed by the Circuit Court of Appeals. ...

It is contended that there was insufficient evidence to implicate Daniel in the conspiracy. But we think there was enough evidence for submission of the issue to the jury.

There is, however, no evidence to show that Daniel participated directly in the commission of the substantive offenses on which his conviction has been sustained, although there was evidence to show that these substantive offenses were in fact committed by Walter in furtherance of the unlawful agreement or conspiracy existing between the brothers. The question was submitted to the jury on the theory that each petitioner could be found guilty of the substantive offenses, if it was found at the time those offenses were committed petitioners were parties to an unlawful conspiracy and the substantive offenses charged were in fact committed in furtherance of it.[6]

Daniel relies on United States v. Sall (C.C.A. 3d) 116 F.2d 745. That case held that participation in the conspiracy was not itself enough to sustain a conviction for the substantive offense even though it was committed in furtherance of the conspiracy. The court held that, in addition to evidence that the offense was in fact committed in furtherance of the conspiracy, evidence of

---

6. ... Daniel was not indicted as an aider or abetter (see Criminal Code, §332, 18 U.S.C.A. 550), nor was his case submitted to the jury on that theory.

direct participation in the commission of the substantive offense or other evidence from which participation might fairly be inferred was necessary.

We take a different view. We have here a continuous conspiracy. There is here no evidence of the affirmative action on the part of Daniel which is necessary to establish his withdrawal from it. Hyde v. United States, 225 U.S. 347, 369. As stated in that case, "Having joined in an unlawful scheme, having constituted agents for its performance, scheme and agency to be continuous until full fruition be secured, until he does some act to disavow or defeat the purpose he is in no situation to claim the delay of the law. As the offense has not been terminated or accomplished, he is still offending. And we think, consciously offending, offending as certainly, as we have said, as at the first moment of his confederation, and consciously through every moment of its existence." And so long as the partnership in crime continues the partners act for each other in carrying it forward. It is settled that "an overt act of one partner may be the act of all without any new agreement specifically directed to that act." Motive or intent may be proved by the acts or declarations of some of the conspirators in furtherance of the common objective. The governing principle is the same when the substantive offense is committed by one of the conspirators in furtherance of the unlawful project. The criminal intent to do the act is established by the formation of the conspiracy. Each conspirator instigated the commission of the crime. The unlawful agreement contemplated precisely what was done. It was formed for the purpose. The act done was in execution of the enterprise. The rule which holds responsible one who counsels, procures, or commands another to commit a crime is founded on the same principle. That principle is recognized in the law of conspiracy when the overt act of one partner in crime is attributable to all. An overt act is an essential ingredient of the crime of conspiracy under §37 of the Criminal Code, 18 U.S.C.A. §88 [now §371]. If that can be supplied by the act of one conspirator, we fail to see why the same or other acts in furtherance of the conspiracy are likewise not attributable to the others for the purpose of holding them responsible for the substantive offense.

A different case would arise if the substantive offense committed by one of the conspirators was not in fact done in furtherance of the conspiracy, did not fall within the scope of the unlawful project, or was merely a part of the ramifications of the plan which could not be reasonably foreseen as a necessary or natural consequence of the unlawful agreement. But as we read this record, that is not this case.

Affirmed.

JUSTICE RUTLEDGE, dissenting in part.

The judgment concerning Daniel Pinkerton should be reversed. In my opinion it is without precedent here and is a dangerous precedent to establish.

Daniel and Walter, who were brothers living near each other, were charged in several counts with substantive offenses, and then a conspiracy count was added naming those offenses as overt acts. The proof showed that Walter alone committed the substantive crimes. There was none to establish that Daniel participated in them, aided and abetted Walter in committing them, or knew that he had done so. Daniel in fact was in the penitentiary . . . when some of Walter's crimes were done.

There was evidence, however, to show that over several years Daniel and Walter had confederated to commit similar crimes concerned with unlawful possession, transportation, and dealing in whiskey, in fraud of the federal revenues. On this evidence both were convicted of conspiracy. Walter also was convicted on the substantive counts on the proof of his committing the crimes charged. Then, on that evidence without more than the proof of Daniel's criminal agreement with Walter and the latter's overt acts, which were also the substantive offenses charged, the court told the jury they could find Daniel guilty of those substantive offenses. They did so. . . .

Daniel has been held guilty of the substantive crimes committed only by Walter on proof that he did no more than conspire with him to commit offenses of the same general character. There was no evidence that he counseled, advised or had knowledge of those particular acts or offenses. There was, therefore, none that he aided, abetted or took part in them. There was only evidence sufficient to show that he had agreed with Walter at some past time to engage in such transactions generally. As to Daniel this was only evidence of conspiracy, not of substantive crime.

The Court's theory seems to be that Daniel and Walter became general partners in crime by virtue of their agreement and because of that agreement without more on his part Daniel became criminally responsible as a principal for everything Walter did thereafter in the nature of a criminal offense of the general sort the agreement contemplated, so long as there was not clear evidence that Daniel had withdrawn from or revoked the agreement. Whether or not his commitment to the penitentiary had that effect, the result is a vicarious criminal responsibility as broad as, or broader than, the vicarious civil liability of a partner for acts done by a co-partner in the course of the firm's business. . . .

State v. Bridges, 133 N.J. 447, 628 A.2d 270 (1993) (Handler, J.): [At a birthday party for a 16-year-old friend, defendant got into a heated argument with another guest, Andy Strickland. Defendant left, yelling that he would return with help. He recruited two acquaintances, Bing and Rolle, to accompany him back to the party, where he expected a confrontation. On the way back, they stopped at Bing's house and picked up guns, to be used to hold Strickland's supporters at bay while defendant fought it out with him. When they returned to the party, defendant began fighting with a friend of Strickland's, while Bing and Rolle stood by. A member of the crowd hit Bing in the face, whereupon Bing and Rolle drew their guns and began firing—first into the air and then into the crowd, as onlookers tried to flee. One of the onlookers was fatally wounded. At trial defendant was convicted of conspiracy to commit aggravated assault and of several substantive crimes including murder. On the murder count defendant was sentenced to life imprisonment, with parole ineligibility for a minimum of 30 years. The intermediate appellate court (the Appellate Division) held that defendant was not responsible for the murder committed by Rolle and Bing in the course of the conspiracy. The prosecution appealed to the New Jersey Supreme Court.]

The Appellate Division majority determined that the Code of Criminal Justice, which provides that the involvement in a conspiracy can be the basis for criminal liability for the commission of substantive crimes, N.J.S.A. 2C:2-6b(4), requires a level of culpability and state of mind that is identical to that required of accomplice liability. The Appellate Division therefore ruled that a conspirator is vicariously liable for the substantive crimes committed by co-conspirators only when the conspirator had the same intent and purpose as the co-conspirator who committed the crimes.

The provision of the New Jersey Code of Criminal Justice . . . that posits criminal liability on the basis of participation in a conspiracy is silent with respect to its culpability requirement. It provides:

> A person is legally accountable for the conduct of another person when: . . . He is engaged in a conspiracy with such other person.

The majority below concluded that the Code contemplated "complete congruity" between accomplice and vicarious conspirator liability. . . . The Appellate Division majority reasoned that *Pinkerton* . . . mandates that a crime "must have been within [a co-conspirator's] contemplation when he entered into the agreement and reasonably comprehended by his purpose and intention in entering into the agreement."

. . . That understanding of *Pinkerton* is not supported. . . . [I]t has not been disputed that [*Pinkerton*] purported to impose vicarious liability on each conspirator for the acts of others based on an objective standard of reasonable foreseeability. . . . [I]t was understood that the liability of a co-conspirator under the objective standard of reasonable foreseeability would be broader than that of an accomplice, where the defendant must actually foresee and intend the result of his or her acts.

That understanding of *Pinkerton* is also widely accepted by commentators and treatises, whether they are critical of its rule, or only expounding the existing law. . . .

We appreciate the concern of the concurring opinion that such a standard of vicarious liability for conspirators differs from that of accomplices. Although conspirator liability is circumscribed by the requirement of a close causal connection between the conspiracy and the substantive crime, that standard concededly is less strict than that defining accomplice accountability. It is, however, evident that the Legislature chose to address the special dangers inherent in group activity and therefore intended to include the crime of conspiracy as a distinctive basis for vicarious criminal liability.[a] . . .

---

a. N.J. Stat. §2C:2-6(b)-(c) provides:

> b. A person is legally accountable for the conduct of another person when: . . .
> (3) He is an accomplice of such other person in the commission of an offense; or
> (4) He is engaged in a conspiracy with such other person.—Eds.

Accordingly, we conclude, and now hold, that a co-conspirator may be liable for the commission of substantive criminal acts that are not within the scope of the conspiracy if they are reasonably foreseeable as the necessary or natural consequences of the conspiracy. . . .

The conspiracy [here] did not have as its objective the purposeful killing of another person. Nevertheless, the evidence discloses that the conspiratorial plan contemplated bringing loaded guns to keep a large contingent of young hostile partygoers back from a beating of one of their friends, and that it could be anticipated that the weapon might be fired at the crowd. . . .

From that evidence a jury could conclude that a reasonably foreseeable risk and a probable and natural consequence of carrying out a plan to intimidate the crowd by using loaded guns would be that one of the gunslingers would intentionally fire at somebody, and, under the circumstances, that act would be sufficiently connected to the original conspirational plan to provide a just basis for a determination of guilt for that substantive crime.

[Reversed.]

O'HERN, J., concurring in part and dissenting in part. An interpretation of the provisions of the Code of Criminal Justice that would allow a sentence of life imprisonment to be imposed on the basis of the negligent appraisal of a risk that another would commit a homicide, conflicts with the internal structure of the Code. . . . If we assume, as the majority does, that Bridges did not intend that Shawn Lockley be killed, he could not have been convicted of attempted murder.

Nor could defendant have been convicted as an accomplice to the murder. . . .

And finally, defendant could not even have been found guilty of conspiracy to commit murder. A person is guilty of a conspiracy to commit an offense only if "*with the purpose* of promoting or facilitating its commission he" or she agrees with another person that they will "engage in conduct which constitutes such crime" or agrees to aid such person "in the planning or commission of such crime." N.J.S.A. 2C:5-2a (emphasis added).

The Code establishes a carefully-measured grid of criminal responsibility. . . . Thus, one who causes the death of another with the knowledge or purpose to kill will be guilty of murder and can be sentenced to death in certain circumstances or to life imprisonment with a minimum of thirty years without parole. . . .

The manslaughter offenses require a finding that an actor causing death has exhibited a reckless disregard for human life. When that recklessness is in disregard of a *probability* that death may occur, the offense is aggravated manslaughter and carries a penalty of up to thirty years in prison. When the proof shows reckless disregard of a possibility of causing death, the offense is reckless manslaughter and carries the penalty of a first-degree crime, up to twenty years in prison. Except for one form of vehicular homicide, N.J.S.A. 2C:11-4b(3), *no negligent homicide* exists under New Jersey law, much less a crime of negligent murder.

... This case is an example of the most extreme sort—life imprisonment with no possibility of parole for thirty years on the basis of a negligent mental state. ... The most reasonable construction of N.J.S.A. 2C:2-6b(4) is that the Legislature intended that the conspirator to the commission of an offense, like an accomplice to the commission of an offense, be punished as a principal. ... No liability is foreseen [under the statute] other than for the crime or crimes that were the object of the conspiracy.

NOTE ON THE MERITS OF PINKERTON

1. In favor of **Pinkerton.** Consider the statement of Deputy Assistant Attorney General Kenney to a Senate subcommittee considering this issue in the context of a revision of the federal criminal law (quoted in Note, 75 Colum. L. Rev. 1122, 1152 (1975)):

> The ever-increasing sophistication of organized crime presents a compelling reason against abandonment of *Pinkerton*. Complicated and highly refined stock frauds ... and narcotics conspiracies represent a substantial and ever-increasing threat to society justifying retention of the *Pinkerton* doctrine. Empirical evidence has repeatedly demonstrated that those who form and control illegal enterprises are generally well insulated from prosecutions, with the exception of prosecutions predicated upon the theory of conspiracy. To preclude uniformly their exposure to additional sanctions, regardless of the circumstances, for the very crimes which sustain their illegal ventures, would have the most unfortunate and inequitable consequences.

Questions: Is Kenney correct that overruling *Pinkerton* would preclude liability for those who "form and control illegal enterprises"? Wouldn't they be liable under traditional accomplice liability?

Scholarly commentators have echoed Kenney's suggestion that the functional justification for *Pinkerton* derives from the same source as the functional justification for conspiracy law more generally—the need to counteract the special advantages (to the criminal) of group organization:

> Thinking of conspiracy and related doctrines as a collective sanction regime casts light on several functional advantages they might bring to law enforcement. ... First, where individual members of conspiracies are difficult to apprehend, conspiracy law makes it possible to inflict costs on them indirectly by punishing other members who are more accessible. For example, if high-level managers of a drug organization are difficult to identify or reach, conspiracy law allows the government to punish lower-level drug dealers, who will in turn demand higher compensation from the managers in exchange for bearing greater liability risks. Second, like other forms of collective sanctions, conspiracy liability can serve as an information-forcing tool. Conspiracy law makes it possible for prosecutors to threaten low-level conspirators with severe sentences and then offer them reductions in exchange for inculpatory evidence about higher-level conspirators. ... Third, conspiracy law, along with other accomplice liability doctrines, gives criminal groups an incentive

to monitor and control excessively harmful activity. Under *Pinkerton*, every member of a drug organization is liable for every [foreseeable] murder committed by another member of the organization [in furtherance of the drug conspiracy] and therefore has an incentive to police unnecessary violence.

Daryl J. Levinson, Collective Sanctions, 56 Stan. L. Rev. 345, 398-399 (2003). See also Neal Kumar Katyal, Conspiracy Theory, 112 Yale L.J. 1307, 1372-1375 (2003).

Questions: Is it realistic to expect low-level drug dealers "to monitor and control" "unnecessary violence" by those higher up in the organization? Even if so, is it legitimate to uphold *Pinkerton* for functional reasons such as these, if doing so will mean that some individuals in a conspiracy will face criminal sanctions beyond their personal fault? Are there any limits to using the criminal law in this way? For example, should parents be liable for the crimes of their children, if there is a functional reason for believing that they can to some degree control the behavior of their children? Or is individual fault too important a principle to abandon in the name of utilitarian goals?

Another argument in favor of *Pinkerton* rests on the notion of a "group will." Consider Jens David Ohlin, Group Think: The Law of Conspiracy and Collective Reason, 98 J. Crim. L. & Criminology 147, 180, 182-183 (2007):

> When an individual joins a group deliberation, she makes a commitment to submit her reasons to collective rationality in order to achieve rational unity at the group level. . . . This is hardly a difficult phenomenon to visualize; every soldier who joins a military unit understands that [he gives up his] autonomy (in some matters) in pursuit of collective goals.

This view of *Pinkerton* liability would require greater attention to the cohesion of the group and the nature of decision making within the group, id. at 197-198:

> It should be clear now that [liability] should be reserved for tightly knit conspiracies with shared decision-making . . . because the agent in question closely participates in the deliberative structure of the [organization] and helps form the collective intention. It is this fact that generates culpability, for the simple reason that he participated closely in the decision-making process and, in a sense, made it his own.

2. Against **Pinkerton.** Compare People v. McGee, 399 N.E.2d 1177, 1181-1182 (N.Y. 1979), where the court observed, in rejecting the *Pinkerton* doctrine:

> It is not offensive to permit a conviction of conspiracy to stand on the overt act committed by another, for the act merely provides corroboration of the existence of the agreement and indicates that the agreement has reached a point where it poses a sufficient threat to society to impose sanctions. . . . But it is repugnant to our system of jurisprudence, where guilt is generally personal to the defendant, . . . to impose punishment, not for the socially harmful

agreement to which the defendant is a party, but for substantive offenses in which he did not participate. . . .

The MPC also rejects *Pinkerton*, imposing accomplice liability on conspirators for the substantive crimes of their co-conspirators only when the strict conditions for accomplice liability are met. Supporting that position, the drafters of the MPC explain (Model Penal Code and Commentaries, Comment to §2.06(3) at 307 (1985)):

> [T]here appears to be no better way to confine within reasonable limits the scope of liability to which conspiracy may theoretically give rise. In People v. Luciano [14 N.E.2d 433 (N.Y. 1938)], for example, Luciano and others were convicted of sixty-two counts of compulsory prostitution, each count involving a specific instance of placing a girl in a house of prostitution, receiving money for so doing or receiving money from the earnings of a prostitute—acts proved to have been committed pursuant to a combination to control commercialized vice in New York City.
>
> Liability was properly imposed with respect to these defendants, who directed and controlled the combination. They solicited and aided the commission of numberless specific crimes. . . . But would so extensive a liability be just for each of the prostitutes or runners involved in the plan? They have, of course, committed their own crimes; they may actually have assisted in others but they exerted no substantial influence on the behavior of a hundred other prostitutes or runners, each pursuing his own ends within the shelter of the combination. A court would and should hold that they are parties to a conspiracy. . . . And they should also be held for those crimes they actually committed, or . . . for those to which they were accomplices. However, law would lose all sense of just proportion if simply because of the conspiracy itself each were held accountable for thousands of additional offenses of which he was completely unaware and which he did not influence at all. . . .

3. Continuing controversy over **Pinkerton.** Although the federal courts and many states continue to permit vicarious liability for the substantive offenses of co-conspirators, the doctrine is far from settled. State supreme courts continue to reconsider their acceptance or rejection of the *Pinkerton* rule. For example, the Connecticut Supreme Court reaffirmed its embrace of *Pinkerton*, rejecting a defendant's constitutional challenge to the doctrine under the Due Process Clause. State v. Coltherst, 620 A.2d 1024 (Conn. 2003). The court stated, "When the defendant has 'played a necessary part in setting in motion a discrete course of criminal conduct,' he cannot reasonably complain that it is unfair to hold him vicariously liable, under the *Pinkerton* doctrine, for the natural and probable result of . . . conduct that, although he did not intend, he should have foreseen." Id. at 1039-1040. In contrast, the Washington Supreme Court rejected the *Pinkerton* doctrine as inconsistent with the mens rea requirements of Washington's statutory provisions on accomplice liability. State v. Stein, 27 P.3d 184 (Wash. 2001). And, in a Solomonic decision, the Nevada Supreme Court overturned the defendant's convictions under *Pinkerton* for a co-conspirator's "specific intent" offenses (burglary and kidnapping), while upholding the defendant's convictions for "general intent" offenses (such as home invasion). The court reasoned that permitting *Pinkerton* liability for specific intent crimes would allow the state to "sidestep" the statutory mens rea requirement for those offenses. Bolden v. State, 124 P.3d 191 (Nev. 2005).

NOTES ON APPLICATIONS OF PINKERTON

1. Liability of a new conspirator for prior acts of co-conspirators. It is often said that upon joining an ongoing conspiracy, a person becomes liable for all acts committed by co-conspirators in furtherance of the conspiracy, including acts committed prior to his joining. See, e.g., 16 Am. Jur. 2d Conspiracy §20 (1979). Such statements are sometimes misinterpreted to suggest that a defendant is liable under *Pinkerton* for *substantive crimes* that co-conspirators committed before he joined the conspiracy. But *Pinkerton* liability is not retroactive. As explained in United States v. Blackmon, 839 F.2d 900, 908-909 (2d Cir. 1988):

> The confusion here is that with regard to liability for *conspiracy,* a defendant may be legally responsible for acts of co-conspirators prior to that defendant's entry into the conspiracy [in the sense that such acts may be used as evidence against him in the prosecution for the crime of conspiracy], whereas, with regard to *substantive offenses,* a defendant cannot be retroactively liable for offenses committed prior to his joining the conspiracy.

2. Conspiracy and accomplice liability compared. Under the traditional view of accomplice liability, as discussed in the *Bridges* case, liability as an *accomplice* requires proof that the accomplice intended to promote or facilitate the specific offense for which the prosecution seeks to hold him accountable. In jurisdictions adhering to this view, liability as a co-conspirator under a *Pinkerton* theory represents a considerable expansion of the liability that the co-conspirator would face under the normal rules of accomplice liability. See, e.g., United States v. Shea, 150 F.3d 44, 49-51 (1st Cir. 1998).

But, as we saw in the section on Complicity, pages 681-686 supra, some jurisdictions now use an objective foreseeability test to determine the liability of an accomplice for originally unintended crimes committed by the principal in the course of the criminal endeavor. In these jurisdictions, the objective theory of accomplice liability often produces results similar to those produced by *Pinkerton.* Indeed, in such jurisdictions, accomplice liability may reach even further than *Pinkerton* liability. Consider the *Luparello* case, supra page 682. Recall that the defendant, who was attempting to locate his former girlfriend, Terri, agreed with several friends to beat up a man named Martin, in order to force Martin to disclose Terri's whereabouts. When one of the conspirators lured Martin out of his house, another conspirator, who was waiting in a parked car, fired six shots at Martin and killed him. Luparello, who was not present at the scene, was convicted of first-degree murder. The *Luparello* court found murder liability under its expansive doctrine of accomplice liability because the killing of Martin was a reasonably foreseeable consequence of Luparello's conceded offense of assault. But could liability be sustained under *Pinkerton* in such a situation? Was the shooter's action "in furtherance" of the conspiratorial agreement?

3. *Expansive applications of* **Pinkerton.** In People v. Brigham, 265 Cal. Rptr. 486 (Cal. App. 1989), the defendant and one Bluitt set out to kill a man named "Chuckie." They saw a teenager on the street, the defendant said, "That is Chuckie," and the two men walked toward the teenager, carrying their weapons. When they got closer, the defendant said to Bluitt, "[T]hat is not Chuckie. . . . Don't do it. . . . That's not the dude." Bluitt rejected the defendant's advice, saying that he wanted to let people "know we [are] serious." Bluitt fired twice, killing the teenager. Because of Bluitt's "hardheaded and erratic nature," the prosecution argued and the jury found that the defendant could "reasonably foresee" that Bluitt, once set in motion, might knowingly kill someone other than his assigned target. On this basis the defendant was convicted of first-degree murder. Is the conviction proper under the *Pinkerton* doctrine? Under any other doctrine?

In United States v. Wall, 225 F.3d 858 (7th Cir. 2000), the defendant, who had a prior felony conviction, was charged with violating 18 U.S.C. §922(g)(1), which made it a felony for a person with a previous felony conviction to possess a gun that had traveled in interstate commerce. The government sought to establish possession under a vicarious liability theory premised on *Pinkerton.* It argued that since the defendant's co-conspirator possessed a gun, its possession could also be attributed to the defendant, even though the co-conspirator's possession of the gun was not a crime. Is this a legitimate application of *Pinkerton?* The court thought not, concluding:

> [T]he government uses a cut-and-paste approach, taking the firearm possession by one conspirator, adding it to the felon status of another conspirator, and thereby creating a substantive offense for that second conspirator. It is a significant expansion of the *Pinkerton* doctrine that appears to be difficult to limit.

Do you agree?

United States v. Alvarez, 755 F.2d 830 (11th Cir. 1985) (Kravitch, J.):
[A run-down motel in Miami, Florida, was the scene of a drug "buy" that had been arranged after long negotiation. Undercover agents from the Bureau of Alcohol, Tobacco, and Firearms (BATF) were in the motel room with the drug dealers, waiting for another dealer to return with a quantity of cocaine that the agents had agreed to buy for $147,000. On the arrival of the cocaine, other agents outside began to converge on the motel and a shoot-out started in the motel room. One of the BATF agents was killed and the other agent, along with two of the cocaine dealers, was seriously wounded. All the dealers were convicted of conspiracy to commit and commission of various drug offenses.

Two of them, Alvarez and Simon, who shot the agents, were also convicted of first-degree murder of a federal agent. Three of the dealers, Portal, Concepcion, and Hernandez, were convicted of second-degree murder, though they played no part in the shooting.] Appellants Portal, Concepcion, and Hernandez contend that their murder convictions . . . were based on an unprecedented and improper extension of Pinkerton v. United States, 328 U.S. 640 (1946). . . . The[y] argue that murder is not a reasonably foreseeable consequence of a drug conspiracy, and that their murder convictions therefore should be reversed. We conclude that, although the murder convictions of the three appellants may represent an unprecedented application of *Pinkerton,* such an application is not improper. . . .

Upon reviewing the record, we find ample evidence to support the jury's conclusion that the murder was a reasonably foreseeable consequence of the drug conspiracy alleged in the indictment. In making this determination, we rely on two critical factors. First, the evidence clearly established that the drug conspiracy was designed to effectuate the sale of a large quantity of cocaine. . . .

Second, based on the amount of drugs and money involved, the jury was entitled to infer that, at the time the cocaine sale was arranged, the conspirators must have been aware of the likelihood (1) that at least some of their number would be carrying weapons, and (2) that deadly force would be used, if necessary, to protect the conspirators' interests. . . . In our opinion, these two critical factors provided ample support for the jury's conclusion that the murder was a reasonably foreseeable consequence of the drug conspiracy alleged in the indictment. . . .

The three appellants also contend that, even if the murder was reasonably foreseeable, their murder convictions nevertheless should be reversed. The appellants argue that the murder was sufficiently distinct from the intended purposes of the drug conspiracy, and that their individual roles in the conspiracy were sufficiently minor, that they should not be held responsible for the murder. We are not persuaded. . . .

We acknowledge that the instant case is not a typical *Pinkerton* case. Here, the murder of Agent Rios was not within the originally intended scope of the conspiracy, but instead occurred as a result of an unintended turn of events. We have not found, nor has the government cited, any authority for the proposition that all conspirators, regardless of individual culpability, may be held responsible under *Pinkerton* for reasonably foreseeable but originally unintended substantive crimes.[25]

---

25. The imposition of *Pinkerton* liability for such crimes is not wholly unprecedented. See, e.g., Government of Virgin Islands v. Dowling, 633 F.2d 660, 666 (3d Cir.) (1980) (conspiracy to commit bank robbery; substantive crime of assault with deadly weapons against police officers, committed during escape attempt); Park v. Huff, 506 F.2d 849, 859 (5th Cir.) (1975) (liquor conspiracy; substantive crime of first degree murder of local district attorney, committed in attempt to stop investigation of illegal liquor sales). In each of the aforementioned cases, however, vicarious liability was imposed only on "major" participants in the conspiracy.

Furthermore, we are mindful of the potential due process limitations on the *Pinkerton* doctrine in cases involving attenuated relationships between the conspirator and the substantive crime.

Nevertheless, these considerations do not require us to reverse the murder convictions of Portal, Concepcion, and Hernandez. . . . All three were more than "minor" participants in the drug conspiracy. Portal served as a lookout in front of the Hurricane Motel during part of the negotiations that led to the shoot-out, and the evidence indicated that he was armed. Concepcion introduced the agents to Alvarez, the apparent leader of the conspiracy, and was present when the shoot-out started. Finally, Hernandez, the manager of the motel, allowed the drug transactions to take place on the premises and acted as a translator during part of the negotiations that led to the shoot-out.

In addition, all three appellants had actual knowledge of at least some of the circumstances and events leading up to the murder. The evidence that Portal was carrying a weapon demonstrated that he anticipated the possible use of deadly force to protect the conspirators' interests. Moreover, both Concepcion and Hernandez were present when Alvarez stated that he would rather be dead than go back to prison, indicating that they, too, were aware that deadly force might be used to prevent apprehension by Federal agents.

. . . We therefore hold that *Pinkerton* liability for the murder of Agent Rios properly was imposed on the three appellants. . . .[27]

NOTE ON PINKERTON AND MINOR PARTICIPANTS

The limitation suggested by the *Alvarez* court in its footnote 27—that *Pinkerton* liability might be negated by a defendant's minor role in a conspiracy or lack of knowledge about the unintended substantive offense—has been developed by other courts as a restraint on the reach of the *Pinkerton* doctrine. For example, when the Connecticut Supreme Court first explicitly adopted the *Pinkerton* rule, it suggested that the rule might apply only when the defendant was a "leader" of the conspiracy. State v. Walton, 630 A.2d 990 (Conn. 1993). In a later case, a defendant sought to avoid substantive liability under this limitation. He argued that although he was one of several men who ambushed a truck and fired multiple shots into it, killing an 8-year-old boy, he was neither the actual shooter of the boy nor the leader of the conspiracy to ambush and thus should not be held liable under Connecticut's version of

---

At trial in the instant case, the government's attorney argued that *Pinkerton* liability for Agent Rios's murder properly could be imposed on all of the conspirators, and expressed the view that prosecutorial discretion would protect truly "minor" participants, such as appellants Rios and Raymond, from liability for the far more serious crimes committed by their coconspirators. We do not find this argument persuasive. In our view, the liability of such "minor" participants must rest on a more substantial foundation than the mere whim of the prosecutor.

27. Although our decision today extends the *Pinkerton* doctrine to cases involving reasonably foreseeable but originally unintended substantive crimes, we emphasize that we do so only within narrow confines. Our holding is limited to conspirators who played more than a "minor" role in the conspiracy, or who had actual knowledge of at least some of the circumstances and events culminating in the reasonably foreseeable but originally unintended substantive crime.

Pinkerton for the boy's murder. The Connecticut Supreme Court rejected this argument, but in doing so cautioned:

> [T]here may be occasions when it would be unreasonable to hold a defendant criminally liable for offenses committed by his coconspirators even though the state has demonstrated technical compliance with the *Pinkerton* rule. [T]he nexus between the defendant's role in the conspiracy and the illegal conduct of a coconspirator [may be] so attenuated or remote . . . that it would be unjust to hold the defendant responsible for the criminal conduct of his coconspirator.

State v. Diaz, 679 A.2d 902, 911 (Conn. 1996).

Question: What would it take to show that a defendant's role was "so attenuated . . . that it would be unjust to hold [him] responsible for the criminal conduct of his coconspirator"? For example, in *Alvarez*, why didn't Concepcion or Hernandez qualify as "minor" participants?

4. The Duration and Scope of a Conspiracy

NOTES

Particularly in jurisdictions where a defendant is liable for crimes committed in furtherance of the conspiracy by co-conspirators, questions of a conspiracy's scope and duration become critically important.

1. Duration of a conspiracy. Conspiracy traditionally has been viewed as a continuing offense. The basic rule is that once formed, a conspiracy remains in effect until its objectives have either been achieved or abandoned. See United States v. Kissel, 218 U.S. 601 (1910). Thus, unlike most criminal offenses, the statute of limitations for conspiracy begins to run not when the offense is committed (that is, when the agreement is made), but when the conspiracy terminates. One effect of this concept is that a conspiracy often can remain subject to prosecution long after the initial agreement was made and long after some of its members have ceased any active participation in the activities. In addition, because the various collateral consequences of conspiracy come into play only with respect to the period when the conspiracy is in existence, it may be crucial for defendants to try to shorten that period or for prosecutors to try to extend it.

2. The breadth of the conspiratorial objectives. In Krulewitch v. United States, 336 U.S. 440 (1949), the government argued that defendants who conspired to violate the Mann Act, a statute prohibiting interstate transportation for the purposes of prostitution, continued their conspiracy long after the transportation itself was completed. The government urged that conspirators always implicitly agree with each other to conceal facts in order to prevent detection and prosecution for the principal offense. The Supreme Court rejected the government's theory. In Grunewald v. United States, 353 U.S. 391, 404 (1957), the Court held that a conspiracy cannot be treated as including a cover-up agreement unless there is "direct evidence [of] an express original agreement among the conspirators to continue to act in concert in order to cover up . . . traces of the crime. . . ." Thus, the Court explained (id. at 402):

> [A] subsidiary conspiracy to conceal may not be implied from circumstantial evidence showing merely that the conspiracy was kept a secret and that the conspirators took care to cover up their crime. . . . Acts of covering up, even though done in the context of a mutually understood need for secrecy, cannot themselves constitute proof that concealment of the crime after its commission was part of the initial agreement. . . .

In accord with *Krulewitch* and *Grunewald*, most courts today refuse to infer that an implicit agreement to cover up the crime is inherent in every conspiracy. See United States v. Turner, 548 F.3d 1094, 1097-1098 (D.C. Cir. 2008). If coconspirators do agree to help each other cover-up the crime, when would the objective of such a conspiracy be achieved? When would the statute of limitations begin to run?

Note that agreements to conceal are not the only way for conspiracies to continue beyond the commission of the object crime. The conspirators may engage in further activities in pursuit of the conspiratorial scheme—such as the distribution of proceeds, or the pawning or fencing of stolen goods, or the dismantling of a stolen car for parts—even after the object crime has been committed. For example, in United States v. Franklin, 415 F.3d 537 (6th Cir. 2005), one Stinson, a former employee of an armored car company, conspired with Franklin and Clarke to rob an armored truck. Stinson provided the others with keys to the truck and recommended where to rob it so as to reap the most cash and avoid capture. The day after Franklin and Clarke committed the robbery, Stinson went to Franklin's apartment to pick up his share of the proceeds. Franklin then recounted details of the crime and cautioned Stinson not to get caught. The court held that Franklin's statements, uttered "only hours after the robbery and in the context of dispersing the ill-gotten proceeds," were made "during the course and in furtherance of the conspiracy." Id. at 552.

3. *Criminalizing non-criminal objectives.* At common law, an agreement became punishable as a conspiracy if the objectives were criminal or "unlawful." See Commonwealth v. Hunt, 45 Mass. 111 (1842). "Unlawful" objectives could include acts deemed offensive to "public morals" and acts that violate civil law regulations or precedents. As Justice Jackson noted in his concurrence in *Krulewitch*, this means that "at common law and under some statutes a combination may be a criminal conspiracy even if it contemplates only acts which are not crimes at all when perpetrated by an individual." Krulewitch v. United States, 336 U.S. at 449.

(a) *Public morals.* In Shaw v. Director of Public Prosecutions, [1962] A.C. 220, the House of Lords upheld a conviction for "conspiracy to corrupt public morals," on the basis of a defendant's agreement to publish a directory listing prostitutes and their services. In the United States, most states reject this doctrine and confine criminal conspiracy to those agreements whose objectives are themselves criminal. See Note, Conspiracy: Statutory Reform Since the Model Penal Code, 75 Colum. L. Rev. 1122, 1129 (1975). But in some states an agreement to pursue noncriminal objectives can be a criminal conspiracy. For example, Cal. Penal Code §182(a)(5) (2011) makes it a punishable conspiracy for two or more persons to agree "[t]o commit any act injurious to the public health, to public morals, or to pervert or obstruct justice, or the due administration of the laws. . . ."

Question: Can a prosecution under §182(a)(5) survive a challenge for unconstitutional vagueness? Reconsider *City of Chicago v. Morales*, page 171 supra.

(b) Other noncriminal objectives. Even where the "public morals" doctrine is not invoked, statutes may use the conspiracy concept to punish those who agree to pursue objectives that are unlawful because they violate the civil code but not the criminal law. Consider Cal. Penal Code §182(a)(3) (2011), which makes it a punishable conspiracy "[t]o falsely move or maintain any suit, action or proceeding."

4. Impossibility. What if the government intervenes to frustrate the success of a conspiracy, without alerting all of the conspirators? Should a conspiracy be considered terminated whenever its object becomes impossible to achieve? In United States v. Jimenez Recio, 537 U.S. 270 (2003), the police stopped a truck carrying illegal drugs, seized the drugs, and with the assistance of the truck's drivers, set up a sting. The drivers paged two other men who arrived and drove away with the truckload of drugs. When these two other men were prosecuted for conspiracy to possess and distribute the drugs, the Ninth Circuit held that their convictions could not be sustained absent evidence that they had joined the conspiracy before the drug seizure. The Supreme Court unanimously rejected this rule of automatic termination as "inconsistent with . . . basic conspiracy law." Id. at 274-275.

> The crime of conspiracy "poses a threat to the public" over and above the threat of the commission of the relevant substantive crime—both because the "combination in crime makes more likely the commission of [other] crimes" and because it "decreases the probability that the individuals involved will depart from their path of criminality." Callanan v. United States, 364 U.S. 587, 593-594 (1961). . . . Where police have frustrated a conspiracy's specific objective but conspirators (unaware of that fact) have neither abandoned the conspiracy nor withdrawn, these special conspiracy-related dangers remain. . . . So too remains the essence of the conspiracy—the agreement to commit the crime.

The Court also noted that the Ninth Circuit's rule would threaten the viability of properly run sting operations. It reasoned that the potential for abuse in such sting operations could be addressed by the defense of entrapment, see supra page 697, rather than by limiting the appropriate scope of conspiracy doctrine.

5. *Abandonment and withdrawal.* A conspiracy is generally considered to be abandoned when none of the conspirators is engaging in any action to further the conspiratorial objectives. If such inactivity continues for a period equal to the statute of limitations, prosecution will be barred. See Model Penal Code §5.03(7)(b). But what if a particular defendant "wants out" of an ongoing conspiracy? Can a conspirator cut off his responsibility for *later* acts and statements of his co-conspirators by terminating his own participation? When should withdrawal by a particular defendant start the statute of limitations running as to him? A defendant's "[a]ffirmative acts inconsistent with the object of the conspiracy and communicated in a manner reasonably calculated to reach co-conspirators have generally been regarded as sufficient to establish withdrawal or abandonment." United States v. United States Gypsum Co., 438 U.S. 422, 464-465 (1978). See also Model Penal Code §5.03(7)(c), Appendix; United States v. Carrazana, 362 Fed. Appx. 973, 976 (11th Cir. 2010).

Courts typically require a defendant to disclose the scheme to law enforcement authorities or communicate his withdrawal to his co-conspirators. But the communication must be direct. The Tenth Circuit, for example, recently rejected a defendant's argument that withdrawal from a criminal gang could be established by a long period of activities inconsistent with gang membership. The court explained (United States v. Randall, 661 F.3d 1291 (10th Cir. 2011)):

> [Withdrawal] requires more than implied dissociation. It must be sufficiently clear and delivered to those with authority in the conspiracy such that a jury could conclude that it was reasonably calculated to make the dissociation known to the organization. Simply not spending time with coconspirators is not enough to satisfy this standard.
>
> Randall argues that [gang] members could withdraw from the gang not "so much by words as by actions." Randall relies on the testimony of a gang expert who explained at trial that gang members could leave by "maturing out," or in other words "getting a good job, having children, or just getting more involved in other activities in life." Thus, Randall argues that he did not need to communicate his withdrawal to other Crips members because he matured out of the gang.
>
> Randall's argument is unavailing. . . . "Maturing out" of a gang, without more, does not meet the legal definition of withdrawal from a conspiracy. If Randall matured out of the gang and explicitly communicated to the [gang] members that he no longer would be involved with the gang in any way, then this would be a different case. . . . Merely hoping that the Crips organization would infer his withdrawal from his absence is not enough. The communication must be unambiguous and effective.

6. *Renunciation as a complete defense.* While a successful withdrawal might shield a conspirator from punishment for acts and statements of co-conspirators that take place after the withdrawal, should it also afford a defense to the conspiracy charge itself? As in the case of abandoned attempts, the common-law answer was no. See pages 621-622 supra. The theory was that once the crime was committed, it could not be "uncommitted." Post-offense conduct was considered relevant only to sentencing. Today, most states, following the lead of the MPC, allow a complete defense for

renunciation under some circumstances. See Evan Tsen Lee, Cancelling Crime, 30 Conn. L. Rev. 117, 121 (1997). The Code allows the defense only if the circumstances manifest renunciation of the actor's criminal purpose *and* the actor succeeds in preventing commission of the criminal objectives. Model Penal Code §5.03(6). Some states consider this latter requirement too severe and therefore require only that the actor make a substantial effort to prevent the crime. See, e.g., Ark. Code Ann. §5-3-405(2)(B) (2011).

7. *Scope of Punishment.* What should be the appropriate level of punishment when the conspirators have committed the object crimes? The traditional view permits separate punishments, with consecutive sentences, for the object crime and the conspiracy to commit it. In Callanan v. United States, 364 U.S. 587 (1961), the defendant was convicted of obstructing interstate commerce by extortion and of conspiring to obstruct commerce by that same extortion. The maximum punishment for obstructing commerce was 20 years. The trial court imposed a sentence of 12 years on the obstruction count and another 12 years to run consecutively on the conspiracy count. The defendant alleged that Congress did not intend to authorize punishment for both the conspiracy and the obstruction itself. The Court rejected the claim, stating (id. at 593-594):

> Concerted action both increases the likelihood that the criminal object will be successfully attained and decreases the probability that the individuals involved will depart from their path of criminality. Group association for criminal purposes often, if not normally, makes possible the attainment of ends more complex than those which one criminal could accomplish. Nor is the danger of a conspiratorial group limited to the particular end toward which it has embarked. Combination in crime makes more likely the commission of crimes unrelated to the original purpose for which the group was formed. In sum, the danger which a conspiracy generates is not confined to the substantive offense which is the immediate aim of the enterprise.

The MPC takes a different position. Section 1.07(1)(b) provides that a defendant may not be convicted of more than one offense if "one offense consists only of a conspiracy or other form of preparation to commit the other." But when an agreement is to achieve various criminal objectives and is not limited to a specific crime, the MPC allows for cumulative sentences. See Model Penal Code and Commentaries, Comment to §5.03, at 390 (1985):

> When a conspiracy is declared criminal because its object is a crime, it is entirely meaningless to say that the preliminary combination is more dangerous than the forbidden consummation; the measure of its danger is the risk of such a culmination. On the other hand, the combination may and often does have criminal objectives that transcend any particular offenses that have been committed in pursuance of its goals. In the latter case, cumulative sentences for conspiracy and substantive offenses ought to be permissible, subject to the general limits on cumulation that the Code prescribes. In the former case, when the preliminary agreement does not go beyond the consummation, double conviction and sentence are barred.

Developments in federal sentencing law reflect the continuing controversy over the imposition of separate punishments for conspiracy and the object offense. The Federal Sentencing Guidelines in effect rejected separate punishments for conspiracy and the object offense. Some have lauded this aspect of the Guidelines for limiting the unfair treatment that might flow from count manipulation. Jacqueline E. Ross, Damned Under Many Headings: The Problem of Multiple Punishment, 29 Am. J. Crim. L. 245, 257 (2002). Despite the Guidelines, however, the proliferation of conspiracy-like statutory offenses—such as RICO (see infra page 760) and the crime of operating a "continuing criminal enterprise" (CCE)—continue to allow prosecutors to impose separate punishments by "stacking" charges for substantive offenses on top of charges for these conspiracy-like enterprise crimes, resulting in "compound liability" in which a single act can sustain liability for multiple offenses. See Susan W. Brenner, RICO, CCE, and Other Complex Crimes: The Transformation of American Criminal Law, 2 Wm. & Mary Bill Rts. J. 239 (1993).

5. *Single or Multiple Conspiracies*

Model Penal Code and Commentaries, Comment to §5.03 at 422-423 (1985): Much of the most perplexing litigation in conspiracy has been concerned less with the essential elements of the offense than with the scope to be accorded to a combination, i.e., the singleness or multiplicity of the conspiratorial relationships typical in a large, complex and sprawling network of crime. . . . [I]n most of these cases it is clear that each defendant has committed or conspired to commit one or more crimes; the question now is, to what extent is he a conspirator with each of the persons involved in the larger criminal network to commit the crimes that are its objects. . . .

KOTTEAKOS v. UNITED STATES

Supreme Court of the United States
328 U.S. 750 (1946)

JUSTICE RUTLEDGE delivered the opinion of the Court.

The only question is whether petitioners have suffered substantial prejudice from being convicted of a single general conspiracy by evidence which the Government admits proved not one conspiracy but some eight or more different ones of the same sort executed through a common key figure, Simon Brown. Petitioners were convicted under the general conspiracy section of the Criminal Code, 18 U.S.C.A. §88 [now §371], of conspiring to violate the provisions of the National Housing Act. The judgments were affirmed by the Circuit Court of Appeals. . . .

The indictment named thirty-two defendants, including the petitioners. The gist of the conspiracy, as alleged, was that the defendants had sought to induce various financial institutions to grant credit, with the intent that the loans for advances would then be offered to the Federal Housing Administration for insurance upon applications containing false and fraudulent information.

Of the thirty-two persons named in the indictment nineteen were brought to trial and the names of thirteen were submitted to the jury. Two were acquitted; the jury disagreed as to four; and the remaining seven, including petitioners, were found guilty.

The government's evidence may be summarized briefly, for the petitioners have not contended that it was insufficient, if considered apart from the alleged errors relating to the proof and the instructions at the trial.

Simon Brown, who pleaded guilty, was the common and key figure in all of the transactions proven. He was president of the Brownie Lumber Company. Having had experience in obtaining loans under the National Housing Act, he undertook to act as broker in placing for others loans for modernization and renovation, charging a five per cent commission for his services. Brown knew, when he obtained the loans, that the proceeds were not to be used for the purposes stated in the applications. [The Court then summarized the evidence against several defendants.]

The evidence against the other defendants whose cases were submitted to the jury was similar in character. They too had transacted business with Brown relating to National Housing Act loans. But no connection was shown between them and petitioners, other than that Brown had been the instrument in each instance for obtaining the loans. In many cases the other defendants did not have any relationship with one another, other than Brown's connection with each transaction. As the Circuit Court of Appeals said, there were "at least eight, and perhaps more, separate and independent groups, none of which had any connection with any other, though all dealt independently with Brown as their agent." As the Government puts it, the pattern was "that of separate spokes meeting at a common center," though we may add without the rim of the wheel to enclose the spokes.

The proof therefore admittedly made out a case, not of a single conspiracy, but of several, notwithstanding only one was charged in the indictment. The Court of Appeals aptly drew analogy in the comment, "Thieves who dispose of their loot to a single receiver—a single 'fence'—do not by that fact alone become confederates; they may, but it takes more than knowledge that he is a 'fence' to make them such." It stated that the trial judge "was plainly wrong in supposing that upon the evidence there could be a single conspiracy; and in the view which he took of the law, he should have dismissed the indictment." Nevertheless the appellate court held the error not prejudicial, saying among other things that "especially since guilt was so manifest, it was 'proper' to join the conspiracies," and "to reverse the conviction would be a miscarriage of justice." This is indeed the Government's entire position. . . .

[T]he trial court itself was confused in the charge which it gave to guide the jury in deliberation. The court instructed:

> The indictment charges but one conspiracy, and to convict each of the defendants of a conspiracy the Government would have to prove, and you would

have to find, that each of the defendants was a member of that conspiracy. You cannot divide it up. It is one conspiracy, and the question is whether or not each of the defendants or which of the defendants, are members of that conspiracy.

On its face, as the Court of Appeals said, this portion of the charge was plainly wrong in application to the proof made; and the error pervaded the entire charge, not merely the portion quoted. The jury could not possibly have found, upon the evidence, that there was only one conspiracy. The trial court was of the view that one conspiracy was made out by showing that each defendant was linked to Brown in one or more transactions, and that it was possible on the evidence for the jury to conclude that all were in a common adventure because of this fact and the similarity of purpose presented in the various applications for loans.

The view . . . confuses the common purpose of a single enterprise with the several, though similar purposes of numerous separate adventures of like character. It may be that, notwithstanding the misdirection, the jury actually understood correctly the purport of the evidence, as the Government now concedes it to have been, and came to the conclusion that the petitioners were guilty only of the separate conspiracies in which the proof shows they respectively participated. But, in the face of the misdirection and in the circumstances of this case, we cannot assume that the lay triers of fact were so well informed upon the law or that they disregarded the permission expressly given to ignore that vital difference.

As we have said, the error permeated the entire charge, indeed the entire trial. Not only did it permit the jury to find each defendant guilty of conspiring with thirty-five other potential co-conspirators, . . . when none of the evidence would support such a conviction. . . . It had other effects. . . . Carrying forward his premise that the jury could find one conspiracy on the evidence, the trial judge further charged that, if the jury found a conspiracy,

> then the acts or the statements of *any* of those whom you so find to be conspirators between the two dates that I have mentioned, may be considered by you in evidence as against *all* of the defendants whom you so find to be members of *the* conspiracy.

(Emphasis added.) . . .

On those instructions it was competent not only for the jury to find that all of the defendants were parties to a single common plan, design and scheme, where none was shown by the proof, but also for them to impute to each defendant the acts and statements of the others without reference to whether they related to one of the schemes proven or another, and to find an overt act affecting all in conduct which admittedly could only have affected some. . . .

Here toleration went too far. . . .

Reversed.

Anderson v. Superior Court, 78 Cal. App. 2d 22, 24-25, 177 P.2d 315, 317 (1947): [Petitioner challenged her indictment for conspiring to commit abortions. Evidence before the grand jury revealed that petitioner was one of several people who, in exchange for a fee, referred women to Stern for abortions. The indictment alleged that the conspiracy embraced not only Stern and petitioner but the greater enterprise among Stern and the others who referred women to him. She was also indicted for the substantive offenses of abortions performed on women she had referred to Stern and abortions committed by Stern upon women referred by others. Denying the challenge, the court stated:] The inference is almost compelled, if the evidence is believed, that this petitioner knew that Stern was engaged in the commission of abortions not casually but as a regular business and that others, like herself, had conspired with him to further his operations. If the grand jury concluded that, with this knowledge, she saw fit to join with him and those others, even though unknown to her, in furthering the unlawful activities of the group we cannot say that the grand jury did not have substantial evidence upon which to find the indictment.

If she did join the conspiracy she is responsible for the substantive offenses later committed as a part of the conspiracy.

Questions: Is the result in *Anderson* consistent with the reasoning of *Kotteakos?* Was there a "rim" to the "wheel" that united Anderson and the other "spokes" who referred abortion patients to Stern? As a prosecutor, what kind of evidence would you look for to establish a rim uniting all of the spokes and the center in a single conspiracy in a case like *Kotteakos* or *Anderson?*

UNITED STATES v. BRUNO

United States Court of Appeals, 2d Circuit
105 F.2d 921, rev'd on other grounds, 308 U.S. 287 (1939)

PER CURIAM. Bruno and Iacono were indicted along with 86 others for a conspiracy to import, sell and possess narcotics; some were acquitted; others, besides these two, were convicted, but they alone appealed. They complain . . . that if the evidence proved anything, it proved a series of separate conspiracies, and not a single one, as alleged in the indictment. . . .

The evidence allowed the jury to find that there had existed over a substantial period of time a conspiracy embracing a great number of persons, whose object was to smuggle narcotics into the Port of New York and distribute them to addicts both in this city and in Texas and Louisiana. This required the cooperation of four groups of persons: the smugglers who imported the drugs; the middlemen who paid the smugglers and distributed to retailers; and two groups of retailers—one in New York and one in Texas and Louisiana—who supplied the addicts. The defendants assert that there were, therefore, at least three separate conspiracies: one between the smugglers and the middlemen, and one between the middlemen and each group of retailers. The evidence did not disclose any cooperation or communication between the smugglers and either group of retailers, or between the two groups of retailers themselves; however, the smugglers knew that the middlemen must sell to retailers, and the retailers knew that the middlemen must buy from importers of one sort or another. Thus the conspirators at one end of the chain knew that the unlawful business would not, and could not, stop with their buyers; and those at the other end knew that it had not begun with their sellers. That being true, a jury might have found that all the accused were embarked upon a venture, in all parts of which each was a participant, and an abettor in the sense that the success of that part with which he was immediately concerned, was dependent upon the success of the whole. . . . It might still be argued that there were two conspiracies; one including the smugglers, the middlemen and the New York group, and the other, the smugglers, the middlemen and the Texas & Louisiana group, for there was apparently no privity between the two groups of retailers. That too would be fallacious. Clearly, quoad the smugglers, there was but one conspiracy, for it was of no moment to them whether the middlemen sold to one or more groups of retailers, provided they had a market somewhere. So too of any retailer; he knew that he was a necessary link in a scheme of distribution, and the others, whom he knew to be convenient to its execution, were as much parts of a single undertaking or enterprise as two salesmen in the same shop. We think therefore that there was only one conspiracy.

United States v. Borelli, 336 F.2d 376 (2d Cir. 1964): [In this case, dealing with an elaborate heroin importing and distributing operation, Judge Friendly wrote:] As applied to the long-term operation of an illegal business, the common pictorial distinction between "chain" and "spoke" conspiracies can obscure as much as it clarifies. The chain metaphor is indeed apt in that the links of a narcotics conspiracy are inextricably related to one another, from grower, through exporter and importer, to wholesaler, middleman, and retailer, each depending for his own success on the performance of all the others. But this simple picture tends to obscure that the links at either end are likely to consist of a number of persons who may have no reason to know that others are performing a role similar to theirs—in other words the extreme links of a chain conspiracy may have elements of the spoke conspiracy.[2] Moreover, whatever the value of the chain concept where the problem is to trace a single operation from the start through its various phases to its successful conclusion, it becomes confusing when, over a long period of time, certain links continue to play the same role but with new counterparts, as where importers who regard their

---

2. Thus, in the oft-cited *Bruno* case, although it is clear enough that "quoad the smugglers, there was but one conspiracy . . . ," it is not so clear why the New York and Texas groups of retailers were not in a "spoke" relation with the smugglers and the middleman, so that there would be two conspiracies unless the evidence permitted the inference that each group of retailers must have known the operation to be so large as to require the other as an outlet.

partnership as a single continuing one, having successfully distributed one cargo through *X* distributing organization, turn, years later, to moving another cargo obtained from a different source through *Y*. . . .

The basic difficulty arises in applying the seventeenth century notion of conspiracy, where the gravamen of the offense was the making of an *agreement* to commit a readily identifiable crime or series of crimes, such as murder or robbery, to what in substance is the conduct of an illegal business over a period of years. . . . Although it is usual and often necessary in conspiracy cases for the agreement to be proved by inference from acts, the gist of the offense remains the agreement, and it is therefore essential to determine what kind of agreement or understanding existed as to each defendant. It is a great deal harder to tell just *what* agreement can reasonably be inferred from the purchase, even the repeated purchase, of contraband, than from the furnishing of dynamite to prospective bank robbers or the exchange of worthless property for securities to be subsequently distributed. . . . A seller of narcotics in bulk surely knows that the purchasers will undertake to resell the goods over an uncertain period of time, and the circumstances may also warrant the inference that a supplier or a purchaser indicated a willingness to repeat. But a sale or a purchase scarcely constitutes a sufficient basis for inferring agreement to cooperate with the opposite parties for whatever period they continue to deal in this type of contraband, unless some such understanding is evidenced by other conduct. . . .

PROBLEM

What degree of interdependence between parties should be necessary to show that they are part of the same "agreement"? When should antagonism or indifference between two parties be considered inconsistent with their membership in a single "conspiracy"? The issue has proved especially troublesome in drug conspiracy prosecutions. In United States v. Swafford, 512 F.3d 833 (6th Cir. 2008), defendant Swafford sold iodine, a key ingredient in the production of methamphetamine, to different meth "cooks." The government charged Swafford with two conspiracies: one to aid and abet the manufacture of meth, and another to distribute iodine to be used in the production of meth. Swafford successfully argued on appeal that there were instead multiple conspiracies because the cooks who purchased the iodine had no relationship with each other, and there was no collective venture with a common goal. The rim was therefore absent.

Question: How could one establish some interdependence between the various cooks?

The Seventh Circuit in United States v. Torres-Ramirez, 213 F.3d 978, 981-982 (7th Cir. 2000), addressed the question of how far the relationship extends between a drug supplier and one of his distributors. Torres-Ramirez, "a big-time drug dealer" in California, sold two kilos of cocaine to Hardin in Los Angeles. He invited Hardin to make future purchases when he was in California but would not commit to specific terms. Hardin returned to Indiana and sold the cocaine there. Torres-Ramirez was convicted of conspiracy to distribute cocaine in the latter state, but the court of appeals reversed, explaining:

> The district court told the jury . . . : "To establish [that] the seller has joined a conspiracy . . . , the government must [prove] an enduring relationship that directly or indirectly shows the seller has knowledge of the conspiracy to distribute drugs." This sentence is . . . false. . . . *Knowing* of a conspiracy differs from *joining* a conspiracy. Every seller of large quantities knows that his buyer intends to resell, and thus knows that his buyer is involved in a criminal conspiracy. No one distributes two kilograms on the street by himself. [But the] district judge needed to tell the jury to look for an agreement to join the Indiana distribution network, not just for knowledge of its existence.
>
> [W]e conclude [moreover] that the evidence would not have supported a conviction under the proper legal standard. [T]his is a one-sale case. . . . Torres-Ramirez did not care whether the [Indiana] redistribution venture succeeded; he had his money already.

Contrast *Swafford* and *Torres-Ramirez* with United States v. Morris, 46 F.3d 410, 416 (5th Cir. 1995), in which various suppliers had sold cocaine to Costa, who in turn distributed it to dealers. The participants, some 23 individuals, were convicted of being members of a single conspiracy. One of the suppliers challenged that finding on appeal. The court wrote:

> The success of this conspiracy depended on the continued willingness of each member to perform his function. If the [suppliers] discontinued selling, there would be no cocaine for Costa and the [dealers] to buy. . . . If [the dealers] ceased to buy, there would be no reason for Costa to buy from the [suppliers].
>
> . . . Munoz, [however], argues that his organization could not have been in the same conspiracy as the other suppliers, such as the Laredo Organization, which were [his] competitors. [Costa] stated that he initially approached the Laredo Organization for cocaine after becoming unhappy with Munoz. . . . We are not persuaded by this argument. [T]he larger, common plan was the purchase and sale of drugs through Costa for profit. Munoz is no less a part of this larger, common plan because Costa also purchased from others. . . . Indeed such purchases may in fact be necessary from time to time to keep the larger, common plan in existence.

Question: Which court's analysis is more consistent with *Kotteakos* and *Bruno*?

UNITED STATES v. McDERMOTT

United States Court of Appeals, 2d Circuit
245 F.3d 133 (2001)

OAKES, Senior Circuit Judge. Defendant James J. McDermott appeals from a judgment . . . convicting him of conspiracy to commit insider trading in violation of 18 U.S.C. §371 [among other counts]. . . . On appeal, McDermott contends principally that . . . the evidence was insufficient as a matter of law to support his convictions. . . . We agree that there is insufficient evidence to support the conspiracy count. . . .

The present prosecution arose out of a triangulated love affair involving the president of a prominent investment bank, a pornographic film star and a New Jersey businessman.

Until May 1999, McDermott was the president, CEO and Chairman of Keefe Bruyette & Woods ("KBW"), an investment bank headquartered in New York City. . . . Around 1996, McDermott began having an extramarital affair with Kathryn Gannon[,] an adult film star and an alleged prostitute. . . . During the course of their affair, McDermott made numerous stock recommendations to Gannon. Unbeknownst to McDermott, Gannon was simultaneously having an affair with Anthony Pomponio and passing these recommendations to him. Although neither Gannon nor Pomponio had extensive training or expertise in securities trading, together they earned around $170,000 in profits during the period relevant to this case.

The government indicted McDermott, Gannon and Pomponio for conspiracy to commit insider trading. . . . McDermott and Pomponio were tried together, but Gannon was not present. . . . The Government built its case against McDermott almost entirely on circumstantial evidence linking records of telephone conversations between McDermott and Gannon with records of Gannon's and Pomponio's trading activities. Telephone records revealed that McDermott and Gannon engaged in approximately 800 telephone calls during the charged period, including up to 29 calls in one day. Trading records revealed correlations between the telephone calls and stock trades. In addition to these records, the sensational highlight of the government's evidence . . . consisted of audiotape recordings of Pomponio's SEC deposition. These tapes undermined Pomponio's defense and credibility, as they recorded him poorly telling lies, evading questions and affecting incredulous reactions. . . .

McDermott challenges the sufficiency of the evidence to establish his conviction . . . for a single conspiracy. . . . [W]e find that the evidence was insufficient as a matter of law on the conspiracy count. . . .

The government argues that from the perspective of Gannon and Pomponio, albeit not from McDermott's perspective, there was a unitary purpose to commit insider trading based on information furnished by McDermott. According to the government, therefore, McDermott was part of the conspiracy even though he did not agree to pass information to both Gannon and Pomponio.

United States v. Carpenter, 791 F.2d 1024 (2d Cir. 1986), aff'd, 484 U.S. 19 (1987), forecloses the government's argument. In Carpenter, we reversed the conspiracy conviction of defendant Winans, a Wall Street Journal reporter who participated in a scheme with his friends Felis and Brant to misappropriate insider information and to use it for personal gain. . . . Felis then passed the insider information to Spratt. . . . We reversed Winans' conspiracy conviction to the extent that it involved Spratt's trades. . . . Because Winans' original trading agreement with Felis and Brant was narrowly limited to specific persons not including Spratt, about whom Winans had no knowledge, we found that by passing the information to Spratt, Felis had "used the information obtained from Winans beyond the scope of the original agreement." . . .

In *Carpenter*, we left open three hypothetical avenues of liability against Winans. First, we emphasized that Winans "might have been liable for the Spratt trades had the scope of the trading agreement been broader, to include trading by or for persons other than the small group of conspirators herein." . . . Second, we noted that Winans might have been liable for the Spratt trades had the trades been "part of the ramifications of the plan which could . . . be reasonably forseen [sic] as a necessary or natural consequence of the unlawful agreement." . . . Third, we suggested that Winans might have been liable had he "at least known of the Felis-Spratt relationship." . . . Because none of these avenues of liability is applicable to this case, we find that McDermott is not liable for the trades made by Pomponio. [A]s a matter of law, no rational jury could find McDermott guilty beyond a reasonable doubt of a single conspiracy with Pomponio to commit insider trading. The government has failed to show the most basic element of a single conspiracy, namely, an agreement to pass insider information to Gannon and possibly to another person, even if unknown. . . .

QUESTIONS

1. *Nonreciprocal conspiracy?* Could Pomponio be charged with conspiring with McDermott, even though McDermott could not be charged with conspiring with him? On the one hand, Pomponio knew that McDermott was the source of the tips. On the other hand, a conspiracy requires an agreement, and McDermott certainly never *agreed* to tip Pomponio. Without much discussion, Judge Oakes resolved Pomponio's appeal on the conspiracy issue in the same way he had resolved McDermott's, noting only that "the government failed to prove a single conspiracy amongst all three co-defendants." United States v. McDermott, 277 F.3d 240, 242 (2d Cir. 2002). Compare the doctrine of "unilateral" conspiracy, pages 754-758 infra.

2. *Insider trading and drug conspiracies compared.* The hypothetical avenues of liability generated by the Second Circuit in its insider trading cases seem very broad. This doctrine would hold a tipster liable whenever it is reasonably foreseeable that the information would be passed along. Should these broad avenues of liability be applicable in other chain conspiracies? For example, in a drug distribution case, should a drug supplier be guilty of conspiring with a remote purchaser whenever that purchase could be "reasonably foreseen" as the natural consequence of selling to a middleman? Or do the differences between the two contexts call for different liability requirements? Note that an insider trading defendant is unlikely to want the information passed along to others, because further use of the information makes it more likely that he will get caught. Thus, when the tipster knows of the likelihood of further use, one can infer that the agreed relationship has a

broader scope than the ordinary tipster-tipee transaction. In contrast, drug suppliers always expect a buyer of large quantities to resell to others, and these further sales are always, directly or indirectly, in the original supplier's interest. Should every drug supplier therefore be considered a party to an "agreement" with all remote purchasers?

NOTE ON MULTIPLE OBJECTIVES

In all of the foregoing cases, prosecutors sought to establish a single, inclusive conspiracy, while defendants attempted to break up the alleged relationship into smaller conspiracies. In United States v. Braverman, 317 U.S. 49 (1942), the positions were reversed: The Government indicted a group of defendants on seven counts, each charging a conspiracy to violate a separate provision of the internal revenue laws. The applicable statute carried a maximum penalty of two years on each count. Defendants were convicted on all seven counts and each defendant was sentenced to eight years' imprisonment. The Supreme Court reversed:

> The gist of the crime of conspiracy as defined by the statute is the agreement to commit one or more unlawful acts. . . . Whether the object of a single agreement is to commit one or many crimes, it is in either case that agreement which constitutes the conspiracy which the statute punishes. The one agreement cannot be taken to be several agreements and hence several conspiracies because it envisages the violation of several statutes rather than one. . . . For such a violation, only the single penalty prescribed by the statute can be imposed.

Question: If conspiracy is regarded as an inchoate offense, punishing combinations that threaten a substantive harm, does it make sense to treat an agreement to commit seven different crimes as only a single offense?

Albernaz v. United States, 450 U.S. 333 (1981), sharply limited the *Braverman* rule. In *Albernaz*, the defendant had conspired with others to import and distribute marijuana. He was convicted on two counts, one charging conspiracy to import and the other conspiracy to distribute. Accepting the premise that there was only a single agreement, the Court nonetheless upheld the two convictions, emphasizing that, unlike cases involving only the general conspiracy statute, here separate statutes proscribed conspiracy to import and conspiracy to distribute. The Court held that by enacting two statutes, each with its own penalties, Congress had manifested its intention to authorize separate convictions and punishments. The Court distinguished *Braverman* on the ground that "the conspiratorial agreement in *Braverman*, although it had many objectives, violated but a single statute." Id. at 339.

NOTE ON THE MODEL PENAL CODE APPROACH

The MPC proposes an innovative solution to the problems of defining the scope of a conspiratorial relationship.

Model Penal Code and Commentaries, Comment to §5.03 at 425-431 (1985): ... Subsections (1) and (2) limit the scope of his conspiracy both in terms of its criminal objectives, to those crimes that he had the purpose of promoting or facilitating, and in terms of parties, to those with whom he agreed, except when the same crime that he conspired to commit is, to his knowledge, also the object of a conspiracy between one of his co-conspirators and another person or persons. Subsection (3) provides that his conspiracy is a single one despite a multiplicity of criminal objectives, as long as such crimes are the object of the same agreement or continuous conspiratorial relationship. ...

The Model Code provision would require a different approach to a case such as *Bruno* and might produce different results. Since the overall operation involved the separate crimes of importing by the smugglers and possession and sale by each group [smugglers, distributors, and retailers], the question as to each defendant would be whether and with whom he conspired to commit *each* of these crimes, under the criteria set forth in Subsections (1) and (2). The conspiratorial objective for the purpose of this inquiry could not be characterized in the manner of the *Bruno* court, as "to smuggle narcotics into the Port of New York and distribute them to addicts both in [New York] and in Texas and Louisiana." This is indeed the overall objective of the entire operation. It also may be true that *some* of the participants conspired to commit all of the crimes involved in the operation; under Subsection (3), as under prevailing law, they would be guilty of only one conspiracy if all these crimes were the object of the same agreement or continuing conspiratorial relationship, and the objective of *that* conspiracy or relationship could fairly be phrased in terms of the overall operation. But this multiplicity of criminal objectives affords a poor referent for testing the culpability of each individual who is in any manner involved in the operation.

With the conspiratorial objectives characterized as the particular crimes and the culpability of each participant tested separately, it would be possible to find ... that the smugglers conspired to commit the illegal sales of the retailers, but that the retailers did not conspire to commit the importing of the smugglers. Factual situations warranting such a finding may easily be conceived. For example, the smugglers might depend upon and seek to foster their retail markets, while the retailers might have many suppliers and be indifferent to the success of any single source. The court's approach in *Bruno* does not admit of such a finding, for treating the conspiratorial objective as the entire series of crimes involved in smuggling, distributing, and retailing requires a finding either of no conspiracy or of a single conspiracy in which all three links in the chain conspired to commit all of each other's crimes.

It also would be possible to find, with the inquiry focused on each individual's culpability as to each criminal objective, that some of the parties in a chain conspired to commit the entire series of crimes while others conspired to commit only some of these crimes. Thus the smugglers and the middlemen in *Bruno* may have conspired to commit, promote, or facilitate the importing and the possession and sales of all of the parties down to the final retail sale; the retailers might have conspired with them as to their own possession and sales, but might be indifferent to all the steps prior to their receipt of the narcotics. In this situation, a smuggler or a middleman might have conspired with all three groups to commit the entire series of crimes, while a retailer might have conspired with the same parties but to achieve fewer criminal objectives. Such results are conceptually difficult to reach under existing doctrine not only because of the frequent failure to focus separately on the different criminal objectives, but also because of the traditional view of the agreement as a bilateral relationship between each of the parties, congruent in scope both as to its party and its objective dimensions.

6. Parties

INTRODUCTORY NOTE

Because conspiracy liability shares with accomplice liability the need for the participation of another party, both doctrines pose similar issues concerning the nature of the required relationship between the parties. Consider the parallels and differences in the legal treatment of these issues in the two kinds of liability.

GEBARDI v. UNITED STATES

Supreme Court of the United States
287 U.S. 112 (1932)

JUSTICE STONE delivered the opinion of the Court.

This case is here on certiorari to review a judgment of conviction for conspiracy to violate the Mann Act. [At the time this case was decided, the Mann Act read as follows: "Whoever knowingly persuades, induces, entices, or coerces any woman or girl to go from one place to another in interstate or foreign commerce . . . for the purpose of prostitution or debauchery, or for any other immoral purpose . . . whether with or without her consent, and thereby knowingly causes such woman or girl to go and to be carried or transported as a passenger . . . in interstate or foreign commerce . . . shall be fined not more than $5,000 or imprisoned not more than five years, or both."] Petitioners, a man and a woman, not then husband and wife, were indicted in the District Court for Northern Illinois, for conspiring together, and with others not named, to transport the woman from one state to another for the purpose of engaging in sexual intercourse with the man. At the trial without a jury there was evidence from which the court could have found that the petitioners had engaged in illicit sexual relations in the course of each of the journeys alleged; that the man purchased the railway tickets for both petitioners for at least one journey, and that in each instance the woman, in advance of the purchase of the tickets, consented to go on the journey and did go on it voluntarily for the specified immoral purpose. There was no evidence supporting the allegation that any other person had conspired. The trial court . . . gave judgment of conviction, which the Court of Appeals . . . affirmed.

Congress set out in the Mann Act to deal with cases which frequently, if not normally, involve consent and agreement on the part of the woman to the forbidden transportation. In every case in which she is not intimidated or forced into the transportation, the statute necessarily contemplates her acquiescence. Yet this acquiescence, though an incident of a type of transportation specifically dealt with by the statute, was not made a crime under the Mann Act itself. Of this class of cases we say that the substantive offense contemplated by the statute itself involves the same combination or community of purpose of two persons only which is prosecuted here as conspiracy. If this were the only case covered by the Act, it would be within those decisions which hold, consistently with the theory upon which conspiracies are punished, that where it is impossible under any circumstances to commit the substantive offense without cooperative action, the preliminary agreement between the same parties to commit the offense is not an indictable conspiracy either at common law or under the federal statute. . . . But criminal transportation under the Mann Act may be effected without the woman's consent as in cases of intimidation or force (with which we are not now concerned). We assume, therefore, . . . that the decisions last mentioned do not in all strictness apply. We do not rest our decision upon the theory of those cases. . . . We place it rather upon the ground that we perceive in the failure of the Mann Act to condemn the woman's participation in those transportations which are effected with her mere consent, evidence of an affirmative legislative policy to leave her acquiescence unpunished. . . . It would contravene that policy to hold that the very passage of the Mann Act effected a withdrawal by the conspiracy statute of that immunity which the Mann Act itself confers.

It is not to be supposed that the consent of an unmarried person to adultery with a married person, where the latter alone is guilty of the substantive offense, would render the former an abettor or a conspirator, or that the acquiescence of a woman under the age of consent would make her a co-conspirator with the man to commit statutory rape upon herself. The principle, determinative of this case, is the same.

On the evidence before us the woman petitioner has not violated the Mann Act and, we hold, is not guilty of a conspiracy to do so. . . .

As there is no proof that the man conspired with anyone else to bring about the transportation, the convictions of both petitioners must be reversed.

NOTES

1. The Gebardi rule. The general principle reflected in Gebardi is widely accepted. See Glanville Williams, Criminal Law: The General Part 673 (2d ed. 1961): "One may submit with some confidence that a person cannot be convicted of conspiracy when there is a recognized rule of justice or policy exempting him from prosecution from the substantive crime." For a statutory statement of a similar principle, see Model Penal Code §5.04(2), Appendix.

The Supreme Court relied on *Gebardi*'s analysis in rejecting the government's claim that a defendant who uses a cell phone to buy drugs can be guilty of "facilitating" drug distribution. The Court noted that "where a statute treats one side of a bilateral transaction more leniently, adding to the penalty of the party on that side for facilitating the action by the other would upend the calibration of punishment set by the legislature." Abuelhawa v. United States, 129 S. Ct. 2102, 2106 (2009).

2. The acquitted co-conspirator. A related question is what to do when all the co-conspirators but one are acquitted. The general trend is to reject a rule of consistency and allow a co-conspirator to be convicted even if all others have been acquitted. Commonwealth v. Campbell, 539 Pa. 212, 217-221 (1994).

3. Wharton's rule. Justice Stone notes that the *Gebardi* case was not governed by the line of precedent holding that "where it is impossible under any circumstances to commit the substantive offense without cooperative action, the preliminary agreement between the same parties to commit the offense is not an indictable conspiracy." That line of precedent exemplifies what has become known as "Wharton's rule." It was explained as follows (2 F. Wharton, Criminal Law §1604 at 1862 (12th ed. 1932)):

> [When] plurality of agents is logically necessary, conspiracy, which assumes the voluntary accession of a person to a crime of such a character that it is aggravated by a plurality of agents, cannot be maintained. . . . In other words, . . . when the law says, such an offense—e.g., adultery—shall have a certain punishment, it is not lawful for the prosecution to evade this limitation by indicting the offense as conspiracy.

Compare the MPC, which rejects Wharton's rule. See Model Penal Code and Commentaries, Comment to §5.04 at 482-483 (1985):

> The classic Wharton's rule cases involve crimes such as dueling, bigamy, adultery, and incest, but it has also been said to apply to gambling, the giving and receiving of bribes, and the buying and selling of contraband goods. The rule has been unevenly applied and has been subject to a number of exceptions and limitations.
>
> It seems clear that Wharton's rule . . . completely overlooks the functions of conspiracy as an inchoate crime. That an offense inevitably requires concert is no reason to immunize criminal preparation to commit it. Further, the rule operates to immunize from a conspiracy prosecution *both* parties to *any* offense that inevitably requires concert, thus disregarding the legislative judgment that at least one should be punishable and taking no account of the varying policies that ought to determine whether the other should be. The rule is supportable only insofar as it avoids cumulative punishment for conspiracy and the completed substantive crime, for it is clear that the legislature would have taken the factor of concert into account in grading a crime that inevitably requires concert. This consideration is of course irrelevant under the Model Code, which precludes cumulative punishment in any case for a conspiracy with a single criminal objective and the completed substantive crime.

Although the MPC commentary describes bribery as an instance where Wharton's rule may apply, many courts have disagreed. See United States v. Jefferson, 2009 WL 4547691 (E.D. La. 2009); United States v. Aubrey, 2010 WL 5314802 (D. Nev. 2010). Which approach makes more sense?

How should courts treat the relationship between a buyer and a seller of drugs? The Sixth Circuit recently concluded that the sale alone is insufficient to establish a conspiracy because conspiracy requires "not just the presence of any agreement, but an agreement with the same joint criminal objective—here the joint objective of distributing drugs." United States v. Delgado, 631 F.3d 685, 695 (5th Cir. 2011). According to the court, the seller's objective was distribution, whereas the buyer's was possession. The dissenting opinion disagreed on the facts of the case because the drugs involved were of such a large quantity that the jury could infer the buyer was also involved in distribution. Id. at 714-715 (Clement, J., dissenting).

4. *Problems. (a)* 21 U.S.C. §861 makes it a crime "for any person at least 18 years of age to knowingly and intentionally [employ] a person under 18 years of age" to sell or distribute drugs. Palmer and Harris organized a group of juveniles to sell cocaine. They both knew that the youngsters working for them were under 18. The prosecution proved that Palmer was over 18, and he was therefore liable under §861. But because the prosecution did not prove Harris's age, Harris could not be convicted of violating §861 personally. Can Harris be convicted of conspiring with Palmer to violate §861? Cf. United States v. Harris, 959 F.2d 246, 262-264 (D.C. Cir. 1992).

(b) The Foreign Corrupt Practices Act (FCPA) makes it a crime for any U.S. citizen to bribe a foreign government official, but it does not make it an offense for such an official to accept the bribe. Can Canadian officials who took bribes from U.S. citizens be convicted of conspiracy to violate the FCPA? See United States v. Castle, 925 F.2d 831 (5th Cir. 1991).

(c) Arizona criminalizes human smuggling, which it defines as "the transportation [of] persons [who] are not United States citizens [or] permanent resident aliens." Ariz. Rev. Code §13-2319(F)(3). Should Wharton's rule bar a prosecution against the person being smuggled for conspiracy to commit human smuggling? See State v. Barragan-Sierra, 196 P.3d 879 (Ariz. Ct. App. 2008).

GARCIA v. STATE

Supreme Court of Indiana
271 Ind. 510, 394 N.E.2d 106 (1979)

PRENTICE, J. Defendant was convicted in a trial by jury of conspiracy to commit murder.... On appeal she raises the ... issue ... whether the defendant can be convicted of conspiracy when the only person with whom the defendant conspired was a police informant who only feigned his acquiescence in the scheme. . . .

The evidence introduced at trial consisted of the following: On September 30, 1977, State's witness, Allen Young, was first contacted by the defendant with regard to certain marital problems that she was having. She stated that her husband constantly beat her and her children and . . . that she wanted her husband killed. [After several subsequent conversations with defendant,] Young went to the [police] and discussed the matter with two detectives. He offered to call the defendant and let them listen and record the conversation, which they did. During the conversation, Young again asked the defendant if she wanted him to help her find someone to kill her husband, and she responded affirmatively. Young replied that he would try to find someone. Several more conversations took place. . . . At their final meeting, Young, accompanied by a plain-clothed detective, introduced the defendant to the detective, stating that here was a man who might be willing to do the job. The defendant then produced $200, a picture of her husband, and a record of his daily habits and gave them to the detective. She agreed to pay the balance of the contract price when the "job" was completed. Defendant was subsequently arrested. At trial, Young testified that he only feigned his acquiescence in the plan and at no time did he intend to actually carry it out.

The issue is whether the conspiracy section of our new penal code adopts the Model Penal Code's "unilateral" concept or whether it retains the traditional "bilateral" concept.

The bilateral concept is the traditional view of conspiracy as derived from common law. It is formulated in terms of two or more persons agreeing to commit a crime, each with intent to do so. In cases where the person or persons with whom the defendant conspired only feigned his acquiescence in the plan, the courts have generally held that neither person could be convicted of conspiracy because there was no "conspiratorial agreement." . . .

Reacting to criticism of this viewpoint, the drafters of the Model Penal Code, though not without internal disagreement, adopted a "unilateral" concept, as follows: [The court then quoted Model Penal Code §§5.03(1) and 5.04(1). See Appendix.]

In explanation of their new approach, the Drafters of the Model Penal Code commented:

> . . . The definition of the Draft departs from the traditional view of conspiracy as an entirely bilateral or multilateral relationship. . . . Attention is directed instead to each individual's culpability by framing the definition in terms of the conduct which suffices to establish the liability of any given actor, rather than the conduct of a group of which he is charged to be a part—an approach which in this comment we have designated "unilateral."
>
> One consequence of this approach is to make it immaterial to the guilt of a conspirator whose culpability has been established that the person or all of the persons with whom he conspired have not been or cannot be convicted. . . . Under the unilateral approach of the Draft, the culpable party's guilt would not be affected by the fact that the other party's agreement was feigned. . . .

True enough, the project's chances of success have not been increased by the agreement; indeed, its doom may have been sealed by this turn of events. But the major basis of conspiratorial liability—the unequivocal evidence of a firm purpose to commit a crime—remains the same. . . .

M.P.C. §5.03 [Tent. Draft No. 10,] Comments at pp. 104-105. . . .

This concept has been adopted, in whole or in part, in at least 26 states and is under consideration in most of the remaining states. See Note, Conspiracy: Statutory Reform Since the Model Penal Code, 75 Colum. L. R. 1122, 1125 (1975).

In 1976, our Indiana Legislature repealed the existing conspiracy statute and adopted Ind. Code §35-41-5-2 . . . which [provides:]

> (c) It is no defense that the person with whom the accused person is alleged to have conspired:
> (1) has not been prosecuted;
> (2) has not been convicted;
> (3) has been acquitted;
> (4) has been convicted of a different crime;
> (5) cannot be prosecuted for any reason; or
> (6) lacked the capacity to commit the crime.

. . . [I]t is clear upon the face of the act that defenses available under the multilateral concept were to be eliminated. The inclusion of the "catch-all" sub-proviso (5) can leave no doubt. Clearly "any reason," as recited therein, includes the absence of criminal culpability on the part of a co-conspirator— including a sole co-conspirator. The words "agrees" and "agreement" have not been used as words of art denoting a "meeting of the minds" and "contract." Rather, the former is descriptive of the defendant's state of mind at the time he communicated with another in furtherance of the felony; and the latter refers to the defendant's understanding.

Defendant has cited us . . . numerous cases supporting the bilateral concept requiring "concurrence of sentiment and cooperative conduct in the unlawful and criminal enterprise"; however, those cases were not decided under statutes remotely similar to our own. . . . Her argument that, by definition, an agreement requires the concurrence of sentiment of at least two individuals . . . is not persuasive in the light of the express wording of the entire enactment. . . .

The judgment of the trial court is affirmed.

NOTES

1. *The traditional offense of conspiracy.* In jurisdictions that have not reformulated their definition of conspiracy, the requirement of bilateral agreement remains, and conspiracy charges will not lie when the defendant's only collaborators are undercover informants or other feigned participants. See, e.g., United States v. Delgado, 631 F.3d 685 (5th Cir. 2011); Longley v. State, 32 So. 3d 736 (Fla. Dist. Ct. App. 2010).

2. Modern conspiracy statutes. In jurisdictions that have adopted definitions of conspiracy similar to that proposed by the MPC, many courts have held, in accord with *Garcia*, that a defendant can be guilty of conspiracy if he agrees to commit a crime with a feigned accomplice or with a person who otherwise lacks the requisite intent for conspiracy. E.g., State v. Roldan, 714 A.2d 351, 355 (N.J. Super. Ct. 1998); Suding v. State, 945 N.E.2d 731 (Ind. Ct. App. 2011). Recently, prosecutors brought conspiracy charges against a single individual, whose only other contacts were law enforcement agents, for having plotted to build and detonate bombs in New York. See Joseph Goldstein & William K. Rashbaum, City Bomb Plot Suspect Called Fan of Qaeda Cleric, N.Y. Times, Nov. 21, 2011, at A1. But in Connecticut and Illinois, two states with conspiracy statutes patterned on the MPC, courts have held that the requirement of bilateral agreement survives. See State v. Grullon, 562 A.2d 481 (Conn. 1989); People v. Foster, 457 N.E.2d 405, 407 (Ill. 1983). The Illinois statute states that a "person commits conspiracy when, with intent that an offense be committed, he agrees with another to the commission of that offense." Ill. Rev. Stat. ch. 720, §5/8-2(a). In *Foster*, the Illinois Supreme Court held that the required "agree[ment]" could not exist unless at least two parties genuinely intended to carry out the plan. Rejecting the reasoning of the *Garcia* case, the court said (457 N.E.2d at 407): "We doubt . . . that the drafters could have intended what represents a rather profound change in the law of conspiracy without mentioning it. . . ." The court noted, however, that the Illinois solicitation statute would (like the corresponding MPC provision) "embrace virtually every situation in which one could be convicted of conspiracy under the unilateral theory." Id. at 408.

3. Rationale for the traditional approach. The case in favor of the traditional view is stated as follows in United States v. Escobar De Bright, 742 F.2d 1196, 1198-1200 (9th Cir. 1984):

> Criminal conspiracy is an offense separate from the actual criminal act because of the perception "that collective action toward an antisocial end involves a greater risk to society than individual action toward the same end." In part, this view is based on the perception that group activity increases the likelihood of success of the criminal act and of future criminal activity by members of the group, and is difficult for law enforcement officers to detect. . . .
>
> Such dangers, however, are non-existent when a person "conspires" only with a government agent. There is no continuing criminal enterprise and ordinarily no inculcation of criminal knowledge and practices. Preventive intervention by law enforcement officers also is not a significant problem in such circumstances. The agent, as part of the "conspiracy," is quite capable of monitoring the situation in order to prevent the completion of the contemplated criminal plan; in short, no cloak of secrecy surrounds any agreement to commit the criminal acts.
>
> Finally, the [traditional] rule responds to the same concern that underlies the entrapment defense: the legitimate law enforcement function of crime prevention "does not include the manufacturing of crime." Allowing a government agent to form a conspiracy with only one other party would create the

potential for law enforcement officers to "manufacture" conspiracies when none would exist absent the government's presence.

4. Attempted conspiracy? In states that adhere to the bilateral approach, can a defendant who "agrees" to commit a crime with an undercover agent be convicted of *attempting* to conspire? In State v. Kihnel, 488 So. 2d 1238, 1241 (La. Ct. App. 1986), the court held in the negative:

> Attempt and conspiracy are both inchoate crimes. Just as there can be no attempt to commit an attempt, such as "attempted assault" . . . we conclude that under the bilateral formulation of conspiracy there can be no "attempted conspiracy."
>
> As part of the very foundation of criminal law, crimes include both a criminal act (or omission) and a criminal intent. "Attempted conspiracy" suggests a crime formed only of criminal intent, as it is the agreement which constitutes the act. We are not prepared to judicially legislate such a crime.

For thorough discussion of this problem, see Ira Robbins, Double Inchoate Crimes, 26 Harv. J. on Legis. 1, 54-58, 80-83, 91-94 (1989). See also Wilson v. State, 53 Ga. 205, 206 (1874), where the court rejected liability for attempted assault as "absurd." But some courts and commentators have found nothing wrong with liability for attempted assault, even though assault (like conspiracy) is an inchoate offense in the nature of an attempt. One scholar noted that "[a]lthough no jurisdiction recognizes the crime of attempted simple assault, an increasing number of state courts have convicted defendants of attempted aggravated assaults." Robbins, supra, at 39. Are there good reasons to permit attempt liability in such cases? Should courts also permit liability for an attempt to conspire, if the crime intended is a serious one?

7. Reassessing the Law of Conspiracy

Compare the following observations on the fairness and utility of conspiracy doctrine:

Phillip Johnson, The Unnecessary Crime of Conspiracy, 61 Cal. L. Rev. 1137, 1139-1140 (1973): The law of criminal conspiracy is not basically sound. It should be abolished, not reformed.

The central fault of conspiracy law and the reason why any limited reform is bound to be inadequate can be briefly stated. What conspiracy adds to the law is simply confusion, and the confusion is inherent in the nature of the doctrine. The confusion stems from the fact that conspiracy is not only a substantive inchoate crime in itself, but the touchstone for invoking several independent procedural and substantive doctrines. We ask whether a defendant agreed with another person to commit a crime initially for the purpose of determining whether he may be convicted of the offense of conspiracy even when the crime itself has not yet been committed. If the answer to that question is in the affirmative, however, we find that we have also answered a number of other questions that would otherwise have to be considered independently. Where there is evidence of conspiracy, the defendant may be tried jointly with his criminal partners and possibly with many other persons whom he has never met or seen, the joint trial may be held in a place he may never have visited, and hearsay statements of other alleged members of the conspiracy may be used to prove his guilt. Furthermore, a defendant who is found guilty of conspiracy is subject to enhanced punishment and may also be found guilty of any crime committed in furtherance of the conspiracy, whether or not he knew about the crime or aided in its commission.

Each of these issues involves a separate substantive or procedural area of the criminal law of considerable importance and complexity. The essential vice of conspiracy is that it inevitably distracts the courts from the policy questions or balancing of interests that ought to govern the decision of specific legal issues and leads them instead to decide those issues by reference to the conceptual framework of conspiracy. Instead of asking whether public policy or the interests of the parties require a particular holding, the courts are led instead to consider whether the theory of conspiracy is broad enough to permit it. What is wrong with conspiracy, in other words, is much more basic than the overbreadth of a few rules. The problem is not with particular results, but with the use of a single abstract concept to decide numerous questions that deserve separate consideration in light of the various interests and policies they involve.

Neal Kumar Katyal, Conspiracy Theory, 112 Yale L.J. 1307, 1309-1314 (2003): Psychologists have made many advances in understanding the ways in which people in groups act differently than they do as individuals. So, too, economists have developed sophisticated explanations for why firms promote efficiency, leading to new theories in corporate law. These insights can be "reverse-engineered" to make conspiracies operate less efficiently. [In other words, if we understand the features that make groups efficient, we can work backwards to undermine those features.—EDS.] In reverse engineering corporate law principles and introducing lessons from psychology, a rich account of how government should approach conspiracy begins to unfold. . . .

[Conspiracy] law strives to prevent conspiracies from forming with high up-front penalties for those who join, but also uses mechanisms to obtain information from those who have joined and decide to cooperate with the government. Federal law itself has come to recognize [the advantages of this dual approach], although scholars have not, and this can explain the function of doctrines such as Pinkerton liability and the exclusion from merger [resulting in the separate punishment for conspiracy and the object offense]. These doctrines not only further information extraction, they also make conspiracies more difficult to create and maintain by forcing them to adopt inefficient practices. The possibility of defection forces the syndicate to use expensive monitoring of its employees for evidence of possible collusion with the government. Mechanisms for defection also erode trust within the group and lead members to think that others are acting out of self-interest. This analysis will suggest that other doctrines in criminal law ... have information-extraction advantages; today, however, conspiracy law is a primary vehicle equipped for the task. ...

[T]his Article does not aspire to defend every aspect of federal conspiracy law. Rather, it contends that the criticism of some of the doctrine's various features (such as its inchoate nature, Pinkerton liability, the exclusion from merger, and its extension to agreements whose successes are "factually impossible") has not appreciated their functional benefits.

8. Criminal Enterprises and RICO

INTRODUCTORY NOTE

In response to a growing concern over organized crime in America and the perception that traditional conspiracy law provided inadequate tools for combating sophisticated criminal enterprises, Congress in 1970 passed the Racketeer Influenced and Corrupt Organizations Act, popularly known as RICO. But RICO's substantive reach goes well beyond the initial target of organized crime. RICO is now used to prosecute everything from business fraud to street gangs. The growing body of RICO law and its importance in modern law enforcement have made RICO a distinctive branch of conspiracy law that is worth careful study in its own right.

The RICO statute has become one of the most controversial provisions in the federal criminal code. RICO bases criminal liability on new, potentially elastic concepts such as "enterprise." The penalties imposed for a violation of RICO can be far higher than those that would apply when the underlying criminal acts are not part of a "pattern" of "racketeering activity," and the statute provides powerful prosecutorial tools to compel forfeiture of assets derived from racketeering. In addition, RICO permits individuals harmed by racketeering to bring civil suits, and it awards treble damages for injuries resulting from RICO violations. By including a provision for treble damage lawsuits, the statute creates a fertile field for civil litigation. In addition, Congress instructed the courts to give RICO a broad reading: "The provisions of this title shall be liberally construed to effectuate its remedial purposes." Organized Crime Control Act of 1970, Pub. L. No. 91-452, §904(a), 84 Stat. 922, 947. And the courts have followed that command. See Boyle v. United States, 129 S. Ct. 2237, 2243 (2009).

In examining the RICO statute, reprinted below, consider to what extent its provisions reach activities that could not be punished under traditional conspiracy doctrines, and to what extent its provisions change the treatment of activities that remain punishable under the traditional doctrines. Do the changes wrought by RICO raise problems of disproportionality by imposing overly severe sanctions on conduct that ordinarily is subject to much lower penalties? In the same vein, to what extent does RICO apply to small-scale criminal conspiracies that lack the special dangers of "organized crime"? Finally, note the broad list of criminal conduct that qualifies as "racketeering activity" within the meaning of RICO (and how it covers a host of traditional state crimes), as well as the tendency for that list to expand over time. Crimes that have been added to the definition of "racketeering activity" since 1988, as well as the date that each crime was added, are shown in italics in §1961(1)(B) below. In many cases, RICO provides a way for federal prosecutors to seek longer federal sentences for crimes already recognized by states but subject to lesser penalties. This raises the question whether RICO legitimately targets crimes where the federal government can play a unique role because of the interstate nature of the activity or the complexity of the investigations, or whether RICO federalizes too much local criminal activity in the name of longer sentences.

RACKETEER INFLUENCED AND CORRUPT ORGANIZATIONS ACT

18 U.S.C. ch. 96

§1961. DEFINITIONS

As used in this chapter—

(1) "racketeering activity" means (A) any act or threat involving murder, kidnapping, gambling, arson, robbery, bribery, extortion, dealing in obscene matter, or dealing in a controlled substance . . . , which is chargeable under State law and punishable by imprisonment for more than one year; (B) any act which is indictable under any of the following provisions of title 18, United States Code: [References are to sections relating to bribery, counterfeiting, theft from interstate shipment, embezzlement from pension and welfare funds, extortionate credit transactions, the transmission of gambling information, fraud, *fraud in connection with identification documents [April 1996], unlawful procurement of passports [April 1996], unlawful procurement of citizenship or citizenship papers [Sept. 1996],* obscenity, obstruction of justice, *misuse of passports, visas and other documents [April 1996], peonage and slavery [April 1996], trafficking in persons [Dec. 2003 and Jan. 2006],* interference with commerce by robbery or extortion, racketeering, interstate transportation of wagering paraphernalia, unlawful welfare fund payments, prohibition of illegal gambling businesses, money laundering, *prohibition of illegal money transmitting businesses [March 2006], sexual exploitation of children [1988],* interstate transportation of stolen property, *trafficking in counterfeit labels for computer programs, recordings or audiovisual works [July 1996], criminal copyright infringement [July 1996],* trafficking in motor vehicles or their parts, and trafficking in contraband cigarettes, *developing or possessing biological weapons [Dec. 2004], developing or possessing chemical weapons [Dec. 2004], and developing or possessing nuclear weapons [Dec. 2004]],* (C) any act which is indictable under title 29, United States Code, section 186 (dealing with restrictions on payments and loans to labor organizations) or section 501(c) (relating to embezzlement from union funds), (D) any offense involving [bankruptcy fraud], fraud in the sale of securities, or the felonious manufacture, importation, receiving, concealment, buying, selling, or otherwise dealing in a controlled substance . . . punishable under any law of the United States, (E) any act which is indictable

under the Currency and Foreign Transactions Reporting Act, (F) any act which is indictable under [certain sections of] the Immigration and Nationality Act [if indictable act is done for financial gain], or *(G) any act that is indictable under any provision listed in section 2332b(g)(5)(B) [relating to international terrorism [Oct. 2001]].* . . .

(4) "enterprise" includes any individual, partnership, corporation, association, or other legal entity, and any union or group of individuals associated in fact although not a legal entity;

(5) "pattern of racketeering activity" requires at least two acts of racketeering activity, one of which occurred after the effective date of this chapter [Oct. 15, 1970] and the last of which occurred within ten years (excluding any period of imprisonment) after the commission of a prior act of racketeering activity. . . .

§1962. Prohibited Activities

(a) It shall be unlawful for any person who has received any income derived, directly or indirectly, from a pattern of racketeering activity or through collection of an unlawful debt . . . to use or invest [any part of such income in acquisition of] any enterprise . . . the activities of which affect interstate or foreign commerce. . . .

(b) It shall be unlawful for any person through a pattern of racketeering activity or through collection of an unlawful debt to acquire or maintain [any interest in any enterprise the activities of which affect] interstate or foreign commerce.

(c) It shall be unlawful for any person employed by or associated with any enterprise engaged in, or the activities of which affect, interstate or foreign commerce, to conduct or participate, directly or indirectly, in the conduct of such enterprise's affairs through a pattern of racketeering activity or collection of unlawful debt.

(d) It shall be unlawful for any person to conspire to violate any of the provisions of subsection (a), (b), or (c) of this section.

§1963. Criminal Penalties

(a) Whoever violates any provision of section 1962 of this chapter shall be fined under this title or imprisoned not more than 20 years (or for life if the violation is based on a racketeering activity for which the maximum penalty includes life imprisonment), or both and shall forfeit to the United States, irrespective of any provision of State law [any interest the person has acquired or maintained in violation of section 1962 and any proceeds which the person obtained from racketeering activity or unlawful debt collection. . . .

PROBLEM

A and *B* burn down a building in order to help *C* defraud its owners. The following year, *A, D,* and *E* sell cars stolen by a car theft ring and continue doing so for several years. *A* has *B* kill a suspected police informant and has *F* help sell a shipment of stolen canned goods. Throughout the time period, drug transactions are engaged in by *A* and *B* together, by *D* and *E* together, and by *F* alone. Who has conspired with whom?

(a) Traditional conspiracy law. Consider first whether, under traditional principles, all six defendants can be tied together in a single conspiracy. All are connected in the sense that they have committed some crime with *A*. But has *C* conspired with *D* and *E*, when they did not commit any crimes together or even know of each other's existence? Is the drug dealing connected to the fencing of stolen cars? Or are the defendants who conspired with *A* like the defendants in *Kotteakos*, supra page 740, where the Supreme Court found that the "wheel" surrounding Simon Brown had no "rim" to make it a single conspiracy?

(b) RICO. Now consider the possibilities for applying the RICO statute to these facts. Note the four categories of "prohibited activities" under §1962. Can the six defendants be charged with violating §1962(c)? All of the underlying crimes qualify as "racketeering activity," so the only questions that remain are whether there was an "enterprise" and whether the defendants "conducted or participated in [its affairs]," through a "pattern" of such activity. Are these requirements met in the Problem case? The separate requirements of "enterprise," "pattern," "conduct," and "participation" are examined below.

NOTES ON THE ENTERPRISE REQUIREMENT

1. The criminal enterprise. The principal type of criminal organization legislators had in mind in drafting RICO was the Mafia. Thus, Congress passed RICO thinking about the bread-and-butter mob activities of "infiltrating unions and their pension funds, investing in and skimming profits from casinos, muscling in on trash collection companies, and actually committing crimes like distributing drugs or running prostitution rings." Randy D. Gordon, Clarity and Confusion: RICO's Recent Trips to the United States Supreme Court, 85 Tul. L. Rev. 677 (2011). The term "enterprise" in RICO reflects this image and includes both legal organizations like corrupted unions and illegal "associat[ions] in fact" like the Mafia. Because much of RICO's original focus was on preventing organized crime from infiltrating and capturing control of legitimate businesses, some courts held that the "enterprise" must be an organization engaged in some legal activities. These courts reasoned that an ordinary criminal conspiracy, in which individuals associate for the sole and specific purpose of committing criminal acts, could not by itself constitute the kind of "enterprise" with which RICO was concerned. But in United States v. Turkette, 452 U.S. 576 (1981), the Supreme Court held that an "enterprise" for RICO purposes can include an exclusively criminal organization.

The defendants in the Problem are undoubtedly a "group of individuals," but are they "associated in fact" based on a shared intention to make money through illegal activities? In an early RICO case with similar facts, United States v. Elliott, 571 F.2d 880 (5th Cir. 1978), the court concluded that defendants like *A* through *E* were in a single "enterprise":

This enterprise can best be analogized to a large business conglomerate. Metaphorically speaking, [A] was the chairman of the board, . . . overseeing the operations of many separate branches of the corporation. An executive committee in charge of the "Counterfeit Title, Stolen Car, and Amphetamine Sales Department" was comprised of [A, D, and E], who supervised the operations of lower employees. . . . Another executive committee, comprised of [A, B, and C], controlled the "Thefts From Interstate Commerce Department," arranging the purchase, concealment and distribution of [various stolen goods]. An offshoot of this department handled subsidiary activities, such as murder and obstruction of justice, intended to facilitate the smooth operation of its primary activities. . . . The thread tying all of these departments, activities, and individuals together was the desire to make money. [A] might have been voicing the corporation's motto when he [declared], "If it ain't a pretty damn good bit of money, I ain't going to f— with it."

Questions: Did the "business conglomerate" described by the court involve any specific organizational arrangements, or was it simply inferred from the defendants' general intention to make money? If the latter, should a more specific enterprise structure be required? If a common purpose to make money is enough, couldn't such an intention be considered sufficient to create a "rim" and thus a single conspiracy under pre-RICO law as well?

2. Distinguishing the enterprise requirement from the pattern requirement. In response to the argument that the holding in *Turkette* would make the required "enterprise" synonymous with the required "pattern of racketeering activity," the Supreme Court said (452 U.S. at 583):

> The enterprise is an entity, for present purposes a group of persons associated together for a common purpose of engaging in a course of conduct. The pattern of racketeering activity is, on the other hand, a series of criminal acts as defined by the statute. The former is proved by evidence of an ongoing organization, formal or informal, and by evidence that the various associates function as a continuing unit. The latter is proved by evidence of the requisite number of acts of racketeering committed by the participants in the enterprise. While the proof used to establish these separate elements may in particular cases coalesce, proof of one does not necessarily establish the other. The "enterprise" is not the "pattern of racketeering activity"; it is an entity separate and apart from the pattern of activity in which it engages. The existence of an enterprise at all times remains a separate element which must be proved by the Government.

3. The requisite structure. *Turkette* left unresolved the question of whether the association-in-fact enterprise (as opposed to formal business organizations like partnerships or corporations) must have "continuity of both structure and personality" and "an 'ascertainable structure' distinct from that inherent in the conduct of a pattern of racketeering activity." In *Boyle v. United States*, the Supreme Court held that an association-in-fact enterprise must have a "structure," but the Court required very little to establish it. It held that "an association-in-fact enterprise must have at least three structural features: a purpose, relationships among those associated with the enterprise, and longevity sufficient to permit these associates to pursue the enterprise's purpose." 129 S. Ct. 2237, 2244 (2009). The Court made clear that an association-in-fact enterprise need not have a hierarchical structure, fixed roles for members, sophisticated organization, or "a name, regular meetings, dues, established rules and regulations, disciplinary procedures, or induction or initiation ceremonies." Id. at 2245-2246. The ascertainable structure is established as long as the group "function[s] as a continuing unit and remain[s] in existence long enough to pursue a course of conduct." Id. "[P]eriods of quiescence" do not negate a finding of an enterprise. "Nor is the statute limited to groups whose crimes are sophisticated, diverse, complex, or unique." Id. The expanded conception of "enterprise" in *Turkette* and *Boyle* has paved the way for the federal government to use RICO to address the activities of street gangs. Joseph Wheatley, The Flexibility of RICO and its Use on Street Gangs Engaging in Organized Crime in the United States, 2 Policing 82 (2008).

NOTES ON THE PATTERN REQUIREMENT

1. Identifying a pattern. Should an ongoing desire to make money create a "pattern" out of discrete criminal acts? The *Elliott* court found that the racketeering crimes of defendants like *A* through *E* constituted a "pattern" (571 F.2d at 899):

> [W]e find nothing in the Act excluding from its ambit an enterprise engaged in diversified activity. . . . As in a firm with a real estate department and an insurance department, the fact that partners bring in two kinds of business on the basis of their different skills and connections does not affect the fact that they are partners in a more general business venture. [T]he two or more predicate crimes must be related to the affairs of the enterprise but need not otherwise be related to each other.

Questions: Is it justified to find a RICO "pattern" merely because two unrelated crimes both generate income for their instigator? If so, can the same reasoning be applied to defendant *F*? He played a minor role in a single theft planned by *A*, and his drug transactions were not connected to the activities of the other defendants. Even if *F* on one occasion "participate[d] in the affairs of the enterprise," did he participate through a *pattern* of activity?

2. Continuity and relationship. In H.J. Inc. v. Northwestern Bell Telephone Co., 492 U.S. 229 (1989), phone company customers sued for treble damages, alleging that Northwestern and several of its employees had violated RICO by bribing members of the Minnesota Public Utilities Commission (MPUC) to approve excessive rates. The court of appeals upheld the dismissal of the case, on the ground that the acts of alleged bribery did not constitute a "pattern" because they were all part of a "single scheme" to influence the MPUC. The Supreme Court reversed. The Court held that a RICO "pattern" must involve something more than just two predicate acts, but that a pattern need not involve separate illegal schemes and need not involve conduct indicative of organized crime activity in the traditional sense. Drawing on RICO's legislative history, the Court interpreted the "pattern" element to require proof "that the racketeering predicates are related, *and* that they . . . pose a threat of continued criminal activity." 492 U.S. at 239 ("It is this factor of continuity plus relationship which combines to produce a pattern."). The Court also held that Congress intended courts to define "relatedness" by referring to 18 U.S.C. §3575(e), which specifies that criminal conduct is related "if it embraces criminal acts that have the same or similar purposes, results, participants, victims, or methods of commission, or otherwise are interrelated by distinguishing characteristics and are not isolated events." Id. at 240.

In an opinion concurring only in the judgment, Justice Scalia, joined by Chief Justice Rehnquist and Justices O'Connor and Kennedy, commented (492 U.S. at 252-256):

> Elevating to the level of statutory text a phrase taken from the legislative history, the Court counsels the lower courts: "continuity plus relationship." This seems to me about as helpful to the conduct of their affairs as "life is a fountain." . . . It hardly closes in on the target to know that "relatedness" refers to acts that are related by "purposes, results, participants, victims, . . . methods of commission, *or* [just in case that is not vague enough] *otherwise*." Is the fact that the victims of both predicate acts were women enough? Or that both acts had the purpose of enriching the defendant? Or that the different coparticipants of the defendant in both acts were his co-employees? I doubt that the lower courts will find the Court's instructions much more helpful than telling them to look for a "pattern"—which is what the statute already says.
>
> The Court finds "continuity" more difficult to define precisely. "Continuity," it says, "is both a closed- and open-ended concept, referring either to a closed period of repeated conduct, or to past conduct that by its nature projects into the future with a threat of repetition." I have no idea what this concept of a "closed period of repeated conduct" means. Virtually all allegations of racketeering activity, in both civil and criminal suits, will relate to past periods that are "closed" (unless one expects plaintiff or the prosecutor to establish that the defendant not only committed the crimes he did, but is still committing them), and all of them *must* relate to conduct that is "repeated," because of RICO's multiple-act requirement. . . .
>
> It is clear to me . . . that the word "pattern" in the phrase "pattern of racketeering activity" was meant to import some requirement beyond the mere existence of multiple predicate acts. . . . But what that something more is, is beyond me. As I have suggested, it is also beyond the Court. Today's opinion has added nothing to improve our prior guidance, which has created a kaleidoscope of circuit positions, except to clarify that RICO may in addition be violated when there is a "threat of continuity." It seems to me this increases rather than removes the vagueness. . . .
>
> No constitutional challenge to this law has been raised in the present case, and so that issue is not before us. That the highest Court in the land has been unable to derive from this statute anything more than today's meager guidance bodes ill for the day when that challenge is presented.

NOTES ON THE CONDUCT AND PARTICIPATION REQUIREMENT

1. "Conduct" and "participation." Does the commission of racketeering crimes suffice to establish that the defendants in the Problem "conduct[ed] or participate[d] in the conduct of" the enterprise's affairs? Assuming that there was an enterprise at all, *A*—as the ringleader—was certainly in charge of conducting its affairs. But did any of the other defendants help *conduct* those affairs? If a defendant like *B* takes orders from the boss, does he thereby "*participate* in the conduct" of the enterprise's affairs, either directly or indirectly?

2. The "operation or management" test. Reves v. Ernst & Young, 507 U.S. 170 (1993), involved a civil suit growing out of the insolvency of an Arkansas farmers' cooperative. In auditing the co-op's books, the Arthur Young accounting firm (which later merged into Ernst & Young) permitted one of the co-op's major assets to be carried at its original cost of $4.5 million rather than its market value of $1.5 million, and failed to disclose the problematic nature of the $4.5 million valuation. When the co-op became insolvent in 1984, the trustee in bankruptcy sued Arthur Young and several individual accountants, alleging that the co-op's noteholders had been defrauded by misrepresentations that violated various securities laws and RICO. The Supreme Court held that Arthur Young and its accountants had not violated §1962(c) because, in order to "conduct or participate directly or indirectly in the conduct of [an] enterprise's affairs," an individual must have some role in directing or managing the enterprise's affairs (which in this case was the co-op). Justice Blackmun wrote for the Court (507 U.S. at 179, 184):

> In order to "participate, directly or indirectly, in the conduct of such enterprise's affairs," one must have some part in directing those affairs. Of course, the word "participate" makes clear that RICO liability is not limited to those with primary responsibility for the enterprise's affairs, just as the phrase "directly or indirectly" makes clear that RICO liability is not limited to those with a formal position in the enterprise, but *some* part in directing the enterprise's affairs is required. The "operation or management" test expresses this requirement in a formulation that is easy to apply.
>
> . . . We agree that liability under §1962(c) is not limited to upper management, but we disagree that the "operation or management" test is inconsistent with this proposition. An enterprise is "operated" not just by upper management but also by lower-rung participants in the enterprise who are under the direction of upper management. An enterprise also might be "operated" or "managed" by others "associated with" the enterprise who exert control over it as, for example, by bribery.

Question: Does the "operation or management" test protect low-level employees and outside professionals from conviction of racketeering offenses under RICO? Consider Daniel R. Fischel & Alan O. Sykes, Civil RICO After *Reves:* An Economic Commentary, [1993] Sup. Ct. Rev. 157, 190-194:

> On first reading, the [*Reves*] opinion provides considerable comfort to professionals. . . . Only those who have "some part in directing the enterprise's affairs" can be liable. . . . [But] there is sufficient contradictory language in *Reves* to make the issue murky at best. . . . The Court [stated] that: "An enterprise is 'operated' not just by upper management but also by lower-rung participants in the enterprise who are under the direction of upper management." With this one sentence, the Court undercut much of its earlier emphasis on the importance of "directing" an enterprise's affairs. Now the "direction" requirement includes both those who direct, as well as those who take direction. For a Court that prides itself on the importance of the plain language of [statutes], this contorted interpretation of the words "operated" and "direction" is, at the very least, paradoxical. . . .
>
> Why was it "clear" that Arthur Young was not acting "under the direction" of the Co-op's management? Presumably the Court was referring to the absence of any direct evidence [that] Co-op management instruct[ed] Arthur Young to use fraudulent numbers. For Arthur Young's liability to turn on this point, however, is to exalt form over substance. The sale of the Co-op notes at inflated prices benefited the Co-op, not Arthur Young. Why else would Arthur Young knowingly participate and assist in the Co-op's fraud except at the behest of management? And even if Arthur Young somehow decided to participate in the fraud independently as opposed to being directed to do so by management, why should this be exonerating? The more the fraud can be attributed to Arthur Young and management as opposed to just management, the stronger the case for imposing liability on both. . . .
>
> To determine whether a defendant played a role in directing an enterprise's affairs also requires a definition of "enterprise." In *Reves,* the enterprise was the Co-op but this is not the only possibility. . . . What if the plaintiff in *Reves* had alleged that an association in fact consisting of Arthur Young, Jack White [Co-op's general manager], and the Co-op constituted the racketeering enterprise and that Arthur Young directed the affairs of this "enterprise"?
>
> Such an allegation might be sufficient if the plaintiff could demonstrate that the alleged association in fact was, as *Turkette* requires, "ongoing" and functioned "as a continuing unit." . . . In future cases, courts' attitude toward association in fact enterprises will be critical in light of the obvious incentives of plaintiffs to allege such associations in fact to satisfy *Reves*'s "operation or management" test.

After *Reves*, many courts upheld liability under §1962(c) for low-level employees who carried out instructions issued by managers of a RICO enterprise, provided that the employees had some degree of importance or autonomy. United States v. Urban, 404 F.3d 754 (3d Cir. 2005), involved inspectors who worked for Philadelphia's Construction Services Department (CSD) and who accepted bribes from the plumbers whose work they were supposed to be inspecting. They challenged their conviction for racketeering under §1962(c) by arguing that the government failed to prove that they directed the affairs of the CSD or otherwise engaged in its operation or management. The Third

Circuit rejected their challenge, stating that the participation requirement is satisfied where there is a "nexus between the person and the conduct in the affairs of an enterprise." Id. at 770 (internal quotation and citation omitted).

Questions: Is the *Urban* court's reasoning consistent with *Reves*? Is it a sound interpretation of the statutory language?

NOTES ON RICO CONSPIRACIES

1. *Conspiracies to conspire?* Section 1962(c) can be viewed as a kind of conspiracy statute: By imposing criminal liability on those who "participate . . . in the conduct of [an] enterprise's affairs through a pattern of racketeering activity," §1962(c) reaches what is inherently a type of group crime. But the RICO statute also includes a provision, §1962(d), that expressly punishes conspiracies. Specifically, §1962(d) covers conspiracies to violate §1962(a), (b), or (c). See page 762 supra. As it relates to §1962(c), does §1962(d) in effect prohibit conspiring to engage in a conspiracy?

2. *Comparing RICO conspiracy with ordinary conspiracy.* What are the effects of §1962(d), and how does it change the traditional law of conspiracy? One basic difference is that RICO conspiracies do not require proof of any overt act. Salinas v. United States, 522 U.S. 52, 64 (1997). The *Elliott* case, see Problem, supra page 762, shows a more profound distinction. The Fifth Circuit in that case found that the RICO statute transformed what would have been multiple conspiracies under traditional law into a single conspiracy under §1962(d), the conspiracy provision of the RICO statute. But how is such alchemy possible? If under pre-RICO law there would be insufficient proof to tie A, B, C, D, and E together in a single agreement, how does passage of the RICO statute create a single agreement between them? Conversely, if—as the *Elliott* court held—these conspirators agreed "to associate for the purpose of making money from repeated criminal activity," then why would pre-RICO law pose any barrier to finding a single agreement? Consider Michael Goldsmith, RICO and Enterprise Criminality: A Response to Gerard E. Lynch. 88 Colum. L. Rev., 174, 798 (1988):

> The answer [to this question] is that the enterprise itself is an important link in the evidentiary chain: a defendant's knowledge of the enterprise's existence is probative of a central purpose. Thus, upon proof that such an enterprise exists, the enterprise itself provides the basis for inferring one large conspiracy instead of many smaller ones. The objective of this conspiracy, which potentially encompasses many crimes, is to conduct enterprise affairs through a pattern of racketeering activity. In contrast, because ordinary conspiracy cases do not involve proof of enterprise, this unifying function is absent.

Goldsmith's defense of RICO's expansive notion of what qualifies as a single conspiracy under §1962(d) rests on the notion that the "enterprise" is well defined. If Goldsmith is correct that the existence of the "enterprise" is critical to RICO conspiracies, should the Court demand more than it currently does to establish an enterprise with an "ascertainable structure"? See supra pages 764-765.

3. RICO conspiracies and predicate offenses. In Salinas v. United States, 522 U.S. 52 (1997), the Court addressed whether a defendant must personally commit or agree to commit "the two predicate acts requisite for a substantive RICO offense under §1962(c)" in order to be guilty of conspiracy under §1962(d). Id. at 61. Salinas was convicted under §1962(d) for conspiring to accept bribes from a federal prisoner, even though the jury had acquitted him of the underlying substantive offense of violating §1962(c). The bribery scheme was run by the county sheriff; Salinas was the chief deputy responsible for managing the jail. The Court noted that conspiracy in "its conventional sense" may be charged "even if a conspirator does not agree to commit or facilitate each and every part of the substantive offense." Id. at 63. Applying this conventional understanding of conspiracy law, the Court explained (id. at 66):

> In the case before us, even if Salinas did not accept or agree to accept two bribes, there was ample evidence that he conspired to violate subsection (c). The evidence showed that [the county sheriff] committed at least two acts of racketeering activity when he accepted numerous bribes and that Salinas knew about and agreed to facilitate the scheme. This is sufficient to support a conviction under §1962(d). . . .

Does *Salinas* create a way to avoid the "operation or management" requirement announced in *Reves*, supra pages 767-768? Can a peripheral actor be convicted of a RICO conspiracy under §1962(d), even if he isn't guilty of conducting or participating in conducting an enterprise within the meaning of *Reves*? Consider the following scenario: The Mexican Mafia (known as La Eme) was running a large-scale drug-smuggling ring in California prisons. The wife of an imprisoned Eme member smuggled drugs and money to him during her visits to him in prison. Though she had no role in organizing the Eme's affairs, she did collect money on behalf of her husband from those outside of prison and passed messages to her husband and other Eme members. Could the wife be convicted of a substantive RICO offense under §1962(c)? Of a RICO conspiracy under §1962(d)? In United States v. Fernandez, 388 F.3d 1199, 1228 (9th Cir. 2004), the Ninth Circuit upheld the wife's conviction under §1962(d) because she "knowingly agree[d] to facilitate a scheme which include[d] the operation or management of a RICO enterprise," even if she did not operate or manage the enterprise herself. See also United States v. Wilson, 605 F.3d 985, 1019 (D.C. Cir. 2010). Following *Salinas*, every court of appeals to consider the question has held that the *Reves* operation or management test does not apply to conspiracy under §1962(d). For an argument that the *Reves* operation or management test should extend to §1962(d), thereby requiring proof that the defendant conspired "*to* operate or manage an enterprise" and not simply conspired "*with* someone who is operating or managing an enterprise," see Sarah Baumgartel, The Crime of Associating with Criminals? An Argument for Extending the Reves "Operation or Management" Test to RICO Conspiracy, 97 J. Crim. L. & Criminology 1, 24-31 (2006).

4. *Scope of RICO conspiracies.* Some commentators have worried that RICO might create single conspiracies whenever multiple, unrelated crimes involve the same RICO "enterprise," which might be an otherwise legitimate business or governmental entity. See, e.g., Barry Tarlow, RICO: The New Darling of the Prosecutor's Nursery, 49 Fordham L. Rev. 165, 243, 251-252 (1980). Consider United States v. Sutherland, 656 F.2d 1181 (5th Cir. 1981). Sutherland was a traffic court judge who allegedly conspired with two others (Walker and Maynard) in a scheme to fix traffic tickets. The government conceded that neither Walker nor Maynard knew of the other's activities; under pre-RICO law there would have been two separate conspiracies—spokes of a wheel without a "rim." But the government claimed that the affairs of the traffic court constituted the RICO "enterprise" and that the three defendants could be charged with a single "enterprise conspiracy" under RICO. The Fifth Circuit acknowledged that some of its language in *Elliott* might appear to support this argument, but it went on to clarify its earlier holding (id. at 1192-1194):

> *Elliott* does indeed hold that on the facts of that case a series of agreements that under pre-RICO law would constitute multiple conspiracies could under RICO be tried as a single "enterprise" conspiracy. But the language of *Elliott* explains that what ties these conspiracies together is not the mere fact that they involve the same enterprise, but is instead—as in any other conspiracy—an "agreement on an overall objective." What RICO does is to provide a new criminal objective by defining a new substantive crime. . . .
>
> In this case the government has not attempted to prove that Walker and Maynard agreed with each other to participate in a bribery scheme with Sutherland, nor has it contended that the nature of each defendant's agreement with Sutherland was such that he or she must necessarily have known that others were also conspiring to commit racketeering offenses in the conduct of the Municipal Court. We must conclude, therefore, that the multiple conspiracy doctrine precluded the joint trial of the two multiple conspiracies involved in this case on a single RICO conspiracy count.

Other circuits, however, have been willing to find a single RICO conspiracy on similar facts. In United States v. Castro, 89 F.3d 1443 (11th Cir. 1996), another judicial bribery case, three lawyers were charged with paying kickbacks to judges in exchange for receiving appointments as public defenders in a Florida circuit court. Despite the absence of evidence that the lawyers cooperated or benefited from appointments obtained by each other, the court held that the lawyers and judges were properly convicted of engaging in a single RICO conspiracy involving a single enterprise (the Circuit Court). Disagreeing on this point, Judge Barkett noted (id. at 1458-1459):

> To prove the existence of a single overarching conspiracy, rather than multiple independent conspiracies, it is not enough that the defendants were simply participating in the conduct of the same enterprise or had knowledge of other criminal activity; the gravamen of a RICO conspiracy, like any other conspiracy, is that the defendant not only knows about the conspiracy, but also *agrees to participate* in it to accomplish an overall objective.

[The evidence,] while possibly establishing knowledge [by some lawyers] of other criminal activity within the Circuit Court, [is] insufficient to establish ... that [they] agreed to accomplish anything more than the receipt of court appointments for their own monetary gain. Nothing suggests ... that they would be interested in or benefit from the similar activities of others.

Question: Given the dangers posed by organized crime, should the existence of a criminal "enterprise" replace the traditional requirement of conspiracy doctrine that defendants agree to a mutually advantageous course of criminal conduct? Or does doing so risk disproportionate punishment and "guilt by association"?

NOTE ON THE CONTROVERSY OVER RICO

The RICO statute has remained controversial. Some of the principal issues concern its potential for distorting civil litigation; also prominent in the debate are concerns about RICO's provisions for pretrial seizure of a defendant's assets, forfeiture of assets connected to the "enterprise," and related procedural matters. These strands in the RICO debate cannot be pursued in depth here, but many of the most important themes in the debate raise problems of substantive criminal law—the breadth and potential vagueness of the RICO offense, the risk of guilt by association, and the possibility for criminal liability greatly disproportionate to personal fault. These issues are central to conspiracy law in general and to other topics that pervade the subject of criminal law. Compare the Fifth Circuit's defense of RICO's constitutionality in the next excerpt with the criticisms offered by Judges David Sentelle and Gerard Lynch in the excerpts that follow.

UNITED STATES v. ELLIOTT

United States Court of Appeals, 5th Circuit
571 F.2d 880 (1978)

SIMPSON, J. In this case we deal with the question of whether and, if so, how a free society can protect itself when groups of people, through division of labor, specialization, diversification, complexity of organization, and the accumulation of capital, turn crime into an ongoing business.

... The "enterprise conspiracy" is a legislative innovation in the realm of individual liability for group crime. We need to consider whether this innovation comports with the fundamental demand of due process that guilt remain "individual and personal." *Kotteakos*, supra, 328 U.S. at 772. ...

The substantive proscriptions of the RICO statute apply to insiders *and outsiders*—those merely "associated with" an enterprise—who participate directly *and indirectly* in the enterprise's affairs through a pattern of racketeering activity. Thus, the RICO net is woven tightly to trap even the smallest fish, those peripherally involved with the enterprise. This effect is enhanced by principles of conspiracy law also developed to facilitate prosecution of conspirators at all levels. Direct evidence of agreement is unnecessary: "proof of such an agreement may rest upon inferences drawn from relevant and competent circumstantial evidence—ordinarily the acts and conduct of the alleged conspirators themselves." United States v. Morado, 454 F.2d at 174. . . .

Undeniably, then, under the RICO conspiracy provision, remote associates of an enterprise may be convicted as conspirators on the basis of purely circumstantial evidence. We cannot say, however, that this section of the statute . . . offends the rule that guilt be individual and personal. The Act does not authorize that individuals "be tried en masse for the conglomeration of distinct and separate offenses committed by others." *Kotteakos*, supra. Nor does it punish mere association with conspirators or knowledge of illegal activity; its proscriptions are directed against conduct, not status. . . .

Our society disdains mass prosecutions because we abhor the totalitarian doctrine of mass guilt. We nevertheless punish conspiracy as a distinct offense because we recognize that collective action toward an illegal end involves a greater risk to society than individual action toward the same end. That risk is greatly compounded when the conspirators contemplate not a single crime but a career of crime. "There are times when of necessity, because of the nature and scope of the particular federation, large numbers of persons taking part must be tried together or perhaps not at all. . . . When many conspire, they invite mass trial by their conduct." *Kotteakos*, supra, 328 U.S. at 773.

We do not lightly dismiss the fact that under this statute four defendants who did not commit murder have been forced to stand trial jointly with, and as confederates of, two others who did. Prejudice inheres in such a trial; . . . But the Constitution does not guarantee a trial free from the prejudice that inevitably accompanies any charge of heinous group crime; it demands only that the potential for transference of guilt be minimized to the extent possible under the circumstances. . . . The RICO statute does not offend this principle. Congress, in a proper exercise of its legislative power, has decided that murder, like thefts from interstate commerce and the counterfeiting of securities, qualifies as racketeering activity. This, of course, ups the ante for RICO violators who personally would not contemplate taking a human life. Whether there is a moral imbalance in the equation of thieves and counterfeiters with murderers is a question whose answer lies in the halls of Congress, not in the judicial conscience.

DAVID SENTELLE, RICO: THE MONSTER THAT ATE JURISPRUDENCE[8]

Lecture to the CATO Institute, Oct. 18, 1989, pp. 5-13

The [RICO] monster is . . . hungrily devouring traditional concepts of American jurisprudence. Among the traditional concepts the monster is

---

8. David Sentelle is the Chief Judge of the U.S. Court of Appeals for the D.C. Circuit.

eating, I would include federalism, the separation of powers, . . . repose of actions and perhaps even the basic concept of government of laws, not of men.

As to federalism: . . . look back to the language of section 1961(1) defining "racketeering activity." Within the incredible compass of that definition, Section (1)(A) adopts wholesale great areas of State criminal law encompassing "any act or threat involving murder, kidnapping, gambling, arson, robbery, bribery, extortion, dealing in obscene matter, or dealing in narcotic or other dangerous drugs, which is chargeable under *State* law and punishable by imprisonment for more than one year." (Emphasis added.)

. . . The almost boundless breadth of RICO, invites, perhaps requires, the Article II Executive in the form of the prosecutor and the Judiciary in the form of Article III Judges to undertake the Article I Legislative role of defining federal crimes. . . .

[D]efenders of RICO . . . tell us that we should rely on prosecutorial discretion to protect against the overbreadth of RICO. Even some of those who seek to reform RICO by the repeal of its civil remedy would retain criminal RICO because they are willing to rely on the discretion of prosecutors despite their distrust of civil plaintiffs' attorneys. But we are not given angels in the form of men to make prosecutorial decisions. If we can rely on the discretion of Executive Branch officials to protect our liberties, why did we need a Constitution creating a limited government and a Bill of Rights protecting our liberties in the first place? . . .

Finally, we see the RICO monster violently attacking traditional principles of repose of actions. . . . The definition of "pattern of racketeering activity" permits the use of "at least two acts of racketeering activity, one of which occurred after the effective date of this chapter and the last of which occurred within ten years (excluding any period of imprisonment) after the commission of a prior act of racketeering activity." . . .

In other words, RICO creates an essentially perpetual cause of action alien to our traditional jurisprudence. . . . Congress, of course, has the power to make determinations as to the period of limitations. Nonetheless, one must wonder if Congress in the RICO statute really made a conscious decision to create a perpetual cause of action or simply unwittingly unleashed a monster. . . .

GERARD E. LYNCH, RICO: THE CRIME OF BEING A CRIMINAL[9]

87 Colum. L. Rev. 661, 920, 932-955, 967-970 (1987)

Fundamental to our traditional law of crimes, criminal procedure and evidence is a conception of crime that is transaction-bound. [T]he core of any definition of crime is a particular act or omission. That act or omission

---

9. Gerard E. Lynch, a former federal prosecutor, was a law professor when he wrote this article. He currently serves as a judge on the U.S. Court of Appeals for the Second Circuit.

is conceived as taking place in an instant of time so precise that it can be associated with a particular mental state of intention, awareness of risk, or neglect of due care. . . . Even the crime of conspiracy, which in practice may permit an examination of an extended course of conduct by one or more individuals, does so in the guise of using that course of conduct as evidence from which to infer that a particular act of "agreement" occurred. . . .

The requirement that criminal punishment be based on a specific act has deep roots. The very nature of criminal punishment, as distinct from other uses of the compulsive power of the state (such as mandatory treatment for physical or mental illness), requires that a person not be punished for bad character, tendency to commit crime, or even a specifically formulated intention to commit some particular prohibited act. . . . Even for those accused of committing what is unquestionably a concrete, particular offense, we are careful to guard against the possibility that a defendant may be convicted and punished for bad character rather than for the particular act charged. The insistence on incident-based liability thus has important consequences for our rules of procedure and evidence. . . .

RICO prosecutions of criminal enterprises present a serious challenge to . . . this transaction-based model of crime. . . . Suppose, for example, the authorities develop evidence that the same defendant from whom they have recently made an undercover purchase of narcotics is a member of an organized crime family who committed a contract killing three years earlier. . . . In a trial on the narcotics charge alone . . . the evidence of a prior homicide committed by the defendant would likely be excluded as irrelevant and highly prejudicial. . . . If the case could be indicted and tried under RICO, however, all of the evidence regarding this defendant's activities could easily be presented in the same trial. Since the government would have to allege and prove a pattern of racketeering activity . . . evidence of the homicide would not be evidence of a *prior* crime, but evidence of the very offense charged in the indictment. . . .

One value served by the transaction model of crime is its preclusion of punishment in the absence of behavior manifesting a concrete threat of harm. . . . "Character" or "predicted danger" are flexible and unpredictable standards of decision, too easily used as tools of oppression.

These substantive concerns, however, are not directly violated by RICO. Although the distinguishing features of RICO are its somewhat amorphous associational and course of conduct elements, a fundamental prerequisite of a substantive RICO violation is the commission of particular criminal acts. These predicate racketeering acts are themselves conventional, transactionally defined crimes. . . .

Recognizing the importance of context to the gravity of individual criminal acts, increasing the possibility of convicting racketeers who might otherwise slip through the cracks in a transaction-based model of procedure, and utilizing the dramatic context of the criminal trial to educate the public to models of criminal activity more significant than the isolated derelictions of particular individuals are important and appropriate goals for criminal law. . . .

Such arguments are tenable, however, only if the RICO trial affords due process. . . . [I]s it within the physical and mental capacity of a jury to recall accurately the separate evidence relating to so many different individuals and so many separate incidents? What is the effect on a jury pool of the elimination of all potential jurors who cannot serve in a trial that may last over a year? . . . The threat of substantive injustice in RICO cases may come far more from such practical concerns than from the conceptual issues discussed above.

NOTE ON ENTERPRISE LIABILITY UNDER STATE LAW

At least 33 states have enacted anti-racketeering statutes closely tracking the structure and terminology of the federal RICO statute. See Susan W. Brenner, RICO, CCE, and Other Complex Crimes: The Transformation of American Criminal Law?, 2 Wm. & Mary Bill Rts. J. 239, 273 (1992). Because these statutes are similar to the federal model, state courts often look to federal RICO precedent in interpreting them. For example, in State v. Rodriguez-Roman, 297 Conn. 66, 81-83 (2010), the Supreme Court of Connecticut, in interpreting the state's racketeering law, followed the U.S. Supreme Court's analysis in *Boyle* that an enterprise does not require a "structure separate from that inherent in the pattern of criminal activity." In some jurisdictions, however, state statutes have been interpreted to reach even more broadly than federal RICO. The Ohio Supreme Court, for example, has held that the "pattern of racketeering activity" required under that state's version of RICO can be satisfied by conviction on several misdemeanor counts involving strict liability violations of a state regulatory statute. State v. Schlosser, 681 N.E.2d 911 (Ohio 1997). In accepting the prosecution's argument that these no-fault misdemeanors could be used to establish a felony RICO violation, the court reasoned that whatever the defendant's mental state might be, "the effect of his activities on the local and national economy is the same. Requiring the finding of a specific culpable mental state for a RICO violation obstructs the purpose of the statute. . . ." Id. at 914.

In contrast, the analogous New York provisions are more cautious. The New York offense of "enterprise corruption" requires proof of a "pattern" consisting of at least three predicate felonies, and each defendant must personally participate in three predicate crimes. N.Y. Penal Law §460.10(4) (2011). The New York statute includes a statement of "[l]egislative findings" that "more rigorous definitions" were adopted, in order to place "reasonable limitations on the law's applicability, and [ensure] due regard for the rights of innocent persons." Id. §460.00. See Martin Marcus, Enterprise Corruption, in R. Greenberg et al., New York Criminal Law 1407-1444 (1996).

Questions: Do the threats posed by racketeering and organized crime call for the breadth and flexibility of the broadest of the state RICO statutes? On the other hand, do such statutes pose dangers of their own as tools of law enforcement? The New York legislature, supra, was concerned that a broad RICO statute might endanger "the rights of innocent persons." See Marcus, supra. How might it do so? Are there any other reasons, aside from fear of conviction of the innocent, to be concerned about the breadth of state or federal RICO provisions?

C. LIABILITY WITHIN THE CORPORATE FRAMEWORK

A special case of group crime occurs within the context of corporations, which raises three main problems:

The first problem of corporate liability is when the company should be punished as a supplement or substitute for punishment of the individual actors; it also involves the legal criteria for determining which actions, of which employees and officials, render the corporation criminally liable.

The second question raised by corporate criminal responsibility is how to punish an organization. With imprisonment not an option, what can be done? If fines are the main weapon, does that sufficiently distinguish criminal penalties from civil ones?

The third issue deals with the *personal* criminal liability of individual employees and officials who act for the corporation. The lesser employees present no special issue; the normal legal doctrines of personal and accomplice liability suffice. The difficulty concerns the individual liability of high officials of corporations, who arguably should sometimes be accountable for the actions of lower-echelon employees even though they would not be liable under the rigorous requirements imposed by the usual doctrines of accomplice liability.

1. Liability of the Corporate Entity

NEW YORK CENTRAL & HUDSON RIVER RAILROAD CO. v. UNITED STATES

United States Supreme Court
212 U.S. 481 (1909)

JUSTICE DAY delivered the opinion of the court.

[The federal Elkins Act, passed in 1903, required common carriers such as railroads to post rates and forbade them from charging less than their posted rates. In this case, both the railroad company and one of its employees, an assistant traffic manager, were convicted for paying rebates to certain companies who shipped products with them, thus effectively lowering the shipping rate in violation of the Elkins Act.]

The principal attack in this court is upon the constitutional validity of certain features of the Elkins act. 32 Stat. 847. That act, among other things, provides:

(1) That anything done or omitted to be done by a corporation common carrier subject to the act to regulate commerce, and the acts amendatory thereof, which, if done or omitted to be done by any director or officer thereof, or any receiver, trustee, lessee, agent or person acting for or employed by such corporation, would constitute a misdemeanor under said acts, or under this act, shall also be held to be a misdemeanor committed by such corporation, and upon conviction thereof it shall be subject to like penalties as are prescribed in said acts, or by this act, with reference to such persons, except as such penalties are herein changed. . . . In construing and enforcing the provisions of this section, the act, omission or failure of any officer, agent or other person acting for or employed by any common carrier, acting within the scope of his employment, shall in every case be also deemed to be the act, omission or failure of such carrier, as well as of that person.

It is contended that these provisions of the law are unconstitutional because Congress has no authority to impute to a corporation the commission of criminal offenses, or to subject a corporation to a criminal prosecution by reason of the things charged. The argument is that to thus punish the corporation is in reality to punish the innocent stockholders, and to deprive them of their property without opportunity to be heard, consequently without due process of law. . . . As no action of the board of directors could legally authorize a crime, and as indeed the stockholders could not do so, the arguments come to this: that owing to the nature and character of its organization and the extent of its power and authority, a corporation cannot commit a crime of the nature charged in this case.

Some of the earlier writers on common law held the law to be that a corporation could not commit a crime. . . . In Blackstone's Commentaries, chapter 18, §12, we find it stated: "A corporation cannot commit treason, or felony, or other crime in its corporate capacity, though its members may in their distinct individual capacities." The modern authority, universally, so far as we know, is the other way. In considering the subject, Bishop's New Criminal Law, §417, devotes a chapter to the capacity of corporations to commit crime, and states the law to be: "Since a corporation acts by its officers and agents their purposes, motives, and intent are just as much those of the corporation as are the things done. If, for example, the invisible, intangible essence of air, which we term a corporation, can level mountains, fill up valleys, lay down iron tracks, and run railroad cars on them, it can intend to do it, and can act therein as well viciously as virtuously." . . .

It is now well established that in actions for tort the corporation may be held responsible for damages for the acts of its agent within the scope of his employment. And this is the rule when the act is done by the agent in the course of his employment, although done wantonly or recklessly or against the express orders of the principal. In such cases the liability is not imputed because the principal actually participates in the malice or fraud, but because the act is done for the benefit of the principal, while the agent is acting within the scope of his employment in the business of the principal, and justice requires that the latter shall be held responsible for damages to the individual who has suffered by such conduct. . . .

It is true that there are some crimes, which in their nature cannot be committed by corporations. But there is a large class of offenses, of which rebating under the Federal statutes is one, wherein the crime consists in purposely doing the things prohibited by statute. In that class of crimes we see no good reason why corporations may not be held responsible for and charged with the knowledge and purposes of their agents, acting within the authority conferred upon them. . . .

It is a part of the public history of the times that statutes against rebates could not be effectually enforced so long as individuals only were subject to punishment for violation of the law, when the giving of rebates or concessions inured to the benefit of the corporations of which the individuals were but the instruments. This situation, developed in more than one report of the Interstate Commerce Commission, was no doubt influential in bringing about the enactment of the Elkins Law, making corporations criminally liable. . . .

We see no valid objection in law, and every reason in public policy, why the corporation, which profits by the transaction, and can only act through its agents and officers, shall be held punishable by fine because of the knowledge and intent of its agents to whom it has intrusted authority to act in the subject-matter of making and fixing rates of transportation, and whose knowledge and purposes may well be attributed to the corporation for which the agents act. [T]he law . . . cannot shut its eyes to the fact that the great majority of business transactions in modern times are conducted through [corporations], and particularly that interstate commerce is almost entirely in their hands, and to give them immunity from all punishment because of the old and exploded doctrine that a corporation cannot commit a crime would virtually take away the only means of effectually controlling the subject-matter and correcting the abuses aimed at. . . .

QUESTIONS

1. Corporate liability in tort vs. crime. As the Court in *New York Central* notes, corporations must pay damages to tort victims for the acts of corporate agents within the scope of their employment. Are the considerations that support criminal liability for corporations the same or different from those that support tort liability? In *New York Central*, which victims would be in a position to sue the defendant for damages? How would damages be measured? If New York Central had destroyed documents, which victims would be in a position to sue for damages? How would *those* damages be measured?

2. Corporate criminal liability for which crimes? The Court states that "It is true there are some crimes, which in their nature cannot be committed by corporations." But as the Court acknowledges, a corporation can act only through its agents, so in theory, a corporation could commit any act that an individual agent could commit, as long as the corporation itself benefits from the crime. To be sure, some crimes (such as murder and rape) are far less likely than others (such as financial crimes) to benefit corporate entities, but that does not mean that they cannot be committed by corporations in some situations.

UNITED STATES v. HILTON HOTELS CORP.

United States Court of Appeals, 9th Circuit
467 F.2d 1000 (1972)

BROWNING, J. This is an appeal from a conviction under an indictment charging a violation of section 1 of the Sherman Act, 15 U.S.C. §1.

Operators of hotels, restaurants, hotel and restaurant supply companies, and other businesses in Portland, Oregon, organized an association to attract conventions to their city. To finance the association, members were asked to make contributions in predetermined amounts. Companies selling supplies to hotels were asked to contribute an amount equal to one per cent of their sales to hotel members. To aid collections, hotel members, including appellant [Hilton Hotels], agreed to give preferential treatment to suppliers who paid their assessments, and to curtail purchases from those who did not. [The Sherman Antitrust Act, passed by Congress in 1890, prohibits all combinations in restraint of trade. In this case, the court of appeals noted that the alleged boycott by the hotel members of suppliers who refused to pay their assessments, if proved, would constitute a per se violation of the Sherman Act. The court then went on to address the separate claim that the hotel could not be liable because it had not authorized the acts of the hotel's purchasing agent who participated in the boycott.]

[The president of Hilton Hotels] testified that it would be contrary to the policy of the corporation for the manager of one of its hotels to condition purchases upon payment of a contribution to a local association by the supplier. The manager of appellant's Portland hotel and his assistant testified that it was the hotel's policy to purchase supplies solely on the basis of price, quality, and service. They also testified that on two occasions they told the hotel's purchasing agent that he was to take no part in the boycott. The purchasing agent confirmed the receipt of these instructions, but admitted that, despite them, he had threatened a supplier with loss of the hotel's business unless the supplier paid the association assessment. He testified that he violated his instructions because of anger and personal pique toward the individual representing the supplier.

Based upon this testimony, appellant requested certain instructions bearing upon the criminal liability of a corporation for the unauthorized acts of its agents. These requests were rejected by the trial court. The court instructed the jury that a corporation is liable for the acts and statements of its agents "within the scope of their employment," defined to mean "in the corporation's behalf in performance of the agent's general line of work," including "not only that which has been authorized by the corporation, but also that which outsiders could reasonably assume the agent would have authority to do." The court added:

> A corporation is responsible for acts and statements of its agents, done or made within the scope of their employment, even though their conduct may be contrary to their actual instructions or contrary to the corporation's stated policies.

Appellant objects only to the court's concluding statement.

Congress may constitutionally impose criminal liability upon a business entity for acts or omissions of its agents within the scope of their employment. Such liability may attach without proof that the conduct was within the agent's actual authority, and even though it may have been contrary to express instructions.

The intention to impose such liability is sometimes express, New York Central & Hudson R.R. Co. v. United States, 212 U.S. 481, but it may also be implied. The text of the Sherman Act does not expressly resolve the issue. For the reasons that follow, however, we think the construction of the Act that best achieves its purpose is that a corporation is liable for acts of its agents within the scope of their authority even when done against company orders. . . .

Legal commentators have argued forcefully that it is inappropriate and ineffective to impose criminal liability upon a corporation, as distinguished from the human agents who actually perform the unlawful acts. . . . But it is the legislative judgment that controls, and "the great mass of legislation calling for corporate criminal liability suggests a widespread belief on the part of legislators that such liability is necessary to effectuate regulatory policy." ALI Model Penal Code, Comment on §2.07, Tentative Draft No. 4, p. 149 (1956). Moreover, the strenuous efforts of corporate defendants to avoid conviction, particularly under the Sherman Act, strongly suggest that Congress is justified in its judgment that exposure of the corporate entity to potential conviction may provide a substantial spur to corporate action to prevent violations by employees.

Because of the nature of Sherman Act offenses and the context in which they normally occur, the factors that militate against allowing a corporation to disown the criminal acts of its agents apply with special force to Sherman Act violations.

Sherman Act violations are commercial offenses. They are usually motivated by a desire to enhance profits.[4] They commonly involve large, complex, and highly decentralized corporate business enterprises, and intricate business processes, practices, and arrangements. More often than not they also involve basic policy decisions, and must be implemented over an extended period of time.

---

4. A purpose to benefit the corporation is necessary to bring the agent's acts within the scope of his employment. Standard Oil Co. v. United States, 307 F.2d 120, 128-129 (5th Cir. 1962).

Complex business structures, characterized by decentralization and delegation of authority, commonly adopted by corporations for business purposes, make it difficult to identify the particular corporate agents responsible for Sherman Act violations. At the same time, it is generally true that high management officials, for whose conduct the corporate directors and stockholders are the most clearly responsible, are likely to have participated in the policy decisions underlying Sherman Act violations, or at least to have become aware of them.

Violations of the Sherman Act are a likely consequence of the pressure to maximize profits that is commonly imposed by corporate owners upon managing agents and, in turn, upon lesser employees. In the face of that pressure, generalized directions to obey the Sherman Act, with the probable effect of foregoing profits, are the least likely to be taken seriously. And if a violation of the Sherman Act occurs, the corporation, and not the individual agents, will have realized the profits from the illegal activity.

In sum, identification of the particular agents responsible for a Sherman Act violation is especially difficult, and their conviction and punishment is peculiarly ineffective as a deterrent. At the same time, conviction and punishment of the business entity itself is likely to be both appropriate and effective.

For these reasons we conclude that as a general rule a corporation is liable under the Sherman Act for the acts of its agents in the scope of their employment, even though contrary to general corporate policy and express instructions to the agent.

Thus the general policy statements of appellant's president were no defense. Nor was it enough that appellant's manager told the purchasing agent that he was not to participate in the boycott. The purchasing agent was authorized to buy all of appellant's supplies. Purchases were made on the basis of specifications, but the purchasing agent exercised complete authority as to source. He was in a unique position to add the corporation's buying power to the force of the boycott. Appellant could not gain exculpation by issuing general instructions without undertaking to enforce those instructions by means commensurate with the obvious risks. . . . Affirmed.

NOTES

1. *The case for corporate liability.* Proponents of corporate criminal liability embrace it for expressive and instrumental reasons. Peter Henning explains the expressive function of corporate criminal liability, observing that "the application of the criminal law to an actor in society is a means to express a moral judgment about that actor's conduct. Corporations are as much a part of modern society as individuals, and so this expressive function of the criminal law is particularly worthwhile when applied to organizations that play such a significant role in the economy and indeed throughout society." Peter J. Henning, Corporate Criminal Liability and the Potential for Rehabilitation, 46 Am. Crim. L. Rev. 1417, 1420 (2009). He further observes

that criminal sanctions are appropriately used when the goal of bringing criminal charges is to rehabilitate the company by changing its corporate culture. Peter Henning, Should the Perception of Corporate Punishment Matter?, 19 J.L. & Pol'y 83, 87 (2010). Samuel Buell argues that, in order to more fully exploit criminal law's expressive power, the blameworthiness of the corporate entity should play a larger role in shaping the prerequisites for corporate criminal liability, as well as the manner in which prosecutorial discretion is exercised. Samuel W. Buell, The Blaming Function of Entity Criminal Liability, 81 Ind. L.J. 473 (2006). The instrumental view emphasizes that corporate criminal liability provides incentives for managers to patrol lower ranking officers and employers and to create a law-abiding corporate culture. This view is reflected in the Department of Justice Manual for United States Attorneys, which states that "[i]ndicting corporations for wrongdoing enables the government to be a force for positive change of corporate culture, and a force to prevent, discover, and punish serious crimes." Dept. of Justice, U.S. Attorneys' Manual, §9-28.200(A).

The Department of Justice is currently investigating whether criminal charges should be brought in relation to the Deepwater Horizon oil spill in the Gulf of Mexico in 2010—the largest marine oil spill in history, which resulted in the deaths of 11 workers. It remains to be seen whether individual or corporate charges will be brought, but those advocating for prosecution highlight these arguments. Thus, David M. Uhlmann argues that "criminal prosecution of the Gulf oil spill is appropriate under a deterrence theory of criminal law and because it expresses societal condemnation of the spill," see David M. Uhlmann, After the Spill is Gone: The Gulf of Mexico, Environmental Crime, and the Criminal Law, 109 Mich. L. Rev. 1413, 1420 (2011). Are criminal charges necessary to express condemnation of the spill? Is it relevant that BP has a record of past incidents resulting in criminal fines?

2. *The case against corporate liability.* Critics of corporate criminal liability question both the expressive and instrumental lines of analysis. Albert Alschuler condemns the expressive view, arguing that "attributing blame to a corporation is no more sensible than attributing blame to a dagger, a fountain pen, a Chevrolet, or any other instrumentality of crime." Albert W. Alschuler, Two Ways to Think About the Punishment of Corporations, 46 Am. Crim. L. Rev. 1359, 1392 (2009). Is Alschuler correct that corporations are mere instrumentalities? The Supreme Court has recognized constitutional rights for corporations, including free speech rights, most recently in Citizens United v. FEC, 130 S. Ct. 876 (2010). If corporations enjoy constitutional protections as entities, why shouldn't they be subject to criminal penalties as well? Sara Sun Beale argues that accepting corporations as separate legal entities dictates that shareholders take the bad with the good. Sara Sun Beale, A Response to Critics of Corporate Criminal Liability, 46 Am. Crim. L. Rev. 1481, 1485 (2009). Is there a meaningful difference between the criteria for conferring privileges and the criteria for importing blame? If so, what is it?

The instrumental view of corporate criminal liability has also come under attack, with critics questioning whether punishment of the corporation deters crime. Some commentators argue that corporate criminal liability spurs excessive monitoring and litigation costs. Daniel R. Fischel & Alan O. Sykes, Corporate Crime, 25 J. Legal Stud. 319 (1996). They argue for a scheme of government-imposed civil penalties based on a claim that civil sanctions will deter wrongdoing more cost-effectively, due to lower procedural hurdles and sanctioning costs. Jennifer Arlen, Corporate Crime and Its Control, in The New Palgrave Dictionary of Economics and the Law 492-497 (Peter Newman ed., 1998). Jennifer Arlen makes an even stronger claim that criminal liability may increase rather than decrease corporate crime because it may lead corporations to relax their monitoring efforts in order to prevent information from coming to the attention of government prosecutors. Jennifer Arlen, The Potentially Perverse Effects of Corporate Criminal Liability, 23 J. Legal Stud. 833 (1994).

3. *Collateral consequences.* While the imposition of criminal liability in other contexts is debated along similar lines, some view corporate criminal liability as raising unique issues because the corporate entity itself, as well as its shareholders, employees, customers, and suppliers, may be a victim of the criminal wrongdoing of corporate agents. Criminal prosecution and punishment of the corporation, which is designed to deter such wrongdoing, will also harm the corporation and these additional (and often wholly innocent) individuals and entities. The case of Arthur Andersen provides one of the most notable examples of these collateral consequences. The criminal conviction of Arthur Andersen, a limited liability partnership that had been one of the largest global accounting firms, for its shredding of audit documents during the Enron scandal, destroyed that firm by ruining its reputation, even though the actual sentence that it received was relatively minor and even though its conviction was later reversed by the Supreme Court. See United States v. Arthur Andersen LLP, 544 U.S. 696 (2005).

Consider the following observations on collateral consequences in Model Penal Code and Commentaries, Comment to §2.07 at 335-339 (1985):

> [Imposing] criminal penalties on corporate bodies results in a species of vicarious liability. . . . In most cases, the shareholders have not participated in the criminal conduct and lack the practical means of supervision of corporate management to prevent misconduct by corporate agents. [T]he fact that the direct impact of corporate fines is felt by a group ordinarily innocent of criminal conduct underscores the point that such fines ought not to be authorized except where they clearly may be expected to accomplish desirable social purposes.
>
> [T]he ultimate justification of corporate criminal responsibility must rest in large measure on an evaluation of the deterrent effects of corporate fines on the conduct of corporate agents. Is there a reason for anticipating a substantially higher degree of deterrence from fines levied on corporate bodies than . . . from proceeding directly against the guilty officer or agent or from other feasible sanctions of a noncriminal character?

. . . If the agent cannot be prevented from committing an offense by the prospect of personal liability, he ordinarily will not be prevented by the prospect of corporate liability. [Yet] there are probably cases in which the economic pressures within the corporate body are sufficiently potent to tempt individuals to hazard personal liability for the sake of company gain, especially where the penalties threatened are moderate and where the offense does not involve behavior condemned as highly immoral by the individual's associates.

Are the problems with corporate criminal liability unique, or are they endemic to criminal law? For an argument that corporate criminal liability is no different from the rest of criminal law in terms of the issues it raises, see Sara Sun Beale, Is Corporate Criminal Liability Unique?, 44 Am. Crim. L. Rev. 1503 (2007).

4. The respondeat superior approach. The use of the tort doctrine of respondeat superior to define the prerequisites of corporate criminal liability, as developed in the *New York Central* and *Hilton Hotels* cases, is one of the two main approaches to corporate liability in the United States. (The other is the more restrictive doctrine of the MPC, which is discussed infra page 794.) The requirements of liability under the respondeat superior approach are summarized in Note, Developments in the Law—Corporate Crime: Regulating Corporate Behavior Through Criminal Sanctions, 92 Harv. L. Rev. 1227, 1247-1251 (1979):

> Under the doctrine of respondeat superior, a corporation may be held criminally liable for the acts of any of its agents if an agent (1) commits a crime (2) within the scope of employment (3) with the intent to benefit the corporation.
>
> First, it must be proved that an illegal act was committed by an agent of the corporation, and that the agent acted with the specific intent required by the governing statute. [I]t is not necessary to prove that a specific person acted illegally, only that *some* agent of the corporation committed the crime. Thus, proving that a corporate defendant committed the illegal act is in practice substantially easier than an individual prosecution. . . .
>
> Second, to establish corporate liability under the doctrine of respondeat superior, the prosecution must show that the illegal act was committed within the agent's scope of employment. The traditional agency definition limits scope of employment to conduct that is authorized, explicitly or implicitly, by the principal or that is similar or incidental to authorized conduct. However, courts generally find conduct to fall within the scope of employment even if it was specifically forbidden by a superior and occurred despite good faith efforts on the part of the corporation to prevent the crime. Thus, scope of employment in practice means little more than that the act occurred while the offending employee was carrying out a job-related activity. . . .
>
> Third, it must be proved that the agent committed the crime with the intent to benefit the corporation. The corporation may be held criminally liable even if it received no actual benefit from the offense, although the existence or absence of benefit is relevant as evidence of an intent to benefit.
>
> The requirements of scope of employment and intent to benefit the corporation can also be met through ratification. When an employee commits a

crime with no intent to benefit the corporation, or while acting outside the scope of his employment, subsequent approval of the act by his supervisor will be sufficient to hold the corporation liable for the employee's criminal act. In a sense, under the doctrine of ratification, a corporation is culpable for approving the criminal act, rather than committing it.

5. *Intent to benefit the corporation.* The reach of the respondeat superior doctrine is exhibited in United States v. Sun-Diamond Growers of California, 138 F.3d 961 (D.C. Cir. 1997). Defendant Sun-Diamond (an agricultural cooperative entity) was charged with wire fraud and illegal campaign contributions. Douglas, an officer of the defendant with some responsibility for lobbying, devised a fraudulent scheme to conceal his misappropriation of the defendant's funds to support the congressional campaign of the brother of the secretary of agriculture, Mike Espy. The court upheld a conviction of Douglas's employer, stating at 970:

> Sun-Diamond says Douglas's scheme was designed to—and did in fact— defraud his employer, not benefit it. In this circumstance, it strenuously argues, there can be no imputation: "[T]o establish precedent holding a principal criminally liable for the acts of an agent who defrauds and deceives the principal while pursuing matters within his self-interest merely because the agent's conduct may provide some incidental benefit to the principal serves to punish innocent principals with no countervailing policy justifications."
>
> This argument has considerable intuitive appeal—Sun-Diamond does look more like a victim than a perpetrator, at least on the fraud charges. The facts in the record, however—that Douglas hid the illegal contribution scheme from others at the company and used company funds to accomplish it—do not preclude a valid finding that he undertook the scheme to benefit Sun-Diamond. Part of Douglas's job was to cultivate his, and Sun-Diamond's, relationship with Secretary Espy. By responding to the Secretary's request to help his brother, Douglas may have been acting out of pure friendship, but the jury was entitled to conclude that he was instead, or also, with an intent (however befuddled) to further the interests of his employer. The scheme came at some cost to Sun-Diamond but it also promised some benefit. . . . Where there is adequate evidence for imputation (as here), the only thing that keeps deceived corporations from being indicted for the acts of their employee-deceivers is not some fixed rule of law or logic but simply the sound exercise of prosecutorial discretion.
>
> And the answer to Sun-Diamond's claim of the absence of any "countervailing policy justification" is simply the justification usually offered in support of holding corporate principals liable for the illegal acts of their agents: to increase incentives for corporations to monitor and prevent illegal employee conduct.

6. *The exercise of prosecutorial discretion.* Despite the potential breadth of the doctrine of respondeat superior, prosecutors can and do use their charging discretion to forgo corporate prosecution in some cases. For example, prosecutors may choose not to prosecute the company when they believe the corporation itself is the primary victim of the offense, as was clear in the stunning collapse of Enron Corporation in the wake of massive fraud committed by several of its chief officers. In the prosecution of Andrew

Fastow, Enron's chief financial officer, the indictment listed Enron as the first "victim" of the offense. Though several of Fastow's alleged actions could be viewed as benefiting the company by defrauding investors, many of them also defrauded Enron itself. As a result, the government declined to prosecute Enron. See Alan C. Michaels, Fastow and Arthur Andersen: Some Reflections on Corporate Criminality, Victim Status, and Retribution, 1 Ohio St. J. Crim. L. 551 (2004). Reconsider, supra pages 700-701, the decision of the MPC and many jurisdictions to adopt a formal rule of law exempting victims of crime from criminal liability as accomplices, regardless of their technical eligibility under ordinary accomplice liability principles. Should the same rule apply in the context of corporate criminal liability?

The status of the corporation as "victim" is not the only consideration relevant to the exercise of prosecutorial discretion. Because the doctrine of respondeat superior is so broad that it allows criminal prosecution of corporations in vastly more cases than the government could possibly wish to pursue, prosecutors consider other factors as well. A Justice Department memo authored by then-Deputy Attorney General Eric H. Holder, Jr., offering line prosecutors guidance on "Bringing Charges Against Corporations," stated that among the factors to be considered are the "pervasiveness of wrongdoing within the corporation, including the complicity in, or condonation of, the wrongdoing by corporate management" and any "collateral consequences, including disproportionate harm to shareholders and employees not proven personally culpable," as well as the "adequacy of non-criminal remedies, such as civil or regulatory enforcement actions."[10]

In the wake of the Enron scandal and other large-scale corporate wrong-doing, the Justice Department in 2002 created the Corporate Fraud Task Force with a mission to strengthen the efforts to investigate and prosecute corporate crime. The Department also released a follow-up memo to the Holder Memo on corporate charging considerations. Authored by then-Deputy Attorney General Larry D. Thompson, the "Thompson Memo" reaffirmed factors from the Holder Memo and also asked prosecutors to consider "whether the corporation, while purporting to cooperate, has engaged in conduct that impedes the investigation (whether or not rising to the level of criminal obstruction)."[11] The Thompson Memo thus focused on the corporation's cooperation as a key factor in deciding whether or not to prosecute. See generally Harry First, Branch Office of the Prosecutor: The New Role of the Corporation in Business Crime Prosecutions, 89 N.C. L. Rev. 23 (2010); Lisa Kern Griffin, Compelled Cooperation and the New Corporate Criminal Procedure, 82 N.Y.U. L. Rev. 311, 332 (2007).

How should corporate cooperation be assessed? The Thompson Memo allowed prosecutors to consider the corporation's "willingness to cooperate in the investigation of its agents, including, if necessary, the waiver of

---

10. Justice Department Guidance on Prosecutions of Corporations, 66 Crim. L. Rep. 189, 190 (Dec. 8, 1999).

11. Memorandum from Larry D. Thompson, Deputy Attorney General, to Heads of Department Components on Principles of Federal Prosecution of Business Organizations 9 (Jan. 20, 2003).

corporate attorney-client and work product protection." Corporations responded by waiving attorney-client privilege and limiting payments for employees' legal fees. The Justice Department, in turn, used such corporate assistance to secure over 1,000 indictments and convictions against individuals since the creation of the Corporate Fraud Task Force. But recent developments establish that there are lines federal prosecutors cannot cross in these negotiations. In 2005, the accounting firm KPMG entered into an agreement with the federal government in which it admitted to using fraudulent tax shelters and resolved to "clean house" by refusing to pay its employees' legal fees and by threatening to fire them unless they cooperated with the government's investigation. The Second Circuit held that the company's refusal to pay legal fees deprived the employees of their right to counsel under the Sixth Amendment. United States v. Stein, 541 F.3d 130, 137, 151 (2d Cir. 2008). In 2006, Senator Arlen Specter proposed legislation that would prohibit the Department of Justice from insisting on the waiver of attorney-client privilege.[12] To ward off the legislation and answer its critics, the Department of Justice updated its corporate charging policy to discourage prosecutors from requesting that corporations withhold employee legal fees or from seeking waivers of attorney-client privilege. The Department now emphasizes that the question of corporate cooperation should turn on the "disclosure of relevant *facts*," regardless of whether the corporation waived attorney-client privilege.[13]

Since the issuance of the Thompson Memo, the Department has curtailed indictments against corporations themselves, opting instead to pursue deferred prosecution agreements (DPAs) or non-prosecution agreements (NPAs) with corporations. These agreements have become the preferred course for federal prosecutors. See Leonard Orland, The Transformation of Corporate Criminal Law, 1 Brook. J. Corp. Fin. & Com. L. 45, 45 (2006) (observing in 2006 that since 2003, "every major federal case of corporate misconduct has been resolved without filing an indictment against the corporation"). Pursuant to these agreements, the government agrees not to prosecute the company in exchange for corporate concessions. With NPAs, the government does not file charges in court but retains the right to prosecute later if the company does not meet the terms of the agreement. With DPAs, charges are filed, but once the company fulfills the terms of the agreement, the government dismisses the charges.

7. Collective knowledge. Although the preceding Notes indicate that the respondeat superior test for liability often is arguably over-inclusive, that test sometimes can present the opposite problem. In Corporate Culpability Under

---

12. Attorney-Client Privilege Protection Act of 2006, S.30, 109th Cong. (2006). The bill was reintroduced in subsequent sessions but has not become law as of this writing.

13. U.S. Dept. of Justice, Memorandum from Mark Filip, Deputy Attorney General, to Heads of Department Components and United States Attorneys, Principles of Federal Prosecution of Business Organizations, Aug. 28, 2008, available at http://www.justice.gov/dag/readingroom/dag-memo-08282008.pdf.

the Federal Sentencing Guidelines, 34 Ariz. L. Rev. 743 (1992), Jennifer Moore criticizes the doctrine of respondeat superior in part for being under-inclusive in some circumstances:

> There are some situations in which corporate policies or procedures do cause a crime, yet the doctrine of respondeat superior is unable to find the corporation culpable because there is no individual culpability to impute.
>
> A . . . way in which courts have coped with the problem of underinclu-siveness is the development of the "collective knowledge" doctrine. This doc-trine enables courts to find liability in cases in which the corporation seems "justly to blame" for the crime, but no single individual has the required mens rea. It permits a finding of corporate mens rea to be derived from the collective knowledge of the corporation's members. In United States v. Bank of New England, N.A., for example, the bank was found guilty of "willfully" violating the Currency Transaction Reporting Act even though no one of its agents was found to have had the required "willfulness." . . . The fact that some employees were aware of the Act's reporting requirements, while other employees were aware of the transactions, was enough to constitute willfulness on the part of the Bank.

Is aggregating the knowledge of individuals within an entity, to establish the culpability (knowledge) of the entity itself, consistent with the derivative nature of entity liability?

PROBLEM

A nursing home patient, McCauley, suffered from dementia and had attempted to leave through the facility's front doors on numerous occasions. A doctor concluded that McCauley was at risk of leaving the nursing home again if left unattended, so he ordered that she wear a security bracelet at all times that would have set off an alarm and locked the front doors when she approached them. An employee of the nursing home mistakenly removed the physician's order from McCauley's treatment sheet, and the omission of the order was not discovered during the monthly editing process of the patients' charts. One spring evening, a nurse from a unit other than McCauley's was on duty and did not realize McCauley was supposed to be wearing a bracelet because it was not in her chart. When McCauley was placed in her wheelchair near the front doors, no nurse stood guard. McCauley went through the front doors, fell down the stairs, and died from the injuries she sustained. Could the nursing home, as a corporation, be charged under the theory of involuntary manslaughter discussed in *Welansky*, supra page 464, based upon a theory of collective knowledge, even in the absence of a specific employee with the requisite mens rea under *Welansky*? The court in Commwealth v. Life Care Centers of America, 926 N.E.2d 206, 212 (Mass. 2010), rejected the collective knowledge theory, holding that "a corporation acts with a given mental state in a criminal context only if at least one employee who acts (or fails to act) possesses the requisite mental state at the time of the act (or failure to act)." The breadth of respondeat superior liability is premised on the idea that the entity generally bears responsibility for the acts of its agents. If no individual agent is responsible, how can the entity be responsible?

COMMONWEALTH v. BENEFICIAL FINANCE CO.

Supreme Judicial Court of Massachusetts
360 Mass. 188, 275 N.E.2d 33 (1971)

SPIEGEL, J. [Individual and corporate defendants, including Beneficial Finance Co., were convicted of bribing, and conspiring to bribe, state banking officials in order to obtain favorable treatment from the state Small Loans Regulatory Board. The corporate convictions were based on acts committed by employees who were neither officers nor directors of the corporation. One of the employees, Farrell, was an officer and director of Beneficial Management Co., a wholly owned subsidiary of BFC. Another, Glynn, reported to Farrell but was on the payroll of Industrial Bankers, another wholly owned BFC subsidiary. Glynn had direct contact with the state officials who were bribed. Farrell supervised Glynn's activities and also chaired an inter-corporate meeting at which the bribery plan was adopted.]

The defendants and the Commonwealth have proposed differing standards upon which the criminal responsibility of a corporation should be predicated. The defendants argue that a corporation should not be held criminally liable for the conduct of its servants or agents unless such conduct was performed, authorized, ratified, adopted or tolerated by the corporations' directors, officers or other "high managerial agents" who are sufficiently high in the corporate hierarchy to warrant the assumption that their acts in some substantial sense reflect corporate policy. This standard is that adopted by [the MPC]. . . . Section 2.07 of the Code provides that, except in the case of regulatory offences and offences consisting of the omission of a duty imposed on corporations by law, a corporation may be convicted of a crime if "the commission of the offence was authorized, requested, commanded, performed or recklessly tolerated by the board of directors or by a high managerial agent acting in behalf of the corporation within the scope of his office or employment." The section proceeds to define "high managerial agent" as "an officer of a corporation . . . or any other agent . . . having duties of such responsibility that his conduct may fairly be assumed to represent the policy of the corporation."

The Commonwealth, on the other hand, argues that the standard applied by the judge in his instructions to the jury was correct. These instructions, which prescribe a somewhat more flexible standard than that delineated in the Model Penal Code, state in part, as follows:

[T]he Commonwealth does not have to prove that the individual who acted criminally was expressly requested or authorized in advance by the corporation to do so, nor must the Commonwealth prove that the corporation expressly ratified or adopted that criminal conduct on the part of that individual or those individuals. [Nor must the Commonwealth prove] that the individual who acted criminally was a member of the corporation's board of directors, or that he was a high officer in the corporation, or that he held any office at all. [Rather, the jury] should consider what the authority of that person was as such officer in relation to the corporation. The mere fact that he has a title is not enough to make the corporation liable for his criminal conduct. The Commonwealth must prove that the individual for whose conduct it seeks to charge the corporation criminally was placed in a position by the corporation where he had enough power, duty, responsibility and authority to act for and in behalf of the corporation to handle the particular business . . . of the corporation in which he was engaged at the time that he committed the criminal act, with power of decision as to what he would or would not do while acting for the corporation, and that he was acting for and in behalf of the corporation in the accomplishment of that particular business. . . .

The difference between the judge's instructions to the jury and the Model Penal Code lies largely in the latter's reference to a "high managerial agent" and in the Code requirement that to impose corporate criminal liability, it at least must appear that its directors or high managerial agent "authorized . . . or recklessly tolerated" the allegedly criminal acts. The judge's instructions focus on the authority of the corporate agent in relation to the particular corporate business in which the agent was engaged. The Code seems to require that there be authorization or reckless inaction by a corporate representative having some relation to framing corporate policy, or one "having duties of such responsibility that his conduct may fairly be assumed to represent the policy of the corporation." Close examination of the judge's instructions reveals that they preserve the underlying "corporate policy" rationale of the Code by allowing the jury to infer "corporate policy" from the position in which the corporation placed the agent in commissioning him to handle the particular corporate affairs in which he was engaged at the time of the criminal act.

[The court then analyzed prior Massachusetts cases concerning vicarious criminal liability and found "a long line of decisions in this Commonwealth holding that before criminal responsibility can be imposed on the master, based on a master-servant relationship under the doctrine of respondeat superior, actual participation in, or approval of, the servant's criminal act must be shown." The court then distinguished the cases from the case of corporate liability where liability is necessarily vicarious:]

[T]he very nature of a corporation as a "person" before the law renders it impossible to equate the imposition of vicarious liability on a human principal with the imposition of vicarious liability on a corporate principal. . . . Thus, the issue is not whether vicarious liability should be imposed on a corporation under the "direct participation and assent rule" of the master-servant cases cited above, but rather, whether the acts and intent of natural persons . . . can be treated as the acts and intent of the corporation itself. For the foregoing reasons, despite the strenuous urging of the defendants, we are unconvinced that the standard for imposing criminal responsibility on a human principal adequately deals with the evidentiary problems which are inherent in ascribing the acts of individuals to a corporate entity. . . .

[The court then addressed one defendant's objection that applying a rule of corporate responsibility for the acts of low-level employees imposes criminal liability based upon a civil law standard.]

It may be that the theoretical principles underlying this standard are, in general, the same as embodied in the rule of respondeat superior. Nevertheless, as we observed at the outset, the judge's instructions, as a whole and in context, required a greater quantum of proof in the practical application of this standard than is required in a civil case. In focusing on the "kinship" between the authority of an individual and the act he committed, the judge emphasized that the jury must be satisfied "beyond a reasonable doubt" that the act of the individual "*constituted*" the act of the corporation. Juxtaposition of the traditional criminal law requirement of ascertaining guilt beyond a reasonable doubt (as opposed to the civil law standard of the preponderance of the evidence), with the rule of respondeat superior, fully justifies application of the standard enunciated by the judge to a criminal prosecution against a corporation for a crime requiring specific intent.

The foregoing is especially true in view of the particular circumstances of this case. In order to commit the crimes charged in these indictments, the defendant corporations either had to offer to pay money to a public official or conspire to do so. The disbursal of funds is an act peculiarly within the ambit of corporate activity. These corporations by the very nature of their business are constantly dealing with the expenditure and collection of moneys. It could hardly be expected that any of the individual defendants would conspire to pay, or would pay, the substantial amount of money here involved, namely $25,000, out of his own pocket. The jury would be warranted in finding that the disbursal of such an amount of money would come from the corporate treasury. A reasonable inference could therefore be drawn that the payment of such money by the corporations was done as a matter of corporate policy and as a reflection of corporate intent, thus comporting with the underlying rationale of the Model Penal Code, and probably with its specific requirements.

Moreover, we do not think that the Model Penal Code standard really purports to deal with the evidentiary problems which are inherent in establishing the quantum of proof necessary to show that the directors or officers of a corporation authorize, ratify, tolerate, or participate in the criminal acts of an agent when such acts are apparently performed on behalf of the corporation. Evidence of such authorization or ratification is too easily susceptible of concealment. As is so trenchantly stated by the judge: "Criminal acts are not usually made the subject of votes of authorization or ratification by corporate Boards of Directors; and the lack of such votes does not prevent the act from being the act of the corporation." . . .

Additional factors of importance are the size and complexity of many large modern corporations which necessitate the delegation of more authority to lesser corporate agents and employees. As the judge pointed out: "There are not enough seats on the Board of Directors, nor enough offices in a corporation, to permit the corporation engaged in widespread operations to give such a title or office to every person in whom it places the power, authority, and responsibility for decision and action." This latter consideration lends credence to the view that the title or position of an individual in a corporation should not be conclusively determinative in ascribing criminal responsibility. In a large corporation, with many numerous and distinct departments, a high ranking corporate officer or agent may have no authority or involvement in a particular sphere of corporate activity, whereas a lower ranking corporate executive might have much broader power in dealing with a matter peculiarly within the scope of his authority. Employees who are in the lower echelon of the corporate hierarchy often exercise more responsibility in the *everyday operations* of the corporation than the directors or officers. Assuredly, the title or office that the person holds may be considered, but it should not be the decisive criterion upon which to predicate corporate responsibility. . . .

[W]e are of opinion that the quantum of proof necessary to sustain the conviction of a corporation for the acts of its agents is sufficiently met if it is shown that the corporation has placed the agent in a position where he has enough authority and responsibility to act for and in behalf of the corporation in handling the *particular* corporate business, operation or project in which he was engaged at the time he committed the criminal act. The judge properly instructed the jury to this effect and correctly stated that this standard does not depend upon the responsibility or authority which the agent has with respect to the entire corporate business, but only to his position with relation to the particular business in which he was serving the corporation.

[The court then held there was sufficient evidence to support a finding of a liability based on the conduct of Farrell and Glynn.]

Question: Is the Massachusetts Supreme Judicial Court right that even a low-level employee's criminal acts may reflect "corporate policy"? Consider how this approach compares with the "high managerial agent" standard as discussed in the opinions in the case that follows.

State v. Community Alternatives Missouri, Inc., 267 S.W.3d 735 (Mo. Ct. App. 2008): [The court upheld the conviction of a corporation that operated a group home facility for resident neglect after a resident of the home died as a result of medical complications from untreated bed sores. Resident neglect is a crime in Missouri defined in relevant part as knowingly failing to provide reasonable and necessary medical care. The defendant corporation operated more than 30 group homes, which were divided among three major divisions in the company (North, Central, and South). Turtle Creek, the group home facility where the resident died, was in the South division, which was run by an executive director and an associate director who oversaw the 13 different homes in that division. Mary Collura was the lead staff person at Turtle Creek, and her responsibilities included managing residents' medical care and supervising the staff at both Turtle Creek and a second group home. The issue in the case was whether the corporation's criminal liability could be based on the fact that Collura knowingly tolerated the lack of medical treatment for the resident. In order to uphold liability against the corporation under state law, Collura had to be a "high managerial agent," which was defined as "an officer of a corporation or any other agent in a position of comparable authority with respect to . . . the supervision in a managerial capacity of subordinate employees." The corporation argued that Collura was not a high managerial agent because she was a low-level employee in the overall structure of the sprawling company. The court rejected this argument:] In this case, defendant operated many facilities, or business units, under a single corporate ownership. Each business unit had personnel responsible for the care of the residents at its facility. This court does not perceive the legislative intent . . . to have been to treat large corporations with numerous operating units different from those that operate a single or a few business units. . . . Mary Collura managed and supervised the employees responsible for providing patient care. She determined what medical care would be afforded [the victim] pursuant to the business structure prescribed by the defendant. She was defendant's "lead staff person" at Turtle Creek. . . . [She] gave job evaluations, disciplined support staff through written reprimands, and made recommendations regarding hiring and firing of support staff. . . . Collura was the only manager who was regularly present at Turtle Creek.

[Judge Scott wrote a concurring opinion explaining his difficulty defining "high managerial agent":] Research has not settled my difficulties interpreting our "high managerial agent" (HMA) definition or applying it to this case, in which the State focuses on definitional language about supervising subordinate employees, while Defendant emphasizes the clause about authority comparable to a corporate officer. [Judge Scott then explained his research, which included looking at the MPC provision defining a HMA as one whose "conduct may fairly be assumed to represent the policy of the corporation." Judge Scott noted that Missouri, like other states, has opted for a broader definition of HMA that includes "persons who manage and supervise employees."] [C]orporations range from one-man shows to multinational enterprises with thousands of branch locations. Even in the latter scenario, the flexibility of modern corporate laws and structures could enable "branch managers" to exercise authority comparable to that of a corporate officer, at least within their sphere of influence and with respect to their subordinate employees. To the extent a corporation authorized or permitted branch managers to so act, it would seem appropriate to impute corporate criminal responsibility arising from or relating to those actions.[3]

NOTES

1. *The Model Penal Code approach.* The MPC provisions, like the Missouri approach, represent an attempt to cut back on the traditional scope of

---

3. That said, I reject the State's arguments to the extent they suggest that any manager who supervises subordinate employees could be deemed a HMA. I believe this interpretation could extend corporate criminal liability far beyond our legislature's intent.

corporate liability based on respondeat superior. Their influence may be seen in a number of state revisions. See Model Penal Code and Commentaries, Comment to §2.07 at 340, n.18 (1985). Professor Brickey summarizes the Model Penal Code proposals as follows (Kathleen F. Brickey, Rethinking Corporate Liability Under the Model Penal Code, 19 Rutgers L.J. 593, 596-598 (1988)):

> The Code adopts a trifurcated scheme of corporate liability that draws intersecting lines between acts and omissions, between true crimes and regulatory offenses, and between the operatives who are the "hands" of the corporation and the policy makers who constitute its "mind."
>
> Among the most expansive of the three rules is section 2.07(1)(a), which adopts a broad respondeat superior theory of liability. Under this rule, a corporation may incur liability for minor infractions and for non-Code penal offenses when a legislative purpose to impose liability on corporations "plainly appears," provided that the conduct constituting the offense is performed by a corporate agent acting within the scope of his employment and on behalf of the corporation.
>
> The potential reach of the (1)(a) liability rule is limited, however, by the availability of a due diligence defense. Proof that "the high managerial agent having supervisory responsibility over the subject matter of the offense employed due diligence to prevent its commission" exonerates the corporation from criminal liability.
>
> The second rule of corporate liability pertains to omissions as opposed to acts. Subsection (1)(b) provides that a corporation is accountable for failure to discharge specific duties imposed on corporations by law. Neither the text of this provision nor the comments address the question of whose omission may lead to liability.
>
> The third rule of liability is by far the most restrictive. Under subsection (1)(c), a corporation will incur liability for true crimes—that is, for an offense defined in the Penal Code—only if the conduct constituting the offense is authorized, commanded, solicited, performed, or recklessly tolerated by the board of directors or a "high managerial agent" whose acquiescence to the wrongdoing—by virtue of his position of authority—may fairly be regarded as reflecting corporate policy.

The MPC proposals have been criticized for providing both too much and too little criminal liability for corporations. As for providing too much liability, some argue that the broad respondeat superior liability proposed for certain minor offenses under §2.07(1)(a) inappropriately extends corporate liability for acts of those outside the "inner circle" of management who make up the "mens" or mind of the corporation. Gerhard O.W. Mueller, Mens Rea and the Corporation: A Study of the Model Penal Code Position on Corporate Criminal Liability, 19 U. Pitt. L. Rev. 21, 41 (1957). As for providing too little liability, some contend that, because of insurmountable difficulties of proof, "a liability rule requiring proof that a high managerial agent ratified a subordinate's misconduct is apt to be, in practice, a rule of no liability at all." Brickey, supra, 19 Rutgers L.J. at 626.

Questions: (a) Reconsider the *Hilton Hotels* case, supra. Would criminal liability be imposed on the corporation under the MPC approach? *(b)* Assuming that corporate liability should be limited to those acts by high-level officials, what is the best way to define those officials? Is the MPC approach too restrictive? Does the broadening to individuals with supervisory authority make sense, or does defining a high managerial agent as anyone with supervisory responsibility sweep too far?

2. *Other alternatives.* Missouri, along with other states, relies on the high managerial agent approach of the MPC, but defines those agents more expansively. Commentators have floated a number of other alternatives to the MPC and respondeat superior approaches for dealing with corporate criminality. One alternative involves strategies to influence the internal functioning of the corporation. For instance, to encourage compliance programs, some commentators argue that "where it seeks to charge a corporation as a defendant, the government should bear the burden of establishing as an additional element that the corporation failed to have reasonably effective policies and procedures to prevent the conduct." Andrew Weissmann & David Newman, Rethinking Criminal Corporate Liability, 82 Ind. L.J. 411, 414 (2007). A related proposal would replace entity-based criminal liability with "compliance insurance," in which "insurance carriers would encourage organizations to monitor and police their employees through privately negotiated insurance policies." Under this scheme, insurance carriers would set their premiums to reflect the risk that a corporation's employees would commit a crime. The higher the risk, the higher the premiums, thus encouraging companies to monitor and deter misconduct through compliance programs. In return, the insurance companies would cover any civil penalties that resulted from employee misconduct. Miriam Hechler Baer, Insuring Corporate Crime, 83 Ind. L.J. 1035, 1041 (2008).

The recognition that the internal functioning of a corporation plays a significant role in promoting or preventing the criminal behavior of individual corporate agents has led some theorists to generate yet another model of corporate criminal liability that is not derivative of an agent's individual liability, but rather based on a conception of the corporation itself as the culpable entity, as "a true, independent player in the system, with powers and identity of its own . . . a living cell, possessing an identity that is separate from the molecules forming it." Eli Lederman, Models for Imposing Corporate Criminal Liability: From Adaptation and Imitation Toward Aggregation and the Search for Self-Identity, 4 Buff. Crim. L. Rev. 641, 646 (2000). Consider the following proposal to base corporate liability on systemic conditions of corporate operation:

> [E]ach corporate entity has a distinct and identifiable personality or "ethos." The government can convict a corporation under this standard only if it proves that the corporate ethos encouraged agents of the corporation to commit the criminal act. Central to this approach is the assumption that organizations possess an identity that is independent of specific individuals who control or work for the organization.
>
> [In determining] whether there existed a corporate ethos that encouraged the criminal conduct . . . factfinders should examine the corporation's internal

structure. . . . Beginning with the corporate hierarchy, the factfinders should determine whether the directors' supervision of officers, or management's supervision of employees was dilatory. Next, factfinders should examine the corporate goals, as communicated to the employees, to determine whether these goals could be achieved only by disregarding the law. The third and fourth factors focus on the corporation's affirmative steps to educate and monitor employees and are more relevant in some fields than others. . . . The factfinders should [also] assess . . . how the corporation has reacted to past violations, to further evaluate whether the corporation encourages or discourages illegal behavior. . . .

The . . . corporate ethos standard . . . rewards those corporations that make efforts to educate and motivate their employees to follow the letter and spirit of the law. This encourages responsible corporate behavior. This advantage is in sharp contrast to the Model Penal Code's standard of liability that discourages higher echelon employees from properly supervising lower echelon employees. This advantage also contrasts with the minimal deterrence achieved by imposing criminal liability on individuals within the corporation. Convicting individual agents and employees of a corporation does not stop other corporate employees from committing future criminal acts if sufficient internal corporate pressure to violate the law continues to exist. In such an environment, the agents are cogs in a wheel. Those convicted are simply replaced by others whose original propensity to obey the law is similarly overcome by a corporate ethos that encourages illegal acts. Unless inside or outside forces change the lawless ethos, it will corrupt each generation of corporate agents. The proposed standard of liability addresses this problem by punishing any corporation that establishes a lawless ethos which overcomes its employees' propensity to obey the law.

Pamela H. Bucy, Corporate Ethos: A Standard for Imposing Corporate Criminal Liability, 75 Minn. L. Rev. 1095, 1099-1101, 1145 (1991). A related approach is to require as a prerequisite to criminal liability that the corporation encourage or actively abet criminal conduct by an employee, thus imposing for entity criminal liability the same actus reus standard of accomplice liability that applies to individuals. Corporations would thus be liable, for example, when "[o]fficers of the firm instigated and finalized the unlawful course of conduct, and corporate policies rewarded employees for engaging in it." Geraldine Scott Moohr, Of Bad Apples and Bad Trees: Considering Fault-Based Liability for the Complicit Corporation, 44 Am. Crim. L. Rev. 1343, 1353 (2007).

2. Punishing the Corporate Entity: The Problem of Sanctions

INTRODUCTORY NOTE

Baron Thurlow, a Lord Chancellor of England, observed that a corporation has "no soul to damn, no body to kick." John C. Coffee, "No Soul to Damn, No Body to Kick": An Unscandalized Inquiry into the Problem of Corporate Punishment, 79 Mich. L. Rev. 386, 386 (1981). Thus, one of the traditional means of criminal punishment—incarceration—is not an option. What sanctions are available?

UNITED STATES v. GUIDANT LLC

United States District Court, District of Minnesota
708 F. Supp. 2d 903 (2010)

FRANK, J. On April 5, 2010, Guidant, LLC ("Guidant") entered pleas of guilty on two misdemeanor counts charged by the Government in the Information. [F]or the reasons set forth below, the Court declines to accept the Plea Agreement as currently drafted.

[Guidant developed, manufactured, and sold implantable cardioverter defibrillators ("ICDs"), which are medical devices implanted in a patient to treat abnormally fast heart rhythms that could result in sudden cardiac death. Two of Guidant's ICD models had a defect that could cause short-circuiting, rendering the device nonfunctional. Guidant discovered and later fixed the defects, but did not notify the Food and Drug Administration ("FDA") in the time and manner required by law. Guidant agreed to a plea agreement with the Government whereby it would plead guilty to two misdemeanor counts: (1) making materially false and misleading statements on reports required to be filed with the FDA, and (2) failing to promptly notify the FDA of a medical device correction.]

[In addition to the guilty pleas, the] Plea Agreement further provides that the parties "recommend jointly that the Court impose a sentence requiring Guidant to pay the United States a criminal fine of $253,962,251 pursuant to 18 U.S.C. §3571(d)." The Plea Agreement also provides that Guidant will agree to a "criminal forfeiture to the United States in the amount of $42,079,675" and a special assessment of $250 pursuant to 18 U.S.C. §3013. In the Plea Agreement, the parties jointly agreed not to include a provision that ordered restitution or probation. . . .

In addition to the alleged victims, Drs. Hauser and Maron urge the Court to reject any plea agreement that does not contain a probation provision:

> Also at issue in this case is the safety of future generations of patients who receive medical devices. Manufacturers control the quality of their products. Manufacturers are the first to know when a medical device is dangerous or underperforming. Thus, it is in the best interest of patients, and society in general, for manufacturers to be liable for the safety and effectiveness of their products. To allow a repeat offender, like Guidant, to escape with a fine (that is entirely borne by the shareholders of Boston Scientific [which acquired Guidant]) does not hold the guilty parties fully accountable and inevitably undermines patient safety.

There is no dispute concerning the validity, in general, of placing a corporation on probation. The Court respectfully disagrees with the Government's view that probation would be a waste of the taxpayers' money, especially given that Guidant could be required, as a condition of probation, to reimburse the Government for any costs associated with its probation. The Court also disagrees with the Government's position that Guidant's current corporate structure renders any probation meaningless. . . . The interests of justice are not served by allowing a company to avoid probation simply by changing their corporate form. At a minimum, the public's interest in accountability would be served by Guidant and Boston Scientific being placed on probation, regardless of the fact that Boston Scientific acquired Guidant after the events in question. And, the Court believes that a period of probation would likely benefit, rather than harm, Guidant's and Boston Scientific's public image. . . .

The Court believes that a term of probation would be appropriate in this case and could be fashioned in a manner to serve the public's interest and address the accountability concerns raised by Drs. Hauser and Maron and likely shared by many others. For instance, as a condition of probation, Guidant, through Boston Scientific, could be ordered to perform community service designed to repair the harm caused by its offenses, namely to help build the public's confidence in the FDA regulation process, the medical device manufacturers' quality control efforts, and the cardiac healthcare industry in general. Indeed, Boston Scientific could be ordered, as a condition of probation and in addition to a criminal fine, to dedicate a certain amount of its resources to some of its already-established charitable programs. . . .

Guidant, through Boston Scientific, could also be required to establish a compliance and ethics program, or if one is already established, to dedicate additional resources to that program to address the specific crimes in this case. Such a program could be overseen by a compliance officer skilled in the regulatory area and who perhaps could work in coordination with either the FDA or the Heart Rhythm Society, or both. . . .

As Guidant alluded to at the plea hearing, sophisticated medical devices, such as the ones at issue in this case, generally have a very high rate of reliability and provide life-saving benefits to many people. Advances in medical technology have, unfortunately, inflated the public's expectations so much so that when any device fails, many assume that there must have been a crime committed or that someone is at fault. This is not necessarily always the case. . . .

IT IS ORDERED that . . . [t]he Court declines to accept the Plea Agreement.

NOTES

1. Fines. The most obvious possible sanction for a corporation, and one at issue in *Guidant*, is a criminal fine. Fines, however, present the dilemma of their spillover effects on innocent shareholders, creditors, employees, and consumers, which can lead sentencing judges to refuse to impose substantial fines even in cases of serious corporate wrongdoing. Coffee, supra, at 400-402, 405-407. Weak fines, however, do not provide sufficient deterrence; when the anticipated fine is less than the expected benefit to the corporation from criminal wrongdoing, it will be cheaper to pay the fine than to refrain from crime. Ilene H. Nagel & Winthrop M. Swenson, The Federal Sentencing Guidelines for Corporations: Their Development, Theoretical

Underpinnings, and Some Thoughts About Their Future, 71 Wash. U. L.Q. 205, 215 (1993). Moreover, even when substantial fines are in fact imposed, they will not sufficiently deter employees whose personal interests do not align with the organization's interests. Thus, such individuals may commit crimes even though the crimes will prove extremely costly to the organization. See Richard Gruner, To Let the Punishment Fit the Organization: Sanctioning Corporate Offenders Through Corporate Probation, 16 Am. J. Crim. L. 1, 5 (1988).

2. *Compliance programs.* Because of the shortcomings of fines, the government has sought to change corporation behavior through other means. A central approach has been the creation of carrots and sticks for corporations to adopt compliance and ethics programs, another option discussed in *Guidant.*

The Federal Sentencing Guidelines take the carrot approach, offering sentencing reductions for companies that have such programs. The commentary to Chapter Eight of the Federal Sentencing Guidelines ("Sentencing of Organizations") explains:

> These guidelines offer incentives to organizations to reduce and ultimately eliminate criminal conduct by providing a structural foundation from which an organization may self-police its own conduct through an effective compliance and ethics program. The prevention and detection of criminal conduct, as facilitated by an effective compliance and ethics program, will assist an organization in encouraging ethical conduct and in complying fully with all applicable laws.

More specifically, under the Guidelines, a convicted corporation is entitled to a three-point deduction from its culpability score, "if the offense occurred even though the organization had in place at the time of the offense an effective compliance and ethics program," provided that the organization reported all detected violations within a reasonable time after becoming aware of them. U.S. Sentencing Guidelines Manual §8C2.5(f) (2005). Moreover, the Guidelines provide for "probation" for corporations in certain cases, and one condition of probation may be that the organization "develop and submit to the court an effective compliance and ethics program." Id. §8.D1.4(c). The Guidelines explain that an effective program should demonstrate "the exercise of due diligence to prevent and detect criminal conduct" and "promote an organizational culture that encourages ethical conduct and commitment to compliance with the law." Id. at §8B2.1. The Guidelines further specify that these general exhortations entail establishing standards and procedures to prevent and detect crime; educating the board of directors, employees, and agents about the compliance and ethics program; assigning specific high-level individuals responsibility for the programs; evaluating the program periodically; and creating a well-publicized, confidential mechanism for internal reporting of potential criminal conduct. If criminal conduct is detected, the organization should respond appropriately and take steps to prevent further criminal conduct. Id.

The Department of Justice seeks to encourage compliance programs by using the stick of a threatened indictment. The Department takes into account whether an organization has a compliance program in deciding whether to file criminal charges. U.S. Attorneys' Manual §9-28.300(A). Thus, although the "corporate ethos" model of corporate criminal liability has not been formally adopted as matter of substantive law, it has made substantial inroads in sentencing law and prosecutorial practice.

The increasing reliance on corporate compliance programs in federal sentencing has received mixed reviews. For a theoretical defense of "composite liability regimes" such as the Federal Sentencing Guidelines (which base liability on the doctrine of respondeat superior, but allow mitigation of punishment for compliance efforts), see Jennifer Arlen & Reinier Kraakman, Controlling Corporate Misconduct: An Analysis of Corporate Liability Regimes, 72 N.Y.U. L. Rev. 687 (1997). Jennifer Arlen has gone on to criticize the Federal Sentencing Guidelines as they currently exist for failing to provide sufficient mitigation to entice companies to adopt compliance programs, to self-report, and to cooperate. Jennifer Arlen, The Failure of the Organizational Sentencing Guidelines, 66 U. Miami L. Rev. 321 (2012). For another skeptical view, see Frank O. Bowman, III, Drifting Down the Dnieper with Prince Potemkin: Some Skeptical Reflections About the Place of Compliance Programs in Federal Criminal Sentencing, 39 Wake Forest L. Rev. 671 (2004). For a defense of these Sentencing Guidelines provisions, see Diana E. Murphy, The Federal Sentencing Guidelines for Organizations: A Decade of Promoting Compliance and Ethics, 87 Iowa L. Rev. 697 (2002).

3. *Regulation through DPAs and NPAs.* As noted above (see supra page 788), prosecutors are increasingly opting not to charge corporations criminally and instead to negotiate agreements to change company practices. Although the precise terms of these agreements vary, prosecutors often demand that companies adopt compliance programs policed by independent monitors, pay fines and restitution, cooperate with investigations against employees, make personnel changes, and alter business practices. See Brandon L. Garrett, Structural Reform Prosecution, 93 Va. L. Rev. 853, 894-901 (2007). Many NPAs and DPAs go quite far into the operation of companies, requiring companies to eliminate lawful lines of business, fire corporate officers, or make other dramatic shifts in operation, including changing fee structures or imposing disclosure obligations where none exist under law. Prosecutors in the Boardroom: Using Criminal Law To Regulate Corporate Conduct 3 (Anthony Barkow & Rachel Barkow eds., 2011). NPAs and DPAs have the benefit of avoiding the collateral consequences of conviction while forcing the company to change its practices. The Department of Justice explains their value as follows (U.S. Attorneys' Manual §9-28.1000):

> Such agreements are a third option, besides a criminal indictment, on the one hand, and a declination, on the other. Declining prosecution may allow a corporate criminal to escape without consequences. Obtaining a conviction

may produce a result that seriously harms innocent third parties who played no role in the criminal conduct. Under appropriate circumstances, a deferred prosecution or non-prosecution agreement can help restore the integrity of a company's operations and preserve the financial viability of a corporation that engaged in criminal conduct, while preserving the government's ability to prosecute a recalcitrant corporation that materially breaches the agreement.

Questions: What are the downsides to this approach to criminal law enforcement? Do prosecutors have too much leverage when negotiating DPAs and NPAs? Is this leverage any different from the rest of criminal law? See infra Chapter 10 for a general discussion of prosecutorial discretion. For analysis of the use of prosecutorial discretion to obtain DPAs and NPAs and proposed reforms to the practice, see Prosecutors in the Boardroom, supra. For an examination of how the current practice of using NPAs and DPAs comports with optimal deterrence, see Jennifer Arlen, Corporate Criminal Liability: Theory and Evidence, in Research Handbook on Criminal Law (Keith Hylton & Alon Harel eds., forthcoming). Are prosecutors well positioned to regulate business practices and decide which officers should stay or go? Is it appropriate for prosecutors to use the threat of criminal liability to get corporations to change the way they operate, even when the operation of the business itself is not a crime?

4. The corporate death penalty. In the wake of Arthur Andersen's collapse after indictment and conviction, the prospect of criminal charges "killing" a company has loomed large in the debate over corporate criminal liability. Most companies survive criminal charges, but some do not, either because they rely on government contracts and their conviction means disqualification, or they lose a necessary license or permit, or the adverse publicity is just too much of a reputational hit. See Beale, A Response to the Critics, supra, at 1501-1503. One of the reasons for the rise in DPAs and NPAs is prosecutorial concern that a conviction could mean the end of a company. Should these collateral consequences of punishment drive prosecutorial charging decisions? In the case of individual liability, collateral consequences (such as to family members) are not ordinarily considered. Why are the collateral consequences to corporations given greater significance than those that affect individuals facing criminal liability?

3. Liability of Corporate Agents

INTRODUCTORY NOTE

Personal liability of corporate officers and agents has not been much affected by the conceptual concerns that hindered development of criminal liability of the corporate entity. One argument against criminal liability was that corporate agents should not be criminally liable for their actions when they acted for the corporation in a representative capacity. But this argument never drew much support in the case law. See 3A W. Fletcher, Encyclopedia of the Law of Private Corporations §1348, at 630 (1975). The prevailing view is reflected in §2.07(6) of the MPC:

> (a) A person is legally accountable for any conduct he performs or causes to be performed in the name of the corporation or an unincorporated association or in its behalf to the same extent as if it were performed in his own name or behalf.
>
> (b) Whenever a duty to act is imposed by law upon a corporation or an unincorporated association, any agent of the corporation or association having primary responsibility for the discharge of the duty is legally accountable for reckless omission to perform the required act to the same extent as if the duty were imposed by law directly upon himself.

A major problem in seeking to impose criminal liability on individual corporate actors derives from the bureaucratic arrangement of corporate activities, with lower employees responsible to higher-level employees in a hierarchy leading up to the highest officers. This arrangement often makes it difficult to fasten liability upon the upper-echelon employees and officers under the prevailing standards of accomplice liability requiring intentional aiding or encouraging criminal conduct of another, for these doctrines are designed for personal rather than bureaucratic relationships. The doctrine of vicarious liability would be one solution, but its use entails potential unfairness and injustice. The materials that follow explore these problems.

GORDON v. UNITED STATES

United States Court of Appeals, 10th Circuit
203 F.2d 248 (1953), rev'd, 347 U.S. 909 (1954)

[Defendant partners in a sewing-machine and appliance business were convicted of violating the Defense Production Act by selling sewing machines on credit terms prohibited by that act and regulations issued thereunder. Section 601 provided that any person who "willfully" violated its provisions or any regulation or order issued thereunder should upon conviction be punished as therein specified. The case was not submitted to the jury on the question whether the partners had actual notice of the transactions. Instead, it was tried and submitted on the theory that knowledge of one partner regarding the transactions was "imputable, attributable and chargeable" to the other and that the knowledge and acts of the salespeople who made the sales and kept the records while acting in the course of their employment were imputable and chargeable to the employing partners. On the "very perplexing question whether the partners can be held criminally responsible for the knowledge and acts of their agents and employees, who the evidence shows, while acting in the course of their employment, actually made the sales without having collected the required down payment," the court, per Murrah, J., answered in the affirmative, stating:]

Deeply rooted in our criminal jurisprudence is the notion that criminal guilt is personal to the accused; that wilfulness or a guilty mind is an essential ingredient of a punishable offense, and that one cannot intend an act in which he did not consciously participate, acquiesce, or have guilty knowledge. Morissette v. United States, 342 U.S. 246.

Amenable to this notion, the courts have been reluctant to hold the master or the employer criminally responsible for the acts of his agent or employee which he did not authorize, counsel, advise, approve or ratify.

It is only in the so-called public welfare offenses usually involving police regulation of food, drink and drugs that the courts have relaxed the necessity for proof of a wilful intent.

In our case wilfulness is specifically made a prerequisite to guilt. Indeed it is the gist of the offenses charged in all of the counts in the information. And the trial court instructed the jury that in every crime or public offense there must be a "union or joint operation of act and intent" but "that the intent or intention is manifest by the circumstances connected with the offense as well as by direct testimony."

What the court did in effect was to make wilfulness an essential element of the offenses charged in the information, and to charge the employers with the guilty knowledge and acts of the employees in determining the question of willfulness. . . .

The effect of this is not to dispense with wilfulness or guilty knowledge as an element of the offense. It is to charge the employer with knowledge of records he is required to keep and acts he is required or forbidden to do, and which he necessarily keeps, does or omits to do by and through his agents and employees. To be sure, the knowledge with which he is charged is not direct; it is constructive. If it be called vicarious responsibility, it is nevertheless a responsibility of him on whom the law places the duty. It is permissible proof of a wilfulness which in its proper context denotes more than mere negligence but less than bad purpose or evil motive. It connotes a course of conduct which may be construed by the triers of facts as deliberate and voluntary, hence intentional; or it may be construed as negligent, inadvertent and excusable. The act or omission itself is not inexorably penalized. The ultimate question of guilt is left to the ameliorating influence of those who sit in judgment. Considered in this light, we do not think the instructions of the court fall short of the traditional standards for guilt.

HUXMAN, J. dissenting: . . . The partners denied intent to violate the law or any knowledge that their employees were violating it. They were entitled to have their testimony weighed and evaluated under proper instructions by the court together with all other relevant evidence. They were entitled to have the jury told that they were not criminally liable for the acts of their employees, although committed within the scope of their employment, unless they directed such activities or had guilty knowledge thereof. It is a principle embedded in the English law from time immemorial that the sins of the father shall not be visited upon the son merely because the father is the agent of the son and his unlawful acts were committed within the scope of his employment, under a criminal statute making wilfulness an element of the offense when the son had no knowledge of or part in such violations.

Strong reliance is placed upon Inland Freight Lines v. United States, 191 F.2d 313, by this court. But that case is clearly distinguishable. There the sole defendant was the corporation charged with keeping false records and it was held that the knowledge of its agents was the knowledge of the corporation. That is the well-established principle of criminal law as applied in the case of a corporation. It is, as the law recognizes, the only way a corporation can be held criminally responsible for violations of penal statutes. While a corporation is recognized as a separate legal entity, such separate entity is a pure fiction of the law. As a separate entity and aside from its agents and employees a corporation can do nothing. It has no conscience, will, or power of thought. It acts only through its agents. Their acts are the only acts it can commit and their knowledge of necessity is the only knowledge it can have.

The only cases in which a principal without actual intent or knowledge of criminal acts of wrong-doing by his employees has been held criminally responsible for such acts arose under welfare statutes such as the Pure Food and Drug Laws, Liquor Laws and Weight and Measure Acts. But under all of these acts where a principal was held guilty because of the acts of his agents without knowledge or intent on his part wilfulness was not an element of the offense and the statute made the doing of the act the offense.

NOTE

The U.S. Supreme Court granted certiorari and reversed the Tenth Circuit's decision in *Gordon* in the following per curiam opinion (347 U.S. 909, 909 (1954)):

> Petitioners are business partners in the sale of appliances. They were convicted under Section 603 of the Defense Production Act of 1950 . . . which provides that "Any person who willfully violates" regulations promulgated under the Act shall be guilty of crime. The jury was instructed that the knowledge of petitioners' employees was chargeable to petitioners in determining petitioners' willfulness. Because of the instruction, the government has confessed error. We agree, and accordingly reverse the judgment and remand the case to the district court for retrial.

Four years later, the Supreme Court held a partnership liable for the "knowing and willful" violation of the Motor Carrier Act, 18 U.S.C. §835, 49 U.S.C. §332(a), based on the conduct of an employee, and distinguished *Gordon* by explaining, "here the government does not seek to hold the individual partners, but only the partnership as an entity." United States v. A & P Trucking Co., 358 U.S. 121, 126 (1958).

UNITED STATES v. PARK

Supreme Court of the United States
421 U.S. 658 (1975)

CHIEF JUSTICE BURGER delivered the opinion of the Court. . . .

Acme Markets, Inc., is a national retail food chain with approximately 36,000 employees, 874 retail outlets, 12 general warehouses, and four special warehouses. Its headquarters, including the office of the president, respondent Park, who is chief executive officer of the corporation, are located in Philadelphia, Pa. [T]he Government charged Acme and respondent with violations of the Federal Food, Drug, and Cosmetic Act. [T]he information alleged that the defendants had received food that had been shipped in interstate commerce and that, while the food was being held for sale in Acme's Baltimore warehouse following shipment in interstate commerce, they caused it to be held in a building accessible to rodents and to be exposed to contamination by rodents. These acts were alleged to have resulted in the food's being adulterated within the meaning of [the statute].

Acme pleaded guilty. . . . Respondent pleaded not guilty. The evidence at trial demonstrated that in April 1970 the Food and Drug Administration (FDA) advised respondent by letter of insanitary conditions in Acme's Philadelphia warehouse. In 1971 the FDA found that similar conditions existed in the firm's Baltimore warehouse. An FDA consumer safety officer testified concerning evidence of rodent infestation and other insanitary conditions discovered during a 12-day inspection of the Baltimore warehouse in November and December 1971. He also related that a second inspection of the warehouse had been conducted in March 1972. On that occasion the inspectors found that there had been improvement in the sanitary conditions, but that "there was still evidence of rodent activity in the building and in the warehouses and we found some rodent-contaminated lots of food items."

The Government also presented testimony by the Chief of Compliance of the FDA's Baltimore office, who informed respondent by letter of the conditions at the Baltimore warehouse after the first inspection.[6] There was testimony by Acme's Baltimore division vice president, who had responded to the letter on behalf of Acme and respondent and who described the steps taken to remedy the insanitary conditions discovered by both inspections. The Government's final witness, Acme's vice president for legal affairs and assistant secretary, identified respondent as the president and chief executive officer of

---

6. The letter, dated January 27, 1972, included the following:

> We note with much concern that the old and new warehouse areas used for food storage were actively and extensively inhabited by live rodents. Of even more concern was the observation that such reprehensible conditions obviously existed for a prolonged period of time without any detection, or were completely ignored. . . .
>
> We trust this letter will serve to direct your attention to the seriousness of the problem and formally advise you of the urgent need to initiate whatever measures are necessary to prevent recurrence and ensure compliance with the law.

the company and read a bylaw prescribing the duties of the chief executive officer.[7] He testified that respondent functioned by delegating "normal operating duties," including sanitation, but that he retained "certain things, which are the big, broad, principles of the operation of the company," and had "the responsibility of seeing that they all work together." . . .

Respondent was the only defense witness. He testified that, although all of Acme's employees were in a sense under his general direction, the company had an "organizational structure for responsibilities for certain functions" according to which different phases of its operation were "assigned to individuals who, in turn, have staff and departments under them." He identified those individuals responsible for sanitation, and related that upon receipt of the January 1972 FDA letter, he had conferred with the vice president for legal affairs, who informed him that the Baltimore division vice president "was investigating the situation immediately and would be taking corrective action and would be preparing a summary of the corrective action to reply to the letter." Respondent stated that he did not "believe there was anything [he] could have done more constructively than what [he] found was being done."

On cross-examination, respondent conceded that providing sanitary conditions for food offered for sale to the public was something that he was "responsible for in the entire operation of the company." . . .

The relevant portion of the trial judge's instructions to the jury challenged by respondent is set out in the margin.[9] Respondent's counsel objected to the instructions on the ground that they failed fairly to reflect our decision in United States v. Dotterweich, [320 U.S. 277 (1943)], and to define " 'responsible relationship.' " The trial judge overruled the objection. The jury found

---

7. The bylaw provided in pertinent part:

    The Chairman of the board of directors or the president shall be the chief executive officer of the company as the board of directors may from time to time determine. He shall, subject to the board of directors, have general and active supervision of the affairs, business, offices and employees of the company. . . .

    He shall, from time to time, in his discretion or at the order of the board, report the operations and affairs of the company. He shall also perform such other duties and have such other powers as may be assigned to him from time to time by the board of directors.

9. [The jury instructions stated as follows:

    . . . "The main issue for your determination is . . . whether the Defendant held a position of authority and responsibility in the business of Acme Markets. . . .

    "The statute makes individuals, as well as corporations, liable for violations. An individual is liable if it is clear, beyond a reasonable doubt, that . . . the individual had a responsible relation to the situation, even though he may not have participated personally.

    "The individual is or could be liable under the statute, even if he did not consciously do wrong. However, the fact that the Defendant is [president] and is a chief executive officer of the Acme Markets does not require a finding of guilt. Though, he need not have personally participated in the situation, he must have had a responsible relationship to the issue. The issue is, in this case, whether the Defendant, John R. Park, by virtue of his position in the company, had a position of authority and responsibility in the situation out of which these charges arose."]

respondent guilty on all counts of the information, and he was subsequently sentenced to pay a fine of $50 on each count.[10]

The Court of Appeals reversed the conviction and remanded for a new trial. That court viewed the Government as arguing "that the conviction may be predicated solely upon a showing that [respondent] was the President of the offending corporation," and it stated that as "a general proposition, some act of commission or omission is an essential element of every crime." It reasoned that, although our decision in United States v. Dotterweich had construed the statutory provisions under which respondent was tried to dispense with the traditional element of " 'awareness of some wrongdoing,' " the Court had not construed them as dispensing with the element of "wrongful action." The Court of Appeals concluded that the trial judge's instructions "might well have left the jury with the erroneous impression that Park could be found guilty in the absence of 'wrongful action' on his part," and that proof of this element was required by due process. It . . . directed that on retrial the jury be instructed as to "wrongful action," which might be "gross negligence and inattention in discharging . . . corporate duties and obligations or any of a host of other acts of commission or omission which would 'cause' the contamination of food." . . .

The question presented by the Government's petition for certiorari in *United States v. Dotterweich*, [supra page 283 this casebook] . . . was whether "the manager of a corporation, as well as the corporation itself, may be prosecuted under the Federal Food, Drug, and Cosmetic Act of 1938 for the introduction of misbranded and adulterated articles into interstate commerce." . . .

In . . . reinstating Dotterweich's conviction, this Court looked to the purposes of the Act and noted that they "touch phases of the lives and health of people which, in the circumstances of modern industrialism, are largely beyond self-protection."

Central to the Court's conclusion that individuals other than proprietors are subject to the criminal provisions of the Act was the reality that "the only way in which a corporation can act is through the individuals who act on its behalf." . . .

At the same time, however, the Court was aware of the concern which was the motivating factor in the Court of Appeals' decision, that literal enforcement "might operate too harshly by sweeping within its condemnation any person however remotely entangled in the proscribed shipment." A limiting principle, in the form of "settled doctrines of criminal law" defining those who "are responsible for the commission of a misdemeanor," was available. In this context, the Court concluded, those doctrines dictated that the offense was committed "by all who . . . have . . . a responsible share in the furtherance of the transaction which the statute outlaws."

---

10. Sections 303(a) and (b) of the Act, 21 U.S.C. §§333(a) and (b), provide:

(a) Any person who violates a provision of section 331 of this title shall be imprisoned for not more than one year or fined not more than $1,000, or both. . . .

The Court recognized that, because the Act dispenses with the need to prove "consciousness of wrongdoing," it may result in hardship even as applied to those who share "responsibility in the business process resulting in" a violation. It regarded as "too treacherous" an attempt "to define or even to indicate by way of illustration the class of employees which stands in such a responsible relation." The question of responsibility, the Court said, depends "on the evidence produced at the trial and its submission—assuming the evidence warrants it—to the jury under appropriate guidance." The Court added: "In such matters the good sense of prosecutors, the wise guidance of trial judges, and the ultimate judgment must be trusted." . . .

Dotterweich and the cases which have followed reveal that in providing sanctions which reach and touch the individuals who execute the corporate mission—and this is by no means necessarily confined to a single corporate agent or employee—the Act imposes not only a positive duty to seek out and remedy violations when they occur but also, and primarily, a duty to implement measures that will insure that violations will not occur. The requirements of foresight and vigilance imposed on responsible corporate agents are beyond question demanding, and perhaps onerous, but they are no more stringent than the public has a right to expect of those who voluntarily assume positions of authority in business enterprises whose services and products affect the health and well-being of the public that supports them. . . .

The Act does not, as we observed in *Dotterweich*, make criminal liability turn on "awareness of some wrongdoing" or "conscious fraud." The duty imposed by Congress on responsible corporate agents is, we emphasize, one that requires the highest standard of foresight and vigilance, but the Act, in its criminal aspect, does not require that which is objectively impossible. The theory upon which responsible corporate agents are held criminally accountable for "causing" violations of the Act permits a claim that a defendant was "powerless" to prevent or correct the violation to "be raised defensively at a trial on the merits." United States v. Wiesenfeld Warehouse Co., 376 U.S. 86, 91 (1964). If such a claim is made, the defendant has the burden of coming forward with evidence, but this does not alter the Government's ultimate burden of proving beyond a reasonable doubt the defendant's guilt, including his power, in light of the duty imposed by the Act, to prevent or correct the prohibited condition. . . .

We cannot agree [that it was necessary to] instruct the jury that the Government had the burden of establishing "wrongful action" in the sense in which the Court of Appeals used that phrase. The concept of a "reasonable relationship" to, or a "reasonable share" in, a violation of the Act indeed imports some measure of blameworthiness; but it is equally clear that the Government establishes a prima facie case when it introduces evidence sufficient to warrant a finding by the trier of the facts that the defendant had, by reason of his position in the corporation, responsibility and authority either to prevent in the first instance, or promptly to correct, the violation complained of, and that he failed to do so. . . .

Reading the entire charge satisfies us that the jury's attention was adequately focused on the issue of respondent's authority with respect to the conditions that formed the basis of the alleged violations. Viewed as a whole, the charge did not permit the jury to find guilt solely on the basis of respondent's position in the corporation. . . .

Reversed.

JUSTICE STEWART, with whom JUSTICE MARSHALL and JUSTICE POWELL join, dissenting.

Although agreeing with much of what is said in the Court's opinion, I dissent from the opinion and judgment, because the jury instructions in this case were not consistent with the law as the Court today expounds it.

As I understand the Court's opinion, it holds that in order to sustain a conviction under §301(k) of the Federal Food, Drug, and Cosmetic Act the prosecution must at least show that by reason of an individual's corporate position and responsibilities, he had a duty to use care to maintain the physical integrity of the corporation's food products. A jury may then draw the inference that when the food is found to be in such condition as to violate the statute's prohibitions, that condition was "caused" by a breach of the standard of care imposed upon the responsible official. This is the language of negligence, and I agree with it.

To affirm this conviction, however, the Court must approve the instructions given to the members of the jury who were entrusted with determining whether the respondent was innocent or guilty. Those instructions did not conform to the standards that the Court itself sets out today.

The trial judge instructed the jury to find Park guilty if it found beyond a reasonable doubt that Park "had a responsible relation to the situation. . . . The issue is . . . whether the Defendant, John R. Park, by virtue of his position in the company, had a position of authority and responsibility in the situation out of which these charges arose." Requiring, as it did, a verdict of guilty upon a finding of "responsibility," this instruction standing alone could have been construed as a direction to convict if the jury found Park "responsible" for the condition in the sense that his position as chief executive officer gave him formal responsibility within the structure of the corporation. But the trial judge went on specifically to caution the jury not to attach such a meaning to his instruction, saying that "the fact that the Defendant is pres-[id]ent and is a chief executive officer of the Acme Markets does not require a finding of guilt." "Responsibility" as used by the trial judge therefore had whatever meaning the jury in its unguided discretion chose to give it.

The instructions, therefore, expressed nothing more than a tautology. They told the jury: "You must find the defendant guilty if you find that he is to be held accountable for this adulterated food." In other words: "You must find the defendant guilty if you conclude that he is guilty." . . .

[B]efore a person can be convicted of a criminal violation of this Act, a jury must find—and must be clearly instructed that it must find—evidence beyond a reasonable doubt that he engaged in wrongful conduct amounting at least to common-law negligence. There were no such instructions, and clearly, there-fore, no such finding in this case. . . .

NOTES

1. *Vicarious liability?* Reconsider the *Guminga* case, supra page 292. Guminga's objection was to the kind of vicarious liability exemplified in the tort doctrine of respondeat superior; namely, where the liability of A for the acts of B is based solely on some relationship between them rather than on any culpable conduct of A. Are Park and Dotterweich being held liable for *their own* misconduct, or are they being held liable for the misconduct of others? Consider Friedman v. Sebelius, 755 F. Supp. 2d 98, 110-111 (D.D.C. 2010):

> Under the "responsible corporate officer" doctrine as described in [*Dotterweich* and *Park*], a corporate official can be convicted of a misdemeanor under the FDCA if he or she had a "responsible share in the furtherance of the trans-action which the statute outlaws, namely, to put into the stream of interstate commerce adulterated or misbranded drugs." *Dotterweich*, 320 U.S. at 284. Although the doctrine "dispenses with the conventional requirement for criminal conduct—awareness of some wrongdoing," id. at 281, liability under the FDCA remains subject to a "limiting principle," namely that the defendant had the "power . . . to prevent or correct the prohibited condition" but failed to do so. *Park*, 421 U.S. at 669. Corporate officials are thus subject to prosecution under the doctrine *only* if they stand in some "responsible rela-tionship" to a specific violation of the Act, meaning that their "failure to exercise the authority and supervisory responsibility reposed in them by the business organization resulted in the violation complained of." Id. at 671. . . .
>
> As made clear by the Supreme Court, it is simply not the case that a defendant can be convicted of a misdemeanor under the responsible corporate officer doctrine based solely on his position within the corporate hierarchy. Rather, to establish a prima facie case, the government must introduce evidence demonstrating that "the defendant had, by reason of his position in the corporation, responsibility and authority either to prevent in the first instance, or promptly to correct, the violation complained of, and that he failed to do so." *Park*, 421 U.S. at 673-74. A defendant's position within a company is certainly relevant, but it is no more than one link in the causal chain to establish liability. Indeed, the Court went to great lengths in *Park* to clarify that the trial court's instructions (which the Court affirmed) did *not* permit the jury to convict the defendant based solely on his position as President and CEO of the company, as such instructions would have been legally erroneous.

Officers may also be held responsible under laws that require them to report the crimes of employees. For example, a Roman Catholic bishop was recently indicted for failing to report child abuse by one of the priests in his diocese. A.G. Sulzberger & Laurie Goodstein, Bishop Indicted; Charge Is Failing to Report Abuse, N.Y. Times, Oct. 15, 2011, at A1.

2. The responsible corporate officer doctrine and the "powerless" defendant. Although a defendant can raise as a defense that the "defendant was 'powerless' to prevent or correct the violation," federal courts have been slow to recognize situations in which it was "objectively impossible" to avoid the harm. See United States v. Gel Spice Co., 773 F2d. 427 (2d Cir. 1985). The court in United States v. New England Grocers Supply Co., 488 F. Supp. 230 (D. Mass. 1980), addressed the difficulty in "ascertain[ing] from [*Park*] the exact nature and scope of the impossibility defense":

> One interpretation . . . is that it relates only to the power of the corporate officer, by virtue of his position in the corporation, to correct or prevent violations of the Act. Under this interpretation, the evidence introduced by the defendant at trial to sustain his impossibility defense would serve only to rebut the evidence introduced by the government in establishing its prima facie case. [T]he impossibility defense would not serve as an affirmative defense, but would merely provide corporate officers a defense open to all who are criminally accused, that is, rebuttal of the government's proof.
>
> An alternative interpretation of the impossibility defense is that it is satisfied by evidence that the corporate officer exercised "extraordinary care" and was still unable to prevent violations. Under this interpretation, the impossibility defense would serve as an affirmative defense, incorporating an objective element—use of extraordinary care—into a strict liability offense.
>
> In light of the severe penalties which may be imposed for a second violation under the Act, I am inclined to adopt [the latter] more lenient position of the impossibility defense. Id. at 235-236.

New England Grocers makes clear that the impossibility defense is available only to individuals and not to corporations. Should it be extended to corporations?

3. Severity of penalties. In *Park*, the responsible corporate officer doctrine led to the defendant's conviction, but only a minor penalty (several fines of $50) was imposed. Most public welfare offenses are misdemeanor offenses that carry neither serious stigma nor substantial punishment. Should the responsible corporate officer doctrine be applied equally to crimes that require mens rea and impose significant punishment? Consider the case that follows, which involves an environmental statute requiring a mens rea of knowledge whose violation constitutes a felony carrying possible imprisonment for five years, and, for a second offense, ten years.

UNITED STATES v. MacDONALD & WATSON WASTE OIL CO.

United States Court of Appeals, 1st Circuit
933 F.2d 35 (1991)

CAMPBELL, C.J. [MacDonald & Watson Waste Oil Co., a corporation engaged in the business of transporting and disposing of contaminated wastes, operated a disposal facility at the Poe Street Lot, a facility leased from the Narragansett

Improvement Company (NIC). Neither MacDonald nor NIC held a permit authorizing them to dispose of solid hazardous wastes in that site, although NIC did have a permit to dispose of *liquid* wastes there.

[MacDonald was hired to remove solid waste (toluene-contaminated soil) from the grounds of the Master Chemical Company. An employee of MacDonald supervised the transportation of the contaminated soil from Master Chemical to the Poe Street Lot. Subsequently Eugene K. D'Allesandro, president of MacDonald, was convicted of knowingly transporting and causing the transportation of hazardous waste to a facility that did not have a permit, in violation of the Resource Conservation and Recovery Act (RCRA), §3008(d)(1). The company was also convicted, but discussion of its liability is omitted.]

D'Allesandro . . . contends that his conviction . . . must be vacated because the district court incorrectly charged the jury regarding the element of knowledge in the case of a corporate officer. Section 3008(d)(1) penalizes "Any person who . . . (1) knowingly transports or causes to be transported any hazardous waste identified or listed under this subchapter . . . to a facility which does not have a permit. . . ." In his closing, the prosecutor conceded that the government had "no direct evidence that Eugene D'Allesandro actually knew that the Master Chemical shipments were coming in," i.e., were being transported to the Poe Street Lot under contract with his company. The prosecution did present evidence, however, that D'Allesandro was not only the President and owner of MacDonald & Watson but was a "hands-on" manager of that relatively small firm. There was also proof that . . . D'Allesandro's subordinates had contracted for and transported the Master Chemical waste for disposal at [the Poe Street] site. The government argued that D'Allesandro was guilty of violating §3008(d)(1) because, as the responsible corporate officer, he was in a position to ensure compliance with RCRA and had failed to do so even after being warned by a consultant on two earlier occasions that other shipments of toluene-contaminated soil had been received from other customers, and that such material violated NIC's permit. In the government's view, any failure to prove D'Allesandro's actual knowledge of the Master Chemical contract and shipments was irrelevant to his criminal responsibility under §3008(d)(1) for those shipments.

The court apparently accepted the government's theory. It instructed the jury as follows:

> When an individual Defendant is also a corporate officer, the Government may prove that individual's knowledge in either of two ways. The first way is to demonstrate that the defendant had actual knowledge of the act in question. The second way is to establish that the defendant was what is called a responsible officer of the corporation committing the act. In order to prove that a person is a responsible corporate officer three things must be shown.
>
> First, it must be shown that the person is an officer of the corporation, not merely an employee.
>
> Second, it must be shown that the officer had direct responsibility for the activities that are alleged to be illegal. Simply being an officer or even the

president of a corporation is not enough. The Government must prove that the person had a responsibility to supervise the activities in question.

And the third requirement is that the officer must have known or believed that the illegal activity of the type alleged occurred. . . .

We agree with D'Allesandro that the jury instructions improperly allowed the jury to find him guilty without finding he had actual knowledge of the alleged transportation of hazardous waste on July 30 and 31, 1986, from Master Chemical Company, Boston, Massachusetts, to NIC's site, knowledge being an element the statute requires. We must, therefore, reverse his conviction.

The seminal cases regarding the responsible corporate officer doctrine are United States v. Dotterweich, 320 U.S. 277 (1943), and United States v. Park, 421 U.S. 658 (1975). These cases concerned misdemeanor charges . . . [that] dispensed with a scienter requirement. . . . But while *Dotterweich* and *Park* thus reflect what is now . . . well-established law in respect to public welfare statutes and regulations lacking an express knowledge or other *scienter* requirement, we know of no precedent for failing to give effect to a knowledge requirement that Congress has expressly included in a criminal statute. Especially is that so where, as here, the crime is a felony carrying possible imprisonment of five years and, for a second offense, ten. . . .

[T]he district court charged, in effect, that proof that D'Allesandro was a responsible corporate officer would conclusively prove the element of his knowledge of the Master Chemical shipments. . . . In a crime having knowledge as an express element, a mere showing of official responsibility under *Dotterweich* and *Park* is not an adequate substitute for direct or circumstantial proof of knowledge. . . .

We vacate the conviction of Eugene D'Allesandro . . . and remand for a new trial. . . .

NOTES

1. RCRA, mens rea, and the responsible corporate officer doctrine. RCRA imposes liability on any person who "knowingly transports . . . any hazardous waste . . . to a facility which does not have a permit." Why were the jury instructions insufficient to satisfy the requirements of RCRA? Note that the judge explicitly told the jury it must find that the "officer must have known or believed that the illegal activity of the type alleged occurred." Why was this instruction not equivalent to proof of knowledge? Is the problem that the instruction allowed the jury to find activity "of the type" as opposed to the specific activity at issue?

The knowledge requirements in various environmental statutes have divided the courts in terms of what they require of responsible corporate officers. Henry Klementowicz et al., Environmental Crimes, 48 Am. Crim. L. Rev. 541, 549-550 (2011). For a general discussion of the issues raised by knowledge requirements in regulatory areas such as this, see supra pages 316-318.

2. *Should officers be liable?* A critical view of the increasing practice of seeking convictions of corporate officers for the crimes of their corporations is taken in Margaret Graham Tebo, Guilty by Reason of Title, 86 A.B.A. J. 44 (May 2000). She notes at 45:

[A] number of former U.S. attorneys say [the] Justice [Department] subscribes to the view that holding high-level executives criminally liable will often bring changes in the behavior of their companies. Prosecutors and regulators at the state and local levels seem to agree. Apparently, so do legislators, who have incorporated criminal penalties into an increasing number of regulatory statutes, such as the federal clean air and water acts, aimed at carrying out public policy priorities. Typically, those provisions make the highest-ranking official involved in a particular company activity the ultimately responsible party, even where that person's direct participation in the violation cannot be shown.

Many federal environmental, antitrust and health care statutes have been interpreted by courts to be public welfare legislation, meaning that no showing of direct personal involvement is necessary to convict a manager for company violations. Courts have consistently held that these public welfare statutes do not require findings of intent, or even negligence, to support convictions. The courts have repeatedly denied attempts to challenge such laws as unconstitutional due process violations.[a]

Such was the case with Edward Hanousek, a project manager for the White Pass & Yukon Railroad in Alaska. One day in 1994, an employee of a subcontractor on the project struck an oil pipeline with his backhoe, spilling several thousand gallons of oil into the Skagway River. Hanousek, who was off duty and at home when the spill occurred, was convicted under the Clean Water Act of negligently discharging oil into a navigable waterway. He was sentenced consecutively to six months in jail, six months in a halfway house and six months of supervised release, plus a $5,000 fine.

The U.S. Supreme Court rejected Hanousek's petition for certiorari [letting] stand a decision that Hanousek suffered no due process violation.

The decision the author is referring to is United States v. Hanousek, 176 F.3d 1116 (9th Cir. 1999), in which the court held that, because the criminal provisions of the Clean Water Act constitute public welfare legislation, they did not violate due process in imposing liability for ordinary as opposed to gross negligence. The court rejected the defendant's argument that he was being held vicariously liable for the negligence of the backhoe operators, pointing out that the trial court did in fact instruct the jury that the discharge must have been "caused by the negligence of the particular defendant," presumably Hanousek's negligence in failing to adequately protect the pipeline.

Questions: Given that the jury *was* instructed that a finding of negligence on the part of Hanousek himself was required for liability, is the author's criticism of the decision well grounded? On the other hand, is the author right to be concerned about imposing criminal liability in the absence of direct personal involvement? Is liability for a negligent failure to act significantly more troubling than liability for negligent action?

---

a. [For a discussion of these issues, see supra pages 294-303.—Eds.]

3. *Expanding the responsibilities of corporate officers after* Enron. What environmental crime was to the 1990s, Enron became to the first decade of the twenty-first century. The massive fraud allegedly perpetrated by Enron's corporate officers and the catastrophic collapse of Enron Corporation (and other corporate scandals) generated widespread concern about whether criminal law offered adequate tools to prosecute and thus deter financial fraud. In response to these concerns, Congress passed the Sarbanes-Oxley Act of 2002, H.R. 3763, 107th Congress, 116 Stat. 745, 807 (2002). The Act did not alter the fundamental structure of criminal liability for either corporate officers or corporations. Rather, the Act's changes were more in the nature of gap-filling: It created several new obstruction-of-justice offenses; increased maximum penalties for existing crimes; and imposed new obligations on chief executive officers and chief financial officers to personally certify the accuracy of their companies' financial statements, subject to severe criminal penalties for false certifications. These certification provisions make it more difficult for CEOs and CFOs responsible for their firms' accounting practices to later try to claim that they were unaware of the relevant accounting facts when they are charged with issuing misleading financial reports.

Some commentators were optimistic that these changes would be effective in deterring corporate fraud, Kathleen F. Brickey, From Enron to WorldCom and Beyond: Life and Crime After Sarbanes-Oxley, 81 Wash. U. L.Q. 357 (2003), whereas others expressed doubt in light of the fact that many criminal laws addressing financial fraud were already on the books when these companies engaged in their frauds, Geraldine Scott Moohr, An Enron Lesson: The Modest Role of Criminal Law in Preventing Corporate Crime, 55 Fla. L. Rev. 937 (2003).

The financial meltdown of 2008 brings these issues to the forefront once again. There is uncertainty about what, if any, crimes were committed, and so far few criminal cases have been brought. See N.Y. Times, Tracking Financial Crisis Cases, available at http://www.nytimes.com/interactive/business/financial-crisis-cases.html. The crisis raises the question whether the laws are reasonably effective, and we are witnessing the level of non-compliance that is to be expected, or whether there is a larger systemic and structural problem with the way the criminal law addresses fraud and corporate malfeasance. Are the problems of demonstrating criminal fraud comparable in the individual and the corporate settings, or does the problem change when fraud occurs within a larger organization? Miriam Baer, for example, points out that corporate fraud is unique in the sense that once a corporate employee has lied to shareholders about a firm's financial state, he or she cannot refrain from lying in the future without raising red flags about the earlier lies. She therefore suggests that increasing sanctions alone will do little to address the dynamic and other mechanisms, such as amnesties or surveillance techniques, might be necessary. Miriam H. Baer, Linkage and the Deterrence of Corporate Fraud, 94 Va. L. Rev. 1295 (2008). For a broader discussion of the difficulties associated with defining and criminalizing fraud, see infra pages 1057-1069.

chapter 8

Exculpation

A. INTRODUCTION: THE CONCEPTS OF JUSTIFICATION AND EXCUSE

Three distinct sorts of defenses can be invoked to bar conviction for an alleged crime. The first asserts that the prosecution has failed to establish one or more required elements of the offense. The defendant may, for example, deny that he was anywhere near the scene of the crime, or he may concede that he fired the fatal shot but deny that he acted intentionally. We have considered defenses of this sort throughout the first seven chapters of this book. They are simply efforts to refute (or raise a reasonable doubt about) whatever the prosecution must prove. Of course, the prosecution always retains the burden of proving its own case—and disproving any such rebuttal efforts—beyond a reasonable doubt.

The present chapter deals with two sorts of defenses that have a different character. Justifications and excuses do not seek to refute any required element of the prosecution's case; rather they suggest considerations that negate culpability even when all elements of the offense are present. For example, successful claims of self-defense and insanity suggest reasons to bar conviction even when the defendant undoubtedly killed someone intentionally. It is customary, moreover, to distinguish sharply between these two groups of defenses (justifications and excuses). Self-defense, for example, is traditionally considered a justification, while insanity is considered an excuse. Pragmatists sometimes argue that this distinction is not important—whether labeled a justification or an excuse, the defense, once proved, requires acquittal.[1] But as J.L. Austin explains in the excerpt below, the distinction is essential for clear thinking because it points to a fundamental difference in the reasons *why* culpability is lacking.

---

1. Justifications and excuses are sometimes treated differently from other defenses for purposes of assigning the burden of proof. See *Patterson v. New York*, Chapter 1, supra.

J.L. AUSTIN, A PLEA FOR EXCUSES

57 Proceedings Aristotelian Soc'y 1, 2-3 (1956-1957)

One way of [defending conduct] is to admit flatly that he, *X*, did do that very thing, *A*, but to argue that it was a good thing, or the right or sensible thing, or a permissible thing to do, either in general or at least in the special circumstances of the occasion. To take this line is to *justify* the action, to give reasons for doing it. . . .

A different way of going about it is to admit that it wasn't a good thing to have done, but to argue that it is not quite fair or correct to say *baldly* "*X* did *A*." We may say it isn't fair just to say *X* did it; perhaps he was under somebody's influence, or was nudged. Or, it isn't fair to say baldly he *did A*; it may have been partly accidental or an unintentional slip. Or, it isn't fair to say he did simply *A*—he was really doing something quite different and *A* was only incidental, or he was looking at the whole thing quite differently. Naturally these arguments can be combined or overlap or run into each other.

In the one defence, briefly, we accept responsibility but deny that it was bad: in the other, we admit that it was bad but don't accept full, or even any, responsibility.

By and large, justifications can be kept distinct from excuses. . . . But the two certainly can be confused, and can *seem* to go very near to each other, even if they do not perhaps actually do so. [W]hen we plead, say, provocation, there is genuine uncertainty or ambiguity as to what we mean—is *he* partly responsible, because he roused a violent impulse or passion in me, so that it wasn't truly or merely me acting "of my own accord" (excuse)? Or is it rather that, he having done me such injury, I was entitled to retaliate (justification)? . . . But that the defences I have for convenience labelled "justification" and "excuse" are in principle distinct can scarcely be doubted.

B. PRINCIPLES OF JUSTIFICATION

1. *Protection of Life and Person*

UNITED STATES v. PETERSON

United States Court of Appeals, District of Columbia Circuit
483 F.2d 1222 (1973)

ROBINSON, J. . . . Self-defense, as a doctrine legally exonerating the taking of human life, is as viable now as it was in Blackstone's time. . . . But "[t]he law of self-defense is a law of necessity"; the right of self-defense arises only when the necessity begins, and equally ends with the necessity; and never must the necessity be greater than when the force employed defensively is deadly. The "necessity must bear all semblance of reality, and appear to admit of no other alternative, before taking life will be justifiable as excusable." Hinged on the exigencies of self-preservation, the doctrine of homicidal self-defense emerges from the body of the criminal law as a limited though important exception to legal outlawry of the arena of self-help in the settlement of potentially fatal personal conflicts.

So it is that necessity is the pervasive theme of the well-defined conditions which the law imposes on the right to kill or maim in self-defense. There must have been a threat, actual or apparent, of the use of deadly force against the defender. The threat must have been unlawful and immediate. The defender must have believed that he was in imminent peril of death or serious bodily harm, and that his response was necessary to save himself therefrom. These beliefs must not only have been honestly entertained, but also objectively reasonable in light of the surrounding circumstances. It is clear that no less than a concurrence of these elements will suffice.

NOTE ON SELF-DEFENSE AS A JUSTIFICATION

When the use of defensive force against an aggressor is necessary to protect the actor from serious bodily harm, that action is *justified*—because it was the right thing to do. But the *Peterson* court, stating the widely accepted view, does not require that the use of force be *truly* necessary; self-defense is available when the actor *reasonably believes* defensive force to be necessary. But if the actor's reasonable belief turns out to be mistaken, we cannot really say that her use of force was the right thing to do; it would be more precise to say that her action is not justified but merely *excused*—because her mistake was reasonable. From this perspective, we have to say that self-defense can be *either* a justification or an excuse, depending on whether the actor's reasonable belief is in fact well-founded. Nonetheless, courts and commentators conventionally refer to self-defense in both settings as a justification, and we follow that somewhat oversimplified convention in the organization of this book. Of course, regardless of the label used (justification or excuse), a defendant who meets the *Peterson* requirements is entitled to an acquittal.

PEOPLE v. GOETZ

New York Court of Appeals
68 N.Y.2d 96, 497 N.E.2d 41 (1986)

WACHTLER, C.J. A Grand Jury has indicted defendant on attempted murder, assault, and other charges for having shot and wounded four youths on a New York City subway train after one or two of the youths approached him and asked for $5. The lower courts, concluding that the prosecutor's charge to the Grand Jury on the defense of justification was erroneous,[a] have dismissed the

---

a. Because a judge typically is not present at grand jury proceedings, the prosecutor usually takes responsibility for explaining to the jurors the applicable law.—EDS.

lower court dismissed charges

attempted murder, assault and weapons possession charges. We now reverse and reinstate all counts of the indictment.

The precise circumstances of the incident giving rise to the charges against defendant are disputed, and ultimately it will be for a trial jury to determine what occurred. We feel it necessary, however, to provide some factual background to properly frame the legal issues before us. Accordingly, we have summarized the facts as they appear from the evidence before the Grand Jury. . . .

On Saturday afternoon, December 22, 1984, Troy Canty, Darryl Cabey, James Ramseur, and Barry Allen boarded an IRT express subway train in The Bronx and headed south toward lower Manhattan. The four youths rode together in the rear portion of the seventh car of the train. Two of the four, Ramseur and Cabey, had screwdrivers inside their coats, which they said were to be used to break into the coin boxes of video machines.

Defendant Bernhard Goetz boarded this subway train at 14th Street in Manhattan and sat down on a bench towards the rear section of the same car occupied by the four youths. Goetz was carrying an unlicensed .38 caliber pistol loaded with five rounds of ammunition in a waistband holster. The train left the 14th Street station and headed towards Chambers Street.

It appears from the evidence before the Grand Jury that Canty approached Goetz, possibly with Allen beside him, and stated "give me five dollars." Neither Canty nor any of the other youths displayed a weapon. Goetz responded by standing up, pulling out his handgun and firing four shots in rapid succession. The first shot hit Canty in the chest; the second struck Allen in the back; the third went through Ramseur's arm and into his left side; the fourth was fired at Cabey, who apparently was then standing in the corner of the car, but missed, deflecting instead off of a wall of the conductor's cab. After Goetz briefly surveyed the scene around him, he fired another shot at Cabey, who then was sitting on the end bench of the car. The bullet entered the rear of Cabey's side and severed his spinal cord.

All but two of the other passengers fled the car when, or immediately after, the shots were fired. The conductor, who had been in the next car, heard the shots and instructed the motorman to radio for emergency assistance. The conductor then went into the car where the shooting occurred and saw Goetz sitting on a bench, the injured youths lying on the floor or slumped against a seat, and two women who had apparently taken cover, also lying on the floor. Goetz told the conductor that the four youths had tried to rob him.

While the conductor was aiding the youths, Goetz headed towards the front of the car. The train had stopped just before the Chambers Street station and Goetz went between two of the cars, jumped onto the tracks and fled. Police and ambulance crews arrived at the scene shortly thereafter. Ramseur and Canty, initially listed in critical condition, have fully recovered. Cabey remains paralyzed, and has suffered some degree of brain damage.

On December 31, 1984, Goetz surrendered to police in Concord, New Hampshire. . . . [A]fter receiving *Miranda* warnings, he made two lengthy statements, both of which were tape recorded with his permission. In the statements . . . Goetz admitted that he had been illegally carrying a handgun in New York City for three years. He stated that he had first purchased a gun in 1981 after he had been injured in a mugging. Goetz also revealed that twice between 1981 and 1984 he had successfully warded off assailants simply by displaying the pistol.

According to Goetz's statement, the first contact he had with the four youths came when Canty, sitting or lying on the bench across from him, asked "how are you," to which he replied "fine." Shortly thereafter, Canty, followed by one of the other youths, walked over to the defendant and stood to his left, while the other two youths remained to his right, in the corner of the subway car. Canty then said "give me five dollars." Goetz stated that he knew from the smile on Canty's face that they wanted to "play with me." Although he was certain that none of the youths had a gun, he had a fear, based on prior experiences, of being "maimed."

Goetz then established "a pattern of fire," deciding specifically to fire from left to right. His stated intention at that point was to "murder [the four youths], to hurt them, to make them suffer as much as possible." When Canty again requested money, Goetz stood up, drew his weapon, and began firing, aiming for the center of the body of each of the four. Goetz recalled that the first two he shot "tried to run through the crowd [but] they had nowhere to run." Goetz then turned to his right to "go after the other two." One of these two "tried to run through the wall of the train, but . . . he had nowhere to go." The other youth (Cabey) "tried pretending that he wasn't with [the others]" by standing still, holding on to one of the subway hand straps, and not looking at Goetz. Goetz nonetheless fired his fourth shot at him. He then ran back to the first two youths to make sure they had been "taken care of." Seeing that they had both been shot, he spun back to check on the latter two. Goetz noticed that the youth who had been standing still was now sitting on a bench and seemed unhurt. As Goetz told the police, "I said '[y]ou seem to be all right, here's another,'" and he then fired the shot which severed Cabey's spinal cord. Goetz added that "if I was a little more under self-control . . . I would have put the barrel against his forehead and fired." He also admitted that "if I had had more [bullets], I would have shot them again, and again, and again." . . .

Penal Law article 35 recognizes the defense of justification, which "permits the use of force under certain circumstances." One such set of circumstances pertains to the use of force in defense of a person, encompassing both self-defense and defense of a third person. Penal Law §35.15 (1) sets forth the general principles governing all such uses of force: "[a] person may . . . use physical force upon another person when and to the extent he *reasonably believes* such to be necessary to defend himself or a third person from what he *reasonably believes* to be the use or imminent use of unlawful physical force by such other person" (emphasis added).

Section 35.15 (2) sets forth further limitations on these general principles with respect to the use of "deadly physical force": "A person may not use deadly physical force upon another person under circumstances specified in subdivision one unless (a) He *reasonably believes* that such other person is using or about to use deadly physical force . . . or (b) He *reasonably believes* that such other person is committing or attempting to commit a kidnapping, forcible rape, forcible sodomy or robbery" (emphasis added). . . .

Because the evidence before the [Grand Jury] included statements by Goetz that he acted to protect himself from being maimed or to avert a robbery, the prosecutor correctly chose to charge the justification defense in section 35.15 to the Grand Jury . . . essentially by reading or paraphrasing the language in Penal Law §35.15. The defense does not contend that he committed any error in this portion of the charge.

When the prosecutor had completed his charge, one of the grand jurors asked for clarification of the term "reasonably believes." The prosecutor responded by instructing the grand jurors that they were to consider the circumstances of the incident and determine "whether the defendant's conduct was that of a reasonable man in the defendant's situation." It is this response by the prosecutor—and specifically his use of "a reasonable man"—which is the basis for the dismissal of the charges by the lower courts. As expressed repeatedly in the Appellate Division's plurality opinion, because section 35.15 uses the term *he* reasonably believes, the appropriate test, according to that court, is whether a defendant's beliefs and reactions were "reasonable to *him*." Under that reading of the statute, a jury which believed a defendant's testimony that he felt that his own actions were warranted and were reasonable would have to acquit him, regardless of what anyone else in defendant's situation might have concluded. Such an interpretation defies the ordinary meaning and significance of the term "reasonably" in a statute, and misconstrues the clear intent of the Legislature, in enacting section 35.15, to retain an objective element as part of any provision authorizing the use of deadly physical force. . . .

In 1961 the Legislature established a Commission to undertake a complete revision of the Penal Law. . . . The impetus for the decision to update the Penal Law came in part from the drafting of the Model Penal Code. . . . While using the Model Penal Code provisions on justification as general guidelines . . . the drafters of the new Penal Law did not simply adopt them verbatim.

The provisions of the Model Penal Code with respect to the use of deadly force in self-defense reflect the position of its drafters that any culpability which arises from a mistaken belief in the need to use such force should be no greater than the culpability such a mistake would give rise to if it were made with respect to an element of a crime. Accordingly, under Model Penal Code §3.04 (2) (b), a defendant charged with murder (or attempted murder) need only show that he "*believe[d]* that [the use of deadly force] was necessary to protect himself against death, serious bodily injury, kidnapping or [forcible] sexual intercourse" to prevail on a self-defense claim (emphasis added). If the defendant's belief was wrong, and was recklessly, or negligently formed, however, he may be convicted of the type of homicide charge requiring only a reckless or negligent, as the case may be, criminal intent (see, Model Penal Code §3.09 . . .).

New York did not follow the Model Penal Code's equation of a mistake as to the need to use deadly force with a mistake negating an element of a crime, choosing instead to use a single statutory section which would provide either a complete defense or no defense at all to a defendant charged with any crime involving the use of deadly force. The drafters of the new Penal Law adopted in large part the structure and content of Model Penal Code §3.04, but, crucially, inserted the word "reasonably" before "believes." . . . Had the drafters of section 35.15 wanted to adopt a subjective standard, they could have simply used the language of section 3.04. "Believes" by itself requires an honest or genuine belief by a defendant as to the need to use deadly force. Interpreting the statute to require only that the defendant's belief was "reasonable to *him*," as done by the plurality below, would hardly be different from requiring only a genuine belief; in either case, the defendant's own perceptions could completely exonerate him from any criminal liability.

We cannot lightly impute to the Legislature an intent to fundamentally alter the principles of justification to allow the perpetrator of a serious crime to go free simply because that person believed his actions were reasonable and necessary to prevent some perceived harm. To completely exonerate such an individual, no matter how aberrational or bizarre his thought patterns, would allow citizens to set their own standards for the permissible use of force. . . . We can only conclude that the Legislature retained a reasonableness requirement to avoid giving license for such actions. . . .

Goetz also argues that the introduction of an objective element will preclude a jury from considering factors such as the prior experiences of a given actor and thus, require it to make a determination of "reasonableness" without regard to the actual circumstances of a particular incident. This argument, however, falsely presupposes that an objective standard means that the background and other relevant characteristics of a particular actor must be ignored. To the contrary, we have frequently noted that a determination of reasonableness must be based on the "circumstances" facing a defendant or his "situation." Such terms encompass more than the physical movements of the potential assailant. [T]hese terms include any relevant knowledge the defendant had about that person. They also necessarily bring in the physical attributes of all persons involved, including the defendant. Furthermore, the defendant's circumstances encompass any prior experiences he had which could provide a reasonable basis for a belief that another person's intentions were to injure or rob him or that the use of deadly force was necessary under the circumstances. . . . The prosecutor's instruction . . . was thus essentially an accurate charge. . . .

Accordingly, . . . the dismissed counts of the indictment [are] reinstated.

NOTES ON THE GOETZ CASE

The jury subsequently convicted Goetz on the charge of carrying an unlicensed concealed weapon, but acquitted him on all other counts. N.Y. Times, June 18, 1987, at B6. He was sentenced on the weapons count to one year in jail, with the possibility of release after 60 days. N.Y. Times, Jan. 14, 1989, at 1. In a subsequent civil suit, the jury—applying the same test for the right to use deadly force in self-defense—found Goetz's actions unjustified, and it awarded Darryl Cabey $43 million in damages. See N.Y. Times, Sept. 10, 2000, at 39.

The *Goetz* case became a cause célèbre. Two book-length studies appeared. George Fletcher, A Crime of Self-Defense: Bernhard Goetz and the Law on Trial (1988); Lilian Rubin, Quiet Rage: Bernie Goetz in a Time of Madness (1988). Consider the following reactions.

Joseph Berger, Goetz *Case: Commentary on Nature of Urban Life, N.Y. Times, June 18, 1987, at B6:* The acquittal of Mr. Goetz on charges of attempted murder broke no dramatic new legal ground, in the opinion of legal experts. But in the context of the national debate on the balance between self-defense and social order, it appeared to widen the circumstances that justify the use of deadly force. . . .

There was almost no evidence presented that any of the four youths who approached Mr. Goetz had actually tried to rob him before he shot them. Thus the jury, by rejecting the charge of attempted murder, seemed to be saying that in the nervousness that courses through much of urban experience, from riding the subway at night to walking a darkened street, such evidence may not matter all that much. Perceptions, the jury suggested, can attain the power of facts.

"The jury decided that no man is reasonable when he's surrounded by four thugs," said Alan Dershowitz, professor of law at Harvard Law School. "It's hard to pay attention to lines drawn by academics in a classroom."

Mr. Dershowitz, noting that jurors often nullify self-defense standards set by the law, said he believed that what Mr. Goetz did was by definition illegal in New York State and every other state. It is illegal, he said, to shoot a person after the immediate danger has passed. "It doesn't change the law," he said of the verdict. "It may show the law is somewhat out of line with people's passions today."

The jury's decision also seemed to be a back-handed commentary on the effectiveness of the police and the courts. Burt Neuborne, a professor at New York University Law School, said, "The jurors had so little faith in the criminal justice system, both to protect us and to bring the guilty to justice, that they were willing to tolerate a degree of vigilante behavior that I think rationally cannot be justified." . . .

Crime has become such a daily feature of urban life that several of the jurors had themselves been victims. It is often on people's minds, determining where they live, how and when they travel, and how they spend their time.

The jury seemed to be saying that the fear of crime, in someone who has been a previous mugging victim like Mr. Goetz, can weigh so heavily on one's emotions that it can lead to conduct that might normally be considered wrongful. The jury in the Goetz case apparently believed there was not enough evidence to show that Mr. Goetz acted out of any motive other than fear. . . .

Underlying the issue of crime in this case was the issue of race. Scholars such as Dr. Kenneth B. Clark, professor emeritus of psychology at the City

University of New York, have expressed doubt that Mr. Goetz would have shot four white youths asking him for money.

However, Marvin E. Wolfgang, a criminologist at the University of Pennsylvania, said that perceptions about who is more likely to commit a crime have some statistical basis. The rates of crime for four violent offenses—homicide, rape, robbery and aggravated assault—are at least ten times as high for blacks as they are for whites, he said. "The expectation that four young black males are going to do you harm is indeed greater than four young whites," he said. "I can understand the black position that this is a racist attitude, but it's not unrealistic."

It is possible that jurors have absorbed such racially based perceptions about who is going to commit a crime. Elijah Anderson, a black sociologist at the University of Pennsylvania who spent three years studying street-corner life in a tough, black neighborhood in Philadelphia, said law-abiding people, black and white, have a distinctive way of relating "to people they assume to be members of the black underclass." People, he said, "can be very intimidated by young black males or people who seem to represent this so-called underclass by their dress or comportment, very intimidated." . . .

Because it raises such issues, the jury verdict may pose some hard questions for the American public to deal with. Will some New Yorkers come to feel that they can now make hair-trigger assumptions about the character of people who somehow threaten them, and if they have a gun, use it in self-defense? Will blacks have to fear that if they look at someone the wrong way or dress too casually they may be mistaken for criminals? . . .

Stephen L. Carter, When Victims Happen to Be Black, 97 Yale L.J. 420, 425-426 (1988): Shortly after a New York jury acquitted Bernhard Goetz [a cartoon appeared of a] post-*Goetz* subway car: two elderly women seated side-by-side in a car empty of other passengers, a screwdriver lying nearby, and outside, a crowd of people, eyes widened with fear, running away from the car. One of the women says to the other: "Heavens! . . . I was just reaching for my lipstick."

[T]he artist managed . . . to capture the shuddering tensions apparent in public reactions to the Goetz incident and the verdict in his trial, and much more besides. Mr. Goetz's public—those who declared him a hero from the first—can find in this cartoon a portrait of salvation of a sort. The people fleeing are thugs and toughs, the anonymous yet ubiquitous individuals who frequent New York's subway trains and cast terror with a glance. . . .

[T]he story of the subway car as perceived by Mr. Goetz's public—the choice of transgressor, the choice of victim—might have been starkly different had Mr. Goetz been black and the others white, and had Mr. Goetz cried "self-defense" while the others insisted that when he pulled the gun, they had been minding their own business. For in that event, a public with no real knowledge of the facts other than the stories told by the participants and the skin colors of the shooter and his victims would not have raced at once to Mr. Goetz's defense. . . .

Against this background, consider once more the cartoon [just described], this time from the point of view of Mr. Goetz's critics, the ones who have condemned the verdict as opening the hunting season on young black men. Now the people fleeing the car are frightened innocents, victims themselves, probably black or brown, who can no longer be certain which gesture of impatience or annoyance someone else will take as a threat, who are now loathe to ask directions or change of a dollar for fear of a fatal misinterpretation. The elderly women left alone in the car are . . . aging, they are women, they are white. . . . And because in society's eyes they are the archetypal victims, were they to shoot and to testify to their fear, their story would be readily believed; the tale told by their tormenters would surely be doubted. . . .

Jody D. Armour, Race Ipsa Loquitur: Of Reasonable Racists, Intelligent Bayesians, and Involuntary Negrophobes, 46 Stan. L. Rev. 781, 787-788, 790, 792, 794, 795 (1994): [E]ven if the "typical" American believes that blacks' "propensity" toward violence justifies a quicker and more forceful response when a suspected assailant is black, this fact is legally significant only if the law defines *reasonable* beliefs as *typical* beliefs. The reasonableness inquiry, however, extends beyond typicality to consider the social interests implicated in a given situation. Hence not all "typical" beliefs are per se reasonable. . . . If we accept that racial discrimination violates contemporary social morality, then an actor's failure to overcome his racism for the sake of another's health, safety, and personal dignity is blameworthy and thus unreasonable, independent of whether or not it is "typical." . . .

A second argument which a defendant may advance to justify acting on race-based assumptions is that, given statistics demonstrating blacks' disproportionate involvement in crime, it is reasonable to perceive a greater threat from a black person than a white person. . . .

Although biases in the criminal justice system exaggerate the differences in rates of violent crime by race, it may, tragically, still be true that blacks commit a disproportionate number of crimes. Given that the blight of institutional racism continues to disproportionately limit the life chances of African-Americans, and that desperate circumstances increase the likelihood that individuals caught in this web may turn to desperate undertakings, such a disparity, if it exists, should sadden but not surprise us. . . .

To the extent that socioeconomic status explains the overinvolvement of blacks in robbery and assault (assuming that there is, in fact, such overinvolvement), race serves merely as a proxy for socioeconomic status. But if race is a proxy for socioeconomic factors, then race loses its predictive value when one controls for those factors. . . .

The use of race-based generalizations in the self-defense context has an especially grievous effect: . . . Ultimately, race-based evidence of reasonableness impairs the capacity of jurors to rationally and fairly strike a balance between the costs of waiting (increased risk for the person who perceives imminent attack) and the costs of not waiting (injury or death to the immediate victim, exclusion of blacks from core community activities, and, ultimately, reduction of individuals to predictable objects). In fact, such evidence may be so effective at tapping the racism—conscious or unconscious—which has been proven to infect jury deliberations, that it should arguably be excluded under the "more prejudicial than probative" standard of most states' evidence codes, of which the provisions in section 403 of the Federal Rules of Evidence are illustrative.[55]

NOTES ON DEADLY FORCE

"Deadly force" plays a crucial role on both sides of the self-defense equation, because a defender can *use* deadly force in response to a *threat* of deadly force. But in the law, the two concepts are not identical.

1. When does a person *use* deadly force? Goetz obviously did so, even though he did not kill any of his victims, because he shot directly at them, "aiming for the center of the body of each." Could a person in Goetz's position avoid the limits on using deadly force by aiming for the feet of his attackers? If that person had defended himself in that way, would he (should he) be able to claim that he had not used *deadly* force? Under current law, that move would not work because a person is deemed to use deadly force whenever he or she knowingly creates a substantial risk of inflicting great bodily harm, and shooting in the direction of another person always qualifies as a use of deadly force. See MPC §3.11(2). Force of this sort is therefore unjustified unless the person attacked can show that he or she faced a threat of force that was not only unlawful but exceptionally serious.

2. Which threats rise to that level? Goetz said he was "certain that none of the youths had a gun" but was afraid of being "maimed." If reasonable, is such a fear sufficient to justify the use of deadly force in response? The general rule is that any threat to inflict great bodily harm (such as a threat to maim) qualifies, even if the harm might not be life-threatening. The New York formula, quoted in *Goetz*, also includes "kidnapping, forcible rape, forcible sodomy or robbery." Under the MPC, threats of kidnapping and rape are likewise included (§3.04(2)(b)), but the Code addresses the use of force to prevent robbery as a defense of *property* rather than *self*-defense, and in that setting it imposes stricter limits on the use of deadly force. See §3.06(3)(d). We examine defense of property in the materials beginning at page 872 infra.

NOTES ON STANDARDS OF JUDGMENT

1. A subjective test? The prevailing American rule is that a self-defense claim can succeed only when the defendant's fear and use of defensive force were both reasonable. But if a defendant perceives that he faces a threat of

---

55. See Fed. R. Evid. 403. Rule 403 reads, in relevant part: "Although relevant, evidence may be excluded if its probative value is substantially outweighed by the danger of unfair prejudice, confusion of the issues, or misleading the jury. . . ." [See pages 25-26 supra].

imminent death or great bodily harm, is it reasonable to require a "reasonable" response? Consider Justice Holmes's oft-quoted epigram: "Detached reflection cannot be demanded in the presence of an uplifted knife." Brown v. United States, 256 U.S. 335, 343 (1921). Professor Glanville Williams (quoted in Model Penal Code and Commentaries, Comment to §3.09 at 152, n.10 (1985)) advanced the following argument in support of a wholly subjective test:

> The criminal law of negligence works best when it gives effect to the large number of rules of prudence which are commonly observed though not directly incorporated into the law. Such rules include the rule against pulling out on a blind corner, . . . the rule against deliberately pointing a gun at another person, even in play, and so on. These rules are not part either of enacted or of common law, but as customary standards of behavior they become binding via the law of negligence. Are there any similar rules of behavior applicable when a person acts in self-defense or in making an arrest? It must be recollected that the injury he inflicts on the other is in itself intentional, so that the usual rules of prudence in respect to the handling of weapons are not in question. The only question is whether the defendant was negligent in arriving at the conclusion that the use of the force in question was called for. It is hard to imagine what rules of prudence could normally serve in this situation. Either the defendant is capable of drawing the inferences that a reasonable man would draw or he is not. If he is not, and he is a peace officer, his tendency to make miscalculations would certainly justify his dismissal from the police force. But there is no obvious case for the intervention of the criminal courts.
>
> The only common situation in which a person makes an unreasonable mistake in what he believes to be self-defense is when he is drunk or otherwise in an abnormal mental state. For example, a drunken person may misconstrue a gesture as an attempt to kill, and, acting under this misconception, he may take a knife and kill or nearly kill the person whom he mistakenly supposes to be an assailant. It is submitted that the solution of this problem lies in provisions directed specifically to it. There should be a specific offense of being drunk and dangerous. . . . Where the defendant is insane or feebleminded, the problem of treatment belongs to the wider problem of insanity and feeble-mindedness in the criminal law.

Consider the following critique of the reasonableness requirement. R. Restak, The Fiction of the "Reasonable Man," Wash. Post, Sunday, May 17, 1987, at C3:

> As a neurologist and neuropsychiatrist with over a decade of experience in conducting pretrial interviews of individuals who have acted violently, the "reasonable person" argument seems an illogical and outdated approach to fully understanding events such as occurred on the New York subway in December of 1984 when Bernhard Goetz shot and injured four teenagers.
>
> On the basis of what I know about the human brain I'm convinced that there are no reasonable people under conditions in which death or severe bodily harm are believed imminent.
>
> Deep within the brain of every reasonable person resides the limbic system: an ancient interconnected network of structures that anatomically and

chemically haven't changed much over hundreds of thousands of years. We share these structures with jungle animals as well as animals that many reasonable people keep as pets. Moreover, the limbic system is capable under conditions of extreme duress of overwhelming the cerebral cortex wherein are formulated many of the reasonable person's most reasonable attributes, like interpretation, judgment and restraint.

. . . Emotions are not incidental and subsidiary to rational processes. Instead, the reasonable person, even at his or her most reasonable moments, is influenced by emotional processes. . . .

In view of what we now know of such cases, the logic of the "reasonable man" standard—in the Bernhard Goetz case or similar cases in the future—may be inherently flawed. . . . The firing of a second shot into Darrell Cabey—after, as the prosecution has contended, the immediate threat was over—is crucial to the state's argument. . . . The prosecutor's logic is this: Once Goetz coolly discerned that he was out of danger, he should have calmed down, put away his gun and awaited the arrival of the police.

[S]uch expectations are neurologically unrealistic. Once aroused, the limbic system can become a directive force for hours, sometimes days, and can rarely be shut off like flipping a switch. The heart keeps pounding, the breathing—harsh and labored—burns in the throat; the thoughts keep churning as fear is replaced by anger and finally, murderous rage. . . .

Consider Goetz' response to the question "Did you just shoot each one of these people just once?"

Goetz: "Well, you see that's why I, that's, that's one of the things that puzzles me. . . . I was out of control. [M]aybe you should always be in control, but if you, if you put people in a situation where they're threatened with mayhem, several times, and then if, then if something happens, and if a person acts, turns into a vicious animal. . . . That's not the end of the shooting. . . . I ran back to the first two, to make sure."

Is that what a reasonable person would do under such circumstances?

Although lawyers and judges love to explore such questions, [they place] an overemphasis on empty intellectualization to the exclusion of those deep and powerful emotional currents of fear, self-preservation or territoriality that can surface in any one of us and overpower the cogitations of reason. . . .

Isn't it preferable therefore to face up courageously to these sometimes frightening and unpleasant realities instead of pretending that questions such as those being asked about Bernhard Goetz can be answered by courtroom speculations about how a reasonable person would have responded in his place?

To expect reasonable behavior in the face of perceived threat, terror and rage is itself a most unreasonable expectation.

Questions: What would it mean for the law "to face up courageously to these . . . realities"? Should the law allow a complete defense whenever the defendant honestly fears for his life, regardless of the circumstances?

2. Qualifications to the objective test. As in other instances in which the law employs an objective standard, there is always the question of just how objective the standard is to be—that is, which features of the defendant's particular situation should be taken into account in determining whether the choice of defensive force was reasonable? Compare the discussion of the reasonable-provocation standard, page 458 supra, and the discussion of the definition of negligence, pages 478-480 supra. Recall the MPC standard (§2.02), calling for a judgment whether the defendant's conduct "involves a gross deviation from the standard of care that a reasonable person would observe *in the actor's situation.*" (Italics added.) Thus, the MPC partially individualizes the objective standard. Likewise, "a majority of jurisdictions adopt some form of 'hybrid' standard: the jury must judge the defendant by the standards of the reasonable person . . . in the 'situation.'" Victoria Nourse, After the Reasonable Man: Getting over the Subjectivity/Objectivity Question, 11 New Crim. L. Rev. 33, 36 (2008).

3. *Specifying the actor's "situation."* Which features of a defendant's background, experiences, and personality can properly be taken into account in determining whether his assessment of a threat and his response to it were "reasonable"? Consider the following issues:

(a) In the *Goetz* case, would it be proper to instruct the jury to determine the reaction of a reasonable person who, like Goetz, had been mugged in the past? If Goetz had previously been approached on the subway by four youths who asked him for money and then mugged and severely injured him, would it be proper to instruct the jury to determine the reaction of a reasonable person who had had that experience in the past? In People v. Carrillo, 2010 WL 4371047 (Cal. App. Nov. 5, 2010), the court held in the affirmative. Do you agree?

(b) People v. Romero, 69 Cal. App. 4th 846, 848 (1999), involved a heated street confrontation in which the defendant stabbed and killed a person who had endangered his younger brother. At his trial for murder, he sought to introduce expert testimony concerning "the role of honor, paternalism, and street fighters in the Hispanic culture," in order to support his claims that he believed he was in imminent danger of great bodily harm and that his belief was objectively reasonable. The trial judge ruled the evidence inadmissible on the ground that it was irrelevant to both claims, and the defendant was convicted of second-degree murder. The appellate court affirmed. Do you agree? Why isn't the culture that shapes the defendant's perceptions relevant to his "situation"? For detailed assessment of the role of culture in determinations of reasonableness in this context, see Eugene R. Milhizer, Group Status and Criminal Defenses, 71 Mo. L. Rev. 547 (2006).

(c) An elderly woman riding in a nearly empty subway car late at night is approached by a homeless man who asks her for $5. Believing that she is about to be mugged, she tells him to back off and when he hesitates, she shoots and kills him. A psychologist offers to testify that the woman suffers from acute neurotic fears that lead her to misjudge situations and to perceive mortal threats when none are present. Is the evidence admissible? Should the jury be instructed to determine the reaction of a reasonable person who is in the situation of being (a) elderly, or (b) frail, or (c) neurotically fearful? In

People v. Maggio, 2009 WL 330915 (Cal. App. Feb. 11, 2009), the court held that the circumstance of having a fearful delusion cannot be considered as a part of the defendant's "situation." Do you agree?

4. *A grading problem.* Where reasonableness is required for total exculpation, how should the law deal with a person who holds an honest but unreasonable belief in the need to use lethal force? Assume such a person kills because she genuinely believes it is the only way to save her life, but she comes to her conclusion on grossly unreasonable grounds. She has killed intentionally and, under the prevailing objective test, she has no defense of self-defense. Thus, she would be guilty of murder, just like the person who kills for revenge or gain. This appears to be the generally prevailing view.[2] But several states avoid this result through various doctrines of mitigation. One, known as the doctrine of "imperfect self-defense," classifies the crime as voluntary manslaughter, on the theory that "malice" is lacking and that the lesser culpability in a killing of this sort is similar to that in a killing in a heat of passion.[3] The other approach, even less common, is to classify the killing as involuntary manslaughter.[4] A problem for this theory is that involuntary manslaughter presupposes an unintentional killing, while a killing in self-defense is ordinarily intentional. The justification, nonetheless, is that the actor's culpability most closely approximates that of a person whose criminal negligence causes an unintentional death.

The MPC is similar to this last approach: A person who kills in the honest but unreasonable belief in the need to kill would be guilty of negligent homicide. The Code achieves this result through the interaction of two distinct requirements. First, in the various justification provisions, the Code states that the justification is available whenever the actor herself subjectively believes that the necessary circumstances are present. See, e.g., §3.04(1), stating that the use of force for self protection "is justifiable when the actor believes that such force is immediately necessary. . . ." Second, to deal with situations involving mistaken beliefs, the Code provides in §3.09(2):

> When the actor believes that the use of force upon or toward the person of another is necessary for any of the purposes for which such belief would establish a justification under §§3.03 to 3.08 but the actor is reckless or negligent in having such belief or acquiring or failing to acquire any knowledge or belief which is material to the justifiability of his use of force, the justification afforded by those Sections is unavailable in a prosecution for an offense for which recklessness or negligence, as the case may be, suffices to establish culpability.

The MPC approach has not been influential in state statutory reform. See Note, Justification: The Impact of the Model Penal Code on State Law Reform,

---

2. E.g., State v. Griffin, 2010 WL 292878 (Vt. Jan. 15, 2010).

3. See, e.g., Wilson v. State, 30 A.3d 955 (Md. 2011). Some state statutes also take this approach, e.g., 18 Pa. Cons. Stat. tit. §2503(b) (2011), supra page 424.

4. E.g., Elliott v. Commonwealth, 976 S.W.2d 416, 420 n.3 (Ky. 1998).

75 Colum. L. Rev. 914, 920 (1975). What disadvantages of the MPC approach might have influenced jurisdictions not to accept it?

5. *Problem.* As we have seen, the MPC and the New York self-defense formulations differ in the way they deal with the reasonableness requirement. Consider how the following hypothetical should be analyzed under each formulation: The defendant shoots to kill *Z* in the honest but unreasonable belief that it is necessary to do so to save the defendant's life. He misses, and *Z* escapes unharmed. Is the defendant guilty of attempted murder? Of attempt to commit manslaughter?

STATE v. KELLY

Supreme Court of New Jersey
97 N.J. 178, 478 A.2d 364 (1984)

WILENTZ, C.J. . . . Gladys Kelly, stabbed her husband, Ernest, with a pair of scissors. He died shortly thereafter. . . .

Ms. Kelly was indicted for murder. At trial, she did not deny stabbing her husband, but asserted that her action was in self-defense. To establish the requisite state of mind for her self-defense claim, Ms. Kelly called Dr. Lois Veronen as an expert witness to testify about the battered-woman's syndrome. After hearing a lengthy voir dire examination of Dr. Veronen, the trial court ruled that expert testimony concerning the syndrome was inadmissible on the self-defense issue. . . . Ms. Kelly was convicted of reckless manslaughter. [We] reverse.

The Kellys had a stormy marriage. Some of the details of their relationship, especially the stabbing, are disputed. The following is Ms. Kelly's version of what happened—a version that the jury could have accepted and, if they had, a version that would make the proffered expert testimony not only relevant, but critical.

The day after the marriage, Mr. Kelly got drunk and knocked Ms. Kelly down. Although a period of calm followed the initial attack, the next seven years were accompanied by periodic and frequent beatings, sometimes as often as once a week. During the attacks, which generally occurred when Mr. Kelly was drunk, he threatened to kill Ms. Kelly and to cut off parts of her body if she tried to leave him. Mr. Kelly often moved out of the house after an attack, later returning with a promise that he would change his ways. Until the day of the homicide, only one of the attacks had taken place in public.

The day [of] the stabbing, [Ernest] left for work. Ms. Kelly next saw her husband late that afternoon at a friend's house. She had gone there with her daughter, Annette, to ask Ernest for money to buy food. He told her to wait until they got home, and shortly thereafter the Kellys left. After walking past several houses, Mr. Kelly, who was drunk, angrily asked "What the hell did you come around here for?" He then grabbed the collar of her dress, and the two fell to the ground. He choked her by pushing his fingers against her throat, punched or hit her face, and bit her leg.

A crowd gathered on the street. Two men from the crowd separated them, just as Gladys felt that she was "passing out" from being choked. Fearing that Annette had been pushed around in the crowd, Gladys then left to look for her. . . .

After finding her daughter, Ms. Kelly then observed Mr. Kelly running toward her with his hands raised. Within seconds he was right next to her. Unsure of whether he had armed himself while she was looking for their daughter, and thinking that he had come back to kill her, she grabbed a pair of scissors from her pocketbook. She tried to scare him away, but instead stabbed him.[1]

The central question in this case is whether the trial court erred in its exclusion of expert testimony on the battered-woman's syndrome. That testimony was intended to explain defendant's state of mind and bolster her claim of self-defense. We shall first examine the nature of the battered-woman's syndrome and then consider the expert testimony proffered in this case and its relevance. . . . *[margin note: issue]*

As the problem of battered women has begun to receive more attention, sociologists and psychologists have begun to focus on the effects a sustained pattern of physical and psychological abuse can have on a woman. The effects of such abuse are what some scientific observers have termed "the battered-woman's syndrome," a series of common characteristics that appear in women who are abused physically and psychologically over an extended period of time by the dominant male figure in their lives. Dr. Lenore Walker, a prominent writer on the battered-woman's syndrome, defines the battered woman as one

> who is repeatedly subjected to any forceful physical or psychological behavior by a man in order to coerce her to do something he wants her to do without concern for her rights. Battered women include wives or women in any form of intimate relationships with men. Furthermore, in order to be classified as a battered woman, the couple must go through the battering cycle at least twice. Any woman may find herself in an abusive relationship with a man once. If it occurs a second time, and she remains in the situation, she is defined as a battered woman. *[margin note: what constitutes a battered woman]*

[L. Walker, The Battered Woman (1979) at xv.]

According to Dr. Walker, relationships characterized by physical abuse tend to develop battering cycles. Violent behavior directed at the woman occurs in three distinct and repetitive stages that vary both in duration and intensity depending on the individuals involved. [As summarized by the court, the expert testimony maintained that phase one of the battering cycle, the

---

1. This version of the homicide—with a drunk Mr. Kelly as the aggressor both in pushing Ms. Kelly to the ground and again in rushing at her with his hands in a threatening position after the two had been separated—is sharply disputed by the State. The prosecution presented testimony intended to show that the initial scuffle was started by Gladys; that upon disentanglement, while she was restrained by bystanders, she stated that she intended to kill Ernest; that she then chased after him, and upon catching up with him stabbed him with a pair of scissors taken from her pocketbook.

explanation of the three stage cycle

"tension-building stage," involves minor battering incidents and verbal abuse during which the woman, beset by fear, attempts to be placating in order to stave off more serious violence. Phase two involves an "acute battering incident" typically triggered by an event in the life of the battering male, although the testimony also suggested that provocation for more severe violence is sometimes provided by the woman, who can no longer control her phase-one anger and anxiety. Phase three of the cycle is characterized by extreme contrition and loving behavior on the part of the battering male, who will often mix pleas for forgiveness with promises to stop drinking and seek professional help. Dr. Walker testified that for some couples, this period of relative calm may last as long as several months, but that the contrition of the man will eventually fade and phase one of the cycle will start anew.]

The cyclical nature of battering behavior helps explain why more women simply do not leave their abusers. The loving behavior demonstrated . . . during phase three reinforces whatever hopes these women might have for their mate's reform and keeps them bound to the relationship. Some women may even perceive the battering cycle as normal, especially if they grew up in a violent household. . . . Other women, however, become so demoralized and degraded by the fact that they cannot predict or control the violence that they sink into a state of psychological paralysis and become unable to take any action at all to improve or alter the situation. There is a tendency in battered women to believe in the omnipotence or strength of their battering husbands and thus to feel that any attempt to resist them is hopeless.

In addition . . . , [lack of material and social resources] often make[s] it difficult for some women to extricate themselves from battering relationships. [T]here may be no place [for them] to go. Moreover, the stigma that attaches to a woman who leaves the family unit without her children undoubtedly acts as a further deterrent to moving out. [B]attered women, when they want to leave the relationship, are typically unwilling to reach out and confide in their friends, family, or the police, either out of shame and humiliation, fear of reprisal by their husband, or the feeling they will not be believed.

Dr. Walker and other commentators have identified several common personality traits of the battered woman(low self-esteem, traditional beliefs about the home, the family, and the female sex role, tremendous feelings of guilt that their marriages are failing, and the tendency to accept responsibility for the batterer's actions.]

Finally, battered women are often hesitant to leave a battering relationship because . . . they harbor a deep concern about the possible response leaving might provoke in their mates. They literally become trapped by their own fear. Case histories are replete with instances in which a battered wife left her husband only to have him pursue her and subject her to an even more brutal attack.

The combination of all these symptoms—resulting from sustained psychological and physical trauma compounded by aggravating social and economic factors—constitutes the battered-woman's syndrome. Only by understanding these unique pressures that force battered women to remain with their mates, despite their long-standing and reasonable fear of severe bodily harm and the isolation that being a battered woman creates, can a battered woman's state of mind be accurately and fairly understood.

The voir dire testimony of Dr. Veronen, sought to be introduced by defendant Gladys Kelly, conformed essentially to this outline of the battered-woman's syndrome. . . . In addition, Dr. Veronen was prepared to testify as to how, as a battered woman, Gladys Kelly perceived her situation . . . , and why, in her opinion, defendant did not leave her husband despite the constant beatings she endured.

Whether expert testimony on the battered-woman's syndrome should be admitted in this case depends on whether it is relevant to defendant's claim of self-defense. . . . The use of force against another in self-defense is justifiable "when the actor reasonably believes that such force is immediately necessary for the purpose of protecting himself against the use of unlawful force by such other person on the present occasion." N.J.S.A. 2C:3-4(a). Further limitations exist when deadly force is used in self-defense. The use of such deadly force is not justifiable

> unless the actor reasonably believes that such force is necessary to protect himself against death or serious bodily harm. . . . [N.J.S.A. 2C:3-4(b)(2).]

Gladys Kelly claims that she stabbed her husband in self-defense, believing he was about to kill her. The gist of the State's case was that Gladys Kelly was the aggressor, that she consciously intended to kill her husband, and that she certainly was not acting in self-defense.

The credibility of Gladys Kelly is a critical issue in this case. If the jury does not believe Gladys Kelly's account, it cannot find she acted in self-defense. The expert testimony offered was directly relevant to one of the critical elements of that account, namely, what Gladys Kelly believed at the time of the stabbing, and was thus material to establish the honesty of her stated belief that she was in imminent danger of death. . . . Specifically, by showing that her experience, although concededly difficult to comprehend, was common to that of other women who had been in similarly abusive relationships, Dr. Veronen would have helped the jury understand that Gladys Kelly could have honestly feared that she would suffer serious bodily harm from her husband's attacks, yet still remain with him. . . . On the facts of this case, we find that the expert testimony . . . was admissible to show she *honestly* believed she was in imminent danger of death. . . .

We also find the expert testimony relevant to the reasonableness of defendant's belief that she was in imminent danger of death or serious injury. We do not mean that the expert's testimony could be used to show that it was understandable that a battered woman might believe that her life was in danger when indeed it was not and when a reasonable person would not have so believed. . . . Expert testimony in that direction would be relevant solely to the honesty of defendant's belief, not its objective reasonableness. Rather, our conclusion is that the expert's testimony, if accepted by the jury, would

[handwritten margin note: Should allow expert testimony to establish D state of mind]

have aided it in determining whether, under the circumstances, a reasonable person would have believed there was imminent danger to her life.

At the heart of the claim of self-defense was defendant's story that she had been repeatedly subjected to "beatings" over the course of her marriage. . . . When that regular pattern of serious physical abuse is combined with defendant's claim that the decedent sometimes threatened to kill her, defendant's statement that on this occasion she thought she might be killed when she saw Mr. Kelly running toward her could be found to reflect a reasonable fear; that is, it could so be found if the jury believed Gladys Kelly's story. . . .

The crucial issue of fact on which this expert's testimony would bear is why, given such allegedly severe and constant beatings, combined with threats to kill, defendant had not long ago left decedent. Whether raised by the prosecutor as a factual issue or not, our own common knowledge tells us that most of us, including the ordinary juror, would ask himself or herself just such a question. [O]ne of the common myths, apparently believed by most people, is that battered wives are free to leave. To some, this misconception is followed by the observation that the battered wife is masochistic, proven by her refusal to leave despite the severe beatings; to others, however, the fact that the battered wife stays on unquestionably suggests that the "beatings" could not have been too bad for if they had been, she certainly would have left. The expert could clear up these myths, by explaining that one of the common characteristics of a battered wife is her *inability* to leave despite such constant beatings; her "learned helplessness"; her lack of anywhere to go; her feeling that if she tried to leave, she would be subjected to even more merciless treatment; her belief in the omnipotence of her battering husband; and sometimes her hope that her husband will change his ways. . . .

The difficulty with the expert's testimony is that it *sounds* as if an expert is giving knowledge to a jury about something the jury knows as well as anyone else, namely, the reasonableness of a person's fear of imminent serious danger. That is not at all, however, what this testimony is *directly* aimed at. It is aimed at an area where the purported common knowledge of the jury may be very much mistaken, an area where jurors' logic, drawn from their own experience, may lead to a wholly incorrect conclusion. . . . After hearing the expert, instead of saying Gladys Kelly could not have been beaten up so badly for if she had, she certainly would have left, the jury could conclude that her failure to leave was very much part and parcel of her life as a battered wife. The jury could conclude that instead of casting doubt on the accuracy of her testimony about the severity and frequency of prior beatings, her failure to leave actually reinforced her credibility.

Since a retrial is necessary, we think it advisable to indicate the limit of the expert's testimony on this issue of reasonableness. It would not be proper for the expert to express the opinion that defendant's belief on that day was reasonable, not because this is the ultimate issue, but because the area of *expert* knowledge relates, in this regard, to the reasons for defendant's failure to leave her husband. Either the jury accepts or rejects that explanation and, based on that, credits defendant's stories about the beatings she suffered. No expert is needed, however, once the jury has made up its mind on those issues, to tell the jury the logical conclusion, namely, that a person who has in fact been severely and continuously beaten might very well reasonably fear that the imminent beating she was about to suffer could be either life-threatening or pose a risk of serious injury. What the expert could state was that defendant had the battered-woman's syndrome, and could explain that syndrome in detail, relating its characteristics to defendant, but only to enable the jury better to determine the honesty and reasonableness of defendant's belief. Depending on its content, the expert's testimony might also enable the jury to find that the battered wife, because of the prior beatings, numerous beatings, as often as once a week, for seven years, from the day they were married to the day he died, is particularly able to predict accurately the likely extent of violence in any attack on her. That conclusion could significantly affect the jury's evaluation of the reasonableness of defendant's fear for her life. . . .

[The court remanded for a new trial.[a]]

NOTES ON THE BATTERED WOMAN'S SYNDROME

1. *The problem of domestic violence.* Justice Department surveys indicate that the incidence of domestic violence has been declining modestly in recent years but continues to affect large numbers of women. Over the period 2001-2005, an average of more than half a million women annually were severely beaten by their spouses or other domestic partners, and in 2005, 1,181 were killed.[5] There is also a substantial overlap between battering and intimate-partner rape; some surveys suggest that sexual assault and forcible rape are involved in 40-45 percent of battering relationships. See Emily J. Sack, Is Domestic Violence a Crime? Intimate Partner Rape as Allegory, 24 St. John's J. Legal Comment. 535, 547 (2010). Men are frequently slapped, kicked, or beaten by their spouses or girlfriends, but they are much less likely to be victims of the most serious assaults; in the Justice Department surveys, 104,000 men annually were victims of significant domestic violence, and in 2005, 329 were killed.[6] Thus, women are almost five times more likely to be the victim of a serious domestic assault. And although the debate about battered spouse syndrome has focused attention on women who kill their

---

a. On remand, the prosecution did not challenge the admissibility of the expert's evidence on the battered woman's syndrome. Instead it offered its own experts to support the conclusion that the defendant did not meet the criteria of the syndrome. Apparently the strategy was successful because at the second trial she was again convicted of reckless manslaughter. See Bergen (N.J.) Rec., June 27, 1985, p. A21; Elizabeth Schneider, Describing and Changing: Women's Self-Defense Work and the Problem of Expert Testimony on Battering, 9 Women's Rts. L. Rep. 195, 205 n.59 (1986).—Eds.

5. U.S. Dept. of Justice, Bureau of Justice Statistics, Intimate Partner Violence in the United States 1993-2005 (Dec. 2007), p. 24, available at http://bjs.ojp.usdoj.gov/index.cfm?ty=pbdetail&iid=1000; U.S. Dept. of Justice, Nat'l Institute of Justice, Practical Implications of Current Domestic Violence Research (June 2009), pp. 1, 3, available at https://www.ncjrs.gov/pdffiles1/nij/225722.pdf.

6. Id.

spouses, men are three times more likely than women to kill their spouses or partners.

Wife beating has a long, ignominious history; at one time the common law explicitly granted the husband a legal privilege to chastise and punish his wife.[7] This prerogative disappeared in the nineteenth century, but police and prosecutors continued to ignore or tolerate the practice (and more severe physical abuses) until very recent times. Until the 1980s, many police departments had rules expressly discouraging officers from making an arrest in response to a domestic violence complaint. The battered woman's perception that legal authorities offered no recourse often was well grounded in fact.

This picture began to change in the 1980s.[8] Many police departments began to encourage or even mandate an arrest in domestic violence cases. Advocates for battered women urged the adoption of mandatory-arrest policies and "no-drop" policies to prevent prosecutors from declining to prosecute such cases. An initial empirical study, conducted in Minneapolis, provided strong support for the hypothesis that mandatory arrest would deter battering, but subsequent studies raised concern about possible countervailing effects. Because battered women often are economically dependent on, and fearful of, their male partners, mandatory-arrest policies in some instances seemed to deter reporting and calls for help by women, more than they deterred violence by men. There was also some evidence that mandatory-arrest policies sometimes prompted the arrested men to be *more* violent toward their spouses afterward. One scholar who initially supported mandatory arrest cautioned that in light of later studies, the mandatory-arrest approach to domestic violence "may make as much sense as fighting a fire with gasoline."[9]

The jury is still out on this issue, but in the meantime many advocates for battered women also have begun to question mandatory-arrest and no-drop policies, arguing that these approaches give too little weight to the victim's own sense of what kind of official intervention would be best for her[10] and "preclude the legal system from being able to respond contextually to the needs of individual women." Leigh Goodmark, Reframing Domestic Violence Law and Policy: An Anti-Essentialist Proposal, 31 Wash. U. J.L. & Pol'y 39, 52 (2009).[11] In some jurisdictions, those problems are aggravated when

---

7. See Reva B. Siegel, "The Rule of Love": Wife Beating as Prerogative and Privacy, 105 Yale L.J. 2117 (1996).

8. See Lawrence W. Sherman, Policing Domestic Violence: Experiments and Dilemmas (1992); Stephen J. Schulhofer, The Feminist Challenge in Criminal Law, 143 U. Pa. L. Rev. 2151, 2158-2170 (1994); Joan Zorza, The Criminal Law of Misdemeanor Domestic Violence, 83 J. Crim. L. & Criminology 46 (1992).

9. Sherman, supra, at 210.

10. See Lisa A. Goodman & Deborah Epstein, Listening to Battered Women: A Survivor-Centered Approach to Advocacy, Mental Health, and Justice 90 (2008); Linda G. Mills, Killing Her Softly: Intimate Abuse and the Violence of State Intervention, 113 Harv. L. Rev. 550 (1999).

11. Others, however, believe that "victim empowerment" often undermines effective enforcement and the interests of victims themselves. See Jane Aiken & Katherine Goldwasser, The Perils of Empowerment, 20 Cornell J.L. & Pub. Pol'y 139, 152 (2010). See also Cheryl Hanna, No Right to Choose: Mandated Victim Participation in Domestic Violence Prosecutions, 109 Harv. L. Rev. 1849,

prosecutors, in an effort to keep victims safe, seek to combine criminal sanctions with orders of protection that bar the abuser from returning home or going anywhere near the victim. The result can be "state-imposed de facto divorce," often against the wishes of the domestic violence victim herself. See Jeannie Suk, At Home in the Law 35 (2009).

Few professionals in this field believe that vigorous prosecution and punishment of batterers can be sufficient by themselves. And women's advocates have noted another dilemma (Deborah Epstein, Procedural Justice: Tempering the State's Response to Domestic Violence, 43 Wm. & Mary L. Rev. 1843, 1846-1847 (2002)):

> [D]iscretionless policies [reduce] the likelihood that defendants will . . . feel that state authorities are attempting to be fair [and the resulting likelihood that they will comply with court orders]. [Because] reformers have sought to protect victims regardless of the impact on batters, and have paid little attention to the potentially close connection between victim safety and abuser's sense of fair treatment[,] . . . a new focus is necessary for victims' long-term protection.

Reflecting these concerns, current proposals often seek to coordinate criminal-justice responses with improved shelter systems and better social and economic support for battered women and their children.[12] Since the 1990s, moreover, most major cities have established specialized domestic violence courts to avoid contradictory court rulings by consolidating before a single judge all legal matters affecting a single family, from criminal assault charges and civil orders of protection to child custody, property settlement, and divorce.[13] Another important initiative has been to require social/psychological treatment for batterers. But the effectiveness of such programs is unclear and, like prosecution, these programs can sometimes backfire. One domestic violence victim, for example, reported that she had been beaten every Monday night because her husband "would come home madder than hell because he had to go to that place. . . . I told the judge, 'I don't care what you do to him, but don't send him to counseling,' " which she called "the worst help ever."[14]

Approaches like these and the resources devoted to them vary widely from community to community. Awareness of what help is available can vary among abused women as well. Although substantial progress has been made, the problems of domestic violence are still a long way from being solved.

1909 (1996), concluding that "leaving the choice of prosecution to the victim . . . creates more problems than it solves."

12. See Goodman & Epstein, supra footnote 10; Nina W. Tarr, Employment and Economic Security for Victims of Domestic Abuse, 16 S. Cal. Rev. L. & Soc. Just. 371 (2007). A related "survivor-centered" approach places the victim's emotional needs at the center of attention. Mills, supra footnote 10.

13. See Eve S. Buzawa & Carl G. Buzawa, Domestic Violence: The Criminal Justice Response 247-255 (3d ed. 2003).

14. Quoted in Goodmark, supra, at 50-51.

Thus, as in the past, women at times may in some sense be trapped in an abusive relationship, or have reasons to believe they are.

2. Same-sex domestic violence. The incidence of violence in same-sex relationships is less well studied and is subject to widely varying estimates, but there is little doubt that the problem is significant. See Same-Sex Domestic Violence: Strategies for Change (Beth Levanthal & Sandra E. Lundy eds., 1999). Some authorities believe that the dynamics of domestic violence are similar in same-sex and heterosexual relationships, but others believe that there are distinctive features in different contexts, including differential risks of exposure to HIV infection, the increased sense of isolation felt by victims in same-sex relationships, and greater difficulty obtaining police intervention and other official help. For a useful overview of the empirical research and policy issues, see Shannon Little, Note, Challenging Changing Legal Definitions of Family in Same-Sex Domestic Violence, 19 Hastings Women's L.J. 259 (2008); Ryiah Lilith, Reconsidering the Abuse that Dare Not Speak Its Name: A Criticism of Recent Legal Scholarship Regarding Same-Gender Domestic Violence, 7 Mich. J. Gender & L. 181 (2001).

3. When battered women kill. The idea of a battered woman's syndrome and its use to support a criminal-law defense are subjects discussed in an extensive literature.[15] We focus here on the issues that arise when testimony about the effects of battering is invoked in connection with a claim of justified self-defense. But we should note that such testimony may also be used in an effort to establish a partial excuse. See page 460 supra, discussing heat-of-passion manslaughter, page 931 infra, discussing duress, and page 998 infra, discussing diminished capacity.

4. The issue of reasonableness. Is evidence of battered woman's syndrome relevant to whether the defendant's response to the situation was reasonable? The *Kelly* court appears to say yes, but *not* because the standard is that of the reasonable battered woman. Most courts agree that the syndrome evidence is relevant to reasonableness, but only in a limited way. Explaining the appropriate standard, the California Supreme Court has said (People v. Humphrey, 13 Cal. 4th 1073, 1086-1087 (1996)):

> [T]he jury, in determining objective reasonableness, must view the situation from the *defendant's perspective*. [T]he prosecutor argued that, "from an objective, reasonable man's standard, there was no reason for her to go get that gun. This threat that she says he made was like so many threats before. There was no reason for her to react that way." Dr. Browker's testimony supplied a response that the jury might not otherwise receive. As violence

---

15. See Regina A. Schuller & Neil Vidmar, BWS Evidence in the Courtroom: A Review of the Literature, 16 Law & Hum. Behav. 273 (1992). Important contributions to the debate, in addition to those cited in the text, include Cynthia Gillespie, Justifiable Homicide: Battered Women, Self Defense and the Law (1989); Holly Maguigan, Battered Women and Self-Defense: Myths and Misconceptions in Court Reform Proposals, 140 U. Pa. L. Rev. 379 (1991); Martha R. Mahoney, Legal Images of Battered Women: Redefining the Issue of Separation, 90 Mich. L. Rev. 1 (1991).

increases over time, and threats gain credibility, a battered person might become sensitized and thus able reasonably to discern when danger is real and when it is not. . . .

The Attorney General concedes that Hampton's behavior towards defendant, including prior threats and violence, was relevant to reasonableness, but distinguishes between evidence of this *behavior*—which the trial court fully admitted—and *expert testimony* about its effects on defendant. The distinction is untenable. "To effectively present the situation as perceived by the defendant, and the reasonableness of her fear, the defense has the option to explain her feelings to enable the jury to overcome stereotyped impressions about women who remain in abusive relationships. It is appropriate that the jury be given a professional explanation of the battering syndrome and its effects on the woman through the use of expert testimony." (State v. Allery (1984), 682 P.2d 312, 316.)

Contrary to the Attorney General's argument, we are not changing the standard from objective to subjective, or replacing the reasonable "person" standard with a reasonable "battered woman" standard. Our decision would not, in another context, compel adoption of a " 'reasonable gang member' standard." . . . The jury must consider defendant's situation and knowledge, which makes the evidence relevant, but the ultimate question is whether a reasonable *person*, not a reasonable battered woman, would believe in the need to kill to prevent imminent harm. Moreover, it is the *jury*, not the expert, that determines whether defendant's belief and, ultimately, her actions, were objectively reasonable.

Compare People v. Romero, 149 Cal. App. 4th 29 (Cal. App. 2007). The defendant, who claimed he had been repeatedly threatened in an abusive same-sex relationship, had killed his male partner. In connection with standard jury instructions on self-defense, he requested an instruction that (id. at 43):

> A person who suffers from battered person's syndrome has a greater sensitivity to danger than does the ordinary person. . . . Evidence has been received in this case that the defendant suffers from battered person's syndrome and has a greater sensitivity to danger. If you believe that the defendant has a greater sensitivity to danger, and because of such sensitivity, had reasonable cause to fear greater peril in the event of an altercation with [the victim], you are to consider such sensitivity in determining whether the defendant acted reasonably in protecting his life or bodily safety.

The trial judge refused this instruction, and the defendant was convicted of involuntary manslaughter. The appellate court affirmed, holding that the instruction above was properly rejected and that "the ultimate question is whether a reasonable person, not a reasonable battered [person], would believe in the need to kill to prevent imminent harm." Id. at 44.

A few courts have moved closer to a fully subjective standard. In State v. Edwards, 60 S.W.3d 602 (Mo. Ct. App. 2001), after a trial in which the defendant introduced extensive evidence that she was suffering from battered spouse syndrome, the judge instructed the jury to consider whether the defendant "reasonably believed she was in imminent danger." The appellate court found this instruction "contradictory . . . and misleading" because (id. at 615):

> A battered woman is a terror-stricken person whose mental state is distorted. Thus, a more accurate statement of the law is that, if the jury believes the defendant was suffering from battered spouse syndrome, it must weigh the evidence in light of how an otherwise reasonable person who is suffering from battered spouse syndrome would have perceived and reacted in view of the prolonged history of physical abuse.

State v. Leidholm, 334 N.W.2d 811, 818 (N.D.1983) goes even further in this direction, holding that the jury should be told that the "defendant's conduct is not to be judged by what a reasonably cautious person might or might not do"; juries instead should "assume the physical *and psychological* properties peculiar to the accused . . . and then decide whether or not the particular circumstances . . . were sufficient to create [a] reasonable belief that the use of force was necessary. . . ." (emphasis added). This approach, the court said, "allows the jury to judge the reasonableness of the accused's actions against the accused's subjective impressions of the need to use force rather than against those impressions . . . that a hypothetical reasonably cautious person would have."

Is it appropriate to individualize the standard to this extent? Professor Stephen Morse thinks not (The "New Syndrome Excuse" Syndrome, 14 Crim. Just. Ethics, 3, 12-13 (Winter/Spring 1995)):

> [I]t is almost impossible to assert sensibly that [barriers to escape] always exist when the syndrome sufferer is in no immediate danger. . . . In response, advocates [for battered women who kill] argue that the battered victim syndrome affects the sufferer's cognitive and volitional functioning, making it difficult or impossible for [her] to recognize or to utilize the alternatives. [I]f these assertions are true, and I believe that they often are, the defendant is really claiming an excuse based on impaired rationality or volition. [P]artial excuses, such as "extreme emotional disturbance" or "imperfect self-defense" [can be] employ[ed]. [But killing] was not the right thing to do, and it should not be justified. . . .
>
> To avoid this logic, [advocates for battered women] sometimes argue that the reasonable person standard should be subjectivized to "the reasonable battered victim syndrome sufferer." . . . But this claim makes a mockery of objective standards. . . . Talk of the "the reasonable battered victim syndrome sufferer" is akin to talk of the "reasonable person suffering from paranoia." . . . Such relativization of ethical standards is . . . impossible for the law to adopt if it is to maintain its moral basis.

Do you agree? Consider the following views on the issue:

Elizabeth Schneider, Describing and Changing: Women's Self-Defense Work and the Problem of Expert Testimony on Battering, 9 Women's Rts. L. Rep. 195, 211-212 (1986): Expert testimony . . . does not address the basic defense problem that the battered woman faces. [If it] is limited, or perceived as limited to the issue of why the woman does not leave, it highlights a contradiction implicit in the message of battered woman syndrome—if the battered woman was so helpless and passive, why did she kill the batterer? [Yet the *Kelly* court holds] that the expert testimony is not relevant to the jury's determination of the reasonableness of a person's fear of imminent severe danger because this is "something the jury knows as well as anyone else." . . .

The reasonableness of the woman's fear and the reasonableness of her act are *not* issues which the jury knows as well as anyone else. The jury needs expert testimony on reasonableness precisely because the jury may not understand that the battered woman's prediction of the likely extent and imminence of violence is particularly acute and accurate.

Susan Estrich, Defending Women (Book Review, Cynthia Gillespie, Justifiable Homicide: Battered Women, Self-Defense and the Law (1989)), 88 Mich. L. Rev. 1430, 1434-1437 (1990): To apply a purely objective standard is unduly harsh because it ignores the characteristics which inevitably and justifiably shape the defender's perspective, thus holding him (or her) to a standard he simply cannot meet. If the defender is young or crippled or blind, we should not expect him to behave like a strapping, sighted adult. On the other hand, if the reasonable person has all of the defender's characteristics, the standard loses any normative component and . . . would give free rein to the short-tempered, the pugnacious, and the foolhardy who see threats of harm where the rest of us would not and who blind themselves to opportunities for escape that seem plainly available. These unreasonable people may not be as wicked as (although perhaps more dangerous than) cold-blooded murderers . . . but neither are they, in practical or legal terms, justified in causing death. . . .

In this context, "reasonableness" can have two possible meanings. First, . . . her experience as a battered woman, and the syndrome from which she suffers, [may make] her a better judge than us of the seriousness of the situation she actually faces. . . . But what of the woman who shoots her husband while he is sound asleep, and not, by anyone's account, about to do anything? What of the woman who faces a beating, but not—even within her own or her expert's description of the cycles of violence—serious bodily harm? Put aside the woman who has tried to escape in the past and been beaten for it, or who has called the police and been rebuffed, or who would be leaving her young children defenseless if she left. In these cases, properly applied, the retreat requirement cannot be met with the necessary "complete safety." But what of the woman who has never tried any of these alternatives? What of the woman who could walk out the back door and into a neighbor's house?

In such cases, the "reasonableness" inquiry, and the evidence of battered woman's syndrome, does not really go to the rightness of the woman's belief in the need for deadly force. It is, instead, a request to abandon the limits on self-defense out of empathy for the circumstances of the defender and disgust for the acts of her abuser. We can find her belief in the imminence of danger "reasonable" only by deciding that these standards mean less in the home than outside it, mean less when applied to cruel husbands who torment defenseless wives than to others.

On its face, that is a very uncomfortable request—at least for those of us who see in the rules of self-defense a laudable recognition of the value of human life and a desirable effort to articulate a normative standard which protects even aggressors and wrongdoers from instant execution or vigilante justice.

5. The issue of scientific reliability.

(a) The law. At the time *Kelly* was decided, courts were divided over whether expert testimony on the battered woman's syndrome (BWS) was sufficiently reliable to allow it to go to the jury. Today its admissibility is overwhelmingly accepted by courts and legislatures. See Rogers v. State, 616 So. 2d 1098, 1100 (Fla. Dist. Ct. App. 1993). In some jurisdictions the issue is resolved by statute. See, e.g., Cal. Evid. Code §1107(b) (2011) ("Expert opinion testimony on intimate partner battering and its effects shall not be considered a new scientific technique whose reliability is unproven"). Texas has an even broader provision, as it is not restricted to intimate partner cases. Tex. Pen. Code §19.06 (2011):

> In a prosecution for murder or manslaughter . . . the defendant, in order to establish the defendant's reasonable belief that use of force or deadly force was immediately necessary, shall be permitted to offer: (1) relevant evidence that the defendant had been the victim of acts of family violence committed by the deceased, . . . and (2) relevant expert testimony regarding the condition of the mind of the defendant at the time of the offense, including those relevant facts and circumstances relating to family violence that are the basis of the expert's opinion.

(b) The science. Concerns about the methodology of the BWS research were raised from the start. In a prescient student note, the author pointed to several problems, observing that the pivotal research of Lenore Walker left unclear the nature of the "loving contrition" phase in the "cycle of violence" and did not indicate whether battered women felt unable to leave during the periods when intimidation was in abeyance. See Note (David L. Faigman), The Battered Woman Syndrome and Self-Defense: A Legal and Empirical Dissent, 72 Va. L. Rev. 619 (1986). Similarly, the Walker research did not specify which groups of women experienced which phases of the cycle of violence, and her data implied that at most only 58 percent of those considered battered women experienced all three phases. As a result, the Note argued, the claim that becomes central in self-defense cases—that battered women develop "learned helplessness" and believe themselves unable to flee—lacked verifiable empirical support.

Subsequent studies reinforce these misgivings. Professor Leigh Goodmark observes that "[e]xperts in the field have largely abandoned the theory of learned helplessness and its conception of women who experience violence as passive non-actors." Goodmark, supra, at 44. See Robert F. Schopp, Barbara J. Sturgis & Megan Sullivan, Battered Woman Syndrome, Expert Testimony, and the Distinction Between Justification and Excuse, [1994] U. Ill. L. Rev. 45, 63-64:

> The complete body of [research] provides neither any clear conception of learned helplessness nor any good reason to believe that it regularly occurs in battered women. . . . Collectively, the data reviewed supports the proposition that battered women do not suffer learned helplessness, at least as well as it supports the claim that they do. Finally, it would be more consistent with the theoretical and empirical foundations of learned helplessness to contend that battered women who kill their batterers differ from those who remain in the battering relationships without killing their batterers precisely because those who kill do *not* manifest learned helplessness.

Despite these developments, however, statutes and case law largely continue to look favorably on expert testimony about BWS.

From a different direction, an emerging body of data suggests that battering, especially when it causes a concussion, can alter the victim's brain chemistry, prompting increased aggressiveness and enhancing fears of future battering. See Jozsef Meszaros, Achieving Peace of Mind: The Benefits of Neurobiological Evidence for Battered Women Defendants, 23 Yale J.L. & Feminism 117, 151-152 (2011).

Questions: If corroborated by additional research, should such evidence be admissible in support of a self-defense claim when a battered woman demonstrates these neurobiological effects? In what way would such evidence be relevant to the claim of self-defense?

6. Feminist perspectives. Some of the criticism of the BWS defense has come from an avowedly feminist perspective. See, e.g., Anne M. Coughlin, Excusing Women, 82 Calif. L. Rev. 1 (1994):

> [T]he battered woman syndrome defense . . . institutionalizes within the criminal law negative stereotypes of women. [I]t relieves the accused woman of the stigma and pain of criminal punishment only if she embraces another kind of stigma and pain: she must advance an interpretation of her own activity that labels it the irrational product of a "mental health disorder."
>
> . . . None of those who advocate, or, for that matter, criticize, adoption of the battered woman syndrome defense has noticed that, for many centuries, the criminal law has been content to excuse women for criminal misconduct on the ground that they cannot be expected to, and, indeed, should not, resist the influence exerted by their husbands. No similar excuse has ever been afforded to men; to the contrary, the criminal law consistently has demanded that men withstand any pressures in their lives that compel them to commit crimes, including pressures exerted by their spouses. In this way, the theory of criminal responsibility has participated in the construction of marriage and, indeed, of gender, as a hierarchical relationship. By construing wives as incapable of choosing lawful conduct when faced with unlawful influence from

their spouses, the theory invests men with the authority to govern both themselves and their irresponsible wives. The battered woman syndrome defense rests on and reaffirms this invidious understanding of women's incapacity for rational self-control.

Questions: Does the partial excuse of provocation (available most classically when a man discovers sexual infidelity by his spouse, see page 447 supra) contradict Coughlin's claim that men have never been afforded an excuse for inability to withstand pressures in their lives? Or is the BWS defense qualitatively different?

7. *Other syndrome evidence.* Many courts that permit the use of BWS to support a claim of self-defense accept similar evidence in cases involving a battered or abused child who kills the abusive parent.[16] Some, however, do not. See Bautista v. Small, 2010 U.S. Dist. LEXIS 141158 (C.D. Cal., Dec. 16, 2010). And courts have generally been unreceptive to evidence of Post Traumatic Stress Disorder (PTSD) offered by military veterans seeking to bolster their claims of self-defense. See Thomas L. Hafemeister & Nicole A. Stockey, Last Stand? The Criminal Responsibility of War Veterans Returning from Iraq and Afghanistan with Posttraumatic Stress Disorder, 85 Ind. L.J. 87 (2010). In the PTSD cases, unlike the battered spouse cases, the defendant's self-defensive action typically is not directed toward an unsympathetic victim who has committed many abusive acts in the past. Should that difference be significant? If a person in the defendant's "situation" would reasonably believe it was necessary to use deadly force to save his own life, shouldn't a self-defense claim be viable regardless of whether, unbeknownst to him, the person killed was innocent of wrongdoing? See Robert P. Mosteller, Syndromes and Politics in Criminal Trials and Evidence Law, 46 Duke L.J. 461 (1996).

How far should the logic of such "syndrome" defenses be extended? In Werner v. State, 711 S.W.2d 639 (Tex. Crim. App. 1986), the defendant appealed his conviction of murder, complaining that the trial court erred in refusing to permit the jury to hear the testimony of his expert witness. He had raised the issue of self-defense, and the witness would have testified that the defendant, as the son of a Nazi concentration camp survivor, was a victim of a so-called "Holocaust Syndrome," which causes people to be unusually assertive in confrontational settings, as a reaction to the memory of Jewish concentration camp victims who did not fight back. The court rejected his argument, stating: "The evidence excluded only tended to show that possibly appellant was not an ordinary and prudent man with respect to self-defense. This did not entitle appellant to an enlargement of the statutory defense on account of his psychological peculiarities" (id. at 646). The dissent observed:

---

16. See, e.g., State v. MacLennan, 702 N.W.2d 219 (Minn. 2005); Nancy Wright, Voice for the Voiceless: The Case for Adopting the Domestic Abuse Syndrome for Self Defense Purposes for All Victims of Domestic Violence Who Kill Their Abusers, 4 Crim. L. Brief 76 (2009).

Dr. Roden's testimony was highly relevant . . . and would have aided the jury, all of whom were probably totally unfamiliar with this type syndrome, in better deciding . . . how his suffering from "The Holocaust Syndrome" affected the condition of his mind. . . .

When a relatively large number of persons, having the same symptoms, exhibit a combination or variation of functional psychiatric disorders that lead to purely emotional stress that causes intense mental anguish or emotional trauma, . . . the psychiatrists put those persons under one or more labels. Today, we have the following labels: "The Battered Wife Syndrome"; "The Battered Child Syndrome"; "The Battered Husband Syndrome"; "The Battered Parent Syndrome"; "The Battle Fatigue Syndrome"; "The Policeman's Syndrome"; and "The Holocaust Syndrome." Tomorrow, there will probably be additions to the list, such as "The Appellate Court Judge Syndrome." . . .

If scientific, technical, or other specialized knowledge will assist the trier of fact to better understand the evidence or determine a fact in issue, a witness . . . qualified as an expert by knowledge, skill, experience, training, or education, . . . should be able to testify in the form of opinion evidence.

In this instance, I find that the subject "The Holocaust Syndrome" was beyond the ken of the average lay person. The jury was entitled to know that when the appellant fired the fatal shot [his] state of mind . . . was affected, not only by that which he visually saw on the night in question, but also [by] his belief that it was necessary for him to defend himself because he comes from a family who did not defend themselves, thus causing them to perish in the Holocaust.

NOTE ON NONPSYCHOLOGICAL DEFENSES

In part because of the problems canvassed in the preceding Notes, defense strategies for battered women have undergone significant change in recent years. See Alafair Burke, Rational Actors, Self-Defense, and Duress: Making Sense, Not Syndromes, Out of the Battered Woman, 81 N.C. L. Rev. 211, 266-267 (2002):

A woman's participation in an abusive relationship can be understood without depicting domestic violence victims as homogeneous, irrational, and cognitively impaired. [A] domestic violence victim's decision to remain in a battering relationship . . . may in fact demonstrate that the woman is a rational actor making a reasoned decision based upon an evaluation of her viable escape options and the value she assigns to competing priorities.

Consider Sue Ostroff & Holly Maguigan, Explaining Without Pathologizing: Testimony on Battering and Its Effects, in D.R. Loseke et al., Current Controversies on Family Violence 225, 227, 229-232 (2005):

In the overwhelming majority of [battered woman] cases where expert testimony is used, this testimony . . . does not focus on the woman's incapacity or lack or reason. . . . Over the years, experiences in criminal courts persuaded advocates, lawyers, and researchers to move beyond the "battered woman syndrome" formulation to more comprehensive testimony. They came to understand that BWS fails to capture the full experience of battered women, and that it risks subjecting women who are battered to labels . . . that portray them as helpless and incapacitated. [E]xpert testimony couched only in terms of battered woman syndrome stigmatizes . . . battered women because the terminology implies a mental illness. The "syndrome" label may encourage jurors to perceive the defendant as pathological.

[Thus,] BWS is no longer the appropriate term to describe either the state of our knowledge or the content of expert testimony. The phrase "testimony on battering and its effects" more accurately describes the expert evidence because it focuses on battered women's experiences [and] moves their social context to the foreground. . . .

Questions: Evidence focused on the social context seems most useful when it serves to show that a self-defensive killing was necessary and that the defendant made no mistake. But when a defendant *errs* in assessing the need for using deadly force (as in *Kelly*, page 832 supra, for example), doesn't psychological evidence remain crucial for an effective defense? And if so, *should* such psychological evidence affect the judgment about reasonableness?

STATE v. NORMAN

Supreme Court of North Carolina
324 N.C. 253, 378 S.E.2d 8 (1989)

MITCHELL, J. The defendant was tried [for] the first degree murder of her husband. The jury found the defendant guilty of voluntary manslaughter. The defendant appealed from the trial court's judgment sentencing her to six years imprisonment. The Court of Appeals granted a new trial, citing as error the trial court's refusal to submit a possible verdict of acquittal by reason of perfect self-defense.

[The defendant's evidence tended to show the following: The 39-year-old defendant was badly abused by her husband during most of their 25-year marriage. He frequently punched and kicked her, threw beer bottles and other objects at her, and burned her with cigarettes or hot coffee. He forced her into prostitution at a local truck stop and then humiliated her in public and at home by calling her "dog," "bitch," or "whore" and forcing her to eat pet food from a bowl on the floor. For years he threatened to maim her and to kill her.

[The day before she killed him, defendant's husband beat her so badly that she called the police. When they arrived, however, they would not arrest him unless she filed a complaint, which she was afraid to do. An hour later she tried to kill herself. When paramedics came to assist her, her husband tried to interfere, insisting that they let her die. He was chased back into the house by a sheriff's deputy but was not arrested.

[The next morning she went to the local mental health center to talk about filing charges and possibly having her husband committed. When she confronted him with this possibility, he threatened to cut her throat before he was taken away. Later, defendant went to the social services office to sign up for welfare so that she would no longer have to prostitute herself to feed her children. Her husband followed her to the office and dragged her from the interview, forcing her to return home. There he beat her and burned her with cigarettes. He refused to let her eat and forced her to sleep on the floor. When her grandchild began to cry, defendant crept out of the house, and took the baby to her mother's home so that it would not wake up defendant's husband. She returned with a pistol, went to the bedroom, and tried to shoot her husband in the back of the head. The gun jammed, but she fixed it and shot him. After she determined that he was still moving, she fired two more shots into the back of his head.]

Based on the evidence that the defendant exhibited battered wife syndrome, that she believed she could not escape her husband nor expect help from others, that her husband had threatened her, and that her husband's abuse of her had worsened in the two days preceding his death, the Court of Appeals concluded that a jury reasonably could have found that . . . the defendant killed her husband lawfully in perfect self-defense, even though he was asleep when she killed him. We disagree. . . .

In North Carolina, a defendant is entitled to have the jury consider acquittal by reason of *perfect* self-defense when the evidence, viewed in the light most favorable to the defendant, tends to show that at the time of the killing it appeared to the defendant and she believed it to be necessary to kill the decedent to save herself from imminent death or great bodily harm. That belief must be reasonable, however, in that the circumstances as they appeared to the defendant would create such a belief in the mind of a person of ordinary firmness. . . . A killing in the proper exercise of the right of *perfect* self-defense is always completely justified in law and constitutes no legal wrong.

Our law also recognizes an *imperfect* right of self-defense in certain circumstances, including, for example, when the defendant is the initial aggressor, but without intent to kill or to seriously injure the decedent, and the decedent escalates the confrontation to a point where it reasonably appears to the defendant to be necessary to kill the decedent to save herself from imminent death or great bodily harm.[a] Although the culpability of a defendant who kills in the exercise of *imperfect* self-defense is reduced, such a defendant is *not justified* in the killing so as to be entitled to acquittal, but is guilty at least of voluntary manslaughter.

The defendant in the present case was not entitled to a jury instruction on either perfect or imperfect self-defense. . . .

The killing of another human being is the most extreme recourse to our inherent right of self-preservation and can be justified in law only by the utmost real or apparent necessity brought about by the decedent. . . . Only [where defendant] killed due to a reasonable belief that death or great bodily

---

a. Imperfect self-defense, as we have seen, supra page 831, more commonly applies when the jury concludes that the defendant truly believed she had to kill to avoid an imminent threat to her life, but that her belief was not reasonable.—EDS.

harm was imminent can the justification for homicide remain clearly and firmly rooted in necessity. . . .

The term "imminent," as used to describe such perceived threats . . . , has been defined as "immediate danger, such as must be instantly met, such as cannot be guarded against by calling for the assistance of others or the protection of the law." Black's Law Dictionary 676 (5th ed. 1979). . . .

The evidence in this case did not tend to show that the defendant reasonably believed that she was confronted by a threat of imminent death or great bodily harm. [H]er husband had been asleep for some time when she [shot him] three times in the back of the head. [A]ll of the evidence tended to show that the defendant had ample time and opportunity to resort to other means of preventing further abuse by her husband. There was no action underway by the decedent from which the jury could have found that the defendant had reasonable grounds to believe either that a felonious assault was imminent. . . .

[T]he lack of any belief by the defendant—reasonable or otherwise—that she faced a threat of imminent death or great bodily harm from the drunk and sleeping victim in the present case was illustrated by the defendant and her own expert witnesses. . . .

Dr. Tyson . . . testified that the defendant "believed herself to be doomed . . . to a life of the worst kind of torture and abuse, degradation that she had experienced over the years in a progressive way; that it would only get worse, and that death was inevitable." [A] defendant's subjective belief of what might be "inevitable" at some indefinite point in the future does not equate to what she believes to be "imminent." Dr. Tyson's opinion that the defendant believed it was necessary to kill her husband for "the protection of herself and her family" was similarly indefinite and devoid of time frame. . . .

The defendant testified that, "I knowed when he woke up, it was going to be the same thing, and I was scared when he took me to the truck stop that night it was going to be worse than he had ever been." She also testified, when asked if she believed her husband's threats: "Yes. . . . [H]e would kill me if he got a chance. If he thought he wouldn't a had to went to jail, he would a done it." Testimony about such indefinite fears concerning what her sleeping husband might do at some time in the future did not tend to establish a fear—reasonable or otherwise—of *imminent death or great bodily harm* at the time of the killing.

We are not persuaded by the reasoning of our Court of Appeals in this case that when there is evidence of battered wife syndrome, neither an actual attack nor threat of attack by the husband at the moment the wife uses deadly force is required to justify the wife's killing of him in perfect self-defense. The Court of Appeals concluded that to impose such requirements would ignore the "learned helplessness," meekness and other realities of battered wife syndrome and would effectively preclude such women from exercising their right of self-defense. . . .

The reasoning of our Court of Appeals in this case proposes to change the established law of self-defense by giving the term "imminent" a meaning substantially more indefinite and all-encompassing than its present meaning. This would result in a substantial relaxation of the requirement of real or apparent necessity to justify homicide. Such reasoning proposes justifying the taking of human life not upon the reasonable belief it is necessary to prevent death or great bodily harm—which the imminence requirement ensures—but upon purely subjective speculation that the decedent probably would present a threat of life at a future time and that the defendant would not be able to avoid the predicted threat.

The Court of Appeals suggests that such speculation would have been particularly reliable in the present case because the jury, based on the evidence of the decedent's intensified abuse during the thirty-six hours preceding his death, could have found that the decedent's passive state at the time of his death was "but a momentary hiatus in a continuous reign of terror by the decedent [and] the defendant merely took advantage of her first opportunity to protect herself." Requiring jury instructions on perfect self-defense in such situations, however, would still tend to make opportune homicide lawful as a result of mere subjective predictions of indefinite future assaults and circumstances. Such predictions . . . would be entirely speculative, because there was no evidence that her husband had ever inflicted any harm upon her that approached life-threatening injury, even during the "reign of terror." It is far from clear in the defendant's poignant evidence that any abuse by the decedent had ever involved the degree of physical threat required to justify the defendant in using deadly force, even when those threats were imminent. The use of deadly force in self-defense to prevent harm other than death or great bodily harm is excessive as a matter of law.

[The court also ruled that the defendant was not entitled to instructions on *imperfect* self-defense because there was no evidence that she actually believed the use of deadly force against her was imminent. The court also noted, however, that the failure to instruct on imperfect self-defense, even if error, was harmless because the defendant was convicted only of voluntary manslaughter; an instruction on imperfect self-defense would have given her nothing more, because in North Carolina killings in cases of imperfect self-defense are treated as voluntary manslaughter.]

[W]e conclude that the defendant's conviction for voluntary manslaughter and the trial court's judgment sentencing her to a six-year term of imprisonment were without error. Therefore, we must reverse the decision of the Court of Appeals which awarded the defendant a new trial.

MARTIN, J., dissenting. . . . Defendant does not seek to expand or relax the requirements of self-defense and thereby "legalize the opportune killing of allegedly abusive husbands by their wives," as the majority overstates. Rather, defendant contends that the evidence as gauged by the existing laws of self-defense is sufficient to require the submission of a self-defense instruction to the jury. . . .

Evidence presented by defendant described a twenty-year history of beatings and other dehumanizing and degrading treatment by her husband. In his expert testimony a clinical psychologist . . . described the defendant as a woman incarcerated by abuse, by fear, and by her conviction that her husband was invincible and inescapable:

> Mrs. Norman didn't leave because she believed, fully believed that escape was totally impossible. There was no place to go. He, she had left before; he had come and gotten her. She had gone to the Department of Social Services. He had come and gotten her. The law, she believed the law could not protect her; no one could protect her, and I must admit, looking over the records, that there was nothing done that would contradict that belief. . . .

Evidence presented in the case sub judice revealed no letup of tension or fear, no moment in which the defendant felt released from impending serious harm, even while the decedent slept. . . . For the battered wife, if there is no escape, if there is no window of relief or momentary sense of safety, then the next attack, which could be the fatal one, is imminent. . . . Properly stated, the . . . [question] is not whether the threat was *in fact* imminent, but whether defendant's belief in the impending nature of the threat, given the circumstances as she saw them, was reasonable in the mind of a person of ordinary firmness.

Defendant's intense fear, based on her belief that her husband intended not only to maim or deface her, as he had in the past, but to kill her, was evident in the testimony of witnesses who recounted events of the last three days of the decedent's life. This testimony could have led a juror to conclude that defendant reasonably perceived a threat to her life as "imminent," even while her husband slept. . . . And from this evidence a juror could find defendant's belief in the necessity to kill her husband not merely reasonable but compelling.

Richard A. Rosen, On Self-Defense, Imminence, and Women Who Kill Their Batterers, 71 N.C. L. Rev. 371, 375-376 (1993): On one level, the view of the [*Norman* court] is unassailable—the threat of death or great bodily harm was not imminent when Ms. Norman shot her husband, not, at least, by any reasonable interpretation of the word imminent. [T]o the extent the court was simply applying the settled law of North Carolina, its decision was surely correct [and was] consistent with the law of self-defense as it . . . is most commonly applied throughout the country today. . . .

At a deeper level, however, the decision is disturbing. [The court] never answered the question whether it was *necessary* for Ms. Norman to kill her husband to avoid great bodily harm or death. And is not *this* the proper question . . . ? If it is true . . . that either a call to the police or an attempt to run away would have resulted in a risk of death or further torture, then is it proper for society to brand Ms. Norman, and others similarly situated, as criminals?

David McCord & Sandra K. Lyons, Moral Reasoning and the Criminal Law: The Example of Self-Defense, 30 Am. Crim. L. Rev. 97, 110 (1992): There are at least ten significant facts which our common sense and life experience tell us are highly significant in this case but which seem not to be considered by the traditional law. In no particular order these ten are:

(1) J.T. and Judy [Norman] were not equally matched in terms of physical prowess ... ; (2) Judy was distraught because of the actions of J.T.; (3) Judy's mental state was colored not merely by one single incident of abuse, but by the culmination of twenty years of abuse; (4) Because J.T. lived in the same house as Judy, he had virtually constant access to her to inflict abuse on her; (5) Having Judy at his disposal in this manner, J.T. thus was able to decide when, where, and how to inflict the abuse—he took advantage of the option which the law apparently ceded to him to launch nondeadly attacks on her at his whim, without fear of a justifiable deadly response; (6) Judy's future was bleak—there was no basis for her to believe that J.T. would be content to live without her or that he had any intent to stop abusing her; (7) Judy apparently had no viable alternative but to stay in the vicinity—she had no job skills to support herself elsewhere, and her support network was in that community; (8) Judy had no reasonable prospect of being able to stay in that community outside the presence of J.T., since he would find her anywhere in the vicinity; (9) The governmental authorities failed to take any action to protect Judy ... ; and (10) J.T.'s actions prevented Judy from doing anything further to invoke the help of the governmental authorities.

These ignored facts have no place in the moral reasoning mandated by the traditional law of self-defense, yet they cause us to suffer moral disquiet with the result.

Questions: How could the law of self-defense take account of these morally relevant factors? Would it be desirable to allow self-defense not only in the traditionally designated circumstances but also: "in any other circumstance in which the defendant's killing of the victim was morally justified"? Compare Jahnke v. State, 682 P.2d 991 (Wyo. 1984), a case in which a badly abused 16-year-old boy killed his father after lying in wait for him and shooting him without warning. The boy, prosecuted as an adult, was convicted of voluntary manslaughter after the trial judge excluded evidence of battered child syndrome that the defendant had sought to introduce in support of his claim of self-defense. The appellate court, upholding the exclusion of the evidence, observed:

> It is difficult enough to justify capital punishment as an appropriate response of society to criminal acts even after the circumstances have been carefully evaluated by a number of people. To permit capital punishment to be imposed upon the subjective conclusion of the individual that prior acts and conduct of the deceased justified the killing would amount to a leap into the abyss of anarchy. [If battered person] evidence has any role at all it is in assisting the jury to evaluate the reasonableness of the defendant's fear in a case involving the recognized circumstances of self-defense which include a confrontation or conflict with the deceased not of the defendant's instigation.

A concurring judge commented:

> This is a textbook case of first-degree murder. . . . In his defense, appellant employed the oldest, most common and most successful tactic in homicide

cases. He put the deceased on trial. . . . There was no one to speak for the deceased. . . . [But by] no stretch of the imagination was this a case of self-defense.

Commonwealth v. Sands, 262 Va. 724, 553 S.E.2d 733 (2001): [Victoria Sands was convicted of the first-degree murder of her husband, Thomas. Thomas began beating his wife approximately two years after they were married in 1983. Over time, the abuse grew more severe, finally becoming a daily occurrence. Thomas was not lawfully employed; instead he sold cocaine, marijuana, and "bootleg" whiskey. The defendant repeatedly asked for a divorce, but he responded by beating her and by threatening to kill her and her family if she did so. In August 1998, Victoria sought the assistance of her parents in an attempt to have Thomas arrested. However, shortly thereafter, her parents were critically injured in an automobile accident. She was afraid to take other action herself because she believed her husband would kill her if he discovered her plans. On the morning of the killing, a neighbor observed the defendant's husband follow her onto the back porch where the couple again fought. Thomas pushed his wife down several concrete steps, seized a gun, and fired two shots into the ground near her.]

Soon thereafter, the defendant's aunt, Sallie Hodges, arrived. . . . Thomas would not allow her to leave with Hodges. He kept pacing the floor . . . , while stating, "I'll kill you and your whole family. . . . I've knocked off a few and I can knock off a few more." . . .

For the rest of the day, Thomas drank beer, used cocaine, physically abused his wife, and threatened to kill her. . . . Around 10:00 P.M., [Victoria] telephoned her sister-in-law, Angela Shelton, and asked her to come to the house. After that telephone call, Thomas beat his wife again. During that episode, which the defendant described as "the longest," Thomas used his fists and the butt of a gun to attack her. He also pushed the barrel of the gun up into his wife's nose. When Shelton arrived, the defendant [told her], "He's the devil. I got to get this devil out of my house. He's evil. He [is] gonna kill me." The defendant then [got a gun, went to the bedroom, and] shot her husband five times while he was lying in bed, watching television. . . .

At trial, the . . . circuit court [ruled] that there was "insufficient evidence for a self-defense instruction." . . . [Virginia's intermediate appellate court disagreed and reversed the murder conviction. The prosecution appealed to the Virginia Supreme Court.]

We agree that the defendant reasonably believed that she was in danger of serious bodily harm or death. Nevertheless, [e]ven when viewed in the light most favorable to the defendant, the evidence fails to reveal any overt act by her husband that presented an imminent danger at the time of the shooting. . . . While we do not doubt the defendant's genuine fear for her life or minimize the atrocities inflicted upon her, we cannot point to any evidence of an overt act indicating imminent danger, or indeed any act at all by her husband, when she shot him five times while he reclined on the bed. . . . Thus, the defendant was not entitled to an instruction on self-defense. . . .

For these reasons, we will reverse the judgment of the Court of Appeals and enter final judgment reinstating the conviction. . . .

NOTES ON THE IMMINENT DANGER REQUIREMENT

1. *Nonconfrontational self-defense.* The great majority of battered-spouse prosecutions   involve women who kill their abusers in the course of a direct confrontation that they perceive as involving a threat of immediate harm. In one study, only 20 percent of the cases involved abusers killed in noncon-frontational settings—8 percent while they slept, 8 percent caught unawares during a lull in the violence, and 4 percent killed by a third party at the abused woman's behest. See Holly Maguigan, Battered Women and Self-Defense: Myths and Misconceptions in Current Reform Proposals, 140 U. Pa. L. Rev. 379, 397 (1991).

The nonconfrontational cases nonetheless pose the greatest challenge to traditional conceptions of self-defense. In cases like *Norman*, where the abuser is killed in his sleep, most courts remain unwilling to admit battered-spouse evidence or to permit jury instructions on the possibility of legitimate self-defense.[17] A few decisions are more flexible. In Robinson v. State, 417 S.E.2d 88, 91 (S.C. 1992), the court, citing the *Norman* dissent, held that even when the batterer is asleep, "[w]here torture appears interminable and escape impossible, the belief that only the death of the batterer can provide relief may be reasonable in the mind of a person of ordinary firmness." Do you agree? Should such cases go to the jury on the self-defense issue, when escape *appears* impossible to the battered woman but is possible in fact? What are the dangers of that approach?

In a comprehensive survey of imminence cases decided over a 20-year period, Professor Victoria Nourse discovered that contrary to the conventional assumption, nonconfrontational cases were only a small minority of the cases in which imminence issues affected the result. Instead, 84 percent of the cases involving an alleged lack of imminence were cases in which the parties were fighting, the defendant allegedly saw a weapon, or the defendant claimed that the victim was advancing toward her. Victoria F. Nourse, Self-Defense and Subjectivity, 68 U. Chi. L. Rev. 1235, 1253 (2001). As a result, she concludes (id. at 1236), "imminence often operates as a proxy for any number of other self-defense factors—for example, strength of the threat, [the opportunity to] retreat, proportionality, and aggression."

Question: Would the law of self-defense produce better results if juries were instructed to more explicitly consider the totality of such circumstances?

---

17. E.g., Evans v. State, 2011 WL 2323016 (Miss. App. June, 14 2011); Hernandez v. State, 2006 WL 397922 (Tex. App. Feb. 22, 2006).

2. When the battered woman seeks help. A small but significant number of battered-spouse prosecutions (4 percent in Professor Maguigan's study) involve women who hire or persuade a third party to commit the killing. Do the arguments that favor a self-defense instruction for the woman who kills her abuser while he sleeps extend to this situation as well? To date, all the cases addressing the issue have ruled the woman's claim of self-defense untenable.[18] Why should it be? If "a person of ordinary firmness" can reasonably believe it necessary to shoot her husband in his sleep, why is it unreasonable for her to enlist the help of a third party in catching him unawares? Consider Stephen J. Schulhofer, The Gender Question in Criminal Law, 7 Soc. Phil. & Pol'y 105, 119-120 (1990):

> [In] non-confrontational cases . . . the Walker approach turns traditional intuitions inside out. In traditional terms, the strongest . . . of the nonconfrontational cases [is] that of the woman who filed for divorce, fled, and sought outside help. But such behavior does not fit the typical pattern of learned helplessness. [P]rosecution experts could testify that the defendant, even if abused, did not display the battered wife *syndrome,* and therefore could be expected to avoid resort to deadly force.
>
> Conversely, . . . the contract killing begins to look like the strongest case of all. The . . . inability to act even when the abuser is sleeping, the apparent dependence on the intervention of a male support figure, all reinforce a diagnosis of battered wife syndrome. In fact, Lenore Walker is very explicit in challenging traditional assumptions about contract killing. She writes with irritation that under the traditional approach, "hiring someone else to kill an abusive mate is seen as evidence of premeditation, even though many women, because of sex role conditioning or other factors, cannot use sufficient force to protect themselves."[47] Walker concludes that this traditional view is just evidence of the criminal law's "[b]iases . . . against women."

Does this argument imply that self-defense should be available *both* to the battered woman who commits the killing herself and to the one who hires another to do it for her? Or does the argument imply that in the absence of an imminent threat of great bodily harm, the defense should be available to *neither?*

3. Defense of another. Suppose that Judy Norman had persuaded a neighbor to help her kill her husband. If, as the dissenting judge argues, she could reasonably believe that killing him was necessary, would the neighbor who helps her have a defense as well? If Judy or the neighbor, being poor shots, hires a hitman to do the job (as in People v. Yaklich, 833 P.2d 758 (Colo. Ct. App. 1991)), should the hitman have a valid defense?

The widely accepted rule is that someone who comes to the aid of a person in peril can use deadly force to prevent the attack, under the same

---

18. E.g., Varner v. Stovall, 500 F.3d 491 (6th Cir. 2007); People v. Yaklich, 833 P.2d 758 (Colo. App. 1991).

47. Lenore E. Walker, A Response to Elizabeth M. Schneider's Describing and Changing, 9 Women's Rts. L. Rep. 223 (1986).

circumstances that would justify the use of deadly force by the endangered person herself. See, e.g., State v. Bryan, 126 Conn. App. 597 (2011); Model Penal Code §3.05, Appendix.[19] In the context of the prosecution of a third-party helper, how should we assess the facts in *Norman*? If Judy's lethal action was indeed justified, should it matter who carried out the necessary act? Would a belief in the need to kill J.T. Norman, though reasonable for Judy, not be reasonable for someone observing the situation from outside? Or was such a belief equally reasonable for both?

4. Imminence in other contexts. Is the imminence requirement subject to special criticism in the context of battered-spouse cases, or is it flawed in a more general way? Consider these situations:

(a) In State v. Schroeder, 261 N.W.2d 759 (Neb. 1978), a 19-year-old inmate stabbed his older cell-mate at 1 A.M. while the latter was asleep. He was convicted of assault with intent to inflict great bodily harm. The deceased had a reputation for sex and violence, the defendant had incurred a large gambling debt to the deceased who threatened to make a "punk" out of him by selling his debt to another prisoner, and before going to bed the morning of the incident the deceased said he might walk in his sleep and "collect" some of the money owed.

The majority found no error in the trial court's failure to give any instruction on self-defense (id. at 761):

> [T]here was no evidence to sustain a finding that the defendant could believe an assault was imminent except the threat that Riggs had made before he went to bed. . . . There is a very real danger in a rule which would legalize preventive assaults involving the use of deadly force where there has been nothing more than threats.

The dissent stated (id. at 761-762):

> The defendant could not be expected to remain awake all night, every night, waiting for the attack that Riggs had threatened to make. The defendant's evidence here was such that the jury could have found the defendant was justified in believing the use of force was necessary to protect himself against an attack by Riggs "on the present occasion."

(b) In Ha v. State, 892 P.2d 184 (Alaska App. 1995), the victim, Buu, beat the defendant severely, but was pulled away by bystanders. Buu left, returned with a hammer, and tried to strike the defendant, but again a bystander intervened. Before leaving, Buu shouted several times that he would kill the

---

19. Traditionally, the third party was said to "stand in the shoes" of the person in danger. If that person did *not* have the right to use force, then the third party had no defense, even if he reasonably thought that force was necessary. People v. Young, 183 N.E.2d 319 (N.Y. 1962). Many jurisdictions now reject this instance of strict liability and allow the mistaken third party a defense, provided that his belief in the need to use defensive force was reasonable. E.g., State v. Beeley, 653 A.2d 722 (R.I. 1995). Conversely, if the third party knows that deadly force is *not* really necessary (for example, if he knows that the assailant is using an unloaded gun), he would not be justified in killing the assailant, even if the person attacked might be.

defendant. Ha spent a sleepless night thinking about Buu's "violent criminal clan" and their reputation for carrying out their threats. He concluded that Buu or the relatives would someday carry out the threat and that "because of his cultural background and poor command of English, . . . it would be useless to go to the police for help" (id. at 191, 195). He then got a rifle, caught Buu unawares, and shot him from behind, killing him. At trial the judge withheld the self-defense issue from the jury, and Ha was convicted of murder.

On appeal, the court concluded that "a reasonable person in Ha's position would have feared death or serious physical injury from Buu," and that the evidence could support a conclusion that "there was no escape. . . . Buu comes from . . . a family of thugs who have a reputation for violence and extortion. . . . Today or tomorrow they would stalk him down" (id. at 191). Nonetheless, the court upheld the conviction, stressing that " 'inevitable harm' is not the same as 'imminent' harm. [A] reasonable fear of future harm does not authorize a person to hunt down and kill an enemy" (id.).

Is the result sound? If so, does the same principle bar a self-defense claim on the facts of *Norman* and *Schroeder*, or are the situations distinguishable?

5. *The Model Penal Code.* The MPC modestly relaxes the imminence requirement, providing that self-defense can be available if the actor reasonably believed that the use of defensive force was "immediately necessary" §3.04(1). Several states have adopted similar language. E.g., N.J. §2C:3-4a (2011); Pa. tit. 18, §505 (2011). Some courts have loosened the imminence requirement on their own authority. In State v. Janes, 121 Wash. 2d 220, 241-242 (1993), for example, the court interpreted the statutory imminence requirement as follows:

> A threat, or its equivalent, can support self-defense when there is a reasonable belief that the threat will be carried out. Especially in abusive relationships, patterns of behavior become apparent which can signal the next abusive episode. . . . Even an otherwise innocuous comment which occurred days before the homicide could be highly relevant when the evidence shows that such a comment inevitably signaled the beginning of an abusive episode.

Question: Would a self-defense instruction have been required in *Norman* if North Carolina had interpreted imminence in this way?

6. *Assessing the imminence requirement.*

(a) *Imminence in fact.* Are courts and commentators justified in assuming that the strict imminence requirement invariably defeats a self-defense claim in nonconfrontational settings? Consider Joan H. Krause, Distorted Reflections of Battered Women Who Kill: A Response to Professor Dressler, 4 Ohio St. J. Crim. L. 555, 563 (2007):

> Unless actually comatose, a sleeping abuser is merely seconds away from being an *awakened* abuser—and . . . abusers (particularly when intoxicated) tend to sleep lightly, demand that their partners be present when they awaken, and resume the abuse immediately. Is it truly unreasonable for a woman who has

repeatedly experienced the violent aftermath of her abuser's naps to believe that the next severe attack is about to begin?

(b) Imminence and necessity. Why *should* imminence be required? One answer is that in the absence of imminence, the killing was not strictly necessary. Imminence, in other words, serves as a proxy for necessity. But if this is the rationale for requiring imminence, why should imminence and necessity be independent requirements? One could justifiably say that lack of imminence creates a presumption that the killing was unnecessary. But note that most courts treat this no-necessity presumption as irrebuttable. Why shouldn't a defendant in cases like *Norman, Sands, Schroeder,* and *Ha* be permitted to argue that the killing *was* necessary even in the absence of imminence?

Compare Kimberly Kessler Ferzan, Defending Imminence: From Battered Women to Iraq, 46 Ariz. L. Rev. 213, 255-256, 260-262 (2004):

> [The critical question is not when the defender needs to act but what kind of threat triggers the right to self-defense. [T]he possession of nuclear weapons by North Korea is a threat to the United States and a sleeping husband is a threat to a battered woman. [I]f two people are stuck in a cave with limited oxygen, each poses a "threat" to the other simply because one individual's survival is dependent on limiting the chances of the other's. [Yet] the right to self-defense cannot be this broad. [Otherwise] India and Pakistan [two mutually hostile nations armed with nuclear weapons] may attack each other. Indeed, during the Cold War, could the Soviet Union have struck the United States in self-defense? Jettisoning imminence in the name of necessity leaves [no] standard for the type of conduct sufficient to warrant defensive force.
>
> It is the aggressor's actions, and not the defender's need, that grounds the right to self-defense. . . . Without aggression, there is no self-defense, only self-preference. . . . Self-defense is uniquely justified by the fact that the defender is responding to aggression. Imminence, far from simply establishing necessity, is conceptually tied to self-defense by staking out the type of threats that constitute aggression. We cannot simply discard imminence in the name of necessity.

(c) Self-defense without *necessity?* The law of self-defense generally operates on what may be called "pacifist" principles;[20] the actor is normally expected to "avoid violence at all costs." See Nourse, supra, at 1271. But some argue that in a case like *Norman,* a number of morally relevant factors, taken together, call for exoneration even when the defendant did have alternatives to the use of violence. See the comments of McCord & Lyons, supra page 852. In addition, existing law already includes exceptions to the "pacifist" principle. For example, as we shall see (infra page 865), many jurisdictions permit an actor to use deadly force even when he could avoid the need to do so, simply by

---

20. See Stephen J. Schulhofer, The Gender Question in Criminal Law, 7 Soc. Phil & Pol'y 105, 115 (1990).

retreating to a readily available place of safety. Professor Joan Krause suggests (supra, at 561-562) that these exceptions to the "pacifist" principle can be explained by:

> an equally compelling "libertarian" theory of self-defense, [under which] the genesis of the [self-defense] doctrine is found instead in the right of each individual citizen to take "self-help" measures in response to unlawful aggression. From this alternative perspective, a battered woman who engages in self-help against her abuser, when all other measures have failed, might have a strong justification claim even under nonconfrontational circumstances.

Questions: Does the "libertarian" theory provide a better grounding for the law of self-defense than the "pacifist" principle? What are its implications for the permissible scope of a valid self-defense claim?

7. *Comparing individual and national self-defense.* In international law, a nation's right to use force in self-defense traditionally has been limited to situations involving either an armed attack or an "imminent" threat. More recently, the National Security Strategy of the United States, as newly formulated in 2002, claims the right to attack "rogue states" preemptively, even when aggression against America is neither imminent nor highly likely, provided that such aggression, if it occurred, would cause devastating harm. Are there good reasons to have a different imminence requirement in international than in domestic law? If not, should the imminence requirement be flexible in both contexts or in neither? See Jane Campbell Moriarty, "While Dangers Gather": The Bush Preemption Doctrine, Battered Women, Imminence, and Anticipatory Self-Defense, 30 N.Y.U. Rev. L. & Soc. Change 15 (2005).

NOTES AND QUESTIONS ON OTHER ISSUES OF SELF-DEFENSE

1. *Limits on the use of deadly force.* As we have seen, page 819 supra, a defender can use deadly force only in response to a threat of "death, serious bodily harm, kidnapping or sexual intercourse compelled by force or threat." MPC §3.04(2)(b). In John Q. La Fond, The Case for Liberalizing the Use of Deadly Force in Self-Defense, 6 U. Puget Sound L. Rev. 237 (1983), the author criticizes this limitation because it leaves many law-abiding citizens (including most female victims) without a practically effective means of defense against a nondeadly assault by a stronger attacker. The author proposes instead that resort to deadly force be permissible whenever "necessary to protect [the defendant] effectively" against unlawful physical violence (id. at 280).

Note the significance of this issue for the battered woman's defense. In *Norman*, the court said "there was no evidence that her husband had ever inflicted any harm upon her that approached life-threatening injury," and accordingly that "it is far from clear ... that [his abuse] ever involved the degree of physical threat required to justify the defendant in using deadly force, *even when those threats were imminent*" (emphasis added). Do you agree on the facts? Did any of J.T.'s abuse meet the MPC standard for using deadly force in self-defense? If not, could Judy Norman have reasonably feared more serious assaults in the future? And apart from the specific facts of *Norman*, is the legal rule sound in requiring a reasonable fear of *great bodily harm*? If a battering husband uses only nondeadly force against a spouse who cannot readily escape the relationship, what are her options?

2. The risk of injury to others. Is a person who is privileged to use deadly force criminally responsible if his defensive actions injure innocent persons? In People v. Adams, 291 N.E.2d 54, 55-56 (Ill. App. 1972), the defendant, acting in self-defense, shot and killed his assailant, Robinson, who was threatening his life. One of the defendant's bullets passed through Robinson's body and struck and killed Mary Davis, who was sitting nearby. The defendant was convicted of manslaughter for killing Davis. The appellate court reversed the conviction, stating:

> [I]f the circumstances are such that they would excuse the killing of an assailant in self-defense, the emergency will be held to excuse the person assailed from culpability, if in attempting to defend himself he unintentionally kills or injures a third person.
>
> [T]he above rule is not absolute and . . . may be subject to modification depending on the circumstances involved. But we do not believe such circumstances present themselves in the case before us. [I]t was dark and defendant was being fired on at close range. . . . He had to act immediately to protect himself from a man . . . who was not just threatening him but was shooting at him. Even under such circumstances defendant did not shoot wildly or carelessly. [H]e hit his assailant with every shot and . . . the innocent victim was killed only as a result of a bullet passing through the body of the assailant. We conclude that under the circumstances of this case the killing of Mary Davis constituted no crime.

What actions should the law allow if a person facing a lethal threat knows that defensive measures pose a grave threat to innocent bystanders? Some courts would permit a self-defense claim even under such circumstances, because they analyze the issue as a problem of "transferred intent." As we have seen (page 584 supra), if a defendant shoots, intending to kill *A*, and the bullet accidentally strikes and kills bystander *B*, the defendant can be convicted of murdering *B*, because his intent to kill *A* is "transferred" to *B*. Applying the same logic, some courts hold that the justification transfers along with the intent, so that if the defendant, acting in justified self-defense, shoots at assailant *A* and accidentally kills *B*, the killing of *B* is deemed to be intentional but justified. See, e.g., Rogers v. State, 994 So. 2d 792, 802 (Miss. App. 2008); People v. Reyes, 2010 WL 5175486, at *3 (Cal. App. Dec. 22, 2010).

Does this approach leave too much room for reckless measures by persons acting in self-defense? Consider Commonwealth v. Fowlin, 710 A.2d 1130 (Pa. 1998). Fowlin, a nightclub patron, was approached by three men, one of whom sprayed pepper gas in his eyes while a second pulled a gun. Thinking that he was about to be killed, Fowlin drew his own handgun and fired more than seven times in the general direction of his attackers. Though nearly blinded by pepper spray, he managed to kill one of his assailants and wound another, but 200 other people were present in the club, and Fowlin also wounded one of these bystanders. No charges were pressed with respect to the shooting of the two assailants, but Fowlin was charged with aggravated assault and reckless endangerment for shooting the bystander. The Pennsylvania Supreme Court dismissed the charges. The court held that if a defendant reasonably believes that deadly force is necessary to avoid death or serious bodily harm, he cannot be deemed reckless, regardless of the extent to which he endangers innocent bystanders. A dissenting judge conceded that Fowlin had been justified in shooting his assailants but argued that the question whether he had acted recklessly toward the bystanders was a matter for the jury to determine under all the circumstances. The dissenting judge added (id. at 1136):

> The holding of the majority effectively allows an actor to respond in any manner and with whatever amount of force he chooses no matter [whom] he injures, so long as he is justified in acting in self-defense. [S]uch blanket authority for the use of self-defense defies logic, especially in contemporary society where possession of lethal weapons and confrontations involving them have become all too commonplace. Under the majority's reasoning, one would be justified [in] detonating a hand-grenade in a crowded shopping mall in order to defend himself against an attacker.

The MPC approach is in accord with that of the dissenting judge in *Fowlin*—the defendant could conceivably be convicted of reckless endangerment, and if the bystander died, the defendant could be convicted of homicide. See §3.09(3). Which approach makes more sense? If the defendant in *Fowlin* knew his desperate acts of self-defense might injure or kill several innocent people, should a lawyer standing at his side advise him to do nothing? If not—if the defendant had a right to use the only defensive measures available to save his life—how can we convict him of a serious felony for doing so? See the material on choice of evils and taking life to save life, page 900 infra, and Sanford H. Kadish, Blame and Punishment 122-126 (1987).

3. Burden of proof. Most jurisdictions place the burden on the prosecution to disprove self-defense beyond a reasonable doubt, once the issue is raised by the evidence. E.g., Commonwealth v. Walker, 820 N.E.2d 195, 201-202 (Mass. 2005); see Annot., 43 A.L.R.3d 221 (2005). Ohio, however, requires the defendant to prove self-defense by a preponderance of the evidence. Ohio Rev. Code. Ann. §2901.05(A) (2011); State v. Dykas, 925 N.E.2d 685 (Ohio App. 2010). In Martin v. Ohio, 480 U.S. 228 (1987), the Supreme Court upheld the constitutionality of this practice, on the ground that the absence of the conditions of self-defense was not among the elements of the crime charged (aggravated murder) as defined by the Ohio statute.

Does this mean that a state could abolish the plea of self-defense completely? Would it be constitutional to punish as a murderer someone who had killed when it was immediately necessary to save herself from an unlawful aggressor? See pages 43-44 supra.

4. Exceptions to the right of self-defense. In a number of situations, the law disallows the use of defensive force, even though the defendant faces an imminent threat of death from the unlawful action of another. These situations are explored in the cases that follow.

STATE v. ABBOTT

Supreme Court of New Jersey
36 N.J. 63, 174 A.2d 881 (1961)

WEINTRAUB, C.J. . . . . Abbott shared a common driveway with his neighbors, Michael and Mary Scarano. The Scaranos engaged a contractor to pave their portion. Abbott obtained some asphalt from the contractor and made a doorstop to keep his garage door from swinging onto the Scaranos' property. Nicholas Scarano, who was visiting with the Scaranos, his parents, objected to Abbott's innovation. After some words between them a fist fight ensued.

Although Abbott managed to land the first punch, with which he sent Nicholas to the ground, a jury could find Nicholas was the aggressor. At this point Michael Scarano came at Abbott with a hatchet. Michael . . . denied he meant to use it as a weapon. According to Abbott, Mary Scarano followed, armed with a carving knife and large fork. The actors gave varying versions of what happened, but the end result was that all of the Scaranos were hit by the hatchet. Nicholas received severe head injuries. Abbott claimed he too suffered a laceration. Abbott admitted he finally wrested the hatchet from Michael but denied he wielded it at all. Rather he insisted that the Scaranos were injured during a common struggle for the instrument. A jury could, however, find Abbott intentionally inflicted the blows.

Abbott was separately indicted for atrocious assault and battery upon each of the Scaranos. . . . The jury acquitted Abbott of the charges relating to Michael and Mary, but found him guilty as to Nicholas. The principal question is whether the trial court properly instructed the jury upon . . . the subject of retreat. . . .

The question whether one who is neither the aggressor nor a party to a mutual combat must retreat has divided the authorities. [O]ne could readily say there was no necessity to kill in self-defense if the use of deadly force could have been avoided by retreat. The critics of the retreat rule do not quarrel with the theoretical validity of this conclusion, but rather condemn it as unrealistic. The law of course should not denounce conduct as criminal when it accords with the behavior of reasonable men. [A]dvocates of no-retreat say the manly thing is to hold one's ground and hence society should not demand what smacks of cowardice. Adherents of the retreat rule reply it is better that the assailed shall retreat than that the life of another be needlessly spent. They add that not only do right-thinking men agree, but further a rule so requiring may well induce others to adhere to that worthy standard of behavior. . . .

Other jurisdictions are closely divided upon the retreat doctrine. . . . The Model Penal Code embraces the retreat rule while acknowledging that on numerical balance a majority of the precedents oppose it.

We are not persuaded to depart from the principle of retreat. We think it salutary if reasonably limited. Much of the criticism goes not to its inherent validity but rather to unwarranted applications of the rule. For example, it is correctly observed that one can hardly retreat from a rifle shot at close range. But if the weapon were a knife, a lead of a city block might well be enough. . . . Such considerations, however, do not demand that a man should have the absolute right to stand his ground and kill in any and all situations. . . .

We believe the following principles are sound:

1. The issue of retreat arises only if the defendant resorted to a deadly force. . . . Model Penal Code §3.04(2)(b)(ii). As defined in §3.11(2) a deadly force means "force which the actor uses with the purpose of causing or which he knows to create a substantial risk of causing death or serious bodily harm."

Hence it is not the nature of the force defended against which raises the issue of retreat, but rather the nature of the force which the accused employed in his defense. If he does not resort to a deadly force, one who is assailed may hold his ground whether the attack upon him be of a deadly or some lesser character. Although it might be argued that a safe retreat should be taken if thereby the use of *any* force could be avoided, yet, as the comment in the Model Penal Code observes, "The logic of this position never has been accepted when moderate force is used in self-defense; here all agree that the actor may stand his ground and estimate necessity upon that basis." . . . Hence, in a case like the present one, the jury should be instructed that Abbott could hold his ground when Nicholas came at him with his fists, and also when Michael and Mary came at him with the several instruments mentioned, and that the question of retreat could arise only if Abbott intended to use a deadly force.

2. What constitutes an opportunity to retreat which will defeat the right of self-defense? As §3.04(2)(b)(ii) of the Model Penal Code states, deadly force is not justifiable "if the actor *knows* that he can avoid the necessity of using such force *with complete safety* by retreating. . . ." We emphasize "knows" and "with complete safety." One who is wrongfully attacked need not risk injury by retreating, even though he could escape with something less than serious bodily injury. It would be unreal to require nice calculations as to the amount of hurt, or to ask him to endure any at all. And the issue is not whether in retrospect it can be found the defendant could have retreated unharmed. Rather the question is whether he knew the opportunity was there, and of course in that inquiry the total circumstances including the attendant excitement must be considered. . . .

[The court reversed the conviction because it found that the trial court's instructions on retreat were ambiguous and confusing.]

NOTES ON THE DUTY TO RETREAT

1. *The traditional view.* The English common law imposed a strict duty to retreat; a person could use deadly force in self-defense only after exhausting every chance to flee, when he had his "back to the wall."[21] In the nineteenth century, American courts began rejecting the English doctrine as unsuited to American values. In a widely quoted decision, Erwin v. State, 29 Ohio St. 186, 199 (1876), the Ohio Supreme Court said that the law "will not permit the taking of [human life] to repel mere trespass, . . . but a true man who is without fault is not obliged to fly from an assailant." Some contemporary scholars continued to defend the retreat requirement; Professor Beale wrote in 1903 that despite the "apparent cowardice, [a] really honorable man . . . would regret ten times more, after the excitement of the contest was past, the thought that he had the blood of a fellow-being on his hands."[22] Many states, especially those on the east coast, retained a retreat requirement, but by the late nineteenth or early twentieth century, the majority had adopted the "true man" or no-retreat rule. Historian Richard Maxwell Brown describes the result:[23]

> The centuries-long English legal severity against homicide was replaced in our country by a proud new tolerance for killing in situations where it might have been avoided. . . . This undoubtedly had an impact on our homicide rate, helping to make it the highest on earth among . . . modern, industrialized nations.

2. *Current controversies.* As the *Abbott* decision notes, most states at that time followed the no-retreat approach. Since then, the law on retreat has been in a state of flux. Ohio, where the "true man" concept originated, rejected that approach in 1979.[24] Tennessee, which had long rejected the no-retreat rule, adopted it by legislation in 1989, and as recently as 2006, its courts approvingly referred to that approach as "the 'true man' doctrine."[25]

Although contemporary cases and commentators sometimes identify no-retreat as the majority rule, the situation is more complex. In decisions based on common-law principles, there has been a distinct tendency to favor a requirement of retreat in settings outside the home, with many decisions requiring retreat when possible and courts in half a dozen additional states treating the possibility of retreat as a factor to be considered in judging necessity.[26] Among the minority of courts that still choose a no-retreat rule under common-law principles, many expressly reject the old justification for it—that the law should not require what looks like cowardice. Rather, these courts argue that a rule requiring retreat tends to confuse the jury because it is

---

21. See Richard Maxwell Brown, No Duty to Retreat 4-30 (1991).
22. Joseph Beale, Retreat from a Murderous Assault, 16 Harv. L. Rev. 567, 681 (1903).
23. Brown, supra footnote 21.
24. State v. Robbins, 388 N.E.2d 755, 758-759 (Ohio 1979).
25. See State v. Clark, 2006 WL 2191255 (Tenn. Crim. App. Aug. 2, 2006); Tenn. Code Ann. §39-11-611 (2011).
26. E.g., State v. James, 867 So. 2d 414 (Fla. Dist. Ct. App. 2003); Commonwealth v. Pasteur, 850 N.E.2d 1118 (Mass. App. 2006); State v. Hall, 764 N.W.2d 837 (Minn. 2009).

so difficult to determine whether the defendant knew he could retreat with complete safety.[27]

Recently, however, judicial decisions reaffirming the retreat requirement have often been trumped by legislation abolishing it. Many states have passed so-called "stand your ground" laws that permit the actor to meet force with force, including deadly force, even when retreat is possible. See Adam Liptak, 15 States Expand Right to Shoot in Self-Defense, N.Y. Times, Aug. 7, 2006. Explaining the rationale for these enactments, a spokesman for the National Rifle Association, one of the organizations lobbying for them, said they send a needed message to law-abiding citizens: "If they make a decision to save their lives in the split second they are being attacked, the law is on their side. . . . Good people make good decisions. That's why they're good people. If you're going to empower someone, empower the crime victim." See Liptak, supra.

In assessing the moral and practical implications of a retreat requirement, consider State v. Smiley, 927 So. 2d 1000 (Fla. Dist. Ct. App. 2006). The defendant, a cab driver, was paid in advance to drive an intoxicated man home from a bar.[28] When they arrived at their destination the man got out of the cab, but then he allegedly started an argument, pulled a knife, and began advancing toward Smiley. Smiley apparently could have driven away in complete safety, but he chose to stand his ground, drew his gun, and shot his customer dead. At the time of the shooting, Florida's common-law decisions required retreat, and Smiley was convicted of first-degree murder. But he might have a strong defense under the "stand your ground" statute enacted shortly after the shooting, which provides (Fla. Stat. §776.013(3) (2006)):

> A person who is not engaged in an unlawful activity and who is attacked in any . . . place where he or she has a right to be has no duty to retreat and has the right to stand his or her ground and meet force with force, including deadly force if he or she reasonably believes it is necessary to do so to prevent death or great bodily harm to himself or herself or another or to prevent the commission of a forcible felony.

Question: Should the law require retreat in a situation like the *Smiley* case, or does the Florida statute set a better standard for determining the scope of the privilege to use deadly force in self-defense?

3. The "castle" exception. (a) Intruders. In jurisdictions requiring retreat before deadly force may be used, an exception is invariably made when the defendant is attacked in his own home by an intruder. Thus, in People v. Tomlins, 107 N.E. 496, 497 (1914), Judge Cardozo stated:

> It is not now and never has been the law that a man assailed in his own dwelling is bound to retreat. If assailed there, he may stand his ground and resist the attack. He is under no duty to take to the fields and the highways, a

---

27. See Culverson v. State, 797 P.2d 238, 240 (Nev. 1990).

28. The facts set out above are drawn from the reported decision and supplementary details described in Liptak, supra.

fugitive from his own home. . . . Flight is for sanctuary and shelter, and shelter, if not sanctuary, is in the home. That there is, in such a situation, no duty to retreat is, we think, the settled law in the United States as in England.

Is the castle exception sound in principle, or is it just a concession to human instinct? Suppose that a distraught teenager pushes her way into the home of her teacher, pulls a knife, cuts the phone lines, and threatens to kill the teacher. If the teacher can easily get to his car and go for help, should he be entitled to ignore that option, pull his gun, and kill the teenager on the spot? All American jurisdictions hold that he may do so. What is the justification for that result?

(b) Guests. Should the castle exception also be available (so that retreat is not required) when the homeowner kills a guest? For example, suppose that the owner and a friend are drinking heavily and get into an argument over dinner; the guest grabs a kitchen knife and advances in a menacing way. If the homeowner can easily escape and get help, should he nonetheless be entitled to draw his gun and kill the guest? Only a few states would require the homeowner to retreat in this situation; the great majority permit the homeowner to kill in self-defense. Do you agree? See Catherine L. Carpenter, Of the Enemy Within, the Castle Doctrine, and Self-Defense, 86 Marq. L. Rev. 653 (2003).

(c) Co-occupants. The greatest disagreement arises in situations in which one occupant kills another, such as a spouse or child. In *Tomkins*, supra, Judge Cardozo held that a father being threatened by his son could kill the son rather than retreat. MPC §3.04 (2)(b)(ii)(1) endorses this view, as do most of the recent decisions on the issue, but some courts require the homeowner to flee if possible when the attacker is a co-occupant. E.g., State v. Gartland, 694 A.2d 564 (N.J. 1997).

Until recently, Minnesota took the latter approach, requiring retreat in cases of attack by a co-occupant, but not in cases of attack by an intruder or guest. What, then, should be the rule when a homeowner is attacked by a girlfriend who visits and sleeps over several nights a week? The difficulty of distinguishing between a co-occupant and a mere guest led the Minnesota Supreme Court to relax its restrictions on using defensive force and to hold that the homeowner was entitled to stand his ground and use deadly force even against a full-fledged co-resident. State v. Glowacki, 630 N.W.2d 392 (Minn. 2001).

An additional concern for courts that follow this approach is fear that a duty to retreat would adversely affect victims of domestic violence, because for battered women "separation or retreat can be the most dangerous time in the relationship." Weiand v. State, 732 So. 2d 1044, 1053 (Fla. 1999). But will some women (and abused teenage children) be placed in even greater danger by a gender-neutral privilege *not* to retreat? Consider State v. Shaw, 441 A.2d 561 (Conn. 1981). The statute in *Shaw*, patterned after the MPC, stated: "[T]he actor shall not be required to retreat if he is in his dwelling . . . and

was not the initial aggressor. . . ." Nevertheless, the court, noting the overriding policy favoring human life and stressing that in the great majority of
homicides the killer and victim are relatives or close acquaintances, chose to
read into the statute a requirement of retreat from co-occupants. The court
stated: "We cannot conclude that the Connecticut legislature intended to
sanction the reenactment of the climactic scene from 'High Noon' in the
familial kitchens of this state."

   Questions: In jurisdictions that require retreat from one's home when the
aggressor is also a lawful occupant, can a battered woman's defense succeed?
How could the defendant show that the retreat duty is inapplicable in her
situation?

UNITED STATES v. PETERSON

United States Court of Appeals, District of Columbia Circuit
483 F.2d 1222 (1973)

ROBINSON, J. Indicted for second-degree murder, and convicted by a jury of
manslaughter as a lesser included offense, Bennie L. Peterson [complains] that
the judge . . . erred in the instructions given the jury in relation to his claim
[of] self-defense. [W]e affirm Peterson's conviction.

   The events immediately preceding the homicide are not seriously in dispute. . . . Charles Keitt, the deceased, and two friends drove in Keitt's car to
the alley in the rear of Peterson's house to remove the windshield wipers from
the latter's wrecked car. While Keitt was doing so, Peterson came out of the
house . . . to protest. After a verbal exchange, Peterson went back into the
house, obtained a pistol, and returned to the yard. In the meantime, Keitt
had reseated himself in his car, and he and his companions were about to
leave.

   Upon his reappearance in the yard, Peterson paused briefly to load the
pistol. . . . He walked to a point in the yard slightly inside a gate in the rear
fence and, pistol in hand, said [to Keitt], "If you come in here I will kill you."
Keitt alighted from his car, took a few steps toward Peterson and exclaimed,
"What the hell do you think you are going to do with that?" Keitt then made an
about-face, walked back to his car and got a lug wrench. With the wrench in a
raised position, Keitt advanced toward Peterson, who stood with the pistol
pointed toward him. Peterson warned Keitt not to "take another step" and,
when Keitt continued onward shot him in the face from a distance of about ten
feet. Death was apparently instantaneous. . . .

   Peterson's complaint centers upon an instruction that the right to use
deadly force in self-defense is not ordinarily available to one who provokes
a conflict or is the aggressor in it. . . . Peterson contends that there was no
evidence that he either caused or contributed to the conflict, and that the
instructions on the topic could only [have] misled the jury.

   It has long been accepted that one cannot support a claim of self-defense by
a self-generated necessity to kill. The right of homicidal self-defense is granted

only to those free from fault in the difficulty; it is denied to slayers who incite the fatal attack, encourage the fatal quarrel or otherwise promote the necessitous occasion for taking life. The fact that the deceased struck the first blow, fired the first shot or made the first menacing gesture does not legalize the self-defense claim if in fact the claimant was the actual provoker. In sum, one who is the aggressor in a conflict culminating in death cannot invoke the necessities of self-preservation. Only in the event that he communicates to his adversary his intent to withdraw and in good faith attempts to do so is he restored to his right of self-defense.

This body of doctrine traces its origin to the fundamental principle that a killing in self-defense is excusable only as a matter of genuine necessity. Quite obviously, a defensive killing is unnecessary if the occasion for it could have been averted.

[T]he trial judge's charge fully comported with these governing principles. The remaining question, then, is whether there was evidence to make them applicable to the case. . . .

The evidence is uncontradicted that when Peterson reappeared in the yard with his pistol, Keitt was about to depart the scene. . . . The uncontroverted fact that Keitt was leaving shows plainly that so far as he was concerned the confrontation was ended. [E]ven if he had previously been the aggressor, he no longer was.

Not so with Peterson, however. . . . Emerging from the house with the pistol, he paused in the yard to load it, and to command Keitt not to move. He then walked through the yard to the rear gate and, displaying his pistol, dared Keitt to come in, and threatened to kill him if he did. While there appears to be no fixed rule on the subject, the cases hold, and we agree, that an affirmative unlawful act reasonably calculated to produce an affray foreboding injurious or fatal consequences is an aggression which, unless renounced, nullifies the right of homicidal self-defense. We cannot escape the abiding conviction that the jury could readily find Peterson's challenge to be a transgression of that character.

The situation at bar is not unlike that presented in *Laney* [294 Fed. 412 (1923)]. There the accused, chased along the street by a mob threatening his life, managed to escape through an areaway between two houses . . . and then returned to the areaway. The mob beset him again, and during an exchange of shots one of its members was killed by a bullet from the accused's gun. In affirming a conviction of manslaughter, the court reasoned: "It is clearly apparent . . . that, when defendant escaped from the mob into the back yard . . . he was in a place of comparative safety, from which, if he desired to go home, he could have gone by the back way. [W]hen he adjusted his gun and stepped out into the areaway, he had every reason to believe that his presence there would provoke trouble. We think his conduct in adjusting his revolver and going into the areaway was such as to deprive him of any right to invoke the plea of self-defense." . .

We are brought much the readier to the same conclusion here. We think the evidence plainly presented an issue of fact as to whether Peterson's conduct was an invitation to and provocation of the encounter which ended in the fatal shot. We sustain the trial judge's action in remitting that issue for the jury's determination.

NOTES AND QUESTIONS

1. Can the nonlethal aggressor respond? In *Peterson*, the defendant became the initial aggressor when he obtained a pistol, reentered his yard, and threatened to shoot. Keitt's response (getting the lug wrench) was arguably a legitimate act of self-protection under these circumstances; if so, it is easy to see why Peterson should not have a right to use deadly force in return. But suppose that Peterson had threatened only nonlethal force and then was met by Keitt's excessive, potentially lethal response. Should the initial aggressor still be denied any right to defend his life, when his initial aggression may have consisted only of provocative words, a shove, or a punch?

In a few states, the nonlethal aggressor can regain his right to self-defense if he is met by an excessive, life-threatening response, provided that he then "exhaust[s] every reasonable means to escape such danger other than the use of [deadly] force."[29] But most jurisdictions tend to deny the initial aggressor even this limited means of escape. On the ground that self-defense is available only to the person who is "free from fault," most states hold that the initial aggressor has no self-defense privilege even when his minor provocation is met by a grossly excessive response.[30] Apparently, the initial aggressor's only choices are to run (if possible), to forgo self-defense (and be killed), or to fight back unlawfully (and face homicide charges if he is forced to kill his attacker). Does this make sense?

Consider Allen v. State, 871 P.2d 79, 92-93 (Okla. Crim. App. 1994). After the defendant and her intimate partner quarreled, the partner, Gloria Leathers, collected her possessions and prepared to move out. As Leathers went to her car, Allen pursued her, asking her to stay, but Leathers grabbed a multiple-pronged garden rake and struck Allen in the face, causing extensive bleeding. Leathers drove off, and Allen got in her own car to pursue Leathers. When Allen caught up, she parked her car and walked toward Leathers's vehicle, hoping (she claimed) to persuade Leathers to reconsider. At that point Allen saw Leathers coming toward her holding the rake. She returned to her car and retrieved a gun from the glove compartment; when she turned around and saw Leathers standing very near her, holding the rake, she fired. Leathers died from a single gunshot wound to the abdomen. Allen was convicted of first-degree murder and sentenced to death. The appellate court noted that in Oklahoma, "a party has no obligation to retreat from a confrontation; she can stand her ground and defend herself"; nonetheless the court

---

29. E.g., Ill. Comp. Stat. Ann. ch. 720 §5/7-4(c)(1) (2011); Kan. Stat. Ann. §21-3214(3)(a) (2011).

30. See, e.g., N.Y. Penal Law §35.15(1)(b) (2011), requiring the nonlethal aggressor to withdraw completely in order to regain his right to self-defense.

affirmed the conviction and the sentence, after finding the no-retreat privilege unavailable to Allen:

> If a person by provocative behavior initiates a confrontation, even with no intention of killing the other person, she loses the right of self-defense. Here, even assuming Appellant did not intend to provoke an argument when she pursued the decedent . . . , she re-initiated the encounter. . . . She knew the decedent was upset, yet she pursued her anyway, knowing the possibility of a confrontation was strong. [E]ven limiting review to Appellant's version of events, we find the Appellant was not entitled to instructions on self-defense.

Questions: Did Allen commit a punishable offense in pursuing Leathers in order to persuade her to reconsider her decision to move out? Even if Allen had thrown the first punch, what should be the appropriate punishment for that offense?

2. *What kinds of fault suffice?* How far should courts extend the doctrine that fault forfeits the privilege of self-defense? Suppose that Uriah catches David in flagrante delicto with Uriah's wife. Uriah, enraged, tries to kill David. Can David defend himself with deadly force, or has he become the aggressor, and therefore lost his right to self-defense, by committing adultery with Uriah's wife? What should be the result under *Allen v. State*, Note 1, supra?

Some courts hold that David cannot defend himself with deadly force in this situation. See Dabney v. State, 21 So. 211 (1897). More recent cases addressing the issue tend to reject this approach. See Atkins v. State, 339 S.E.2d 782 (Ga. 1986). Which is the better view? Is it wrong to permit David to have an affair and then kill the husband who is understandably enraged by his provocative conduct? Or is it worse to make David, whose most serious offense is adultery, either face a homicide conviction (if he defends himself) or pay with his life (if he does not)?

Some courts take this "free from fault" requirement even further, holding that commission of any crime causally related to the fatal result will forfeit the privilege of self-defense, even when the crime itself does not *provoke* the victim's threatening conduct. Consider Mayes v. State, 744 N.E.2d 390 (Ind. 2001). The defendant and his girlfriend Mary were having a bitter argument. Mary left the house, and the defendant pursued her into the street. When she reached for her purse, the defendant, who claimed she was about to pull a gun, drew his own weapon and fired, killing her. Whether the circumstances would support a claim of self-defense was hotly disputed. But the prosecution argued that because the defendant had committed a misdemeanor by carrying a handgun without a license, he had, in any event, forfeited his right to self-defense. The trial judge instructed the jury that, as specified in the applicable Indiana statute, the defendant was not entitled to use force in self-defense if he was "committing [or] escaping after the commission [of] a crime." The jury convicted Mayes of murder, and the Indiana Supreme Court affirmed. The court acknowledged that a literal application of the statute would produce absurd results, and stressed that there must be "an immediate causal connection between the crime and the confrontation." Id. at 394. But, the court held, "the jury could have concluded that but for Mayes' possession of the unlicensed handgun, Mary would still be alive because Mayes' unlicensed handgun [which he had carried into the street] was required, by law, to be kept at his dwelling." Id.

Is the result sound? Recall the felony-murder doctrine, under which the commission of certain felonies can sometimes be a basis for murder liability when death results. If Mayes's possession of the handgun was a felony, would he be guilty of murder under the felony-murder rule? If not, is there good reason to attach murder penalties when death is proximately caused by the commission of a misdemeanor?

3. The Model Penal Code. The traditional common-law rule reflected in *Peterson* and *Allen* differs from MPC §3.04. See Model Penal Code and Commentaries, Comment to §3.04 at 49-51 (1985):

> Subsection (2)(b)(i) denies justification for the use of deadly force if the actor, with the purpose of causing death or serious bodily harm, provoked the use of force against himself in the same encounter. This is a narrower forfeiture of the privilege of self-defense than commonly obtains. [However,] it is sufficient to resolve the problem, in view of the adoption in Subsection (2)(b)(ii) of a general duty to retreat before resorting to deadly force.
>
> The typical case to be imagined is this: A attacks B with his fists; B defends himself, and manages to subdue A to the extent of pinning him to the floor. B then starts to batter A's head savagely against the floor. A manages to rise, and since B is still attacking him and A now fears that if he is thrown again to the floor he will be killed, A uses a knife. B is killed or seriously wounded.
>
> [Under] this section . . . B is entitled to defend himself against A's attack, but only to the extent of using moderate, nondeadly force. . . . B exceeds the bounds of "necessary" force . . . , however, when, after reducing A to helplessness, he batters A's head on the floor. Since this excessive force is, in its turn, unlawful, under Subsection (1) A is entitled to defend himself against it and, if he believes that he is then in danger of death or serious bodily harm without apparent opportunity for safe retreat, A is also entitled to use his knife in self-protection. A of course is criminally liable for his initial battery on B, but would have a justifying defense that he could raise against prosecution for the ultimate homicide or wounding. Subsection (2)(b)(i), depriving A of his justification on the ground of initial aggression, would not become operative unless A entered the encounter with the purpose of causing death or serious bodily harm. . . .

2. Protection of Property and Law Enforcement

Actual or apparent threats to property not person

PEOPLE v. CEBALLOS

Supreme Court of California
12 Cal. 3d 470, 526 P.2d 241 (1974)

BURKE, J. Don Ceballos was found guilty by a jury of assault with a deadly weapon (Pen. Code, §245). Imposition of sentence was suspended and he was placed on probation. . . .

Defendant lived alone in a home in San Anselmo. The regular living quarters were above the garage, but defendant sometimes slept in the garage and had about $2,000 worth of property there.

In March 1970 some tools were stolen from defendant's home. On May 12, 1970, he noticed the lock on his garage doors was bent and pry marks were on one of the doors. The next day he mounted a loaded .22 caliber pistol in the garage. The pistol was aimed at the center of the garage doors and was connected by a wire to one of the doors so that the pistol would discharge if the door was opened several inches.

The damage to defendant's lock had been done by a 16-year-old boy named Stephen and a 15-year-old boy named Robert. On the afternoon of May 15, 1970, the boys returned to defendant's house while he was away. Neither boy was armed with a gun or knife. After looking in the windows and seeing no one, Stephen succeeded in removing the lock on the garage doors with a crowbar, and, as he pulled the door outward, he was hit in the face with a bullet from the pistol.

Stephen testified: He intended to go into the garage "[f]or musical equipment" because he had a debt to pay to a friend. His "way of paying that debt would be to take [defendant's] property and sell it" and use the proceeds to pay the debt. He "wasn't going to do it [i.e., steal] for sure, necessarily." He was there "to look around," and "getting in, I don't know if I would have actually stolen."

Defendant, testifying in his own behalf, admitted having set up the trap gun. He stated that after noticing the pry marks on his garage door on May 12, he felt he should "set up some kind of a trap, something to keep the burglar out of my home." When asked why he was trying to keep the burglar out, he replied, "[. . .] Because somebody was trying to steal my property . . . and I don't want to come home some night and have the thief in there . . . usually a thief is pretty desperate . . . and . . . they just pick up a weapon . . . if they don't have one . . . and do the best they can." [D]efendant [also] stated that "he didn't have much and he wanted to protect what he did have."

[*what he was afraid of*]

[T]he jury found defendant guilty of assault with a deadly weapon. An assault is "an unlawful attempt, coupled with a present ability, to commit a violent injury on the person of another." (Pen. Code, §240.)

Defendant contends that had he been present he would have been justified in shooting Stephen since Stephen was attempting to commit burglary, that under cases such as United States v. Gilliam, 25 Fed. Cas. p. 1319, defendant had a right to do indirectly what he could have done directly, and that therefore any attempt by him to commit a violent injury upon Stephen was not "unlawful" and hence not an assault. The People argue that the rule in *Gilliam* is unsound, that as a matter of law a trap gun constitutes excessive force, and that in any event the circumstances were not in fact such as to warrant the use of deadly force. . . .

[*Δ's contends*]

[*The PP1*]

In the United States, courts have concluded that a person may be held criminally liable . . . or civilly liable, if he sets upon his premises a deadly mechanical device and that device kills or injures another. . . . However, an exception to the rule that there may be criminal and civil liability for death or injuries caused by such a device has been recognized where the intrusion is, in fact, such that the person, were he present, would be justified in taking the life or inflicting the bodily harm with his own hands. . . .

Allowing persons, at their own risk, to employ deadly mechanical devices imperils the lives of children, firemen and policemen acting within the scope of their employment, and others. Where the actor is present, there is always the possibility he will realize that deadly force is not necessary, but deadly mechanical devices are without mercy or discretion. Such devices "are silent instrumentalities of death. They deal death and destruction to the innocent as well as the criminal intruder without the slightest warning. The taking of human life [or infliction of great bodily injury] by such means is brutally savage and inhuman." (See State v. Plumlee, . . . 149 So. 425, 430).

It seems clear that the use of such devices should not be encouraged. Moreover, whatever may be thought in torts, the foregoing rule setting forth an exception to liability for death or injuries inflicted by such devices "is inappropriate in penal law for it is obvious that it does not prescribe a workable standard of conduct; liability depends upon fortuitous results." (See Model Penal Code (Tent. Draft No. 8), §3.06, com. 15.) We therefore decline to adopt that rule in criminal cases.

Furthermore, even if that rule were applied here, as we shall see, defendant was not justified in shooting Stephen. Penal Code section 197 provides:

> Homicide is . . . justifiable . . . 1. When resisting any attempt to murder any person, or to commit a felony, or to do some great bodily injury upon any person; or, 2. When committed in defense of habitation, property, or person, against one who manifestly intends or endeavors, by violence or surprise, to commit a felony. . . .

By its terms subdivision 1 of Penal Code section 197 appears to permit killing to prevent any "felony," but in view of the large number of felonies today and the inclusion of many that do not involve a danger of serious bodily harm, a literal reading of the section is undesirable. People v. Jones, 191 Cal. App. 2d 478, 481, . . . read into section 197, subdivision 1, the limitation that the felony be "some atrocious crime attempted to be committed by force." *Jones* further stated, "the punishment provided by a statute is not necessarily an adequate test as to whether life may be taken. . . . We must look further into the character of the crime and the manner of its perpetration. . . . *When these do not reasonably create a fear of great bodily harm, . . . there is no cause for the exaction of a human life.*" (italics added. . . .)

Jones involved subdivision 1 of Penal Code section 197, but subdivision 2 of that section is likewise so limited. The term "violence or surprise" in subdivision 2 is found in common law authorities . . . and, whatever may have been the very early common law . . . the rule developed at common law that killing or use of deadly force to prevent a felony was justified only if the offense was a forcible and atrocious crime. . . . "Surprise" means an unexpected attack— which includes force and violence . . . and the word thus appears redundant.

Examples of forcible and atrocious crimes are murder, mayhem, rape and robbery. . . . In such crimes "from their atrocity and violence human life [or personal safety from great harm] either is, or is presumed to be, in peril" (see United States v. Gilliam, supra, 25 Fed. Cas. pp. 1319, 1320 . . .).

Burglary has been included in the list of such crimes. . . . However, in view of the wide scope of burglary under Penal Code section 459, as compared with the common law definition of that offense, in our opinion it cannot be said that under all circumstances burglary under section 459 constitutes a forcible and atrocious crime.[2] Where the character and manner of the burglary do not reasonably create a fear of great bodily harm, there is no cause for exaction of human life . . . or for the use of deadly force. . . . In the instant case the asserted burglary did not threaten death or serious bodily harm, since no one but Stephen and Robert was then on the premises. A defendant is not protected from liability merely by the fact that the intruder's conduct is such as would justify the defendant, were he present, in believing that the intrusion threatened death or serious bodily injury. . . . We thus conclude that defendant was not justified under Penal Code section 197, subdivisions 1 or 2, in shooting Stephen to prevent him from committing burglary. [I]n view of the supreme value of human life, we do not believe deadly force can be justified to prevent all [burglaries of a dwelling], including ones in which no person is, or is reasonably believed to be, on the premises except the would-be burglar.

Defendant also argues that had he been present he would have been justified in shooting Stephen under subdivision 4 of Penal Code section 197, which provides, "Homicide is . . . justifiable . . . 4. When necessarily committed in *attempting,* by lawful ways and means, to *apprehend* any person for any felony committed. . . ." (italics added.) The argument cannot be upheld. [N]o showing was made that defendant's intent in shooting was to apprehend a felon. Rather it appears . . . his intent was to prevent a burglary, to protect his property, and to avoid the possibility that a thief might get into defendant's house and injure him upon his return. . . .

We conclude that as a matter of law the exception to the rule of liability for injuries inflicted by a deadly mechanical device does not apply under the circumstances here appearing. . . .

The judgment is affirmed.

NOTES ON DEFENSE OF HABITATION

1. Variations on **Ceballos.** Suppose that instead of using a spring gun, Ceballos had put a curtain over the window to prevent anyone from looking in, had then seated himself inside the garage, facing the door, and had fired at

---

2. A common law burglary was the breaking and entering of a mansion house in the night with the intent to commit a felony. . . . Burglary under Penal Code section 459 differs from common law burglary in that the entry may be in the daytime and of numerous places other than a mansion house . . . and breaking is not required. . . . For example, under section 459 a person who enters a store with the intent of committing theft is guilty of burglary. . . . It would seem absurd to hold that a store detective could kill that person if necessary to prevent him from committing that offense. . . .

the boys as they raised the door. On these facts would the California court still consider his actions unjustified? Would it matter whether Ceballos knew that the boys were unarmed?

2. Other statutory approaches. (a) MPC §3.06(3)(d), like the *Ceballos* court, strictly limits the use of deadly force against an intruder in the home. But §3.06(3)(d)(ii)(2) nonetheless permits the use of deadly force when "the use of force other than deadly force to prevent the commission or the consummation of the crime would expose the actor . . . to substantial danger of serious bodily harm." Would Ceballos have a defense under this provision? Aside from the tactic he actually employed, how else could Ceballos have prevented the burglary?

(b) In 1984, ten years after the decision in *Ceballos*, California enacted a "Home Protection Bill of Rights," which provides (Cal. Penal Code §198.5):

> Any person using [deadly] force . . . within his or her residence shall be presumed to have held a reasonable fear of imminent peril of death or great bodily injury . . . when that force is used against another person, not a member of the family or household, who unlawfully and forcibly enters . . . and the person using the force knew or had reason to believe that an unlawful and forcible entry occurred.

Would Ceballos have had a defense under this provision? Would he have a defense under this provision if the shooting had occurred as specified in Note 1, supra?

(c) Many states have gone further. Some permit deadly force to prevent or terminate any felonious entry or even any unlawful entry. See Stuart P. Green, Castles and Carjackers: Proportionality and the Use of Deadly Force in Defense of Dwellings and Vehicles, 1999 U. Ill. L. Rev. 1. The Colorado statute, referred to in that state as its "Make-My-Day" law, provides (Colo. Rev. Stat. 18-1-704.5 (2011)):

> (1) [T]he citizens of Colorado have a right to expect absolute safety within their own homes.
>
> (2) [A]ny occupant of a dwelling is justified in using any degree of physical force, including deadly physical force, against another person when that other person has made an unlawful entry into the dwelling, and when the occupant has a reasonable belief that such other person has committed [or intends to commit] a crime in the dwelling in addition to the uninvited entry, . . . and when the occupant reasonably believes that such other person might use any physical force, no matter how slight, against any occupant.
>
> (3) Any occupant of a dwelling using physical force, including deadly physical force, in accordance with the provisions of subsection (2) of this section shall be immune from criminal prosecution [and civil liability] for the use of such force.

The Florida "stand your ground" law, enacted in 2005, is even broader. It applies to vehicles as well as dwellings and to attempted as well as completed entries. Moreover, it does not require the person using defensive force to believe that the suspected intruder is about to commit any other crime. See Fla. Stat. §776.013(1) (2011):

> A person is presumed to have held a reasonable fear of imminent peril of death or great bodily harm to himself or herself or another . . . if:
>
> (a) The person against whom the defensive force was used was in the process of unlawfully and forcefully entering, or had unlawfully and forcibly entered, a dwelling . . . or occupied vehicle . . . ; and
>
> (b) The person who uses defensive force knew or had reason to believe that an unlawful and forcible entry . . . was occurring or had occurred.

Compare these broad privileges to defend property with the strictly limited privilege to use deadly force in defense of one's life (see supra pages 819-832). Suppose that an uninvited guest (a drunken student) crashes a fraternity party, refuses to leave, and takes another beer from the refrigerator. Under Florida law, could a resident of the fraternity house shoot the unwelcome student and kill him? Some argue that in the event of an unlawful intrusion, the danger of serious injury is so high that it is reasonable to presume such a threat in all cases. Is this convincing? The possible justifications for laws like these are summarized and criticized in Green, supra, at 18-41.

3. Problem. On the night of October 17, 1992, Yoshihiro Hattori, a 16-year-old Japanese exchange student, was with a friend looking for a Halloween party, and he was dressed in a "Saturday Night Fever" costume. He mistakenly rang Mr. Peairs's doorbell, and when Mrs. Peairs came to the door and saw them, she became frightened and screamed. Apparently neither Hattori nor his friend could speak enough English to reassure her. At this point Peairs grabbed his laser-scoped .44-magnum handgun from his bedroom and went to the carport door. The two boys had retreated to the sidewalk, but when the carport door opened, Hattori began walking towards Peairs, waving his arms as he often did when trying to communicate. Peairs yelled "freeze," but Hattori did not understand him. Hattori continued forward; he had recently lost a contact lens and presumably did not see the gun. When Hattori was less than five feet away, Mr. Peairs fired one shot into his chest, killing him.

Rodney Peairs was indicted for manslaughter. He claimed that the shooting, though mistaken, was justified under La. Rev. Stat. Ann. §14:20(3), which allows the use of deadly force based on a reasonable belief that an intruder is "likely to use any unlawful force against a person [in the dwelling] while committing . . . a burglary of that dwelling. . . ." Peairs's lawyer argued that Peairs saw an intruder who kept advancing "with absolutely no respect for [Peairs's] home, his gun, or his warning." During closing arguments, Peairs's lawyer proclaimed "You have the absolute legal right in this country to answer your door with a gun. In your house, if you want to do it, you have the legal right to answer everybody that comes to your door with a gun." The prosecutor emphasized the fact that Peairs acted without investigating why his wife screamed; Peairs's alleged negligence was "his conduct in going to the closet and getting the biggest handgun made by human beings and never ever asking what it's for." After a seven-day trial and three hours of deliberation,

Peairs was acquitted. The acquittal sparked outrage in Japan where owning a handgun is illegal (with minor exceptions), but many people in Peairs's community supported his actions. See N.Y. Times, May 23, 1993, at A1; May 20, 1993, at A10.

In a subsequent development, a judge in a civil case found "no justification whatsoever" for the shooting and awarded the estate of Mr. Hattori $650,000 in damages against Mr. Peairs. N.Y. Times, Sept. 16, 1994, at A7.

For close analysis of the role of cultural misunderstanding and language barriers in determining reasonableness in the context of the *Peairs* cases, see Caroline Forell, What's Reasonable?: Self-Defense and Mistake in Criminal and Tort Law, 14 Lewis & Clark L. Rev. 1401 (2010).

Questions: Was the result of the criminal prosecution justified under Louisiana law? Would the defendant's case be stronger if it arose in Florida or in Colorado? If so, does that argue for or against such statutes?

NOTE ON DEFENSE OF OTHER TYPES OF PROPERTY

In Sydnor v. State, 776 A.2d 669, 671 (Md. 2001), the defendant was sitting on a stoop when Anthony Jackson approached, pulled a gun, and told him to hand over a gold chain he was wearing. After hitting Sydnor on the head and threatening to kill him, Jackson took $30 and was about to take the gold chain when Sydnor, assisted by friends, grabbed the gun and took it away. Jackson then attempted to flee, but Sydnor fired five shots, hitting him four times. Jackson collapsed and died 40 to 50 yards from where the robbery occurred. At Sydnor's trial for murder and manslaughter, the judge instructed the jury that before using deadly force, the defendant was required to retreat unless "at the moment that the shots were fired the defendant was being robbed," and the prosecution contended that the jury was entitled to view the robbery and the shooting as separate incidents. Sydnor was convicted of voluntary manslaughter. The Maryland Court of Appeals affirmed, rejecting the defense argument that the robbery was "a continuous transaction that is not complete until the perpetrator reaches a place of temporary safety." Id. at 676. Acknowledging that under felony-murder precedents, a robbery does not end until the robber has made good his escape, the court said (id. at 676-677):

> That principle does not, however, expand or trump the rule that limits the right to use deadly force to the time and circumstance that such force is necessary. The issue . . . is not whether the criminal enterprise is still in operation, but whether deadly force is then and there necessary to avoid imminent danger of death or serious bodily harm to the victim of the offense. If it is not, deadly force may not be used because its use . . . would be excessive and not required by the exigency of the moment. . . .

A dissenting judge commented (id. at 681-682):

> I am a believer in the rule of law. But I do not believe that it requires victims of violent crimes to submit to being robbed and beaten at gunpoint, without the

right to respond with all necessary force during the act. . . . The law should not . . . require complacent and compliant victims. . . .

This is not a case where Mr. Sydnor saw Mr. Jackson on the street a week after the robbery, and shot him in order to get his money back. In the present case, Mr. Jackson . . . was still attempting to complete the robbery, by carrying the stolen money away. . . . The majority does not sufficiently address the fact that robbery is not only a taking of property by force, but it is a forcible taking *and carrying away* of property. At the time he was shot, Mr. Jackson was carrying away property he had, just seconds before, taken by force and at gunpoint.

Questions: (a) Which is the better approach to a case like *Sydnor*? The MPC position is closer to that of the dissenting judge. See §3.06(3)(d)(ii). But if a person is required to retreat, when possible, in the face of a deadly threat to life, why should he be entitled to pursue and kill his assailant in order to recover $30?

(b) Putting aside Sydnor's desire to recover his property, should his use of deadly force be justifiable as a means of apprehending a dangerous felon? Consider the material that follows.

DURHAM v. STATE

Supreme Court of Indiana
199 Ind. 567, 159 N.E. 145 (1927)

[Defendant, a deputy game warden, arrested one Long for illegal fishing. Long jumped into his boat in an attempt to escape. Defendant pursued him, grabbing first the gunwale and then the anchor chain. While Long was beating defendant about the head with an oar, defendant shot him in the arm. Defendant was convicted of assault and battery and appealed.]

MARTIN, J. . . . Instruction 12 was to the effect . . . that human life is too precious to be imperiled by the arrest of one who is only guilty of a misdemeanor; that, if appellant, in order to overcome Long's resistance, used a dangerous and deadly weapon, and in such manner as to endanger his life, and thereby inflict serious wounds, then the appellant would be guilty of assault and battery, at least. This instruction . . . did not correctly state the law. . . .

The general rules . . . may be stated to be: (a) That an officer having the right to arrest a misdemeanant may use all the force that is reasonably necessary to accomplish the arrest, except (b) that he . . . may not kill or shed blood in attempting to arrest a misdemeanant who is fleeing, but not resisting. (c) That, if the defendant physically resists, the officer need not retreat but may press forward and repel the resistance with such force, short of taking life, as is necessary to effect the arrest; and, if in so doing the officer is absolutely obliged to seriously wound or take the life of the accused, in order to prevent the accused from seriously wounding, or killing him, he will be justified.[3]

To adopt the rule . . . stated by the court in instruction 12 [would] render the state powerless to use extreme force when extreme resistance is offered, and would permit misdemeanants to stay the power of the state by unlawful resistance. "To say to a defendant, 'You may measure strength with the arresting officer, and avoid being taken if you are the stronger or after your arrest you may break away unless he can prevail over you in a wrestle,' is to elevate mere brute force to a position of command over the wheels of justice." 1 Bishop's Cr. Proc. (2d Ed.) §16. . . . The judgment is reversed, with directions to sustain appellant's motion for a new trial. . . .

TENNESSEE v. GARNER

Supreme Court of the United States
471 U.S. 1 (1985)

WHITE, J., delivered the opinion of the Court.

This case requires us to determine the constitutionality of the use of deadly force to prevent the escape of an apparently unarmed suspected felon. We conclude that such force may not be used unless it is necessary to prevent the escape and the officer has probable cause to believe that the suspect poses a significant threat of death or serious physical injury to the officer or others.

At about 10:45 P.M. on October 3, 1974, Memphis Police Officers Elton Hymon and Leslie Wright were dispatched to answer a "prowler inside call." Upon arriving at the scene they saw a woman standing on her porch and gesturing toward the adjacent house. She told them she had heard glass breaking and that "they" or "someone" was breaking in next door. While Wright radioed the dispatcher to say that they were on the scene, Hymon went behind the house . . . and saw someone run across the back yard. The fleeing suspect, who was appellee-respondent's decedent, Edward Garner, stopped at a 6-feet-high chain link fence at the edge of the yard. With the aid of a flashlight, Hymon was able to see Garner's face and hands. He saw no sign of a weapon, and, though not certain, was "reasonably sure" . . . that Garner was unarmed. He thought Garner was 17 or 18 years old and about 5′5″ or 5′7″ tall.[2] While Garner was crouched at the base of the fence, Hymon called out "police, halt" and took a few steps toward him. Garner then began to climb over the fence.

---

3. [T]he protection which an officer is entitled to receive in making an arrest is a different thing from self-defense, for it is his duty to push forward and make the arrest and to secure and retain custody of the prisoner. . . .

2. In fact, Garner, an eighth-grader, was 15. He was 5′4″ tall and weighed somewhere around 100 or 110 pounds.

Convinced that if Garner made it over the fence he would elude capture,[3] Hymon shot him. The bullet hit Garner in the back of the head. Garner was taken by ambulance to a hospital, where he died on the operating table. Ten dollars and a purse taken from the house were found on his body.

In using deadly force to prevent the escape, Hymon was acting under the authority of a Tennessee statute and pursuant to Police Department policy. The statute provides that "[i]f, after notice of the intention to arrest the defendant, he either flee or forcibly resist, the officer may use all the necessary means to effect the arrest." Tenn. Code Ann. §40-7-108 (1982).[5] The Department policy was slightly more restrictive than the statute, but still allowed the use of deadly force in cases of burglary. The incident was reviewed by the Memphis Police Firearm's Review Board and presented to a grand jury. Neither took any action.

Garner's father then brought this action in the Federal District Court . . . , seeking damages . . . for asserted violations of Garner's constitutional rights. . . . [T]he district court entered judgment for all defendants. . . . The Court of Appeals reversed and remanded. It reasoned that the killing of a fleeing suspect is a "seizure" under the Fourth Amendment,[6] and is therefore constitutional only if "reasonable." . . .[7] The State of Tennessee, which had intervened to defend the statute, appealed to this Court. . . .

A police officer may arrest a person if he has probable cause to believe that person committed a crime. Petitioners and appellant argue that if this require-ment is satisfied the Fourth Amendment has nothing to say about *how* that seizure is made. This submission ignores the many cases in which this Court, by balancing the extent of the intrusion against the need for it, has examined the reasonableness of the manner in which a search or seizure is conducted. . . .

[N]otwithstanding probable cause to seize a suspect, an officer may not always do so by killing him. The intrusiveness of a seizure by means of deadly force is unmatched. The suspect's fundamental interest in his own life need not be elaborated upon. The use of deadly force also frustrates the interest of the individual, and of society, in judicial determination of guilt and punish-ment. Against these interests are ranged governmental interests in effective law enforcement. It is argued that overall violence will be reduced by encour-aging the peaceful submission of suspects who know that they may be shot if

---

3. When asked at trial why he fired, Hymon stated:

> Well, first of all it was apparent to me . . . that he was going to get away because, number 1, I couldn't get to him. . . . I couldn't get to him because of the fence here, I couldn't have jumped this fence . . . and caught him before he got away because he was already up on the fence, just one leap and he was already over the fence, and so there is no way that I could have caught him. . . .

5. Although the statute does not say so explicitly, Tennessee law forbids the use of deadly force in the arrest of a misdemeanant.

6. "The right of the people to be secure in their persons . . . against unreasonable searches and seizures, shall not be violated. . . ." U.S. Const., Amdt. 4.

7. The Court of Appeals concluded that the rule set out in the Model Penal Code "accurately states Fourth Amendment limitations on the use of deadly force against fleeing felons." . . .

they flee. . . . "Being able to arrest such individuals is a condition precedent to the state's entire system of law enforcement."

Without in any way disparaging the importance of these goals, we are not convinced that the use of deadly force is a sufficiently productive means of accomplishing them to justify the killing of nonviolent suspects. . . . [W]hile the meaningful threat of deadly force might be thought to lead to the arrest of more live suspects by discouraging escape attempts, the presently available evidence does not support this thesis. The fact is that a majority of police departments in this country have forbidden the use of deadly force against nonviolent suspects. [T]here is [thus] a substantial basis for doubting that the use of such force is an essential attribute of the arrest power in all felony cases. . . . It is not better that all felony suspects die than that they escape. It is no doubt unfortunate when a suspect who is in sight escapes, but the fact that the police arrive a little late or are a little slower afoot does not always justify killing the suspect. A police officer may not seize an unarmed, non-dangerous suspect by shooting him dead. The Tennessee statute is unconstitutional insofar as it authorizes the use of deadly force against such fleeing suspects.

It is not, however, unconstitutional on its face. Where the officer has probable cause to believe that the suspect poses a threat of serious physical harm, either to the officer or to others, it is not constitutionally unreasonable to prevent escape by using deadly force. . . . As applied in such circumstances, the Tennessee statute would pass constitutional muster.

It is insisted that the Fourth Amendment must be construed in light of the common-law rule, which allowed the use of whatever force was necessary to effect the arrest of a fleeing felon, though not a misdemeanant. . . . Because of sweeping change in the legal and technological context, reliance on the common-law rule in this case would be a mistaken literalism that ignores the purposes of a historical inquiry. [The common-law rule] arose at a time when virtually all felonies were punishable by death. . . . Courts have also justified the common-law rule by emphasizing the relative dangerousness of felons. Neither of these justifications makes sense today. Almost all crimes formerly punishable by death no longer are or can be. . . . Many crimes classified as misdemeanors . . . at common law are now felonies. These changes have . . . made the assumption that a "felon" is more dangerous than a misdemeanant untenable. . . . Officer Hymon could not reasonably have believed that Garner—young, slight, and unarmed—posed any threat. Indeed, Hymon never attempted to justify his actions on any basis other than the need to prevent an escape. . . .

The dissent argues that the shooting was justified by the fact that Officer Hymon had probable cause to believe that Garner had committed a nighttime burglary. While we agree that burglary is a serious crime, we cannot agree that it is so dangerous as automatically to justify the use of deadly force. . . . Although the armed burglar would present a different situation, the fact that an unarmed suspect has broken into a dwelling at night does not automatically mean he is physically dangerous. This case demonstrates as much. In fact, the available statistics demonstrate that burglaries only rarely involve physical violence. During the 10-year period from 1973-1982, only 3.8 percent of all burglaries involved violent crime. . . .

The judgment of the Court of Appeals is affirmed. . . .

O'CONNOR, J., with whom THE CHIEF JUSTICE and REHNQUIST, J., join, dissenting. . . .

Victims of a forcible intrusion into their home by a nighttime prowler will find little consolation in the majority's confident assertion that "burglaries only rarely involve physical violence." Moreover, even if a particular burglary, when viewed in retrospect, does not involve physical harm to others, the "harsh potentialities for violence" inherent in the forced entry into a home preclude characterization of the crime as "innocuous, inconsequential, minor, or 'nonviolent.'" Solem v. Helm, [463 U.S. 277 (1983)], at 316 (Burger, C.J., dissenting).

Because burglary is a serious and dangerous felony, the public interest in the prevention and detection of the crime is of compelling importance. Where a police officer has probable cause to arrest a suspected burglar, the use of deadly force as a last resort might well be the only means of apprehending the suspect. . . . Although some law enforcement agencies may choose to assume the risk that a criminal will remain at large, the Tennessee statute reflects a legislative determination that the use of deadly force in prescribed circumstances will serve generally to protect the public. . . .

Without questioning the importance of a person's interest in his life, I do not think this interest encompasses a right to flee unimpeded from the scene of a burglary. . . . The legitimate interests of the suspect in these circumstances are adequately accommodated by the Tennessee statute: to avoid the use of deadly force and the consequent risk to his life, the suspect need merely obey the valid order to halt. . . .

The Court's [holding] invites second-guessing of difficult police . . . decisions that must be made quickly in the most trying of circumstances. Police are given no guidance for determining which objects, among an array of potentially lethal weapons ranging from guns to knives to baseball bats to rope, will justify the use of deadly force. The Court also declines to outline the additional factors necessary to provide "probable cause" for believing that a suspect "poses a significant threat of death or serious physical injury." . . .

Whatever the constitutional limits on police use of deadly force in order to apprehend a fleeing felon, I do not believe they are exceeded in a case in which a police officer has probable cause to arrest a suspect at the scene of a residential burglary, orders the suspect to halt, and then fires his weapon as a last resort to prevent the suspect's escape into the night. I respectfully dissent.

NOTES

1. Deadly force. Which police measures for effectuating an arrest constitute the sort of deadly force that *Garner* restricts? Are choke holds, electric cattle prods, night sticks, and pepper spray included? In a recent California incident, a police officer pursuing a suspect threatened to unleash his K-9 companion unless the suspect stopped. When the suspect refused to do so, the officer released the dog, who effected the arrest by catching up to the suspect, biting onto his right arm, and holding him until the officer ordered the dog to release its grip. The suspect sustained severe wounds to his upper arm, requiring surgery and eight days of hospitalization. Was this a use of "deadly force"? Was it permissible under *Garner*? See Vera Cruz v. City of Escondido, 139 F.3d 659 (9th Cir. 1997). Compare the definition of deadly force in Model Penal Code §3.11(2).

2. *Private citizens.* Because the rule announced in *Garner* is based on the Fourth Amendment, this constitutional limit on the use of deadly force applies only to the police and others acting under state authority. (A much-debated question is whether a private person who uses defensive force is "acting under state authority" when state law creates a privilege to use force under those circumstances.) Apart from the technical "state-action" issue under constitutional law, what limits should apply when private citizens use deadly force to protect their property? What limits should apply when the state authorizes conduct that will deprive certain citizens of their life? Reconsider the "Make-My-Day" statutes and other laws permitting homeowners to shoot intruders who do not pose a lethal threat, page 876 supra.

Suppose a teenager cuts a bicycle chain, gets on the bike, and starts to ride off on it. We have discussed above the bicycle owner's right to shoot the teenager in order to recoup his property. See page 878 supra and MPC §3.06(d)(ii). But if the teenager abandons the bicycle and flees on foot, may the owner shoot to prevent his escape? Should the answer be different if the teenager flees after trying unsuccessfully to rob the owner at gunpoint?

MODEL PENAL CODE

§3.07(2)(b). Use of Force in Law Enforcement

[See Appendix.]

Model Penal Code and Commentaries, Comment to §3.07 at 111-120 (1985): The common law [authorized deadly force] where necessary to prevent the escape of one fleeing from arrest for felony, but not for misdemeanor. . . .

The extreme breadth of the privilege apparently induced some courts and legislatures to limit its application in the very worst way—by imposing a rule of strict liability. Thus, the privilege was at times said to attach only when the deceased had in fact committed a felony, apart from all considerations of good faith and reasonable belief on the part of the arresting officer. . . . Still other jurisdictions appeared to adhere to a rule of reasonable belief, but the law was in a state of considerable ambiguity and uncertainty on this vital point. . . .

Like the common law rule, Paragraph (i) of Subsection (2)(b) restricts the use of extreme force to arrests for felonies. . . . But unlike the common law rule, Subsection (2)(b) imposes certain additional qualifications on the privilege.

First, the use of deadly force is restricted by Paragraph (ii) of Subsection (2)(b) to those who, under the law of the jurisdiction, are authorized to act as peace officers and to those who are assisting persons whom they believe are authorized to act as peace officers. Where the purpose to be served is the apprehension of persons to answer criminal charges, it has seemed important, in an age of firearms, to restrict the use of deadly force to situations where official personnel are . . . believed to be involved. . . .

[Second,] the public interest is poorly served if the use of deadly force creates a substantial risk of injury to innocent bystanders. The privilege is accordingly withheld unless the actor believes that there is no such risk. . . .

[Third,] the character of the offender . . . , rather than [the] abstract classification of the offense he is thought to have committed, should be determinative as to the use of deadly force. [Thus,] the use of deadly force [is permissible] only in cases where the offender is thought to pose such a danger to life or limb that his immediate apprehension overrides competing considerations.

3. Choice of the Lesser Evil—The Residual Principle of Justification

PEOPLE v. UNGER

Supreme Court of Illinois
66 Ill. 2d 333, 362 N.E.2d 319 (1977)

RYAN, J. Defendant, Francis Unger, was [convicted of] the crime of escape and was . . . sentenced to a term of three to nine years to be served consecutively to the remainder of the sentence for which he was imprisoned at the time of the escape. The conviction was reversed upon appeal and the cause was remanded for a new trial. . . . We granted leave to appeal and now affirm the judgment of the appellate court.

At the time of the present offense, the defendant was confined at the Illinois State Penitentiary in Joliet, Illinois. Defendant was serving a one- to three-year term as a consequence of a conviction for auto theft. . . . On February 23, 1972, the defendant was transferred to the prison's minimum security, honor farm. It is undisputed that on March 7, 1972, the defendant walked off the honor farm. Defendant was apprehended two days later in a motel room in St. Charles, Illinois.

At trial, defendant testified that prior to his transfer to the honor farm he had been threatened by a fellow inmate. This inmate allegedly brandished a six-inch knife in an attempt to force defendant to engage in homosexual *facts.*

activities. Defendant was 22 years old and weighed approximately 155 pounds. He testified that he did not report the incident to the proper authorities due to fear of retaliation. Defendant also testified that he is not a particularly good fighter.

Defendant stated that after his transfer to the honor farm he was assaulted and sexually molested by three inmates, and he named the assailants at trial. The attack allegedly occurred on March 2, 1972, and from that date until his escape defendant received additional threats from inmates he did not know. On March 7, 1972, the date of the escape, defendant testified that he received a call on an institution telephone. Defendant testified that the caller, whose voice he did not recognize, threatened him with death because the caller had heard that defendant had reported the assault to prison authorities. *Ha!* → Defendant said that he left the honor farm to save his life and that he planned to return once he found someone who could help him. None of these incidents were reported to the prison officials. As mentioned, defendant was apprehended two days later still dressed in his prison clothes. . . .

The following instruction (People's Instruction No. 9) was given by the trial court over defendant's objection. "The reasons, if any, given for the alleged escape are immaterial and not to be considered by you as in any way justifying or excusing, if there were in fact such reasons." . . . The principal issue in the present appeal is whether it was error for the court to instruct the jury that it must disregard the reasons given for defendant's escape and to conversely refuse to instruct the jury on the statutory defenses of compulsion and necessity. . . .

Traditionally, the courts have been reluctant to permit the defenses of compulsion and necessity to be relied upon by escapees. This reluctance appears to have been primarily grounded upon considerations of public policy. Several recent decisions, however, have recognized the applicability of the compulsion and necessity defenses to prison escapes. In People v. Harmon (1974), 220 N.W.2d 212, the defense of duress was held to apply in a case where the defendant alleged that he escaped in order to avoid repeated homosexual attacks from fellow inmates. In People v. Lovercamp (1974), 43 Cal. App. 3d 823, a limited defense of necessity was held to be available to two defendants whose escapes were allegedly motivated by fear of homosexual attacks.

As illustrated by *Harmon* and *Lovercamp*, different courts have reached similar results in escape cases involving sexual abuse, though the question was analyzed under different defense theories. A certain degree of confusion has resulted from the recurring practice on the part of the courts to use the terms "compulsion" (duress) and "necessity" interchangeably, though the defenses are theoretically distinct. . . .

In our view, the defense of necessity . . . is the appropriate defense in the present case. [T]he defendant here was not deprived of his free will by the threat of imminent physical harm which, according to the Committee Comments, appears to be the intended interpretation of the defense of compulsion as set out in section 7-11 of the Criminal Code. . . . Rather, if defendant's testimony is believed, he was forced to choose between two admitted evils by the situation which arose from actual and threatened homosexual assaults and fears of reprisal. Though the defense of compulsion would be applicable in the unlikely event that a prisoner was coerced by the threat of imminent physical harm to perform the specific act of escape, no such situation is involved in the present appeal. . . .

The defendant's testimony was clearly sufficient to raise the affirmative defense of necessity [as] defined by statute (Ill. Rev. Stat. 1971, ch. 38, par. 7-13):

> Conduct which would otherwise be an offense is justifiable by reason of necessity if the accused was without blame in occasioning or developing the situation and reasonably believed such conduct was necessary to avoid a public or private injury greater than the injury which might reasonably result from his own conduct.

Defendant testified that he was subjected to threats of forced homosexual activity and that, on one occasion, the threatened abuse was carried out. He also testified that he was physically incapable of defending himself and that he feared greater harm would result from a report to the authorities. Defendant further testified that just prior to his escape he was told that he was going to be killed, and that he therefore fled the honor farm in order to save his life. Though the State's evidence cast a doubt upon the defendant's motives for escape and upon the reasonableness of defendant's assertion that such conduct was necessary, the defendant was entitled to have the jury consider the defense on the basis of his testimony. . . .

The State, however, would have us apply a more stringent test to prison escape situations. The State refers to the *Lovercamp* decision, where . . . it was held that the defense of necessity need be submitted to the jury only where five conditions had been met. Those conditions are: "(1) The prisoner is faced with a specific threat of death, forcible sexual attack or substantial bodily injury in the immediate future; (2) There is no time for a complaint to the authorities or there exists a history of futile complaints . . .; (3) There is no time or opportunity to resort to the courts; (4) There is no evidence of force or violence used towards prison personnel or other 'innocent' persons in the escape; and (5) The prisoner immediately reports to the proper authorities when he has attained a position of safety from the immediate threat."

The State correctly points out that the defendant never informed the authorities of his situation and failed to report immediately after securing a position of safety. Therefore, it is contended that, under the authority of *Lovercamp*, defendant is not entitled to a necessity instruction. We agree . . . that the above conditions are relevant factors to be used in assessing claims of necessity. We cannot say, however, that the existence of each condition is, as a matter of law, necessary to establish a meritorious necessity defense.

The preconditions set forth in *Lovercamp* are, in our view, matters which go to the weight and credibility of the defendant's testimony. . . . The absence of one or more of the elements listed in *Lovercamp* would not necessarily mandate a finding that the defendant could not assert the defense of necessity.

[I]n the present case . . . defendant never voluntarily turned himself in to the proper officials. However, defendant testified that he intended to return to the prison upon obtaining legal advice from an attorney and claimed that he was attempting to get money from friends to pay for such counsel. Regardless of our opinion as to the believability of defendant's tale, this testimony, if accepted by the jury, would have negated any negative inference which would arise from defendant's failure to report to proper authorities after the escape. The absence of one of the *Lovercamp* preconditions does not alone disprove the claim of necessity and should not, therefore, automatically preclude an instruction on the defense. We therefore reject the contention that the availability of the necessity defense be expressly conditioned upon the elements set forth in *Lovercamp*.

In conclusion, we hold that under the facts and circumstances of the present case the defendant was entitled to submit his defense of necessity to the jury. It was, therefore, reversible error to give People's Instruction No. 9 to the jury and to refuse to give an appropriate instruction defining the defense of necessity, such as the instruction tendered by the defendant. . . .

UNDERWOOD, J., dissenting: My disagreement with my colleagues stems from an uneasy feeling that their unconditional recognition of necessity as a defense to the charge of escape carries with it the seeds of future troubles. Unless narrowly circumscribed, the availability of that defense could encourage potential escapes, disrupt prison discipline, and could even result in injury to prison guards, police or private citizens. . . .

I am not totally insensitive to the sometimes brutal and unwholesome problems faced by prison inmates, and the frequency of sexually motivated assaults. Prisoner complaints to unconcerned or understaffed prison administrations may produce little real help to a prisoner or may actually increase the hazard from fellow inmates of whose conduct complaint has been made. Consequently, and until adequate prison personnel and facilities are realities, I agree that a necessity defense should be recognized. The interests of society are better served, however, if the use of that defense in prison-escape cases is confined within well-defined boundaries such as those in *Lovercamp*. In that form it will be available, but with limitations precluding its wholesale use.

It is undisputed that defendant here did not meet those conditions. . . . Rather, he stole a truck some nine hours after his escape, drove to Chicago, and later drove to St. Charles, using the telephone to call friends in Canada. This conduct, coupled with his admitted intent to leave in order to gain publicity for what he considered an unfair sentence, severely strain the credibility of his testimony regarding his intention to return to the prison.

NOTES

1. In United States v. Bailey, 444 U.S. 394 (1980), the Supreme Court held, contrary to *Unger* but in accord with *Lovercamp*, that a prerequisite for invoking the necessity defense in a federal prosecution for prison escape is that the defendant make a bona fide effort to surrender or return "as soon as the duress or necessity had lost its coercive force."

2. Consider the following comment on the task of weighing the evils in a prison escape case (Model Penal Code and Commentaries, Comments to §3.02 at 12, n.5 (1985): "The harm sought to be prevented by the law defining the offense may be viewed broadly. . . . For example, a court could consider whether recognition of the defense when a prisoner has escaped to avoid assault would have the effect of substantially encouraging unjustified escapes."

Question: Under this approach could a court deny a necessity defense in an otherwise justified circumstance, on the ground that other defendants might abuse the defense by invoking it when their conduct was *not* justified?

3. What perils are created by the elasticity of the necessity defense? We saw earlier, in the section on the principle of legality, page 171 supra, that vagueness is regarded as a serious evil in the criminal law. Is vagueness less offensive when it affects defenses to, rather than definitions of, criminal conduct?

MODEL PENAL CODE

§3.02. JUSTIFICATION GENERALLY: CHOICE OF EVILS

[See Appendix.]

Model Penal Code and Commentaries, Comment to §3.02 at 9-14 (1985): This section accepts the view that a principle of necessity, properly conceived, affords a general justification for conduct that would otherwise constitute an offense. . . . Under this section, property may be destroyed to prevent the spread of a fire. . . . An ambulance may pass a traffic light. Mountain climbers lost in a storm may take refuge in a house or may appropriate provisions. . . . A developed legal system must have better ways of dealing with such problems than to refer only to the letter of particular prohibitions, framed without reference to cases of this kind. . . .[3]

---

3. A contrary view is expressed in Brown Comm'n. Final Report §601 Comment, which suggests that any general "choice of evils" codification would be "a potential source of unwarranted difficulty in ordinary cases," and that case by case prosecutive discretion is preferable. But reliance on prosecutorial discretion alone leaves the matter to be decided in the absence of governing principles and by an executive official who must act without legislative guidance or judicial check. . . .

The Code's principle of necessity is subject to a number of limitations. . . . It is not enough that the actor believes that his behavior possibly may be conducive to ameliorating certain evils; he must believe it is "necessary" to avoid the evils. [Moreover,] the balancing of evils is not committed to the private judgment of the actor; . . . . Subsection (1)(a) . . . requires that the harm or evil sought to be avoided be greater than that which would be caused by the commission of the offense, not that the defendant believe it to be so. What is involved may be described as an interpretation of the law of the offense, in light of the submission that the special situation calls for an exception to the criminal prohibition that the legislature could not reasonably have intended to exclude, given the competing values to be weighed. The Code does not resolve the question of how far the balancing of values should be determined by the court as a matter of law or submitted to the jury. . . .

NEW YORK PENAL LAW (2011)

§35.05. JUSTIFICATION; GENERALLY

Unless otherwise limited by the ensuing provisions of this article defining justifiable use of physical force, or with some other provision of law, conduct which would otherwise constitute an offense is justifiable and not criminal when: . . .

2. Such conduct is necessary as an emergency measure to avoid an imminent public or private injury which is about to occur by reason of a situation occasioned or developed through no fault of the actor, and which is of such gravity that, according to ordinary standards of intelligence and morality, the desirability and urgency of avoiding such injury clearly outweigh the desirability of avoiding the injury sought to be prevented by the statute defining the offense in issue. The necessity and justifiability of such conduct may not rest upon considerations pertaining only to the morality and advisability of the statute, either in its general application or with respect to its application to a particular class of cases arising thereunder. Whenever evidence relating to the defense of justification under this subdivision is offered by the defendant, the court shall rule as a matter of law whether the claimed facts and circumstances would, if established, constitute a defense.

NOTES ON STATUTORY STANDARDS

1. An imminence requirement? Recall that Unger's necessity claim was based on a death threat he had received over the prison telephone. But at the time he escaped, the caller was not about to strike; if Unger had identified the potential assailant and approached him from behind, he would not have been entitled to kill in self-defense because the execution of the threat was not "imminent." See page 855 supra. Instead, however, Unger took a less extreme self-protective measure—in a sense, he simply chose to "retreat." Should he nonetheless lose a necessity defense on the ground that the harm he faced was

not imminent at the moment of escape? Compare the prerequisites for the necessity defense under the New York and MPC formulations. Which approach is preferable? Consider Model Penal Code and Commentaries, Comment to §3.02 at 17, 19-21 (1985):

> [The New York requirement that conduct be an "emergency measure to avoid an imminent . . . injury."] unduly emphasizes one ingredient in the judgment that is called for. . . . It is true that genuine necessity rests on the unavailability of alternatives that would avoid both evils, and that typically when the evil is not imminent some such alternative will be available; but it is a mistake to erect imminence as an absolute requirement, since there may be situations in which an otherwise illegal act is necessary to avoid an evil that may occur in the future. . . .

Questions: Is the New York approach more consistent with the imminence requirement typically imposed in self-defense cases? Or is there good reason to eliminate that requirement in the context of a "necessity" claim?

2. *When does the law* preclude *a choice of evils?* Note that under both the New York and MPC formulations, "the general choice of evils defense cannot succeed if the issue of competing values has been previously foreclosed by a deliberate legislative choice, as when some provision of the law deals explicitly with the specific situation that presents the choice of evils or a legislative purpose to exclude the claimed justification otherwise appears."[31] Consider Commonwealth v. Leno, 616 N.E.2d 453 (Mass. 1993):

> Massachusetts is one of ten States that prohibit distribution of hypodermic needles without a prescription. In the face of those statutes the defendants operated a needle exchange program in an effort to combat the spread of acquired immuno-deficiency syndrome (AIDS). [They were] convicted of . . . unlawful distribution of an instrument to administer controlled substances. . . . On appeal, [they] challenge the judge's refusal to instruct the jury on the defense of necessity. . . . We affirm. . . . That some States prohibit the distribution of hypodermic needles without a prescription, and others do not, merely indicates that the best course to take to address the long-term hazard of the spread of AIDS remains a matter of debate. . . . Whether a statute is wise or effective is not within the province of courts. . . . The defendants argue that the increasing number of AIDS cases constitutes a societal problem of great proportions, and that their actions were an effective means of reducing the magnitude of that problem; they assert that their possession, transportation and distribution of hypodermic needles eventually will produce an overall reduction in the spread of HIV and in the future incidence of AIDS. The defendants' argument raises the issue of jury nullification, not the defense of necessity. . . .

3. *Necessity and "clean hands."* Suppose that one of Unger's fellow prisoners had threatened to kill him because Unger had (a) accused the other man of being a sexual pervert; or (b) assaulted the other man. Would Unger still

---

31. Model Penal Code and Commentaries, Comment to §3.02 at 14 (1985).

have a defense under the Illinois necessity provision? *Should* he have a necessity defense? Like Illinois, New York denies the defense when a necessity arises as a result of some fault of the actor. Is this always a sensible result? If commission of an offense can avert serious harm in an unforeseen emergency, why should the law seek to prevent the defendant from taking steps that would leave society better off? Consider Model Penal Code and Commentaries, supra:

> [T]he New York provision [requires] that the situation that gives rise to the necessity for action be occasioned or developed "through no fault of the actor." Thus, an actor who negligently starts a fire is deprived of any defense for destroying property or breaking traffic regulations in an effort to prevent its spread or to notify the proper authorities. . . . By contrast, [under] the Code . . . the actor [could] be prosecuted for offenses for which negligence would suffice, but would not be deprived of the choice of evils defense for offenses committed in the attempt to put out the fire that require a higher culpability level. . . .

4. Necessity and mens rea. Lawrence Tiffany & Carl Anderson, Legislating the Necessity Defense in Criminal Law, 52 Den. L.J. 839, 861-862 (1975), write:

> A question which needs to be clarified is posed by LaFave and Scott: "*A*, driving a car, suddenly finds himself in a predicament where he must either run down *B* or hit *C*'s house and he reasonably chooses the latter, unfortunately killing two people in the house who by bad luck happened to be just at that place inside the house where *A*'s car struck. . . ."
>
> Of course, the defendant [charged with reckless or negligent homicide] is guilty of no crime to begin with. . . . Defendant needs no general justification defense when charged with a crime based on recklessness or negligence since it is implicit in the charge itself that the defendant's conduct was not justified; unjustifiability of conduct becomes an element of the charge itself and must be proved by the state.

Compare State v. Rasmussen, 524 N.W.2d 843 (N.D. 1994). The defendant's license to drive had been suspended. On a bitterly cold night, during a snowstorm, he found himself stranded on a highway in North Dakota. His car had broken down, and the person driving him had left to get help. When the driver did not return, Rasmussen managed to get the car started, took the wheel, and drove away. He was caught and prosecuted for driving while suspended—a strict liability offense. Should he be able to assert a necessity defense when the underlying crime does not require mens rea? If the necessity defense is designed to identify cases in which blame for a wrongful act should not be imposed, then it would seem that the defense should not be available in *Rasmussen*, because a strict liability offense is—by definition—an offense in which liability for wrongful conduct is imposed even in the absence of fault. But if the necessity defense is designed to identify cases in which the defendant's conduct is not wrongful at all, then it would seem that a claim of necessity *should* be considered in a context like *Rasmussen*, because the claim seeks to show that the defendant's conduct was not wrongful. Which is it?

NOTES ON MEDICAL NECESSITY

1. Consider Commonwealth v. Hutchins, 575 N.E.2d 741 (Mass. 1991). Defendant was charged with illegal cultivation of marijuana. At trial he offered to prove that he was a victim of progressive systemic sclerosis, a serious and sometimes fatal disease with frightful symptoms for which no cure exists, and that ingestion of marijuana had produced a remarkable remission. The judge denied the offer of proof on the ground that it would not support a necessity defense, and the defendant was convicted. On appeal, the Massachusetts Supreme Judicial Court affirmed, stating:

> In our view, the alleviation of the defendant's medical symptoms, the importance to the defendant of which we do not underestimate, would not clearly and significantly outweigh the potential harm to the public were we to declare that the defendant's cultivation of marihuana and its use for his medicinal purposes may not be punishable. We cannot dismiss the reasonably possible negative impact of such a judicial declaration on the enforcement of our drug laws, including but not limited to those dealing with marihuana, nor can we ignore the government's overriding interest in the regulation of such substances.

Chief Justice Liacos, dissenting, protested:

> [T]he common law defense of necessity . . . is based on the recognition that, under very limited circumstances, "the value protected by the law is, as a matter of public policy, eclipsed by a superseding value which makes it inappropriate and unjust to apply the usual criminal rule." The superseding value in a case such as the present one is the humanitarian and compassionate value in allowing an individual to seek relief from agonizing symptoms caused by a progressive and incurable illness in circumstances which risk no harm to any other individual. In my view, the harm to an individual in having to endure such symptoms may well outweigh society's generalized interest in prohibiting him or her from using the marihuana in such circumstances.

The dissent added in a footnote:

> There is no reason to believe, as the court suggests, that allowing a defendant to present evidence of medical necessity to a jury will have a negative impact on the enforcement of drug laws. I am confident that juries would apply their wisdom and common sense in making sure that the necessity defense is not successfully utilized by defendants who use marihuana for purposes other than to alleviate agonizing and painful medical symptoms.

2. Courts remain divided over whether to permit a necessity defense for medical uses of marijuana to alleviate the symptoms of severe illness. Compare Sowell v. State, 738 So. 2d 205 (Fla. App. 1998) (allowing the defense), with State v. Poling, 531 S.E.2d 678 (W. Va. 2000) (holding that the state legislature implicitly intended to preclude the defense). Several states have statutory exceptions to their antidrug laws for such cases. In California, the Compassionate Use Act authorizes the possession and use of marijuana when recommended by a physician. Other states have taken a narrower approach. Virginia legislation permits the use of marijuana for glaucoma and cancer patients; because other diseases are not mentioned, the necessity defense was denied to a man who used marijuana to treat debilitating migraine headaches that did not respond to prescription medications. Murphy v. Commonwealth, 521 S.E.2d 301 (Va. App. 1999).

Even in states that recognize a medical necessity exception to their state antidrug laws, there remains a risk of federal prosecution. Federal law prohibits distribution of any "controlled substance," 28 U.S.C. §841(a)(1), and posits that as a matter of federal law, marijuana is a controlled substance for which there is "[no] currently accepted medical use." As a result, the Supreme Court has held that Congress intended to preclude any medical necessity defense to a prosecution under §841(a)(1) and that the federal prohibition takes precedence over any more permissive standards under state law. United States v. Oakland Cannabis Buyers' Cooperative, 532 U.S. 483 (2001). Three concurring justices stressed, however, that the decision to preclude a necessity defense applies only to prosecutions under §841(a)(1) for drug distribution; accordingly, the defense may remain available in other contexts, such as the prosecution of individual users. But if a cancer patient is *justified* in buying and using marijuana to alleviate her extreme pain, how can the seller *not* be justified in selling the drug to her for that purpose?

NOTES ON ECONOMIC NECESSITY

1. Consider Borough of Southwark v. Williams, [1971] 2 All E.R. 175. Defendants were homeless families in London at a time when the city suffered an extreme housing shortage. Obtaining no help from local government, they made an orderly entry into some empty houses belonging to the Borough and became squatters there. The Borough brought an action to oust them. The squatters resisted by raising the defense of necessity. The court rejected the defense:

> [I]n case of great and imminent danger, in order to preserve life, the law will permit of an encroachment on private property. . . . The doctrine so enunciated must, however, be carefully circumscribed. . . . If homelessness were once admitted as a defence to trespass, no one's house could be safe. Necessity would open a door which no man could shut. It would not only be those in extreme need who would enter. . . . There would be others who would imagine that they were in need, or would invent a need, so as to gain entry. Each man would say his need was greater than the next man's. The plea would be an excuse for all sorts of wrongdoing. So the courts must, for the sake of law and order, take a firm stand. They must refuse to admit the plea of necessity to the hungry and the homeless; and trust that their distress will be relieved by the charitable and the good. . . . We can sympathise with the plight in which [these squatters] find themselves. We can recognise the orderly way in which they made their entry. But we can go no further. They must make their appeal for help to others, not to us. [W]e must, in the interest of law and order itself, . . . and order the defendants to go out.

2. Many American courts are similarly hostile to claims of economic necessity. In People v. Fontes, 89 P.3d 484 (Colo. App. 2003), a defendant was convicted of attempting to cash a forged check in the amount $454.75, after the trial court rejected his offer to prove: that he intended to use the money to buy food for his three young children, who suffered from severe health problems; that they had not eaten for more than 24 hours; that three different food banks had turned down his requests for food; and that he feared that with continued lack of food, his children faced "malnutrition and death." The appellate court affirmed the conviction, holding that his effort to raise a necessity defense was properly rejected:

> While we are not without sympathy for the downtrodden, the law is clear that economic necessity alone cannot support a choice of crime. Although economic necessity may be an important issue in sentencing, a choice of evils defense cannot be based upon economic necessity.

Questions: Would this result be correct under the MPC or New York formulations of the necessity defense? Is it correct as a matter of principle?

3. In the wake of Hurricane Katrina, with many New Orleans businesses shuttered and with supplies short, some residents broke into stores to take food, water, and medications needed for themselves or their children. If prosecuted for theft or "looting,"[32] should they be able to raise a necessity defense? How should we compare the benefits of their conduct to the harm caused? Professor Stuart P. Green argues (Looting, Law, and Lawlessness, 81 Tul. L. Rev. 1129, 1152-1153 (2007)) that assessing the harm of looting is quite complicated, in part precisely because the offense, by definition, occurs under emergency conditions:

> Although the most direct harms . . . are those suffered by the person or entity whose premises are looted, less direct harms accrue to the community generally, including the loss of civil order and the sense of fear that such loss is likely to cause. We must also consider the possibility that looting tends to be contagious: others in the community might be encouraged . . . to engage in similar, perhaps less clearly justified, conduct. And such looting might also cause more remote, but still significant, harms. [T]he store whose goods were looted might . . . even close for good; the premises might remain vacant and boarded up; the incident might mark the beginning of the community's slide into decline. . . . It is easy to see that, other things being equal, it should be permissible to cause ten dollars in property damage in order to prevent a million dollars of damage. But by what yardstick are we to compare . . . on the one hand, the hunger that is alleviated by the looter's stealing food, and, on the other, the disorder in the community to which her looting might contribute?

---

32. La. R.S. §14:62.5 (2011) defines looting as the "intentional entry [without authorization] into . . . any structure belonging to another . . . , in which normal security of property is not present by virtue of a hurricane, flood, fire, [or] act of God, . . . and the obtaining [of] property of the owner." Violations are punishable by "imprison[ment] at hard labor for [up to] fifteen years." Id.

UNITED STATES v. SCHOON

United States Court of Appeals, 9th Circuit
971 F.2d 193 (1992)

BOOCHEVER, J.: Gregory Schoon, Raymond Kennon, Jr., and Patricia Manning appeal their convictions for obstructing activities of the Internal Revenue Service Office in Tucson, Arizona. [The] charges stem from their activities in protest of United States involvement in El Salvador. They claim the district court improperly denied them a necessity defense. Because we hold the necessity defense inapplicable in cases like this, we affirm.

On December 4, 1989, thirty people, including appellants, gained admittance to the IRS office in Tucson, where they chanted "keep America's tax dollars out of El Salvador," splashed simulated blood on the counters, walls, and carpeting, and generally obstructed the office's operation. After a federal police officer ordered the group, on several occasions, to disperse or face arrest, appellants were arrested.

At a bench trial, appellants proffered testimony about conditions in El Salvador as the motivation for their conduct. They attempted to assert a necessity defense, essentially contending that their acts in protest of American involvement in El Salvador were necessary to avoid further bloodshed in that country. While finding appellants motivated solely by humanitarian concerns, the court nonetheless precluded the defense as a matter of law. . . .

To invoke the necessity defense . . . the defendants colorably must have shown that: (1) they were faced with a choice of evils and chose the lesser evil; (2) they acted to prevent imminent harm; (3) they reasonably anticipated a direct causal relationship between their conduct and the harm to be averted; and (4) they had no legal alternatives to violating the law. The district court denied the necessity defense on the grounds that (1) the requisite immediacy was lacking; (2) the actions taken would not abate the evil; and (3) other legal alternatives existed. Because the threshold test for admissibility of a necessity defense is a conjunctive one, a court may preclude invocation of the defense if "proof is deficient with regard to any of the four elements."

While we could affirm substantially on those grounds relied upon by the district court, we find a deeper, systemic reason for the complete absence of federal case law recognizing a necessity defense in an indirect civil disobedience case. As used in this opinion, "civil disobedience" is the wilful violation of a law, undertaken for the purpose of social or political protest. Indirect civil disobedience involves violating a law or interfering with a government policy that is not, itself, the object of protest. Direct civil disobedience, on the other hand, involves protesting the existence of a law by breaking that law or by preventing the execution of that law in a specific instance in which a particularized harm would otherwise follow. This case involves indirect civil disobedience because these protestors were not challenging the laws under which they were charged. In contrast, the civil rights lunch counter sit-ins, for example, constituted direct civil disobedience because the protestors were challenging the rule that prevented them from sitting at lunch counters. . . . Today, we conclude, for the reasons stated below, that the necessity defense is inapplicable to cases involving indirect civil disobedience.

Necessity is, essentially, a utilitarian defense . . . , maximizing social welfare by allowing a crime to be committed where the social benefits of the crime outweigh the social costs of failing to commit the crime. . . . What all the traditional necessity cases have in common is that the commission of the "crime" averted the occurrence of an even greater "harm." In some sense, the necessity defense allows us to act as individual legislatures, amending a particular criminal provision or crafting a one-time exception to it, subject to court review, when a real legislature would formally do the same under those circumstances. For example, by allowing prisoners who escape a burning jail to claim the justification of necessity, we assume the lawmaker, confronting this problem, would have allowed for an exception to the law proscribing prison escapes.

Because the necessity doctrine is utilitarian, however, strict requirements contain its exercise so as to prevent nonbeneficial criminal conduct. . . .

Analysis of three of the necessity defense's four elements leads us to the conclusion that necessity can never be proved in a case of indirect civil disobedience. We do not rely upon the imminent harm prong of the defense because we believe there can be indirect civil disobedience cases in which the protested harm is imminent.

. . . Indirect civil disobedience seeks first and foremost to bring about the repeal of a law or a change of governmental policy, attempting to mobilize public opinion through typically symbolic action. These protestors violate a law, not because it is unconstitutional or otherwise improper, but because doing so calls public attention to their objectives. . . . However, the mere existence of a constitutional law or governmental policy cannot constitute a legally cognizable harm.

[A] court [must also] judge the likelihood that an alleged harm will be abated by the taking of illegal action. . . . In the traditional cases, a prisoner flees a burning cell and averts death, or someone demolishes a home to create a firebreak and prevents the conflagration of an entire community. The nexus between the act undertaken and the result sought is a close one. . . .

In political necessity cases involving indirect civil disobedience against congressional acts, however, the act alone is unlikely to abate the evil precisely because the action is indirect. Here, the IRS obstruction [is] unlikely to abate the killings in El Salvador, or immediately change Congress's policy; instead, it takes another volitional actor not controlled by the protestor to take a further step; Congress must change its mind.

A final reason the necessity defense does not apply to these indirect civil disobedience cases is that . . . the harm indirect civil disobedience aims to prevent is the continued existence of a law or policy. [T]he "possibility" that Congress will change its mind is sufficient in the context of the democratic process to make lawful political action a reasonable alternative to indirect civil disobedience. [P]etitioning Congress to change a policy is always a legal alternative in such cases, regardless of the likelihood of the plea's success. . . .

Thus, we see the failure of any federal court to recognize a defense of necessity in a case like ours not as coincidental, but rather as the natural consequence of the historic limitation of the doctrine. Indirect protests of congressional policies can never meet all the requirements of the necessity doctrine. Therefore, we hold that the necessity defense is not available in such cases.

Affirmed.

NOTE

The necessity defense has been raised in many sit-in, vandalism, trespass, and related prosecutions. The causes have ranged from nuclear power protests to anti-abortion protests. See Matthew Lippman, The Necessity Defense and Political Protest, 26 Crim. L. Bull. 317 (1990). Though the defense has sometimes prevailed with juries and magistrates, appellate courts have overwhelmingly refused necessity instructions or barred defendants from introducing evidence on the issue in civil disobedience situations. See Note, Political Protest and the Illinois Defense of Necessity, 54 U. Chi. L. Rev. 1070 (1987).

REGINA v. DUDLEY AND STEPHENS

Queen's Bench Division
14 Q.B.D. 273 (1884)

[For the opinion in this case, see page 83 supra.]

NOTES

1. James Fitzjames Stephen, Digest of the Criminal Law 25 n.1 (5th ed. 1894):

> I can discover no principle in the judgment in *R. v. Dudley*. It depends entirely on its peculiar facts. The boy was deliberately put to death with a knife in order that his body might be used for food. This is quite different from any of the following cases—(1) The two men on a plank. Here the successful man does no direct bodily harm to the other. He leaves him the chance of getting another plank. (2) Several men are roped together on the Alps. They slip, and the weight of the whole party is thrown on one, who cuts the rope in order to save himself. Here the question is not whether some shall die, but whether one shall live. (3) The choice of evils. The captain of a ship runs down a boat, as the only means of avoiding shipwreck. A surgeon kills a child in the act of birth, as the only way to save the mother. A boat being too full of passengers to float, some are thrown overboard. Such cases are best decided as they arise.

2. A modern variant on *Dudley and Stephens* occurred in a 1987 tragedy at Zeebrugge, Belgium. The ferry *Herald of Free Enterprise*, lacking an adequate system to signal when its doors were properly shut, suddenly sank as it left port, trapping dozens of passengers inside. The safety problems were attributed to "tough competition" and "the reluctance of the ferry operators . . . to incur extra costs."[33] Almost 200 passengers drowned, but before the ship went down, many of them attempted to escape by climbing a rope ladder to the deck. At one point a passenger climbing the ladder froze in panic and refused repeated commands to move. Those below him then pulled him off the ladder, and he drowned. A coroner mentioned the possibility of murder charges but concluded that the actions taken were "a reasonable act of what is known as self-preservation." See Neil Hanson, The Custom of the Sea 301 (2000).

Would Judge Stephen (Note 1, supra) agree? What legal advice would he have given if passengers, seeing their escape route blocked, had asked whether they had the right to pull the fearful man out of the way? Were those passengers legally (or morally) in the wrong?

3. The American case referred to in Lord Coleridge's opinion was United States v. Holmes, 26 F. Cas. 360 (C.C.E.D. Pa. 1842). Following a shipwreck, the first mate, eight seamen, and 32 passengers were cast adrift on a life boat. The boat was grossly overcrowded and sprang a leak making it necessary to bail constantly in order to stay afloat. Rough seas made bailing difficult, and after a day and half, the boat was in danger of sinking. To lighten the boat, the first mate ordered all male passengers whose wives were not in the boat to be thrown overboard. Eighteen passengers were jettisoned before a rescue ship arrived. Subsequently Holmes, one of the crew who assisted in ejecting the passengers, was charged with manslaughter, after the grand jury declined to indict for murder. The trial judge charged the jury that if two persons face a situation in which only one can survive "neither is bound to save the other's life by sacrificing his own, nor would either commit a crime in saving his own life for the only means of safety"; that while this principle prevailed between sailor and sailor it did not prevail between sailor and passenger because of the special duty owed the latter by the former; that absent this special relationship the choice of who should be sacrificed must be made by lot, since, "In no other way than this or some like way are those having equal rights put on an equal footing, and in no other way is it possible to guard against partiality and oppression, violence and conflict. . . ." Holmes was convicted and sentenced to six months' imprisonment and a fine of $20. Shortly thereafter the penalty was remitted.

4. In his opinion in *Dudley and Stephens*, Lord Coleridge argues that it was not certain the defendants had to kill Parker, and that "they might possibly have been picked up next day by a passing ship; they might possibly not have been picked up at all; in either case it is obvious that the killing of the boy would have been an unnecessary and profitless act." But suppose there had been certainty on the key points? Professor Glanville Williams puts the following case (Textbook of Criminal Law 606 (2d ed. 1983)):

> [S]uppose that the boat was equipped with [a] radio transmitter. . . . The crew were able to make contact with Whitehall, which arranged for a ship to go to

---

33. Jeremy Lovell, Ferry Safety Still an Issue 10 Years After *Herald*, J. Com., Mar. 13, 1997, at 3B.

the rescue, but it could not arrive for seven days. . . . The crew had reached such a stage of exhaustion that very soon none of them would be able to wield a knife. In these circumstances they asked . . . the Home Secretary . . . : should they all accept death, or may they draw lots, kill the one with the unlucky number, and live on his body? In this way all but one will be saved. What should the Home Secretary reply?

For a tour de force of hypothetical opinions in a fictional case involving a similar scenario, see Lon Fuller, The Case of the Speluncean Explorers, 62 Harv. L. Rev. 616 (1949).

NOTE ON TAKING LIFE TO SAVE LIFE

May the choice-of-evils principle ever justify the intentional killing of an innocent person who is not an aggressor? The Model Penal Code plainly anticipates an affirmative answer. In the commentary on the necessity proposal, the drafters state (Model Penal Code and Commentaries, Comment to §3.02 at 14-15 (1985)):

> It would be particularly unfortunate to exclude homicidal conduct from the scope of the defense. For, recognizing that the sanctity of life has a supreme place in the hierarchy of values, it is nonetheless true that conduct that results in taking life may promote the very value sought to be protected by the law of homicide. Suppose, for example, that the actor makes a breach in a dike, knowing that this will inundate a farm, but taking the only course available to save a whole town. If he is charged with homicide of the inhabitants of the farm house, he can rightly point out that the object of the law of homicide is to save life, and that by his conduct he has effected a net saving of innocent lives. The life of every individual must be taken in such a case to be of equal value and the numerical preponderance in the lives saved compared to those sacrificed surely should establish legal justification for the act. So too, a mountaineer, roped to a companion who has fallen over a precipice, who holds on as long as possible but eventually cuts the rope, must certainly be granted the defense that he accelerated one death slightly but avoided the only alternative, the certain death of both. Although the view is not universally held that it is ethically preferable to take one innocent life than to have many lives lost,[15] most persons probably think a net saving of lives is ethically warranted if the choice among lives to be saved is not unfair. Certainly the law should permit such a choice.

How sound is the use of a numerical calculus to justify the intentional killing of an innocent, nonthreatening person? Resistance to the MPC position

---

15. Roman Catholic moralists have generally taken the position that one should not cause effects that are directly evil even if they are thought to be a necessary means to a greater good. . . . Thus, it is considered wrong to terminate the life of a fetus even if that is the only way the mother can be saved and even if the fetus will die in any event. On the other hand, an ordinary operation designed directly to protect the mother's health is permissible, even if an inevitable effect is the death of the fetus, under the so-called principle of "double effect" that death is only permitted, not intended, and is not itself a means to saving the mother's life. . . .

is evident; many statutes and commentators explicitly reject it.[34] One scholar observes that "[e]ven though many lives could be saved by the sacrifice of one, this would hardly be justifiable. It would conflict with the general attitude toward the inviolability of human life to interfere in this way with the course of events."[35] But if it is better, when accidents happen, that fewer lives be lost, why is it wrong for a person to bring this about by his action? How can it be wrong to make things better? Consider the Note that follows.

NOTE ON RIGHTS VERSUS LIVES

The one circumstance in which the MPC arguably justifies killing an innocent, nonthreatening bystander is that in which the killing is necessary to avoid the death of several; killing one person is deemed a lesser evil than the death of more than one. See the MPC Commentary, supra page 900.

The same reasoning can be applied to the famous "trolley problem": D, a trolley car driver, sees five workers in front of him repairing the track and applies the brakes, but the brakes fail and the trolley appears certain to crush all five. Luckily, D can divert the trolley onto a spur and save the five, but if he does so, a sixth worker, repairing the spur, is certain to be crushed. If D diverts the trolley, he will have intentionally killed the sixth worker. Is he morally or legally entitled to do so?[36] Apparently, the MPC choice-of-evils principle would give him a justification defense to a charge of homicide. Should we applaud that result or be troubled by it? What should be the result under the holding in *Dudley and Stephens*? The difficulties are discussed in Judith Jarvis Thompson, The Trolley Problem, 94 Yale L.J. 1395 (1985).

Regardless of our analysis of cases like these, the maximizing-lives principle clearly does not limit the use of defensive force when several assailants threaten a single person's life. The privilege of self-defense justifies the person attacked in taking the lives of his attackers to save his own, no matter how many attackers there are. So maximizing lives here yields to the person's right to resist aggression. Moreover that right exists even if the assailants are innocent: Even when they have a defense of mental incapacity, duress or youth, the victim is permitted to kill them if necessary to save his life. See Model Penal Code §3.11(1).[37]

But hypotheticals, even farfetched ones, cast doubt on these propositions. Suppose a terrorist and her insane husband and eight-year-old son are operating a machine gun from an apartment building. They are about to shoot down a government official. His only chance is to throw a hand grenade

---

34. See John M. Taurek, Should the Numbers Count?, 6 Phil. & Pub. Aff. 293 (1977); Jeffrie G. Murphy, The Killing of the Innocent, 57 Monist 527 (1973).

35. Johannes Andenaes, The General Part of the Criminal Law of Norway 169 (1965).

36. See Philippa Foot, Utilitarianism and the Virtues, 94 Mind 196 (1985).

37. For a forceful challenge to the MPC position that a person under attack can defend by killing several *innocent* aggressors, see Alec Walen, Consensual Sex Without Assuming the Risk of Carrying an Unwanted Fetus; Another Foundation for the Right to an Abortion, 63 Brook. L. Rev. 1051, 1095-1100 (1997).

through his assailants' window. Under the MPC and American law he will be legally justified in doing so. His right to resist the aggressors' threat is determinative. The lives of the terrorist's legally insane husband and their child carry no weight because they are aggressors who threaten his right to life.

But what if the victim knows there is a woman in an adjoining flat who will surely be killed by the blast? Now under the MPC, the official arguably is *not* legally justified in throwing the grenade (though he might be excused), for his action will not result in a net saving of nonaggressor lives.[38]

Finally, what if the terrorists are directing the machine gun against *two* government officials? Now, the MPC's lesser-evil doctrine *does* allow the first official to throw the grenade. The right of the person in the adjoining flat is the same, but her claim of right would yield to the social valuation that the two other innocent lives are to be preferred over her one life.

This last case reveals an anomaly in the MPC approach: Rights prevail over lives (even multiple innocent lives) in the aggression cases, but lives prevail over rights in the bystander cases like this last one or the flood-deflection and trolley cases. We must conclude that, to the extent this is the law, a bystander's right against aggression sometimes yields to a utilitarian assessment in terms of net saving of lives. Yet, it should be added, this is not always so, for there are some killings fairly within the net-saving-of-lives, lesser-evil doctrine that we can be sure courts would not permit—for example, killing a person to obtain his organs, even when that step might be necessary to save the lives of several other people, or even removing one of his organs for that purpose against his will without killing him. This evidences an acute moral unease with reliance on a utilitarian calculus for assessing the justification of intended killings, even when a net savings of lives is achieved.

Questions: Should it matter whether the net savings of life is achieved by steps *designed* to kill innocent bystanders, rather than just by steps that the actor knows will kill them as an undesired but inevitable side effect? In *Dudley and Stephens*, the defendants maximized their chances of survival by cutting Parker's throat. Many condemn this action but nonetheless think it is not necessarily wrong for a ship's passenger who falls overboard to grasp the only plank in sight and push another man off of it, hoping that the other man will be rescued but knowing that he will almost certainly drown. Similarly, in armed conflict, it is unquestionably a war crime to shoot civilians in order to coerce an opposing army to surrender, but it is often permissible to bomb a vital ammunition dump, even when doing so will inevitably kill just as many civilians. Does it make sense to view these two situations (killing on purpose and killing knowingly but unintention- ally) so differently? There is a large literature on whether the distinction is

---

38. Compare the cases that invoke the doctrine of "transferred intent" (and its corollary of transferred privilege) to allow a person in this situation to claim self-defense in connection with acts that cause the death of an innocent bystander. See page 861 supra.

sound,[39] but there is no doubt that many moral intuitions—not to mention the entire structure of rules governing lethal force in warfare—depend on it.

Consider the implications of the distinction: The right to maximize the number of lives saved presumably allows two men under attack to throw a grenade at their assailants, even when it is certain to kill the lone bystander in an adjoining apartment. Does it follow that it is permissible to forcibly take one of a person's two healthy kidneys, against that person's will, in order to save an injured motorist who otherwise will certainly die? For reflections on these problems, see George C. Christie, The Defense of Necessity Considered from the Legal and Moral Points of View, 48 Duke L.J. 975 (1999).

PROBLEMS

1. Can the innocent victim of a lesser-evil choice use force to protect himself? For example, *A*'s house stands just outside the main village. A storm threatens to break the levee protecting the village from flooding by a nearby river. *B*, seeking to avert the danger to the village residents, prepares to explode a hole in the levee at a point calculated to cause the flood to miss the town but to inundate *A*'s house, which has been evacuated. *A* holds *B* off with a loaded gun, preventing *B* from setting the explosion. The village is flooded, with loss of life and property. Is *A* guilty of assault with a deadly weapon? Of murder or manslaughter of the dead villagers? Consider 2 James Fitzjames Stephen, History of the Criminal Law of England 108-109 (1883):

> In an American case in which sailors threw passengers overboard to lighten a boat it was held that the sailors ought to have been thrown overboard first unless they were required to work the boat, and that at all events the particular persons to be sacrificed ought to have been decided on by ballot [sic]. Such a view appears to me to be over refined. Self-sacrifice may or may not be a moral duty, but it seems hard to make it a legal duty, and it is impossible to state its limits or the principle on which they can be determined. Suppose one of the party in the boat had a revolver and was able to use it, and refused either to draw lots or to allow himself or his wife or daughter to be made to do so or to be thrown overboard, could any one deny that he was acting in self-defence and the defence of his nearest relations, and would he violate any legal duty in so doing?

2. The case of Re A (children), [2000] 9 BHRC 261 (Ct. App., Civil Div.), involved conjoined twins, connected at the lower abdomen. Each had all her own vital organs, but they shared a common artery that enabled the stronger twin (Jodie) to circulate blood to both of them. If they were separated, the weaker twin (Mary) would die almost immediately, but if they were not

---

39. See, e.g., Thomas Nagel, The View from Nowhere 175-185 (1986); Alex J. Bellamy, Supreme Emergencies and the Protection of Non-Combatants in War, 80 Int'l Aff. 829, 849 (2004); Alison McIntyre, Doing Away with Double Effect, 111 Ethics 219 (2001).

separated, both would die within three to six months, because the strain of supporting both bodies would eventually cause Jodie's heart to fail. The parents refused to consent to the operation because "as devout Roman Catholics they sincerely believe that their children . . . must be left in God's hands." Id. at 268. Convinced that the parents' decision was not in the best interest of the children, doctors petitioned for a court order permitting them to perform surgery in order to save Jodie's life. The English Court of Appeal acknowledged that "the operation will be an active invasion of Mary's body and by that act the doctors will kill her" (id. at 312). But the court nonetheless authorized the procedure as the lesser evil, and the parents chose not to seek review in the House of Lords. Doctors then carried out the operation, and Mary died a few moments later.

Questions: Does the court of appeal decision in effect overrule *Dudley and Stephens*, or are the situations distinguishable? Either way, how *should* the dilemma of Jodie and Mary be resolved?

PUBLIC COMMITTEE AGAINST TORTURE v. STATE OF ISRAEL

Supreme Court of Israel
H.C. 5100/94 (Sept. 6, 1999)

Justice Barak, President: The General Security Service (hereinafter, the "GSS") investigates individuals suspected of committing crimes against Israel's security. [Administrative directives] authorize investigators to apply physical means against those undergoing interrogation (for instance, shaking the suspect,[a] [sleep deprivation, and forcing the suspect to wait in painful positions]). The basis for permitting such methods is that they are deemed immediately necessary for saving human lives.

[Israeli authorities had issued "directives" authorizing GSS interrogators to use physical means under restricted circumstances. The directives instructed the officer in charge to weigh the severity and urgency of the attack that an interrogation was intended to prevent and to seek alternative means of

---

a. Elsewhere in its opinion the Court described "shaking" as follows:

"Among the investigation methods outlined in the GSS' interrogation regulations, shaking is considered the harshest. The method is defined as the forceful shaking of the suspect's upper torso, back and forth, repeatedly, in a manner which causes the neck and head to dangle and vacillate rapidly. According to an expert opinion submitted in one of the applications, the shaking method is likely to cause serious brain damage, harm the spinal cord, cause the suspect to lose consciousness, vomit and urinate uncontrollably and suffer serious headaches."

"The State [offered] several countering expert opinions. . . . To its contention, there is no danger to the life of the suspect inherent to shaking; the risk to life as a result of shaking is rare; there is no evidence that shaking causes fatal damage; and medical literature has not to date listed a case in which a person died directly as a result of having been only shaken. In any event, they argue, doctors are present in all interrogation compounds, and instances where the danger of medical damage presents itself are investigated and researched."—Eds.

averting the danger. They also required that before using such measures, the investigator would evaluate the suspect's health and "ensure that no harm comes to him." The GSS argued that such measures had helped thwart specific bombing attempts in the past and were "indispensable to its ability to thwart deadly terrorist attacks" in the future.

[The applicants, representing suspects arrested and interrogated by the GSS, petitioned the court for an order prohibiting the use of these physical means against the applicants during their interrogations.]

The State of Israel has been engaged in an unceasing struggle for both its very existence and security, from the day of its founding. Terrorist organizations have established as their goal Israel's annihilation. . . . They carry out terrorist attacks in which scores are murdered in . . . public transportation, city squares and centers, theaters and coffee shops. They do not distinguish between men, women and children. They act out of cruelty and without mercy. . . .

The facts presented before this Court reveal that one hundred and twenty one people died in terrorist attacks between 1.1.96 to 14.5.98. Seven hundred and seven people were injured. A large number of those killed and injured were victims of harrowing suicide bombings in the heart of Israel's cities. Many attacks . . . were prevented due to the measures taken by the authorities responsible for fighting . . . terrorist activities, [mainly] the GSS.

[The court addressed two issues: whether GSS's general mandate to conduct interrogations encompassed the authority to use physical means and, if not, whether in exceptional situations such an authority could be based on the concept of "necessity." On the first issue, the court noted that "a reasonable investigation is likely to cause discomfort" for the suspect but concluded nonetheless that in ordinary cases interrogation must be "free of torture, free of cruel, inhuman treatment of the subject and free of any degrading handling whatsoever." Under both Israeli law and International Law, the court said, "[t]hese prohibitions are 'absolute.' There are no exceptions to them and there is no room for balancing."[b] Applying these requirements to the interrogation methods at issue, the court held:]

[Shaking] harms the suspect's body. It violates his dignity. [T]here is no doubt that shaking is not to be resorted to . . . as part of an "ordinary" investigation. [Similarly,] there is no inherent investigative need for seating the suspect on a chair so low and tilted forward towards the ground, in a manner that causes him real pain and suffering [the so-called Shabach position]. These methods . . . impinge upon the suspect's dignity, his bodily integrity and his basic rights in an excessive manner. They are not to be deemed as included within the general power to conduct interrogations.

---

b. The court referred here to Ireland v. United Kingdom, 2 EHRR 25 (1978), a case in which the European Court of Human Rights held that similar physical means used by English authorities to investigate suspected terrorism in Northern Ireland constituted "inhuman and degrading" treatment and therefore were prohibited by the European Convention on Human Rights.—EDS.

[Nonetheless,] the authority to employ these interrogation methods . . . can, in the State's opinion, be obtained in specific cases by virtue of the criminal law defense of "necessity" [Penal Law Article 34 (1)]:

> A person will not bear criminal liability for committing any act immediately necessary for the purpose of saving the life, liberty, body or property, of either himself or his fellow person, from substantial danger of serious harm, imminent from the particular circumstances, at the requisite [time], and absent alternative means for avoiding the harm.

The State's position is that by virtue of this "defence" to criminal liability, GSS investigators are also authorized to apply physical means, such as shaking, in the appropriate circumstances, in order to prevent serious harm to human life or body, in the absence of other alternatives. The State maintains that an act committed under conditions of "necessity" [is] a deed that society has an interest in encouraging. . . . Not only is it legitimately permitted to engage in the fighting of terrorism, it is our moral duty to employ the necessary means for this purpose. . . . As this is the case, there is no obstacle preventing the investigators' superiors from instructing and guiding them with regard to when the conditions of the "necessity" defence are fulfilled.

[T]he State's attorneys submitted the "ticking time bomb" argument. A given suspect . . . holds information respecting the location of a bomb that [will] imminently explode. There is no way to defuse the bomb without this information. . . . If the bomb is not defused, scores will be killed and maimed. Is a GSS investigator authorized to employ physical means in order to elicit information regarding the location of the bomb? . . .

We are prepared to assume that—although this matter is open to debate— . . . the "necessity" exception is likely to arise in instances of "ticking time bombs," and that the immediate need [required by the statute] refers to the imminent nature of the act rather than that of the danger. Hence, the imminence criteria is satisfied even if the bomb is set to explode in a few days, or perhaps even after a few weeks, provided the danger is certain to materialize and there is no alternative means of preventing its materialization. . . .

A long list of arguments, from both the fields of Ethics and Political Science, may be raised for and against the use of the "necessity" defence. This matter, however, has already been decided. . . . Israel's Penal Law recognizes the "necessity" defence.

[Thus, we] accept that in the appropriate circumstances, GSS investigators may avail themselves of the "necessity" defence, if criminally indicted. [But here,] we are not dealing with the potential criminal liability of a GSS investigator. . . . The question before us is whether it is possible to infer the authority to, in advance, establish permanent directives setting out the physical interrogation means that may be used under conditions of "necessity." . . .

In the Court's opinion, [the necessity defence] is the result of an improvisation given the unpredictable character of the events. Thus, the very nature of the defence does not allow it to serve as the source of a general administrative power. [Therefore,] neither the government nor the heads of security services possess the authority to [authorize] the use of liberty infringing physical means during the interrogation of suspects. . . .

This decision opens with a description of the difficult reality in which Israel finds herself securitywise. . . . We are aware that this decision does not ease dealing with that reality. This is the destiny of democracy, as not all means are acceptable to it, and not all practices employed by its enemies are open before it. Although a democracy must often fight with one hand tied behind its back, it nonetheless has the upper hand. Preserving the Rule of Law and recognition of an individual's liberty constitutes an important component in its understanding of security. At the end of the day, they [add to] its strength. . . . If it will nonetheless be decided that it is appropriate for Israel, in light of its security difficulties, to sanction physical means in interrogations . . . , this is an issue that must be decided by the legislative branch . . . , provided, of course, that a law infringing upon a suspect's liberty "befitting the values of the State of Israel," is enacted for a proper purpose, and to an extent no greater than is required. (Article 8 to the Basic Law: Human Dignity and Liberty). . . .

Our apprehension[,] that this decision will hamper the ability to properly deal with terrorists and terrorism, disturbs us. We are, however, judges. [W]e must act according to our purest conscience when we decide the law. . . . [We have] rejected the "ways of the hypocrites, who remind us of their adherence to the Rule of Law, while being willfully blind to what is being done in practice." . . .

Consequently, it is decided that the order *nisi* [prohibiting physical means of interrogation] be made absolute, as we declare that the GSS does not have the authority to "shake" a man, hold him in the "Shabach" position [or] deprive him of sleep in a manner other than that which is inherently required by the interrogation. . . . Our decision does not negate the possibility that the "necessity" defence be available to GSS investigators . . . if criminal charges are brought against them, as per the Court's discretion.

JUSTICE J'KEDMI: [I]t is difficult for me to accept [that] the State should be helpless from a legal perspective, in those rare emergencies . . . defined as "ticking time bombs." [A]n authority exists in those circumstances, deriving from the basic obligation of being a State . . . to defend its existence, its well-being, and to safeguard its citizens. [I]n those circumstances, the State—as well as its agents—will have the natural right of "self-defence," in the larger meaning of the term.

[Therefore,] I suggest that the judgment be suspended from coming into force for a period of one year. During that year, the GSS could employ exceptional interrogative methods in those rare cases of "ticking time bombs." . . . During the suspension period, the Knesset [legislature] will be given an opportunity to consider the issue. . . . The GSS will be given the opportunity to cope with emergency situations [and] have an opportunity to adapt itself . . . to the new state of things . . . concerning the status and weight of human rights.

I, therefore, join in the judgment of the President subject to my proposal regarding the suspension of the judgment ... for a period of one year. ...
[Decided According to the President's Opinion.]

NOTES AND QUESTIONS

1. *The tactics used.* Do you agree that the necessity defense should be available to an interrogator who uses physical means against a suspected terrorist, in hopes of locating a "ticking time bomb"? If such means fail to elicit the needed information, would the logic of the necessity defense permit the use of even more brutal methods, in order to avert the death of many hundreds of individuals?

2. *The Bybee Memorandum.* The question whether a necessity defense could ever be available when interrogators use severe physical and psychological coercion was given an affirmative answer in the "Bybee Memorandum," an analysis submitted to White House Counsel Alberto R. Gonzales by Assistant Attorney General Jay S. Bybee, head of the Justice Department's Office of Legal Counsel, on August 1, 2002.[40] When the document became public, it triggered a political firestorm, and soon thereafter it was withdrawn "in its entirety."[41] Nonetheless, the issues raised by the Bybee Memorandum continue to be debated on their merits and are worth examining in detail. This Note therefore takes a close look at the Memorandum. Are its arguments sound? If not, why not?

Note that torture, a criminal offense under 18 U.S.C. §2340A, is defined in 18 U.S.C. §2340(1) as "an act committed by a person acting under the color of law specifically intended to inflict severe physical or mental pain or suffering (other than pain or suffering incidental to lawful sanctions) upon a person within his custody or physical control." In one of its most controversial sections, the Bybee Memorandum set an exceptionally high threshold for the degree of pain necessary to constitute torture. But it also went on to argue that even if a government interrogator were to use methods of that especially painful sort, a necessity defense could still be available. There being no federal statutory provision specifically authorizing or foreclosing a necessity defense, the Memorandum discusses the defense in terms of general common-law principles:

> It appears to us that under the current circumstances the necessity defense could be successfully maintained in response to an allegation of a Section 2340A violation. [A] detainee may possess information that could enable the United States to prevent attacks that potentially could equal or surpass the September 11 attacks in their magnitude. Clearly, any harm that might occur during an interrogation would pale to insignificance compared to the

---

40. Reprinted in Karen J. Greenberg & Joshua L. Dratel eds., The Torture Papers 172, 208-209 (2005).

41. Memorandum for James B. Comey, Deputy Attorney General, from Daniel Levin, Acting Assistant Attorney General, Dec. 30, 2004, reprinted in Karen J. Greenberg ed., The Torture Debate in America 361, 362 (2006).

harm avoided by preventing such an attack, which could take hundreds or thousands of lives.

Under this calculus, two factors will help indicate when the necessity defense could appropriately be invoked. First, the more certain that government officials are that a particular individual has information needed to prevent an attack, the more necessary interrogation will be. Second, the more likely it appears to be that a terrorist attack is likely to occur, and the greater the amount of damage expected from such an attack, the more that an interrogation to get information would become necessary. Of course, the strength of the necessity defense depends on the circumstances that prevail, and the knowledge of the government actors involved when the interrogation is conducted.

Questions: (a) Scope of the defense. The necessity defense outlined in the Bybee Memorandum does not appear limited to "ticking time bomb" scenarios. Should it be? Under the logic of a cost-benefit calculus, society could arguably gain, on balance, even when the probability of an attack is not high, provided that the loss of life, if the attack occurs, would be extensive. If so, does that conclusion suggest that the necessity defense should not be confined to "ticking time bomb" cases? Or does that conclusion suggest that the logic of ordinary cost-benefit calculus is flawed in this context?

(b) Potential benefits? Note the two factors that the Bybee Memorandum identifies as governing the cost-benefit equation: the likelihood that an individual has information and the likelihood that a damaging attack will occur. But what of the possibility that the individual subjected to torture, even if he has information, may not reveal it in time for it to be of value? The Memorandum may be assuming that this is only a minor qualification— most interrogation experts agree that torture almost always succeeds in getting individuals to talk. Experts are by no means agreed, however, about the likelihood that information given under torture will be true. How should we account for the instances in which torture produces only useless information or causes investigators to waste precious time pursuing false leads?

(c) Potential harms? Does the Bybee Memorandum properly describe the harms of permitting torture in circumstances of "necessity"? The Memorandum compares the benefit of averting a catastrophic terror attack to "the harm that might occur during an interrogation." Is this the right way to identify the harm sought to be prevented by the law defining the offense? Compare *Unger*, the Model Penal Code Commentaries, and the material on economic necessity, pages 885-895 supra, all considering broad systemic harms that could result from accepting a claim of necessity in an isolated case. As applied to the problem of torture, what broader harms, in addition to the pain inflicted on a particular suspect, could be entailed in allowing highly coercive methods of questioning?

(d) The legislative judgment. Note that torture, as defined in 18 U.S.C. §2340(1), is not simply an extreme form of aggravated assault but "an act

committed by a person *acting under the color of law* . . . upon a person *within his custody.* . . ."[42] In other words, the statute specifically targets law enforcement tactics typically, if not invariably, used to get information from uncooperative suspects. Should this fact have a bearing on the necessity analysis? Reconsider *Leno*, supra page 891, and *Schoon*, supra page 896, both refusing to permit cost-benefit arguments to override a policy judgment made by the legislature. Should the terms of §2340(1) and its background (including legislative awareness of the circumstances in which governments have sought to justify torture throughout history[43]) limit the availability of a cost-benefit exception to the statutory prohibition? Or should the nature of contemporary threats supersede that "pre-9/11 thinking"? If §2340(1) was intended to preclude a necessity defense, should it be amended to permit one?[44]

3. Culpability of the person targeted for torture. Both the Israel Supreme Court decision and the Bybee Memorandum contemplate the use of torture against a known terrorist who has, or probably has, vital information. Should the case for permitting torture change if the person under interrogation is merely a *suspected* terrorist—for example, a villager accused by two of his neighbors? The lack of certainty that the suspect is involved reduces the likelihood that he has vital information, but the Bybee Memorandum makes that probability only one of several factors, and the probability need not be high if the potential attack would have catastrophic effects. Shouldn't the possible innocence of the person under interrogation make the resort to torture absolutely unacceptable? But why should it, if the logic of ordinary cost-benefit calculus is sound in this context?

Should it ever be permissible to torture a person *known* to be innocent? Such a scenario is readily imaginable. Suppose that an admitted terrorist, who has acknowledged involvement in planning a still-impending attack, is captured and brutally interrogated. But he refuses to reveal vital details of the plot. Should interrogators be permitted, on necessity grounds, to torture the terrorist's six-year-old daughter, on the plausible assumption that this is the most

---

42. The statute was enacted to comply with obligations the United States assumed when it adhered to the International Convention Against Torture and Other Cruel, Inhuman, or Degrading Treatment, 1465 U.N.T.S. 85 (1984).

43. The Convention Against Torture, supra footnote 42, states explicitly in article 2.2 that "[n]o exceptional circumstances whatsoever . . . may be invoked as a justification of torture." Similarly, the official U.S. government position, prior to 9/11, was that under U.S. law (including §§2340(1), 2340A), "[n]o exceptional circumstances may be invoked as a justification of torture." U.S. Dept. of State, Initial Report of the United States of America to the UN Committee Against Torture, Oct. 15, 1999. The Bybee Memorandum does not address the previous U.S. Government position. For the argument that the Convention was "deliberately crafted to leave room for states to engage in coercive treatment in compelling circumstances, so long as the conduct falls short of torture," see John T. Parry, The Shape of Modern Torture: Extraordinary Rendition and Ghost Detainees, 6 Melbourne J. Int'l L. 516, 526 (2005).

44. It should not be overlooked that such an amendment, if enacted, would seem to put the United States in violation of its obligations under the Convention Against Torture. See footnote 43, supra. But for present purposes our concern is not with international law but with the appropriate moral and legal boundaries of the necessity principle.

likely means, and perhaps the only means, of getting the terrorist to talk and thus averting the potentially catastrophic attack?

4. *Procedures and oversight.* If the Israel Supreme Court was right to hold that a necessity defense should sometimes be available to an interrogator who uses physical means, wasn't it wrong to hold that administrative authorities cannot regulate the use of such methods by rules promulgated in advance? If necessity is a genuine justification, indicating that the action taken is beneficial on balance, why must the circumstances justifying that action always be assessed on an ad hoc basis?

One proposal hotly debated since 9/11 has been to permit torture if, but only if, investigators first obtain a judicial warrant authorizing it. Compare Alan M. Dershowitz, Why Terrorism Works 158-163 (2002) (advocating this approach), with Oren Gross, Are Torture Warrants Warranted?, 88 Minn. L. Rev. 1481 (2004) (opposing it). Would administrative regulations and independent oversight tend to make the use of torture and other severely coercive methods less frequent? Or would official legitimation of those practices lead them to be used even more frequently? If torture is going to occur anyway, is it better for society to acknowledge the practice or to treat it as something that is never condoned?

5. *Further reading.* Prior to the decision of the Israel Supreme Court, the issues in the case were explored in depth by an official commission (the Landau Commission) in 1988. For the commission's report and a wide range of views commenting on it, see Symposium, 23 Israel L. Rev., Nos. 2 & 3 (Spring-Summer 1989). See also Michael Moore, Torture and the Balance of Evils, in Michael Moore, Placing Blame 669-736 (1997). The 9/11 attacks spawned a vast literature. See, e.g., Karen J. Greenberg ed., The Torture Debate in America (2005); Sanford Levinson ed., Torture (2004); Jeremy Waldron, Torture and Positive Law: Jurisprudence for the White House, 105 Colum L. Rev. 1681 (2005). The last article, in addition to analyzing "positive law," argues that "the absolute prohibition on torture should remain in force" and that "any attempt to loosen it . . . would deal a traumatic blow to our legal system and our ability to sustain the law's commitment to human dignity . . . even in areas where torture as such is not involved." Id. at 1681-1682. Do you agree?

4. Euthanasia

INTRODUCTORY NOTE

In the material on omissions, supra page 236, we considered the question whether a physician who withdraws life-sustaining treatment from a terminally ill or permanently comatose patient can avoid criminal liability by arguing that his conduct is not an "act" but merely an omission where there is no duty to act. Here we revisit the subject of what may loosely be called "euthanasia" to consider the case for recognizing an affirmative justification even for *actions* that directly take the life of a consenting person, or that help her to take her own life.

CRUZAN v. DIRECTOR, MISSOURI DEPT. OF HEALTH

Supreme Court of the United States
497 U.S. 261 (1989)

CHIEF JUSTICE REHNQUIST delivered the opinion of the Court.

On the night of January 11, 1983, Nancy Cruzan lost control of her car as she traveled down Elm Road in Jasper County, Missouri. The vehicle over-turned, and Cruzan was discovered lying face down in a ditch without detect-able respiratory or cardiac function. . . . She now lies in a Missouri state hospital in what is commonly referred to as a persistent vegetative state: generally, a condition in which a person exhibits motor reflexes but evinces no indications of significant cognitive function. The State of Missouri is bear-ing the cost of her care.

After it had become apparent that Nancy Cruzan had virtually no chance of regaining her mental faculties, her parents asked hospital employees to ter-minate the artificial nutrition and hydration procedures. All agree that such a removal would cause her death. The employees refused to honor the request without court approval. The parents then sought and received authorization from the state trial court for termination. The court found that a person in Nancy's condition had a fundamental right under the State and Federal Con-stitutions to refuse or direct the withdrawal of "death prolonging procedures." The court also found that Nancy's "expressed thoughts at age twenty-five in somewhat serious conversation with a housemate friend that if sick or injured she would not wish to continue her life unless she could live at least halfway normally suggests that given her present condition she would not wish to continue on with her nutrition and hydration."

The Supreme Court of Missouri reversed by a divided vote. . . . The court found that Cruzan's statements to her roommate regarding her desire to live or die under certain conditions were "unreliable for the purpose of determining her intent," "and thus insufficient to support the co-guardians['] claim to exercise substituted judgment on Nancy's behalf." . . .

We granted certiorari to consider the question whether Cruzan has a right under the United States Constitution which would require the hospital to withdraw life-sustaining treatment from her under these circumstances.

. . . Before the turn of the century, this Court observed that "[n]o right is held more sacred, or is more carefully guarded, by the common law, than the right of every individual to the possession and control of his own person, free from all restraint or interference of others, unless by clear and unquestionable authority of law." Union Pacific R. Co. v. Botsford, 141 U.S. 250, 251 (1891). This notion of bodily integrity has been embodied in the requirement that informed consent is generally required for medical treatment. Justice Cardozo, while on the Court of Appeals of New York, aptly described this doctrine: "Every human being of adult years and sound mind has a right to determine what shall be done with his own body; and a surgeon who performs an operation without his patient's consent commits an assault, for which he is liable in damages." Schloendorff v. Society of New York Hospital, 105 N.E. 92, 93 (N.Y. 1914). The informed consent doctrine has become firmly entrenched in American tort law. . . .

The logical corollary of the doctrine of informed consent is that the patient generally possesses the right not to consent, that is, to refuse treatment. [M]ost courts have based a right to refuse treatment either solely on the common-law right to informed consent or on both the common-law right and a constitutional privacy right.

[T]he common-law doctrine of informed consent is viewed as generally encompassing the right of a competent individual to refuse medical treatment. . . . This is the first case in which we have been squarely presented with the issue whether the United States Constitution grants what is in common parlance referred to as a "right to die." . . .

The Fourteenth Amendment provides that no State shall "deprive any person of life, liberty, or property, without due process of law." The principle that a competent person has a constitutionally protected liberty interest in refusing unwanted medical treatment may be inferred from our prior decisions. . . .

But determining that a person has a "liberty interest" under the Due Process Clause does not end the inquiry; "whether respondent's constitutional rights have been violated must be determined by balancing his liberty interests against the relevant state interests." Youngberg v. Romeo, 457 U.S. 307, 321 (1982).

Petitioners insist that under the general holdings of our cases, the forced administration of life-sustaining medical treatment, and even of artificially delivered food and water essential to life, would implicate a competent person's liberty interest. Although we think the logic of the cases discussed above would embrace such a liberty interest, the dramatic consequences involved in refusal of such treatment would inform the inquiry as to whether the deprivation of that interest is constitutionally permissible. But for purposes of this case, we assume that the United States Constitution would grant a competent person a constitutionally protected right to refuse lifesaving hydration and nutrition.

Petitioners go on to assert that an incompetent person should possess the same right in this respect as is possessed by a competent person. . . .

The difficulty with petitioners' claim is that in a sense it begs the question: An incompetent person is not able to make an informed and voluntary choice to exercise a hypothetical right to refuse treatment or any other right. Such a "right" must be exercised for her, if at all, by some sort of surrogate. Here, Missouri has in effect recognized that under certain circumstances a surrogate may act for the patient in electing to have hydration and nutrition withdrawn in such a way as to cause death, but it has established a procedural safeguard to assure that the action of the surrogate conforms as best it may to the wishes expressed by the patient while competent. Missouri requires that evidence of the incompetent's wishes as to the withdrawal of treatment be proved by clear and convincing evidence. The question, then, is whether the United States Constitution forbids the establishment of this procedural requirement by the State.

[This question] depends in part on what interests the State may properly seek to protect in this situation. Missouri relies on its interest in the protection and preservation of human life, and there can be no gainsaying this interest. . . . We cannot say that the Supreme Court of Missouri committed constitutional error in reaching the conclusion that it did.

The judgment of the Supreme Court of Missouri is affirmed.

WASHINGTON v. GLUCKSBERG

Supreme Court of the United States
521 U.S. 702 (1997)

CHIEF JUSTICE REHNQUIST delivered the opinion of the Court.

[Several terminally ill patients and their physicians sued the State of Washington for a declaratory judgment that the state's ban on assisted suicide violated a fundamental right protected by the Due Process Clause. The courts below agreed that it did.]

The question presented in this case is whether Washington's prohibition against "caus[ing]" or "aid[ing]" a suicide offends the Fourteenth Amendment to the United States Constitution. We hold that it does not. . . .

We begin, as we do in all due-process cases, by examining our Nation's history, legal traditions, and practices. . . . In almost every State—indeed, in almost every western democracy—it is a crime to assist a suicide. The States' assisted-suicide bans are . . . longstanding expressions of the States' commitment to the protection and preservation of all human life. [F]or over 700 years, the Anglo-American common-law tradition has punished or otherwise disapproved of both suicide and assisting suicide. . . .

Though deeply rooted, the States' assisted-suicide bans have in recent years been reexamined and, generally, reaffirmed. . . . The Washington statute at issue in this case . . . was enacted in 1975 as part of a revision of that State's criminal code. . . . In 1991, Washington voters rejected a ballot initiative which, had it passed, would have permitted a form of physician-assisted suicide. . . . California voters rejected an assisted-suicide initiative similar to Washington's in 1993. On the other hand, in 1994, voters in Oregon enacted, also through ballot initiative, that State's "Death With Dignity Act," which legalized physician-assisted suicide for competent, terminally ill adults. Since the Oregon vote, many proposals to legalize assisted-suicide have been and continue to be introduced in the States' legislatures. . . . Against this backdrop of history, tradition, and practice, we now turn to respondents' constitutional claim.

The Due Process Clause ... provides heightened protection against government interference with certain fundamental rights and liberty interests. ... In a long line of cases, we have held that, in addition to the specific freedoms protected by the Bill of Rights, the "liberty" specially protected by the Due Process Clause includes the rights to marry, to have children, to direct the education and upbringing of one's children, to marital privacy, to use contraception, to bodily integrity, and to abortion, Planned Parenthood v. Casey, 505 U.S. 833 (1992). We have also assumed, and strongly suggested, that the Due Process Clause protects the traditional right to refuse unwanted lifesaving medical treatment. Cruzan v. Director, Missouri Department of Health, 497 U.S. 261 (1990).

But we "ha[ve] always been reluctant to expand the concept of substantive due process because guideposts for responsible decision making in this uncharted area are scarce and open-ended." Collins v. City of Harker Heights, 503 U.S. 115 (1992). By extending constitutional protection to an asserted right or liberty interest, we, to a great extent, place the matter outside the arena of public debate and legislative action. ...

The Washington statute at issue in this case prohibits "aid[ing] another person to attempt suicide," Wash. Rev. Code §9A.36.060(1) (1994), and, thus, the question before us is whether the "liberty" specially protected by the Due Process Clause includes a right to commit suicide which itself includes a right to assistance in doing so. ...

To hold for respondents, we would have to reverse centuries of legal doctrine and practice, and strike down the considered policy choice of almost every State. ...

Respondents contend, however, that the liberty interest they assert is consistent with this Court's substantive-due-process line of cases, if not with this Nation's history and practice. Pointing to *Casey* and *Cruzan*, respondents read our jurisprudence in this area as reflecting a general tradition of "self-sovereignty," ... and as teaching that the "liberty" protected by the Due Process Clause includes "basic and intimate exercises of personal autonomy." ...

Respondents contend that ... "the patient's liberty to direct the withdrawal of artificial life support applies at least as strongly to the choice to hasten impending death by consuming lethal medication." ... The right assumed in *Cruzan,* however, was not simply deduced from abstract concepts of personal autonomy. Given the common-law rule that forced medication was a battery, and the long legal tradition protecting the decision to refuse unwanted medical treatment, our assumption was entirely consistent with this Nation's history and constitutional traditions. The decision to commit suicide with the assistance of another may be just as personal and profound as the decision to refuse unwanted medical treatment, but it has never enjoyed similar legal protection. Indeed, the two acts are widely and reasonably regarded as quite distinct. ... That many of the rights and liberties protected by the Due Process Clause sound in personal autonomy does not warrant the sweeping conclusion that any and all important, intimate, and personal decisions are so protected.

[O]ur decisions lead us to conclude that the asserted "right" to assistance in committing suicide is not a fundamental liberty interest protected by the Due Process Clause. The Constitution also requires, however, that Washington's assisted-suicide ban be rationally related to legitimate government interests. This requirement is unquestionably met here. . . . Washington's assisted-suicide ban implicates a number of state interests.

First, Washington has an "unqualified interest in the preservation of human life." . . . This interest is symbolic and aspirational as well as practical. . . .

Relatedly, all admit that suicide is a serious public-health problem, especially among persons in otherwise vulnerable groups. . . . Those who attempt suicide—terminally ill or not—often suffer from depression or other mental disorders. . . . Research indicates, however, that many people who request physician-assisted suicide withdraw that request if their depression and pain are treated.

The State also has an interest in protecting the integrity and ethics of the medical profession. . . . [T]he American Medical Association, like many other medical and physicians' groups, has concluded that "[p]hysician-assisted suicide is fundamentally incompatible with the physician's role as healer." . . . And physician-assisted suicide could, it is argued, undermine the trust that is essential to the doctor-patient relationship by blurring the time-honored line between healing and harming.

Next, the State has an interest in protecting vulnerable groups—including the poor, the elderly, and disabled persons—from abuse, neglect, and mistakes. [T]he New York Task Force warned that ". . . [t]he risk of harm is greatest for the many individuals in our society whose autonomy and well-being are already compromised by poverty, lack of access to good medical care, advanced age, or membership in a stigmatized social group." [New York State Task Force on Life and the Law, When Death is Sought: Assisted Suicide and Euthanasia in the Medical Context (1994) at] 120. . . . If physician-assisted suicide were permitted, many might resort to it to spare their families the substantial financial burden of end-of-life health-care costs. . . . The State's assisted-suicide ban reflects and reinforces its policy that the lives of terminally ill, disabled, and elderly people must be no less valued than the lives of the young and healthy, and that a seriously disabled person's suicidal impulses should be interpreted and treated the same way as anyone else's. . . .

Finally, the State may fear that permitting assisted suicide will start it down the path to voluntary and perhaps even involuntary euthanasia. . . . If suicide is protected as a matter of constitutional right, it is argued, "every man and woman in the United States must enjoy it." The Court of Appeals' decision [below], and its expansive reasoning, provide ample support for the State's concerns. The court noted, for example, that . . . "in some instances, the patient may be unable to self-administer the drugs and . . . administration by the physician . . . may be the only way the patient may be able to receive them"; and that not only physicians, but also family members and loved ones, will inevitably participate in assisting suicide. Thus, it turns out that what is couched as a limited right to "physician-assisted suicide" is likely, in effect, a much broader license, which could prove extremely difficult to police and contain. Washington's ban on assisting suicide prevents such erosion. . . .

We need not weigh exactly the relative strengths of these various interests. They are unquestionably important and legitimate, and Washington's ban on assisted suicide is at least reasonably related to their promotion and protection. We therefore hold that Wash. Rev. Code §9A.36.060(1) (1994) does not violate the Fourteenth Amendment, either on its face or "as applied to competent, terminally ill adults who wish to hasten their deaths by obtaining medication prescribed by their doctors."

NOTES

1. The Oregon approach. Oregon's "Death with Dignity Act," referred to in *Glucksberg,* was the first such legislation in the United States. The ballot description of the Act read as follows:

> This measure would allow an informed and capable adult resident of Oregon, who is terminally ill and within six months of death, to voluntarily request a prescription for medication to take his or her life. The measure allows a physician to prescribe a lethal dose of medication when conditions of the measure are met. . . .
>
> The process begins when the patient makes the request of his or her physician, who shall:
>
> - Determine if the patient is terminally ill, is capable of making health care decisions, and has made the request voluntarily.
> - Inform the patient of his or her diagnosis and prognosis; the risks and results of taking the medication; and alternatives, including comfort care, hospice care, and pain control. . . .
> - Ask that the patient notify next of kin. . . .
> - Refer the patient for counseling, if appropriate.
> - Refer the patient to a consulting physician.
>
> A consulting physician, who is qualified by specialty or experience, must confirm the diagnosis and determine that the patient is capable and acting voluntarily. If either physician believes that the patient might be suffering from a psychiatric or psychological disorder, or from depression causing impaired judgment, the physician must refer the patient to a licensed psychiatrist or psychologist for counseling. The psychiatrist or psychologist must determine that the patient does not suffer from such a disorder before medication may be prescribed. . . .
>
> At least fifteen days must pass from the time of the initial oral request and 48 hours must pass from the time of the written request before the prescription may be written. Before writing the prescription, the attending physician must again verify the patient is making a voluntary and informed request, and offer the patient the opportunity to rescind the request. . . . Those who comply with the requirements of the measure are protected from prosecution and professional discipline. . . . The measure does not authorize lethal injection,

mercy killing or active euthanasia. Actions taken in accordance with this measure shall not constitute suicide, assisted suicide, mercy killing or homicide, under the law.

The U.S. Department of Justice attempted to block implementation of the Oregon measure. In November 2001, Attorney General Ashcroft ruled that under federal laws regulating prescription drugs, there was no "legitimate medical purpose" for prescriptions written to assist suicide pursuant to the Oregon law, and therefore any physician writing such a prescription would be exposed to revocation of her federal drug license and prosecution under the Controlled Substances Act (CSA). In a suit brought by the State of Oregon, however, the Supreme Court held that the CSA was intended to preserve states' traditional powers to regulate the medical profession and that the Attorney General's ruling was invalid. Gonzales v. Oregon, 546 U.S. 243 (2006). Chief Justice Roberts and Justices Scalia and Thomas dissented. By the end of 2010, 525 Oregon patients had chosen to use prescription medication to end their lives.[45]

One concern about measures like Oregon's has been that they could reduce incentives for physicians to treat patients' pain, and that assisted suicide would simply become an easy alternative to effective pain management. There is evidence, however, that the opposite may have occurred; perhaps surprisingly, patients' ability to consider the assisted suicide option apparently has stimulated greater effort to improve pain management. See Kathryn L. Tucker, In the Laboratory of the States: The Progress of *Glucksberg*'s Invitation to States to Address End of Life Choice, 106 Mich. L. Rev. 1593 (2008).[46]

2. Subsequent American developments. Although the *Glucksberg* decision upheld Washington's prohibition of assisted suicide, that state reversed course in 2008 and approved by ballot initiative a law permitting assisted suicide on terms virtually identical to those of the Oregon legislation. See Wash. Rev. Code Ann. §70.245 (2010). Shortly thereafter, the Montana Supreme Court interpreted that state's right-to-refuse-treatment statute as granting immunity from civil or criminal liability to any health care provider who honors a patient's wishes, not only by withdrawing or withholding treatment but also by providing medication that will enable the patient to end her own life. Baxter v. State, 224 P.3d 1211, 1219-1220 (Mont. 2009). For in-depth analysis of legal standards in American jurisdictions, see Katherine Ann Wingfield & Carl S. Hacker, Physician-Assisted Suicide: An Assessment and Comparison of Statutory Approaches Among the States, 32 Seton Hall Legis. J. 13 (2007).

---

45. http://public.health.oregon.gov/ProviderPartnerResources/EvaluationResearch/Deathwith-DignityAct/Documents/yr13-tbl-1.pdf.

46. It should be noted, however, that some who have studied the Oregon experience closely believe that the law's safeguards are often circumvented in practice and that the state agency charged with monitoring the law needs to scrutinize its implementation much more carefully. See Herbert Hendin & Kathleen Foley, Physician-Assisted Suicide in Oregon: A Medical Perspective, 106 Mich. L. Rev. 1613 (2008).

3. Developments abroad.

(a) "Suicide tourism." Switzerland has allowed assisted suicide since 1937, and it is apparently the only jurisdiction in the world that permits non-residents to travel there for this purpose. As a result, a Zurich clinic has become a destination of choice for individuals who desire physician-assisted suicide, and from 1998 through the end of 2009, nearly 1,000 non-Swiss patients chose to end their lives at the clinic.[47]

(b) The British response. Concerns about "suicide tourism" prompted British authorities to threaten prosecution of citizens who helped a family member obtain a physician-assisted suicide in Switzerland, especially after several prominent Britons had done so in widely publicized fashion. That policy, however, was challenged by a victim of multiple sclerosis who hoped to take advantage of the Swiss clinic. In a landmark decision, the House of Lords ruled that uncertainty about the risk of prosecution unacceptably interfered with her right to respect for her private life, and accordingly it ordered the Director of Public Prosecutions (DPP) to publicly identify the factors he would consider deciding whether to prosecute in such a case. Regina (Purdy) v. Director of Public Prosecutions, [2009] UKHL 45. In response, the DPP promulgated a draft policy, and after extensive public comment, announced final guidelines that largely limit prosecution to cases involving underage or incompetent victims and cases in which a person persuades or pressures someone to kill themselves or benefits from their death.[48] Although assisted suicide remains a crime in England (and is punishable by up to 14 years' imprisonment), the DPP guidelines effectively decriminalize the practice when someone acts out of compassion to help a terminally ill patient who has a "clear, settled and informed wish to die." See Haroon Siddique, DPP Releases Assisted Suicide Guidelines, Guardian, Feb. 25, 2010.

4. For discussion of the issues, see the symposium articles in 106 Mich. L. Rev. 1453 (2008) and 109 Ethics 497-642 (April 1999); Yale Kamisar, Physician-Assisted Suicide: The Problems Presented by the Compelling, Heartwrenching Case, 88 J. Crim. L. & Criminology 1121 (1998); John Deigh, Physician-Assisted Suicide and Voluntary Euthanasia: Some Relevant Differences, id. at 1155. Consider these comments:

New York State Task Force on Life and the Law, When Death Is Sought— Assisted Suicide in the Medical Context ix, xiii-xiv (1994): In light of the pervasive failure of our health care system to treat pain and diagnose and treat depression, legalizing assisted suicide and euthanasia would be profoundly dangerous for many individuals who are ill and vulnerable. . . . No matter how

---

47. See http://www.guardian.co.uk/news/datablog/2010/feb/25/assisted-suicide-dignitas-statistics? INTCMP=ILCNETTXT3487.

48. See Crown Prosecution Service, Policy for Prosecutors in Respect of Cases of Encouraging or Assisting Suicide (Feb. 2010), available at http://www.cps.gov.uk/publications/prosecution/ assisted_suicide_policy.html.

carefully any guidelines are framed, assisted suicide and euthanasia will be practiced through the prism of social inequality and bias that characterizes the delivery of services in all segments of our society, including health care. The practices will pose the greatest risks to those who are poor, elderly, members of a minority group, or without access to good medical care. The growing concern about health care costs increases the risks presented by legalizing assisted suicide and euthanasia. . . .

The clinical safeguards that have been proposed to prevent abuse and errors would not be realized in many cases. For example, most doctors do not have a long-standing relationship with their patients or information about the complex personal factors relevant to evaluating a request for suicide assistance or a lethal injection. In addition, neither treatment for pain nor the diagnosis of and treatment for depression is widely available in clinical practice.

The Task Force members feel deep compassion for patients in those rare cases when pain cannot be alleviated even with aggressive palliative care. They also recognize that the desire for control at life's end is widely shared and deeply felt. As a society, however, we have better ways to give people greater control and relief from suffering than by legalizing assisted suicide and euthanasia.

Depression accompanied by feelings of hopelessness is the strongest predictor of suicide for both individuals who are terminally ill and those who are not. Most doctors, however, are not trained to diagnose depression, especially in complex cases such as patients who are terminally ill. Even if diagnosed, depression is often not treated. In elderly patients as well as the terminally and chronically ill, depression is grossly underdiagnosed and undertreated.

The presence of unrelieved pain also increases susceptibility to suicide. The undertreatment of pain is a widespread failure of current medical practice, with far-reaching implications for proposals to legalize assisted suicide and euthanasia.

If assisted suicide and euthanasia are legalized [and those] practices are incorporated into the standard arsenal of medical treatments, the sense of gravity about the practices would dissipate. . . . Policies limiting suicide to the terminally ill, for example, would be inconsistent with the notion that suicide is a compassionate choice for patients who are in pain or suffering. As long as the policies hinge on notions of pain or suffering, they are uncontainable; neither pain nor suffering can be gauged objectively. . . .

Joel Feinberg, Overlooking the Merits of the Individual Case: An Unpromising Approach to the Right to Die, 4 Ratio Juris 131, 150-151 (1991): [Some] of the arguments against the legalization of voluntary euthanasia . . . candidly concede that judged on the merits, many individual cases do deserve euthanasia. Rather, these arguments favour deliberately overlooking the merits of individual cases, and [maintain that] the inevitability of honest mistakes and not-so-honest abuses will create evils that outweigh the evils of sustaining the comatose and the pain-wracked against their presumed wills. Convincing as the argument from abusable discretion may be in some contexts, . . . it fails in its application to the euthanasia situation. . . . The enemy of voluntary euthanasia errs in minimizing the evils of human suffering and overrating the value of merely biological life in the absence of a human person, or in the presence of a human person whose sufferings are too severe for him to have a human life, even though his heart beats on.

Sanford H. Kadish, Letting Patients Die: Legal and Moral Reflections, 80 Calif. L. Rev. 857, 867-868 (1992): One ground on which courts have sought to distinguish letting-die situations from conventional suicide is that the latter requires affirmative life-taking actions. On this view a patient refusing to be attached to an apparatus necessary for his survival is not taking his life, but is simply letting nature take its course. [But this] distinction between intentionally killing oneself and intentionally submitting to an avoidable death is suspect. [The] basic argument [for] the right to refuse treatment . . . is that the choice between medical treatment and death is so fundamental that it is protected against state control by a constitutional right of autonomy. That being the case, however, there is no principled basis for denying the same freedom of choice to those not dependent on medical treatment for survival. The failure of efforts to distinguish suicide from refusal of treatment is attributable not simply to usage and definition, but to the equivalence between the two. The moral case for autonomy extends to both if it extends to one.

C. PRINCIPLES OF EXCUSE

INTRODUCTORY NOTE

Unlike justifications, excuses do not assert that what the accused did was a good thing, or that society is better off, on balance, because of his actions. Instead, an excuse seeks to show that although the acts of the accused were harmful, he or she could not fairly have been expected to do otherwise. The materials in this section focus on the three most important excuses—duress, intoxication, and mental disorder. Then, in a final subsection we turn to the ongoing efforts to test the boundaries of the traditional excuses and extend them to include such problems as drug addiction, childhood abuse, and economic deprivation. But first, we focus on the underlying puzzle of why excuses are ever accepted as a defense to harmful conduct and what underlying rationales are common to this group of criminal law doctrines.

1. Introduction: What Are Excuses and Why Do We Have Them?

Eugene R. Milhizer, Justification and Excuse: What They Were, What They Are, and What They Ought to Be, 78 St. John's L. Rev. 725, 816-818 (2004): Excuse defenses focus on the actor and not the act. A defendant is excused when he is judged to be not blameworthy for his conduct, even though the conduct itself is improper and harmful. . . .

The diversity among excuse defenses—procedurally, substantively, and philosophically—is in many respects far greater than that found among justification defenses. [But] several general observations can be made about the structure and content of excuse defenses. All excuse defenses are predicated upon the presence of some disability or disabling condition affecting the actor claiming the defense. The disability can arise from a number of sources, both internal and external to the actor, and may be temporary or permanent. . . .

Excuse defenses can be organized into three categories: involuntary actions, actions related to cognitive deficiencies, and actions related to volitional deficiencies. Involuntary actions are those acts, i.e., bodily movements, that are not willed by the actor.[a] When used in this narrow sense, the term "involuntary" does not include behavior that is a consequence of exerted will that has been overborne. Rather, it refers only to those acts that are caused by the actor's brain but are not the product of the actor's mind. Reflex actions and convulsions are examples of involuntary actions, while actions performed in response to a threat are not. . . .

The second group of excusing conditions involves conduct relating to a cognitive impairment or deficiency. "Cognition" concerns an actor's ability to know certain things, which, in a broad sense, includes both facts and law.[b] When used in connection with a criminal defense based on excuse, cognitive impairment is concerned with an actor's knowledge of the nature of his conduct and whether it is right or wrong, and legal or illegal.

The third group of excusing conditions involves impairments or deficiencies in volition, which concern an actor's ability to make unencumbered choices [free from external threats] or to meaningfully control his behavior. A volitionally deficient actor is a voluntary actor, at least insofar as his behavior is a product of his effort or determination. Since a volitionally deficient actor's cognition need not be impaired, he also may be fully aware of the nature of his conduct and whether it is right or wrong, and legal or illegal. Put differently, because most defenses based on a volitional deficiency require only some impairment of an actor's will, the actor's conduct remains voluntary in a strict sense and is usually informed by some degree of awareness.

Sanford H. Kadish, Excusing Crime, 75 Calif. L. Rev. 257, 263-265 (1987): Why we have excuses is less obvious than why we have other defenses. [Jeremy Bentham] saw the point of excuses to be that they identified situations in which conduct is nondeterrable, so that punishment would be so much unnecessary evil. [S]ince only the nondeterrable are excused, withholding punishment offers no comfort to those who are deterrable. The trouble is . . . that this [conclusion] does not follow, for punishing all, whether or not they happen to be deterrable, closes off any hope a deterrable offender

---

a. Reconsider the treatment of involuntary acts in Chapter 3, supra pages 205-216, as a form of excuse as well as the negation of the actus reus element of a criminal offense.—EDS.

b. Reconsider the defenses of mistake of fact and mistake of law, see Chapter 3, supra pages 266-282 and 303-329, as excuses as well as the negation of the mens rea element of a criminal offense.—EDS.

might otherwise harbor that he could convince a jury that he was among the nondeterrable.[a] Moreover, without excuses, prosecutions would be faster and cheaper, convictions more reliable, and the deterrent threat more credible. Indeed, strict liability offenses [dispense] with mens rea requirements on just these grounds. [Yet, doesn't the effectiveness of strict liability give up] something of value . . . , something that is not captured in Bentham's rationale?

Professor [H.L.A.] Hart . . . offered a different account of excuses. He argued that by confining liability to cases in which persons have freely chosen, excuses serve to maximize the effect of a person's choices within the framework of coercive law, thereby furthering the satisfaction people derive in knowing that they can avoid the sanction of the law if they choose.

This rationale is an improvement over Bentham, inasmuch as Hart gives us a reason why we might want to put up with the loss of deterrence caused by excuses. But does this account capture the full force of a system of excuses? Suppose we preferred the risk of accidentally being victims of law enforcement to the increased risk of being victims of crime. That would be a plausible choice, particularly for a public obsessed with rising crime rates. Would we then feel there was nothing more problematic in giving up excuses than that we would be trading one kind of satisfaction for another? I think not. Something is missing in this account.

Hart's account focuses on the interests and satisfactions of the great majority of us who never become targets of law enforcement—our security in knowing we will not be punished if we do not choose to break the law. What is missing is an account of the concern for the innocent person who is the object of a criminal prosecution. . . . To blame a person is to express a moral criticism, and if the person's action does not deserve criticism, blaming him is a kind of falsehood and is, to the extent the person is injured by being blamed, unjust to him. It is this feature of our everyday moral practices that lies behind the law's excuses. Excuses . . . represent no sentimental compromise with the demands of a moral code; they are, on the contrary, of the essence of a moral code. . . .

Of course, one might escape excuses altogether by withdrawing the element of blame from a finding of criminality. Indeed, [some people] would prefer that the criminal law reject all backward-looking judgments of punishment, blame, and responsibility, and concern itself exclusively with identifying and treating those who constitute a social danger. Whether it would be desirable to loosen [official coercion] from its mooring in blame is a large and much discussed question.[b] I will confine myself here to two observations.

---

a. Compare Donald A. Dripps, Rehabilitating Bentham's Theory of Excuses, 42 Tex. Tech L. Rev. 383, 411 (2009).—Eds.:

> [This] critique of Bentham is unsound. The situational excuses are hedged by safeguards that include factual skepticism, discretion, and partial excuse. Rational actors have very little incentive to fabricate the excuses, and Bentham's basic point that punishment will not achieve much general deterrence when applied to crimes powerfully impelled by infancy, insanity, intoxication, provocation, and duress seems perfectly plausible.

b. For the leading defense of the view that punishment should be wholly forward-looking and divorced from blame, see Barbara Wooton, Crime and the Criminal Law (1963). For a critique, see H.L.A. Hart, Book Review, 74 Yale L.J. 1325 (1965).—Eds.

First, such a dissociation would not likely succeed. People would continue to see state coercion as punishment, notwithstanding official declarations that the state's only interest is the individual's welfare and social protection. Second, it is very doubtful that we should want it to succeed, since blame and punishment give expression to the concept of personal responsibility which is a central feature of our moral culture.

2. *Duress*

STATE v. TOSCANO

Supreme Court of New Jersey
74 N.J. 421, 378 A.2d 755 (1977)

PASHMAN, J. [Dr. Joseph Toscano, a chiropractor, was charged with conspiring to obtain money by false pretenses from the Kemper Insurance Company. The charges were part of a larger indictment alleging that 11 named defendants and two unindicted co-conspirators had participated in a scheme to defraud various insurance companies by staging accidents in public places and obtaining payments in settlement of fictitious injuries. William Leonardo, the alleged architect of the conspiracy and the organizer of each of the separate incidents, pleaded guilty, as did several other defendants. Toscano went to trial, admitting that he had aided in the preparation of a fraudulent insurance claim by making out a false medical report, but arguing that he had acted under duress. The trial judge ruled that the threatened harm was not sufficiently imminent to justify charging the jury on the defense of duress. The jury convicted, and Toscano was fined $500. His conviction was affirmed on appeal, and the New Jersey Supreme Court granted certification to consider the status of duress as an affirmative defense.]

The State attempted to show that Toscano agreed to fill out the false medical report because he owed money to Richard Leonardo [William's brother] for gambling debts. It also suggested that Toscano subsequently sought to cover up the crime by fabricating office records of non-existent office visits by Hanaway.[a] Defendant sharply disputed these assertions and maintained that he capitulated to William Leonardo's demands only because he was fearful for his wife's and his own bodily safety. Since it is not our function here to assess these conflicting versions, we shall summarize only those facts which, if believed by the jury, would support defendant's claim of duress. . . .

[The court recited a number of overtures made by William Leonardo to defendant, which defendant refused, to prepare a false medical report for submission to a claims adjuster.]

The third and final call occurred on Friday evening. Leonardo was "boisterous and loud" repeating, "You're going to make this bill out for me." Then he said: "Remember, you just moved into a place that has a very dark entrance and you leave there with your wife. . . . You and your wife are going to jump at

---

a. Hanaway was an unindicted coconspirator who acted as the victim in a number of staged accidents.—EDS.

shadows when you leave that dark entrance." Leonardo sounded "vicious" and "desperate" and defendant felt that he "just had to do it" to protect himself and his wife. He thought about calling the police, but failed to do so in the hope that "it would go away and wouldn't bother me any more."

In accordance with Leonardo's instructions, defendant left a form in his mailbox on Saturday morning for Leonardo to fill in with the necessary information about the fictitious injuries. It was returned that evening and defendant completed it. On Sunday morning he met Hanaway at a prearranged spot and delivered a medical bill and the completed medical report. He received no compensation for his services, either in the form of cash from William Leonardo or forgiven gambling debts from Richard Leonardo. He heard nothing more from Leonardo after that Sunday.

Shortly thereafter, still frightened by the entire episode, defendant moved to a new address and had his telephone number changed to an unlisted number in an effort to avoid future contacts with Leonardo. He also applied for a gun permit but was unsuccessful. His superior at his daytime job with the Newark Housing Authority confirmed that the quality of defendant's work dropped so markedly that he was forced to question defendant about his attitude. After some conversation, defendant explained that he had been upset by threats against him and his wife. He also revealed the threats to a co-worker at the Newark Housing Authority.

After defendant testified, the trial judge granted the State's motion to exclude any further testimony in connection with defendant's claim of duress, and announced his decision not to charge the jury on that defense. . . .

After stating that the defense of duress is applicable only where there is an allegation that an act was committed in response to a threat of present, imminent and impending death or serious bodily harm, the trial judge charged the jury:

> Now, one who is standing and receiving instructions from someone at the point of a gun is, of course, in such peril. . . .
>
> Now, where the peril is not imminent, present and pending to the extent that the defendant has the opportunity to seek police assistance for himself and his wife as well, the law places upon such a person the duty not to acquiesce in the unlawful demand and any criminal conduct in which he may thereafter engage may not be excused. Now, this principle prevails regardless of the subjective estimate he may have made as to the degree of danger with which he or his wife may have been confronted. Under the facts of this case, I instruct you, as members of the jury, that the circumstances described by Dr. Toscano leading to his implication in whatever criminal activities in which you may find he participated are not sufficient to constitute the defense of duress.

. . . Since New Jersey has no applicable statute defining the defense of duress,[b] we are guided only by common law principles which conform to the purposes of our criminal justice system and reflect contemporary notions of justice and fairness.

---

b. New Jersey does have such a statute at the present time, because the legislature eventually enacted the draft proposal discussed later in the court's opinion.—EDS.

At common law the defense of duress was recognized only when the alleged coercion involved a use or threat of harm which is "present, imminent and pending" and "of such a nature as to induce a well grounded apprehension of death or serious bodily harm if the act is not done."

It was commonly said that duress does not excuse the killing of an innocent person even if the accused acted in response to immediate threats. Aside from this exception, however, duress was permitted as a defense to prosecution for a range of serious offenses. . . .

To excuse a crime, the threatened injury must induce "such a fear as a man of ordinary fortitude and courage might justly yield to." Although there are scattered suggestions in early cases that only a fear of death meets this test, . . . [8] an apprehension of immediate serious bodily harm has been considered sufficient to excuse capitulation to threats. Thus, the courts have assumed as a matter of law that neither threats of slight injury nor threats of destruction to property are coercive enough to overcome the will of a person of ordinary courage. [The court then referred to cases in which threats of loss of job, denial of food rations, economic need, and prospect of financial ruin were held inadequate.] . . . When the alleged source of coercion is a threat of "future" harm, courts have generally found that the defendant had a duty to escape from the control of the threatening person or to seek assistance from law enforcement authorities.

Assuming a "present, imminent and impending" danger, however, there is no requirement that the threatened person be the accused. [C]oncern for the well-being of another, particularly a near relative, can support a defense of duress if the other requirements are satisfied. . . .

The insistence under the common law on a danger of immediate force causing death or serious bodily injury may be ascribed to . . . judicial fears of perjury and fabrication of baseless defenses. We do not discount [this] concern as a reason for caution in modifying this accepted rule, but we are concerned by its obvious shortcomings and potential for injustice. Under some circumstances, the commission of a minor criminal offense should be excusable even if the coercive agent does not use or threaten force which is likely to result in death or "serious" bodily injury. Similarly, it is possible that authorities might not be able to prevent a threat of future harm from eventually being carried out. . . .

[S]ome commentators have advocated a flexible rule which would allow a jury to consider whether the accused actually lost his capacity to act in accordance with "his own desire, or motivation, or will" under the pressure of real or imagined forces. See Fletcher, "The Individualization of Excusing Conditions," 47 S. Cal. L. Rev. 1269, 1288-1293 (1974). The inquiry here would focus on the weaknesses and strengths of a particular defendant, and his subjective reaction to unlawful demands. Thus, the "standard of heroism"

---

8. Several states, by statute, continue to require that the actor have reasonable cause to believe that his life was in danger. . . . Minnesota limits the defense to situations in which "instant death" is threatened. Minn. Stat. 609.08 (1965).

of the common law would give way, not to a "reasonable person" standard, but to a set of expectations based on the defendant's character and situation.

The drafters of the Model Penal Code and the [proposed] New Jersey Penal Code ... focus[ed] on whether the standard imposed upon the accused was one with which "normal members of the community will be able to comply." ...

They substantially departed from the existing statutory and common law limitations requiring that the result be death or serious bodily harm, that the threat be immediate and aimed at the accused, or that the crime committed be a non-capital offense. While these factors would be given evidential weight, the failure to satisfy one or more of these conditions would not justify the trial judge's withholding the defense from the jury. ...

Although they are not entirely identical, under both model codes defendant would have had his claim of duress submitted to the jury.[12] Defendant's testimony provided a factual basis for a finding that Leonardo threatened him and his wife with physical violence if he refused to assist in the fraudulent scheme. Moreover, a jury might have found from other testimony adduced at trial that Leonardo's threats induced a reasonable fear in the defendant. Since he asserted that he agreed to complete the false documents only because of this apprehension, the requisite elements of the defense were established. Under the model code provisions, it would have been solely for the jury to determine whether a "person of reasonable firmness in his situation" would have failed to seek police assistance or refused to cooperate, or whether such a person would have been, unlike defendant, able to resist.

Exercising our authority to revise the common law, we have decided to adopt this approach as the law of New Jersey. Henceforth, duress shall be a defense to a crime other than murder if the defendant engaged in conduct because he was coerced to do so by the use of, or threat to use, unlawful force against his person or the person of another, which a person of reasonable firmness in his situation would have been unable to resist. ...

Defendant's conviction of conspiracy to obtain money by false pretenses is hereby reversed and remanded for a new trial.

MODEL PENAL CODE

§2.09. DURESS

[See Appendix for text of this section.]

Model Penal Code and Commentaries, Comment to §2.09 at 372-375 (1985): The problem of how far duress should exculpate conduct that otherwise would constitute a crime is much debated. ... [Sir James] Stephen

---

12. The most significant difference between the two provisions is the treatment of duress as a defense to murder. The Model Penal Code permits it as an affirmative defense, while the New Jersey Penal Code allows it only to reduce a crime from murder to manslaughter.

argued, for example, that "compulsion by threats ought in no case whatever to be admitted as an excuse for crime, though it may and ought to operate in mitigation of punishment in most though not in all cases." His reason was, in substance, that "it is at the moment when temptation to crime is strongest that the law should speak most clearly and emphatically to the contrary."[29] Jerome Hall is less hostile to allowing the defense, but he would limit it with rigor to the situation where the actor rightly chose the lesser of two evils; and even then he gives such weight to the moral duty to resist the evil-doing author of the duress that he does not commit himself beyond the proposition that "coercion should not exculpate in the most serious crimes but . . . should be a defense where, e.g., it is a question of imminent death or the commission of relatively minor harm."[30]

Much of the issue posed by these competing views is resolved . . . in Section 3.02, which provides a general defense in cases where the actor believed his conduct necessary to avoid an evil to himself or to another and the evil sought to be avoided is greater than that sought to be prevented by the law defining the offense charged. The Institute saw no reason why this principle should be denied full application when the evil apprehended has its source in the action or the threatened action of another person, rather than the forces and perils of the physical world. . . .

The problem of Section 2.09, then, reduces to the question of whether there are cases where the actor cannot justify his conduct under Section 3.02, as when his choice involves an equal or greater evil than that threatened, but where he nonetheless should be excused because he was subjected to coercion. If he is so far overwhelmed by force that his behavior is involuntary, as when his arm is physically moved by someone else, Section 2.01(1) stands as a barrier to liability. . . . The case of concern here is that in which the actor makes a choice, but claims in his defense that he was so intimidated that he was unable to choose otherwise. . . .

In favor of allowing the defense, it may be argued that the legal sanction cannot be effective in the case supposed and that the actor may not properly be blamed for doing what he had to choose to do. It seems clear, however, that the argument in its full force must be rejected. The crucial reason is the same as that which elsewhere leads to an unwillingness to vary legal norms with the individual's capacity to meet the standards they prescribe, absent a disability that is both gross and verifiable, such as the mental disease or defect that may establish irresponsibility. The most that it is feasible to do with lesser disabilities is to accord them proper weight in sentencing. To make liability depend upon the fortitude of any given actor would be no less impractical or otherwise impolitic than to permit it to depend upon such other variables as intelligence or clarity of judgment, suggestibility or moral insight.

Moreover, the legal standard may gain in its effectiveness by being unconditional in this respect. It cannot be known what choices might be different if

---

29. 2 J. Stephen, History of the Criminal Law of England 108 (1883).
30. General Principles of Criminal Law 448 (2d ed. 1960).

the actor thought he had a chance of exculpation on the ground of his peculiar disabilities instead of knowing that he does not. No less important, legal norms and sanctions operate not only at the moment of climactic choice, but also in the fashioning of values and of character.

Though, for the foregoing reasons, the submission that the actor lacked the fortitude to make the moral choice should not be entertained as a defense, a different situation is presented if the claimed excuse is based upon the incapacity of men in general to resist the coercive pressures to which the individual succumbed. . . . [L]aw is ineffective in the deepest sense, indeed . . . it is hypocritical, if it imposes on the actor who has the misfortune to confront a dilemmatic choice, a standard that his judges are not prepared to affirm that they should and could comply with if their turn to face the problem should arise. Condemnation in such a case is bound to be an ineffective threat; what is, however, more significant is that it is divorced from any moral base and is unjust. . . .

The Model Code accordingly provides for the defense in cases where the actor was coerced by force or threats of force "that a person of reasonable firmness in his situation would have been unable to resist." The standard is not, however, wholly external in its reference; account is taken of the actor's "situation," a term that should here be given the same scope it is accorded in appraising recklessness and negligence. Stark, tangible factors that differentiate the actor from another, like his size, strength, age, or health, would be considered in making the exculpatory judgment. Matters of temperament would not.

NOTES ON THE MODEL PENAL CODE

1. *Partial vs. complete excuse.* In a homicide case, the common law denies the defense of duress entirely, see infra page 939, while under the MPC, duress excuses homicide altogether. The New Jersey statute, enacted after the decision in *Toscano* (see page 925 n.b and page 927 n.12, supra), takes an intermediate position—a successful claim of duress (like a successful claim of provocation) only reduces murder to manslaughter. If the MPC rationale for the duress defense is sound, should it apply as well to the defense of provocation, so that a successful claim of provocation (or "extreme emotional disturbance") would be a complete defense to a homicide charge? Alternatively, if the MPC is sound in its treatment of provocation as a *partial* excuse, why shouldn't the same approach apply to duress? Should provocation and duress be treated similarly? If so, which way? Or are there differences in the rationales for the two defenses that justify the different treatment that they usually receive? See Jeremy Horder, Autonomy, Provocation and Duress, [1992] Crim. L. Rev. 70.

2. *The objective standard.* MPC §2.09(1) requires a defendant claiming duress to meet an objective standard of "a person of reasonable firmness in his situation." But as in other areas where a norm of reasonableness is set (for

example, in the law defining criminal negligence and adequate provocation), it remains necessary to determine how the norm should be tailored to the particular actor's "situation." As we have seen, the MPC drafters deliberately chose a term that was undefined and ambiguous, in order "to leave the issue to the courts."[49] But courts sometimes duck the issue as well. In State v. Helmedach, 8 A.3d 514 (Conn. App. 2010), the jury sent the trial judge a note asking for "[a] further explanation in [layman's] terms" of the "situation" standard, but the judge merely replied that he "could only provide you with the instruction on duress that you already had." Id. at 518. The appellate court held that this was a proper response: "Because the term situation does not have a statutory definition ... , it is taken that the jury, as a matter of common knowledge, comprehends the term." Id. at 520. Is this a plausible response? How can the court posit that "the jury, as a matter of common knowledge, comprehends the term" when the jury itself expressly indicates otherwise? If the judge was wrong to duck the issue, what explanation should he have given? Helmedach claimed to be under duress from a domestic partner who had subjected her to years of abuse. Was her status as a battered woman relevant to her situation? Courts are divided on the issue (see Note 2(b), infra). Under these circumstances, is it better for the trial judge to leave the issue unexplained, on the ground that the jury knows the answer "as a matter of common knowledge"? Consider these aspects of the problem:

(a) *Immaturity and mental retardation.* In State v. Heinemann, 920 A.2d 278 (Conn. 2007), the court rejected the 16-year-old defendant's effort to have the jury instructed that differences in maturity "make it more difficult for adolescents to resist pressures [which included death threats] because of their limited decision-making capacity and their susceptibility to outside influences." Id. at 295. The court acknowledged that adolescents are "more vulnerable to all sorts of pressure, including ... duress" (id. at 296), but concluded that the defendant's argument was precluded by "[t]he legislature's determination to treat sixteen year olds as adults for purposes of [eligibility for trial in juvenile court.]" (Id. at 297). In United States v. Johnson, 416 F.3d 464 (6th Cir. 2005), the court held that evidence of low IQ, even if sufficient to establish mental retardation, should not be admitted to modify the "reasonable person" standard for the purposes of a duress defense: "Unlike ... non-mental physical disabilities, mental deficiency or retardation is difficult to identify, more difficult to quantify, and more easily feigned. For these reasons and others, it was the common law rule going back at least to 1616, and still is, that an adult suffering from a mental deficiency is nevertheless held to a reasonable person standard." Id. at 469.

In contrast, the Pennsylvania Supreme Court held that mental retardation should be considered as part of an actor's "situation" for the purposes of duress: "While the trier of fact must consider whether an objective person

---

49. Model Penal Code and Commentaries, Comment to §2.02 at 242 (1985) (discussing the analogous issue with respect to the reasonableness requirement in the definition of negligence).

of reasonable firmness would have been able to resist the threat, it must ultimately base its decision on whether that person would have been able to resist the threat if he was subjectively placed in the defendant's situation. . . . [T]he fact that a defendant suffers from 'a gross and verifiable' mental disability . . . is a relevant consideration." Commonwealth v. DeMarco, 570 Pa. 263, 273 (2002). Should individualization of standards for duress extend even beyond "gross and verifiable" mental disabilities? The English Law Commission has argued that it should:[50]

> Threats directed against a weak, immature or disabled person may well be much more compelling than the same threats directed against a normal healthy person. . . . Relative timidity, for example, may be an inseparable aspect of a total personality that is in turn part cause and part product of its possessor's life situation; and thus may itself be one of the "circumstances" in the light of which . . . the duress is to be assessed.

Compare John Gardner, The Gist of Excuses, 2 Buff. Crim. L. Rev. 1 (1997), questioning a highly individualized standard. Which approach is more in accord with basic principles of just punishment?

(b) Battered woman's syndrome. Courts now uniformly hold that evidence of battered woman's syndrome (BWS) is admissible to support a claim of self-defense when a woman facing an immediate threat kills her abuser (see pages 844-845 supra). But courts do *not* agree about whether BWS evidence is admissible when the woman claims duress as an excuse for participating in a robbery or drug deal under pressure from her abuser. Is there a valid basis for this distinction?

One commentator suggests that in claims of duress, the standard of reasonableness should not take into account that a woman suffers from BWS, in part because "[i]n self-defense, the woman avoids the imminent danger by responding in kind against its source—her batterer. In duress, however, the woman avoids her abuser's threat by misconduct directed against an innocent third party." Laurie Kratky Doré, Downward Adjustment and the Slippery Slope: The Use of Duress in Defense of Battered Offenders, 56 Ohio St. L.J. 665, 749 (1995). Do you agree that the innocence of the victim should be a relevant consideration? Does the defendant's degree of culpability change with the identity of the victim?

If BWS evidence is admissible in cases of duress at all, to which factual issues is it relevant? The reasonableness of the defendant's fear? The recklessness or negligence of the defendant in placing herself in a position where she might be subjected to duress? The degree of firmness that the defendant should be expected to exhibit under the circumstances? Most courts have not distinguished among these issues. Some hold that BWS evidence is not admissible at all in duress cases. E.g., United States v. Willis, 38 F.3d 170 (5th Cir. 1994). In Pickle v. State, 635 S.E.2d 197, 206 (Ga. App. 2006), the court said

---

50. Law Commission, Consultation Paper No. 122, at 55 (1992).

that "as the reasonableness standard . . . is purely objective, evidence of [the defendant's] subjective cognitive reasoning as it relates to the battered person syndrome is simply not relevant." Compare Dando v. Yukins, 461 F.3d 791, 801 (6th Cir. 2006), holding that BWS is admissible and relevant to the entire defense of duress.

At least one court has held that the requirement of "reasonable firmness" should be treated differently from the other issues. In State v. B.H., 183 N.J. 171 (2005), the defendant admitted to engaging in sexual activity with her seven-year-old stepson while S.H., her husband and father of the child, watched. The defendant raised a defense of duress, claiming that S.H. had often physically and sexually assaulted her in the past, and that he held his hand to her throat during her sexual activity with the boy and said that if she refused he would make her pay and she would never see her daughter again. The trial court allowed the defendant to present BWS evidence, but instructed the jury that the evidence was *not* relevant to whether "a person of reasonable firmness in the defendant's situation would have been unable to resist" the threat, but rather was relevant only to the issue of whether the defendant had "recklessly placed herself in a situation that it was probable that she would be subjected to duress." Id. at 181. The New Jersey Supreme Court affirmed, stating: "Because N.J.S.A. 2C:2-9a embodies an objective standard for the evaluation of a defendant's conduct in response to a threat by another, we can discern no place for battered woman syndrome evidence in that assessment. In applying the statute's objective measure, it is a person of reasonable firmness that the jury must consider. . . . The evidence is relevant, however, to a defendant's subjective perception of a threat from her abuser, and in that respect, can be relevant to her credibility. It also helps in explaining why she would remain with her abuser and, therefore, why such a defendant ought not to be perceived as acting recklessly." Id. at 199-201.

Question: Why should BWS be considered irrelevant when assessing whether a battered woman acted with "reasonable firmness" in responding to her abuser's threats?

NOTE: NECESSITY AND DURESS COMPARED

The relationship between the defenses of necessity and duress can be confusing. Partly the reason is terminological: Courts and commentators don't always use the terms the same way. But, more significantly, the confusion is analytical. See Peter Westen & James Mangiafico, The Criminal Defense of Duress: A Justification, Not an Excuse—And Why It Matters, 6 Buff. Crim. L. Rev. 833 (2003); Claire O. Finkelstein, Duress: A Philosophical Account of the Defense in Law, 37 Ariz. L. Rev. 251 (1995).

Two separate concepts are at work here. What is usually called necessity refers to a defense resting on the rationale of justification. One can see this most clearly in the MPC defense of the choice of evils (§3.02), which we explored in the preceding section: The defendant violated a criminal prohibition, but in the circumstances it was good that she did, because doing so was the lesser evil. The other concept rests on the rationale of excuse. The defendant is accorded a defense not because it was good to violate the law, but because the circumstances were so compelling that normally law-abiding people might well have done the same. This is the spirit behind the MPC defense of duress.

But the lines between these two distinguishable concepts are often blurred in the way the law is formulated and discussed. For example, Wayne R. LaFave, Criminal Law 467 (3d ed. 2000), summarizes the law of duress as requiring not only that the defendant be threatened by another with imminent serious unlawful harm, but that the defendant's choice to break the law was the lesser evil in the circumstances.

In those jurisdictions where the law of duress is as LaFave summarizes it, duress becomes a species of justification. But why is it needed? Wouldn't the defense of justification (necessity) cover all the cases duress covers? The answer might be no, because the law in some jurisdictions accords significance to the source of the peril. Under this view, if the source of the peril was the "do-it-or-else" command of another person, the only possible defense is duress, not necessity; but if the source of the peril is something else (for example, a natural disaster), the only possible defense may be necessity, not duress. Recall, for example, the dictum in *People v. Unger*, supra page 885, that the defense of compulsion (duress) would be available only if someone commanded the prisoner to escape by threatening him with serious harm if he did not.

These ways of formulating the defenses of duress and necessity—that *both* are justification defenses, but that only a do-it-or-else command of another can establish duress—are problematic in that they preclude the possibility of a defense when conduct is harmful on balance and therefore not *justifiable.* The MPC §2.09 addresses this difficulty by defining duress purely as an excuse. The defense is established when the defendant acted under a threat a person of reasonable firmness would have been unable to resist. If the circumstances would also make the defendant's act the lesser evil, the MPC permits the justification defense (§3.02) as well, but he can claim duress even if he did not choose the lesser evil.

Even when a defendant's duress claim can plausibly be framed in terms of either justification or excuse, the difference between the two can have significant practical consequences. Consider United States v. Lopez, 662 F. Supp. 1083 (N.D. Cal. 1987). Defendant McIntosh landed a helicopter in the recreation yard of a federal prison and then flew off with Lopez, who had been an inmate there. Prosecuted for escape, Lopez asserted the defenses of duress and necessity, on the basis of her fear that she faced threats of death or serious injury at the hands of other inmates. McIntosh was charged with aiding and abetting Lopez's escape. Does he have a good justification defense if Lopez does? Does he have a good duress defense if Lopez does?

The difference between choice-of-evils *justification* and the duress *excuse* can be important for another reason, because the MPC allows the justification defense regardless of the *source of the peril*, but it makes the duress excuse available only when the peril arises from the do-it-or-else command of another person. The MPC thus adheres to the tradition of attributing importance to the source of the peril. The following Notes explore this issue and other major issues in the law of duress.

NOTES ON DURESS

1. *Source of the threat.* What is the basis for the MPC distinction depending on the source of the threat? If the peril is great enough that a person of reasonable firmness would be unable to resist, why should it matter whether the peril is from another person or from some natural event? Consider the following cases.

(a) X, under the command of *Y,* an armed escaping felon, is unwillingly driving a car along a narrow and precipitous mountain road that drops off sharply on both sides. The headlights pick out two drunken persons lying across the road in such a position as to make passage impossible without running over them. *X* is prevented from stopping by *Y*'s threat to shoot him dead if he does not drive straight on. If *X* kills the drunks in order to save himself, he would not be justified under the lesser-evil principle of §3.02, but he would be excused under §2.09 if the jury found that "a person of reasonable firmness in his situation would have been unable to resist."

(b) The same situation as above except that *X* is driving alone and is prevented from stopping by suddenly inoperative brakes. His alternatives are either to run down the drunks or to run off the road and down the mountainside. If *X* chooses the first alternative to save his own life and kills the drunks, he would not be excused under §2.09 even if a jury decided that a person of reasonable firmness would have been unable to do otherwise.

Can the difference between these two cases be defended? Shouldn't an actor have an excuse whenever she commits a criminal act that most people would lack the fortitude to resist? But if so, could every criminal defendant argue that reasonable people in her situation would lack the willpower to resist the act she committed? Would such a defense be too easily abused? One way to avoid that danger would be to limit the defense to situations in which the peril (whether from an unlawful threat or natural causes) posed a risk of death or great bodily harm. But the MPC does not permit a duress defense for *any* naturally arising peril, no matter how severe. The Commentary justifies this position as follows (Model Penal Code and Commentaries, Comment to §2.09 at 378-379 (1985)):

> [T]here is a significant difference between the situations in which an actor makes the choice of an equal or greater evil under the threat of unlawful human force and when he does so because of a natural event. In the former situation, the basic interests of the law may be satisfied by prosecution of the agent of unlawful force; in the latter circumstance, if the actor is excused, no one is subject to the law's application.

What "basic interests of the law" does the MPC Commentary have in mind? If in principle the defendant in the latter case should be excused, why should it matter that there is no one else to prosecute?

2. Nature of the threat. At common law only a threat of death or serious bodily harm could give rise to a duress defense. The MPC is broader, but its duress defense still is available only for threats of unlawful force *against the person.* Why should other coercive threats be categorically excluded? Consider the comment of Lord Simon dissenting in D.P.P. for Northern Ireland v. Lynch, [1975] A.C. 653, 686:

> [A] threat to property may, in certain circumstances, be as potent in overbearing the actor's [will] as a threat of physical harm. For example, the threat may be to burn down his house unless the householder merely keeps watch against interruption while a crime is committed. Or a fugitive from justice may say, "I have it in my power to make your son bankrupt. You can avoid that merely by driving me to the airport." Would not many ordinary people yield to such threats . . . ?

3. Imminence. Both *Toscano* and MPC §2.09 treat the imminence of the threatened harm as one factor to be weighed in determining whether the defendant's conduct was that of "a person of reasonable firmness in his situation." Accord, Bates v. Commonwealth, 145 S.W.3d 845, 847 (Ky. Ct. App. 2004). In contrast, many common-law decisions treat imminence as an absolute prerequisite to a duress defense, and some statutes limit the defense to situations involving threats of "instant" death. The majority of recent statutory revisions also reject the MPC's flexible approach and preserve some requirement that the threatened harm be "immediate," "imminent," or "instant." See Model Penal Code and Commentaries, Comments to §2.09 at 369, 382 (1985). Many recent judicial decisions likewise insist on strict temporal imminence. E.g., United States v. Shryock, 342 F.3d 948 (9th Cir. 2003); Davis v. State, 18 So. 2d 842, 848 (Miss. 2009).

What is the justification for this inflexible imminence requirement? Consider the following cases:

United States v. Fleming, 23 C.M.R. 7 (1957): [Defendant, an army officer, was court-martialed for violating the Uniform Code of Military Justice while a prisoner of war in Korea. The charges against him rested on his having collaborated with the enemy by helping prepare propaganda designed to promote disaffection among U.S. troops, and by making numerous English-language broadcasts criticizing American war objectives and calling upon U.S. authorities to withdraw or surrender. In describing the circumstances leading up to the acts of collaboration, the court noted that after being captured, defendant suffered numerous interrogations, forced marches, and physical abuse. It characterized the prison camp conditions as "extremely bad." The court then described specific threats that occurred in response to defendant's initial refusals to cooperate (id. at 15-16):]

[T]he accused testified that he was constantly harangued and pressured by Colonel Kim. According to Kim, there were two kinds of people: those for peace and those against peace. Those against peace were war criminals and not fit to live. If the accused fitted into that category he would be put in a "hole" and would never come out. But if he were for peace, he was a friend. . . . When the accused initially refused to do the acts to prove his "friendliness," he was asked if he wanted to return to the previous camp up north. The accused replied in the affirmative and Kim informed him that he could start walking the 150-200 mile distance. It was midwinter, the accused's shoes had been stolen, and he was wearing rags wrapped around his feet. These factors, plus his greatly weakened physical condition, led the accused to the conclusion that he would never reach the north camp alive. Thereafter, on each occasion when the accused objected to Kim's propaganda efforts, he was threatened with the walk north. . . .

Also Kim's subsequent threat of the caves . . . undoubtedly affected prisoner cooperation. [The caves] were recesses in the hillside. They were wet and muddy with little or no heating facilities. The prisoners lived in the muck and mire like animals. . . . The mortality rate in the indescribable filth and privation of these holes in the ground was extremely high. The prisoners felt that a sentence to the caves was almost tantamount to a sentence of death. . . . According to the accused, whenever he balked on the propaganda, Kim reminded him of the Americans in the caves and again took him to see them.

[At the court-martial, the trier of fact was instructed that defendant's acts could be excused on grounds of duress only if he had "a well-grounded apprehension of immediate and impending death or of immediate, serious, bodily harm." Defense counsel argued that the insistence on a fear of *immediate* death was error under the circumstances, that fear of "a delayed, or a wasting death from starvation, deprivation or other like conditions can just as well spell coercion and compulsion as the fear of immediate death." Rejecting this argument, the court upheld the conviction (id. at 24-25):]

We are not unmindful of the hardships or the pressures to which the accused and his fellow prisoners were subjected prior to the time of his collaboration with the enemy, [but] we cannot overlook the fact that accused cooperated with his captors upon the mere assertion of the threats. . . . It was not at all certain at the time the threat was made that walking north to Pyoktong would cause death at all, much less immediately. By way of comparison, if, for example, accused's captors had actually made him start on foot for Camp Five, and it then became evident that he could not survive the march, a valid defense of duress might have arisen for capitulation at that point. . . . Here the danger of death was problematical and remote. . . . As the court stated in *D'Aquino v. United States*, "The person claiming the defense of coercion and duress must be a person whose resistance has brought him to the last ditch" (182 F.2d at 359). Accused's resistance had not "brought him to the last ditch"; the danger of death or great bodily harm was not *immediate*. Accused can not now avail himself of the defense of duress.

United States v. Contento-Pachon, 723 F.2d 691 (9th Cir. 1984): [Defendant, a native of Bogota, Colombia, was employed there as a taxicab driver. One of his passengers, Jorge, proposed] that Contento-Pachon swallow cocaine-filled balloons and transport them to the United States. Contento-Pachon agreed to consider the proposition. He was told not to mention the proposition to anyone, otherwise he would "get into serious trouble." Contento-Pachon testified that he did not contact the police because he believes that the Bogota police are corrupt and that they are paid off by drug traffickers. Approximately one week later, Contento-Pachon told Jorge that he would not carry the cocaine. In response, . . . Jorge told Contento-Pachon that his failure to cooperate would result in the death of his wife and three-year-old child.

The following day the pair met again. Contento-Pachon's life and the lives of his family were again threatened. At this point, Contento-Pachon agreed to take the cocaine into the United States. The pair met two more times. At the last meeting, Contento-Pachon swallowed 129 balloons of cocaine. He was informed that he would be watched at all times during the trip, and that if he failed to follow Jorge's instruction he and his family would be killed.

After leaving Bogota, Contento-Pachon's plane landed in Panama. Contento-Pachon asserts that he did not notify the authorities there because he felt that the Panamanian police were as corrupt as those in Bogota. Also, he felt that any such action on his part would place his family in jeopardy. When he arrived at the customs inspection point in Los Angeles, Contento-Pachon consented to have his stomach x-rayed, which led to the discovery of the cocaine.

[At trial, the government's motion to exclude the duress defense was granted. The District Court held that two necessary elements of the defense are the immediacy and the inescapability of the threat. It concluded that neither element was satisfied. The court of appeals reversed:] [T]he defendant was dealing with a man who was deeply involved in the exportation of illegal substances. Large sums of money were at stake and, consequently, Contento-Pachon had reason to believe that Jorge would carry out his threats. . . . These were not vague threats of possible future harm. According to the defendant, if he had refused to cooperate, the consequences would have been immediate and harsh. . . . Contento-Pachon's contention that he was operating under the threat of immediate harm was supported by sufficient evidence to present a triable issue of fact.

The defendant must show that he had no reasonable opportunity to escape. . . . The trier of fact should decide whether one in Contento-Pachon's position might believe that some of the Bogota police were paid informants for drug traffickers and that reporting the matter to the police did not represent a reasonable opportunity of escape.

If he chose not to go to the police, Contento-Pachon's alternative was to flee. We reiterate that the opportunity to escape must be reasonable. To flee, Contento-Pachon, along with his wife and three year-old child, would have been forced to pack his possessions, leave his job, and travel to a place beyond the reaches of the drug traffickers. A juror might find that this was not a reasonable avenue of escape. Thus, Contento-Pachon presented a triable issue on the element of escapability.

Regina v. Ruzic, [1998] D.L.R.4th 358: The defendant was a 21-year-old woman who had traveled from Belgrade, Yugoslavia, to Toronto with two kilos of heroin strapped to her body. At trial she admitted bringing the heroin into Canada but argued duress. She claimed that a man named Mirkovic, a known killer, had stabbed and burned her arm and had threatened to "do something" to her mother if she would not carry heroin to Canada. She claimed she did not tell the police because she no longer trusted the Yugoslav authorities. A defense expert testified that in Yugoslavia large paramilitary groups engaged in mafia-like coercive activities and that people perceived the police to have lost control.

Section 17 of the Canadian Criminal Code provides:

> A person who commits an offence under compulsion by threats of immediate death or bodily injury from a person who is present when the offense is committed is excused for committing the offense if the person believes that the threats will be carried out.

The trial court instructed the jury on compulsion as a defense but, contrary to the Canadian statute, refused to specify that the threat had to be immediate, had to be made against the defendant herself, and had to be made by a person who was present when the offense was committed. The jury acquitted, and the prosecution appealed. The Ontario Court of Appeal upheld the acquittal on the ground that the restrictive conditions in the duress statute violated Section 7 of the Canadian Charter of Rights and Freedoms, a general provision stating:

> Everyone has the right to life, liberty, and security of the person, and the right not to be deprived thereof except in accordance with the principles of fundamental justice.

The court reasoned that if the defendant's story were believed, the threat left her no realistic choice, even though the threat was not immediate and the threatener was not present when she committed the offense. To convict her in such a situation would amount to convicting the innocent in violation of the principles of fundamental justice. She would be innocent because her actions were in effect involuntary—not physically, but morally—because she had no realistic choice but to comply.

Questions: Should a U.S. court be willing to reject the immediacy requirement and similar restrictions on the duress defense, on the ground that a defendant like Ruzic cannot be considered morally innocent? Are such restrictions explained by practical concerns? If so, do such practical concerns (if any) justify the conviction of a person who is morally innocent?

4. Duress and Mens Rea. Because cases of imminent duress involve a lack of moral culpability, it makes sense for duress to be defense to crimes like assault or damage to property, which require a culpable mens rea (for example, an intent to cause harm). But does the same logic suggest that duress *should not* be available as a defense to strict liability crimes? For example, in many states, driving under the influence of alcohol (DUI) is a strict liability offense; it is no defense that the defendant was unaware of being intoxicated. What should be the result if a defendant who knows he is intoxicated is forced at gunpoint to drive a fleeing felon away from the scene of a crime? Since a DUI conviction does not require moral culpability, should the defendant's claim of duress be considered irrelevant for the same reasons that a mistake of fact would be considered irrelevant? Or conversely, if a duress defense is permitted in this situation (as it apparently is in most states), does that willingness suggest that the refusal to permit a mistake-of-fact defense is fundamentally unsound? For a careful analysis, see Vera Bergelson, A Fair Punishment for Humbert Humbert: Strict Liability and Affirmative Defenses, 14 New Crim. L. Rev. 55 (2011).

5. *Contributory fault.* Should it matter whether the defendant is in some way to blame for being in a position that leads to duress? Suppose a defendant joins a gang engaged in petty thefts. When the leader decides to rob a bank, the defendant refuses to go along, but is threatened with death if he fails to cooperate. If the defendant participates in the robbery, should he have a duress defense? A common approach is to hold that, where a defendant "voluntarily, and with knowledge of its nature, joined a criminal organization or gang which he knew might bring pressure on him to commit an offense and was an active member when he was put under such pressure, he cannot avail himself of the defense of duress." Regina v. Sharp, [1987] 3 W.L.R. 1, 8-9. If, however, the nature of the criminal enterprise is such that the defendant has no reason to suspect he will be forcibly prevented from withdrawing, and if trouble materializes unexpectedly, the defense remains available. Regina v. Shepherd, 86 Cr. App. R. 47 (1988). See also MPC §2.09(2), withdrawing the defense where the defendant "recklessly placed himself in a situation in which it is probable that he would be subjected to duress."

Questions: Is it fair for the defense to remain available, as it does under the MPC, even though the defendant negligently ran an unreasonable risk of incurring duress? Conversely, is the MPC defense too restrictive in precluding the defense whenever the defendant has been reckless? For example, suppose that a defendant was aware that his involvement with a gang exposed him to a vague risk that he might be pressured to participate in various unspecified crimes. If the defendant is later threatened with death if he does not help in a bank robbery, is it fair to deny him the duress defense to the specific intent crime of bank robbery? What if the choice to join the gang was itself coerced? See David Rutkowski, A Coercion Defense for the Street Gang Criminal: Plugging the Moral Gap in Existing Law, 10 Notre Dame J.L. Ethics & Pub. Pol'y 137 (1999).

6. *Duress as a defense to murder.* Prior to the MPC, most jurisdictions held the duress defense inapplicable in prosecutions for murder (and

s for other very serious crimes) even when the stringent require-
an imminent, inescapable lethal threat were satisfied. The MPC
this exclusion of murder cases, as have a few states that adopted
provisions derived from the MPC. E.g., Commonwealth v. Markman,
d 586, 606 (Pa. 2007); N.Y. Penal Law §40.00 (2011). But most recent
nd statutory revisions continue to exclude the defense in murder prosecutions. E.g., State v. Brown, 646 S.E.2d 775 (N.C. App. 2007); People v.
Anderson, 28 Cal. 4th 767 (2002). In England, the defense is precluded in
cases of murder and attempted murder, but not in cases of aircraft hijacking.
See Regina v. Abdul-Hussain, [1999] Crim. L. R. 570 (Ct. App.).

Questions: (a) Duress as a defense to felony murder. Suppose that a
defendant is compelled to participate in a robbery, and during the course of
that crime a bystander is shot and killed by one of the other robbers. If duress
is available in a prosecution for robbery but not in a murder prosecution,
should the defendant be able to invoke the duress defense in a prosecution
for felony murder? Logically, the answer should be yes: A well-founded claim
of duress will defeat the robbery charge, and any allegation of murder must
therefore rest upon independent proof of malice, without regard to the underlying felony. Most courts accept this analysis. E.g., McMillan v. State, 956 A.2d
716 (Md. App. 2008; People v. Sims, 869 N.E.2d 1115 (Ill. App. 2007). But
some courts hold that duress is not available as a defense to any homicide
charge. See Russell Shankland, Comment, Duress and the Underlying Felony,
99 J. Crim. L. & Criminology 1227 (2009); Steven J. Mulroy, The Duress
Defense's Uncharted Terrain, 43 San Diego L. Rev. 159 (2006).

(b) The defendant's role in a homicidal offense. Where, as in most jurisdictions, duress cannot be a defense to a murder charge, should the defense
nonetheless remain available if the coerced defendant's participation in the
crime was relatively minor? Consider the observations of Chief Justice Bray,
dissenting in Regina v. Brown, [1968] S.A.S.R. 467, 494:

> The reasoning generally used to support the proposition that duress is no
> defence to a charge of murder is, to use the words of Blackstone cited above, that
> "he ought rather to die himself, than escape by the murder of an innocent."
> Generally speaking I am prepared to accept this position. Its force is obviously
> considerably less where the act of the threatened man is not the direct act of
> killing but only the rendering of some minor form of assistance, particularly
> when it is by no means certain that if he refuses the death of the victim will be
> averted, or conversely when it is by no means certain that if he complies the
> death will be a necessary consequence. It would seem hard, for example, if an
> innocent passer-by seized in the street by a gang of criminals visibly engaged in
> robbery and murder in a shop and compelled at the point of a gun to issue
> misleading comments to the public, or an innocent driver compelled at the
> point of a gun to convey the murderer to the victim, were to have no defence. . . .

When is a defendant's role sufficiently limited to justify the availability of a
duress defense to homicide?

PROBLEM

The question whether duress should be available as a defense to murder or other serious offenses has assumed new importance in international efforts to prosecute individuals involved in perpetrating atrocities, such as the mass killings that took place in the 1990s in the former Yugoslavia and in Rwanda.

Drazen Erdemović was charged before the International Criminal Tribunal for the Former Yugoslavia (ICTY) with crimes against humanity and war crimes for his participation in the mass execution of 1,200 unarmed Muslim men and boys in Srebrenica during a five-hour period in July 1995. At the time of the massacre, Erdemović was a low-ranking soldier in the Serbian army. He testified that when members of his unit were ordered to shoot the civilians, he refused, only to be threatened with instant death: "If you don't wish to do it, stand in the line with the rest of them and give others your rifle so that they can shoot you." Prosecutor v. Erdemović, No. IT-96-22-A (ICTY, Appeals Chamber, Oct. 7, 1997), at p.6. The prosecution did not dispute Erdemović's account of the facts; rather, it argued that duress could not constitute a complete defense to such crimes, but could be considered only as a mitigating factor in sentencing. Consider these issues:

1. *The question of guilt.* The Appeals Chamber of the ICTY, in a 3–2 vote, agreed with the prosecution that duress can only be a mitigating factor, not a complete defense to such charges. Two judges in the majority insisted that "he ought rather to die himself, than kill an innocent."[51] The House of Lords has taken a similar position (Abbott v. The Queen [1976] 3 All E.R. 140, 146):

> A terrorist of notorious violence might, e.g., threaten death to A and his family unless A obeys his instructions to put a bomb with a time fuse set by A in a certain passenger aircraft and/or in a thronged market, railway station or the like. . . . Is there any limit to the number of people you may kill to save your own life and that of your family?

Is the reasoning persuasive? The dissent in *Erdemović* castigated this approach for setting "standards of behaviour which require mankind to perform acts of martyrdom, and brand as criminal any behaviour falling below those standards"; it offered this example, drawn from an actual case before the ICTY:[52]

> An inmate of a concentration camp, starved and beaten for months, is then told, after a savage beating, that if he does not kill another inmate, who has already been beaten with metal bars and will certainly be beaten to death before long, then his eyes will, then and there, be gouged out. He kills the other inmate as a result. Perhaps a hero could accept a swift bullet in his skull to avoid having to kill, but it would require an extraordinary—and perhaps impossible act of courage to accept one's eyes being plucked out.

---

51. Prosecutor v. Erdemović, No. IT-96-22-A, Joint Separate Opinion of Judge McDonald and Judge Vohrah at ¶71 (ICTY, Appeals Chamber, Oct. 7, 1997).

52. *Erdemović*, supra, Separate and Dissenting Opinion of Judge Cassese, at p. 18.

Does the dissent have the stronger argument, or is it simply making a different point? Professor Alexander K.A. Greenawalt notes (The Pluralism of International Criminal Law, 86 Ind. L.J. 1063, 1118 (2011)):

> [T]he majority's reasoning . . . reflects the concern that granting Erdemović's defense would somehow endorse his behavior. The criminal law is more nuanced than that, however. . . . The law may maintain that Erdemović's actions were regrettable . . . while at the same time acknowledging [that] self-sacrifice may be too much to expect under the circumstances. [This] perspective does not require downgrading duress into a mere partial defense that offers only mitigation of punishment. Instead, if the law does not expect self-sacrifice on Erdemović's part, it should afford a complete defense while recognizing that his behavior is merely excused, rather than justified.

2. *A possible* **justification?** There was an important complicating factor for Erdemović: It was virtually certain that if he had refused to execute the innocent civilians, he himself would have been immediately killed, and the massacre would then have been carried out by others. In other words, *more* people would have died if he had *resisted* the threat. A dissenting judge argued that the decision to succumb to the threat and kill the innocent victims therefore was the lesser evil.

Is that analysis sound? Professor Luis E. Chiesa observes (Duress, Demanding Heroism, and Proportionality, 41 Vand. J. Transnat'l L. 741, 769 (2008)):

> [This] contention presupposes an oversimplified calculus of what constitutes the lesser evil. [B]y giving way to the threats, the actor is aiding someone else in the commission of a wrongful and heinous act. This collaboration in the perpetration of a crime is, in and of itself, an evil that should weigh against yielding to the threats. [T]hese types of decisions are "not merely a matter of weighing the lives saved versus the life lost," for the agent's moral integrity is compromised by his forced involvement in the production of evil. [Thus,] a coerced actor who harms an innocent victim may act wrongfully despite the fact that she could not have prevented the harm.

Nonetheless, Professor Chiesa continues (id. at 771):

> [B]ecause the actor effectively lacked the capacity to prevent the harm threatened from occurring, punishing [her] for deciding to save her own life instead of dying to protect innocent people who were going to die anyway would be unfair. [Y]ielding to the coercive threats in this case is wrongful but perfectly understandable and, hence, not punishable.

3. *The appropriate sentence.* Erdemović ultimately served a five-year prison term. Do the arguments for denying the duress defense altogether suggest that this relatively lenient sentence (for having helped murder 1,200 persons) was inappropriate? How can a sentence of this sort possibly deter people in his situation from participating in a mass atrocity? Or does official condemnation through a criminal conviction suffice even without severe sanctions?

4. Professor Rosa Ehrenreich Brooks offers this thought on the issues (Law in the Heart of Darkness: Atrocity & Duress, 43 Va. J. Int'l L. 861, 888 (2003)):

> [Our law and philosophy] were [not] of much use to Drazen Erdemović as he faced his commander on the farm outside Srebrenica. Reason and law still seem to lack sufficient normative force in the face of violence and terror: they provide us with what appears to be prospective guidance on how we should behave in some hypothetical future, and retrospective guidance on how we ought to have behaved in the past, but little guidance when we're actually on the spot.

NOTE ON POSITIVE INDUCEMENTS

Should there be a defense when a crime is committed in response to *inducements* (as opposed to *threats*) that would overcome the resistance of a person of ordinary firmness? Sir James Stephen, reflecting the prevailing common-law view, thought not: "It is at the moment when temptation to crime is strongest that the law should speak most clearly and emphatically to the contrary." 2 James Fitzjames Stephen, A History of the Criminal Law of England 107 (1983). But since some inducements can affect ordinary, law-abiding people as powerfully as forcible threats, why should the two be treated differently? Consider the offer of employment, housing, or medical care to a person in desperate need. Wouldn't an offer to donate a kidney to a seriously ill person who otherwise lacked access to one be as difficult for that person to resist as a threat to inflict serious bodily injury on a healthy person?

The only inducement defense that exists in American law is that of entrapment, which applies only to excessive inducements offered by *government* agents. See the discussion of entrapment in the section on accomplice liability in Chapter 7, page 697 supra. It is widely accepted that the primary purpose of the defense is to deter government overreaching in undercover operations. See Model Penal Code & Commentaries, Comment to §2.13 at 413-415 (1985). Yet the most common version of the defense is considerably narrower, because it is available only to a supposedly "innocent" defendant—someone not "predisposed" to offend. See Jacobson v. United States, 503 U.S. 540, 553 (1992). Given this focus on the particular defendant's culpability or predisposition, why shouldn't the excuse be available for similarly "innocent" defendants whose lack of predisposition is overcome by nongovernmental inducements?

3. Intoxication

a. Voluntary Intoxication

Glanville Williams, Criminal Law: The General Part 564 (2d ed. 1961): If a man is punished for doing something when drunk that he would not have done when sober, is he not in plain truth punished for getting drunk?

Roberts v. People, 19 Mich. 401, 419 (1870): [A defendant] must be presumed to have intended the obscuration and perversion of his faculties which followed from his voluntary intoxication. He must be held to have purposely blinded his moral perceptions, and set his will free from the control of reason—to have suppressed the guards and invited the mutiny; and should therefore be held responsible as well for the vicious excesses of the will, thus set free, as for the acts done by its prompting.

PEOPLE v. HOOD

Supreme Court of California
1 Cal. 3d 444, 462 P.2d 370 (1969)

TRAYNOR, C.J. [The evidence showed that defendant, who had been drinking heavily, resisted an effort by a police officer to subdue and arrest him, and in the course of the struggle seized the officer's gun and shot him in the legs. Defendant was convicted at trial of assault with a deadly weapon. Because the trial court had given the jury "hopelessly conflicting instructions on the effect of intoxication," the California Supreme Court reversed and attempted to clarify the issue for re-trial. The court explained that the relevance of intoxication generally had been held to turn on whether the charged offense was a crime of "specific intent" or "general intent," but that lower courts were in conflict about which category properly described crimes of assault. The court then continued:]

The distinction between specific and general intent crimes evolved as a judicial response to the problem of the intoxicated offender. That problem is to reconcile two competing theories of what is just in the treatment of those who commit crimes while intoxicated. On the one hand, the moral culpability of a drunken criminal is frequently less than that of a sober person effecting a like injury. On the other hand, it is commonly felt that a person who voluntarily gets drunk and while in that state commits a crime should not escape the consequences.

Before the nineteenth century, the common law refused to give any effect to the fact that an accused committed a crime while intoxicated. The judges were apparently troubled by this rigid traditional rule, however, for there were a number of attempts during the early part of the nineteenth century to arrive at a more humane, yet workable, doctrine. The theory that these judges explored was that evidence of intoxication could be considered to negate intent, whenever intent was an element of the crime charged. . . . To limit the operation of the doctrine and achieve a compromise between the conflicting feelings of sympathy and reprobation for the intoxicated offender, later courts both in England and this country drew a distinction between so-called specific intent and general intent crimes.

Specific and general intent have been notoriously difficult terms to define and apply, and a number of text writers recommended that they be abandoned altogether. Too often the characterization of a particular crime as one of specific or general intent is determined solely by the presence or absence of words describing psychological phenomena—"intent" or "malice," for example—in the statutory language defining the crime. When the definition of a crime consists of only the description of a particular act, without reference to intent to do a further act or achieve a future consequence, we ask whether the defendant intended to do the proscribed act. This intention is deemed to be a general criminal intent. When the definition refers to defendant's intent to do some further act or achieve some additional consequence, the crime is deemed to be one of specific intent. There is no real difference, however, only a linguistic one, between an intent to do an act already performed and an intent to do that same act in the future.

The language of Penal Code section 22, drafted in 1872 when "specific" and "general" intent were not yet terms of art, is somewhat broader than those terms:

> No act committed by a person while in a state of voluntary intoxication is less criminal by reason of his having been in such condition. But whenever the actual existence of any particular purpose, motive, or intent is a necessary element to constitute any particular species or degree of crime, the jury may take into consideration the fact that the accused was intoxicated at the time, in determining the purpose, motive, or intent with which he committed the act.

Even this statement of the relevant policy is no easier to apply to particular crimes. We are still confronted with the difficulty of characterizing the mental element of a given crime as a particular purpose, motive, or intent necessary to constitute the offense, or as something less than that to which evidence of intoxication is not pertinent. . . . The difficulty with applying such a test to the crime of assault or assault with a deadly weapon is that no word in the relevant code provisions unambiguously denotes a particular mental element, yet the word "attempt" in Penal Code section 240 strongly suggests goal-directed, intentional behavior.[6] This uncertainty accounts for the conflict over whether assault is a crime only of intention or also of recklessness.

. . . Even if assault requires an intent to commit a battery on the victim, it does not follow that the crime is one in which evidence of intoxication ought to be considered in determining whether the defendant had that intent. It is true that in most cases specific intent has come to mean an intention to do a future act or achieve a particular result, and that assault is appropriately characterized as a specific intent crime under this definition. An assault, however, is equally well characterized as a general intent crime under the definition of general intent as an intent merely to do a violent act. Therefore, whatever reality the distinction between specific and general intent may have in other contexts, the difference is chimerical in the case of assault with a deadly weapon or simple assault. Since the definitions of both specific intent and general intent cover the requisite intent to commit a battery, the decision

---

6. Penal Code, section 240 provides: "An assault is an unlawful attempt, coupled with a present ability, to commit a violent injury on the person of another."

whether or not to give effect to evidence of intoxication must rest on other considerations.

A compelling consideration is the effect of alcohol on human behavior. A significant effect of alcohol is to distort judgment and relax the controls on aggressive and antisocial impulses. Alcohol apparently has less effect on the ability to engage in simple goal-directed behavior, although it may impair the efficiency of that behavior. In other words, a drunk man is capable of forming an intent to do something simple, such as strike another, unless he is so drunk that he has reached the stage of unconsciousness. What he is not as capable as a sober man of doing is exercising judgment about the social consequences of his acts or controlling his impulses toward antisocial acts. He is more likely to act rashly and impulsively and to be susceptible to passion and anger. It would therefore be anomalous to allow evidence of intoxication to relieve a man of responsibility for the crimes of assault with a deadly weapon or simple assault, which are so frequently committed in just such a manner. . . .

Those crimes that have traditionally been characterized as crimes of specific intent [such as assault with intent to rape or assault with intent to kill] are not affected by our holding here. The difference in mental activity between formulating an intent to commit a battery and formulating an intent to commit a battery for the purpose of raping or killing may be slight, but it is sufficient to justify drawing a line between them and considering evidence of intoxication in the one case and disregarding it in the other. Accordingly, on retrial the court should not instruct the jury to consider evidence of defendant's intoxication in determining whether he committed assault with a deadly weapon on a peace officer or any of the lesser assaults included therein. . . .

State v. Stasio, 78 N.J. 467, 396 A.2d 1129 (1979): [The defendant was convicted of assault with intent to rob. Conceding that this was a "specific intent" crime, the court nonetheless ruled that evidence of voluntary intoxication was inadmissible:] [D]istinguishing between specific and general intent gives rise to incongruous results by irrationally allowing intoxication to excuse some crimes but not others. In some instances if the defendant is found incapable of formulating the specific intent necessary for the crime charged, such as assault with intent to rob, he may be convicted of a lesser included general intent crime, such as assault with a deadly weapon. In other cases there may be no related general intent offense so that intoxication would lead to acquittal. . . .

The [traditional] approach may free defendants of specific intent offenses even though the harm caused may be greater than in an offense held to require only general intent. This course thus undermines the criminal law's primary function of protecting society from the results of behavior that endangers the public safety. This should be our guide rather than concern with logical consistency in terms of any single theory of culpability, particularly in view of the fact that alcohol is significantly involved in a substantial number of offenses. The demands of public safety and the harm done are identical irrespective of the offender's reduced ability to restrain himself due to his drinking. . . .

Our holding today does not mean that voluntary intoxication is always irrelevant in criminal proceedings. Evidence of intoxication may be introduced to demonstrate that premeditation and deliberation have not been proven so that a second degree murder cannot be raised to first degree murder or to show that the intoxication led to a fixed state of insanity. Intoxication may be shown to prove that a defendant never participated in a crime. Thus it might be proven that a defendant was in such a drunken stupor and unconscious state that he was not a part of a robbery. . . . Under some circumstances intoxication may be relevant to demonstrate mistake. However, in the absence of any basis for the defense, a trial court should not in its charge introduce that element. A trial court, of course, may consider intoxication as a mitigating circumstance when sentencing a defendant.

[PASHMAN, J., dissenting:] [T]he majority rules that a person may be convicted of the crimes of assault *with intent* to rob and breaking and entering *with intent* to steal even though he never, in fact, intended to rob anyone or steal anything. The majority arrives at this anomalous result by holding that voluntary intoxication can never constitute a defense to any crime other than first-degree murder even though, due to intoxication, the accused may not have possessed the mental state specifically required as an element of the offense. This holding . . . defies logic and sound public policy. . . .

A person who intentionally commits a bad act is more culpable than one who engages in the same conduct without any evil design. The intentional wrongdoer [also] constitutes a greater threat to societal repose. A sufficiently intoxicated defendant is thus subject to less severe sanctions not because the law "excuses" his conduct but because the circumstances surrounding his acts have been deemed by the Legislature to be less deserving of punishment. . . .

Just as the lack of premeditation, willfulness, or deliberation precludes a conviction for first-degree murder, so should the lack of intent to rob or steal be a defense to assault and battery with intent to rob, or breaking and entering with intent to steal. The principle is the same in both situations. If voluntary intoxication negates an element of the offense, the defendant has not engaged in the conduct proscribed by the criminal statute, and hence should not be subject to the sanctions imposed by that statute.

The majority . . . professes to be concerned with protecting society from drunken offenders. There are several problems with this approach. First, the majority's opinion is not even internally consistent. Although intoxication is not to be given the status of a defense, the majority states that it can be considered to "buttress the affirmative defense of reasonable mistake." It is difficult to comprehend why the public would be less endangered by persons who become intoxicated and, as a result, commit alcohol-induced "mistakes" . . . than by persons who get so intoxicated that they commit the same acts without any evil intent. . . .

The most important consideration, however, is that the standards for establishing the defense are extremely difficult to meet. Contrary to the implications contained in the majority opinion, it is not the case that every defendant who has had a few drinks may successfully urge the defense. The mere intake of even large quantities of alcohol will not suffice. Moreover, the defense cannot be established solely by showing that the defendant might not have committed the offense had he been sober. What is required is a showing of such a great prostration of the faculties that the requisite mental state was totally lacking. That is, to successfully invoke the defense, an accused must show that he was so intoxicated that he did not have the intent to commit an offense. Such a state of affairs will likely exist in very few cases. I am confident that our judges and juries will be able to distinguish such unusual instances. . . .

NOTES ON VOLUNTARY INTOXICATION AS EVIDENCE NEGATING MENS REA

Why try to distinguish between whole classes of offenses for which voluntary intoxication can serve as a defense and those for which it cannot? Wouldn't it be simpler and more straightforward to admit evidence of voluntary intoxication whenever it is relevant to a fact in dispute? Decisions like *Hood* and *Stasio* reflect widespread resistance to this approach: In a number of jurisdictions, courts and legislatures have long specified that evidence of intoxication sometimes is inadmissible even when it is logically relevant. These Notes explore the reasons for this reluctance and the doctrinal forms that it takes.

1. Developments after **Hood** *and* **Stasio.** In California and New Jersey, subsequent statutes superseded the tests applied in *Hood* and *Stasio.* California, at the time of *Hood*, allowed intoxication evidence to be considered in determining "purpose, motive or intent," and in 1994, the California Supreme Court ruled, applying similar language then in effect, that intoxication evidence was admissible on the question whether a defendant had formed the malice ("depraved heart" recklessness) required for second-degree murder. The legislative response was swift. As amended in 1995, Cal. Penal Code §22(b) states that "[e]vidence of voluntary intoxication is admissible solely on the issue of whether or not the defendant actually formed a required specific intent," including, in murder cases, the issues of premeditation, deliberation, and express malice (i.e., intent to kill) but not the issue of implied malice ("depraved heart" recklessness).

The New Jersey legislature moved in the opposite direction. After *Stasio* held that intoxication evidence was not admissible to negate specific *or* general intent (except in cases of first-degree murder), the legislature enacted a provision specifying that intoxication evidence could be considered in determining purpose or knowledge but not in determining recklessness or negligence. N.J.S.A. §2C:2-8 (2011).

Looking more widely, the law is far from uniform. Many federal courts follow the "specific intent" versus "general intent" approach described in *Hood.* In United States v. Veach, 455 F.3d 628 (6th Cir. 2006), U.S. Park

Rangers arrested a motorist for driving while intoxicated. The motorist shoved one of the officers, and once in the patrol car, he said "[I]f I get a shot at you[,] . . . I'll kill you[;] I'm going to cut off your head." He was convicted of two offenses: assaulting a federal officer (18 U.S.C. §111), and threatening to assault a federal officer "with intent to impede [such] officer while engaged in the performance of official duties." 18 U.S.C. §115(a)(1)(B). The court held that the ample evidence of defendant's intoxication was properly ruled irrelevant to the charge of simple assault under §111, but that the trial judge had erred in ruling this evidence irrelevant on the question whether the defendant had formed the specific "intent to impede" required for conviction under §115.

Roughly two-thirds of the states likewise make the distinction between "specific intent" and "general intent" crimes decisive. But several, following the *Stasio* approach, exclude logically relevant intoxication evidence even on the issue of specific intent, except in first-degree murder cases (e.g., Swisher v. Commonwealth, 506 S.E.2d 763 (Va. 1998)), and 14 states bar defense use of intoxication evidence on *all* mens rea issues. See Mitchell Keiter, Just Say No Excuse: The Rise and Fall of the Intoxication Defense, 87 J. Crim. L. & Criminology 482, 518-520 (1997).

2. Why should intoxication be treated differently from other logically relevant evidence? Some of the reluctance to give intoxication its normal significance in rebutting evidence of mens rea is explained by the close connection between alcohol consumption and crime. In a 2002 national survey, 33 percent of jail inmates reported being under the influence of alcohol at the time of their offense, and for those convicted of violent crimes, the figure rose to 38 percent.[53] Numerous studies find a close association between alcohol consumption and homicide.[54]

3. Identifying "general intent" crimes. If assault were defined as an act that recklessly creates a risk of injury, all courts would classify the offense as a "general intent" crime, and then, under the majority rule set out in Note 1, supra, intoxication evidence would not be admissible to negate the required mens rea. But because California (and many other states) define assault as a kind of attempt and require proof of *intent* to inflict injury (not just recklessness), how can assault be a general intent crime? If assault requires proof of a purpose to accomplish a particular result, the offense seems to meet one of the classic definitions of a *specific intent* crime. See the Note on "specific intent" and "general intent," Chapter 3, page 247 supra. Did the court in *Hood* decide that assault nonetheless was *not* a specific intent crime, or did it decide that intoxication evidence should be inadmissible even though assault *is* a specific intent crime?

---

53. U.S. Dept. of Justice, Bureau of Justice Statistics, Substance Dependence, Abuse, and Treatment of Jail Inmates, 2002, at 5-6 (July 2005).

54. E.g., Robert N. Parker & Randi S. Cartmill, Alcohol and Homicide in the United States 1934-1995, 88 J. Crim. L. & Criminology 1369, 1374-1377 (1998).

In People v. Rocha, 479 P.2d 372 (Cal. 1971), the California Supreme Court noted the confusion generated by *Hood* and announced that assault with a deadly weapon is a "general intent" crime as to which intoxication evidence is inadmissible. This approach preserves the traditional general intent–specific intent test for determining the admissibility of intoxication evidence, but only at the cost of confounding the traditional test for determining what is a general intent crime. In California, assault is considered a general intent crime even though recklessness is insufficient and intention to injure must be proved.

Do the concepts of general and specific intent really aid the analysis, or are they simply labels used to announce conclusions reached on other grounds? Why shouldn't a court focus directly on the question whether intoxication evidence *should* be admissible, without attempting to determine whether the crime is properly classified as one of "general intent"?

4. The Model Penal Code. The MPC, and many of the recent court decisions, reject the controlling significance of the general intent–specific intent distinction and instead focus directly on the question of when intoxication evidence should be admissible.

MODEL PENAL CODE

§2.08. INTOXICATION

[See Appendix for text of this section.]

Model Penal Code and Commentaries, Comment to §2.08 at 357-359 (1985): Two major issues are . . . presented by the Model Code's provisions. The first . . . is the question of whether intoxication ought to be accorded a significance that is entirely coextensive with its relevance to disprove purpose or knowledge when they are the requisite mental elements of a specific crime. The answer ought to be affirmative. . . . For when purpose or knowledge, as distinguished from recklessness, is made essential for conviction, the reason very surely is that in the absence of such states of mind the conduct involved does not present a comparable danger. . . . If the mental state that is the basis of the law's concern does not exist, the reason for its nonexistence is usually immaterial. So it is that in the case of crimes of violence against the person, purpose or knowledge rarely is required to establish liability, though their presence may have weight in aggravating the degree of the offense or in sentencing; recklessness or even negligence is ordinarily sufficient.

The second and more difficult question relates to recklessness, where awareness of the risk created by the actor's conduct ordinarily is requisite for liability under Section 2.02. The problem is whether intoxication ought to be accorded a significance coextensive with its relevance to disprove such awareness, as in the case of purpose or knowledge that has previously been discussed. . . .

Those who oppose a special rule for drunkenness in relation to awareness of the risk in recklessness draw strength . . . from the proposition that it is precisely the awareness of the risk in recklessness that is the essence of its moral culpability—a culpability dependent upon the magnitude of the specific risk knowingly created. When that risk is greater in degree than that which the actor perceives at the time of getting drunk, as is frequently the case, the result of a special rule is bound to be a liability disproportionate to culpability. Hence the solution urged is to dispense with any special rule, relying rather on the possibility of proving foresight at the time of drinking and, when this cannot be proved, upon a generalized prohibition of being drunk and dangerous, with sanctions appropriate for such behavior. This approach would also permit prosecution for negligence if negligent commission of the act in question was sufficient to establish criminal liability. With respect to negligence, the essence of the culpability is the failure to perceive a risk that the actor should have perceived. The actor's culpability in failing to perceive a risk would be judged against the standard of a man in normal possession of his faculties. Thus, the fact that the defendant was drunk will not exculpate him from a charge of negligence. . . .

The case thus made is worthy of respect, but there are strong considerations on the other side. There is first the weight of the antecedent law which . . . has tended toward a special rule for drunkenness in this context. Beyond this, there is the fundamental point that awareness of the potential consequences of excessive drinking on the capacity of human beings to gauge the risks incident to their conduct is by now so dispersed in our culture that it is not unfair to postulate a general equivalence between the risks created by the conduct of the drunken actor and the risks created by his conduct in becoming drunk. Becoming so drunk as to destroy temporarily the actor's powers of perception and judgment is conduct that plainly has no affirmative social value to counterbalance the potential danger. The actor's moral culpability lies in engaging in such conduct. Added to this are the impressive difficulties posed in litigating the foresight of any particular actor at the time when he imbibes and the relative rarity of cases where intoxication really does engender unawareness as distinguished from imprudence. These considerations led to the conclusion, on balance, that the Model Code should declare that unawareness of a risk, of which the actor would have been aware had he been sober, is immaterial. Most states with revised codes have taken a similar position.

5. *The recklessness "equation."* Is the Model Penal Code right to equate drunkenness with recklessness? Suppose a defendant has several drinks at a party, assuming that his roommate (the designated driver) will take him home afterwards. On the way home, the roommate becomes sick and is unable to drive, so the defendant takes over the wheel. Shortly afterwards, he fails to stop in time to avoid a pedestrian crossing the road and the pedestrian is killed. The defendant could perhaps be convicted of negligent homicide or involuntary manslaughter, but should he be considered guilty of murder? Is the

MPC approach sound in equating his willingness to get drunk at the party with the reckless mens rea necessary to establish murder? Consider Stephen J. Morse, Fear of Danger, Flight from Culpability, 4 Psychol. Pub. Pol'y & L. 250, 254 (1998):

> As an empirical matter, . . . this equation is often preposterous. An agent will not be consciously aware while becoming drunk that there is a substantial and unjustifiable risk that he or she will commit a particular crime when drunk, unless the person has a previous history of . . . committing this specific crime [while drunk]. If such a prior history . . . exists, then the prosecution is capable of proving [the] previous awareness. The prosecution should not be able to rely on what is, in effect, the conclusive presumption that becoming drunk demonstrates the same culpability as the actual conscious awareness of a substantial and unjustifiable risk that the defendant would commit the specific harm.

6. Intoxication and due process. Once a state decides to require a particular mens rea (for example, knowledge or recklessness) as an element of an offense, how can the state legitimately deny a defendant the opportunity to present relevant exculpatory evidence that bears on the question whether, in fact, he had the required mens rea?

Montana v. Egelhoff, 518 U.S. 37 (1996), involved a state law defining "deliberate homicide" as a killing committed "purposely" or "knowingly." But Mont. Penal Code §45-2-203 provided that "an intoxicated condition . . . may not be taken into consideration in determining the existence of a mental state which is an element of the offense unless [the intoxication was involuntary]." Egelhoff was convicted of deliberate homicide after a trial at which the judge told the jury, in accordance with §45-2-203, that it could not consider his intoxicated condition in determining whether he had acted purposely or knowingly. The Montana Supreme Court reversed and held the statute unconstitutional. The court said that the evidence of Egelhoff's intoxication was "clear[ly] . . . relevant to the issue of whether [he] acted knowingly and purposely," and that the rule precluding consideration of that evidence had in effect "relieved [the State] of part of its burden to prove [guilt] beyond a reasonable doubt."

Do you agree? The U.S. Supreme Court did not, but the Court produced five separate opinions and was unable to agree on a single rationale. Justice Scalia, writing for four members of the Court, emphasized that the State must still offer evidence sufficient to prove purpose or knowledge beyond a reasonable doubt. He acknowledged that "by excluding a significant line of evidence that might refute mens rea, the statute made it easier for the State to meet [that] requirement." "But," Justice Scalia continued, "*any* evidentiary rule can have that effect. 'Reducing' the State's burden in this manner is not unconstitutional, unless the rule of evidence itself violates a fundamental principle of fairness (which . . . this one does not)." Id. at 55. Justice O'Connor, also writing for four members of the Court, reached the opposite conclusion. She reasoned that "to impede the defendant's ability to throw doubt on the State's case, [makes] the State's burden to prove its case . . . correspondingly easier," and that the statute therefore violated the due process requirement that the prosecution prove each element of an offense beyond a reasonable doubt. Id. at 61.

Justice Ginsburg, casting the deciding vote, found it unnecessary to resolve this disagreement and upheld the Montana statute on a different ground. She concluded that the Montana rule did *not* exclude evidence relevant to a required element of the offense, because §45-2-203 had in effect redefined deliberate homicide. As she interpreted Montana law, a deliberate-homicide conviction required the prosecution to prove *either* (1) that the defendant had killed purposely or knowingly, *or* (2) "that the defendant killed under circumstances that would otherwise establish knowledge or purpose 'but for' [the defendant's] voluntary intoxication." Id. at 58. She reasoned that Montana had not excluded relevant exculpatory evidence, because the intoxication evidence was irrelevant to an accusation based on the second theory, which the prosecution had proved beyond a reasonable doubt.

Questions: Is Justice Ginsburg's interpretation of the Montana statute workable? In the case of an intoxicated actor, how should the jury go about determining whether his act of killing *would have been* knowing or purposeful " 'but for' [his] voluntary intoxication"? Which of the opinions offers the best way of implementing the requirement of proof beyond a reasonable doubt? For incisive critiques of the opinions in *Egelhoff*, see Ronald J. Allen, Forward: *Montana v. Egelhoff*—Reflections on the Limits of Legislative Imagination and Judicial Authority, 87 J. Crim. L. & Criminology 633 (1997); Larry Alexander, The Supreme Court, Dr. Jekyll, and the Due Process of Proof, 1996 Sup. Ct. Rev. 191.

7. *A separate offense?* In his critique of the MPC's recklessness "equation" (the notion that knowingly drinking to excess is equivalent to knowingly creating a risk of harm), Professor Morse argues that this notion confuses the vague and relatively minor culpability involved in choosing to get drunk with the much more serious culpability involved in the mens rea required for crimes like rape and murder. But what criminal charges would be available if the prosecution must restrict its attention to the defendant's conduct in choosing to get drunk? At present, such behavior usually is not in itself a crime. Should it be? A German statute creates a separate offense applicable to any person who commits a wrongful act after intentionally or negligently getting intoxicated. Although the act of getting drunk must be committed intentionally or negligently, no additional culpability is required with respect to the subsequent wrongful act that brings the statute into play. See George Fletcher, Rethinking Criminal Law 846-848 (1978). Is this kind of law preferable to the American approach? And if so, what punishment would be appropriate for the crime of intentionally or negligently getting drunk?

8. *Voluntary intoxication and insanity.* Is evidence of voluntary intoxication admissible for any purpose other than to refute the existence of the mens rea of the charged offense? Severe intoxication, even if voluntary, might

produce a state in which culpability in the broader sense—the ability to under-stand the consequences of one's actions or to meaningfully choose to engage in them—is entirely absent. The common-law rule, still widely in effect, allows voluntary intoxication to be a defense in such circumstances only when it produces a permanent condition sufficient to meet the test for legal insanity—that is, a substantial incapacity either to appreciate the criminality of the actor's conduct or to conform to the law. See Model Penal Code §2.08. As explained in State v. Booth, 169 N.W.2d 869, 873 (Iowa 1969):

> Voluntary temporary intoxication does not excuse one for the criminal con-sequences of his conduct. . . . A distinction is made when prolonged extensive use of alcohol damages the brain and "settled or established" insanity results therefrom. This is treated the same as insanity from any other cause. However, a temporary condition caused by voluntary intoxication . . . does not excuse one from responsibility for his conduct.

Is this rule so restrictive because it is unlikely that someone might become temporarily insane through intoxication? Or because it would be too difficult to detect false assertions of such a condition? Why should a defendant's choice to become drunk deprive him of an insanity defense, if his assertion of temporary insanity is factually true?

b. Involuntary Intoxication

Should evidence of intoxication be treated differently if the defendant did not choose to become intoxicated, but instead became drunk by accident or through the stratagem of another? The common-law approach is marginally more generous to defendants asserting a defense of involuntary intoxication, in that it allows the defendant to assert a defense of temporary legal insanity. But if a defendant is involuntarily impaired to a degree insufficient to meet the test for legal insanity, no defense is available (beyond the limited mens rea defense that we explored above in the context of voluntary intoxication). As the Commentaries to the Model Penal Code section on insanity explain (at 363): "The actor whose personality is altered by intoxication to a lesser degree [than legal insanity] is treated like others who may have difficulty in conform-ing to the law and yet are held responsible for violation." Consider the con-trasting views of two English courts on the availability of a defense for involuntary intoxication.

REGINA v. KINGSTON

Court of Appeal, Criminal Division
[1993] 4 All E.R. 373, rev'd, *House of Lords [1994] 3 All E.R. 353*

LORD TAYLOR OF GOSFORTH, C.J. [for the Court of Appeal]: [In order to blackmail defendant, Penn lured a 15-year-old boy to his (Penn's) flat and then invited defendant over to abuse the boy sexually. Penn photographed and audiotaped defendant committing the act. At trial for indecent assault, defendant said he could not remember drinking anything before going to the bedroom, but stated that he sometimes drank coffee at Penn's flat. In addition, defendant could be heard to say on the tape "I don't know why, am I falling asleep?" and "Have you put something in my coffee?"

[At trial, the judge instructed the jury it should acquit the defendant only if it found that because of the drug he did not intend to commit an indecent assault upon the boy, but so long as he did have that intent, it was irrelevant that he had been drugged, because "a drugged intent is still an intent." The jury convicted.

[Defendant's counsel argued on appeal that "an accused person may be entitled to be acquitted if there is a possibility that although his act was intentional, the intent itself arose out of circumstances for which he bears no blame." After noting that there was little authority for this proposition, the court turned to first principles:]

[T]he purpose of the criminal law is to inhibit, by proscription and by penal sanction, anti-social acts which individuals may otherwise commit. . . . Having paedophiliac inclinations and desires is not proscribed; putting them into practice is. If the sole reason why the threshold between the two has been crossed is or may have been that the inhibition which the law requires has been removed by the clandestine act of a third party, the purposes of the criminal law are not served by nevertheless holding that the person performing the act is guilty of an offence. . . . If therefore drink or drug, surreptitiously administered, causes a person to lose his self-control and for that reason to form an intent which he would not otherwise have formed, . . . the law should exculpate him because the operative fault is not his. [I]nvoluntary intoxication negatives the mens rea. . . .

By . . . summing up as he did, the judge effectively withdrew the issue from the jury. In our judgment, that amounted to a material misdirection. . . . [Conviction set aside and appellant discharged.]

LORD MUSTILL [for the House of Lords]: [W]e are concerned here with a case of disinhibition. The drug is not alleged to have created the desire to which the respondent gave way, but rather to have enabled it to be released.

. . . The decision [below] was explicitly founded on [the] general principle . . . that if blame is absent the necessary mens rea must also be absent. My Lords, with every respect I must [reject the] argument which treats the absence of moral fault on the part of the appellant as sufficient in itself to negative the necessary mental element of the offence. . . .

To recognize a new defense of this type would be a bold step. . . . So one must turn to consider just what defence is now to be created. The judgment under appeal implies [several] characteristics.

1. The defence applies to all offences, except perhaps to absolute [strict liability] offences. It therefore differs from other defences such as provocation and diminished responsibility.

2. The defence is a complete answer to a criminal charge. If not rebutted it leads to an outright acquittal, and unlike provocation and diminished

responsibility leaves no room for conviction and punishment for a lesser offence. The underlying assumption must be that the defendant is entirely free from culpability. . . .

5. The defence is subjective in nature. Whereas provocation and self-defence are judged by the reactions of the reasonable person in the situation of the defendant, here the only question is whether this particular defendant's inhibitions were overcome by the effect of the drug. The more susceptible the defendant to the kind of temptation presented, the easier the defence is to establish.

[T]he defence appears to run into difficulties at every turn. . . . Before the jury could form an opinion on whether the drug might have turned the scale witnesses would have to give a picture of the defendant's personality and susceptibilities, for without it the crucial effect of the drug could not be assessed; pharmacologists would be required to describe the potentially dis-inhibiting effect of a range of drugs whose identity would, if the present case is anything to go by, be unknown; psychologists and psychiatrists would express opinions, not on the matters of psychopathology familiar to those working within the framework of the Mental Health Acts but on altogether more elusive concepts. No doubt as time passed those concerned could work out techniques to deal with these questions. Much more significant would be the opportunities for a spurious defence. Even in the field of road traffic the "spiked" drink as a special reason for not disqualifying from driving is a regular feature. Transferring this to the entire range of criminal offences is a disturbing prospect. The defendant would only have to assert, and support by the evidence of well-wishers, that he was not the sort of person to have done this kind of thing, and to suggest an occasion when by some means a drug might have been administered to him for the jury to be sent straight to the question of a possible disinhibition. The judge would direct the jurors that if they felt any legitimate doubt on the matter—and by its nature the defence would be one which the prosecution would often have no means to rebut—they must acquit outright. . . .

My Lords, the fact that a new doctrine may require adjustment of existing principles to accommodate it, and may require those involved in criminal trials to learn new techniques, is not of course a ground for refusing to adopt it, if that is what the interests of justice require. Here, however, justice makes no such demands, for the interplay between the wrong done to the victim, the individual characteristics and frailties of the defendant, and the pharmacological effects of whatever drug may be potentially involved can be far better recognised by a tailored choice from the continuum of sentences available to the judge than by the application of a single Yea-or-Nay jury decision. [Court of Appeal reversed.]

NOTES

1. Problems of culpability or proof? The House of Lords offered two different grounds for rejecting the defense of involuntary intoxication—that involuntary "disinhibition" does not negate mens rea because an intoxicated defendant still possesses the intent to perform the criminal act, and that such a defense would create insurmountable evidentiary problems. Is the court right that the defendant's preexisting illegal desires require that his actions be viewed as voluntary to some degree? Or was the lower court right that in such cases the purposes of the criminal law are not served by punishment? If no purposes of punishment are served, are problems of proof nonetheless sufficient reason to deny a defense?

2. *Pushing the boundaries of intoxication.* While alcohol and illegal drugs are the most common intoxicating substances, defendants have also asserted defenses of involuntary intoxication from taking prescription medication. In People v. Garcia, 113 P.3d 775 (Colo. 2005), the defendant had assaulted his wife a few days after she asked for a divorce; the court held that he was entitled to present a defense of involuntary intoxication based on insulin shock from his own injection of a large dose of insulin for his diabetic condition. In Cobb v. State, 884 So. 2d 437 (Fla. App. 2004), a defendant who shot her former lover was not allowed to present evidence of involuntary intoxication based on the effects of the antidepressants Xanax and Paxil, because she had knowingly taken higher-than-prescribed doses. For an account of a defendant's unsuccessful attempt to assert involuntary intoxication—based on severe dehydration while camping in the desert—as a defense to charges of murder after he stabbed a fellow camper to death, see Shawn Marie Boyne & Gary C. Mitchell, Death in the Desert: A New Look at the Involuntary Intoxication Defense in New Mexico, 32 N.M. L. Rev. 243 (2002). The preference of these defendants to claim involuntary intoxication rather than insanity may reflect the fact that involuntary intoxication is the more complete defense. As noted in the *Garcia* case, supra (113 P.3d at 783):

> While, in theory, both an involuntarily intoxicated person and a legally insane person are absolved of responsibility for all crimes, the consequence to an accused who successfully asserts involuntary intoxication is dramatically different. [An] accused found to be legally insane . . . is committed to the custody of the Department of Human Services until determined eligible for release. An accused who successfully asserts the defense of involuntary intoxication is held morally blameless, and is at once returned to society as a free person.

Is there a legitimate basis for this difference in the consequences of the two defenses? If a defendant's intoxication were truly involuntary, why should he be held in confinement after his acquittal?

3. *Recent trends.* For a critique of legal trends that have been increasingly inhospitable to the defenses of both voluntary and involuntary intoxication, see Meghan Paulk Ingle, Law on the Rocks: The Intoxication Defenses Are Being Eighty-Sixed, 55 Vand. L. Rev. 607, 631 (2002), arguing that narrowing legal standards and jury hostility to intoxication defenses have rendered them "essentially unavailable."

4. Mental Disorder

a. The Defense of Legal Insanity

INTRODUCTORY NOTES

Mental incapacity has legal significance in a variety of settings; for example, it may render a contract unenforceable or a will void. In the criminal process, mental incapacity can be a defense to a criminal charge, or it can preclude the guilty plea, trial, sentencing, or execution of a defendant. Our principal focus is on the appropriate contours of the insanity defense: What forms of mental incapacity should provide a complete defense to criminal responsibility? Note how the insanity defense differs from the excuses we have considered thus far: While the basis for excuses such as duress is that the actor has shown herself no different from the rest of us, the basis for the insanity excuse is that she has shown herself *very* different from the rest of us. Before wrestling with the complexities of competing legal standards for insanity, consider the following accounts of two seriously mentally ill defendants, both of whom were deemed competent to stand trial and whose defenses of insanity were rejected by juries.

1. A tale of two insanity defenses.

(a) Steven Green (facts reported in State v. Green, 643 S.W.2d 902 (Tenn. 1982)). Steven Green was 18 years old when he shot and killed a Chattanooga police officer with the officer's own revolver in a city park where the homeless Green was apparently residing. A bizarre note left on the victim's body led the police to an FBI agent, who reported that Green had walked into the FBI building a few weeks before the murder complaining of "voices" that were "directing" him. In response, the agent suggested to Green that he seek mental health assistance at a city hospital, advice that Green did not follow.

Green's mental illness had become apparent early in his life. He first received psychiatric treatment at the age of seven, when he was diagnosed with paranoia and treated for more than two years. At age 12, Green attacked his mother with a knife and again received short-term psychiatric treatment. As a teenager, Green reported hearing voices and exhibited increasingly bizarre behavior, which led to his hospitalization for more than a month, until his family's insurance coverage ran out. He continued to receive out-patient care, but because the medications he received made him feel like a "zombie," he stopped taking them and refused to return to the out-patient clinic. Although Green managed to graduate from high school and enlisted in the Navy, he was soon thereafter discharged for failure to adapt to regulations. Continuing to hear voices, he attacked his brother with a knife and ran away from his parents' home in New York City to Tennessee, where he stayed first with an uncle and then with an aunt; both relatives ejected him from their homes because of his bizarre and potentially dangerous behavior. His father traveled to Tennessee and tried to persuade Green to return home to New York, but Green refused, so his father left him in Memphis with some money and a new pair of shoes. Two months later, Green was arrested for murder. On the day Officer Wilcox was killed, Green was found carrying what was apparently his only possession at that time, a pair of shiny black shoes.

Although initially found incompetent to stand trial and committed to a mental health facility, Green's ability to think coherently gradually improved in response to intensive drug therapy, and he was found competent to stand trial. At trial, mental health experts testified that they and all the other professional staff members who had contact with Green after his arrest agreed unanimously that he was insane at the time the offense. The prosecution offered no experts in rebuttal, but instead presented police officers who had contact with Green at around the time of the offense; they testified that Green appeared "normal" to them. The jury rejected Green's insanity defense and convicted him of first-degree murder.

(b) Andrea Yates (facts reported in Yates v. State, 171 S.W.3d 215 (Tex. App. 2005)). Andrea Yates drowned her five children, ranging in age from seven months to seven years, in a bathtub in an attempt, she said, to save them from Satan. After giving birth to three children in three-and-a-half years, Yates moved with her family into a converted bus in a trailer park in the Houston area. When she told her husband that she felt depressed and overwhelmed, he suggested that she talk to her mother and a friend. After the birth of her fourth child a year later, Yates suffered from severe depression and tried to commit suicide. She was admitted to the psychiatric unit of a hospital for a week and continued to see a psychiatrist after her release. A month later, her husband found her holding a knife to her own throat in the bathroom, and she was again hospitalized. During this hospitalization, Yates told a psychologist that she had been having visions and hearing voices since the birth of her first child. Her treating psychiatrist ranked Yates as one of the five sickest patients he had ever seen at the time of this second hospitalization, and he warned both Yates and her husband that she had a high risk of another psychotic episode if she had another baby.

Fifteen months later, Yates gave birth to her fifth child. A few months after that, Yates's father died, and she began to suffer from depression again. She was again hospitalized. During this hospitalization, Yates was placed on suicide watch and was observed as being catatonic or nearly catatonic and possibly delusional. Two weeks later, Yates was discharged at her own and her husband's request, though she continued to receive out-patient care. The psychiatrist who discharged her recommended that someone stay with her at all times and that she not be left alone with her children. Yates's mother-in-law came to help with the children, and reported that Yates was almost catatonic, stared into space, scratched her head until she created bald spots, and did not eat. Three weeks later, Yates was hospitalized again but discharged after ten days, refusing her doctor's recommendation that she receive electroconvulsive therapy. During the next month, Yates did not report any suicidal or psychotic thoughts, and her psychiatrist decided to taper her off of

Haldol, the powerful antipsychotic drug that had been previously prescribed, though she remained on other antidepressant medication. Five weeks after her most recent hospital discharge, Yates drowned her children.

At trial, 12 mental health professionals testified regarding Yates's mental state. All agreed that she was psychotic at the time of her offense, and only one testified that Yates's mental state did not meet the state's insanity standard. The jury nonetheless rejected her insanity defense and found her guilty of capital murder, though she was sentenced to life imprisonment instead of death.

(c) *The sequels.* Despite the rejection of their insanity defenses by their trial juries, Green and Yates each prevailed in different ways on appeal. The appellate court reversed Green's conviction on the ground that the prosecution had failed to carry its burden of disproving insanity, as was then (but no longer is) required by Tennessee law. The appellate court reversed Yates's conviction on the ground that the lone expert who testified against her insanity plea had suggested that Yates fabricated her defense after watching a Law & Order television episode about a woman who drowned her children and was found to be insane; in fact, no such episode existed. On retrial before a new jury in 2006, Yates was found not guilty by reason of insanity.

(d) *Thoughts and questions.* The *Yates* and *Green* cases, though not "typical" (perhaps no insanity case is), offer some insight into the dynamics of criminal justice in insanity- defense cases. Before considering the details of legal doctrine, we can reflect on several broader issues:

First, it should be noted that Green's and Yates's appellate victories are as rare as their initial trial defeats are common: The insanity defense is rarely asserted and even more rarely accepted. See infra page 981. Why are juries so reluctant to accept an insanity plea, and is that reluctance appropriate or misplaced? Should our legal system run the risk of imposing criminal punishment on those who are as impaired as Green and Yates undeniably were?

Next, note that both Green and Yates were able to offer extensive expert testimony in support of their insanity pleas. Should a successful defense require so much medical (as opposed to lay) testimony? Does the necessity of producing expert witnesses unduly limit the defense to defendants wealthy enough to hire such experts (or lucky enough to have court appointed lawyers who have the inclination and resources to do so)? Are juries right to approach such expert testimony with great skepticism? Or should our rules encourage juries to give more deference to the weight of expert opinion?

Finally, consider how easily (at least in hindsight) we can identify so many missed opportunities to prevent the tragic deaths that occurred: Steven Green could have received more consistent mental health treatment throughout his childhood; that he did not is largely explained simply by the fact that his own family lacked adequate health insurance coverage. Green's homelessness could have been addressed by his family, or by local charities, or by the City of Chattanooga. The FBI agent to whom Green turned could have done something to assure that he received treatment. Andrea Yates could have received more aggressive treatment from the many mental health professionals who saw her and recognized the seriousness of her illness. Or she could have gotten more help from family members. Perhaps she and her husband should have heeded the warning about not having more children or been offered counseling on how to avoid future pregnancies.

Do these missed opportunities suggest that it is unjust to hold people like Green and Yates responsible for their criminal acts, given how clear their mental illness was to all around them? Or does the proper response lie in the provision of better social services rather than in changes within the criminal justice system? After all, non-insane offenders who have suffered severe abuse are routinely held accountable for their criminal acts. Should these offenders have grounds to assert a defense of nonresponsibility? See infra pages 1026-1031 (considering the defense of "rotten social background").

2. *Terminology defined.* In considering the relevance of mental incapacity in the criminal process, it is helpful to distinguish among three distinct concepts: mental illness, insanity, and incompetence. "Mental illness" is a medical rather than a legal term, used by clinicians to refer to a disorder recognized by the therapeutic community for purposes of diagnosis and treatment. In contrast, "insanity" is a legal term that refers to a mental state, existing at the time of a criminal offense, that is considered sufficient to preclude criminal responsibility. "Incompetence" is a legal term that refers to a person's mental state at the time of a legal proceeding. A person who lacks sufficient mental capacity to understand or participate in the relevant legal proceeding is deemed incompetent (to stand trial, or enter a guilty plea, or be sentenced, or even to be executed). Because the medical category of mental illness is far broader than the legal categories of insanity or incompetence, it is possible and indeed common for people suffering from mental illness to be held neither insane nor incompetent. Because the determinations of insanity and incompetence refer to different time periods (time of offense vs. time of legal proceeding), and because the legal standards for insanity and incompetence are different, it is possible that a person could be deemed insane and yet competent, or conversely, sane and yet incompetent to stand trial or participate in other legal proceedings. For probing analysis of the distinct legal doctrines relating to mental disorder at various stages of the criminal process (and in related processes that lead to confinement for purposes of social protection), see Stephen J. Morse, Mental Disorder and Criminal Law, 101 J. Crim. L. & Criminology 885 (2011).

3. *Competence to stand trial.* Although precise wording varies across jurisdictions, Model Penal Code §4.04 states the generally accepted test of competence to be tried and sentenced: "No person who as a result of mental disease or defect lacks capacity to understand the proceedings against him or to assist in his own defense shall be tried, convicted or sentenced for the commission of an offense so long as such incapacity endures." In Dusky v. United States, 362 U.S. 402 (1960), the Court stated: "[T]he test must be whether [the defendant] has sufficient present ability to consult with his lawyer with a reasonable

degree of rational understanding—and whether he has a rational as well as factual understanding of the proceedings against him." This focus on "rational" and "factual" understanding, however, typically neglects mood disorders and certain forms of organic brain damage that can "unreasonably [interfere] with decision-relevant emotional perception, processing, and expression." Terry A. Maroney, Emotional Competence, "Rational Understanding," and the Criminal Defendant, 43 Am. Crim. L. Rev. 1375, 1381 (2006).

May defendants be forcibly medicated in order to render them competent to stand trial? The Supreme Court held in Sell v. United States, 539 U.S. 166 (2003), that the Constitution sometimes permits forced medication to render a defendant competent to stand trial, but suggested that those instances may well be "rare" in light of the constitutional right to refuse medical treatment in the absence of unusual circumstances. To uphold such involuntary treatment, a court must find that (1) the government's interest in trying the defendant for the crime at issue is important; (2) forced medication is substantially likely to render the defendant competent and substantially unlikely to have side effects that will interfere with her ability to assist defense counsel; (3) alternative, less intrusive treatments are unlikely to achieve substantially the same results; and (4) the treatment is medically appropriate (i.e., in the defendant's best medical interest in light of her condition).

Is a finding of incompetence to stand trial warranted when a defendant suffers from memory impairment? If the defendant is suffering from total amnesia concerning the alleged crime but is otherwise in full command of her faculties, most courts hold that the defendant is competent to stand trial. See State v. Wynn, 490 A.2d 605 (Del. Super. 1985); People v. Francobandera, 310 N.E.2d 292, 295 (N.Y. 1974). What is the basis for this view? Doesn't an inability to recall the events charged seriously impede a defendant's ability to mount a defense? Compare State v. McClendon, 419 P.2d 69 (Ariz. 1966) (improper to hold trial if continuance might enable amnesiac to recover); See also People v. Palmer, 9 P.3d 1156 (Colo. App. 2000) (careful inquiry required on the issue).

4. Execution. In Ford v. Wainwright, 477 U.S. 399 (1986), the Supreme Court held that the Eighth Amendment's proscription of "cruel and unusual punishment" bars execution of the insane, but the Court offered no definition of what constitutes insanity for purposes of the Eighth Amendment requirement. Nor did the Court pinpoint the specific reasons *why* execution of the "insane" would be cruel and unusual. Justice Marshall, speaking for five members of the Court, concluded:

> Unanimity of rationale . . . we do not find. "But whatever the reason of the law is, it is plain the law is so." Hawles, [Remarks on the Trial of Mr. Charles Bateman, [1685] 11 HOW. St. Tr. *477 (1816)]. We know of virtually no authority condoning the execution of the insane at English common law. . . . And the intuition that such an execution simply offends humanity is evidently shared across this Nation. Faced with such widespread evidence of a

restriction upon sovereign power, this Court is compelled to conclude that the Eighth Amendment prohibits a State from carrying out a sentence of death upon a prisoner who is insane. Whether its aim be to protect the condemned from fear and pain without comfort of understanding, or to protect the dignity of society itself from the barbarity of exacting mindless vengeance, the restriction finds enforcement in the Eighth Amendment.

Justice Powell, in a concurring opinion, commented as follows:

> [S]ome authorities contended that the prohibition against executing the insane was justified as a way of preserving the defendant's ability to make arguments on his own behalf. Other authorities suggest, however, that the prohibition derives from more straightforward humanitarian concerns. . . .
>
> The first of these justifications has slight merit today. Modern practice provides far more extensive review of convictions and sentences than did the common law, including not only direct appeal but ordinarily both state and federal collateral review. . . . It is thus unlikely indeed that a defendant today could go to his death with knowledge of undiscovered trial error that might set him free. . . .
>
> The more general concern of the common law—that executions of the insane are simply cruel—retains its vitality. It is as true today as when Coke lived that most men and women value the opportunity to prepare, mentally and spiritually, for their death. Moreover, today as at common law, one of the death penalty's critical justifications, its retributive force, depends on the defendant's awareness of the penalty's existence and purpose. . . . For precisely these reasons, Florida requires the Governor to stay executions of those who "d[o] not have the mental capacity to understand the nature of the death penalty and why it was imposed" on them. Fla. Stat. §922.07 (1985). A number of States have more rigorous standards, but none disputes the need to require that those who are executed know the fact of their impending execution and the reason for it.
>
> Such a standard appropriately defines the kind of mental deficiency that should trigger the Eighth Amendment prohibition.

Most jurisdictions now define insanity for purposes of execution along the lines endorsed by Justice Powell in *Ford*. See, e.g., Ark. Code Ann. §16-90-506(d) (2011). A few states have adopted stricter tests. The Washington and South Carolina Supreme Courts have declared that sanity for purposes of execution requires that the prisoner not only understand the nature of the death penalty and why it is being imposed, but also have the ability to communicate rationally with defense counsel. See Singleton v. State, 437 S.E.2d 53 (S.C. 1993); State v. Harris, 789 P.2d 60, 64-65 (Wash. 1990).

At least one court has held that the state may not subject an insane death-row prisoner to antipsychotic medication, against his will, in order to restore his sanity so that he may be executed. See State v. Perry, 610 So. 2d 746 (La. 1992). The problem is a recurrent one, because antipsychotic drugs are an increasingly popular means of treating mental disorder, and up to 70 percent of death-row inmates are estimated to suffer some form of mental illness. See Robert Johnson, Death Work 50 (1990). Does the *Perry* approach mean that the incompetent prisoner (or someone acting on his behalf) must choose between continued insanity and death by execution? Is there any way to escape this dilemma? See Kristen Wenstrup Crosby, Comment, *State v. Perry*, 77 Minn. L. Rev. 1193 (1993).

The Supreme Court held in Atkins v. Virginia, 536 U.S. 304 (2002), that the Eighth Amendment forbids the execution of persons with mental retardation, even if they are not "insane" under the *Ford* standard. See supra page 548. As in *Ford*, the Court discerned a societal consensus (though not unanimity) against the execution of those with mental retardation. But whereas the *Ford* Court had based the exemption from execution on the condemned inmate's mental state at the time of execution, the *Atkins* Court explained that mental retardation precludes execution because it undermines the defendant's culpability for the charged crime and places such defendants at a special risk of wrongful execution. Id. at 319-321.

NOTES ON ADMINISTERING THE INSANITY DEFENSE

1. Who may raise the defense? In most jurisdictions the decision to raise the insanity issue must be left entirely within the defendant's control. Courts have stressed that a properly counseled defendant may prefer to be found guilty rather than not guilty by reason of insanity, because the latter verdict can lead to longer confinement, more intrusive treatment, or greater stigma. See, e.g., Frendak v. United States, 408 A.2d 364 (D.C. App. 1979). And a competent defendant may decline to plead insanity even against the advice of his attorney. See, e.g., Commonwealth v. Federici, 696 N.E.2d 111 (Mass. 1998). Compare Hughes v. State, 2011 Ark. LEXIS 134 (Apr. 7, 2011). In a prosecution for making terroristic threats, the defendant pled not guilty, but the state insisted on a bench trial and introduced evidence that he was suffering from a mental disease at the time of the offense. The judge found the defendant not guilty by reason of insanity, and ordered him committed; the Arkansas Supreme Court then dismissed his appeal on the ground that state statutes granted an appeal in a criminal case only when the defendant had been "convicted." And see Bratty v. Attorney-General, [1963] A.C. 386, 411, where Lord Denning, speaking of the English practice, said: "The old notion that only the defence can raise a defence of insanity is now gone. The prosecution are entitled to raise it and it is their duty to do so rather than allow a dangerous person to be at large."

2. Disposition after acquittal. How should the law deal with defendants who have been   acquitted on grounds of legal insanity? As they have been found not guilty, they cannot be blamed for their actions. On the other hand, those actions have done harm and the public demands protection against any repetition. Consider the following:

(a) Civil commitment. One approach to protecting the public while also respecting the person's innocence is to rely on the processes for civil commitment. In these processes, a judge, after a hearing, decides whether to commit a

person indefinitely to a mental institution because he is suffering from a mental disability that makes him a danger to himself or others. In states that adopt this approach, insanity acquittees may be committed only in compliance with the procedural and substantive standards for any mentally disturbed person in the community. But there are constitutional restrictions on civil commitment. For example, the standard of proof is high—both mental illness and dangerousness must be proven by clear and convincing evidence. Addington v. Texas, 441 U.S. 418 (1979). That high threshold in civil commitment serves to reduce the risk of confining members of the public who are simply idiosyncratic. But is that concern equally applicable to those who have been shown to be irresponsible authors of criminal acts? Many states have thought not and have enacted special commitment procedures for insanity acquittees in which the crucial factual findings (mental illness and dangerousness) can be made by a preponderance of the evidence. See Jan Brakel, After the Verdict: Dispositional Decisions Regarding Criminal Defendants Acquitted by Reason of Insanity, 37 DePaul L. Rev. 181 (1988).

Other jurisdictions follow a different approach: Commitment is automatic and mandatory for all insanity acquittees. In defense of this approach, it has been observed that it "not only provides the public with the maximum immediate protection, but may also work to the advantage of mentally diseased or defective defendants by making the defense of irresponsibility more acceptable to the public and to the jury." Model Penal Code and Commentaries, Comment to §4.08 at 256 (1985). But is a finding that the defendant was insane at the time of the offense sufficiently probative of present mental illness and dangerousness to justify confinement?

In Jones v. United States, 463 U.S. 354 (1983), the Supreme Court upheld the constitutionality of mandatory commitment. The court asserted as a matter of common sense that the mental disorder and dangerousness of an insanity acquittee are likely to continue through to the time of trial and thereafter. Do you agree? Even if a presumption of continuing insanity is plausible, what is the justification for making that presumption in effect irrebuttable, by requiring automatic commitment without any hearing on the present mental disorder and dangerousness of the defendant? The Court in *Jones* also noted that the committed person was given an opportunity to demonstrate his recovery at a hearing within 50 days of commitment. Does this allay the reservations about the justification for the initial commitment? One court noted "the practical difficulties of requiring a mental patient to overcome the effects of his confinement, his closed environment, his possible incompetence and the debilitating effects of drugs or other treatment. . . ." Fasulo v. Arafeh, 378 A.2d 553, 557 (Conn. 1997). These practical difficulties often mean that the initial commitment becomes an indefinite one.

(b) Duration of confinement. Regardless of the procedure used to support an initial commitment, how long may the person committed be held? Under regular civil commitment statutes, the medical facility may release the patient when satisfied he has recovered and is no longer dangerous to himself or

others. Provisions for commitment of insanity acquittees, however, require that the appropriate finding be made by a judge, usually with the burden on the inmate to prove that he meets the conditions for release. As a result, the person committed after winning acquittal may in practice be held indefinitely, sometimes for his entire life. Should extended commitment of this sort be permissible even when the crime charged was a minor property offense punishable by no more than a short prison term? In *Jones*, supra, the Supreme Court held that an insanity acquittee subjected to automatic commitment could be held indefinitely, even when the period he had spent in confinement exceeded the maximum sentence authorized for the underlying offense. The Court reasoned that dangerousness warranting indefinite commitment may be established by proof of a nonviolent act against property, in that case, shoplifting. Do you agree? Is there a case for requiring release at the maximum term for the offense of which the person was acquitted, unless the state can then meet the ordinary criteria for civil commitment by establishing by clear and convincing evidence that the inmate continues to be mentally ill and a danger to himself or others? This is the law in roughly a dozen states. See, e.g., In Re Commitment of W.K., 731 A.2d 482 (N.J. 1999); Brakel, supra, at 196.

(c) Guilty but mentally ill. One major concern in states using standard civil commitment is that a committed insanity acquittee may be released too soon. In Michigan, an acquittee committed under the ordinary civil commitment laws was released, as the law required, upon a medical determination that he was no longer mentally ill and dangerous. His recovery, however, was dependent upon his continuing to take his prescribed medicine, which he failed to do, resulting in a crime spree that shocked the community. This led to the enactment in Michigan of the first "Guilty but Mentally Ill" statute. See Sharon M. Brown & Nicholas J. Wittner, Criminal Law (1978 Annual Survey of Michigan Law), 25 Wayne L. Rev. 335 (1978). This statute allowed the jury a third option—it could find the defendant guilty, not guilty by reason of insanity, or guilty but mentally ill at the time of the offense. If the jury returns the last mentioned verdict, the court retains the same sentencing authority it has in cases of guilty verdicts, but if the court sentences the defendant to prison, he is to be given treatment "as is psychiatrically indicated for his mental illness." Such statutes are now found in about a dozen states, almost always as an addition to, rather than a replacement for, the traditional insanity defense. What is the practical effect of such laws? They do establish a cap on how long the defendant can be held without a fresh judicial determination of dangerousness and mental disorder. But in practice, are they likely to make an insanity acquittal less likely and thereby make conviction of morally innocent persons more likely? For a critique, see Christopher Slobogin, The Guilty but Mentally Ill Verdict: An Idea Whose Time Should Not Have Come, 53 Geo. Wash. L. Rev. 494 (1985).

The experiment with "Guilty but Mentally Ill" statutes also suggests a broader problem—the pervasive perception that public safety considerations make some dilution of the insanity defense a practical necessity. Of course, many would dispute this view. But if public opinion insists on some such dilution, what is the best way to achieve it? Is it preferable to dilute the insanity defense in the way that the "Guilty but Mentally Ill" laws do (by encouraging juries not to vote an insanity acquittal) or in the way that *Jones*, supra, does (by depriving insanity acquittees of the full benefits of an ordinary acquittal)? See Stephen J. Schulhofer, Two Systems of Social Protection, 7 J. Contemp. Legal Issues 69 (1996); Paul H. Robinson, Forward: The Criminal-Civil Distinction and Dangerous Blameless Offenders, 83 J. Crim. L. & Criminology 693 (1993).

3. *Instructing the jury on the consequences of an insanity acquittal.* In jurisdictions that provide for mandatory commitment following an insanity acquittal, defendants have pressed to have the jury informed of that fact because the jury may otherwise assume that an insanity acquittal will lead to the release of a dangerous, mentally unstable individual. Yet most courts have held that the jury should not be instructed on the procedures that follow an insanity verdict, on the ground that what will happen to the defendant is not relevant to whether the defendant met the test of legal insanity. See, e.g., People v. Goad, 364 N.W.2d 584 (Mich. 1984). For federal prosecutions, the Supreme Court has held that juries should not be informed of the mandatory commitment provisions applicable under federal law. Shannon v. United States, 512 U.S. 573 (1994). The Court said that "the principle that juries are not to consider the consequences of their verdicts is a reflection of the basic division of labor in our legal system between judge [as sentencer] and jury [as factfinder]"; the Court also noted that "[even if] some jurors will harbor the mistaken belief that defendants found [not guilty by reason of insanity] will be released into society immediately . . . [there is] no reason to depart from 'the almost invariable assumption of the law that jurors follow their instructions.'" However, a number of courts have taken a less formalistic view, holding that when commitment is mandatory, a jury should be informed that a defendant found not guilty by reason of insanity must be detained until she is no longer mentally ill and dangerous. See, e.g., Commonwealth v. Mutina, 323 N.E.2d 294, 301-302 (Mass. 1975) ("If jurors can be entrusted with responsibility for a defendant's life and liberty . . . they are entitled to know what protection they and their fellow citizens will have if they conscientiously apply the law to the evidence and arrive at a verdict of not guilty by reason of insanity.").

Question: If commitment is *not* mandatory, should the jury be informed of that fact?

4. *Burden of proof.* All jurisdictions create a presumption of legal sanity at the trial. The effect of this presumption is that, in the absence of evidence on the issue, the sanity of the accused is presumed for all legal purposes. American jurisdictions, however, differ on two issues: (1) How much evidence must be presented before the effect of the presumption disappears and the question of the defendant's insanity becomes an issue that must be established by the evidence? (2) Who bears the burden of persuasion, and how is that burden defined?

As to the first question, some states require only "some evidence" of legal insanity in order to eliminate the presumption of sanity, e.g., People v. Hill, 934 P.2d 821 (Colo. 1997). Others require more, usually that the evidence raise a reasonable doubt about the sanity of the accused, e.g., Jamezic v. State, 723 So. 2d 355 (Ala. 1996). For discussion of this issue, see Abraham S. Goldstein, The Insanity Defense ch. 8 (1967); Julian Eule, The Presumption of Sanity: Bursting the Bubble, 25 UCLA L. Rev. 637 (1978).

As to the second question, once insanity becomes an issue, roughly a dozen states continue to adhere to what once was the majority rule requiring the prosecution to prove the sanity of the defendant beyond a reasonable doubt. See Commonwealth v. Keita, 712 N.E.2d 65, 73 (Mass. 1999), where the court supported this rule on the ground that, "[t]here is no theoretical justification for maintaining a lower standard for the proof of sanity than for the proof of guilt." This approach was widely abandoned in the aftermath of the *Hinckley* verdict, see pages 980-982 infra. About three-quarters of the states now place the burden of proof of insanity on the defense. *Keita*, supra at 71. For the federal courts, the question is governed by 18 U.S.C. §17(b) (2011): "The defendant has the burden of proving the defense of insanity by clear and convincing evidence."

i. Competing Formulations

M'NAGHTEN'S CASE

House of Lords
10 Cl. & F. 200, 8 Eng. Rep. 718 (1843)

[Defendant was indicted for the murder of Edward Drummond, secretary to the prime minister, Sir Robert Peel. Apparently M'Naghten had mistaken Drummond for Peel and had shot Drummond by mistake. Upon his arrest he told police that he had come to London to murder the prime minister because "[t]he tories in my city follow and persecute me wherever I go, and have entirely destroyed my peace of mind. [T]hey do everything in their power to harass and persecute me; in fact they wish to murder me." The defense introduced extensive expert and lay testimony indicating that M'Naghten was obsessed with delusions and suffered from acute insanity.[a] The presiding judge, Lord Chief Justice Tindal, in his charge to the jury stated:

> The question to be determined is whether at the time the act in question was committed, the prisoner had or had not the use of his understanding, so as to know that he was doing a wrong or wicked act. If the jurors should be of opinion that the prisoner was not sensible, at the time he committed it, that he was violating the laws both of God and man, then he would be entitled to a

---

a. At the time of his arrest, M'Naghten was found in possession of £750, and as a result he "probably had the best-financed defense in the history of the Old Bailey." He had the assistance of "four of the most able barristers in Britain [and] nine prominent medical experts." No expert witnesses appeared for the prosecution. See Richard Moran, Knowing Right from Wrong 90 (1981), which provides a fascinating, detailed account of *M'Naghten's Case.*—EDS.

verdict in his favour: but if, on the contrary, they were of opinion that when he committed the act he was in a sound state of mind, then their verdict must be against him.

[The jury returned a verdict of "not guilty, on the ground of insanity." The verdict attracted great public attention and aroused considerable alarm. The press suggested that the insanity defense left madmen free to kill with impunity. Queen Victoria was particularly concerned: She herself had been the object of three recent assassination attempts, and one of her attackers had also benefited from an insanity acquittal. Both the *M'Naghten* verdict and the general problem of the insanity defense were debated in the House of Lords. As a result, the English judiciary (there were some 15 judges at the time) were invited to attend the House of Lords for the purpose of delivering answers to certain questions propounded to them. The famous *M'Naghten* Rule is found in the answer to the second and third questions delivered by Lord Chief Justice Tindal.]

Your Lordships are pleased to inquire of us, secondly, "What are the proper questions to be submitted to the jury, where a person alleged to be afflicted with insane delusion respecting one or more particular subjects or persons, is charged with the commission of a crime (murder, for example), and insanity is set up as a defence?" And, thirdly, "In what terms ought the question to be left to the jury as to the prisoner's state of mind at the time when the act was committed?" And as these two questions appear to us to be more conveniently answered together, we have to submit our opinion to be, that the jurors ought to be told in all cases that every man is to be presumed to be sane, and to possess a sufficient degree of reason to be responsible for his crimes, until the contrary be proved to their satisfaction; and that to establish a defence on the ground of insanity, it must be clearly proved that, at the time of the committing of the act, the party accused was labouring under such a defect of reason, from disease of the mind, as not to know the nature and quality of the act he was doing; or, if he did know it, that he did not know he was doing what was wrong. The mode of putting the latter part of the question to the jury on these occasions has generally been, whether the accused at the time of doing the act knew the difference between right and wrong: which mode, though rarely, if ever, leading to any mistake with the jury, is not, as we conceive, so accurate when put generally and in the abstract, as when put with reference to the party's knowledge of right and wrong in respect to the very act with which he is charged. If the question were to be put as to the knowledge of the accused solely and exclusively with reference to the law of the land, it might tend to confound the jury, by inducing them to believe that an actual knowledge of the law of the land was essential in order to lead to a conviction; whereas the law is administered upon the principle that every one must be taken conclusively to know it, without proof that he does know it. If the accused was conscious that the act was one which he ought not to do, and if the act was at the same time contrary to the law of the land, he is punishable; and the usual course therefore has been to leave the question to the jury, whether the party accused

· Knowledge of the law of land.

had a sufficient degree of reason to know that he was doing an act that was wrong: and this course we think is correct, accompanied with such observations and explanations as the circumstances of each particular case may require.

The King v. Porter, 55 Commw. L.R. 182, 186-188 (1933): [Presiding at trial, Justice Dixon explained the *M'Naghten* Rule in his charge to the jury:] There is a legal standard of disorder of mind which is sufficient to afford a ground of irresponsibility for crime, and a ground for your finding [a verdict of not guilty on the ground of insanity].

Before explaining what that standard actually is, I wish to draw your attention to some general considerations affecting the question of insanity in the criminal law in the hope that by so doing you may be helped to grasp what the law prescribes. The purpose of the law in punishing people is to prevent others from committing a like crime or crimes. Its prime purpose is to deter people from committing offences. It may be that there is an element of retribution in the criminal law, so that when people have committed offences the law considers that they merit punishment, but its prime purpose is to preserve society from the depredations of dangerous and vicious people. Now, it is perfectly useless for the law to attempt, by threatening punishment, to deter people from committing crimes if their mental condition is such that they cannot be in the least influenced by the possibility or probability of subsequent punishment; if they cannot understand what they are doing or cannot understand the ground upon which the law proceeds. The law is not directed, as medical science is, to curing mental infirmities. The criminal law is not directed, as the civil law of lunacy is, to the care and custody of people of weak mind. . . . This is quite a different thing from the question, what utility there is in the punishment of people who, at a moment, would commit acts which, if done when they were in sane minds, would be crimes. What is the utility of punishing people if they be beyond the control of the law for reasons of mental health? In considering that, it will not perhaps, if you have ever reflected upon the matter, have escaped your attention that a great number of people who come into a Criminal Court are abnormal. They would not be there if they were the normal type of average everyday people. Many of them are very peculiar in their dispositions and peculiarly tempered. That is markedly the case in sexual offences. Nevertheless, they are mentally quite able to appreciate what they are doing and quite able to appreciate the threatened punishment of the law and the wrongness of their acts, and they are held in check by the prospect of punishment. It would be very absurd if the law were to withdraw that check on the ground that they were somewhat different from their fellow creatures in mental make-up or texture at the very moment when the check is most needed. You will therefore see that the law, in laying down a standard of mental disorder sufficient to justify a jury in finding a prisoner not guilty on the ground of insanity at the moment of offence, is addressing itself to a somewhat difficult task. It is attempting to define what are the classes of people who should not be punished although they have done actual things which in others would amount to crime. . . . With that explanation I shall tell you what that standard is.

The first thing which I want you to notice is that you are only concerned with the condition of the mind at the time the act complained of was done. . . .

The next thing which I wish to emphasize is that his state of mind must have been one of disease, disorder or disturbance. Mere excitability of a normal man, passion, even stupidity, obtuseness, lack of self-control, and impulsiveness, are quite different things from what I have attempted to describe as a state of disease or disorder or mental disturbance arising from some infirmity, temporary or of long standing. If that existed it must then have been of such a character as to prevent him from knowing the physical nature of the act he was doing or of knowing that what he was doing was wrong. . . .

BLAKE v. UNITED STATES

United States Court of Appeals, 5th Circuit
407 F.2d 908 (1969)

BELL, Circuit Judge: . . . Blake was charged with bank robbery, 18 U.S.C.A. §2113. He was arrested on the day following the robbery and his trial began some six months later. The evidence that he committed the robbery was overwhelming; his principal defense was insanity at the time of the commission of the offense. He was convicted and . . . this appeal followed. . . . Appellant urges that the definition of insanity given the jury in charge for determining the issue of not guilty by reason of insanity was outmoded and prejudicial. . . .

[Blake came from a well-to-do family, completed two years of college, and briefly served on active duty with the Navy until he was given a medical discharge after suffering an epileptic seizure. The following year, he received his first course of electroshock therapy, and the year after that he was hospitalized for psychiatric treatment for the first time. Over the next 20 years, Blake continued to need extensive psychiatric care, including numerous periods of in-patient treatment and further electroshock therapy. During this time, he was a heavy drinker who also used stimulants and drugs. In his 20s, Blake managed to work for his father's construction company and marry and start a family. As his drinking and irrational behavior increased, however, he was no longer able to work, and in his 30s Blake was twice adjudged incompetent and hospitalized in mental institutions for periods of six months. He was divorced from his first wife, though he married three more times. In addition to his repeated hospitalizations, Blake served a brief prison sentence when his probation for shooting his second wife was revoked because of a further charge of aggravated assault. While in prison, Blake was hospitalized several times, and he was released from prison less than three months before the robbery for which he was convicted in the instant case. As the Fifth Circuit summarized: "To this point Blake's adult life had been one long round of confinement for mental problems and drinking when not confined."]

The facts of the robbery are rather bizarre. Blake committed the robbery within a matter of two or three hours after making an attempt to obtain a legal hearing before the United States District Court . . . apparently seeking a writ of habeas corpus to relieve him of certain state prison release restrictions which kept him from going to the Miami area. He was registered at a Jacksonville hotel. He obtained a hotel employee as a chauffeur for the purpose of driving him about town. He stopped by a bar en route to the robbery, had several drinks and told a waitress that he would be back later with a large sum of money. The waitress jokingly asked him if he planned to rob a bank. He said, "That's possible."

The bank which was robbed was one of two under consideration. Each was a member of the bank group which he claimed had mishandled a trust which was established either by or for him several years earlier. His quarrel with the bank over the trust had gone on for some years and was bitter. He did not case the bank. He selected the bank, ordered his driver to take him to the bank and wait, walked in during rush hour, demanded the money, obtained it, and walked out. He had no trouble getting away immediately to Tampa in the same car and with the same driver. He returned from Tampa to Jacksonville the very next day with an attorney to press his petition for the writ in the district court and was arrested for the robbery.

There was psychiatric testimony that Blake was suffering from the mental disease of schizophrenia, marked with psychotic episodes, and that his behavior on the occasion of the robbery indicated that appellant was in a psychotic episode. This was described as a form of severe mental illness. There was testimony that in such a period his actions would not be subject to his will. On the other hand, there was psychiatric testimony that he had a sociopathic personality and was not suffering from a mental disease. [T]he burden was on the prosecution, once the hypothesis of insanity was established, to prove beyond a reasonable doubt that Blake was sane at the time of the commission of the crime. . . .

We come then to the definition of insanity given in charge. The district court charge was based on the dictum in Davis v. United States, 165 U.S. 373, 378 (1897). [The defense objected to the *Davis* standard and proposed substitution of the MPC instead.] The *Davis* standard is as follows:

The term "insanity" as used in this defense means such a perverted and deranged condition of the mental and moral faculties as to render a person incapable of distinguishing between right and wrong, or unconscious at the time of the nature of the act he is committing, or where, though conscious of it and able to distinguish between right and wrong and know that the act is wrong, yet his will, by which I mean the governing power of his mind, has been otherwise than voluntarily so completely destroyed that his actions are not subject to it, but are beyond his control.

Section 4.01 of the ALI Model Penal Code is as follows:

(1) A person is not responsible for criminal conduct if at the time of such conduct as a result of mental disease or defect he lacks substantial capacity

either to appreciate the criminality (wrongfulness) of his conduct or to conform his conduct to the requirements of law.

(2) As used in this Article, the terms "mental disease or defect" do not include an abnormality manifested only by repeated criminal or otherwise antisocial conduct. . . .

The facts of this case point up the difference in the standards. Here the facts are such, read favorably to the government as they must be, as not to show complete mental disorientation under the absolutes of *Davis*. The record does show evidence which, if believed, would indicate that Blake suffered from a severe mental disease which the jury might have found impaired his control over the conduct in question. He could not prevail under a *Davis* charge. He might have prevailed under a substantial lack of capacity type charge.

We think that a substantiality type standard is called for in light of current knowledge regarding mental illness. A person, as Blake here, may be a schizophrenic or may merely have a sociopathic personality. The evidence could go either way. He may or may not have been in a psychotic episode at the time of the robbery. But, he was not unconscious, incapable of distinguishing right and wrong nor was his will completely destroyed in terms of the *Davis* definition. Modifying the lack of mental capacity by the adjective "substantial," still leaves the matter for the jury under the evidence, lay and expert, to determine mental defect vel non and its relationship to the conduct in question. . . .

MODEL PENAL CODE AND COMMENTARIES (1985)

§4.01, pp. 164-172

No problem in the drafting of a penal code presents greater intrinsic difficulty than that of determining when individuals whose conduct would otherwise be criminal ought to be exculpated on the ground that they were suffering from mental disease or defect when they acted as they did. The problem is the drawing of a line between the use of public agencies and force (1) to condemn the offender by conviction, with resulting sanctions in which the ingredient of reprobation is present no matter how constructive one may seek to make the sentence and the process of correction, and (2) modes of disposition in which the condemnatory element is absent, even though restraint may be involved. . . . Stating the matter differently, the problem is to etch a decent working line between the areas assigned to the authorities responsible for public health and those responsible for the correction of offenders. . . .

As far as its principle extends, the *M'Naghten* rule is right. Those who are irresponsible under the test are plainly beyond the reach of the restraining influence of the law, and their condemnation would be both futile and unjust. A deranged person who believes he is squeezing lemons when he chokes his wife, or who kills in supposed self-defense on the basis of a delusion that another is attempting to kill him, is plainly beyond the deterrent influence of the law; he needs restraint but condemnation is meaningless and ineffective. Moreover, the category defined by the rule is so extreme that to the ordinary person the exculpation of those it encompasses bespeaks no weakness in the law. He does not identify such persons with himself; they are a world apart.

The question remains, however, whether the *M'Naghten* rule goes far enough to draw a fair and workable distinction. In two respects, this question must be answered in the negative. The *M'Naghten* test addresses itself to the actor's "knowledge," which can naturally be understood as referring to a simple awareness by the actor of his wrongdoing such as would be manifested by a verbal acknowledgment on his part of the forbidden nature of his conduct. One shortcoming of this criterion is that it authorizes a finding of responsibility in a case in which the actor is not seriously deluded concerning his conduct or its consequences, but in which the actor's appreciation of the wrongfulness of his conduct is a largely detached or abstract awareness that does not penetrate to the affective level. Insofar as a formulation centering on "knowledge" does not readily lend itself to application to emotional abnormalities, the *M'Naghten* test appears less than optimal as a standard of responsibility in cases involving affective disorder.

A second and more pervasive difficulty with the *M'Naghten* standard appears in cases in which the defendant's disorder . . . destroys or overrides the defendant's power of self-control. . . .

Responding to the *M'Naghten* formulation's inadequacy in connection with claims that emphasize a defendant's volitional incapacity rather than his inability to understand, a minority of jurisdictions . . . explicitly supplemented the *M'Naghten* rule by what was commonly called the "irresistible impulse" test. . . .

The Model Code formulation is based on the view that a sense of understanding broader than mere cognition, and a reference to volitional incapacity should be achieved directly in the formulation of the defense. . . .

In contrast to the *M'Naghten* and "irresistible impulse" criteria, the Model Code formulation reflects the judgment that no test is workable that calls for complete impairment of ability to know or to control. The extremity of these conceptions had posed the largest difficulty for the administration of the old standards. Disorientation, psychiatrists indicated, might be extreme and still might not be total; what clinical experience revealed was closer to a graded scale with marks along the way. . . . To meet these difficulties, it was thought that the criterion should ask if the defendant, as a result of mental disease or defect, was deprived of "substantial capacity" to appreciate the criminality (or wrongfulness) of his conduct or to conform his conduct to the requirements of law, meaning by "substantial" a capacity of some appreciable magnitude when measured by the standard of humanity in general, as opposed to the reduction of capacity to the vagrant and trivial dimensions characteristic of the most severe afflictions of the mind.

The adoption of the standard of substantial capacity may well be the Code's most significant alteration of the prevailing tests. It was recognized, of course, that "substantial" is an open-ended concept, but its quantitative connotation was believed to be sufficiently precise for purposes of practical administration. The law is full of instances in which courts and juries are explicitly authorized to confront an issue of degree. Such an approach was deemed to be no less essential and appropriate in dealing with this issue than in dealing with the questions of recklessness and negligence.

UNITED STATES v. LYONS

United States Court of Appeals, 5th Circuit, en banc
731 F.2d 243, 739 F.2d 994 (1984)

GEE, J. Defendant Robert Lyons was indicted on twelve counts of knowingly and intentionally securing controlled narcotics. . . . Lyons proffered evidence that in 1978 he began to suffer from several painful ailments, that various narcotics were prescribed to be taken as needed for his pain, and that he became addicted to these drugs. He also offered to present expert witnesses who would testify that his drug addiction affected his brain both physiolog- *· drug addict* ically and psychologically and that as a result he lacked substantial capacity to conform his conduct to the requirements of the law. . . .

[The trial court excluded the proffered evidence, and Lyons was convicted.]
Today the great weight of legal authority clearly supports the view that evidence of mere narcotics addiction, standing alone and without other phys- iological or psychological involvement, raises no issue of such a mental defect or disease as can serve as a basis for the insanity defense. . . .

We do not doubt that actual physical damage to the brain itself falls within the ambit of "mental disease or defect." . . . Because the proffer offers evidence tending to suggest such damage, that evidence should have been submitted to the jury. And although we today withdraw our recognition of the volitional prong of [the insanity defense]—that as to which such evidence has usually been advanced—we also conclude that should Lyons wish to offer such evidence in an attempt to satisfy the remaining cognitive prong, fairness demands that we afford him an opportunity to do so.

. . . We last examined the insanity defense in Blake v. United Sates, 407 F.2d 908 (5th Cir. 1969) (en banc), where we adopted the ALI Model Penal Code definition of insanity. [W]e concluded that then current knowledge in the field of behavioral science supported such a result. Unfortunately, it now appears our conclusion was premature. . . .

Reexamining the *Blake* standard today, we conclude that the volitional prong of the insanity defense—a lack of capacity to conform one's conduct to the requirements of the law—does not comport with current medical and scientific knowledge, which has retreated from its earlier, sanguine expecta- tions. Consequently, we now hold that a person is not responsible for criminal conduct on the grounds of insanity only if at the time of that conduct, as a result of a mental disease or defect, he is unable to appreciate the wrongfulness of that conduct.

We do so for several reasons. First, as we have mentioned, a majority of psychiatrists now believe that they do not possess sufficient accurate scientific bases for measuring a person's capacity for self-control or for calibrating the impairment of that capacity. Bonnie, The Moral Basis of the Insanity Defense, 69 A.B.A.J. 194, 196 (1983). "The line between an irresistible impulse and an impulse not resisted is probably no sharper than between twilight and dusk." American Psychiatric Association Statement on the Insanity Defense, 11 (1982) [APA Statement]. Indeed, Professor Bonnie [supra] states:

> There is, in short, no objective basis for distinguishing between offenders who were undeterrable and those who were merely undeterred, between the impulse that was irresistible and the impulse not resisted, or between substantial impairment of capacity and some lesser impairment.

In addition, the risks of fabrication and "moral mistakes" in administering the insanity defense are greatest "when the experts and the jury are asked to speculate whether the defendant had the capacity to 'control' himself or whether he could have 'resisted' the criminal impulse." Bonnie, supra, at 196. Moreover, psychiatric testimony about volition is more likely to produce confusion for jurors than is psychiatric testimony concerning a defendant's appreciation of the wrongfulness of his act. It appears, moreover, that there is considerable overlap between a psychotic person's inability to understand and his ability to control his behavior. Most psychotic persons who fail a volitional test would also fail a cognitive test, thus rendering the volitional test superfluous for them. Finally, [case law currently] requires that such proof be made by the federal prosecutor beyond a reasonable doubt, an all but impossible task in view of the present murky state of medical knowledge.[a]

[W]e see no prudent course for the law to follow but to treat all criminal impulses—including those not resisted—as resistible. To do otherwise in the present state of medical knowledge would be to cast the insanity defense adrift upon a sea of unfounded scientific speculation, with the palm awarded case by case to the most convincing advocate of that which is presently unknown— and may remain so, because unknowable. . . .

RUBIN, J., with whom TATE, J., joins, dissenting. . . . An adjudication of guilt is more than a factual determination that the defendant pulled a trigger, took a bicycle, or sold heroin. It is a moral judgment that the individual is blameworthy. "Our collective conscience does not allow punishment where it cannot impose blame." . . . "[H]istorically, our substantive criminal law is based on a theory of punishing the [vicious] will. It postulates a free agent confronted with a choice between doing right and wrong, and choosing freely to do wrong."[3] . . . An acquittal by reason of insanity is a judgment that the

---

a. For recent changes in the law governing the burden of proof, see supra page 967, Note 4.—EDS.
3. Morissette v. United States, 342 U.S. 246, 250 n.4 (1952) (quoting Pound, Introduction to Sayre, Cases on Criminal Law (1927)).

defendant is not *guilty* because, as a result of his mental condition, he is unable to make an effective choice regarding his behavior.

The majority does not controvert these fundamental principles; indeed it accepts them as the basis for the defense when the accused suffers from a disease that impairs cognition. It rests its decision to redefine insanity and to narrow the defense on "new policy considerations." ...

The first is the potential threat to society created by the volitional prong of the insanity defense. Public opposition to any insanity-grounded defense is often based, either explicitly or implicitly, on the view that the plea is frequently invoked by violent criminals who fraudulently use it to evade just punishment. ... This perception depicts an insanity trial as a "circus" of conflicting expert testimony that confuses a naive and sympathetic jury. And it fears insanity acquittees as offenders who, after manipulating the criminal justice system, are soon set free to prey once again on the community.

Despite the prodigious volume of writing devoted to the plea, the empirical data that are available provide little or no support for these fearsome perceptions and in many respects directly refute them. Both the frequency and the success rate of insanity pleas are grossly overestimated by professionals and lay persons alike; the plea is rarely made, and even more rarely successful.[8] The number of insanity pleas based on control defects, as compared to those based on lack of cognition, must have been almost negligible.

The perception that the defendant who successfully pleads insanity is quickly released from custody is also based only on assumption. ... "The truth is that in almost every case, the acquittee is immediately hospitalized and evaluated for dangerousness. Usually, the acquittee remains hospitalized for an extended time."[9]

Another set of objections to the plea is based on the thesis that factfinders—especially juries—are confused and manipulated by the vagueness of the legal standards of insanity and the notorious "battle of the experts" who present conclusory, superficial, and misleading testimony. These conditions, the argument runs, conspire to produce inconsistent and "inaccurate" verdicts.

Let us first put these objections in perspective. Most cases involving an insanity plea do not go to trial; instead, like most other criminal cases, they are settled by a plea bargain. In many of the cases that do go to trial, psychiatric testimony is presented by deposition, without disagreement among experts, and without opposition by the prosecution. And in the few cases in which a contest does develop, the defendant is usually convicted. ...

---

8. For example, one extensive study examined the opinions held by college students, the general public, state legislators, law enforcement officers, and mental health personnel in Wyoming. Estimates of the frequency with which [felony] defendants entered the plea ranged from 13% to 57%. During the time period considered, however, the actual frequency was only 0.47%: one case in 200. Similarly, although estimates of its success rate varied from 19% to 44%, during the relevant period only one of the 102 defendants who entered the plea was acquitted by reason of insanity. ...

9. Rappeport, The Insanity Plea Scapegoating the Mentally Ill—Much Ado about Nothing?, 24 So. Tex. L.J. 687, 698 (1983). ...

The manipulated-jury argument is supported largely by declamation, not data. [N]o source has been cited to the court to support the conclusion that, as an empirical matter, pleas based upon the volitional prong present an especially problematic task for the jury.

Indeed, the majority opinion does not assert that the insanity defense, particularly the control test, *doesn't* work; it contends that the defense *can't* work. The principal basis for this contention is the belief, held by "a majority of psychiatrists," that they lack "sufficient accurate scientific bases for measuring a person's capacity for self-control or for calibrating the impairment of that capacity." . . . [B]ut the absence of useful expert evidence, if indeed there is none, does not obviate the need for resolving the question whether the defendant ought to be held accountable for his criminal behavior. . . .

Our concept of responsibility in this sense is not limited to observable behavior: it embraces *meaningful* choice, and necessarily requires inferences and assumptions regarding the defendant's unobservable mental state. . . . The difference between the concepts of excusing circumstances such as coercion and the insanity defense is that the former is based on objective assumptions about human behavior and is tested against hypothetical-objective standards such as "the reasonable person." "The insanity defense [on the other hand] marks the transition from the adequate man the law demands to the inadequate man he may be."[17]

The relevant inquiry under either branch of the insanity test is a subjective one that focuses on the defendant's actual state of mind. Our duty to undertake that inquiry is not based on confidence in the testimony of expert witnesses, but on the ethical precept that the defendant's mental state is a crucial aspect of his blameworthiness. . . . The availability of expert testimony and the probative value of such testimony are basically evidentiary problems that can be accommodated within the existing test. . . .

[A] defendant pleading insanity typically faces both a judge and a jury who are skeptical about psychiatry in general and the insanity plea in particular. . . . The formal allocation of the persuasion burden notwithstanding, the defendant to prevail must convince the doubting factfinder that, despite present outward appearances, he was insane at the time he committed the crime.

The majority's fear that the present test invites "moral mistakes" is difficult to understand. The majority opinion concedes that some individuals cannot conform their conduct to the law's requirements. . . . [T]he majority embraces a rule certain to result in the conviction of at least some who are not morally responsible and the punishment of those for whom retributive, deterrent, and rehabilitative penal goals are inappropriate. A decision that virtually ensures undeserved, and therefore unjust, punishment in the name of avoiding moral mistakes rests on a peculiar notion of morality. . . .

Judges are not, and should not be, immune to popular outrage over this nation's crime rate. Like everyone else, judges watch television, read

---

17. A. Goldstein, The Insanity Defense 18 (1967).

newspapers and magazines, listen to gossip, and are sometimes themselves victims. They receive the message trenchantly described in a recent book criticizing the insanity defense: "Perhaps the bottom line of all these complaints is that *guilty people go free.* ... These are not cases in which the defendant is *alleged* to have committed a crime. *Everyone knows he did it.*"[25] Although understandable as an expression of uninformed popular opinion, such a viewpoint ought not to serve as the basis for judicial decisionmaking; for it misapprehends the very meaning of guilt.

... By definition, guilt cannot be attributed to an individual unable to refrain from violating the law. When a defendant is properly acquitted by reason of insanity under the control test, the guilty does not go free. ...

NOTES ON THE "VOLITIONAL PRONG" CONTROVERSY

1. Practical concerns. Professor Michael Corrado has challenged the claim that it is impossible to tell the difference between those who can't control their behavior and those who can but won't. He writes (The Case for a Purely Volitional Insanity Defense, 42 Tex. Tech L. Rev. 481, 502) (2009)) that "recent studies have shown that the line between those who can't ... and those who won't ... can be very clear indeed." Professor Corrado adds that "those who advanced [the contrary claim] should be a little red-faced, ... especially if their argument was that the possibility of abuse was too great." In making that point, he refers to Supreme Court decisions upholding the constitutionality of "sexually violent predator" (SVP) statutes. Those decisions (discussed at pages 81-82 supra) stress that SVP confinement is constitutionally permissible for offenders who largely *can't* control their behavior, but not for those who simply won't; as a result the Court has upheld such statutes only on the premise that it is possible to reliably distinguish between those two sorts of offenders. See Kansas v. Crane, 534 U.S. 407, 413 (2002) (SVP commitment is permissible only on "proof of serious difficulty in controlling behavior ... sufficient to distinguish the dangerous sexual offender [who is subject to preventive confinement] from the dangerous but typical recidivist convicted in an ordinary criminal case.")[55]

2. Moral culpability. For careful development of the argument that, even aside from practical concerns, a purely cognitive test for insanity is the appropriate test as a matter of moral principle, see Stephen J. Morse, Rationality and Responsibility, 74 So. Cal. L. Rev. 251 (2000). Professor Morse argues (id. at 252-253):

[T]he law's concept of the person is a creature who acts for reasons and is potentially able to be guided by reason. ... When we want to know why an

---

25. W. Winslade & J. Ross, The Insanity Plea 2-3 (1983) (emphasis added).

55. On the other side of this debate, however, many observers argue that the Court's decisions upholding SVP commitment are unsound, precisely because the effort to distinguish those who can't from those who won't is, in their view, inherently "vague and not operationalizable." See, e.g., Stephen J. Morse, Mental Disorder and Criminal Law, 101 J. Crim. L. & Criminology 885, 953 (2011).

agent intentionally behaved as she did, we do not desire a biophysical explanation, as if the person were simply biophysical flotsam and jetsam. Instead, we seek the reason she acted, the desires and beliefs that formed the practical syllogism that produced intentional conduct. . . . The law's concept of responsibility follows from its view of the person. . . . Legally responsible agents [are] people who have the general capacity to grasp and be guided by good reason in particular legal contexts.

Professor Corrado, in contrast, argues (supra at 509) that the essence of an insanity defense should lie not in cognitive but in volitional incapacity:

Where a person, whether or not he knows the nature of his act, cannot avoid performing the act, he should be excused-unless he himself is responsible for not being able to avoid it. [T]he defining characteristic of a mental condition that moves its victim from the category of the sane to the category of the legally insane is that it deprives her of the ability to choose to conform her behavior to the law. It may do that through depriving her of the ability to reason; it may do that through depriving her of the ability to appreciate the wrongfulness of her action, but even when it does neither of those things, it may rob her of her responsibility for her actions by depriving her of the ability to act in accordance with her best judgment.

NOTES ON CHANGES IN THE LAW

The change from *Blake* to *Lyons* exemplifies the changing attitudes toward the insanity defense beginning in the early 1980s. Before then, the MPC formulation of the defense had captured a good deal of the field. About half the states adopted some version of the MPC, either by statute or judicial decision, as did all but one of the U.S. Courts of Appeal. But this trend in favor of the Model Penal Code approach was abruptly reversed following the 1982 trial of John W. Hinckley, Jr., who shot and wounded President Reagan (and several people accompanying the president) in an abortive assassination attempt that was witnessed on national television. When the jury, applying the MPC test, found Hinckley not guilty by reason of insanity, there were widespread expressions of concern about the insanity defense and an outpouring of outraged reactions to the verdict. See Valerie P. Hans & Dan Slater, John W. Hinckley, Jr. & the Insanity Defense: The Public's Verdict, 47 Pub. Opinion Q. 202 (1983).

Proposals to restrict defenses based on mental illness included adjustments in the burden of proof, changes in the disposition of insanity acquittees, introduction of a separate verdict of "Guilty but Mentally Ill," and complete abolition of the insanity defense. The choice of which approach (if any) to take involves a complex mixture of substantive and tactical judgments. For helpful discussions, see Ralph Slovenko, The Insanity Defense in the Wake of the *Hinckley* Trial, 14 Rutgers L.J. 373 (1983); Peter Arenella, Reflections on Current Proposals to Abolish or Reform the Insanity Defense, 8 Am. J.L. & Med. 271 (1982).

Developments in each of the areas just mentioned are explored in the appropriate places in this chapter. The present Note focuses on the formulation of the insanity test itself.

1. State law. Although a substantial minority of the states still adhere to the MPC test, several important jurisdictions have returned to the *M'Naghten* Rule. California adopted the MPC formula by judicial decision in 1978 but returned to *M'Naghten* as a result of a voter initiative approved in 1982. See People v. Skinner, 704 P.2d 752 (Cal. 1985). At least seven other states, including Texas and Indiana, likewise dropped the MPC test in the wake of the *Hinckley* verdict and adopted *M'Naghten* in its place. See John Q. LaFond & Mary L. Durham, Back to the Asylum 64 (1992). According to one count, by 2004, 30 states had returned to some form of the *M'Naghten* Rule, while only 15 states continued to use the MPC approach. See Michael Louis Corrado, Responsibility and Control, 34 Hofstra L. Rev. 59, 61-62 (2005).

2. Federal law. As part of the Comprehensive Crime Control Act of 1984, Congress enacted a provision that supersedes the *Lyons* decision and narrows the insanity test even further. 18 U.S.C. §17(a) (2011) provides:

> It is an affirmative defense to a prosecution under any Federal statute that, at the time of the commission of the acts constituting the offense, the defendant, as a result of a severe mental disease or defect, was unable to appreciate the nature and quality or the wrongfulness of his acts. Mental disease or defect does not otherwise constitute a defense.

3. Legislative proposals. Three influential bodies have, in similar language, proposed retention of the cognitive branch of the MPC test and rejection of the volitional branch. See American Bar Association, Criminal Justice Mental Health Standards §7-6.1(a) (approved Feb. 9, 1983); American Psychiatric Association, Statement on the Insanity Defense, 140 Am. J. Psychiatry 6 (1983); National Conf. of Commissioners on Uniform State Laws, Model Insanity Defense and Post-Trial Disposition Act §201 (1984). The ABA standard provides:

> A person is not responsible for criminal conduct if, at the time of such conduct, and as a result of mental disease or defect, that person was unable to appreciate the wrongfulness of such conduct.

The American Psychiatric Association standard provides:

> A person charged with a criminal offense should be found not guilty by reason of insanity if it is shown that as a result of mental disease or mental retardation he was unable to appreciate the wrongfulness of his conduct at the time of the offense.

4. Rates of use and success of the insanity defense. As noted in Judge Rubin's dissenting opinion in *Lyons*, supra, the frequency and success rate of insanity pleas are often overestimated. The actual use of the insanity defense varies markedly from jurisdiction to jurisdiction. Colorado had an average of one insanity plea for every 5,000 arrests, while the rate was one in 480 arrests for Michigan and one in 200 arrests for Wyoming. As might be expected, success rates for insanity pleas tend to be higher where the plea is infrequently used. Success rates ranged from 44 percent of all insanity pleas tendered in Colorado to 7 percent in Michigan and 2 percent in Wyoming. The two largest states, California and New York, had only 63 and 88 successful insanity pleas per year, a ratio of one for every 27,000 arrests in California and one for every 11,000 arrests in New York.[56] Nationally, insanity acquittals probably represent no more than 0.25 percent of terminated felony prosecutions.[57] The overall figures have varied very little over time; the overall success rate for the insanity plea was virtually identical in the early 1980s, before the post-*Hinckley* reforms took effect.[58]

5. *The effect of different versions of the insanity defense.* There is little evidence that different formulations of the insanity defense produce different results in practice. In one attempt to study this question empirically,[59] the researcher assembled roughly 100 experimental jury panels from actual jury pools in Chicago, St. Louis, and Minneapolis. The juries listened to the transcript of an actual insanity defense case, then deliberated until they reached a unanimous verdict. One-third of the juries were given the *M'Naghten* instruction, one-third a more liberalized test, and one-third were simply told to find the defendant not guilty by reason of insanity "[i]f you believe the defendant was insane" at the time of the offense. It turned out the differences in instruction made much less difference than the composition of the jury. Other researchers reached similar conclusions from studies using mock juries to read case summaries. Asked whether to acquit under *M'Naghten*, the irresistible impulse test, the MPC, and "their own best lights," no significant differences in acquittal rates were found.[60]

Another approach relies on before-and-after comparisons in jurisdictions that have enacted statutory changes. In Wyoming, legislation replaced *M'Naghten* with the MPC test; the change had no significant effect on the rate of insanity pleas tendered, the rate of insanity acquittals, or in the characteristics of defendants invoking the defense.[61] California moved in the opposite direction, replacing the MPC test with *M'Naghten*; again, there

---

56. Hugh McGinley & Richard A. Pasewark, National Survey of the Frequency and Success of the Insanity Plea and Alternate Pleas, 17 J. Psychiatry & L. 205, 208-214 (1989).

57. See Andrew Blum, Debunking Myths of the Insanity Plea, Natl. L.J., Apr. 20, 1992, at 9, reporting a 1992 study by the American Academy of Psychiatry and the Law.

58. See National Commission on the Insanity Defense, Myths and Realities 14-15 (1983); Borum & Fulero, Empirical Research on the Insanity Defense and Attempted Reforms, 23 Law & Hum. Behav. 375 (1999).

59. Rita James Simon, The Jury and the Defense of Insanity (1967).

60. See Norman J. Finkel, The Insanity Defense: A Comparison of Verdict Schemas, 15 Law & Hum. Behav. 533 (1991); Norman J. Finkel, The Insanity, Defense Reform Act of 1984: Much Ado About Nothing, 7 Behav. Sci. & L. 399 (1989).

61. Paseward & Bieber, Insanity Plea: Statutory Language and Trial Procedure, 12 J. Psychiatry & L. 399 (1984).

was no significant change in the rate of insanity pleas and acquittals or in the types of defendants invoking the defense.[62]

6. Prospects for reform. Professor Alan A. Stone, who served on the committee that prepared the American Psychiatric Association's formulation of a proposed insanity defense, supra page 981, Note 3, has offered some pessimistic reflections on the possibility of successfully reforming the insanity defense. He writes in his Law, Psychiatry, and Morality 94-96 (1984):

> Despite the endless attempts of law to define precise tests of criminal responsibility, the ordinary psychiatrist typically asks: Is the person psychotic? If the diagnosis is psychosis, particularly schizophrenia, the person is insane. If a personality disorder is diagnosed, the person is sane. The new APA proposal has gone back to that time-honored clinical distinction, noting that we now have 80 percent reliability [in diagnosis] of psychosis. But . . . Hinckley apparently fell into the 20 percent nonreliability category. We should not be surprised by that. Rather, we should expect that in most cases where the prosecution would want to contest an insanity defense, the defendant will not be obviously psychotic. The obviously psychotic defendant can be readily identified even by a prosecutor. Thus it may be that contested cases raising the insanity defense will be those about which we can expect diagnostic disagreement by psychiatrists. . . .
>
> [The] APA proposal involves going back to an essentially cognitive test— again in part because psychiatric testimony relevant to cognitive matters such as appreciation and understanding "is more reliable, and has a stronger scientific base" than testimony relevant to volition. Here again the hopes of the APA proposal fail. The defense [in *Hinckley*] found ample evidence of thought disorder, including ideas of reference, magical thinking, bizarre ideas, and a break with reality. The prosecution found none of this. Thus testimony limited to the cognitive issue did not prove reliable in the courtroom. . . .
>
> Changing the insanity defense is like chipping away at the tip of the iceberg. . . . An exchange between defense and prosecution psychiatrists will illustrate one aspect of these deeper and more basic theoretical problems. Doctor Biological Psychiatry said that the Valium Hinckley took may well have produced "paradoxical rage," thus causing him to be unable to control himself. Doctor Corrections said it was "appropriate" for Hinckley to take Valium if he was anxious about assassinating the President. Put aside the fact that these are both conjectures. They are conjectures which are part of two quite different kinds of discourse.
>
> The theory of paradoxical rage is part of a discourse about organisms with brains, enzymes, and physical chemical reactions. The theory of appropriate behavior is part of a discourse about persons with minds, intentions, and motivated actions. In the discourse about organisms, the self disappears and paradoxical rage is *caused* by the chemical release of the inhibitory neural system. In the discourse about persons, the self is the agent who chooses, who intends, and who assumes a firing position and pulls the trigger. Morality

---

62. McGreevy, Steadman & Callahan, The Negligible Effects of California's 1982 Reform of the Insanity Defense Test, 148 Am. J. Psychiatry 744 (1991).

does not enter the discourse of organisms because free will and choice are not part of that language. To say that a *person* had a paradoxical rage reaction is to confuse the two discourses. . . . Psychiatry has not yet found a unified discourse about organisms and persons. That is the giant iceberg against which the insanity defense inevitably is wrecked. Neither psychiatry nor law nor moral philosophy has found a sure way past this barrier. It does no good to pretend the barrier does not exist or to ask the jury to deal with it. These are not questions for which common sense has an answer.

NOTE ON ABOLITION OF THE INSANITY DEFENSE

While the defense of legal insanity has long been an established feature of American law, there have been movements to abolish it. Several states attempted to do so in the early decades of the past century, but these efforts were usually held unconstitutional under state constitutions guaranteeing a jury trial and due process of law. See, e.g., Sinclair v. State, 132 So. 581 (Miss. 1931); State v. Strasburg, 110 P. 1020 (Wash. 1910). There was renewed interest in abolition in the latter decades of the century, leading to abolition of the defense in five states—Idaho, Kansas, Montana, Nevada, and Utah. These more recent statutes differed from the earlier ones in that they allowed evidence of mental disease to be introduced on the issue of whether the defendant possessed the mens rea required by the crime charged. Some also authorized the court, after conviction, to determine at sentencing whether the defendant suffered from a mental disease, and if so, to commit him for institutional care and treatment for a period not to exceed the maximum sentence. See, e.g., Kansas Stat. Ann. §22-3220 (2011); Mont. Code Ann. §§46-14-311, 46-14-312(2) (2011). Rejecting constitutional challenges to four of these statutes, state supreme courts have held that the insanity defense has been so controversial and so variable over time that it does not possess the historical pedigree necessary to establish it as a fundamental right under the Due Process Clause. See State v. Korell, 690 P.2d 992 (Mont. 1984); State v. Searcy, 798 P.2d 914 (Idaho 1990); State v. Herrera, 895 P.2d 359 (Utah 1995); State v. Bethel, 66 P.3d 840 (Kan. 2003).

In Finger v. State, 27 P.3d 66 (Nev. 2001), however, the Nevada Supreme Court struck down that state's statute abolishing the insanity defense, holding that the defense is "a well-established and fundamental principle" under the Due Process Clauses of both the United States and the Nevada constitutions. Id. at 84. Finger was charged with the murder of his mother. He acknowledged that he had intended to kill her; his defense—unavailable under the Nevada statute—was that his longstanding paranoid schizophrenia, which included visual and auditory hallucinations, precluded criminal responsibility because it led him to believe that his mother was plotting to kill him. The Nevada Supreme Court held that allowing admission of Finger's mental illness only to negate his intent to kill was not sufficient; due process required that he be able to contest his guilt on the ground that he did not know that his intentional killing was wrong.

The U.S. Supreme Court has never ruled on whether statutes abolishing the insanity defense are unconstitutional. However, in Clark v. Arizona, 548 U.S. 735 (2006), the Court rejected a due process challenge to Arizona's very limited insanity statute, which accepts only half of the *M'Naghten* test, defining insanity solely in terms of the defendant's capacity to tell whether the criminal act was right or wrong (and not in terms of the defendant's capacity to know the nature or quality of the act committed). "History shows no deference to *M'Naghten* that could elevate its formula to the level of fundamental principle, so as to limit the traditional recognition of a State's capacity to define crimes and defenses. . . ." Id. at 749. After canvassing the diversity of approaches among the states, the Court concluded "that no particular formulation has evolved into a baseline for due process and that the insanity rule, like the conceptualization of criminal offenses, is substantially open to state choice." Id. at 752. As for the constitutionality of complete abolition of the insanity defense, the Court observed, "This case does not call upon us to decide the matter." Id. at 752 n.20. For consideration of the constitutional issues, see Daniel J. Nusbaum, The Craziest Reform of Them All: A Critical Analysis of the Constitutional Implications of "Abolishing" the Insanity Defense, 87 Cornell L. Rev. 1509 (2002).

The desirability of abolition remains controversial, and the issue tends to flare up with widespread media coverage of an insanity acquittal of a highly unsympathetic defendant, like Hinckley. Is abolition a good idea? Will it promote or impair public safety? Consider these comments.

Chief Justice Joseph Weintraub, Insanity as a Defense: A Panel Discussion, 37 F.R.D. 365, 369-372 (1964): [I]nsanity should have nothing to do with the adjudication of guilt but rather should bear upon the disposition of the offender after conviction[;] the contest among *M'Naghten* and its competitive concepts . . . is simply a struggle over an irrelevancy. . . . Upon the psychiatric view the distinction between the sick and the bad is . . . an illusion. . . . The thrust of the psychiatric thesis must be to reject insanity as a defense and to deal with all transgressors as unfortunate mortals. . . . [The problem] is that the psychiatry-based critics of *M'Naghten* will not accept [this] inevitable answer, . . . but rather they urge that *M'Naghten* be abandoned in favor of some other concept of insanity. . . . And I think that debate just has to be fruitless. It's a quixotic attempt to draw a line that just doesn't exist. No definition of criminal responsibility and hence of legal insanity can be valid unless it truthfully separates the man who is personally blameworthy for his makeup from the man who is not, and I submit to you that there is just no basis in psychiatry to make a differentiation between the two.

Professor Herbert Wechsler, id. at 381-383: I suggest you think about [the distinction between the sick and the bad] not in terms of the effort to do absolute justice to individuals (we must agree with the Chief Justice, this is for God and not for man) but rather in terms of asking ourselves this question: how would you feel about living in a society in which a differentiation of this sort were not attempted? For example, your elderly father in an advanced arteriosclerotic state is taken to the hospital and while in the hospital experiences . . . a delusion . . . and knocks over a lamp, with the result that an attendant is killed. Now, would you be satisfied with a legal system in which he could be indicted and convicted of a homicidal crime and his condition regarded as relevant only on the question of what to do with him? Everybody would say no to this. That is why the criterion of responsibility as affected by disease or a defect parallels the traditional mens rea rules in requiring a determination of blameworthiness in the ordinary moral sense, in the sense of working morality, not in the sense of man's responsibility for his nature or his nurture but in the sense that the afflictive sanctions of the law will not be visited on anyone unless he does something which is the product of a choice, unless in traditional jurisprudential terms he performs a juridical act. Now, general confidence that this is so seems to me quite central to the sense of security that is one of the greatest values in a law abiding society. . . . So I don't think that it's just a question of whether you get sent away and for how long. I rather think that the distinctive feature of the entire criminal process is the element of condemnation that it marshals, of social condemnation. And, indeed, is it not the mark of a healthy society that the criminal law marshal an appropriate moral condemnation?

Norval Morris, Psychiatry and the Dangerous Criminal, 41 S. Cal. L. Rev. 514, 519-521 (1968): Overwhelmingly, criminal matters are disposed of by pleas of guilty and by bench trials. Only the exceptional case goes to trial by jury. And of these exceptional cases, in only two of every hundred is this defense raised. Does anyone believe that this percentage measures the actual significance of gross psychopathology to crime? Let him visit the nearest criminal court or penitentiary if he does. Clearly this defense is a sop to our conscience, a comfort for our failure to address the difficult arena of psychopathology and crime.

    . . . It too often is overlooked that one group's exculpation from criminal responsibility confirms the inculpation of other groups. . . . You argue that insanity destroys, undermines, diminishes man's capacity to reject what is wrong and to adhere to what is right. So does the ghetto—more so. But surely, you reply, I would not have us punish the sick. Indeed I would, if you insist on punishing the grossly deprived. To the extent that criminal sanctions serve punitive purposes, I fail to see the difference between these two defenses. To the extent that they serve rehabilitative, treatment, and curative purposes I fail to see the need for the difference. . . .

Model Penal Code and Commentaries, Comment to §4.01, at 182-186 (1985): A variety of reasons for abolition have been advanced from quite different ideological perspectives. . . . The first position is perhaps epitomized by President Nixon's support of abolition, which he said was "the most significant feature" of the codification of general defenses in the Administration's proposed criminal code and was designed to curb "unconscionable abuse" of the insanity defense. . . . This position . . . has little empirical support. The insanity defense is in fact infrequently invoked and then only for very serious crimes. When it has been invoked, jurors have not shown themselves ready to accept attenuated claims. Those who do successfully claim the defense are often committed for long periods of time. Unfounded fears of "abuse" are hardly a sufficient reason for abolishing a defense that has properly come to be viewed as fundamental.

The other attack on the insanity defense is more complex and it goes to the roots of the criminal law. It shares with the first position a skepticism that distinctions can sensibly be made between those who are responsible and those who are not. Critics taking this view cite the rarity of the employment of the defense as evidence that most mentally ill defendants are being convicted despite the availability of the defense. They doubt that the stigma of those convicted and subsequently treated as mentally disturbed is any worse than the stigma of those who commit criminal acts and are committed to high security institutions for the mentally ill without undergoing trial or after being acquitted on grounds of insanity. They argue that there is little basis for withholding condemnation of those whose mental illness causes them to act criminally when those whose deprived economic and social background causes them to act criminally are condemned. They regard the adversarial debate over the responsibility of particular defendants as wasteful, confusing for the jury, and possibly harmful for those defendants who are mentally disturbed. They think psychiatric diagnosis should be employed primarily after conviction to determine what sort of correctional treatment is appropriate instead of prior to conviction to determine criminal responsibility. Ideally, in the view of some of these critics, criminal convictions generally should not be regarded as stigmatizing, but as determinants of dangerousness to which the community must respond.

When properly understood, this attack is a challenge to the basic notion that a criminal conviction properly reflects moral condemnation by the community of the act performed. Yet those who advance the attack do not provide persuasive reasons for believing it would benefit society if the association between moral wrongdoing and criminal conviction were dissipated. Nor do they give reasons for supposing that the association will be dissipated in the near future. Yet they propose labeling as criminal many persons whom society at large would clearly not regard as morally blameworthy.

For further development of the case for abolishing the insanity defense, see Abraham L. Halpern, The Politics of the Insanity Defense, 14 Am. J. Forensic Psychiatry 3 (1993). For criticism of the arguments for abolishing the insanity defense, see Stephen J. Morse, Excusing the Crazy: The Insanity Defense Reconsidered, 58 S. Cal. L. Rev. 777 (1985). For an "intermediate" proposal that would consider mental disorder only if relevant to other criminal defenses, such as self-defense, duress, and lack of mens rea, see Christopher Slobogin, An End to Insanity: Recasting the Role of Mental Illness in Criminal Cases, 86 Va. L. Rev. 1199 (2000).

TRANSITIONAL NOTE

Despite the differences in the prevailing formulations of the insanity defense, they generally incorporate two basic concepts. First, these tests generally excuse when the defendant is unable to know (or appreciate) that her action was "wrong"; second, they generally require that the disabling condition, however defined, be attributable to "a mental disease or defect." The following two subsections explore the meaning of these two concepts.

ii. The Meaning of Wrong

STATE v. CRENSHAW

Washington Supreme Court
98 Wash. 2d 789, 659 P.2d 488 (1983)

BRACHTENBACH, J. . . . While defendant and his wife were on their honeymoon in Canada, petitioner was deported as a result of his participation in a brawl. He secured a motel room in Blaine, Washington, and waited for his wife to join him. When she arrived 2 days later, he immediately thought she had been unfaithful—he sensed "it wasn't the same Karen . . . she'd been with someone else."

Petitioner did not mention his suspicions to his wife, instead he took her to the motel room and beat her unconscious. He then went to a nearby store, stole a knife, and returned to stab his wife 24 times, inflicting a fatal wound. He left again, drove to a nearby farm where he had been employed and borrowed an ax. Upon returning to the motel room, he decapitated his wife with such force that the ax marks cut into the concrete floor under the carpet and splattered blood throughout the room.

Petitioner then proceeded to conceal his actions. He placed the body in a blanket, the head in a pillowcase, and put both in his wife's car. Next, he went to a service station, borrowed a bucket and sponge, and cleaned the room of blood and fingerprints. Before leaving, petitioner also spoke with the motel manager about a phone bill, then chatted with him for a while over a beer.

When Crenshaw left the motel he drove to a remote area 25 miles away where he hid the two parts of the body in thick brush. He then fled, driving to the Hoquiam area, about 200 miles from the scene of the crime. There he picked up two hitchhikers, told them of his crime, and enlisted their aid in disposing of his wife's car in a river. The hitchhikers contacted the police and Crenshaw was apprehended shortly thereafter. He voluntarily confessed to the crime.

The defense of not guilty by reason of insanity was a major issue at trial. Crenshaw testified that he followed the Moscovite religious faith, and that it would be improper for a Moscovite not to kill his wife if she committed adultery. Crenshaw also has a history of mental problems, for which he has been hospitalized in the past. The jury, however, rejected petitioner's insanity defense, and found him guilty of murder in the first degree. . . .

Petitioner assigned error to insanity defense instruction 10 which reads: . . .

> For a defendant to be found not guilty by reason of insanity you must find that, as a result of mental disease or defect, the defendant's mind was affected to such an extent that the defendant was unable to perceive the nature and quality of the acts with which the defendant is charged or was unable to tell right from wrong with reference to the particular acts with which defendant is charged.
>
> What is meant by the terms "right and wrong" refers to knowledge of a person at the time of committing an act that he was acting contrary to the law.

But for the last paragraph, this instruction tracks the language of . . . the *M'Naghten* test as codified in RCW 9A.12.-010. Petitioner contends, however, that the trial court erred in defining "right and wrong" as legal right and wrong rather than in the moral sense. . . .

The definition of the term "wrong" in the *M'Naghten* test has been considered and disputed by many legal scholars. . . . This court's view has been [as follows]:

> [O]nly those persons "who have lost contact with reality so completely that they are beyond any of the influences of the criminal law," may have the benefit of the insanity defense in a criminal case.

State v. McDonald, 89 Wash. 2d 256, 272, 571 P.2d 930 (1977). Given this perspective, the trial court could assume that one who knew the illegality of his act was not necessarily "beyond any of the influences of the criminal law," thus finding support for the statement in instruction 10.

Alternatively, the statement in instruction 10 may be approved because, in this case, legal wrong is synonymous with moral wrong. [I]t is important to note that it is society's morals, and not the individual's morals, that are the standard for judging moral wrong under *M'Naghten*. If wrong meant moral wrong judged by the individual's own conscience, this would seriously undermine the criminal law, for it would allow one who violated the law to be excused from criminal responsibility solely because, in his own conscience, his act was not morally wrong. . . .

There is evidence on the record that Crenshaw knew his actions were wrong according to society's standards, as well as legally wrong. Dr. Belden testified:

> I think Mr. Crenshaw is quite aware on one level that he is in conflict with the law *and with people*. However, this is not something that he personally invests his emotions in.

We conclude that Crenshaw knew his acts were morally wrong from society's viewpoint and also knew his acts were illegal. His personal belief that it was his duty to kill his wife for her alleged infidelity cannot serve to exculpate him from legal responsibility for his acts.

A narrow exception to the societal standard of moral wrong has been drawn for instances wherein a party performs a criminal act, knowing it is morally and legally wrong, but believing, because of a mental defect, that the act is ordained by God: such would be the situation with a mother who kills her infant child to whom she is devotedly attached, believing that God has spoken to her and decreed the act. Although the woman knows that the law and society condemn the act, it would be unrealistic to hold her responsible for the crime, since her free will has been subsumed by her belief in the deific decree.

Reasoning

This exception is not available to Crenshaw, however. Crenshaw argued only that he followed the Moscovite faith and that Moscovites believe it is their duty to kill an unfaithful wife. This is not the same as acting under a deific command. Instead, it is akin to "[t]he devotee of a religious cult that enjoins . . . human sacrifice as a duty [and] is *not* thereby relieved from responsibility before the law." Crenshaw's personal "Moscovite" beliefs are not equivalent to a deific decree and do not relieve him from responsibility for his acts. . . .

NOTES

1. Legal vs. moral wrong. American courts are divided on the issue presented in *Crenshaw*. Several jurisdictions hold, in accord with *Crenshaw*, that an insanity acquittal requires the defendant to be unaware that his conduct was *legally* wrong. Although ignorance of the law is not, of course, a defense, *knowledge* of the law will be sufficient in these jurisdictions to defeat any claim under *M'Naghten.* See, e.g., State v. Hollis, 731 P.2d 260 (Kan. 1987); State v. Hamann, 285 N.W.2d 180 (Iowa 1979). In contrast, a number of decisions hold that "wrong" means "morally wrong." E.g., People v. Coddington, 2 P.3d 1081 (Cal. 2000); People v. Serravo, 823 P.2d 128 (Colo. 1992). Many jurisdictions leave the issue to the jury without specifying whether "wrong" means legally or morally wrong. E.g., State v. Morgan, 863 So. 2d 520, 525 n.5 (La. 2004) (identifying this practice as the predominant American approach).

Which approach to the *Crenshaw* issue is more consistent with the purposes of an insanity defense? On the one hand, if a defendant has sufficient awareness to realize the illegality of his conduct and to attempt to conceal his crime, doesn't he fall, by definition, among those whose behavior is potentially deterrable? On the other hand, consider James F. Stephen, 2 History of the Criminal Law of England 167 (1883):

> [T]he question whether "wrong" means "morally wrong," or only "illegal," may be important. In Hadfield's case, for instance, knowledge of the illegality of his act was the very reason why he did it. He wanted to be hung for it. He no doubt knew it to be wrong in the sense that he knew that other people would disapprove of it, but he would also have thought, had he thought at all, that if they knew all the facts (as he understood them) they would approve of him, and see that he was sacrificing his own interest for the common good. I could not say that such a person knew that such an act was wrong. His delusion would prevent anything like an act of calm judgment in the character of the act.

In *Serravo*, supra, expert testimony established that due to either brain damage or paranoid schizophrenia, defendant suffered from the delusion that God had told him to construct a multimillion dollar sports facility to teach people the path to perfection and that he believed he had to stab his wife to achieve that goal. At his trial for her murder, psychiatric experts for both the state and the defense agreed that Serravo was unable to distinguish moral right from wrong, though he probably knew that his act was illegal. Holding that knowledge of the act's illegality will not defeat a defense under *M'Naghten*, the court said (823 P.2d at 135-139):

> We acknowledge that some cases subsequent to *M'Naghten* have interpreted the right-wrong test as limiting the insanity defense to a cognitive inability to distinguish legal right from legal wrong, with the result that a person's simple awareness that an act is illegal is a sufficient basis for finding criminal responsibility. We believe, however, that such an analysis injects a formalistic legalism into the insanity equation to the disregard of the psychological underpinnings of legal insanity. A person in an extremely psychotic state, for example, might be aware that an act is prohibited by law, but due to the overbearing effect of the psychosis may be utterly without the capacity to comprehend that the act is inherently immoral. A standard of legal wrong would render such a person legally responsible and subject to imprisonment for the conduct in question notwithstanding the patent injustice of such a disposition. Conversely, a person who, although mentally ill, has the cognitive capacity to distinguish right from wrong and is aware that an act is morally wrong, but does not realize that it is illegal, should nonetheless be held responsible for the act, as ignorance of the law is no excuse. . . . A clarifying instruction on the definition of legal insanity, therefore, should clearly state that, as related to the conduct charged as a crime, the phrase "incapable of distinguishing right from wrong" refers to a person's cognitive inability, due to a mental disease or defect, to distinguish right from wrong as measured by a societal standard of morality, even though the person may be aware that the conduct in question is criminal. Any such instruction should also expressly inform the jury that the phrase "incapable of distinguishing right from wrong" does not refer to a purely personal and subjective standard of morality.

For a helpful review of the possible meanings of "wrong" as contrary to law, against prevailing morality, or against one's conscience, see Herbert Fingarette, The Meaning of Criminal Insanity 123 (1972).

2. The "deific decree" exception. Why does the court in *Crenshaw* suggest that the result would be different if the defendant had said that his acts were "ordained by God" rather than merely by his "Moscovite" religion? In a later case, State v. Cameron, 674 P.2d 650 (Wash. 1983), where there was evidence the defendant believed God was instructing him, the court reversed for failure to give a "deific decree" instruction. A concurring judge observed, "Both *Crenshaw* and the subject case were almost factually identical; both involved outrageous, vicious, messy murders. . . . I frankly don't see much or any distinction, however, in carrying out or executing a murder under the direction of God or Crenshaw's Moscovite religious beliefs, or under the beliefs of a prophet, Buddha, etc. . . ."

Why do courts distinguish deific decrees from nonreligious command hallucinations and even from less specific religious beliefs? Is the significance of a deific decree that no defendant can be expected to withstand a threat from God (a sort of deific duress defense)? Or that obedience to a deific decree (by a person who believed God really had issued it) would be morally correct—a direct application of *M'Naghten*? For an argument that the deific decree doctrine is unworkable because it is impossible to distinguish insane delusions from sincere religious beliefs, see Grant H. Morris & Ansar Haroun, "God Told Me to Kill" : Religion or Delusion?, 38 San Diego L. Rev. 973 (2001).

ii. The Meaning of "Mental Disease or Defect"

STATE v. GUIDO

New Jersey Supreme Court
40 N.J. 191, 191 A.2d 45 (1963)

WEINTRAUB, C.J., Adele Guido was convicted of murder in the second degree and sentenced to imprisonment for a minimum of 24 years and a maximum of 27 years. She appeals directly to this Court. . . .

The victim was defendant's husband. When they first met, she was a young girl and he a professional fighter of some success. . . . All the details of the marital discord need not be stated. [Defendant] wanted a divorce, while decedent insisted upon holding on to her notwithstanding he would not or could not end his extra marital romance. . . . In the early morning of April 17, 1961, after deceased fell asleep on a couch in the living room while watching television, defendant, according to her testimony, took the gun and went into her room, intending to end her life. Deciding that suicide would be no solution, she returned to the living room to put the weapon back in the suitcase, but when her eyes fell upon Guido, she raised the weapon and fired until it was empty.

With respect to physical abuse, the jury could find that although there were only a few incidents of actual injury, there was the constant threat of it. . . . It appears that on several occasions shortly before the homicide defendant called the local police to express her fear of harm. . . .

Defendant . . . was examined by two court-appointed psychiatrists. [Their] report contained sundry medical findings and ultimately the opinion that defendant was "legally" sane at the time of the shooting. Mr. Saltzman [defense counsel] met with the psychiatrists, and after some three hours of debate the psychiatrists changed their opinion as to "legal" insanity although their underlying medical findings remained the same. They then retyped the last page of their report. . . .

[During closing argument, the prosecutor, who had discovered this change in the psychiatric reports, charged that the insanity defense had been "concocted" and that defense counsel had "perpetrated a fraud on this Court." Defendant sought reversal of her conviction on the ground that this line of argument was unjustified and inexcusably prejudicial.]

When the basis of the change in the experts' opinion was explored, it quickly appeared that the change was thoroughly consistent with honesty however mistaken it might be. . . . Specifically, the doctors originally understood that the "disease of the mind" required by [*M'Naghten*] means a *psychosis* and not some lesser illness or functional aberration. As the result of their pretrial debate with Mr. Saltzman, the doctors concluded they had had too narrow a view of *M'Naghten* and that the "anxiety neurosis" they had found *anxiety neurosis.* did qualify as a "disease" within the legal rule, and hence . . . defendant did not know right from wrong and she did not know what she was doing was wrong because of that "disease." . . .

The change in the opinions of the defense psychiatrists simply focuses attention upon an area of undeniable obscurity. [T]he *M'Naghten* rule requires a "disease of the mind." The competing [tests] of legal insanity also require a disease (or defect) of the mind. . . . But the hard question under any concept of legal insanity is, What constitutes a "disease"? . . . The postulate is that some wrongdoers are sick while others are bad, and that it is against good morals to stigmatize the sick. Who then are the sick whose illness shows they are free of moral blame? We cannot turn to the psychiatrist for a list of illnesses which have that quality because, for all his insight into the dynamics of behavior, he has not solved the riddle of blame. The question remains an ethical one, the answer to which lies beyond scientific truth.

[A]lthough emphasis [in the *M'Naghten* Rule is] upon a state of mind, it is nonetheless required that that state be due to "disease" and not something else. So our cases contrast that concept of insanity with "emotional insanity" or "moral insanity" which, upon the dichotomy mentioned above, is attributed to moral depravity or weakness and hence will not excuse the offender even if his rage was so blinding that he did not really appreciate what he was doing or that it was wrong. . . . Yet the traditional charge of the *M'Naghten* rule to the jury does not attempt to say what is meant by "disease," and [there is a] rather universal reluctance to assay a definition. . . .

We have described the problem, not to resolve it, but simply to reveal the room for disputation, to the end of demonstrating the unfairness of charging defendant, her attorney, and her witnesses with a fraud when the change in the experts' opinion . . . involved no departure from prior medical findings but rather a change in the witnesses' understanding of what the law means by "disease." . . .

The judgment is reversed. . . .

NOTES AND QUESTIONS

1. Questions on **Guido.** If "mental disease" is a legal concept, why were the psychiatrists allowed to express their conclusions about it at all? In what sense were they "experts" in the meaning of a legal concept?

2. The legal definition of "disease." In agreement with *Guido*, most courts treat "mental disease" for purposes of the insanity defense as a legal, not a medical concept, but few indicate the criteria that determine when this legal element is present. When they do, the tests typically give little guidance. Consider whether the following formulation is helpful (McDonald v. United States, 312 F.2d 847, 850-851 (D.C. Cir. 1962)):

> What psychiatrists may consider a "mental disease or defect" for clinical purposes, where their concern is treatment, may or may not be the same as mental disease or defect for the jury's purpose in determining criminal responsibility. Consequently, for that purpose the jury should be told that a mental disease or defect includes any abnormal condition of the mind which substantially affects mental or emotional processes and substantially impairs behavior controls.

Compare the definition proposed by the American Psychiatric Association (140 Am. J. Psychiatry 6 (1980)):

> [T]he terms mental disease or mental retardation include only those severely abnormal mental conditions that grossly and demonstrably impair a person's perception or understanding of reality and that are not attributable primarily to the voluntary ingestion of alcohol or other psychoactive substances.

Another attempt at definition, offered by the American Bar Association, states (A.B.A., Crim. Just. Mental Health Stand. §7-6.1(a) (1983)):

> [The term mental disease or defect] refers to impairments of mind, whether enduring or transitory, or to mental retardation which substantially affected the mental or emotional processes of the defendant at the time of the alleged offense.

3. Specific applications. Suppose that psychiatric examination indicates that the defendant, because of "explosive personality disorder," lacks the capacity to "appreciate" the wrongfulness of his aggressive, violent reactions. Does he qualify for the insanity defense? Should the answer depend on whether the psychiatric profession classifies this abnormality as a "personality disorder" rather than as a psychosis?

Does the *McDonald* definition help resolve the difficulties. The defendant's situation presumably is "abnormal," but is it a "condition of the mind" within the meaning of *McDonald*? Is this a legal or a medical question? Apart from the *McDonald* formulation, what is the "right" result in the preceding example? If a defendant suffers from an impairment of cognition or control sufficiently serious to satisfy the prevailing insanity test, why should it matter that the impairment results not from disease but only from a "personality disorder"? Isn't blame inappropriate (and deterrence unlikely) in either case? In other words, why *bother* to define disease?

The disease requirement has often defeated defense efforts to introduce evidence of a great variety of mental abnormalities, including battered spouse syndrome,[63] compulsive gambling disorder,[64] premenstrual

---

63. E.g., Bechtel v. State, 840 P.2d 1,7 (Okla. Cr. App. 1992).
64. E.g., United States v. Gould, 741 F.2d 45 (4th Cir. 1984).

syndrome,[65] postpartum disorders,[66] multiple personality,[67] post-traumatic stress disorders,[68] alcohol and drug addictions,[69] homosexual panic,[70] and sexual disorders such as pedophilia, sadism, and masochism.[71] Is this obstacle to a successful insanity defense good or bad? For discussion, see Stephen J. Morse, Excusing and the New Excuse Defenses: A Legal and Conceptual Review, 23 Crime & Just. 329 (1998); Alan M. Dershowitz, The Abuse Excuse (1994).

NOTE ON THE PSYCHOPATH

A major issue of policy for the insanity defense concerns its application to the psychopath—the offender with a long history of antisocial conduct. Many persistent offenders "know" (in a purely verbal way) that their conduct is illegal, but they experience little or no empathy and have no apparent capacity to "understand" (at the "affective," emotional level) the rights of others. Their behavior brings them repeatedly into conflict with others and with the law. Often, psychiatrists diagnose them as suffering from "psychopathic personality" or "sociopathic personality," now more commonly designated "antisocial personality disorder," and many mental health professionals regard the disorder as a "mental disease." Is such an offender legally insane?

MPC §4.01(2), commonly referred to as the "caveat paragraph," was designed to exclude from the concept of "mental disease or defect" the case of the so-called psychopathic personality. It states that "the terms 'mental disease or defect' do not include an abnormality manifested only by repeated criminal or otherwise antisocial conduct." Consider State v. Werlein, 401 N.W.2d 848 (Wis. App. 1987), decided in a state that had adopted the caveat paragraph. The defendant, for no apparent reason, opened fire with a semiautomatic rifle, inflicting serious injury on the victim. He was convicted of attempted first-degree murder. At trial, he had called Dr. Albert Lorenz, who diagnosed him as suffering from antisocial personality disorder:

> Lorenz testified that Werlein's [symptoms] included an inability to handle work, squandering money, lack of attachment to people or groups, and reckless behavior. Lorenz stated that Werlein has no personality of his own, cannot plan for the future, and follows others much like a little child would. Lorenz concluded that as a result of Werlein's illness, he could not conform his conduct to the requirements of law.

---

65. See Christopher Boorse, Premenstrual Syndrome and Criminal Responsibility, in Premenstrual Syndrome 81-124 (B.E. Ginsburg & B.F. Carter eds., 1987).

66. See Jessie Manchester (Comment), Beyond Accommodation: Reconstructing the Insanity Defense to Provide an Adequate Remedy for Postpartum Psychotic Women, 93 J. Crim. L. & Criminology 713 (2003).

67. See Elyn R. Saks, Jekyll on Trial: Multiple Personality Disorder and Criminal Law (1997).

68. E.g., People v. Babbitt, 755 P.2d 253 (Cal. 1998). See C. Peter Erlinder, Paying the Price for Vietnam: Post-Traumatic Stress Disorder and Criminal Behavior, 25 B.C. L. Rev. 305 (1984).

69. E.g., Commonwealth v. Sheehan, 383 N.E.2d 1115 (Mass. 1978).

70. See Kara S. Suffredini (Note), Pride and Prejudice: The Homosexual Panic Defense, 21 B.C. Third World L.J. 279 (2001).

71. E.g., State v. Armstrong, 789 N.E.2d 657 (Ohio App. 2003).

The trial court struck Dr. Lorenz's testimony and precluded the jury from considering whether Werlein was mentally irresponsible. The court of appeals reversed, holding that caveat paragraph was inapplicable, since Dr. Lorenz's diagnosis went far beyond that of an abnormality manifested only by repeated criminal or otherwise antisocial conduct. Cf. Wade v. United States, 426 F.2d 64, 73 (9th Cir. 1970): "[I]t is practically inconceivable that a mental disease or defect would, in the terms of paragraph (2), be 'manifested *only* by repeated criminal or otherwise antisocial conduct'" (emphasis added). If the MPC text is inadequate to achieve the broad exclusion intended by its drafters, should it be amended? How?

For arguments that psychopathy should be considered a mental disease for purposes of the defense of insanity, see Charles Fischette (Note), Psychopathy and Responsibility, 90 Va. L. Rev. 1423 (2004); the author argues that empirical evidence linking emotional brain states and ethical motivations suggests that psychopaths are not full moral agents for whom punishment is appropriate. In United States v. Currens, 290 F.2d 751 (3d Cir. 1961), the court asserted that it is possible to distinguish psychopaths from those who merely demonstrate recurrent criminal behavior and that juries should be allowed to consider all pertinent symptoms of a defendant in considering whether the insanity defense is warranted in such cases. In contrast, some experts argue that psychopathy should be excluded from the ambit of the insanity defense. Samuel Perry, Allen Frances & John Clarkin suggest (in A DSM-III Casebook of Differential Therapeutics 304-305 (1985)) that because the capacity of mental health professionals to treat psychopathy is limited, and because psychopathic defendants will prey on other vulnerable mental patients, such defendants should not avoid punishment by being referred for a treatment that does not exist. See also People v. Fields, 673 P.2d 690 (Cal. 1983), where the court expressed concern that because psychopaths are defined by their recurring criminal behavior, permitting them to assert the insanity defense would open up the defense to a substantial proportion of serious criminal offenders.

Questions: Do these disagreements flow from differing perceptions about the relevant *facts* (such as whether psychopaths feel emotion, whether they respond to deterrent measures, and whether they are treatable)? Or do these disagreements flow from different *judgments* about values and policy? If the latter, does the disagreement center on the impact that the insanity defense will have on social protection in these cases, or does it center on whether the psychopath can justly be blamed?

NOTES ON AUTOMATISM—SANE AND INSANE

Should the insanity defense apply to acts performed by a defendant who is not conscious of performing them, such as acts performed while sleepwalking, under hypnosis, during an epileptic seizure, or following extreme physical or emotional trauma? Like defendants who are insane, defendants in a state of automatism do not seem proper subjects for either blame or deterrence. But unlike insanity, automatism is not always the product of "a mental disease or defect." Should the criminal law treat automatism as a species of insanity? Or should the law attempt to distinguish between automatism that is a result of a mental disease or defect ("insane automatism") and automatism that has some other source ("sane automatism")? Note what is at stake in choosing among these options: Automatism may give rise to the complete defense of involuntary action, see page 212 supra; whereas the insanity defense generally results in a prolonged period of incapacitation and treatment, see pages 964-966 supra.

1. Defendant's option? Most American courts hold that the defendant may elect to plead either insanity, involuntariness, or both. See, e.g., State v. Jenner, 451 N.W.2d 710 (S.D. 1990). The English rule, in contrast, holds that when automatism results from a mental disease or defect, the only defense available is the plea of not guilty by reason of insanity. See Bratty v. Attorney-General for Northern Ireland, [1963] A.C. 386. A minority of American jurisdictions follow the English approach. See, e.g., Loven v. State, 831 S.W.2d 387 (Tex. App. 1992).

2. Distinguishing sane from insane automatisms. Where insanity and automatism are mutually exclusive defenses, courts must decide whether the claimed automatism results from a mental disorder. For example, in Wyoming, where the insanity defense is available for impairments resulting from "mental illness or deficiency," the definition of "mental deficiency" is "a defect attributable to intellectual disability, brain damage and cognitive disabilities." Wyo. Stat. §7-11-301(a)(iii) (2011). In Fulcher v. State, 633 P.2d 142 (Wyo. 1981), the defendant was charged with aggravated assault. With the support of expert medical testimony, he claimed that his actions were committed in a state of automatism resulting from traumatic head injuries inflicted in a brawl shortly before the alleged offense. Should such injuries be regarded as a form of "brain damage," which Wyoming law would require to be raised solely in terms of the insanity defense? The Wyoming Supreme Court held that the defendant's injuries did not represent "brain damage" within the meaning of the statute and accordingly that the automatism defense remained available. The court said (id. at 146):

> It is our view that the "brain damage" contemplated in the statute is some serious and irreversible condition having an impact upon the ability of the person to function. It is undoubtedly something far more significant than a temporary and transitory condition.

A dissenting judge commented (id. at 155, 162-163):

> There is no basis whatsoever that supports the proposition the majority espouses that, . . . "the 'brain damage' contemplated in the statute is some serious and irreversible condition . . . ." To the contrary, the only material condition is that which exists at the moment of the crime. How long should the condition exist before it comes within the cloak of the statute—a minute,

an hour, a day, a week, two weeks, a month, a year, five years, a lifetime? The statute says nothing about a temporary condition or one that is "serious and irreversible."

Question: What considerations might have led the majority to reach its interpretation of the statute?

3. Sleep. Relatively few cases have dealt with criminal conduct during various states of sleep. The courts appear to be divided on the question whether the defendant in such a case is entitled to outright acquittal due to the absence of a volitional act, or whether the defendant must plead insanity and face commitment to a mental hospital. In McClain v. State, 678 N.E.2d 104 (Ind. 1997), the court held that the defendant's sleep disorder could form the basis of an automatism defense. Noting that Indiana law required commitment proceedings to follow an insanity acquittal, the court observed that merging the automatism and insanity defenses, as the state urged, would force a sane but automatistic defendant to face "a choice of possible commitment or effectively presenting no defense at all." Id. at 108. An English case reached the opposite conclusion. In Regina v. Burgess, [1991] 2 All E.R. 769, the defendant fell asleep while watching a videotape with his neighbor. He awoke to find himself hitting her on the head with a bottle and attempting to strangle her. He quickly came to his senses and called an ambulance for her, but he was charged with assault. He had no history of mental illness and had been on completely friendly terms with the victim. Because the defendant's automatism derived from an "internal" source, the court concluded that it was the result of a "mental disease" and that therefore the defendant could raise only a defense of insanity and not a defense of automatism. Burgess was found not guilty by reason of insanity. For a trenchant criticism of the result, see Irene Mackay, The Sleepwalker Is Not Insane, 55 Mod. L. Rev. 714 (1992).

Sleep disorder experts study "parasomnias" (involuntary behaviors during sleep) through clinical observations in "sleep labs" and animal experimentation. Such research has suggested a distinction between "REM behavior disorder," which is the result of altered brain-stem activity and can be treated with a sedative, and "nocturnal dissociative disorder," which may appear similar, but is technically a waking state and a psychiatric disorder rather than a sleep disorder. See Chip Brown, the Man Who Mistook His Wife For a Deer, N.Y. Times Mag., Feb. 2, 2003, at 34. Should clinical distinctions such as these be dispositive of the legal questions?

b. Diminished Capacity

UNITED STATES v. BRAWNER

United States Court of Appeals, District of Columbia Circuit
471 F.2d 969 (1972)

LEVENTHAL, J. [After examining the test of legal insanity as a complete defense, the court considered whether mental health evidence should be admissible apart from its bearing on the insanity issue.] [E]xpert testimony as to a defendant's abnormal mental condition may be received and considered, as tending to show . . . that defendant did not have the specific mental state required for a particular crime or degree of crime—even though he was aware that his act was wrongful and was able to control it, and hence was not entitled to complete exoneration.

Some of the cases following this doctrine use the term "diminished responsibility," but we prefer [to] avoid this term, for its convenience is outweighed by its confusion: Our doctrine has nothing to do with "diminishing" responsibility of a defendant because of his impaired mental condition, but rather with determining whether the defendant had the mental state that must be proved as to all defendants.

Procedurally, the issue of abnormal mental condition negativing a person's intent may arise in different ways: For example, the defendant may offer evidence of mental condition not qualifying as mental disease. . . . Or he may tender evidence that qualifies [as a mental disease], yet the jury may conclude from all the evidence that defendant has knowledge and control capacity sufficient for responsibility. . . .

The issue often arises with respect to mental condition tendered as negativing the element of premeditation in a charge of first degree premeditated murder. . . . An offense like deliberated and premeditated murder requires a specific intent that cannot be satisfied merely by showing that defendant failed to conform to an objective standard. This is plainly established by the defense of voluntary intoxication. In Hopt v. Utah, 104 U.S. 631 (1881), the Court, after stating the familiar rule that voluntary intoxication is no excuse for crime, said: "[W]hen a statute establishing different degrees of murder requires deliberate premeditation in order to constitute murder in the first degree, the question of whether the accused is in such a condition of mind, by reason of drunkenness or otherwise, as to be capable of deliberate premeditation, necessarily becomes a material subject of consideration by the jury. . . ."

Neither logic nor justice can tolerate a jurisprudence . . . such that one defendant can properly argue that his voluntary drunkenness removed his capacity to form the specific intent but another defendant is inhibited from a submission of his contention that an abnormal mental condition, for which he was in no way responsible, negated his capacity to form a particular specific intent, even though the condition did not exonerate him from all criminal responsibility. . . .

The pertinent reasoning was succinctly stated by the Colorado Supreme Court as follows [Battalino v. People, 199 P.2d 897, 901 (Colo. 1948)]:

> A claim of insanity cannot be used for the purpose of reducing a crime of murder in the first degree to murder in the second degree or from murder to manslaughter. If the perpetrator is responsible at all in this respect, he is responsible in the same degree as a sane man; and if he is not responsible at all, he is entitled to an acquittal in both degrees. However, . . . *evidence of the*

condition of the mind of the accused at the time of the crime, together with the surrounding circumstances, may be introduced, not for the purpose of establishing insanity, but to prove that the situation was such that a specific intent was not entertained—that is, *to show absence of any deliberate or premeditated design.* Emphasis in original.) . . .

Our rule permits the introduction of expert testimony as to abnormal condition if it is relevant to negative, or establish, the specific mental condition that is an element of the crime. The receipt of this expert testimony to negative the mental condition of specific intent requires careful administration by the trial judge. . . . The judge will . . . determine whether the testimony is grounded in sufficient scientific support to warrant use in the courtroom, and whether it would aid the jury in reaching a decision on the ultimate issues. . . .

CLARK v. ARIZONA

Supreme Court of the United States
548 U.S. 735 (2006)

JUSTICE SOUTER delivered the opinion of the Court.

[Defendant shot and killed Jeffrey Moritz, a police officer who had pulled him over for a traffic stop. He was charged under an Arizona statute making it first-degree murder to "intentionally or knowingly" kill a police officer in the line of duty. He waived his right to a jury. At a bench trial, the prosecutor offered circumstantial evidence that Clark knew he was killing a law enforcement officer—the officer was in uniform, in a marked police car with emergency lights flashing, and Clark had acknowledged these symbols of police authority when he stopped.]

Clark claimed mental illness, which he sought to introduce for two purposes. First, he raised the affirmative defense of insanity, [which under Arizona law put] the burden on himself to prove by clear and convincing evidence that "at the time of the commission of the criminal act [he] was afflicted with a mental disease or defect of such severity that [he] did not know the criminal act was wrong." Second, he aimed to rebut the prosecution's evidence . . . that he had acted intentionally or knowingly to kill a law enforcement officer.

The trial court ruled that Clark could not rely on evidence bearing on insanity to dispute the *mens rea*[, citing state precedent holding that] "Arizona does not allow evidence of a defendant's mental disorder short of insanity . . . to negate the *mens rea* element of a crime."

As to his insanity, then, Clark presented testimony from classmates, school officials, and his family describing his increasingly bizarre behavior over the year before the shooting. Witnesses testified, for example, that paranoid delusions led Clark to rig a fishing line with beads and wind chimes at home to alert him to intrusion by invaders. . . . There was lay and expert testimony that Clark thought Flagstaff was populated with "aliens" [and] the "aliens" were trying to kill him. . . . A psychiatrist testified that Clark was suffering from paranoid schizophrenia, [that he was incapable of] understanding right from wrong and that he was thus insane at the time of the killing. In rebuttal, a psychiatrist for the State gave his opinion that Clark's paranoid schizophrenia did not keep him from appreciating the wrongfulness of his conduct, as shown by his actions before and after the shooting (such as . . . , evading the police after the shooting, and hiding the gun).

[The trial judge concluded that Clark did intend to kill the officer and rejected Clark's insanity defense because he found that Clark had failed to prove that his schizophrenia prevented him from knowing his actions were wrong. Accordingly, he found Clark guilty of first-degree murder and sentenced him to life imprisonment, without the possibility of release for 25 years. The Arizona Court of Appeals affirmed. The Supreme Court granted certiorari to examine two principal issues. First it considered and rejected Clark's challenge to the narrowness of Arizona's formulation of the insanity defense. We discuss this aspect of the *Clark* decision at page 985 supra. The Court then turned to the question whether Arizona violated due process in barring consideration of Clark's mental illness in determining whether the evidence established the mens rea that was a required element of the offense charged.]

Understanding Clark's claim requires attention to the categories of evidence with a potential bearing on mens rea. First, there is "observation evidence" . . . , testimony from those who observed what Clark did and heard what he said; this category would also include testimony that an expert witness might give about Clark's tendency to think in a certain way and his behavioral characteristics. This . . . kind of evidence [can] be relevant to show what in fact was on Clark's mind when he fired the gun. Observation evidence in the record covers Clark's behavior at home and with friends [and] his expressions of belief around the time of the killing that "aliens" were inhabiting the bodies of local people (including government agents).[27] . . .

Second, there is "mental-disease evidence" in the form of opinion testimony that Clark suffered from a mental disease with features described by the witness. As was true here, this evidence characteristically but not always comes from professional psychologists or psychiatrists who . . . base their opinions in part on examination of a defendant, usually conducted after the events in question. The thrust of this evidence was that . . . Clark was psychotic at the time in question, with a condition that fell within the category of schizophrenia.

Third, there is evidence we will refer to as "capacity evidence" about a defendant's capacity for cognition and moral judgment (and ultimately also his capacity to form mens rea). This, too, is opinion evidence. Here . . . this

---

27. Clark's parents testified that, in the months before the shooting and even days beforehand, Clark called them "aliens" and thought that "aliens" were out to get him. One night before the shooting, according to Clark's mother, Clark repeatedly viewed a popular film characterized by her as telling a story about "aliens" masquerading as government agents, a story Clark insisted was real despite his mother's protestations to the contrary. . . .

testimony came from the same experts and concentrated on those specific details of the mental condition that make the difference between sanity and insanity under the Arizona definition. . . .

[Arizona imposes] no restriction on considering . . . observation evidence. [Rather, its restrictions apply to] testimony that characteristically comes only from . . . expert witnesses: mental-disease evidence . . . and capacity evidence. . . .

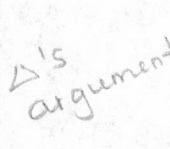

Clark's argument is [that Arizona's restrictions violate] a defendant's right as a matter of simple due process to present evidence favorable to himself on an element that must be proven to convict him.[39] . . . Clark claims a right to require the factfinder in this case to consider testimony about his mental illness and his incapacity directly, when weighing the persuasiveness of other evidence tending to show mens rea. [H]owever, the right to introduce relevant evidence can be curtailed if there is a good reason for doing that. ". . . [W]ell-established rules of evidence permit trial judges to exclude evidence if its probative value is outweighed by certain other factors such as unfair prejudice, confusion of the issues, or potential to mislead the jury." Holmes v. South Carolina, 547 U.S. 319 (2006). [In Arizona,] mental-disease and capacity evidence [is] channeled or restricted to one issue and given effect only if the defendant carries the burden to convince the factfinder of insanity; the evidence is not being excluded entirely, and the question is whether reasons for requiring it to be channeled and restricted are good enough to satisfy the standard of fundamental fairness that due process requires. . . . We think there are [such reasons]: in the controversial character of some categories of mental disease, in the potential of mental-disease evidence to mislead, and in the danger of according greater certainty to capacity evidence than experts claim for it.

To begin with, the diagnosis may mask vigorous debate within the profession about the very contours of the mental disease itself. . . .

Next, [e]ven when a category of mental disease is broadly accepted . . . , the classification may suggest something very significant about a defendant's capacity, when in fact the classification tells us little or nothing about the ability of the defendant to form mens rea. . . . The limits of the utility of a professional disease diagnosis are evident in the dispute between the two testifying experts in this case; they agree that Clark was schizophrenic, but they come to opposite conclusions on whether the mental disease in his particular case left him bereft of cognitive or moral capacity. [I]t is very easy to slide from evidence that an individual with a professionally recognized mental disease is very different, into doubting that he has the capacity to form mens rea, whereas that doubt may not be justified. . . . Because allowing mental-disease evidence on mens rea can thus easily mislead, it is not unreasonable to address that tendency by confining consideration of this kind of

---

39. Clark's argument assumes that Arizona's rule is a rule of evidence, rather than a redefinition of mens rea. We have no reason to view the rule otherwise, and on this assumption, it does not violate due process.

evidence to insanity, on which a defendant may be assigned the burden of persuasion.

There are, finally, particular risks inherent in the opinions of the experts who supplement the mental-disease classifications with opinions on incapacity. . . . Unlike observational evidence bearing on mens rea, capacity evidence consists of judgment, and judgment fraught with multiple perils. . . . Although such capacity judgments may be given in the utmost good faith, [they have a] potentially tenuous character. [J]udgment addressing the basic categories of capacity requires a leap from the concepts of psychology, which are devised for thinking about treatment, to the concepts of legal sanity, which are devised for thinking about criminal responsibility. [There is] a real risk that an expert's judgment in giving capacity evidence will come with an apparent authority that psychologists and psychiatrists do not claim to have. We think that this risk, like the difficulty in assessing the significance of mental-disease evidence, supports the State's decision to channel such expert testimony to consideration on the insanity defense, on which the party seeking the benefit of this evidence has the burden of persuasion.

It bears repeating that not every State will find it worthwhile to make the judgment Arizona has made, and the choices the States do make about dealing with the risks posed by mental-disease and capacity evidence will reflect their varying assessments about the presumption of sanity as expressed in choices of insanity rules. The point here simply is that Arizona has sensible reasons to assign the risks as it has done by channeling the evidence.[45] . . .

The judgment of the Court of Appeals of Arizona is, accordingly, affirmed.

JUSTICE KENNEDY, with whom JUSTICE STEVENS and JUSTICE GINSBURG join, dissenting. . . .

Clark's defense was that his schizophrenia made him delusional. He lived in a universe where the delusions were so dominant, the theory was, that he had no intent to shoot a police officer or knowledge he was doing so. It is one thing to say he acted with intent or knowledge to pull the trigger. . . . If the trier of fact were to find Clark's evidence sufficient to discount the case made by the State, which has the burden to prove knowledge or intent as an element of the offense, Clark would not be guilty of first-degree murder under Arizona law. . . . The issue is not, as the Court insists, whether Clark's mental illness acts as an "excuse from customary criminal responsibility," but whether his mental illness, as a factual matter, made him unaware that he was shooting a

---

45. Arizona's rule is supported by a further practical reason, though not as weighty as those just considered. [I]f substantial mental-disease and capacity evidence is accepted as rebutting mens rea in a given case, the affirmative defense of insanity will probably not be reached or ruled upon; the defendant will simply be acquitted (or perhaps convicted of a lesser included offense). If an acquitted defendant suffers from a mental disease or defect that makes him dangerous, he will neither be confined nor treated psychiatrically unless a judge so orders after some independent commitment proceeding. But if a defendant succeeds in showing himself insane, Arizona law . . . will require commitment and treatment as a consequence of that finding. . . . It makes sense, then, to channel capacity evidence to the issue structured to deal with mental incapacity when such a claim is raised successfully.

police officer. If it did, Clark needs no excuse, as then he did not commit the crime as Arizona defines it. [Arizona's evidentiary restriction] excludes evidence no matter how credible and material it may be in disproving an element of the offense. . . .

In the instant case Arizona's proposed reasons are insufficient to support its categorical exclusion. While the State contends that testimony regarding mental illness may be too incredible or speculative for the jury to consider, this does not explain why the exclusion applies in all cases to all evidence of mental illness. . . . States have certain discretion to bar unreliable or speculative testimony and to adopt rules to ensure the reliability of expert testimony. Arizona has done so, and there is no reason to believe its rules are insufficient to avoid speculative evidence of mental illness.

The risk of jury confusion also fails to justify the rule. . . . The difficulty of resolving a factual issue . . . does not present a sufficient reason to take evidence away from the jury even when it is crucial for the defense. . . .

The reliability rationale has minimal applicability here. . . . Schizophrenia . . . is a well-documented mental illness, and no one seriously disputes either its definition or its most prominent clinical manifestations. The State's own expert conceded that Clark had paranoid schizophrenia and was actively psychotic at the time of the killing. . . .

Contrary to the Court's suggestion, the fact that the state and defense experts drew different conclusions about the effect of Clark's mental illness on his mental state only made Clark's evidence contested; it did not make the evidence irrelevant or misleading. The trial court was capable of evaluating the competing conclusions, as factfinders do in countless cases where there is a dispute among witnesses. In fact, the potential to mislead will be far greater under the Court's new evidentiary system, where jurors will receive observation evidence without the necessary explanation from experts.

The fact that mental-illness evidence may be considered in deciding criminal responsibility does not compensate for its exclusion from consideration on the mens rea elements of the crime. . . . Criminal responsibility involves an inquiry into whether the defendant knew right from wrong, not whether he had the mens rea elements of the offense. While there may be overlap between the two issues, "the existence or nonexistence of legal insanity bears no necessary relationship to the existence or nonexistence of the required mental elements of the crime." Mullaney v. Wilbur, 421 U.S. 684, 706 (1975) (Rehnquist, J., concurring).

Even if the analyses were equivalent, there is a different burden of proof for insanity than there is for mens rea. Arizona requires the defendant to prove his insanity by clear and convincing evidence. The prosecution, however, must prove all elements of the offense beyond a reasonable doubt. The shift in the burden on the criminal responsibility issue, while permissible under our precedent, cannot be applied to the question of intent or knowledge without relieving the State of its responsibility to establish this element of the offense. . . .

Future dangerousness is not, as the Court appears to conclude, [supra] n.45, a rational basis for convicting mentally ill individuals of crimes they did not commit. Civil commitment proceedings can ensure that individuals who present a danger to themselves or others receive proper treatment without unfairly treating them as criminals. [T]he Court ought not to imply otherwise. . . .

While Arizona's rule is not unique . . . , this fact does not dispose of Clark's constitutional argument. . . . While 13 States still impose significant restrictions on the use of mental-illness evidence to negate mens rea, a substantial majority of the States currently allow it. The fact that a reasonable number of States restrict this evidence weighs into the analysis, but applying the rule as a per se bar, as Arizona does, is so plainly unreasonable that it cannot be sustained. [I]ts irrationality is apparent when considering the evidence that is allowed. Arizona permits the defendant to introduce, for example, evidence of "behavioral tendencies" to show he did not have the required mental state. [The State allows] unexplained and uncategorized tendencies to be introduced while excluding relatively well-understood psychiatric testimony regarding well-documented mental illnesses. It is unclear, moreover, what would have happened in this case had the defendant wanted to testify that he thought Officer Moritz was an alien. If disallowed, it would be tantamount to barring Clark from testifying on his behalf to explain his own actions. If allowed, then Arizona's rule would simply prohibit the corroboration necessary to make sense of Clark's explanation. In sum, the rule forces the jury to decide guilt in a fictional world with undefined and unexplained behaviors but without mental illness. This rule has no rational justification and imposes a significant burden upon a straightforward defense: He did not commit the crime with which he was charged.

NOTES ON MENTAL DISORDER TO NEGATE MENS REA

1. *State of the law.* As Justice Kennedy's dissent notes, most states do not impose special restrictions on the use of mental health evidence to rebut a required mens rea. The MPC takes this view as well. See MPC §4.02(1) ("Evidence that the defendant suffered from a mental disease or defect is admissible whenever it is relevant to prove that the defendant did or did not have a state of mind which is an element of the offense.").

2. *The variety of restrictions.* Jurisdictions imposing restrictions have done so in different ways.

(a) Total ban. Arizona is one of the few states that bar all use of mental health evidence to negate mens rea. Putting the constitutional issue aside, how can a total ban on using mental health evidence to negate mens rea be justified as a matter of policy? If a jury can be trusted to deal with such evidence on the issue of legal insanity, why can't it be trusted to deal properly with such evidence on the issue of the required mental state? For discussion, see Peter Arenella, The Diminished Capacity and Diminished Responsibility Defenses: Two Children of a Doomed Marriage, 77 Colum. L. Rev. 827, 860 (1977).

(b) Capacity evidence. Other jurisdictions prohibit the use of mental health evidence to establish lack of *capacity* to form a mental state, but allow such evidence on the issue of whether the defendant in fact had the relevant mental state. E.g., State v. Flattum, 122 Wis. 2d 282, 303 (1985).

Questions: Why shouldn't a defendant be allowed to show that he *didn't have* a required mental state by introducing evidence that he lacked the *capacity to form* that mental state? Consider the argument of Professor Stephen J. Morse, Undiminished Confusion in Diminished Capacity, 75 J. Crim. L. & Criminology, 1, 42-42 (1984):

> A mens rea is a relatively simple mental state; it requires little cognitive capacity to intend to do something or to know legally relevant facts, such as that the car one is driving across the border contains contraband in a hidden compartment. A mentally abnormal person may not form a requisite intent or have the required knowledge, but it will rarely be because he lacked the capacity to form the mens rea. For example, suppose a mentally disordered person abroad [becomes] lost in a deserted part of town on a cold evening. Lacking the resources to find his way to proper shelter, he breaks into a building to get out of the cold. Caught by the police while doing so, he is charged with burglary on the theory that he intended to steal. Our poor defendant is innocent of burglary because he lacks the mens rea for theft— he only wanted to stay warm, not to steal—but [the reason he lacks] mens rea [is not that] he did not have the capacity to form it. He was perfectly capable of intending to steal; [he simply] did not intend to do so on this occasion. The defendant's mental disorder is relevant to proving that he lacked mens rea, for it is the reason he . . . got lost, and needed to get warm, but his mental disorder did not affect his capacity to form the mens rea.

(c) Specific intent. In several states, as in federal courts that follow the *Brawner* approach, mental health evidence is admissible to negate a required specific intent but not a general intent.[72]

Question: What is the basis for allowing mental health evidence to rebut mens rea only in prosecutions for specific intent crimes? In McCarthy v. State, 372 A.2d 180, 183 (Del. 1977), the court suggests a rationale applicable to certain specific intent crimes. Upholding a refusal to give diminished capacity instructions in a prosecution for the specific intent offenses of kidnapping and attempted rape, the court stated:

> This specific intent–general intent dichotomy explains [the] application of the doctrine in such cases as assault and battery with intent to kill; first degree forgery, requiring specific intent to defraud; . . . and entering a building with intent to commit theft. In each of these instances, the requisite specific intent

---

72. Federal law was potentially muddied by enactment in 1984 of 18 U.S.C. §17, which adopted the *M'Naghten* test of insanity and then declared that "mental disease or defect does not otherwise constitute a defense." However, as observed in United States v. Twine, 853 F.2d 676, 679 (9th Cir. 1988), "a careful reading of the 1984 Act and its history [shows] that Congress . . . did not intend to eliminate a defendant's ability to disprove guilt with mental defect evidence [that negates mens rea]." This is now the prevailing view. See United States v. Veach, 455 F.3d 628 (6th Cir. 2006).

constituted an aggravating factor to an otherwise general mens rea offense and the doctrine was applied to permit a finding of the lesser offense. [A]cceptance of the doctrine requires that there be some lesser-included offense which lacks the requisite specific intent of the greater offense charged. Otherwise, the doctrine of diminished responsibility becomes an impermissible substitute test of criminal responsibility. . . . In the instant case, there are no such lesser-included offenses within those for which the defendant was charged and tried. The acceptance of the doctrine in this case, therefore, would be inconsistent with the theory's basic purpose.

Compare People v. Wetmore, 583 P.2d 1308, 1315 (Cal. 1978):

[I]f a crime requires specific intent, a defendant who, because of mental disease or defect lacks that intent, cannot commit that crime. The presence or absence of a lesser included offense within the charged crime cannot affect the result. [W]e do not perceive how a defendant who has in his possession evidence which rebuts an element of the crime can logically be denied the right to present that evidence merely because it will result in his acquittal. [If the charged crime lacks a lesser included offense, the] solution to this problem [lies] in providing [legislation] for the confinement and treatment of defendants with diminished capacity arising from mental disease or defect.

3. *Criticism of* Clark. For probing critique of the majority and dissenting opinions in *Clark v. Arizona*, see Ronald J. Allen, *Clark v. Arizona*: Much (Confused) Ado About Nothing, 4 Ohio St. L.J. 135 (2006); Peter Westen, The Supreme Court's Bout with Insanity: *Clark v. Arizona*, 4 Ohio St. L.J. 143 (2006).

NOTE ON MENTAL DISORDER AS A GROUND FOR MITIGATION

The diminished capacity issue in cases like *Brawner* and *Clark* (the use of evidence of mental disorder to negate a required mens rea) must be distinguished from what is sometimes called "diminished responsibility" or "partial responsibility." According to the latter doctrine, the fact that the defendant was mentally disturbed entitles him to a reduction in the severity of the sentence, even though the prosecution has proved all the legal elements required for conviction. Such a doctrine has been recognized by some European countries. In the United Kingdom, for example, a partial-responsibility doctrine is available to reduce murder to manslaughter. The English Homicide Act, 1957, 5 & 6 Eliz. II, ch. II, §2(1).

Should this approach be adopted in the United States? Given the convoluted American rules on the admissibility of mental disorder to negate mens rea, would it be more straightforward to create an explicit affirmative defense for cases in which mens rea requirements are technically present but a mental disorder suggests greatly reduced culpability? See Stephen J. Morse, Diminished Rationality, Diminished Responsibility, 1 Ohio St. J. Crim. L. 289 (2003), proposing that a verdict of "Guilty but Partially Responsible" for defendants with diminished responsibility should result in a fixed sentencing reduction inversely proportional to the seriousness of the crime.

The nearest thing to a comparable doctrine in American law appears in sentencing provisions authorizing courts to use their discretion to impose a lesser sentence in cases of reduced capacity. An example is §5K2.13 of the Federal Sentencing Guidelines, which provides (U.S. Sentencing Guidelines Manual (2011)):

> A downward departure may be warranted if (1) the defendant committed the offense while suffering from a significantly reduced mental capacity; and (2) the significantly reduced mental capacity contributed substantially to the commission of the offense. . . . However, the court may not depart below the applicable guideline range if (1) the significantly reduced mental capacity was caused by the voluntary use of drugs or other intoxicants; (2) the facts and circumstances of the defendant's offense indicate a need to protect the public because the offense involved actual violence or a serious threat of violence; (3) the defendant's criminal history indicates a need to incarcerate the defendant to protect the public. . . .

Questions: If the principle behind §5K2.13 is sound, why should a reduced sentence be limited to cases of *non*-violent crimes and to defendants *without* serious criminal histories? If Professor Morse is right that defendants who are less culpable, because of mental impairment short of legal insanity, should receive less severe punishment, why should the amount of their sentencing reduction be inversely proportional to the seriousness of their crime—in other words, the smallest reduction for defendants facing the longest sentences? Consider the comments of Judge Richard Posner in United States v. Garthus, 652 F.3d 715 (7th Cir. 2011):

> Why diminished capacity . . . should be a mitigating factor in sentencing is obscure. The diminution makes a defendant more likely to repeat his crime when he is released from prison. That is especially so when the crime involves compulsive behavior, such as behavior driven by sexual desire. [D]iminished capacity weakens the ability to resist. . . . From a "just deserts" standpoint, diminished capacity argues for a lighter sentence, but from the standpoint of preventing recidivism it argues for a heavier one. The heavier sentence may not deter a criminal from repeating his crime when he is released (that is implied by saying he has diminished capacity), but it will reduce his lifetime criminal activity by incapacitating him for a longer time than if he received a lighter sentence.

The MPC, as we have seen (see page 1005 supra, Note 1), permits the use of mental health evidence to rebut a required mens rea, but for cases in which the elements of an offense are proved, the Code rejects a statutory reduction of punishment for reduced mental capacity. The Commentary explains (Model Penal Code and Commentaries, Comment to §210.3 at 71-72 (1980)):

> [Allowing] the defendant's own mental disorder or emotional instability as a basis for partially excusing his conduct [would] undoubtedly [achieve] a closer relation between criminal liability and moral guilt. . . . But this approach has

its costs. By evaluating the abnormal individual on his own terms, it decreases the incentives for him to behave as if he were normal. It blurs the law's message that there are certain minimal standards of conduct to which every member of society must conform. . . . And the factors that call for mitigation under this doctrine are the very aspects of an individual's personality that make us most fearful of his future conduct. In short, diminished responsibility brings formal guilt more closely into line with moral blameworthiness, but only at the cost of driving a wedge between dangerousness and social control.

Many jurisdictions leave each sentencing judge free to decide, without "guidelines," what significance (if any) to attach to mental illness when it neither establishes insanity nor negates a mens rea in a particular case. Does this approach provide an appropriate way to enable judges to tailor punishment to the defendant's moral fault? Or in this approach, is diminished mental capacity more likely to be treated as an aggravating factor? *Should it* be treated as an aggravating factor?

5. *Changing Patterns of Excuse*

ROBINSON v. CALIFORNIA

Supreme Court of the United States
370 U.S. 660 (1962)

JUSTICE STEWART delivered the opinion of the Court.

A California statute makes it a criminal offense for a person to "be addicted to the use of narcotics." This appeal draws into question the constitutionality of that provision of the state law, as construed by the California courts in the present case. . . .

[The prosecution's evidence was principally the testimony of policemen that defendant had scar tissue, discoloration, and needle marks that indicated his frequent use of narcotics.]

The judge . . . instructed the jury that the appellant could be convicted under a general verdict if the jury agreed *either* that he was of the "status" *or* had committed the "act" denounced by the statute. "All that the People must show is either that the defendant did use a narcotic in Los Angeles County, or that while in the City of Los Angeles he was addicted to the use of narcotics. . . ."

Under these instructions the jury returned a verdict finding appellant "guilty of the offense charged." . . .

The broad power of a State to regulate the narcotic drugs traffic within its borders is not here in issue. . . . This statute is not one which punishes a person for the use of narcotics, for their purchase, sale or possession, or for antisocial or disorderly behavior resulting from their administration. It is not a law which even purports to provide or require medical treatment. Rather, we deal with a statute which makes the "status" of narcotic addiction a criminal offense, for which the offender may be prosecuted "at any time before he reforms." California has said that a person can be continuously guilty of this offense, whether or not he has ever used or possessed any narcotics within the State, and whether or not he has been guilty of any antisocial behavior there.

It is unlikely that any State at this moment in history would attempt to make it a criminal offense for a person to be mentally ill, or a leper, or to be afflicted with a venereal disease. A State might determine that the general health and welfare require that the victims of these and other human afflictions be dealt with by compulsory treatment, involving quarantine, confinement, or sequestration. But, in the light of contemporary human knowledge, a law which made a criminal offense of such a disease would doubtless be universally thought to be an infliction of cruel and unusual punishment in violation of the Eighth and Fourteenth Amendments.

We cannot but consider the statute before us as of the same category. In this Court counsel for the State recognized that narcotic addiction is an illness. Indeed, it is apparently an illness which may be contracted innocently or involuntarily.[9]

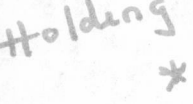

We hold that a state law which imprisons a person thus afflicted as a criminal, even though he has never touched any narcotic drug within the State or been guilty of any irregular behavior there, inflicts a cruel and unusual punishment in violation of the Fourteenth Amendment. To be sure, imprisonment for ninety days is not, in the abstract, a punishment which is either cruel or unusual. But the question cannot be considered in the abstract. Even one day in prison would be a cruel and unusual punishment for the "crime" of having a common cold. . . .

Reversed.

JUSTICE DOUGLAS, concurring. . . .

The addict is a sick person. He may, of course, be confined for treatment or for the protection of society. Cruel and unusual punishment results not from confinement, but from convicting the addict of a crime. . . . A prosecution for addiction, with its resulting stigma and irreparable damage to the good name of the accused, cannot be justified as a means of protecting society, where a civil commitment would do as well. . . . We would forget the teachings of the Eighth Amendment if we allowed sickness to be made a crime and permitted sick people to be punished for being sick. The age of enlightenment cannot tolerate such barbarous action.

JUSTICE HARLAN, concurring.

I am not prepared to hold that on the present state of medical knowledge it is completely irrational and hence unconstitutional for a State to conclude that narcotics addiction is something other than an illness, nor that it amounts to

_____

9. Not only may addiction innocently result from the use of medically prescribed narcotics, but a person may even be a narcotics addict from the moment of his birth. . . .

cruel and unusual punishment for the State to subject narcotics addicts to its criminal law. . . . But in this case the trial court's instructions permitted the jury to find the appellant guilty on no more proof than that he was present in California while he was addicted to narcotics. Since addiction alone cannot reasonably be thought to amount to more than a compelling propensity to use narcotics, the effect of this instruction was to authorize criminal punishment for a bare desire to commit a criminal act. . . .

JUSTICE WHITE, dissenting. . . .

The Court clearly does not rest its decision upon the narrow ground that the jury was not expressly instructed not to convict if it believed appellant's use of narcotics was beyond his control. The Court recognizes no degrees of addiction. The Fourteenth Amendment is today held to bar any prosecution for addiction regardless of the degree of frequency of use, and the Court's opinion bristles with indications of further consequences. If it is "cruel and unusual punishment" to convict appellant for addiction, it is difficult to understand why it would be any less offensive to the Fourteenth Amendment to convict him for use on the same evidence of use which proved he was an addict. . . .

The Court has not merely tidied up California's law by removing some irritating vestige of an outmoded approach to the control of narcotics. At the very least, it has effectively removed California's power to deal effectively with the recurring case under the statute where there is ample evidence of use but no evidence of the precise location of use. Beyond this it has cast serious doubt upon the power of any State to forbid the use of narcotics under threat of criminal punishment. I cannot believe that the Court would forbid the application of the criminal laws to the use of narcotics under any circumstances. But the States, as well as the Federal Government, are now on notice. They will have to await a final answer in another case. . . .

NOTES

1. *Competing rationales.* Justice Douglas and Justice Harlan offer different reasons for concurring in the reversal of Robinson's conviction. Which of their views, if either one, is endorsed by Justice Stewart's opinion for the Court? Justice Stewart notes that the California statute creates a form of continuous criminal liability, that it fails to require that any criminal act actually be performed within the jurisdiction, and that it imposes punishment for a disease. Are all of these failings necessary for constitutional invalidation, or would any one of them suffice? What if a statute criminalized a specific act (such as drug use) that could be considered the involuntary product of a disease (drug addiction)? Or what if a statute criminalized a status (such as being a member of a criminal organization) that was entirely voluntary?

2. *Status vs. act.* In considering why a status crime may sometimes impose "cruel and unusual punishment" in violation of the Eighth Amendment, review the materials on the requirement of voluntary conduct,

pages 205-218 supra. Those materials considered the act requirement as a component of "culpability," one of the core "elements of just punishment" in any legal system. To what extent should culpability be viewed as a *constitutional* requirement for criminal punishment? How would constitutionalizing the culpability requirement affect the nature of permissible criminal laws and the scope of required excuses? The cases that follow explore these questions.

POWELL v. TEXAS

Supreme Court of the United States
392 U.S. 514 (1968)

JUSTICE MARSHALL announced the judgment of the Court and delivered an opinion in which THE CHIEF JUSTICE, JUSTICE BLACK, and JUSTICE HARLAN join.

In late December 1966, appellant was arrested and charged with being found in a state of intoxication in a public place, in violation of Texas Penal Code, Art. 477 (1952), which reads as follows: "Whoever shall get drunk or be found in a state of intoxication in any public place, or at any private house except his own, shall be fined not exceeding one hundred dollars." . . .

The trial judge . . . , sitting without a jury, . . . ruled as a matter of law that chronic alcoholism was not a defense to the charge. He found appellant guilty, and fined him $50. There being no further right to appeal within the Texas judicial system, appellant appealed to this Court. . . .

The principal testimony was that of Dr. Davis Wade, a Fellow of the American Medical Association, duly certified in psychiatry. . . . Dr. Wade sketched the outlines of the "disease" concept of alcoholism; noted that there is no generally accepted definition of "alcoholism"; alluded to the ongoing debate within the medical profession over whether alcohol is actually physically "addicting" or merely psychologically "habituating"; and concluded that in either case a "chronic alcoholic" is an "involuntary drinker," who is "powerless not to drink," and who "loses his self-control over his drinking." He testified that he had examined appellant, and that appellant is a "chronic alcoholic," who "by the time he has reached [the state of intoxication] is not able to control his behavior, and [who] has reached this point because he has an uncontrollable compulsion to drink." . . . He added that in his opinion jailing appellant without medical attention would operate neither to rehabilitate him or lessen his desire for alcohol.

On cross-examination, Dr. Wade admitted that when appellant was sober he knew the difference between right and wrong, and he responded affirmatively to the question whether appellant's act of taking the first drink in any given instance when he was sober was a "voluntary exercise of his will." Qualifying his answer, Dr. Wade stated that

> these individuals have a compulsion, and this compulsion, while not completely overpowering, is a very strong influence, an exceedingly strong

influence, and this compulsion, coupled with the firm belief in their mind that they are going to be able to handle it from now on causes their judgment to be somewhat clouded.

Appellant testified concerning the history of his drinking problem. He reviewed his many arrests for drunkenness; testified that he was unable to stop drinking; stated that when he was intoxicated he had no control over his actions and could not remember them later, but that he did not become violent; and admitted that he did not remember his arrest on the occasion for which he was being tried. On cross-examination, appellant admitted that he had had one drink on the morning of the trial and had been able to discontinue drinking. . . .

The State made no effort to obtain expert psychiatric testimony of its own, or even to explore with appellant's witness the question of appellant's power to control the frequency, timing, and location of his drinking bouts, or the substantial disagreement within the medical profession concerning the nature of the disease, the efficacy of treatment and the prerequisites for effective treatment. . . . Instead, the State concerned itself with a brief argument that appellant had no defense to the charge because he "is legally sane and knows the difference between right and wrong."

Following this abbreviated exposition of the problem before it, the trial court indicated its intention to disallow appellant's claimed defense of "chronic alcoholism." Thereupon defense counsel submitted, and the trial court entered, the following "findings of fact":

> (1) That chronic alcoholism is a disease which destroys the afflicted person's will power to resist the constant, excessive consumption of alcohol.
> (2) That a chronic alcoholic does not appear in public by his own volition but under a compulsion symptomatic of the disease of chronic alcoholism.
> (3) That Leroy Powell, a defendant herein, is a chronic alcoholic who is afflicted with the disease of chronic alcoholism.

Whatever else may be said of them, those are not "findings of fact" in any recognizable, traditional sense in which that term has been used in a court of law; they are the premises of a syllogism transparently designed to bring this case within the scope of this Court's opinion in Robinson v. California, 370 U.S. 660 (1962). Nonetheless, the dissent would have us adopt these "findings" without critical examination; it would use them as the basis for a constitutional holding that "a person may not be punished if the condition essential to constitute the defined crime is part of the pattern of his disease and is occasioned by a compulsion symptomatic of the disease."

The difficulty with that position, as we shall show, is that it goes much too far on the basis of too little knowledge. In the first place, the record in this case is utterly inadequate to permit the sort of informed and responsible adjudication which alone can support the announcement of an important and wide-ranging new constitutional principle. We know very little about the circumstances surrounding the drinking bout which resulted in this conviction, or about Leroy Powell's drinking problem, or indeed about alcoholism itself. . . .

[T]he inescapable fact is that there is no agreement among members of the medical profession about what it means to say that "alcoholism" is a "disease." One of the principal works in this field states that the major difficulty in articulating a "disease concept of alcoholism" is that "alcoholism has too many definitions and disease has practically none." This same author concludes that "*a disease is what the medical profession recognizes as such.*" In other words, there is widespread agreement today that "alcoholism" is a "disease," for the simple reason that the medical profession has concluded that it should attempt to treat those who have drinking problems. There the agreement stops. . . .

The trial court's "finding" that Powell "is afflicted with the disease of chronic alcoholism, which destroys the afflicted person's will power to resist the constant, excessive consumption of alcohol" covers a multitude of sins. Dr. Wade's testimony [is] more carefully stated, if no less mystifying. . . .

Dr. Wade [testified] that once appellant began drinking he appeared to have no control over the amount of alcohol he finally ingested. Appellant's own testimony concerning his drinking on the day of the trial would certainly appear, however, to cast doubt upon the conclusion that he was without control over his consumption of alcohol when he had sufficiently important reasons to exercise such control. . . . Dr. Wade testified that when appellant was sober, the act of taking the first drink was a "voluntary exercise of his will," but that this exercise of will was undertaken under the "exceedingly strong influence" of a "compulsion" which was "not completely overpowering." Such concepts, when juxtaposed in this fashion, have little meaning. . . .

It is one thing to say that if a man is deprived of alcohol his hands will begin to shake, he will suffer agonizing pains and ultimately he will have hallucinations; it is quite another to say that a man has a "compulsion" to take a drink, but that he also retains a certain amount of "free will" with which to resist. It is simply impossible, in the present state of our knowledge, to ascribe a useful meaning to the latter statement. This definitional confusion reflects, of course, not merely the undeveloped state of the psychiatric art but also the conceptual difficulties inevitably attendant upon the importation of scientific and medical models into a legal system generally predicated upon a different set of assumptions. . . .

Despite the comparatively primitive state of our knowledge on the subject, it cannot be denied that the destructive use of alcoholic beverages is one of our principal social and public health problems. . . .

There is as yet no known generally effective method for treating the vast number of alcoholics in our society. . . . [I]t is entirely possible that, even were the manpower and facilities available for a full-scale attack upon chronic alcoholism, we would find ourselves unable to help the vast bulk of our "visible"—let alone our "invisible"—alcoholic population. . . . The medical profession cannot, and does not, tell us with any assurance that, even if the buildings, equipment and trained personnel were made available, it could provide anything more than slightly higher-class jails for our indigent habitual inebriates. Thus we run the grave risk that nothing will be accomplished beyond the hanging of a new sign—reading "hospital"—over one wing of the jailhouse.

One virtue of the criminal process is, at least, that the duration of penal incarceration typically has some outside statutory limit; this is universally true in the case of petty offenses, such as public drunkenness, where jail terms are quite short on the whole. "Therapeutic civil commitment" lacks this feature; one is typically committed until one is "cured." Thus, to do otherwise than affirm might subject indigent alcoholics to the risk that they may be locked up for an indefinite period of time under the same conditions as before, with no more hope than before of receiving effective treatment and no prospect of periodic "freedom."

Faced with this unpleasant reality, we are unable to assert that the use of the criminal process as a means of dealing with the public aspects of problem drinking can never be defended as rational. . . .

Appellant claims that his conviction on the facts of this case would violate the Cruel and Unusual Punishment Clause [as applied] in Robinson v. California, 370 U.S. 660 (1962). . . .

On its face the present case does not fall within that holding, since appellant was convicted, not for being a chronic alcoholic, but for being in public while drunk on a particular occasion. The State of Texas thus has not sought to punish a mere status, as California did in *Robinson*; nor has it attempted to regulate appellant's behavior in the privacy of his own home. Rather, it has imposed upon appellant a criminal sanction for public behavior which may create substantial health and safety hazards, both for appellant and for members of the general public, and which offends the moral and aesthetic sensibilities of a large segment of the community. This seems a far cry from convicting one for being an addict, being a chronic alcoholic, being "mentally ill or a leper. . . ."

Robinson so viewed brings this Court but a very small way into the substantive criminal law. And unless *Robinson* is so viewed it is difficult to see any limiting principle that would serve to prevent this Court from becoming, under the aegis of the Cruel and Unusual Punishment Clause, the ultimate arbiter of the standards of criminal responsibility, in diverse areas of the criminal law, throughout the country.

It is suggested in dissent that *Robinson* stands for the "simple" but "subtle" principle that "[c]riminal penalties may not be inflicted on a person for being in a condition he is powerless to change." . . . In that view, appellant's "condition" of public intoxication was "occasioned by a compulsion symptomatic of the disease" of chronic alcoholism, and thus, apparently, his behavior lacked the critical element of mens rea. Whatever may be the merits of such a doctrine of criminal responsibility, it surely cannot be said to follow from *Robinson.* The entire thrust of *Robinson*'s interpretation of the Cruel and Unusual Punishment Clause is that criminal penalties may be inflicted only if the accused has committed some act, has engaged in some behavior, which society has an interest in preventing, or perhaps in historical common law terms, has committed some actus reus. It thus does not deal with the question of whether certain conduct cannot constitutionally be punished because it is, in some sense, "involuntary" or "occasioned by a compulsion." . . . .

Ultimately, then, the most troubling aspects of this case, were *Robinson* to be extended to meet it, would be the scope and content of what could only be a constitutional doctrine of criminal responsibility. In dissent it is urged that the decision could be limited to conduct which is "a characteristic and involuntary part of the pattern of the disease as it afflicts" the particular individual, and that "it is not foreseeable" that it would be applied "in the case of offenses such as driving a car while intoxicated, assault, theft, or robbery." That is limitation by fiat. . . . If Leroy Powell cannot be convicted of public intoxication, it is difficult to see how a State can convict an individual for murder, if that individual, while exhibiting normal behavior in all other respects, suffers from a "compulsion" to kill, which is an "exceedingly strong influence," but "not completely overpowering." Even if we limit our consideration to chronic alcoholics, it would seem impossible to confine the principle within the arbitrary bounds which the dissent seems to envision. . . .

Traditional common-law concepts of personal accountability and essential considerations of federalism lead us to disagree with appellant. We are unable to conclude, on the state of this record or on the current state of medical knowledge, that chronic alcoholics in general, and Leroy Powell in particular, suffer from such an irresistible compulsion to drink and to get drunk in public that they are utterly unable to control their performance of either or both of these acts and thus cannot be deterred at all from public intoxication. And in any event this Court has never articulated a general constitutional doctrine of mens rea.

We cannot cast aside the centuries-long evolution of the collection of interlocking and overlapping concepts which the common law has utilized to assess the moral accountability of an individual for his antisocial deeds. The doctrines of actus reus, mens rea, insanity, mistake, justification, and duress have historically provided the tools for a constantly shifting adjustment of the tension between the evolving aims of the criminal law and changing religious, moral, philosophical, and medical views of the nature of man. This process of adjustment has always been thought to be the province of the States.

Nothing could be less fruitful than for this Court to be impelled into defining some sort of insanity test in constitutional terms. Yet, that task would seem to follow inexorably from an extension of *Robinson* in this case. If a person in the "condition" of being a chronic alcoholic cannot be criminally punished as a constitutional matter for being drunk in public, it would seem to follow that a person who contends that, in terms of one test, "his unlawful act was the product of mental disease or mental defect," Durham v. United States, 214 F.2d 862, 875 (C.A.D.C. Cir. 1954), would state an issue of constitutional dimension with regard to his criminal responsibility had he been tried under some different and perhaps lesser standard, e.g., the right-wrong test of *M'Naghten*'s Case. . . . But formulating a constitutional rule would reduce, if not eliminate, that fruitful experimentation, and freeze the developing productive dialogue between law and psychiatry into a rigid constitutional mold. It is simply not yet the time to write into the Constitution formulas cast in terms whose meaning, let alone relevance, are not yet clear either to doctors or to lawyers.

Affirmed.

JUSTICE BLACK, whom JUSTICE HARLAN joins, concurring. . . .

I agree with Justice Marshall that the findings of fact in this case are inadequate to justify the sweeping constitutional rule urged upon us. I could not, however, consider any findings that could be made with respect to "voluntariness" or "compulsion" controlling on the question whether a specific instance of human behavior should be immune from punishment as a constitutional matter. When we say that appellant's appearance in public is caused not by "his own" volition but rather by some other force, we are clearly thinking of a force that is nevertheless "his" except in some special sense.[1] The accused undoubtedly commits the proscribed act and the only question is whether the act can be attributed to a part of "his" personality that should not be regarded as criminally responsible. Almost all of the traditional purposes of the criminal law can be significantly served by punishing the person who in fact committed the proscribed act, without regard to whether his action was "compelled" by some elusive "irresponsible" aspect of his personality. [P]unishment of such a defendant can clearly be justified in terms of deterrence, isolation, and treatment. On the other hand, medical decisions concerning the use of a term such as "disease" or "volition," based as they are on the clinical problems of diagnosis and treatment, bear no necessary correspondence to the legal decision whether the overall objectives of the criminal law can be furthered by imposing punishment. For these reasons, much as I think that criminal sanctions should in many situations be applied only to those whose conduct is morally blameworthy, see Morissette v. United States, 342 U.S. 246 (1951), I cannot think the States should be held constitutionally required to make the inquiry as to what part of a defendant's personality is responsible for his actions and to excuse anyone whose action was, in some complex, psychological sense, the result of a "compulsion." . . .

JUSTICE WHITE, concurring in the result.

If it cannot be a crime to have an irresistible compulsion to use narcotics, Robinson v. California, 370 U.S. 660, I do not see how it can constitutionally be a crime to yield to such a compulsion. Punishing an addict for using drugs convicts for addiction under a different name. Distinguishing between the two crimes is like forbidding criminal conviction for being sick with flu or epilepsy but permitting punishment for running a fever or having a convulsion. Unless *Robinson* is to be abandoned, the use of narcotics by an addict must be beyond the reach of the criminal law. Similarly, the chronic alcoholic with an irresistible urge to consume alcohol should not be punishable for drinking or

---

1. If an intoxicated person is actually carried into the street by someone else, "he" does not do the act at all, and of course he is entitled to acquittal. E.g., Martin v. State, 31 Ala. App. 334 (1944) [page 205 supra].

for being drunk. [But] I cannot say that the chronic who proves his disease and a compulsion to drink is shielded from conviction when he has knowingly failed to take feasible precautions against committing a criminal act, here the act of going to or remaining in a public place. On such facts the alcoholic is like a person with smallpox, who could be convicted for being on the street but not for being ill, or like the epileptic, punishable for driving a car but not for his disease.

JUSTICE FORTAS, with whom JUSTICE DOUGLAS, JUSTICE BRENNAN, and JUSTICE STEWART join, dissenting. . . .

Robinson stands upon a principle which, despite its subtlety, must be simply stated and respectfully applied because it is the foundation of individual liberty and the cornerstone of the relations between a civilized state and its citizens: Criminal penalties may not be inflicted upon a person for being in a condition he is powerless to change. In all probability, Robinson at some time before his conviction elected to take narcotics. But the crime as defined did not punish this conduct. The statute imposed a penalty for the offense of "addiction"—a condition which Robinson could not control. Once Robinson had become an addict, he was utterly powerless to avoid criminal guilt. He was powerless to choose not to violate the law.

In the present case, appellant is charged with a crime comprised of two elements—being intoxicated and being found in a public place while in that condition. The crime, so defined, differs from that in *Robinson*. The statute covers more than a mere status. But the essential constitutional defect here is the same as in *Robinson*, for in both cases the particular defendant was accused of being in a condition which he had no capacity to change or avoid. The trial judge [found] that Powell is a "chronic alcoholic [who] does not appear in public by his own volition but under a compulsion symptomatic of the disease of chronic alcoholism." I read these findings to mean that appellant was powerless to avoid drinking; that having taken his first drink, he had "an uncontrollable compulsion to drink" to the point of intoxication; and that, once intoxicated, he could not prevent himself from appearing in public places. . . . The findings in this case, read against the background of the medical and sociological data to which I have referred, compel the conclusion that the infliction upon appellant of a criminal penalty for being intoxicated in a public place would be "cruel and inhuman punishment." . . .

State ex rel. Harper v. Zegeer, 296 S.E.2d 873 (W. Va. 1982): We believe that criminally punishing alcoholics for being publicly intoxicated violates the prohibition against cruel and unusual punishment. W. Va. Const. art. III, §5. In Powell v. Texas, 392 U.S. 514 (1968), five Justices [were] unwilling to extend *Robinson*'s rationale to public intoxication. . . . Since *Powell*, no state court has held that alcoholics could not be punished criminally for public intoxication, except Minnesota.[a]

---

a. State v. Fearon, 166 N.W.2d 720 (Minn. 1969).—EDS.

Most states have adopted the Uniform Alcoholism and Intoxication Treatment Act that deals with alcoholism as a disease. Others stopped short of decriminalization, and instead developed diversionary systems for both alcoholics and public drunks. . . . We urge our Legislature to enact a comprehensive plan for dealing with alcoholics in a humane and beneficial manner.

Criminal punishment of chronic alcoholics violates constitutional prohibitions against cruel and unusual punishment. However, their public presence is a potential threat to their own and others' well-being, is often offensive, even obnoxious to other people, and the State has a legitimate right to get them off the streets or out of whatever public area in which they may be gamboling. . . .[10]

If the arresting officer has knowledge that the accused has a previous history of arrests for public intoxication, he has a duty to bring these facts to the attention of the judicial officer, or to make application for involuntary hospitalization for examination of an accused who, because of his inebriated state, is likely to harm himself or others if allowed to remain at liberty. . . . Upon a showing that an accused is a chronic alcoholic, he is to be accorded all of the procedural safeguards that surround those with mental disabilities who are accused of crime.

NOTES

1. Alcoholism. The medical and scientific premises of the defense position in *Powell* are questioned in Herbert Fingarette, Heavy Drinking (1988). Professor Fingarette characterizes the disease concept of alcoholism as a "myth" that attained ever wider public acceptance just at the time that its empirical foundations were being discredited by researchers. He notes that E.M. Jellinek's early articles and his influential 1960 book, *The Disease Concept of Alcoholism*, upon which Justice Fortas relied heavily in *Powell*, drew on preliminary data subject to limitations that Jellinek himself acknowledged. The research of the next two-and-a-half decades consistently contradicted Jellinek's hypotheses, and Fingarette states (id. at 3) that today "*no* leading research authorities accept the classic disease concept."

The notion that alcoholics cannot "control" their drinking similarly has gained wide acceptance, and Fingarette observes (id. at 32) that "[a]nyone who has ever observed the behavior of a chronic heavy drinker cannot help feeling a sense of powerful momentum at work." Nonetheless, Fingarette notes (id. at 34), researchers have published "decisive evidence disproving the myth." The studies show that on any particular occasion heavy drinkers, including those labeled chronic alcoholics, may drink heavily, moderately, or not at all, and the choice depends on a wide variety of situational factors including the rewards or penalties the drinker believes likely to follow.

---

10. The State has a right and duty to prosecute people who, while drunk, commit crimes: drunken drivers, for example, . . . assaulters, and such. This opinion is about people who are charged solely with public intoxication. . . .

For a discussion more sympathetic to the view of alcoholism as a disease, see L. Tiffany & M. Tiffany, Nosologic Objection to the Criminal Defense of Pathological Intoxication: What Do the Doubters Doubt?, 13 Int'l J.L. & Psychiatry 49 (1990). Professor Michael Louis Corrado challenges the notion that claims about an addict's inability to exercise self-control are incoherent. In Addiction and the Theory of Action, 25 Quinnipiac L. Rev. 117 (2006), he notes that the law often recognizes defenses (like provocation) that are based on judgments about a defendant's lack of control. As a result, he argues (id. at 145-146):

> the idea of a defect of will is essential [in many areas of the law]. That means that we must recognize the possibility that the addict suffers from such a defect, from such great difficulty in controlling his behavior that he is entitled to an excuse. Whether the facts support an addiction excuse remains an empirical question, but the idea that evidence of such difficulty is impossible to come by, . . . seems to have no basis in fact.

2. Other "status" offenses. A Los Angeles ordinance, discussed in Chapter 3 in connection with the actus reus requirement (see page 207 supra), makes it an offense for any person to "sit, lie or sleep in or upon any street, sidewalk or other public way." In a suit brought by homeless individuals who proved that the city had too few beds to accommodate them, the U.S. Court of Appeals held that the Eighth Amendment, as interpreted in *Robinson* and *Powell*, barred enforcement of the ordinance against these individuals (Jones v. City of Los Angeles, 444 F.3d 1118, 1136-1137 (9th Cir. 2006)):

> Whether sitting, lying, and sleeping are defined as acts or conditions, they are universal and unavoidable consequences of being human. . . . In contrast to Leroy Powell, Appellants have made a substantial showing that they are "unable to stay off the streets on the night[s] in question." [T]he conduct at issue here is involuntary and inseparable from status— . . . given that human beings are biologically compelled to rest, whether by sitting, lying, or sleeping.

A dissenting judge objected that the Eighth Amendment claim was untenable because the ordinance "targets *conduct*—sitting, lying or sleeping on city sidewalks." Id. at 1139 (Rymer, J., dissenting).[73] Other courts are divided about whether such ordinances are constitutional as applied to the homeless. Which result follows from the principles articulated in *Robinson* and *Powell*?

3. Mens rea and the Constitution. Justice Marshall's plurality opinion rejected Robinson's defense of chronic alcoholism not only because of the insufficiency of the empirical case for the "disease" concept of alcoholism, but also because of the undesirability of "a general constitutional doctrine of mens rea," supra page 1016. What would such a constitutional doctrine look like, and what consequences would it have? Canada offers one answer to this question, having interpreted the "fundamental justice" provision of its Charter of Rights

---

73. As indicated in our earlier discussion of *Jones*, the parties subsequently settled the case, and the Ninth Circuit then dismissed the litigation as moot. See page 207 n.6 supra.

and Freedoms to require mens rea as a condition for a criminal conviction. See, e.g., Reference Re Section 94(2) of the Motor Vehicle Act, R.S.B.C. 1979 [1985] 2 S.C.R. 486 (holding strict liability unconstitutional on the ground that protection of the morally innocent is required by "principles of fundamental justice"). See page 299 supra. For discussion of the Canadian experience on this issue, see Bruce P. Archibald, The Constitutionalization of the General Part of Criminal Law, 67 Can. Bar Rev. 403 (1998).

4. Non-criminal incarceration of the dangerous. Justice Marshall worried that accepting Robinson's defense would lead to the civil commitment of offending alcoholics that would be non-criminal in name only—in essence, "the hanging of a new sign reading 'hospital'—over one wing of the jailhouse." The Supreme Court has upheld the constitutionality of preventive civil commitment of the dangerous when there is a mental disorder of some sort and "proof of serious difficulty in controlling behavior." Kansas v. Crane, 534 U.S. 407, 413 (2002) (upholding that state's provision for the commitment of "sexually violent predators"). Would non-criminal incapacitation and treatment be a preferable disposition for alcoholics who commit criminal offenses? For drug addicts? For anyone who has "serious difficulty in controlling behavior" because of genetic factors or environmental deprivation? For probing criticism of preventive confinement on the basis of this "serious difficulty in controlling behavior" standard, see Stephen J. Morse, Mental Disorder and Criminal Law, 101 J. Crim. L. & Criminology 885, 951-960 (2011). Consider the materials that follow.

UNITED STATES v. MOORE

United States Court of Appeals, District of Columbia Circuit
486 F.2d 1139 (1973)

WILKEY, J. . . . Appellant contends that his conviction [for possession of heroin] was improper because he is a heroin addict with an overpowering need to use heroin and should not, therefore, be held responsible for being in possession of the drug. After careful consideration, we must reject appellant's contention. . . .

[The prosecution conceded that Moore was an addict. The evidence was in conflict as to whether he was a trafficking addict. The trial court refused to permit defendant's expert witnesses to testify on the nature of defendant's heroin addiction, and declined to instruct the jury that a nontrafficking addict could not be convicted under the statutes charged.]

We believe it is clear from the evidence that Moore was not a mere nontrafficking addict but was in fact engaged in the drug trade. Yet even if we were to assume that appellant was a simple addict and nothing more, we believe that his conviction must be sustained. . . .

According to appellant this case has one central issue:

Is the proffered evidence of Appellant's long and intensive dependence on (addiction to) injected heroin, resulting in substantial impairment of his behavior controls and a loss of self-control over the use of heroin, relevant to his criminal responsibility for unlawful possession . . . ?

In other words, is appellant's addiction a defense to the crimes, involving only possession, with which he is charged? Arguing that he has lost the power of self-control with regard to his addiction, appellant maintains that by applying "the broad principles of common law criminal responsibility" we must decide that he is entitled to dismissal of the indictment or a jury trial on this issue. The gist of appellant's argument here is that "the common law has long held that the capacity to control behavior is a prerequisite for criminal responsibility." . . .

Drug addiction of varying degrees may or may not result in loss of self-control, depending on the strength of character opposed to the drug craving. Under appellant's theory, adopted by the dissenters, only if there is a resulting loss of self-control can there be an absence of *free will* which, under the extension of the common law theory, would provide a valid defense to the addict. If there is a demonstrable absence of free will (loss of self-control), the illegal acts of possession and acquisition cannot be charged to the user of the drugs.

But if it is absence of free will which excuses the mere possessor-acquirer, the more desperate bank robber for drug money has an even more demonstrable lack of free will and derived from precisely the same factors as appellant argues should excuse the mere possessor.

. . . [T]he peculiar nature of the problem of the heroin traffic makes certain policies necessary that should not be weakened by the creation of this defense. There is no compelling policy requiring us to intervene here. . . .

Robinson is no authority for the proposition that the Eighth Amendment prevents punishment of an addict for acts he is "compelled" to do by his addiction. . . . *Robinson* simply illustrates repugnance at the prospect of punishing one for his status as an addict. . . .

The Eighth Amendment defense for chronic alcoholics advanced by some members of the Court in *Powell v. Texas*, that is, the interpretation that *Robinson* held that it was not criminal to give in to the irresistible compulsions of a "disease," weaves in and out of the *Powell* opinions, but there is definitely no Supreme Court holding to this effect. . . .

[Conviction affirmed.]

LEVENTHAL, J., with whom MCGOWAN, J., concurs. . . .

Appellant's presentation rests, in essence, on the premise that the "mental disease or defect" requirement of [the insanity defense] is superfluous. He discerns a broad principle that excuses from criminal responsibility when conduct results from a condition that impairs behavior control. . . . The broad assertion is that in general the mens rea element of criminal responsibility requires freedom of will, which is negatived by an impairment of behavioral control and loss of self-control. . . .

It does not follow that because one condition (mental disease) yields an exculpatory defense if it results in impairment of and lack of behavioral controls the same result follows when some other condition impairs behavior controls. . . .

The legal conception of criminal capacity cannot be limited to those of unusual endowment or even average powers. A few may be recognized as so far from normal as to be entirely beyond the reach of criminal justice, but in general the criminal law is a means of social control that must be potentially capable of reaching the vast bulk of the population. Criminal responsibility is a concept that not only extends to the bulk of those below the median line of responsibility, but specifically extends to those who have a realistic problem of substantial impairment and lack of capacity due, say, to weakness of intellect that establishes susceptibility to suggestion; or to a loss of control of the mind as a result of passion, whether the passion is of an amorous nature or the result of hate, prejudice or vengeance; or to a depravity that blocks out conscience as an influence on conduct. The criminal law cannot "vary legal norms with the individual's capacity to meet the standards they prescribe, absent a disability that is both gross and verifiable, such as the mental disease or defect that may establish irresponsibility. The most that it is feasible to do with lesser disabilities is to accord them proper weight in sentencing."[65]

Only in limited areas have the courts recognized a defense to criminal responsibility, on the basis that a described condition establishes a psychic incapacity negativing free will in the broader sense. These are areas where the courts have been able to respond to a deep call on elemental justice, and to discern a demarcation of doctrine that keeps the defense within verifiable bounds that do not tear the fabric of the criminal law as an instrument of social control. . . .

Our analysis has revealed that there is no broad common law principle of exculpation on ground of lack of control, but rather a series of particular defenses staked out in manageable areas, with the call for justice to the individual confined to ascertainable and verifiable conditions, and limited by the interest of society in control of conduct. . . .

WRIGHT, J., dissenting: . . . I suggest that the development of the common law of mens rea has reached the point where it should embrace a new principle: a drug addict who, by reason of his use of drugs, lacks substantial capacity to conform his conduct to the requirements of the law may not be held criminally responsible for mere possession of drugs for his own use. . . .

[C]riminal responsibility is assessed only when through "free will" a man elects to do evil, and if he is not a free agent, or is unable to choose or to act voluntarily, or to avoid the conduct which constitutes the crime, he is outside the postulate of the law of punishment. . . . Moreover, recognition of a defense of "addiction" for crimes such as possession of narcotics is consistent . . . with the traditional goals of penology—retribution, deterrence, isolation and

---

65. ALI Model Penal Code §2.09, Comment (Tent. Draft No. 10, 1960), at 6.

rehabilitation. .... Revenge, if it is ever to be legitimate, must be premised on moral blameworthiness, and what segment of our society would feel its need for retribution satisfied when it wreaks vengeance upon those who are diseased because of their disease? It is of course true that there may have been a time in the past before the addict lost control when he made a conscious decision to use drugs. But imposition of punishment on this basis would violate the longstanding rule that "[t]he law looks to the immediate, and not to the remote cause; to the actual state of the party, and not to the causes, which remotely produced it." ...

The most widely employed argument in favor of punishing addicts for crimes such as possession of narcotics is that such punishment or threat of punishment has a substantial deterrent effect. Given our present knowledge, however, the merits of this argument appear doubtful. Deterrence presupposes rationality— it proceeds on the assumption that the detriments which would inure to the prospective criminal upon apprehension can be made so severe that he will be dissuaded from undertaking the criminal act. In the case of the narcotic addict, however, the normal sense of reason, which is so essential to effective functioning of deterrence, is overcome by the psychological and physiological compulsions of the disease. As a result, it is widely agreed that the threat of even harsh prison sentences cannot deter the addict from using and possessing the drug.

A similar situation prevails insofar as deterrence of *potential* addicts is concerned. [N]othing in this opinion would in any way affect the criminal responsibility of non-addict users for crimes they may commit—including illegal possession of narcotics. ...

Shifting our focus now to the goal of isolating the offender, we arrive here at not only a justifiable basis for action but one which, in some cases at least, may be vital to the interests of society. ... This does not mean, however, that the goal of isolation justifies infliction of criminal punishment upon the addict. On the contrary, this interest may be fully vindicated through a program of civil commitment with treatment. ...

This, then, brings us to the final and most important goal of modern penology—to rehabilitate the offender. In this age of enlightened correctional philosophy, we now recognize that society has a responsibility to both the individual and the community to treat the offender so that upon his release he may function as a productive, law-abiding citizen. ...

Perhaps the most troublesome question arising out of recognition of the addiction defense I suggest is whether it should be limited only to those acts— such as mere possession for use—which are inherent in the disease itself. It can hardly be doubted that, in at least some instances, an addict may in fact be "compelled" to engage in other types of criminal activity in order to obtain sufficient funds to purchase his necessary supply of narcotics. ... Nevertheless, I am convinced that Congress has manifested a clear intent to preclude common law extension of the defense beyond those crimes which, like the act of possession, cause direct harm only to the addict himself. ... The essential inquiry, then, is simply whether, at the time of the offense, the defendant, as a result of his repeated use of narcotics, lacked substantial capacity to conform his conduct to the requirements of the law.

BAZELON, C.J. (concurring in part and dissenting in part): . . . On the issue of guilt or innocence, Judge Wright's views are closest to my own. I cannot, however, accept his view that the addiction/responsibility defense should be limited to the offense of possession. I would also permit a jury to consider addiction as a defense to a charge of, for example, armed robbery or trafficking in drugs, to determine whether the defendant was under such duress or compulsion, because of his addiction, that he was unable to conform his conduct to the requirements of the law. . . .

Meir Dan-Cohen, Actus Reus, in Encyclopedia of Criminal Justice 15, 18-19 (1983)*: For punishment to serve as an effective deterrent, the law must preserve a sufficiently wide range of cases where punishment can be imposed. The law, therefore, can and does recognize involuntariness only when the defendant's determinist account of the criminal event is both of a rare kind and is generally perceived to be clearly convincing. By insisting on these two conditions, the law affirms its commitment to fairness (or justice) without significantly diminishing its effectiveness.

From this perspective, the compromise struck by the law is extremely precarious. There is no escaping the recognition that the requirement of voluntariness is locked in a deadly, and possibly losing, battle with determinism. Scientific (psychological, biological, or medical) explanations, it is argued, almost invariably increase the deterministic element in our view of human conduct. An epileptic seizure supports a claim of involuntariness because the acts in question are accounted for by a determinist medical theory. The more such accounts we possess, the greater the encroachment on the presupposition of voluntariness that underlies the criminal law. Any recognition of a case of involuntariness is bound to take us down a slippery slope, at the end of which we would have nullified the entire criminal law. On the other hand, a refusal to go down the slope, or any attempt to stop somewhere along the way, is bound to be arbitrary and unfair. . . .

NOTES

1. For close analysis of the opinions in the *Moore* case, see Richard Boldt, The Construction of Responsibility in the Criminal Law, 140 U. Pa. L. Rev. 2245, 2285-2294 (1992). The author observes:

> In the nearly two decades since *Moore*, other state courts have considered the question referred to them in general terms by Justice Marshall in the *Powell* case. With few significant exceptions, they have declined to recognize any version of the involuntariness or lack-of-choice defense pressed by alcoholic or drug-addicted defendants. The relative paucity of cases in which defendants have pressed a loss-of-control defense, together with the near universal hostility accorded such arguments by the few courts to reach the issue, is

*From Dressler (editor). Encyclopedia of Crime & Justice, 2E. ©2001 Gale, a part of Cengage Learning, Inc. Reproduced by permission. www.cengage.com/permissions.

significant evidence that a judicially created involition doctrine is unlikely to emerge in the foreseeable future.

For a review of the cases, see Annot., 73 A.L.R.3d 16 (2009).

2. From drug addiction to societal deprivation. Judge Bazelon's position in *Moore* (that drug addiction should allow a defense to any crime when it could be shown that the defendant could not conform his behavior to law) was but one application of a general principle to which he subscribed—that impaired behavior controls, whatever their source, should provide a defense to criminal charges. The same year as *Moore*, Judge Bazelon dissented in United States v. Alexander, 471 F.2d 923 (D.C. Cir. 1973), a case about the excusing potential of societal deprivation. The next Note examines this issue.

NOTE ON ENVIRONMENTAL DEPRIVATION

Richard Delgado, "Rotten Social Background": Should the Criminal Law Recognize a Defense of Severe Environmental Deprivation? 3 Law & Inequality 9, 20-23 (1985): Judge Bazelon first raised the possibility that extreme poverty might give rise to an RSB [Rotten Social Background] defense in *United States v. Alexander* [page 1026 supra, Note 2]. . . . In *Alexander*, one of the defendants shot and killed a marine in a tavern after the marine called him a "black bastard." The defense attempted to show that the youth's action stemmed from an irresistible impulse to shoot, which they, in turn, traced to an emotionally and economically deprived childhood in Watts, California. The defendant reported that when he was young, his father deserted the family and the boy grew up with little money or attention. He was subjected to racist treatment and learned to fear and hate white persons.

A psychiatrist testified that the defendant suffered from impaired behavior controls rooted in his "rotten social background." The psychiatrist refused to label the defendant insane, however. The trial judge instructed the jury to disregard the testimony about the defendant's deprived background and to consider only whether or not his mental condition met the legal standard of insanity. The jury found him sane and the defendant was sentenced to twenty years to life.

The court of appeals affirmed. In a lengthy, troubled opinion that concurred in part and dissented in part, Judge Bazelon laid out his early thoughts on the RSB defense. For Bazelon, the trial judge erred in instructing the jury to disregard the testimony about defendant's social and economic background. That testimony might well have persuaded the jury that the defendant's behavioral controls were so impaired as to require acquittal, even though that impairment might not render him clinically insane. Apart from this, exposure to the testimony would benefit society. As a result of learning about the wretched conditions in which some of its members live, society would presumably decide to do something about them.

Nevertheless, Bazelon was not prepared to abandon all the trappings of the "disease" model. Among other things, that model provides a rationale for detaining dangerous persons following acquittal. Bazelon reviewed other possible dispositions for the RSB defendant—outright release, preventive detention, and psychological reprogramming—finding each unacceptable. According to Bazelon, the ultimate solution to the problem of violent crime in our society is some form of income redistribution coupled with other social reform measures. The current narrow insanity test conceals the need for such reform and thus should be broadened, although disposition of offenders not "sick" in any classic sense remained a problem for Bazelon. Judge Bazelon further developed his views on an RSB defense in his Hoover lecture[87] and in a reply article. . . .[88]

In a response to Judge Bazelon[95] and a short rejoinder,[96] Professor Stephen Morse argued against Judge Bazelon's position. For Morse, all environments affect choice, making some choices easy and others hard. Rarely, however, will environmental adversity completely eliminate a person's power of choice. Poor persons are free to choose or not choose to commit crimes, and the criminal law may justifiably punish them when they give in to temptation and break the law. Although he conceded a statistical correlation between poverty and crime, Morse denied that poverty causes crime. He pointed out that some poor persons are law-abiding, while some wealthy persons break the law, and that economic improvements often result in more, not less, crime. Moreover, Bazelon's social-welfare suggestions would be impractical because there is not enough money to eradicate all poverty; giving money to the poor would entail higher taxation, thus endangering such goals as free accumulation and disposition of wealth; and though eradicating poverty may eliminate some crime, it is a wasteful way to do it. Consequently, Bazelon's broadened inquiry into culpability could exonerate dangerous criminals without generating socially useful knowledge or experience. Indeed, Bazelon's defense skirts paternalism. When an individual has freely broken the law, respect for that individual's personhood *demands* punishment; any other treatment demeans the defendant, and treats him or her as something less than an autonomous individual.

The Bazelon-Morse debate thus raises, but does not answer, a number of key questions concerning a "rotten social background" defense. Does economic and cultural disadvantage impair controls or otherwise cause crime, and if so, how? If severe impairment can be shown in a particular case, what effect should this have on criminal responsibility? What should be done with the successful RSB defendant?

---

87. David Bazelon, The Morality of the Criminal Law, 49 S. Cal. L. Rev. 385 (1976).

88. David Bazelon, The Morality of the Criminal Law: A Rejoinder to Professor Morse, 49 S. Cal. L. Rev. 1269 (1976).

95. Stephen Morse, The Twilight of Welfare Criminology: A Reply to Judge Bazelon, 49 S. Cal. L. Rev. 1247 (1976).

96. Stephen Morse, The Twilight of Welfare Criminology: A Reply to Judge Bazelon, 49 S. Cal. L. Rev. 1275 (1976).

NOTE

Professor Delgado goes on to argue that the criminal law *should* recognize a defense of severe environmental deprivation. In accord, Professor George Wright suggests (in The Progressive Logic of Criminal Responsibility and the Circumstances of the Most Deprived, 43 Cath. U. L. Rev. 459 (1994)) that by failing to allow for the dire economic and social circumstances of the most deprived elements of the population, the criminal law departs from its professed principle that only the morally responsible may be punished for their acts. See also Theodore Y. Blumoff, The Problems with Blaming, in Law, Mind, and Brain 127, 129 (M. Freeman & O. Goodenough eds., 2009). Professor Blumoff challenges the prevalent social attitude that "accepts without much debate that the wrongdoing actor virtually always posses-ses . . . sufficient cognitive and volitional capacity to [avoid] the crime they have committed"; he argues that, to the contrary, "poor environmental con-ditions do in fact effect changes within an individual's cognitive and volitional control."

On whether it is just to blame and punish an individual who commits criminal acts because his genes or his upbringing were the cause of his bad character, see Sanford H. Kadish, Blame and Punishment 102-103 (1987); Peter Arenella, Convicting the Morally Blameless: Reassessing the Relation-ship Between Legal and Moral Accountability, 39 UCLA L. Rev. 1511 (1992); Samuel H. Pillsbury, The Meaning of Deserved Punishment: An Essay on Choice, Character, and Responsibility, 67 Ind. L.J. 719 (1992); Stephen J. Morse, Culpability and Control, 142 U. Pa. L. Rev. 1587, 1652 (1994).

H.L.A. Hart, Punishment and Responsibility 31-33 (1968): [N]o legal sys-tem in practice admits without qualification the principle that *all* criminal responsibility is excluded by *any* of the excusing conditions. . . . This is so for a variety of reasons.

For one thing, it is clear that not only lawyers but scientists and plain men differ as to the relevance of some excusing conditions, and this lack of agree-ment is usually expressed as a difference of view regarding what kind of factor limits the human *capacity* to control behaviour. Views so expressed have indeed changed with the advance of knowledge about the human mind. Perhaps most people are now persuaded that it is possible for a man to have volitional control of his muscles and also to know the physical character of his movements and their consequences for himself and others, and yet be *unable* to resist the urge or temptation to perform a certain act; yet many think this incapacity exists only if it is associated with well-marked physiological or neurological symptoms or independently definable psycho-logical disturbances. . . .

Another reason limiting the scope of the excusing conditions is difficulty of *proof.* Some of the mental elements involved are much easier to prove than others. It is relatively simple to show that an agent lacked, either generally or on a particular occasion, volitional muscular control; it is somewhat more difficult to show that he did not know certain facts . . . ; it is much more difficult to establish whether or not a person was deprived of "self-control" by passion provoked by others, or by partial mental disease. As we consider these different cases not only do we reach much vaguer concepts, but we become progressively more dependent on the agent's own statements about himself, buttressed by inferences from "common-sense" generalizations about human nature, such as that men are capable of self-control when confronted with an open till but not when confronted with a wife in adultery. The law is accordingly much more cautious in admitting "defects of the will" than "defect in knowledge" as qualifying or excluding criminal responsibility.

Clarence Thomas, Punishment and Personhood, The City Journal, Autumn 1994, at 31: How did the ideas underlying [the legal revolution in individual rights] affect the functioning of the criminal justice system?

Many began questioning whether the poor and minorities could be blamed for the crimes they committed. Our legal institutions and popular culture began identifying those accused of wrongdoing as victims of upbringing and circumstances. Many argued that human actions and choices, like events in the natural world, are often caused by factors beyond one's control. No longer was an individual identified as the cause of a harmful act. Rather, societal conditions or the actions of institutions or other people became the responsible causes of harm. These external causes might include poverty, poor education, a faltering family structure, systemic racism or other forms of bigotry, and spousal or child abuse, just to name a few. . . .

As a further extension of these ideas, some began challenging society's moral authority to hold many of our less fortunate citizens responsible for their harmful acts. Punishment is an expression of society's disapproval or reprobation. . . . Critics insisted, though, that an individual's harmful conduct is not the only relevant factor in deciding whether punishment is justified. The individual's conduct must be judged in relation to how society has acted toward that individual in the past. Many began to hesitate to hold responsible those individuals whose conduct might be explained as a response to societal injustice. How can we hold the poor responsible for their actions, some asked, when our society does little to remedy the social conditions of the ill-educated and unemployed in our urban areas? Similarly, others questioned how we could tell blacks in our inner cities to face the consequences for breaking the law when the very legal system—and indeed the society—that will judge their conduct had perpetuated years of racism and unequal treatment under the law.

Once our legal system accepted the general premise that social conditions and upbringing could be excuses for harmful conduct, the range of cases that might prevent society from holding anyone accountable for his actions became potentially limitless. Do we punish a drunk driver who has a family history of alcoholism? A bigoted employer reared in a segregationist environment, who was taught that blacks are inferior? The fraudulent and manipulative busi-nessman who was raised in a poor family and who had never experienced the good life? The abusive father or husband whose parents mistreated him? A thief or drug pusher who was raised in a dysfunctional family and who received a poor education? A violent gang member, rioter or murderer who attributes his rage, aggression, and lack of respect for authority to a racist society that has oppressed him since birth? Which of these individuals, if any, should be excused for his conduct? Can we really make any principled distinctions among them?

An effective criminal justice system—one that holds people accountable for harmful conduct—cannot be sustained when there are boundless excuses for violent behavior and no moral authority for the state to punish. If people know that they are not going to be held accountable because of a myriad of excuses, how will our society be able to influence behavior and provide incentives to follow the law? How can we teach future generations right from wrong if the idea of criminal responsibility is riddled with exceptions and our governing institutions and courts lack moral self-confidence? A society that does not hold someone accountable for harmful behavior can be viewed as condoning, even endorsing, such conduct. In the long run, a society that abandons personal responsibility will lose its moral sense, destroying, above all, the lives of the urban poor.

This is not surprising. A system that does not hold individuals accountable for their harmful acts treats them as less than full citizens. In such a world, people are reduced to the status of children or, even worse, treated as though they were animals without a soul. There may be a hard lesson here. In the face of societal injustice, it is natural and easy to demand recompense or a dispensation from conventional norms. But all too often, doing so involves the individual accepting diminished responsibility for his future. Doesn't the acceptance of diminished responsibility shackle the human spirit from rising above the tragedies of one's condition? When we demand something from our oppressors—more lenient standards of conduct, for example—are we merely going from a state of slavery to a more deceptive, but equally destructive, state of dependency?

What's more, efforts to rehabilitate criminals will never work in a system that often neglects to assign blame to individuals for their harmful acts. How can we encourage criminals not to return to crime if our justice system fosters the idea that it is the society that has perpetuated racism and poverty that is to blame for aggression and crime, not the individual who engaged in harmful conduct? Thus, it is society, not the wrongdoer, that is in greatest need of rehabilitation and reform. . . .

Doubtless the rights revolution had a noble purpose: to stop society from treating blacks, the poor, and others as if they were invisible, not worthy of attention. But the revolution missed a larger point by merely changing their status from invisible to victimized. Minorities and the poor are human beings—capable of dignity as well as shame, folly as well as success. [They] should be treated as such.

Questions: If the substantive criminal law does not offer an excuse to a criminal defendant when environmental deprivation has contributed to his misconduct, should other aspects of the criminal justice process fill this gap?

(a) Should prosecutors, for example, take into account defendants' race or socioeconomic status in exercising their charging discretion or in offering plea-bargains? Compare Memorandum of Attorney General John Ashcroft (September 22, 2003)[74] (directing that "federal prosecutors must charge and pursue the the most serious, readily provable offense or offenses" in the absence of exceptional circumstances), with Memorandum of Attorney General Eric H. Holder, Jr. (May 19, 2010)[75] (noting that "discretion is essential to the fair, effective, and even-handed administration of the federal criminal laws" and directing that "a federal prosecutor should ordinarily charge 'the most serious offense . . . that is likely to result in a sustainable conviction'" but only after "an individualized assessment of the extent to which particular charges fit the specific circumstances of the case" and "fairly represent the defendant's criminal conduct").

(b) Should juries consider the race or socioeconomic status of the defendants before them in deciding whether to vote to acquit despite the evidence (i.e., to nullify the criminal law)? For an argument that jurors are sometimes legally and morally justified in voting to nullify charges against African-American defendants in cases involving drug possession and other nonviolent crime, see Paul Butler, Racially Based Jury Nullification: Black Power in the Criminal Justice System, 105 Yale L.J. 677 (1995), excerpted at page 66 supra.

(c) Should sentencing judges or sentencing guidelines take race or socioeconomic status into account in determining levels of punishment? Compare United States Sentencing Guidelines §SRI.10 (stating that race and socioeconomic status are never relevant in the determination of a sentence).

---

74. Available at http://www.crimelynx.com/ashchargememo.html.
75. Available at http://www.justice.gov/oip/holder-memo-charging-sentencing.pdf.

chapter 9

Theft Offenses

Taking something belonging to another is at the root of a multitude of offenses that fall under the umbrella of theft. The nature of these crimes varies along two dimensions: how the item in question is acquired and what is taken. The law has changed dramatically on both levels. The means of acquisition separate the various common-law offenses of larceny, embezzlement, obtaining by false pretenses, fraud, and blackmail, but modern statutes tend to consolidate these into general theft statutes. Similarly, the property subject to theft has also evolved over time. There is no controversy about how to treat the unauthorized taking of tangible property, but what about other valuable rights and interests? Here, too, we must ask what is appropriately treated as a criminal offense and where to draw the lines.

A. THE MEANS OF ACQUISITION

MODEL PENAL CODE AND COMMENTARIES
Comment to §223.1 at 128-131 (1980)

Distinctions among larceny, embezzlement, obtaining by false pretenses, extortion, and the other closely related theft offenses are explicable in terms of a long history of expansion of the role of the criminal law in protecting property. That history begins with a concern for crimes of violence—in the present context, the taking of property by force from the possession of another, i.e., robbery. The criminal law then expanded, by means of the ancient quasi-criminal writ of trespass, to cover all taking of another's property from his possession without his consent, even though no force was used. This misconduct was punished as larceny. The law then expanded once more, through some famous judicial manipulation of the concept of possession, to embrace misappropriation by a person who with the consent of the owner already had physical control over the property, as in the case of servants. . . .

At this point in the chronology of the law of theft, about the end of the 18th century, . . . the initiative pass[ed] from the courts to the legislature. . . .

The earliest statutes dealt with embezzlement by such narrowly defined groups as bank clerks. Subsequent laws extended coverage to agents, attorneys, bailees, fiduciaries, . . . until at last a few American legislatures enacted fraudulent-conversion statutes penalizing misappropriation by anyone who received or had in his possession or control the property of another. . . .

The fraud aspects of theft, never regarded with such abhorrence as larceny, begin with the common-law misdemeanor of cheat. This offense required use of false weights or similar "tokens," thus limiting criminal deception to certain special techniques conceived as directed against the public generally. One may suspect that this development was an outgrowth of guild regulation of unfair competition as much as it reflected a desire to protect the buying public. . . . A mere lie for the purpose of deceiving another in a business transaction did not become criminal until the Statute of 30 Geo. 2, ch. 24 (1757), created the misdemeanor of obtaining property by false pretenses. Even this statute was not at first believed to make mere misrepresentation criminal. Instead, it was thought to require some more elaborate swindling stratagem. . . . Eventually it was settled in Anglo-American law that false representations of "fact," if "material," would suffice. Today's battleground is over such matters as misrepresentation of "opinion," "law," or "value," as well as "misleading omissions" and "false promises." . . .

The criminal law reached larceny first and embezzlement later because of real distinctions between theft by a stranger and the peculations of a trusted agent. . . . The ordinary trespass-theft was committed by a stranger, an intruder with no semblance of right even to touch the object taken. The offender was easily recognized by the very taking, surreptitious or forceful, and so set apart from the law-abiding community. . . . In contrast, the embezzler stands always in a lawful as well as in an unlawful relation to the victim and the property. He is respectable; indeed, some tend to identify with him rather than with the bank or insurance company from which he embezzles. The line between lawful and unlawful activity is for the embezzler a question of the scope of his authority, which may be ill-defined. Not every deviation from the authority conferred will be civilly actionable, much less a basis for criminal liability. . . .

The embezzlement problem is complicated further by the necessity of distinguishing between defalcation by one who has "property of another" and failure of a debtor to pay his debts. Modern society is opposed to imprisonment for debt, however committed it may be to punishment for betrayal of trust. Yet when property is entrusted to a dealer for sale, with the expectation that he will receive the proceeds, deduct his commission, and remit the balance, the dealer's criminal liability if he fails to remit may turn on refinements of the civil law of contracts, agency, sales, or trusts. Such refinements, designed to allocate financial risks or to determine priorities among creditors of an insolvent, are hardly a relevant index to the harm done the owner or to the character of the defaulting dealer and thus may be entirely inappropriate as a measure of criminal liability.

1. *Trespassory Takings*

COMMONWEALTH v. TLUCHAK

Superior Court of Pennsylvania
166 Pa. Super. 16, 70 A.2d 657 (1950)

RENO, J. Appellants, husband and wife . . . appealed from convictions for larceny. . . . The husband was sentenced to pay a fine of $50 and make restitution. Sentence was suspended in the wife's case. . . .

By a written instrument appellants agreed to sell their farm to the prosecutor and his wife. The agreement did not include any personal property but it did cover: "All buildings, plumbing, heating, lighting fixtures, screens, storm sash, shades, blinds, awnings, shrubbery and plants." The purchasers took possession . . . and discovered that certain articles which had been on the premises at the time the agreement of sale was executed were missing. [These included:] an unattached washstand, . . . a hay carriage, . . . and 30 or 35 peach trees. These articles were charged in the indictment as subjects of the larceny.

The Commonwealth contended that the articles which were not covered by the written contract had been sold by an oral agreement between the parties. Appellants denied the oral agreement; denied the sale of the personal property; denied taking the trees; admitted they took the hay carriage; and as to all the articles which they took they contended that they were taken under a claim of right and therefore not feloniously. The jury found against them and, although they contend that the evidence is not sufficient in law to sustain a conviction, we shall assume, for the purpose of this decision, that the testimony established a *sale* of the personal property by appellants to the prosecutor and his wife. That is, that appellants sold but failed or refused to deliver the goods to the purchasers. Are sellers who refuse or fail to deliver goods sold to their purchasers guilty of larceny?

. . . Appellants had possession of the goods, not mere custody of them. The evidence indicates that they were allowed to retain possession without trick or artifice and without fraudulent intent to convert them. Presumably title passed upon payment of the purchase price; nevertheless appellants had lawful possession thereafter. "One who is in lawful possession of the goods or money of another cannot commit larceny by feloniously converting them to his own use, for the reason that larceny, being a criminal trespass on the right of possession, . . . cannot be committed by one who, being invested with that right, is consequently incapable of trespassing on it." 52 C.J.S., Larceny, §31; and see §1.

[Similarly,] in Com. v. Quinn, 19 A.2d 526, 530 (Pa. Super Ct. 1941), this Court approved instructions to a jury wherein it was said:

> But a person may come into possession of somebody else's property in a legal way and if he, being so in possession of the property in a legal way converts it to his own use or withholds it from the owner so that the owner is deprived of

the use thereof which he should have, then, though the defendant could not be guilty of larceny because he received it legally, he may be guilty of fraudulent conversion because after having received it he has deprived the owner of his use of it. . . .

As suggested, appellants may have been guilty of fraudulent conversion, or of larceny by bailee *if* the theory is accepted that a vendor retaining possession of goods sold by him becomes constructively a bailee of the purchaser, and criminally culpable for failure to deliver them to his purchaser. Appellants were indicted for larceny only, and of that they clearly were not guilty. . . .

Judgments and sentences reversed and appellants discharged without delay.

NOTES

1. Traditional asportation and its statutory variants. Both at common law and under statutory formulations, larceny requires a trespassory taking as well as a carrying away (asportation). While courts have substantially minimized the significance of this requirement by holding that any movement of the thing, no matter how slight, is sufficient, problems still may arise. Consider McAlevy v. Commonwealth, 605 S.E.2d 283 (Va. Ct. App. 2004). The defendant purported to sell farm equipment, not his own, to an innocent purchaser, who himself carried the equipment away. May the defendant be held for larceny? A few courts would answer in the negative because of the absence of an asportation. See, e.g., State v. Laborde, 11 So. 2d 404 (La. 1942). The majority, however, as in *McAlevy*, supra, resolve the issue by finding the purchaser to be the innocent agent of the seller and imputing his acts to the defendant. Can this be analytically defended?

The New York Court of Appeals, in People v. Alamo, 358 N.Y.S.2d 375 (1974), dispensed with the requirement of an actual movement of the object in a case where the defendant entered a stranger's car, turned on the lights, and started the engine. The court upheld the trial court's instruction that the jury might find theft of the car in these circumstances even if the defendant had not moved the vehicle (assuming, of course, they found the requisite intent to steal it). The court read the traditional doctrine requiring an asportation as reflecting a concern that the crucial elements of possession and control were established. Comparing pickpocket cases where some movement of the seized object had been held to be required, the court stated (358 N.Y.S.2d at 379):

A wallet, or a diamond ring, or a safe are totally inert objects susceptible of movement only by physical lifting or shoving by the thief. An automobile, however, is itself an instrument of transportation and when activated comes within the total possession and control of the operator. In this situation movement or motion is not essential to control. Absent any evidence that the vehicle is somehow fastened or immovable because of a mechanical defect, the thief has taken command of the object of the larceny.

Congress makes it a federal crime when one "intentionally accesses a computer without authorization or exceeds authorized access, and thereby obtains . . . information from any protected computer." Should it count as "obtain[ing] information" if a person reads or views information without downloading or copying it? The legislative history rejects an asportation requirement: "[T]he term 'obtaining information' includes merely reading it. There is no requirement that the information be copied or transported. This is critically important because, in an electronic environment, information can be 'stolen' without asportation, and the original usually remains intact." S. Rep. No. 104-357, at 7 (1996).

The MPC eliminates the requirement of an asportation and substitutes the requirement that the defendant "exercise unlawful control" over the movable property. Section 223.2(1), Model Penal Code and Commentaries, Comment to §223.2(1), at 164 (1980) states:

> Since larceny was generally a felony and attempt a misdemeanor, important differences in procedure and punishment turned on the criminologically insignificant fact of slight movement of the object of the theft. Under Section 5.01 of the Model Code, and in modern criminal law generally, differences in penal consequences between attempt and completed crime are minimized, so that it becomes less important where the line is drawn between them. . . .

Most revised codes follow this lead. Id. at 165.

2. Problem. The defendant removed a price label for £2.73 from a piece of meat in a supermarket and affixed the label to a piece of meat that should have cost £6.91. His act was detected at the checkout counter before he paid for the mislabeled package. Could the defendant be convicted of larceny? See Regina v. Morris, [1983] 3 All E.R. 288, [1984] A.C. 320 (H.L. 1983).

Compare People v. Olivo, 52 N.Y.2d 309 (1981), a consolidated appeal from several petit larceny convictions for shoplifting from department stores and a bookstore. In one case the defendant took objects on display and secreted them in his clothing, while furtively looking around. In another case the defendant removed a sensor device from a jacket, put the jacket on, and leaving his own jacket on the table, walked toward the exit. N.Y. Pen. Code §155.05 provides that one commits larceny when "he wrongfully takes" another's property, with the intent to steal. The defendant argued that a customer cannot "wrongfully take" an article in a self-service store so long as he remains in the store. The court disagreed and affirmed all the convictions, holding that these defendants could be held for larceny even though they were apprehended before leaving the store. The court stated (52 N.Y.2d at 317-318):

> [I]n modern self-service stores . . . customers are impliedly invited to examine, try on, and carry about the merchandise on display. . . . That the owner has consented to that possession does not, however, preclude a conviction for larceny. If the customer exercises dominion and control wholly inconsistent with the continued rights of the owner, and the other elements of the crime are

present, a larceny has occurred. Such conduct on the part of a customer satisfies the "taking" element of the crime.

TOPOLEWSKI v. STATE

Supreme Court of Wisconsin
130 Wis. 244, 109 N.W. 1037 (1906)

[The accused arranged with Dolan, who owed him money and was an employee of the Plankinton Packing Company, to place three barrels of the company's meat on the loading platform, the plan being that accused would load the barrels on his wagon and drive away as if he were a customer. Dolan carried out his end of the plan after informing the company's representatives and receiving their instructions to feign cooperation. Accused took the barrels as planned and was arrested, charged, and convicted of stealing the barrels of meat.]

MARSHALL, J. . . . Did [Dolan's agreement] with the accused to place the property of the packing company on the loading platform, where it could be appropriated by the accused . . . constitute consent to such appropriation?

The case is very near the border line, if not across it, between consent and nonconsent to the taking of the property. [In] Reg. v. Lawrence, 4 Cox C.C. 438, it was held that if the property was delivered by a servant to the defendant by the master's direction the offense cannot be larceny, regardless of the purpose of the defendant. In this case the property was not only placed on the loading platform, as was usual in delivering such goods to customers, with knowledge that the accused would soon arrive, having a formed design to take it, but the packing company's employee in charge of the platform, Ernst Klotz, was instructed that the property was placed there for a man who would call for it. Klotz from such statement had every reason to infer, when the accused arrived and claimed the right to take the property, that he was the one referred to and that it was proper to make delivery to him and he acted accordingly. While he did not physically place the property, or assist in doing so, in the wagon, his standing by, witnessing such placing by the accused, and then assisting him in arranging the wagon, as the evidence shows he did, and taking the order, in the usual way, from the accused as to the disposition of the fourth barrel, and his conduct in respect thereto amounted, practically, to a delivery of the three barrels to the accused.

In Rex v. Egginton, 2 P. & P. 508, [a] servant informed his master that he had been solicited to aid in robbing the latter's house. By the master's direction the servant opened the house, gave the would-be thieves access thereto and took them to the place where the intended subject of the larceny had been laid in order that they might take it. All this was done with a view to the apprehension of the guilty parties after the accomplishment of their purpose. The servant by direction of the master not only gave access to the house but afforded the would-be thieves every facility for taking the property, and yet the court held that the crime of larceny was complete, because there was no direction to the servant to deliver the property to the intruders or consent to their taking it. [T]he way was made easy for them to do so, but they were neither induced to commit the crime, nor was any act essential to the offense done by any one but themselves. . . .

[W]here the owner of property by himself or his agent, actually or constructively, aids in the commission of the offense, as intended by the wrongdoer, by performing or rendering unnecessary some act in the transaction essential to the offense, the would-be criminal is not guilty of all the elements of the offense. . . .

The logical basis for the doctrine above discussed is that there can be no larceny without a trespass. So if one procures his property to be taken by another intending to commit larceny, or delivers his property to such other, the latter purposing to commit such crime, the element of trespass is wanting and the crime not fully consummated however plain may be the guilty purpose of the one possessing himself of such property. That does not militate against a person's being free to set a trap to catch one whom he suspects of an intention to commit the crime of larceny, but the setting of such trap must not go further than to afford the would-be thief the amplest opportunity to carry out his purpose, formed without such inducement on the part of the owner of the property, as to put him in the position of having consented to the taking. If I induce one to come and take my property and then place it before him to be taken, and he takes it with criminal intent, or if knowing that one intends to take my property I deliver it to him and he takes it with such intent, the essential element of trespass involving nonconsent requisite to a completed offense of larceny does not characterize the transaction, regardless of the fact that the moral turpitude involved is no less than it would be if such essential were present. Some writers in treating this subject give so much attention to condemning the deception practiced to facilitate and encourage the commission of a crime . . . that the condemnation is liable to be viewed as if the deception were sufficient to excuse the would-be criminal, or to preclude his being prosecuted; . . . and that the wrongful participation of the owner of the property renders him and the public incapable of being heard to charge the person he has entrapped with the offense of larceny. That is wrong. [The obstacle to convicting the would-be thief] is the removal from the completed transaction . . . of the element of trespass or nonconsent. [Determining whether such element is absent] is often not free from difficulty and courts of review should incline quite strongly to support the decision of the trial judge in respect to the matter and not disturb it except in a clear case. It seems that there is such a case before us.

The judgment is reversed, and the cause remanded for a new trial.

NOTES

1. Feigned accomplices and consent. An informant told a police officer that the defendant, Jarrott, proposed that he join him in stealing and selling cars. The informant was instructed to play along. Later, the informant informed the police officer of the general time and place that Jarrott, with his ostensible help, planned to steal a car. The police officer thereupon arranged for his own car to be present at that time and place. He left it with the key in the ignition, concealing himself in the back end. This was known to the informant. Jarrott and the informant later appeared. Jarrott saw the car and proposed they steal it. They entered and drove the car to a car lot. While Jarrott and the buyer were haggling over the price, the policeman climbed out from the car and made his arrest. Defendant appealed his larceny conviction on the grounds (1) that the car was never taken from the personal possession of the owner and (2) that the taking occurred with the owner's consent. What should be the result? Jarrott v. State, 1 S.W.2d 619 (Tex. Crim. 1927). Concerning the defense of entrapment by police agents, see page 697 supra, and Model Penal Code §2.13, Appendix.

2. Statutory modifications. In United States v. Bryan, 483 F.2d 88 (3d Cir. 1973), U.S. Lines, on the instruction of the FBI, permitted its agents to deliver a shipment of whiskey to Echols, who allegedly intended to steal it. The court rejected the argument that Echols committed no crime because U.S. Lines consented to the taking, stating (at 90-91):

> The crime alleged here is [stealing in] violation of 18 U.S.C. §659, [which] has been given a broad construction, free from the technical requirements of common law larceny. United States v. DeNormand, 149 F.2d 622, 624 (2d Cir. 1945). A trial court instruction that the jury need only find "an unlawful taking of the goods by the defendants," was found sufficient in *DeNormand.* The consent to the removal of the goods by U.S. Lines personnel in this case does not demonstrate the absence of an unlawful taking. [T]he relevant question involves not the state of mind of personnel of U.S. Lines, but rather the state of mind of defendants. . . .
>
> In cases where the lawful possessor indicated to the taker that permission was granted for the taking, a finding of commission of a crime would be unlikely. That, however, is not the case sub judice. There is no proof that U.S. Lines led defendants to believe they had permission to take the goods.

3. Non-consent and attempt. In the *Topolewski* case, would it have been possible to convict the defendant of an attempt to commit larceny? See The Case of Lady Eldon's French Lace, page 649 supra.

NOTE ON ROBBERY AND EXTORTION

Note, A Rationale of the Law of Aggravated Theft, 54 Colum. L. Rev. 84, 84-86 (1954): [T]o protect not only against misappropriation but also against injuries which may result from peculiarly dangerous means devised for accomplishing misappropriation, there developed the law of aggravated theft. At common law the only substantive crime embodied within this law was robbery, a larceny accomplished by violence or threat of immediate violence to the person of the victim. In time it was acknowledged that men may be intimidated by threats other than those foreboding bodily harm. As a result, modern legislation has extended the substantive content of aggravated theft, complementing robbery with the crime of extortion. . . .

The first inquiry, then, concerns the manner in which these crimes differ. The statutory definitions of robbery restate in essence the common law definition: the felonious and forcible taking of property from the person of another or in his presence, against his will, by violence or putting in fear. Extortion statutes are generally of two types. The majority of jurisdictions treat as the substantive crime of extortion the making of certain specified threats for the purpose of obtaining property, but a substantial number require an actual misappropriation with the owner's consent. . . . In jurisdictions following either extortion pattern, robbery requires a taking from the person or in his presence, while for extortion the intimidation is crucial and the place of the taking immaterial. In states which do not require more than the threat for extortion, the fact of misappropriation is relevant only to robbery. And in those states where misappropriation is essential to extortion, there is a distinction based on the factor of consent. The robbery statutes speak of the absence of consent; the extortion statutes require its presence. But the willingness to surrender the property in any case is only an apparent willingness since in both instances the victim must choose between alternative evils, namely, the surrender of his property or the execution of the threat. Only if the taking is accomplished by violence to the person of the victim is this apparent consent precluded, for then the victim is presented with no choice. Thus the definitional distinctions between robbery and extortion are extremely tenuous. . . .

California Penal Code (2010) §211. Robbery Defined: Robbery is the felonious taking of personal property in the possession of another, from his person or immediate presence, and against his will, accomplished by means of force or fear [punishable by imprisonment for two, three, or five years; or, in aggravated cases, by imprisonment for three, six, or nine years].

California Penal Code (2010) §212. Fear Defined: The fear mentioned in Section 211 may be either:

> 1. The fear of an unlawful injury to the person or property of the person robbed, or of any relative of his or member of his family; or,
> 2. The fear of an immediate and unlawful injury to the person or property of anyone in the company of the person robbed at the time of the robbery.

California Penal Code (2010) §518. [Extortion Defined:] Extortion is the obtaining of property from another, with his consent, or the obtaining of an official act of a public officer, induced by a wrongful use of force or fear, or under color of official right [punishable by imprisonment for two, three, or four years].

California Penal Code (2010) §519. Fear Used to Extort: Threats Inducing: Fear, such as will constitute extortion, may be induced by a threat, either:

1. To do an unlawful injury to the person or property of the individual threatened or of a third person; or,
2. To accuse the individual threatened, or any relative of his, or member of his family, of any crime; or,
3. To expose, or to impute to him or them any deformity, disgrace or crime; or,
4. To expose any secret affecting him or them.

Model Penal Code §222.1. Robbery: [See Appendix.]

Model Penal Code §223.4. Theft by Extortion: [See Appendix.]

Model Penal Code and Commentaries, Comment to §223.4 at 202 n.1, 208 (1980): At common law, robbery included taking not only by force but also by threat of force or even by threat of certain other serious harms. To be guilty of robbery under the Model Penal Code, the defendant must threaten immediate and serious harm. Other coercive deprivation falls under Section 223.4. . . .

There is no requirement in Section 223.4 that the threatened harm be "unlawful." The actor may be privileged or even obligated to inflict the harm threatened; yet, if he employs the threat to coerce a transfer of property for his own benefit, he clearly belongs among those who should be subject to punishment for theft. The case of the policeman who has a duty to arrest illustrates the point. His threat to arrest unless the proposed subject of the arrest pays him money should be treated as extortionate even though the failure to arrest would be dereliction of duty.

For more on extortion (also called blackmail), see page 1070 infra.

Questions: (a) Note that the threats sufficient to establish robbery are defined much more broadly in California than under the MPC. Is that a strength or a weakness of the California scheme? *(b)* In California, if an offender threatens to slash a motorist's tires unless the motorist pays him $200, is the offender guilty of robbery, extortion, or both? What would be the answer in a state following the MPC approach? How *should* the offense be classified? *(c)* In California, if an offender threatens to assault a man's wife unless the man pays him $200, is the offender guilty of robbery, extortion, or both? What would be the answer in a state following the MPC approach? How *should* that offense be classified? *(d)* In California, an offender stole a car from a parking lot and ran over the owner as the offender was driving away. The offender conceded that he intended to steal the car, but insisted that he did not intend to strike or frighten the owner. Is this robbery? In People v. Anderson, 252 P.3d 968 (Cal. 2011), the California Supreme Court reinstated the offender's conviction, holding that "the intent element of robbery does not include an intent to apply force against the victim or to cause the victim to feel fear. It is robbery if the defendant committed a forcible act against the victim motivated by the intent to steal, even if the defendant did not also intend for the victim to experience force or fear." Do you agree with the court's approach to the mens rea for robbery?

2. Misappropriation

NOLAN v. STATE

Maryland Court of Appeals
213 Md. 298, 131 A.2d 851 (1957)

[Defendant was convicted of embezzlement. He was the office manager of the Federal Discount Corporation, a finance company engaged in the business of making loans and collections. The evidence showed that he appropriated money from his employer as follows: As payments were received from customers, the payments would be placed in the cash drawer. At the end of the day, an accomplice would prepare a report showing the daily cash receipts. Defendant would then take some of the cash from the drawer, and his accomplice would recompute the adding tapes to equal the remaining cash.]

COLLINS, J. . . . The appellant . . . contends that . . . the evidence produced made the crime larceny and not embezzlement, as charged in the indictment.

. . . The embezzlement statutes were passed, not to cover any cause within the common law range of larceny, but to cover new cases outside of that range. If the goods were taken from the owner's possession, the crime is larceny, not embezzlement. Goods which have reached their destination are constructively in the owner's possession although he may not yet have touched them and, hence, after such termination of transit, the servant who converts them is guilty of larceny, not of embezzlement. [As stated in 2 Wharton's Criminal Law, 12th ed.,] at page 1591: "No inconvenience can arise from the maintenance of this distinction, since it is allowable *as well as prudent* to join a count for larceny to that for embezzlement. But great inconvenience would follow from the acceptance of the principle that the embezzlement statutes absorb all cases of larceny by servants." (Italics supplied.) . . .

The money was not taken by Mr. Nolan until it had been placed in the cash drawer and balanced at the end of the day. When taken by appellant, as alleged, the cash was in the possession of Federal. We must therefore conclude that under the authorities cited and under the testimony in this case there was not sufficient evidence to find the defendant guilty of embezzlement. The case will be remanded for further proceedings in order that the State, if it deems proper, may try the defendant on an indictment for embezzlement and larceny, if such an indictment is returned against the defendant.

PRESCOTT, J. (concurring). [I]t seems to me that [the court's opinion] reestablishes many of the tenuous niceties between larceny and embezzlement with which the early English cases are replete, and that it unnecessarily will embarrass many future prosecutions although the accused palpably may be guilty. . . .

Our statute, Art. 27, §154 of the Maryland Code (1951), reads:

> Whosoever being a . . . servant . . . shall fraudulently embezzle any money . . . which . . . shall be . . . taken into possession by him, for . . . his master or employer, shall be deemed to have feloniously stolen the same from his master or employer, although such money . . . was not received into the possession of such master . . . otherwise than by the actual possession of his . . . servant. . . .

A simple down-to-earth application of the facts presented in the record discloses that every element required in the statute is fully and completely covered. . . . But the majority of the Court feel that the English decisions and other authorities . . . require a holding that because the money went into the drawers before its fraudulent conversion, the offense was larceny and not embezzlement. If this be so, it seems to place the law in an unfortunate and somewhat indefensible position. [W]e find ourselves in the peculiar position of following the subtle reasoning developed in the English decisions for the purpose of bringing the guilty to the bar of justice; but, in so doing, we directly come to their aid and comfort. Probably the solution of this rather difficult problem lies in the course followed by several of our sister States (and as was done in England) where the legislative power has provided that under an indictment for larceny, or for larceny in one count and embezzlement in another, there may be a conviction of either offense.

NOTE ON EMBEZZLEMENT

The early conception of larceny as a trespassory taking from the possession of the owner against his will was thought to preclude conviction of persons who physically and lawfully held property of the owner, such as servants, guests, and employees. Since they had "possession" of the owner's goods, their making off with them could not constitute larceny.

This was changed through judicial development of the concept that, in some situations the servant merely had *custody*, while *possession*—"legal" or "constructive" possession—remained in the employer. The development was gradual, and there was considerable disagreement over such issues as whether a servant had mere custody or legal possession when the master entrusted property to him to be taken a distance from the house. Such doubts were resolved by statute in 1529, and by later cases it was established that "a servant, whether at the master's home or elsewhere, never has legal possession of such property of his master as he controls in his capacity as servant." 2 Wm. Oldnall Russell, A Treatise on Crimes and Misdemeanors (11th ed., Turner, 1958). A servant, therefore, who made off with his master's goods, committed larceny from the possession of the master. By analogous reasoning, similar results were reached with guests.

What about the case in which the servant is given goods by a third party for delivery to his master? Could it be said here that when a servant misappropriated the goods, he was taking them from someone's possession? The answer was no, since the master did not have possession and the third party voluntarily gave up possession. As a result, the servant could not be convicted of larceny.

The courts found a way to fill part of this gap, too. They reasoned that if the servant deposited the goods or money he had received in a place provided by the master and subject to the master's control (as in *Nolan*, supra), then *possession* passed to the master; the servant retained only *custody*. In that scenario, therefore, a dishonest appropriation was larceny. The solution, however, was far from perfect, as became clear in Bazeley's Case, 168 Eng. Rep. 517 (1799).

Bazeley was a bank teller who pocketed a £100 note received from a customer for deposit. The court found no larceny because at the time of the conversion, the note was in the legal possession of the teller. To fill the gap in the law dramatized by this case, the first embezzlement statute was passed in 1799 (39 Geo. III, ch. 85) providing:

> If ... any person employed ... in the capacity of a servant or clerk, to any person or persons whomsoever, or to any body corporate or politick, shall, by virtue, of such employment, receive or take into his possession any money, goods, bond, bill, note, banker's draft, or other valuable security, or effects, for or in the name or on the account of his master or masters, or employer or employers, and shall fraudulently embezzle, secrete, or make away with the same, or any part thereof, every such offender shall be deemed to have feloniously stolen the same.

Modern cases, such as *Nolan*, supra, are products of this history of larceny and embezzlement as mutually exclusive offenses. Following the common-law rule, State v. Weaver, 607 S.E.2d 599 (N.C. 2005), held that a defendant could not be convicted of aiding and abetting embezzlement because his wife, who allegedly used company checks for personal expenses, did not have the authority to sign for the checks. By contrast, State v. Willard-Freckleton, 939 A.2d 416 (Vt. 2007), rejected the common-law distinction between larceny and embezzlement. It distinguished *Weaver* and found all employee conversions to constitute embezzlement when the employee has custody or control of the property by virtue of his or her employment, even if the employee does not have lawful possession.

Additional enactments have gradually extended the categories of persons capable of embezzling to brokers, merchants, bankers, attorneys, trustees, and similar positions of trust. American embezzlement statutes still bear the mark of this piecemeal legislative development. See *Riggins*, page 1051 infra.

Because misappropriation cases involve individuals with lawful possession of property (or at least lawful custody), they often raise questions of when an employee's use goes too far and crosses the line into criminality. For example, when does the employee's use of a company car for personal use cross the line from accepted personal use into criminal embezzlement? John L. Diamond, Reviving Lenity and Honest Belief at the Boundaries of Criminal Law, 44 U. Mich. J.L. Reform 1, 4-5 (2010). How should prosecutors determine when to bring charges in these cases where they will undoubtedly have broad discretion because of the nature of the charge? Note that similar concerns are raised in other contexts involving theft, including extortion, bribery, and theft of services. See pages 1070-1079, 1083-1084 infra. Does this question of line-drawing exist to the same degree with larceny? Why or why not?

BURNS v. STATE

Supreme Court of Wisconsin
145 Wis. 373, 128 N.W. 987 (1911)

[A constable taking an insane man, Adamsky, into custody after pursuit received from another of the pursuers a roll of money that Adamsky had thrown away in his flight. The jury convicted the constable of larceny by bailee under a Wisconsin statute reproduced in the opinion. The court rejected the argument that a bailment was not established because there was no contract between the constable and Adamsky:]

MARSHALL, J. . . . No particular ceremony or actual meeting of minds is necessary to the creation of a bailment. If one, without the trespass which characterizes ordinary larceny, comes into possession of any personalty of another and is in duty bound to exercise some degree of care to preserve and restore the thing to such other or to some person for that other, or otherwise account for the property as that of such other, according to circumstances,—he is a bailee. It is the element of lawful possession, however created, and duty to account for the thing as the property of another, that creates the bailment, regardless of whether such possession is based on contract in the ordinary sense or not. . . . The mutuality essential to the contractual feature may be created by operation of law as well as by the acts of the parties with intention to contract.

So it makes no difference whether the thing be intrusted to a person by the owner, or another, or by some one for the owner or by the law to the same end. Taking possession without present intent to appropriate raises all the contractual elements essential to a bailment. So the person who bona fide recovers the property of another which has been lost, or irresponsibly cast away by an insane man, as in this case, is a bailee as much as if the same property were intrusted to such person by contract inter partes. In the latter case the contract creates the duty. In the former the law creates it. Such a situation is to be distinguished from that where one knowingly receives money paid him by mistake and fraudulently retains it. There the element of bona fide possession may be said not to exist and so the duty accompanied by such possession essential to a bailment not to have been created. . . .

So the finder here of the cast-away money was clearly a bailee, and when his duties were voluntarily assumed by the accused he became such. . . .

[Burns next argues that if he] was guilty of any offense, it was that of having broken the package and extracted therefrom part of the contents for the purpose of appropriating it to his own use, and executed such purpose, thus committing the offense of larceny, not of conversion by a bailee. It is a sufficient answer thereto that the purpose of the statute [containing provisions on traditional larceny and on takings by bailees] was to abolish the distinction between conversion by a bailee of an entire thing, as a quantity of property in a package of some kind, and the unlawful breaking of the package and conversion of part or all of the contents—whether preceded by the element of breaking bulk with intent to permanently deprive the owner of the thing appropriated or not,—making the latter a statutory class of larcenies, differing only from ordinary larcenies, by absence in the former of the element of trespass in gaining original possession, which is essential to the latter. The meaning of the statute, as indicated, seems very plain:

> Whoever being a bailee of any chattel, money or valuable security shall fraudulently take or fraudulently convert the same to his own use or to the use of any person other than the owner thereof, although he shall not break bulk or otherwise determine the bailment, shall be guilty of larceny. . . .

It follows that the acquittal of the accused of the offense of larceny is not inconsistent with his conviction of the statute offense of larceny as bailee. . . .

NOTE ON THE MISAPPROPRIATING BAILEE

The Note following *Nolan*, supra, described the development of the possession-custody distinction as a means whereby certain kinds of misappropriation by persons lawfully holding the property of another came to be treated as larceny. The enactment of embezzlement statutes eliminated the need for such judicial gap filling. However, just as this distinction proved inadequate to deal with the servant who received goods for his master from a third person, it proved inadequate to deal with the bailee who misappropriated his bailor's property, because the crucial significance of a bailment relation was the transfer of *possession* and not mere custody. The early common law therefore sought to bring at least some bailee misappropriations within the scope of larceny. In the Carrier's Case, decided in 1473 (Y.B. 13 Edw. IV, f. 9, pl. 5), a carrier to whom a foreign merchant delivered a shipment for delivery broke into the bales and made off with the contents. The case was argued before the judges in the Exchequer Chamber. A majority agreed that if a bailment has terminated, the former bailee who then takes the goods may be guilty of larceny. What was unclear was the theory on which the defendant could be said to have terminated the bailment. The judges, without stating their reasons, reported that a majority found that defendant had committed larceny. Later courts interpreted the result as establishing that by "breaking bulk," the bailee terminated the bailment, somehow lost possession of the property bailed to him, and therefore became a trespasser when he took the contents.

James Fitzjames Stephen observed:

> This has always appeared an extraordinary decision, as, to all common apprehension, theft of the whole thing bailed must [terminate] the bailment quite as much as a theft of part of it. I think it obvious from the report that the decision was a compromise intended to propitiate the chancellor, and perhaps the King. This required a deviation from the common law, which was accordingly made, but was as slight as the judges could make it.

3 James Fitzjames Stephen, A History of the Criminal Law of England 139 (1883). The pragmatic basis for the decision was explained by Jerome Hall in his classic study of the case, Theft, Law and Society (2d ed. 1952). Professor Hall concludes (at 93):

> On the one hand, the criminal law at the time is clear. On the other hand, the whole complex aggregate of political and economic conditions described above thrusts itself upon the court. The more powerful forces prevailed—that happened which in due course must have happened under the circumstances. . . . The great forces of an emerging modern world, [such as the mercantile class, the wool and textile industry, and the Italian merchants who bought English wool], necessitated the elimination of a formula which had outgrown its usefulness. A new set of major institutions required a new rule. The law, lagging behind the needs of the times, was brought into more harmonious relationship with the other institutions by the decision rendered in the Carrier's Case.

The breaking-bulk device proved only a stopgap. It left without criminal sanction appropriations without breaking bulk as well as cases where the requirement of breaking was difficult to establish, as where the shipment consisted of separable units. The remedy was again statutory, an act of 1857 (20 & 21 Vict., ch. 54, §4) creating the new crime of larceny by bailee, which placed the dishonest bailee on a par with the dishonest servant. American statutes today either retain similar provisions as a separate crime of larceny by bailee or include misappropriation by a bailee as an instance of embezzlement.

NOTES ON APPROPRIATION OF LOST PROPERTY AND PROPERTY TRANSFERRED BY MISTAKE

Sometimes property comes into a defendant's possession through mistake: A delivery person may give a package to a person standing in front of a house, thinking (incorrectly) that the person is the homeowner to whom the package is addressed. A person may find a wallet containing both cash and a driver's license that shows the owner's name and address. In these cases, the person who comes into possession of the property may dishonestly decide to keep it for himself. Yet in these situations there seems to be no trespass that interferes with possession, as is required for larceny. Nor is there the employee or fiduciary relationship or the "entrusting" required by the usual embezzlement statute. Of what crime, then, may the dishonest person be convicted?

1. Found property. As for property found by a person who fails to return it, an early partial solution was the distinction between *lost* property (property unintentionally placed where found) and *mislaid* property (property deliberately placed where found, the owner forgetting where he or she put it). In the latter case, the courts often found that "possession" never left the owner, so that when the finder appropriated it, the finder "took" it from the owner's possession. Even as to the former, however, it was eventually determined that the finder took the property from the constructive possession of the owner, and if at the time the finder appropriated the lost property he or she intended to convert it, even though he might be able to discover the owner's identity, the finder was guilty of larceny. Penny v. State, 159 S.W. 1127 (Ark. 1913). It is generally held, however, that the felonious intent to appropriate must accompany the original finding and appropriation—otherwise there is no felonious taking. Long v. State, 33 So. 2d 382 (Ala. App. 1948). Suppose, for example, that a restaurant patron's wallet falls out of his pocket and the patron leaves the restaurant without knowing it. A waitress finds the wallet and takes it with her, fully intending to return it to the owner. But when the waitress gets home, she discovers she needs to pay a bill. At that point, she looks in the wallet and decides she is going to keep the money inside it. Is she guilty of larceny?

Consider the solution to this problem proposed by the MPC and now adopted by many states. Section 223.5 provides:

> A person who comes into control of property of another that he knows to have been lost, mislaid, or delivered under a mistake as to the nature or amount of the property or the identity of the recipient is guilty of theft if, with purpose to deprive the owner thereof, he fails to take reasonable measures to restore the property to a person entitled to have it.

See Model Penal Code and Commentaries, Comment to §223.5 at 228 (1980):

> The common-law view of larceny as an infringement of the possession of another required a determination of the actor's state of mind at the moment of finding. . . . The search for an initial fraudulent intent appears to be largely fictional, and in any event poses the wrong question. The realistic objective in this area is not to prevent initial appropriation but to compel subsequent acts to restore to the owner. The section therefore permits conviction even where the original taking was honest in the sense that the actor then intended to restore; if he subsequently changes his mind and determines to keep the property, he will then be guilty of theft.

2. Found information. In 2010, an Apple engineer left a prototype of the soon-to-be-released iPhone 4 at a California bar. Brian Hogan found the prototype and brought it home. Weeks later, Hogan sold the prototype to Gizmodo .com, a tech website, for $5,000; Gizmodo published a preview of the device, and the story spread like wildfire across the Internet. (The iPhone 4 was extraordinarily popular: When released two months later, Apple sold over 1 million phones on the first day). When the story ran, Apple claimed the story was damaging to the company because customers would not purchase its existing phones and instead opt to wait for the iPhone 4. Gizmodo later returned the phone to Apple.

Hogan was subsequently charged with misdemeanor theft; he pleaded no contest and received probation. Gizmodo was not charged. Would you have brought charges against either Hogan or Gizmodo? On what theory? What precisely did Hogan (mis)appropriate? See also Section B.2, Theft of Information, beginning on page 1085 infra.

3. *Misdelivered property.* In the case of dishonest appropriation of property delivered by mistake, there is again a twofold problem: first, finding the necessary taking from possession, and second, finding a felonious intent coincident with the taking. The solution of the MPC, also now followed in many states, is §223.5, just quoted. The supporting Commentary states as follows (Model Penal Code and Commentaries, Comment to §223.5 at 225-226 (1980)):

> [O]ne who accepts a $10 bill knowing that the other person thinks he is handing over a $1 bill acquires it without trespass or false pretense. Moreover, he may not be in any of the employee or fiduciary relations that were enumerated in the typical older embezzlement statutes. Consequently, special legislation or judicial sleight-of-hand was required to reach persons taking advantage of such mistakes. . . . Yet the recipient, knowing that the transfer to him is inadvertent, is in a moral and physical situation with respect to the property much like that of the finder of lost property. Moreover, he knows who is rightfully entitled to the property and can easily take steps to restore the property. Accordingly, Section 223.5 imposes theft sanctions against one in this situation who fails to take reasonable measures to restore. . . .
>
> It is necessary to limit the reach of Section 223.5, on the other hand, in order to avoid impinging on certain types of tolerated sharp trading. For example, it is not proposed to punish the purchase of another's property at a bargain price on a mere showing that the buyer was aware that the seller was misinformed regarding the value of what he sold. The language of Section 223.5 is accordingly limited to situations where the mistake is as to "the nature or amount of the property or the identity of the recipient."

PROBLEM

S.F. Chronicle, Nov. 14, 1964, at 4, contained the following story:

MONTGOMERY, Ala.—A man who withdrew $43,000 mistakenly credited to his bank account and refused to give it back was convicted yesterday by a jury in Federal Court. . . . It was Thaggard's second trial. The first ended with a deadlocked jury.

Thaggard was tried under a Federal law which prohibits taking anything worth more than $100 from a bank "with intent to steal or purloin." . . .

The dispute began in March 1963 when the Union Bank & Trust Co. erroneously credited a $43,000 deposit to the account of Alabama Motors, a used car business operated by Thaggard. The money belonged to Alabama Power Co.

On March 6, Thaggard asked for his balance, then drew out the $43,000 after the teller had three times verified the amount, at his request.

He finally signed a withdrawal slip and tellers spent 30 minutes counting out the bills and putting them in a brown paper sack.

In the first trial, Thaggard's lawyer, Ira De Ment, contended his client was not guilty of larceny since the money was voluntarily handed over. "I'm not saying he did right. I'm saying he's not guilty of larceny," De Ment said.

U.S. Attorney Ben Hardeman said, "Cotton Thaggard entered that bank with a heart full of larceny and left there with a sack full of money." . . .

Thaggard was first arrested on a state charge of false pretense. But that charge was dropped when the State Supreme Court ruled that it wasn't false pretense to get the money after three times asking the bank to recheck his balance.

Later, a Federal grand jury indicted Thaggard on a larceny charge involving a bank whose funds were insured by the Federal Deposit Insurance Corporation.

The bank has won a civil judgment against Thaggard in state court and some $10,575 worth of property belonging to him has been sold to satisfy the judgment.

Question: Was the criminal conviction appropriate as well?

STATE v. RIGGINS

Supreme Court of Illinois
8 Ill. 2d 78, 132 N.E.2d 519 (1956)

HERSHEY, C.J. [The defendant was convicted by a jury of embezzlement and sentenced to a term of not less than two nor more than seven years.]

[T]he defendant was the owner and operator of a collection agency . . . and during 1953 and 1954 had a clientele of some 500 persons and firms for whom he collected delinquent accounts.

In February, 1953, he called on the complaining witness, Dorothy Tarrant, who operated a firm known as Cooper's Music and Jewelry. He said he was in the collection business and asked to collect the firm's delinquent accounts. As a result, they reached an oral agreement whereby the defendant was to undertake the collections. By this agreement, the defendant was to receive one third on city accounts and one half on out-of-city accounts. It was further agreed that he need not account for the amounts collected until a bill was paid in full, at which time he was to remit by check.

There is a conflict in the evidence as to whether the defendant was to give a check for the whole amount collected and then receive his commission, or whether he was authorized to deduct his commission and account only for the net amount due.

It was further agreed that the defendant would be liable for court costs in the event he chose to file suit on any of the accounts, but the first money collected was to be applied to those costs. If no collection was made, however, the defendant was to stand the loss.

The parties operated under this agreement for almost two years. During that time the complaining witness exercised no control over the defendant as to the time or manner of collecting the accounts, and with her knowledge he commingled funds collected for all his clients in a single bank account. He also used this as a personal account, from which he drew for business, family and personal expenses.

In October, 1954, the complaining witness became aware that the defendant had collected several accounts for her in full, but had not accounted to her. . . . Thereafter, the complaining witness preferred the charges against the defendant which resulted in his indictment and conviction for embezzlement.

To decide whether the defendant, a collection agent, can be guilty of embezzlement in Illinois, it is helpful to consider our embezzlement statutes in the historical context of this crime.

Embezzlement, unknown at common law, is established by statute, and its scope, therefore, is limited to those persons designated therein. . . .

[O]ur laws relating to embezzlement are broad and comprehensive. The following persons are included in those statutes making the crime of embezzlement a felony: "Whoever embezzles or fraudulently converts to his own use" (Ill. Rev. Stat. 1953, chap. 38, par. 207); "a clerk, agent, servant or apprentice of any person" (par. 208); "any banker or broker, or his agent or servant, or any officer, agent or servant of any banking company, or incorporated bank" (par. 209); "any clerk, agent, servant, solicitor, broker, apprentice or officer . . . receiving any money . . . in his fiduciary capacity" (par. 210); public officers (par. 214); administrators, guardians, conservators and other fiduciaries (par. 216); and certain members and officers of fraternal societies (par. 218). . . .

In this instance, we are particularly interested in the general embezzlement statute (par. 208), and the special statute under which defendant was indicted (par. 210). The former, applying to any "clerk, agent, servant or apprentice of any person," was originally enacted in 1827, and has existed in its present form since 1874. [Par. 210] was not passed until 1919. For present purposes, this latter enactment is very significant, for it also provides as follows: such person

> shall be punished as provided by the criminal statutes of this state for the punishment of larceny, *irrespective of whether any such* officer, agent, clerk, servant, solicitor, broker or apprentice *has or claims to have any commission or interest in such money*, substitute for money, or thing of value so received by him.

(Italics added.)

[A] 1903 decision of this court reversed the conviction of an agent who was employed to solicit subscriptions on commission and who was authorized to deduct her commissions from the amounts collected, for the reason that she was joint owner with the principal in the amounts collected. McElroy v. People, 66 N.E. 1058 (Ill. 1903). . . .

Briefly, then, this was the status of the law in 1919 when the special statute (par. 210) . . . expressly abrogated [that] doctrine.[a] . . .

[T]he defendant acted as agent for the complaining witness in collecting her accounts. . . . He had no right to collect from anyone except as authorized by her and was required to render a full account of all matters entrusted to him, the same as any agent. . . . The prevailing view of the courts in construing embezzlement statutes is succinctly expressed in 18 Am. Jur., Embezzlement, §30, as follows: "The term 'agent' as used in embezzlement statutes is construed in its popular sense as meaning a person who undertakes to transact some business or to manage some affair for another by the latter's authority and to render an account of such business or affair. . . ."

We conclude that the defendant was an "agent" of the complaining witness, receiving money in a "fiduciary capacity" and, therefore, within the purview of said embezzlement statute. . . .

Reversed [on other grounds].

SCHAEFER, J., dissenting. . . . The critical question is whether the defendant was the agent of the complaining witness. Upon the record it seems to me that he was not. He maintained his own office, had his own employees, and collected accounts for approximately 500 other individuals and firms. He was subject to no control whatsoever by any of his customers in making his collections. His customers knew that he kept all of his collections in a single account. That the defendant was not an agent would be clear, I think, if vicarious liability was sought to be asserted against Dorothy Tarrant on account of the defendant's conduct in the course of his collection activities.

The conclusion of the majority that the defendant was an agent rests upon the assertion that "[t]he term 'agent' as used in embezzlement statutes is construed in its popular sense. . . ." That generalization runs counter to the basic rule that criminal statutes are strictly construed.

. . . The statute under which the defendant was indicted refers to "any clerk, agent, servant, solicitor, broker, apprentice, or officer." If "agent" has the broad meaning which the majority gives it, each of the other terms is superfluous because all are embraced within the single term "agent." Many of the specific enumerations in the other statutes referred to by the majority likewise become largely, if not entirely, meaningless, for the particular relationships they seek to reach are also swallowed up in the expanded definition of the term "agent."

It is arguable of course that the conduct of the defendant in this case should be regarded as criminal. The General Assembly might wish to make it so. But it might not. It might regard the collection agency as a desirable service enterprise which should not be made unduly perilous. If the defendant in this case,

---

a. Many cases have taken the view that, even absent such a specific statute, the fact that a collector is entitled to deduct a commission out of the funds collected does not preclude an embezzlement conviction for appropriation of the entire proceeds.—EDS.

with his little agency, is guilty of one embezzlement, he is guilty of 500. The General Assembly might not want to make the enterprise so hazardous. It has not done so, in my opinion, by the statute before us.[b]

MODEL PENAL CODE

§223.8. THEFT BY FAILURE TO MAKE REQUIRED DISPOSITIONS OF FUNDS RECEIVED [See Appendix.]

Model Penal Code and Commentaries, Comment to §223.8 at 256-262 (1980): The challenge . . . is to distinguish default that should be assimilated to theft from non-performance that should be left to the traditional remedies for breach of contract.

The difficulty that has troubled courts in the past may be illustrated by the decisions in *Commonwealth v. Mitchneck*[1] and *State v. Polzin.*[2] The *Mitchneck* case involved a mine operator whose employees signed written authorizations for him to deduct from their wages the amounts of their grocery bills. Mitchneck made the deductions but failed to pay the grocer. He was convicted under the Pennsylvania fraudulent-conversion statute, which at the time covered anyone who

> having received or having possession, in any capacity or by any means or manner whatever, of any money or property, of any kind whatsoever, of or belonging to any other person, firm, or corporation, or which any other person, firm, or corporation is entitled to receive and have, who fraudulently withholds, converts, or applies the same, or any part thereof, . . . to and for his own use and benefit, or to and for the use and benefit of any other person.

The conviction was reversed on the ground that Mitchneck did not have in his possession

> any money *belonging* to his employees. True he owed them money. . . . Defendant's liability for the unpaid wages due his employees was, and remained, civil, not criminal. His liability for the amount due [the grocer] after his agreement to accept or honor the assignments of his employees' wages was likewise civil and not criminal.

If the miners in the *Mitchneck* case had drawn their pay at one window and passed part of it back to Mitchneck's cashier at the next window, conviction for embezzlement or fraudulent conversion could have been obtained. The premise of Section 223.8 is that liability should also follow

---

b. The statutes at issue in *Riggins* have been replaced by §5/16-1 of the Illinois Revised Criminal Code, reprinted at page 1080 infra.—EDS.

1. 198 A. 463 (Pa. Super Ct. 1938).

2. 85 P.2d 1057 (Wash. 1939).

on the facts of the case as they occurred. The bookkeeping shortcut actually used hardly serves as a rational basis for exculpating Mitchneck from criminal liability. . . .

The *Polzin* case presents a more complex variation of the same situation. Polzin was a money lender who took a note from a Mrs. Braseth under an arrangement by which, instead of paying the cash to her, he agreed to pay off certain of her creditors. Instead of doing so, he made out a check to a collection agency which he owned. He then approached the creditors with a proposal to act for them in collecting their claim from Mrs. Braseth for a 33 percent collection fee. They accepted the arrangement, after which Polzin paid the creditors and withheld $19 as his agreed-upon collection fee.

Polzin was convicted of petty larceny, the jury having evidently taken the view that what was stolen was the $19 fee which Polzin had withheld. The Supreme Court of Washington reversed the conviction. The court held first that there could be no misappropriation of any "property" belonging to Mrs. Braseth, because she never gave Polzin anything other than her note. Since Polzin held no "property" belonging to Mrs. Braseth but had merely promised to make certain payments, he was her debtor rather than her trustee. Second, with respect to the $19 withheld from the creditors, Mrs. Braseth "lost nothing"; the bills had been completely discharged and Polzin had therefore performed his agreement as far as she was concerned.

Section 223.8 was designed in part to provide a theory for reaching cases like *Mitchneck* and *Polzin*. Both were thought to illustrate situations that properly should be assimilated to theft rather than treated as mere breach of contract. . . .

There is a long tradition, deriving to some extent from the harsh days of the debtors' prison and to some extent enshrined in constitutional provisions, against enforcing individual consensual obligations by criminal sanctions. . . . Among the valid objections[:] that the invocation of criminal sanctions in cases of non-performance involves the impairment of the incentive to make wise risk selections and thus impairment of the social functions of contract-making . . . ; the unlikelihood of deterring honest insolvency by criminal threats, since insolvency is so often a result of factors beyond the control of the individual; the dangers, in attempting to punish insolvency for which the actor may properly be viewed as at fault, of discouraging the kind of speculation that is properly a part of a free-enterprise system and of securing unjust convictions by hindsight; and the futility, from the creditors' standpoint, of imprisoning a debtor who is unable to pay.

None of the foregoing considerations was thought applicable to cases such as *Mitchneck* and *Polzin*. In neither of those cases was there an ordinary credit transaction or an understanding that involves an assessment of risks at some future date. Mitchneck and Polzin were not supposed to use the funds in any way for their own purposes nor even to retain them for any substantial period. They were merely conduits for the transmission of money to persons designated by the real owner of the money. . . .

It should be noted, however, that the *Mitchneck* and *Polzin* situations are not free from difficulty even under such a formulation as Section 223.8. The text of the offense requires that the actor "obtain" property from another. The term "obtain" is defined in Section 223.0(5) to mean, in relation to property, "to bring about a transfer or purported transfer of a legal interest in the property, whether to the obtainer or another." The problem in both *Mitchneck* and *Polzin* was that the defendant was not perceived as having "obtained" anything from the victim in this sense, and that perception might be no less applicable to Section 223.8. Indeed, if the property were regarded as having been "obtained" as that term is defined, Section 223.2(1) would be an adequate basis for prosecution. If Mitchneck and Polzin obtained property of another under an understanding and then "exercised unlawful control over" that property, there would seem to be no bar to an ordinary embezzlement prosecution. Even if this is true, however, there may be an important value in addressing a specific formulation to situations of this kind. Convictions of embezzlement are not easily obtained under the broader standards embodied in the general definition of theft.

It is important, nevertheless, to emphasize the point that Section 223.8 must not be construed so broadly that a bright line between theft and breach of contract is obscured. [Consider] credit-card purchases, a practice that has assumed enormous proportions in today's economy. Typically, the purchaser of goods "obtains" property by becoming the drawee-acceptor of a draft, drawn by the merchant in favor of the credit-card company as payee. If unauthorized use of the card is involved, or if forged or stolen cards are used, Section 224.6 is adequate to handle the problem. If the actor intended from the beginning not to pay, Section 223.3 covers the situation. But if the actor . . . simply cannot pay his bills, it is inappropriate to make him a thief; the risk that he cannot pay is a cost of doing business that credit-card companies should assume. . . .

The path to avoiding such undue extensions of Section 223.8 is to accord proper weight to the limitation embodied in the words "to be reserved," so that Section 223.8 is deemed applicable only in cases of a promise to turn over property actually received in kind or an equivalent sum of money specifically reserved in the sense that a trustee reserves a fiduciary account. It is true that such a construction would seem to limit Section 223.8 to classic instances of embezzlement. [T]here may be some cases beyond ordinary embezzlement to which the provision could be applied by a broad construction of "obtains" to deal with situations where property was not physically exchanged. But in order to eliminate application of the section to cases where civil remedies alone should be permitted, something approaching an explicit agreement to "reserve" would seem to be required.

NOTE

Only nine states followed the MPC's lead in this section. See Model Penal Code and Commentaries, Comment to §223.8 at 266 (1980). What might be the reasons for the reluctance?

3. *Fraud*

INTRODUCTORY NOTE

The hallmark of theft by fraud is the use of deception to obtain either possession or title of another's property. The difficulty is drawing a line between deception that rises to the level of criminality and, as Samuel Buell puts it, "acceptable behavior in the rough-and-tumble of markets." Samuel W. Buell, Good Faith and Law Evasion, 58 UCLA L. Rev. 611, 638 (2011). See also Stuart P. Green, Lying, Cheating, and Stealing: A Moral Theory of White Collar Crime (2006). Even after conduct is identified as falling on the criminal side of the line, there remains a similarly complex question of how it stacks up against other criminal frauds and should be graded for punishment.

Here, too, history plays an important role in making sense of the current state of the law. The early common law, influenced by the ethic of caveat emptor, did not criminalize situations in which a person acquired another's property through simple deception. The classic justification was given by Lord Chief Justice John Holt in 1703: "[W]e are not to indict one man for making a fool of another." Regina v. Jones, 91 Eng. Rep. 330.[1] But through the development of common-law "cheats," the principle was modified as to certain kinds of fraud aimed indiscriminately at any member of the public rather than at a particular person, when ordinary prudence was an insufficient protection: for example, using a false token, false weights or measures. See Rex. v. Wheatley, 97 Eng. Rep. 746, 748-749 (1761).

A more far-reaching innovation came in 1757 with the enactment of what became the prototype false pretense statute, 30 Geo. II, ch. 24, making it a misdemeanor to obtain "money, goods, wares or merchandizes" by false pretenses with intent to cheat or defraud. There originally was some doubt whether the false pretense statute reached any and all misrepresentations or was to be narrowly read. It was not until 1789 that the broader meaning was established. See Jerome Hall, Theft, Law and Society 45-52 (2d ed. 1952). In a false pretenses case, ownership of the property transfers, not merely possession.

In the meantime, the landmark case of The King v. Pear, decided in 1779, 1 Leach 212, 168 Eng. Rep. 208, created what came to be known as "larceny by trick" as a distinct form of common-law larceny where possession of property is obtained by trickery. The defendant was indicted for stealing Finch's horse. Finch was a stablekeeper, and the defendant hired a horse from him, claiming he would return later that same day. In fact, he did not return but instead sold the horse. The following report of the case is taken from 168 Eng. Rep. 208:

> The learned Judge said: There had been different opinions on the law of this class of cases; that the general doctrine then was that if a horse be let for a particular portion of time, and after that time is expired, the party hiring,

---

1. Cf. 1 W. Hawkins, Pleas of the Crown 344 (6th ed. 1788): "[It is] needless to provide severe laws for such mischiefs, against which common prudence and caution may be a sufficient security."

instead of returning the horse to its owner, sell it and convert the money to his own use, it is felony, because there is then no privity of contract subsisting between the parties. . . . He therefore left it with the Jury to consider, Whether the prisoner meant at the time of the hiring to take such journey, but was afterwards tempted to sell the horse? for if so he must be acquitted; but that if they were of opinion that at the time of the hiring the journey was a mere pretense to get the horse into his possession, and he had no intention to take such journey but intended to sell the horse, they would find that fact specially for the opinion of the Judges.

The Jury found that the facts above stated were true; and also that the prisoner had hired the horse with a fraudulent view and intention of selling it immediately.

The question was referred to the Judges, Whether the delivery of the horse by the prosecutor to the prisoner, had so far changed the possession of the property, as to render the subsequent conversion of it a mere breach of trust, or whether the conversion was felonious?

The Judges differed greatly in opinion on this case. . . . The majority of them thought, That the question, as to the original intention of the prisoner in hiring the horse, had been properly left to the jury; and as they had found, that his view in so doing was fraudulent, the parting with the property had not changed the nature of the possession, but that it remained unaltered in the prosecutor at the time of the conversion; and that the prisoner was therefore guilty of felony.

Use was made, therefore, of the notion that possession never passes to a fraudulent bailee to stretch the concept of larceny to include an act otherwise not subject to proper criminal sanction. Jerome Hall, Theft, Law and Society 42 (2d ed. 1952).

When the false pretense statute was subsequently extended to all misrepresentations of fact, regardless of the technique of deception, there were two crimes, larceny by trick (a felony) and statutory false pretenses (only a misdemeanor), covering much the same conduct but distinguished on whether possession (larceny by trick) or ownership (false pretenses) was transferred.

Question: Why should it be a more serious crime to trick someone into transferring possession of property temporarily than to trick someone into parting with something greater, namely the ownership of it?

HUFSTETLER v. STATE

Alabama Court of Appeals
37 Ala. App. 71, 63 So. 2d 730 (1953)

CARR, J. The accused was convicted by the court without a jury on a charge of petit larceny. The property involved was 6½ gallons of gasoline. [The defendant drove up to a gas station and asked the owner of the station to "fill it up." After the owner put 6½ gallons in the car, the defendant asked for a quart of oil and drove off when the attendant left to get it without paying the $1.94 for the gas.]

The only question of critical concern is whether, on the basis of the above proof, the judgment of conviction can be sustained. . . .

Confusion sometimes arises in an effort to distinguish the kindred criminal offenses of larceny, false pretenses, and embezzlement.

The Massachusetts Supreme Court in Commonwealth v. Barry, 124 Mass. 325, gave a distinction that is clear and comprehensive:

> If a person honestly receives the possession of the goods, chattels or money of another upon any trust, express or implied, and, after receiving them, fraudulently converts them to his own use, he may be guilty of the crime of embezzlement, but cannot be of that of larceny, except as embezzlement is by statute made larceny. If the possession of such property is obtained by fraud, and the owner of it intends to part with his title as well as his possession, the offence is that of obtaining property by false pretenses, provided the means by which they are acquired are such as, in law, are false pretenses. If the possession is fraudulently obtained, with intent on the part of the person obtaining it, at the time he receives it, to convert the same to his own use, and the person parting with it intends to part with his possession merely, and not with his title to the property, the offence is larceny.

In the case at bar the circumstances disclose that . . . appellant secured the possession of the gasoline by a trick or fraud. The obtaining of the property by the consent of the owner under such conditions will not necessarily prevent the taking from being larceny. In other words, an actual trespass is not always required to be proven. The trick or fraud vitiates the transaction, and it will be deemed that the owner still retained the constructive possession.

What we have said relates to the possession. It is certainly a logical conclusion that [the gas station owner] had no intention of parting with the ownership of the property until he had received pay therefor. The element of the intent of the appellant is inferable from the factual background. . . .

Affirmed. . . .

GRAHAM v. UNITED STATES

United States Court of Appeals for the District of Columbia Circuit
187 F.2d 87 (1950)

WASHINGTON, J. The appellant, an attorney, was indicted in two counts for grand larceny under section 2201 of Title 22 of the District of Columbia Code. . . . He appeals from a judgment and conviction entered upon a verdict of guilty.

The complaining witness, Francisco Gal, consulted appellant in his professional capacity. Gal had been arrested and charged with disorderly conduct, and had forfeited $25 as collateral. He was seeking American citizenship and was apprehensive that the arrest would impede or bar his attainment of that goal. An immigrant employed as a cook, his command of the English language was far from complete. He testified that appellant Graham told him that he wasn't sure what he could do, that Graham would "have to talk to the policeman. You have to pay money for that, because the money is talk." He further testified that Graham told him he would charge him $200 for a fee; that he would have to pay an additional $2,000 for the police; that Graham said "don't mention the money for nobody and for the police either." As a result, Gal testified that he paid the appellant $300 on February 2, 1950 (of which, he said, $200 was paid as a legal fee), and $1,900 on February 3, 1950. The police officer who originally had arrested Gal testified that he came to appellant's office, and after talking with Graham, told Gal that he wasn't in any trouble. . . . The officer testified that Graham did not then or at any other time offer or give him money. The appellant testified that the entire payment was intended as a fee for legal services; that he had never mentioned money for the police; that no part of the money was in fact paid to the police or anyone else, but was kept by the appellant. . . .

Section 2201 of Title 22 of the District of Columbia Code provides as follows:

> Whoever shall feloniously take and carry away anything of value of the amount or value of $50 or upward, including things savoring of the realty, shall suffer imprisonment of not less than one nor more than ten years.

Interpreting this statute, this court has held that "one who obtains money from another upon the representation that he will perform certain service therewith for the latter, intending at the time to convert the money, and actually converting it, to his own use, is guilty of larceny." In classic terminology, "the distinction drawn by the common law is between the case of one who gives up possession of a chattel for a special purpose to another who by converting it to his own use is held to have committed a trespass, and the case of one who, although induced by fraud or trick, nevertheless actually intends that title to the chattel shall pass to the wrongdoer." United States v. Patton, 3 Cir., 1941, 120 F.2d 73, 76.

We now turn to appellant's first contention, that under the evidence in the case the court should have directed a verdict for the defendant. We think this contention without merit. If the jury believed Gal's testimony, and did not believe that of the defendant, it was possible for the jury to conclude beyond a reasonable doubt that the defendant fraudulently induced Gal to give him $2,000 to be used for a special purpose, i.e., to bribe the police, that the defendant did not intend so to use the money, and converted it to his own use. Under the rule stated above, this would be larceny by trick.

Thus, in the *Means* case [Means v. United States, 65 F.2d 206], the defendant was convicted of the crime of larceny under the following circumstances: After the kidnapping of the infant son of Charles Lindbergh, the defendant in an interview with Mrs. McLean persuaded her that he could assist in locating and recovering the kidnapped baby, stating that if Mrs. McLean would give him $100,000 he would use that sum to pay the ransom and secure the return of the child. On the basis of these representations he secured the money from Mrs. McLean. His representations were fraudulent and he intended at the time to convert the money to his own use, and actually so converted it. [U]nder these circumstances "title would remain in [the complainant] until the accomplishment of the purpose for which she gave [the defendant] the money." . . .

The judgment of the District Court is affirmed.

NOTES AND QUESTIONS

1. *Gal's intent.* How can the court defend its decision that Gal did not intend to pass his whole interest in the money to the defendant, title and all, when Gal himself testified that he gave the money to the defendant to be given to the police officer as a bribe? But if the court had held otherwise, thus precluding a larceny-by-trick conviction, could the defendant have been convicted of obtaining money by false pretenses? Note that a false *promise* is often regarded as inadequate to sustain a false pretense conviction, although it suffices for larceny by trick. See *People v. Ashley*, infra.

2. *Possession versus ownership.* In Bourbonnaise v. State, 248 P.2d 640 (Okla. Crim. App. 1952), the defendant bootlegger obtained money from Bean as payment for a bottle of whiskey that defendant claimed he would buy from another bootlegger. He said he would return in 30 minutes with the bottle but never did. Affirming a conviction of larceny, the court stated (248 P.2d at 642):

> This money was not given the defendant to consummate a purchase of liquor represented by defendant to be in his possession. . . . If such had been the case, then the money would have become defendant's money, and if the defendant had failed to turn over the liquor . . . such facts would have supported a charge of obtaining money under false pretense. But here defendant . . . merely agreed to take Bean's money and go purchase the liquor from another bootlegger. The money was not his. He was to pay it over for Bean. It was Bean's money until paid over, and then the whiskey would be Bean's.

3. *Problem.* The defendant went to an auto dealership, took a vehicle for a test drive, and failed to return it. He was convicted of larceny by false pretenses. Is the case distinguishable from *Hufstetler*? Should the conviction be affirmed? See Baker v. Commonwealth, 300 S.E.2d 788 (Va. 1983).

PEOPLE v. ASHLEY

Supreme Court of California
42 Cal. 2d 246, 267 P.2d 271 (1954)

TRAYNOR, J. . . . [Defendant, the business manager of a corporation, was convicted of grand theft under §404 of the California Penal Code. Defendant obtained a loan of $7,200 from an elderly woman, Mrs. Russ, by promising that the loan would be secured by a first mortgage on property owned by the corporation and that the money would be used to build a theater. In fact, the corporation leased but did not own the property, and no theater was ever built, the money having been used to meet the corporation's operating expenses. After defendant received the money, Mrs. Russ quarreled with him over his failure to deliver the promised first mortgage. After it became apparent that the loan would not be paid, defendant requested an extension. Mrs. Russ granted the extension after defendant had threatened to kill himself if she refused, so that she might be paid from the proceeds of his life insurance policies.

[Defendant also obtained $13,590 from a Mrs. Neal, representing that the corporation intended to use the money to buy a theater. She was initially told that the loan would be secured by a trust deed on the theater and that she would have good security for her loan because the corporation was worth a half million dollars. Subsequently, she loaned the corporation an additional $4,470. Mrs. Neal testified that when she hesitated in making the additional loan, defendant placed a gun on his desk and said: "Now look here, Mrs. Neal, I don't want no monkey business out of you. Do you understand that?" The corporation did not buy the theater; Mrs. Neal never received the trust deed; and the money was deposited to the corporation's account.]

Although the crimes of larceny by trick and device and obtaining property by false pretenses are much alike, they are aimed at different criminal acquisitive techniques. Larceny by trick and device is the appropriation of property, the possession of which was fraudulently acquired; obtaining property by false pretenses is the fraudulent or deceitful acquisition of both title and possession. . . . In the present case, it is clear from the record that each of the prosecuting witnesses intended to pass both title and possession, and that the type of theft, if any, in each case, was that of obtaining property by false pretenses. [Defendant's] defense was not based on distinctions between title and possession, but rather he contends that there was no unlawful taking of any sort.

To support a conviction of theft for obtaining property by false pretenses, it must be shown that the defendant made a false pretense or representation with intent to defraud the owner of his property, and that the owner was in fact defrauded. It is unnecessary to prove that the defendant benefited personally from the fraudulent acquisition. The false pretense or representation must have materially influenced the owner to part with his property, but the false pretense need not be the sole inducing cause. If the conviction rests primarily on the testimony of a single witness that the false pretense was made, the making of the pretense must be corroborated. . . .

[O]ur statute, like those of most American states, is directly traceable to 30 Geo. II, ch. 24, section 1. In an early Crown Case Reserved, Rex v. Goodhall, Russ. & Ry. 461 (1821), the defendant obtained a quantity of meat from a merchant by promising to pay at a future day. The jury found that the promise was made without intention to perform. The judges concluded, however, that the defendant's conviction was erroneous because the pretense "was merely a promise of future conduct, and common prudence and caution would have prevented any injury arising from it." . . . By stating that the "promise of future conduct" was such that "common prudence and caution" could prevent any injury arising therefrom, the new offense was confused with the old common law "cheat." [This opinion] was completely misinterpreted in the case of Commonwealth v. Drew, 1837, 19 Pick. 179, 185, 36 Mass. 179,

185, in which the Supreme Judicial Court of Massachusetts declared by way of dictum, that under the statute "naked lies" could not be regarded as "false pretenses." On the basis of these two questionable decisions, Wharton formulated the following generalization: ". . . the false pretense to be within the statute, must relate to a state of things averred to be at the time existing, and not to a state of things thereafter to exist." Wharton, American Criminal Law 542 [1st ed. 1846]. This generalization has been followed in the majority of American cases, almost all of which can be traced to reliance on Wharton or the two cases mentioned above. [But] other courts have repudiated the majority rule. . . . [3]

The Court of Appeals for the District of Columbia has, however, advanced the following reasons in defense of the majority rule: ". . . [W]here, as here, the act complained of—namely, failure to repay money or use it as specified at the time of borrowing—is as consonant with ordinary commercial default as with criminal conduct, the danger of applying this technique to prove the crime is quite apparent. Business affairs would be materially incumbered by the ever present threat that a debtor might be subjected to criminal penalties if the prosecutor and jury were of the view that at the time of borrowing he was mentally a cheat. The risk of prosecuting one who is guilty of nothing more than a failure or inability to pay his debts is a very real consideration. . . ." Chaplin v. United States, 157 F.2d 697, 698-699.

. . . We do not find this reasoning persuasive. In this state, and in the majority of American states as well as in England, false promises can provide the foundation of a civil action for deceit. In such actions something more than nonperformance is required to prove the defendant's intent not to perform his promise. Nor is proof of nonperformance alone sufficient in criminal prosecutions based on false promises. In such prosecutions the People must . . . prove [the defendant's fraudulent intent] beyond a reasonable doubt. . . . Moreover, in cases of obtaining property by false pretenses, it must be proved that any misrepresentations of fact alleged by the People were made knowingly and with intent to deceive. . . .

If false promises were not false pretenses, the legally sophisticated, without fear of punishment, could perpetrate on the unwary fraudulent schemes like that divulged by the record in this case. . . . The inclusion of false promises within sections 484 and 532 of the Penal Code will not "materially encumber" business affairs. . . .

The judgment and the order denying the motion for a new trial are affirmed.

SCHAUER, J. I concur in the judgment solely on the ground that the evidence establishes, with ample corroboration, the making by the defendant of false representations as to existing facts. On that evidence the convictions should be sustained pursuant to long accepted theories of law. . . . I dissent from all that

---

3. The majority rule was also rejected by the United States Supreme Court in the construction of the federal mail fraud statute. See Durland v. United States, 161 U.S. 306, 313. . . .

portion of the opinion which discusses and pronounces upon the theories which in my view are extraneous to the proper disposition of any issue actually before us. . . .

In a prosecution for obtaining property by the making of a false promise, knowingly and with intent to deceive, the matter to be proved . . . is purely subjective. It is not, like the specific intent in such a crime as burglary, a mere element of the crime; it is, in any significant sense, all of the crime. The proof will necessarily be of objective acts, entirely legal in themselves, from which inferences as to the ultimate illegal subjective fact will be drawn. But, whereas in burglary the proof of the subjective element is normally as strong and reliable as the proof of any objective element, in this type of activity the proof of such vital element can almost never be reliable; it must inevitably (in the absence of confession or something tantamount thereto) depend on inferences drawn by creditors, prosecutors, jurors, and judges from facts and circumstances which by reason of their nature cannot possibly exclude innocence with any certainty. . . . I am unwilling to accept as a premise the scholastic redaction of the majority that rules of proof may be set aside because appellate judges will always know when a jury has been misled and the proof is not sufficient. . . .

With the rule that the majority opinion now enunciates, no man, no matter how innocent his intention, can sign a promise to pay in the future, or to perform an act at a future date, without subjecting himself to the risk that at some later date others, in the light of differing perspectives, philosophies and subsequent events, may conclude that, after all, the accused *should* have known that at the future date he could not perform as he promised—and if he, as a "reasonable" man from the point of view of the creditor, district attorney and a grand or trial jury—*should* have known, then, it may be inferred, he did know. And if it can be inferred that he knew, then this court and other appellate courts will be bound to affirm a conviction. . . .

NOTES AND QUESTIONS

1. In accord with *Ashley*, see Commonwealth v. Parker, 564 A.2d 246 (Pa. Super. 1989); Kennedy v. State, 342 S.E.2d 251 (W. Va. 1986). In contrast, some courts continue to hold that a false promise cannot constitute false pretenses. E.g., State v. Allen, 505 So. 2d 1024 (Miss. 1987); People v. Reigle, 566 N.W.2d 21, 24 (Mich. Ct. App. 1997).

2. Federal fraud statutes. In its original 1872 enactment, the federal mail fraud statute criminalized use of the mails to advance "any scheme or artifice to defraud." McNally v. United States, 483 U.S. 350, 356 (1987). Congress subsequently expanded the statute to cover an even wider range of conduct, and enacted the federal wire fraud statute, 18 U.S.C. §1343, to proscribe fraud conducted over interstate telecommunications in addition to mail. The modern mail fraud statute, 18 U.S.C. §1341, reads:

> Whoever, having devised or intending to devise any scheme or artifice to defraud, or for obtaining money or property by means of false or fraudulent

pretenses, representations, or promises ... for the purpose of executing such scheme or artifice or attempting so to do ... [causes] any matter or thing whatever to be sent or delivered by the Postal Service, or [causes] any matter or thing whatever to be sent or delivered by any private or commercial inter-state carrier ... shall be fined under this title or imprisoned not more than 20 years, or both.

The breadth of the mail fraud statute's coverage to include false promises and "any scheme or artifice to defraud" that involves the use of federal mail—a sweeping expansion of federal jurisdiction over fraud—has led one federal pro-secutor (and now federal judge) to call §1341 the white collar prosecutor's "true love." Jed S. Rakoff, The Federal Mail Fraud Statute (Part I), 18 Duq. L. Rev. 771, 771 (1980). Why might fraud statutes be more ambiguous than other criminal statutes? See Samuel W. Buell, Novel Criminal Fraud, 81 N.Y.U. L. Rev. 1971 (2006). Other aspects of the federal mail and wire fraud statutes are discussed begininning on page 1093 infra. For a comprehensive overview, see Elizabeth Wagner Pittman, Mail and Wire Fraud, 47 Am. Crim. L. Rev. 797 (2010).

Recall Judge Schauer's concern in dissent that an action based on false promises could potentially turn any breach of a promise into a crime. The federal statute by its terms makes no effort to police against such an outcome, but other statutory schemes use more care. Consider, for example, N.Y. Penal Law §155.05(2)(d), which makes clear that "the defendant's intention or belief that the promise would not be performed may not be established by or inferred from the fact alone that such promise was not performed. Such a finding may be based only upon evidence establishing that the facts and cir-cumstances of the case are wholly consistent with guilty intent or belief and wholly inconsistent with innocent intent or belief, and excluding to a moral certainty every hypothesis except that of the defendant's intention or belief that the promise would not be performed. . . ." Section 223.3(1) of the MPC similarly provides that "deception as to a person's intention to perform a promise shall not be inferred from the fact alone that he did not subsequently perform the promise."

As you read the following case, consider whether these evidentiary rules are necessary or advisable to ensure that theft based on false promises does not sweep too broadly.

NELSON v. UNITED STATES

United States Court of Appeals for the District of Columbia Circuit
227 F.2d 21 (1955)

DANAHER, J. This is an appeal from a conviction for obtaining goods by false pretenses in violation of D.C. Code §22-1301 (1951). The trial court entered judgment of acquittal on a second count charging grand larceny. Evidence was offered to show that appellant from time to time over a period of months, for purposes of resale, had purchased merchandise from Potomac Distributors. . . . By September 18, 1952, his account was said to be in arrears more than thirty days. Late that afternoon, appellant sought immediate possession of two television sets and a washing machine, displayed his customers' purchase contracts to support his statement that he had already sold such merchandise and had taken payment therefor, and told one Schneider, secretary-treasurer of Potomac Distributors, "I promised delivery tonight." Appellant was told no further credit could be extended to him because of his overdue indebtedness in excess of $1,800, whereupon appellant offered to give security for the desired items as well as for the delinquent account. He represented himself as the owner of a Packard car for which he had paid $4,260.50, but failed to disclose an outstanding prior indebtedness on the car of $3,028.08 secured by a chattel mortgage in favor of City Bank. Instead, he represented that he owed only one payment of some $55, not then due. Relying upon such representations, Potomac Distributors delivered to appellant two television sets each worth $136, taking in return a demand note for the entire indebtedness, past and present, in the total, $2,047.37, secured by a chattel mortgage on the Packard and the television sets. Appellant promised to make a cash payment on the note within a few days for default of which the holder was entitled to demand full payment. When the promised payment was not forthcoming, Schneider, by telephone calls and a personal visit to appellant's home, sought to locate appellant but learned he had left town. The Packard about that time was in a collision, incurring damage of about $1,000, and was thereupon repossessed in behalf of the bank which held the prior lien for appellant's car purchase indebtedness. . . .

Appellant argues that Potomac Distributors could not have been defrauded for the car on September 18, 1952, "had an equity of between $900 and $1,000 and roughly five times the value of the two television sets." That fact is immaterial. . . .

This appellant has sold two television sets, and apparently had taken payment therefor although he had no television sets to deliver to his customers. He could not get the sets from Potomac Distributors without offering security for his past due account as well as for his present purchase. In order to get them he lied. He represented that his car acquired at a cost of more than $4,000 required only one further payment of $55. He now complains because his victim believed him when he lied. He argues that the misrepresentations were not material although the victim testified, and the jury could properly find, that he would not have parted with his goods except in reliance upon appellant's statements. . . .

He argues that there was no proof of an intent upon his part to defraud his victim.

> Wrongful acts knowingly or intentionally committed can neither be justified nor excused on the ground of innocent intent. . . . The intent to injure or defraud is presumed when the unlawful act, which results in loss or injury, is proved to have been knowingly committed. It is a well-settled rule, which the law applies in both criminal and civil cases, that the intent is presumed and inferred from the result of the action.

This quotation from a challenged charge was found by the Supreme Court to be "unexceptionable as matter of law" in Agnew v. United States, 1897, 165 U.S. 36, 53. . . .

Affirmed.

MILLER, J. (dissenting). . . . Nelson did make a false representation; but the question is whether there was evidence from which the jury could properly be permitted to infer that he intended to defraud, and to conclude that Potomac was thereby defrauded. . . .

Differing definitions of the word "defraud" probably cause the difference in opinion between the majority and me. They seem to think it means, in connection with a purchase, to make a false pretense in the process of obtaining goods even though the purchase price is well secured. I think the word means, in connection with a purchase, to make a false pretense as a result of which the seller is deprived of his goods or of the purchase price. . . . A purchaser can be said to have defrauded the seller of his goods only if he intended to defraud him of the purchase price for which the seller was willing to exchange them. It seems to me to follow that a purchaser who makes a false statement in buying on credit has not defrauded the seller of his goods if he nevertheless amply secures the debt. . . .

In considering the criminality vel non of the false statement, it must be remembered that the past due indebtedness of $1,697.87 is to play no part. That credit had already been extended generally, and with respect to it Potomac parted with nothing on September 18. Nelson was only charged with defrauding Potomac by obtaining through false pretense the articles then delivered, which had a total value of only $349.50.

What was the actual value on September 18 of the property upon which Potomac took a lien, on the strength of which it parted with property worth $349.50? The bank collection manager, testifying for the Government, said that although on September 18 Nelson still owed the bank $3,028.08, he had on that day an equity in the car worth from $900 to $1,000. The mortgaged television sets were, I suppose, worth their price of $272. Adding to this the minimum equity in the automobile proved by the prosecution, it appears that Potomac had a lien on property worth at least $1,172 to protect a debt of $349.50. The proportion was more than three to one.

Such is the evidence as to what happened September 18, from which the jury was permitted to infer that Nelson then intended to defraud. [I]t is wholly irrational to presume or infer that one intends to defraud when he buys goods on credit and safeguards that credit by giving more than triple security for it— no matter if he does falsely pretend that the security is even greater. It is equally illogical to conclude that the creditor was thereby defrauded. For that reason, my opinion is that the proof I have outlined—which was the only pertinent proof—did not warrant the trial court in submitting the case to the jury. . . .

Nelson was guilty of a moral wrong in falsely and grossly misrepresenting his debt to the bank, but in the circumstances he should not have been indicted and convicted because of it. The . . . statute under which he was prosecuted does not make mere falsehood felonious; it only denounces as criminal a false pretense which was intended to defraud and which in fact had that result. Even a liar is entitled to the full protection of the law. I am afraid a grave injustice has been done in this case.

PROBLEM

In United States v. Regent Office Supply Co., 421 F.2d 1174 (2d Cir. 1970), the defendant company sold business supplies through agents who solicited orders by telephone. In order to get secretaries to put their calls through to the purchasing agents of potential customers, and in order to get the purchasing agents to listen to their pitch, Regent's sales agents told secretaries and purchasing agents a variety of lies, stating, for example, that they had been referred by one of the customer company's officers or that they had a large volume of supplies that needed to be disposed of because of the death of another customer. These tactics generated a substantial volume of sales, but there was no claim that the merchandise sold by Regent was in any way unacceptable to the purchasers. The government conceded that sales agents always discussed the price and quality of the merchandise honestly, and that customers were free to return any goods found to be unsatisfactory.

Regent was convicted of mail fraud under 18 U.S.C. §1341. Regent argued that its misrepresentations merely deceived but did not "defraud" the customers. The court of appeals agreed and reversed the conviction, stating:

> We do not . . . condone the deceitfulness such business practices represent nor do we approve [Regent's] cynical view . . . that such blatant dishonesty should be encouraged by reason of its "social utility" and . . . "worthy competitive enterprise." . . . We find these "white lies" repugnant. . . . Nevertheless, the facts . . . do not, in our view, constitute a scheme to defraud. . . .
>
> [W]e have said that "it is not essential that the Government allege or prove that purchasers were in fact defrauded." [T]he government cannot escape the burden of showing that some actual harm or injury was *contemplated* by the schemer. . . . Where the false representations are directed to the quality, adequacy or price of the goods themselves, . . . the intent of the schemer is to injure another to his own advantage by withholding or misrepresenting material facts. Although proof that the injury was accomplished is not required to convict under §1341, we believe the statute does require evidence from which it may be inferred that some actual injury to the victim, however slight, is a reasonably probable result of the deceitful representations if they are successful. [B]ecause the falsity of [Regent's] representations was not shown to be capable of affecting the customer's understanding of the bargain, . . . no injury was shown to flow from the deception.

Questions: Do you agree? When does lying become fraud? Consider the contrasting implications of the court's approach and the alternative position advanced by the government:

(a) The government's view. Suppose that a storeowner in an area frequented by tourists posts this sign in her window: "GOING OUT OF

BUSINESS. ALL MERCHANDISE MUST GO." In fact, the store is not going out of business, and the sign has been in its window for over a year. If the conviction had been upheld in *Regent Office Supply*, would the storeowner be guilty of obtaining money by fraud? Should she be?

(b) The court's view. Suppose that a student goes door-to-door selling magazine subscriptions, and tells potential customers that he is donating half of his commission on each sale to an agency that helps famine victims in Africa. The subscription prices are the same as those available elsewhere, and subscribers have the right to cancel their subscriptions, for a full refund, after receiving the first issue of the magazine. The student, however, keeps all of the commissions for himself. Under the holding in *Regent Office Supply*, is he guilty of obtaining money by fraud? Should he be?

Suppose that a resort development company offers "beautiful designer luggage worth $500" to each prospective customer who attends a "brief, one-hour" sales talk about new condominiums the company is offering for sale in the Caribbean. In fact, the sales talk lasts all day (with a break for lunch), customers cannot claim their luggage unless they stay to the end of the presentation, and the luggage turns out to be a single cheap suitcase worth no more than $50. Apart from these facts, no customer is pressured to buy a condo, customers who do sign a purchase contract are given the right to revoke it within 30 days (with full refund of their deposit), and no customer who made a purchase has expressed any regret. Under the holding in *Regent Office Supply*, is the development company guilty of obtaining money by fraud? Should it be?

Alternatively, could we say that the resort development company (or the sales company in *Regent Office Supply*) perpetrated a "scheme to defraud" by obtaining the potential purchasers' *time* under false pretenses? (For further consideration of the kinds of interests that constitute "property" protected by the law of theft, see pages 1081-1101 infra.)

(c) The Model Penal Code approach. How would the foregoing cases be decided under MPC §223.3 (Theft by Deception)?

For helpful discussions of the scope of the legal concept of fraud, see Buell, Novel Criminal Fraud, supra; Ellen S. Podgor, Criminal Fraud, 48 Am. U. L. Rev. 729 (1999). Differences between varying forms of dishonesty and the relationship of moral to legal norms are explored in Stuart P. Green, Lying, Cheating, and Stealing: A Moral Theory of White Collar Crime (2006).

(d) Lying. False pretenses and fraud are theft crimes where lying is critical to culpability. Should lying that causes "egregious social harm" be criminalized even when it does not involve the appropriation of property? For an affirmative argument, see Bryan H. Druzin & Jessica Li, The Criminalization of Lying: Under What Circumstances, If Any, Should Lies Be Made Criminal?, 101 J. Crim. L. & Criminology 529 (2011). What problems would such an offense present? The Stolen Valor Act, 18 U.S.C. §704(b), makes it a crime punishable by up to a year in prison to falsely claim that one received a military medal or decoration for service. Is that a form of theft? From whom?

4. *Blackmail*

STATE v. HARRINGTON

Supreme Court of Vermont
128 Vt. 242, 260 A.2d 692 (1969)

HOLDEN, C.J. [The respondent, John B. Harrington, was an attorney retained by Mrs. Norma Morin to obtain a divorce from her husband, Mr. Armand Morin. As Mrs. Morin was without funds, respondent agreed to work on a contingent fee basis. The couple owned assets worth approximately $500,000, including a motel in New Hampshire where the two had previously lived.

[Together with his client, Harrington arranged to obtain evidence of Mr. Morin's infidelity by hiring a woman, armed with a tape recorder, to entice him into having sex with her in one of his motel rooms. She succeeded, and at the appropriate moment Harrington and his associates entered the room and took pictures of Mr. Morin and the woman naked in bed.

[Several days later Harrington, in the presence of Mrs. Morin, dictated a letter to Mr. Morin proposing a settlement of the divorce action in which Mrs. Morin would receive her divorce, give up her interest in the marital assets, waive alimony, and receive a lump sum of $175,000. The letter also provided that

> any such settlement would include the return to you of all tape recordings, all negatives, all photographs and copies of photographs that might in any way, bring discredit upon yourself. Finally, there would be an absolute undertaking on the part of your wife not to divulge any information of any kind or nature which might be embarrassing to you in your business life, your personal life, your financial life, or your life as it might be affected by the Internal Revenue Service, the United States Customs Service, or any other governmental agency.

The letter stressed Mrs. Morin's current state of insolvency, and requested a prompt reply. The letter went on to say that:]

> Unless the writer has heard from you on or before March 22, we will have no alternative but to withdraw the offer and bring immediate divorce proceedings. . . . If we were to proceed under New Hampshire laws, without any stipulation, it would be necessary to allege, in detail, all of the grounds that Mrs. Morin has in seeking the divorce. The writer is, at present, undecided as to advising Mrs. Morin whether or not to file for "informer fees" with respect to the Internal Revenue Service and the United States Customs Service. In any event, we would file, alleging adultery, including affidavits, alleging extreme cruelty and beatings, and asking for a court order enjoining you from disposing of any property, including your stock interests, during the pendency of the procee- ding. . . . With absolutely no other purpose than to prove to you that we have all of the proof necessary to prove adultery beyond a reasonable doubt, we are enclosing a photograph taken by one of my investigators on the early morning of March 8. The purpose of enclosing the photograph as previously stated, is simply to show you that cameras and equipment were in full operating order.

13 V.S.A. §1701 provides: "A person who maliciously threatens to accuse another of a crime or offense, or with an injury to his person or property, with intent to extort money or other pecuniary advantage, or with intent to compel the person so threatened to do an act against his will, shall be imprisoned in the state prison not more than two years or fined not more than $500.00." . . .

[T]he respondent maintains his letter does not constitute a threat to accuse Morin of the crime of adultery. He argues the implicit threats contained in the communication were "not to accuse of the CRIME of adultery but to bring an embarrassing, reputation-ruining divorce proceeding in Mr. Morin's county of residence unless a stipulation could be negotiated."

In dealing with a parallel contention in State v. Louanis, 79 Vt. 463, 467, 65 A. 532, 533, the Court answered the argument in an opinion by Chief Judge Rowell. "The statute is aimed at blackmailing, and a threat of any public accusation is as much within the reason of the statute as a threat of a formal complaint, and is much easier made, and may be quite as likely to accomplish its purpose. There is nothing in the statute that requires such a restricted meaning of the word 'accuse'; and to restrict it thus, would well nigh destroy the efficacy of the act."

The letter, marked "personal and confidential," makes a private accusation of adultery in support of a demand for a cash settlement. An incriminating photograph was enclosed for the avowed purpose of demonstrating "we have all of the proof necessary to prove adultery beyond a reasonable doubt." According to the writing itself, cost of refusal will be public exposure of incriminating conduct in the courts of New Hampshire where the event took place.

In further support of motion for acquittal, the respondent urges that the totality of the evidence does not exclude the inference that he acted merely as an attorney, attempting to secure a divorce for his client on the most favorable terms possible. . . .

At the time of the writing, the respondent was undecided whether to advise his client to seek "informer fees." One of the advantages tendered to Morin for a "quiet" and "undamaging" divorce is an "absolute undertaking" on the part of the respondent's client not to inform against him in any way. The Internal Revenue Service, the United States Customs Service and other governmental agencies are suggested as being interested in such information. Quite clearly, these veiled threats exceeded the limits of the respondent's representation of his client in the divorce action. Although these matters were not specified in the indictment, they have a competent bearing on the question of intent.

Apart from this, the advancement of his client's claim to the marital property, however well founded, does not afford legal cause for the trial court to direct a verdict of acquittal in the background and context of his letter to Morin. A demand for settlement of a civil action, accompanied by a malicious threat to expose the wrongdoer's criminal conduct, if made with intent to extort payment, against his will, constitutes the crime alleged in the indictment.

The evidence at hand establishes beyond dispute the respondent's participation was done with preconceived design. The incriminating evidence which his letter threatens to expose was wilfully contrived and procured by a temptress hired for that purpose. These factors in the proof are sufficient to sustain a finding that the respondent acted maliciously and without just cause, within the meaning of our criminal statutes. The sum of the evidence supports the further inference that the act was done with intent to extort a substantial contingent fee to the respondent's personal advantage. . . . The evidence of guilt is ample to support the verdict and the trial was free from errors in law.

Judgment affirmed.

NOTES AND QUESTIONS

1. Consider whether the Vermont statute quoted in the principal case makes criminal the following threats:

(a) Employee, who has been directing a crucial project for employer, to employer: "Give me a raise, or I will quit." Without employee the project will likely fail, possibly placing employer in bankruptcy.

(b) A to his lover B: "If you stop having sexual relations with me, I will require that you leave my house and sue you for all of that money you owe me." See Lovely v. Cunningham, 796 F.2d 1 (1st Cir. 1986).

(c) Storeowner to shoplifter: "I saw you steal that radio last week. Pay me the $50 it costs, or I'll report you to the police." See People v. Fichtner, 118 N.Y.S.2d 392 (1952), reprinted infra page 1074.

(d) Storeowner to shoplifter: "I saw you steal that radio last week. Pay me the $50 it costs, plus a $350 fine, or I'll post your picture on the store's 'wall of shame.'" See Corey Kilgannon & Jeffrey E. Singer, Shoplifting Suspects' Choice: Pay or Be Shamed, N.Y. Times, June 22, 2010, at A1.

(e) Customer to online retailer: "Every time I buy one of your appliances, it breaks within two weeks. Now my dishwasher has broken down so many times it's worthless. Give me a new one, or I'll post negative comments about the product I've purchased from you in my online review on your website and blog about how awful you have been, and you'll never see another customer."

2. Model Penal Code. Consider how the foregoing hypotheticals and the *Harrington* case would come out under Model Penal Code §223.4, Appendix, and the California Penal Code, supra pages 1041-1042.

3. Consider the following criticism of the decision in *Harrington*:

[V]ery serious problems are created for every lawyer. Any time a cause of action involves behavior that is either criminal or embarrassing, a threat to bring the action would be extortionate. Obviously this would effectively preclude many lawyer demand letters. Anomalously, it would be permissible to destroy reputation by bringing suit but not to allow the defendant to avoid that destruction by paying the claim. Not only would this mean a net loss to the privacy that the extortion statute is, in part, aimed at protecting, but it would also involve significantly expanded litigation costs and burdens on efficient utilization of judicial resources. So read, the *Harrington* rule is obviously absurd.

Joseph M. Livermore, Lawyer Extortion, 20 Ariz. L. Rev. 403, 406 (1978).
Question: How could that decision be read more narrowly?

4. Victims who threaten lawsuits. Should what Harrington did be considered a crime, or merely aggressive advancement of his client's interests? Consider Rex v. Dymond, [1920] 2 K.B. 260, where defendant, who had been sexually assaulted, demanded that her attacker pay her reparations upon threat of "let[ting] the town knowed all about your going on." Glanville Williams criticized her conviction for blackmail:

> [H]ow fine is the line dividing proper from improper threats. Dymond was an illiterate girl, trying to obtain what she may have believed to be her rights without legal aid. Had she the [money] . . . with which to consult a solicitor, instead of writing herself, he would have written a letter to the [attacker] on her behalf in something like the following terms. "Dear Sir, We have been consulted by . . . who states that . . . Our client claims . . . compensation for the wrong committed against her, and unless we have your cheque for [the requested] amount we are instructed to commence legal proceedings against you." Such a letter would not constitute a criminal offense.

Glanville Williams, Blackmail, [1954] Crim. L. Rev. 162, 165-166. Williams suggests that had Dymond simply hired a lawyer who threatened to sue, the resulting settlement would not be subject to criminal sanction. But can a threat to sue sometimes be extortionate? The answer turns on statutory construction. In State v. Rendelman, 947 A.2d 546, 547 (Md. 2008), the Maryland high court held that threats of litigation were not "wrongful" within the meaning of the state extortion statute, regardless of bad faith or legal merit. But in State v. Hynes, 978 A.2d 264, 271, 275 (N.H. 2009), the New Hampshire high court distinguished *Rendelman* because its state extortion statute did not require "wrongful" means, but rather a comparison of the harm to the recipient against the benefit to the threatener. On the *Hynes* court's analysis, a threat to sue can be extortion if it fails to provide "actual advantage that is real and definite." Like *Rendelman*, the federal extortion statute, 18 U.S.C. §1951, requires "wrongful" conduct, but as may be expected, determining what is "wrongful" is a matter of continuing dispute. See United States v. Pendergraft, 297 F.3d 1198 (11th Cir. 2002).

5. Blackmail (often termed extortion) statutes vary a great deal. A useful review may be found in the Commentaries to Model Penal Code §223.4 at 201-224 (1980). There are important variations in the types of threats required. Threats of personal and property injury or to accuse of crime are always enough. Also commonly included are threats to make disclosures that would defame the victim. But how about threats to expose matters that are not defamatory? Some statutes include threats of this nature. See, e.g., Cal. Penal Code §519 (threats to expose any secret affecting the victim); Ill. Cons.

Stat. ch. 720, §5/15-5 (threats to reveal any information sought to be concealed by the victim). The MPC would seem to exclude such threats, unless they are picked up in the catchall provision that includes "any other harm which would not benefit the actor." Should they be excluded?

Statutes also vary in how they define what the blackmailer seeks to obtain by his threats. Many statutes, like the MPC, limit the purpose of the threats to obtaining property or other things of value and rely on other code provisions to deal with the use of coercive threats to obtain other benefits for the person who threatens. See, e.g., Model Penal Code §212.5 (criminal coercion offense that covers threats made with the "purpose unlawfully to restrict another's freedom of action to his detriment"). Some statutes, on the other hand, define the object of the threat more comprehensively. E.g., Minn. Penal Code §609.27 (threats that cause another against his will to do any act or forbear doing a lawful act).

Should blackmail extend beyond using threats to obtain the property of someone else? Consider the case of Toby the bunny. Toby's owner posted pictures of Toby on his website and announced that he would kill and eat Toby unless his website's readers sent $50,000 to save Toby's life. Should the criminal law recognize a form of blackmail that includes the destruction of one's own property under certain circumstances? What social interest would such a statute serve? Would it punish conduct that should not be criminalized? For an affirmative argument, see Stephen E. Sachs, Comment, Saving Toby: Extortion, Blackmail, and the Right To Destroy, 24 Yale L. & Pol'y Rev. 251 (2006).

PEOPLE v. FICHTNER

New York Supreme Court, Appellate Division, Second Department
281 A.D. 159, 118 N.Y.S.2d 392 (1952), aff'd without opinion,
305 N.Y. 864, 114 N.E.2d 212 (1953)

JOHNSTON, J. Section 850 of the Penal Law provides: "Extortion is the obtaining of property from another, . . . with his consent, induced by a wrongful use of . . . fear. . . ." Section 851 of the Penal Law provides:

> Fear, such as will constitute extortion, may be induced by an oral or written threat: . . . 2. To accuse him, or any relative of his or any member of his family, of any crime; or, 3. To expose, or impute to him, or any of them, any . . . disgrace. . . .

Defendant Fichtner is the manager, and defendant McGuinness the assistant manager, of the Hill Supermarket. . . . [Defendants were charged] with the crime of extortion in that on January 18, 1951, defendants, aiding and abetting each other, obtained $25 from one Smith, with his consent, which consent defendants induced by a wrongful use of fear by threatening to accuse Smith of the crime of petit larceny, and to expose and impute to him a disgrace unless Smith paid them $25.

Smith testified that on January 18, 1951, he purchased a number of articles in the Hill store for a total of about $12, but left the store without paying for a fifty-three-cent jar of coffee, which he had concealed in his pocket. After Smith left the store he returned at defendant Fichtner's request. Defendants then threatened to call a policeman, to arrest Smith for petit larceny, with resulting publicity in the newspapers and over the radio, unless he paid $75 and signed a paper admitting that during the course of several months he had unlawfully taken merchandise from the store in that amount. Although Smith admitted he had shopped in Hill's [stores for years and on numerous occasions], he insisted that the only merchandise he had ever stolen was the fifty-three-cent jar of coffee on the evening in question, and a sixty-five-cent roll of bologna one week previously. However, he finally signed the paper admitting that he had unlawfully taken $50 worth of merchandise from the store during a period of four months. That evening Smith paid $25 in cash and promised to pay the balance in weekly installments of $5. He testified he was induced to sign the paper and make the payment because defendants threatened to accuse him of petit larceny and to expose him to the disgrace of the criminal charge and the resulting publicity. It is not disputed that the $25 taken from Smith was "rung up" on the store register; that the money went into the company funds and that defendants received no part of the money. During the following week Smith reported the incident to the police, and defendants were arrested on January 25, 1951, when Smith, accompanied by a detective, returned to the store and paid the first $5 installment.

Defendants testified that over the course of several weeks, they saw Smith steal merchandise amounting to $5.61, and they honestly believed that during the several months that Smith had been shopping, he had stolen merchandise of the value of $75; that on January 18, 1951, Smith freely admitted that during the four-month period he stole merchandise of the value of $50, and that he voluntarily signed the paper admitting thefts in that amount; that on that date he paid $25 on account and promised to pay the balance in weekly installments.

That the Smith incident was not an isolated one, but rather part of a course of conduct pursued by defendants, even after warning by the police to discontinue the practice, was not only clearly established but admitted by defendant Fichtner. . . .

In my opinion, the verdict is amply supported by the evidence. Implicit in the verdict is a finding that Smith stole only $1.18 in merchandise as he admitted, or at most the $5.61 which defendants claimed they actually saw him steal, and that he was induced to pay the $25 on January 18, 1951, by defendants' threats to accuse him of crime and to expose him to disgrace. By its verdict, the jury rejected defendants' contention that Smith voluntarily admitted having stolen $50 worth of merchandise and that they demanded from Smith only what was rightfully due.

Defendants requested the court to charge that

> if in the judgment of the jury the defendants honestly believed that the amount which the complainant paid or agreed to pay represented the approximate amount of the merchandise which he . . . had previously stolen from the Hill Supermarket, then the defendants must be acquitted.

... [W]e believe that the portion of the main charge to the effect that, under the circumstances of this case, extortion is committed only when one obtains property from another by inducing fear in that other by threatening to accuse him of crime unless he pays an amount over and above what was rightfully due was more favorable to defendants than that which they were entitled to receive. In our opinion, the extortion statutes were intended to prevent the collection of money by the use of fear induced by means of threats to accuse a debtor of crime, and it makes no difference whether the debtor stole any goods, nor how much he stole, and that defendants may properly be convicted even though they believed that the complainant was guilty of the theft of their employer's goods in an amount either equal to or less, or greater than any sum of money obtained from the complainant. Nor is defendants' good faith in thus enforcing payment of the money alleged to be due to their employer a defense. . . .

The law does not authorize the collection of just debts by threatening to accuse the debtor of crime, even though the complainant is in fact guilty of the crime. In my opinion, it makes no difference whether the indebtedness for which a defendant demands repayment is one arising out of the crime for the prosecution of which he threatens the complainant, or is entirely independent and having no connection with the crime which forms the basis of the accusation. The result in both cases is the concealment and compounding of a felony to the injury of the State. It is that result which the extortion statutes were intended to prevent.

[Conviction affirmed.]

WENZEL, J. (dissenting). [T]he jury was permitted to convict defendants of the crime of extortion on proof that they had induced complainant, by the threats alleged, to pay to defendants more than he rightfully owed for goods which he had stolen, even though defendants might have honestly believed that the amount demanded from complainant was the amount which he rightfully owed. In my opinion, although the question is one as to which there is a conflict of authority, if defendants, acting without malice and in good faith, made an honest mistake, they were not guilty of the crime charged. There would then be no criminal intent. The defendants were not acting in their own behalf but in that of their employer, in recovering what they believed to be rightfully due it. . . .

NOTE

Under the New York Penal Law enacted subsequent to *Fichtner*, extortion remains excluded from the class of larceny-type crimes for which a claim of right is a defense. See *People v. Reid*, page 1108 infra. However, a special provision applicable to extortion, N.Y. Pen. Law §155.15(2) provides:

In any prosecution for larceny by extortion committed by instilling in the victim a fear that he or another person would be charged with a crime, it is an affirmative defense that the defendant reasonably believed the threatened charge to be true and that his sole purpose was to compel or induce the victim to take reasonable action to make good the wrong which was the subject of such threatened charge.

Section 215.45 provides:

> 1. A person is guilty of compounding a crime when: (a) He solicits, accepts or agrees to accept any benefit upon an agreement or understanding that he will refrain from initiating a prosecution for a crime; or (b) He confers, or offers or agrees to confer, any benefit upon another person upon an agreement or understanding that such other person will refrain from initiating a prosecution for a crime.
>
> 2. In any prosecution under this section, it is an affirmative defense that the benefit did not exceed an amount which the defendant reasonably believed to be due as restitution or indemnification for harm caused by the crime.

NOTE ON THE RATIONALE OF BLACKMAIL

In *Unraveling the Paradox of Blackmail*, 84 Colum. L. Rev. 670, 670 (1984), James Lindgren identifies the puzzle about blackmail:

> [B]lackmail is unique among major crimes: no one has yet figured out why it ought to be illegal. [T]he heart of the problem is that two separate acts, each of which is a moral and legal right, can combine to make a moral and legal wrong. For example, if I threaten to expose a criminal act unless I am paid money, I have committed blackmail. Or if I threaten to expose a sexual affair unless I am given a job, once again I have committed blackmail. I have a legal right to expose or threaten to expose the crime or affair, and I have a legal right to seek a job or money, but if I combine these rights it is blackmail. If both a person's ends—seeking a job or money—and his means—threatening to expose—are otherwise legal, why is it illegal to combine them? Therein lies what has been called the "paradox of blackmail."

Consider the following attempts to explain this paradox.

James Lindgren, Unraveling the Paradox of Blackmail, 84 Colum. L. Rev. 670, 672 (1984): [T]he key to the wrongfulness of the blackmail transaction is its triangular structure. The transaction implicitly involves not only the blackmailer and his victim but always a third party as well. This third party may be, for example, the victim's spouse or employer, the authorities or even the public at large. . . . If the blackmail victim pays the blackmailer, it is to avoid the harm that those others would inflict. Thus blackmail is a way that one person requests something in return for suppressing the actual or potential interests of others. . . . Selling the right to go to the police involves suppressing the state's interests. Selling the right to tell a tort victim who committed the tort involves suppressing the tort victim's interests. . . . [T]he criminalization of informational and noninformational blackmail represents a principled decision that advantages may not be gained by extra leverage belonging more to a third party than to the threatener.

George P. Fletcher, Blackmail: The Paradigmatic Crime, 141 U. Pa. L. Rev. 1617, 1626(1993): The proper test, I submit, is whether the transaction with the suspected blackmailer generates a relationship of dominance and subordination. If *V*'s paying money or rendering a service to *D* creates a situation in which *D* can or does dominate *V,* then the action crosses the line from permissible commerce to criminal wrongdoing. The essence of *D*'s dominance over *V* is the prospect of repeated demands. . . . Blackmail occurs when, by virtue of the demand and the action satisfying the demands, the blackmailer knows that she can repeat the demand in the future. Living with that knowledge puts the victim of blackmail in a permanently subordinate position.

Douglas H. Ginsburg & Paul Shechtman, Blackmail: An Economic Analysis of the Law, 141 U. Pa. L. Rev. 1849, 1873-1874 (1993): [T]he apparent paradox of blackmail, that one may not threaten to do what one has a lawful right to do, is an economically rational rule. If such threats were lawful, there would be an incentive for people to expend resources to develop embarrassing information about others in the hope of then selling their silence. In that case, some people would be deterred from engaging in embarrassing (but lawful) conduct, while some others who were undeterred would find that their business or social acquaintances or family were informed of their activity. Neither such deterrence nor such information can be counted as a good in many situations, however. These particularly include social and family relations in which the concern of one individual for another is altruistic rather than self-interested; i.e., where one might be distressed to learn another's secret, but was not harmed by ignorance of it. It is precisely these relationships that are threatened with disruption by the prototypical blackmail threat, and that would be protected by an economically rational law. The general principle of the Model Penal Code closely approximates this result by prohibiting threats that it would not benefit the actor to carry out.

Wendy J. Gordon, Truth and Consequences: The Force of Blackmail's Central Case, 141 U. Pa. L. Rev. 1741, 1758, 1770, 1776-1777 (1993): [P]olicymakers prohibit blackmail less because of economic waste or inefficiency than because they perceive the act of blackmail to be wrong in itself. . . . One person deliberately seeks to harm another to serve her own ends—to exact money or other advantage—and does so in a context where she has no conceivable justification for her act. . . .

Libertarians who recommend the legalization of blackmail sometimes claim that there is no way to distinguish blackmail from an ordinary commercial transaction. . . . I suggest [these] distinctions . . . : first, that the blackmailer intends to harm; and second, that regardless of intent, the buyer of silence in an extortion transaction suffers a net harm, while the buyer in an ordinary commercial transaction is benefitted. . . .

It is important to note that criminalization also has an impact on blackmail victims, providing them with . . . tools to encourage and assist them in resisting the blackmailer's demands. . . . By threatening to go to the authorities if and only if disclosure is made, victims can discourage blackmailers from disclosing the contested information. This is what Joel Feinberg terms "counterblackmail."

For a careful critique of the preceding arguments, see Mitchell N. Berman, The Evidentiary Theory of Blackmail: Taking Motives Seriously, 65 U. Chi. L. Rev. 795 (1998). Professor Berman argues that none of these efforts provides a persuasive account of why blackmail is a crime. He notes, however, that unconditional disclosure of information ordinarily is not illegal because it may be done for legitimate reasons. In contrast, he argues, a conditional threat to disclose (in the event of nonpayment) is made illegal because it provides strong evidence that any disclosure would be morally blameworthy—"the actor would be inflicting harm knowingly and without good motives." Id. at 848. A recent empirical study of subjects' intuitions about hypothetical blackmail scenarios suggests that Berman's account of blackmail most closely mirrors people's moral intuitions about when threats should be criminalized. Paul H. Robinson et al., Competing Theories of Blackmail: An Empirical Research Critique of Criminal Law Theory, 89 Tex. L. Rev. 291, 339-340 (2010).

5. *Consolidation*

INTRODUCTORY NOTE

Insofar as the pattern of discrete theft offenses covering fundamentally similar kinds of acquisitive conduct has left gaps in the law, only legislative or judicial revision of the definitions of criminal conduct can supply an effective remedy. Another and more direct consequence of this condition of the law of theft is procedural in character. A defendant convicted of one of these theft offenses, say, embezzlement, may be able to obtain a reversal on appeal through the curious device of proving that the evidence technically established another offense, say, larceny. See, e.g., *Nolan v. State*, page 1043 supra. This possibility is a constant threat to the efficient administration of criminal justice. The distinctions between many of the discrete theft offenses (1) are without criminological significance, and (2) turn on highly technical legal characterizations of basically similar fact situations rather than real differences in conduct, so that in these cases a defendant is not likely to be prejudiced (though he may be) by a variance between charge and proof.

The principal means of reform, which has gained widespread acceptance, is to consolidate the variety of common-law forms of wrongful acquisition of another's property into one single crime, which might be called "theft" or "larceny," and to deprive of any legal significance the differences in modes of acquisition. Some examples of consolidation statutes follow.

Model Penal Code §223.1: Consolidation of Theft Offenses; Grading; Provisions Applicable to Theft Generally. [See Appendix.]

New York Penal Law (2010) §155.05: Larceny; Defined.

1. A person steals property and commits larceny when, with intent to deprive another of property or to appropriate the same to himself or to a third person, he wrongfully takes, obtains or withholds such property from an owner thereof.

2. Larceny includes a wrongful taking, obtaining or withholding of another's property, with the intent prescribed in subdivision one of this section, committed in any of the following ways:

    (a) By conduct heretofore defined or known as common law larceny by trespassory taking, common law larceny by trick, embezzlement, or obtaining property by false pretenses;

    (b) By acquiring lost property. . . .

    (c) By committing the crime of issuing a bad check. . . .

    (d) By false promise. . . .

    (e) By extortion. . . .

New York Penal Law (2010) §155.45: Larceny; Pleading and Proof.

1. Where it is an element of the crime charged that property was taken from the person or obtained by extortion, an indictment for larceny must so specify. In all other cases, an indictment, information or complaint for larceny is sufficient if it alleges that the defendant stole property of the nature or value required for the commission of the crime charged without designating the particular way or manner in which such property was stolen or the particular theory of larceny involved.

2. Proof that the defendant engaged in any conduct constituting larceny as defined in section 155.05 is sufficient to support any indictment, information or complaint for larceny other than one charging larceny by extortion. An indictment charging larceny by extortion must be supported by proof establishing larceny by extortion.

Illinois Compiled Statutes (2010) Chapter 720, §5/16-1: Theft.

    (a) A person commits theft when he knowingly:

        (1) Obtains or exerts unauthorized control over property of the owner; or

        (2) Obtains by deception control over property of the owner; or

        (3) Obtains by threat control over property of the owner; or

        (4) Obtains control over stolen property knowing the property to have been stolen or under such circumstances as would reasonably induce him to believe that the property was stolen . . . and

        (A) Intends to deprive the owner permanently of the use or benefit of the property; or

        (B) Knowingly uses, conceals or abandons the property in such manner as to deprive the owner permanently of such use or benefit; or

        (C) Uses, conceals, or abandons the property knowing such use, concealment or abandonment probably will deprive the owner permanently of such use or benefit. . . .

California Penal Code (2010) §484(a): Every person who shall feloniously steal, take, carry, lead, or drive away the personal property of another, or who shall fraudulently appropriate property which has been entrusted to him or her, or who shall knowingly and designedly, by any false or fraudulent representation or pretense, defraud any other person of money, labor or real or personal property, . . . is guilty of theft.

California Penal Code (2010) §952: In charging an offense, each count shall contain, and shall be sufficient if it contains in substance, a statement that the accused has committed some public offense therein specified. . . . In charging theft it shall be sufficient to allege that the defendant unlawfully took the labor or property of another.

B. THE PROPERTY SUBJECT TO THEFT

1. Traditional Theft

STATE v. MILLER

Supreme Court of Oregon
192 Or. 188, 233 P.2d 786 (1951)

LUSK, J. [Defendant induced complaining witness to agree to guarantee his indebtedness to another on his false representation that he owned a tractor free of encumbrance and on his executing a chattel mortgage thereto as security. In fact, defendant was purchasing the tractor under a conditional sales contract. He was convicted of obtaining property (the complaining witness's guarantee) by false pretenses.

[Defendant was charged under §23-537, O.C.L.A:]

> If any person shall, by any false pretenses or by any privity [sic] or false token, and with intent to defraud, obtain or attempt to obtain, from any other person any money or property whatsoever, or shall obtain or attempt to obtain with the like intent the signature of any person to any writing, the false making whereof would be punishable as forgery, such person, upon conviction thereof, shall be punished by imprisonment.

. . . Reduced to its simplest terms, this indictment means that by false pretenses the defendant induced the Hub Lumber Company to agree to pay his indebtedness to the Howard Cooper Corporation if he should fail to pay it. The question is whether this amounts to an allegation that, in the sense of the statute, the defendant obtained "any property" from the Hub Lumber Company. . . .

The source of the false pretenses statute in this country is the common law and the statute law of England. The English courts hold that the thing obtained must be the subject of larceny at common law, and accordingly a conviction for obtaining two dogs by false pretenses was quashed because at common law dog stealing is not larceny; so likewise of an indictment for obtaining food and lodging by false pretenses. Under statutes like ours many of the courts of this country take the same view of the law. The California statute covers "money or property." Pen. Code, §532. The court in People v. Cummings, 46 P. 284, in holding that the word "property" did not include real property [relied on the fact that real property was not recognized under the English law as the subject of false pretenses.] . . .

It should be observed at this point that our statute in respect of the present question is not as broad as those in some of the other states. It reads "any money or property whatsoever." In some of the states, as stated in Burdick [Law of Crime], 481, §640, the statutes, "after enumerating various classes of personal property, conclude the list with what is apparently intended as an all inclusive term, such as 'other things of value,' 'any other valuable thing,' or 'any other valuable thing or effects whatsoever.'" The Kansas statute includes "any money, personal property, right in action, or any other valuable thing or effects whatsoever." G.S. 1949, 21-551. Notwithstanding the comprehensiveness of this provision, the [Kansas] court held, in the light of the origin and history of the crime of false pretenses, that obtaining an extension of time in which to pay a matured debt was not a "valuable thing" within the meaning of the section. [State v. Tower, 251 Pac. 401.] The term "personal property" was said "to denote personal movable things generally." "Mere pecuniary advantage, devoid of any physical attribute of money, chattel, or valuable security, in the sense of the English statute, was not included."

[Similarly, in] State v. Eicher, 140 So. 498, 499, . . . the court [said] that "The privilege of having a note renewed or the time of its payment extended may be and frequently is a valuable one to the debtor. But such privilege or advantage is neither money nor property in the sense those terms are ordinarily used and understood." The court further said: "'Property' . . . means worldly goods or possessions, tangible things, and things which have an exchangeable or commercial value." . . .

The provisions of the statute which make unlawful the obtaining of the signature of any person with intent to defraud . . . rather definitely indicate that such an intangible thing as credit was not considered by the legislature to be property.

Moreover, this court [has] recognized that "property" under the statute must be something capable of being possessed and the title to which can be transferred. . . . It need hardly be said that the thing which the defendant is charged with obtaining in the present indictment, the guaranty, or, to be more accurate, the benefit of the guaranty which the Hub Lumber Company gave to the Howard Cooper Corporation, could not be possessed, and that there could be no such thing as holding title to it.

Had the indictment alleged that the defendant obtained the signature of the Hub Lumber Company or its agent to a guaranty of the defendant's indebtedness, we would have had an entirely different question. The failure so to allege was not due to an oversight of the pleader but to the facts themselves, for the proof is that no written guaranty was ever executed but merely an oral one. . . .

It is doubtless true, as the state's brief asserts, that "a guaranty is a chose in action, a right to indemnity from the guarantor," but it is the right of the creditor who extends credit on the faith of the guaranty, not of the debtor to whom credit is given. The defendant did not receive even a chose in action from the Hub Lumber Company. . . .

The state argues that . . . the obtaining of a loan by fraud is a violation of the statute and asserts that this is a similar case. But in the loan cases, as the state's brief itself points out, the victim parts with his money. And, while it is true (although not alleged in the indictment) that, just as in the loan cases, the accused obtained credit, he obtained it, not from the victim of his false representations, but from another.

The state's argument of "policy" that the public are entitled to the protection of the law against immoral and reprehensible conduct such as that with which the accused was charged, and of which, no doubt, he was guilty, is appealing, but should be addressed to the legislature, not to the courts. The legislature has not undertaken to make every fraud a crime, but has set boundaries around the crime of false pretenses which the courts must respect and have no authority to pass. . . .

[T]he judgment must therefore be reversed and the action dismissed.

NOTES

1. The Model Penal Code approach. On the facts of *Miller*, what would be the result if the applicable definition of "property" were that set forth in MPC §223.0(6)?

2. Theft of services. In Chappell v. United States, 270 F.2d 274 (9th Cir. 1959), the defendant, an Air Force sergeant, was convicted of knowingly converting property of the United States by making use of the services and labor of an airman to paint his own private dwellings during the airman's on-duty hours. The statute, 18 U.S.C. §641, making it criminal to knowingly convert to one's own use anything of value of the United States, was construed as intending no such revolutionary change in the common law as would be entailed, in the Ninth Circuit's view, in holding that an employee's services were property which could be stolen. The conviction was reversed.

The Seventh Circuit reached a contrary conclusion in a case involving a professor who used the services of a research assistant, paid for out of his grant from the Environmental Protection Agency, to perform work for him on a research contract unrelated to his EPA grant. United States v. Croft, 750 F.2d 1354 (7th Cir. 1984). Affirming his conviction under 18 U.S.C. §641, the court held that the section is designed to punish "intentional conduct by which a person either misappropriates or obtains a wrongful advantage from government property," and that the defendant "obtained a wrongful advantage by converting and misappropriating the services of [the assistant] for his personal research project while allowing those services to be paid for by the EPA." Id. at 1362. In United States v. Schwartz, 785 F.2d 673, 681 n.4 (9th Cir. 1986), the Ninth Circuit expressed agreement with *Croft* and overruled its earlier decision in *Chappell*. For a criticism of such results as an unwarranted judicial extension of a statute concerned with traditional property offenses, see Ralph G. Picardi, Comment, Theft of Employee Services Under the United States Penal Code, 23 San Diego L. Rev. 897 (1986).

With respect to theft of services, see MPC §223.7, Appendix. Under Ill. Comp. Stat. ch. 720, §5/16-3, a person commits theft of services when he obtains "labor or services of another which are available only for hire, by means of threat or deception or knowing that such use is without the consent of the person providing the . . . labor or services." In People v. Davis, 561 N.E.2d 165 (Ill. 1990), the defendants were city officials who were supervising a construction project being performed for the city by an independent contractor. They were responsible for giving job assignments to the contractor's employees when the employees reported for work. The defendants asked several of the employees to participate in political campaigning instead of working on the construction project. The employees willingly agreed to do so, but their employer was not aware of the arrangement and lost the value of their services. Are the defendants guilty of theft under the Illinois statute? The court held in the negative. Was there any way, under this statute, to support the opposite result? The Illinois Supreme Court thought so, overruling *Davis* in People v. Perry, 864 N.E.2d 196 (Ill. 2007).

3. Theft of use of property. In State v. McGraw, 480 N.E.2d 552 (Ind. 1985), a city employee used a city computer and services for his personal business and was convicted of theft under Ind. Code §35-43-4-2: "A person who knowingly or intentionally exerts unauthorized control over property of another person, with intent to deprive the other person of its value or use, commits theft. . . ." It appeared that the defendant's unauthorized use cost the city nothing, since the computer service was leased at a fixed charge and the tapes and discs he had used could be erased and reused. The court held that these facts could not support a conviction, even assuming arguendo that the use of the computer was "property" under the theft statute. The court reasoned that the city was not deprived of any part of the value or use of the property. The court said: "Defendant has likened his conduct to the use of an employer's vacant bookshelf, for the temporary storage of one's personal items, and to the use of an employer's telephone facilities for toll-free calls. The analogies appear to us to be appropriate." Id. at 554.

Questions: (a) What should be the result under the MPC? *(b)* How should the law treat the unauthorized use, termed "joyriding," of unsecured wireless networks? Consider the case of Benjamin Smith, who was arrested and charged after twice parking his SUV outside a stranger's house in order to access the Internet. See Matthew Bierlein, Policing the Wireless World: Access Liability in the Open Wi-Fi Era, 67 Ohio St. L.J. 1123, 1123-1125 (2006). New York criminal law makes it a misdemeanor to "knowingly use[], cause[] to be used, or access . . . a computer network without authorization," N.Y. Penal Law §156.05 (McKinney 2006), and defines "without authorization" to mean that the criminal defendant either knew she lacked permission to access the network or that the defendant knowingly circumvented an installed security measure. See, e.g., People v. Klapper, 902 N.Y.S.2d 305, 309 (N.Y. Crim. Ct. 2010). Could a prosecutor show that Smith knew he lacked permission to access the network by virtue of the fact that Smith had no preexisting relationship with the resident of the house? Should the default rule be that one acts without authorization whenever there is no affirmative grant of permission? Or should the doctrine of consent protect the joyrider if the resident of the house could have easily set up the wireless network with password protection but chose not to apply any security settings? And does the consent problem change if the joyrider's operating system is configured to connect automatically to unsecured networks? Who is the victim of the potential theft—the resident who set up the unsecured network or the Internet Service Provider (ISP) who is likely missing out on additional subscription revenues? See S. Gregory Herman, One or More Wireless Networks Are Available: Can ISPs Recover for Unauthorized Wi-Fi Use Under Cable Television Piracy Laws, 55 Cath. U. L. Rev. 1095 (2006).

4. Sex as property. Recall that false representations to obtain sex generally cannot be the basis for criminal liability, pages 337-342 supra. Courts that have rejected sex as "property" under federal extortion statutes have focused on the fact that a sexual act is not an "alienable economic or contractual right that carries forward into the future." United States v. Warme, 2010 WL 125846 (W.D.N.Y., Jan. 7, 2010). Is this the right definition of property for purposes of criminal law and its coverage? What result in a prosecution for fraud?

2. Theft of Information

UNITED STATES v. GIRARD

United States Court of Appeals for the Second Circuit
601 F.2d 69 (1979)

VAN GRAAFEILAND, J. Appellants have appealed from judgments convicting them of the unauthorized sale of government property (18 U.S.C. §641) and of conspiring to accomplish the sale (18 U.S.C. §371). . . .

In May 1977, appellant Lambert was an agent of the Drug Enforcement Administration, and Girard was a former agent. During that month, Girard and one James Bond began to discuss a proposed illegal venture that involved smuggling a planeload of marijuana from Mexico into the United States. Girard told Bond that for $500 per name he could, through an inside source, secure reports from the DEA files that would show whether any participant in the proposed operation was a government informant. Unfortunately for

Mr. Girard, Bond himself became an informant and disclosed his conversations with Girard to the DEA. . . . Bond asked Girard to secure reports on four men whose names were furnished him by DEA agents. DEA records are kept in computerized files, and the DEA hoped to identify the inside source by monitoring access to the four names in the computer bank. In this manner, the DEA learned that Girard's informant was Lambert, who obtained the reports through a computer terminal located in his office. The convictions . . . are based on the sale of this information.

Section 641, so far as pertinent, provides that whoever without authority sells any "record . . . or thing of value" of the United States or who "receives . . . the same with intent to convert it to his use or gain, knowing it to have been embezzled, stolen, purloined or converted," shall be guilty of a crime. Appellants contend that the statute covers only tangible property or documents and therefore is not violated by the sale of information. [The district court rejected this argument, and we agree.]

[W]e are impressed by Congress' repeated use of the phrase "thing of value" in section 641 and its predecessors. These words are found in so many criminal statutes throughout the United States that they have in a sense become words of art. The word "thing" notwithstanding, the phrase is generally construed to cover intangibles as well as tangibles. For example, amusement is held to be a thing of value under gambling statutes. Sexual intercourse, or the promise of sexual intercourse, is a thing of value under a bribery statute. So also are a promise to reinstate an employee and an agreement not to run in a primary election. The testimony of a witness is a thing of value under 18 U.S.C. §876. . . .

The existence of a property in the contents of unpublished writings was judicially recognized long before the advent of copyright laws. . . . Although we are not concerned here with the laws of copyright, we are satisfied, nonetheless, that the Government has a property interest in certain of its private records which it may protect by statute as a thing of value. It has done this by the enactment of section 641. [If] conversion is the "misuse or abuse of property" or its use "in an unauthorized manner," the defendants herein could properly be found to have converted DEA's computerized records.

The District Judge also rejected appellants' constitutional challenge to section 641 based upon alleged vagueness and overbreadth, and again we agree with his ruling. Appellants, at the time of the crime a current and a former employee of the DEA, must have known that the sale of DEA confidential law enforcement records was prohibited. The DEA's own rules and regulations forbidding such disclosure may be considered as both a delimitation and a clarification of the conduct proscribed by the statute. Where, as here, we are not dealing with defendants' exercise of a First Amendment freedom, we should not search for statutory vagueness that did not exist for the defendants themselves. Neither should we find a constitutional infirmity simply because the statute might conceivably trespass upon the First Amendment rights of others. In view of the statute's plainly legitimate sweep in regulating conduct, . . . any overbreadth that may exist [can] be cured on a case by case basis. . . .

The judgments . . . are affirmed.

NOTES

1. An Official Secrets Act? Anthony Lewis of the *New York Times* had some harsh things to say about such an interpretation of §641. Speaking about the same theory sanctioned by a federal trial court in another case, he said (Whisper Who Dares, N.Y. Times, June 19, 1978, at A19):

> The two men were charged—and convicted—under Section 641. . . . What was the property? The Justice Department said it was information, and Judge Albert V. Bryan Jr. followed that view of the law when he charged the jury.
>
> "Information may be government property," the judge said, "apart from the document or the sheets of paper themselves." Thus it does not matter if the original government document remains in the files. Anyone who copies it or makes notes from it without official approval has still stolen "property."
>
> For advocates of secrecy, the beauty of that legal theory is that it applies no matter what kind of government information is involved. National security need not have a thing to do with it. The price of food in the White House mess, the Amtrak deficit—any fact that leaked could be the subject of a criminal prosecution.
>
> In short, the government property theory of information would give this country an Official Secrets Act. It would be potentially as devastating to the press and public knowledge as much-criticized Britain's secrecy law.

2. Photocopies. In United States v. Bottone, 365 F.2d 389 (2d Cir. 1966), the defendants purchased documents, for ultimate exportation to Europe, from several former employees of Lederle Laboratories, knowing that the employees had temporarily removed and copied the documents. The documents described secret processes for manufacturing antibiotics. The court upheld their convictions on a charge of violating 18 U.S.C. §2314, which prohibits transporting in interstate or foreign commerce "any goods, wares, merchandise, securities or money, of the value of $5,000 or more, knowing the same to have been stolen, converted or taken by fraud." The court, per Judge Henry Friendly, said (id. at 393-394):

> The serious question is whether, on the facts of this case, the papers showing Lederle processes . . . were "goods" which had been "stolen, converted or taken by fraud" in view of the lack of proof that any of the physical materials so transported came from Lederle's possession. The standard procedure was for [the defendants] to remove documents from Lederle's files . . . take these . . . home within New York state, make photocopies, microfilms or notes, and then restore the purloined papers to the files; only the copies and notes moved or were intended to move in interstate or foreign commerce. . . .
>
> To be sure, where no tangible objects were ever taken or transported, a court would be hard pressed to conclude that "goods" had been stolen and transported within the meaning of §2314; the statute would presumably not extend to the case where a carefully guarded secret formula was memorized, carried away in the recesses of a thievish mind and placed in writing only after a boundary had been crossed. The situation, however, is quite different where tangible goods are stolen and transported and the only obstacle to

condemnation is a clever intermediate transcription or use of a photocopy machine. In such a case, when the physical form of the stolen goods is secondary in every respect to the matter recorded in them, the transformation of the information in the stolen papers into a tangible object never possessed by the original owner should be deemed immaterial. It would offend common sense to hold that these defendants fall outside the statute simply because, in efforts to avoid detection, their confederates were at pains to restore the original papers to Lederle's files and transport only copies or notes, although an oversight would have brought them within it.

3. Ordinary business practices. In Carpenter v. United States, 484 U.S. 19 (1987), the Supreme Court upheld the view, reflected in cases like *Girard* and *Bottone*, that confidential information is protected by the law of theft. Consider John C. Coffee, Jr., Hush!: The Criminal Status of Confidential Information After *McNally* and *Carpenter* and the Enduring Problem of Overcriminalization, 26 Am. Crim. L. Rev. 121, 122-123, 140, 142 (1988):

[These cases rest] on an analogy that broadly characterizes the unauthorized communication of trade secrets as equivalent to the crime of embezzlement. [T]his view of "confidential information" as a form of property covered by the laws against larceny is (a) historically unsound, [and] (b) inconsistent with most statutory law dealing with the subject of trade secrets. [The] logic [of these cases] has the potential to alter significantly the relationship between employers and employees across the landscape of American business life. . . .

To see this, consider the case of . . . a broker at a major securities firm [who] is fired [and told that] he may not take with him any list or address book listing his clients, as such information is a trade secret belonging to the firm. As a practical matter, if this broker cannot contact his former clients, he is unemployable with other firms and forfeits valuable "human capital" that he may have developed over a career. [I]t is clear as a civil law matter that the customer lists are confidential trade secrets. To criminalize this civil law rule then effectively arms the employer with a weapon that the legislature never intended to grant. . . .

[It] is not just that civil wrongs are being casually converted into criminal offenses, but that the equivalent of a covenant not to compete is being created by operation of law. [S]uch covenants are . . . generally enforceable only if they have a brief duration and limited scope. [If *Carpenter* and similar cases] mean that, in order to avoid potential entanglement with the criminal law, the employee . . . must desist from using any particularized knowledge about his customers that he gained in his former employment, then [these cases have] given the employer a very powerful weapon to stifle competition. . . .

[Another] illustration raises an even darker prospect. . . . Suppose a corporate employee reveals to the press that internal corporate studies show some serious environmental consequences of a specific corporate activity. [G]ood motives do not excuse embezzlement. Under [the] logic [of these cases,] the employee is arguably in the same position as if he stole corporate funds to aid a worthy cause.

[M]ost adult Americans are employees; most possess some form of confidential information about their employer; and most will at some point in their careers change employers. Do all departing employees potentially face entanglement with the federal criminal law?

4. Problems:

(a) Jones was visiting the United States Attorney's office when he over-heard conversations between government personnel concerning an ongoing criminal investigation of an employee at Barclays Bank. The conversations took place in a reception area and in an individual office. Jones subsequently told officials at Barclays that he had information relating to a criminal inves-tigation and offered to sell it to them for $100; ultimately he received $60 for revealing what he knew. The court held that these facts were sufficient to support an indictment for larceny under 18 U.S.C. §641. United States v. Jones, 677 F. Supp. 238 (S.D.N.Y. 1988). Do you agree?

(b) Dreiman repeatedly called and harassed his ex-girlfriend. In defense she obtained an unlisted telephone number. Dreiman then broke into her trailer, so that he could copy down the unlisted number. He was convicted of burglary, on the theory that he had entered with the intent to commit a crime (larceny). The court held that copying the unlisted number consti-tuted larceny, and it therefore upheld the burglary conviction. Dreiman v. State, 825 P.2d 758 (Wyo. 1992). Is the result sound? If so, does the same principle justify the results in *Girard* and *Jones*, or are those situations distinguishable?

(c) While making repairs in a woman's apartment, the defendant picked up intimate photographs he found in her bedroom, scanned them into his computer, and quickly returned the photographs to their original location. Though he obviously borrowed the photographs temporarily, did he perma-nently take any "property of another"? Of what, if anything, did he deprive the victim? See State v. Nelson, 842 A.2d 83 (N.H. 2004).

5. Statutory interpretation. The criminality of dishonest appropriation can depend on distinctions in statutory wording. The statute involved in *Girard*, 18 U.S.C. §641, broadly protects tangible and intangible property, including any "record . . . or thing of value," but the property involved must belong to the U.S. Government. Taking of information from a private firm may or may not violate state laws against theft, depending on the extent to which those laws protect intangibles. The statute involved in *Bottone*, 18 U.S.C. §2314, may apply, but that statute only protects "goods, wares, merchan-dise, securities or money." To take another example, a computer password is protected by an Oregon statute that punishes "theft of proprietary infor-mation," State v. Schwartz, 21 P.3d 1128 (Or. Ct. App. 2001). A PIN code is considered "property" under California laws prohibiting extortion. People v. Kozlowski, 96 Cal. App. 4th 853 (2002). But a similar password does not qualify as "goods, wares [or] merchandise" protected under §2314; in United States v. Stafford, 136 F.3d 1109, 1115 (7th Cir. 1998), the court said: "Given the [1934] statute's age . . . and wording, and the principle that the definition of federal crimes is a legislative rather than a judicial func-tion . . . we don't think the [wording] of section 2314 will stretch this far." For examination of these issues, see Geraldine Szott Moohr, Federal

Criminal Fraud and the Development of Intangible Property Rights in Information, 2000 U. Ill. L. Rev. 683.

6. *Intellectual property theft.* U.S. companies lose $250 billion from intellectual property theft each year.[2] In an effort to strengthen federal protection of trade secrets, Congress in 1996 enacted the Economic Espionage Act, 18 U.S.C. §§1831-1839. The Act prohibits unauthorized conveying of trade secrets either (1) with intent to provide economic or strategic benefit to a foreign government, or (2) with intent to provide economic benefit to a third party and to harm the owner of the trade secret. Trade secrets are broadly defined to include "all forms and types of financial, business, scientific, technical, economic, or engineering information." Id. §1839(3). For discussion of the statute, see Kent B. Alexander & Kristen L. Wood, The Economic Espionage Act: Setting the Stage for a New Commercial Code of Conduct, 15 Ga. St. U. L. Rev. 907 (1999).

Problem: The defendant, a paralegal working for a firm representing plaintiffs in a class action suit, e-mailed to opposing attorneys an excerpt from the plaintiff firm's 400-page "trial plan," and offered to sell them the entire plan for $2 million. The defense attorneys contacted the FBI, and an undercover agent arranged a meeting that led to the defendant's arrest. Could the defendant be charged with violating the Economic Espionage Act, on the theory that the trial plan excerpt was "business [or] economic . . . information"? The government chose instead to prosecute under §2314. Did the defendant's e-mail message transmit "goods, wares [or] merchandise"? See United States v. Farraj, 142 F. Supp. 2d 484 (S.D.N.Y. 2001).

7. *Identity theft.* Identity theft—the unauthorized use of identifying information such as a person's name, social security number, or credit—is the number one consumer fraud complaint and one of the fastest growing crimes in America. Samuel H. Johnson, Who We Really Are: On the Need for the United States to Adopt the European Paradigm for Identity Fraud Protection, Currents: Int'l Trade L.J., Winter 2006, at 123. The federal aggravated identity theft statute, 18 U.S.C. §1028A, imposes additional penalties on an individual who, during the commission of certain crimes, "knowingly transfers, possesses, or uses, without lawful authority, a means of identification of another person." Conviction requires that the defendant know that the identification actually belongs to someone else (and is not fake, for instance). Thus, the Supreme Court reversed the conviction of an illegal immigrant who presented a counterfeit social security card whose number, allegedly unbeknownst to the defendant, belonged to someone else. Flores-Figueroa v. United States, 129 S. Ct. 1886 (2009). In the ordinary prosecution, of course, proof of knowledge is easy because the defendant's aim was precisely to exploit the

---

2. U.S. Dept. of Justice, Progress Report of the Department of Justice's Task Force on Intellectual Property 13 (2006), available at http://www.justice.gov/criminal/cybercrime/2006IPTFProgressReport(6-19-06).pdf.

victim's real identity. Consider United States v. Blixt, 548 F.3d 882 (3d Cir. 2008), where an employee forged her employer's signature on 352 bank checks. The court upheld the aggravated identity theft conviction for the forgery on the theory that forging another person's signature is the use of that person's name and therefore a "means of identification." Should the theft of identify be recognized as a form of property crime?

REGINA v. STEWART

Supreme Court of Canada, 1988
50 D.L.R.4th 1, 41 C.C.C.3d 481

LAMER, J.: . . . A union attempting to organize the approximately 600 [hotel] employees . . . was unable to obtain the names, addresses and telephone numbers of the employees because of a hotel policy that such information be treated as confidential. . . . The appellant, Wayne John Stewart, a self-employed consultant, was hired by somebody he assumed to be acting for the union to obtain the [employee information]. Stewart offered a security guard [Hart] at the hotel a fee to obtain this information. . . . The security guard reported the offer to his security chief and the police; as a result, a subsequent telephone conversation between Hart and Stewart was recorded, and Stewart was indicted for, [inter alia, counseling the offense of theft, defined in §283 of the Criminal Code as the taking of "anything whether animate or inanimate" with the required intention. The accused was acquitted by a single-judge court, but on appeal the Ontario Court of Appeal reversed and entered a verdict of conviction.[a] The defendant then appealed to the Supreme Court of Canada.]

We are here dealing not with the theft of a list or any other tangible object containing confidential information, but with the theft of confidential information per se, a pure intangible. [The meaning of "anything"] must be determined within the context of §283 of the Code.

[I]t is clear that to be the object of theft, "anything" must be property in the sense that to be stolen, it has to belong in some way to someone. For instance, no conviction for theft would arise out of a taking or converting of the air that we breathe, because air is not property. . . .

It is possible that, with time, confidential information will come to be considered as property in the civil law or even be granted special legal protection by statutory enactment. Even if confidential information were to be considered as property under civil law, it does not, however, automatically follow that it qualifies as property for the purposes of criminal law. Conversely, the fact that something is not property under civil law is likewise not conclusive for the purpose of criminal law. . . .

a. In Canada, unlike the United States, a prosecutor may appeal such an acquittal and have the appellate court enter a judgment of conviction.—EDS.

[T]he qualification of confidential information as property must be done in each case by examining the purposes and context of the civil and criminal law. It is understandable that one who possesses valuable information would want to protect it from unauthorized use and reproduction. In civil litigation, this protection can be afforded by the courts because they simply have to balance the interests of the parties involved. However, criminal law is designed to prevent wrongs against society as a whole. From a social point of view, whether confidential information should be protected requires a weighing of interests much broader than those of the parties involved. As opposed to the alleged owner of the information, society's best advantage may well be to favour the free flow of information and greater accessibility by all. Would society be willing to prosecute the person who discloses to the public a cure for cancer, although its discoverer wanted to keep it confidential?

The criminalization of certain types of conduct should not be done lightly. If the unauthorized appropriation of confidential information becomes a criminal offence, there would be farreaching consequences that the courts are not in a position to contemplate. For instance, the existence of such an offence would have serious implications with respect to the mobility of labour. . . .

Moreover, because of the inherent nature of information, treating confidential information as property simpliciter for the purposes of the law of theft would create a host of practical problems. For instance, what is the precise definition of "confidential information"? Is confidentiality based on the alleged owner's intent or on some objective criteria? . . . Should only confidential information be protected under the criminal law, or any type of information deemed to be of some commercial value? . . . The choices to be made rest upon political judgments that, in my view, are matters of legislative action and not of judicial decision. . . .

Appeal allowed; acquittal restored.

NOTE

In Oxford v. Moss, [1978] 68 Crim. App. 183 (B.D.), the defendant, an engineering student, managed to obtain the page proof to the civil engineering exam to be given at his university the following month. He was caught and charged with theft. It was stipulated that the defendant intended only to "borrow" the proofs and hoped to return them undetected after acquiring advance knowledge of the questions to be asked. Section 1(1) of the English Theft Act of 1968 provided that "[a] person is guilty of theft if he dishonestly appropriates property belonging to another with the intention of permanently depriving the other of it." Section 4(1) defined "property" to include "money and all other property, real or personal, including things in action and other intangible property." The court held that the confidential information contained in the exam paper was not "intangible property" within the meaning of the statute. As the *Girard* case indicates, however, the result could be different in the United States, at least if the test had been sponsored by a federal agency.

Question: Are the *Oxford v. Moss* and *Stewart* cases distinguishable?

3. *Honest Services*

The federal mail fraud statute, 18 U.S.C. §1341, as noted above, pages 1064-1065, prohibits "any scheme or artifice to defraud, or for obtaining money or property by means of false or fraudulent pretenses, representations, or promises" using the U.S. mail.[3] Over time, courts interpreted §1341's "any scheme or artifice to defraud" language to cover the deprivation of not just tangible property, but also the deprivation of intangible rights and fiduciary duties by public and corporate officials. The Supreme Court described these cases as follows in McNally v. United States, 483 U.S. 350, 362-362 (1987):

> In the public sector . . . officials have secretly made governmental decisions with the objective of benefiting themselves or promoting their own interests, instead of fulfilling their legal commitment to provide the citizens of the State or local government with their loyal service and honest government . . . In the private sector, purchasing agents, brokers, union leaders, and others with clear fiduciary duties to their employers or unions have been found guilty of defrauding their employers or unions by accepting kickbacks or selling confidential information. In other cases, defendants have been found guilty of using the mails to defraud individuals of their rights to privacy and other nonmonetary rights.

The victims in these cases—shareholders or the public—do not lose tangible property or money, but their right to honest services. Courts accepted this loss of intangible rights as a substitute for economic loss. In addition, although the defendants in many of these cases did not typically engage in express deceit or misrepresentation, courts found the element of fraud was satisfied through a failure to disclose their dishonest or corrupt actions. Courts justified the honest services doctrine "by positing that the public has an intangible right to the honest services of government officials," such that the "official's failure to disclose his crookedness may then constitute the basis of a mail fraud conviction." Thomas J. Miles, Dupes and Losers in Mail Fraud, 77 U. Chi. L. Rev. 1111, 1135 (2010). For example, in United States v. Margiotta, 688 F.2d 108 (2d Cir. 1982), the Second Circuit affirmed the mail fraud conviction of a local chair of a political party committee who distributed thousands of dollars in insurance commissions to numerous brokers, lawyers, and friends who failed to do legitimate work. The court held that Margiotta breached a fiduciary duty owed to the public by failing to disclose material information about the commissions. Judge Winter's dissent criticized the sweep of the honest services theory: "[T]here is no end to the common political practices which may now

---

3. The wire fraud statute, 18 U.S.C. §1343, contains comparable language, and the legal analysis for both is largely the same. Margaret Ryznar, The Honest-Services Doctrine in White-Collar Criminal Law, 34 Hamline L. Rev. 83, n.8 (2010).

be swept within the ambit of mail fraud," including "[a]n elected official who for political purposes performs an act imposing unnecessary costs on taxpayers" without making disclosure, "[a] partisan political leader who throws decisive support behind a candidate known to the leader to be less qualified than his or her opponent," and "[a] partisan political leader who causes elected officials to fail to modernize government to retain jobs for the party faithful." Id. at 140 (Winter, J., concurring in part and dissenting in part).

In the private context, honest services cases included violations of duties of loyalty, such as securities brokers trading for their own accounts based on their employer's information. Miles, supra, at 1135-1136. This, too, sparked criticism, with some courts concluding that honest services was "problematic" in the private sector because it could potentially turn any kind of dishonesty by an employee into a crime. These courts thus demanded a showing of some risk of economic harm to the party to whom the duty of honest services was owed. See, e.g., United States v. Frost, 125 F.3d 346 (6th Cir. 1997).

The Supreme Court rejected the broad reading of honest services in 1987 in *McNally*, concluding that a deprivation of money or tangible property was necessary under §1341. Justice Stevens dissented and questioned the logic of criminalizing schemes to defraud that involved trivial sums of money but not allowing prosecutions to go forward when citizens were deprived of honest government. 483 U.S. at 366 (Stevens, J., dissenting). Congress seemed to agree with Justice Stevens, for it quickly responded by passing a revised statute, 18 U.S.C. §1346, that expressly stated that the "'scheme or artifice to defraud' includes a scheme or artifice to deprive another of the intangible right of honest services." In the wake of that statute, courts continued to recognize honest services deprivation as a form of mail and wire fraud. But the scope of §1346 raised questions of its own, which are addressed in the following case.

SKILLING v. UNITED STATES

Supreme Court of the United States
130 S. Ct. 2896 (2010)

GINSBURG, J., delivered the opinion of the Court.

Founded in 1985, Enron Corporation grew ... into one of the world's leading energy companies. [Defendant] Skilling steadily rose through the corporation's ranks, serving as president and chief operating officer, and then, beginning in February 2001, as chief executive officer. Six months later, on August 14, 2001, Skilling resigned from Enron.

Less than four months after Skilling's departure, Enron spiraled into bankruptcy. The company's stock, which had traded at $90 per share in August 2000, plummeted to pennies per share in late 2001. Attempting to comprehend what caused the corporation's collapse, the U.S. Department of Justice formed an Enron Task Force, comprising prosecutors and FBI agents from around the Nation. The Government's investigation uncovered an elaborate conspiracy to prop up Enron's short-run stock prices by overstating the company's financial well-being. In the years following Enron's bankruptcy, the Government prosecuted dozens of Enron employees who participated in the scheme. In time, the Government worked its way up the corporation's chain of command: On July 7, 2004, a grand jury indicted Skilling, [Ken Lay, the CEO,] and Richard Causey, Enron's former chief accounting officer.

These three defendants, the indictment alleged, "engaged in a wide-ranging scheme to deceive the investing public, including Enron's shareholders, . . . about the true performance of Enron's businesses by: (a) manipulating Enron's publicly reported financial results; and (b) making public statements and representations about Enron's financial performance and results that were false and misleading."

Skilling and his co-conspirators, the indictment continued, "enriched themselves as a result of the scheme through salary, bonuses, grants of stock and stock options, other profits, and prestige."[a]

Count 1 of the indictment charged Skilling with conspiracy to commit securities and wire fraud[, alleging] that Skilling had sought to "depriv[e] Enron and its shareholders of the intangible right of [his] honest services." The indictment further charged Skilling with more than 25 substantive counts of securities fraud, wire fraud, making false representations to Enron's auditors, and insider trading. . . .

Following a 4-month trial and nearly five days of deliberation, the jury found Skilling guilty of 19 counts, including the honest-services-fraud conspiracy charge. . . . [The court of appeals affirmed the conviction, finding that the jury was entitled to convict] "on these elements": "(1) a material breach of a fiduciary duty . . . (2) that results in a detriment to the employer," including one occasioned by an employee's decision to "withhold material information, i.e., information that he had reason to believe would lead a reasonable employer to change its conduct."

Was Skilling's conspiracy conviction . . . premised on an improper theory of honest-services wire fraud[?] The honest-services statute, §1346, Skilling maintains, is unconstitutionally vague. Alternatively, he contends that his conduct does not fall within the statute's compass.

To place Skilling's constitutional challenge in context, we first review the origin and subsequent application of the honest-services doctrine.

Enacted in 1872, the original mail-fraud provision, the predecessor of the modern-day mail- and wire-fraud laws, proscribed, without further elaboration, use of the mails to advance "any scheme or artifice to defraud." . . . In 1909, Congress amended the statute to prohibit, as it does today, "any scheme or artifice to defraud, *or for obtaining money or property by means of false or fraudulent pretenses, representations, or promises.*" §1341 (emphasis added). Emphasizing Congress' disjunctive phrasing, the Courts of Appeals, one after the other, interpreted the term "scheme or artifice to defraud" to include deprivations not only of money or property, but also of intangible rights.

---

a. Skilling's "compensation was tied directly to the value of the company's stock." Brief for the United States at 2, Skilling v. United States, 130 S. Ct. 2896 (2010).—Eds.

In an opinion credited with first presenting the intangible-rights theory, *Shushan v. United States*, 117 F.2d 110 (1941), the Fifth Circuit reviewed the mail-fraud prosecution of a public official who allegedly accepted bribes from entrepreneurs in exchange for urging city action beneficial to the bribe payers. "It is not true that because the [city] was to make and did make a saving by the operations there could not have been an intent to defraud," the Court of Appeals maintained. "A scheme to get a public contract on more favorable terms than would likely be got otherwise by bribing a public official," the court observed, "would not only be a plan to commit the crime of bribery, but would also be a scheme to defraud the public."

The Fifth Circuit's opinion in *Shushan* stimulated the development of an "honest-services" doctrine. Unlike fraud in which the victim's loss of money or property supplied the defendant's gain, with one the mirror image of the other, the honest-services theory targeted corruption that lacked similar symmetry. While the offender profited, the betrayed party suffered no deprivation of money or property; instead, a third party, who had not been deceived, provided the enrichment. For example, if a city mayor (the offender) accepted a bribe from a third party in exchange for awarding that party a city contract, yet the contract terms were the same as any that could have been negotiated at arm's length, the city (the betrayed party) would suffer no tangible loss. Even if the scheme occasioned a money or property *gain* for the betrayed party, courts reasoned, actionable harm lay in the denial of that party's right to the offender's "honest services."

[C]ourts also recognized private-sector honest-services fraud. In perhaps the earliest application of the theory to private actors, a District Court, reviewing a bribery scheme, explained:

> "When one tampers with [the employer-employee] relationship for the purpose of causing the employee to breach his duty [to his employer,] he in effect is defrauding the employer of a lawful right. The actual deception that is practiced is in the continued representation of the employee to the employer that he is honest and loyal to the employer's interests." United States v. Procter & Gamble Co., 47 F. Supp. 676, 678 (D. Mass. 1942).

. . . [B]y 1982, all Courts of Appeals had embraced the honest-services theory of fraud.

In 1987, this Court, in *McNally v. United States*, stopped the development of the intangible-rights doctrine in its tracks. *McNally* involved a state officer who, in selecting Kentucky's insurance agent, arranged to procure a share of the agent's commissions via kickbacks paid to companies the official partially controlled. The prosecutor did not charge that, "in the absence of the alleged scheme[,] the Commonwealth would have paid a lower premium or secured better insurance." Instead, the prosecutor maintained that the kickback scheme "defraud[ed] the citizens and government of Kentucky of their right to have the Commonwealth's affairs conducted honestly."

We held that the scheme did not qualify as mail fraud. "Rather than constru[ing] the statute in a manner that leaves its outer boundaries ambiguous and involves the Federal Government in setting standards of disclosure and good government for local and state officials," we read the statute "as limited in scope to the protection of property rights." "If Congress desires to go further," we stated, "it must speak more clearly."

. . . The following year, [Congress] enacted a new statute "specifically to cover one of the 'intangible rights' that lower courts had protected . . . prior to *McNally*: 'the intangible right of honest services.'" Cleveland v. United States, 531 U.S. 12, 19-20 (2000). . . .

Congress, Skilling charges, reacted quickly but not clearly: He asserts that §1346 is unconstitutionally vague. . . . We [believe] that §1346 should be construed rather than invalidated. First, we look to the doctrine developed in pre-*McNally* cases in an endeavor to ascertain the meaning of the phrase "the intangible right of honest services." Second, to preserve what Congress certainly intended the statute to cover, we pare that body of precedent down to its core: In the main, the pre-*McNally* cases involved fraudulent schemes to deprive another of honest services through bribes or kickbacks supplied by a third party who had not been deceived. Confined to these paramount applications, §1346 presents no vagueness problem.

There is no doubt that Congress intended §1346 to refer to and incorporate the honest-services doctrine recognized in Courts of Appeals' decisions before *McNally* derailed the intangible-rights theory of fraud. . . . [W]e acknowledge that Skilling's vagueness challenge has force, for honest-services decisions preceding *McNally* were not models of clarity or consistency. . . .

Although some applications of the pre-*McNally* honest-services doctrine occasioned disagreement among the Courts of Appeals, these cases do not cloud the doctrine's solid core: The "vast majority" of the honest-services cases involved offenders who, in violation of a fiduciary duty, participated in bribery or kickback schemes.

. . . In view of this history, there is no doubt that Congress intended §1346 to reach *at least* bribes and kickbacks. Reading the statute to proscribe a wider range of offensive conduct, we acknowledge, would raise the due process concerns underlying the vagueness doctrine. To preserve the statute without transgressing constitutional limitations, we now hold that §1346 criminalizes *only* the bribe-and-kickback core of the pre-*McNally* case law.

The Government urges us to go further by locating within §1346's compass another category of proscribed conduct: "undisclosed self-dealing by a public official or private employee—*i.e.*, the taking of official action by the employee that furthers his own undisclosed financial interests while purporting to act in the interests of those to whom he owes a fiduciary duty."

[We are not] persuaded that the pre-*McNally* conflict-of-interest cases constitute core applications of the honest-services doctrine. Although the Courts of Appeals upheld honest-services convictions for "some schemes of nondisclosure and concealment of material information," they reached no consensus on which schemes qualified. In light of the relative infrequency of conflict-of-interest prosecutions in comparison to bribery and kickback charges, and the intercircuit inconsistencies they produced, we conclude that a reasonable limiting construction of §1346 must exclude this amorphous category of cases. . . .

SCALIA, J., with whom Justice THOMAS joins, and with whom Justice KENNEDY joins except as to Part III, concurring in part and concurring in the judgment.

. . . The Court maintains that "the intangible right of honest services" "means the right not to have one's fiduciaries accept "bribes or kickbacks." . . . I agree that Congress used the novel phrase to adopt the lower-court case law that had been disapproved by *McNally*—what the Court calls "the pre-*McNally* honest-services doctrine." The problem is that that doctrine . . . is not limited to "bribes or kickbacks."

[T]he first step in the Court's analysis—holding that "the intangible right of honest services" refers to "the honest-services doctrine recognized in Court of Appeals' decisions before *McNally*"—is a step out of the frying pan into the fire. The pre-*McNally* cases provide no clear indication of what constitutes a denial of the right of honest services. The possibilities range from any action that is contrary to public policy or otherwise immoral, to only the disloyalty of a public official or employee to his principal, to only the secret use of a perpetrator's position of trust in order to harm whomever he is beholden to. The duty probably did not have to be rooted in state law, but maybe it did. It might have been more demanding in the case of public officials, but perhaps not. At the time §1346 was enacted there was no settled criterion for choosing among these options, for conclusively settling what was in and what was out.

[Justice Scalia went on to criticize the Court's approach as failing to address the vagueness argument, noting that the Court's approach] would not solve the most fundamental indeterminacy: the character of the "fiduciary capacity" to which the bribery and kickback restriction applies. Does it apply only to public officials? Or in addition to private individuals who contract with the public? Or to everyone, including the corporate officer here? The pre-*McNally* case law does not provide an answer. Thus, even with the bribery and kickback limitation the statute does not answer the question "What is the criterion of guilt?"

[Justice Alito's concurrence is omitted.]

NOTES

1. Corruption as theft. As the Court observes in *Skilling*, the honest services doctrine grew out of a desire to promote good government and business behavior by targeting corrupt behavior on the part of public officials and corporate officers in situations where "the offender profited, [but] the betrayed party suffered no deprivation of money or property; instead, a third party, who had not been deceived, provided the enrichment." Defining what, exactly, the betrayed party has lost when there is no tangible property or money loss therefore presents difficult definitional questions and explains the ongoing dialogue between the Supreme Court and Congress over the sweep of the theory of honest services. The Court in *Skilling* opted to limit the statute to bribes and kickbacks, relying heavily on an amicus brief by Albert W. Alschuler submitted in a companion case that explained this limiting principle as follows:

[Limiting honest-services liability to quid pro quo bribes and kickbacks would] obviate the need for a distinction between public-sector and private-sector cases—a distinction that only some circuits have found appropriate. Because accepting bribes and kickbacks constitutes hard-core corruption whether the recipients are public officials or private fiduciaries, there would be no need to distinguish between these classes of defendants. . . . [This standard would also] effectively resolve a circuit conflict over whether the law of honest-services fraud should focus on gain to the defendant or economic harm to the victim. . . . Under the statute, a person who has taken a bribe or kickback cannot assert as a defense that his wrongful act caused no economic harm.[4]

But just as Congress rejected the Court's limiting efforts in *McNally*, it appears poised to reject the limit established in *Skilling*. In September 2010, Senator Patrick Leahy responded to *Skilling* by introducing a bill entitled the Honest Services Restoration Act, which would criminalize the kind of undisclosed self-dealing that the Court refused to reach. Elizabeth R. Sheyn, Criminalizing the Denial of Honest Services After *Skilling*, 11 Wis. L. Rev. 27, 48-51 (2011). Testifying in support of such legislation, Assistant Attorney General Lanny A. Breuer argued that "a public official who conceals his financial interests and then takes official action to advance those interests engages in behavior every bit as corrupt as if he accepts a clear bribe from a third party."Ashley Southall, Justice Department Seeks a Broader Law to Cover Self-Dealing, N.Y. Times, Sept. 29, 2010, at B3. One critic believes any new legislation should require proof of actual economic harm to avoid overcriminalization. Sheyn, supra, at 57-61. As of the time of this writing, the legislation remains in committee.

2. The scope of honest services. Why is capturing a broader notion of honest services than the one acknowledged by the Court—bribes and kickbacks—so important as a matter of public policy? What gap does honest services attempt to fill? To some extent, the answer depends on how broadly the courts view bribery and kickbacks. While bribery may be limited to a quid pro quo, where a public or private official accepts a payment with the intent that it will influence his or her duties, United States v. Ganim, 510 F.3d 134, 149 (2d Cir. 2007), there are broader theories of bribery that allow prosecutions when a stream of benefits is given to curry favor with a public official and there is no need to show that a specific benefit was given in exchange for a specific act. United States v. Ryan, 759 F. Supp. 2d 975, 984 (N.D. Ill. 2010). But whatever the scope of bribery and kickbacks, some element of undisclosed self-dealing will fall outside its purview. Imagine, for example, that *A*, the CEO of Acme, owns zero shares in Acme but 40 percent of the shares of Acme's supplier, Widget. *A* convinces the board of Acme to acquire Widget, even though he

---

4. Brief of Albert W. Alschuler as Amicus Curiae in Support of Neither Party at 29, 32, Weyrauch v. United States, 130 S. Ct. 2971 (2009).

knows Widget is having issues with some of its other customers, who may not renew their contracts next year. *A* does not disclose his financial interest in the transaction, and Acme buys Widget. Because *A* breached his fiduciary duty to Acme, *A* may be subject to criminal liability under the self-dealing theory, even though he engaged in no bribes or kickbacks.

If the law seeks to target the breach of a duty to disclose self-dealing, where is the content of that duty to be located for public officials? For private actors? Apart from written contracts, where are the courts supposed to look to determine what the employee's duty of loyalty entails? For example, should it be deemed fraud for an employee to use the Internet for personal reasons during job hours without disclosing it to his or her employer? As Samuel Buell points out, the scope of fiduciary duties admits of no easy answer. Samuel W. Buell, The Court's Fraud Dud, 6 Duke J. Const. L. & Pub. Pol'y 31, 38-39 (2010). And the Court in *Skilling*, 130 S. Ct. at 2933 n.45, sounded a note of caution should Congress opt to amend §1346 in the wake of the decision to include undisclosed self-dealing:

> If Congress were to take up the enterprise of criminalizing "undisclosed self-dealing by a public official or private employee," it would have to employ standards of sufficient definiteness and specificity to overcome due process concerns. The Government proposes a standard that prohibits the "taking of official action by the employee that furthers his own undisclosed financial interests while purporting to act in the interests of those to whom he owes a fiduciary duty," so long as the employee acts with a specific intent to deceive and the undisclosed conduct could influence the victim to change its behavior. That formulation, however, leaves many questions unanswered. How direct or significant does the conflicting financial interest have to be? To what extent does the official action have to further that interest in order to amount to fraud? To whom should the disclosure be made and what information should it convey?

Vagueness concerns thus continue to cast a shadow over congressional efforts in this area. A penetrating assessment of the expansion of mail fraud as a threat to rule-of-law values may be found in two articles by Professor John Coffee: From Tort to Crime: Some Reflections on the Criminalization of Fiduciary Breaches and the Problematic Line Between Law and Ethics, 19 Am. Crim. L. Rev. 117 (1981), and The Metastasis of Mail Fraud: The Continuing Story of the "Evolution" of a White-Collar Crime, 21 Am. Crim. L. Rev. 1 (1983).

3. Prosecutorial Discretion. Given its breadth of coverage, even as limited by *Skilling*, the mail fraud statute vests prosecutors with tremendous discretion. Consider Francis A. Allen, The Erosion of Legality in American Criminal Justice: Some Latter-Day Adventures of the *Nulla Poena* Principle, 29 Ariz. L. Rev. 387, 407-409 (1987):

> The expansion of coverage of the Mail Fraud Act by the courts . . . exacerbates the problems of prosecutorial discretion . . . [which is] particularly troublesome . . . in cases involving immoral and corrupt behavior by persons engaged

in state and local governments. The incidents of serious improprieties in these areas are so numerous and ubiquitous that federal prosecution is incapable of responding to more than a small fraction of the total. Because choosing cases for prosecution must necessarily be highly selective, there is the ever-present danger of choices being made that promise the greatest political advantage to the national administration or to political and economic groups at the local level. Almost equally serious, suspicions of politicizing the processes of justice are engendered, whether or not justified in the particular case.

Does §1346 sweep too broadly, as Allen argues, or is it necessary to be that broad to allow prosecutors to reach the variety of self-dealing behaviors that deprive voters and shareholders of the services to which they are entitled?

C. MENS REA

PEOPLE v. BROWN

Supreme Court of California
105 Cal. 66, 38 P. 518 (1894)

GAROUTE, J. [Appellant, a 17-year-old, was convicted of burglary on an information charging that he entered a house with intent to commit larceny. He entered an acquaintance's house and took a bicycle. He testified: "I didn't intend to keep it. I just wanted to get even with him. The boy was throwing oranges at me in the evening, and he would not stop when I told him to, and it made me mad. . . . I intended to take it back Sunday night; but, before I got back, they caught me."]

[T]he court gave the jury the following instruction: . . .

In defining to you the crime of grand larceny, [defense counsel says] that you must find that the taker intended to deprive him of it permanently. I do not think that is the law. I think in this case, for example, if the defendant took this bicycle, we will say for the purpose of riding twenty-five miles, for the purpose of enabling him to get away, and then left it for another to get it, and intended to do nothing else except to help himself away for a certain distance, it would be larceny, just as much as though he intended to take it all the while. . . . He converts it to that extent to his own use and purpose feloniously.

This instruction is erroneous, and demands a reversal of the judgment. If the boy's story be true, he is not guilty of larceny in taking the machine. . . . The court told the jury that larceny may be committed, even though it was only the intent of the party taking the property to deprive the owner of it temporarily. We think the authorities form an unbroken line to the effect that the felonious intent must be to deprive the owner of the property permanently. [If the defendant] did not intend so to do, there is no felonious intent, and his acts constitute but a trespass. While the felonious intent of the party taking need not necessarily be an intention to convert the property to his own use, still it must in all cases be an intent to wholly and permanently deprive the owner thereof.

For the foregoing reasons, it is ordered that the judgment and order be reversed, and the cause remanded for a new trial.

NOTE

Some limited exceptions to the requirement of an intent to take permanently have been made judicially and by statute. The courts early found that, where the taker of property recklessly exposed it to loss or abandoned it, this fact was not only evidence of an intent to effect a permanent deprivation but would sustain larceny even if a permanent taking was not the object of the defendant's acts. State v. Davis, 38 N.J.L. 176 (1875). See N.Y. Penal Law §155.00(3): "To 'deprive' another of property means . . . to dispose of the property in such manner or under such circumstances as to render it unlikely that an owner will recover such property." Similarly, courts and statutes commonly provide that the requirement of an intent to deprive permanently can be satisfied by an intent to take the property for an extended period sufficient to deprive the owner of a major portion of the item's value. E.g., People v. Avery, 38 P.3d 1 (Cal. 2002). Thus, a defendant who "borrows" a season pass to her team's home baseball games could not defend on the ground that she had returned the pass after the season was over. See also MPC §223.0(1).

Significant gaps remain when a defendant keeps the property for a significant period but nonetheless brings it back in time for the owner to benefit from it in the future. To fill part of this gap, many states have long enacted "joy ride" statutes, which make criminal the temporary taking of an automobile and sometimes other vehicles. See, e.g., Cal. Penal Code §499b.

Question: Why should the law of theft confine itself to cases where the intent of the taker is to effect a permanent deprivation? As Holmes observed (The Common Law 71 (1881)): "A momentary loss of possession is not what has been guarded against with such severe penalties. What the law means to prevent is the loss of it wholly and forever. . . ." But should interference with possession that is more than momentary, though less than permanent, be protected against by the law of theft? Following MPC §223.0(1), N.Y. Penal Law §155.00(3) now provides: "To 'deprive' another of property means (a) to withhold it or cause it to be withheld . . . for so extended a period or under such circumstances that the major portion of its economic value or benefit is lost to him. . . ." §155.00(4) provides: "To 'appropriate' property of another to oneself or a third person means (a) to exercise control over it . . . permanently or for so extended a period or under such circumstances as to acquire the major portion of its economic value or benefit. . . ." These provisions were construed in the following case.

People v. Jennings, 69 N.Y.2d 103, 504 N.E.2d 1079 (1986): [Defendants, Sentry Armored Courier Corp. and its officers, had an agreement with Chemical Bank to pick up, "fine count," and deliver Chemical's bulk deposits to

Chemical's account at the Federal Reserve Bank within 72 hours. Since it took only 24 hours to count the money, defendants used the extra 48 hours to obtain interest on the money by arrangement with the Hudson Valley Bank. The scheme involved little risk, since the "loan" to Hudson, which was a key element in the arrangement, was secured by A-rated bonds. The majority found these facts not to constitute a deprivation or appropriation of Chemical's money.]

What is lacking here . . . is evidence demonstrating an "intent to deprive . . . or to appropriate." The gist of the People's claim is that by investing Chemical's money for periods up to 48 hours, defendants evinced an intent to deprive its true owner of the money's "economic value or benefit," that is, the interest that the money was capable of generating. The mens rea element of larceny, however, is simply not satisfied by an intent temporarily to use property without the owner's permission, or even an intent to appropriate outright the benefits of the property's short-term use.

. . . [T]he evidence . . . indicates only that defendants exercised control over Chemical's money to the extent of using it to make short-term, profitable investments and, as a result, appropriated some portion of its economic benefit for themselves. However, in light of the fact that their unauthorized use of Chemical's money extended over no more than a series of discrete 48-hour periods, the proof was insufficient to show that they intended to use Chemical's money "for so extended a period or under such circumstances as to acquire the *major portion* of its economic value or benefit" (emphasis supplied).

Moreover, [i]nasmuch as Chemical had ceded possession of its money to Sentry for various 72-hour periods, it had no legal rights during those periods to the money's "economic value or benefit," which is an incident of possession. . . . It is clear that an individual who "joy-rides" and thereby deprives the automobile's owner of the value arising from its temporary use is not liable in larceny for stealing that intangible "value" under article 155 of the Penal Law. By parity of reasoning, an individual who temporarily invests another's money and thereby gains interest or profit cannot be deemed guilty of larceny for appropriating that interest or profit. . . .

Finally, we note that neither Sentry's patently false response to Chemical's inquiry concerning the rerouting of its money through Hudson nor Sentry's disobedience when ordered by Chemical to deliver the money directly are sufficient to establish that Sentry was acting with the larcenous intent required by Penal Law §155.00(3), (4) and §155.05(1). At worst, Sentry's conduct demonstrates its unwillingness to relinquish what was obviously a profitable short-term use of Chemical's money. It does not, however, alter the inescapable and uncontradicted inference that Sentry was merely emulating the behavior of many reputable financial institutions by taking advantage of the "float" on the temporarily idle money in its possession.

. . . [H]owever unethical defendants' conduct may have been, it did not constitute the crimes of larceny . . . [and] the indictments charging those crimes were properly dismissed.

REGINA v. FEELY

Court of Appeal [1973]
Q.B. 530, 2 W.L.R. 201

LAWTON, L.J. . . . . The appeal raises an important point of law, namely, can it be a defence *in law* for a man charged with theft and proved to have taken money to say that when he took the money he intended to repay it and had reasonable grounds for believing and did believe that he would be able to do so.

[Defendant was a branch manager for a firm of bookmakers. In September 1971, the firm sent a circular to all branch managers that the practice of borrowing from tills was to stop. Defendant nevertheless took about £30 from a branch safe on October 4. When discovered, he said he borrowed the £30 intending to pay it back and that his employers owed him about £70 from which he wanted them to deduct the money. Trial testimony showed that the firm did owe him that amount. He was convicted of theft of the £30.]

[The trial judge directed the jury] that if the defendant had taken the money from either the safe or the till . . . it was no defence for him to say that he had intended to repay it and that his employers owed him more than enough to cover what he had taken. The trial judge put his direction in stark terms: . . .

> As a matter of law, members of the jury, I am bound to direct you, even if he were prepared to pay back the following day and even if he were a millionaire, it makes no defence in law to this offence. If he took the money, that is the essential matter for you to decide.

At no stage of his summing up did he leave the jury to decide whether the prosecution had proved that the defendant had taken the money dishonestly. This was because he seems to have thought that he had to decide as a matter of law what amounted to dishonesty and he expressed his concept of dishonesty as follows: ". . . if someone does something deliberately knowing that his employers are not prepared to tolerate it, is that not dishonest?"

Should the jury have been left to decide whether the defendant had acted dishonestly? The search for an answer must start with the Theft Act 1968, under section 1 of which the defendant had been indicted. . . . [Under the Act,] nearly all the old legal terms to describe offences of dishonesty have been left behind; larceny, embezzlement and fraudulent conversion have become theft. . . . Words in everyday use have replaced legal jargon in many parts of the Act. . . .

"Theft" . . . is defined . . . as follows: "A person is guilty of theft if he dishonestly appropriates property belonging to another with the intention of permanently depriving the other of it. . . ."

In section 1(1) of the Act of 1968, the word "dishonestly" can only relate to the state of mind of the person who does the act which amounts to appropriation. . . . The Crown did not dispute this proposition, but it was submitted that in some cases (and this, it was said, was such a one) it was necessary for the trial judge to define "dishonestly." . . .

We do not agree that judges should define what "dishonestly" means. . . . Jurors, when deciding whether an appropriation was dishonest can be reasonably expected to, and should, apply the current standards of ordinary decent people.

[T]he jury should have been left to decide whether the defendant's alleged taking of the money had been dishonest. . . .

This would suffice for the appeal were it not for . . . Reg. v. Williams [1953] 1 Q.B. 660, [where] the two appellants, who were husband and wife, carried on a general shop, part of which was a sub-post office. The wife was the sub-postmistress. The business of the shop got into difficulties and in order to get out of them the wife . . . took money from the Post Office till to discharge some of the debts of the business. [S]he said that she thought she would be able to repay the money out of her salary from the Post Office and from sales from the business. The husband said that he knew it was wrong to do what they had done, but he thought that it would all come right in the end. They were found guilty on a number of counts and in respect of two the jury added a rider that the appellants had intended to repay the money and honestly believed that they would be able to do so. . . .

The question in the case which is relevant for the purposes of this appeal was whether the facts found by the jury and recorded in their riders afforded any defence. [The court held they did not, stating]: "They knew that they had no right to take the money which they knew was not their money. The fact that they may have had a hope or expectation in the future of repaying that money is a matter which at most can go to mitigation and does not amount to a defence." . . .

We find it impossible to accept that a conviction for stealing, whether it be called larceny or theft, can reveal no moral obloquy. A man so convicted would have difficulty in persuading his friends and neighbours that his reputation had not been gravely damaged. . . .

If the principle enunciated in [*Williams*] was right, there would be a strange divergence between the position of a man who obtains cash by passing a cheque on an account which has no funds to meet it and one who takes money from a till. The man who passes the cheque is deemed in law not to act dishonestly if he genuinely believes on reasonable grounds that when it is presented to the paying bank there will be funds to meet it. But, according to [*Williams*], the man who takes money from a till intending to put it back and genuinely believing on reasonable grounds that he will be able to do so should be convicted of theft. Lawyers may be able to appreciate why one man should be adjudged to be a criminal and the other not; but we doubt whether anyone else would. People who take money from tills and the like without permission are usually thieves; but if they do not admit that they are by pleading guilty, it is for the jury, not the judge, to decide whether they have acted dishonestly. . . .

For these reasons we allowed the appeal.

NOTES AND QUESTIONS ON INTENT TO RESTORE OR PAY

1. Intent to restore and embezzlement. In State v. Pratt, 220 P. 505, 506-507 (Kan. 1923), the defendant was convicted of embezzlement on the following facts:

> [T]he Building & Loan Association purchased $10,000 worth [of bonds], which passed into the custody of the appellant as secretary-treasurer of the association. Without any authority to do so, and without the knowledge of the directors and other officers of the association, appellant sold these bonds in January, 1920. . . . The money was not used for the benefit of the association. In fact, appellant concealed his disposition of these bonds from the association until some time in May or June, 1921.

On appeal the defendant contended "that before he could be convicted of the crime of embezzlement the state must prove beyond a reasonable doubt that at the time he wrongfully converted the bonds he had the intent to deprive the owner, not temporarily, but permanently, of its property," and that error was committed in refusing evidence of his intent to restore the bonds or their equivalent and in failing to instruct that such an intent was a good defense. The court affirmed, resting on the weight of authority that as long as "the money of the principal is knowingly used by the agent in violation of his duty," it is still embezzlement even if "at the time he intended to restore it." Similarly, in People v. Sisuphan, 104 Cal. Rptr. 3d 654, 662 (Cal. Ct. App. 2010), the Court held that the intent to restore is not a defense, even if it is present at the time the property is taken and the property is restored before criminal charges are filed.

2. Intent to restore and false pretenses. The intent to restore is likewise held to be no defense to a false pretense charge. See People v. Weiger, 34 P. 826 (Cal. 1893). The defendant obtained goods on credit from the complaining witness on false representations concerning his financial position. The court affirmed a conviction of obtaining by false pretenses, holding it immaterial that the defendant intended to pay for the goods he purchased.

Questions: Suppose the goods the defendant obtained in the *Weiger* case were a set of law books and that his defense was that he was an attorney expecting a visit from a potential client of substance whom he wanted to impress. He obtained the books for this purpose, fully intending to ship them back to the seller after the client's visit. Would it follow from *Weiger* that he would be guilty of obtaining by false pretenses? If so, consider the liability of the attorney if he secretly removed the books from another attorney's office for the same purpose and with the same intent to return them after the client's visit. This, presumably, would be a temporary taking, a circumstance inconsistent with larceny. Why should he have a defense if charged with physically taking the books by stealth but not if charged with obtaining the books by a false representation?

3. *Intent to restore and federal law.* Courts have concluded that the intent to repay is irrelevant when defendants are charged with federal statutes prohibiting "conversion" and "steal[ing]." United States v. Van Elsen, 652 F.3d 955, 961 (8th Cir. 2011). In *Van Elsen*, the defendant's intent to repay funds misappropriated from his employer's retirement accounts did not preclude his conviction under 18 U.S.C. §664, which imposes criminal liability on "[a]ny person who embezzles, steals, or unlawfully and willfully abstracts or converts to his own use or to the use of another, any of the moneys, funds, securities, premiums, credits, property or other assets of any employee welfare benefit plan or employee pension benefit plan, or of any fund connected therewith."

4. *The Model Penal Code.* In connection with these issues, consider the following observations in Model Penal Code §206.1(2)(c), Comment at 72-73 (Tent. Draft No. 1, 1953):

> Deprivation accompanied by an intent to make good later, by payment of money or by the actor's repurchasing an equivalent article for restoration to the owner, is quite different in effect from the taking of a thing for temporary use of the taker. In the latter situation, the actor's retention of the property offers some assurance of his ability to restore, beyond his general credit. In the former situation, the man who takes money intending to repay or the broker who sells his client's bonds meaning to repurchase and restore the bonds later, substitutes his own credit for the owner's property in hand. Even if the actor carries out his intent to restore, he is simply paying off a liability from his own assets, rather than restoring property which has continued to belong to the owner during the interval of deprivation.

Questions: Does this account suffice to explain why the young attorney who obtains a discrete item of physical property under false pretenses should not have a defense when she intends to restore the property after a brief interval? Does it explain why a person *does* have a defense if she steals cash and spends it, but can prove that she intended to repay the money later?

The MPC addresses these issues by defining theft by *unlawful taking* in slightly different terms from those used to define theft by *deception.* The former offense is committed when the defendant has a purpose to "deprive" the owner of his or her property, while the latter offense is committed when the defendant purposely "obtains" another person's property. See Model Penal Code §§223.2, 223.3. The definitions of "deprive" and "obtain" are distinct. See Model Penal Code §223.0(1), (5). Consider how these provisions apply to the case of the young attorney who dishonestly acquires a set of law books for temporary use, intending to return them? If he secretly removes the books from another office, is he guilty of theft by unlawful taking? If he tricks a distributor into selling them to him under false pretenses, is he guilty of theft by deception?

PEOPLE v. REID

New York Court of Appeals
69 N.Y.2d 469, 508 N.E.2d 661 (1987)

SIMONS, J. [Appellants Reid and Riddles were convicted of armed robberies of money from their victims, despite evidence that they were only trying to recover money owed to them. In one case, the trial court, conducting a trial without a jury, stated that it credited the testimony of defendant that he had taken the money to satisfy a debt, but the court denied him the defense of claim of right because he used force.]

The common issue presented by these two appeals is whether a good-faith claim of right, which negates larcenous intent in certain thefts . . . also negates the intent to commit robbery by a defendant who uses force to recover cash allegedly owed him. We hold that it does not [and affirm the convictions]. . . .

A person "commits robbery when, in the course of committing a larceny, he uses or threatens the immediate use of physical force." The larceny statute, in turn, provides that an assertion that "property was appropriated under a claim of right made in good faith" is a defense to larceny. Since a good-faith claim of right is a defense to larceny, and because robbery is defined as forcible larceny, defendants contend that claim of right is also a defense to robbery. They concede the culpability of their forcible conduct, but maintain that because they acted under a claim of right to recover their own property, they were not guilty of robbery, but only some lesser crime, such as assault or unlawful possession of a weapon.

[Lower courts in New York] have uniformly ruled that claim of right is not a defense to robbery . . . based upon the interpretation of the applicable statutes and a policy decision to discourage self-help and . . . consistent with what appears to be the emerging trend of similar appellate court decisions from other jurisdictions. For similar reasons, we conclude that the claim of right defense is not available in these cases. We need not decide the quite different question of whether an individual who uses force to recover a specific chattel which he owns may be convicted of robbery. It should be noted, however, that because taking property "from an owner thereof" is an element of robbery, a person who recovers property which is his own (as compared to the fungible cash taken to satisfy a claimed debt in the cases before us) may not be guilty of robbery.

The claim of right defense is found in the larceny article of the Penal Law, . . . (see Penal Law §155.15[1])[a] [but it] does not apply to all forms of larceny. For example, extortion is a form of larceny, but the Legislature, consistent with a prior decision of this court, has not authorized a claim of right defense to extortion (see People v. Fichtner, 118 N.Y.S.2d 159). The exception is significant for extortion entails the threat of actual or potential force or some form of coercion. Thus, the inference may reasonably be drawn that in failing to authorize a claim of right defense for extortion in Penal Law §155.15(1),

---

a. N.Y. Penal Law §155.15(1) provides: "1. In any prosecution for larceny committed by trespassory taking or embezzlement, it is an affirmative defense that the property was appropriated under a claim of right made in good faith."—EDS.

and by failing to incorporate it in article 160 of the statute, which governs robbery, the Legislature recognized that an accused should not be permitted to invoke it in crimes involving force. We assume that if the Legislature intended to excuse forcible taking, it would have said so.

Our decision also rests upon policy considerations against expanding the area of permissible self-help. . . . [F]orcible conduct is not merely a transgression against property, but also entails the risk of physical or mental injury to individuals, [and] it should be subjected to criminal sanctions. Consequently, we find the courts in both [cases] correctly denied defendants' requests to assert claim of right defenses.

NOTES

1. *Chattels versus cash.* In accord with *Reid*, courts routinely distinguish between the use of force to reclaim a specific chattel and the use of force to obtain cash as repayment for an alleged debt, normally allowing a claim-of-right defense in the former situation but not the latter. See People v. Tufunga, 987 P.2d 168 (Cal. 1999).

2. *The Model Penal Code.* MPC §223.1(3)(b) provides a claim-of-right defense that is available to all forms of theft, including robbery and extortion, and regardless of whether the property appropriated is money or a discrete physical item. The Commentaries offer this justification for allowing claim-of-right as a defense to robbery (Model Penal Code and Commentaries, Comment to §223.1(3) at 157 n.99 (1980)):

> [I]t should be emphasized that the provisions of Article 211 dealing with assault and Section 212.5 dealing with criminal coercion would be fully applicable to such conduct. . . . It ought to be the objective of the criminal law to describe the character deficiencies of those subjected to it in accord with the propensities that they actually manifest. One who is prepared to use violence to regain what he regards as his own property is, properly viewed, one who should be subjected to the laws designed to regulate violence and not to the laws designed to regulate the misappropriation of property of another.

That view has not proved popular. The New Jersey Supreme Court in State v. Mejia, 662 A.2d 308, 319 (N.J. 1995), rejected such a defense, arguing that the position claim of right negates the felonious intent in robbery

> has no place in an ordered and orderly society such as ours, which eschews self-help through violence. Adoption of the proposition would be but one step short of accepting lawless reprisal as an appropriate means of redressing grievances, real or fancied.

Who has the better of the argument? See Danielle R. Newton, Comment, What's Right with a Claim of Right?, 33 U.S.F. L. Rev. 673 (1999).

chapter 10

Discretion

The subject matter of criminal law, broadly speaking, is the framework of rules and principles that defines certain conduct as crimes and determines the degree of punishment attached to any given instance of criminal behavior. Because the media tends to focus on the cases that go to trial, the image of this process is usually of an adversarial battle in a courtroom, with opposing counsel putting forward their strongest arguments before a decision maker (a jury or a trial judge) who resolves all disputed questions, in order to arrive at the decision that best reflects the requirements of established law.

But that image ignores the reality and complexity of how substantive law and punishment typically gets implemented. At crucial points, the binding force of this body of law is qualified, and may even be nullified completely, by discretion. Discretion allows decisions concerning culpability and punishment to be made outside the ordinary doctrinal framework, in a process that often can be described as unilateral and administrative rather than adversarial and adjudicative. This chapter provides an opportunity to examine this phenomenon systematically and to reflect upon its implications.

"Discretion," for present purposes, exists when the institutions charged with implementing criminal law doctrine are endowed with authority—*legitimate* authority—to ignore established rules and decide questions of liability and punishment on different grounds or on no particular grounds at all.[1] We have already examined one example—the jury's unreviewable power to render a verdict of acquittal in the face of incontrovertible evidence of guilt. See pages 56-68 supra. Jury nullification has been enshrined in Anglo-American criminal procedure for more than 200 years. But its importance has faded to some extent, as jury trials have become increasingly rare, with only 2 percent of state court convictions coming after a jury trial.[2]

At the same time, developments have increased the significance of discretion at other points in the process. The potential reach of criminal law has

---

1. An early exploration of this problem appears in Sanford H. Kadish, Legal Norm and Discretion in the Police and Sentencing Process, 75 Harv. L. Rev. 904 (1962).

2. Bureau of Justice Statistics, U.S. Dept. of Justice, Sourcebook for Criminal Justice Statistics Online tbl. 5.46.2002 (2004), http://ww.albany.edu/sourcebook/pdf/t5462002.pdf.

widened because the number of criminal laws has exponentially increased, and their scope is ever broader—covering "more conduct than any jurisdiction could possibly punish."[3] The abundance of legislated crimes permits prosecutors to file a multiplicity of serious charges or to pick and choose among possible statutes. Authorized sentences have become increasingly severe, and nominally "mandatory" sentences have been attached to more and more offenses. These transformations have combined to give charging decisions, plea bargaining, and the sentencing process a growing importance in determining culpability and punishment. In many ways, prosecutors in the modern era of criminal justice are now the key adjudicators, and not simply advocates, because of the power they wield.[4] And at each of these points, discretion is pervasive; the formal doctrines of criminal law must compete for influence with unofficial norms and the decision maker's personal motivations.

A common intuition is that formal adjudications of guilt at trial require stronger moral justification than charge dismissals, plea bargaining, and jury nullification because the last three processes involve the exercise of leniency. The thought seems to be that decisions to *impose* pains and penalties require better reasons and more oversight than decisions to *withhold* sanctions.

In assessing this intuition, two points must be stressed. First, as Professor Kenneth Culp Davis insisted, "the power to be lenient is the power to discriminate."[5] Second, whatever may have been true in the past, we can no longer describe charging and bargaining discretion as simply the discretion to *withhold* deserved punishment. Criminal statutes now commonly permit (or purport to require) draconian punishments that no one expects to be imposed in the typical case. Indeed, prisons are already filled to capacity and beyond capacity, even in a world where the most severe available sentences are inflicted on a mere 5-10 percent of the offenders actually eligible. "Leniency" has therefore become not merely common but a systemic imperative. Under these circumstances, as we shall see in this chapter, the decision to "withhold leniency" is effectively a decision to *impose* severe punishment, and to do so selectively, on grounds that need not be adjudicated or even disclosed.

This chapter reflects the view that examination of these practices has become an important complement to the study of criminal law:[6]

> [A] rounded treatment of substantive rules and doctrines of the criminal law should include treatment of those features of the working system that tend to frustrate or distort the system's design. One would want to look at those features critically. To what extent are they dispensable irrationalities, adhered to because of economy or sheer expedience or inertia . . . ?

---

3. William J. Stuntz, The Pathological Politics of Criminal Law, 100 Mich. L. Rev. 505, 507 (2001). Not all scholars agree, however, that the scope of criminalized conduct constantly expands. See Darryl K. Brown, Democracy and Decriminalization, 86 Tex. L. Rev. 223, 225 (2007).

4. Gerard E. Lynch, Our Administrative System of Criminal Justice, 66 Fordham L. Rev. 2117 (1998).

5. Kenneth Culp Davis, Discretionary Justice 170 (1969).

6. Sanford H. Kadish, Why Substantive Criminal Law—A Dialogue, 29 Clev. St. L. Rev. 1, 8 (1980).

To what extent do they represent a judgment that equity and discretion are indispensable to a just criminal law . . . ? In either event, what should be done differently in formulating criminal doctrines to account for these discretionary features?

This chapter does not deal with criminal *procedure* in the conventional sense. Rather, its focus is on the quintessentially *substantive* problem of understanding the criteria (or lack of criteria) by which culpability and punishment are determined in contemporary America. Section A examines the charging decision, Section B considers plea bargaining, and Section C explores the sentencing process.[7] This division, though necessary for purposes of exposition, is somewhat artificial. Charging decisions are often shaped by the prospect of plea negotiation, and plea negotiation is almost always shaped by expectations about the potential sentence. We take up the three processes in the order that they arise in litigation, but it must be remembered that they are interdependent.

A. THE DECISION TO CHARGE

INTRODUCTORY NOTES

1. The existence of discretion. The rules of professional responsibility permit prosecutors to file criminal charges only when they can establish "probable cause,"[8] and usually the prosecutor will file charges only when there is legally admissible evidence sufficient to prove guilt beyond a reasonable doubt.[9] Are there situations where prosecutors should file charges when they have probable cause but are concerned whether a jury will find the defendant guilty? Consider the rape allegations against Dominique Strauss-Kahn, the former head of the International Monetary Fund. A maid at a hotel where Strauss-Kahn was staying alleged that he sexually assaulted her. At the time the alleged assault was initially reported, prosecutors believed the maid's story. Later, however, several facts undermined the housekeeper's credibility, including her ties to individuals with drug convictions, false information on her immigration forms, and recordings where she discussed a desire to profit from the allegations. The prosecutors ultimately dismissed the charges, stating that "for generations, before determining whether a case should proceed to trial, felony prosecutors in New York County have insisted that they be *personally* convinced beyond a reasonable doubt of the defendant's guilt, and

---

7. Although these three sites of official discretion are probably the most significant ones for purposes of substantive criminal law, there are (in addition to jury discretion) several others, most importantly police discretion whether to investigate or arrest, and executive discretion to parole, pardon, or grant clemency.

8. American Bar Assn. Model Rules of Professional Conduct, Rule 3.8 (5th ed. 2003).

9. American Bar Assn. Standards: The Prosecution Function §3-3.9(a) (3d ed. 1993).

believe themselves able to prove that guilt to a jury."[10] Because prosecutors did not believe the complainant beyond a reasonable doubt, their view was they could "not ask a jury to do so."[11]

The ABA has proposed a revised standard that comports with the standard applied by the prosecutors in the Strauss-Kahn case, requiring a prosecutor to dismiss charges when he or she "reasonably believes that proof of guilt beyond reasonable doubt is lacking." Standards for Criminal Justice: Prosecution Function §3-5.5(c) (Proposed Revisions 2009). Does a standard that requires prosecutors themselves to believe in guilt beyond a reasonable doubt properly protect defendants' rights, or does it risk disadvantaging certain types of victims when credibility is a central issue in the case? The Department of Justice authorizes prosecutors to bring charges when they have "probable cause" that a person committed a federal offense. U.S. Attorney Manual §9-27-200. That threshold has been criticized as too low "barring exceptional circumstances such as the need to interdict an immediate threat to public safety or national security." Anthony S. Barkow & Beth George, Prosecuting Political Defendants, 44 Ga. L. Rev. 953, 1014-1015 (2010). Are those exceptions warranted? Are there other circumstances where probable cause should be sufficient?

Even when there is evidence that prosecutors believe shows guilt beyond a reasonable doubt, they still often choose not to pursue all legally sustainable charges. Two reasons commonly offered are limited available enforcement resources and the need to individualize justice. See Wayne R. LaFave, The Prosecutor's Discretion in the United States, 18 Am. J. Comp. L. 532, 533 (1970). Josh Bowers argues that prosecutors are well positioned to assess the first but not the second. Prosecutors understand the office's strategic priorities and resource limits, but there are reasons to doubt their ability "to reach commonsense determinations of whether defendants normatively ought to be charged." Josh Bowers, Legal Guilt, Normative Innocence, and the Equitable Decision Not to Prosecute, 110 Colum. L. Rev. 1655, 1657 (2010). Why might prosecutors be ill-positioned to make assessments about individual blameworthiness?

Another factor that supports discretion is "overcriminalization." Legislators have many incentives to cast criminal prohibitions in broad terms and to authorize severe punishments. Legislation expanding the reach of the criminal law and raising penalties is relatively easy to enact and often virtually impossible to repeal. See LaFave, supra; Stuntz, supra footnote 3. This one-way ratchet produces an ever-expanding body of criminal prohibitions that often overlap and that contain ever-increasing sanctions. Such laws presuppose discretion; often they are intended primarily as symbolic expressions of

---

10. New York v. Strauss-Kahn, Recommendation for Dismissal 4, Aug. 22, 2011, available at http://www.nytimes.com/interactive/2011/08/22/nyregion/dsk-recommendation-to-dismiss-case.html (emphasis added).
11. Id. at 2.

disapproval, or as options for use in unusual situations, rather than as efforts to prevent the designated behavior under any and all circumstances.

Questions: If we were designing a criminal justice system from scratch, would it be better to narrow the reach of criminal law and provide resources sufficient to permit consistent, full enforcement? Or would prosecutorial discretion remain desirable (and perhaps impossible to eliminate) in any event?

Even if enforcement discretion is inevitable, not every legal system accepts the kind of *broad, unstructured* discretion commonly found in the United States. Is it desirable to channel prosecutorial discretion by formal standards and to control it by some system of supervision or review? Consider the Notes that follow.

2. Standards. What factors justify a decision not to prosecute a legally provable case? The current standards of the American Bar Association (ABA) recommend that prosecutors consider the strength of the evidence, the harm caused, the possible disproportion between the authorized punishment and the gravity of a particular crime, the defendant's willingness to cooperate in the prosecution of others, and the likelihood of prosecution in another jurisdiction.[12] Proposed revisions to the ABA standards would include additional factors, such as the collateral impact on third parties, "the particulars of the offender's character, or his situation," and "changes . . . in the larger cultural context, including that the statute has fallen into desuetude."[13] Are these suggested revisions advisable? Will failing to consider these factors ignore important differences between offenders that should be considered in making charging decisions? Or are the standards so malleable as to lead to disparate results in similarly situated cases based on the varying views of the prosecutors applying the standards? For the latter view, see Bennett L. Gershman, Prosecutorial Decisionmaking and Discretion in the Charging Function, 62 Hastings L.J. 1259, 1276 (2011).

For federal prosecutors, the United States Attorney's Manual lists in some detail the circumstances to be considered in making decisions to charge, but many are obvious (e.g., the strength of the evidence) and all are essentially open-ended, nonbinding examples of factors to be weighed.[14] A few U.S. Attorneys and local prosecutors have more specific rules for handling recurring issues, such as the appropriate charging of various kinds of assault, theft, and drug cases. See, e.g., Ronald Wright & Marc Miller, The Screening/Bargaining Tradeoff, 55 Stan. L. Rev. 29 (2002) (describing charging standards in New Orleans). Most, however, give their subordinates no rule books or manuals sufficiently concrete to constrain the front-line prosecutor's

---

12. American Bar Assn. Standards: The Prosecution Function §3-3.9(b) (3d ed. 1993).
13. Standards for Criminal Justice: Prosecution Function §3-5.6(d) (Proposed Revisions 2009).
14. See U.S. Attorney's Manual, Principles of Federal Prosecution, available online at http://www.usdoj.gov/usao/eousa/foia_reading_room/usam/title9/27mcrm.htm.

discretion to do whatever she thinks best. What are the advantages and disadvantages of establishing detailed standards in advance?

When a prosecutor's office has established detailed charging guidelines, as many scholars recommend, should it then make those guidelines available to the general public and the defense bar? Will publication allow wrongdoers to exploit loopholes? But without publication, can consistency and political accountability be achieved? For a discussion, see Norman Abrams, Internal Policy: Guiding the Exercise of Prosecutorial Discretion, 19 UCLA L. Rev. 1, 34 (1971).

These issues arose recently in Britain when a woman asked the Director of Public Prosecutions whether the prosecutor would bring charges against the woman's husband if he helped her travel to Switzerland for physician-assisted suicide (which is permitted there). The Director declined to answer, but the House of Lords ordered the Director to provide guidance on his "general approach towards the exercise of his discretion regarding the prosecution of this most sensitive and distressing class of cases." Regina (Purdy) v. Director of Public Prosecutions, [2009] UKHL 45, 76. The Director did so, after first submitting a draft policy for public comment. See supra page 919 for a description of the final policy statement.

Questions: Should courts in the United States similarly require prosecutors to provide guidance in advance when the scope of a law is unclear? Is the case of assisted suicide and end-of-life decision making unique, or is the need for advance planning and notice sufficiently strong in other situations as well? Is there excessive risk of evasion in the case of assisted suicide, or is that danger outweighed by the rights at stake? Regardless of whether the ultimate guidelines are published, is obtaining public comment on enforcement policies a good idea for prosecutors?

3. Federal versus state prosecution. The last factor mentioned in the ABA Standards—the likelihood of prosecution in another jurisdiction—is especially important for federal prosecutors, because many of the most important federal crimes (drug distribution, firearms offenses, bank robbery, and mail fraud) also can be charged as state crimes and prosecuted by local district attorneys. State penalties, however, typically are much lower. Indeed, the decision to bring a federal case is often driven by the desire to obtain a longer sentence than could be obtained in state court. Rachel E. Barkow, Federalism and Criminal Law: What the Feds Can Learn from the States, 109 Mich. L. Rev. 519, 573-578 (2011). As a result, the decision to refer a case for state rather than federal prosecution can be as significant as the decision whether to prosecute the case at all. See Daniel C. Richman, Federal Criminal Law, Congressional Delegation, and Enforcement Discretion, 46 UCLA L. Rev. 757 (1999). Should there be formal criteria to determine when federal prosecutors take the lead in cases of overlapping federal/state crimes? Is the difference in punishment an appropriate basis for federal jurisdiction? What should be done to ensure that any criteria established are consistently applied? The important issue of potential racial bias in the decision to charge a federal rather than a state crime is explored in connection with *United States v. Armstrong*, page 1126 infra.

4. Internal review. In several prosecutors' offices, supervisors systematically review the charging recommendations of front-line prosecutors. See, e.g., Wright & Miller, supra. In most, however, the charging decision is left to the assistant district attorney assigned to the case. Although these front-line prosecutors are often inexperienced, supervisory review of their charging recommendations is typically perfunctory or nonexistent. This tradition seems to have developed without much conscious thought about its merits. One senior federal prosecutor claimed that his "office cannot hire excellent attorneys unless they are granted unfettered control over their cases." See Stephen J. Schulhofer & Ilene H. Nagel, Plea Negotiations under the Federal Sentencing Guidelines, 91 Nw. U. L. Rev. 1284, 1295 (1997). Another—more plausible—explanation may simply be that supervisory review takes time. The charging decision is only the first step in a potentially lengthy process of examining and reexamining a case. Does the initial charging decision, by itself, have implications sufficiently important to justify the resources required for a systematic process of review? If the prosecutor making the charging decision also investigated the case, can she objectively review the evidence? One observer argues that the potential for bias is strong.[15] In offices that keep good data on dismissals, prosecutors might be able to track potential areas of racial bias. Consider Marc L. Miller & Ronald F. Wright, The Black Box, 94 Iowa L. Rev. 125, 165 (2008):

> [A] well-functioning data-management system in a prosecutor's office allows a manager to run reports for sub-areas of crimes. Based on these reports, managers can note racial patterns in particular crime areas, diagnose the point in the office process where the racial gap appears, and then consult reasons listed to get a sharper picture of what might be creating the pattern. The objective is not to find some individual line prosecutor who is intentionally or unintentionally biased. Instead, the manager aims to uncover practices built into the system—into the articulated and unspoken priorities and habits of the office—that turn out to have a racial impact.

5. Independent checks. Should some institution independent of the prosecution have power to ensure that charging decisions in fact conform to applicable office guidelines and other legitimate charging criteria? Aside from the trial process, there are few additional mechanisms to police prosecutorial overreaching or misconduct in bringing charges. State bars almost never impose sanctions, criminal charges are virtually unheard of, even when the prosecutorial misconduct is egregious, and civil suits typically fail because prosecutors enjoy absolute immunity when their misconduct is associated with "the judicial phase of the criminal process." Imbler v. Pachtman, 424 U.S. 409, 430 (1976). As discussed below, selective and vindictive prosecution is similarly difficult to

---

15. See Rachel E. Barkow, Institutional Design and the Policing of Prosecutors: Lessons from Administrative Law, 61 Stan. L. Rev. 869 (2009).

establish. Should the system do more to check against prosecutorial overcharging, or does the trial process provide an adequate check?

What remedies should be available in the opposite situation, where a prosecutor drops a readily provable case or fails to bring charges in the first place? Consider the material that follows.

INMATES OF ATTICA CORRECTIONAL FACILITY v. ROCKEFELLER

United States Court of Appeals, 2d Circuit
477 F.2d 375 (1973)

MANSFIELD, J.: [Plaintiffs] are certain present and former inmates of New York State's Attica Correctional Facility ("Attica") [and] the mother of an inmate who was killed when Attica was retaken after the inmate uprising in September 1971.... The complaint alleges that before, during, and after the prisoner revolt ... [which resulted in the killing of 29 inmates and 10 civilians who were held hostage by the inmates, as well as the wounding of many others] the defendants, including the Governor of New York, the State Commissioner of Correctional Services, ... and other officials, either committed, conspired to commit, or aided and abetted in the commission of various crimes against the complaining inmates.... It is charged [that] State Police, Troopers, and Correction Officers ... intentionally killed some of the inmate victims without provocation during the recovery of Attica, that state officers ... assaulted and beat prisoners after the prison had been successfully retaken ... and that medical assistance was maliciously denied to over 400 inmates wounded during the recovery of the prison.

The complaint further alleges that [a Deputy State Attorney General specially appointed by the Governor] to investigate [these crimes] "has not investigated, nor does he intend to investigate, any crimes committed by state officers." ... With respect to the sole federal defendant, the United States Attorney for the Western District of New York, the complaint simply alleges that he has not arrested, investigated, or instituted prosecutions against any of the state officers accused of criminal violation of plaintiffs' federal civil rights.... [P]laintiffs request relief in the nature of mandamus (1) against state officials, requiring the State of New York to submit a plan for the independent and impartial investigation and prosecution of the offenses charged ... and (2) against the United States Attorney, requiring him to investigate, arrest and prosecute the same state officers for having committed the federal offenses....

The motions of the federal and state defendants to dismiss the complaint [were granted by the court below]....

[W]e believe that even if [the plaintiffs] may properly present their claims for judicial resolution, they seek relief which cannot, in this case at least, be granted either against the state or federal prosecuting authorities.

With respect to the defendant United States Attorney, plaintiffs seek mandamus to compel him to investigate and institute prosecutions against state officers. . . . Federal mandamus is, of course, available only "to compel an officer or employee of the United States . . . to perform a duty owed to the plaintiff." 28 U.S.C. §1361. And [federal courts have] uniformly refrained from overturning, at the instance of a private person, discretionary decisions of federal prosecuting authorities not to prosecute persons regarding whom a complaint of criminal conduct is made. This judicial reluctance to direct federal prosecutions at the instance of a private party . . . has been applied even in cases such as the present one where . . . serious questions are raised as to the protection of the civil rights and physical security of a definable class of victims. . . .

The primary ground upon which this traditional judicial aversion to compelling prosecutions has been based is the separation of powers doctrine. . . . Although a leading commentator has criticized this [doctrine as] incompatible with the normal function of the judiciary in reviewing for abuse or arbitrariness administrative acts that fall within the discretion of executive officers, K.C. Davis, Administrative Law Treatise §28.16(4) at 982-990 (1970 Supp.), he has also recognized . . . that the manifold imponderables which enter into the prosecutor's decision to prosecute or not to prosecute make the choice not readily amenable to judicial supervision.

In the absence of statutorily defined standards, . . . the problems inherent in the task of supervising prosecutorial decisions do not lend themselves to resolution by the judiciary. . . . In the normal case of review of executive acts of discretion, the administrative record is open, public and reviewable on the basis of what it contains. The decision not to prosecute, on the other hand, may be based upon the insufficiency of the available evidence, in which event the secrecy of the grand jury and of the prosecutor's file may serve to protect the accused's reputation from public damage based upon insufficient, improper, or even malicious charges. [R]eview would not be meaningful without access by the complaining party to the evidence before the grand jury or U.S. Attorney. . . . Any person, merely by filing a complaint [alleging] unlawful failure to prosecute, could gain access to the prosecutor's file and the grand jury's minutes, notwithstanding the secrecy normally attaching to the latter by law.

Nor is it clear what the judiciary's role of supervision should be were it to undertake such a review. At what point would the prosecutor be entitled to call a halt to further investigation as unlikely to be productive? . . . How much judgment would the United States Attorney be allowed? . . . With limited personnel and facilities at his disposal, what priority would the prosecutor be required to give to cases in which investigation or prosecution was directed by the court? . . . On balance, we believe that substitution of a court's decision to compel prosecution for the U.S. Attorney's decision not to prosecute, even upon an abuse of discretion standard of review and even if limited to directing that a prosecution be undertaken in good faith, would be unwise.

Plaintiffs urge, however, that Congress withdrew the normal prosecutorial discretion for the kind of conduct alleged here by providing in 42 U.S.C. §1987 that the United States Attorneys are "authorized and *required* . . . to institute prosecutions against all persons violating any of [the criminal statutes protecting civil rights]" (emphasis supplied). . . . This contention must be rejected. The mandatory nature of the word "required" as it appears in §1987 is insufficient to evince a broad Congressional purpose to bar the exercise of executive discretion in the prosecution of federal civil rights crimes. Similar mandatory language is contained in [many statutes]. Such language has never been thought to preclude the exercise of prosecutorial discretion. . . .

With respect to the state defendants, plaintiffs . . . have pointed to no statutory language even arguably creating any mandatory duty upon the state officials to bring such prosecutions. To the contrary, New York law reposes in its prosecutors a discretion to decide whether or not to prosecute in a given case, which is not subject to review in the state courts. . . . The serious charge that the state's investigation is proceeding against inmates but not against state officers, if shown to be accurate, might lead the Governor to supplement or replace those presently in charge of the investigation. . . . But the gravity of the allegation does not reduce the inherent judicial incapacity to supervise. . . .

The order of the district court is affirmed.

NOTES ON CHECKING THE DECISION NOT TO PROSECUTE

1. Special prosecutors. The Attica circumstances involved at least the appearance of a potential conflict of interest, with respect to state prosecutors, because they are part of the same government as the corrections officers who were being investigated. This is not unusual: In many cases, an actual or perceived conflict of interest might give one reason to doubt whether a prosecutor can make a fair assessment of whether to bring charges because the prospective defendant is a government employee or has some other connection to the prosecutor's office. At the federal level, the Ethics in Government Act was passed to deal with this situation by allowing a panel of three federal judges to appoint a special prosecutor (known as the "Independent Counsel") to pursue charges against high officials of the federal executive branch, with guarantees against interference or control by the attorney general.[16] In Morrison v. Olson, 487 U.S. 654 (1988), the Supreme Court upheld the constitutionality of this regime. The Act lapsed in 1999, and there is currently no federal statute requiring the appointment of a special prosecutor in high-profile political cases. The attorney general nonetheless retains, and on occasion has exercised, the discretion to appoint a special prosecutor, outside the ordinary Justice Department chain of command, to handle politically sensitive cases, such as the investigation and 2005 indictment on perjury and obstruction-of-justice charges of former vice presidential chief of staff Lewis Libby.

In many states, the law permits the governor or state attorney general to appoint a special prosecutor to assume responsibility when a case is especially

---

16. See Independent Counsel Reauthorization Act of 1994, 28 U.S.C. §§591-599 (1994).

complicated or when the local district attorney faces a conflict of interest (as, for example, when serious criminal allegations are made against the district attorney's child or spouse). Such situations present no separation-of-powers problems, however, because the special prosecutor remains an official of the executive branch, with discretion not to file charges, even when strong evidence is available to sustain them; the *Attica* case itself was an effort to compel prosecution in a case under the responsibility of a special prosecutor.

2. *Prosecutions initiated by judges and victims.* American courts have uniformly held that separation-of-powers requirements prohibit judges from compelling an unwilling prosecutor to file charges. A Wisconsin statute, for example, provided that if a judge finds probable cause to believe that an individual has committed an offense and the district attorney nonetheless refuses to file a complaint, the judge can direct the commencement of a prosecution. The statute was tested in State ex rel. Unnamed Petitioners v. Connors, 401 N.W.2d 782 (Wis. 1987), where a female dancer alleged that she had been assaulted by two professional football players in her dressing room at a Milwaukee night club. When the prosecutor acknowledged the existence of probable cause but refused to proceed, because he had doubts about his ability to win convictions at trial, a circuit judge invoked the statute and ordered the prosecution to go forward. The Wisconsin Supreme Court reversed, holding that the statute violated the separation-of-powers requirements of the state constitution.

Private prosecution, like the judge-initiated prosecution in *Connors*, supra, likewise violates American separation-of-powers principles. People v. Municipal Court, 103 Cal. Rptr. 645 (Ct. App. 1972). The Supreme Court of South Carolina in In re Richland County Magistrate's Court, 389 S.C. 408, 412 (2010), offers additional functional arguments against the practice:

> If a private party is permitted to prosecute a criminal action, we can no longer be assured that the powers of the State are employed only for the interest of the community at large. In fact, we can be absolutely certain that the interests of the private party will influence the prosecution, whether the self-interest lies in encouraging payment of a . . . debt, influencing settlement in a civil suit, or merely seeking vengeance.

In contrast, in Great Britain and in many countries of continental Europe, a private person can initiate a criminal prosecution, become a formal party, or retain counsel to prosecute the case on her own behalf. See Carsten Stahn, Héctor Olásolo & Kate Gibson, Participation of Victims in Pre-Trial Proceedings of the ICC, 4 J. Int'l Crim. Just. 219, 220 (2006).

Despite the formal prohibition on private prosecutions in the United States, Roger Fairfax documents the many ways in which prosecution has been "outsourced" to private actors, including state contracts with private attorneys to bring prosecutions, part-time prosecutors who maintain a private practice on the side, and victim-funded prosecutions. Roger A. Fairfax, Jr., The Delegation of the Criminal Prosecution Function to Private Actors, 43 U.C. Davis L. Rev. 411, 416-444 (2009).

Questions: (a) Would granting the victims of serious crimes a formal right to compel prosecution (when there is sufficient legally admissible evidence) give victims undue control over the prosecutor's resource-allocation decisions and result in less effective law enforcement? Or would such a right tend to correct resource allocation decisions that disfavor minorities and other disadvantaged groups? How could we ensure that, in practice, victims' rights of this sort do not serve merely to enhance the leverage of groups that may already have disproportionate influence?

(b) Granting victims a right to compel prosecution could lead to much more common use of the very long prison sentences attached to the highest grades of many offenses. Would that outcome represent progress, in the sense that the legislative will was being more fully respected? Or would society consider the results intolerable, because it does not really intend for such sentences to be imposed on a regular basis? Are victims well placed to make those decisions in individual cases?

3. Victim participation in the prosecutor's charging decision. Every American jurisdiction grants victims a right to be kept informed about the course of the investigation and to discuss the case with the prosecutor. The federal statute, the Crime Victims' Rights Act of 2004, is typical. It provides victims with the right to notice of hearings, the right to attend those hearings, and a "reasonable right to confer with the attorney for the Government," 18 U.S.C. §3771(a) (2005); Paul G. Cassell, Protecting Crime Victims in Federal Appellate Courts: The Need to Broadly Construe the Crime Victims' Rights Act's Mandamus Provision, 87 Denv. U. L. Rev. 599 (2010). But victims cannot control or challenge the charging decision, a limitation that exists in state victims' rights statutes as well. Gansz v. People, 888 P.2d 256, 257 (Colo. 1995). Courts typically stress that the victim's individual interest in "safety and redress" must be subordinate to "the effective and efficient administration of law enforcement." Dix v. Superior Court, 807 P.2d 1063, 1067 (Cal. 1991). One observer asks why victims should play a large role in charging decisions when they "would be instantly disqualified from serving on the defendant's jury."[17] But if victims are given only the right to confer, will that serve as an effective means of checking the prosecutor's charging discretion, or are there reasons prosecutors may not sufficiently take victims' concerns into account? See Erin Ann O'Hara, Victim Participation in the Criminal Process, 13 J.L. & Pol'y 229, 233 (2005).

Questions: How could states ensure that the victim's right to participate is not reduced to a mere formality? Would efforts to strengthen the right to participate in practice prevent prosecutors from setting different but justified priorities and leave victims with *too much* influence?

---

17. See Stephen J. Schulhofer, The Trouble with Trials; The Trouble with Us, 105 Yale L.J. 825, 847 (1995).

4. *Domestic violence cases.* Domestic violence has posed a distinctive set of challenges. Until the 1980s, many police departments discouraged officers from making arrests in such cases and as a result, prosecutors seldom had to deal with them. In response to widespread concern that this approach was dangerous to women, police departments began to encourage or mandate an arrest, and some district attorneys' offices adopted policies to encourage or mandate the filing of charges. The traditional problem—excessive use of the discretion not to prosecute—was largely erased.

Concerns began to emerge, however, about whether victims were now being hurt by the opposite problem—*over*enforcement. See Stephen J. Schulhofer, The Feminist Challenge in Criminal Law, 143 U. Pa. L. Rev. 2151, 2158-2170 (1995). Mandatory arrest and "no-drop" prosecution policies typically require that charges must be pursued even without the victim's consent, because of the danger that a battered woman, succumbing to intimidation, might (against her own real desires or interests) tell officials that she was opposed to the arrest or prosecution of her abuser. Although some studies suggest that mandatory arrest and prosecution deters batterers more effectively than discretionary policies do, other evidence suggests the reverse—that mandatory policies deter calls for help by women more than they deter violence by men, and that such policies may even aggravate subsequent violence by some types of defendants. (We consider this problem in more detail in connection with our discussion of battered woman's syndrome, at page 832 supra.)

There continues to be a broad consensus that prosecutors should press charges when the domestic violence victim supports this step. But when the victim opposes prosecution or simply fails to cooperate, prosecutors disagree over whether they should respect the victim's wishes or press charges anyway. Some victims' advocates protest that the legal system endangers and in effect re-victimizes the battered woman if it fails to respect the victim's own sense of what would be best for her. See, e.g., Linda G. Mills, Killing Her Softly: Intimate Abuse and the Violence of State Intervention, 113 Harv. L. Rev. 550 (1999). Many argue that the better approach is to provide social services to victims and to pay greater attention to victims' wishes about criminal prosecution in order to get victims to trust the system and therefore cooperate with law enforcement in future cases. See, e.g., Laurie S. Kohn, The Justice System and Domestic Violence: Engaging the Case but Divorcing the Victim, 32 N.Y.U. Rev. L. & Soc. Change 191, 246-249 (2008). Others argue that a successful attack on domestic violence requires mandatory prosecution, and that "leaving the choice of prosecution to the victim . . . creates more problems than it solves." Cheryl Hanna, No Right to Choose: Mandated Victim Participation in Domestic Violence Prosecutions, 109 Harv. L. Rev. 1848, 1909 (1996).

The possibly distinctive features of violence in intimate relationships make the relevance of victim preferences for prosecutorial discretion especially complex. But domestic violence cases also illustrate a more general problem: As the person most affected by a criminal offense, should the victim who desires leniency be given a decisive voice? Or are there substantial public interests that can justify prosecution even when the victim, after careful thought, decides that she prefers otherwise?

5. *Victimless crimes.* If victim participation provides a valuable safeguard against misguided prosecutorial priorities or "selective indifference" to the concerns of particular groups, what safeguards can serve this function in the case of so-called victimless crimes? Drug cases represent a substantial segment of the workload in most prosecutors' offices, and concerns about discriminatory patterns of investigation and enforcement are probably more prominent in this area than in any other. What mechanisms should be available to prevent the abuse of discretion in the large volume of selective judgments that prosecutors inevitably must make with respect to drug crimes?

NOTES ON "COMPULSORY" PROSECUTION IN EUROPE

1. Absent special circumstances, prosecutors in many European countries are required to file and pursue all charges for which there is evidence sufficient to support a conviction. The European prosecutor does have discretion, but that discretion is typically limited by statute and subject to judicial oversight. When a prosecuting attorney decides not to prosecute, he must give a written explanation for his action and obtain approval of his superior. Regina E. Rauxloh, Formalization of Plea Bargaining in Germany: Will The New Legislation Be Able To Square the Circle, 34 Fordham Int'l L.J. 296 (2011). Most decisions to forgo prosecution are subject to judicial review in Europe. See Joachim Herrman, Bargaining Justice—A Bargain for German Criminal Justice, 53 U. Pitt. L. Rev. 755 (1995). Some observers doubt that judicial review imposes truly significant constraints. See id. at 759 ("a judge consents as a matter of course"). Nonetheless, such review, even if a mere formality, provides a degree of accountability unknown in American criminal justice. In addition, aggrieved victims have standing to file a mandamus action that serves to compel prosecution when a dismissal is found to be unwarranted. See Richard S. Frase & Thomas Weigend, German Criminal Justice as a Guide to American Law Reform, 18 B.C. Int'l & Comp. L. Rev. 317, 338 (1995).

2. M.C. v. Bulgaria, [2003] ECHR 39272/98 (Eur. Ct. Hum. Rts.), illustrates common European practice. A prosecutor initially rebuffed a date-rape victim's efforts to press criminal charges. She then lodged a formal objection that required prosecutors to reopen the investigation. After more evidence was gathered, the local prosecutor decided that criminal charges were not warranted, but he was required to support this conclusion by a written opinion, which the victim then appealed to higher levels within the supervising state prosecutor's office. Senior prosecutors concurred in the initial decision, supporting their views in two lengthy written opinions. Those opinions, in turn, formed the basis of the victim's complaint to the European Court of

Human Rights, which held that the prosecutors' restrictive interpretation of their rape law, and their failure to go forward with a criminal prosecution, violated the victim's right to protection of her bodily integrity, as guaranteed by the European Convention on Human Rights. That procedural background and the substantive rape law issues raised by the case are considered in detail in Chapter 4, page 369 supra.

Questions: What social and systemic factors might make broad prosecutorial discretion not to charge more (or less) justifiable in the United States than in Europe? In proportion to caseloads, the resources available to the European prosecutor are greater than those available to American state prosecutors, but not significantly greater than those available to U.S. federal prosecutors. The resource constraint arguably makes charging discretion more necessary in American states than in Europe, though of course states and localities *choose* the level of funding they provide to their prosecutors and courts. Another contrast is that sentences authorized or mandated are far more severe in America than in Europe. And whereas European prosecutors tend to be professional bureaucrats with extensive training and merit-based selection on the basis of competitive national exams, American prosecutors in charge of offices are typically elected, and "cannot count on promotion within a bureaucratic hierarchy . . . [t]hus prosecutors with experience in white collar crimes often enter private practice . . . and others run for [other] political office[s]." Geraldine Szott Moohr, Prosecutorial Power in an Adversary System: Lessons from Current White Collar Cases and the Inquisitorial Model, 8 Buff. Crim. L. Rev. 165, 194-196 (2004). Do these factors make it more desirable—or less desirable—for prosecutors in America to have broad discretion not to pursue legally provable cases?

NOTE ON SELECTIVE PROSECUTION

When a prosecutor decides to file charges, our system of criminal procedure provides checks (both prior to and during any trial) to ensure that there is sufficient evidence of guilt. What safeguards should be available to the defendant who cannot dispute the sufficiency of the evidence but claims that he or she was unfairly singled out for prosecution? While serving as attorney general of the United States, Robert H. Jackson, later a justice of the Supreme Court, observed (Jackson, The Federal Prosecutor, 31 J. Crim. L. Criminology & Police Sci. 3, 5 (1940)):

> With the law books filled with a great assortment of crimes, a prosecutor stands a fair chance of finding at least a technical violation of some [statute] on the part of almost anyone. In such a case, it is not a question of discovering the commission of a crime and then looking for the man who has committed it, it is a question of picking the man and then searching the law books, or putting investigators to work, to pin some offense on him. It is in this realm—in which the prosecutor picks some person whom he dislikes or desires to embarrass, or

selects some group of unpopular persons and then looks for an offense, that the greatest danger of abuse of prosecuting power lies.

Although courts cannot be asked (as in *Attica*, page 1118 supra) to compel a prosecution, they clearly have the power to dismiss one. The following case considers problems that arise even when the prosecutor's decision allegedly was based on a clearly impermissible consideration, such as race.

UNITED STATES v. ARMSTRONG

Supreme Court of the United States
517 U.S. 456 (1996)

CHIEF JUSTICE REHNQUIST delivered the opinion of the Court. . . .

In April 1992, respondents were indicted in [federal court] on charges of conspiring to possess with intent to distribute more than 50 grams of cocaine base (crack) . . . and federal firearms offenses. [Informants for federal and state agents] had bought a total of 124.3 grams of crack from respondents and witnessed respondents carrying firearms during the sales. [Agents seized crack and a loaded gun from the hotel room in which the sales were transacted and arrested respondents Armstrong and Hampton.]

[R]espondents filed a motion for discovery or for dismissal of the indictment, alleging that they were selected for federal prosecution because they are black. In support . . . they offered only an affidavit by a "Paralegal Specialist," employed by the Office of the Federal Public Defender representing one of the respondents. The only allegation in the affidavit was that, in every one of the 24 [drug] cases closed by the office during 1991, the defendant was black. Accompanying the affidavit was a "study" listing the 24 defendants, their race, whether they were prosecuted for dealing cocaine as well as crack, and the status of each case. . . .

The District Court . . . ordered the Government (1) to provide a list of all cases from the last three years in which the Government charged both cocaine and firearms offenses, (2) to identify the race of the defendants in those cases, (3) to identify what [state and federal agencies] were involved in the investigations of those cases, and (4) to explain its criteria for deciding to prosecute those defendants for federal cocaine offenses.

The Government moved for reconsideration of the District Court's discovery order. [I]t submitted affidavits and other evidence to explain why it had chosen to prosecute respondents and why respondents' study did not support the inference that the Government was singling out blacks for cocaine prosecution. . . . An Assistant United States Attorney explained in an affidavit that the decision to prosecute met the general criteria for prosecution, because "there was over 100 grams of cocaine base involved, over twice the threshold necessary for a ten year mandatory minimum sentence; there were multiple sales involving multiple defendants, thereby indicating a fairly substantial crack cocaine ring; . . . there were multiple federal firearms violations intertwined with the narcotics trafficking; the overall evidence in the case was extremely strong, including audio and videotapes of defendants; . . . and several of the defendants had criminal histories including narcotics and firearms violations." The Government also submitted sections of a published 1989 Drug Enforcement Administration report which concluded that "large-scale, interstate trafficking networks controlled by Jamaicans, Haitians and Black street gangs dominate the manufacture and distribution of crack."

In response, one of respondents' attorneys submitted an affidavit alleging that an intake coordinator at a drug treatment center had told her that there are "an equal number of caucasian users and dealers to minority users and dealers." Respondents also submitted an affidavit from a criminal defense attorney alleging that in his experience many nonblacks are prosecuted in state court for crack offenses, and a newspaper article reporting that federal "crack criminals . . . are being punished far more severely than if they had been caught with powder cocaine, and almost every single one of them is black."

The District Court denied the motion for reconsideration [of its discovery order]. When the Government indicated it would not comply with [that] order, the court dismissed the case. [The Court of Appeals for the Ninth Circuit affirmed.] We granted certiorari to determine the appropriate standard for discovery for a selective-prosecution claim. . . .

Our cases delineating the necessary elements to prove [such a claim] have taken great pains to explain that the standard is a demanding one. [T]he showing necessary to obtain discovery should itself be a significant barrier to the litigation of insubstantial claims.

A selective-prosecution claim asks a court to exercise judicial power over a "special province" of the Executive. The Attorney General and United States Attorneys . . . are designated by statute as the President's delegates to help him discharge his constitutional responsibility to "take Care that the Laws be faithfully executed." U.S. Const., Art. II, §3. As a result, . . . "in the absence of clear evidence to the contrary, courts presume that they have properly discharged their official duties." . . .

Judicial deference to the decisions of these executive officers rests in part on an assessment of the relative competence of prosecutors and courts. "Such factors as the strength of the case, the prosecution's general deterrence value, the Government's enforcement priorities, and the case's relationship to the Government's overall enforcement plan are not readily susceptible to the kind of analysis the courts are competent to undertake." It also stems from a concern not to unnecessarily impair the performance of a core executive constitutional function. "Examining the basis of a prosecution delays the criminal proceeding, threatens to chill law enforcement by subjecting the prosecutor's motives and decisionmaking to outside inquiry, and may undermine prosecutorial effectiveness by revealing the Government's enforcement policy."

The requirements for a selective-prosecution claim draw on "ordinary equal protection standards." The claimant must demonstrate that the federal prosecutorial policy "had a discriminatory effect and that it was motivated by a discriminatory purpose." To establish a discriminatory effect in a race case, the claimant must show that similarly situated individuals of a different race were not prosecuted. . . .

[W]e turn to the showing necessary to obtain discovery in support of such a claim. If discovery is ordered, the Government must assemble from its own files documents which might corroborate or refute the defendant's claim. . . . It will divert prosecutors' resources and may disclose the Government's prosecutorial strategy. The justifications for a rigorous standard for the elements of a selective-prosecution claim thus require a correspondingly rigorous standard for discovery in aid of such a claim. . . .

The vast majority of the Courts of Appeals require the defendant to produce some evidence that similarly situated defendants of other races could have been prosecuted, but were not. . . . The Court of Appeals [in this case] reached its decision [to the contrary] in part because it started "with the presumption that people of all races commit all types of crimes—not with the premise that any type of crime is the exclusive province of any particular racial or ethnic group." It cited no authority for this proposition, which seems contradicted by the most recent statistics of the United States Sentencing Commission. . . . More than 90% of the persons sentenced in 1994 for crack cocaine trafficking were black, 93.4% of convicted LSD dealers were white, and 91% of those convicted for pornography or prostitution were white. . . .

The Court of Appeals also expressed concern about the "evidentiary obstacles defendants face." But . . . if the claim of selective prosecution were well founded, it should not have been an insuperable task to prove that persons of other races were being treated differently. . . . [R]espondents could have investigated whether similarly situated persons of other races were prosecuted by the State of California and were known to federal law enforcement officers, but were not prosecuted in federal court. We think the required threshold—a credible showing of different treatment of similarly situated persons—adequately balances the Government's interest in vigorous prosecution and the defendant's interest in avoiding selective prosecution.

[R]espondents' "study" did not constitute "some evidence." . . . The study failed to identify individuals who were not black and could have been prosecuted. . . . The newspaper article, which discussed the discriminatory effect of federal drug sentencing laws, was not relevant to an allegation of discrimination in decisions to prosecute. Respondents' affidavits, which recounted one attorney's conversation with a drug treatment center employee and the experience of another attorney defending drug prosecutions in state court, recounted hearsay and reported personal conclusions based on anecdotal evidence. The judgment of the Court of Appeals is therefore reversed. . . .

JUSTICE STEVENS, dissenting. . . .

The District Judge's order should be evaluated in light of three circumstances that underscore the need for judicial vigilance over certain types of drug prosecutions. First, the Anti-Drug Abuse Act of 1986 and subsequent legislation established a regime of extremely high penalties for the possession and distribution of so-called "crack" cocaine. Those provisions treat one gram of crack as the equivalent of 100 grams of powder cocaine. . . . These penalties result in sentences for crack offenders that average three to eight times longer than sentences for comparable powder offenders.

Second, the disparity between the treatment of crack cocaine and powder cocaine is matched by the disparity between the severity of the punishment imposed by federal law and that imposed by state law for the same conduct. . . . For example, if respondent Hampton is found guilty, his federal sentence might be as long as a mandatory life term. Had he been tried in state court, his sentence could have been as short as 12 years, less worktime credits of half that amount.

Finally, it is undisputed that the brunt of the elevated federal penalties falls heavily on blacks. While 65% of the persons who have used crack are white, in 1993 they represented only 4% of the federal offenders convicted of trafficking in crack. Eighty-eight percent of such defendants were black. . . . The Sentencing Commission acknowledges that the heightened crack penalties are a "primary cause of the growing disparity between sentences for Black and White federal defendants."

The extraordinary severity of the imposed penalties and the troubling racial patterns of enforcement give rise to a special concern about the fairness of charging practices for crack offenses. [T]he District Judge . . . acted well within her discretion to call for the development of facts that would demonstrate what standards, if any, governed the choice of forum where similarly situated offenders are prosecuted. . . .

The majority discounts the probative value of [respondents'] affidavits, claiming that they recounted "hearsay." . . . But the [affidavit of defense attorney] Reed offered information based on his own extensive experience in both federal and state courts. . . . The criticism that the affidavits were based on "anecdotal evidence" is also unpersuasive. [D]efendants do not need to prepare sophisticated statistical studies in order to receive mere discovery in cases like this one. Certainly evidence based on a drug counselor's personal observations or on an attorney's practice in two sets of courts, state and federal, can "tend to show the existence" of a selective prosecution.

Even if respondents failed to carry their burden of showing that there were individuals who were not black but who could have been prosecuted in federal court for the same offenses, it does not follow that the District Court abused its discretion in ordering discovery. There can be no doubt that such individuals exist, and indeed the Government has never denied the same. . . . I fail to see why the District Court was unable to take judicial notice of this obvious fact and demand information from the Government's files to support or refute respondents' evidence. The presumption that some whites are prosecuted in state court is not "contradicted" by the statistics the majority cites, which show only that high percentages of blacks are convicted of certain federal crimes, while high percentages of whites are convicted of other federal crimes. Those figures are entirely consistent with the allegation of selective prosecution. . . . The District Court, therefore, was entitled to find the evidence before her significant and to require some explanation from the Government.[6] . . .

Pamela Karlan, Race, Rights, and Remedies in Criminal Adjudication, 96 Mich. L. Rev. 2001, 2023-2025 (1998): When it comes to suspect classes [like race], the Court generally rejects stereotypes whether or not they are true. The very act of stereotyping is constitutionally illegitimate. . . . By contrast, when it came to "the presumption that people of all races commit all types of crimes," . . . the Court [in *Armstrong*] took precisely the opposite tack. Relying on a somewhat circular set of statistics that showed that more than ninety percent of the defendants sentenced for crack-related offenses were black, it declared that "presumptions at war with presumably reliable statistics have no proper place in the analysis of this issue." [In no other area is the Court] prepared to assume, based on ambiguous statistics, that blacks and whites differ in a legally cognizable way. That the Court adopts such a position here illustrates a broader point. . . . Whatever the Court says about its commitment to ridding the criminal justice process of racial discrimination, it is in fact quite skeptical that this can be done, at least at an acceptable social cost. [T]he Court tacitly accepts the level of disparate impact that discretion seems to produce.

NOTES AND QUESTIONS

1. Disparate patterns. In *Armstrong*, the lower courts inferred a pattern of discriminatory enforcement based on two factual assumptions—that both whites and blacks were committing crack offenses and that only the blacks were being prosecuted in federal court. Which of these alleged facts does the Supreme Court seem to question? Does the Court consider it possible that significant numbers of whites *were* being prosecuted in federal court, or does the Court believe that no significant numbers of whites were committing crack offenses? Note the statistics cited by the Court—that more than 90 percent of those convicted on federal crack charges were black,[18] while 93 percent of those convicted on federal LSD charges were white. The Court concludes that these statistics contradict the lower courts' assumption that whites are also committing crack cocaine offenses. Do they? Under what circumstances would these statistics be *irrelevant* to the lower courts' analysis?

---

6. Also telling was the Government's response to respondents' evidentiary showing. [It] offered the names of 11 nonblack defendants whom it had prosecuted for crack offenses. All 11, however, were members of other racial or ethnic minorities. The District Court was authorized to draw adverse inferences from the Government's inability to produce a single example of a white defendant, especially when the very purpose of its exercise was to allay the Court's concerns about the evidence of racially selective prosecutions. As another court has said: "Statistics are not, of course, the whole answer, but nothing is as emphatic as zero. . . ."

18. The 90 percent figure technically refers to those sentenced on crack charges, but for this purpose there is no significant difference between the percentage of those convicted and the percentage of those sentenced.

2. Armstrong's *impact*. Does *Armstrong* pose a significant barrier to obtaining discovery in aid of a selective prosecution claim? The Court says that in order to establish the prima facie case of discrimination required to get discovery, a complainant must offer evidence that "similarly situated persons of other races were prosecuted by the State of California and were known to federal law enforcement officers, but were not prosecuted in federal court." But evidence of unprosecuted violations is difficult to obtain without access to government files, since these violations often occur in private and cannot be uncovered without police work. Richard H. McAdams, Race and Selective Prosecution, Discovering the Pitfalls of Armstrong, 73 Chi.-Kent L. Rev. 605, 618-623 (1998). And courts have held that providing one or two cases where someone of a different race was treated differently is not sufficient to establish the prima facie case.

In addition, courts seem to interpret the "similarly situated" language to require defendants to identify uncharged individuals who are virtually identical to themselves. Consider the facts in United States v. Lewis, 517 F.3d 20 (1st Cir. 2008), involving a defendant charged with false statements on a federal firearms application. Lewis sought discovery to demonstrate that he was singled out for prosecution because he is African American and Muslim. To meet the threshold for discovery, Lewis "introduced a series of analyses showing that over a three-year period no one else [who had no prior record] had been prosecuted in the District of Massachusetts for a weapons-related offense as picayune as misstating an address on a federal firearms application. [He argued] that statistical probability indicates that while white non-Muslims quite probably have committed such minor infractions, they have not been prosecuted." Id. at 26. The appellate court affirmed the trial court's decision that the "pool of offenders situated similarly to the defendant consisted of non-African-Americans and/or non-Muslims who had committed multiple misrepresentation offenses in connection with firearms paperwork, who posed a danger of violence, and who may have had links to terrorism." Was this an appropriate way to define the pool? Or did the court set the bar too high?

3. *The federalism issue*. The selective prosecution claim in *Armstrong* is atypical in a sense, because the complaint is not that white defendants are not prosecuted at all, but only that they are prosecuted in state courts, where penalties generally are lower. What considerations and what features of a case should legitimately affect the federal prosecutor's judgment about whether federal rather than state prosecution is appropriate? See pages 1116-1117 supra.

4. *The transparency issue*. The immediate goal of the defendants in *Armstrong* was simply to get discovery, in order to reveal the criteria being used to make charging decisions. The Court's approach to that issue was governed by its sense that exposure of such information can be harmful; as a result, the Court insisted, the threshold showing required to obtain such information should be "demanding," so that it will pose "a significant barrier." One could, of course, argue the opposite—that the public would be well served by making such information available on a routine basis, even when no one is alleging an egregious abuse of discretion. Are there good reasons to protect the confidentiality of information about the prosecutor's charging criteria? If so, should such information be protected across the board, or should the public interest in disclosure prevail at least with respect to some aspects of the prosecutor's charging policies?

5. *Crack reform.* The Fair Sentencing Act of 2010, Pub. L. §2, 124 Stat. 2372, reduced the disparity between federal penalties for crack cocaine and powder cocaine offenses from a 100:1 ratio to an 18:1 ratio. The law also eliminated the five-year mandatory minimum for simple possession. Does Congress's passage of this law show that judicial involvement was unnecessary? Or does the long period of time before Congress addressed the issue (more than two decades after the crack/powder disparity was put into place) and the continued disparity in the 18:1 ratio suggest that the political process is a poor outlet for resolving discriminatory effects?

PROBLEM

In highly publicized congressional testimony, Attorney General John Ashcroft proclaimed his intention to use every available means to combat terrorists operating in the United States. He likened his approach to the one Attorney General Robert F. Kennedy used in cracking down on organized crime—tracking terror suspects and arresting them for any offense they commit, no matter how trivial. He said he would prosecute them even for "spitting on the sidewalk."[19]

Should this tactic be considered legitimate? If citizens considered above suspicion are never prosecuted for spitting on the sidewalk, then the only people prosecuted and jailed will be those whom the attorney general suspects of doing or planning something else. Should it matter whether the attorney general can show any basis for his suspicions? Should it matter what penalty is authorized for spitting on the sidewalk? Suppose a state law authorizes a penalty of up to two years in prison for spitting on the sidewalk, jaywalking, or driving even one mile per hour faster than the posted speed limit. When someone happens to violate one of these provisions, is it appropriate to file criminal charges and seek the maximum prison sentence only because a prosecutor suspects the person of more serious wrongdoing? For discussion, see Daniel C. Richman & William J. Stuntz, Al Capone's Revenge: An Essay on the Political Economy of Pretextual Prosecution, 105 Colum. L. Rev. 583 (2005); Harry Litman, Pretextual Prosecution, 92 Geo. L.J. 1135 (2004).

---

19. See "Transforming the Federal Government to Protect America from Terrorism," Hearing Before the H. Select Comm. on Homeland Sec., 107th Cong., 2d Sess. 23-25 (2002) (statement of John Ashcroft).

B. PLEA BARGAINING

BRADY v. UNITED STATES

Supreme Court of the United States
397 U.S. 742 (1970)

Mr. Justice White delivered the opinion of the Court.

In 1959, petitioner was charged with kidnaping in violation of 18 U.S.C. 1201(a). Since the indictment charged that the victim of the kidnaping was not liberated unharmed, petitioner faced a maximum penalty of death if the verdict of the jury should so recommend. Petitioner, represented by competent counsel throughout, first elected to plead not guilty. . . . Upon learning that his codefendant, who had confessed to the authorities, would plead guilty and be available to testify against him, petitioner changed his plea to guilty. His plea was accepted after the trial judge twice questioned him as to the voluntariness of his plea. Petitioner was sentenced to 50 years' imprisonment, later reduced to 30.

[Petitioner sought postconviction relief, claiming that his plea of guilty was not voluntary because he faced the death penalty if he exercised his right to a jury trial. The lower courts denied relief, and the Supreme Court granted certiorari.]

Waivers of constitutional rights not only must be voluntary but must be knowing, intelligent acts done with sufficient awareness of the relevant circumstances and likely consequences. On neither score was Brady's plea of guilty invalid. . . .

The State to some degree encourages pleas of guilty at every important step in the criminal process. . . . [A]pprehension and charge, [or] the post-indictment accumulation of evidence may convince the defendant and his counsel that a trial is not worth the agony and expense to the defendant and his family. All these pleas of guilty are valid in spite of the State's responsibility for some of the factors motivating the pleas. . . .

Of course, the agents of the State may not produce a plea by actual or threatened physical harm or by mental coercion overbearing the will of the defendant. But nothing of the sort is claimed in this case; nor is there evidence that Brady was so gripped by fear of the death penalty or hope of leniency that he did not or could not, with the help of counsel, rationally weigh the advantages of going to trial against the advantages of pleading guilty. Brady's claim is of a different sort: [T]hat a guilty plea is coerced and invalid if influenced by the fear of a possibly higher penalty for the crime charged if a conviction is obtained after the State is put to its proof.

Insofar as the voluntariness of his plea is concerned, there is little to differentiate Brady from (1) the defendant, in a jurisdiction where the judge and jury have the same range of sentencing power, who pleads guilty because his lawyer advises him that the judge will very probably be more lenient than the jury; (2) the defendant, in a jurisdiction where the judge alone has sentencing power, who is advised by counsel that the judge is normally more lenient with defendants who plead guilty than with those who go to trial; (3) the defendant who is permitted by prosecutor and judge to plead guilty to a lesser offense included in the offense charged; and (4) the defendant who pleads guilty to certain counts with the understanding that other charges will be dropped. In each of these situations,[8] as in Brady's case, the defendant might never plead guilty absent the possibility or certainty that the plea will result in a lesser penalty than the sentence that could be imposed after a trial and a verdict of guilty. We decline to hold, however, that a guilty plea is compelled and invalid under the Fifth Amendment whenever motivated by the defendant's desire to accept the certainty or probability of a lesser penalty rather than face a wider range of possibilities extending from acquittal to conviction and a higher penalty authorized by law for the crime charged.

The issue we deal with is inherent in the criminal law and its administration because guilty pleas are not constitutionally forbidden, because the criminal law characteristically extends to judge or jury a range of choice in setting the sentence in individual cases, and because both the State and the defendant often find it advantageous to preclude the possibility of the maximum penalty authorized by law. For a defendant who sees slight possibility of acquittal, the advantages of pleading guilty and limiting the probable penalty are obvious—his exposure is reduced, the correctional processes can begin immediately, and the practical burdens of a trial are eliminated. For the State there are also advantages—the more promptly imposed punishment after an admission of guilt may more effectively attain the objectives of punishment; and with the avoidance of trial, scarce judicial and prosecutorial resources are conserved for those cases in which there is a substantial issue of the defendant's guilt or in which there is substantial doubt that the State can sustain its burden of proof. It is this mutuality of advantage that perhaps explains the fact that at present well over three-fourths of the criminal convictions in this country rest on pleas of guilty, a great many of them no doubt motivated at least in part by the hope or assurance of a lesser penalty than might be imposed if there were a guilty verdict after a trial to judge or jury.

Of course, that the prevalence of guilty pleas is explainable does not necessarily validate those pleas or the system which produces them. But we cannot hold that it is unconstitutional for the State to extend a benefit to a defendant who in turn extends a substantial benefit to the State and who demonstrates by his plea that he is ready and willing to admit his crime and to enter the correctional system in a frame of mind that affords hope for success in rehabilitation over a shorter period of time than might otherwise be necessary. . . .

Bram v. United States, 168 U.S. 532 (1897), held that the admissibility of a confession depended upon whether it was compelled within the meaning of the Fifth Amendment. To be admissible, a confession must be "'free and

---

8. We here make no reference to the situation where the prosecutor or judge, or both, deliberately employ their charging and sentencing powers to induce a particular defendant to tender a plea of guilty. In Brady's case there is no claim that the prosecutor threatened prosecution on a charge not justified by the evidence or that the trial judge threatened Brady with a harsher sentence if convicted after trial in order to induce him to plead guilty.

voluntary: that is, must not be extracted by any sort of threats or violence, nor obtained by any direct or implied promises, however slight, nor by the exertion of any improper influence.'" . . . *Bram* dealt with a confession given by a defendant in custody, alone and unrepresented by counsel. In such circumstances, even a mild promise of leniency was deemed sufficient to bar the confession, not because the promise was an illegal act as such, but because defendants at such times are too sensitive to inducement and the possible impact on them too great to ignore and too difficult to assess. . . .

Brady's situation bears no resemblance to Bram's. . . . He had competent counsel and full opportunity to assess the advantages and disadvantages of a trial as compared with those attending a plea of guilty; there was no hazard of an impulsive and improvident response to a seeming but unreal advantage. His plea of guilty was entered in open court and before a judge obviously sensitive to the requirements of the law with respect to guilty pleas. Brady's plea, unlike Bram's confession, was voluntary.

The standard as to the voluntariness of guilty pleas must be essentially that defined by Judge Tuttle of the Court of Appeals for the Fifth Circuit: "'[A] plea of guilty entered by one fully aware of the direct consequences, including the actual value of any commitments made to him by the court, prosecutor, or his own counsel, must stand unless induced by threats (or promises to discontinue improper harassment), misrepresentation (including unfulfilled or unfulfillable promises), or perhaps by promises that are by their nature improper as having no proper relationship to the prosecutor's business (e.g. bribes).'"[13] Under this standard, a plea of guilty is not invalid merely because entered to avoid the possibility of a death penalty.

The record before us also supports the conclusion that Brady's plea was intelligently made. He was advised by competent counsel, he was made aware of the nature of the charge against him, and there was nothing to indicate that he was incompetent or otherwise not in control of his mental faculties. . . .

This is not to say that guilty plea convictions hold no hazards for the innocent or that the methods of taking guilty pleas presently employed in this country are necessarily valid in all respects. This mode of conviction is no more foolproof than full trials to the court or to the jury. . . . We would have serious doubts about this case if the encouragement of guilty pleas by offers of leniency substantially increased the likelihood that defendants, advised by competent counsel, would falsely condemn themselves. But our view is to the contrary and is based on our expectations that courts will satisfy themselves that pleas of guilty are voluntarily and intelligently made by competent defendants with adequate advice of counsel and that there is nothing to question the accuracy and reliability of the defendants' admissions that they committed the crimes with which they are charged. . . .

Affirmed.

[The concurring opinions of Justices Black and Brennan are omitted.]

---

13. Shelton v. United States, 246 F.2d 571, 572 n.2 (5th Cir. 1957) (en banc), *rev'd on confession of error on other grounds*, 356 U.S. 26 (1958).

Albert W. Alschuler, The Supreme Court, the Defense Attorney, and the Guilty Plea, 47 U. Colo. L. Rev. 1, 55-58 (1975): [I]t may be reasonable to equate a competently counseled guilty plea with a knowing guilty plea. . . . In *Brady,* however, the Supreme Court seemed to conclude that a competently counseled guilty plea would ordinarily be, not only a knowing plea, but a voluntary plea as well. [But] the presence of counsel has little relevance to the question of voluntariness. A guilty plea entered at gunpoint is no less involuntary because an attorney is present to explain how the gun works.

Under today's guilty-plea system, the basic function of the defense attorney is indeed to explain "how the gun works"—something that was illustrated by the record in *Brady.* . . . The defense attorney had two allies in his effort to persuade the defendant to plead guilty. The trial judge announced from the bench that he thought the defendant "might get the death penalty." Moreover, when the defense attorney told the judge in chambers that he thought that a guilty plea would probably be entered at a later date, the judge replied, "Well, I think you are very wise, because I was certainly going to submit the death penalty to the jury." The attorney dutifully reported this comment to the defendant.

The defendant's mother may also have been influential in altering the defendant's choice of plea. She attempted to visit the defendant in jail but found that "it wasn't visiting hours." She testified:

> I went through the alley of the city jail where he was being held and I kept yelling, "Brady. Brady." Then—then there was somebody, some fellow up there that yelled, "Is there a Brady here?" So then Brady came to the window. It was upstairs. I don't know how many floors. Brady came to the window and he said, "Mom what are you doing? You are going to get yourself in trouble," and I just said, "For God's sake, plead guilty. They are going to give you the death sentence."

When it became apparent that a codefendant would probably testify against him, the defendant agreed to plead guilty. The defense attorney reported that he "felt very gratified when [the defendant] decided to change his plea in that we saved him from a death penalty in my opinion."

The defense attorney was, I think, entitled to feel gratified; he had done a capable job and may indeed have saved the defendant from a death sentence. The defendant's principal complaint did not, however, concern his attorney's performance; it was directed to the fact that exercise of the right to trial might have incurred an awesome penalty. This underlying reality was beyond the defense attorney's control but not beyond the control of the Supreme Court.

Contrary to the Supreme Court's suggestion, the presence of the defense attorney in *Brady* did not "dissipate" the "possibly coercive impact" of this reality. Indeed, the record in *Brady* suggests that the principal function of a competent attorney in the guilty-plea system is exactly the opposite of the function suggested by the Supreme Court. Rather than dispel the coercive impact of a promise of leniency, the attorney must make the defendant realize with full clarity the coercive power of the alternatives that he faces. In that way, the attorney may persuade the defendant to choose the course that within the confines of a cynical system, is likely to injure him least.

NOTES ON PLEA BARGAINING

1. *Guilty plea procedure.* As *Brady* indicates, a guilty plea, to be valid, must be the product of a knowing and intelligent choice, and it must be "voluntary," in the sense that it does not result from threats or promises *other than* those involved in any plea agreement. Before accepting a guilty plea, the trial judge typically will address the defendant in open court, in a colloquy that makes explicit the elements of the offense, the potential sentence, and the three principal rights being waived by the plea (the privilege against self-incrimination, the right to jury trial, and the right to confront one's accusers). See, e.g., Fed. R. Crim. Pro., Rule 11(c), (d).

2. *Knowing and intelligent.* The Supreme Court in *Brady* stated that defendants need "sufficient awareness of relevant circumstances" and any "direct consequences" of a guilty plea for it to be knowing and intelligent. *Brady*, 397 U.S. at 748, 755. What are those relevant circumstances and direct consequences? Courts are clear that maximum sentence exposure is one. Should defendants also be told of mandatory minimum sentences? The Third Circuit believes so, reasoning that "the mandatory minimum sentence may be far more relevant than the theoretical maximum because that is rarely imposed." See Jamison v. Klem, 544 F.3d 266, 277 (3d Cir. 2008). Why did the Court in *Brady* focus on "direct" consequences and not collateral consequences? Note that collateral consequences, such as termination of federal benefits or the loss of a professional license, can be enormously significant, especially if the "direct" consequence is only a small fine. See Am. Bar Ass'n, Internal Exile: Collateral Consequences of Conviction in Federal Laws and Regulations (2009).

3. *Effective assistance of counsel.* In Padilla v. Kentucky, 130 S. Ct. 1473 (2010), the Supreme Court held that criminal defense attorneys provide ineffective assistance of counsel if they fail to advise noncitizen clients, before they plead guilty, about possible deportation. The Court concluded that deportation is "uniquely difficult to classify as either a direct or a collateral consequence." Id. at 1482. For an argument that *Padilla* may signal the beginning of greater constitutional oversight of the guilty plea process, see Gabriel J. Chin & Margaret Love, Status as Punishment, 25 Crim. Just. 21 (2010).

When counsel is ineffective at the plea bargaining stage, there remains the question of what remedy is appropriate if the defendant ultimately rejects the plea offer and receives a longer sentence after being convicted at a fair trial. The Supreme Court recently rejected the argument that a subsequent trial automatically cures any defect at the plea-bargaining stage so that no additional remedy is necessary. Instead, the Court held that trial courts should have the discretion to determine whether the appropriate remedy is to require the prosecution to reoffer the plea proposal, to adhere to the post-trial sentence, or to issue a sentence somewhere in between. Lafler v. Cooper, No. 10-209, slip op. at 12-13 (U.S. Mar. 21, 2012).

4. *The extent of plea bargaining.* At the time of the *Brady* decision, 70-85 percent of American felony convictions were obtained by guilty plea. The guilty plea rate has risen substantially since the Court expressly endorsed the process. Nationally, about 95 percent of state court felony convictions are currently obtained by guilty plea, and in the federal courts, the figure is about 96 percent.[20] These statistics led the Supreme Court to concede that "[i]n today's criminal justice system . . . the negotiation of a plea bargain, rather than the unfolding of a trial, is almost always the critical point for a defendant." Missouri v. Frye, No. 10-444, slip op. at 8 (U.S. Mar. 21, 2012). Nonetheless, there are wide variations in guilty plea rates, both among states and among jurisdictions within states. Moreover, the variations do not seem to correspond to differences in population or other factors indicative of case-load pressure. In some states, for example, guilty plea rates are more prevalent in rural than in urban counties, and guilty plea rates are much greater in some large cities than in others. One study found that for cities with populations over 500,000, the mean guilty plea rate was 93 percent in New York State but only 65 percent in Pennsylvania.[21] The guilty plea rate, moreover, cannot be equated with the *bargaining* rate. Studies suggest that many defendants plead guilty even though they have no expectation of receiving more lenient treatment in return.

Suppose the defendant and his counsel do not *negotiate* for a specific sentencing concession; instead they decide on a guilty plea because they believe, in light of past experience, that the judge will probably impose a more lenient sentence than he would impose if the defendant is convicted at trial. Should a guilty plea tendered for that reason be considered the product of "plea bargaining"? Is a practice of tacit or indirect inducements preferable to one in which parties negotiate explicitly and the defendant knows in advance the precise difference between the sentences to be imposed after a plea and after conviction at trial?

5. *The nature of the bargain.* In Santobello v. New York, 404 U.S. 257 (1971), the Court held that if the prosecution fails to honor commitments made to the defendant in exchange for his or her plea, then the defendant

---

20. Bureau of Justice Statistics, U.S. Dept. of Justice, Sourcebook of Criminal Justice Statistics Online tbl.5.46.2002 (2004), http://www.albany.edu/sourcebook/pdf/t5462002.pdf; Id. at tbl.5.17.2003 (2005), http://www.albany.edu/sourcebook/pdf/t5172003.pdf.

21. See H. Miller, W. McDonald & J. Cramer, Plea Bargaining in the United States 16-24 (1978). See also Stephen J. Schulhofer, Is Plea Bargaining Inevitable?, 97 Harv. L. Rev. 1037, 1051 (1984) (reporting a guilty plea rate of 45 percent for Philadelphia, where most felony cases received fully contested bench trials).

must be allowed to withdraw the plea. This safeguard does not, however, mean that the defendant who pleads guilty will receive precisely the sentence he or she expects. The prosecutor's commitment might take the form of a promise to dismiss certain counts or to "recommend" a certain sentence to the judge; the bargain is therefore fulfilled if the prosecutor takes the action promised, even if the judge then imposes a different sentence from the one the defendant expected. Defendants who seek a commitment that a specific sentence *will* be imposed are sometimes told that local practice forbids that sort of offer because it intrudes upon the sentencing authority of the judge. Are nonbinding recommendations a preferable form of guilty plea inducement, because they preserve the judge's role in setting the appropriate punishment? Or are they undesirable because they can mislead a defendant about the actual value of his plea bargain? For discussion, see Wes R. Porter, The Pendulum in Federal Sentencing Can Also Swing Toward Predictability: A Renewed Role for Binding Plea Agreements Post-*Booker*, 37 Wm. Mitchell L. Rev. 469, 515-523 (2011).

How large are the concessions given to defendants who plead guilty? (Or, to put it another way, how large is the penalty imposed on those who stand trial?) In the 1970s, when the official acknowledgement and endorsement of plea bargaining was still recent, statistics suggested that, on average, the sentencing concession received for a guilty plea was small or nonexistent. See Stephen J. Schulhofer, Due Process of Sentencing, 128 U. Pa. L. Rev. 733, 757 & n.97 (1980). Current data indicate, however, that "the trial penalty has ballooned in magnitude" and is now substantial; controlling for relevant differences among cases, sentences after jury trial were on average three times longer than sentences imposed in comparable cases after a plea. Candace McCoy, Plea Bargaining as Coercion: The Trial Penalty and Plea Bargaining Reform, 50 Crim. L.Q. 67, 89, 91 (2005). There is some evidence that trial penalties are greater in large urban counties. Jeffrey T. Ulmer & Mindy S. Bradley, Variation in Trial Penalties Among Serious Violent Offenses, 44 Criminology 631, 656 (2006). Nonetheless, there is still considerable evidence that defendants sometimes plead guilty, believing they are getting a "good deal," only to receive a sentence just as severe as the one they would have received if convicted at trial. Is this phenomenon unfair, or does it give society "the best of both worlds"? Conversely, consider the situation in jurisdictions where sentences imposed after jury trials routinely are three times longer than those imposed in comparable cases after pleas. Is that phenomenon reassuring or worrisome?

Note that the number of acquittals after a trial has declined dramatically in many jurisdictions in recent decades, raising the possibility that many defendants who previously would have elected a trial and won acquittal are now pleading guilty instead. Ronald F. Wright, Trial Distortion and the End of Innocence in Federal Criminal Justice, 154 U. Pa. L. Rev. 79 (2005). Is the correlation between the decrease in the number of acquittals and the increase in the sentencing penalty for taking a case to trial merely a coincidence, or has the risk of a much longer sentence after conviction at trial prompted innocent defendants to plead guilty? See Richard A. Oppel, Jr., Sentencing Shift Gives New Leverage to Prosecutors, N.Y. Times, Sept. 25, 2011, at A1.

Should jurisdictions limit the differential between sentences offered in pleas and those given after trial? One commentator argues for plea-based ceilings to guarantee that defendants would not receive a sentence following a trial conviction that is more severe than any plea offer made to them—except by a "modest, pre-determined amount." Russell D. Covey, Fixed Justice: Reforming Plea Bargaining with Plea-Based Ceilings, 82 Tul. L. Rev. 1237 (2008). Similarly, Máximo Langer suggests that, during the plea colloquy, the trial judge should ask the defendant what the prosecutor threatened the sentence would be after trial, and advocates that the judge should reject the plea if the potential trial sentence is "clearly disproportionate." Máximo Langer, Rethinking Plea Bargaining: The Practice and Reform of Prosecutorial Adjudication in American Criminal Procedure, 33 Am. J. Crim. L. 223, 284 (2006).

6. The trial judge's role. ABA standards provide that the trial judge may not initiate plea discussions, but if the parties request her to become involved, she is free to meet and indicate the plea concessions that she would consider appropriate. ABA Standards: Pleas of Guilty, §14-3.3(c). The Federal Rules of Criminal Procedure forbid judicial participation in plea negotiation (Fed. R. Crim. Pro., Rule 11(e)(1)), but they also provide that the judge must explicitly accept or reject an agreement and must inform the parties whether she is willing to be bound by it. Id., Rule 11(e)(3),(4). As a result, the judge in federal cases is inevitably an unseen but important presence in negotiations, with decisive power to control the contours of any bargain if she wishes to do so. For discussion of the issues, see Albert W. Alschuler, The Trial Judge's Role in Plea Bargaining, Part I, 76 Colum. L. Rev. 1059 (1976).

To what extent is it desirable for the judge who will try a case to discuss with the defendant the sentence reduction she will grant in return for a guilty plea? Is judicial involvement of this sort unduly coercive? Or is it beneficial because it allows the defendant to find out what his plea bargain is really worth? Should the judge seek to provide unambiguous information without coercion, or are these features just two sides of the same coin?

Jenia Iontcheva Turner analyzed three jurisdictions (Connecticut, Florida, and Germany) that permit greater judicial involvement in plea negotiations than the federal system does, and she is optimistic that safeguards can guard against judicial coercion. Jenia Iontcheva Turner, Judicial Participation in Plea Negotiations: A Comparative View, 54 Am. J. Comp. L. 199 (2006). Some of the safeguards she discusses are (1) placing all plea discussions with the judge on the record and having appellate courts closely monitor the exchanges for coercion; (2) prohibiting judges from initiating plea discussions; and (3) precluding a judge who is involved with plea discussions from presiding over the trial or sentencing of the case should the defendant ultimately decide not to plead guilty or withdraw his plea. Id.

at 262-263. Are these sound policies? What are the tradeoffs with adopting these measures?

Are there other mechanisms of judicial involvement that could curb abuses in plea bargaining? For suggestions, see Mary Sue Backus, The Adversary System is Dead; Long Live the Adversary System: The Trial Judge as the Great Equalizer in Criminal Trials, 2008 Mich. St. L. Rev. 945.

NOTES ON THE POLICY DEBATE

A voluminous literature discusses the supposed merits and demerits of plea bargaining.[22] These notes examine several of the most important issues.

1. Necessity. Compare these viewpoints:

Santobello v. New York, 404 U.S. 257, 260 (1971) (Burger, C.J.): [Plea bargaining] is an essential component of the administration of justice. . . . If every criminal charge were subjected to a full-scale trial, the States and the Federal Government would need to multiply by many times the number of judges and court facilities.

[More explicitly, in a speech to the American Bar Association,[a] the Chief Justice declared, "The consequence of what might seem on its face a small percentage change in the rate of guilty pleas can be tremendous. A reduction from 90 percent to 80 percent in guilty pleas requires the assignment of twice the judicial manpower and facilities—judges, court reporters, bailiffs, clerks, jurors and courtrooms. A reduction to 70 percent trebles this demand."]

Albert W. Alschuler, Book Review, 12 Crim. L. Bull. 629, 632 (1976): The prospect of multiplying current criminal court resources several times over may seem unthinkable until one realizes how limited these resources are. The situation in my own jurisdiction, however, seems typical. [In] a county of more than 250,000 people, one judge hears felony cases full-time, and another hears felony cases part-time. To multiply these resources five times, or ten . . . would require no more than the building and staffing of a single new courthouse, a task that might be almost as difficult as the building and staffing of a new hospital or a new high school. If the need were in the area of medicine or education, however, responsible citizens would at least talk about meeting it. They would not insist that "practical necessity" required bargaining with patients to "waive" their operations or with students to "waive" their classes.

---

22. The starting point for any consideration of the issues is Professor Albert W. Alschuler's groundbreaking portrait of the system, as conducted by its three most important practitioners. See The Prosecutor's Role in Plea Bargaining, 36 U. Chi. L. Rev. 50 (1968); The Defense Attorney's Role in Plea Bargaining, 84 Yale L.J. 1179 (1975); The Trial Judge's Role in Plea Bargaining, Part I, 76 Colum. L. Rev. 1059 (1976).

a. Burger, The State of the Judiciary—1970, 56 A.B.A. J. 929, 931 (1970).—Eds.

Questions: If a trial with the full package of due process safeguards is simply too time-consuming and expensive to provide in every criminal case, should jurisdictions seek, in lieu of plea bargaining, to solve that problem by streamlining their trial procedures while ensuring that these more efficient trials are afforded without penalty to every defendant who wants one? Would the dangers to the innocent of reducing our traditional due process safeguards be greater than the dangers of preserving those safeguards while making them costly for defendants to invoke?

In one approach to the resource problem, pioneered in Philadelphia, defendants typically receive no inducement to plead guilty but gain sentencing concessions by waiving their right to a jury and accepting a bench trial. Commenting on this solution, one observer notes (Stephen J. Schulhofer, Is Plea Bargaining Inevitable?, 97 Harv. L. Rev. 1037, 1083-1084 (1984)):

> By waiving a jury, the defendant [often reduces] the probability of an acquittal on grounds of reasonable doubt. . . . [But e]ven when the jury waiver does deprive the defendant of a valuable procedural right, it does not deprive him of *all* valuable procedural rights. . . . The defendant retains the rights to confront the witnesses against him, to object on constitutional or other grounds to the admissibility of evidence, to cross-examine witnesses, to develop factual defenses, to have his guilt determined on the basis of the testimony presented in open court, to have that testimony evaluated under applicable substantive law, and to test by appeal any of the trial judge's rulings on matters of admissibility, legal interpretation, or evidentiary weight. . . . [A]part from isolated aberrations, all the bench trials we observed were genuinely contested proceedings. The lawyers remained within their traditional adversary roles, and the judges took seriously their obligation to adjudicate. Participants were (normally) courteous to one another, but they did not cooperate at the expense of their separate institutional responsibilities. Cases were not compromised but were decided on the governing law and the evidence.

Questions: Is the Philadelphia solution preferable to a two-tier system that offers most defendants either a full-fledged jury trial or a guilty plea with a substantially reduced sentence? Nearly all American jurisdictions prefer the two-tier approach. What might explain the unpopularity of the Philadelphia solution?

2. The propriety of sentencing concessions. Is there a legitimate justification for imposing a lower sentence on a defendant who pleads guilty than on a defendant whose offense and other relevant circumstances are identical, except that he was found guilty at trial? In United States v. Rodriguez, 162 F.3d 135 (1st Cir. 1998), three members of a cocaine distribution conspiracy pleaded guilty and were sentenced to time served, 17 months and 60 months respectively, with the differences primarily reflecting differences in their prior records. Two of their coconspirators, whose records were comparable and whose alleged roles in the offense were essentially identical, pleaded not guilty; after conviction at trial, they were sentenced to 235 months and 260 months respectively. Why should the defendants who chose to go to trial have received longer sentences? Why should they have received sentences that were *that much* longer?

Courthouse legend has it that many a judge will justify these kinds of sentence differentials by explaining openly and without embarrassment, "He takes some of my time; I take some of his." Are there better reasons? The American Bar Association has noted that concessions are appropriate when a defendant is "genuinely contrite;" when concessions allow for "alternative correction measures;" when "the defendant, by making public trial unnecessary, has demonstrated genuine remorse or consideration for the victims;" and when the defendant's cooperation results in the prosecution of others who have committed equally serious or more serious crimes. American Bar Association, Standards: Pleas of Guilty, §14-1.8(a) (3d ed. 1999).

For another view, consider the following:

Scott v. United States, 419 F.2d 264, 271, 276-277 (D.C. Cir. 1969) (Bazelon, C.J.): [The court first rejected the "contrition" rationale for sentencing concessions, but then offered a different justification for them.] If the defendant were unaware that a proper display of remorse might affect his sentence, his willingness to admit the crime might offer the sentencing judge some guidance. But with the inducement of a lighter sentence dangled before him, the sincerity of any cries of mea culpa becomes questionable.

[It may seem that] the defendant who insists upon a trial and is found guilty pays a price for the exercise of his right when he receives a longer sentence than his less venturesome counterpart who pleads guilty. In a sense he has. . . . After the fact, the defendant who pleads innocent and is convicted receives a heavier sentence. But, by the same token, the defendant who pleads innocent and is acquitted receives no sentence. To the extent that the bargain struck reflects only the uncertainty of conviction before trial, the "expected sentence before trial"—length of sentence discounted by probability of conviction—is the same for those who decide to plead guilty and those who hope for acquittal but risk conviction by going to trial. . . . If the sentence expectations of those two classes at that time are the same, then there will be no chilling effect upon exercise of the right to trial, and it is accurate to say that no "price" has been placed upon exercise of the right. . . .

The situation is quite different when the prosecutor engages in bargaining not because he is willing to take a sure half loaf rather than to await the outcome of a trial, but because his limited resources convince him he must deter defendants from demanding a trial. The divide between the two situations may be difficult to locate for even the best-intentioned prosecutor, and even more difficult for a trial judge to review. . . . But this reality imposes a special duty upon courts to provide what guidance they can for prosecutors entrusted with such discretion. In the area of plea bargaining, the lodestar must be the realization that our law solemnly promises each man accused his day in court. If a prosecutor enters plea and charge negotiations not with the purpose of adjusting the charge to reflect the uncertainties of litigation but with the goal of deterring the defendant from the exercise of his right to a trial, the chasm between promise and reality is no narrower because the trial court affects a righteous air of non-involvement.

3. *Cooperation.* The ABA highlights cooperation as an appropriate ground for making a sentencing concession in a plea deal. At the federal level, the number one basis for a departure below the recommended sentencing guideline is a prosecution motion that the defendant provided substantial assistance to the government.[23] Offering substantial assistance to the government is also the only way for most defendants to avoid an otherwise applicable mandatory minimum sentence. 18 U.S.C. §3553(e). On what theory of punishment is cooperation worthy of a sentencing discount? Are cooperation discounts different in principle from discounts for waiving the right to trial? If so, which practice is more dubious?

What are the costs of giving discounts to cooperators? For a general discussion, see Miriam Hechler Baer, Cooperation's Cost, 88 Wash. U. L. Rev. 903 (2011). Note that only defendants who know about other offenders can obtain this discount. As a result, a bigger fish in a criminal organization, because he knows of lots of other criminal activity, often can obtain a significant discount, yet those at the lowest level may have nothing to offer and receive a much higher sentence. Is there adequate justification for imposing more severe sentences on the defendants at the lowest levels of criminal responsibility?

4. *Criminal history.* Sentencing laws that mandate long sentences for repeat offenders increase the bargaining power of prosecutors because offenders with criminal histories face especially long sentences if convicted at trial. As a result, one scholar argues, prosecutors effectively bear a lower burden of proof in cases involving recidivists than cases with first-time offenders. Russell D. Covey, Longitudinal Guilt: Repeat Offenders, Plea Bargaining, and the Variable Standard of Proof, 63 Fla. L. Rev. 431 (2011). Is this situation justified by the offender's criminal past or should greater protections be in place to ensure that an offender with a criminal history is not coerced into pleading guilty to a crime he or she did not commit?

5. *Freedom of choice.* Many critics of plea bargaining believe that defendants are harmed by sentencing concessions that pressure them to waive their trial rights. But to the defendants, those rights presumably were worth less than the leniency they gained by "selling" them; if not, they would have rejected the offer. As in a commercial transaction, when each party can choose whether to accept or reject a proposal, an agreement they both prefer to accept

---

23. U.S. Sentencing Comm'n, Preliminary Quarterly Data Report, tbl. 1 (2011), available at http://www.ussc.gov/Data_and_Statistics/Federal_Sentencing_Statistics/Quarterly_Sentencing_Updates/USSC_2011_3rd_Quarter_Report.pdf.

seems, by definition, to leave them better off (in their own best judgment) than they would be without the deal. Consider Robert E. Scott & William J. Stuntz, Plea Bargaining as Contract, 101 Yale L.J. 1909, 1914-1915 (1992):

> The defendant has the right to ... force the prosecutor to prove the case at trial. The prosecutor has the right to seek the maximum sentence. ... It is easy to imagine some circumstances where each party values the other's entitlement more than his own. If so, the conditions exist for an exchange that benefits both parties and harms neither. The defendant will trade the right to ... force a trial for the prosecutor's right to seek the maximum sentence. ...
>
> Moreover, the gains the participants realize from the exchange presumably have *social* value, not just value to the bargaining parties. Plea bargaining provides a means by which prosecutors can obtain a larger net return from criminal convictions, holding resources constant. Criminal defendants, as a group, are able to reduce the risk of the imposition of maximum sanctions. ... In short, the existence of entitlements implies the right to exploit those entitlements fully, which in turn implies the right to trade the entitlement or any of its associated risks.

Questions: (a) Given that prosecutors are entitled to seek the maximum sentence for any provable offense, does it follow that the existence of those entitlements "implies the right to exploit those entitlements fully"? Or are there considerations, independent of the plea, that should guide the prosecutor's judgment about the appropriate sanction?

(b) As applied to a defendant like Brady (page 1133 supra), who faced the death penalty, is it plausible to consider his guilty plea a voluntary choice? Or, as Alschuler puts it (page 1136 supra), was his decision in effect made "at gunpoint," like a robbery victim who agrees to turn over his cash to avoid physical violence? Does it make a meaningful difference that Brady's predicament resulted only because there was a significant chance of *lawfully* sentencing him to death after conviction at trial?

(c) If a bargain is beneficial to a particular defendant (because of the severe sentence he would face after conviction at trial), does it follow that the institution of plea bargaining benefits defendants *as a group*? The unconstitutional conditions doctrine forbids bargains in which parties agree to abandon their constitutional rights, because such bargains may detract from overall social welfare. Absent such a doctrine, individuals might nevertheless agree to such socially destructive bargains. Richard A. Epstein, Unconstitutional Conditions, State Power, and the Limits of Consent, 102 Harv. L. Rev. 4 (1988). Because of the government's monopoly in many domains (it does not face meaningful competition), it therefore has great leverage when it bargains with individuals. In addition, individuals face a problem of collective action when bargaining, because it is difficult to coordinate their behavior. Finally, these bargains may impose costs—or externalities—on third parties whose interests are insufficiently represented in the bargaining process. The Court's willingness to accept plea bargaining appears to be an exception to the general

rule against bargaining away constitutional rights. Why should criminal trial rights be treated differently from other constitutional rights?

The plea-bargaining system presumably benefits defendants generally if—after abolition of plea bargaining—defendants convicted at trial would face the same severe sentences that they had faced before abolition; such defendants would be worse off after abolition than when they were able to plead guilty in exchange for leniency. But if guilty plea concessions were abolished, would society impose on *all* defendants the relatively severe sentences that are now reserved for defendants who refuse to plead guilty? What would happen to prison populations and state budgets in that event? Alternatively, if the abolition of guilty plea concessions required a substantial reduction of average sentences imposed after conviction at trial, would defendants *as a group* be better or worse off than they were in the system that permits plea bargaining?

(*d*) Josh Bowers argues that the system of plea bargaining helps one common type of innocent defendant: an innocent recidivist in a low-stakes case. He argues that such a defendant is better off with the option of a plea bargain than not having such an option because the guilty plea often gets that defendant out of pretrial detention quickly and avoids an unwelcome pretrial process. Josh Bowers, Punishing the Innocent, 156 U. Pa. L. Rev. 1117 (2008). But is the plea-bargaining system—the practice of imposing higher sentences on defendants who go to trial—necessary for the innocent defendant to realize those benefits? Why can't jurisdictions abolish plea *bargaining* without insisting that every defendant go through a full trial? See also Ronald F. Wright, Guilty Pleas and Submarkets, 157 U. Pa. L. Rev. PEN-Numbra 68 (2008), arguing that plea bargaining is especially *dis*advantageous for defendants facing serious felony charges; he advocates a regulatory approach that would separately govern plea bargaining in different "submarkets" of criminal justice consisting of different types of offenders and offenses. Id.

6. Structural problems. Can we be reasonably confident that defendants considering a plea offer will make the choice that is in their own best interest? Of course, "buyer's remorse" is a common phenomenon in ordinary commercial transactions; it does not in itself suggest that consumers should be prohibited from buying what they think they want. But plea bargaining presents an additional complication because—unlike a contract negotiation between a single buyer and seller—the relevant parties to a plea bargain (the defendant and the public) are each represented by agents (the defense attorney and the prosecutor). And those agents may be influenced by personal interests at odds with the best interests of the party they represent. Are there times when a plea bargain could be to the advantage of a prosecutor, even though it was not in the best interests of the public? Prosecutors, particularly in large counties and districts, face crushing caseloads. Some commentators argue that these resource pressures create an environment where prosecutors are "asked to commit malpractice on a daily basis by handling far more cases than any lawyer can competently manage," which can lead to errors that harm defendants, victims, and the public. Adam M. Gershowitz & Laura R. Killinger, The State (Never) Rests: How Excessive Prosecutorial Caseloads Harm Criminal Defendants, 105 Nw. U. L. Rev. 261, 263-265 (2011). For a discussion of cognitive factors that may distort prosecutorial priorities, see Barbara O'Brien, A Recipe for Bias: An Empirical Look at the Interplay Between Institutional Incentives and Bounded Rationality in Prosecutorial Decision Making, 74 Mo. L. Rev. 999 (2009); Alafair S. Burke, Prosecutorial Passion, Cognitive Bias, and Plea Bargaining, 91 Marq. L. Rev. 183 (2007).

Could a plea bargain benefit a defense attorney even though it was not advantageous to her client? Stephanos Bibas discusses some biases that may affect defense counsel, including financial incentives and psychological irrationalities. Stephanos Bibas, Plea Bargaining Outside the Shadow of Trial, 117 Harv. L. Rev. 2463 (2004).

Consider Stephen J. Schulhofer, Plea Bargaining as Disaster, 101 Yale L.J. 1979, 1987-1990 (1992):

> Both the chief prosecutor (the District Attorney) and her assistants have numerous incentives to pursue goals that diverge from the public's interest in optimal [punishment]. [For example, the D.A. may seek] a high conviction rate, a good relationship with influential private attorneys, and an absence of high-profile trial losses. [Often] she will want to ensure settlement, even if this requires overly generous plea offers. . . . Front-line prosecutors . . . may or may not share the District Attorney's [goals]. Hence, there is an additional layer of [conflicting interests] in the relationship between the chief prosecutor and her assistants. . . .
>
> Like prosecutors, defense attorneys [often] have powerful incentives to avoid trial, even when a trial would be in the client's interest. . . . [N]early all [retained] attorneys work for a flat fee paid in advance. Since court rules usually prohibit defense counsel from withdrawing once an appearance has been entered, a retained attorney is obliged to take her case to trial if settlement negotiations fail, and in that event, her additional services are rendered free of charge. Accordingly, financial pressure to settle is intense.
>
> Counsel appointed for the indigent [sometimes] are conscripted from the list of those admitted to the bar and are required to serve without any compensation [or at rates far below market value]. Understanding the impact of such systems on the attorney's incentives to settle does not require a Ph.D. in economics. . . . Appointed attorneys in many jurisdictions volunteer for criminal defense work and are paid for their services. But in nearly all cases, compensation takes the form of either a flat fee per case, or a low hourly rate coupled with a ceiling on total compensation [that is] almost invariably identical for guilty plea cases and those that go to trial. [T]he attorney who counsels his client against accepting a plea must do so knowing that his time spent preparing and trying the case will be provided entirely free of charge. . . .

Conflict of interest problems are less dramatic for public defenders because they have no immediate financial incentive to avoid trial. But defender organizations, which are typically run as agencies of state or county government, ... develop a strong priority for moving their caseloads.

[B]ecause both prosecutors and defense counsel have interests that diverge from those of the parties they represent, *both* sides may lack sufficient zeal. ... But we have no reason to expect that conflict of interest effects neatly balance one another in any particular case. More likely, [conflicts of interest] generate inadequate deterrence in some cases and harm to defendants, especially innocent defendants, in others.

Questions: If criminal defense services are typically underfunded and infected by conflicts of interest, won't those problems undermine the fairness and reliability of the trial process as well? Judge Frank Easterbrook writes (Criminal Procedure as a Market System, 12 J. Legal Stud. 289, 309 (1983)) that conflict-of-interest problems in plea bargaining are "trivial" because "[l]awyers may cut corners at trial too." In what ways, specifically, can conflicts of interest affect an attorney's performance at trial? Are the conflict-of-interest effects more serious (or less serious) than those at work in the plea-bargaining context? How do the opportunities for monitoring poor representation differ in the two contexts? See Stephen J. Schulhofer, Criminal Justice Discretion as a Regulatory System, 17 J. Legal Stud. 43, 57-59 (1988).

7. *Penalties and coercion.* Part of the argument in favor of plea bargaining is the claim that the sentence imposed after trial will represent a punishment appropriate to the defendant's crime, not a punishment for having contested his guilt or a weapon to coerce him to waive his rights. But how can we ensure that a prosecutor does not threaten the defendant with a sentence that, even after discounting for the possibility of acquittal, is much more severe than the sentence the defendant can guarantee himself by pleading guilty? And what steps should a court take when a threat of that sort appears to have been made? Consider the case that follows.

BORDENKIRCHER v. HAYES

Supreme Court of the United States
434 U.S. 357 (1978)

JUSTICE STEWART delivered the opinion of the Court....

The respondent, Paul Lewis Hayes, was indicted by a Fayette County, Ky., grand jury on a charge of uttering a forged instrument in the amount of $88.30, an offense then punishable by a term of 2 to 10 years in prison. After arraignment, Hayes, his retained counsel, and the Commonwealth's Attorney met in the presence of the Clerk of the Court to discuss a possible plea agreement. During these conferences the prosecutor offered to recommend a sentence of five years in prison if Hayes would plead guilty to the indictment. He also said that if Hayes did not plead guilty and "save[] the court the inconvenience and necessity of a trial," he would return to the grand jury to seek an indictment under the Kentucky Habitual Criminal Act, which would subject Hayes to a mandatory sentence of life imprisonment by reason of his two prior felony convictions. Hayes chose not to plead guilty, and the prosecutor did obtain an indictment charging him under the Habitual Criminal Act. . . . A jury found Hayes guilty on the principal charge of uttering a forged instrument and [as] required by the habitual offender statute, he was sentenced to a life term in the penitentiary. The Kentucky Court of Appeals [affirmed].

On Hayes' petition for a federal writ of habeas corpus, [the court of appeals] thought that the prosecutor's conduct during the bargaining negotiations had violated the principles . . . which "protect[ed] defendants from the vindictive exercise of a prosecutor's discretion." Accordingly, the court ordered that Hayes be discharged "except for his confinement under a lawful sentence imposed solely for the crime of uttering a forged instrument." We granted certiorari. . . .

This Court held in North Carolina v. Pearce, 395 U.S. 711, 725, that the Due Process Clause of the Fourteenth Amendment "requires that vindictiveness against a defendant for having successfully attacked his first conviction must play no part in the sentence he receives after a new trial." . . . To punish a person because he has done what the law plainly allows him to do is a due process violation of the most basic sort. . . . But in the "give-and-take" of plea bargaining, there is no such element of punishment or retaliation so long as the accused is free to accept or reject the prosecution's offer.

Plea bargaining flows from "the mutuality of advantage" to defendants and prosecutors, each with his own reasons for wanting to avoid trial. Defendants advised by competent counsel and protected by other procedural safeguards are presumptively capable of intelligent choice in response to prosecutorial persuasion, and unlikely to be driven to false self-condemnation. . . .

While confronting a defendant with the risk of more severe punishment clearly may have a "discouraging effect on the defendant's assertion of his trial rights, the imposition of these difficult choices [is] an inevitable"—and permissible—"attribute of any legitimate system which tolerates and encourages the negotiation of pleas." It follows that, by tolerating and encouraging the negotiation of pleas, this Court has necessarily accepted as constitutionally legitimate the simple reality that the prosecutor's interest at the bargaining table is to persuade the defendant to forgo his right to plead not guilty. [So] long as the prosecutor has probable cause to believe that the accused committed an offense defined by statute, the decision whether or not to prosecute, and what charge to file or bring before a grand jury, generally rests entirely in his discretion.[8] Within the limits set by the legislature's constitutionally valid

---

8. This case does not involve the constitutional implications of a prosecutor's offer during plea bargaining of adverse or lenient treatment for some person *other* than the accused, which might pose a greater danger of inducing a false guilty plea by skewing the assessment of the risks a defendant must consider.

definition of chargeable offenses, "the conscious exercise of some selectivity in enforcement is not in itself a federal constitutional violation" so long as "the selection was [not] deliberately based upon an unjustifiable standard such as race, religion, or other arbitrary classification." To hold that the prosecutor's desire to induce a guilty plea is an "unjustifiable standard," which, like race or religion, may play no part in his charging decision, would contradict the very premises that underlie the concept of plea bargaining itself. Moreover, a rigid constitutional rule that would prohibit a prosecutor from acting forthrightly in his dealings with the defense could only invite unhealthy subterfuge that would drive the practice of plea bargaining back into the shadows from which it has so recently emerged.

There is no doubt that the breadth of discretion that our country's legal system vests in prosecuting attorneys carries with it the potential for both individual and institutional abuse. And broad though that discretion may be, there are undoubtedly constitutional limits upon its exercise. We hold only that the course of conduct engaged in by the prosecutor in this case, which no more than openly presented the defendant with the unpleasant alternatives of forgoing trial or facing charges on which he was plainly subject to prosecution, did not violate the Due Process Clause of the Fourteenth Amendment. . . .

JUSTICE BLACKMUN, with whom JUSTICE BRENNAN and JUSTICE MARSHALL join, dissenting. . . .

In *Pearce*, as indeed the Court notes, it was held that "vindictiveness against a defendant for having successfully attacked his first conviction must play no part in the sentence he receives after a new trial." . . . Yet in this case vindictiveness is present to the same extent as it was thought to be in *Pearce* . . . ; the prosecutor here admitted, that the sole reason for the new indictment was to discourage the respondent from exercising his right to a trial.[1] . . .

It might be argued that it really makes little difference how this case, now that it is here, is decided. The Court's holding gives plea bargaining full sway despite vindictiveness. A contrary result, however, merely would prompt the aggressive prosecutor to bring the greater charge initially in every case, and only thereafter to bargain. The consequences to the accused would still be adverse, for then he would bargain against a greater charge, face the likelihood of increased bail, and run the risk that the court would be less inclined to accept a bargained plea. Nonetheless, it is far preferable to hold the prosecution to the charge it was originally content to bring and to justify in the eyes of its public.[2]

---

1. In Brady v. United States, 397 U.S. 742 (1970), where the Court as a premise accepted plea bargaining as a legitimate practice, it nevertheless observed: "We here make no reference to the situation where the prosecutor or judge, or both, deliberately employ their charging and sentencing powers to induce a particular defendant to tender a plea of guilty."

2. That prosecutors . . . sometimes bring charges more serious than they think appropriate for the ultimate disposition of a case, in order to gain bargaining leverage with a defendant, does not add

JUSTICE POWELL, dissenting. . . .

The deference that courts properly accord the exercise of a prosecutor's discretion perhaps would foreclose judicial criticism if the prosecutor originally had sought an indictment under [the Habitual Criminal] Act, as unreasonable as it would have seemed. But here the prosecutor evidently made a reasonable, responsible judgment not to subject an individual to a mandatory life sentence when his only new offense had societal implications as limited as those accompanying the uttering of a single $88 forged check. . . . I think it may be inferred that the prosecutor himself deemed it unreasonable and not in the public interest to put this defendant in jeopardy of a sentence of life imprisonment.[a] . . .

[If the plea-bargaining] system is to work effectively, prosecutors must be accorded the widest discretion, within constitutional limits, in conducting bargaining. [But i]mplementation of a strategy calculated solely to deter the exercise of constitutional rights is not a constitutionally permissible exercise of discretion. I would affirm the opinion of the Court of Appeals on the facts of this case.

David Lynch, The Impropriety of Plea Agreements: A Tale of Two Counties, 19 Law & Soc. Inquiry 115, 125 (1994): After spending three years as a public defender, [I was hired] as an assistant district attorney . . . in nearby Lincoln County [the author's pseudonym for a county of 350,000 people in a large Eastern state]. . . . I quickly learned that prosecutors in Lincoln County were the real judges when it came to sentencing decisions. By allowing plea bargaining, . . . Lincoln County judges successfully dumped the burdens of sentencing most criminal defendants onto prosecutors. How did prosecutors in Lincoln County handle this sentencing burden? The answer, I quickly learned, was "any way they wanted to." There were no official rules that bound me or my fellow prosecutors in the making of plea-bargaining offers. And though some counties here and there do have them, there were no internal office guidelines in Lincoln County either. . . . Prosecutors, then, had nearly complete discretion in deciding what offers to make to defense counsel.

Unlike judges, who in Lincoln County were required by law to consider sentences in light of official guidelines developed by the state legislature, Lincoln County prosecutors merely used such guidelines as general starting points. If their "gut" told them that the guidelines weren't appropriate, they

---

support to today's decision, for this Court, in its approval of the advantages to be gained from plea negotiations, has never openly sanctioned such deliberate overcharging or taken such a cynical view of the bargaining process. Normally, of course, it is impossible to show that this is what the prosecutor is doing, and the courts necessarily have deferred to the prosecutor's exercise of discretion in initial charging decisions.

Even if overcharging is to be sanctioned, there are strong reasons of fairness why the charges should be presented at the beginning of the bargaining process, rather than as a fillliped threat at the end. . . . Visibility is enhanced if the prosecutor is required to lay his cards on the table with an indictment of public record at the beginning of the bargaining process, rather than making use of unrecorded verbal warnings of more serious indictments yet to come. . . .

a. In a footnote, Justice Powell added, "The majority's view confuses the propriety of a particular exercise of prosecutorial discretion with its unreviewability. In the instant case, however, we have no problem of proof."—EDS.

could ignore them entirely, or else re[-]label one crime as something else, so that it would fit neatly into the sentence guideline range they desired. There were many instances in which prosecutors would decide the appropriate sentence; offer it to defense counsel who then accepted; then search the crimes code for some offense that would produce the "correct" sentence.

This is not to say that prosecutors spent long periods of time agonizing over appropriate sentences. A prosecutor would often work through a pile of cases in machine-gun fashion, making snap decisions as to appropriate punishments in just a few minutes per case. These few minutes (perhaps 3 or so for misdemeanors and 10 for serious felonies) included all the time devoted to (1) examining police reports and all the evidence; (2) reviewing the defendant's prior criminal history; (3) deciding the defendant's fate as to sentencing; and (4) putting the plea offer into a form letter to be sent to defense counsel. [W]hat was also noteworthy was the surprising lack of training we prosecutors received for our sentencing roles. . . .

There were, in fact, people who were equipped to help the court decide appropriate sentences—presentence investigators who constituted a specialized unit within the probation office. They would, when asked, carefully prepare sophisticated, lengthy presentence reports [which] included detailed background information on the defendant, . . . sentencing recommendations, and other vital information. But these reports were typically prepared only when judges were going to be doing the sentencing. Since prosecutors did most of the real sentencing, this crucial resource was grossly underutilized.

NOTES

1. The environment described in the preceding excerpt appears to be common. Most district attorneys' offices do not significantly constrain the plea-agreement terms that front-line prosecutors can negotiate. The prevailing pattern in U.S. Attorneys' offices seems to be somewhat different. Nearly all offices require that plea agreements be in writing, and most have review procedures of some sort. See Mary Patrice Brown & Stevan E. Bunnell, Negotiating Justice: Prosecutorial Perspectives on Federal Plea Bargaining in the District of Columbia, 43 Am. Crim. L. Rev. 1063 (2006). But in practice supervisory review is often cursory, and the review procedures leave considerable room for evasion. In some U.S. Attorneys' offices, for example, prosecutors must seek approval to dismiss readily provable counts, but need not seek approval to dismiss a count that the front-line prosecutor deems not readily provable. See Stephen J. Schulhofer & Ilene H. Nagel, Plea Negotiations Under the Federal Sentencing Guidelines, 91 Nw. U. L. Rev. 1284, 1295 (1997).

Questions: (a) David Lynch is skeptical of the value of allowing front-line prosecutors the kind of unsupervised discretion that he himself was permitted to exercise in "Lincoln County." Does such a system have any advantages? Why do so many chief district attorneys accept it?

(b) If district attorneys' offices are unwilling to channel or supervise the plea-bargaining practices of their front-line prosecutors, should the courts themselves impose some guidelines or review procedures? Would doing so violate the separation of powers, by interfering with a legitimate prosecutorial function? Or would it preserve the separation of powers, by protecting the judicial authority to determine appropriate punishment? Consider State v. Lagares, 601 A.2d 698 (N.J. 1991). The case involved a statute allowing prosecutors complete discretion in deciding whether to seek an extended sentence for drug offenders with a previous drug conviction. The court required the state attorney general to develop guidelines for determining when it was permissible for a prosecutor to seek the extended sentence. Did this measure violate or preserve an appropriate separation of powers?

2. For another possible approach for promoting the proper exercise of prosecutorial discretion in plea bargaining, consider William J. Stuntz, The Political Constitution of Criminal Justice, 119 Harv. L. Rev. 780, 838, 841 (2005):

> For all crimes with a sentence of incarceration, prosecutors should be required to show that some number of other defendants in factually similar cases within the same state have been convicted of the same crime. [T]his rule would limit prosecutors' ability to threaten unusual criminal liability in order to extract guilty pleas. . . . For prosecutors, the message [of *Bordenkircher*] is: threaten everything in your arsenal in order to get the plea you want. [L]egislators [then] have every reason to vote for harsh penalties, secure in the knowledge that prosecutors need not and will not enforce them as written. [T]he only way to break this cycle is to require that the laws be enforced regularly or not at all.

Questions: What does it mean to require a law to be enforced "regularly"? Would this requirement get to the root problem of plea bargaining or simply give prosecutors an incentive to threaten harsh penalties more often, in order to get to "some number" of convictions that would be sufficient to establish a regular practice?

GERARD E. LYNCH, OUR ADMINISTRATIVE SYSTEM OF CRIMINAL JUSTICE[24]

66 Fordham L. Rev. 2117 (1998)

Because our governing ideology does not admit that prosecutors adjudicate guilt and set punishments, the procedures by which they do so are neither formally regulated nor invariably followed. . . . The rules conceive of the prosecutor as an autonomous party to an adversary proceeding, who has no more

---

24. This article, written before Judge Lynch's appointment to the bench, is based in part on his experience as an assistant U.S. Attorney in the Southern District of New York.

obligation to listen to his adversary's arguments before acting than does any civil litigant. . . .

[In practice, however,] prosecutors are generally prepared to [listen]. [F]ederal white-collar criminal investigations involving well-financed defendants . . . represent the system in its most elaborate form. . . . Defense counsel's contacts with the prosecutor during the preliminary stages of an investigation range from informal contacts designed to find out the nature of the allegations, . . . to elaborate formal presentations arguing that prosecution is not appropriate. . . . As the investigation reaches its conclusion, defense counsel will often make extensive, formal arguments. . . . [I]f the line prosecutor rejects the defense's contentions, counsel may seek "appellate review" by the prosecutor's supervisors, at ascending levels of prosecutorial bureaucracy. . . .

Although both the defense lawyers and the prosecutorial bureaucracy may operate with one eye on the eventual litigation that may result at the end of the internal process . . . it would be a mistake to analogize these decisions too closely to settlement discussions involving private parties. [P]rosecutors are not seeking simply to maximize the amount of jail time that can be extracted from their adversaries, regardless of guilt or innocence; rather, they undertake to determine, in response to the defendant's arguments, whether the evidence truly demonstrates guilt, and if so, what sentence is appropriate. . . .

That such procedures exist, and that they undertake a quasi-judicial function, does not mean that they are necessarily fair. . . . Unlike a judge or jury, the prosecutor remains free to speak ex parte with either the defense lawyer or the police, and frequently does so. Moreover, the extent and nature of these ex parte contacts are hardly symmetrical. . . . Law enforcement agencies and prosecutors are . . . part of the same "team," and their discussions, unlike those between prosecutors and defense lawyers, are affirmatively concerned with accomplishing shared goals. . . . [a] Even more importantly, the usual burdens of production and persuasion tend to be reversed. . . . The precise nature of the charges has not usually been specified, and the evidence on which they will be based is not often disclosed. . . . The decisionmaker, moreover, is under no obligation to give reasons for a rejection of the defendant's arguments. [W]hen the process operates at its best, . . . the process cannot be dismissed as arbitrary. It is not, however, an adversarial or judicial system. It is an inquisitorial and administrative one, characterized by informality and ad hoc flexibility of procedure.

Seen in the light of this administrative adjudicatory structure, it becomes apparent that the very term "plea bargaining" is something of a misnomer. . . . First of all, in many courts not all that much haggling goes on. [Y]ou will get no farther "bargaining" with the prosecutor than you will by making a counteroffer on the price of a can of beans at the grocery.

---

a. For in-depth analysis of these relationships, see Daniel C. Richman, Prosecutors and Their Agents, Agents and Their Prosecutors, 103 Colum. L. Rev. 749 (2003).—Eds.

On the other hand, not every case comes off the rack; some need, and receive, custom tailoring. [I]n a typical white-collar fraud investigation, defense counsel . . . will often spend hour after hour in the prosecutor's office, making presentations and arguments. [B]ecause [the prosecutor] does not see herself as an interested party seeking personal advantage [but] as a public official, seeking "justice" . . . [,] the self-definition of the prosecutor affects the nature of the arguments that can be used. . . . The ideology of at least some marketplaces permits the merchant openly to rely on superior bargaining power and to reject arguments from fairness; prosecutors, who will often have the power to impose terms, would be sharply criticized if they declined to consider arguments that the terms imposed are unjust. . . .

The frequent disparity of power between the prosecutor and the defendant makes the role-definition of the prosecutor particularly important to the outcome of the negotiation. [T]he prosecutor may hold the virtually unilateral power to inflict pain on the defendant. In many cases, for example, potential defendants perceive that an indictment alone, even if it ultimately results in acquittal, is an unbearable outcome. . . . In other situations, conviction [and a] harsh outcome at trial [may be a certainty], given the elastic definitions of substantive crimes, the severe and unpredictable (or in the case of mandatory sentences, all too predictable) sentences that may be applicable. . . . In such cases, the defendant is often likely to take, in the end, whatever plea the prosecutor can be persuaded to offer. Defense counsel's bargaining posture may implicitly threaten a trial, but both sides may know that the defense is very likely arguing to the ultimate decisionmaker about the nature of a fair outcome, rather than proposing an exchange of values based on relative bargaining strength. . . .

Because American lawyers have a large investment in the myth of the adversarial system, it is hard for us even to see this administrative system of punishment, let alone to approve of it. . . . Because the prosecutor represents one side in an anticipated adversarial proceeding, to acknowledge her role as a de facto adjudicator would be to make her the judge in her own case. Of course, if we continue to see the prosecutor as an adversarial "bargainer," settling her client's dispute with the defendant, this problem disappears, for this kind of bargaining between adversaries is an accepted part of an adversarial system. Legitimizing plea bargaining by insisting on the prosecutor's role as an adversarial bargainer, however, may encourage prosecutors to indulge exactly the wrong aspects of their divided mentality. . . . Treating pre-indictment decisionmaking and plea bargaining as an aspect of the adversary process makes it inevitable that decisions that ought to be taken in a spirit of judgment will be heavily influenced by considerations of adversarial tactics. Justice is much better served when prosecutors determining whether to indict or making plea offers see themselves as quasi-judicial decisionmakers, obligated to reach the fairest possible results, rather than as partisan negotiators looking to extract every ounce of advantage for their client. . . .

We should not [of course] abandon the due process model in favor of a formalized administered system, that would substitute for judicial judgment in criminal cases an administrative finding by a "Criminal Adjudication Agency." . . . So long as the de facto administrative process operates within the shell of the due process model, defendants retain the power to opt out of that process and submit themselves instead to a formal judicial procedure that is bound strictly by due process rules. That is a much stronger protection for the innocent than a deferential reasonableness review of prosecutorial decisions. . . .

An understanding of the different functions of the administrative and judicial aspects of our current system, [however], should help us to identify areas in need of change—and areas where change is not needed. First, an appreciation of the true role of the jury trial in our system might make us a little more cautious about efforts to streamline courtroom procedure in the interest of more efficient law enforcement. In our actual system, [the] jury trial serves . . . as the fail-safe appellate process that promotes the reasonableness of prosecutorial-administrative determinations by setting the limits within which it operates. That trials are cumbersome does not directly harm the efficiency of criminal procedure, because most cases do not involve trials at all. . . .

Second, . . . greater formality of procedure could enhance the fairness of the [plea bargaining] process. . . . Defendants should have a right to be heard, both by the prosecutor in charge of a case and by supervisory prosecutors. . . . Greater attention should also be paid to the selection of prosecutors, and to the nature of their career paths. In [European] systems, both prosecutors and judges are career civil servants, selected at an early age by merit-based criteria, and then advanced over the course of their careers by normal bureaucratic processes. American prosecutors [often] are more transient, seeking a few years of excitement, public service, or intense trial experience before pursuing private sector opportunities as criminal defense lawyers or civil litigators. The district attorneys and United States Attorneys who direct their efforts may be elected or appointed, and constitute a mix of career prosecutors, prominent members of the bar, and politically active lawyers. . . . Some greater measure of independence and judiciousness would seem suited to officials who have the awesome and often final power wielded by prosecutors today. . . .

[W]e should not be entirely cynical about the possibility that government officials can conduct themselves with fairness and in the broadest public interest. [M]ost do. [But we] need institutional checks, . . . not primarily to detect those who act in bad faith, but to prevent the excesses that can be committed with good intentions.

NOTES AND QUESTIONS

1. *The administrative law/criminal law contrast.* If charging and the making of plea offers have indeed become administrative processes of the sort Judge Lynch describes, should they be subject to the safeguards we routinely require for other administrative actions affecting individuals? In formal administrative proceedings, individuals get notice of charges, a right to be heard, a written decision supported by reasons and evidence, and a right of appeal to higher levels within the agency. Should all of these rights be available

in the context of charging decisions and plea offers? Would giving defendants these rights increase the perceived legitimacy of the criminal justice system? See Michael O'Hear, Plea Bargaining and Procedural Justice, 42 Ga. L. Rev. 407 (2008). Or would such requirements prove so cumbersome that prosecutors would evade them—moving decisions about charges and plea offers even farther into the shadows than they are now? Which safeguards are both required for fairness and workable in practice?

Administrative law suggests other caveats for plea bargaining. Judge Lynch observes that prosecutors essentially "adjudicate guilt and set punishments." If one takes seriously the notion that charging and bargaining are an administrative process, should criminal law follow the administrative-law principle that those who investigate a case should be barred from adjudicating—in this case, from deciding what to charge or what plea to accept? Some scholars argue that this is a workable means to police plea bargaining.[25] For additional institutional-design proposals, see Stephanos Bibas, Prosecutorial Regulation versus Prosecutorial Accountability, 157 U. Pa. L. Rev. 959 (2009).

2. *The federal/state contrast.* Judge Lynch focuses especially on the dynamics of charging and bargaining in federal prosecutions for white-collar crime. That setting has several distinctive features. First, although no prosecutor's resources are ever unlimited, the U.S. Attorney's Office, together with the federal agencies that investigate white-collar crime—for example, the Securities and Exchange Commission and the Environmental Protection Agency—have enormous resources at their disposal for investigating and trying cases. Second, the federal prosecutor has more freedom to set priorities and choose cases than her state counterpart does. Some white-collar cases (such as fraud) can be referred out for prosecution in the state courts, and nearly all cases can be downgraded to civil enforcement actions or dropped completely; in state courts, in contrast, much of the caseload consists of traditional crimes against persons and property that may be more difficult to disregard. Finally, the white-collar defendant in a federal case is typically represented by experienced, well-compensated counsel.

What safeguards would be appropriate to ensure that an "administrative" system functions properly when (as in more than 80 percent of all criminal cases) the defendant is represented by the public defender or by court-appointed counsel paid under a schedule of strictly limited fees?

C. SENTENCING

In no area of contemporary criminal law is there as much controversy, as much doctrinal movement, and as much diversity of approach throughout

---

25. E.g., Rachel E. Barkow, Institutional Design and the Policing of Prosecutors: Lessons from Administrative Law, 61 Stan. L. Rev. 869 (2009).

the country as there is in matters relating to sentencing. In historical perspective, this is a comparatively recent phenomenon. Until the 1970s, sentencing at the federal level and in almost all states took largely the same discretionary and indeterminate form. Trial judges could select any sentence within wide statutory boundaries, subject to few if any constraints. After the defendant had served some proportion of a sentence behind bars, parole officials could determine the ultimate release date. Regimes with these parole powers were deemed indeterminate sentencing schemes because defendants sentenced to prison did not learn their actual date of release until a parole board made its decision, usually many years later. Today, some form of discretionary sentencing scheme—with or without indeterminate powers in a parole board—remains in effect in more than half the American states.[26] But dissatisfaction with so much discretion from across the political spectrum triggered fundamental change in many places. Numerous jurisdictions have replaced their traditional systems with alternatives that limit—sometimes drastically—the discretion of the sentencing judge and parole officials.

In Chapter 2 we considered sentencing from a strictly substantive angle. We sought to examine the justification of punishment and to discuss which facts about an offender or his offense should be deemed relevant in determining the kind and degree of punishment imposed. We considered these issues as they would be confronted by any decision maker, in any legal setting, who was empowered to select an optimally appropriate sentence. Embedded in those issues, of course, is the problem of determining who the decision maker should be and what should be the constraints under which that decision maker operates. Accordingly, we touched briefly on recent developments that modify the traditional discretion of the sentencing judge. See pages 124-130 supra.

Here we examine these developments in depth. We consider the concerns that prompted them, the legal issues they have spawned, and their implications for the rule of law. Section C.1 examines the traditional discretionary approach and Section C.2 discusses the newer determinate systems, including the federal sentencing guidelines and the recent round of problems and reforms prompted by the Supreme Court's renewed attention to the relationship between the jury's role and sentencing.

1. Discretionary Sentencing Systems

WILLIAMS v. NEW YORK

Supreme Court of the United States
337 U.S. 241 (1949)

JUSTICE BLACK delivered the opinion of the Court.

A jury in a New York state court found appellant guilty of murder in the first degree. The jury recommended life imprisonment, but the trial judge

---

26. Rachel E. Barkow, Administering Crime, 52 UCLA L. Rev. 715, 741 n.74 (2005).

imposed sentence of death. In giving his reasons . . . the judge discussed in open court the evidence upon which the jury had convicted, stating that this evidence had been considered in the light of additional information obtained through the court's "Probation Department, and through other sources." . . .

The Court of Appeals of New York affirmed the conviction and sentence over the contention that . . . the controlling penal statutes are in violation of the due process clause of the Fourteenth Amendment . . . "in that the sentence of death was based upon information supplied by witnesses with whom the accused had not been confronted and as to whom he had no opportunity for cross-examination or rebuttal." . . .

The evidence [at trial] proved a wholly indefensible murder committed by a person engaged in a burglary. The judge instructed the jury that if it returned a verdict of guilty as charged, without recommendation for life sentence, "The Court must impose the death penalty," but if such recommendation was made, "the Court may impose a life sentence." The judge went on to emphasize that "the Court is not bound to accept your recommendation."

About five weeks after the verdict of guilty with recommendation of life imprisonment, and after a statutory pre-sentence investigation report to the judge, the defendant was brought to court to be sentenced. [T]he judge . . . narrated the shocking details of the crime as shown by the trial evidence, [and] stated that the pre-sentence investigation revealed many material facts concerning appellant's background which though relevant to the question of punishment could not properly have been brought to the attention of the jury. . . . He referred to the experience appellant "had had on thirty other burglaries in and about the same vicinity" where the murder had been committed. The appellant had not been convicted of these burglaries although the judge had information that he had confessed to some and had been identified as the perpetrator of some of the others. The judge also referred to certain activities of appellant as shown by the probation report that indicated appellant possessed "a morbid sexuality" and classified him as a "menace to society." The accuracy of the statements made by the judge as to appellant's background and past practices were not challenged by appellant or his counsel, nor was the judge asked to disregard any of them or to afford appellant a chance to refute or discredit any of them by cross-examination or otherwise.

The case presents a serious and difficult question [concerning] the manner in which a judge may obtain information to guide him in the imposition of sentence upon an already convicted defendant. Within limits fixed by statutes, New York judges are given a broad discretion to decide the type and extent of punishment for convicted defendants. . . . To aid a judge in exercising this discretion intelligently the New York procedural policy encourages him to consider information about the convicted person's past life, health, habits, conduct, and mental and moral propensities. The sentencing judge may consider such information even though obtained outside the courtroom from persons whom a defendant has not been permitted to confront or cross-examine. . . .

Appellant urges that the New York statutory policy is in irreconcilable conflict with . . . the due process of law clause of the Fourteenth Amendment [and its requirement] that no person shall be tried and convicted of an offense unless he is given reasonable notice of the charges against him and is afforded an opportunity to examine adverse witnesses. . . .

Tribunals passing on the guilt of a defendant always have been hedged in by strict evidentiary procedural limitations. But both before and since the American colonies became a nation, courts in this country and in England practiced a policy under which a sentencing judge could exercise a wide discretion in the sources and types of evidence used to assist him in determining the kind and extent of punishment to be imposed within limits fixed by law. Out-of-court affidavits have been used frequently, and of course in the smaller communities sentencing judges naturally have in mind their knowledge of the personalities and backgrounds of convicted offenders. . . .

In addition to the historical basis for different evidentiary rules governing trial and sentencing procedures there are sound practical reasons for the distinction. . . . Rules of evidence have been fashioned for criminal trials which narrowly confine the trial contest to evidence that is strictly relevant to the particular offense charged. These rules rest in part on a necessity to prevent a time-consuming and confusing trial of collateral issues. They were also designed to prevent tribunals concerned solely with the issue of guilt of a particular offense from being influenced . . . by evidence that the defendant had habitually engaged in other misconduct. A sentencing judge, however, is not confined to the narrow issue of guilt. . . . Highly relevant—if not essential—to his selection of an appropriate sentence is the possession of the fullest information possible concerning the defendant's life and characteristics. And modern concepts individualizing punishment have made it all the more necessary that a sentencing judge not be denied an opportunity to obtain pertinent information by a requirement of rigid adherence to restrictive rules of evidence properly applicable to the trial.

Undoubtedly the New York statutes emphasize a prevalent modern philosophy of penology that the punishment should fit the offender and not merely the crime. The belief no longer prevails that every offense in a like legal category calls for an identical punishment without regard to the past life and habits of a particular offender. This whole country has traveled far from the period in which the death sentence was an automatic and commonplace result of convictions—even for offenses today deemed trivial. Today's philosophy of individualizing sentences makes sharp distinctions for example between first and repeated offenders. Indeterminate sentences, the ultimate termination of which are sometimes decided by nonjudicial agencies have to a large extent taken the place of the old rigidly fixed punishments. The practice of probation which relies heavily on nonjudicial implementation has been accepted as a wise policy. . . . Retribution is no longer the dominant objective of the criminal law. Reformation and rehabilitation of offenders have become important goals of criminal jurisprudence.

Modern changes in the treatment of offenders make it more necessary now than a century ago for observance of the distinctions in the evidential procedure in the trial and sentencing processes. For indeterminate sentences and probation have resulted in an increase in the discretionary powers exercised in fixing punishments. [A] strong motivating force for the changes has been the belief that by careful study of the lives and personalities of convicted offenders many could be less severely punished and restored sooner to complete freedom and useful citizenship. This belief to a large extent has been justified.

. . . Probation workers making reports of their investigations have not been trained to prosecute but to aid offenders. Their reports have been given a high value by conscientious judges who want to sentence persons on the best available information rather than on guesswork. . . . We must recognize that most of the information now relied upon by judges to guide them in the intelligent imposition of sentences would be unavailable if information were restricted to that given in open court by witnesses subject to cross-examination. And the modern probation report draws on information concerning every aspect of a defendant's life. The type and extent of this information make totally impractical if not impossible open court testimony with cross-examination. Such a procedure could endlessly delay criminal administration in a retrial of collateral issues.

The considerations we have set out admonish us against treating the due process clause as a uniform command that courts throughout the Nation abandon their age-old practice of seeking information from out-of-court sources to guide their judgment toward a more enlightened and just sentence. [W]e do not think the Federal Constitution restricts the view of the sentencing judge to the information received in open court. The due process clause should not be treated as a device for freezing the evidential procedure of sentencing in the mold of trial procedure. So to treat the due process clause would hinder if not preclude all courts—state and federal—from making progressive efforts to improve the administration of criminal justice. . . . We hold that appellant was not denied due process of law.

JUSTICE MURPHY, dissenting. . . . Due process of law includes at least the idea that a person accused of crime shall be accorded a fair hearing through all the stages of the proceedings against him. I agree with the Court as to the value and humaneness of liberal use of probation reports as developed by modern penologists, but, in a capital case, against the unanimous recommendation of a jury, where the report would concededly not have been admissible at the trial, and was not subject to examination by the defendant, I am forced to conclude that the high commands of due process were not obeyed.

Note, Due Process and Legislative Standards in Sentencing, 101 U. Pa. L. Rev. 257, 276-277 (1952): The practical problem which is posed is not that of admissibility but the utilization of procedural devices to ensure accuracy and allow argument on the relevancy of the disclosed information to the particular circumstances of the case. The presentence probation report in *Williams v. New York* illustrates this problem. The probation department there concluded that Williams was a "psychopathic liar" whose ideas "revolve around a morbid sexuality," that he was "a full time burglar," "emotionally unstable," "suffers no remorse," and was deemed to be "a menace to society." His criminal record, confined to a charge of theft when he was 11 years old and a conviction as a wayward minor, did not support such generalizations. The conclusions of the probation department were apparently based upon (1) stolen goods found in his room, (2) identification of Williams by a woman whose apartment he allegedly burglarized and a seven-year-old girl he had allegedly raped, (3) allegations that he had committed "about 30 burglaries," and (4) ". . . information" that he had acted as a "pimp" and had been observed taking indecent photographs of young children. Aside from the truth or falsity of these statements or their adequacy as a basis for a death sentence, in this case life or death turned upon conclusions drawn by probation officers from hearsay and from unproven allegations. Such information is highly relevant to the question of sentence, but its accuracy depends upon the ability and fairness of the probation officer, who must weigh evidence, judge the credibility of the informants and be zealous in closely examining them. [A]t best this method of ascertaining facts has serious deficiencies because it relies for cross-interrogation and cross-investigation upon one "who has neither the strong interest nor the full knowledge that are required," and which usually only the defendant can provide.

NOTES

1. Developments in sentencing law after **Williams.** Some aspects of *Williams* have not withstood the test of time. In *capital* cases, *Williams* has in effect been overruled. In Gardner v. Florida, 430 U.S. 349 (1977), a jury recommended life imprisonment, but the judge, relying on a confidential presentence report, sentenced the murder defendant to death. The Court found the procedure constitutionally defective and vacated the death sentence. A plurality emphasized that constitutional developments since *Williams* now mandate heightened care in death penalty sentencing and rejected the state's argument that confidentiality was necessary to "enable investigators to obtain relevant but sensitive disclosures from persons unwilling to comment publicly." The Court has also since made clear that sentencing hearings must comport with many due process requirements; the defendant must, for example, be afforded the effective assistance of counsel. Mempa v. Rhay, 389 U.S. 128 (1967).

But in most particulars, the holding in *Williams* has proved durable. For non-capital cases, the central holding of *Williams*—that the federal Constitution does not bar reliance on confidential information at sentencing—remains undisturbed. And judges relying on such information continue to make critical factual findings that dictate a defendant's sentence.

Nonetheless, most states now allow felony defendants to review the presentence report, or at least most portions of it, prior to imposition of sentence. Federal practice affords less disclosure. Fed. R. Crim. Pro. Rule 32(d), guarantees the defense unrestricted access to a document called "the presentence report," (PSR) but it allows the judge to receive other information in a separate document that is not made available to the defense. The report supplied to the defendant "must exclude" three types of information that the judge receives confidentially: a diagnostic opinion that, if disclosed, might disrupt a rehabilitation program; "information obtained on a promise of confidentiality"; and "information that, if disclosed, might result in physical or other harm to the defendant or others." The defendant receives only the trial judge's summary of information excluded from the report. Rule 32 gives the defense an opportunity to comment on the report, and at the court's discretion, to offer evidence to rebut alleged factual inaccuracies. But in cases of factual dispute, the prosecution needs to prove its version only by a preponderance of the evidence. Moreover, the defendant usually is afforded no opportunity to confront or cross-examine those who may have provided adverse information. See Alan Michaels, Trial Rights at Sentencing, 81 N.C. L. Rev. 1771 (2003).

For a sense of what these rules can mean in practice, consider United States v. Weston, 448 F.2d 626 (9th Cir. 1971). The defendant was convicted of transporting 537 grams of heroin. The PSR asserted that federal agents "feel that she ... has been the chief supplier to the Western Washington area," making trips to Mexico every two weeks and earning up to $140,000 in profit on each trip. Their source for these conclusions, presumably a confidential informant, was not disclosed. Defense counsel hotly denied the accusation, saying that he "had never seen Weston display any sign of wealth," and "can't conceive of what type of investigation I can do to come back and say that she isn't [a major dealer]." Nonetheless, the trial judge stated that, with nothing more than the defendant's vehement denial, he had "no alternative ... but to accept as true the information [obtained from] the Federal Bureau of Narcotics." He then imposed the maximum sentence, 20 years' imprisonment. Was the judge's action justified, or should he have disregarded the accusation and treated Weston as a low-level dealer? Which approach runs the greater risk of an inappropriate sentence?

One solution, endorsed in the Second Circuit, has become known as the *Fatico* hearing. In United States v. Fatico, 603 F.2d 1053 (2d Cir. 1979), the defendant had been convicted of conspiracy to possess stolen furs. The presentence report described him as an "upper echelon" figure in organized crime. The FBI refused to identify its source, a confidential informant, "for the obvious reasons that both his life and usefulness as an informant would be jeopardized." The sentencing judge held an evidentiary hearing on the allegations but allowed the FBI agents to report the hearsay accusations only if the government also offered significant corroboration. Seven FBI agents testified that 17 informants had independently told them of Fatico's high-level involvement in organized crime, and the judge, accepting their testimony, imposed a sentence close to the applicable maximum. The court of appeals upheld this approach, confirming the district judge's discretion to hold such a hearing "where there is reason to question the reliability of material facts having in the judge's view direct bearing on the sentence to be imposed, especially where those facts are essentially hearsay." Id. at 1057 n.9 (1979). This approach, of course, falls far short of the evidentiary requirements for proving guilt at trial, and even this modest safeguard is left to the discretion of the trial court. In practice, judges often decline to take even this limited step towards assuring factual reliability.

Questions: Is the *Fatico* hearing too burdensome? Insufficient to protect against unreliable accusations? Both?

2. *Discretion and the rationale of punishment.* What purposes of punishment call for individualized sentencing and wide discretion for the decision maker? In *Williams*, the Court defends individualization on the ground that "[r]etribution is no longer the dominant objective of the criminal law. Reformation and rehabilitation have become important goals." Indeed, the premise of indeterminate sentences, with broad discretion for judges and parole officials, rests on the aim of rehabilitation.

Indeterminate sentencing fell into disfavor in the 1970s both because of a concern with disparity and because of doubts that rehabilitation was effective and that parole officials could identify when a prisoner was, in fact, rehabilitated. See Tapia v. United States, 131 S. Ct. 2382, 2387 (2011); Michelle S. Phelps, Rehabilitation in the Punitive Era: The Gap Between Rhetoric and Reality in U.S. Prison Programs, 45 Law & Soc'y Rev. 33, 36-38 (2011). When Congress overhauled federal sentencing with the Sentencing Reform Act in 1984, it eliminated parole and cabined judicial discretion based on these concerns. And although judges are charged under 18 U.S.C. §3553(a)(2)(D) with considering what sentence will provide the defendant with "needed educational or vocational training, medical care, or other correctional treatment in the most effective manner," the Sentencing Reform Act also made clear that judges must "recognize[e] that imprisonment is not an appropriate means of promoting correction and rehabilitation." 18 U.S.C. §3582(a). Thus, while rehabilitation may still be a goal of sentencing in the federal system, it cannot be used as a justification for imposing or extending a term of incarceration. *Tapia*, 131 S. Ct. at 2388-2389. Although the rhetoric around rehabilitation has changed over time, the amount of actual programming in prisons has stayed relatively modest and constant from the 1970s until today; its emphasis, however, has changed from academic programs to reentry-related counseling. Phelps, supra, at 56-59. Sharon Dolovich argues that whatever benefit flows from the minimal rehabilitation programming that is offered in prison, it is outweighed by the harm to rehabilitation caused by the dehumanizing experience of incarceration itself. Sharon Dolovich, Foreword: Incarceration American-Style, 3 Harv. L. & Pol'y Rev. 237, 245-254 (2009).

Is rehabilitation the only theory of punishment that requires individualized determinations? If we understand retribution to mean punishment tailored to the culpability of the offender, doesn't retribution also require a highly individualized, discretionary judgment? Even if we understand retribution and deterrence to mandate a punishment set solely as a function of the seriousness of the offense, don't these goals still require a highly individualized, discretionary judgment about the nature of the offense in that particular case? Conversely, can a highly discretionary system *undermine* any goals of punishment? Consider the comments that follow:

Francis Allen, The Borderland of Criminal Justice 32-36 (1964): [The] rehabilitative ideal has been debased in practice and . . . the consequences . . . are serious and, at times, dangerous. [U]nder the dominance of the rehabilitative ideal, the language of therapy is frequently employed, wittingly or unwittingly, to disguise [a] fixation on problems of custody. . . . Even more disturbing [is] the tendency of the staff to justify these custodial measures in therapeutic terms. . . . Surprisingly enough, the therapeutic ideal has often led to increased severity of penal measures.

[A] study of criminal justice is fundamentally a study in the exercise of political power. No such study can properly avoid the problem of the abuse of power. The obligation of containing power within the limits suggested by a community's political values has been considerably complicated by the rise of the rehabilitative ideal. For the problem today is one of regulating the exercise of power by men of good will, whose motivations are to help, not to injure. . . . There is a tendency for such persons to claim immunity from the usual forms of restraint and to insist that professionalism and a devotion to science provide sufficient protection against unwarranted invasion of individual rights. . . .

Measures which subject individuals to the substantial and involuntary deprivation of their liberty contain an inescapable punitive element. . . . As such, these measures must be closely scrutinized to insure that power is being applied consistently with those values of the community that justify interference with liberty for only the most clear and compelling reasons.

Marvin Frankel, Criminal Sentencing: Law Without Order 5, 9-11, 17-23, 98-102 (1973): [T]he almost wholly unchecked and sweeping powers we give to judges in the fashioning of sentences are terrifying and intolerable for a society that professes devotion to the rule of law. . . .

The ideal of individualized justice is by no means an unmitigated evil, but it must be an ideal of justice *according to law*. This means we must reject individual distinctions—discriminations, that is—unless they can be justified by relevant tests capable of formulation and application with sufficient objectivity to ensure that the results will be more than the idiosyncratic ukases of particular officials, judges or others.

[S]weeping penalty statutes allow sentences to be "individualized" not so much in terms of defendants but mainly in terms of the wide spectrums of character, bias, neurosis, and daily vagary encountered among occupants of the trial bench. It is no wonder that wherever supposed professionals in the field—criminologists, penologists, probation officers, and, yes, lawyers and judges—discuss sentencing, the talk inevitably dwells upon the problem of "disparity." . . . The evidence is conclusive that judges of widely varying attitudes on sentencing, administering statutes that confer huge measures of discretion, mete out widely divergent sentences where the divergences are explainable only by the variations among the judges, not by material differences in the defendants or their crimes.

[T]he tragic state of disorder in our sentencing practices is not attributable to any unique endowments of sadism or bestiality among judges as a species. [J]udges in general, if only because of occupational conditioning, may be somewhat calmer, more dispassionate, and more humane than the average of people across the board. But nobody has the experience of being sentenced by "judges in general." The particular defendant on some existential day confronts a specific judge. The occupant of the bench on that day may be punitive, patriotic, self-righteous, guilt-ridden, and more than customarily dyspeptic. The vice in our system is that all such qualities have free rein as well as potentially fatal impact upon the defendant's finite life.

Such individual, personal powers are not evil only, or mainly, because evil people may come to hold positions of authority. The more pervasive wrong is that a regime of substantially limitless discretion is by definition arbitrary, capricious, and antithetical to the rule of law.

Twentieth Century Fund, Task Force on Criminal Sentencing, Fair and Certain Punishment 33 (1976): [T]he vagaries of sentencing—one convicted robber being sentenced to life and another placed on probation—have seriously affected the deterrent value of criminal sanctions. For many convicted offenders, there is what amounts to amnesty. And for other offenders, often undistinguishable from the first group in terms of past record, current crime, or future dangerousness, there is the injustice of the exemplary sentence. The judge, aware that most persons who commit the particular crime are not sentenced to prison, determines to make an example of this offender and thus sentences him to an unfairly long term. Such haphazard sentencing does little to increase the deterrent impact of the criminal law, since the potential criminal is likely to calculate his potential sentence by reference to what most similarly situated offenders receive.

2. *Sentencing Reform*

INTRODUCTORY NOTES

In response to the concerns raised by a broad range of critics—with those on the left decrying discrimination in sentencing (particularly against the poor and minorities) and those on the right arguing that judges and parole boards were using their discretion to undermine the deterrent and retributive purposes of criminal punishment by releasing offenders too early—many jurisdictions abandoned their traditional discretionary systems. Some states addressed the perceived injustice of indeterminate sentencing systems either by requiring the parole-release date to be fixed early in the prisoner's term or by abolishing parole altogether. This system provides certainty for the offender sentenced to prison but does nothing to make the critical decisions more uniform or predictable; indeed complete abolition of parole actually aggravates the problem of broad judicial discretion by removing the countervailing power of the parole board. More commonly, reform proposals have treated judicial discretion as the principal evil. Several distinct approaches to reform emerged.

1. Mandatory minimums. A solution increasingly popular with lawmakers has been enactment of mandatory minimum sentences for specified crimes. Congress introduced stiff mandatory minimums for drug offenses in 1956, but soon concluded that they were a failure, and in 1970, it repealed virtually all the drug mandatories. Among those supporting the 1970 repeal was Congressman George H.W. Bush (R-TX), who argued that mandatories were ineffective and unjust. See Stephen J. Schulhofer, Rethinking Mandatory Minimums, 28 Wake Forest L. Rev. 199, 200-201 (1993). Just as Congress was repealing its mandatories, New York turned to them, enacting long mandatory drug sentences (the so-called Rockefeller drug laws) in 1973. In 1984, Congress once more enacted severe mandatory minimums for drug offenses (as well as for certain firearms offenses), and has continued to pass statutes with mandatory minimum sentences on a regular basis ever since. More than one-quarter of offenders sentenced in federal court in fiscal year 2010 were convicted of an offense carrying a mandatory minimum penalty.[27] Most of these—more than 75 percent—are for drug offenses, and firearms offenses make up another 12 percent.[28] And roughly 40 percent of the offenders in federal prison as of 2010 were subject to a mandatory minimum penalty at sentencing.[29] The tide might be turning on mandatory minimums again, however, as several states (including New York) have repealed some of their mandatory sentencing laws in the wake of fiscal pressures. Marc Mauer, Sentencing Reform: Amid Mass Incarcerations—Guarded Optimism, 26

---

27. United States Sentencing Commission, Report to the Congress: Mandatory Minimum Penalties in the Federal Criminal Justice System 120 (Oct. 2011), available at http://www.ussc.gov/Legislative_and_Public_Affairs/Congressional_Testimony_and_Reports/Mandatory_Minimum_Penalties/20111031_RtC_Mandatory_Minimum.cfm. [hereafter cited as 2011 Report].

28. Id. at 122.

29. Id. at xxix.

Crim. Just. 27, 28 (Spring 2011). Still, many mandatory minimum laws remain on the books in the states, and Congress has done little to reform mandatory minimums at the federal level, with a notable exception being the repeal of the five-year mandatory minimum for possession of crack cocaine in the Fair Sentencing Act of 2010.

Although a major stated goal of mandatory minimum sentences was to eliminate discrimination on the basis of race, racial disparities have increased with the proliferation of mandatory minimum laws. Although it is difficult to pin down a direct causal link between the racial disparities in the prison population and these mandatory minimum laws, there are signs of a connection. In a 2004 report, the United States Sentencing Commission concluded that "[t]oday's sentencing policies, crystallized into sentencing guidelines and mandatory minimum statutes, have a greater adverse impact on Black offenders than did the factors taken into account by judges in the [prior] discretionary system. . . ."[30] The Commission's 2011 report finds that black offenders make up 38 percent of the offenders convicted of an offense carrying a mandatory minimum penalty, even though black offenders represent 21 percent of the total offender population.[31]

One possible reason for this disparity is that mandatory minimum schemes are usually a misnomer. They are truly mandatory only when they require filing of the most serious charge and prohibit bargaining, or when they require judges to ignore the formal charge and base the sentence on the actual conduct, as revealed by a presentence investigation. Even if some jurisdictions—such as the federal system—espouse this view, in practice they fail to achieve it. A recent study of the federal mandatory minimums showed, for example, that among defendants who entered into plea agreements, almost half were sentenced below the mandatory level for which they appeared eligible, because they provided substantial assistance to the government or qualified for a statutory safety valve provision, or both.[32] This made an enormous difference in an offender's sentence, with "[o]ffenders who were convicted of an offense carrying a mandatory minimum penalty and remained subject to that penalty at sentencing receiv[ing] an average sentence of 139 months," compared to 63 months for those offenders who received relief from a mandatory penalty.[33] More disturbingly, the distribution of cases did not fall proportionately on all offenders. Black offenders convicted of an offense carrying a mandatory minimum penalty remained subject to it at the highest rate—65 percent of the cases—of any racial group.[34]

Most jurisdictions do not even claim to insist on the mandatory filing of available charges that carry a mandatory minimum. Far more common are

---

30. United States Sentencing Commission, Fifteen Years of Guidelines Sentencing 135 (2004).
31. 2011 Report, supra, at 124 tbl. 7-1.
32. Id. at xxviii.
33. Id. at 136.
34. Id. (white offenders followed at 53.5%, and then Hispanic offenders at 44.3%). This pattern replicates an earlier finding, United States Sentencing Commission, Mandatory Minimum Penalties in the Federal Criminal Justice System: A Special Report to Congress 58, 76-82 (1991).

mandatories that require a given sentence only in the event of conviction on a given charge. Such "discretionary mandatories" constrain judges but not prosecutors, who are sometimes perceived as less likely to be "soft on crime." As a result, in most places, the greatest impact of mandatory minimums is to give prosecutors a powerful bargaining chip for use in plea negotiation. Consider the following example:

United States v. Vasquez, 2010 WL 1257359 (E.D.N.Y.) Statement of Reason for Sentence (Gleeson, J.): [Roberto Vasquez had a troubled history that included sexual abuse by his older brother, drug addiction, and treatment for depression and bi-polar disorder. Aside from the drug trafficking at issue in this case, his only criminal history involved his ex-wife, Ingrid Melendez, with whom he had three children. When that relationship ended, Melendez would not let him see their children, and he reacted by menacing her with a knife. Six months later, he violated an order of protection by threatening to kill her. A year later, Vasquez once again showed up at Melendez's home, and as a result was convicted of harassment. Since 2005, he had a stable relationship with another woman, Caraballo, with whom he has a three-year-old daughter. But Melendez continued to deny Vasquez access to their three children, even though Vasquez was complying with his court-ordered child support obligations. Under the stress of this situation, he began using cocaine again. That development established the groundwork for his involvement in his offense of conviction.]

To support his expensive cocaine habit, Vasquez . . . personally assisted in the distribution of 300 grams of heroin. He was aware of the distribution of 350 additional grams by others, so he was responsible under the sentencing guidelines for 650 grams. . . . After his arrest, Vasquez tried to cooperate with the government. He provided information about two individuals, but it could not be corroborated. . . .

The government had it within its power to charge Vasquez with a standard drug trafficking charge, which carries a maximum sentence of 20 years. Instead, it included him in a conspiracy charge with his brother and three others and cited . . . a sentence-enhancing provision that carries a maximum of life in prison and a mandatory minimum of ten years upon conviction. During plea negotiations, the government refused to drop that charge unless Vasquez pled guilty to a lesser-included sentencing enhancement that carried a maximum of 40 years and a mandatory minimum of five years.

. . . Most people, including me, agree that the kingpins, masterminds, and mid-level managers of drug trafficking enterprises deserve severe punishment. But right from the start Congress made a mistake: it made a drug defendant's eligibility for the mandatory sentences depend not on his or her role in the offense, but on the quantity of drugs involved in the crime. Thus, if the crime involved one kilogram of heroin, five kilograms of cocaine, or only 50 grams of crack, every defendant involved in that crime, irrespective of his or her actual role, is treated as a kingpin or mastermind and must get at least ten years in jail.

If they want to, prosecutors can decide that street-level defendants like Vasquez—the low-hanging fruit for law enforcement—must receive the harsh sentences that Congress intended for kingpins and managers, no matter how many other factors weigh in favor of less severe sentences. The government concedes, as it must, that Vasquez played a *minor* role in his brother's modest drug operation, not the mid-level managerial role the five-year mandatory sentence was enacted to punish. . . . Yet, by the simple act of invoking the sentence-enhancing provision of the statute, the government has dictated the imposition of the severe sentence intended only for those with an aggravating role.

When the case was first called . . . I pointed out the obvious: the five-year mandatory sentence in this case would be unjust. The prosecutor agreed, and welcomed my direction that she go back to the United States Attorney with a request from the Court that he withdraw the aspect of the charge that required the imposition of the five-year minimum. . . .

[When the prosecutor returned, s]he reported that the United States Attorney would not relent. She offered two reasons. The first was that I might have failed to focus on the fact that Vasquez . . . was allowed to plead to the five-year mandatory minimum rather than to the ten-year mandatory minimum that he, his brother, and three other co-defendants were originally charged with. I think this means that Vasquez should be grateful the government did not insist on a ten-year minimum sentence based on additional quantities of cocaine it concedes he knew nothing about. . . . I suppose there is some consolation in the fact that the government did not pursue that absurd course. . . . But that hardly explains, let alone justifies, the government's insistence on the injustice at hand.

Second, the prosecutor suggested that I had failed to "focus" on the seriousness of Vasquez's crimes against his ex-wife, Melendez. Implicit in that assertion is the contention that even if Vasquez does not deserve the five-year minimum because he was not a mid-level manager of a drug enterprise, he deserves it because of his past crimes. This rings especially hollow. Those past crimes have been front and center at all times. . . .

I recognize that the United States Attorney is not required to explain to judges the reasons for decisions like this one, and for that reason I did not ask for them. But the ones that were volunteered do not withstand the slightest scrutiny.

As a result of the decision to insist on the five-year mandatory minimum, there was no judging going on at Vasquez's sentencing. . . . The defendant's difficult childhood and lifelong struggle with mental illness were out of bounds, as were the circumstances giving rise to his minor role in his brother's drug business, . . . the fact that he tried to cooperate but was not involved enough in the drug trade to be of assistance, the effect of his incarceration on his three-year-old daughter and the eight-year-old child of Caraballo he is raising as his own, the fact that he has been a good father to them for nearly five years, the fact that his prior convictions all arose out of his ex-wife's refusal to permit him to see their three children. Sentencing is not a science, and I don't pretend to be better than anyone else at assimilating these and the numerous other factors, both aggravating and mitigating, that legitimately bear on an appropriate sentence. But I try my best ... to do justice for the individual before me and for our community. In this case, those efforts would have resulted in a prison term of 24 months, followed by a five-year period of supervision with conditions including both other forms of punishment (home detention and community service) and efforts to assist Vasquez with the mental health, substance abuse, and anger management problems that have plagued him, in some respects for his entire life. If he had failed to avail himself of those efforts, or if, for example, he intentionally had contact with Melendez without the prior authorization of his supervising probation officer, he would have gone back to jail on this case.

The mandatory minimum sentence ... supplanted any effort to do justice, leaving in its place the heavy wooden club that was explicitly meant only for mid-level managers of drug operations. The absence of fit between the crude method of punishment and the particular set of circumstances before me was conspicuous; when I imposed sentence on the weak and sobbing Vasquez on March 5, everyone present, including the prosecutor, could feel the injustice. . . .

Questions: How should we appraise the value and drawbacks of mandatory minimums? *(a)* For "discretionary mandatories," are the risks of unequal treatment and disproportionate punishment outweighed by potential deterrence gains? For that matter, are potential gains in deterrence dissipated by the uncertainty that these nominally mandatory sentences will actually be applied? For a discussion of the merits of mandatory minimum sentences and a proposal that judges be allowed to depart from them whenever the federal guidelines provide for a lower sentence than the statutory minimum, see Erik Luna & Paul G. Cassell, Mandatory Minimalism, 32 Cardozo L. Rev. 1, 10-17, 60 (2010).

(b) Should a jurisdiction try to avoid these difficulties by making its mandatory minimums truly mandatory, for prosecutors as well as for judges? Is there a way to ensure that prosecutors will fully comply with the requirements of a mandatory minimum? If they do comply, will the result be *too much* equality—equal treatment of offenders who committed their offenses under very different circumstances? Is Vasquez an example of too much equality, or were prosecutors correct to charge him as they did? If a mandatory minimum is truly mandatory, why would any defendant who commits one of the subject crimes ever be willing to plead guilty?

(c) In addition to their power to withhold charges that carry a mandatory minimum sentence, prosecutors often can enable a defendant to avoid the mandatory minimum by filing a motion with the court attesting to the defendant's cooperation. See, e.g., 18 U.S.C. §3553(e). In multi-defendant cases, will this just reward the defendant who gets to the prosecutor's office first? Luna &

Cassell, supra, at 15. For further discussion of the pros and cons of sentence reductions in return for cooperation, see page 1144 supra.

2. *"Presumptive" and guideline sentencing.* Given the drawbacks of mandatory minimums, no American legislature has attempted to extend that approach to all crimes; rather, legislatures have targeted selected crimes, such as drug distribution, firearms offenses, and sex offenses against children. To address the problems of sentencing discretion more generally, reformers have turned to more flexible techniques. California, for example, adopted legislation specifying within narrow limits the normal sentence for each offense and tightly restricted the trial judge's discretion to depart from the specified terms.[35]

Most states, unlike California, were not prepared to undertake the complex task of identifying appropriate sentences in detail and making the statutory revisions and refinements necessary to keep them current. Several jurisdictions therefore opted to create an expert body—a sentencing commission—charged with drafting guidelines that judges would be required or encouraged to follow in making sentencing decisions. The commissions are administrative agencies accountable to the legislature but insulated to some degree from immediate political pressures, and they are afforded the time and resources to deal with the complex array of sentencing problems. A 2006 study found that of 17 states with sentencing guidelines, nine use guidelines that are presumptively binding on the judge, and eight use guidelines that are voluntary. John F. Pfaff, The Continued Vitality of Structured Sentencing Following Blakely: The Effectiveness of Voluntary Guidelines, 54 UCLA L. Rev. 235, 244 (2006). In its tentative draft of new sentencing provisions to the MPC, the American Law Institute has endorsed the view that the best approach is to have a sentencing commission adopt presumptive guidelines. Model Penal Code, Sentencing, Tentative Draft No. 1 (Apr. 9, 2007).

Developments in the federal system have received the most attention and generated the most controversy because Congress enacted a guideline system that is far less flexible than any of the systems used to control judicial discretion in the states. In 1984, in addition to abolishing parole, Congress created a United States Sentencing Commission charged with promulgating guidelines for judges to use in federal sentencing decisions. See 28 U.S.C. §§991-998. The Commission was directed to establish sentencing categories based on specific combinations of offense and offender characteristics and to identify a narrow range of authorized sentences (with no more than a 25 percent spread between maximum and minimum terms of imprisonment) for each category. See 28 U.S.C. §994(b). Except under restricted conditions, judges were required to impose a sentence within the authorized range. See 18 U.S.C. §3553:

---

35. See People v. Black, 113 P.3d 534 (Cal. 2005).

(a) *Factors To Be Considered in Imposing a Sentence.*—The court shall impose a sentence sufficient, but not greater than necessary, to comply with the purposes set forth in paragraph (2) of this subsection. The court, in determining the particular sentence to be imposed, shall consider—

(1) the nature and circumstances of the offense and the history and characteristics of the defendant;

(2) the need for the sentence imposed—

(A) to reflect the seriousness of the offense, to promote respect for the law, and to provide just punishment for the offense;

(B) to afford adequate deterrence to criminal conduct;

(C) to protect the public from further crimes of the defendant; and

(D) to provide the defendant with needed educational or vocational training, medical care, or other correctional treatment in the most effective manner. . . .

(4) the kinds of sentence and the sentencing range established for the applicable category of offense committed by the applicable category of defendant as set forth in the guidelines that are issued by the Sentencing Commission. . . .

(b) *Application of Guidelines in Imposing a Sentence.*—The court shall impose a sentence of the kind, and within the range, referred to in subsection (a)(4) unless the court finds that there exists an aggravating or mitigating circumstance of a kind, or to a degree, not adequately taken into consideration by the Sentencing Commission in formulating the guidelines that should result in a sentence different from that described. . . .

The guidelines promulgated by the Commission took effect in 1987. This complex set of rules for calculating federal sentences runs over 400 pages, and for years it was amended annually. For a useful introduction, see Stephen Breyer, The Federal Sentencing Guidelines and the Key Compromises upon which They Rest, 17 Hofstra L. Rev. 1 (1988). In the article that follows, Professor Frank Bowman outlines the background of the federal legislation and provides an overview of the system it put in place.

FRANK O. BOWMAN, III, THE FAILURE OF THE FEDERAL SENTENCING GUIDELINES: A STRUCTURAL ANALYSIS

105 Colum. L. Rev. 1315, 1322-1328 (2005)

The SRA . . . created [a] Sentencing Commission for three basic reasons. First, the substantive federal criminal law is sprawling and unorganized. [L]egislators recognized that a body of experts was needed to draft reasonable sentencing rules. Second, Congress realized that the first set of rules would certainly be imperfect and would require monitoring, study, and modification over time. For this task, too, a body of experts was required. Third, creating sentencing rules requires not only expertise, but some insulation from the distorting pressures of politics. Thus, the Sentencing Commission was situated outside both of the political branches of government and made independent even of the normal chain of command in the judicial branch in which it formally resides.

The federal sentencing guidelines are, in a sense, simply a long set of instructions for one chart: the sentencing table[,] a two-dimensional grid which measures the seriousness of the current offense on its vertical axis and the defendant's criminal history on its horizontal axis.[a] The goal of guidelines calculations is to determine an offense level and a criminal history category, which together generate an intersection in the body of the grid. Each intersection designates a sentencing range expressed in months. Most American sentencing guidelines systems use some form of sentencing grid [employing] measurements of offense seriousness and criminal history to place defendants within a sentencing range. The federal system, however, is unique in the complexity of its sentencing table, which has 43 offense levels, 6 criminal history categories, and 258 sentencing range boxes.

The criminal history category reflected on the horizontal axis of the sentencing table attempts to quantify the defendant's disposition to criminality. The offense level reflected on the vertical axis of the sentencing table is a measurement of the seriousness of the present crime. The offense level has three components: (1) the "base offense level," which is a seriousness ranking based purely on the fact of conviction of a particular statutory violation, (2) a set of "specific offense characteristics," which are factors not included as elements of the offense that cause us to think of one crime as more or less serious than another,[47] and (3) additional adjustments under chapter three of the guidelines.[48]

A unique and controversial aspect of the guidelines is "relevant conduct." The guidelines require that a judge calculating the applicable offense level and any chapter three adjustments must consider not only a defendant's conduct directly related to the offense or offenses for which he was convicted, but also the foreseeable conduct of his criminal partners, as well as his own uncharged, dismissed, and sometimes even acquitted conduct[51]

---

a. The table, as it currently stands, is reproduced immediately following the extract from this article.—Eds.

47. For example, the guidelines differentiate between a mail fraud in which the victim loses $1,000 and a fraud with a loss of $1,000,001. A loss of $1,000 would produce no increase in the base offense level for fraud of seven, while a loss of $1,000,001 would add sixteen levels and thus increase the offense level from seven to twenty-three. [Other "specific offense characteristics" for which the guidelines mandate upward adjustments of the offense level include the extent of a victim's physical injury, the quantity of drugs sold, and use of a firearm to commit the offense.—Eds.]

48. Chapter three adjustments include the defendant's role in the offense; whether the defendant engaged in obstruction of justice; commission of an offense against a particularly vulnerable victim; and the existence of multiple counts of conviction. A defendant's offense level may be reduced based on factors such as his "mitigating role" in the offense, or on "acceptance of responsibility."

51. See United States v. Watts, 519 U.S. 148, 155, 157 (1997) (finding that sentencing court was not barred from considering acquitted conduct because burden of proof at sentencing is preponderance of evidence, rather than trial standard of beyond a reasonable doubt).

undertaken as part of the same transaction or common scheme or plan as the offense of conviction. The primary purpose of the relevant conduct provision is to prevent the parties (and to a lesser degree the court itself) from circumventing the guidelines through charge bargaining or manipulation. . . .

Once a district court has determined a defendant's sentencing range, the judge retains effectively unfettered discretion to sentence within that range. However, to sentence outside the range, the judge must justify the departure on certain limited grounds. [Specifically, there must be "an aggravating or mitigating circumstance of a kind, or to a degree, not adequately taken into consideration by the Sentencing Commission in formulating the guidelines."] Critically, both the rules determining the guideline range and those governing the judge's departure authority are made enforceable by a right of appeal given to both parties. . . .

In many important respects, the federal sentencing system fulfilled the objectives of its framers. First, the SRA abandoned the rehabilitative or medical model of punishment. . . . Second, the SRA [achieved] "truth in sentencing" by abolishing parole and requiring that federal defendants sentenced to incarceration serve at least eighty-five percent of the term imposed by the court. . . . Third, the SRA addressed the problem of unwarranted disparity. . . . The available evidence suggests that the guidelines have succeeded in reducing judge-to-judge disparity within judicial districts. On the other hand, researchers have found significant disparities between sentences imposed on similarly situated defendants in different districts and different regions of the country, and inter-district disparities appear to have grown larger in the guidelines era, particularly in drug cases. The question of whether the guidelines reduced or exacerbated racial disparities in federal sentencing remains unresolved.

Finally, the SRA and the guidelines brought law and due process to federal sentencing by requiring that sentencing judges find facts and apply the guidelines' rules to those findings, and by making the guidelines legally binding and enforceable through a process of appellate review. Not all forms of guidelines accomplish this end. Some states have voluntary guidelines systems in which judges need not apply the rules at all. Other states have advisory guidelines systems in which judges are required to perform guidelines calculations, but are not required to sentence in conformity with the result. In neither voluntary nor advisory guidelines systems is the judge's sentencing decision subject to meaningful appellate review. In theory, bringing law to sentencing makes sentencing outcomes more predictable and gives the parties a fair opportunity to present and dispute evidence bearing on legally relevant sentencing factors. Relatedly, bringing law to sentencing promotes transparency, such that one can ascertain from the record many, if not all, of the factors which were dispositive in generating the final sentence.

SENTENCING TABLE[b]
(in months of imprisonment)

Offense Level	Criminal History Category (Criminal History Points)					
	I (0 or 1)	II (2 or 3)	III (4, 5, 6)	IV (7, 8, 9)	V (10, 11, 12)	VI (13 or more)
1	0-6	0-6	0-6	0-6	0-6	0-6
2	0-6	0-6	0-6	0-6	0-6	1-7
3	0-6	0-6	0-6	0-6	2-8	3-9
4	0-6	0-6	0-6	2-8	4-10	6-12
5	0-6	0-6	1-7	4-10	6-12	9-15
6	0-6	1-7	2-8	6-12	9-15	12-18
7	0-6	2-8	4-10	8-14	12-18	15-21
8	0-6	4-10	6-12	10-16	15-21	18-24
9	4-10	6-12	8-14	12-18	18-24	21-27
10	6-12	8-14	10-16	15-21	21-27	24-30
11	8-14	10-16	12-18	18-24	24-30	27-33
12	10-16	12-18	15-21	21-27	27-33	30-37
13	12-18	15-21	18-24	24-30	30-37	33-41
14	15-21	18-24	21-27	27-33	33-41	37-46
15	18-24	21-27	24-30	30-37	37-46	41-51
16	21-27	24-30	27-33	33-41	41-51	46-57
17	24-30	27-33	30-37	37-46	46-57	51-63
18	27-33	30-37	33-41	41-51	51-63	57-71
19	30-37	33-41	37-46	46-57	57-71	63-78
20	33-41	37-46	41-51	51-63	63-78	70-87
21	37-46	41-51	46-57	57-71	70-87	77-96
22	41-51	46-57	51-63	63-78	77-96	84-105
23	46-57	51-63	57-71	70-87	84-105	92-115
24	51-63	57-71	63-78	77-96	92-115	100-125
25	57-71	63-78	70-87	84-105	100-125	110-137
26	63-78	70-87	78-97	92-115	110-137	120-150
27	70-87	78-97	87-108	100-125	120-150	130-162
28	78-97	87-108	97-121	110-137	130-162	140-175
29	87-108	97-121	108-135	121-151	140-175	151-188
30	97-121	108-135	121-151	135-168	151-188	168-210
31	108-135	121-151	135-168	151-188	168-210	188-235
32	121-151	135-168	151-188	168-210	188-235	210-262
33	135-168	151-188	168-210	188-235	210-262	235-293
34	151-188	168-210	188-235	210-262	235-293	262-327
35	168-210	188-235	210-262	235-293	262-327	292-365
36	188-235	210-262	235-293	262-327	292-365	324-405
37	210-262	235-293	262-327	292-365	324-405	360-life
38	235-293	262-327	292-365	324-405	360-life	360-life
39	262-327	292-365	324-405	360-life	360-life	360-life
40	292-365	324-405	360-life	360-life	360-life	360-life
41	324-405	360-life	360-life	360-life	360-life	360-life
42	360-life	360-life	360-life	360-life	360-life	360-life
43	life	life	life	life	life	life

Zones:
- Zone A: Offense Levels 1–8 (approximately)
- Zone B: Offense Levels 9–10
- Zone C: Offense Levels 11–12
- Zone D: Offense Levels 13–43

b. For sentencing ranges in Zone A, the judge is authorized to grant probation without imposing any term of confinement. For sentences in Zone B, the judge is permitted to substitute for the minimum term of confinement an equivalent term of home detention or intermittent confinement. In Zone C, the judge may substitute home detention or intermittent confinement for up to six months of the minimum term, but must impose incarceration for the balance of that term. In Zone D, neither probation nor substitute sanctions are permitted; the judge must impose a prison sentence for at least the term at the low end of the guideline range. The zone applicable to each case is the one in which the case falls after taking into account any decision to depart upward or downward from the presumptively applicable guideline range.—Eds.

NOTES ON THE SENTENCING GUIDELINE APPROACH

From one perspective, sentencing guidelines appear to offer an ideal solution to the problems of unguided judicial sentencing discretion. The sentence must fall within a predetermined range that varies according to the specific details of the offense and the offender. At the same time, flexibility is preserved because the judge can depart from that range when unusual circumstances present themselves. Appellate review is available to ensure that the judge stays within these boundaries, takes the required factors into account, and departs (if she does) only for legitimate reasons. The governing principles become visible and can be tested and progressively refined through the time-honored common-law process. Is there any downside to this optimistic scenario? Is it too good to be true? The complicated dynamics of criminal law and criminal justice examined in previous chapters of this book, and especially in the previous sections of this chapter, should alert us to several potential sources of trouble. What could go wrong? Consider some of the possible dangers of the sentencing guidelines approach:

1. *Is equity predictable?* What, precisely, makes a sentence appropriate? Is it possible to identify all the relevant factors in advance, without squeezing out an essential but intangible human element? Recall that in capital sentencing, the Supreme Court has held it unconstitutional to "treat[] all persons convicted of a designated offense not as uniquely individual human beings, but as members of a faceless, undifferentiated mass to be subjected to the blind imposition of the penalty. . . ." Woodson v. North Carolina, 428 U.S. 280, 303-304 (1976), discussed at page 543 supra. The Court has not recognized this constitutional imperative outside the death penalty context. But if a guidelines system can indeed succeed in making sentencing wholly predictable, will the resulting process become so mechanical that the criminal law will lose some of its ability to communicate moral condemnation of the individual offender? Professor Erik Luna observes (Gridland: An Allegorical Critique of Federal Sentencing, 96 J. Crim. L. & Criminology 25, 28 (2005)) that "the language and practice of formulaic sentencing [now] reign in U.S. district courts[, resulting in] the purging of moral judgment in punishment." Do you agree? Does a largely mechanical process forfeit its moral credibility, or does it gain credibility by providing assurance of evenhandedness and consistency?

2. *Are "soft" factors less important?* Under the federal guidelines system, the guideline ranges are particularly narrow and the system attempts to make especially detailed provision for the diverse circumstances that a well-conceived sentencing system should take into account.[36] But can any system take into account all relevant factors? Because the variables that can legitimately influence the severity of a punishment are almost limitless, a sentencing commission inevitably must choose which ones will enter into

---

36. All of the state guideline systems adopted to date are considerably more flexible. See Rachel E. Barkow, Federalism and the Politics of Sentencing, 105 Colum. L. Rev. 1276 (2005).

the guideline calculus and which ones will not. In making this decision, factors that are easily quantified, like dollar losses and drug quantities, are especially attractive because it is easy to assign "points" to them on a continuous scale, and because it is relatively easy to ensure that different judges make the required computation in a consistent way. In contrast, factors that depend on subjective impression—like a defendant's previous contributions to his community or (in the other direction) the fact that he is known to have an explosive temper—are hard to integrate into a numerical calculation. And judges can easily manipulate these subjective considerations to reintroduce unwarranted disparities. To the extent that consistency is important, therefore, "soft" factors almost inevitably must be allowed less influence. Yet if such factors are excluded from consideration (or allowed little weight) in the interest of eliminating disparity, the guidelines would tend toward a *false* uniformity, with offenders receiving identical sentences when their circumstances were not truly comparable. See Stephen J. Schulhofer, Assessing the Federal Sentencing Process: The Problem Is Uniformity, Not Disparity, 29 Am. Crim. L. Rev. 833 (1992). In determining a defendant's sentence, is it more important to know the exact value of a car that he stole or the circumstances that prompted the theft? How can a guideline approach eliminate *unwarranted* disparity without eliminating *justified* disparity as well? If we must choose, are we better off eliminating both forms of disparity or neither?

3. *Can visibility be dangerous?* Reconsider the federal sentencing grid at page 1176 supra. A simple robbery case would normally be assigned an offense level of 20,[37] so if the perpetrator is a first-time offender, his guideline range would be 33-41 months—a maximum of less than 3½ years. Does that severity level seem about right? Once Congress or a state legislature gets a look at a grid like this, will the legislators be tempted to change the numbers—and if so, in what direction? As William Stuntz, supra, has documented, when punishment levels are made highly visible and easily understandable, the political process generates strong pressure to push the levels upward, subject only to the haphazard constraints of a state's budget. That process has been especially marked in connection with the federal guidelines. See Bowman, supra, at 1328-1350. Is this phenomenon a good or a bad thing? Without "truth in sentencing," where you know the punishment clearly in advance of its imposition, punishment policies are obscured, which could allow criminal justice insiders to implement their own preferences, whether or not voters approve. Stephanos Bibas, Transparency and Participation in Criminal Procedure, 81 N.Y.U. L. Rev. 911 (2006). Should greater visibility and accountability be counted as improvements? Or will the emotions attached to crime control politics and media coverage of criminal cases make highly visible sentencing policies worse than policies that remain obscure to the general public?

---

37. U.S.S.G. §2B3.1.

4. Can discretion increase in one part of the system when it is eliminated in another? Discretion so thoroughly pervades the criminal justice system that eliminating it *completely* cannot be considered an option. The only plausible goal of reform, therefore, is to tackle the extent of discretion and how it is allocated among different actors. Thus, sentencing reform typically seeks to control the discretion of sentencing judges and, perhaps, that of parole boards as well. If prosecutors retain their discretion over charging and plea-bargaining discretion, while the discretion of judges is eliminated, is it accurate to say that there is less discretion in the system? Or is there *more* discretion, because judges and parole boards have lost their ability to oversee and offset abuses of discretion by the prosecutor? For a discussion of this issue, see Kate Stith, The Arc of the Pendulum: Judges, Prosecutors, and the Exercise of Discretion, 117 Yale L.J. 1420 (2008).

Consider also the institutional environment in which discretionary decisions are made. If discretion *moves* from judges to prosecutors, should we expect the quality and consistency of the decisions to improve or deteriorate? If we have to choose between having largely unregulated discretion in the hands of either prosecutors or judges, which arrangement is preferable? Why?

One hope of sentencing reformers was to control the discretion of *both* judges and prosecutors. As Professor Bowman explains, the U.S. Sentencing Commission instructed judges to base their guideline calculations on all "relevant conduct," that is, on what is sometimes called the "real offense" as opposed to the charged offense. The expectation was that federal probation officers would become a "truth squad," providing judges with a complete picture of the crime, even if prosecutors agreed, in order to induce a plea, that they would withhold or fudge crucial details. The prosecutors, of course, could try to counter that check by dismissing most of the counts and accepting a plea to an offense that carried a low statutory maximum; whatever the guideline calculation might suggest, the judge could never impose a sentence greater than the statutory maximum for the offense of conviction. The Commission in turn attempted to neutralize that maneuver by instructing judges to reject any guilty plea when the terms of the proposed charge dismissal or plea agreement did not "adequately reflect the seriousness of the underlying offense behavior." U.S.S.G. §6B1.2.

Should judges reject a plea agreement if the inevitable effect of doing so would be to force compliance with a guideline sentencing calculation that all the parties consider too severe? Is it appropriate for judges to force the parties to go to trial on charges more serious than the prosecutor considers warranted? For one view, suggesting that such an action violates the separation of powers (and principles of efficient government), see United States v. O'Neill, 437 F.3d 654, 658, (7th Cir. 2006) (Posner, J., concurring). But if judges should not (or will not) reject plea agreements that are inconsistent with guideline calculations, does a guideline system really reduce discretion? Or, once again, does it simply transfer discretion from judges to prosecutors? And in the latter event, do the guideline reforms improve the sentencing process or make it worse?

To date, no state sentencing guidelines scheme has attempted to follow the federal "real offense" system. One reason states have rejected this approach is that it leaves important determinations that can affect a sentence to be made by a judge in the sentencing phase (by a preponderance of the evidence), rather than by a jury at trial (beyond a reasonable doubt). This worry is particularly pronounced when a jury acquits a defendant of a charge, but a judge nonetheless finds the conduct to have occurred by a preponderance of the evidence and therefore uses that conduct as a basis to increase a defendant's sentence. The use of so-called acquitted conduct to increase a defendant's sentence has been widely criticized, but it remains an accepted part of the federal "real offense" framework. United States v. Waltower, 643 F.3d 572, 577 (7th Cir. 2011).

5. *Advisory versus mandatory guidelines.* The Sentencing Reform Act specified that judges had to follow the federal guidelines whenever the case fell within the heartland of typical or ordinary cases on which the guidelines were based. Koon v. United States, 518 U.S. 81, 92-94 (1996). That constraint was substantially relaxed in 2005 when the Supreme Court held that it ran afoul of the jury trial guarantee because the Guidelines system allowed judges, as opposed to jurors, to find facts that "the law makes essential" to a defendant's punishment by mandating that they must increase a sentence in a particular way. United States v. Booker, 543 U.S. 220, 232 (2005). The Court distinguished facts that are *necessary* as a matter of law to authorize a new sentence from facts that have *no pre-determined legal significance.* Id. at 233. The remedy adopted by the Court was therefore to make the federal guidelines "advisory" and to allow an appellate court to set aside the decision of the sentencing judge, whether within the guideline range or not, only when the sentence was "unreasonable." For discussions of appellate review under the post-*Booker* federal regime, see Carissa Byrne Hessick & F. Andrew Hessick, Appellate Review of Sentencing Decisions, 60 Ala. L. Rev. 1 (2008); Lindsay C. Harrison, Appellate Discretion and Sentencing After *Booker*, 62 U. Miami L. Rev. 1115 (2008).

Many states also have advisory or voluntary guidelines, some with less appellate review than the post-*Booker* federal guidelines or even no appellate review at all. Are such guidelines likely to be effective in reducing disparity, or will judges ignore them? Empirical studies of voluntary and advisory guidelines show that judges follow these guidelines in roughly 75 percent of cases, a rate of within-guideline sentencing that is similar to the rate of within-guideline sentencing in mandatory guideline jurisdictions that allow for departures.[38] Why might judges sentence within the guidelines in advisory and

---

38. Professor Ronald F. Wright, Statement Before the United States Sentencing Commission, Regional Hearing, at 6-7 (Feb. 11, 2009); Virginia Sentencing Commission, 2008 Annual Report 16 (2008), available at http://leg2.state.va.us/dls/h&sdocs.nsf/By+Year/RD4152008/$file/RD415.pdf; National Association of Sentencing Commissions, The Sentencing Guideline 7 (Feb. 2009), available at http://www.ussc.gov/STATES/NASC_2009_02.pdf; Missouri Sentencing Advisory Commission, Using the New Sentencing Tools 5 (June 26, 2006), available at http://www.mosac.mo.gov/file/ Using%2520the%2520New%2520Sentencing%2520Tools%2520-%2520SAR%2520Implementation%20Report%20June%202006.pdf.

voluntary regimes even if they do not face reversal for ignoring them? For a discussion, see Pfaff, supra at 238-239.

As for the federal guidelines, reports since *Booker* was decided suggest that most district judges continue to take the guidelines seriously, with judges initiating a departure in 19 percent of cases (2% of cases involve upward departures; 17% involve downward departures).[39] There is also evidence of increased inter-judge sentencing disparity in some districts. Amy Farrell & Geoff Ward, Examining District Variation in Sentencing in the Post-*Booker* Period, 23 Fed. Sent. Rep. 318 (2011); Ryan W. Scott, Inter-judge Sentencing Disparity After *Booker*: A First Look, 63 Stan. L. Rev. 1 (2010).

6. Adding it up. The foregoing Notes suggest some of the many risks that sentencing reform entails, but we should not lose sight of the possible benefits. How could the details of a guidelines system be fine-tuned to minimize the dangers? Are the potential gains worth the uncertainties and potential costs?

7. An example. In operation, any jurisdiction's guideline system is bound to raise dozens of distinct problems, all of them important to assessing the potential of the sentencing reform enterprise. The decision that follows illustrates several of the issues that can arise in the course of using guidelines—in this instance the federal guidelines—to determine the appropriate sentence in a concrete case.

UNITED STATES v. DEEGAN

605 F.3d 625 (8th Cir. 2010)

COLLTON, J. [Dana Deegan gave birth to a baby boy in her home on the Fort Berthold Indian Reservation. She fed, cleaned, and dressed the baby, and placed him in a basket. She then left the house, intentionally leaving the baby alone without food or a caregiver. When she returned two weeks later, she found the baby dead, placed his remains in a suitcase, and put the suitcase in a ditch, where it was later discovered. Pursuant to a plea agreement, she pled guilty to second-degree murder and was sentenced to ten years in prison, the bottom of the advisory guidelines range.]

[Deegan] urged the court to vary from the advisory guidelines and sentence her to probation or to a very short period of incarceration [because of] what she described as her "psychological and emotional condition" at the time of the offense, her history as a victim of abuse, and the fact that she acted impulsively. . . .

---

39. United States Sentencing Commission Preliminary Quarterly Data Report Through June 30, 2011, tbl. 1, available at http://www.ussc.gov/Data_and_Statistics/Federal_Sentencing_Statistics/Quarterly_Sentencing_Updates/USSC_2011_3rd_Quarter_Report.pdf.

As support, she submitted a report prepared by Dr. Phillip Resnick, an expert in "neonaticide[,]" a term coined by Resnick to describe the killing of an infant within the first twenty-four hours following birth. The report addressed what Resnick viewed as an "extraordinary number of mitigating circumstances," and expressed the opinion that a prison sentence was not necessary to deter other women from committing neonaticide. The report concluded that Deegan suffered from an extensive history of abuse . . . [and] major depression and dissociation at the time of the homicide, acted impulsively in leaving her baby alone, presented a very low risk of reoffending, and did not merit a lengthy prison sentence, especially because other women convicted in state court of committing similar offenses were usually sentenced to no more than three years in prison.

. . . On appeal, Deegan argues that the sentence is unreasonable, because the advisory guideline for second-degree murder is not based on empirical data and national experience, and because the sentence imposed is greater than necessary to comply with the statutory purposes of sentencing set forth in 18 U.S.C. §3553(a)(2). . . .

In explaining why it chose a sentence of 121 months' imprisonment rather than a greater punishment, the court acknowledged that Deegan's life had not been "easy," and that it had been plagued with physical abuse and sexual abuse. . . . The court said that it "underst[ood] why [Deegan] took the steps that she did . . ." and that "under the circumstances," a sentence under the 2007 guidelines in effect at the time of sentencing, i.e., 19.5 to 24.5 years' imprisonment, would not have been fair. But the court also thought a lesser sentence would not be sufficient, explaining that . . . it could not "ignore the fact that there was an innocent life that was lost."

. . . Where, as here, a sentence imposed is within the advisory guideline range, we typically accord it a presumption of reasonableness. The presumption "simply recognizes . . . that when the judge's discretionary decision accords with the Commission's view of the appropriate application of §3553(a) in the mine run of cases, it is probable that the sentence is reasonable." But even if we do not apply such a presumption here, on the view that Deegan's offense is not a "mine run" second-degree murder, the district court did not abuse its considerable discretion. . . .

The record . . . includes evidence in aggravation and mitigation. [A] court reasonably could view Deegan's offense as "unusually heinous, cruel, and brutal," and deserving of harsh punishment. . . . Deegan also presented evidence of her troubled personal history and family circumstances, and of course we share our dissenting colleague's condemnation of violence against American Indian women.

[W]e are firm in our view that the district court did not abuse its discretion by refusing to impose a more lenient sentence. Whatever the deterrent effect of this sentence, general or specific, and whatever Deegan's personal history, the court was entitled to consider the need for the sentence imposed to "reflect the seriousness of the offense, to promote respect for the law, and to provide just punishment for the offense." 18 U.S.C. §3553(a)(2)(A). . . .

... We disagree, moreover, with the dissent's contention that the district court should have considered the "disparity" between Deegan's sentence and the sentence that may have been imposed if Deegan ... had been prosecuted in state court. [It is well-settled] that "the need to avoid unwarranted sentence disparities ..." 18 U.S.C. §3553(a)(6), refers only to disparities among *federal* defendants. It would have been error for the district court to consider potential federal/state sentencing disparities under §3553(a)(6). ...

BRIGHT, J., dissenting. [This case] represents the most clear sentencing error that this dissenting judge has ever seen. ...

Ms. Deegan's life is marked by a history of extensive and cruel abuse. Her alcoholic father beat her on an almost daily basis. ... Some of the beatings were so severe that her father kept her home from school to avoid reports to Child Protective Services. She and her siblings were eventually removed from her parents' house due to the abuse, placed in a variety of foster homes, and periodically returned to her parents' house. While in foster care, Ms. Deegan was separated from her siblings and experienced physical abuse from some of her foster family members. ...

Ms. Deegan also suffered extensive and cruel sexual abuse. At five years of age, her father's drinking buddies began sexually abusing her. ... At age eleven, the sexual abuse ended when Ms. Deegan finally disclosed the abuse to her mother. Her father responded by beating her for being a "slut and allowing it to happen." Ms. Deegan spent much of her childhood caring for and protecting her six younger siblings. ... As an adult the abuse continued [and] her father [once] attacked her while she was pregnant with her second child. She jumped through a window to escape.

At age fifteen, Ms. Deegan began a relationship with Shannon Hale, the son of one of her foster parents. ... She bore four children fathered by Mr. Hale, including the infant victim in this case.

After Ms. Deegan's third child was born, she became depressed. ... Hale was physically abusing her two to three times per week, forcing her to have sexual intercourse with him, and refusing to care for their children. ...

Despite the abuse, Ms. Deegan did not leave Mr. Hale permanently because he repeatedly assured her that he would reduce his drinking and stop abusing her. Ms. Deegan reported that she sometimes went to live with her parents when the abuse was most severe, but then her father would physically and verbally abuse her. Ms. Deegan also explained that she did not feel that she could leave Mr. Hale because [she] feared that if she left Mr. Hale, his mother, a prominent member of the Indian community, would acquire custody of her children. ... Ms. Deegan's state of despair and depression was [aggravated by additional factors. She and Hale were unemployed, and she] lived in extreme poverty and isolation.. ... When Ms. Deegan obtained any money, Mr. Hale took it and bought methamphetamine. ...

Ms. Deegan's crime of neonaticide was ... completely unlike the usual and ordinary killings that constitute second-degree murder under federal law. . . . Only because this neonaticide occurred on an Indian reservation does this case become one of federal jurisdiction. . . .

Congress recognized that the goals of certainty and uniformity must in some instances yield to unique circumstances. . . . Despite the seemingly obvious fact that neonaticide is an unusual crime in federal court, the presentence report makes no mention that this is an "atypical" case. Even more distressing, the presentence report fails to indicate much in the way of the abusive circumstances Ms. Deegan faced during her childhood and at the time she gave birth to the infant victim. . . .

[In] Koon v. United States, 518 U.S. 81 (1996), the Court explained that the then-mandatory guidelines carve out a "heartland" of typical cases and the Court provided an approach for delineating which cases fall within that heartland. . . . Applying this rationale, whether Ms. Deegan's conduct fell outside the heartland . . . depends on whether her conduct significantly differed from the norm. "The norm" is certainly not what we have here—an American Indian woman so beset by the serious problems in her life she cannot cope with another child, cannot think with logic, and believes she has no alternative but to run away and abandon her newborn child. Tragic yes, typical no!

. . . To determine whether the Commission contemplated neonaticide . . . in its guidelines for second-degree murder, this writer inquired of the Sentencing Commission [and it responded that its records since 2006 contain no other case involving neonaticide.] Thus, a neonaticide case clearly falls outside the "heartland" for second-degree murder sentences. . . .

[The dissent then went through the §3553(a) factors. It relied on Dr. Resnick's testimony that incarcerating Deegan would not likely deter others from committing neonaticide, in part because, after Deegan committed her crime, all 50 states enacted safe haven laws allowing women to drop off a baby at a hospital or police station with no questions asked. Resnick also explained that Deegan is a low recidivism risk because she had a tubal ligation, so she won't have more children; she has no criminal record; no substance abuse history; and is remorseful. Moreover, a study of women who commit neonaticide found that most of them go on to be good mothers, suggesting, Resnick said, that "this is a crime based upon circumstances as opposed to bad character in the perpetrator." The dissent also considered Deegan's family ties:]

While the guidelines do not ordinarily consider matters such as family ties, such a consideration is permissible under §3553(a). . . . Deegan spoke of her children's needs for her. . . . Instead of the prosecutor acknowledging that the children's needs [their ages were one, two, and five] can play a role in reducing a federal sentence, he justified the guideline sentence saying, "[T]he punishment that comes to those siblings as well comes at the hand of the defendant. Basically her choice is what has caused all of this." . . . But what blame should be placed on Mr. Hale who did not support the children he fathered and consistently abused Ms. Deegan? And what about the failures of society to assist Ms. Deegan in her travail? . . .

[The dissent then addressed the need to avoid disparity:] A district court should consider . . . the need to avoid unwarranted disparity among defendants who have been found guilty of similar conduct. 18 U.S.C. §3553(a)(2)(A) and (a)(6). [The record revealed another neonaticide crime in North Dakota, but committed off the Indian reservation and, thus, subject only to state law. That defendant was sentenced to three years' probation.] Dr. Resnick informed the court that women who plead guilty to neonaticide are "infrequently sentenced to more than three years in prison." These are all state sentences and, as observed by the majority, ordinarily state sentences are not germane to showing disparities in sentencing. But here, we ought to consider the difference in sentence between (1) Ms. Deegan, a woman living in North Dakota [but subject to] federal law because of her residency on an Indian reservation, and (2) a North Dakota woman who committed a neonaticide crime off the reservation. . . .

[The judge quoted a letter from Deegan's sister:] "The cultural deprivations and discriminations of our people merely because of our heritage has contributed to the psychological deficits that Dana, at that particular low time in her life, was unable to overcome. *I fear that these same cultural factors may also contribute to harsher penalties of an already oppressed woman.*"

Reading this letter should give us all pause. How many of us can really comprehend the misery of Ms. Deegan's situation as described in this record? None of these matters made any difference to the district court when sentencing under the guidelines. I ask what respect should be given to this guideline sentence? . . .

NOTES AND QUESTIONS

1. Guidelines and the purposes of punishment. As *Deegan* illustrates, under the current federal scheme, judges first determine the appropriate guideline sentence and whether a departure is warranted because a case falls outside the heartland. Next, judges are to determine whether the sentence is warranted under 18 U.S.C. §3553(a), which requires judges to consider, among other things, whether the sentence serves retributive and utilitarian goals of punishment. Will the consideration of these broad factors undercut the goals of the more specific and finely tuned guidelines? Is Judge Bright's approach to §3553(a) an example of how that approach can undermine those goals, or does his opinion illustrate the value of keeping the overall goals of sentencing in mind to determine which cases are, in fact, alike?

2. Family circumstances. The Sentencing Commission, when it promulgated the guidelines, concluded that family and community ties are "not ordinarily relevant." What justifies that conclusion? Is this factor ruled out because it is not relevant to penal law objectives or only because it is likely to be applied inconsistently? If the latter, is consistency important enough to trump the substantive objectives of punishment? Judge Bright thought family circumstances (the three preschool children whose mother would be taken away if she is sentenced to prison) could be relevant under §3553(a), even though those circumstances are not ordinarily relevant under the guidelines. Which of the §3553(a) factors is implicated by family circumstances? What theory of punishment justifies a reduced sentence when a defendant's incarceration will harm third parties such as the defendant's children?

If the innocent victims of an offense are relevant third parties whose interests should be taken into account, does that mean the defendant's innocent family members should also have their interests factored into a sentence? One commentator argues that the children of incarcerated parents have First Amendment freedom of association and due process liberty interests at stake in sentencing determinations and that those interests should be considered. Chesa Boudin, Children of Incarcerated Parents: The Child's Constitutional Right to the Family Relationship, 101 J. Crim. L. & Criminology 77, 92-97 (2011). For a general discussion, see Dan Markel, Jennifer M. Collins & Ethan J. Lieb, Criminal Justice and the Challenge of Family Ties, 2007 U. Ill. L. Rev. 1147, 1171-1178 (2007).

3. *Other offender circumstances.* Now that the federal guidelines are merely advisory, many judges have used their greater flexibility to sentence defendants below the applicable guideline range, in the manner urged by Judge Bright in dissent. The Sentencing Commission followed some of these cues and changed its course on certain offender characteristics. Before 2010, a defendant's age, mental and emotional conditions, physical condition, and military service were deemed "not ordinary relevant." Now the Commission's policy statement provides that these factors "may be relevant" in determining whether a departure is permitted—if these factors are "present to an unusual degree and distinguish the case from the typical cases." The Commission did not, however, change its views on family circumstances and community service. Was the Commission correct to distinguish between these two groups of offender characteristics? What might justify its approach? Why should military service be a factor in a defendant's sentence? Should it count only when the military service creates a condition—such as post-traumatic stress disorder—that is related to the criminal behavior? Or is service relevant even if it does not bear such a relationship, because it demonstrates prior good acts by the defendant? Every sentencing regime takes into account a defendant's prior bad acts (i.e., past criminal conduct) at sentencing; is there a principled reason for not taking into account prior good acts as well? See Carissa Byrne Hessick, Why are Only Bad Acts Good Sentencing Factors?, 88 B.U. L. Rev. 1109 (2008).

4. *Culture.* Judge Bright included an appendix to his dissent entitled "Lifting the Curtain on Assaults Against Women and Children in Indian Country." It quoted at length from Mark J. MacDougall & Katherine Deming Brodie, Strange Justice in Indian Country, Nat. L.J. (Sept. 28, 2009), which contains some sobering statistics, including the fact that one in three women living on reservations will be raped in her lifetime, a rate roughly double that found in surveys of American adult women generally.[40] Such statistics led Judge Bright

---

40. Justice Department surveys find that roughly 15 percent of American adult women have experienced one or more completed rapes in their lifetimes, and another 3 percent have been victims of attempted rape. See page 333 supra.

to conclude: "The violence against women and children on Indian reservations is a national scandal. . . . If the violence against Ms. Deegan had been
stopped . . . and she had been given moral and societal assistance in raising the
three children in her family, this crime of neonaticide might never have
occurred." Id. at 664. How, if at all, should the prevalence of violence on
reservations in general and in Deegan's life in particular affect her sentence?
For the debate about the relevance of environmental deprivation to just punishment, see supra page 1026. How would Justice Thomas (page 1029 supra)
assess the appropriate punishment for Deegan?

5. *The defendant's personal experience.* Should a sentencing court take
into account how a particular defendant will experience his or her sentence?
Consider State v. Thompson, 735 N.W.2d 818 (Neb. 2007). The defendant
had sexually assaulted a child, and the trial court imposed a sentence of probation. One factor in that decision was the defendant's relatively small stature.
Thompson is 5 feet 2 inches tall and weighs 125-130 pounds, and those facts
led the trial court to observe: "I look at your physical size . . . and, quite
frankly, I shake to think of what might happen to you in prison. . . . I am
going to try to put together some kind of order that will keep you out of
prison." Assuming that Thompson's physical size would increase his risk
of being the victim of physical or sexual abuse in prison, was that an appropriate consideration in setting the sentence?

Should a defendant's *subjective* experience of punishment be relevant? For
an argument that proportionality requires one to consider variations in how
defendants experience the suffering associated with punishment, see Adam J.
Kolber, The Subjective Experience of Punishment, 109 Colum. L. Rev. 182
(2009); John Bronsteen, Christopher Buccafusco & Jonathan Masur, Happiness and Punishment, 76 U. Chi. L. Rev. 1037 (2009). What are the dangers of
a subjectivist approach? For critiques, see Dan Markel & Chad Flanders,
Bentham on Stilts: The Bare Relevance of Subjectivity to Retributive Justice,
98 Calif. L. Rev. 907 (2010); David Gray, Punishment as Suffering, 63 Vand.
L. Rev. 1619 (2010). Even if judges do not consider the subjective experience
of punishment, should prison officials? For a probing, in-depth account of a
special unit established in the Los Angeles County Jail to protect the personal
security of gay men and trans women, see Sharon Dolovich, Strategic Segregation in the Modern Prison, 48 Am. Crim. L. Rev. 1 (2011).

NOTES ON THE JURY'S ROLE IN SENTENCING

1. *The constitutional right to jury factfinding.* As noted supra page 31,
the defendant has a constitutional right to require the prosecution to prove
every *element* of the offense to a jury beyond a reasonable doubt. But as
Williams v. New York, supra page 1158, makes clear, judges can consider a
wide range of factors, and reach judgments about what the facts were, when
deciding how severe a sentence to impose. The line between offense elements
and sentencing factors is therefore important for delineating the respective

province of the judge and the jury. In a series of cases, beginning with Apprendi v. New Jersey, 530 U.S. 466 (2000), the Supreme Court has taken an active role in policing the line between the jury's province and that of the judge. The Court has held that "[o]ther than the fact of a prior conviction, any fact that increases the penalty for a crime beyond the pre-scribed statutory maximum must be submitted to a jury, and proved beyond a reasonable doubt." Id. at 490. The Court then concluded in Blakely v. Washington, 542 U.S. 296, 303 (2004), that "the 'statutory maximum' for *Apprendi* purposes is the maximum sentence a judge may impose *solely on the basis of the facts reflected in the jury verdict or admitted by the defendant*[,] . . . *without* any additional findings." The Court in *Blakely* held that the defendant's sentence, which Washington state guidelines made manda-tory on the basis of facts determined by the sentencing judge, ran afoul of the Sixth Amendment. The Court required the trial judge either to sentence the defendant within the sentencing range supported by the jury's findings or to hold a separate sentencing hearing before a jury.

2. *The implications for sentencing under guidelines.* In light of *Blakely*, a number of state courts—after holding their sentencing guideline systems unconstitutional—have required jury findings, beyond a reasonable doubt, for facts necessary to trigger a higher sentencing range. E.g., State v. Shattuck, 704 N.W.2d 131 (Minn. 2005); State v. Schofield, 876 A.2d 43 (Me. 2005).

A year after *Blakely*, the U.S. Supreme Court, as noted (page 1180 supra), held the federal sentencing guidelines unconstitutional as well, but adopted a different remedy. The Court simply made the federal guidelines "advisory" rather than mandatory, and allowed the court of appeals to set aside the sentencing decision of a lower court, whether within the guideline range or not, only when the sentence was found "unreasonable." The upshot is that the federal guidelines, though no longer mandatory, remain an important factor in the sentencing process. And on the heels of *Booker*, several states likewise adopted this approach, made their guidelines "advisory," and held that this step was sufficient to save their constitutionality. E.g., State v. Foster, 845 N.E.2d 470 (Ohio 2006); State v. Natale, 878 A.2d 724 (N.J. 2005). Some commentators view *Booker* as a welcome restoration of balance in a system that had previously tilted too heavily toward prosecutors. E.g., Paul J. Hofer, Has *Booker* Restored Balance? A Look at Data on Plea Bargaining and Senten-cing, 23 Fed. Sent. Rep. 326 (2011). Others have argued that without stringent appellate review, trial judges will have too much discretion under *Booker*. See Stephanos Bibas, Max M. Schanzenbach & Emerson H. Tiller, Policing Pol-itics at Sentencing, 103 Nw. U. L. Rev. 1371 (2009).

3. *The implications for mandatory minimums.* In McMillan v. Pennsyl-vania, 477 U.S. 79 (1986), and Harris v. United States, 536 U.S. 545 (2002), the Supreme Court held that, although a jury must find any facts necessary to increase the *maximum* term of a sentence, the right to jury trial does not apply to facts that increase only the *minimum* term. Recall that the Framers viewed the jury as "in estimable safeguard against the corrupt or overzealous

prosecutor and against the compliant, biased, or eccentric judge." *Duncan*, supra page 47. Can the jury adequately fulfill its function as a check against the government if it authorizes only the upper bound of a sentence? At least one court has held that the Sixth Amendment is violated when the facts triggering a mandatory minimum sentence (a particular quantity of drugs, for example) are neither admitted nor proved before a jury at trial but instead are established by a mere preponderance of the evidence at the sentencing hearing. State v. Barker, 705 N.W.2d 768 (Minn. 2005).

4. Problem. Where in the criminal justice system should sentencing discretion be located, and how should it be channeled? With or without mandatory minimums, how can a sentencing system simultaneously ensure consistency, effective deterrence, and punishments proportionate to individual culpability?

American Law Institute
Model Penal Code
Official Draft, 1962

[The American Law Institute (ALI), a private nonprofit association founded in 1923, consists of prominent lawyers, judges, and academics committed to clarifying and simplifying the law and improving the administration of justice. Among its early products were a series of "restatements" that sought systematically to organize and summarize the law of torts, contracts, and other common law fields, as that law had emerged from the common law process of judicial decisionmaking. In 1935 the Institute, acting on a suggestion from President Roosevelt, approved a project to attempt something similar in the field of criminal law.[1] But because of the Depression and World War II, the project was postponed, and it did not begin in earnest until 1950. The advisory committee formed for that purpose quickly concluded, however, that the "restatement" approach was ill-suited to a project in the field of criminal law. Unlike the law of torts and contracts, criminal law, a complex mixture of statutory and judicial doctrines, had developed with enormous variation from state to state and little coherence or consistency in its underlying principles. An accurate restatement accordingly was neither possible nor desirable. The advisory committee decided instead to begin from first principles and attempt to draft a "model" code that could serve as a basis for comprehensive legislative reform in every American jurisdiction.

[Under the leadership of a Chief Reporter, Professor Herbert Wechsler of Columbia Law School, and an Associate Reporter, Professor Louis B. Schwartz of the University of Pennsylvania Law School, the ALI assembled teams of academics and practitioners who labored over the next 10 years to produce a series of "tentative drafts," followed by an Official Draft that was approved by the ALI in 1962.

[This Model Penal Code achieved a success that is unprecedented for a project of its kind. ALI approval of the Official Draft triggered a wave of criminal law codification throughout the United States. Over the next 20 years, 34 states enacted codes based to some degree on the Model Penal Code.[2] Many of these codes (including those of New Jersey, New York, Pennsylvania, and Oregon) adhere closely to the Model Penal Code text; others, though they diverge from it, make significant use of Model Penal Code concepts and vocabulary. In addition, courts have come to rely heavily on the Model Penal Code and its accompanying commentaries, even in jurisdictions (such as California and the federal system) that have not recodified their criminal law. Thus, although the Model Penal Code is not, in itself, "law," and is not legally binding anywhere, it exerts a powerful influence on the content and development of criminal law rules and principles throughout the United States. It has become an essential point of reference in any discussion of what the doctrines of criminal law are or should be.]

---

1. See Sanford H. Kadish, Fifty Years of Criminal Law: An Opinionated Review, 87 Cal. L. Rev. 943, 947-948 (1999); Sanford H. Kadish, The Model Penal Code's Historical Antecedents, 19 Rutgers L. Rev. 521 (1988).

1. Kadish, Fifty Years, supra, at 948-949.

PART I.   GENERAL PROVISIONS

PART II.   DEFINITION OF SPECIFIC CRIMES
Offenses Involving Danger to the Person

PART III.   TREATMENT AND CORRECTION [OMITTED]

PART IV.   ORGANIZATION OF CORRECTION [OMITTED]

PART I.   GENERAL PROVISIONS

Article 1.   Preliminary

SECTION 1.01.   TITLE AND EFFECTIVE DATE [omitted]

SECTION 1.02.   PURPOSES; PRINCIPLES OF CONSTRUCTION

(1) The general purposes of the provisions governing the definition of offenses are:

(a) to forbid and prevent conduct that unjustifiably and inexcusably inflicts or threatens substantial harm to individual or public interests;

(b) to subject to public control persons whose conduct indicates that they are disposed to commit crimes;

(c) to safeguard conduct that is without fault from condemnation as criminal;

(d) to give fair warning of the nature of the conduct declared to constitute an offense;

(e) to differentiate on reasonable grounds between serious and minor offenses.

(2) The general purposes of the provisions governing the sentencing and treatment of offenders are:

(a) to prevent the commission of offenses;

(b) to promote the correction and rehabilitation of offenders;

(c) to safeguard offenders against excessive, disproportionate or arbitrary punishment;

(d) to give fair warning of the nature of the sentences that may be imposed on conviction of an offense;

(e) to differentiate among offenders with a view to a just individualization in their treatment;

(f) to define, coordinate and harmonize the powers, duties and functions of the courts and of administrative officers and agencies responsible for dealing with offenders;

(g) to advance the use of generally accepted scientific methods and knowledge in the sentencing and treatment of offenders;

(h) to integrate responsibility for the administration of the correctional system in a State Department of Correction [or other single department or agency].

(3) The provisions of the Code shall be construed according to the fair import of their terms but when the language is susceptible of differing constructions it shall be interpreted to further the general purposes stated in this Section and the special purposes of the particular provision involved. The discretionary powers conferred by the Code shall be exercised in accordance with the criteria stated in the Code and, insofar as such criteria are not decisive, to further the general purposes stated in this Section.

SECTION 1.03.　TERRITORIAL APPLICABILITY

(1) Except as otherwise provided in this Section, a person may be convicted under the law of this State of an offense committed by his own conduct or the conduct of another for which he is legally accountable if:

(a) either the conduct which is an element of the offense or the result which is such an element occurs within this State; or

(b) conduct occurring outside the State is sufficient under the law of this State to constitute an attempt to commit an offense within the State; or

(c) conduct occurring outside the State is sufficient under the law of this State to constitute a conspiracy to commit an offense within the State and an overt act in furtherance of such conspiracy occurs within the State; or

(d) conduct occurring within the State establishes complicity in the commission of, or an attempt, solicitation or conspiracy to commit, an offense in another jurisdiction which also is an offense under the law of this State; or

(e) the offense consists of the omission to perform a legal duty imposed by the law of this State with respect to domicile, residence or a relationship to a person, thing or transaction in the State; or

(f) the offense is based on a statute of this State which expressly prohibits conduct outside the State, when the conduct bears a reasonable relation to a legitimate interest of this State and the actor knows or should know that his conduct is likely to affect that interest.

(2) Subsection (1)(a) does not apply when either causing a specified result or a purpose to cause or danger of causing such a result is an element of an offense and the result occurs or is designed or likely to occur only in another jurisdiction where the conduct charged would not constitute an offense, unless a legislative purpose plainly appears to declare the conduct criminal regardless of the place of the result.

(3) Subsection (1)(a) does not apply when causing a particular result is an element of an offense and the result is caused by conduct occurring outside the State which would not constitute an offense if the result had occurred there, unless the actor purposely or knowingly caused the result within the State.

(4) When the offense is homicide, either the death of the victim or the bodily impact causing the death constitutes a "result," within the meaning of Subsection (1)(a) and if the body of the homicide victim is found within the State, it is presumed that such result occurred within the State.

(5) This State includes the land and water and the air space above such land and water with respect to which the State has legislative jurisdiction.

SECTION 1.04.　CLASSES OF CRIMES; VIOLATIONS

(1) An offense defined by this Code or by any other statute of this State, for which a sentence of [death or of] imprisonment is authorized, constitutes a crime. Crimes are classified as felonies, misdemeanors or petty misdemeanors.

(2) A crime is a felony if it is so designated in this Code or if persons convicted thereof may be sentenced [to death or] to imprisonment for a term which, apart from an extended term, is in excess of one year.

(3) A crime is a misdemeanor if it is so designated in this Code or in a statute other than this Code enacted subsequent thereto.

(4) A crime is a petty misdemeanor if it is so designated in this Code or in a statute other than this Code enacted subsequent thereto or if it is defined by a statute other than this Code which now provides that persons convicted thereof may be sentenced to imprisonment for a term of which the maximum is less than one year.

(5) An offense defined by this Code or by any other statute of this State constitutes a violation if it is so designated in this Code or in the law defining the offense or if no other sentence than a fine, or fine and forfeiture or other civil penalty is authorized upon conviction or if it is defined by a statute other than this Code which now provides that the offense shall not constitute a crime. A violation does not constitute a crime and conviction of a violation shall not give rise to any disability or legal disadvantage based on conviction of a criminal offense.

(6) Any offense declared by law to constitute a crime, without specification of the grade thereof or of the sentence authorized upon conviction, is a misdemeanor.

(7) An offense defined by any statute of this State other than this Code shall be classified as provided in this Section and the sentence that may be imposed upon conviction thereof shall hereafter be governed by this Code.

SECTION 1.05.   ALL OFFENSES DEFINED BY STATUTE: APPLICATION OF GENERAL PROVISIONS
            OF THE CODE

(1) No conduct constitutes an offense unless it is a crime or violation under this Code or another statute of this State.

(2) The provisions of Part I of the Code are applicable to offenses defined by other statutes, unless the Code otherwise provides.

(3) This Section does not affect the power of a court to punish for contempt or to employ any sanction authorized by law for the enforcement of an order or a civil judgment or decree.

SECTION 1.06.   TIME LIMITATIONS

(1) A prosecution for murder may be commenced at any time.

(2) Except as otherwise provided in this Section, prosecutions for other offenses are subject to the following periods of limitation:

(a) a prosecution for a felony of the first degree must be commenced within six years after it is committed;

(b) a prosecution for any other felony must be commenced within three years after it is committed;

(c) a prosecution for a misdemeanor must be commenced within two years after it is committed;

(d) a prosecution for a petty misdemeanor or a violation must be commenced within six months after it is committed.

(3) If the period prescribed in Subsection (2) has expired, a prosecution may nevertheless be commenced for:

(a) any offense a material element of which is either fraud or a breach of fiduciary obligation within one year after discovery of the offense by an aggrieved party or by a person who has legal duty to represent an aggrieved party and who is himself not a party to the offense, but in no case shall this provision extend the period of limitation otherwise applicable by more than three years; and

(b) any offense based upon misconduct in office by a public officer or employee at any time when the defendant is in public office or employment or within two years thereafter, but in no case shall this provision extend the period of limitation otherwise applicable by more than three years.

(4) An offense is committed either when every element occurs, or, if a legislative purpose to prohibit a continuing course of conduct plainly appears, at the time when the course of conduct or the defendant's complicity therein is terminated. Time starts to run on the day after the offense is committed.

(5) A prosecution is commenced either when an indictment is found [or an information filed] or when a warrant or other process is issued, provided that such warrant or process is executed without unreasonable delay.

(6) The period of limitation does not run:

(a) during any time when the accused is continuously absent from the State or has no reasonably ascertainable place of abode or work within the State, but in no case shall this provision extend the period of limitation otherwise applicable by more than three years; or

(b) during any time when a prosecution against the accused for the same conduct is pending in this State.

SECTION 1.07.   METHOD OF PROSECUTION WHEN CONDUCT CONSTITUTES MORE THAN ONE OFFENSE

(1) *Prosecution for Multiple Offenses; Limitation on Convictions.* When the same conduct of a defendant may establish the commission of more than one offense, the defendant may be prosecuted for each such offense. He may not, however, be convicted of more than one offense if:

(a) one offense is included in the other, as defined in Subsection (4) of this Section; or

(b) one offense consists only of a conspiracy or other form of preparation to commit the other; or

(c) inconsistent findings of fact are required to establish the commission of the offenses; or

(d) the offenses differ only in that one is defined to prohibit a designated kind of conduct generally and the other to prohibit a specific instance of such conduct; or

(e) the offense is defined as a continuing course of conduct and the defendant's course of conduct was uninterrupted, unless the law provides that specific periods of such conduct constitute separate offenses.

(2) *Limitation on Separate Trials for Multiple Offenses.* Except as provided in Subsection (3) of this Section, a defendant shall not be subject to separate trials for multiple offenses based on the same conduct or arising from the same criminal episode, if such offenses are known to the appropriate prosecuting officer at the time of the commencement of the first trial and are within the jurisdiction of a single court.

(3) *Authority of Court to Order Separate Trials.* When a defendant is charged with two or more offenses based on the same conduct or arising from the same criminal episode, the Court, on application of the prosecuting attorney or of the defendant, may order any such charge to be tried separately, if it is satisfied that justice so requires.

(4) *Conviction of Included Offense Permitted.* A defendant may be convicted of an offense included in an offense charged in the indictment [or the information]. An offense is so included when:

(a) it is established by proof of the same or less than all the facts required to establish the commission of the offense charged; or

(b) it consists of an attempt or solicitation to commit the offense charged or to commit an offense otherwise included therein; or

(c) it differs from the offense charged only in the respect that a less serious injury or risk of injury to the same person, property or public interest or a lesser kind of culpability suffices to establish its commission.

(5) *Submission of Included Offense to Jury.* The Court shall not be obligated to charge the jury with respect to an included offense unless there is a rational basis for a verdict

acquitting the defendant of the offense charged and convicting him of the included offense.

SECTION 1.08.   WHEN PROSECUTION BARRED BY FORMER PROSECUTION FOR THE SAME OFFENSE [OMITTED]

SECTION 1.09.   WHEN PROSECUTION BARRED BY FORMER PROSECUTION FOR DIFFERENT OFFENSE [OMITTED]

SECTION 1.10.   FORMER PROSECUTION IN ANOTHER JURISDICTION: WHEN A BAR [OMITTED]

SECTION 1.11.   FORMER PROSECUTION BEFORE COURT LACKING JURISDICTION OR WHEN FRAUDULENTLY PROCURED BY THE DEFENDANT [OMITTED]

SECTION 1.12.   PROOF BEYOND A REASONABLE DOUBT; AFFIRMATIVE DEFENSES; BURDEN OF PROVING FACT WHEN NOT AN ELEMENT OF AN OFFENSE; PRESUMPTIONS

(1) No person may be convicted of an offense unless each element of such offense is proved beyond a reasonable doubt. In the absence of such proof, the innocence of the defendant is assumed.

(2) Subsection (1) of this Section does not:

(a) require the disproof of an affirmative defense unless and until there is evidence supporting such defense; or

(b) apply to any defense which the Code or another statute plainly requires the defendant to prove by a preponderance of evidence.

(3) A ground of defense is affirmative, within the meaning of Subsection (2)(a) of this Section, when:

(a) it arises under a section of the Code which so provides; or

(b) it relates to an offense defined by a statute other than the Code and such statute so provides; or

(c) it involves a matter of excuse or justification peculiarly within the knowledge of the defendant on which he can fairly be required to adduce supporting evidence.

(4) When the application of the Code depends upon the finding of a fact which is not an element of an offense, unless the Code otherwise provides:

(a) the burden of proving the fact is on the prosecution or defendant, depending on whose interest or contention will be furthered if the finding should be made; and

(b) the fact must be proved to the satisfaction of the Court or jury, as the case may be.

(5) When the Code establishes a presumption with respect to any fact which is an element of an offense, it has the following consequences:

(a) when there is evidence of the facts which give rise to the presumption, the issue of the existence of the presumed fact must be submitted to the jury, unless the Court is satisfied that the evidence as a whole clearly negatives the presumed fact; and

(b) when the issue of the existence of the presumed fact is submitted to the jury, the Court shall charge that while the presumed fact must, on all the evidence, be proved beyond a reasonable doubt, the law declares that the jury may regard the facts giving rise to the presumption as sufficient evidence of the presumed fact.

(6) A presumption not established by the Code or inconsistent with it has the consequences otherwise accorded it by law.

SECTION 1.13.   GENERAL DEFINITIONS

In this Code, unless a different meaning plainly is required:

(1) "statute" includes the Constitution and a local law or ordinance of a political subdivision of the State;

(2) "act" or "action" means a bodily movement whether voluntary or involuntary;

(3) "voluntary" has the meaning specified in Section 2.01;

(4) "omission" means a failure to act;

(5) "conduct" means an action or omission and its accompanying state of mind, or, where relevant, a series of acts and omissions;

(6) "actor" includes, where relevant, a person guilty of an omission;

(7) "acted" includes, where relevant, "omitted to act";

(8) "person," "he" and "actor" include any natural person and, where relevant, a corporation or an unincorporated association;

(9) "element of an offense" means (i) such conduct or (ii) such attendant circumstances or (iii) such a result of conduct as

(a) is included in the description of the forbidden conduct in the definition of the offense; or

(b) establishes the required kind of culpability; or

(c) negatives an excuse or justification for such conduct; or

(d) negatives a defense under the statute of limitations; or

(e) establishes jurisdiction or venue;

(10) "material element of an offense" means an element that does not relate exclusively to the statute of limitations, jurisdiction, venue or to any other matter similarly unconnected with (i) the harm or evil, incident to conduct, sought to be prevented by the law defining the offense, or (ii) the existence of a justification or excuse for such conduct;

(11) "purposely" has the meaning specified in Section 2.02 and equivalent terms such as "with purpose," "designed" or "with design" have the same meaning;

(12) "intentionally" or "with intent" means purposely;

(13) "knowingly" has the meaning specified in Section 2.02 and equivalent terms such as "knowing" or "with knowledge" have the same meaning;

(14) "recklessly" has the meaning specified in Section 2.02 and equivalent terms such as "recklessness" or "with recklessness" have the same meaning;

(15) "negligently" has the meaning specified in Section 2.02 and equivalent terms such as "negligence" or "with negligence" have the same meaning;

(16) "reasonably believes" or "reasonable belief" designates a belief which the actor is not reckless or negligent in holding.

Article 2.   General Principles of Liability

SECTION 2.01.   REQUIREMENT OF VOLUNTARY ACT; OMISSION AS BASIS OF LIABILITY;
 POSSESSION AS AN ACT

(1) A person is not guilty of an offense unless his liability is based on conduct which includes a voluntary act or the omission to perform an act of which he is physically capable.

(2) The following are not voluntary acts within the meaning of this Section:

(a) a reflex or convulsion;

(b) a bodily movement during unconsciousness or sleep;

(c) conduct during hypnosis or resulting from hypnotic suggestion;

(d) a bodily movement that otherwise is not a product of the effort or determination of the actor, either conscious or habitual.

(3) Liability for the commission of an offense may not be based on an omission unaccompanied by action unless:

(a) the omission is expressly made sufficient by the law defining the offense; or

(b) a duty to perform the omitted act is otherwise imposed by law.

(4) Possession is an act, within the meaning of this Section, if the possessor knowingly procured or received the thing possessed or was aware of his control thereof for a sufficient period to have been able to terminate his possession.

SECTION 2.02. GENERAL REQUIREMENTS OF CULPABILITY

(1) *Minimum Requirements of Culpability.* Except as provided in Section 2.05, a person is not guilty of an offense unless he acted purposely, knowingly, recklessly or negligently, as the law may require, with respect to each material element of the offense.

(2) *Kinds of Culpability Defined.*

(a) *Purposely.* A person acts purposely with respect to a material element of an offense when:

(i) if the element involves the nature of his conduct or a result thereof, it is his conscious object to engage in conduct of that nature or to cause such a result; and

(ii) if the element involves the attendant circumstances, he is aware of the existence of such circumstances or he believes or hopes that they exist.

(b) *Knowingly.* A person acts knowingly with respect to a material element of an offense when:

(i) if the element involves the nature of his conduct or the attendant circumstances, he is aware that his conduct is of that nature or that such circumstances exist; and

(ii) if the element involves a result of his conduct, he is aware that it is practically certain that his conduct will cause such a result.

(c) *Recklessly.* A person acts recklessly with respect to a material element of an offense when he consciously disregards a substantial and unjustifiable risk that the material element exists or will result from his conduct. The risk must be of such a nature and degree that, considering the nature and purpose of the actor's conduct and the circumstances known to him, its disregard involves a gross deviation from the standard of conduct that a law-abiding person would observe in the actor's situation.

(d) *Negligently.* A person acts negligently with respect to a material element of an offense when he should be aware of a substantial and unjustifiable risk that the material element exists or will result from his conduct. The risk must be of such a nature and degree that the actor's failure to perceive it, considering the nature and purpose of his conduct and the circumstances known to him, involves a gross deviation from the standard of care that a reasonable person would observe in the actor's situation.

(3) *Culpability Required Unless Otherwise Provided.* When the culpability sufficient to establish a material element of an offense is not prescribed by law, such element is established if a person acts purposely, knowingly or recklessly with respect thereto.

(4) *Prescribed Culpability Requirement Applies to All Material Elements.* When the law defining an offense prescribes the kind of culpability that is sufficient for the commission of an offense, without distinguishing among the material elements thereof, such provision shall apply to all the material elements of the offense, unless a contrary purpose plainly appears.

(5) *Substitutes for Negligence, Recklessness and Knowledge.* When the law provides that negligence suffices to establish an element of an offense, such element also is established if a person acts purposely, knowingly or recklessly. When recklessness suffices to establish an element, such element also is established if a person acts purposely or knowingly. When acting knowingly suffices to establish an element, such element also is established if a person acts purposely.

(6) *Requirement of Purpose Satisfied if Purpose Is Conditional.* When a particular purpose is an element of an offense, the element is established although such purpose is conditional, unless the condition negatives the harm or evil sought to be prevented by the law defining the offense.

(7) *Requirement of Knowledge Satisfied by Knowledge of High Probability.* When knowledge of the existence of a particular fact is an element of an offense, such knowledge is established if a person is aware of a high probability of its existence, unless he actually believes that it does not exist.

(8) *Requirement of Wilfulness Satisfied by Acting Knowingly.* A requirement that an offense be committed wilfully is satisfied if a person acts knowingly with respect to the material elements of the offense, unless a purpose to impose further requirements appears.

(9) *Culpability as to Illegality of Conduct.* Neither knowledge nor recklessness or negligence as to whether conduct constitutes an offense or as to the existence, meaning or application of the law determining the elements of an offense is an element of such offense, unless the definition of the offense or the Code so provides.

(10) *Culpability as Determinant of Grade of Offense.* When the grade or degree of an offense depends on whether the offense is committed purposely, knowingly, recklessly or negligently, its grade or degree shall be the lowest for which the determinative kind of culpability is established with respect to any material element of the offense.

SECTION 2.03.   CAUSAL RELATIONSHIP BETWEEN CONDUCT AND RESULT; DIVERGENCE BETWEEN RESULT DESIGNED OR CONTEMPLATED AND ACTUAL RESULT OR BETWEEN PROBABLE AND ACTUAL RESULT

(1) Conduct is the cause of a result when:

(a) it is an antecedent but for which the result in question would not have occurred; and

(b) the relationship between the conduct and result satisfies any additional causal requirements imposed by the Code or by the law defining the offense.

(2) When purposely or knowingly causing a particular result is an element of an offense, the element is not established if the actual result is not within the purpose or the contemplation of the actor unless:

(a) the actual result differs from that designed or contemplated, as the case may be, only in the respect that a different person or different property is injured or affected or that the injury or harm designed or contemplated would have been more serious or more extensive than that caused; or

(b) the actual result involves the same kind of injury or harm as that designed or contemplated and is not too remote or accidental in its occurrence to have a [just] bearing on the actor's liability or on the gravity of his offense.

(3) When recklessly or negligently causing a particular result is an element of an offense, the element is not established if the actual result is not within the risk of which the actor is aware or, in the case of negligence, of which he should be aware unless:

(a) the actual result differs from the probable result only in the respect that a different person or different property is injured or affected or that the probable injury or harm would have been more serious or more extensive than that caused; or

(b) the actual result involves the same kind of injury or harm as the probable result and is not too remote or accidental in its occurrence to have a [just] bearing on the actor's liability or on the gravity of his offense.

(4) When causing a particular result is a material element of an offense for which absolute liability is imposed by law, the element is not established unless the actual result is a probable consequence of the actor's conduct.

SECTION 2.04.   IGNORANCE OR MISTAKE

(1) Ignorance or mistake as to a matter of fact or law is a defense if:

(a) the ignorance or mistake negatives the purpose, knowledge, belief, recklessness or negligence required to establish a material element of the offense; or

(b) the law provides that the state of mind established by such ignorance or mistake constitutes a defense.

(2) Although ignorance or mistake would otherwise afford a defense to the offense charged, the defense is not available if the defendant would be guilty of another offense had the situation been as he supposed. In such case, however, the ignorance or mistake of the defendant shall reduce the grade and degree of the offense of which he may be convicted to those of the offense of which he would be guilty had the situation been as he supposed.

(3) A belief that conduct does not legally constitute an offense is a defense to a prosecution for that offense based upon such conduct when:

(a) the statute or other enactment defining the offense is not known to the actor and has not been published or otherwise reasonably made available prior to the conduct alleged; or

(b) he acts in reasonable reliance upon an official statement of the law, afterward determined to be invalid or erroneous, contained in (i) a statute or other enactment; (ii) a judicial decision, opinion or judgment; (iii) an administrative order or grant of permission; or (iv) an official interpretation of the public officer or body charged by law with responsibility for the interpretation, administration or enforcement of the law defining the offense.

(4) The defendant must prove a defense arising under Subsection (3) of this Section by a preponderance of evidence.

SECTION 2.05. WHEN CULPABILITY REQUIREMENTS ARE INAPPLICABLE TO VIOLATIONS AND TO OFFENSES DEFINED BY OTHER STATUTES; EFFECT OF ABSOLUTE LIABILITY IN REDUCING GRADE OF OFFENSE TO VIOLATION

(1) The requirements of culpability prescribed by Sections 2.01 and 2.02 do not apply to:

(a) offenses which constitute violations, unless the requirement involved is included in the definition of the offense or the Court determines that its application is consistent with effective enforcement of the law defining the offense; or

(b) offenses defined by statutes other than the Code, insofar as a legislative purpose to impose absolute liability for such offenses or with respect to any material element thereof plainly appears.

(2) Notwithstanding any other provision of existing law and unless a subsequent statute otherwise provides:

(a) when absolute liability is imposed with respect to any material element of an offense defined by a statute other than the Code and a conviction is based upon such liability, the offense constitutes a violation; and

(b) although absolute liability is imposed by law with respect to one or more of the material elements of an offense defined by a statute other than the Code, the culpable commission of the offense may be charged and proved, in which event negligence with respect to such elements constitutes sufficient culpability and the classification of the offense and the sentence that may be imposed therefor upon conviction are determined by Section 1.04 and Article 6 of the Code.

SECTION 2.06. LIABILITY FOR CONDUCT OF ANOTHER; COMPLICITY

(1) A person is guilty of an offense if it is committed by his own conduct or by the conduct of another person for which he is legally accountable, or both.

(2) A person is legally accountable for the conduct of another person when:

(a) acting with the kind of culpability that is sufficient for the commission of the offense, he causes an innocent or irresponsible person to engage in such conduct; or

(b) he is made accountable for the conduct of such other person by the Code or by the law defining the offense; or

(c) he is an accomplice of such other person in the commission of the offense.

(3) A person is an accomplice of another person in the commission of an offense if:

(a) with the purpose of promoting or facilitating the commission of the offense, he

(i) solicits such other person to commit it; or

(ii) aids or agrees or attempts to aid such other person in planning or committing it; or

(iii) having a legal duty to prevent the commission of the offense, fails to make proper effort so to do; or

(b) his conduct is expressly declared by law to establish his complicity.

(4) When causing a particular result is an element of an offense, an accomplice in the conduct causing such result is an accomplice in the commission of that offense, if he acts with the kind of culpability, if any, with respect to that result that is sufficient for the commission of the offense.

(5) A person who is legally incapable of committing a particular offense himself may be guilty thereof if it is committed by the conduct of another person for which he is legally accountable, unless such liability is inconsistent with the purpose of the provision establishing his incapacity.

(6) Unless otherwise provided by the Code or by the law defining the offense, a person is not an accomplice in an offense committed by another person if:

(a) he is a victim of that offense; or

(b) the offense is so defined that his conduct is inevitably incident to its commission; or

(c) he terminates his complicity prior to the commission of the offense and

(i) wholly deprives it of effectiveness in the commission of the offense; or

(ii) gives timely warning to the law enforcement authorities or otherwise makes proper effort to prevent the commission of the offense.

(7) An accomplice may be convicted on proof of the commission of the offense and of his complicity therein, though the person claimed to have committed the offense has not been prosecuted or convicted or has been convicted of a different offense or degree of offense or has an immunity to prosecution or conviction or has been acquitted.

Section 2.07.   Liability of Corporations, Unincorporated Associations and Persons Acting, or Under a Duty to Act, in Their Behalf

(1) A corporation may be convicted of the commission of an offense if:

(a) the offense is a violation or the offense is defined by a statute other than the Code in which a legislative purpose to impose liability on corporations plainly appears and the conduct is performed by an agent of the corporation acting in behalf of the corporation within the scope of his office or employment, except that if the law defining the offense designates the agents for whose conduct the corporation is accountable or the circumstances under which it is accountable, such provisions shall apply; or

(b) the offense consists of an omission to discharge a specific duty of affirmative performance imposed on corporations by law; or

(c) the commission of the offense was authorized, requested, commanded, performed or recklessly tolerated by the board of directors or by a high managerial agent acting in behalf of the corporation within the scope of his office or employment.

(2) When absolute liability is imposed for the commission of an offense, a legislative purpose to impose liability on a corporation shall be assumed, unless the contrary plainly appears.

(3) An unincorporated association may be convicted of the commission of an offense if:

(a) the offense is defined by a statute other than the Code which expressly provides for the liability of such an association and the conduct is performed by an agent of the association acting in behalf of the association within the scope of his office or employment, except that if the law defining the offense designates the agents for whose conduct the association is accountable or the circumstances under which it is accountable, such provisions shall apply; or

(b) the offense consists of an omission to discharge a specific duty of affirmative performance imposed on associations by law.

(4) As used in this Section:

(a) "corporation" does not include an entity organized as or by a governmental agency for the execution of a governmental program;

(b) "agent" means any director, officer, servant, employee or other person authorized to act in behalf of the corporation or association and, in the case of an unincorporated association, a member of such association;

(c) "high managerial agent" means an officer of a corporation or an unincorporated association, or, in the case of a partnership, a partner, or any other agent of a corporation or association having duties of such responsibility that his conduct may fairly be assumed to represent the policy of the corporation or association.

(5) In any prosecution of a corporation or an unincorporated association for the commission of an offense included within the terms of Subsection (1)(a) or Subsection (3)(a) of this Section, other than an offense for which absolute liability has been imposed, it shall be a defense if the defendant proves by a preponderance of evidence that the high managerial agent having supervisory responsibility over the subject matter of the offense employed due diligence to prevent its commission. This paragraph shall not apply if it is plainly inconsistent with the legislative purpose in defining the particular offense.

(6) (a) A person is legally accountable for any conduct he performs or causes to be performed in the name of the corporation or an unincorporated association or in its behalf to the same extent as if it were performed in his own name or behalf.

(b) Whenever a duty to act is imposed by law upon a corporation or an unincorporated association, any agent of the corporation or association having primary responsibility for the discharge of the duty is legally accountable for a reckless omission to perform the required act to the same extent as if the duty were imposed by law directly upon himself.

(c) When a person is convicted of an offense by reason of his legal accountability for the conduct of a corporation or an unincorporated association, he is subject to the sentence authorized by law when a natural person is convicted of an offense of the grade and the degree involved.

SECTION 2.08.   INTOXICATION

(1) Except as provided in Subsection (4) of this Section, intoxication of the actor is not a defense unless it negatives an element of the offense.

(2) When recklessness establishes an element of the offense, if the actor, due to self-induced intoxication, is unaware of a risk of which he would have been aware had he been sober, such unawareness is immaterial.

(3) Intoxication does not, in itself, constitute mental disease within the meaning of Section 4.01.

(4) Intoxication which (a) is not self-induced or (b) is pathological is an affirmative defense if by reason of such intoxication the actor at the time of his conduct lacks substantial capacity either to appreciate its criminality [wrongfulness] or to conform his conduct to the requirements of law.

(5) *Definitions.* In this Section unless a different meaning plainly is required:

(a) "intoxication" means a disturbance of mental or physical capacities resulting from the introduction of substances into the body;

(b) "self-induced intoxication" means intoxication caused by substances which the actor knowingly introduces into his body, the tendency of which to cause intoxication he knows or ought to know, unless he introduces them pursuant to medical advice or under such circumstances as would afford a defense to a charge of crime;

(c) "pathological intoxication" means intoxication grossly excessive in degree, given the amount of the intoxicant, to which the actor does not know he is susceptible.

SECTION 2.09.   DURESS

(1) It is an affirmative defense that the actor engaged in the conduct charged to constitute an offense because he was coerced to do so by the use of, or a threat to use, unlawful force against

his person or the person of another, which a person of reasonable firmness in his situation would have been unable to resist.

(2) The defense provided by this Section is unavailable if the actor recklessly placed himself in a situation in which it was probable that he would be subjected to duress. The defense is also unavailable if he was negligent in placing himself in such a situation, whenever negligence suffices to establish culpability for the offense charged.

(3) It is not a defense that a woman acted on the command of her husband, unless she acted under such coercion as would establish a defense under this Section. [The presumption that a woman, acting in the presence of her husband, is coerced is abolished.]

(4) When the conduct of the actor would otherwise be justifiable under Section 3.02, this Section does not preclude such defense.

SECTION 2.10.   MILITARY ORDERS

It is an affirmative defense that the actor, in engaging in the conduct charged to constitute an offense, does no more than execute an order of his superior in the armed services which he does not know to be unlawful.

SECTION 2.11.   CONSENT

(1) *In General.* The consent of the victim to conduct charged to constitute an offense or to the result thereof is a defense if such consent negatives an element of the offense or precludes the infliction of the harm or evil sought to be prevented by the law defining the offense.

(2) *Consent to Bodily Harm.* When conduct is charged to constitute an offense because it causes or threatens bodily harm, consent to such conduct or to the infliction of such harm is a defense if:

(a) the bodily harm consented to or threatened by the conduct consented to is not serious; or

(b) the conduct and the harm are reasonably foreseeable hazards of joint participation in a lawful athletic contest or competitive sport; or

(c) the consent establishes a justification for the conduct under Article 3 of the Code.

(3) *Ineffective Consent.* Unless otherwise provided by the Code or by the law defining the offense, assent does not constitute consent if:

(a) it is given by a person who is legally incompetent to authorize the conduct charged to constitute the offense; or

(b) it is given by a person who by reason of youth, mental disease or defect or intoxication is manifestly unable or known by the actor to be unable to make a reasonable judgment as to the nature or harmfulness of the conduct charged to constitute the offense; or

(c) it is given by a person whose improvident consent is sought to be prevented by the law defining the offense; or

(d) it is induced by force, duress or deception of a kind sought to be prevented by the law defining the offense.

SECTION 2.12.   DE MINIMIS INFRACTIONS

The Court shall dismiss a prosecution if, having regard to the nature of the conduct charged to constitute an offense and the nature of the attendant circumstances, it finds that the defendant's conduct:

(1) was within a customary license or tolerance, neither expressly negatived by the person whose interest was infringed nor inconsistent with the purpose of the law defining the offense; or

(2) did not actually cause or threaten the harm or evil sought to be prevented by the law defining the offense or did so only to an extent too trivial to warrant the condemnation of conviction; or

(3) presents such other extenuations that it cannot reasonably be regarded as envisaged by the legislature in forbidding the offense.

The Court shall not dismiss a prosecution under Subsection (3) of this Section without filing a written statement of its reasons.

SECTION 2.13.   ENTRAPMENT

(1) A public law enforcement official or a person acting in cooperation with such an official perpetrates an entrapment if for the purpose of obtaining evidence of the commission of an offense, he induces or encourages another person to engage in conduct constituting such offense by either:

(a) making knowingly false representations designed to induce the belief that such conduct is not prohibited; or

(b) employing methods of persuasion or inducement which create a substantial risk that such an offense will be committed by persons other than those who are ready to commit it.

(2) Except as provided in Subsection (3) of this Section, a person prosecuted for an offense shall be acquitted if he proves by a preponderance of evidence that his conduct occurred in response to an entrapment. The issue of entrapment shall be tried by the Court in the absence of the jury.

(3) The defense afforded by this Section is unavailable when causing or threatening bodily injury is an element of the offense charged and the prosecution is based on conduct causing or threatening such injury to a person other than the person perpetrating the entrapment.

Article 3.   General Principles of Justification

SECTION 3.01.   JUSTIFICATION AN AFFIRMATIVE DEFENSE; CIVIL REMEDIES UNAFFECTED

(1) In any prosecution based on conduct which is justifiable under this Article, justification is an affirmative defense.

(2) The fact that conduct is justifiable under this Article does not abolish or impair any remedy for such conduct which is available in any civil action.

SECTION 3.02.   JUSTIFICATION GENERALLY: CHOICE OF EVILS

(1) Conduct which the actor believes to be necessary to avoid a harm or evil to himself or to another is justifiable, provided that:

(a) the harm or evil sought to be avoided by such conduct is greater than that sought to be prevented by the law defining the offense charged; and

(b) neither the Code nor other law defining the offense provides exceptions or defenses dealing with the specific situation involved; and

(c) a legislative purpose to exclude the justification claimed does not otherwise plainly appear.

(2) When the actor was reckless or negligent in bringing about the situation requiring a choice of harms or evils or in appraising the necessity for his conduct, the justification afforded by this section is unavailable in a prosecution for any offense for which recklessness or negligence, as the case may be, suffices to establish culpability.

SECTION 3.03.   EXECUTION OF PUBLIC DUTY

(1) Except as provided in Subsection (2) of this Section, conduct is justifiable when it is required or authorized by:

(a) the law defining the duties or functions of a public officer or the assistance to be rendered to such officer in the performance of his duties; or

(b) the law governing the execution of legal process; or

(c) the judgment or order of a competent court or tribunal; or

(d) the law governing the armed services or the lawful conduct of war; or

(e) any other provision of law imposing a public duty.

(2) The other sections of this Article apply to:

(a) the use of force upon or toward the person of another for any of the purposes dealt with in such sections; and

(b) the use of deadly force for any purpose, unless the use of such force is otherwise expressly authorized by law or occurs in the lawful conduct of war.

(3) The justification afforded by Subsection (1) of this Section applies:

(a) when the actor believes his conduct to be required or authorized by the judgment or direction of a competent court or tribunal or in the lawful execution of legal process, notwithstanding lack of jurisdiction of the court or defect in the legal process; and

(b) when the actor believes his conduct to be required or authorized to assist a public officer in the performance of his duties, notwithstanding that the officer exceeded his legal authority.

SECTION 3.04.   USE OF FORCE IN SELF-PROTECTION

(1) *Use of Force Justifiable for Protection of the Person.* Subject to the provisions of this Section and of Section 3.09, the use of force upon or toward another person is justifiable when the actor believes that such force is immediately necessary for the purpose of protecting himself against the use of unlawful force by such other person on the present occasion.

(2) *Limitations on Justifying Necessity for Use of Force.*

(a) The use of force is not justifiable under this Section:

(i) to resist an arrest which the actor knows is being made by a peace officer, although the arrest is unlawful; or

(ii) to resist force used by the occupier or possessor of property or by another person on his behalf, where the actor knows that the person using the force is doing so under a claim of right to protect the property, except that this limitation shall not apply if:

(1) the actor is a public officer acting in the performance of his duties or a person lawfully assisting him therein or a person making or assisting in a lawful arrest; or

(2) the actor has been unlawfully dispossessed of the property and is making a re-entry or recaption justified by Section 3.06; or

(3) the actor believes that such force is necessary to protect himself against death or serious bodily harm.

(b) The use of deadly force is not justifiable under this Section unless the actor believes that such force is necessary to protect himself against death, serious bodily harm, kidnapping or sexual intercourse compelled by force or threat; nor is it justifiable if:

(i) the actor, with the purpose of causing death or serious bodily harm, provoked the use of force against himself in the same encounter; or

(ii) the actor knows that he can avoid the necessity of using such force with complete safety by retreating or by surrendering possession of a thing to a person asserting a claim of right thereto or by complying with a demand that he abstain from any action which he has no duty to take, except that:

(1) the actor is not obliged to retreat from his dwelling or place of work, unless he was the initial aggressor or is assailed in his place of work by another person whose place of work the actor knows it to be; and

(2) a public officer justified in using force in the performance of his duties or a person justified in using force in his assistance or a person justified in using force in making an arrest or preventing an escape is not obliged to desist from efforts to perform such duty, effect such arrest or prevent such escape because of resistance or threatened resistance by or on behalf of the person against whom such action is directed.

(c) Except as required by paragraphs (a) and (b) of this Subsection, a person employing protective force may estimate the necessity thereof under the circumstances as he believes them to be when the force is used, without retreating, surrendering possession, doing any other act which he has no legal duty to do or abstaining from any lawful action.

(3) *Use of Confinement as Protective Force.* The justification afforded by this Section extends to the use of confinement as protective force only if the actor takes all reasonable measures to terminate the confinement as soon as he knows that he safely can, unless the person confined has been arrested on a charge of crime.

SECTION 3.05.   USE OF FORCE FOR THE PROTECTION OF OTHER PERSONS

(1) Subject to the provisions of this Section and of Section 3.09, the use of force upon or toward the person of another is justifiable to protect a third person when:

(a) the actor would be justified under Section 3.04 in using such force to protect himself against the injury he believes to be threatened to the person whom he seeks to protect; and

(b) under the circumstances as the actor believes them to be, the person whom he seeks to protect would be justified in using such protective force; and

(c) the actor believes that his intervention is necessary for the protection of such other person.

(2) Notwithstanding Subsection (1) of this Section:

(a) when the actor would be obliged under Section 3.04 to retreat, to surrender the possession of a thing or to comply with a demand before using force in self-protection, he is not obliged to do so before using force for the protection of another person, unless he knows that he can thereby secure the complete safety of such other person; and

(b) when the person whom the actor seeks to protect would be obliged under Section 3.04 to retreat, to surrender the possession of a thing or to comply with a demand if he knew that he could obtain complete safety by so doing, the actor is obliged to try to cause him to do so before using force in his protection if the actor knows that he can obtain complete safety in that way; and

(c) neither the actor nor the person whom he seeks to protect is obliged to retreat when in the other's dwelling or place of work to any greater extent than in his own.

SECTION 3.06.   USE OF FORCE FOR THE PROTECTION OF PROPERTY

(1) *Use of Force Justifiable for Protection of Property.* Subject to the provisions of this Section and of Section 3.09, the use of force upon or toward the person of another is justifiable when the actor believes that such force is immediately necessary:

(a) to prevent or terminate an unlawful entry or other trespass upon land or a trespass against or the unlawful carrying away of tangible, movable property, provided that such land or movable property is, or is believed by the actor to be, in his possession or in the possession of another person for whose protection he acts; or

(b) to effect an entry or re-entry upon land or to retake tangible movable property, provided that the actor believes that he or the person by whose authority he acts or a person from whom he or such other person derives title was unlawfully dispossessed of such land or movable property and is entitled to possession, and provided, further, that:

(i) the force is used immediately or on fresh pursuit after such dispossession; or

(ii) the actor believes that the person against whom he uses force has no claim of right to the possession of the property and, in the case of land, the circumstances, as the actor believes them to be, are of such urgency that it would be an exceptional hardship to postpone the entry or re-entry until a court order is obtained.

(2) *Meaning of Possession.* For the purposes of Subsection (1) of this Section:

(a) a person who has parted with the custody of property to another who refuses to restore it to him is no longer in possession, unless the property is movable and was and still is located on land in his possession;

(b) a person who has been dispossessed of land does not regain possession thereof merely by setting foot thereon;

(c) a person who has a license to use or occupy real property is deemed to be in possession thereof except against the licensor acting under claim of right.

(3) *Limitations on Justifiable Use of Force.*

(a) *Request to Desist.* The use of force is justifiable under this Section only if the actor first requests the person against whom such force is used to desist from his interference with the property, unless the actor believes that:

(i) such request would be useless; or

(ii) it would be dangerous to himself or another person to make the request; or

(iii) substantial harm will be done to the physical condition of the property which is sought to be protected before the request can effectively be made.

(b) *Exclusion of Trespasser.* The use of force to prevent or terminate a trespass is not justifiable under this Section if the actor knows that the exclusion of the trespasser will expose him to substantial danger of serious bodily harm.

(c) *Resistance of Lawful Re-entry or Recaption.* The use of force to prevent an entry or re-entry upon land or the recaption of movable property is not justifiable under this Section, although the actor believes that such re-entry or recaption is unlawful, if:

(i) the re-entry or recaption is made by or on behalf of a person who was actually dispossessed of the property; and

(ii) it is otherwise justifiable under paragraph (1)(b) of this Section.

(d) *Use of Deadly Force.* The use of deadly force is not justifiable under this Section unless the actor believes that:

(i) the person against whom the force is used is attempting to dispossess him of his dwelling otherwise than under a claim of right to its possession; or

(ii) the person against whom the force is used is attempting to commit or consummate arson, burglary, robbery or other felonious theft or property destruction and either:

(1) has employed or threatened deadly force against or in the presence of the actor; or

(2) the use of force other than deadly force to prevent the commission or the consummation of the crime would expose the actor or another in his presence to substantial danger of serious bodily harm.

(4) *Use of Confinement as Protective Force.* The justification afforded by this Section extends to the use of confinement as protective force only if the actor takes all reasonable measures to terminate the confinement as soon as he knows that he can do so with safety to the property, unless the person confined has been arrested on a charge of crime.

(5) *Use of Device to Protect Property.* The justification afforded by this Section extends to the use of a device for the purpose of protecting property only if:

(a) the device is not designed to cause or known to create a substantial risk of causing death or serious bodily harm; and

(b) the use of the particular device to protect the property from entry or trespass is reasonable under the circumstances, as the actor believes them to be; and

(c) the device is one customarily used for such a purpose or reasonable care is taken to make known to probable intruders the fact that it is used.

(6) *Use of Force to Pass Wrongful Obstructor.* The use of force to pass a person whom the actor believes to be purposely or knowingly and unjustifiably obstructing the actor from going to a place to which he may lawfully go is justifiable, provided that:

(a) the actor believes that the person against whom he uses force has no claim of right to obstruct the actor; and

(b) the actor is not being obstructed from entry or movement on land which he knows to be in the possession or custody of the person obstructing him, or in the possession or custody of another person by whose authority the obstructor acts, unless the circumstances, as the actor believes them to be, are of such urgency that it would not be reasonable to postpone the entry or movement on such land until a court order is obtained; and

(c) the force used is not greater than would be justifiable if the person obstructing the actor were using force against him to prevent his passage.

SECTION 3.07.   USE OF FORCE IN LAW ENFORCEMENT

(1) *Use of Force Justifiable to Effect an Arrest.* Subject to the provisions of this Section and of Section 3.09, the use of force upon or toward the person of another is justifiable when the actor is making or assisting in making an arrest and the actor believes that such force is immediately necessary to effect a lawful arrest.

(2) *Limitations on the Use of Force.*

(a) The use of force is not justifiable under this Section unless:

(i) the actor makes known the purpose of the arrest or believes that it is otherwise known by or cannot reasonably be made known to the person to be arrested; and

(ii) when the arrest is made under a warrant, the warrant is valid or believed by the actor to be valid.

(b) The use of deadly force is not justifiable under this Section unless:

(i) the arrest is for a felony; and

(ii) the person effecting the arrest is authorized to act as a peace officer or is assisting a person whom he believes to be authorized to act as a peace officer; and

(iii) the actor believes that the force employed creates no substantial risk of injury to innocent persons; and

(iv) the actor believes that:

(1) the crime for which the arrest is made involved conduct including the use or threatened use of deadly force; or

(2) there is a substantial risk that the person to be arrested will cause death or serious bodily harm if his apprehension is delayed.

(3) *Use of Force to Prevent Escape from Custody.* The use of force to prevent the escape of an arrested person from custody is justifiable when the force could justifiably have been employed to effect the arrest under which the person is in custody, except that a guard or other person authorized to act as a peace officer is justified in using any force, including deadly force, which he believes to be immediately necessary to prevent the escape of a person from a jail, prison, or other institution for the detention of persons charged with or convicted of a crime.

(4) *Use of Force by Private Person Assisting an Unlawful Arrest.*

(a) A private person who is summoned by a peace officer to assist in effecting an unlawful arrest, is justified in using any force which he would be justified in using if the arrest were lawful, provided that he does not believe the arrest is unlawful.

(b) A private person who assists another private person in effecting an unlawful arrest, or who, not being summoned, assists a peace officer in effecting an unlawful arrest, is justified in using any force which he would be justified in using if the arrest were lawful, provided that (i) he believes the arrest is lawful, and (ii) the arrest would be lawful if the facts were as he believes them to be.

(5) *Use of Force to Prevent Suicide or the Commission of a Crime.*

(a) The use of force upon or toward the person of another is justifiable when the actor believes that such force is immediately necessary to prevent such other person from committing suicide, inflicting serious bodily harm upon himself, committing or consummating the commission of a crime involving or threatening bodily harm, damage to or loss of property or a breach of the peace, except that:

(i) any limitations imposed by the other provisions of this Article on the justifiable use of force in self-protection, for the protection of others, the protection of property, the effectuation of an arrest or the prevention of an escape from custody shall apply notwithstanding the criminality of the conduct against which such force is used; and

(ii) the use of deadly force is not in any event justifiable under this Subsection unless:

(1) the actor believes that there is a substantial risk that the person whom he seeks to prevent from committing a crime will cause death or serious bodily harm to another unless the commission or the consummation of the crime is prevented and that the use of such force presents no substantial risk of injury to innocent persons; or

(2) the actor believes that the use of such force is necessary to suppress a riot or mutiny after the rioters or mutineers have been ordered to disperse and warned, in any particular manner that the law may require, that such force will be used if they do not obey.

(b) The jurisdiction afforded by this Subsection extends to the use of confinement as preventive force only if the actor takes all reasonable measures to terminate the confinement as soon as he knows that he safely can, unless the person confined has been arrested on a charge of crime.

SECTION 3.08.   USE OF FORCE BY PERSONS WITH SPECIAL RESPONSIBILITY FOR CARE, DISCIPLINE OR SAFETY OF OTHERS

The use of force upon or toward the person of another is justifiable if:

(1) the actor is the parent or guardian or other person similarly responsible for the general care and supervision of a minor or a person acting at the request of such parent, guardian or other responsible person and:

(a) the force is used for the purpose of safeguarding or promoting the welfare of the minor, including the prevention or punishment of his misconduct; and

(b) the force used is not designed to cause or known to create a substantial risk of causing death, serious bodily harm, disfigurement, extreme pain or mental distress or gross degradation; or

(2) the actor is a teacher or a person otherwise entrusted with the care or supervision for a special purpose of a minor and:

(a) the actor believes that the force used is necessary to further such special purpose, including the maintenance of reasonable discipline in a school, class or other group, and that the use of such force is consistent with the welfare of the minor; and

(b) the degree of force, if it had been used by the parent or guardian of the minor, would not be unjustifiable under Subsection (1)(b) of this Section; or

(3) the actor is the guardian or other person similarly responsible for the general care and supervision of an incompetent person; and:

(a) the force is used for the purpose of safeguarding or promoting the welfare of the incompetent person, including the prevention of his misconduct, or, when such incompetent person is in a hospital or other institution for his care and custody, for the maintenance of reasonable discipline in such institution; and

(b) the force used is not designed to cause or known to create a substantial risk of causing death, serious bodily harm, disfigurement, extreme or unnecessary pain, mental distress, or humiliation; or

(4) the actor is a doctor or other therapist or a person assisting him at his direction, and:

(a) the force is used for the purpose of administering a recognized form of treatment which the actor believes to be adapted to promoting the physical or mental health of the patient; and

(b) the treatment is administered with the consent of the patient or, if the patient is a minor or an incompetent person, with the consent of his parent or guardian or other person legally competent to consent in his behalf, or the treatment is administered in an emergency when the actor believes that no one competent to consent can be consulted and that a reasonable person, wishing to safeguard the welfare of the patient, would consent; or

(5) the actor is a warden or other authorized official of a correctional institution, and:

(a) he believes that the force used is necessary for the purpose of enforcing the lawful rules or procedures of the institution, unless his belief in the lawfulness of the rule or procedure sought to be enforced is erroneous and his error is due to ignorance or mistake as to the provisions of the Code, any other provision of the criminal law or the law governing the administration of the institution; and

(b) the nature or degree of force used is not forbidden by Article 303 or 304 of the Code; and

(c) if deadly force is used, its use is otherwise justifiable under this Article; or

(6) the actor is a person responsible for the safety of a vessel or an aircraft or a person acting at his direction, and

(a) he believes that the force used is necessary to prevent interference with the operation of the vessel or aircraft or obstruction of the execution of a lawful order, unless his belief in the lawfulness of the order is erroneous and his error is due to ignorance or mistake as to the law defining his authority; and

(b) if deadly force is used, its use is otherwise justifiable under this Article; or

(7) the actor is a person who is authorized or required by law to maintain order or decorum in a vehicle, train or other carrier or in a place where others are assembled, and:

(a) he believes that the force used is necessary for such purpose; and

(b) the force used is not designed to cause or known to create a substantial risk of causing death, bodily harm, or extreme mental distress.

SECTION 3.09.   MISTAKE OF LAW AS TO UNLAWFULNESS OF FORCE OR LEGALITY OF ARREST; RECKLESS OR NEGLIGENT USE OF OTHERWISE JUSTIFIABLE FORCE; RECKLESS OR NEGLIGENT INJURY OR RISK OF INJURY TO INNOCENT PERSONS

(1) The justification afforded by Sections 3.04 to 3.07, inclusive, is unavailable when:

(a) the actor's belief in the unlawfulness of the force or conduct against which he employs protective force or his belief in the lawfulness of an arrest which he endeavors to effect by force is erroneous; and

(b) his error is due to ignorance or mistake as to the provisions of the Code, any other provision of the criminal law or the law governing the legality of an arrest or search.

(2) When the actor believes that the use of force upon or toward the person of another is necessary for any of the purposes for which such belief would establish a justification under Sections 3.03 to 3.08 but the actor is reckless or negligent in having such belief or in acquiring or failing to acquire any knowledge or belief which is material to the justifiability of his use of force, the justification afforded by those Sections is unavailable in a prosecution for an offense for which recklessness or negligence, as the case may be, suffices to establish culpability.

(3) When the actor is justified under Sections 3.03 to 3.08 in using force upon or toward the person of another but he recklessly or negligently injures or creates a risk of injury to innocent persons, the justification afforded by those Sections is unavailable in a prosecution for such recklessness or negligence towards innocent persons.

SECTION 3.10. JUSTIFICATION IN PROPERTY CRIMES

Conduct involving the appropriation, seizure or destruction of, damage to, intrusion on or interference with property is justifiable under circumstances which would establish a defense of privilege in a civil action based thereon, unless:

(1) the Code or the law defining the offense deals with the specific situation involved; or

(2) a legislative purpose to exclude the justification claimed otherwise plainly appears.

SECTION 3.11. DEFINITIONS

In this Article, unless a different meaning plainly is required:

(1) "unlawful force" means force, including confinement, which is employed without the consent of the person against whom it is directed and the employment of which constitutes an offense or actionable tort or would constitute such offense or tort except for a defense (such as the absence of intent, negligence, or mental capacity; duress; youth; or diplomatic status) not amounting to a privilege to use the force. Assent constitutes consent, within the meaning of this Section, whether or not it otherwise is legally effective, except assent to the infliction of death or serious bodily harm.

(2) "deadly force" means force which the actor uses with the purpose of causing or which he knows to create a substantial risk of causing death or serious bodily harm. Purposely firing a firearm in the direction of another person or at a vehicle in which another person is believed to be constitutes deadly force. A threat to cause death or serious bodily harm, by the production of a weapon or otherwise, so long as the actor's purpose is limited to creating an apprehension that he will use deadly force if necessary, does not constitute deadly force.

(3) "dwelling" means any building or structure, though movable or temporary, or a portion thereof, which is for the time being the actor's home or place of lodging.

Article 4. Responsibility

SECTION 4.01. MENTAL DISEASE OR DEFECT EXCLUDING RESPONSIBILITY

(1) A person is not responsible for criminal conduct if at the time of such conduct as a result of mental disease or defect he lacks substantial capacity either to appreciate the criminality [wrongfulness] of his conduct or to conform his conduct to the requirements of law.

(2) As used in this Article, the terms "mental disease or defect" do not include an abnormality manifested only by repeated criminal or otherwise anti-social conduct.

SECTION 4.02. EVIDENCE OF MENTAL DISEASE OR DEFECT ADMISSIBLE WHEN RELEVANT TO
ELEMENT OF THE OFFENSE; [MENTAL DISEASE OR DEFECT IMPAIRING CAPACITY
AS GROUND FOR MITIGATION OF PUNISHMENT IN CAPITAL CASES]

(1) Evidence that the defendant suffered from a mental disease or defect is admissible whenever it is relevant to prove that the defendant did or did not have a state of mind which is an element of the offense.

[(2) Whenever the jury or the Court is authorized to determine or to recommend whether or not the defendant shall be sentenced to death or imprisonment upon conviction, evidence that the capacity of the defendant to appreciate the criminality [wrongfulness] of his conduct or to conform his conduct to the requirements of law was impaired as a result of mental disease or defect is admissible in favor of sentence of imprisonment.]

SECTION 4.03.   MENTAL DISEASE OR DEFECT EXCLUDING RESPONSIBILITY IS AFFIRMATIVE
                DEFENSE; REQUIREMENT OF NOTICE; FORM OF VERDICT AND JUDGMENT
                WHEN FINDING OF IRRESPONSIBILITY IS MADE

(1) Mental disease or defect excluding responsibility is an affirmative defense.

(2) Evidence of mental disease or defect excluding responsibility is not admissible unless the defendant, at the time of entering his plea of not guilty or within ten days thereafter or at such later time as the Court may for good cause permit, files a written notice of his purpose to rely on such defense.

(3) When the defendant is acquitted on the ground of mental disease or defect excluding responsibility, the verdict and the judgment shall so state.

SECTION 4.04.   MENTAL DISEASE OR DEFECT EXCLUDING FITNESS TO PROCEED

No person who as a result of mental disease or defect lacks capacity to understand the proceedings against him or to assist in his own defense shall be tried, convicted or sentenced for the commission of an offense so long as such incapacity endures.

SECTION 4.05.   PSYCHIATRIC EXAMINATION OF DEFENDANT WITH RESPECT TO MENTAL DISEASE
                OR DEFECT

(1) Whenever the defendant has filed a notice of intention to rely on the defense of mental disease or defect excluding responsibility, or there is reason to doubt his fitness to proceed, or reason to believe that mental disease or defect of the defendant will otherwise become an issue in the cause, the Court shall appoint at least one qualified psychiatrist or shall request the Superintendent of the _____ (3) Hospital to designate at least one qualified psychiatrist, which designation may be or include himself, to examine and report upon the mental condition of the defendant. The Court may order the defendant to be committed to a hospital or other suitable facility for the purpose of the examination for a period of not exceeding sixty days or such longer period as the Court determines to be necessary for the purpose and may direct that a qualified psychiatrist retained by the defendant be permitted to witness and participate in the examination.

(2) In such examination any method may be employed which is accepted by the medical profession for the examination of those alleged to be suffering from mental disease or defect.

(3) The report of the examination shall include the following: (a) a description of the nature of the examination; (b) a diagnosis of the mental condition of the defendant; (c) if the defendant suffers from a mental disease or defect, an opinion as to his capacity to understand the proceedings against him and to assist in his own defense; (d) when a notice of intention to rely on the defense of irresponsibility has been filed, an opinion as to the extent, if any, to which the capacity of the defendant to appreciate the criminality [wrongfulness] of his conduct or to conform his conduct to the requirements of law was impaired at the time of the criminal conduct charged; and (e) when directed by the Court, an opinion as to the capacity of the defendant to have a particular state of mind which is an element of the offense charged.

If the examination can not be conducted by reason of the unwillingness of the defendant to participate therein, the report shall so state and shall include, if possible, an opinion as to whether such unwillingness of the defendant was the result of mental disease or defect.

The report of the examination shall be filed [in triplicate] with the clerk of the Court, who shall cause copies to be delivered to the district attorney and to counsel for the defendant.

SECTION 4.06.   DETERMINATION OF FITNESS TO PROCEED; EFFECT OF FINDING OF UNFITNESS;
                PROCEEDINGS IF FITNESS IS REGAINED[; POST-COMMITMENT HEARING]

(1) When the defendant's fitness to proceed is drawn in question, the issue shall be determined by the Court. If neither the prosecuting attorney nor counsel for the defendant contests

the finding of the report filed pursuant to Section 4.05, the Court may make the determination on the basis of such report. If the finding is contested, the Court shall hold a hearing on the issue. If the report is received in evidence upon such hearing, the party who contests the finding thereof shall have the right to summon and to cross-examine the psychiatrists who joined in the report and to offer evidence upon the issue.

(2) If the Court determines that the defendant lacks fitness to proceed, the proceeding against him shall be suspended, except as provided in Subsection (3) [Subsections (3) and (4)] of this Section, and the Court shall commit him to the custody of the Commissioner of Mental Hygiene [Public Health or Correction] to be placed in an appropriate institution of the Department of Mental Hygiene [Public Health or Correction] for so long as such unfitness shall endure. When the Court, on its own motion or upon the application of the Commissioner of Mental Hygiene [Public Health or Correction] or the prosecuting attorney, determines, after a hearing if a hearing is requested, that the defendant has regained fitness to proceed, the proceeding shall be resumed. If, however, the Court is of the view that so much time has elapsed since the commitment of the defendant that it would be unjust to resume the criminal proceeding, the Court may dismiss the charge and may order the defendant to be discharged or, subject to the law governing the civil commitment of persons suffering from mental disease or defect, order the defendant to be committed to an appropriate institution of the Department of Mental Hygiene [Public Health].

(3) The fact that the defendant is unfit to proceed does not preclude any legal objection to the prosecution which is susceptible of fair determination prior to trial and without the personal participation of the defendant.

[Alternative: (3) At any time within ninety days after commitment as provided in Subsection (2) of this Section, or at any later time with permission of the Court granted for good cause, the defendant or his counsel or the Commissioner of Mental Hygiene [Public Health or Correction] may apply for a special post-commitment hearing. If the application is made by or on behalf of a defendant not represented by counsel, he shall be afforded a reasonable opportunity to obtain counsel, and if he lacks funds to do so, counsel shall be assigned by the Court. The application shall be granted only if the counsel for the defendant satisfies the Court by affidavit or otherwise that as an attorney he has reasonable grounds for a good faith belief that his client has, on the facts and the law, a defense to the charge other than mental disease or defect excluding responsibility.

[(4) If the motion for a special post-commitment hearing is granted, the hearing shall be by the Court without a jury. No evidence shall be offered at the hearing by either party on the issue of mental disease or defect as a defense to, or in mitigation of, the crime charged. After hearing, the Court may in an appropriate case quash the indictment or other charge, or find it to be defective or insufficient, or determine that it is not proved beyond a reasonable doubt by the evidence, or otherwise terminate the proceedings on the evidence or the law. In any such case, unless all defects in the proceedings are promptly cured, the Court shall terminate the commitment ordered under Subsection (2) of this Section and order the defendant to be discharged or, subject to the law governing the civil commitment of persons suffering from mental disease or defect, order the defendant to be committed to an appropriate institution of the Department of Mental Hygiene [Public Health].]

Section 4.07.   Determination of Irresponsibility on Basis of Report; Access to
                 Defendant by Psychiatrist of His Own Choice; Form of Expert Testimony
                 When Issue of Responsibility Is Tried

(1) If the report filed pursuant to Section 4.05 finds that the defendant at the time of the criminal conduct charged suffered from a mental disease or defect which substantially impaired his capacity to appreciate the criminality [wrongfulness] of his conduct or to conform his conduct to the requirements of law, and the Court, after a hearing if a hearing is requested by the prosecuting attorney or the defendant, is satisfied that such impairment was sufficient to

exclude responsibility, the Court on motion of the defendant shall enter judgment of acquittal on the ground of mental disease or defect excluding responsibility.

(2) When, notwithstanding the report filed pursuant to Section 4.05, the defendant wishes to be examined by a qualified psychiatrist or other expert of his own choice, such examiner shall be permitted to have reasonable access to the defendant for the purposes of such examination.

(3) Upon the trial, the psychiatrists who reported pursuant to Section 4.05 may be called as witnesses by the prosecution, the defendant or the Court. If the issue is being tried before a jury, the jury may be informed that the psychiatrists were designated by the Court or by the Superintendent of the _____ (3) Hospital at the request of the Court, as the case may be. If called by the Court, the witness shall be subject to cross-examination by the prosecution and by the defendant. Both the prosecution and the defendant may summon any other qualified psychiatrist or other expert to testify, but no one who has not examined the defendant shall be competent to testify to an expert opinion with respect to the mental condition or responsibility of the defendant, as distinguished from the validity of the procedure followed by, or the general scientific propositions stated by, another witness.

(4) When a psychiatrist or other expert who has examined the defendant testifies concerning his mental condition, he shall be permitted to make a statement as to the nature of his examination, his diagnosis of the mental condition of the defendant at the time of the commission of the offense charged and his opinion as to the extent, if any, to which the capacity of the defendant to appreciate the criminality [wrongfulness] of his conduct or to conform his conduct to the requirements of law or to have a particular state of mind which is an element of the offense charged was impaired as a result of mental disease or defect at that time. He shall be permitted to make any explanation reasonably serving to clarify his diagnosis and opinion and may be cross-examined as to any matter bearing on his competency or credibility or the validity of his diagnosis or opinion.

SECTION 4.08. LEGAL EFFECT OF ACQUITTAL ON THE GROUND OF MENTAL DISEASE OR DEFECT EXCLUDING RESPONSIBILITY; COMMITMENT; RELEASE OR DISCHARGE

(1) When a defendant is acquitted on the ground of mental disease or defect excluding responsibility, the Court shall order him to be committed to the custody of the Commissioner of Mental Hygiene [Public Health] to be placed in an appropriate institution for custody, care and treatment.

(2) If the Commissioner of Mental Hygiene [Public Health] is of the view that a person committed to his custody, pursuant to paragraph (1) of this Section, may be discharged or released on condition without danger to himself or to others, he shall make application for the discharge or release of such person in a report to the Court by which such person was committed and shall transmit a copy of such application and report to the prosecuting attorney of the county [parish] from which the defendant was committed. The Court shall thereupon appoint at least two qualified psychiatrists to examine such person and to report within sixty days, or such longer period as the Court determines to be necessary for the purpose, their opinion as to his mental condition. To facilitate such examination and the proceedings thereon, the Court may cause such person to be confined in any institution located near the place where the Court sits, which may hereafter be designated by the Commissioner of Mental Hygiene [Public Health] as suitable for the temporary detention of irresponsible persons.

(3) If the Court is satisfied by the report filed pursuant to paragraph (2) of this Section and such testimony of the reporting psychiatrists as the Court deems necessary that the committed person may be discharged or released on condition without danger to himself or others, the Court shall order his discharge or his release on such conditions as the Court determines to be necessary. If the Court is not so satisfied, it shall promptly order a hearing to determine whether such person may safely be discharged or released. Any such hearing shall be deemed a civil proceeding and the burden shall be upon the committed person to prove

that he may safely be discharged or released. According to the determination of the Court upon the hearing, the committed person shall thereupon be discharged or released on such conditions as the Court determines to be necessary, or shall be recommitted to the custody of the Commissioner of Mental Hygiene [Public Health], subject to discharge or release only in accordance with the procedure prescribed above for a first hearing.

(4) If, within [five] years after the conditional release of a committed person, the Court shall determine, after hearing evidence, that the conditions of release have not been fulfilled and that for the safety of such person or for the safety of others his conditional release should be revoked, the Court shall forthwith order him to be recommitted to the Commissioner of Mental Hygiene [Public Health], subject to discharge or release only in accordance with the procedure prescribed above for a first hearing.

(5) A committed person may make application for his discharge or release to the Court by which he was committed, and the procedure to be followed upon such application shall be the same as that prescribed above in the case of an application by the Commissioner of Mental Hygiene [Public Health]. However, no such application by a committed person need be considered until he has been confined for a period of not less than [six months] from the date of the order of commitment, and if the determination of the Court be adverse to the application, such person shall not be permitted to file a further application until [one year] has elapsed from the date of any preceding hearing on an application for his release or discharge.

SECTION 4.09.   STATEMENTS FOR PURPOSES OF EXAMINATION OR TREATMENT INADMISSIBLE
                EXCEPT ON ISSUE OF MENTAL CONDITION [omitted]

SECTION 4.10.   IMMATURITY EXCLUDING CRIMINAL CONVICTION; TRANSFER
                OF PROCEEDINGS TO JUVENILE COURT

(1) A person shall not be tried for or convicted of an offense if:

(a) at the time of the conduct charged to constitute the offense he was less than sixteen years of age[, in which case the Juvenile Court shall have exclusive jurisdiction]; or

(b) at the time of the conduct charged to constitute the offense he was sixteen or seventeen years of age, unless:

(i) the Juvenile Court has no jurisdiction over him, or

(ii) the Juvenile Court has entered an order waiving jurisdiction and consenting to the institution of criminal proceedings against him.

(2) No court shall have jurisdiction to try or convict a person of an offense if criminal proceedings against him are barred by Subsection (1) of this Section. When it appears that a person charged with the commission of an offense may be of such an age that criminal proceedings may be barred under Subsection (1) of this Section, the Court shall hold a hearing thereon, and the burden shall be on the prosecution to establish to the satisfaction of the Court that the criminal proceeding is not barred upon such grounds. If the Court determines that the proceeding is barred, custody of the person charged shall be surrendered to the Juvenile Court, and the case, including all papers and processes relating thereto, shall be transferred.

Article 5.   Inchoate Crimes

SECTION 5.01.   CRIMINAL ATTEMPT

(1) *Definition of Attempt.* A person is guilty of an attempt to commit a crime if, acting with the kind of culpability otherwise required for commission of the crime, he:

(a) purposely engages in conduct which would constitute the crime if the attendant circumstances were as he believes them to be; or

(b) when causing a particular result is an element of the crime, does or omits to do anything with the purpose of causing or with the belief that it will cause such result without further conduct on his part; or

(c) purposely does or omits to do anything which, under the circumstances as he believes them to be, is an act or omission constituting a substantial step in a course of conduct planned to culminate in his commission of the crime.

(2) *Conduct Which May Be Held Substantial Step Under Subsection (1)(c).* Conduct shall not be held to constitute a substantial step under Subsection (1)(c) of this Section unless it is strongly corroborative of the actor's criminal purpose. Without negativing the sufficiency of other conduct, the following, if strongly corroborative of the actor's criminal purpose, shall not be held insufficient as a matter of law:

(a) lying in wait, searching for or following the contemplated victim of the crime;

(b) enticing or seeking to entice the contemplated victim of the crime to go to the place contemplated for its commission;

(c) reconnoitering the place contemplated for the commission of the crime;

(d) unlawful entry of a structure, vehicle or enclosure in which it is contemplated that the crime will be committed;

(e) possession of materials to be employed in the commission of the crime, which are specially designed for such unlawful use or which can serve no lawful purpose of the actor under the circumstances;

(f) possession, collection or fabrication of materials to be employed in the commission of the crime, at or near the place contemplated for its commission, where such possession, collection or fabrication serves no lawful purpose of the actor under the circumstances;

(g) soliciting an innocent agent to engage in conduct constituting an element of the crime.

(3) *Conduct Designed to Aid Another in Commission of a Crime.* A person who engages in conduct designed to aid another to commit a crime which would establish his complicity under Section 2.06 if the crime were committed by such other person, is guilty of an attempt to commit the crime, although the crime is not committed or attempted by such other person.

(4) *Renunciation of Criminal Purpose.* When the actor's conduct would otherwise constitute an attempt under Subsection (1)(b) or (1)(c) of this Section, it is an affirmative defense that he abandoned his effort to commit the crime or otherwise prevented its commission, under circumstances manifesting a complete and voluntary renunciation of his criminal purpose. The establishment of such defense does not, however, affect the liability of an accomplice who did not join in such abandonment or prevention.

Within the meaning of this Article, renunciation of criminal purpose is not voluntary if it is motivated, in whole or in part, by circumstances, not present or apparent at the inception of the actor's course of conduct, which increase the probability of detection or apprehension or which make more difficult the accomplishment of the criminal purpose. Renunciation is not complete if it is motivated by a decision to postpone the criminal conduct until a more advantageous time or to transfer the criminal effort to another but similar objective or victim.

SECTION 5.02.　CRIMINAL SOLICITATION

(1) *Definition of Solicitation.* A person is guilty of solicitation to commit a crime if with the purpose of promoting or facilitating its commission he commands, encourages or requests another person to engage in specific conduct which would constitute such crime or an attempt to commit such crime or which would establish his complicity in its commission or attempted commission.

(2) *Uncommunicated Solicitation.* It is immaterial under Subsection (1) of this Section that the actor fails to communicate with the person he solicits to commit a crime if his conduct was designed to effect such communication.

(3) *Renunciation of Criminal Purpose.* It is an affirmative defense that the actor, after soliciting another person to commit a crime, persuaded him not to do so or otherwise prevented the commission of the crime, under circumstances manifesting a complete and voluntary renunciation of his criminal purpose.

SECTION 5.03. CRIMINAL CONSPIRACY

(1) *Definition of Conspiracy.* A person is guilty of conspiracy with another person or persons to commit a crime if with the purpose of promoting or facilitating its commission he:

(a) agrees with such other person or persons that they or one or more of them will engage in conduct which constitutes such crime or an attempt or solicitation to commit such crime; or

(b) agrees to aid such other person or persons in the planning or commission of such crime or of an attempt or solicitation to commit such crime.

(2) *Scope of Conspiratorial Relationship.* If a person guilty of conspiracy, as defined by Subsection (1) of this Section, knows that a person with whom he conspires to commit a crime has conspired with another person or persons to commit the same crime, he is guilty of conspiring with such other person or persons, whether or not he knows their identity, to commit such crime.

(3) *Conspiracy with Multiple Criminal Objectives.* If a person conspires to commit a number of crimes, he is guilty of only one conspiracy so long as such multiple crimes are the object of the same agreement or continuous conspiratorial relationship.

(4) *Joinder and Venue in Conspiracy Prosecutions.*

(a) Subject to the provisions of paragraph (b) of this Subsection, two or more persons charged with criminal conspiracy may be prosecuted jointly if:

(i) they are charged with conspiring with one another; or

(ii) the conspiracies alleged, whether they have the same or different parties, are so related that they constitute different aspects of a scheme of organized criminal conduct.

(b) In any joint prosecution under paragraph (a) of this Subsection:

(i) no defendant shall be charged with a conspiracy in any county [parish or district] other than one in which he entered into such conspiracy or in which an overt act pursuant to such conspiracy was done by him or by a person with whom he conspired; and

(ii) neither the liability of any defendant nor the admissibility against him of evidence of acts or declarations of another shall be enlarged by such joinder; and

(iii) the Court shall order a severance or take a special verdict as to any defendant who so requests, if it deems it necessary or appropriate to promote the fair determination of his guilt or innocence, and shall take any other proper measures to protect the fairness of the trial.

(5) *Overt Act.* No person may be convicted of conspiracy to commit a crime, other than a felony of the first or second degree, unless an overt act in pursuance of such conspiracy is alleged and proved to have been done by him or by a person with whom he conspired.

(6) *Renunciation of Criminal Purpose.* It is an affirmative defense that the actor, after conspiring to commit a crime, thwarted the success of the conspiracy, under circumstances manifesting a complete and voluntary renunciation of his criminal purpose.

(7) *Duration of Conspiracy.* For purposes of Section 1.06(4):

(a) conspiracy is a continuing course of conduct which terminates when the crime or crimes which are its object are committed or the agreement that they be committed is abandoned by the defendant and by those with whom he conspired; and

(b) such abandonment is presumed if neither the defendant nor anyone with whom he conspired does any overt act in pursuance of the conspiracy during the applicable period of limitation; and

(c) if an individual abandons the agreement, the conspiracy is terminated as to him only if and when he advises those with whom he conspired of his abandonment or he informs the law enforcement authorities of the existence of the conspiracy and of his participation therein.

SECTION 5.04.   INCAPACITY, IRRESPONSIBILITY OR IMMUNITY OF PARTY TO SOLICITATION OR CONSPIRACY

(1) Except as provided in Subsection (2) of this Section, it is immaterial to the liability of a person who solicits or conspires with another to commit a crime that:

(a) he or the person whom he solicits or with whom he conspires does not occupy a particular position or have a particular characteristic which is an element of such crime, if he believes that one of them does; or

(b) the person whom he solicits or with whom he conspires is irresponsible or has an immunity to prosecution or conviction for the commission of the crime.

(2) It is a defense to a charge of solicitation or conspiracy to commit a crime that if the criminal object were achieved, the actor would not be guilty of a crime under the law defining the offense or as an accomplice under Section 2.06(5) or 2.06(6)(a) or (b).

SECTION 5.05.   GRADING OF CRIMINAL ATTEMPT, SOLICITATION AND CONSPIRACY; MITIGATION IN CASES OF LESSER DANGER; MULTIPLE CONVICTIONS BARRED

(1) *Grading.* Except as otherwise provided in this Section, attempt, solicitation and conspiracy are crimes of the same grade and degree as the most serious offense which is attempted or solicited or is an object of the conspiracy. An attempt, solicitation or conspiracy to commit a [capital crime or a] felony of the first degree is a felony of the second degree.

(2) *Mitigation.* If the particular conduct charged to constitute a criminal attempt, solicitation or conspiracy is so inherently unlikely to result or culminate in the commission of a crime that neither such conduct nor the actor presents a public danger warranting the grading of such offense under this Section, the Court shall exercise its power under Section 6.12 to enter judgment and impose sentence for a crime of lower grade or degree or, in extreme cases, may dismiss the prosecution.

(3) *Multiple Convictions.* A person may not be convicted of more than one offense defined by this Article for conduct designed to commit or to culminate in the commission of the same crime.

SECTION 5.06.   POSSESSING INSTRUMENTS OF CRIME; WEAPONS

(1) *Criminal Instruments Generally.* A person commits a misdemeanor if he possesses any instrument of crime with purpose to employ it criminally. "Instrument of crime" means:

(a) anything specially made or specially adapted for criminal use; or

(b) anything commonly used for criminal purposes and possessed by the actor under circumstances which do not negative unlawful purpose.

(2) *Presumption of Criminal Purpose from Possession of Weapon.* If a person possesses a firearm or other weapon on or about his person, in a vehicle occupied by him, or otherwise readily available for use, it shall be presumed that he had the purpose to employ it criminally, unless:

(a) the weapon is possessed in the actor's home or place of business;

(b) the actor is licensed or otherwise authorized by law to possess such weapon; or

(c) the weapon is of a type commonly used in lawful sport.

"Weapon" means anything readily capable of lethal use and possessed under circumstances not manifestly appropriate for lawful uses which it may have; the term includes a firearm which is not loaded or lacks a clip or other component to render it immediately operable, and components which can readily be assembled into a weapon.

(3) *Presumptions as to Possession of Criminal Instruments in Automobiles.* Where a weapon or other instrument of crime is found in an automobile, it is presumed to be in the possession of the occupant if there is but one. If there is more than one occupant, it shall be presumed to be in the possession of all, except under the following circumstances:

(a) where it is found upon the person of one of the occupants;

(b) where the automobile is not a stolen one and the weapon or instrument is found out of view in a glove compartment, car trunk, or other enclosed customary depository, in which case it shall be presumed to be in the possession of the occupant or occupants who own or have authority to operate the automobile;

(c) in the case of a taxicab, a weapon or instrument found in the passengers' portion of the vehicle shall be presumed to be in the possession of all the passengers, if there are any, and, if not, in the possession of the driver.

SECTION 5.07.   PROHIBITED OFFENSIVE WEAPONS

A person commits a misdemeanor if, except as authorized by law, he makes, repairs, sells, or otherwise deals in, uses or possesses any offensive weapon. "Offensive weapon" means any bomb, machine gun, sawed-off shotgun, firearm specially made or specially adapted for concealment or silent discharge, any blackjack, sandbag, metal knuckles, dagger, or other implement for the infliction of serious bodily injury which serves no common lawful purpose. It is a defense under this Section for the defendant to prove by a preponderance of evidence that he possessed or dealt with the weapon solely as a curio or in a dramatic performance, or that he possessed it briefly in consequence of having found it or taken it from an aggressor, or under circumstances similarly negativing any purpose or likelihood that the weapon would be used unlawfully. The presumptions provided in Section 5.06(3) are applicable to prosecutions under this Section.

Article 6.   Authorized Disposition of Offenders

SECTION 6.01.   DEGREES OF FELONIES

(1) Felonies defined by this Code are classified, for the purpose of sentence, into three degrees, as follows:

(a) felonies of the first degree;

(b) felonies of the second degree;

(c) felonies of the third degree.

A felony is of the first or second degree when it is so designated by the Code. A crime declared to be a felony, without specification of degree, is of the third degree.

(2) Notwithstanding any other provision of law, a felony defined by any statute of this State other than this Code shall constitute for the purpose of sentence a felony of the third degree.

SECTION 6.02.   SENTENCE IN ACCORDANCE WITH CODE; AUTHORIZED DISPOSITIONS

(1) No person convicted of an offense shall be sentenced otherwise than in accordance with this Article.

[(2) The Court shall sentence a person who has been convicted of murder to death or imprisonment, in accordance with Section 210.6.]

(3) Except as provided in Subsection (2) of this Section and subject to the applicable provisions of the Code, the Court may suspend the imposition of sentence on a person who has been convicted of a crime, may order him to be committed in lieu of sentence, in accordance with Section 6.13, or may sentence him as follows:

(a) to pay a fine authorized by Section 6.03; or

(b) to be placed on probation[, and, in the case of a person convicted of a felony or misdemeanor to imprisonment for a term fixed by the Court not exceeding thirty days to be served as a condition of probation]; or

(c) to imprisonment for a term authorized by Sections 6.05, 6.06, 6.07, 6.08, 6.09, or 7.06; or

(d) to fine and probation or fine and imprisonment, but not to probation and imprisonment[, except as authorized in paragraph (b) of this Subsection].

(4) The Court may suspend the imposition of sentence on a person who has been convicted of a violation or may sentence him to pay a fine authorized by Section 6.03.

(5) This Article does not deprive the Court of any authority conferred by law to decree a forfeiture of property, suspend or cancel a license, remove a person from office, or impose any other civil penalty. Such a judgment or order may be included in the sentence.

SECTION 6.03.   FINES

A person who has been convicted of an offense may be sentenced to pay a fine not exceeding:

(1) $10,000, when the conviction is of a felony of the first or second degree;

(2) $5,000, when the conviction is of a felony of the third degree;

(3) $1,000, when the conviction is of a misdemeanor;

(4) $500, when the conviction is of a petty misdemeanor or a violation;

(5) any higher amount equal to double the pecuniary gain derived from the offense by the offender;

(6) any higher amount specifically authorized by statute.

SECTION 6.04.   PENALTIES AGAINST CORPORATIONS AND UNINCORPORATED ASSOCIATIONS;
                FORFEITURE OF CORPORATE CHARTER OR REVOCATION OF CERTIFICATE
                AUTHORIZING FOREIGN CORPORATION TO DO BUSINESS IN THE STATE

(1) The Court may suspend the sentence of a corporation or an unincorporated association which has been convicted of an offense or may sentence it to pay a fine authorized by Section 6.03.

(2) (a) The [prosecuting attorney] is authorized to institute civil proceedings in the appropriate court of general jurisdiction to forfeit the charter of a corporation organized under the laws of this State or to revoke the certificate authorizing a foreign corporation to conduct business in this State. The Court may order the charter forfeited or the certificate revoked upon finding (i) that the board of directors or a high managerial agent acting in behalf of the corporation has, in conducting the corporation's affairs, purposely engaged in a persistent course of criminal conduct and (ii) that for the prevention of future criminal conduct of the same character, the public interest requires the charter of the corporation to be forfeited and the corporation to be dissolved or the certificate to be revoked.

(b) When a corporation is convicted of a crime or a high managerial agent of a corporation, as defined in Section 2.07, is convicted of a crime committed in the conduct of the affairs of the corporation, the Court, in sentencing the corporation or the agent, may direct the [prosecuting attorney] to institute proceedings authorized by paragraph (a) of this Subsection.

(c) The proceedings authorized by paragraph (a) of this Subsection shall be conducted in accordance with the procedures authorized by law for the involuntary dissolution of a corporation or the revocation of the certificate authorizing a foreign corporation to conduct business in this State. Such proceedings shall be deemed additional to any other proceedings authorized by law for the purpose of forfeiting the charter of a corporation or revoking the certificate of a foreign corporation.

SECTION 6.05.   YOUNG ADULT OFFENDERS

(1) *Specialized Correctional Treatment.* A young adult offender is a person convicted of a crime who, at the time of sentencing, is sixteen but less than twenty-two years of age. A young adult offender who is sentenced to a term of imprisonment which may exceed thirty days

[alternatives: (1) ninety days; (2) one year] shall be committed to the custody of the Division of Young Adult Correction of the Department of Correction, and shall receive, as far as practicable, such special and individualized correctional and rehabilitative treatment as may be appropriate to his needs.

(2) *Special Term.* A young adult offender convicted of a felony may, in lieu of any other sentence of imprisonment authorized by this Article, be sentenced to a special term of imprisonment without a minimum and with a maximum of four years, regardless of the degree of the felony involved, if the Court is of the opinion that such special term is adequate for his correction and rehabilitation and will not jeopardize the protection of the public.

[(3) *Removal of Disabilities; Vacation of Conviction.*

(a) In sentencing a young adult offender to the special term provided by this Section or to any sentence other than one of imprisonment, the Court may order that so long as he is not convicted of another felony, the judgment shall not constitute a conviction for the purposes of any disqualification or disability imposed by law upon conviction of a crime.

(b) When any young adult offender is unconditionally discharged from probation or parole before the expiration of the maximum term thereof, the Court may enter an order vacating the judgment of conviction.]

[(4) *Commitment for Observation.* If, after pre-sentence investigation, the Court desires additional information concerning a young adult offender before imposing sentence, it may order that he be committed, for a period not exceeding ninety days, to the custody of the Division of Young Adult Correction of the Department of Correction for observation and study at an appropriate reception or classification center. Such Division of the Department of Correction and the [Young Adult Division of the] Board of Parole shall advise the Court of their findings and recommendations on or before the expiration of such ninety-day period.]

Section 6.06.　Sentence of Imprisonment for Felony; Ordinary Terms

A person who has been convicted of a felony may be sentenced to imprisonment, as follows:

(1) in the case of a felony of the first degree, for a term the minimum of which shall be fixed by the Court at not less than one year nor more than ten years, and the maximum of which shall be life imprisonment;

(2) in the case of a felony of the second degree, for a term the minimum of which shall be fixed by the Court at not less than one year nor more than three years, and the maximum of which shall be ten years;

(3) in the case of a felony of the third degree, for a term the minimum of which shall be fixed by the Court at not less than one year nor more than two years, and the maximum of which shall be five years.

Alternate Section 6.06.　Sentence of Imprisonment for Felony; Ordinary Terms

A person who has been convicted of a felony may be sentenced to imprisonment, as follows:

(1) in the case of a felony of the first degree, for a term the minimum of which shall be fixed by the Court at not less than one year nor more than ten years, and the maximum at not more than twenty years or at life imprisonment;

(2) in the case of a felony of the second degree, for a term the minimum of which shall be fixed by the Court at not less than one year nor more than three years, and the maximum at not more than ten years;

(3) in the case of a felony of the third degree, for a term the minimum of which shall be fixed by the Court at not less than one year nor more than two years, and the maximum at not more than five years.

No sentence shall be imposed under this Section of which the minimum is longer than one-half the maximum, or, when the maximum is life imprisonment, longer than ten years.

SECTION 6.07.   SENTENCE OF IMPRISONMENT FOR FELONY; EXTENDED TERMS

In the cases designated in Section 7.03, a person who has been convicted of a felony may be sentenced to an extended term of imprisonment, as follows:

(1) in the case of a felony of the first degree, for a term the minimum of which shall be fixed by the Court at not less than five years nor more than ten years, and the maximum of which shall be life imprisonment;

(2) in the case of a felony of the second degree, for a term the minimum of which shall be fixed by the Court at not less than one year nor more than five years, and the maximum of which shall be fixed by the Court at not less than ten nor more than twenty years;

(3) in the case of a felony of the third degree, for a term the minimum of which shall be fixed by the Court at not less than one year nor more than three years, and the maximum of which shall be fixed by the Court at not less than five nor more than ten years.

SECTION 6.08.   SENTENCE OF IMPRISONMENT FOR MISDEMEANORS AND PETTY MISDEMEANORS; ORDINARY TERMS

A person who has been convicted of a misdemeanor or a petty misdemeanor may be sentenced to imprisonment for a definite term which shall be fixed by the Court and shall not exceed one year in the case of a misdemeanor or thirty days in the case of a petty misdemeanor.

SECTION 6.09.   SENTENCE OF IMPRISONMENT FOR MISDEMEANORS AND PETTY MISDEMEANORS; EXTENDED TERMS

(1) In the cases designated in Section 7.04, a person who has been convicted of a misdemeanor or a petty misdemeanor may be sentenced to an extended term of imprisonment, as follows:

(a) in the case of a misdemeanor, for a term the minimum of which shall be fixed by the Court at not more than one year and the maximum of which shall be three years;

(b) in the case of a petty misdemeanor, for a term the minimum of which shall be fixed by the Court at not more than six months and the maximum of which shall be two years.

(2) No such sentence for an extended term shall be imposed unless:

(a) the Director of Correction has certified that there is an institution in the Department of Correction, or in a county, city [or other appropriate political subdivision of the State] which is appropriate for the detention and correctional treatment of such misdemeanants or petty misdemeanants, and that such institution is available to receive such commitments; and

(b) the [Board of Parole][Parole Administrator] has certified that the Board of Parole is able to visit such institution and to assume responsibility for the release of such prisoners on parole and for their parole supervision.

SECTION 6.10.   FIRST RELEASE OF ALL OFFENDERS ON PAROLE; SENTENCE OF IMPRISONMENT INCLUDES SEPARATE PAROLE TERM; LENGTH OF PAROLE TERM; LENGTH OF RECOMMITMENT AND REPAROLE AFTER REVOCATION OF PAROLE; FINAL UNCONDITIONAL RELEASE

(1) *First Release of All Offenders on Parole.* An offender sentenced to an indefinite term of imprisonment in excess of one year under Section 6.05, 6.06, 6.07, 6.09 or 7.06 shall be released conditionally on parole at or before the expiration of the maximum of such term, in accordance with Article 305.

(2) *Sentence of Imprisonment Includes Separate Parole Term; Length of Parole Term.* A sentence to an indefinite term of imprisonment in excess of one year under Section 6.05, 6.06, 6.07, 6.09 or 7.06 includes as a separate portion of the sentence a term of parole or of recommitment for violation of the conditions of parole which governs the duration of parole or recommitment after the offender's first conditional release on parole. The minimum of such term is one year and the maximum is five years, unless the sentence was imposed under Section 6.05(2) or Section 6.09, in which case the maximum is two years.

(3) *Length of Recommitment and Reparole After Revocation of Parole.* If an offender is recommitted upon revocation of his parole, the term of further imprisonment upon such recommitment and of any subsequent reparole or recommitment under the same sentence shall be fixed by the Board of Parole but shall not exceed in aggregate length the unserved balance of the maximum parole term provided by Subsection (2) of this Section.

(4) *Final Unconditional Release.* When the maximum of his parole term has expired or he has been sooner discharged from parole under Section 305.12, an offender shall be deemed to have served his sentence and shall be released unconditionally.

SECTION 6.11.   PLACE OF IMPRISONMENT [omitted]

SECTION 6.12.   REDUCTION OF CONVICTION BY COURT TO LESSER DEGREE OF FELONY
              OR TO MISDEMEANOR

If, when a person has been convicted of a felony, the Court, having regard to the nature and circumstances of the crime and to the history and character of the defendant, is of the view that it would be unduly harsh to sentence the offender in accordance with the Code, the Court may enter judgment of conviction for a lesser degree of felony or for a misdemeanor and impose sentence accordingly.

SECTION 6.13.   CIVIL COMMITMENT IN LIEU OF PROSECUTION OR OF SENTENCE

(1) When a person prosecuted for a [felony of the third degree,] misdemeanor or petty misdemeanor is a chronic alcoholic, narcotic addict [or prostitute] or person suffering from mental abnormality and the Court is authorized by law to order the civil commitment of such person to a hospital or other institution for medical, psychiatric or other rehabilitative treatment, the Court may order such commitment and dismiss the prosecution. The order of commitment may be made after conviction, in which event the Court may set aside the verdict or judgment of conviction and dismiss the prosecution.

(2) The Court shall not make an order under Subsection (1) of this Section unless it is of the view that it will substantially further the rehabilitation of the defendant and will not jeopardize the protection of the public.

Article 7.   Authority of Court in Sentencing

SECTION 7.01.   CRITERIA FOR WITHHOLDING SENTENCE OF IMPRISONMENT AND FOR PLACING
              DEFENDANT ON PROBATION

(1) The Court shall deal with a person who has been convicted of a crime without imposing sentence of imprisonment unless, having regard to the nature and circumstances of the crime and the history, character and condition of the defendant, it is of the opinion that his imprisonment is necessary for protection of the public because:

    (a) there is undue risk that during the period of a suspended sentence or probation the defendant will commit another crime; or

(b) the defendant is in need of correctional treatment that can be provided most effectively by his commitment to an institution; or

(c) a lesser sentence will depreciate the seriousness of the defendant's crime.

(2) The following grounds, while not controlling the discretion of the Court, shall be accorded weight in favor of withholding sentence of imprisonment:

(a) the defendant's criminal conduct neither caused nor threatened serious harm;

(b) the defendant did not contemplate that his criminal conduct would cause or threaten serious harm;

(c) the defendant acted under a strong provocation;

(d) there were substantial grounds tending to excuse or justify the defendant's criminal conduct, though failing to establish a defense;

(e) the victim of the defendant's criminal conduct induced or facilitated its commission;

(f) the defendant has compensated or will compensate the victim of his criminal conduct for the damage or injury that he sustained;

(g) the defendant has no history of prior delinquency or criminal activity or has led a law-abiding life for a substantial period of time before the commission of the present crime;

(h) the defendant's criminal conduct was the result of circumstances unlikely to recur;

(i) the character and attitudes of the defendant indicate that he is unlikely to commit another crime;

(j) the defendant is particularly likely to respond affirmatively to probationary treatment;

(k) the imprisonment of the defendant would entail excessive hardship to himself or his dependents.

(3) When a person who has been convicted of a crime is not sentenced to imprisonment, the Court shall place him on probation if he is in need of the supervision, guidance, assistance or direction that the probation service can provide.

Section 7.02.   Criteria for Imposing Fines

(1) The Court shall not sentence a defendant only to pay a fine, when any other disposition is authorized by law, unless having regard to the nature and circumstances of the crime and to the history and character of the defendant, it is of the opinion that the fine alone suffices for protection of the public.

(2) The Court shall not sentence a defendant to pay a fine in addition to a sentence of imprisonment or probation unless:

(a) the defendant has derived a pecuniary gain from the crime; or

(b) the Court is of opinion that a fine is specially adapted to deterrence of the crime involved or to the correction of the offender.

(3) The Court shall not sentence a defendant to pay a fine unless:

(a) the defendant is or will be able to pay the fine; and

(b) the fine will not prevent the defendant from making restitution or reparation to the victim of the crime.

(4) In determining the amount and method of payment of a fine, the Court shall take into account the financial resources of the defendant and the nature of the burden that its payment will impose.

Section 7.03.   Criteria for Sentence of Extended Term of Imprisonment; Felonies

The Court may sentence a person who has been convicted of a felony to an extended term of imprisonment if it finds one or more of the grounds specified in this Section. The finding of the Court shall be incorporated in the record.

(1) The defendant is a persistent offender whose commitment for an extended term is necessary for protection of the public.

The Court shall not make such a finding unless the defendant is over twenty-one years of age and has previously been convicted of two felonies or of one felony and two misdemeanors, committed at different times when he was over [insert Juvenile Court age] years of age.

(2) The defendant is a professional criminal whose commitment for an extended term is necessary for protection of the public.

The Court shall not make such a finding unless the defendant is over twenty-one years of age and:

(a) the circumstances of the crime show that the defendant has knowingly devoted himself to criminal activity as a major source of livelihood; or

(b) the defendant has substantial income or resources not explained to be derived from a source other than criminal activity.

(3) The defendant is a dangerous, mentally abnormal person whose commitment for an extended term is necessary for protection of the public.

The Court shall not make such a finding unless the defendant has been subjected to a psychiatric examination resulting in the conclusions that his mental condition is gravely abnormal; that his criminal conduct has been characterized by a pattern of repetitive or compulsive behavior or by persistent aggressive behavior with heedless indifference to consequences; and that such condition makes him a serious danger to others.

(4) The defendant is a multiple offender whose criminality was so extensive that a sentence of imprisonment for an extended term is warranted.

The court shall not make such a finding unless:

(a) the defendant is being sentenced for two or more felonies, or is already under sentence of imprisonment for felony, and the sentences of imprisonment involved will run concurrently under Section 7.06; or

(b) the defendant admits in open court the commission of one or more other felonies and asks that they be taken into account when he is sentenced; and

(c) the longest sentences of imprisonment authorized for each of the defendant's crimes, including admitted crimes taken into account, if made to run consecutively would exceed in length the minimum and maximum of the extended term imposed.

SECTION 7.04. CRITERIA FOR SENTENCE OF EXTENDED TERM OF IMPRISONMENT; MISDEMEANORS AND PETTY MISDEMEANORS

The Court may sentence a person who has been convicted of a misdemeanor or petty misdemeanor to an extended term of imprisonment if it finds one or more of the grounds specified in this Section. The finding of the Court shall be incorporated in the record.

(1) The defendant is a persistent offender whose commitment for an extended term is necessary for protection of the public.

The Court shall not make such a finding unless the defendant has previously been convicted of two crimes, committed at different times when he was over [insert Juvenile Court age] years of age.

(2) The defendant is a professional criminal whose commitment for an extended term is necessary for protection of the public.

The Court shall not make such a finding unless:

(a) the circumstances of the crime show that the defendant has knowingly devoted himself to criminal activity as a major source of livelihood; or

(b) the defendant has substantial income or resources not explained to be derived from a source other than criminal activity.

(3) The defendant is a chronic alcoholic, narcotic addict, prostitute or person of abnormal mental condition who requires rehabilitative treatment for a substantial period of time.

The Court shall not make such a finding unless, with respect to the particular category to which the defendant belongs, the Director of Correction has certified that there is a specialized institution or facility which is satisfactory for the rehabilitative treatment of such persons and which otherwise meets the requirements of Section 6.09, Subsection (2).

(4) The defendant is a multiple offender whose criminality was so extensive that a sentence of imprisonment for an extended term is warranted.

The Court shall not make such a finding unless:

(a) the defendant is being sentenced for a number of misdemeanors or petty misdemeanors or is already under sentence of imprisonment for crimes of such grades, or admits in open court the commission of one or more such crimes and asks that they be taken into account when he is sentenced; and

(b) maximum fixed sentences of imprisonment for each of the defendant's crimes, including admitted crimes taken into account, if made to run consecutively, would exceed in length the maximum period of the extended term imposed.

SECTION 7.05.   FORMER CONVICTION IN ANOTHER JURISDICTION; DEFINITION AND PROOF OF CONVICTION; SENTENCE TAKING INTO ACCOUNT ADMITTED CRIMES BARS SUBSEQUENT CONVICTION FOR SUCH CRIMES [omitted]

SECTION 7.06.   MULTIPLE SENTENCES; CONCURRENT AND CONSECUTIVE TERMS [omitted]

SECTION 7.07.   PROCEDURE ON SENTENCE; PRE-SENTENCE INVESTIGATION AND REPORT; REMAND FOR PSYCHIATRIC EXAMINATION; TRANSMISSION OF RECORDS TO DEPARTMENT OF CORRECTION

(1) The Court shall not impose sentence without first ordering a pre-sentence investigation of the defendant and according due consideration to a written report of such investigation where:

(a) the defendant has been convicted of a felony; or

(b) the defendant is less than twenty-two years of age and has been convicted of a crime; or

(c) the defendant will be [placed on probation or] sentenced to imprisonment for an extended term.

(2) The Court may order a pre-sentence investigation in any other case.

(3) The pre-sentence investigation shall include an analysis of the circumstances attending the commission of the crime, the defendant's history of delinquency or criminality, physical and mental condition, family situation and background, economic status, education, occupation and personal habits and any other matters that the probation officer deems relevant or the Court directs to be included.

(4) Before imposing sentence, the Court may order the defendant to submit to psychiatric observation and examination for a period of not exceeding sixty days or such longer period as the Court determines to be necessary for the purpose. The defendant may be remanded for this purpose to any available clinic or mental hospital or the Court may appoint a qualified psychiatrist to make the examination. The report of the examination shall be submitted to the Court.

(5) Before imposing sentence, the Court shall advise the defendant or his counsel of the factual contents and the conclusions of any pre-sentence investigation or psychiatric examination and afford fair opportunity, if the defendant so requests, to controvert them. The sources of confidential information need not, however, be disclosed.

(6) The Court shall not impose a sentence of imprisonment for an extended term unless the ground therefor has been established at a hearing after the conviction of the defendant and on written notice to him of the ground proposed. Subject to the limitation of Subsection (5) of this Section, the defendant shall have the right to hear and controvert the evidence against him and to offer evidence upon the issue.

(7) If the defendant is sentenced to imprisonment, a copy of the report of any pre-sentence investigation or psychiatric examination shall be transmitted forthwith to the Department of Correction [or other state department or agency] or, when the defendant is committed to the custody of a specific institution, to such institution.

SECTION 7.08.   COMMITMENT FOR OBSERVATION; SENTENCE OF IMPRISONMENT FOR FELONY
DEEMED TENTATIVE FOR PERIOD OF ONE YEAR; RE-SENTENCE ON PETITION
OF COMMISSIONER OF CORRECTION

(1) If, after pre-sentence investigation, the Court desires additional information concerning an offender convicted of a felony or misdemeanor before imposing sentence, it may order that he be committed, for a period not exceeding ninety days, to the custody of the Department of Correction, or, in the case of a young adult offender, to the custody of the Division of Young Adult Correction, for observation and study at an appropriate reception or classification center. The Department and the Board of Parole, or the Young Adult Divisions thereof, shall advise the Court of their findings and recommendations on or before the expiration of such ninety-day period. If the offender is thereafter sentenced to imprisonment, the period of such commitment for observation shall be deducted from the maximum term and from the minimum, if any, of such sentence.

(2) When a person has been sentenced to imprisonment upon conviction of a felony, whether for an ordinary or extended term, the sentence shall be deemed tentative, to the extent provided in this Section, for the period of one year following the date when the offender is received in custody by the Department of Correction [or other state department or agency].

(3) If, as a result of the examination and classification by the Department of Correction [or other state department or agency] of a person under sentence of imprisonment upon conviction of a felony, the Commissioner of Correction [or other department head] is satisfied that the sentence of the Court may have been based upon a misapprehension as to the history, character or physical or mental condition of the offender, the Commissioner, during the period when the offender's sentence is deemed tentative under Subsection (2) of this Section shall file in the sentencing Court a petition to re-sentence the offender. The petition shall set forth the information as to the offender that is deemed to warrant his re-sentence and may include a recommendation as to the sentence to be imposed.

(4) The Court may dismiss a petition filed under Subsection (3) of this Section without a hearing if it deems the information set forth insufficient to warrant reconsideration of the sentence. If the Court is of the view that the petition warrants such reconsideration, a copy of the petition shall be served on the offender, who shall have the right to be heard on the issue and to be represented by counsel.

(5) When the Court grants a petition filed under Subsection (3) of this Section, it shall re-sentence the offender and may impose any sentence that might have been imposed originally for the felony of which the defendant was convicted. The period of his imprisonment prior to re-sentence and any reduction for good behavior to which he is entitled shall be applied in satisfaction of the final sentence.

(6) For all purposes other than this Section, a sentence of imprisonment has the same finality when it is imposed that it would have if this Section were not in force.

(7) Nothing in this Section shall alter the remedies provided by law for vacating or correcting an illegal sentence.

SECTION 7.09.   CREDIT FOR TIME OF DETENTION PRIOR TO SENTENCE; CREDIT FOR IMPRISONMENT
UNDER EARLIER SENTENCE FOR THE SAME CRIME [omitted]

PART II. DEFINITION OF SPECIFIC CRIMES

Offenses Involving Danger to the Person

Article 210.   Criminal Homicide

SECTION 210.0.   DEFINITIONS

In Articles 210-213, unless a different meaning plainly is required:

(1) "human being" means a person who has been born and is alive;

(2) "bodily injury" means physical pain, illness or any impairment of physical condition;

(3) "serious bodily injury" means bodily injury which creates a substantial risk of death or which causes serious, permanent disfigurement, or protracted loss or impairment of the function of any bodily member or organ;

(4) "deadly weapon" means any firearm, or other weapon, device, instrument, material or substance, whether animate or inanimate, which in the manner it is used or is intended to be used is known to be capable of producing death or serious bodily injury.

SECTION 210.1.   CRIMINAL HOMICIDE

(1) A person is guilty of criminal homicide if he purposely, knowingly, recklessly or negligently causes the death of another human being.

(2) Criminal homicide is murder, manslaughter or negligent homicide.

SECTION 210.2.   MURDER

(1) Except as provided in Section 210.3(1)(b), criminal homicide constitutes murder when:

(a) it is committed purposely or knowingly; or

(b) it is committed recklessly under circumstances manifesting extreme indifference to the value of human life. Such recklessness and indifference are presumed if the actor is engaged or is an accomplice in the commission of, or an attempt to commit, or flight after committing or attempting to commit robbery, rape or deviate sexual intercourse by force or threat of force, arson, burglary, kidnapping or felonious escape.

(2) Murder is a felony of the first degree [but a person convicted of murder may be sentenced to death, as provided in Section 210.6].

SECTION 210.3.   MANSLAUGHTER

(1) Criminal homicide constitutes manslaughter when:

(a) it is committed recklessly; or

(b) a homicide which would otherwise be murder is committed under the influence of extreme mental or emotional disturbance for which there is reasonable explanation or excuse. The reasonableness of such explanation or excuse shall be determined from the viewpoint of a person in the actor's situation under the circumstances as he believes them to be.

(2) Manslaughter is a felony of the second degree.

SECTION 210.4.   NEGLIGENT HOMICIDE

(1) Criminal homicide constitutes negligent homicide when it is committed negligently.

(2) Negligent homicide is a felony of the third degree.

Section 210.5.   Causing or Aiding Suicide

(1) *Causing Suicide as Criminal Homicide.* A person may be convicted of criminal homicide for causing another to commit suicide only if he purposely causes such suicide by force, duress or deception.

(2) *Aiding or Soliciting Suicide as an Independent Offense.* A person who purposely aids or solicits another to commit suicide is guilty of a felony of the second degree if his conduct causes such suicide or an attempted suicide, and otherwise of a misdemeanor.

Section 210.6.   Sentence of Death for Murder; Further Proceedings
           to Determine Sentence*

(1) *Death Sentence Excluded.* When a defendant is found guilty of murder, the Court shall impose sentence for a felony of the first degree if it is satisfied that:

(a) none of the aggravating circumstances enumerated in Subsection (3) of this Section was established by the evidence at the trial or will be established if further proceedings are initiated under Subsection (2) of this Section; or

(b) substantial mitigating circumstances, established by the evidence at the trial, call for leniency; or

(c) the defendant, with the consent of the prosecuting attorney and the approval of the Court, pleaded guilty to murder as a felony of the first degree; or

(d) the defendant was under 18 years of age at the time of the commission of the crime; or

(e) the defendant's physical or mental condition calls for leniency; or

(f) although the evidence suffices to sustain the verdict, it does not foreclose all doubt respecting the defendant's guilt.

(2) *Determination by Court or by Court and Jury.* Unless the Court imposes sentence under Subsection (1) of this Section, it shall conduct a separate proceeding to determine whether the defendant should be sentenced for a felony of the first degree or sentenced to death. The proceeding shall be conducted before the Court alone if the defendant was convicted by a Court sitting without a jury or upon his plea of guilty or if the prosecuting attorney and the defendant waive a jury with respect to sentence. In other cases it shall be conducted before the Court sitting with the jury which determined the defendant's guilt or, if the Court for good cause shown discharges that jury, with a new jury empanelled for the purpose.

In the proceeding, evidence may be presented as to any matter that the Court deems relevant to sentence, including but not limited to the nature and circumstances of the crime, the defendant's character, background, history, mental and physical condition and any of the aggravating or mitigating circumstances enumerated in Subsections (3) and (4) of this Section. Any such evidence not legally privileged, which the Court deems to have probative force, may be received, regardless of its admissibility under the exclusionary rules of evidence, provided that the defendant's counsel is accorded a fair opportunity to rebut any hearsay statements. The prosecuting attorney and the defendant or his counsel shall be permitted to present argument for or against sentence of death.

The determination whether sentence of death shall be imposed shall be in the discretion of the Court, except that when the proceeding is conducted before the Court sitting with a jury, the Court shall not impose sentence of death unless it submits to the jury the issue whether the defendant should be sentenced to death or to imprisonment and the jury returns a verdict that the sentence should be death. If the jury is unable to reach a unanimous verdict, the Court shall dismiss the jury and impose sentence for a felony of the first degree.

The Court, in exercising its discretion as to sentence, and the jury, in determining upon its verdict, shall take into account the aggravating and mitigating circumstances enumerated in

---

* . . . The brackets are meant to reflect the fact that the Institute took no position on the desirability of the death penalty. . . .

Subsections (3) and (4) and any other facts that it deems relevant, but it shall not impose or recommend sentence of death unless it finds one of the aggravating circumstances enumerated in Subsection (3) and further finds that there are no mitigating circumstances sufficiently substantial to call for leniency. When the issue is submitted to the jury, the Court shall so instruct and also shall inform the jury of the nature of the sentence of imprisonment that may be imposed, including its implication with respect to possible release upon parole, if the jury verdict is against sentence of death.

Alternative formulation of Subsection (2):

(2) *Determination by Court.* Unless the Court imposes sentence under Subsection (1) of this Section, it shall conduct a separate proceeding to determine whether the defendant should be sentenced for a felony of the first degree or sentenced to death. In the proceeding, the Court, in accordance with Section 7.07, shall consider the report of the pre-sentence investigation and, if a psychiatric examination has been ordered, the report of such examination. In addition, evidence may be presented as to any matter that the Court deems relevant to sentence, including but not limited to the nature and circumstances of the crime, the defendant's character, background, history, mental and physical condition and any of the aggravating or mitigating circumstances enumerated in Subsections (3) and (4) of this Section. Any such evidence not legally privileged, which the Court deems to have probative force, may be received, regardless of its admissibility under the exclusionary rules of evidence, provided that the defendant's counsel is accorded a fair opportunity to rebut any hearsay statements. The prosecuting attorney and the defendant or his counsel shall be permitted to present argument for or against sentence of death.

The determination whether sentence of death shall be imposed shall be in the discretion of the Court. In exercising such discretion, the Court shall take into account the aggravating and mitigating circumstances enumerated in Subsections (3) and (4) and any other facts that it deems relevant but shall not impose sentence of death unless it finds one of the aggravating circumstances enumerated in Subsection (3) and further finds that there are no mitigating circumstances sufficiently substantial to call for leniency.

(3) *Aggravating Circumstances.*

(a) The murder was committed by a convict under sentence of imprisonment.

(b) The defendant was previously convicted of another murder or of a felony involving the use or threat of violence to the person.

(c) At the time the murder was committed the defendant also committed another murder.

(d) The defendant knowingly created a great risk of death to many persons.

(e) The murder was committed while the defendant was engaged or was an accomplice in the commission of, or an attempt to commit, or flight after committing or attempting to commit robbery, rape or deviate sexual intercourse by force or threat of force, arson, burglary or kidnapping.

(f) The murder was committed for the purpose of avoiding or preventing a lawful arrest or effecting an escape from lawful custody.

(g) The murder was committed for pecuniary gain.

(h) The murder was especially heinous, atrocious or cruel, manifesting exceptional depravity.

(4) *Mitigating Circumstances.*

(a) The defendant has no significant history of prior criminal activity.

(b) The murder was committed while the defendant was under the influence of extreme mental or emotional disturbance.

(c) The victim was a participant in the defendant's homicidal conduct or consented to the homicidal act.

(d) The murder was committed under circumstances which the defendant believed to provide a moral justification or extenuation for his conduct.

(e) The defendant was an accomplice in a murder committed by another person and his participation in the homicidal act was relatively minor.

(f) The defendant acted under duress or under the domination of another person.

(g) At the time of the murder, the capacity of the defendant to appreciate the criminality [wrongfulness] of his conduct or to conform his conduct to the requirements of law was impaired as a result of mental disease or defect or intoxication.

(h) The youth of the defendant at the time of the crime.]

Article 211.   Assault; Reckless Endangering; Threats

SECTION 211.0.   DEFINITIONS

In this Article, the definitions given in Section 210.0 apply unless a different meaning plainly is required.

SECTION 211.1.   ASSAULT

(1) *Simple Assault.* A person is guilty of assault if he:

(a) attempts to cause or purposely, knowingly or recklessly causes bodily injury to another; or

(b) negligently causes bodily injury to another with a deadly weapon; or

(c) attempts by physical menace to put another in fear of imminent serious bodily injury.

Simple assault is a misdemeanor unless committed in a fight or scuffle entered into by mutual consent, in which case it is a petty misdemeanor.

(2) *Aggravated Assault.* A person is guilty of aggravated assault if he:

(a) attempts to cause serious bodily injury to another, or causes such injury purposely, knowingly or recklessly under circumstances manifesting extreme indifference to the value of human life; or

(b) attempts to cause or purposely or knowingly causes bodily injury to another with a deadly weapon.

Aggravated assault under paragraph (a) is a felony of the second degree; aggravated assault under paragraph (b) is a felony of the third degree.

SECTION 211.2.   RECKLESSLY ENDANGERING ANOTHER PERSON

A person commits a misdemeanor if he recklessly engages in conduct which places or may place another person in danger of death or serious bodily injury. Recklessness and danger shall be presumed where a person knowingly points a firearm at or in the direction of another, whether or not the actor believed the firearm to be loaded.

SECTION 211.3.   TERRORISTIC THREATS

A person is guilty of a felony of the third degree if he threatens to commit any crime of violence with purpose to terrorize another or to cause evacuation of a building, place of assembly, or facility of public transportation, or otherwise to cause serious public inconvenience, or in reckless disregard of the risk of causing such terror or inconvenience.

Article 212.   Kidnapping and Related Offenses; Coercion

SECTION 212.0.   DEFINITIONS

In this Article, the definitions given in Section 210.0 apply unless a different meaning plainly is required.

SECTION 212.1.   KIDNAPPING

A person is guilty of kidnapping if he unlawfully removes another from his place of residence or business, or a substantial distance from the vicinity where he is found, or if he unlawfully confines another for a substantial period in a place of isolation, with any of the following purposes:

    (a) to hold for ransom or reward, or as a shield or hostage; or

    (b) to facilitate commission of any felony or flight thereafter; or

    (c) to inflict bodily injury on or to terrorize the victim or another; or

    (d) to interfere with the performance of any governmental or political function.

Kidnapping is a felony of the first degree unless the actor voluntarily releases the victim alive and in a safe place prior to trial, in which case it is a felony of the second degree. A removal or confinement is unlawful within the meaning of this Section if it is accomplished by force, threat or deception, or, in the case of a person who is under the age of 14 or incompetent, if it is accomplished without the consent of a parent, guardian or other person responsible for general supervision of his welfare.

SECTION 212.2.   FELONIOUS RESTRAINT

A person commits a felony of the third degree if he knowingly:

    (a) restrains another unlawfully in circumstances exposing him to risk of serious bodily injury; or

    (b) holds another in a condition of involuntary servitude.

SECTION 212.3.   FALSE IMPRISONMENT

A person commits a misdemeanor if he knowingly restrains another unlawfully so as to interfere substantially with his liberty.

SECTION 212.4.   INTERFERENCE WITH CUSTODY

(1) *Custody of Children.* A person commits an offense if he knowingly or recklessly takes or entices any child under the age of 18 from the custody of its parent, guardian or other lawful custodian, when he has no privilege to do so. It is an affirmative defense that:

    (a) the actor believed that his action was necessary to preserve the child from danger to its welfare; or

    (b) the child, being at the time not less than 14 years old, was taken away at its own instigation without enticement and without purpose to commit a criminal offense with or against the child.

Proof that the child was below the critical age gives rise to a presumption that the actor knew the child's age or acted in reckless disregard thereof. The offense is a misdemeanor unless the actor, not being a parent or person in equivalent relation to the child, acted with knowledge that his conduct would cause serious alarm for the child's safety, or in reckless disregard of a likelihood of causing such alarm, in which case the offense is a felony of the third degree.

(2) *Custody of Committed Persons.* A person is guilty of a misdemeanor if he knowingly or recklessly takes or entices any committed person away from lawful custody when he is not privileged to do so. "Committed person" means, in addition to anyone committed under judicial warrant, any orphan, neglected or delinquent child, mentally defective or insane person, or other dependent or incompetent person entrusted to another's custody by or through a recognized social agency or otherwise by authority of law.

SECTION 212.5.   CRIMINAL COERCION

(1) *Offense Defined.* A person is guilty of criminal coercion if, with purpose unlawfully to restrict another's freedom of action to his detriment, he threatens to:

(a) commit any criminal offense; or

(b) accuse anyone of a criminal offense; or

(c) expose any secret tending to subject any person to hatred, contempt or ridicule, or to impair his credit or business repute; or

(d) take or withhold action as an official, or cause an official to take or withhold action.

It is an affirmative defense to prosecution based on paragraphs (b), (c) or (d) that the actor believed the accusation or secret to be true or the proposed official action justified and that his purpose was limited to compelling the other to behave in a way reasonably related to the circumstances which were the subject of the accusation, exposure or proposed official action, as by desisting from further misbehavior, making good a wrong done, refraining from taking any action or responsibility for which the actor believes the other disqualified.

(2) *Grading.* Criminal coercion is a misdemeanor unless the threat is to commit a felony or the actor's purpose is felonious, in which cases the offense is a felony of the third degree.

Article 213.   Sexual Offenses

SECTION 213.0.   DEFINITIONS

In this Article, unless a different meaning plainly is required:

(1) the definitions given in Section 210.0 apply;

(2) "Sexual intercourse" includes intercourse per os or per anum, with some penetration however slight; emission is not required;

(3) "Deviate sexual intercourse" means sexual intercourse per os or per anum between human beings who are not husband and wife, and any form of sexual intercourse with an animal.

SECTION 213.1.   RAPE AND RELATED OFFENSES

(1) *Rape.* A male who has sexual intercourse with a female not his wife is guilty of rape if:

(a) he compels her to submit by force or by threat of imminent death, serious bodily injury, extreme pain or kidnapping, to be inflicted on anyone; or

(b) he has substantially impaired her power to appraise or control her conduct by administering or employing without her knowledge drugs, intoxicants or other means for the purpose of preventing resistance; or

(c) the female is unconscious; or

(d) the female is less than 10 years old.

Rape is a felony of the second degree unless (i) in the course thereof the actor inflicts serious bodily injury upon anyone, or (ii) the victim was not a voluntary social companion of the actor upon the occasion of the crime and had not previously permitted him sexual liberties, in which cases the offense is a felony of the first degree. Sexual intercourse includes intercourse per os or per anum, with some penetration however slight; emission is not required.

(2) *Gross Sexual Imposition.* A male who has sexual intercourse with a female not his wife commits a felony of the third degree if:

(a) he compels her to submit by any threat that would prevent resistance by a woman of ordinary resolution; or

(b) he knows that she suffers from a mental disease or defect which renders her incapable of appraising the nature of her conduct; or

(c) he knows that she is unaware that a sexual act is being committed upon her or that she submits because she mistakenly supposes that he is her husband.

SECTION 213.2. DEVIATE SEXUAL INTERCOURSE BY FORCE OR IMPOSITION

(1) *By Force or Its Equivalent.* A person who engages in deviate sexual intercourse with another person, or who causes another to engage in deviate sexual intercourse, commits a felony of the second degree if:

(a) he compels the other person to participate by force or by threat of imminent death, serious bodily injury, extreme pain or kidnapping, to be inflicted on anyone; or

(b) he has substantially impaired the other person's power to appraise or control his conduct, by administering or employing without the knowledge of the other person drugs, intoxicants or other means for the purpose of preventing resistance; or

(c) the other person is unconscious; or

(d) the other person is less than 10 years old.

Deviate sexual intercourse means sexual intercourse per os or per anum between human beings who are not husband and wife, and any form of sexual intercourse with an animal.

(2) *By Other Imposition.* A person who engages in deviate sexual intercourse with another person, or who causes another to engage in deviate sexual intercourse, commits a felony of the third degree if:

(a) he compels the other person to participate by any threat that would prevent resistance by a person of ordinary resolution; or

(b) he knows that the other person suffers from a mental disease or defect which renders him incapable of appraising the nature of his conduct; or

(c) he knows that the other person submits because he is unaware that a sexual act is being committed upon him.

SECTION 213.3. CORRUPTION OF MINORS AND SEDUCTION

(1) *Offense Defined.* A male who has sexual intercourse with a female not his wife, or any person who engages in deviate sexual intercourse or causes another to engage in deviate sexual intercourse, is guilty of an offense if:

(a) the other person is less than [16] years old and the actor is at least [4] years older than the other person; or

(b) the other person is less than 21 years old and the actor is his guardian or otherwise responsible for general supervision of his welfare; or

(c) the other person is in custody of law or detained in a hospital or other institution and the actor has supervisory or disciplinary authority over him; or

(d) the other person is a female who is induced to participate by a promise of marriage which the actor does not mean to perform.

(2) *Grading.* An offense under paragraph (a) of Subsection (1) is a felony of the third degree. Otherwise an offense under this section is a misdemeanor.

SECTION 213.4. SEXUAL ASSAULT

A person who has sexual contact with another not his spouse, or causes such other to have sexual conduct with him, is guilty of sexual assault, a misdemeanor, if:

(1) he knows that the contact is offensive to the other person; or

(2) he knows that the other person suffers from a mental disease or defect which renders him or her incapable of appraising the nature of his or her conduct; or

(3) he knows that the other person is unaware that a sexual act is being committed; or

(4) the other person is less than 10 years old; or

(5) he has substantially impaired the other person's power to appraise or control his or her conduct, by administering or employing without the other's knowledge drugs, intoxicants or other means for the purpose of preventing resistance; or

(6) the other person is less than [16] years old and the actor is at least [four] years older than the other person; or

(7) the other person is less than 21 years old and the actor is his guardian or otherwise responsible for general supervision of his welfare; or

(8) the other person is in custody of law or detained in a hospital or other institution and the actor has supervisory or disciplinary authority over him.

Sexual contact is any touching of the sexual or other intimate parts of the person for the purpose of arousing or gratifying sexual desire.

Section 213.5.   Indecent Exposure

A person commits a misdemeanor if, for the purpose of arousing or gratifying sexual desire of himself or of any person other than his spouse, he exposes his genitals under circumstances in which he knows his conduct is likely to cause affront or alarm.

Section 213.6.   Provisions Generally Applicable to Article 213

(1) *Mistake as to Age.* Whenever in this Article the criminality of conduct depends on a child's being below the age of 10, it is no defense that the actor did not know the child's age, or reasonably believed the child to be older than 10. When criminality depends on the child's being below a critical age other than 10, it is a defense for the actor to prove by a preponderance of the evidence that he reasonably believed the child to be above the critical age.

(2) *Spouse Relationships.* Whenever in this Article the definition of an offense excludes conduct with a spouse, the exclusion shall be deemed to extend to persons living as man and wife, regardless of the legal status of their relationship. The exclusion shall be inoperative as respects spouses living apart under a decree of judicial separation. Where the definition of an offense excludes conduct with a spouse or conduct by a woman, this shall not preclude conviction of a spouse or woman as accomplice in a sexual act in which he or she causes another person, not within the exclusion, to perform.

(3) *Sexually Promiscuous Complainants.* It is a defense to prosecution under Section 213.3 and paragraphs (6), (7) and (8) of Section 213.4 for the actor to prove by a preponderance of the evidence that the alleged victim had, prior to the time of the offense charged, engaged promiscuously in sexual relations with others.

(4) *Prompt Complaint.* No prosecution may be instituted or maintained under this Article unless the alleged offense was brought to the notice of public authority within [3] months of its occurrence or, where the alleged victim was less than [16] years old or otherwise incompetent to make complaint, within [3] months after a parent, guardian or other competent person specially interested in the victim learns of the offense.

(5) *Testimony of Complainants.* No person shall be convicted of any felony under this Article upon the uncorroborated testimony of the alleged victim. Corroboration may be circumstantial. In any prosecution before a jury for an offense under this Article, the jury shall be instructed to evaluate the testimony of a victim or complaining witness with special care in view of the emotional involvement of the witness and the difficulty of determining the truth with respect to alleged sexual activities carried out in private.

Offenses Against Property

Article 220.   Arson, Criminal Mischief, and Other Property Destruction

SECTION 220.1.   ARSON AND RELATED OFFENSES

(1) *Arson.* A person is guilty of arson, a felony of the second degree, if he starts a fire or causes an explosion with the purpose of:
  (a) destroying a building or occupied structure of another; or
  (b) destroying or damaging any property, whether his own or another's, to collect insurance for such loss. It shall be an affirmative defense to prosecution under this paragraph that the actor's conduct did not recklessly endanger any building or occupied structure of another or place any other person in danger of death or bodily injury.

(2) *Reckless Burning or Exploding.* A person commits a felony of the third degree if he purposely starts a fire or causes an explosion, whether on his own property or another's, and thereby recklessly:
  (a) places another person in danger of death or bodily injury; or
  (b) places a building or occupied structure of another in danger of damage or destruction.

(3) *Failure to Control or Report Dangerous Fire.* A person who knows that a fire is endangering life or a substantial amount of property of another and fails to take reasonable measures to put out or control the fire, when he can do so without substantial risk to himself, or to give a prompt fire alarm, commits a misdemeanor if:
  (a) he knows that he is under an official, contractual, or other legal duty to prevent or combat the fire; or
  (b) the fire was started, albeit lawfully, by him or with his assent, or on property in his custody or control.

(4) *Definitions.* "Occupied structure" means any structure, vehicle or place adapted for overnight accommodation of persons, or for carrying on business therein, whether or not a person is actually present. Property is that of another, for the purposes of this section, if anyone other than the actor has a possessory or proprietory interest therein. If a building or structure is divided into separately occupied units, any unit not occupied by the actor is an occupied structure of another.

SECTION 220.2.   CAUSING OR RISKING CATASTROPHE

(1) *Causing Catastrophe.* A person who causes a catastrophe by explosion, fire, flood, avalanche, collapse of building, release of poison gas, radioactive material or other harmful or destructive force or substance, or by any other means of causing potentially widespread injury or damage, commits a felony of the second degree if he does so purposely or knowingly, or a felony of the third degree if he does so recklessly.

(2) *Risking Catastrophe.* A person is guilty of a misdemeanor if he recklessly creates a risk of catastrophe in the employment of fire, explosives or other dangerous means listed in Subsection (1).

(3) *Failure to Prevent Catastrophe.* A person who knowingly or recklessly fails to take reasonable measures to prevent or mitigate a catastrophe commits a misdemeanor if:
  (a) he knows that he is under an official, contractual or other legal duty to take such measures; or
  (b) he did or assented to the act causing or threatening the catastrophe.

SECTION 220.3.   CRIMINAL MISCHIEF

(1) *Offense Defined.* A person is guilty of criminal mischief if he:

(a) damages tangible property of another purposely, recklessly, or by negligence in the employment of fire, explosives, or other dangerous means listed in Section 220.2(1); or

(b) purposely or recklessly tampers with tangible property of another so as to endanger person or property; or

(c) purposely or recklessly causes another to suffer pecuniary loss by deception or threat.

(2) *Grading.* Criminal mischief is a felony of the third degree if the actor purposely causes pecuniary loss in excess of $5,000, or a substantial interruption or impairment of public communication, transportation, supply of water, gas or power, or other public service. It is a misdemeanor if the actor purposely causes pecuniary loss in excess of $100, or a petty misdemeanor if he purposely or recklessly causes pecuniary loss in excess of $25. Otherwise criminal mischief is a violation.

Article 221.   Burglary and Other Criminal Intrusion

SECTION 221.0.   DEFINITIONS

In this Article, unless a different meaning plainly is required:

(1) "occupied structure" means any structure, vehicle or place adapted for overnight accommodation of persons, or for carrying on business therein, whether or not a person is actually present.

(2) "night" means the period between thirty minutes past sunset and thirty minutes before sunrise.

SECTION 221.1.   BURGLARY

(1) *Burglary Defined.* A person is guilty of burglary if he enters a building or occupied structure, or separately secured or occupied portion thereof, with purpose to commit a crime therein, unless the premises are at the time open to the public or the actor is licensed or privileged to enter. It is an affirmative defense to prosecution for burglary that the building or structure was abandoned.

(2) *Grading.* Burglary is a felony of the second degree if it is perpetrated in the dwelling of another at night, or if, in the course of committing the offense, the actor:

(a) purposely, knowingly or recklessly inflicts or attempts to inflict bodily injury on anyone; or

(b) is armed with explosives or a deadly weapon.

Otherwise burglary is a felony of the third degree. An act shall be deemed "in the course of committing" an offense if it occurs in an attempt to commit the offense or in flight after the attempt or commission.

(3) *Multiple Convictions.* A person may not be convicted both for burglary and for the offense which it was his purpose to commit after the burglarious entry or for an attempt to commit that offense, unless the additional offense constitutes a felony of the first or second degree.

SECTION 221.2.   CRIMINAL TRESPASS

(1) *Buildings and Occupied Structures.* A person commits an offense if, knowing that he is not licensed or privileged to do so, he enters or surreptitiously remains in any building or occupied structure, or separately secured or occupied portion thereof. An offense under this Subsection is a misdemeanor if it is committed in a dwelling at night. Otherwise it is a petty misdemeanor.

(2) *Defiant Trespasser.* A person commits an offense if, knowing that he is not licensed or privileged to do so, he enters or remains in any place as to which notice against trespass is given by:

(a) actual communication to the actor; or

(b) posting in a manner prescribed by law or reasonably likely to come to the attention of intruders; or

(c) fencing or other enclosure manifestly designed to exclude intruders.

An offense under this Subsection constitutes a petty misdemeanor if the offender defies an order to leave personally communicated to him by the owner of the premises or other authorized person. Otherwise it is a violation.

(3) *Defenses.* It is an affirmative defense to prosecution under this Section that:

(a) a building or occupied structure involved in an offense under Subsection (1) was abandoned; or

(b) the premises were at the time open to members of the public and the actor complied with all lawful conditions imposed on access to or remaining in the premises; or

(c) the actor reasonably believed that the owner of the premises, or other person empowered to license access thereto, would have licensed him to enter or remain.

Article 222. Robbery

SECTION 222.1. ROBBERY

(1) *Robbery Defined.* A person is guilty of robbery if, in the course of committing a theft, he:

(a) inflicts serious bodily injury upon another; or

(b) threatens another with or purposely puts him in fear of immediate serious bodily injury; or

(c) commits or threatens immediately to commit any felony of the first or second degree.

An act shall be deemed "in the course of committing a theft" if it occurs in an attempt to commit theft or in flight after the attempt or commission.

(2) *Grading.* Robbery is a felony of the second degree, except that it is a felony of the first degree if in the course of committing the theft the actor attempts to kill anyone, or purposely inflicts or attempts to inflict serious bodily injury.

Article 223. Theft and Related Offenses

SECTION 223.0. DEFINITIONS

In this Article, unless a different meaning plainly is required:

(1) "deprive" means: (a) to withhold property of another permanently or for so extended a period as to appropriate a major portion of its economic value, or with intent to restore only upon payment of reward or other compensation; or (b) to dispose of the property so as to make it unlikely that the owner will recover it.

(2) "financial institution" means a bank, insurance company, credit union, building and loan association, investment trust or other organization held out to the public as a place of deposit of funds or medium of savings or collective investment.

(3) "government" means the United States, any State, county, municipality, or other political unit, or any department, agency or subdivision of any of the foregoing, or any corporation or other association carrying out the functions of government.

(4) "movable property" means property the location of which can be changed, including things growing on, affixed to, or found in land, and documents although the rights represented thereby have no physical location. "Immovable property" is all other property.

(5) "obtain" means: (a) in relation to property, to bring about a transfer or purported transfer of a legal interest in the property, whether to the obtainer or another; or (b) in relation to labor or service, to secure performance thereof.

(6) "property" means anything of value, including real estate, tangible and intangible personal property, contract rights, choses-in-action and other interests in or claims to wealth, admission or transportation tickets, captured or domestic animals, food and drink, electric or other power.

(7) "property of another" includes property in which any person other than the actor has an interest which the actor is not privileged to infringe, regardless of the fact that the actor also has an interest in the property and regardless of the fact that the other person might be precluded from civil recovery because the property was used in an unlawful transaction or was subject to forfeiture as contraband. Property in possession of the actor shall not be deemed property of another who has only a security interest therein, even if legal title is in the creditor pursuant to a conditional sales contract or other security agreement.

SECTION 223.1. CONSOLIDATION OF THEFT OFFENSES; GRADING; PROVISIONS APPLICABLE TO THEFT GENERALLY

(1) *Consolidation of Theft Offenses.* Conduct denominated theft in this Article constitutes a single offense. An accusation of theft may be supported by evidence that it was committed in any manner that would be theft under this Article, notwithstanding the specification of a different manner in the indictment or information, subject only to the power of the Court to ensure fair trial by granting a continuance or other appropriate relief where the conduct of the defense would be prejudiced by lack of fair notice or by surprise.

(2) *Grading of Theft Offenses.*

(a) Theft constitutes a felony of the third degree if the amount involved exceeds $500, or if the property stolen is a firearm, automobile, airplane, motorcycle, motorboat or other motor-propelled vehicle, or in the case of theft by receiving stolen property, if the receiver is in the business of buying or selling stolen property.

(b) Theft not within the preceding paragraph constitutes a misdemeanor, except that if the property was not taken from the person or by threat, or in breach of a fiduciary obligation, and the actor proves by a preponderance of the evidence that the amount involved was less than $50, the offense constitutes a petty misdemeanor.

(c) The amount involved in a theft shall be deemed to be the highest value, by any reasonable standard, of the property or services which the actor stole or attempted to steal. Amounts involved in thefts committed pursuant to one scheme or course of conduct, whether from the same person or several persons, may be aggregated in determining the grade of the offense.

(3) *Claim of Right.* It is an affirmative defense to prosecution for theft that the actor:

(a) was unaware that the property or service was that of another; or

(b) acted under an honest claim of right to the property or service involved or that he had a right to acquire or dispose of it as he did; or

(c) took property exposed for sale, intending to purchase and pay for it promptly, or reasonably believing that the owner, if present, would have consented.

(4) *Theft from Spouse.* It is no defense that theft was from the actor's spouse, except that misappropriation of household and personal effects, or other property normally accessible to both spouses, is theft only if it occurs after the parties have ceased living together.

SECTION 223.2. THEFT BY UNLAWFUL TAKING OR DISPOSITION

(1) *Movable Property.* A person is guilty of theft if he unlawfully takes, or exercises unlawful control over, movable property of another with purpose to deprive him thereof.

(2) *Immovable Property.* A person is guilty of theft if he unlawfully transfers immovable property of another or any interest therein with purpose to benefit himself or another not entitled thereto.

SECTION 223.3.   THEFT BY DECEPTION

A person is guilty of theft if he purposely obtains property of another by deception. A person deceives if he purposely:

(1) creates or reinforces a false impression, including false impressions as to law, value, intention or other state of mind; but deception as to a person's intention to perform a promise shall not be inferred from the fact alone that he did not subsequently perform the promise; or

(2) prevents another from acquiring information which would affect his judgment of a transaction; or

(3) fails to correct a false impression which the deceiver previously created or reinforced, or which the deceiver knows to be influencing another to whom he stands in a fiduciary or confidential relationship; or

(4) fails to disclose a known lien, adverse claim or other legal impediment to the enjoyment of property which he transfers or encumbers in consideration for the property obtained, whether such impediment is or is not valid, or is or is not a matter of official record.

The term "deceive" does not, however, include falsity as to matters having no pecuniary significance, or puffing by statements unlikely to deceive ordinary persons in the group addressed.

SECTION 223.4.   THEFT BY EXTORTION

A person is guilty of theft if he obtains property of another by threatening to:

(1) inflict bodily injury on anyone or commit any other criminal offense; or

(2) accuse anyone of a criminal offense; or

(3) expose any secret tending to subject any person to hatred, contempt or ridicule, or to impair his credit or business repute; or

(4) take or withhold action as an official, or cause an official to take or withhold action; or

(5) bring about or continue a strike, boycott or other collective unofficial action, if the property is not demanded or received for the benefit of the group in whose interest the actor purports to act; or

(6) testify or provide information or withhold testimony or information with respect to another's legal claim or defense; or

(7) inflict any other harm which would not benefit the actor.

It is an affirmative defense to prosecution based on paragraphs (2), (3) or (4) that the property obtained by threat of accusation, exposure, lawsuit or other invocation of official action was honestly claimed as restitution or indemnification for harm done in the circumstances to which such accusation, exposure, lawsuit or other official action relates, or as compensation for property or lawful services.

SECTION 223.5.   THEFT OF PROPERTY LOST, MISLAID, OR DELIVERED BY MISTAKE

A person who comes into control of property of another that he knows to have been lost, mislaid, or delivered under a mistake as to the nature or amount of the property or the identity of the recipient is guilty of theft if, with purpose to deprive the owner thereof, he fails to take reasonable measures to restore the property to a person entitled to have it.

SECTION 223.6.   RECEIVING STOLEN PROPERTY

(1) *Receiving.* A person is guilty of theft if he purposely receives, retains, or disposes of movable property of another knowing that it has been stolen, or believing that it has probably been stolen, unless the property is received, retained, or disposed with purpose to restore it to the owner. "Receiving" means acquiring possession, control or title, or lending on the security of the property.

(2) *Presumption of Knowledge.* The requisite knowledge or belief is presumed in the case of a dealer who:

(a) is found in possession or control of property stolen from two or more persons on separate occasions; or

(b) has received stolen property in another transaction within the year preceding the transaction charged; or

(c) being a dealer in property of the sort received, acquires it for a consideration which he knows is far below its reasonable value.

"Dealer" means a person in the business of buying or selling goods including a pawnbroker.

SECTION 223.7.   THEFT OF SERVICES

(1) A person is guilty of theft if he purposely obtains services which he knows are available only for compensation, by deception or threat, or by false token or other means to avoid payment for the service. "Services" includes labor, professional service, transportation, telephone or other public service, accommodation in hotels, restaurants or elsewhere, admission to exhibitions, use of vehicles or other movable property. Where compensation for service is ordinarily paid immediately upon the rendering for such service, as is the case of hotels and restaurants, refusal to pay or absconding without payment or offer to pay gives rise to a presumption that the service was obtained by deception as to intention to pay.

(2) A person commits theft if, having control over the disposition of services of others, to which he is not entitled, he knowingly diverts such services to his own benefit or to the benefit of another not entitled thereto.

SECTION 223.8.   THEFT BY FAILURE TO MAKE REQUIRED DISPOSITION OF FUNDS RECEIVED

A person who purposely obtains property upon agreement, or subject to a known legal obligation, to make specified payment or other disposition, whether from such property or its proceeds or from his own property to be reserved in equivalent amount, is guilty of theft if he deals with the property obtained as his own and fails to make the required payment or disposition. The foregoing applies notwithstanding that it may be impossible to identify particular property as belonging to the victim at the time of the actor's failure to make the required payment or disposition. An officer or employee of the government or of a financial institution is presumed: (i) to know any legal obligation relevant to his criminal liability under this Section, and (ii) to have dealt with the property as his own if he fails to pay or account upon lawful demand, or if an audit reveals a shortage or falsification of accounts.

SECTION 223.9.   UNAUTHORIZED USE OF AUTOMOBILES AND OTHER VEHICLES

A person commits a misdemeanor if he operates another's automobile, airplane, motorcycle, motorboat, or other motor-propelled vehicle without consent of the owner. It is an affirmative defense to prosecution under this Section that the actor reasonably believed that the owner would have consented to the operation had he known of it.

Article 224.   Forgery and Fraudulent Practices

SECTION 224.0.   DEFINITIONS

In this Article, the definitions given in Section 223.0 apply unless a different meaning plainly is required.

SECTION 224.1.   FORGERY

(1) *Definition.* A person is guilty of forgery if, with purpose to defraud or injure anyone, or with knowledge that he is facilitating a fraud or injury to be perpetrated by anyone, the actor:

(a) alters any writing of another without his authority; or

(b) makes, completes, executes, authenticates, issues or transfers any writing so that it purports to be the act of another who did not authorize that act, or to have been executed at a time or place or in a numbered sequence other than was in fact the case, or to be a copy of an original when no such original existed; or

(c) utters any writing which he knows to be forged in a manner specified in paragraphs (a) or (b).

"Writing" includes printing or any other method of recording information, money, coins, tokens, stamps, seals, credit cards, badges, trade-marks, and other symbols of value, right, privilege, or identification.

(2) *Grading.* Forgery is a felony of the second degree if the writing is or purports to be part of an issue of money, securities, postage or revenue stamps, or other instruments issued by the government, or part of an issue of stock, bonds or other instruments representing interests in or claims against any property or enterprise. Forgery is a felony of the third degree if the writing is or purports to be a will, deed, contract, release, commercial instrument, or other document evidencing, creating, transferring, altering, terminating, or otherwise affecting legal relations. Otherwise forgery is a misdemeanor.

SECTION 224.2.   SIMULATING OBJECTS OF ANTIQUITY, RARITY, ETC. [omitted]

SECTION 224.3.   FRAUDULENT DESTRUCTION, REMOVAL OR CONCEALMENT OF
RECORDABLE INSTRUMENTS

A person commits a felony of the third degree if, with purpose to deceive or injure anyone, he destroys, removes or conceals any will, deed, mortgage, security instrument or other writing for which the law provides public recording.

SECTION 224.4.   TAMPERING WITH RECORDS

A person commits a misdemeanor if, knowing that he has no privilege to do so, he falsifies, destroys, removes or conceals any writing or record, with purpose to deceive or injure anyone or to conceal any wrongdoing.

SECTION 224.5.   BAD CHECKS

A person who issues or passes a check or similar sight order for the payment of money, knowing that it will not be honored by the drawee, commits a misdemeanor. For the purposes of this Section as well as in any prosecution for theft committed by means of a bad check, an issuer is presumed to know that the check or order (other than a postdated check or order) would not be paid, if:

(1) the issuer had no account with the drawee at the time the check or order was issued; or

(2) payment was refused by the drawee for lack of funds, upon presentation within 30 days after issue, and the issuer failed to make good within 10 days after receiving notice of that refusal.

Section 224.6. Credit Cards

A person commits an offense if he uses a credit card for the purpose of obtaining property or services with knowledge that:

(1) the card is stolen or forged; or

(2) the card has been revoked or cancelled; or

(3) for any other reason his use of the card is unauthorized by the issuer.

It is an affirmative defense to prosecution under paragraph (3) if the actor proves by a preponderance of the evidence that he had the purpose and ability to meet all obligations to the issuer arising out of his use of the card. "Credit card" means a writing, or other evidence of an undertaking to pay for property or services delivered or rendered to or upon the order of a designated person or bearer. An offense under this Section is a felony of the third degree if the value of the property or services secured or sought to be secured by means of the credit card exceeds $500; otherwise it is a misdemeanor.

Section 224.7. Deceptive Business Practices

A person commits a misdemeanor if in the course of business he:

(1) uses or possesses for use a false weight or measure, or any other device for falsely determining or recording any quality or quantity; or

(2) sells, offers or exposes for sale, or delivers less than the represented quantity of any commodity or service; or

(3) takes or attempts to take more than the represented quantity of any commodity or service when as buyer he furnishes the weight or measure; or

(4) sells, offers or exposes for sale adulterated or mislabeled commodities. "Adulterated" means varying from the standard of composition or quality prescribed by or pursuant to any statute providing criminal penalties for such variance, or set by established commercial usage. "Mislabeled" means varying from the standard of truth or disclosure in labeling prescribed by or pursuant to any statute providing criminal penalties for such variance, or set by established commercial usage; or

(5) makes a false or misleading statement in any advertisement addressed to the public or to a substantial segment thereof for the purpose of promoting the purchase or sale of property or services; or

(6) makes a false or misleading written statement for the purpose of obtaining property or credit; or

(7) makes a false or misleading written statement for the purpose of promoting the sale of securities, or omits information required by law to be disclosed in written documents relating to securities.

It is an affirmative defense to prosecution under this Section if the defendant proves by a preponderance of the evidence that his conduct was not knowingly or recklessly deceptive.

Section 224.8. Commercial Bribery and Breach of Duty to Act Disinterestedly

(1) A person commits a misdemeanor if he solicits, accepts or agrees to accept any benefit as consideration for knowingly violating or agreeing to violate a duty of fidelity to which he is subject as:

(a) partner, agent, or employee of another;

(b) trustee, guardian, or other fiduciary;

(c) lawyer, physician, accountant, appraiser, or other professional adviser or informant;

(d) officer, director, manager or other participant in the direction of the affairs of an incorporated or unincorporated association; or

(e) arbitrator or other purportedly disinterested adjudicator or referee.

(2) A person who holds himself out to the public as being engaged in the business of making disinterested selection, appraisal, or criticism of commodities or services commits a misdemeanor if he solicits, accepts or agrees to accept any benefit to influence his selection, appraisal or criticism.

(3) A person commits a misdemeanor if he confers, or offers or agrees to confer, any benefit the acceptance of which would be criminal under this Section.

SECTION 224.9.   RIGGING PUBLICLY EXHIBITED CONTEST

(1) A person commits a misdemeanor if, with purpose to prevent a publicly exhibited contest from being conducted in accordance with the rules and usages purporting to govern it, he:

(a) confers or offers or agrees to confer any benefit upon, or threatens any injury to a participant, official or other person associated with the contest or exhibition; or

(b) tampers with any person, animal or thing.

(2) *Soliciting or Accepting Benefit for Rigging.* A person commits a misdemeanor if he knowingly solicits, accepts or agrees to accept any benefit the giving of which would be criminal under Subsection (1).

(3) *Participation in Rigged Contest.* A person commits a misdemeanor if he knowingly engages in, sponsors, produces, judges, or otherwise participates in a publicly exhibited contest knowing that the contest is not being conducted in compliance with the rules and usages purporting to govern it, by reason of conduct which would be criminal under this Section.

SECTION 224.10.   DEFRAUDING SECURED CREDITORS

A person commits a misdemeanor if he destroys, removes, conceals, encumbers, transfers or otherwise deals with property subject to a security interest with purpose to hinder enforcement of that interest.

SECTION 224.11.   FRAUD IN INSOLVENCY [omitted]

SECTION 224.12.   RECEIVING DEPOSITS IN A FAILING FINANCIAL INSTITUTION [omitted]

SECTION 224.13.   MISAPPLICATION OF ENTRUSTED PROPERTY AND PROPERTY OF GOVERNMENT
              OR FINANCIAL INSTITUTION [omitted]

SECTION 224.14.   SECURING EXECUTION OF DOCUMENTS BY DECEPTION

A person commits a misdemeanor if by deception he causes another to execute any instrument affecting, purporting to affect, or likely to affect the pecuniary interest of any person.

Offenses Against the Family

Article 230.   Offenses Against the Family

SECTION 230.1.   BIGAMY AND POLYGAMY

(1) *Bigamy.* A married person is guilty of bigamy, a misdemeanor, if he contracts or purports to contract another marriage, unless at the time of the subsequent marriage:
   (a) the actor believes that the prior spouse is dead; or
   (b) the actor and the prior spouse have been living apart for five consecutive years throughout which the prior spouse was not known by the actor to be alive; or
   (c) a Court has entered a judgment purporting to terminate or annul any prior disqualifying marriage, and the actor does not know that judgment to be invalid; or
   (d) the actor reasonably believes that he is legally eligible to remarry.
(2) *Polygamy.* A person is guilty of polygamy, a felony of the third degree, if he marries or cohabits with more than one spouse at a time in purported exercise of the right of plural marriage. The offense is a continuing one until all cohabitation and claim of marriage with more than one spouse terminates. This section does not apply to parties to a polygamous marriage, lawful in the country of which they are residents or nationals, while they are in transit through or temporarily visiting this State.
(3) *Other Party to Bigamous or Polygamous Marriage.* A person is guilty of bigamy or polygamy, as the case may be, if he contracts or purports to contract marriage with another knowing that the other is thereby committing bigamy or polygamy.

SECTION 230.2.   INCEST

A person is guilty of incest, a felony of the third degree, if he knowingly marries or cohabits or has sexual intercourse with an ancestor or descendant, a brother or sister of the whole or half blood [or an uncle, aunt, nephew or niece of the whole blood]. "Cohabit" means to live together under the representation or appearance of being married. The relationships referred to herein include blood relationships without regard to legitimacy, and relationship of parent and child by adoption.

SECTION 230.3.   ABORTION [omitted]

SECTION 230.4.   ENDANGERING WELFARE OF CHILDREN

A parent, guardian, or other person supervising the welfare of a child under 18 commits a misdemeanor if he knowingly endangers the child's welfare by violating a duty of care, protection or support.

SECTION 230.5.   PERSISTENT NON-SUPPORT

A person commits a misdemeanor if he persistently fails to provide support which he can provide and which he knows he is legally obliged to provide to a spouse, child or other dependent.

Offenses Against Public Administration

Article 240.   Bribery and Corrupt Influence [omitted]

Article 241.   Perjury and Other Falsification in Official Matters [omitted]

Article 242.   Obstructing Governmental Operations; Escapes [omitted]

Article 243.   Abuse of Office [omitted]

Offenses Against Public Order and Decency

Article 250.   Riot, Disorderly Conduct, and Related Offenses

SECTION 250.1.   RIOT; FAILURE TO DISPERSE

(1) *Riot.* A person is guilty of riot, a felony of the third degree, if he participates with [two] or more others in a course of disorderly conduct:
   (a) with purpose to commit or facilitate the commission of a felony or misdemeanor;
   (b) with purpose to prevent or coerce official action; or
   (c) when the actor or any other participant to the knowledge of the actor uses or plans to use a firearm or any other deadly weapon.
(2) *Failure of Disorderly Persons to Disperse Upon Official Order.* Where [three] or more persons are participating in a course of disorderly conduct likely to cause substantial harm or serious inconvenience, annoyance or alarm, a peace officer or other public servant engaged in executing or enforcing the law may order the participants and others in the immediate vicinity to disperse. A person who refuses or knowingly fails to obey such an order commits a misdemeanor.

SECTION 250.2.   DISORDERLY CONDUCT

(1) *Offense Defined.* A person is guilty of disorderly conduct if, with purpose to cause public inconvenience, annoyance or alarm, or recklessly creating a risk thereof, he:
   (a) engages in fighting or threatening, or in violent or tumultuous behavior; or
   (b) makes unreasonable noise or offensively coarse utterance, gesture or display, or addresses abusive language to any person present; or
   (c) creates a hazardous or physically offensive condition by any act which serves no legitimate purpose of the actor.
"Public" means affecting or likely to affect persons in a place to which the public or a substantial group has access; among the places included are highways, transport facilities, schools, prisons, apartment houses, places of business or amusement, or any neighborhood.
(2) *Grading.* An offense under this section is a petty misdemeanor if the actor's purpose is to cause substantial harm or serious inconvenience, or if he persists in disorderly conduct after reasonable warning or request to desist. Otherwise disorderly conduct is a violation.

SECTION 250.3.   FALSE PUBLIC ALARMS

A person is guilty of a misdemeanor if he initiates or circulates a report or warning of an impending bombing or other crime or catastrophe, knowing that the report or warning is false or baseless and that it is likely to cause evacuation of a building, place of assembly, or facility of public transport, or to cause public inconvenience or alarm.

SECTION 250.4.   HARASSMENT

A person commits a petty misdemeanor if, with purpose to harass another, he:
(1) makes a telephone call without purpose of legitimate communication; or

(2) insults, taunts or challenges another in a manner likely to provoke violent or disorderly response; or

(3) makes repeated communications anonymously or at extremely inconvenient hours, or in offensively coarse language; or

(4) subjects another to an offensive touching; or

(5) engages in any other course of alarming conduct serving no legitimate purpose of the actor.

SECTION 250.5.   PUBLIC DRUNKENNESS; DRUG INCAPACITATION

A person is guilty of an offense if he appears in any public place manifestly under the influence of alcohol, narcotics or other drugs, not therapeutically administered, to the degree that he may endanger himself or other persons or property, or annoy persons in his vicinity. An offense under this Section constitutes a petty misdemeanor if the actor has been convicted hereunder twice before within a period of one year. Otherwise the offense constitutes a violation.

SECTION 250.6.   LOITERING OR PROWLING

A person commits a violation if he loiters or prowls in a place, at a time, or in a manner not usual for law-abiding individuals under circumstances that warrant alarm for the safety of persons or property in the vicinity. Among the circumstances which may be considered in determining whether such alarm is warranted is the fact that the actor takes flight upon appearance of a peace officer, refuses to identify himself, or manifestly endeavors to conceal himself or any object. Unless flight by the actor or other circumstances makes it impracticable, a peace officer shall prior to any arrest for an offense under this section afford the actor an opportunity to dispel any alarm which would otherwise be warranted, by requesting him to identify himself and explain his presence and conduct. No person shall be convicted of an offense under this Section if the peace officer did not comply with the preceding sentence, or if it appears at trial that the explanation given by the actor was true and, if believed by the peace officer at the time, would have dispelled the alarm.

SECTION 250.7.   OBSTRUCTING HIGHWAYS AND OTHER PUBLIC PASSAGES

(1) A person, who, having no legal privilege to do so, purposely or recklessly obstructs any highway or other public passage, whether alone or with others, commits a violation, or, in case he persists after warning by a law officer, a petty misdemeanor. "Obstructs" means renders impassable without unreasonable inconvenience or hazard. No person shall be deemed guilty of recklessly obstructing in violation of this Subsection solely because of a gathering of persons to hear him speak or otherwise communicate, or solely because of being a member of such a gathering.

(2) A person in a gathering commits a violation if he refuses to obey a reasonable official request or order to move:

(a) to prevent obstruction of a highway or other public passage; or

(b) to maintain public safety by dispersing those gathered in dangerous proximity to a fire or other hazard.

An order to move, addressed to a person whose speech or other lawful behavior attracts an obstructing audience, shall not be deemed reasonable if the obstruction can be readily remedied by police control of the size or location of the gathering.

SECTION 250.8.   DISRUPTING MEETINGS AND PROCESSIONS

A person commits a misdemeanor if, with purpose to prevent or disrupt a lawful meeting, procession or gathering, he does any act tending to obstruct or interfere with it physically, or makes any utterance, gesture or display designed to outrage the sensibilities of the group.

SECTION 250.9.   DESECRATION OF VENERATED OBJECTS [omitted]

SECTION 250.10.   ABUSE OF CORPSE [omitted]

SECTION 250.11.   CRUELTY TO ANIMALS [omitted]

SECTION 250.12.   VIOLATION OF PRIVACY [omitted]

Article 251.   Public Indecency

SECTION 251.1.   OPEN LEWDNESS

A person commits a petty misdemeanor if he does any lewd act which he knows is likely to be observed by others who would be affronted or alarmed.

SECTION 251.2.   PROSTITUTION AND RELATED OFFENSES

(1) *Prostitution.* A person is guilty of prostitution, a petty misdemeanor, if he or she:

(a) is an inmate of a house of prostitution or otherwise engages in sexual activity as a business; or

(b) loiters in or within view of any public place for the purpose of being hired to engage in sexual activity.

"Sexual activity" includes homosexual and other deviate sexual relations. A "house of prostitution" is any place where prostitution or promotion of prostitution is regularly carried on by one person under the control, management or supervision of another. An "inmate" is a person who engages in prostitution in or through the agency of a house of prostitution. "Public place" means any place to which the public or any substantial group thereof has access.

(2) *Promoting Prostitution.* A person who knowingly promotes prostitution of another commits a misdemeanor or felony as provided in Subsection (3). The following acts shall, without limitation of the foregoing, constitute promoting prostitution:

(a) owning, controlling, managing, supervising or otherwise keeping, alone or in association with others, a house of prostitution or a prostitution business; or

(b) procuring an inmate for a house of prostitution or a place in a house of prostitution for one who would be an inmate; or

(c) encouraging, inducing, or otherwise purposely causing another to become or remain a prostitute; or

(d) soliciting a person to patronize a prostitute; or

(e) procuring a prostitute for a patron; or

(f) transporting a person into or within this state with purpose to promote that person's engaging in prostitution, or procuring or paying for transportation with that purpose; or

(g) leasing or otherwise permitting a place controlled by the actor, alone or in association with others, to be regularly used for prostitution or the promotion of prostitution, or failure to make reasonable effort to abate such use by ejecting the tenant, notifying law enforcement authorities, or other legally available means; or

(h) soliciting, receiving, or agreeing to receive any benefit for doing or agreeing to do anything forbidden by this Subsection.

(3) *Grading of Offenses Under Subsection (2).* An offense under Subsection (2) constitutes a felony of the third degree if:

(a) the offense falls within paragraph (a), (b) or (c) of Subsection (2); or

(b) the actor compels another to engage in or promote prostitution; or

(c) the actor promotes prostitution of a child under 16, whether or not he is aware of the child's age; or

(d) the actor promotes prostitution of his wife, child, ward or any person for whose care, protection or support he is responsible.

Otherwise the offense is a misdemeanor.

(4) *Presumption from Living Off Prostitutes.* A person, other than the prostitute or the prostitute's minor child or other legal dependent incapable of self-support, who is supported in whole or substantial part by the proceeds of prostitution is presumed to be knowingly promoting prostitution in violation of Subsection (2).

(5) *Patronizing Prostitutes.* A person commits a violation if he hires a prostitute to engage in sexual activity with him, or if he enters or remains in a house of prostitution for the purpose of engaging in sexual activity.

(6) *Evidence.* On the issue whether a place is a house of prostitution the following shall be admissible evidence: its general repute; the repute of the persons who reside in or frequent the place; the frequency, timing and duration of visits by non-residents. Testimony of a person against his spouse shall be admissible to prove offenses under this Section.

SECTION 251.3.   LOITERING TO SOLICIT DEVIATE SEXUAL RELATIONS

A person is guilty of a petty misdemeanor if he loiters in or near any public place for the purpose of soliciting or being solicited to engage in deviate sexual relations.

SECTION 251.4.   OBSCENITY [omitted]

PART III. TREATMENT AND CORRECTION [OMITTED]

PART IV. ORGANIZATION OF CORRECTION [OMITTED]

Italics indicate principal cases or cases otherwise prominently treated.

Alschuler, Albert W., Book Review, 12 Crim. L. Bull. 629 (1976), 1141

Alschuler, Albert W., Courtroom Misconduct by Prosecutors and Trial Judges, 50 Tex. L. Rev. 629 (1972), 31

Alschuler, Albert W., The Defense Attorney's Role in Plea Bargaining, 84 Yale L.J. 1179 (1975), 1141

Alschuler, Albert W., The Prosecutor's Role in Plea Bargaining, 36 U. Chi. L. Rev. 50 (1968), 15, 1141

Alschuler, Albert W., The Supreme Court, the Defense Attorney, and the Guilty Plea, 47 U. Colo. L. Rev. 1 (1975), 1136

Alschuler, Albert W., The Trial Judge's Role in Plea Bargaining, Part I, 76 Colum. L. Rev. 1059 (1976), 1140, 1141

Alschuler, Albert W., Two Ways to Think About the Punishment of Corporations, 46 Am. Crim. L. Rev. 1359 (2009), 783

Alschuler Albert W. & Schulhofer, Stephen J., Antiquated Procedures or Bedrock Rights?: A Response to Professors Meares and Kahan, 1998 U. Chi. Legal F. 215, 183

Am. Bar Ass'n, Internal Exile: Collateral Consequences of Conviction in Federal Laws and Regulations (2009), 1137

Amir, Menachem, Patterns in Forcible Rape (1971), 336

Amnesty International, Rape and Sexual Violence: Human Rights Law and Standards in the International Criminal Court (2011), 369

Andenaes, Johannes, The General Part of the Criminal Law of Norway 169 (1965), 901

Anderson, Michelle J., All-American Rape, 79 St. John's L. Rev. 625 (2005), 368

Anderson, Michelle J., Diminishing the Legal Impact of Negative Social Attitudes Toward Acquaintance Rape Victims, 13 New Crim. L. Rev. 644 (2010), 412

Anderson, Michelle J., From Chastity Requirement to Sexuality License: Sexual Consent and a New Rape Shield Law, 70 Geo. Wash. L. Rev. 51 (2002), 411

Anderson, Michelle J., Marital Immunity, Intimate Relationships, and Improper Inferences: A New Law on Sexual Offenses by Intimates, 54 Hastings L.J. 1465 (2003), 407

Anderson, Michelle J., Negotiating Sex, 78 S. Cal. L. Rev. 101 (2005), 352, 379

Anderson, Michelle J., Reviving Resistance in Rape Law, 1998 U. Ill. L. Rev. 953 (1999), 352, 353

Anderson, Michelle J., Sex Education and Rape, 17 Mich. J. Gender & L. 83 (2010), 404

Andrews, D.A. et al., Does Correctional Treatment Work?, 28 Criminology 369 (1990), 118

Antonowicz, Daniel H. & Ross, Robert R., Essential Components of Successful Rehabilitation Programs for Offenders, 38 Int'l J. Offender Therapy & Comp. Criminology 97 (1994), 118

Appleman, Laura I., The Lost Meaning of the Jury Trial Right, 84 Ind. L.J. 397 (2009), 54

Archibald, Bruce P., The Constitutionalization of the General Part of Criminal Law, 67 Can. Bar Rev. 403 (1998), 1021

Arenella, Peter, Convicting the Morally Blameless: Reassessing the Relationship Between Legal and Moral Accountability, 39 UCLA L. Rev. 1511 (1992), 1028

Berger, Vivian D., Not So Simple Rape, 7 Crim. J. Ethics 69 (1988), 355

Berger, Vivian D., Rape Law Reform at the Millennium, 3 Buff. Crim. L. Rev. 513 (2000), 377

Berk, Richard, New Claims About Executions and General Deterrence: Déjà Vu All Over Again?, 2 J. Empirical Legal Stud. 303 (2005), 527

Berman, Mitchell N., The Evidentiary Theory of Blackmail: Taking Motives Seriously, 65 U. Chi. L. Rev. 795 (1998), 1079

Berman, Mitchell N., Punishment and Justification, 118 Ethics 258 (2008), 109

Bibas, Stephanos, Plea Bargaining Outside the Shadow of Trial, 117 Harv. L. Rev. 2463 (2004), 15, 1147

Bibas, Stephanos, Prosecutorial Regulation versus Prosecutorial Accountability, 157 U. Pa. L. Rev. 959 (2009), 1157

Bibas, Stephanos, Transparency and Participation in Criminal Procedure, 81 N.Y.U. L. Rev. 911 (2006), 1178

Bibas, Stephanos, Schanzenbach, Max M. & Tiller, Emerson H., Policing Politics at Sentencing, 103 Nw. U. L. Rev. 1371 (2009), 1188

Bierlein, Matthew, Policing the Wireless World: Access Liability in the Open Wi-Fi Era, 67 Ohio St. L.J. 1123 (2006), 1084

Binder, Guyora, The Culpability of Felony Murder, 83 Notre Dame L. Rev. 965 (2008), 495

Binder, Guyora & Smith, Nicholas J., Framed: Utilitarianism and Punishment of the Innocent, 32 Rutgers L.J. 115 (2001), 92

Birdsong, Leonard, The Felony Murder Doctrine Revisited, 33 Ohio N.U. L. Rev. 497 (2007), 520

Blackstone, William, 4 Commentaries on the Laws of England (1765), 33, 38, 217, 240, 338

Blum, Andrew, Debunking Myths of the Insanity Plea, Natl. L.J. (Apr. 20, 1992), 982

Blumoff, Theodore Y., A Jurisprudence for Punishing Attempts Asymmetrically, 6 Buff. Crim. L. Rev. 951 (2003), 610

Blumoff, Theodore Y., On the Nature of the Action-Omission Network, 24 Ga. St. U. L. Rev. 1003 (2008), 223

Blumoff, Theodore Y., The Problems with Blaming, in Law, Mind, and Brain (M. Freeman & O. Goodenough eds., 2009), 1028

Blumstein, Alfred & Nakamura, Kiminori, Paying a Price, Long After the Crime, N.Y. Times (Jan. 9, 2012), 8

Bogira, Steve, Courtroom 302 (2005), 6

Boland, Mary L., Taking Aim at the High-Tech Stalker, Criminal Justice (ABA Criminal Justice Section) (Spring 2005), 630

Boldt, Richard, The Construction of Responsibility in the Criminal Law, 140 U. Pa. L. Rev. 2245 (1992), 1025

Bonnie, Richard, The Moral Basis of the Insanity Defense, 69 A.B.A. J. 194 (1983), 976

Boorse, Christopher, Premenstrual Syndrome and Criminal Responsibility, in Premenstrual Syndrome (B.E. Ginsburg & B.F. Carter eds., 1987), 995

Borum & Fulero, Empirical Research on the Insanity Defense and Attempted Reforms, 23 Law & Hum. Behav. 375 (1999), 982

Fisher, Bonnie S., Cullen, Francis T. & Turner, Michael G., The Sexual Victimization of College Women (Nat'l Inst. of Justice 2000), 333

Fletcher, George P., Blackmail: The Paradigmatic Crime, 141 U. Pa. L. Rev. 1617 (1993), 1078

Fletcher, George, A Crime of Self-Defense: Bernhard Goetz and the Law on Trial (1988), 824

Fletcher, George, The Individualization of Excusing Conditions, 47 S. Cal. L. Rev. 1269 (1974), 926

Fletcher, George, The Place of Victims in the Theory of Retribution, 3 Buff. Crim. L. Rev. 51 (1999), 101

Fletcher, George P., Reflections on Felony-Murder, 12 Sw. U. L. Rev. 413 (1981), 497

Fletcher, George P., Rethinking Criminal Law (1978), 268, 622, 668, 953

Fletcher, W., Encyclopedia of the Law of Private Corporations §1348 (1975), 803

Foderaro, Lisa W., Private Moment Made Public, Then a Fatal Jump, N.Y. Times (Sept. 29, 2010), 146

Fontaine, Reid Griffith, Adequate (Non)Provocation and Heat of Passion as Excuse Not Justification, 43 U. Mich. J.L. Reform 27 (2009), 452

Foot, Philippa, Utilitarianism and the Virtues, 94 Mind 196 (1985), 901

Forell, Caroline, Homicide and the Unreasonable Man, 72 Geo. Wash. L. Rev. 597 (2004), 456

Forell, Caroline, What's Reasonable?: Self-Defense and Mistake in Criminal and Tort Law, 14 Lewis & Clark L. Rev. 1401 (2010), 878

Frankel, Marvin, Criminal Sentencing: Law Without Order (1973), 1165

Frase, Richard, Excessive Prison Sentences, Punishment Goals and the Eighth Amendment: "Proportionality" Relative to What?, 89 Minn. L. Rev. 571 (2005), 202

Frase, Richard, Limiting Excessive Prison Sentences Under Federal and State Constitutions, 11 U. Pa. J. Const. L. 39 (2008), 204

Frase, Richard S., State Sentencing Guidelines: Diversity, Consensus, and Unresolved Policy Issues, 105 Colum. L. Rev. 1190 (2005), 124

Frase, Richard S. & Weigend, Thomas, German Criminal Justice as a Guide to American Law Reform, 18 B.C. Int'l & Comp. L. Rev. 317 (1995), 1124

Freedom's Lamp Dims, Economist (June 23, 2005), 55

French, Peter A., The Virtues of Vengeance (2001), 101

Fuller, Lon, The Case of the Speluncean Explorers, 62 Harv. L. Rev. 616 (1949), 900

Galvin, Harriett R., Shielding Rape Victims in the State and Federal Courts: A Proposal for the Second Decade, 70 Minn. L. Rev. 763 (1986), 411

Gardner, John, The Gist of Excuses, 2 Buff. Crim. L. Rev. 1 (1997), 931

Gardner, John & Macklen, Timothy, Compassion Without Respect? Nine Fallacies in R v. Smith, (2001) Crim. L. Rev. 623, 462

Garland, David, Peculiar Institution: America's Death Penalty in an Age of Abolition (2010), 529, 530, 534

Garrett, Brandon, Convicting the Innocent: Where Criminal Prosecutions Go Wrong (2011), 532

Garrett, Brandon L., Structural Reform Prosecution, 93 Va. L. Rev. 853 (2007), 801

Held, Eliot M. & Fontaine, Reid Griffith, On the Boundaries of Culture as an Affirmative Defense, 51 Ariz. L. Rev. 237 (2009), 329

Hellman, Deborah Prosecuting Doctors for Trusting Patients, 16 Geo. Mason L. Rev. 3 (2009), 264

Hellman, Willfully Blind for Good Reason, 3 Crim. L. & Philosophy 301 (2009), 263

Henderson, Lynne, Getting to Know: Honoring Women in Law and in Fact, 2 Tex. J. Women & L. 41 (1993), 400

Hendin, Herbert & Foley, Kathleen, Physician-Assisted Suicide in Oregon: A Medical Perspective, 106 Mich. L. Rev. 1613 (2008), 918

Henning, Peter, Should the Perception of Corporate Punishment Matter?, 19 J.L. & Pol'y 83 (2010), 783

Henning, Peter J., Corporate Criminal Liability and the Potential for Rehabilitation, 46 Am. Crim. L. Rev. 1417 (2009), 782

Henriques, Diana B. & Healy, Jack, Madoff Goes to Jail After Guilty Pleas, N.Y. Times (Mar. 13, 2009), 125

Herman, S. Gregory, One or More Wireless Networks Are Available: Can ISPs Recover for Unauthorized Wi-Fi Use Under Cable Television Piracy Laws, 55 Cath. U. L. Rev. 1095 (2006), 1085

Herrman, Joachim, Bargaining Justice—A Bargain for German Criminal Justice, 53 U. Pitt. L. Rev. 755 (1995), 1124

Hessick, Carissa Byrne, Why Are Only Bad Acts Good Sentencing Factors?, 88 B.U. L. Rev. 1109 (2008), 1186

Hessick, Carissa Byrne & Hessick, F. Andrew, Appellate Review of Sentencing Decisions, 60 Ala. L. Rev. 1 (2008), 1180

Heyman, Steven J., Foundations of the Duty to Rescue, 47 Vand. L. Rev. 673 (1994), 223

Hoernle, Tatjana, Social Expectations in the Criminal Law: The "Reasonable Person" in a Comparative Perspective, 11 New Crim. L. Rev. 1 (2008), 479

Hofer, Paul J., Has *Booker* Restored Balance? A Look at Data on Plea Bargaining and Sentencing, 23 Fed. Sent'g Rep. 326 (2011), 1188

Holmes Jr., Oliver Wendell, The Common Law 68 (1881), 305, 498, 614, 1102

Home Office U.K., Report of the Committee on Homosexual Offences and Prostitution (Wolfenden Report) (1957), 143

Horder, Jeremy, Autonomy, Provocation and Duress, (1992) Crim. L. Rev. 70. 929

Horowitz, Irwin A. & Kirkpatrick, Laird C., A Concept in Search of a Definition: The Effects of Reasonable Doubt Instructions on Certainty of Guilt Standards and Jury Verdicts, 20 Law & Hum. Behav. 655 (1996), 34

Horowitz, Irwin A. et al., Chaos in the Courtroom Reconsidered: Emotional Bias and Juror Nullification, 30 Law & Hum. Behav. 163 (2006), 60

Horowitz, Irwin A., Jury Nullification: An Empirical Perspective, 28 N. Ill. U. L. Rev. 425 (2008), 60

Hu, Winnie, Bullying Law Puts New Jersey Schools on Spot, N.Y. Times (Aug. 30, 2011), 147

Hughes, Graham, Criminal Omissions, 67 Yale L.J. 590 (1958), 229

Hughes, Graham, Response to Peter Brett in Criminal Responsibility, 16 Stan. L. Rev. 470 (1964), 268

Huigens, Kyron, Homicide in Aretaic Terms, 6 Buff. L. Rev. 97 (2002), 485

Morrison, Trevor W., Fair Warning and Retroactive Judicial Expansion of Federal Criminal Statutes, 74 S. Cal. L. Rev. 455 (2001), 321

Morse, Stephen J., Culpability and Control, 142 U. Pa. L. Rev. 1587 (1994), 1028

Morse, Stephen J., Diminished Rationality, Diminished Responsibility, 1 Ohio St. J. Crim. L. 289 (2003), 1007

Morse, Stephen J., Excusing and the New Excuse Defenses: A Legal and Conceptual Review, 23 Crime & Just. 329 (1998), 995

Morse, Stephen J., Excusing the Crazy: The Insanity Defense Reconsidered, 58 S. Cal. L. Rev. 777 (1985), 987

Morse, Stephen J., Fear of Danger, Flight from Culpability, 4 Psychol. Pub. Pol'y & L. 250 (1998), 952

Morse, Stephen J., Mental Disorder and Criminal Law, 101 J. Crim. L. & Criminology 885 (2011), 961, 979, 1021

Morse, Stephen J., Rationality and Responsibility, 74 S. Cal. L. Rev. 251 (2000), 979

Morse, Stephen J., Reason, Results, and Criminal Responsibility, (2004) U. Ill. L. Rev. 363, 609

Morse, Stephen J., The "New Syndrome Excuse" Syndrome, 14 Crim. Just. Ethics, 3 (Winter/Spring 1995), 842

Morse, Stephen J., The Twilight of Welfare Criminology: A Reply to Judge Bazelon, 49 S. Cal. L. Rev. 1247 (1976), 1026

Morse, Stephen J., Undiminished Confusion in Diminished Capacity, 75 J. Crim. L. & Criminology 1 (1984), 446, 1006

Mosteller, Robert P., Syndromes and Politics in Criminal Trials and Evidence Law, 46 Duke L.J. 461 (1996), 846

Mounts, Suzanne, Premeditation and Deliberation in California: Returning to a Distinction Without a Difference, 36 U.S.F. L. Rev. 261 (2002), 436

Muehlenhard, Charlene L. & Hollabaugh, Lisa C., Do Women Sometimes Say No When They Mean Yes?, 54 J. Personality & Soc. Psych. 872 (1988), 400

Mueller, Gerhard O.W., Mens Rea and the Corporation: A Study of the Model Penal Code Position on Corporate Criminal Liability, 19 U. Pitt. L. Rev. 21 (1957), 795

Muller, Eric L., The Hobgoblin of Little Minds? Our Foolish Law of Inconsistent Verdicts, 111 Harv. L. Rev. 771 (1998), 72

Mulroy, Steven J., The Duress Defense's Uncharted Terrain, 43 San Diego L. Rev. 159 (2006), 940

Murphy, Diana E., The Federal Sentencing Guidelines for Organizations: A Decade of Promoting Compliance and Ethics, 87 Iowa L. Rev. 697 (2002), 801

Murphy, Jeffrie, Getting Even: The Role of the Victim, 7 Soc. Phil. & Pol'y 209 (1990), 101

Murphy, J.G., Involuntary Acts and Criminal Liability, 51 Ethics 332 (1971), 211

Murphy, Jeffrie G., The Killing of the Innocent, 57 Monist 527 (1973), 901

Murphy, Jeffrie G., Legal Moralism and Retributivism Revisited, 1 Crim. L. & Phil. 5 (2007), 143

Murphy, Jeffrie G., Marxism and Retribution, 2 Phil. & Pub. Aff. 217 (1973), 97

Nagel, Ilene H. & Swenson, Winthrop M., The Federal Sentencing Guidelines for Corporations: Their Development, Theoretical Underpinnings, and Some Thoughts About Their Future, 71 Wash. U. L.Q. 205 (1993), 799

Oppel Jr., Richard A., Sentencing Shift Gives New Leverage to Prosecutors, N.Y. Times (Sept. 25, 2011), 1140

Orenstein, Aviva, Deviance, Due Process, and the False Promise of Federal Rules of Evidence, 90 Cornell L. Rev. 1487 (2005), 28

Orland, Leonard, The Transformation of Corporate Criminal Law, 1 Brook. J. Corp. Fin. & Com. L. 45 (2006), 788

Ostroff, Sue & Maguigan, Holly, Explaining Without Pathologizing: Testimony on Battering and Its Effects, in D.R. Loseke et al., Current Controversies on Family Violence 225 (2005), 847

Packer, Herbert, The Limits of the Criminal Sanction (1968), 300

Parker, Robert N. & Cartmill, Randi S., Alcohol and Homicide in the United States, 88 J. Crim. L. & Criminology 1369 (1998), 949

Parry, John T., Culpability, Mistake, and Official Interpretations of Law, 25 Am. J. Crim. L. 1 (1997), 319

Parry, John T., The Shape of Modern Torture: Extraordinary Rendition and Ghost Detainees, 6 Melbourne J. Int'l L. 516 (2005), 910

Paseward & Bieber, Insanity Plea: Statutory Language and Trial Procedure, 12 J. Psychiatry & L. 399 (1984), 982

Pauley, Matthew A., Murder by Premeditation, 36 Am. Crim. L. Rev. 145 (1999), 435

Perkins, Rollin M., Criminal Attempt and Related Problems, 2 UCLA L. Rev. 319 (1955), 650

Perry, Samuel, Frances, Allen & Clarkin, John, A DSM-III Casebook of Differential Therapeutics (1985), 996

Petersilia, Joan, Community Corrections: Probation, Parole, and Prisoner Reentry, in Crime and Public Policy (James Q. Wilson & Joan Petersilia eds., 2011), 8

Pfaff, John F., The Continued Vitality of Structured Sentencing Following Blakely: The Effectiveness of Voluntary Guidelines, 54 UCLA L. Rev. 235 (2006), 1172

Pfaff, John, The Empirics of Prison Growth: A Critical Review and Path Forward, 98 J. Crim. L. & Criminology 547 (2008), 6

Phelps, Michelle S., Rehabilitation in the Punitive Era: The Gap Between Rhetoric and Reality in U.S. Prison Programs, 45 Law & Soc'y Rev. 33 (2011), 1164

Picardi, Ralph G., Comment, Theft of Employee Services Under the United States Penal Code, 23 San Diego L. Rev. 897 (1986), 1084

Pillsbury, Samuel H., Crimes of Indifference, 49 Rutgers L. Rev. 105 (1996), 477

Pillsbury, Samuel H., Judging Evil: Rethinking the Law of Murder and Manslaughter (1998), 436, 448, 476

Pillsbury, Samuel H., Misunderstanding Provocation, 43 U. Mich. J.L. Reform 143 (2009), 444

Pillsbury, Samuel H., The Meaning of Deserved Punishment: An Essay on Choice, Character, and Responsibility, 67 Ind. L.J. 719 (1992), 1028

Pinard, Michael, Collateral Consequences of Criminal Convictions: Confronting Issues of Race and Dignity, 85 N.Y.U. L. Rev. 457 (2010), 8

Pinard, Michael, Freedom in Decline: Reflections and Perspectives on Reentry and Collateral Consequences, 100 J. Crim. L. & Criminology 1213 (2010), 75

Richman, Daniel C., Prosecutors and Their Agents, Agents and Their Prosecutors, 103 Colum. L. Rev. 749 (2003), 1154

Richman, Daniel C. & Stuntz, William J., Al Capone's Revenge: An Essay on the Political Economy of Pretextual Prosecution, 105 Colum. L. Rev. 583 (2005), 1132

Ristroph, Alice, Desert, Democracy, and Sentencing Reform, 96 J. Crim. L. & Criminology 1293 (2006), 99

Ristroph, Alice, Hope, Imprisonment, and the Constitution, 23 Fed. Sent'g Rep. 75 (2010), 202

Ristroph, Alice, Sexual Punishments, 15 Colum. J. Gender & L. 139 (2006), 335

Robbins, Ira P., Attempting the Impossible: The Emerging Consensus, 23 Harv. J. Legis. 377 (1986), 653

Robbins, Ira, Double Inchoate Crimes, 26 Harv. J. Legis. 1 (1989), 758

Roberts, Dorothy E., Motherhood and Crime, 79 Iowa L. Rev. 95 (1993), 232, 693

Roberts, Dorothy E., Race, Vagueness, and the Social Meaning of Order-Maintenance Policing, 89 J. Crim. L. & Criminology 775 (1995), 183

Robertson, John, Respect for Life in Bioethical Dilemmas—The Case of Physician-Assisted Suicide, 45 Clev. St. L. Rev. 329 (1997), 240-241

Robinson, Paul H. et al., Competing Theories of Blackmail: An Empirical Research Critique of Criminal Law Theory, 89 Tex. L. Rev. 291 (2010), 1079

Robinson Paul H. & Darley, John M., The Role of Deterrence in the Formulation of Criminal Code Rules, 91 Geo. L.J. 949, 951 (2003), 112

Robinson Paul H. & Darley, John M., The Utility of Desert, 91 Nw. U. L. Rev. 453 (1997), 113, 530

Robinson, Paul H., Distributive Principles of Criminal Law: Who Should Be Punished How Much? (2008), 99

Robinson, Paul H., Forward: The Criminal-Civil Distinction and Dangerous Blameless Offenders, 83 J. Crim. L.& Criminology 693 (1993), 967

Robinson, Paul H., The Ongoing Revolution in Punishment Theory: Doing Justice as Controlling Crime, 42 Ariz. St. L.J. 1089 (2010), 99

Robinson, Paul, Would You Convict? Seventeen Cases That Challenged the Law 142 (1999), 473

Robinson, Russell K., Masculinity as Prison: Sexual Identity, Race, and Incarceration, 99 Cal. L. Rev. 1309 (2011), 334

Rogers, Audrey, Protecting Children on the Internet: Mission Impossible?, 61 Baylor L. Rev. 323 (2009), 647

Rosen, Richard A., On Self-Defense, Imminence, and Women Who Kill Their Batterers, 71 N.C. L. Rev. 371 (1993), 852

Ross, Jacqueline E., Damned Under Many Headings: The Problem of Multiple Punishment, 29 Am. J. Crim. L. 245 (2002), 740

Roth, Nelson E. & Sundby, Scott E., The Felony-Murder Rule: A Doctrine at Constitutional Crossroads, 70 Cornell L. Rev. 446 (1985), 502

Roxin, C., Täterschaft und Tatherrschaft (1984), 660

Rozelle, Susan D., Controlling Passion: Adultery and the Provocation Defense, 37 Rutgers L.J. 197, (2005), 448

Rubin, Lilian, Quiet Rage: Bernie Goetz in a Time of Madness (1988), 824

Russell, Diana E. H., Rape in Marriage (2d ed. 1990), 406

Russell, Oldnall, A Treatise on Crimes and Misdemeanors (11th ed.,Turner ed., 1958), 1044

Schulhofer, Stephen J., Rethinking Mandatory Minimums, 28 Wake Forest L. Rev. 199 (1993), 1167

Schulhofer, Stephen J., Solving the Drug Enforcement Dilemma: Lessons from Economics, U. Chi. Legal F. 207 (1994), 113

Schulhofer, Stephen J., Taking Sexual Autonomy Seriously: Rape Law and Beyond, 11 Law & Phil. 35 (1992), 337, 378

Schulhofer, Stephen J, The Trouble with Trials; The Trouble with Us, 105 Yale L.J. 825 (1995), 1122

Schulhofer, Stephen J., Two Systems of Social Protection, 7 J. Contemp. Legal Issues 69 (1996), 81, 967

Schulhofer, Stephen J., Unwanted Sex (1998), 79, 337, 359, 368, 383, 389, 402, 404

Schulhofer, Stephen J. & Friedman, David, Rethinking Indigent Defense: Promoting Effective Representation through Consumer Sovereignty and Freedom of Choice for All Criminal Defendants, 31 Am. Crim. L. Rev. 73 (1993), 4

Schulhofer, Stephen J. & Nagel, Ilene H., Plea Negotiations Under the Federal Sentencing Guidelines, 91 Nw. U. L. Rev. 1284 (1997), 1117, 1152

Schuller, Regina A. & Vidmar, Neil, BWS Evidence in the Courtroom: A Review of the Literature, 16 Law & Hum. Behav. 273 (1992), 840

Schwartz, Victoria, The Victims' Rights Amendment, 42 Harv. J. Legis. 525 (2005), 102

Schwartzer, William E., Communicating with Juries: Problems and Remedies, 69 Cal. L. Rev. 731 (1981), 31

Scott, Robert E. & Stuntz, William J., Plea Bargaining as Contract, 101 Yale L.J. 1909 (1992), 1145

Scott, Ryan W., Inter-judge Sentencing Disparity After *Booker*: A First Look, 63 Stan. L. Rev. 1 (2010), 1181

Segal, Uzi & Stein, Alex, Ambiguity Aversion and the Criminal Process, 81 Notre Dame L. Rev. 1495 (2006), 54

Seigel, Michael L., Bringing Coherence to Mens Rea Analysis for Securities-Related Offenses, 2006 Wis. L. Rev. 1563, 252-253

Sellin, Thorsten, "Homicides in Retentionist and Abolitionist States," in Capital Punishment (Thorsten Sellin ed., 1967), 527

Sentelle, David, RICO: The Monster That Ate Jurisprudence: Lecture to the CATO Institute (Oct. 18, 1989), 773

Severance, Lawrence J., Greene, Edith & Loftus, Elizabeth F., Toward Criminal Jury Instructions that Jurors Can Understand, 75 J. Crim. L. & Criminolgy 198 (1984), 31

Shankland, Russell, Comment, Duress and the Underlying Felony, 99 J. Crim. L. & Criminology 1227 (2009), 940

Shedding, Ellis & Heath, The Works of Francis Bacon 343 (1859), 86

Sheketoff, Julia Fong, Note, State Innovations in Noncapital Proportionality Doctrine, 85 N.Y.U. L. Rev. 2209 (2010), 204

Sherman, Lawrence W., Policing Domestic Violence: Experiments and Dilemmas (1992), 838

Sheyn, Elizabeth R., Criminalizing the Denial of Honest Services After *Skilling*, 11 Wis. L. Rev. 27 (2011), 1099

Siddique, Haroon, DPP Releases Assisted Suicide Guidelines, Guardian, Feb. 25, 2010, 919

Thompson, Sandra G., The White Collar Police Force: "Duty to Report" Statutes in Criminal Law Theory, 11 Wm. & Mary Bill of Rts. J. 3 (2002), 228

Tiffany L. & Tiffany M., Nosologic Objection to the Criminal Defense of Pathological Intoxication: What Do the Doubters Doubt?, 13 Int'l J.L. & Psychiatry 49 (1990), 1020

Tiffany, Lawrence & Anderson, Carl, Legislating the Necessity Defense in Criminal Law, 52 Denv. L.J. 839 (1975), 892

Tjaden, Patricia & Thoennes, Nancy, Extent, Nature and Consequences of Rape Victimization: Findings from the National Violence Against Women Survey (Nat'l Institute of Justice 2006), 335

Tomkovicz, James J., The Endurance of the Felony-Murder Rule, 51 Wash. & Lee L. Rev. 1429 (1994), 497, 500

Tomlinson, Edward A., The French Experience with a Duty to Rescue, 20 N.Y.L. Sch. J. Int'l & Comp. L. 451 (2000), 227

Tonry, Michael, Malign Neglect (1995), 7

Trieman, David, Recklessness and the Model Penal Code, 9 Am. J. Crim. L. 283 (1981), 259

Truman, Jennifer L. & Rand, Michael R., National Crime Victimization Survey—2009 (U.S. Dept. of Justice, Bureau of Justice Statistics, 2010), 333

Tucker, Kathryn L., In the Laboratory of the States: The Progress of Glucksberg's Invitation to States to Address End of Life Choice, 106 Mich. L. Rev. 1593 (2008), 918

Turner, Jenia Iontcheva, Judicial Participation in Plea Negotiations: A Comparative View, 54 Am. J. Comp. L. 199 (2006), 1141

Twentieth Century Fund, Task Force on Criminal Sentencing, Fair and Certain Punishment (1976), 1166

Tyler, Tom R., Why People Obey the Law 60 (1990), 114

U.S. Dept of Justice Bureau of Justice Statistics, Homicide Trends by Race, http://bjs.ojp.usdoj.gov/content/homicide/tables/vracetab.cfm, 78

U.S. Dept of Justice, Bureau of Justice Statistics, Census of State and Federal Correctional Facilities (2000), 77

U.S. Dept. of Justice Bureau of Justice Statistics, Federal Justice Statistics, 2008—Statistical Tables at 18 (Nov. 2010), 11

U.S. Dept. of Justice Bureau of Justice Statistics, Felony Convictions in State Courts, 2006 (Dec. 2009), 11

U.S. Dept. of Justice, Bureau of Justice Statistics, Capital Punishment Statistics, http://bjs.ojp.usdoj.gov/index.cfm, 523, 525

U.S. Dept. of Justice, Bureau of Justice Statistics, Characteristics of State Parole Supervising Agencies, 2006 (Aug. 2008), 8

U.S. Dept. of Justice, Bureau of Justice Statistics, Crime in the United States—2009 (2010), 1

U.S. Dept. of Justice, Bureau of Justice Statistics, Criminal Victimization—2004 at 1 (Sept. 2005), 7

U.S. Dept. of Justice, Bureau of Justice Statistics, Prison and Jail Inmates at Midyear 1999 (Apr. 2000), 123

U.S. Dept. of Justice, Bureau of Justice Statistics, Prisoners in 2010 (Dec. 2011), 79

U.S. Dept. of Justice, Bureau of Justice Statistics, Recidivism of Prisoners released in 1994 (2002), 135